谨以此书感恩
亲爱的父母亲人、母校和祖国

Exploring International Economic Law
with Chinese Characteristics *Volume I*

中国特色国际经济法学探索

上册

曾华群◎著

北京大学出版社
PEKING UNIVERSITY PRESS

图书在版编目(CIP)数据

中国特色国际经济法学探索：上、下册/曾华群著. —北京：北京大学出版社，2022.12
ISBN 978-7-301-33811-7

Ⅰ. ①中…　Ⅱ. ①曾…　Ⅲ. ①国际经济法学—文集　Ⅳ. ①D996-53

中国国家版本馆 CIP 数据核字(2023)第 035942 号

书　　　　名	中国特色国际经济法学探索（上、下册）
	ZHONGGUO TESE GUOJI JINGJI FAXUE TANSUO（SHANG、XIACE）
著作责任者	曾华群　著
责 任 编 辑	刘秀芹
标 准 书 号	ISBN 978-7-301-33811-7
出 版 发 行	北京大学出版社
地　　　　址	北京市海淀区成府路 205 号　100871
网　　　　址	http://www.pup.cn　　新浪微博：@北京大学出版社
电 子 邮 箱	zpup@pup.cn
电　　　　话	邮购部 010-62752015　发行部 010-62750672　编辑部 021-62071998
印 刷 者	北京中科印刷有限公司
经 销 者	新华书店
	787 毫米×1092 毫米　16 开本　56.75 印张　彩插 8　1121 千字
	2022 年 12 月第 1 版　2022 年 12 月第 1 次印刷
定　　　　价	228.00 元（上、下册）

参加"第一期国际经济法讲习班"（庐山，1984）

在美国威拉姆特大学（Willamette University）
法学院选修法律博士（J.D.）学位课程（塞伦，
1988）

入选"旅美中国法律学者考察团"（Scholar
Orientation Program），幸会美中关系全国委员
会主席 David M. Lampton 先生（纽约，1988）

在瑞士比较法研究所（Swiss Institute of Comparative Law）作题为："The Development of Hong
Kong's Bilateral Treaties in the Period of Transition"（过渡期香港双边条约的发展）的学术报告（右
为主持人 Bertil Cottier 副所长）（洛桑，1996）

和新加坡国立大学东亚研究所（East Asian Institute）同事聚会（新加坡，1999）

在"首届中韩国际学术研讨会"作题为"Legal Considerations on the China-Korea FTA"（关于建立中国—韩国自由贸易区的法律思考）的大会报告（首尔，2005）

出席"厦门国际法高等研究院首届董事会成立会议"（海牙，2005）

厦门国际法高等研究院"第三届国际法前沿问题研修班"合影（厦门，2008）

在 OECD 和 UNCTAD 主办的"第二届国际投资协定研讨会"作题为"Innovative Path for International Investment Agreements"（国际投资协定的革新之路）的大会报告（巴黎，2010）

出席"海峡两岸法学交流20周年纪念研讨会"（台北，2010）

与新加坡国立大学法学院亚洲法律研究中心（Centre for Asian Legal Studies）联办"中国、东南亚与国际经济法"研讨会（新加坡，2014）

"2016年中国国际经济法学会年会暨学术研讨会"合影（厦门，2016）

在厦门国际法高等研究院"第十二届国际法前沿问题研修班"作题为"International Legal Perspective on China's 'Belt and Road' Initiative"（中国"一带一路"倡议的国际法观察）的开学演讲（厦门，2017）

"第八届WTO法专题研讨会"合影（广州，2017）

在"第九届纽黑文学派国际学术会议"作题为"Towards the 'Common Development' Model: China's Initiative on BIT Practice"（"共同发展"模式：中国双边投资条约实践的创新）的大会报告（杭州，2018）

"第十二届国际投资法专题研讨会"合影（厦门，2018）

感念感恩韩德培老师和姚梅镇老师亲临主持厦门大学首篇法学博士学位论文答辩会（厦门，1990）

厦门大学历史系77级毕业20周年师生合影 2002.2.

厦门大学历史系 77 级毕业 20 周年感恩团聚（厦门，2002）

欢迎世界银行集团成员"多边投资担保机构"（MIGA）总法律顾问 Lorin S. Weisenfeld 先生来家访（厦门，2002）

和陈安老师，廖益新、李国安、徐崇利同学有缘常聚"鹰园"（厦门，2003）

和中国国际经济法学会老师、学友（左二起：王传丽、陈安、陈治东、董世忠、吴焕宁、朱榄叶教授）赴韩国访问交流（朝鲜半岛"三八线"，2005）

感恩联合国国际法院前院长、大法官，厦门国际法高等研究院董事会主席史久镛教授亲临"首届国际法前沿问题研修班"作开学演讲（厦门，2006）

和陈安老师、Andreas F. Lowenfeld 教授相会于和平宫（海牙，2005）

在厦门市人民代表大会内务司法委员会履职（厦门，2007）

感念联合国国际法院小和田恒（Hisashi Owada）大法官亲临厦门国际法高等研究院"第四届国际法前沿问题研修班"讲学（厦门，2009）

拜会联合国国际法院大法官、厦门国际法高等研究院"第五届国际法前沿问题研修班"教授 Abdul G. Koroma 先生（海牙，2010）

祝贺伦敦大学亚非学院（School of Oriental and African Studies）彭文浩（Michael Palmer）教授来华履斯（厦门，2010）

感恩联合国国际法院薛捍勤大法官参访厦门国际法高等研究院（厦门，2013）

访问斯坦福大学法学院国际法与比较法项目
Allen Weiner 主任（斯坦福大学，2013）

感谢外交部乐玉成副部长颁授"外交部国际法
咨询委员会委员聘书"（北京，2019）

祝贺世界贸易组织上诉机构前主席张月姣教授履职载誉
归来（厦门，2016）

向亲临厦门国际法高等研究院"第十四届国际法前沿问题研修班"讲学的联合国国际法院院长A.
A. 优素福（Abdulqawi A. Yusuf）大法官致敬致谢（厦门，2019）

自强不息
且行且享

"旅美中国法律学者考察团"参访惠特曼和芮森法律事务所（Whitman & Ransom）（纽约，1988）

和留学不列颠哥伦比亚大学（University of British Columbia）的淳弟畅游加拿大西部（南北铁路交汇点，1988）

借访学之机，成为日内瓦湖畔流连忘返的"常客"（洛桑，1995）

偕妻林庆兰、子弘毅在好友伦敦大学亚非学院彭文浩教授家做客（伦敦，1996）

"客座东道主"欢迎同窗同事赵德铭（右）、单文华负笈英伦（伦敦，1998）

游学剑桥大学劳特派特国际法研究中心（Lauterpacht Research Centre for International Law）（剑桥，1998）

欧亚行程中顺访欧洲联盟总部（布鲁塞尔，1998）

首战荣获"'贸仲杯'国际商事仲裁模拟辩论赛"亚军的厦门大学首届国际法辩论队（前排左起：池漫郊、曾华群、颜盈盈；后排左起：陈延忠、黄哲、邱冬梅、于湛旻）（北京，2001）

率队参加"Willem C. Vis 国际商事模拟仲裁辩论赛",尝试国际 "第一次搏击"(维也纳,2002)

第二次率队参加"Willem C. Vis 国际商事模拟仲裁辩论赛"的"非典"之旅(罗马,2003)

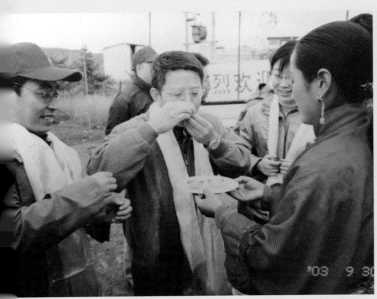

"请喝一杯青稞酒"——学会年会的附加"议程"(甘南草原,03)

漫步原始森林(夏威夷大岛,2013)

参访加州大学伯克利法学院（Berkeley Law School, University of California）（伯克利，2014）

履新出席国庆66周年招待会（北京，2015）

探访神秘的玛雅金字塔（坎昆，2017）

年会期间的校友欢聚（上海，2020）

父母结婚照（晋江安海镇，1949）

母亲与获奖学生（题字为：养小参加全县算术抽考得第一、三名与该科教师合影）（晋江安海镇，1948）

"英雄母亲"和我（厦门，1955）

和解放军辅导员俞叔叔在一起（厦门，1964）

父亲篆刻作品"持之以恒"

厦门一中的同学农友（厦门，1970）

上杭县溪口公社首批荣获"招工"的知青（龙岩上杭县，1970）

上杭县瓷厂原料加工班的"领头人"（龙岩上杭县，1971）

准考证（1977）

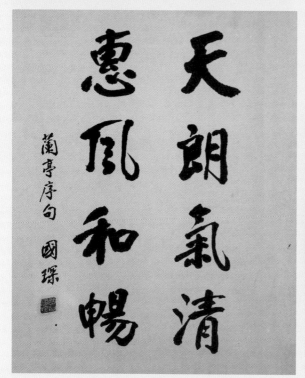

父亲书法作品"天朗气清 惠风和畅"

厦门大学60周年校庆和弟妹合影（厦门，1981）

和父母、民兄家同游鼓浪屿（厦门，1997）

和父母、琦妹欢聚泰晤士河畔（伦敦，1998）

父母、琦妹欧陆五国游（巴黎，1998）

父母、淳弟旅美探望伟弟家（华盛顿特区，1998）

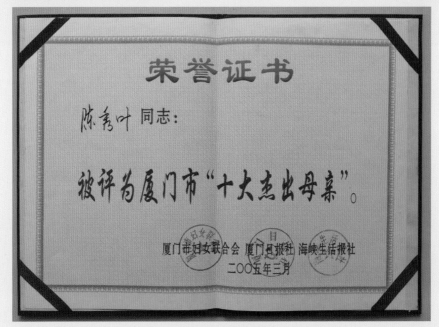

荣誉证书

陈秀叶 同志：

被评为厦门市"十大杰出母亲"。

厦门市妇女联合会 厦门日报社 海峡生活报社
二〇〇五年三月

感恩父母 传承家风

父亲篆刻作品"铅华落尽见真淳"

南洋团聚迎新春（新加坡，1999）

鹭江之滨大团聚（厦门，2007）

弘毅荣获斯坦福大学博士（计算机科学）学位（斯坦福大学，2014）

和伟弟家团聚（斯坦福大学，2019）

✦ 作者简介 ✦

曾华群 毕业于厦门大学,获历史学学士(1982)、法学硕士(1984)和法学博士(1990)学位。1996 年入选为国家"百千万人才工程首批第一、二层次人选"。历任厦门大学法学院助教(1984—1986)、讲师(1986—1988)、副教授(1988—1991)、教授(1991—)、博士生导师(1994—),厦门大学国际经济法研究所所长(2000—2016),厦门国际法高等研究院联席院长(2005—)。主要学术兼职:中国国际经济法学会会长(2011—),《国际经济法学刊》副主编(2018—),《厦门大学学报》(哲学社会科学版)编委会委员(1993—2018),《中国国际法学刊》(英文版)编委会委员(Member of Editorial Board,*Chinese Journal of International Law*,Oxford)(2002—),《中国比较法学刊》(英文版)咨询委员会委员(Member of Advisory Editorial Board,*The Chinese Journal of Comparative Law*,Oxford)(2013—)。主要专业兼职:世界银行集团成员"解决投资争端国际中心"(International Centre for Settlement of Investment Disputes,ICSID)调解员(2017—),中国外交部国际法咨询委员会委员(2017—2020),福建省人民政府法律顾问(2001—),厦门市第十一、十二、十三届人民代表大会法制委员会副主任委员(1998—2002)、内务司法委员会副主任委员(2002—2012),中国国际经济贸易仲裁委员会仲裁员(1995—),厦门第二律师事务所、福建联合信实律师事务所律师(1985—)。

曾在美国威拉姆特大学法学院(1987—1988)、香港大学法律学院(1993)、瑞士比较法研究所(1995—1996)、英国伦敦大学亚非学院(1996、1998)、新加坡国立大学东亚研究所(1999)等研修和讲学。著有《国际经济法导论》(第三版)(法律出版社,2020)、《促进与保护我国海外投资的法制》(北京大学出版社,2017,联合主编)、《WTO 与中国外资法的发展》(厦门大学出版社,2006)、*China-ASEAN Relations: Economic and Legal Dimensions*(World Scientific Publishing Co. Pte.,Ltd.,2006,co-editor)、《国际投资法学》(北京大学出版社,1999,主编)、《香港经贸法》(中国政法大学出版社,1996)、《国际投资法概论》(厦门大学出版社,1995)、《中外合资企业法律的理论与实务》(厦门大学出版社,1991)等。

自 序

敝帚自珍，人之常情。在融媒体时代，出一本自选文集，反映本人有关中国特色国际经济法学的探索，自以为或有"私人定制"式的增进学术、经验和情感交流的意义。

自 1978 年实行改革开放政策以来，我国步入复兴大道，欣欣向荣，举世瞩目。为适应新形势发展的迫切需要，国际经济法学在我国产生和发展，逐渐形成了"中国特色话语"。本书汇集本人教学之余在海内外发表的有关中国特色国际经济法学的代表作。全书分为六编十五章。第一至四编是论文集，分别探讨"国际经济法的'中国特色话语'""国际投资法的中国特色实践""国际贸易法的中国特色实践"和"香港涉外经济法律实践"等四个领域十个专题，合计三十八篇论文。可与大家共勉的是，全部论文均为本人潜心面壁独力完成之作。早期的手抄卡片、复印资料和近期的网上资源收集，亦是亲力亲为。本人以为，主题性文集的独特学术价值是，由于汇集作者持续研究同一主题的成果，较系统反映其学术观点的形成和发展，更有利于深入理解其基本立场和学术理念，引发进一步的研究和交流。

知行合一，功夫在诗外。在汇集学术论文的同时，本书希望为学界同行和广大读者提供多层面、有个性的相关信息，以期深化互动交流。第五编和附编是本书在论文集结构方面的拓展和创新。第五编题为"中国特色国际经济法学科的创建"，选择具有代表性、参考性的信息资料，从学科建设实践、学会工作感悟和治学心得分享等方面反映本人参与创建中国特色国际经济法学科的实践和体会。附编题为"惠风和畅 家国情感"，是本人感念父母亲人、分享成长经历和温馨情感的文字，从一个侧面反映了本人所处的家庭环境、社会背景和时代特色。

人有生命、慧命、使命，贵有自知之明、感恩之心、奉献之志。在一定意义上，本书是一个"50 后"学者对家庭、母校和国家的感恩汇报。梦幻机缘。1978 年初，在经历了三年"文革"和九年农工生活后，本人有幸"由工转学"，成为恢复高考后的首届（1977 级）大学生，在厦门大学历史系攻读历史学。1982 年初，成为厦门大学法律系国际法专业的首届(1981级)研究生,开始了在国际经济法领域学习、教学和研究的漫漫长旅。一直以来,秉持"知识报国,兼济天下"愿景,自信自强,且行且珍惜,内心充满感恩。感恩亲爱的父母亲人,感恩"惠风和畅,敬业奉献"的家风!感恩亲爱的"厦门系"母校厦门第五幼儿园(1959届)、厦门民立小学(1965届)、厦门第一中学(1968届初中)和厦门大学(1981届本科、1984届硕士、1990届博士),厦门大学更是我家四兄妹共同的母校!感恩伟大的祖国,生于斯长于斯,感恩能在实现中华民族伟大复兴的时代担当匹夫之责,奉献一份心力!

十分感谢北京大学出版社杨立范老师第一时间表示支持和悉心安排本书的出版计划。十分感谢刘秀芹编辑的精心编辑。付梓之际,适逢母校厦门大学迎来百年华诞大庆,谨奉献此感恩之作,聊表寸心。

曾华群

2021 年 4 月 6 日

于厦门大学西村

目录

MULU

上　册

第一编

国际经济法的"中国特色话语"

第二编

国际投资法的中国特色实践

下 册

第三编

国际贸易法的中国特色实践

第四编

香港涉外经济法律实践

第五编

中国特色国际经济法学科的创建

附　编

惠风和畅　家国情感

第一编
国际经济法的"中国特色话语"

导　言

本编主要研讨国际经济法的"中国特色话语"。第一章探讨国际经济法的基本理论,较系统论述西方国家国际经济法研究概况、国际经济法的含义及中国国际经济法的产生和发展(第一、二节);以 WTO 体制与国际投资法的关系为例,分析国际经济法各分支的相互关系(第三节);在此基础上,论述中国特色国际经济法的含义(第四、五节)。第二章探讨国际经济法的基本原则,以"外资征收及其补偿标准"和 WTO"特殊与差别待遇条款"为典例,分别探讨经济主权原则和公平互利原则在改革旧国际经济秩序、建立新国际经济秩序中的重要作用(第一、二节);进而探讨富有时代特点的合作发展原则,涉及国际经济法基本原则共同的法律效力问题(第三节);以双边投资条约体制改革为例,提出基于国际经济法基本原则的"中国主张"和"中国进路"(第四节)。

作者的基本观点:

(1) 关于中国特色国际经济法学的确立。 国际经济法学是"舶来品",中国特色国际经济法学可从指导思想、立场意识及基本原则等方面确立和论述。

(2) 关于中国特色国际经济法学的重大理论贡献。 西方学者对国际经济法基本原则鲜有系统涉及。对旨在建立国际经济新秩序的经济主权、公平互利、合作发展等国际经济法基本原则的提炼、论证和发展,是中国特色国际经济法学对国际经济法理论的重大贡献。

(3) 关于中国特色国际经济法学的使命担当。 中国特色国际经济法学的历史使命和中国国际经济法学人的学术担当是,站在中国和广大发展中国家立场,以马克思主义为指导思想,紧密联系中国和国际实践,坚持建立国际经济新秩序的目标,汲取国际社会长期积淀的国际经济法学精华,开拓创新,丰富和革新"国际话语体系",坚定维护和发展国际社会普遍认同的经济主权、公平互利、合作发展等国际经济法基本原则,为促进国际经济法实践的健康发展,为推动构建"人类命运共同体"作出积极的学术贡献。

第一章
国际经济法的基本理论

第一节　论国际经济法学的发展[*]

在世界范围,国际经济法作为独立的法律部门,形成于 19 世纪末;国际经济法学作为独立的法学学科,直至第二次世界大战后才逐渐形成和发展起来。1978 年中国实行改革开放政策以来,国际经济法学在中国应运而生,蓬勃发展,取得了令人瞩目的丰硕成果。本文在评述国际经济法学在西方国家和中国的产生和发展、关于国际经济法的分歧与共识的基础上,初步探讨国际经济法的法律部门地位和中国国际经济法学的进一步发展问题。

一、西方国家国际经济法研究述略

虽然调整国际经济交往活动的法律规范历史悠久,国际经济法(international economic law)作为一个法律分支或法律部门的概念,延至二战后才引起西方国家法学界的普遍重视和承认。相应地,作为一个新兴的法学部门,国际经济法的教学和研究也在西方国家法学界首先发展起来。

（一）英国

英国国际法学界较早将国际经济法作为国际法的新内容进行教学和研究。

在奥本海(Oppenheim)、布莱里(Brierly)、麦克奈尔(McNair)等国际法学者的国际法著作中,尚无国际经济法的内容,因为这些著作出版于国际金融组织和国际贸易体制成立之前。在由沃尔多克(Waldock)编的《布莱里国际法》的最新版本中开始

---

[*] 原载陈安主编:《国际经济法论丛》第 2 卷,法律出版社 1999 年版。

有论述国际劳工组织的内容,国际货币基金组织和世界银行也被列为联合国的专门机构。劳特派特(Lauterpacht)在詹克斯(C. W. Jenks)博士协助下,在《奥本海国际法》的最新版本中,增添了简介国际货币基金组织、世界银行和关税及贸易总协定的附录。

1948 年英国伦敦大学的"国际经济法"教学大纲第一次试图表述国际经济法的内容。其列举的专题包括:待遇标准,特别是国民待遇和最惠国待遇标准;海外财产的保护;商务条约,金融协定,国家贷款和其他国家契约;卡尔沃条款,国际金融管制措施,波特公约(Potter Convention);对敌通商法,军事占领下的国际经济与金融法;中立财产的保护和赔偿的法律;国际经济与金融组织的法律。伦敦大学施瓦曾伯格(Schwarzenberger)教授认为,上述不同专题的共同特征是,均属具有"显著经济因素"(predominant economic element)的国际法专题。[1]

在英国国际法学者中,施瓦曾伯格教授最先阐述国际经济法的概念,其发表于1948 年的论文"国际经济法的原则与标准"在欧洲影响甚广。在 1970 年,他在《经济的世界秩序》中将国际经济法定义为"国际法的分支,它涉及自然资源的所有权和开发,商品的生产与销售,经济或金融性的无形国际交易,货币和金融,有关服务以及参加此种活动的实体的地位和组织"。[2]

詹克斯(Jenks)虽未直接使用"国际经济法"这一用语,也是最早确认国际经济法的国际法学者之一。他在 1954 年发表的论文"国际法的范围"中指出,"调整国家之间经济关系的规则,包括有关金融和一般经济政策的义务、一国对他国造成有关经济损失或损害的责任以及国家之间的金融交易"。他后来在其专著《普通法》中提出了"国际经济关系法"(law of international economic relationships)的三项原则,即:取得外国人权利的原则、事前与他国协商原则、对他国造成损害的责任原则。[3]

曼勒(F. A. Mann)在其专著《货币的法律问题》中论及国际经济法问题。鲍威特(D. W. Bowett)在《国际组织法》(*Law of International Institutions*)中论述了国际组织的制度和结构。

最新的国际经济法著作是福克斯(Hazel Fox)主编、于 1988 年和 1992 年出版的《国际经济法与发展中国家》第 1、2 卷,对国际经济法的定义、渊源、原则等专题作了

---

〔1〕 See F. V. Garcia-Amador, *The Emerging International Law of Development: A New Dimension of International Economic Law*, Oceana Publications, 1990, pp. 18-19.

〔2〕 See Hazel Fox, *International Economic Law and Developing States: Some Aspects*, British Institute of International and Comparative Law, 1988, p. 1.

〔3〕 See F. V. Garcia-Amador, *The Emerging International Law of Development: A New Dimension of International Economic Law*, Oceana Publications, 1990, p. 19.

较全面的理论探讨。

值得注意的是，一些英国国际法学者在研究中虽然也涉及国家之间经济行为，但否认国际法对国家之间经济关系的一般调整。换言之，他们仍然坚持传统国际法只限于调整国家之间政治关系的立场，否认国际法中包含调整国家之间经济关系的规范。如奥康内尔（O'Connell）在其 1970 年出版的《国际法》中以"有关货币主权的责任"为题，专章论述有关货币政策的国际法规则和控制各国金融政策的国际组织机制。他在确认该主题时称："货币是经济的概念，其法律特征是颇有争议的"，"在国际公法著作中，货币被关注的范围仅在于，货币不再成为国内事项而是涉及各国的安全"。显然，这种方式不是研究国际法对国家经济行为的正式调整，而是将国际法局限于对国家违反非经济规范行为的控制。

此后一段时期，尽管通过国际货币基金组织、世界银行和关税及贸易总协定调整各国经济关系已成为国际社会的新特征，英国一些国际法学者仍沿袭上述局限性的研究方法。他们主张，除非经济制裁用于控制威胁或违反国际和平，或者一国对外国人的待遇导致外国人财产被征收和不充分补偿，国际法不得调整贸易或货币事项。这种观点也反映在一些国际法著作中。例如，哈里斯（Harris）和肖（Shaw）的国际法著作未设专章论述国际货币基金组织、世界银行或关贸总协定。布朗里（Brownlie）在其《国际公法原则》中亦循此方式：外国投资和征收问题只是在"对外国人及其财产的损害"中提及；对外国人适用贸易限制只是在管辖权项下简述；对经济制裁未作专门论述；对联合国、国际货币基金组织和世界银行也着墨甚少。可见，作者并未将上述内容作为国际法的重要内容。[1]

（二）法国

法国国际经济法的教学和研究是在法国国际法协会的直接推动下开展起来的。

自 1979 年法国国际法协会举办奥尔良国际经济法研讨会后，相继出版了一些有关国际经济法的教材，例如，卡罗（D. Carreau）、朱亚尔（P. Julliard）和弗洛里（T. Flory）的《国际经济法》，布朗热（M. Belanger）的《国际经济制度》等。一般的国际公法教材也包括有关贸易和金融政策的国际法制导论，例如，在科奥（N. Quoc）、戴利尔（Daillier）和佩莱（A. Pellet）的《国际公法》中，有关贸易和金融的国际法问题的论述占了相当的篇幅。[2]

在法国国际经济法学界中，卡罗等合著的《国际经济法》影响最大。他们主张，

---

〔1〕 See Hazel Fox, *International Economic Law and Developing States*：*An Introduction*，International Economic Law Series Vol. Ⅱ，British Institute of International and Comparative Law，1992，pp. 4-6.

〔2〕 Ibid.，p. 7.

国际经济法是作为国际经济秩序法出现的国际公法新分支,它一方面调整各国领土上来自外国的生产因素,即外国人和外国资本,另一方面也调整各种财产、劳务和资本的国际交易,即对国际经济贸易活动实行国际性的调整。具体而言,国际经济法律规范可划分为国际(跨国)定居创业法,国际(跨国)公、私投资法,国际经济关系法,国际经济组织法和区域经济共同体法。[1]

有关发展的问题成为国际经济合作和组织的主要问题之一,相应地产生了有关的法律制度,因此扩大了国际经济法的范围。在法国国际法协会有关"国际经济法问题"的奥尔良研讨会上,韦伊(P. Weil)认为,国际经济法已成为目标法(droit de finalite),即"发展与评估的经济政策所需的框架"。[2]

(三)德国

与英、法不同,德国的国际经济法研究是在经济法研究的基础上兴起的。

早在战前,德国学者哈姆斯(B. Harms)从 20 世纪以来国民经济与世界经济相互对立这一经济事实出发,试图在原有国际法和国内法体系之外,建立新的法律体系。他把经济法分为世界经济法和国民经济法。世界经济法指调整国家之间经济关系的法律规范,属于国际法范畴。国民经济法则属国内法范畴,分为两类:一是调整各国境内私人之间和私人与其本国之间经济关系的法律规范,称为内部国民经济法;另一类是调整一国私人与他国私人经济关系的法律规范,称为外部国民经济法。国际经济法与传统国际法不同,是包括属于国际法范畴的世界经济法和属于国内法范畴的外部国民经济法的一种新的法律体制。[3]

艾尔勒(G. Erler)也是欧洲最早试图表述国际经济法内容的国际法学者之一。他列举属于国际经济法领域的三方面事项:(1)国际贸易,特别是关税、对外商务和移民的法律以及国际协调和自由化的法律;(2)金融协议的法律,特别是调整货币的法律以及调整货币金融自由化和协调的法律;(3)国际经济干预的法律,特别是调整津贴、投资、卡特尔和销售的法律以及国际经济一体化组织在经济援助、关税优惠等方面的法律。[4]

彼特斯曼(E.-U. Petersmann)将"经济的国际法"(the international law of the economy)与其提出的"国际经济法律"(the law of the international economy)比较,

---

〔1〕 参见陈安主编:《国际经济法总论》,法律出版社 1991 年版,第 80—82 页。

〔2〕 See F. V. Garcia-Amador, *The Emerging International Law of Development: A New Dimension of International Economic Law*, Oceana Publications, 1990, p. 23.

〔3〕 参见〔日〕田中耕太郎:『世界法の理論』,岩波书店 1952 年,第 510 页以下。转引自姚梅镇:《国际投资法》,武汉大学出版社 1985 年版,第 5 页。

〔4〕 See F. V. Garcia-Amador, *The Emerging International Law of Development: A New Dimension of International Economic Law*, Oceana Publications, 1990, p. 20.

认为后者是"世界经济的民间、国家和国际规则的功能性统一体"（a functional unity）。[1]它本身表现为私法（包括"商法"和"跨国商法"）、内国法（包括冲突法）和国际公法（包括欧共体法）的混合物，具有多种形式，诸如多边和双边条约、行政协定、由国际组织通过的"第二级法律"、君子协定、中央银行安排、原则的宣示、决议、建议、习惯法、一般法律原则、事实上命令、国会法令、政府法令、私法判决、私人契约或商务惯例。[2]

（四）美国

战后美国法学界对国际经济法的研究特点是，着重研究私人特别是跨国公司跨国经济活动的法律问题，认为只有"跨国法律问题"（transnational legal problems）这一用语，才能如实反映国际经济关系中法律问题的特点。因为现代国际经济交往活动，不限于在国家之间、国际组织之间进行，更大量的是私人特别是跨国公司跨越国境的经济活动。由于"国际"（international）的本义是指"国家之间"（between nations）或"政府之间"（inter-governments），该用语已不能用于表达包括国家、国际组织和私人为主体的国际经济关系。只有用"跨国"（transnational）这一用语，才能准确概括当前国际经济关系及其活动的特点。

1956年，杰塞普在其著作《跨国法》中，系统阐述了"跨国法"理论。所谓"跨国法"，是指调整跨越国境活动的法律规范，"不仅包括民法和刑法，也包括国际公法和国际私法，而且还可包括国内法中其他公法和私法，乃至不属于上述范围的其他法律规范"，"传统的国际公法、国际私法、关于国家契约的法律以及国际行政法等，均将构成跨国法这一独立法律部门的各个分支"。他通过案例分析，特别是分析外国私人与东道国签订特许协议时所面临的法律选择等困难，指出采用"跨国法"这一概念，"可以广泛地包括调整适用于跨越国境而发生的事件和行为的法律"，"这样，就具体案件来说，就不用担心是适用公法或适用私法"，可获得解决现实问题的最适当最必要的方法。[3]

1964年，沃尔夫冈教授指出，应注意"在许多现代国际经济交往中公与私因素的解释"和公法与私法的混合，并提倡采用处理这种不可逆转现象的国际法新技术。[4]

〔1〕 See Hazel Fox, *International Economic Law and Developing States：An Introduction*, International Economic Law Series Vol. Ⅱ, British Institute of International and Comparative Law,1992, p. 13.

〔2〕 See Sergei A. Voitovich, *International Economic Organizations in the International Legal Process*, Martinus Nijhoff Publishers, 1995, pp. 6-7.

〔3〕 See P. C. Jessup, *Transnational Law*, Yale University Press, 1956, pp. 2,4,7,15,71,106-107. 转引自姚梅镇：《国际投资法》，武汉大学出版社1985年版，第6—7页。

〔4〕 See Stephen Zamora, Is There Customary International Economic Law? *German Yearbook of International Law*, Vol. 32, 1989, p. 14.

斯泰纳和瓦格茨在 1968 年合著的《跨国法律问题》中较具体地阐述了跨国法体系。他们认为，该书论述的课题来自许多学科，以具有"跨国性"（transnational character）和"涉法性"（law-related character）为连结点而融为一体。它们涉及的学科，不仅包括国际公法、国际组织法、冲突法、比较法，还包括了宪法、经济法以及法理学和某些政治学理论。其中许多课题本身具有明显的国际性或跨国性，另一些课题虽属于一国国内的法律体制，但具有涉外性。这些国内法的涉外部分，连同国际公法和国际组织法，共同构成了跨国法的学术领域和有关的法律结构，用于调整国家之间或不同国籍私人之间的法律关系。该书论述的内容涉及各国政府之间的关系，也涉及私人与国家之间的关系；不仅包括跨国投资、贸易等经济方面的法律课题，也包括跨国的人权保护、控制国际违法行为、国际刑法的域外效力、跨国司法协作等课题。[1]

卡茨和布鲁斯特在其 1976 年的著作中指出，传统法学的片面性在于忽视国际法与国内法之间的相互联系和相互作用，国际法只侧重国际法秩序的政治方面。而新的研究方法打破了国际私法、国际公法、比较法之间及其与国内法之间相互隔绝的界限，进而研究国际法秩序的政治和经济两个方面，着重研究国际法与国内法之间相互渗透的作用，把私人、国家和国际组织相互之间的国际交易关系中的一切法律问题作为研究对象。他们提出"国际交易关系法"（law of international transaction and relations）的概念，定义为调整国际经济交往的法律规范的总和。其中包含两类法律规范：第一类是涉外关系法，即国内法（公法和私法）、国际私法和双边条约；第二类是国际行政法，即多边条约。[2]

杰克逊（J. H. Jackson）采用"国际经济法"的概念，认为，用于调整国际（跨国）经济关系的国际经济法，可大体分为三个层次：第一个层次是有关国家用于调整跨国经济交往活动的私法，包括合同法、货物买卖法、冲突法、保险法、公司法和海商法；第二个层次是有关国家用于管理跨国经济交往活动的公法，包括关税法、进出口管制法、产品质量和包装标准法、所得税法、优先采购国货法等；第三个层次是对跨国经济交往活动具有影响的国际公法或国际经济组织法。一般说来，此类法律规范只适用于国家之间的经济交往，但也间接适用于不同国籍的私人之间的经济交往。[3]

---

〔1〕　See H. Steiner, D. Vagts, *Transnational Legal Problems*, 1986, preface, pp.19-20. 转引自陈安主编：《国际经济法总论》，法律出版社 1991 年版，第 84—85 页。

〔2〕　See M. Katz, K. Brewster, *The Law of International Transactions and Relations: Cases and Materials*, Modern Law Review, 1961. 转引自姚梅镇：《国际投资法》，武汉大学出版社 1985 年版，第 7—8 页。

〔3〕　参见陈安主编：《国际经济法总论》，法律出版社 1991 年版，第 85—86 页。

洛文费尔德（A. F. Lowenfeld）于 1976—1979 年间主持编纂了题为《国际经济法》的系列教材，分为《国际私人贸易》《国际私人投资》《政治性贸易管制》《国际货币制度》《国际交易中的税收问题》和《国际贸易的政府管制》6 卷。全套教材立足于美国实际，从国际法和国内法两个方面，对调整国际经济交往活动的重要法律规范，即国际贸易法、国际投资法、国际货币金融法、国际税法作了系统论述，是全面论述美国国际经济法体系的代表作。[1]

（五）日本

战后，随着日本参与国际经济组织和签订双边经济条约实践的发展，日本国际法学界逐渐关注调整国际经济关系的法律规范，开展了对有关通商航海条约的基本结构、不正当竞争等专题的研究。1961、1962 年相继出版了国际事务研究所主编的《国际经济法问题》及续编等著作。从这一时期的著作中，可以看出日本国际法学者为适应解决现实问题的需要，对国际经济法问题进行系统理论研究的初步努力。

60 年代中期以后，国际政治经济形势发生了重要变化，相应地，日本国际经济法的研究对象和范围扩大了，有关国际经济活动的国际法已成为国际法体系中的一个组成部分。当时一般的国际法教科书虽然未设专章论述经济活动的国际法问题，但在国际组织、条约和个人等章节中分别涉及该问题。值得注意的是，在 70 年代中期，一些国际法教科书设立了题为"国际经济活动与国际法"的专章，表明将该专题视为与其他专题同等重要。这一时期国际经济法的研究侧重于国际投资法问题，包括国有化、特许协议、海外投资保证制度、投资争端的解决、区域经济合作与外国投资等。在国际经济法的其他领域，学术研究涉及诸如公司的国际活动与国际法、最惠国待遇条款、国际共同企业、国际贸易法、反垄断、国际货币基金组织、区域性经济活动和工业产权的国际保护等专题。[2]

关于国际经济法的概念和体系，日本学者有不同的见解。

金泽良雄认为，国际经济法是为解决资本主义高度矛盾，各国从国际经济整体立场出发，通过国际条约对国际经济活动进行调整所形成的国际法秩序。[3]其中包括国家之间、国家与国际组织之间、国际组织之间的法律规范。随着国际经济交往的日益频繁和不断扩大，资本主义各国在商品和财富的生产、流通和消费等方面产生

---

〔1〕 关于洛文费尔德主编的《国际经济法》系列教材的概述，参见姚梅镇：《美国〈国际经济法〉丛书评介》，载姚梅镇：《国际经济法的理论与实践》，武汉大学国际法研究所，1984 年，第 36—50 页；陈安主编：《国际经济法总论》，法律出版社 1991 年版，第 86—89 页。

〔2〕 See Yasuo Ishimoto, Kazuya Hirobe, Development of Post-War Japanese Studies in Public International Law, Part 1: 1945-1964; Part 2: 1965-1987, *The Japanese Annual of International Law*, Vol. 30, 1987, pp. 126-127; *The Japanese Annual of International Law*, Vol. 31, 1988, pp. 110-113.

〔3〕 参见姚梅镇：《国际投资法》，武汉大学出版社 1985 年版，第 3—4 页。

了尖锐的利害冲突和矛盾对立。各国政府除凭借实力、通过战争来解决矛盾外,还必须通过国际协商,制定国际性的法律规范,调整和制约相互间的经济关系和利害冲突,这就是国际经济法的本质。其表现形式是各种具有经济内容的双边或多边的国际条约。[1]福光家庆、高田源清教授也有类似的观点。

吉田荣助、小西唯雄教授认为,国际经济法是在国际范围确保竞争法实现的国际法。国际法学者金田近二、山本草二、高桥通敏和横川新也持同样的观点。

田中耕太郎教授认为,调整世界经济关系的法律,分为以国际经济为基础的法律规范(关于国民经济相互间的法律——国际法)和以万民经济为基础的法律规范,即个别经济相互间的法律(如统一法、世界习惯法、国际私法)两大类。前者称为国际经济的法律,后者称为万民经济的法律,总称为世界经济法。虽然他采用的是"世界经济法"的概念,并把"国际经济的法律"限于调整国民经济相互关系的条约,但他把"世界经济关系"视为一个整体,以统一的"世界经济法"调整,这在当时日本国际法学界,是一理论创新。

与前述金泽良雄的观点不同,樱井雅夫认为,国际经济法是现代国际经济新秩序形成以后的产物。世界上存在资本主义国家集团、社会主义国家集团和发展中国家集团,国家、法人、自然人都参与国际经济活动,从事各种带有国际性质的法律行为,产生了传统的"国际的"(international)等用语无法表达的国际社会现象,出现了"国际交易""跨国法"等概念。因此,必须摒弃传统的观念,对国际经济法作综合的考察。在作此考察时,首先应从法学分科理论出发,将国际经济法看成是调整国际经济关系的国际法;其次,应从国际法与国内法两个部门来综合考察跨国经济现象,缺一不可;最后,在考虑跨国经济法的问题时,还必须研究上述三个国家集团内调整跨国经济关系的法律和跨越三个国家集团的调整跨国经济关系的法律。因此,不存在单一的国际经济法,而是并存多层次的交错的国际经济法律状态。

小原喜雄在考察欧美国际经济法主要学说的基础上指出,如果面对国际经济法律调整的现实,国际经济法应当包括两类法律规范:其一是从国民经济利益的观点出发,以国际贸易为调整对象的法律规范,其法律渊源是关于国际贸易的复数国家(包括本国和外国)的国内法(包括公法和私法)、解决法律冲突的国际私法以及双边条约等,统称为涉外关系法;另一类是从世界经济利益的观点出发,由国际经济组织主持缔结的调整各国涉外关系法的抵触或对外经济政策的对立的多边条约,称为国际经济行政法。两类法律规范在形成过程中,前者先出现,后者是为弥补前者的不

---

[1]　参见陈安主编:《国际经济法总论》,法律出版社1991年版,第78—79页。

足和协调前者的矛盾而出现的。两者虽然形成的时期和原理不同，但共同构成了统一的具有复合结构的法律秩序。[1]

大平善梧、佐藤和男教授也主张，国际经济法是包括国际法和国内法的新的法学分科。其主要理由是，根据考察对象国际经济关系的同一性，应避免国际法和国内法分离的认识，理解两者统一的脉络。[2]

二、中国国际经济法学的创立与发展

（一）中国国际经济法学的初步创立

20 世纪 70 年代末 80 年代初，中国法学界的一些学者深切感受到改革开放新形势下的迫切需求，开始进行国际经济法学的研究和传播。这一时期的代表作有武汉大学姚梅镇教授发表在《武汉大学学报》和《中国国际法年刊》的一系列研究国际经济法的论文、译文和厦门大学陈安教授 1982 年编译出版的《国际经济立法的历史和现状》等。

在《中国国际法年刊》(1983)发表的一组"国际经济法讨论"文章中，反映了中国法学界关于国际经济法的概念和体系的不同主张。其中，汪瑄、史久镛教授主张国际经济法是国际公法的一个分支，是"经济的国际法"；姚梅镇、王名扬教授则主张国际经济法是调整国际经济关系的国际法和国内法规范的总称，是独立的新兴的法学部门。上述和其后的继续讨论，在一定程度上促进了全国性国际经济法学习和研究热潮的形成。

1984 年 5 月 8 日至 6 月 5 日，经武汉大学、上海社会科学院、厦门大学、南开大学、安徽大学、中山大学和江西大学发起组织，在庐山举办了"国际经济法讲习班"，来自全国 53 个单位的 90 多名代表参加。我国较早研究国际经济法的学者周子亚、姚梅镇、陈安、董世忠、高尔森、朱学山、盛愉、卢绳祖、方之寅、江振良和王国良等同志作学术讲座。讲题涉及国际经济法各主要分支和重要专题，分别是"一般国际法与国际经济法""国际投资的法律保护""美国对海外美资的法律保护""关于国际商品贸易的法律制度""国际税法""国际技术转让的国内立法""国际货币法""商事仲裁""涉外合同的法律适用问题""经济特区立法问题"和"产品责任法"等。这是全国国际经济法学者的第一次盛会。在讲习班上，代表们倡议筹建成立全国性的国际经济法学术团体。经协商讨论，决定成立"中国国际经济法研究会"，并通过研究会章

---

〔1〕 参见何勤华：《当代日本国际经济法学的发展与特点》，载《法学评论》1991 年第 1 期，第 84—87 页。
〔2〕 参见〔日〕樱井雅夫：《国际投资法》，有信堂 1988 年日文版，第 11—12 页。

程和协商成立第一届理事会,推选姚梅镇教授为会长。[1]

庐山国际经济法讲习班的举办和中国国际经济法研究会的成立标志着中国国际经济法学的初步创立。

(二) 中国国际经济法学的全面发展

中国国际经济法学初步创立之后,在学科体系的确立、学科建设和人才培养、专题研究以及学术团体活动等方面取得了全面的发展,呈现出良好的发展势头。

1. 中国国际经济法学科体系的初步确立

80 年代中期以来,在借鉴和吸收外国有关研究成果的基础上,中国国际经济法学界陆续出版了国际经济法概论性著作、国际经济法各分支的教材或专著和国际经济法系列专著或教材。

1984 年刘丁教授编著的《国际经济法》是我国第一部国际经济法的概论性著作。沈达明、冯大同教授编著的《国际贸易法》(1983)和姚梅镇教授著《国际投资法》(1985)是最早系统论述国际经济法分支的教材或专著。

1987 年陈安教授主编的"国际经济法系列专著",包括《国际贸易法》《国际投资法》《国际货币金融法》《国际税法》和《国际海事法》等 5 部,是中国第一套国际经济法系列专著,对创建中国国际经济法学科体系作出了重要的贡献。1988—1991 年,司法部法学教材编辑部为适应国际经济法专业本科教学的需要,组织编写了一套高等学校法学试用教材,包括《国际经济法总论》《国际贸易法新论》《国际金融法》《国际税法》《国际技术转让》《海商法学》《冲突法》和《涉外法律文书》等 8 种。1996—1998 年,该编辑部又编审出版了"'九五'规划高等学校法学教材·国际经济法系列",包括《国际经济法导论》《国际贸易法》《国际金融法》《国际投资法》《国际技术转让法》《国际税法》《世界贸易组织》《国际商事争议解决程序》和《国际环境法》等 9 种。1999 年,陈安教授总主编的"国际经济法学系列专著",含《国际投资法学》《国际贸易法学》《国际货币金融法学》《国际税法学》和《国际海事法学》等 5 卷,相继推出。该套专著是以陈安教授为学术带头人的厦门大学法学院国际经济法学术梯队,在历年国际经济法专题研究的基础上,系统研究国际经济法学的力作,为确立中国国际经济法学科体系作出了新的贡献。

贯穿于上述论著中的共同观点是,国际经济法学是由调整国际经济关系的国际法和国内法规范构成的学科体系;该体系由国际经济法基本理论和国际贸易法、国际投资法、国际货币金融法、国际税法、国际海事法、国际经济组织法和国际经济争

---

[1] 据国际经济法研究会编:《简报》第 1 期,1984 年 5 月 28 日。

端解决法等主要分支组成；中国国际经济法学应紧密联系中国实际，以中国已经参加或准备参加的国际经济条约、中国涉外经济立法、国际商务惯例和涉外经贸合同实务为研究重点，同时，应站在发展中国家立场，坚持建立国际经济新秩序的目标。

上述论著，大体上确立了具有中国特色的国际经济法学科体系，同时，在相当程度上满足了国际经济法的教学需要和实务参考需要。

2. 具有中国特色的学科建设和人才培养

与西方国家比较，中国国际经济法学的学科建设和人才培养具有明显的特色。主要表现在，由于国家教育行政主管部门重视，学科建设后来居上，发展迅速，国际经济法专门人才培养规范化、系统化。

近十多年来，许多法律院校经国家教委批准，相继设立国际经济法本科专业和国际经济法专业硕士学位授予点。北京大学（1982）、对外经济贸易大学（1984）、武汉大学（1984）和厦门大学（1986）先后获准设立国际经济法博士学位授予点。目前，中国各大学的法律院系、各政法院校（以下统称"高校"）一般都将国际经济法作为一门主要的专业课程。一些高校的国际金融、世界经济、国际经济合作等专业也将国际经济法作为一门主要的专业必修课程。国际经济法各层次专业课程的设置和教材建设渐趋成熟和规范化。国际经济法专业各层次专门人才因其"懂法律、懂经济、懂外语"的优势而受到涉外经贸管理部门、涉外经贸企业和法律实务界等的普遍欢迎和重视。一些较早毕业的国际经济法专业的硕士、博士从事教学和研究工作，逐渐成长为新一代的学术带头人。实践表明，在中国实行对外开放政策、建立社会主义市场经济体制和建立社会主义法治国家的大背景下，国际经济法的专门人才切合市场急需，大有用武之地。

3. 理论联系实际的专题研究

在"七五""八五"和"九五"期间，中国国际经济法学界承担了许多国家和省部级重点科研项目，紧密联系改革开放的实际，在国际经济法基本理论和国际经济法各分支领域进行了开拓性的专题研究。

在此期间出版的国际经济法专题研究著作甚多，仅以国际投资法和国际贸易法领域为例。

国际投资法领域，陈安教授著《美国对海外投资的法律保护及典型案例分析》（1985）以案例研究的方法，对美国海外私人投资保证制度作了深入的研究。姚梅镇教授主编的《比较外资法》（1993）采用比较研究的方法，把中国外资法的研究提高到一个新水平。余劲松博士著《跨国公司法律问题研究》（1989）和笔者所著《中外合资企业法律的理论与实务》（1991）均采取综合研究的方法，从国际法和国内法角度，分别对跨国公司和中外合资企业的法律问题作了系统探讨。陈安教授主编的《"解决投资争端国际中心"述评》(1989)和《MIGA 与中国：多边投资担保机构述评》(1995)对现有两个多边投资法律体制进行了较深入的剖析，对我国是否接受和如何利用该体制提出了建设性意见。

在国际贸易法领域，冯大同教授主编的《国际货物买卖法》(1993)和张玉卿编著的《联合国国际货物销售合同公约释义》(1988)是研究《联合国国际货物销售合同公约》的重要著作。研究关税及贸易总协定和世界贸易组织的主要著作有赵维田教授的《最惠国与多边贸易体制》(1996)、曹建明教授主编的《关税与贸易总协定》(1994)、张克文博士的《关税与贸易总协定及其最惠国待遇制度》(1992)、冯予蜀博士的《国际贸易体制下的关贸总协定与中国》(1992)、曾令良教授的《世界贸易组织法》(1996)和汪尧田、周汉民教授主编的《世界贸易组织总论》(1995)等。

与此同时，我国国际经济法学者还在国内外重要学术刊物上发表了一系列高水平的学术论文，涉及国际经济法的基本理论和国际经济法各分支的重要专题。1998年，中国国际经济法学界的学术著述汇辑《国际经济法论丛》第 1 卷出版，反应热烈。预期每年推出两卷（每卷约 42—45 万字），此举将进一步推动国际经济法的专题研究。

此外，中国国际经济法学界还积极承担国家有关机构委托研究的项目或咨询项目。例如，厦门大学法学院、北京大学法学院、中国社会科学院法学研究所和对外经贸大学等有关专家分别受对外经贸部委托，先后就"中国加入 1965 年《华盛顿公约》的利弊得失""'九七'后中国参加的国际经济条约在香港的适用问题""外资国民待遇问题"和"'解决投资争端国际中心'案例研究""外贸代理制""知识产权保护"和"公司法适用于三资企业"等专题提出咨询报告或研究报告，供有关机构决策参考。

4. 生机勃勃的学术团体活动

自 1984 年庐山国际经济法讲习班以来，中国国际经济法学术团体主持开展了一系列卓有成效的学术交流活动，促进了中国国际经济法研究和教学的发展。

1987 年，在国家教委的领导和大力支持下，全国国际经济法教学研讨会在武汉大学召开，来自全国 30 多所大学和科研机构的 40 多名专家学者参加。会议决定加强中国国际经济法研究会（以下简称"研究会"）的机构建设。姚梅镇教授继续担任会长。研究会秘书处设于武汉大学。1989 年和 1992 年，研究会先后在大连和厦门举办中国国际经济法学术研讨会。1993 年，研究会在珠海召开中国国际经济法学术研讨会暨会员代表大会，选举产生第二届理事会，并一致通过决议将研究会更名为中国国际经济法学会（以下简称"学会"）。陈安教授当选为会长。学会秘书处设于厦门大学。1994—1998年,学会分别在重庆、上海、昆明、杭州和深圳召开学术研讨会。1997年,在杭州召开的中国国际经济法学术研讨会暨会员代表大会上,选举产生了第三届理事会,陈安教授连任会长。

中国国际经济法学术团体的建立和健全,对促进全国国际经济法的教学和研究起了重要的作用。目前,在一年一届的中国国际经济法学术研讨会上,对外经贸部条法司领导均应邀莅临报告有关中国参与国际经济交往的最新发展动态和面临的重要法律问题。来自全国高校和科研机构的国际经济法教学和研究人员以及来自涉外经贸部门管理和实务工作者聚集一堂,相互交流国际经济法学术研究成果和讨论我国对外经济交往中面临的重要法律问题。理论紧密联系实际,成为学会学术活动的重要特色。

三、关于国际经济法的分歧与共识

（一）关于国际经济法的分歧

概括而言,各国法学界关于国际经济法的主要学说有以下三种:

1. 狭义说

国际经济法的早期定义是狭义的。

狭义说认为,国际经济法是国际法的分支,是调整国际法主体之间（即国家之间、国际组织之间和国家与国际组织之间）经济关系的法律规范。传统的国际法,主要调整国际法主体之间的政治关系,忽视它们相互之间的经济关系。随着国际经济交往活动的发展,在国际法的传统体系内,逐渐形成了专门调整国际经济关系的新分支。国际经济法由于主体、调整对象和渊源与国际法完全一致,因此属于国际法的范畴。

狭义说的代表人物有英国的施瓦曾伯格、詹克斯,法国的卡罗、朱亚尔、弗洛里,德国的艾尔勒,日本的金泽良雄等。

在中国,一些国际法学者接受狭义说。他们认为,从国际经济法的产生和发展以及法律规范功能统一性作为法律体系的要素来说,国际经济法是国际公法的一个部门。国际经济法是调整国家之间在经济领域关系的公法体系,其法律规则是通过国家之间协议制定的。具体地说,国际经济法是指调整国际投资、国际货物、服务和资本交易、国际技术转让以及与这些活动密切相关的国际货币、金融和财政制度的国际公法、原则和规则的总合。[1]因此,国际经济法和国际法的原则、规则和规章、制

---

[1] 参见史久镛:《论国际经济法的概念和范围》,载中国国际法学会主办:《中国国际法年刊》(1983),中国对外翻译出版公司1983年版,第359—372页。

度是完全一致的；国际经济法和国际法的主体、渊源是一致的。[1]

关于国际经济法的调整对象，狭义说主张不一。一些学者将国际经济法定义为调整任何包含"显著经济因素"的事项。例如，鲁特（P. Reuter）认为，"国际经济法是有关资源的开发、消费和流通的法律问题的国际法分支"。美国法律协会认为："广义上，国际经济关系法包括调整跨越国境或其他包括一国以上的经济交易的所有国际法和国际协议。此类交易如商品、资金、人员、无形财产、技术、船舶或飞机运输的交易。"类似的定义是，国际经济法指"有关调整跨国经济关系的国际公法（直接或间接基于条约）的所有规范"。[2]帕里（Parry）和格兰特（Grant）编纂的《国际法百科词典》对国际经济法作了更为概括的定义，即："关于跨国经济关系的国际公法（直接或间接基于条约）的全部规范"。[3]在另一些定义中，国际经济法调整的对象极为广泛，包含了国际法其他分支的事项，如"深海自由"和"大陆架"。值得注意的是，当前狭义的国际经济法概念，明示或默示地包含了调整国际经济组织、经济一体化和有关发展的法律。

关于跨国私法规范是否一概排除于国际经济法之外，在狭义说中有不同的见解。例如，根据《美国对外关系法第三次诠释》，调整国际经济关系的法律包括"调整跨越国境或涉及一国以上的经济交往的所有国际法和国际协定"。对此有两种理解：

一种观点认为，跨国私法调整由国内法院审理的私人之间的双边商务，未涉及国际行为者（international actors）。即使跨国商法的有关规则由国际条约进行国际协调，仍然保留私法性质，一般由国内法院适用。因此，有关调整商品销售、供应和运输等的各国商法以及调整此类交往的冲突法应予排除；任何对商人法（*lex mercatoria*）或商人遵循的习惯规则或有关实体规则的国际协调（如《联合国国际货物买卖合同公约》），或者对冲突法规范的国际协调（如《承认和执行外国仲裁裁决的公约》）也应排除。

另一种观点是，调整国际经济关系的法律应包括跨国商法，美国国际贸易法律课程经常采用这种观点。在美国国际法协会国际经济法专门小组搜集的基本文件

---

〔1〕　参见汪瑄：《略论国际经济法》，载中国国际法学会主办：《中国国际法年刊》(1983)，中国对外翻译出版公司 1983 年版，第 393—397 页。

〔2〕　See F. V. Garcia-Amador, *The Emerging International Law of Development: A New Dimension of International Economic Law*, Oceana Publications, 1990, p. 21.

〔3〕　See Hazel Fox, *International Economic Law and Developing States: Some Aspects*, British Institute of International and Comparative Law, 1988, p. 1.

资料库中,也包括了调整私人商务交往、国际诉讼和国际仲裁的文件。[1]

狭义说的显著特征是坚持传统法律部门分类,维护传统国际法体系,把调整国际经济关系的法律规范限于国际法规范。施瓦曾伯格曾指出,如果将国际经济法视为调整国际经济关系的国际法和国内法规范的总和,其代价是很大的,"国际经济法将面临失去其法律统一性(legal unity)的严重危险"。[2]

2. 广义说

广义说认为,国际经济法是调整国家之间、国际组织之间、国家与国际组织之间、国家与他国私人之间、国际组织与私人之间以及不同国籍私人之间经济关系的法律规范。由于国际经济法的主体包括国家、国际组织和私人,其渊源包括国际法和国内法规范,因此已经突破传统国际法体系,成为一个独立的法律部门和法律学科。

广义说的代表人物有德国的哈姆斯、彼特斯曼,美国的杰克逊、洛文费尔德,日本的樱井雅夫、小原喜雄等。

在中国,多数国际经济法学者接受广义说。他们认为,国际经济法是国际社会中关于经济关系和经济组织的法律规范的总和,即关于国际经济交往中商品生产、流通、结算、信贷、投资、税收等关系及国际经济组织等法规和法制的总称,是一个包括国际法规范与国内法规范在内的新兴的独立的法学部门。[3]国际经济法的规范既表现在各国国内法中调整涉外经济关系的法律规范,也表现为国家缔结或参与的调整国际经济关系的双边或多边条约等国际法规范。

广义说对狭义说的主要批评是:首先,在多数国际经济关系涉及私人、国家和国际组织的时代,狭义的国际经济法定义是人为的限制。当前,国家深深介入私人经济活动,私人可能行使高于国家行为的重要权力,而国际组织的作用可能居于国家与私人之间。[4]在此错综复杂的国际经济关系中,狭义的国际经济法所能发挥的作用相当有限。其次,尽管各国政府在私人商务企业的直接参与越来越多(从能源生产到运输和旅游),私人仍然是国际经济关系的最主要当事人,调整私人经济交往的规则如被排除在国际经济法的范围之外,是不符合逻辑的。在现代国际经济交往

---

[1] See Hazel Fox, *International Economic Law and Developing States: An Introduction*, International Economic Law Series Vol. Ⅱ, British Institute of International and Comparative Law, 1992, pp. 20-21.

[2] See F. V. Garcia-Amador, *The Emerging International Law of Development: A New Dimension of International Economic Law*, Oceana Publications, 1990, p. 24.

[3] 参见姚梅镇:《国际经济法是一个独立的法学部门》,载中国国际法学会主办:《中国国际法年刊》(1983),中国对外翻译出版公司1983年版,第374页。

[4] See Stephen Zamora, Is There Customary International Economic Law? *German Yearbook of International Law*, Vol. 32, 1989, pp. 13-14.

中,公法问题经常混合私法问题。如果将两者分别考虑,是徒劳无益的。广义国际经济法虽然不符合传统法律部门分类,但适应了 20 世纪后半期国际经济关系现实的需要。[1]

有的学者进一步区分法律部门与法学部门,认为,由于国内经济关系和国际经济关系性质不同,两者不能简单合并成一个独立的社会关系,从而成为某一法律部门的调整对象,国际经济法作为独立的法律部门是不能成立的。然而,由于国际上存在大量的反映国内法和国际法中各种经济法律规范及其相互之间关系的"跨国经济法律问题",以这些法律问题为研究对象,可形成一个独立的综合性的国际经济法学学科。[2]

3. 混合法说

与广义说相同,混合法说也主张,由于国际经济关系的不可分割性,调整国际经济关系的国际法和国内法也必然是相互联系的。正如特玛(P. Verloren van Themaat)所指出的:"国际经济法应符合各国经济政策和各国经济法律基础的需要"。然而,混合法说认为,法律部门是"单一制规范的总和",鉴于国际法律制度与国内法律制度在其性质、创立模式、主体、客体和调整方法上均不相同,将两者合并为"混合的"法律部门在方法论上是不正确的。更合适的表述应是"国际经济关系法律规则的综合体(the complex of legal regulation of international economic relations),即包含作为国际公法分支的国际经济法和有关的国内法。在此综合体中,不同法律性质的规定通过履行、连结、援引等程序相互联系。[3]

(二) 关于国际经济法的共识

如前所述,狭义说和广义说在国际经济法主体、调整对象以及法律渊源方面均存在重大分歧。值得注意的是,狭义说在其发展过程中,出现了某些与广义说相近的观点,表明两种学说已达成了一定程度的共识。

1. 关于国际经济法的主体

两种学说都认为,国际经济法主体包括国际法主体,即国家和国际组织。分歧在于,广义说认为国际经济法主体还应包括从事跨国经济活动的国内法主体,即法人和自然人等,而传统狭义说一般持否定态度。

---

〔1〕　See Stephen Zamora, Is There Customary International Economic Law? *German Yearbook of International Law*, Vol. 32, 1989, p. 15.

〔2〕　参见徐崇利:《国际经济法与国际经济法学》,载《厦门大学学报》(哲学社会科学版)1996 年第 2 期,第 90—96 页。

〔3〕　See Sergei A. Voitovich, *International Economic Organizations in the International Legal Process*, Martinus Nijhoff Publishers, 1995, p. 7.

鉴于私人（individuals，包括自然人和法人）特别是跨国公司在国际经济交往活动中的重要地位和作用，持狭义说的一些学者相继提出了在国际经济法研究中应重视私人的见解。

近年来，有的"狭义说"学者进一步明确主张，私人应成为国际经济法主体。奥地利霍亨威尔登（Ignaz Seidl Hohenveldern）教授的如下观点最具代表性：

（1）如果忽略跨国公司或政府与他国国民间的合同，就不能妥善处理面临的国际现实问题。鉴此，应遵循将国际法主体的种类扩大为包括私人的现代原则；

（2）在国际经济生活中，私人经常是跨国公司而不是自然人。两者在一定情况下，均可成为国际法权利和义务的直接享有和承担者；此外，非政府组织的一些活动在国际经济生活中也具有重要的意义；

（3）私人同样可从条约直接取得权利。条约如授权私人在其母国未介入的情况下，向国际性机构直接提出其权利请求，私人就成为国际法的积极主体。从国际经济法角度看，承认私人为国际法主体的最重要条约是《解决国家与他国国民间投资争端公约》（以下简称《华盛顿公约》）。[1]

应当指出，霍亨威尔登教授承认私人的国际经济法主体地位是以私人可具有国际法主体地位为前提的。而广义说学者主张私人是国际经济法的主体的依据是，国际经济法包含国际法和国内法规范，作为国内法主体的私人当然也是国际经济法的主体。显然，同样主张私人是国际经济法的主体，狭义说与广义说的立论根据大相径庭。

一般认为，法律关系的主体是法律关系中权利和义务的享有和承担者。特定法律制度的主体需要具备三个要素：（1）承担违反该法律制度而产生的责任；（2）享有从该法律制度取得的权利；（3）具有与该法律制度承认的其他法律人格者建立法律关系的能力。在任何法律制度框架内，各主体不必相同，也不必具有完全相同的性质和特征。[2]随着国际法的发展，当前国际法主体已不限于国家，国际组织的国际法主体地位已得到国际法学界和国际社会的普遍承认。然而，私人能否成为国际法主体，在国际法学界远未达成共识，即使少数持肯定态度者也承认，私人作为国际法主体，与主权国家在权利范围方面有重大的区别，私人一般只享有由国际条约授予

〔1〕 See Ignaz Seidl Hohenveldern，*International Economic Law*，2nd revised edition，Martinus Nijhoff Publishers，1992，pp. 2，11-13，101.

〔2〕 正如国际法院在"履行联合国职务中遭受损害之赔偿"案中指出："任何法律制度的主体在其性质或在其权利范围方面不必是同一的，而其性质取决于该社会的需要。" See P. R. Menon，The Legal Personality of International Organizations，*Sri Lanka Journal of International Law*，Vol. 4，1992，p. 93.

的程序性权利。[1] 国际经贸条约实践表明,私人并不能从条约直接取得权利,进而改变其法律地位。以《华盛顿公约》为例,该公约旨在为解决国家与他国国民间投资争端提供调解和仲裁的便利,从而促进国际投资活动的发展。私人要利用根据该公约成立的"解决投资争端国际中心"(以下简称"中心")的机制,首先要以其所属国加入该公约为前提,在这个意义上,私人显然未能从公约直接取得权利。此外,由于"中心"属国际性常设仲裁机构,其仲裁管辖本身未能改变当事人的法律地位。私人在其母国未介入的情况下成为"中心"的仲裁当事人,这种地位与其在其他国际性或国内常设仲裁机构仲裁的地位并无性质上的区别。1994 年《能源宪章条约》有关缔约国私人仲裁权利的规定亦然。[2]

2. 关于国际经济法的调整对象

两种学说都认为,国际经济法的调整对象是国际经济关系,但在国际经济关系的理解上存在分歧。广义说主张,国际经济关系应理解为国家之间、国际组织之间、不同国籍私人之间、国家与国际组织之间、国家与他国私人之间、国际组织与私人之间的经济关系。传统狭义说则认为,国际经济关系是指国家之间、国际组织之间、国家与国际组织之间的经济关系。

"狭义说"学者英国的施瓦曾伯格,法国的卡罗、朱亚尔、弗洛里(Verloren van Themaat)和奥地利的霍亨威尔登等都认为国际经济法是调整国际经济关系的国际法。[3]

所谓"国际经济关系"究何所指?上述 1948 年伦敦大学的"国际经济法"教学大纲似可作诠释。其所列举的具有"显著经济因素"的一些国际法专题,如待遇标准、海外财产的保护、国家契约、卡尔沃条款等,不仅涉及国家之间的经济关系,也不可避免地涉及国家或国际组织与私人之间或不同国籍私人之间的经济关系。

鉴于国际经济关系的复杂性,一些"狭义说"学者在严守传统法律部门分类,主张国际经济法限于调整国家或国际组织之间经济关系的同时,提出了新的法律部门概念。曼勒(F. A. Mann)和弗里德曼(Fridmann)提出了"万国商法"(commercial

---

〔1〕 在国际场合,私人的地位受到如下限制:(1) 私人只被授予程序性的权利,即向国际性机构提起诉讼的权利,旨在确定该被诉国是否违反有利于私人实体权利的条约规定;(2) 该有关实体权利只能由条约授予,或者,在少数情况下,由国际性决议授予;(3) 对该权利的另一限制是,事实上,有关条约的所有成员国并非都接受对私人负有责任的观点;(4) 私人国际地位的进一步弱点是授予私人起诉的程序与国内法的有关规定大相径庭。See P. K. Menon, The Legal Personality of Individuals, *Sri Lanka Journal of International Law*, Vol. 6, 1994, pp. 148-150.

〔2〕 根据《能源宪章条约》第 26 条,缔约一方私人投资者可将其与缔约另一方(东道国)之间的投资争端提交国际仲裁解决,无须后者同意。

〔3〕 See Hazel Fox, *International Economic Law and Developing States: An Introduction*, International Economic Law Series Vol. Ⅱ, British Institute of International and Comparative Law, 1992, pp. 12-13.

law of nations)的概念,认为该法不仅包括调整某些国家之间契约关系的原则,也包括调整某些国家与他国私人之间契约关系的原则。英国施米托夫(C. M. Schmith-off)教授认为,国际商务法(international business law)不同于作为国际法分支的国际经济法。前者调整私人在私法层次上的交往,主要包括:(1) 国际贸易法,其中,国际货物买卖法是最基本的部分;(2) 国际公司法,即调整跨国公司的法律。他还进一步指出国际商务法与国际经济法的重叠,具体表现在,首先,严格说来,创设区域性贸易集团的安排和避免双重税收协定属于国际经济法,但它们在很大程度上影响进口商或出口商,也是国际商务法的组成部分;其次,在国际商务活动中,国家与私法主体之间的合同并非罕见。例如,资源国授予外国私人石油或矿业特许权的协定,因其"混合"性质,属于"国际商务法和国际经济法"。[1]

另一些狭义说学者进一步提出了国际经济关系分为两个层次的理论。日本金泽良雄教授认为,国际经济法所适用的国际社会,可分为两个层次:第一层次是直接由主权国家和国际组织构成的。在这种意义上的国际社会中所适用的法律,就是国家之间、国际组织之间或国家与国际组织之间所签订的条约;国际社会的第二层次是由各国私人(自然人和法人)组成的。当各国私人跨越国境进行经济交往活动时,上述条约的有关条款一般通过相应的国内法规定而间接地适用于这些活动。其结论是,国际经济法是根据构成国际社会第一层次的国家或国际组织的合意所订立的各种经济条约的总和。同时,他也指出,国际经济法也间接调整构成国际社会第二层次的各国私人之间的跨国经济关系。[2]瓦特维奇(Sergei A. Voitovich)也认为,国际经济关系可分为:(1)国家或国际组织之间层次;(2)隶属不同国家的国民(自然人和法人)之间层次。国家之间层次处理经济政策的协调、原则的具体化和国际经济合作的机制。换言之,国家之间在经济领域的关系是一种比一般经济关系较为政治化的关系。与此同时,商品的生产和交换是在国民之间层次上进行。显然,作为整体的国际经济关系不能单独由国际经济法或国内经济法调整。在这个领域,国际法与国内法之间必然存在相互的密切关系。[3]

以上狭义说学者的各种观点虽然表述不同,实际上不同程度地承认了国际经济关系不仅包括国家或国际组织之间、国家与国际组织之间的经济关系,也包括了国

---

〔1〕 See F. V. Garcia-Amador, *The Emerging International Law of Development : A New Dimension of International Economic Law*, Oceana Publications, 1990, pp. 25-26;F. A. Mann, Reflections on a Commercial Law of Nations,*British Yearbook of International Law* Vol. 33, 1957, p. 20.

〔2〕 参见陈安主编:《国际经济法总论》,法律出版社 1991 年版,第 79—80 页。

〔3〕 See Sergei A. Voitovich, *International Economic Organizations in the International Legal Process*, Martinus Nijhoff Publishers, 1995, p. 4.

家或国际组织与私人之间、不同国籍私人之间的经济关系。更重要的是,有的学者还进一步指出国际经济关系的"混合"性质和国际经济关系"两个层次"的密切关系。这类观点表面上与广义说已相当接近,然而,仍未突破传统法律部门分类的局限,即仍然坚持国际经济法限于直接调整国际法主体之间的经济关系,而不同国籍私人之间的经济关系,则由新的法律部门或国内法规范调整。至于国家或国际组织与私人之间的经济关系,则尚无明确的归属。至此,广义说与狭义说分歧的焦点在于国际经济关系是否可分割为国家或国际组织之间经济关系和不同国籍私人之间经济关系两个层次,分别由两个不同的法律部门调整?

国际经济现实表明,国家或国际组织之间的经济关系与不同国籍私人之间的经济关系往往相互交错,密不可分。一项国家之间的经济谈判,不仅涉及当事国政府之间的经济关系,更多是涉及当事国一方与当事国对方私人之间或当事国双方私人之间经济关系问题。一项国际私人投资或贸易活动,必然涉及当事人所属国之间的经济关系。反映在法律规范上,国际经济条约、例如双边投资保护协定,在很大程度上是"第三人受益安排",涉及缔约国双方私人的权利义务;各国涉外经济法律甚至涉外经济合同也往往和有关国际经济条约相联系;至于国家与他国私人之间的合同,更是常常涉及国际法和国内法规范。显然,由国家或国际组织之间的经济关系、国家或国际组织与私人之间的经济关系以及不同国籍私人之间的经济关系构成的国际经济关系是一个不可分割的统一体。相应地,调整这种国际经济关系的国际经济法,也应该是包含国际法和国内法规范的独立法律部门。

3. 关于国际经济法的渊源

两种学说都认为,国际经济法的渊源包括国际法规范。分歧是,广义说认为,国际经济法的渊源还包括调整国际法主体与国内法主体之间或国内法主体之间跨国经济关系的国内法规范。传统狭义说对此则予以否认。

当前,一些狭义说学者有关国际经济法渊源的论述,并不限于传统的国际法渊源。[1]如霍亨威尔登教授主张,应遵循现代国际法原则,考虑《国际法院规约》第38条第1款表述的国际法渊源以外的其他渊源,或者,至少是重新解释这些渊源。他认为,国际经济法渊源包括:(1)国际法的传统渊源,即国际公约、简式协定(agreements in simplified form)、习惯国际法、法律的一般原则等;(2)联合国大会决议;(3)国际经济软法,如国际组织的宣言、行动守则等;(4)国家与他国投资者之间的

---

[1]　一般认为,《国际法院规约》第38条第1款列举了传统的国际法渊源,即:(1)不论普通或特别国际协约,确立诉讼当事国明白承认之规条者;(2)国际习惯,作为通例之证明而经接受为法律者;(3)一般法律原则为文明各国所承认者;(4)在第59条规定之下,司法判例及各国权威最高之公法学家学说,作为确定法律原则之补助资料者。

协议。[1]狭义说学者虽然普遍认为，国际组织特别是联合国大会的决议是国际经济法的渊源，但对其法律效力评价不一。英国学者福克斯指出，国际组织的决议未被《国际法院规约》第38条第1款明确列为国际法渊源。此类决议有些可从其成员国之间的协议产生法律效力，有些可被视为国家实践的证据并由此成为国际习惯的证据，或者本身构成国际习惯法。[2]霍亨威尔登教授认为，联合国大会决议不是国际法的新渊源，但这不意味着此类决议在任何情况下仅具有建议性质。决议内容如符合传统国际法规则，可具有与习惯国际法同样的拘束力。因此，决议内容应是确立"法律确信"（opinio juris）的证据，而且，有关国家应以其实践表明将决议内容视为习惯国际法的一部分。[3]新加坡学者索纳那扎（M. Sornarajah）反对将联合国大会决议称为"软法"或"拟议法"（lex ferenda）。他主张，联合国大会有关经济主权的决议是主张在国际法中业已确立的领土主权原则，应视为与既存法律一致的有效原则。[4]

以上各说尽管都试图将部分符合一定条件、具有法律拘束力的联合国大会决议纳入传统国际法渊源中的国际习惯范畴，但同时也承认作为整体的联合国大会决议是有别于传统国际法渊源的国际经济法渊源。此外，诸如国家与他国投资者之间的协议，更是传统国际法渊源所无法涵盖的。

应当指出，霍亨威尔登教授虽然提出国家与他国投资者之间的协议也属国际经济法渊源，但与"广义说"学者的一般主张迥然有别：前者是将此类协议视为特殊的国际条约，即作为国际法"不完全主体"（a partial subject）的他国投资者与国家签订的条约；[5]而后者则一般主张此类协议属国内法规范。

综上所述，关于国际经济法概念的两种学说，在仍存在重大分歧的情况下，已达成的重要共识有：（1）私人在国际经济活动中具有重要地位，在国际经济法研究中应重视研究私人特别是跨国公司的经济活动；（2）国际经济法直接或间接调整对象不仅应包括国家或国际组织之间的经济关系，也应包括不同国籍私人之间的经济关系，两类关系密切联系；（3）国际经济法渊源包括国际组织规范性文件，特别是联合国大会决议。

---

[1] See Ignaz Seidl Hohenveldern，*International Economic Law*，2nd revised edition，Martinus Nijhoff Publishers，1992，p. 2.

[2] See Hazel Fox，*International Economic Law and Developing States：An Introduction*，International Economic Law Series Vol. Ⅱ，British Institute of International and Comparative Law，1992，p. 20.

[3] See Ignaz Seidl Hohenveldern，*International Economic Law*，2nd revised edition，Martinus Nijhoff Publishers，1992，p. 42.

[4] See M. Sornarajah，*International Law on Foreign Investment*，Grotius Publishers，1994，pp. 74-77.

[5] See Ignaz Seidl Hohenveldern，*International Economic Law*，2nd revised edition，Martinus Nijhoff Publishers，1992，p. 48.

在此基础上,两种学说能否达成进一步的共识,除了立足国际经济客观现实这一必要前提外,在很大程度上取决于如何对待国际法和国内法两大法律部门的传统分类。广义说已突破了这种传统分类的界限。狭义说以发展的观点,也已对传统国际法本身提出了挑战,即在一定程度上力图淡化国际法与国内法在主体、调整对象以及法律渊源方面的严格区分,客观上也造成了对国际法和国内法传统分类的冲击。这种倾向也许预示着两种学说"分久必合"的前景。

四、国际经济法是独立的法律部门

笔者以为,基于如下理由,似可主张国际经济法是独立的法律部门:

（一）国际经济法作为独立的法律部门是国际经济关系发展的客观反映

国际经济法与各国经济法一样,是资本主义发展到垄断阶段的时代产物。

从资本主义各国国内范围看,当自由资本主义进入垄断阶段,资本主义本身固有的矛盾已达到不可调和、不可克服的程度,随着生产和资本的高度集中,资本主义的市场自动调节作用已无济于事,原来以所谓"私法自治"原则为基础的民商法体系已不能作为调整经济的唯一手段。在此情况下,资本主义各国相继通过经济管制立法,对本国经济活动、包括涉外经济活动直接进行管制。经济法逐渐形成为独立于民商法体系的法律体系。

从国际范围看,随着资本主义世界市场的形成和资本输出的增加,19世纪末,各国垄断资本从控制本国市场,发展为跨越国境组成国际垄断同盟,在经济上瓜分世界,共享垄断利润。各垄断同盟在争夺原料产地、销售市场、投资场所等激烈斗争中,为达成均势,相互之间签订各种世界性的协议。此类协议虽属私人契约,实质上是国家政权在国际范围内同垄断资本结合,对国际经济活动进行干预的结果。各国经济法的产生和发展,进一步加深了资本主义各国之间的矛盾和冲突。列强为争夺世界市场,不惜刀兵相见,诉诸战争。显然,资本主义世界高度发展的矛盾,已不能由各国单独解决,需要谋求国际调整。因此,国际多边、双边经济条约,无论从数量或调整范围看,进入了一个空前发展的阶段。作为独立法律部门的国际经济法的产生,正是反映了国际经济关系这一发展阶段的客观现实。[1]

（二）国际经济法成为独立的法律部门是国际经济关系内在统一性的需要

一般认为,国际经济法的客体是国际经济关系。然而,从法律的角度观察,这种

---

〔1〕 参见姚梅镇:《国际经济法是一个独立的法学部门》,载中国国际法学会主办:《中国国际法年刊》(1983),中国对外翻译出版公司1983年版,第378—380页。

关系就显得复杂了。

"国际"指出了该关系所涵盖的范围和参与主体的特征，即国际经济关系包含了国家之间、国际组织之间、国家与国际组织之间、国家与他国私人之间、国际组织与私人之间以及不同国籍私人之间的经济关系。上述各种关系，特别是国家之间的经济关系同不同国籍私人之间的经济关系是相互影响，密切联系的。从现实情况看，大量国际经济关系都是法人和其他经济实体进行跨国经济活动的产物。归根结底，调整此类国际经济关系的法律规范所调整的客体都是同一的，即以法人为主的各种经济实体的跨国经济活动。例如，世界贸易组织关注各国政府之间的关税谈判，但最终享受减让关税实惠的，是世界贸易组织成员方的私人。国际经济关系的这种内在统一性，决定了各种调整国际经济关系的法律规范的内在统一性。它们统一于共同的主体、客体和为国际市场服务的目标。[1]

"经济"则反映了客体的实际内容和性质，国际经济关系具有其客观的基础，即各国生产一定种类的产品并参与国际交换。国际经济关系包括贸易、投资、货币与金融、税收、交通运输、通信等大量事务。国际经济是一个有机的统一体，各种调整国际经济关系的法律都是使国际经济成为统一体的纽带。

国际经济关系的内在统一性决定了调整它的法律规范的多重性。以一项国际投资活动为例，甲国 A 公司在向本国海外投资保证机构投保后，在同甲国签有双边投资条约的乙国与当地 B 公司举办合营企业。由于这项投资活动，在甲国与 A 公司之间产生海外投资政治风险的保险关系，在 A 公司与 B 公司之间产生合营伙伴关系，在乙国与 A 公司之间产生投资管理关系，在甲国、乙国之间产生基于双边投资条约的关系。上述关系的总和构成了该投资项目的内在统一的国际投资关系。调整该国际投资关系必然涉及的基本法律规范包括：

（1）甲国海外投资保证机构与 A 公司之间的保险合同；

（2）A 公司与 B 公司之间的合营合同；

（3）乙国外商投资法律、外汇管理法律和涉外税法等；

（4）甲国与乙国之间的双边投资条约。

从传统法律部门划分，第（1）（2）项分属甲、乙两国国内法的私法规范，第（3）项属乙国国内法的公法规范，第（4）项属国际法规范，舍弃上述任何一项规范，都不能完整、有效地调整这项国际投资关系。由此可见，包括国内法规范和国际法规范的国际经济法，绝非人为的糅合，而是国际经济关系中跨国活动相互联系的统一的经

---

〔1〕　参见南开大学国际经济法研究所：《论国际经济法与国际公法、国际私法的关系》，第 5 页，1996 年中国国际法学会国际经济法学术研讨会论文。

济现象在法律上的客观反映。无论是国内法规范或国际法规范，只反映这种统一的经济现象的一个侧面，而只有采取综合国内法规范和国际法规范的调整方法，才能全面、有效地解决实际问题。显然，调整国际经济关系的国内法规范和国际法规范是一种有机的组合，将这两者视为统一、独立的法律部门的有机组成部分，正是反映了客观现实的需要。

（三）应以发展的观点看法律部门的划分标准

所谓法律部门，一般是指对法律规范按其所调整的社会关系及与之相适应的调整方法的不同所作的一种分类。任何法律部门均有三个基本的组成部分：（1）法律主体；（2）作为法律客体的特定社会关系；（3）法律主体适用的法律方式的混合（即法律调整机制）。这三部分通过立法和执法两个程序而相互联系。

关于法律部门的划分标准，一般认为主要是法律的调整对象和调整方法。调整对象是指法律所调整的社会关系，即一定的社会主体所活动的特定领域。法律的调整方法，指调整某一领域的法律所特有的实体规则、救济方法和救济程序。

以上述标准衡量，特别是以发展的眼光看待上述标准，国际经济法应属独立的法律部门。

首先，如前所述，国际经济法的调整对象是内在统一的国际经济关系，符合调整特定社会关系的标准。

法律部门的划分不是以人们的主观意志为转移，而主要是由需要调整的社会关系的多样性的客观存在决定的。由于社会关系处于不断发展变化之中，法律部门的划分不是一成不变的。随着新的社会关系和相应的法律规范的产生和发展，必然会出现新的法律部门。[1]

传统法学以法律的调整对象、即特定社会关系为首要标准，特别是考虑到法律主体的不同，首先将法律规范划分为国际法和国内法两大部门，这在当时历史条件下是科学的。在现代条件下，由于国家已深深介入和参与传统上专属于私人的经济领域，这种同一社会关系中的主体多元化使国际法与国内法两大部门已不可能截然分开。[2]以调整对象为标准划分出的法律部门，常常涉及国际法和国内法两种规范，这种情况特别明显地反映在传统的国际私法的新发展和新兴的国际经济法的渊源问题上。在此情况下，如果严守传统的两大法律部门分类，把同一社会关系分解，分别以国际法和国内法规范调整，表面上维护了传统的两大法律部门分类的权威，但

---

〔1〕　在科学发展史上，由于科学技术的发展，对自然现象的研究不断出现新的突破。由多种学科交叉而发展成为独立的新学科，称为边缘学科、交叉学科或综合学科者，屡见不鲜，例如物理化学、生物化学、生物物理等。

〔2〕　主体的多元化在许多法律部门存在，如国内经济法、国际私法的主体都包括了国家和私人。

由于分解了同一社会关系，实际上已破坏或否定了传统的法律部门分类的首要标准。

主张国际经济法是独立的法律部门，正是坚持了以特定社会关系为划分法律部门的首要标准。其对传统标准的突破在于，在国际经济关系深入发展，传统的国际法和国内法规范均无法单独胜任调整功能的情况下，不再拘泥于国际法和国内法两大法律部门的严格界限，主张国际经济法是调整统一的国际经济关系的，包含国际法和国内法规范的综合性的独立法律部门。

值得注意的是，中国学者主张的广义国际经济法只是在研究方法上借鉴美国的"跨国法"学派的理论，两者的重要区别是，后者力图建立所谓独立于国内法和国际法规范之外的"第三法律体系"，这恰恰是前者所坚决反对的。必须注意到，中国主张广义国际经济法的学者虽然称国际经济法是调整国际经济关系的国际法和国内法规范的总称，但无意否定传统国际法与国内法两大法律部门的划分。国际法仍然是调整国家、国际组织之间关系的法律，国内法也仍然是调整一国国内社会关系的法律。把它们作为国际经济法规范的组成部分，只是根据客观实际需要，运用不同功能、不同层次的法律规范，相互配合和补充，来达到调整统一的国际经济关系的目的。在这个意义上，中国学者的上述主张更类似于国外的混合法说。应当进一步明确，国际经济法不同层次规范的法律效力各不相同，国际社会普遍接受的国际法规范具有普遍的效力，区域性的国际法规范主要对该区域国家发生效力，双边国际法规范只对缔约双方有效，而国内法规范则仅适用于该特定国家。

其次，国际经济法的调整方法由于法律主体的多元性、调整对象的复杂性而难以符合传统的"特有的实体规则、救济方法和救济程序"的标准。然而，从发展的观点看，似可认为，由于国际经济关系包含了国际法主体之间、国内法主体之间以及国际法主体与国内法主体之间跨越国境的经济关系，与此相适应，宏观上，国际经济法特有的实体规则和调整方法是国际法与国内法规范的密切结合、相互为用；其特有的救济方法和救济程序是非诉讼的争端解决方式，如调解、仲裁等，取代诉讼方式的优先地位。

再次，调整国际经济关系的相辅相成的法律渊源本身表明存在一个独立的法律部门。[1] 在这些法律渊源中，国际法与国内法规范密切联系，相互补充。当前，调整国际经济关系的法律规范是如此规模庞大，国际经济法已分成许多分支，如国际贸易法、国际投资法、国际货币金融法、国际税法、国际经济组织法等。传统的国际法

---

〔1〕 See Janusz Gilas, Problems of Methodology in International Economic Law, *Polish Yearbook of International Law*, Vol. 13, 1984, pp. 81-82.

体系以调整国家之间的政治关系为主要内容,如包容所有调整国际经济关系的国际法规范,将在很大程度上削弱和冲淡该法律部门和法学部门的主题特色,有尾大不掉之嫌,实际上也不利于该法律部门和法学部门的发展。

最后,应当指出,法律部门的划分不可能是"一刀切"。法律部门或法学部门之间的相互交叉和相互渗透是正常的。这种交叉和渗透以及对法律部门或法学部门划分的分歧并不妨碍对具体法律问题的研究。对同一问题的多角度研究有利于研究的深化。例如,在当前对国际经济法的含义尚未达成共识的情况下,对世界贸易组织的研究,国际法学者着重从国家主权的角度,国际经济法学者从组织机构和成员国的权利义务的角度进行研究;对国际海底资源开发问题,国际法学者主要研究相关的海洋法问题,国际经济法学者则侧重研究有关资源开发的契约性安排。两者并行不悖,相得益彰。

五、促进中国国际经济法学进一步发展

中国国际经济法学虽然已走过了二十年历程,但从历史的观点看,尚处于艰苦创业的阶段。无论是从学科建设本身,还是从改革开放的现实需要看,中国国际经济法学者任重而道远,为争取中国国际经济法学的更大发展,尤其需要从以下三个方面努力:

(一)加强中国国际经济法学基本理论的研究

由于亟待解决的国际经济法实际问题林林总总,中国国际经济法学者在一定程度上忽略了对国际经济法学基本理论的继续研究。在 1996 年中国国际法学会年会上,重新提出了国际经济法学的基本理论问题,特别是国际经济法的学科体系问题,引起了热烈的讨论。这从一个侧面反映了深入进行国际经济法学理论研究的重要性。基本理论的研究是学科发展的前提和基础。作为新兴的学科,中国国际经济法学的基本理论应予以持续的关注和研究,经过长期的努力和积累,才能不断发展和日臻成熟。

冷战结束以来,国际政治经济形势发生了深刻的变化。少数西方大国近年来在理论上鼓吹"人权高于主权"等谬论,在实践中粗暴干涉他国内政,甚至大动干戈,严重践踏了国家主权原则。在经济领域,由于发达国家的优势地位,体现和维护发达国家利益的国际经济旧秩序不仅稳固维持,而且不断发展。国家主权原则和建立国际经济新秩序的事业面临严峻的挑战。鉴于强调建立国际经济新秩序是有中国特色的国际经济法学的重要标志,在中国国际经济法学基本理论研究中,国际经济法

的基本原则和国际经济新秩序理论研究也是重要的课题。

（二）深入进行国际经济法专题研究

在当前国际经济关系迅速发展的情况下，调整国际经济关系的国际法规范和国内法规范不断发展和加强，国家之间、不同国籍私人之间和一国与他国私人之间等不同层面的国际经济合作新形式不断涌现。从理论的角度考虑，只有深入进行国际经济法专题研究，才能丰富国际经济法学各分支的内容，从而进一步确立中国国际经济法的学科体系。从务实的角度考虑，高质量的国际经济法专题研究成果将为我国国际经济条约实践和涉外经济立法提供理论依据和决策参考意见。

在今后一段时期内，中国国际经济法学者需要特别关注和加强研究的国际经济法专题似可大致归纳为如下五个方面：

（1）世界性国际经济组织的法律体制。一些世界性国际经济组织，如国际货币基金组织（IMF）、国际复兴开发银行（IBRD）、解决投资争端国际中心（ICSID）、多边投资担保机构（MIGA）和世界贸易组织（WTO）的法律体制在调整国际经济关系中起了重要的作用，中国作为这些组织的成员或潜在参与者，对这些组织的法律体制及其发展应有全面、深入、持续的跟踪研究。

（2）区域性国际经济组织的法律体制。区域性国际经济组织近年来有了重大的发展，《北美自由贸易区协定》（NAFTA）开了南北国家组成区域性国际经济组织的先河，"欧洲联盟"（EU）的发展超越了区域性经济一体化组织的范畴，"亚太经合组织"（APEC）则创设了区域性经济合作的新模式。中国作为这些组织的经济合作伙伴或成员，有必要深入研究这些组织的法律体制及其对外关系。经合组织（OECD）成员国自1995年5月开始正式谈判的《多边投资协定》（MAI）（草案）是国际投资法的新发展，也需要认真研究和密切注视其发展动向。

（3）中外双边经济条约。中国近十多年来，与外国签订了大量的双边经济条约，主要是双边投资条约和双边税收条约。为了今后能更有效地通过中外双边经济条约维护经济主权和促进中外经济合作，这些条约的内容、依据和利弊得失值得探讨和总结。

（4）涉外经济立法。自1993年以来，中国处于向社会主义市场经济体制过渡的历史时期，随着统一民商法的迅速发展，原有的许多涉外经济法律需要修改和更新，原有的涉外经济法律体制亟须重构，以适应社会主义市场经济体制的需要。应从建立社会主义法治国家的目标出发，借鉴外国的立法经验，就健全和完善我国的涉外经济立法，特别是有关投资、贸易、融资、税收等的监管法律制度进行深入的研究，提出建设性的立法建议。

（5）国际经贸惯例或法律实务。不同国籍私人之间的经济交往是国际经济关系最重要的表现形式，也衍生了一系列法律问题。对国际经贸惯例或法律实务，特别是新的国际经济合作形式，如"建造—经营—转让"（BOT）、外资"并购"（M&A）、"电子数据交换"（EDI）合同等的法律实务，需要进行深入的专题研究。

（三）坚持和发展中国国际经济法学的研究方法

中国属于发展中的社会主义国家，中国国际经济法的研究服务于建立国际经济新秩序和建立社会主义市场经济体制的目标，这决定了中国国际经济法学界在吸收西方国家有关研究成果的同时，应有符合本国国情和目标的研究方法。从中国国际经济法学发展的经验看，今后应继续坚持和发展的研究方法主要是：

（1）立足本国实际的方法。从各国国际经济法的研究现状看，各国学者都是从本国实际出发，研究本国政府和私人在对外经济交往活动中所涉及的国际法和国内法问题。如前所述，中国国际经济法学应改革开放之运而生，也只有紧密联系改革开放的实际才能获得更大的发展。因此，中国国际经济法的研究，应以中国已经参加或准备参加的国际经济条约、中国涉外经济立法与涉外经贸合同实务为重点，为中国的国际经济条约实践、涉外经济立法和涉外经贸合同实务提供科学的理论基础，以维护国家的利益和中外当事人的合法利益，促进中国的改革开放事业进一步发展。

（2）历史和现实结合的方法。国际经济法是历史发展到一定阶段的产物，并随历史的发展而发展。在研究国际经济法的理论问题时，特别应该注重以历史的观点分析现实问题，不能割断历史，不能孤立地就事论事，无原则地迎合所谓"国际惯例"或"时代潮流"。例如，在研究经济主权原则时，应当回顾主权原则的历史发展，了解发展中国家获得和维护经济主权的艰难历程和重要意义，才能认清当前西方国家淡化、贬低甚至否定主权的理论主张的要害，较准确地理解和把握南北矛盾、新旧国际经济秩序斗争的实质和发展方向，较好地站在发展中国家的立场，坚持原则，为争取建立国际经济新秩序的伟大事业作出贡献。

（3）综合研究的方法。国际经济法是包含国际法规范和国内法规范的综合性、边缘性的法律部门。在研究特定国际经济法问题时，应采取综合研究的方法。具体说来，在研究国际经济条约问题时，应同时研究有关国家的国内法规范，以后者作为前者的基础；在研究涉外经济法律或合同实务问题时，也不能忽略有关的国际法规范，以后者作为前者的背景。这样，以问题为中心，不受传统法律部门划分的束缚，才能对研究对象有一个全面、整体的了解和认识，避免顾此失彼，失之偏颇。

（4）比较研究的方法。取决于国际经济关系的复杂性和相互联系的性质，比较研究的方法对国际经济法的研究十分重要。例如，在双边经济条约实践的研究中，比较分析同类双边经济条约的有关规定，可了解该领域普遍的或不同的国家实践及其发展趋向，由此判断是否形成习惯国际经济法，以便根据本国的实际情况采取符合本国利益的立场和原则。在涉外经济法律的研究中，比较分析不同国家的有关法制，有助于借鉴国外先进的立法经验，进一步健全和完善本国的涉外经济法制。此外，对本国和外国涉外经济法的比较研究，可为当事人进行国际经济交往活动的合同实务，特别是在法律选择方面提供必要的指导。

（5）法律与经济相结合的方法。国际经济法是以国际经济关系为调整对象的，因此，国际经济法的研究应注意密切结合国际经济现象、国际经济关系的研究。如果就法论法，忽视决定国际经济法的发展变化的国际经济关系，就不可能深刻了解和掌握国际经济法的发展变化规律，其研究也无法深入和取得成效。

在强调"中国特色"的国际经济法学的同时，还应当明确，国际经济法学是世界性的，中国国际经济法学是世界性国际经济法学的一个重要组成部分。中国国际经济法学的发展和繁荣在一定程度上有赖于世界性国际经济法学的发展和繁荣，世界性国际经济法学的发展和繁荣也不能缺少中国国际经济法学的参与和奉献。因此，中国国际经济法学者理应继续借鉴和吸收外国的相关研究成果，积极主动地开展国际学术交流和合作，在国际学术论坛上，对国际经济法学的重要理论和实践问题提出中国学者的见解，表明中国的立场，为世界性国际经济法学的发展和繁荣作出应有的贡献。

第二节　国际经济法涵义再探
——由杨紫煊教授的"国际经济协调论"引发的思考*

国际经济法是新兴的法律部门和法学学科,许多基本理论问题见仁见智,亟待进一步求索、争鸣。北京大学杨紫煊教授在《法商研究》2000 年第 3 期发表的《论国际经济法基础理论的若干问题》(以下简称"杨文")中,以独创性的"国际经济协调论"对国际经济法的基础理论作了较全面的研讨,提出不少新见,发人深思。限于学力,本文主要针对文中的某些新观点提出个人初步的体会和商榷意见,请教杨教授并期望引起法学界的进一步讨论。

一、关于国际经济法的定义

如所周知,各国法学界关于国际经济法的主要学说有狭义说和广义说两种。狭义说认为,国际经济法是国际法的分支,是调整国际法主体之间(即国家之间、国际组织之间和国家与国际组织之间)经济关系的法律规范。传统的国际法主要调整国际法主体之间的政治关系,忽视它们相互之间的经济关系。随着国际经济交往活动的发展,在国际法的传统体系内,逐渐形成了专门调整国际经济关系的新分支。国际经济法由于主体、调整对象和渊源与国际法完全一致,因此属于国际法的范畴。广义说则认为,国际经济法是调整国家之间、国际组织之间、国家与国际组织之间、国家与他国私人之间、国际组织与私人之间以及不同国籍私人之间经济关系的法律规范。由于国际经济法的主体包括国家、国际组织和私人,其渊源包括国际法和国内法规范,因此已经突破传统国际法体系,成为一个独立的法律部门和法律学科。[1]

杨文对国际经济法所下的定义是:"国际经济法是调整在两个以上国家共同协调国际经济运行过程中发生的经济关系的法律规范的总称。简言之,国际经济法是调整国际经济协调关系的法律规范的总称。"[2]笔者以为,这里值得进一步思考和讨论的主要问题是:

第一,国际经济法定义是否不需要列明主体?

杨文特别指出,在国际经济法的定义中,不需要列举该法的主体。原因有三:一

---

*　原载陈安主编:《国际经济法论丛》第 5 卷,法律出版社 2002 年版。

[1]　关于国际经济法定义的"狭义说""广义说"以及"混合法说",参见曾华群:《国际经济法导论》,法律出版社1999 年版,第 22—36 页。

[2]　杨紫煊:《论国际经济法基础理论的若干问题》,载《法商研究》2000 年第 3 期,第 50 页。

是国际经济法与其他法律部门的根本区别不在于主体的不同,而在于它们各自调整的社会关系的特殊性;二是国际经济法各种主体难以列举完全;三是如列举国际经济法各种主体,会违反逻辑学关于定义简练的要求。[1]

　　一般认为,所谓法律部门,是指对法律规范按其所调整的社会关系及与之相适应的调整方法的不同所作的一种分类。任何法律部门均有三个基本的组成部分:一是法律主体;二是作为法律客体的特定社会关系;三是法律调整机制。这三部分通过立法和执法两个程序而相互联系。显然,在对特定法律部门下定义时,有必要列明法律主体。否则,该定义就缺少了首要的基本组成部分的描述,是不完整的、含糊的。实际上,狭义说对国际经济法主体的表述与国际法主体相同,即国家和国际组织;而广义说只是增加了私人(individuals,包括自然人和法人),因此是可以列举完全,并且符合定义简练的要求的。进而言之,"国际经济协调论"与狭义说的重要区别之一在于,前者指出,国际经济法主体为包括私人的"各种主体",在国际经济法定义中未表明这一区别,与后者殊难分辨。

　　第二,所谓"在两个以上国家共同协调国际经济运行过程中发生的经济关系"的涵义是什么?

　　笔者以为,杨文中所表述的"在两个以上国家共同协调国际经济运行过程中发生的经济关系",当是"国际经济协调论"的基础,其含义需要厘清。该表述比较抽象、艰深,杨文未作具体论证,就简称为"国际经济协调关系"。这种关系,究何所指?何谓"国际经济运行过程"? 两个以上国家如何"共同协调"? 均有必要作进一步阐释。如有可能,似可举例说明,理论联系实际,以求达到深入浅出的效果。

　　第三,国际经济法是否属于国际法体系?

　　杨文在国际经济法定义中采用"法律规范"这一用语,未涉及"国际法规范"和"国内法规范"问题,但在讨论国际经济法的地位时则明确指出,国际经济法是国际法体系中的一个独立的法的部门,而不是国际公法的一个部门。[2]

　　笔者以为,虽然杨文有关"国际经济法不是国际公法的一个部门"的结论与广义说一致,但两者论证的基础和方法是不同的。杨文对国际法、国际法体系和国际公法有其独特的见解,即"由两个以上国家制定或认可的法律规范的总称,就是国际法";"国际法体系是由多层次的、门类齐全的国际法部门组成的有机联系的统一整体";"国际公法主体所参加的法律关系是国际政治关系在法律上的反映"。[3] 应当

---

　　[1]　杨紫烜:《论国际经济法基础理论的若干问题》,载《法商研究》2000 年第 3 期,第 48—49 页。
　　[2]　同上文,第 56—57 页。
　　[3]　同上文,第 56—57、53 页。

指出,在国际上,国际法通常是专指国际公法的。[1] 我国国际法学界普遍接受的定义是,国际法是"部门法之一,即国际公法,旧称万国法,主要是国家之间的法律,即以国家之间关系为主要调整对象的有约束力的原则、规则和制度的总和。"[2]实际上,这一定义也是世界各国国际法学界的共识。虽然长期以来国际法调整的重心是国际政治关系,国际法从来未将其领域局限于政治方面。相反,在早期国际法著作(如格老秀斯 1609 年的《海洋自由论》)中,就已主张各国航海和贸易的普遍权利。[3]目前,国际公法的分支包括国际海洋法、国际空间法、国际刑法、国际行政法、国际组织法、国际人权法等等,当然也可以包括狭义说的国际经济法。由于杨文主张国际经济法属于国际法体系,与"调整国际政治关系"的国际公法相区别,实际上已回到狭义说的立场。这方面值得进一步思考的问题是,以法的创制主体作为划分国内法与国际法的唯一标准,无视适用的主体,是否科学? 由于杨文主张国际经济法属国际法体系,又主张国际经济法的主体包括个人、法人和非法人实体,国际法如何直接或间接适用于此类主体?

二、关于国际经济法的主体

广义说和狭义说都认为,国际经济法主体包括国际法主体,即国家和国际组织。分歧在于,广义说认为国际经济法主体还应包括从事跨国经济活动的国内法主体,即法人和自然人等,而传统狭义说一般持否定态度。

关于国际经济法的主体,杨文指出:"国际经济法主体,即国际经济法律关系的主体,是指国际经济法律关系的参加者或当事人",包括:(1)国家;(2)国际组织;(3)个人;(4)法人;(5)非国家特别行政区,如中国的香港特别行政区、澳门特别行政区;(6)非法人实体,如中外双边投资条约中"投资者"定义所包括的"具有或不具有法人资格的组织或社团"。[4]

由此可见,就国际经济法主体而言,杨文与广义说大同小异,创新之处是列举了"非国家特别行政区"和"非法人实体"两类主体。值得进一步探讨的问题是:

第一,"非国家特别行政区"概念是否科学? 是否单列?

"非国家特别行政区"概念中的"特别行政区"是中国实行"一国两制"的专有概

---

〔1〕　参见韩德培:《论国际公法、国际私法与国际经济法的合并问题》,载陈安主编:《国际经济法论丛》第 1 卷,法律出版社 1998 年版,第 5 页。

〔2〕　参见中国大百科全书出版社编辑部编:《中国大百科全书·法学》,中国大百科全书出版社 1984 年版,第 189 页。

〔3〕　参见〔英〕戴维·M. 沃克:《牛津法律大辞典》,光明日报出版社 1989 年版,第 458 页。

〔4〕　参见杨紫煊:《论国际经济法基础理论的若干问题》,载《法商研究》2000 年第 3 期,第 52—55 页。

念。"特别行政区"概念本身已表明其不是国家，似无必要加上"非国家"，否则，是否也有"国家特别行政区"？事实上，特别行政区的地位是单一制国家的地方性行政实体，虽然经法律授权享有高度自治权（包括一定的对外权），但仍属于国家的"第二级实体"的范畴，似不宜单独列为与国家并列的一类法律主体。[1] 不然，从国际上看，享有一定对外权的其他单一制国家的地方性行政实体和联邦制国家的成员国或州，岂不也应分别列举？

第二，非法人实体是否应有限定词？

一般认为，法律关系的主体是法律关系中权利的享有者和义务的承担者。特定法律制度的主体需要具备三个要素：一是享有从该法律制度取得的权利；二是承担违反该法律制度而产生的责任；三是具有与该法律制度承认的其他法律人格者建立法律关系的能力。在任何特定法律制度框架内，各主体不必相同，也不必具有完全相同的性质和特征。[2]

杨文将"非法人实体"作为国际经济法主体的一种类型，并定义为"指虽不具有法人资格但是能够独立享有财产权利和承担财产义务的社会组织。"笔者以为，此定义似不够准确。"非法人实体"是"法人实体"的对称。所谓"法人实体"是具有法人资格的实体，是能够独立享有权利和承担义务的社会组织。而"非法人实体"则是不具有法人资格的实体，包含能够独立享有权利和承担义务的社会组织和不能独立享有权利和承担义务的社会组织两种类型。可见，对"非法人实体"不宜先定位为国际经济法主体，再作限定。对作为国际经济法主体的"非法人实体"本身就应加上"能够独立享有权利和承担义务"的限定词。

三、关于国际经济法的调整对象

杨文主张，国际经济法具有特定的调整对象。具体说来，一是有一定的范围，而不是"漫无边际、捉摸不定"的。不能强调国际经济法调整对象的综合性，而否定其特定性；二是国际经济法调整对象同其他法的部门的调整对象是有区别的、可分的；三是国际经济法的调整对象是特定的经济关系，即国际经济协调关系。涉外经济关系不是国际经济协调关系。在现实生活中，大量存在不同国家的个人、法人等主体

---

[1]《中华人民共和国香港特别行政区基本法》第12条规定："香港特别行政区是中华人民共和国的一个享有高度自治权的地方行政区域，直辖于中央人民政府。"

[2] 正如国际法院在"履行联合国职务中遭受损害之赔偿"案中指出："任何法律制度的主体在其性质或在其权利范围方面不必是同一的，而其性质取决于该社会的需要。" See P. R. Menon, The Legal Personality of International Organizations, *Sri Lanka Journal of International Law*, Vol. 4, 1992, p. 93.

参与的经济关系。其中,有些关系不属涉外经济关系,而是属国际经济协调关系。[1]

由上述可见,在国际经济法的调整对象方面,"国际经济协调论"与广义说的基本论点是一致的。广义说也是主张国际经济法有一定的调整范围,同其他法的部门的调整对象是有区别的、可分的。两种学说的主要分歧在于"特定的经济关系"的含义和范围。如前所述,作为"国际经济协调论"基石的国际经济协调关系有待进一步明确。尽管杨文在国际经济法定义中不列明国际经济法的主体,但从相关论述中可见,国际经济协调关系包括国家之间、国家与国际组织之间和国际组织之间的经济协调关系,也包括了不同国籍私人之间或国家与他国私人之间的经济协调关系,但不是涉外经济关系。问题是,在理论和实践上如何界定涉外经济关系?有否"在两个以上国家协调国际经济运行过程中发生的"涉外经济关系?如何区分涉外经济关系与国际经济协调关系?特别是,如何区分涉外经济关系与不同国籍私人之间或国家与他国私人之间的经济协调关系?

杨文一方面指出,狭义说学者无视国内法、国际公法调整对象以外的私人参与的国际经济协调关系的客观存在,将这种经济关系排除在国际经济法的调整对象之外,否定了对其进行法律调整的必要性,是脱离实际的。另一方面,也反对广义说关于国际经济法是"边缘性、综合性和独立性"法律部门的主张,[2]认为广义说否定了国际经济法具有特定的调整对象,混淆了民法、经济法与国际经济法的界限,国内法与国际法的界限。[3]

需要澄清的是,第一,考察广义说关于国际经济法调整对象的观点,并未发现有"漫无边际"的表述,与狭义说的区别在于,广义说主张的国际经济关系不限于国家之间的经济关系,而是包括了涉外经济关系,即国家与私人之间、国际组织与他国私人之间和不同国籍的私人之间的经济关系;第二,广义说并未混淆民法、经济法同国际经济法的界限,相反,在广义说著述中,各国民法并未被列为国际经济法的渊源,对经济法与国际经济法的关系也作了严格的区分,能成为国际经济法渊源的只限于专门性的涉外经济法,而在市场经济条件下,专门性的涉外经济法在各国经济法体系中只占较小的比重。因此,总体上,国际经济法与经济法都有其特定的调整对象,各司其职,并行不悖。

进一步的问题是,国际经济法与经济法的调整对象是否容许有交叉或重叠?杨文认为,国际经济法调整的国际经济协调关系所涉及的范围同其他法的部门的调整

---

〔1〕　参见杨紫烜:《论国际经济法基础理论的若干问题》,载《法商研究》2000 年第 3 期,第 46—48 页。

〔2〕　关于国际经济法的边缘性、综合性和独立性的论述,参见陈安:《论国际经济法学科的边缘性、综合性和独立性》,载陈安主编:《国际经济法论丛》第 1 卷,法律出版社 1998 年版,第 9—64 页。

〔3〕　参见杨紫烜:《论国际经济法基础理论的若干问题》,载《法商研究》2000 年第 3 期,第 47—48 页。

对象是能够分开的，而不是交叉的、重叠的。在调整对象方面，广义说与狭义说、"国际经济协调论"的区别在于，前者突破了传统单一、纯粹的由国际法调整的"特定的调整对象"范围，其调整范围是国际经济关系，包括国家或国际组织之间的经济关系和涉外经济关系。就是在涉外经济关系这一点上，国际经济法与经济法的调整对象出现了交叉或重叠。国际经济现实表明，国家或国际组织之间的经济关系与涉外经济关系往往相互交错，密不可分。一项国家之间的经济谈判，不仅涉及当事国政府之间的经济关系，更多是涉及当事国一方与当事国对方私人之间或当事国双方私人之间的经济关系问题。一项国际私人投资或贸易活动，必然涉及当事人所属国之间的经济关系。反映在法律规范上，国际经济条约、例如世界贸易组织协定和双边投资保护协定等，在很大程度上是"第三人受益安排"，涉及缔约国双方私人的权利义务；各国涉外经济法律甚至涉外经济合同也往往和有关国际经济条约相联系；至于国家与他国私人之间的合同，更是常常涉及国际法和国内法规范。显然，由国家或国际组织之间的经济关系和涉外经济关系构成的国际经济关系是一个不可分割的统一体。相应地，调整这种国际经济关系的国际经济法，也应该是包含国际法和国内法规范的独立法律部门。

四、关于国际经济法的渊源

杨文认为，根据法的创制形式的不同，可将法分为制定法与非制定法。国际经济法的渊源包括：(1) 条约，不限于国际经济条约；(2) 国际组织制定的规范性文件，包括联合国大会决议；(3) 国际习惯法，限于经两个以上国家认可并赋予法律约束力的国际习惯。[1] 显然，"国际经济协调论"主张的国际经济法渊源与国际公法渊源、狭义说主张的国际经济法渊源基本雷同。

笔者以为，杨文主张国际经济法渊源中的条约不限于国际经济条约，这无疑是正确的。同时应当指出，国际经济条约毕竟是国际经济法的最主要渊源之一。尽管国际经济条约与国际政治条约等难以"一刀切"，但也有一些典型的国际经济条约，如双边投资协定、双边贸易协定和双边税务协定等。在广义说著述中提及国际经济条约是国际经济法渊源之一，主要是为了凸显国际经济法渊源的特殊性，以利区别于国际公法渊源。

关于联合国大会决议（以下简称为"联大决议"）法律效力的学说，各国学者见仁见智，概括而言，有"传统国际法渊源"说、"其他渊源"（other sources）说、"软法"（soft

---

〔1〕 参见杨紫烜：《论国际经济法基础理论的若干问题》，载《法商研究》2000年第3期，第50—51页。

law)说和区别说等。[1] 杨文认为,国际组织制定的规范性文件,包括联大决议,"不论是一致通过的还是按规定以特别多数或简单多数通过的,对于表明同意该规范性文件的所有成员国来说,表明该规范性文件体现了这些国家的协调意志,表明它们愿意接受该规范性文件的约束。所以,该规范性文件理所当然地对这些国家具有法律约束力,属于国际经济法的渊源。"[2] 笔者以为,由于联合国大会不是立法机构,联大决议一般属于"建议"性质,对联大决议的法律效力问题应作具体分析,不宜一概而论。[3] 有关建立国际经济新秩序的联大决议是国际经济法的重要渊源之一,其法律效力的主要依据是:(1)反映了国际社会的法律确信;(2)其形成遵循了国家主权平等原则和民主原则;(3)其重申的传统国际法原则当然具有法律效力;(4)其确立的国际经济法新规范的法律效力在实践中不断加强。

杨文对"国际习惯法"的定义是,"只有被两个以上国家认可并赋予法律约束力的国际习惯,才对这些国家具有法律约束力,才能被称为国际习惯法,才属于国际经济法的渊源"。[4] 笔者以为,首先,杨文中的"国际习惯法"的内涵需要进一步研究。是否包括习惯国际经济法(Customary International Economic Law)[5]和国际私人商务惯例? 国际经济惯例突出反映了国际经济法作为综合性和边缘性法律部门的特征。从性质上看,它可进一步区分为习惯国际经济法和国际私人商务惯例。前者调整国际法主体、主要是国家之间的经济关系,后者调整不同国籍的私人之间、国家与他国私人之间或国际组织与私人之间的经济关系。其次,一般认为,国家实践和法律确信是形成国际惯例的两个基本要素[6],这同样适用于国际经济惯例。根据杨文,"国际习惯"产生法律约束力的条件是"被两个以上国家认可并赋予法律约束力",不同于上述通说。显然,需要进一步阐明当事国"认可并赋予法律约束力"的方式,并明确国际习惯法的法律效力的范围。

---

〔1〕　参见曾华群:《国际经济法导论》,法律出版社 1999 年版,第 135—140 页。

〔2〕　参见杨紫烜:《论国际经济法基础理论的若干问题》,载《法商研究》2000 年第 3 期,第 51 页。

〔3〕　关于联大决议法律效力的考察和分析,参见秦娅:《联合国大会决议的法律效力》,载中国国际法学会主办:《中国国际法年刊》(1984),中国对外翻译出版公司 1984 年版,第 164—191 页。

〔4〕　参见杨紫烜:《论国际经济法基础理论的若干问题》,载《法商研究》2000 年第 3 期,第 51 页。

〔5〕　关于习惯国际经济法的系统论述,参见 Stephen Zamora, Is There Customary International Economic Law? *German Yearbook of International Law*, Vol. 32, 1989, pp. 8-42.

〔6〕　根据《国际法院规约》第 38 条第 1 款第 2 项规定,国际法的渊源之一为:"国际习惯,作为通例之证明而经接受为法律者"。学说上普遍认为,该条款确立了习惯国际法的两个基本要素:国家实践和法律确信。

第三节　论 WTO 体制与国际投资法的关系[*]

【摘要】　在探讨 WTO 体制与国际投资法在体制上的分立、在内容上的联系及 WTO 体制连结国际投资法的新动向之后，本文指出，由于 WTO 体制与国际投资法是分立的体制，有其特定的调整对象，两者不能相互取代；两者在内容上某种程度的连结、重叠或交叉并不足以否定两者在体制上的分立；当前应注意避免 WTO 体制"与贸易有关的投资措施"规范的过度扩张。

【关键词】　WTO 体制　国际投资法　国际贸易法

在乌拉圭回合协定中，包含了《与贸易有关的投资措施协定》（TRIMs 协定）等涉及投资的规范。随着 WTO 体制"与贸易有关"领域的不断发展，继投资成为"新加坡议题"之后，[1]发达国家进一步力主在 WTO 体制下开展多边投资协定（MAI）的谈判；国际实践中，WTO 体制与国际投资法的连结点亦悄然发展。WTO 体制与国际投资法的关系究竟如何，这个看似不言自明的问题变得模糊不清，值得国际法学界认真关注和探讨。

一、WTO 体制与国际投资法在体制上的分立

（一）国际贸易与国际投资是分立的两种经济活动

众所周知，WTO 体制调整国际贸易关系，国际投资法调整国际直接投资（以下简称"国际投资"）关系。在这个意义上，WTO 体制与国际投资法的关系取决于国际贸易与国际投资的关系的现状和发展趋势。

一般认为，国际投资与国际贸易是国际经济活动的两种主要方式。两者的基本区别在于：首先，从经济活动内容看，国际投资指资本的跨国流动，通常表现为一国私人（包括法人、自然人）在外国投资经营企业，直接或间接地控制其投资企业的经营活动；国际贸易指货物、服务或技术的跨国交易，通常表现为不同国家私人之间的货物、服务或技术的交易。其次，从经营或交易时间看，国际投资一般是长期的经营项目，在投资合同中规定经营期限（如 20 年）或未规定经营期限，意味着永续经营；而

---

　　[*]　原载《厦门大学学报》（哲学社会科学版）2007 年第 6 期。
　　〔1〕　1996 年 12 月，在 WTO 新加坡部长理事会会议上，各成员同意考虑投资、竞争政策、政府采购透明度及贸易便利化等议题。这四个议题统称为"新加坡议题"。

国际贸易则一般是短期或一次性的交易行为,在贸易合同中规定交易期限,取决于交易的标的、环节等因素,在数日或数月内完成交易。再次,从东道国的管制方式看,国际投资活动经历准入和经营两个阶段,涉及外资审批和投资措施等管制方式;而国际贸易活动通常只经历交易一个阶段,一般涉及关税和非关税措施。

另一方面,国际投资与国际贸易又是紧密联系的,有时甚至是相互交融的。从历史上看,国际投资活动是国际贸易活动的发展和延伸;在国际经济实践中,实物投资本身也是一种变相的国际贸易活动,而作为国际服务贸易形式之一的"商业存在"方式本身就是国际投资活动。《1996 年世界投资报告》认为,国际投资和国际贸易都是促进经济增长和发展的重要因素,对于提高各国的经济业绩具有举足轻重的影响。国际贸易和国际投资日益紧密地联系在一起,相互作用,互为因果,促进了世界经济一体化的深化。作为向国外市场交付商品和劳务的主要方式和国际化生产的主要因素,国际投资及有关政策日益影响国际贸易的规模与构成,与此同时,国际贸易及有关政策也对国际投资的规模、流向和构成产生重要的影响。传统理论认为,国际投资与国际贸易既存在替代性的关系,也具有互补性的关系。《1996 年世界投资报告》对不同行业的国际投资与国际贸易之间的关系进行了具体的分析,结论是,国际贸易最终必然导致国际投资,而国际投资将会带来更多的国际贸易。国际贸易政策与国际投资政策的相互影响也是显而易见的。高关税的国际贸易政策可能促进国际投资,而出口要求、外汇平衡的国际投资政策可能促进国际贸易。国际贸易自由化政策必然推动国际投资自由化政策的发展。国际投资与国际贸易的融合和相互联系要求进行国家之间的政策协调以增强国际投资政策与国际贸易政策的一致性,避免政策效应的相互抵触或抵消,提高政策的有效性。反映在法律上,调整国际投资关系和调整国际贸易关系的一些国内法或国际法规范是相互渗透、相互作用的。

由上述可见,无论国际贸易与国际投资如何紧密联系,国际贸易政策与国际投资政策如何相互影响,国际贸易与国际投资毕竟是分立的两种主要经济活动,国际贸易政策与国际投资政策毕竟是分立的两种主要经济政策。这似可作为考察 WTO 体制与国际投资法的关系的基本出发点。

(二)WTO 体制与国际投资法是分立的两个体制

在国际经济法体系中,以"显著的经济特征"为标准,主要有国际贸易法、国际投资法、国际货币金融法、国际税法和国际经济争议解决法等。所谓国际贸易法,指调整跨国货物、服务和技术贸易关系的国际法规范和国内法规范的总称。其渊源首先是国际贸易协定,而 WTO 体制是当前影响最大的国际贸易协定群。WTO 体制属于国际贸易法范畴,应当是没有疑义的。

历史上,GATT/WTO 体制与国际投资法各循其特定的方式发展。虽然,试图调整国际投资的努力可追溯到 1947 年 GATT 成立之初和流产的国际贸易组织(ITO),GATT 作为《哈瓦那宪章》和 ITO 的遗产继承人,显然与国际投资无关。或者更准确地说,GATT 的管辖范围并未扩及东道国对外资准入和外资经营所规定的条件。国际贸易与国际投资的分立,对脆弱的 GATT 是有益的。长期以来,在东方国家与西方国家之间、南方国家与北方国家之间许多最基本的争议问题,诸如东道国对外国投资者的责任、征收的法律后果、国际经济新秩序以及起草《跨国公司行为守则》等,GATT 均置身事外。这些问题曾在联合国大会及其下属机构、世界银行、国际货币基金组织以及旨在签订友好通商航海条约和双边投资条约(BITs)的谈判中辩论,但从未发生于 GATT。[1]

就国际经济法体系而言,WTO 体制属国际贸易法,而国际贸易法与国际投资法分立,同样作为国际经济法的重要分支。两者虽然不是泾渭分明,但具有基本的分界,互不隶属。当前,由于发达国家的强力推动,WTO 已涵盖了"与贸易有关的投资措施"领域,WTO 体制与国际投资法的涵盖内容也出现了一定程度的连结、重叠或交叉。然而,这并不能改变 WTO 体制与国际投资法两种分立体制的基本分野。

二、WTO 体制与国际投资法在内容上的联系

经济全球化的重要特征之一是,作为可获得的投资和金融资产竞争集中的结果,各国特别是发展中国家可选择的范围日益缩小。另一个重要特征是各国受外部力量驱动作出其经济决策。得益于全球自由贸易的国家,控制了充足的政治和经济力量以确保推行其有关自由化、私有化和外国投资的政策。它们通过创设 WTO 等国际组织及其体制和有关投资的双边或区域性条约来达到其目的。[2]

发达国家将投资议题纳入 GATT/WTO 体制的企图由来已久。早在 1982 年 12 月 GATT 部长级会议上,美国作为主要倡议者,首次提出了将投资议题纳入 GATT 体制的建议。由于欧共体成员和发展中国家反对,该提议被取消。在乌拉圭回合中,在美国等发达国家的强力推动下,产生了 TRIMs 协定等涉及投资的规范。随着 WTO 体制"与贸易有关"领域的不断扩张,投资已然成为 WTO 多边贸易谈判的议题之一。WTO 体制与国际投资法的涵盖内容出现了一定程度的连结、重叠或交叉。

---

〔1〕 See Andreas F. Lowenfeld, *International Economic Law*, Oxford University Press, 2002, p. 94.

〔2〕 See M. Sornarajah, A Developing Country Perspective of International Economic Law in the Context of Dispute Settlement, in Asif H. Qureshi, *Perspectives in International Economic Law*, Kluwer Law International, 2002, p. 83.

乌拉圭回合的成果涉及投资的主要规范包括 TRIMs 协定,《服务贸易总协定》(GATS)和《与贸易有关的知识产权协定》(TRIPS 协定)。其中,GATS 和 TRIPS 协定只是部分内容涉及国际投资。GATS 中涉及国际投资的主要内容是,"商业存在"作为服务提供方式,本身也是一种投资方式。而 TRIPS 协定通过对"与贸易有关的知识产权"的保护而与国际投资密切相关。与贸易有关的投资措施(TRIMs)问题,则直接涉及各国外资法的"履行要求"。TRIMs 协定专门调整各成员的 TRIMs,是WTO 体制与国际投资法重叠的最典型实例。顾名思义,TRIMs 协定是规范 TRIMs的协定,不是一个有关投资的综合性多边法律框架,比之 OECD 主导的《多边投资协定》(MAI)和各国普遍接受的 BITs,其适用范围极为有限,只能视为朝向有关投资的多边管制框架迈出的一小步。[1]

WTO 成立之后,WTO 体制有关投资议题有两个重要的发展。其一是根据1996 年 WTO《新加坡部长理事会宣言》第 20 节设立了"贸易与投资关系工作组"(WGTI),专门研讨贸易与投资的关系。在该会议上达成的决议是,WTO 应研究贸易与投资之间的关系,由 WGTI 开展专门研究。其研讨范围限于 WTO 成员提出的同"贸易与投资的关系"相关的议题。其研讨工作虽然不具有立法或立法建议的性质,只是一种启发性、指导性工作,但反映了 WTO 体制内对"贸易与投资的关系"的持续关注。[2] 同时,也反映了 WTO 力图将投资议题纳入其制度性安排的趋向。

第二个重要发展体现于 WTO《多哈部长理事会宣言》有关投资的内容。WTO成员同意多哈回合有关贸易与投资关系的讨论集中于澄清范围与定义、透明度、非歧视、基于 GATS 型"积极清单"(positive list)的设立前承诺、发展的规定、例外与收支平衡的保障以及协商与成员之间争议的解决。在该框架中没有 BITs 等传统国际投资条约包含的重要问题,如给予外国投资者的保护性待遇、货币转移、针对征收的保护以及外国投资者与东道国之间争议的解决。该宣言未规定传统国际投资条约有关投资保护、促进和自由化的宗旨,而是强调其他新目标,即"任何框架应以平衡的方式反映母国和东道国利益,并适当考虑东道国政府的发展政策和目标以及它们为公共利益的管制权利"。上述新目标涉及的三个因素值得注意:一是促进的利益限于国家利益,而未提及私人投资者的利益;二是适当考虑的国家利益主要是东道国的利益,而不是投资者母国的利益;三是坚持"管制权利"意味着界定外资财产权

---

〔1〕 See Yong-Shik Lee, *Reclaiming Development in the World Trading System*, Cambridge University Press, 2006, pp. 116-117.

〔2〕 参见刘笋:《贸易与投资——WTO 法与国际投资法的共同挑战》,载《法学评论》2004 年 1 期。

利与东道国管制外资的权利是多哈回合有关投资议题谈判的争议焦点。[1]

显然，目前 WTO 体制的投资议题仍然限于"与贸易有关"的领域，不能等同于 BITs 等传统国际投资条约或 MAI，两者不能混淆。需要特别引起警惕的是，在 WTO 体制中，发达国家看来是采取"步步为营"和"得陇望蜀"的策略，从投资议题的谈判谈起，一俟时机成熟即转为 MAI 谈判。

应当指出，在贸易谈判中涉及投资，并非 GATT/WTO 的独创。一些涉及投资的多边经济协定，如《北美自由贸易区协定》(NAFTA)和《能源宪章条约》等都是在多边贸易谈判中产生的。其原因是，在多边经济谈判中将贸易与投资问题相联系，提供了支撑条约谈判的宽广的交易基础，这是单纯的多边投资谈判无法企及的谈判方式。这是基于贸易的投资谈判方式。特别是，发展中国家为增加其在发达国家市场的贸易量，将导致它们对外资采取更自由的保护性政策。不仅如此，从谈判理论的观点看，在多边谈判中涉及的问题越多，当事方就可能设计越多的协调点（trade-offs）。而当事方拥有越多的协调点，就越可能发现达成协议的基础。[2]

三、WTO 体制连结国际投资及其规范的新动向

近年来，WTO 体制的基本原则、规则及其相关案例与国际投资活动和国际投资法各种渊源正在形成新的连结点，将对 WTO 体制与国际投资法的关系产生重要而深远的影响。这一新的发展动向值得密切关注和跟踪研究。

（一）WTO 基本原则对国际投资活动的适用问题

WTO 基本原则指 WTO 成员普遍接受的调整相互之间贸易关系的最基本的法律原则。WTO 基本原则是在 GATT 基本原则的基础上发展起来，主要来自历次多边贸易谈判，特别是乌拉圭回合谈判达成的一系列协定。关于 WTO 基本原则，学界有不同的见解。多数学者基于 WTO 是 GATT 的继承和发展的认识，将 GATT 基本原则作为 WTO 基本原则。[3] 少数学者强调 WTO 基本原则的普遍适用性，认为在《WTO 协定》中明文规定并普遍适用于 WTO 各个领域的最惠国待遇原则、国民

---

[1] See Jeswald W. Salacuse, Towards a Global Treaty on Foreign Investment: The Search for a Grand Bargain, in Norbert Horn, *Arbitrating Foreign Investment Disputes*, Kluwer Law International, 2004, p. 86.

[2] Ibid., p. 87.

[3] 曹建明教授认为，WTO 的基本原则包括非歧视原则，互惠原则，最惠国待遇原则，国民待遇原则，市场准入原则，关税减让原则，取消数量限制原则，公平贸易原则和透明度原则。参见曹建明、贺小勇：《世界贸易组织》，法律出版社 1999 年版，第 66—98 页。曾令良教授认为，WTO 的基本原则包括非歧视原则，关税保护原则，公平贸易原则，优惠待遇原则，透明度原则和协商与协商一致原则。参见曾令良：《世界贸易组织法》，武汉大学出版社 1996 年版，第 38—45 页。王贵国教授认为，WTO 的基本原则包括非歧视、互惠、最惠国待遇、国民待遇、透明度等基本原则。参见王贵国：《世界贸易组织法》，法律出版社 2003 年版，第 38 页。

待遇原则和透明度原则是 WTO 体制的三项最基本原则。[1] 尽管对 WTO 基本原则见仁见智,贸易自由化原则、非歧视原则是学者普遍认同的。

WTO 贸易自由化原则包含了市场准入、关税减让和取消数量限制等内容。鉴于前述国际投资与国际贸易的基本区别,不能简单地援引 WTO 的贸易自由化原则,推而广之,主张国际投资自由化。国际投资因涉及国家的经济要害或敏感部门,加之长期性质,可能在更大程度上涉及国家主权问题。鉴此,各国对外国投资的准入,一般保持和行使充分的管辖权。对广大发展中国家而言,对西方国家的投资自由化的要求不能无原则地迁就,更不宜作为多边投资谈判的"首要目标"。[2] 有西方学者指出,OECD 的 MAI 试图对国际投资提供与国际贸易和国际服务相同的自由环境,其失败原因是未能充分考虑不同的非生产商的利益,部分地是由于 OECD 国家的环境和劳工权利倡导者的极力反对。[3]

由最惠国待遇原则和国民待遇原则构成的 WTO 非歧视原则也不能完全适用于国际投资领域。其理由首先是,在 WTO 体制中,除了知识产权保护领域之外,非歧视原则主要适用于国际贸易的"产品"和"服务",两者均为"物",而在国际投资领域,非歧视原则主要适用于"投资"和"投资者",即包括了"物"和"人";其次,国际贸易一般是一次性交易,而国际投资包含外资准入和外资经营两个阶段,在外资准入阶段,可能牵涉国家主权问题,各国对外国投资和外国投资者一般尚无法实行国民待遇原则。

（二）WTO 体制下启动 MAI 谈判问题

制定一个具有普遍约束力的综合性、实体性的多边投资协定,是发达国家长期追求而迄今未能实现的目标。OECD 的 MAI 谈判失败后,随之产生了 WTO 能否接此重任的问题。日本和欧共体极力推动在 1999 年 11 月召开的 WTO 西雅图部长理事会会议上启动 MAI 议题的谈判。这一企图因受到一些发展中国家代表团和非政府组织的反对而偃旗息鼓。2001 年 12 月召开的 WTO 多哈部长理事会会议仍未达成明确启动多边投资规则框架谈判的最后决议,只是提及正式决议留待坎昆部长理事会会议决定。在 2003 年 9 月召开的 WTO 坎昆部长理事会会议上,多数发展中国

---

〔1〕　参见胡振杰、何平:《世贸组织规则与我国新法律法规》,人民法院出版社 2002 年版,第 19 页。

〔2〕　有学者基于投资自由化是一种趋势和为中国扩大海外投资等因素的考虑,主张选择投资自由化作为多边投资谈判的首要目标。参见张庆麟、彭忠波:《晚近多边投资规则谈判的新动向——兼论我国多边投资谈判策略的选择》,载陈安主编:《国际经济法学刊》第 12 卷第 3 期,北京大学出版社 2005 年版,第 125 页。

〔3〕　See Edward Kwakwa, Institutional Perspectives of International Economic Law, in Asif H. Qureshi, *Perspectives in International Economic Law*, Kluwer Law International, 2002, p. 57.

家表示尚未做好 MAI 谈判的准备。[1] 由于各成员在农产品议题和新加坡议题的尖锐矛盾无法调和，坎昆会议重蹈西雅图会议无果而终之覆辙。[2] 2005 年 12 月，在WTO 香港部长理事会会议上，投资议题仍未能取得进展。[3] 尽管发达国家一再强调 MAI 对于促进国际贸易的重要性，在 WTO 体制中是否需要 MAI，尚未达成共识。[4]

值得注意的是，发达国家在 WTO 体制中提出投资议题，只是"投石问路"，其更重要的目标是将 MAI 纳入 WTO 体制。早在 1998 年，时值 OECD 的 MAI 谈判陷入困境，法国政府委托进行的一项有关 MAI 的研究结果认为，OECD 不是 MAI 的适当谈判场所，不能在已有基础上继续该谈判。法国总理进一步指出，MAI 的适当谈判场所不是 OECD，而"很自然地是 WTO"。[5] 面临大多数发展中国家反对的情况，一些主要发达国家提出了看来较弹性的两项建议：一是将 MAI 定位为"复边协定"（Plurilateral Agreement）。[6] 依此定位，对 WTO 投资议题谈判感兴趣的 WTO 成员可启动并持续进行 MAI 谈判，达成协议后，由希望成为 MAI 当事方的 WTO 成员签署并加入。这样，未参与谈判的其他成员不会受到损害，因为它们可自主决定选择保留在 MAI 之外，甚至是 MAI 谈判之外；二是 MAI 采用 GATS"积极清单"的承诺方式。该方式意味着，MAI 的约束力不会自动延伸到缔约方所有行业和所有投资领域。相反，各缔约方可规定承担义务的行业和承担义务的种类。[7]

有西方学者在预见 MAI 谈判的前景时指出，MAI 或类似的条约，最终将在WTO 体制下占有一席之地；如果在 WTO 受阻，则会在其他现有的或未来新设立的

[1] 参见冯军：《从多哈回合议程谈中国多边投资框架谈判立场》，载陈安主编：《国际经济法学刊》第 10 卷，北京大学出版社 2004 年版，第 316 页。

[2] 参见周汉民、邱一川：《坎昆峰会述评与 WTO 多哈回合展望》，载陈安主编：《国际经济法学刊》第 11 卷，北京大学出版社 2004 年版，第 133 页。

[3] See Doha Work Programme, Ministerial Declaration. Adopted on 18 December 2005（WT/MIN(05)/DEC），22/12/2005.

[4] See Yong-Shik Lee, *Reclaiming Development in the World Trading System*, Cambridge University Press, 2006, p. 122.

[5] See Jeswald W. Salacuse, Towards a Global Treaty on Foreign Investment: The Search for a Grand Bargain, in Norbert Horn, *Arbitrating Foreign Investment Disputes*, Kluwer Law International, 2004, p. 84.

[6] 《马拉喀什建立世界贸易组织协定》包含两类附件：第一类为多边贸易协定（Multilateral Trade Agreements），对此类协定，各国或具有单独关税区地位的地区在加入 WTO 时应采取一次性一揽子接受的方式，不得对任何协定或条款采取选择加入或保留。第二类为复边贸易协定（Plurilateral Trade Agreement），对此类协定，仍允许各国或具有单独关税区地位的地区在加入 WTO 时选择加入。因此，此类协定只约束选择加入特定协定的成员，对未加入的成员不产生任何权利和义务。

[7] 参见〔印〕哈吉拉·劳·达斯：《WTO 与多边贸易体系之过去、现在与未来》，第三世界网络（TWN），2004年，第 94—95 页。

体制结构中达成。[1] 还有西方学者更为乐观地预测,很有可能甚至可以肯定,有关投资议题的谈判最终将在 WTO 体制中完成。[2] 显然,一旦发达成员的主张占上风,发展中国家被迫接受,WTO 将成为催生 MAI 的温床。

应当指出,GATT/WTO 体制是发达国家主导的体制。在对 GATT/WTO 体制作历史考察之后,印度 WTO 专家哈吉拉·劳·达斯指出,发达国家,尤其是美国和欧共体一直在 GATT/WTO 体制中追求其自身的发展利益和目标,在很大程度上已获得了成功。历史表明,GATT 体制是由发达国家主导和创建的,[3] 发达国家无论何时意识到某些对其有重要利益的议题,都会将其纳入 GATT/WTO 谈判议程。因此,GATT/WTO 体制一直以来几乎都承载着发达国家的利益主题,而 GATT/WTO 体制的主要特点是依据主要发达国家,尤其是美国的法律和惯例模式而形成。[4] 将 MAI 纳入 WTO 体制,同样反映了发达国家的利益。其主要目的是,通过 WTO 的贸易自由化机制扩大投资的自由化,确保其海外投资者能在发展中国家自由进入和经营,从而消除或削弱发展中国家调整外资准入和外资经营的权力。如果在 WTO 体制中形成 MAI,其义务将如同 WTO 其他协定一样约束各成员。对发展中国家而言,这是十分困难的局面,意味着发展中国家将丧失其在发展过程中调整外国投资政策的所有灵活性。此外,将 MAI 纳入 WTO 体制所产生的严重后果之一是,使发展中国家因外国投资问题而面临交叉报复的风险。[5]

笔者以为,能否在 WTO 体制中启动 MAI 谈判的基本问题在于,该谈判有否 WTO 法上的根据。《马拉喀什建立世界贸易组织协定》(以下简称《WTO 协定》)第 2 条题为"WTO 的范围",第 1 款明确规定:"WTO 在与本协定附件所含协定和相关法律文件有关的事项方面,为处理其成员间的贸易关系提供共同的组织机构。"该基本规定表明,WTO 的管辖范围是"其成员间的贸易关系"。显然,WTO 是调整其成

---

〔1〕 See John H. Jackson, *Sovereignty, the WTO and Changing Fundamentals of International Law*, Cambridge University Press, 2006, p. 243.

〔2〕 See Edward Kwakwa, Institutional Perspectives of International Economic Law, Asif H. Qureshi. *Perspectives in International Economic Law*, Kluwer Law International, 2002, p. 58.

〔3〕 关于美国在创建 GATT 中的作用,参见 Ronald A. Brand, *Fundamentals of International Business Transactions*, Kluwer Law International, 2000, pp. 277-281。

〔4〕 参见〔印度〕哈吉拉·劳·达斯:《WTO 与多边贸易体系之过去、现在与未来》,第三世界网络(TWN),2004,第 16—19 页。

〔5〕 根据《关于争端解决规则与程序的谅解》第 22 条第 3 款:"在考虑中止哪些减让或其他义务时,起诉方应适用下列原则和程序:(a) 总的原则是,起诉方应首先寻求对与专家组或上诉机构认定有违反义务或其他造成利益损失或减损情形的部门相同的部门中止减让或其他义务;(b) 如该方认为对相同部门中止减让或其他义务不可行或无效,则可寻求中止对同一协定项下的其他部门的减让或其他义务;(c) 如该方认为对同一协定项下的其他部门中止减让或其他义务不可行或无效,且情况足够严重,则可寻求中止另一适用协定项下的减让或其他义务……"

员间贸易关系的国际组织，而不是富有夸张意味的所谓"经济联合国"。[1]《WTO协定》第3条进一步规定了WTO的职能，指出WTO"应为其成员间就多边贸易关系进行的谈判提供场所"。关于未来的谈判议题和协定，"WTO还可按部长级会议可能作出的决定，为其成员间的多边贸易关系的进一步谈判提供场所，并提供实施此类谈判结果的体制"。显然，无论是当前或未来的谈判议题，都必须在"多边贸易关系"的涵盖范围之内。由于MAI并非"多边贸易关系"的一部分，MAI谈判显然不属WTO的职能范围。

（三）区域贸易协定中的"WTO适用条款"

早期的区域贸易协定（RTAs）一般只调整缔约方之间的贸易关系。随着RTAs在世界范围的发展，已包含了广泛的经济领域，特别是有关国际投资的规定。有的RTAs甚至专章规定外国投资问题，如NAFTA第11章。

在WTO体制中，有规范RTAs的规定，主要是GATT第24条、《关于解释1994年关税与贸易总协定第24条的谅解》和授权条款、GATS第5条等。WTO通过对RTAs的规范，进一步直接或间接影响了由WTO成员组成的RTAs中的投资规范。

值得注意的是，在近年的RTAs中，出现了涉及WTO的条款，同时对成员之间的贸易和投资产生影响。如2003年7月生效的《东南亚国家联盟与中华人民共和国全面经济合作框架协定》（FACEC）第1条规定的宗旨是：(1) 加强和促进缔约方之间的经济、贸易和投资合作；(2) 逐步促进货物贸易和服务贸易的自由化，并创设透明、自由和便利的投资体制；(3) 开辟新领域和发展缔约方之间的更紧密经济合作的适当措施。由上述宗旨可见，"投资合作""投资体制"表明了投资在FACEC中的重要性。FACEC第5条进一步专门规定投资体制、投资合作与投资保护事项。[2]

在FACEC中，许多条款受WTO规则调整，涉及GATT的传统领域，如货物贸易，或涉及乌拉圭回合的新领域，如服务贸易、与贸易有关的知识产权等。FACEC第6(3)(d)条题为"WTO规定的适用"，明确反映了FACEC将某些WTO规则作为缔约双方直接适用的第一选择。不仅如此，FACEC缔约方还同意根据WTO有关规则谈判建立中国—东盟自由贸易区。可见，FACEC的一些条款与WTO规则之间存在紧密的联系。在一定程度上，FACEC的一些条款是以WTO规则作为依据、基础或补充。鉴于"投资合作"是建立中国—东盟自由贸易区的重要内容及贸易与投资

---

[1] 有学者指出，把WTO称为"经济联合国"在法律上有误导作用。参见张玉卿：《善用WTO规则》，载陈安主编：《国际经济法学刊》第10卷，北京大学出版社2004年版，第8页。

[2] FACEC第5条题为"投资"，规定："为促进投资和创设一个自由、便利、透明和竞争的投资体制，缔约方同意：(a)参与谈判以逐渐使投资体制自由化；(b)加强投资合作，便利投资和改善投资规则和法规的透明度；和(c)提供投资保护。"

的相关性，WTO 规则对 FACEC 货物贸易、服务贸易及知识产权问题的适用也必然直接或间接影响中国—东盟自由贸易区有关投资规范的形成和发展。

在 RTAs 实践中，对 WTO 成员而言，需要区分"WTO 调整范围之内"和"WTO 调整范围之外"的概念。毋庸置疑，在 WTO 规则调整范围之内，各成员应严格遵循规则，履行承诺，在 RTAs 中重申或强化 WTO 规则。另一方面，由于各成员的履约责任以其承担的 WTO 义务为限，在 WTO 规则调整范围之外，如投资领域，各成员可根据一般国际法，通过 RTAs 调整相互之间的经济关系。

（四）BITs 中的"WTO 相符性条款"

在 BITs 中，也出现了涉及 WTO 的条款。如加拿大 2004 年 6 月提出的《某国与加拿大促进和保护投资协定草案》(New text proposed by Canada as of June 2004, Agreement between[……]and Canada for the Promotion and Protection of Investments)第 5 条第 2 款涉及"间接征收"条款的适用范围。该款规定："本条规定不适用于与知识产权有关的授予的强制许可的颁布，或知识产权的撤销、限制或创设，以此种颁布、撤销、限制或创设符合 1994 年 4 月 15 日在马拉喀什签订的世界贸易组织协定为限。"

该条款规定的重要意义首先是，虽然表面上排除了该条款对"与知识产权有关的授予的强制许可的颁布或知识产权的撤销、限制或创设"的适用，但实际上表明了该条款仍具有适用的可能性。换言之，缔约方"与知识产权有关的授予的强制许可的颁布或知识产权的撤销、限制或创设"如不符合《WTO 协定》，特别是 TRIPS 协定的有关规定，可能被认定为"间接征收"。更值得注意的是，该条款的征收认定直接与"WTO 相符性"相联系，反映了 BITs 实践与 WTO 体制挂钩的新动向。

应当指出，BITs 是传统的双边条约安排，是缔约双方平等协商谈判的产物。缔约双方如同为 WTO 成员，愿意在 BITs 引入"WTO 相符性"要求，无可厚非，但缔约双方必须接受者，当以"WTO 调整范围之内"为限。而在"WTO 调整范围之外"的投资领域，是否规定"WTO 相符性"要求，则完全取决于缔约双方的真实意愿，不可强求。

（五）WTO 案例对国际投资案的"先例"价值问题

有学者认为，在近 5 年的实践中，有关法律语境意义的最具争议的问题是，WTO 体制的相关性及 WTO 有关"同类产品"(like products)的案例对 BITs 的解释。近年国际仲裁实践反映了这方面的新发展。

在 S. D. Myers, Pope v. Talbot and Feldman 案中，NAFTA 仲裁庭的裁决看来是主张，WTO 有关案例确实是适于指导 NAFTA 仲裁庭。与此同时，有关国民待遇的理解也有了重要的发展，趋向于反对在 BITs 的解释和适用中考虑 WTO 有关案例。其主要理由是，WTO 争议解决实践是朝一个要求有特定目标的具体方向发展，各成员政府承担了对其政策合法性的举证责任。2004 年，仲裁庭在 OECP v. Ecuador 案中驳回了有关 WTO 争议解决实践应适用于厄瓜多尔与美国之间 BIT 争议的主张。该仲裁庭注意到，与 WTO 有关的是"同类产品"，而 BITs 的相关规定是"同类情况"（a like situation），认为 WTO 有关竞争和替代性产品的政策与 BITs 有关"同类情况"的政策不能同等对待，WTO 规则适用于受来源国措施影响的进口产品，而 BITs 是用于规定外国投资者在东道国的地位的保护。2005 年 8 月，在 Methanex 案中，仲裁庭对 NAFTA 条款与 WTO 条款进行了详细的比较分析，认为 NAFTA 当事方认识到 WTO 体制中"同类产品"与 NAFTA 有关外国投资的"同类情势"（like circumstances）用语的不同。根据传统的国际法解释规则，仲裁庭裁决，外国投资语境中的"同类情势"不能视为与 WTO 体制的"同类产品"概念相同，因此，BITs 应以自主的方式解释，独立于 WTO 争议解决实践。[1]

上述国际仲裁实践否定 WTO 案例对国际投资案的"先例"价值的基本立场是值得肯定的。由于 WTO 体制与国际投资法是分立的两个体制，WTO 争议解决机制与国际投资解决机制是分立的两种机制，主张 WTO 案例对国际投资案的"先例"价值实属牵强附会。

四、结语

诚然，国际贸易与国际投资的关系密切，甚至在某些方面相互融合，相互影响。反映在 WTO 体制与国际投资法的关系上，两者在内容上也出现了某种程度的连结、重叠或交叉。然而，由于 WTO 体制与国际投资法是分立的体制，分别有其特定的调整对象，两者不能相互取代。两者在内容上某种程度的连结、重叠或交叉并不足以否定两者在体制上的分立。正如国际贸易不能取代国际投资一样，WTO 体制也不能取代国际投资法。反之亦然。鉴于 WTO 体制连结国际投资法的种种新动向，WTO 各成员应依据《WTO 协定》的有关规定，坚持将 WTO 体制的投资规范严格限于"与贸易有关"的范围，避免 TRIMs 规则的过度扩张。在当前的相关国际实践中，特别要审视将 MAI 纳入 WTO 体制的法律依据问题，同时关注 WTO 体制对国际投资法的影响问题。

---

[1] See Rudolf Dolzer, Main Substantive Issues Arising from Investment Disputes, National Treatment: New Developments, Paper for Symposium Co-organised by ICSID, OECD and UNCTAD on Making the Most of International Investment Agreements: A Common Agenda, 12 December 2005, Paris.

On the Relationship between WTO Regime and International Investment Law

Abstract: Studying on the division in systems and connection in contents of WTO regime and international investment law, and new trends of WTO regime linking to international investment law, the article points out that as WTO regime and international investment law are different systems, they have specific regulation objects and cannot be substituted each other. The links, overlaps or crosses to some extent in contents of the two systems are not sound grounds to deny the division of the two systems. It should be paid much attention to avoid excessive expansion of the WTO rules for TRIMs.

Key words: WTO regime, international investment law, international trade law

第四节　中国特色国际经济法学的理念与追求

——《陈安论国际经济法学》的学术创新与特色贡献[*]

【摘要】《陈安论国际经济法学》（五卷本）是创建中国特色国际经济法学的奠基之作。其学术创新和贡献主要是：以马克思主义为指导，深刻分析国际经济关系的发展，揭示南北问题的根源和实质，阐释马克思主义主权观；站在中国和发展中国家的立场，坚持和发展"三个世界"理论，坚持建立国际经济新秩序的目标，提出南北矛盾发展的"6C 律"；论证南北矛盾中形成的经济主权原则、公平互利原则和全球合作原则，充分反映了作者创建中国特色国际经济法学的理念和追求。作者强烈的学术使命感、历史与现实结合的研究方法以及学术成果"国际化"的不懈努力，尤其值得学习。

【关键词】　南北矛盾；经济主权；国际经济新秩序

陈安老师积三十年之功蔚为大观的《陈安论国际经济法学》（五卷本），以马克思主义为指导，以南北问题为主线，站在中国和广大发展中国家的立场，坚持建立国际经济新秩序的目标，深刻论证国际经济法的基本原则，充分反映了作者[1]创建中国特色国际经济法学的理念和追求。

一、以马克思主义为指导，论述国际经济法学的基本问题

如所周知，中国特色法学理论是中国特色社会主义理论的重要组成部分之一，其指导思想和理论基础是马克思主义。作为中国特色法学理论的重要组成部分之一，中国特色国际经济法学尽管具有"国际性"和"普世性"，其指导思想和理论基础同样是马克思主义。

早在 20 世纪 40 年代，作者在厦门大学求学时就开始接受马克思主义的启蒙和熏陶；50—70 年代，曾专门从事马克思主义教学和研究。对马克思主义，特别是对马克思主义民族殖民地及主权理论的学养深厚，是其致力创建中国特色国际经济法学的重要思想和理论优势。在 80 年代以来的国际经济法学研究中，作者援引马克思主义原著的精辟论述，科学分析国际经济关系的发展，以殖民掠夺史揭示南北问题的

　＊　原载《西南政法大学学报》2012 年第 2 期。
　〔1〕　为求行文简便，本节中的"作者"均指《陈安论国际经济法学》的作者陈安老师。

根源和实质,并深入阐释马克思主义主权观。

（一）科学分析国际经济关系的发展

国际经济关系既是国际经济法借以产生和发展的主要依据,又是国际经济法调整的主要对象。作者以辩证唯物主义和历史唯物主义详细分析国际经济关系发展的三大主要阶段（即早期的国际经济交往与国际经济关系的初步形成,资本主义世界市场的形成与国际经济关系的重大发展,社会主义国家的出现、众多弱小民族的独立与国际经济关系的本质变化）,深刻指出,历史唯物主义的基本原理"是对人类社会长期发展进程客观事实的科学总结","是对各国社会进行解剖的利器,也是对国际社会实行科学分析的指南"。[1]

（二）以殖民掠夺史揭示南北问题的根源和实质

依据历史事实,作者以激扬文字历数 15 世纪以来列强在亚、非、美地区推行殖民主义的十大罪恶行径,称为"殖民十恶"（即"欺蒙诈骗,以贱易贵""明火执仗,杀人越货""践踏主权,霸占领土""横征暴敛,榨取脂膏""强制劳役,敲骨吸髓""猎取活人,贩卖奴隶""垄断贸易,单一经济""种毒贩毒,戕民攫利""毁灭文化,精神侵略"和"血腥屠杀,种族灭绝"）,[2]进而总结,"漫漫数百年,一部殖民史,就是一部弱肉强食史,也就是欧美列强和全世界众多弱小民族之间的国际经济关系史的主要内容。"[3]"15世纪以来的数百年间,欧洲列强在亚、非、美广大地区实行殖民掠夺的历史,是一部火与剑的历史,也是一部血与泪的历史。"[4]

在中外国际经济法学论著中,居于道义制高点,以如此犀利笔触历数殖民之恶,似为仅见。或有学者认为这是政治学或史学的内容。笔者[5]以为,殖民掠夺史在西方国际经济法学论著中讳莫如深,却是中国特色国际经济法学应有的立论之本。正本清源,温故知新。只有回顾殖民掠夺史,才能深刻理解南北问题的根源和实质,认清西方列强罄竹难书的罪恶"发家史"及其对广大发展中国家所欠下的巨大"历史债务",也才能深刻理解建立国际经济新秩序的正当性、必要性和紧迫性,正确认识社会发展规律和国际经济关系的发展趋势和方向。在法理上,回顾殖民掠夺史是阐述和论证当代经济主权、公平互利和全球合作等国际经济法基本原则必要的史实依据和理论铺垫。

---

〔1〕　陈安:《论国际经济关系的历史发展与南北矛盾》,载陈安:《陈安论国际经济法学》（第 1 卷）,复旦大学出版社 2008 年版,第 40 页。

〔2〕　同上书,第 46—54 页。

〔3〕　同上书,第 53 页。

〔4〕　同上书,第 46 页。

〔5〕　本节中的"笔者"均指本文作者。

（三）深入阐释马克思主义主权观

作者对马克思主义主权观的研究和论述，重点强调民族自决权和批判民族虚无主义。两者相辅相成，构成了作者研讨马克思主义主权观的核心主张，即十分强调尊重和维护广大发展中国家的主权，坚决反对殖民主义、帝国主义和社会帝国主义等形形色色的霸权主义。

在专著《列宁对民族殖民地革命学说的重大发展》(1981年)中，作者系统深入研究马克思、恩格斯关于民族殖民地问题的基本理论、列宁1895—1924年期间关于弱小民族国家主权问题的学说，重点探讨国际共产主义运动史上有关"民族自决"问题的长期论战，研究国际公法上关于弱小民族国家主权学说的争鸣辩论，侧重论述殖民地、半殖民地弱小民族国家主权——民族自决权问题在国际共产主义运动队伍中的论战过程及其发展历史。[1]

在专论"论社会帝国主义主权观的一大思想渊源：民族虚无主义的今昔"(1981年)中，作者回顾和缕述当年马克思、恩格斯和列宁与伪装成"国际主义者"的形形色色的民族虚无主义者论战的历史事实，追本溯源，探讨曾经猖獗一时的社会帝国主义主权观的理论基础和思想渊源，揭露它既是对国际法主权原则的粗暴践踏，又是对马克思主义主权观的彻底背离。[2]

应当指出，马克思主义主权观具有重要的现实指导意义。研究国际共产主义运动中的民族殖民地学说和国际法上的弱小民族国家主权学说，大有助于理解当代发展中国家的历史来由、现实地位、发展趋向以及南北问题的根源和实质。研究近代以来西方列强和社会帝国主义的霸权行径及相关谬论，大有助于认清当前全球化趋势下美国推行的霸权主义的历史渊源，大有助于明辨当代西方学者否定或淡化弱国主权的"理论先导"及其与当年相关谬论的一脉相承，异曲同工。不难看出，作者在国际经济法基本理论研究中强调经济主权原则，深刻批判美国经济霸权及西方学者否定或淡化弱国主权的种种谬论，源于对马克思主义主权观的深刻理解和研究积淀。

二、站在中国和发展中国家立场，提出南北矛盾发展的"6C律"

不容否认，作为法学学科之一，国际经济法学具有普世价值，各国国际经济法学者当有共同的法治理念、价值取向和学术追求。基于此，各国国际经济法学者需要

---

〔1〕 参见陈安：《列宁对民族殖民地革命学说的重大发展》，三联书店1981年版。本部分内容亦可参见陈安：《陈安论国际经济法学》（第1卷），复旦大学出版社2008年版，第136—342页。

〔2〕 参见陈安：《论社会帝国主义主权观的一大思想渊源：民族虚无主义的今昔》，载陈安：《陈安论国际经济法学》（第1卷），复旦大学出版社2008年版，第421—443页。

加强学术交流,增强共识,求同存异,共同促进世界性国际经济法学的发展和繁荣。

同样不容否认,作为法律规范之一,国际经济法既是发达国家巩固国际经济旧秩序的重要工具,也是发展中国家改革国际经济旧秩序、建立国际经济新秩序的重要工具。换言之,国际经济法规范体现了新旧法律规则既同时并存、又相互冲突的现实状况。在国际经济法的发展过程中,始终贯穿维护国际经济旧秩序与建立国际经济新秩序的斗争。相应地,各国国际经济法学者并非居于同一的、纯粹的、超脱的法治立场。在全球化背景下,由于国家利益、历史传统、意识形态、宗教信仰、文化背景等因素,各国特别是南北两类国家的国际经济法学者各有其不同的基本立场、法治理念、价值取向和学术追求。西方国家国际经济法学者对其立场或直言不讳,或"犹抱琵琶"。在国际经济法学研究中,作者一向旗帜鲜明地站在中国和发展中国家的立场,坚持和发展"三个世界"理论,坚持建立国际经济新秩序的目标,体现了"知识报国,兼济天下"的志向和胸怀。

(一)坚持和发展"三个世界"理论

20世纪90年代"东欧剧变"、冷战结束后,世界格局发生了重大变化。作者坚持和发展"三个世界"理论,明确指出:"现在的世界实际上存在着互相联系又互相矛盾着的三个方面,从而使全球划分为三个世界:首先,美国、苏联是第一世界,苏联在1991年瓦解之后,美国遂成为第一世界中唯一的超级大国;亚、非、拉美发展中国家和其他地区的发展中国家,是第三世界;处在这两者之间的发达国家是第二世界。中国是一个社会主义国家,也是一个发展中国家,它和其他发展中国家,曾经有过共同的经历,当前又面临着共同的斗争。过去、现在和将来长时间共同的处境和共同的利害,决定了中国属于第三世界。"[1]作者进一步分析,世纪之交,国际经济秩序破旧立新的争斗进入新的回合。其主要特点有三:一是冷战已告结束,和平与发展成为当代世界主题;二是霸权主义和强权政治在各种新"包装"下有新的发展,"新干涉主义"和"新炮舰政策"不时肆虐;三是经济全球化趋势加速发展,南北矛盾日益突出,广大发展中国家的经济主权面临严峻挑战。[2]

对当前国际经济秩序,西方学界有不同的解读,诸如"新自由主义经济秩序"论、"WTO宪政秩序"论和"经济民族主义扰乱全球化秩序"论等。其共同特点是,总体上回避"三个世界"、南北矛盾和新旧国际经济秩序等理论,试图另辟蹊径,以所谓"经济全球化""法律全球化"理论为先导,创建"国际经济秩序新论",以达到淡化或否定发

---

〔1〕　陈安:《论国际经济关系的历史发展与南北矛盾》,载陈安:《陈安论国际经济法学》(第1卷),复旦大学出版社2008年版,第59页。

〔2〕　同上书,第60—61页。

展中国家主权的目的。作者针对上述各说,逐一辨析,言简意赅,切中肯綮。[1]

针对"新自由主义经济秩序"论,作者指出,"宣扬全面自由化、市场化和私有化的新自由主义和'华盛顿共识'的本质是为国际垄断资本在全球扩张服务的";"'新自由主义经济秩序'的说教及其实践,实质上乃是殖民主义、资本主义、帝国主义三位一体的国际经济旧秩序在当代的更新和翻版,充其量只不过是'新瓶装旧酒'或'换汤不换药'罢了"。[2]

针对"WTO 宪政秩序"论,作者指出,其先天性缺陷和致命性弱点是忽略了当代 WTO 体制及其规则缺乏坚实的、真正的民主基础;WTO 体制虽然素来被称为摆脱了"权力导向",转而实行"规则导向",但其"立法"完全是"权力导向"之下的产物,带着先天的不公胎记,其"司法"和"执法"实践也出现过"财大者力大气粗"、霸权或强权国家不受约束或规避制裁的弊端,实际上体现了"规则导向"向"权力导向"的异化、转化;"要求将贸易自由宪法化、最高化、绝对化的主张是不可取的。[3]

针对"经济民族主义扰乱全球化秩序"论,作者指出,其实质是以莫须有的"罪名",力图迫使国际弱势群体离开原定的建立国际经济新秩序的奋斗目标。他主张,把"经济民族主义"理解为全球各民族,特别是各弱小民族坚持在经济上独立自主,坚持国际经济主权,是基本正确的。[4]

笔者以为,坚持和发展"三个世界"理论,是正确认识新时期中国在国际经济关系和国际体制的立场和战略定位问题的必要前提。基于"三个世界"理论,才能高屋建瓴,入木三分地分析当前西方强势主导的形形色色、似是而非的"国际经济秩序新论",也才能坚持和发展建立国际经济新秩序的理论。鉴于南北矛盾仍然是当前国际经济关系的主要矛盾和国际经济关系发展的重大问题,寻求建立各国普遍认同的公正的"国际经济秩序"和有效的"全球治理体系",[5]不能回避南北矛盾问题,更不

---

[1] 陈安:《论中国在建立国际经济新秩序中的战略定位—兼评"新自由主义经济秩序"论、"WTO 宪政秩序"论、"经济民族主义扰乱全球化秩序"论》,载陈安:《陈安论国际经济法学》(第 1 卷),复旦大学出版社 2008 年版,第 120—134 页。

[2] 同上书,第 121—122 页。

[3] 同上书,第 129 页。关于 WTO 体制的进一步剖析,参见陈安:《中国加入 WTO 十年的法理断想:简论 WTO 的法治、立法、执法、守法与变法》,载《现代法学》2010 年第 6 期。

[4] 陈安:《论中国在建立国际经济新秩序的战略定位——兼评"新自由主义经济秩序"论、"WTO 宪政秩序"论、"经济民族主义扰乱全球化秩序"论》,载陈安:《陈安论国际经济法学》(第 1 卷),复旦大学出版社 2008 年版,第 131—134 页。

[5] 近年来,西方学者除上述"国际经济秩序新论"外,还提出了所谓"全球治理"论。如在国际投资法领域,提出了所谓"外国直接投资的全球治理体系"(the global governance system for FDI)的概念,并指出这一体系主要是由 BITs 构成的。参见 Axel Berger, China's New Bilateral Investment Treaty Programme: Substance, Rational and Implications for Investment Law Making, Paper for the American Society of International Law International Economic Law Group (ASIL IELIG) 2008 biennial conference "The Politics of International Economic Law: The Next Four Years", Washington, D. C., November 14-15, 2008.

能回避改革国际经济旧秩序、建立国际经济新秩序这一根本性问题。

（二）提出南北矛盾发展的"6C 律"

早在《国际经济法总论》（1991 年）中，作者就以马克思主义为指导，指出："在国际经济和国际经济法的发展过程中，始终贯串着强权国家保持和扩大既得经济利益、维护国际经济旧秩序与贫弱国家争取和确保经济平权地位、建立国际经济新秩序的斗争。这些斗争，往往以双方的妥协和合作而告终，妥协合作之后又因新的利害矛盾和利益冲突而产生新的争斗，如此循环往复不已，每一次循环往复，均是螺旋式上升，都把国际经济秩序以及和它相适应的国际经济法规范，推进到一个新的水平或一个新的发展阶段。"[1]

在专论"南南联合自强五十年的国际经济立法反思：从万隆、多哈、坎昆到香港"（2006 年）和专著《国际经济法学专论》（2007 年）中，作者总结万隆会议以来的南北斗争史，进一步提出了南北矛盾发展的"6C 律"及其特点，强调南南联合自强对建立国际经济新秩序的重大意义。其主要观点概述如下：

国际经济秩序的新旧更替和国际经济法的破旧立新是在南北矛盾发展进程中产生的。南北两类国家之间既有互相矛盾、互相斗争的一面，又有互相依存、互相合作的一面。因此，南北矛盾斗争的每一个回合，往往以双方的妥协和国际经济秩序在某种程度上的除旧布新而告终。妥协之后经过一段期间，又在新的历史条件下产生新的矛盾斗争。南北矛盾上述规律性的发展进程，可概括称为螺旋式的"6C 轨迹"或"6C 律"，即 Contradiction（矛盾）→Conflict（冲突或交锋）→Consultation（磋商）→Compromise（妥协）→Cooperation（合作）→Coordination（协调）→Contradiction new（新的矛盾）……而当代国际经济秩序和国际经济法也就是在此种"6C 律"的基础上和支配下，不断经历着新旧交替、吐故纳新、弃旧图新和破旧立新的进程。[2] 南北问题的根本解决取决于国际经济新秩序的建立，取决于南北两类国家基于经济主权、公平互利和全球合作等国际经济法基本原则的真诚合作。发展中国家要在南北经济关系中获得真正平等的地位，只有依靠独立自主和自力更生，提高本国的经济实力，才能提高和增强在南北合作中的谈判地位和能力。与此同时，要大力加强南南

---

[1] 陈安：《国际经济法总论》，法律出版社 1991 年版，第 28—29 页；陈安：《论国际经济法的产生和发展》，载陈安：《陈安论国际经济法学》（第 1 卷），复旦大学出版社 2008 年版，第 64 页。

[2] 参见陈安：《南南联合自强五十年的国际经济立法反思：从万隆、多哈、坎昆到香港》，载陈安：《陈安论国际经济法学》（第 1 卷），复旦大学出版社 2008 年版，第 500—502 页；陈安主编：《国际经济法学专论》（第二版）（上编·总论），高等教育出版社 2007 年版，第 246、324—326 页。

合作，以求联合自强和共同发展。[1]

笔者认为，"6C律"的提出具有重要的理论和实践意义。首先，指明了发展中国家"斗争中求生存，合作中求发展"的必由之路。南北两类国家之间在矛盾、冲突之后继以磋商、妥协、合作和协调，张弛有度，循环往复，反映了南北双方既相互矛盾、冲突，又相互依存、合作的客观现实和南北矛盾运动的发展规律。第二，揭示发展中国家的持续斗争是促进国际经济秩序新旧更替和国际经济法破旧立新的原动力。发达国家为保持和发展其在国际经济交往中的优势地位，自然成为固守和维护国际经济旧秩序的守护神。而发展中国家为改变其在国际经济交往中的劣势地位，必然成为要求改革国际经济旧秩序、建立国际经济新秩序的主力军。第三，强调建立国际经济新秩序和国际经济法新规范的长期性和艰巨性。长远看来，在上述"6C律"的发展过程中，国际经济秩序的新旧更替和国际经济法的破旧立新总体上处于上升态势。但在特定历史时期，由于南北两类国家在矛盾、斗争中彼强此弱，此消彼长，在发达国家占上风的情况下，则可能出现下行态势。对发展中国家而言，如同逆水行舟，每一个进步，都需要艰辛的斗争和努力，稍有懈怠，已取得的成果可能得而复失或名存实亡。对于建立国际经济新秩序和国际经济法新规范的长期性和艰巨性，发展中国家应有战略的眼光和充分的准备。

（三）新时期中国在国际经济关系和国际体制中的立场和战略定位

关于新时期中国在国际经济关系和国际体制中的立场和战略定位，特别是中国在建立国际经济新秩序中的地位与作用，中外学者见仁见智。近年来，随着中国经济的迅速发展和国际影响力的显著提升，某些西方学者热衷于强调中国的"领导作用"和"大国责任"，甚至提出"中国威胁"论，其用意发人深思。[2] 中国是现存国际经济秩序的最大受惠者、维护者？改良者？抑或是改革者、革命者？众说纷纭。对此，作者在国际经济法理论研究中早有涉及，其相关视角和论述富有启迪意义。

首先，是关于研究中国国际经济法问题的角度及对中国的定位。在专论"我国涉外经济立法中可否规定对外资绝不实行国有化"（1986年）中，作者指出："从中国国情与国际舆情的结合上来考虑问题，从南北矛盾的历史与现实的结合上来考虑问

---

〔1〕 关于南南合作问题的系统论述，参见 An Chen, Weak versus Strong at the WTO, The South-South Coalition from Bandung to Hong Kong, The Geneva Post Quarterly, *The Journal of World Affairs*, April 2006, pp. 55-107。

〔2〕 关于"中国威胁"论的历史考察，参见陈安：《"黄祸"论的本源、本质及其最新霸权"变种"："中国威胁"论——中国对外经济交往史的主流及其法理原则的视角》，载《现代法学》2011年第6期。See also An Chen, On the Source, Essence of "Yellow Peril" Doctrine and Its Latest Hegemony "Variant"—the "China Threat" Doctrine: From the Perspective of Historical Mainstream of Sino-Foreign Economic Interactions and Their Inherent Jurisprudential Principles, *The Journal of World Investment & Trade*, Vol. 13, No. 1, 2012.

题，从新、旧两种国际经济秩序的更迭兴替上来考虑问题，作为在世界上具有举足轻重地位的社会主义国家和发展中国家，作为第三世界的一个中坚成员，中国在本国关于经济特区和沿海开放城市的涉外经济立法中，显然不宜、不必、不应、不容明文规定对外资绝对不实行征用或国有化。"[1]由此可见，作者一向主张的研究国际经济法问题的三个角度分别是中国国情与国际舆情的结合、南北矛盾的历史与现实的结合以及新、旧两种国际经济秩序的更迭兴替，对中国的明确定位是"第三世界中坚成员"。

其次，是关于新中国对外经济交往的一贯原则立场。鉴于新时期中国在国际经济关系和国际体制中的立场和战略定位是新中国成立以来的延续，有必要考察新中国对外经济交往的一贯原则立场。作者指出："独立自主和平等互利，乃是新中国对外经济交往中一贯坚持的最基本的法理原则和行为规范，也是中国对外经济交往健康发展的两大基石。"[2]

关于新时期中国在国际经济关系和国际体制中的立场和战略定位，作者在论述古代中国的自我定位、近现代中国历史形成的"中华民族爱国主义"独特内涵及新中国对外经济交往一贯原则立场的基础上，明确指出，中国应成为建立国际经济新秩序的积极推手，应致力于成为南南联合自强的中流砥柱之一，中国与全球弱势群体共同参与建立国际经济新秩序的战略目标，应当坚定不移，韧性斗争，百折不挠，应当既坚持战略原则的坚定性，又坚持策略战术的灵活性。[3]

概言之，历史已然成就了中国作为"第三世界中坚成员"的地位。作为"第三世界中坚成员"，中国的基本立场理应是，奉行独立自主和平等互利原则，成为建立国际经济新秩序的积极推手，致力于成为南南联合自强的中流砥柱之一，坚持建立国

---

　　[1]　陈安：《我国涉外经济立法中可否规定对外资绝不实行国有化》，载陈安：《陈安论国际经济法学》（第3卷），复旦大学出版社2008年版，第1209页。

　　[2]　陈安：《论源远流长的中国对外经济交往及其法理原则》，载陈安：《陈安论国际经济法学》（第1卷），复旦大学出版社2008年版，第98页。

　　[3]　陈安：《论中国在建立国际经济新秩序中的战略定位——兼评"新自由主义经济秩序"论、"WTO宪政秩序"论、"经济民族主义扰乱全球化秩序"论》，载陈安：《陈安论国际经济法学》（第1卷），复旦大学出版社2008年版，第109—120页。在该文发表之后，作者相继发表有关中国在建立国际经济新秩序中战略定位的专论，包括：陈安：《再论旗帜鲜明地确立中国在构建NIEO中的战略定位——兼论与时俱进，完整、准确地理解邓小平"对外28字方针"》，载《国际经济法学刊》2009年第16卷第3期，北京大学出版社2009年版；陈安：《三论中国在构建NIEO中的战略定位："匹兹堡发轫之路"走向何方——G20南北合作新平台的待解之谜以及"守法"与"变法"等理念碰撞》，载《国际经济法学刊》第16卷第4期，北京大学出版社2009年版；陈安：《中国加入WTO十年的法理断想：简论WTO的法治、立法、执法、守法与变法》，载《现代法学》2010年第6期。See also An Chen, What Should Be China's Strategic Position in the Establishment of New International Economic Order? With Comments on Neo-liberalistic Economic Order, Constitutional Order of the WTO and Economic Nationalism's Disturbance of Globalization, *The Journal of World Investment & Trade*, Vol. 10, No. 3, 2009; An Chen, Some Jurisprudential Thoughts upon WTO's Law-governing, Law-making, Law-enforcing, Law-abiding and Law-reforming, *The Journal of World Investment & Trade*, Vol. 11, No. 2, 2010.

际经济新秩序的战略目标。笔者认为，中国无论将来国际经济地位发生怎样的改变，应该有始终如一的、坚定的立场和目标。以国际投资关系为例，中国必须坚持和强调经济主权、公平互利和全球合作原则，将来不能因为居于净资本输出国地位就片面强调资本输出国的权益，苛求资本输入国限制其主权。中国一向反对发达国家"以邻为壑""损人利己"，同样，也要引以为戒，严格自律，言行一致。随着中国国际经济地位的改变，对外经济政策可以根据形势的变化而调整，但基本立场要坚定，不因国际经济地位的转变而变化，不因一国之利而忽略、漠视甚至放弃建立国际经济新秩序的远大目标和历史使命。中国国际经济法学者进行学术研究应有"第三世界中坚成员"学者的"立场"意识，政府主管部门在国际经济实践中也应有"第三世界中坚成员"的坚定立场。

三、论证南北矛盾中形成的国际经济法基本原则

一般而言，国际经济法的基本原则指国际社会普遍接受的调整国际经济关系的最基本的法律原则。作者主张，"国际经济法的基本原则，指的是贯穿于调整国际经济关系的各类法律规范之中的主要精神和指导思想，指的是这些法律规范的基础和核心"；[1]"在当代国际经济法基本规范或基本原则更新发展的全过程中，始终贯穿着强权国家保护既得利益、维护国际经济旧秩序与贫弱国家争取平权地位、建立国际经济新秩序的矛盾和斗争。这种矛盾斗争，乃是当代世界性'南北矛盾'斗争的主要内容。"[2]作者站在发展中国家的立场，论述国际经济法基本原则是在南北矛盾中形成的，旨在强调其"发展性"和"动态性"，特别是强调其与建立国际经济新秩序的密切关联，反映了中国国际经济法学的特色。以下概述作者论述国际经济法三大基本原则，即经济主权原则、公平互利原则和全球合作原则的部分重要观点。

（一）经济主权原则

如所周知，主权是国际法的基石。当前，为推进经济全球化，西方国家以理论为先导，提出了否定或淡化主权的种种理论。[3] 对于广大发展中国家而言，面临的首要任务是坚持和维护《联合国宪章》确立的国家主权原则。[4]

经济主权原则是国家主权原则在经济领域的体现。关于经济主权原则，作者重

---

〔1〕 陈安：《论经济主权原则是当代国际经济法首要的基本规范》，载陈安：《陈安论国际经济法学》（第1卷），复旦大学出版社2008年版，第344页。

〔2〕 同上书，第346页。

〔3〕 关于西方当代主权观的代表作，可参见 John H. Jackson, *Sovereignty, the WTO, and Changing Fundamentals of International Law*, Cambridge University Press, 2006。

〔4〕 See B. B. Ghali, B. Gosovic, *Global Leadership and Global Systemic Issues: South, North and the United Nations in a 21st Century World*, Transcend University Press, 2011.

点研究经济主权原则的形成原因及其基本内容、世纪之交经济主权"攻防战"及中国坚持经济主权原则的实践。

1. 经济主权原则的形成原因及其基本内容

作者指出,发展中国家强调和坚持经济主权有其特定的历史原因和现实原因。从历史上看,大多数发展中国家在第二次世界大战结束之前都处于殖民地、半殖民地地位;战后,殖民地、半殖民地弱小民族相继挣脱殖民枷锁,取得政治独立,但经济上仍然遭受原宗主国的控制,不同程度地处于从属或附庸的地位。政治主权是经济主权的前提,经济主权则是政治主权的保障。发展中国家强调经济主权,实质上是全世界弱小民族反殖民主义斗争的必要继续和必然发展。[1]

根据 1974 年《各国经济权利和义务宪章》的规定,作者概括经济主权的主要内容,包括:各国对本国内部以及本国涉外的一切经济事务享有完全、充分的独立自主权利,不受任何外来干涉;各国对境内一切自然资源享有永久主权;各国对境内的外国投资以及跨国公司的活动享有管理监督权;各国对境内的外国资产有权收归国有或征用;各国对世界性经贸大政享有平等的参与权和决策权。[2]

2. 世纪之交经济主权"攻防战"

近年来,作者以马克思主义主权观为指导,针对当前全球化趋势下西方国家否定或淡化主权的理论和实践,进行了深入细致的专题研究。作者以 WTO 体制运作十年来美国单边主义与 WTO 多边主义交锋的三大回合为中心,综合评析美国"1994年主权大辩论"、1998—2000 年"301 条款"争端案及 2002—2003 年"201 条款"争端案的前因后果和来龙去脉,指出这三次交锋的实质,都是美国经济"主权"(经济霸权)与各国群体经济主权之间限制与反限制的争斗,植根于美国早在 1994 年"入世"之初就已确立的"其单边主义政策高于其 WTO 义务"的既定方针。作者进而提出,这场以经济主权问题为核心的激烈论战对发展中国家的重要启示是:增强忧患意识,珍惜经济主权;力争对全球经贸大政决策权实行公平的国际再分配;善用经济主权保护民族权益,抵御霸权欺凌和其他风险;警惕理论陷阱,摒除经济主权"淡化"论。[3]

针对种种主权"淡化"论,作者深刻指出,"主权'过时'论、主权'废弃'论的主旨

---

〔1〕 陈安:《论经济主权原则是当代国际经济法首要的基本规范》,载《陈安论国际经济法学》,第 1 卷第 1 编第 VIII 部分,复旦大学出版社 2008 年版,第 347—348 页。

〔2〕 同上书,第 351—359 页。

〔3〕 陈安:《世纪之交在经济主权上的新争议与"攻防战":综合评析十年来美国单边主义与 WTO 多边主义交锋的三大回合》,载陈安:《陈安论国际经济法学》,第 1 卷第 1 编第 X 部分,复旦大学出版社 2008 年版,第 366—420 页。

在于彻底解除弱小民族的思想武装，好让当代霸权主义在全球通行无阻；'淡化'论和'弱化'论的'发展方向'，正是归宿于'过时'论和'废弃'论。这种归宿，绝不是弱小民族之福，而是善良的人们不能预见其后果的理论陷阱"。[1]

3. 中国坚持经济主权原则的实践

不言而喻，作为发展中大国，中国理应与广大发展中国家站在一起，坚持经济主权原则。作者主张，无论是国内立法实践，或是国际条约实践，中国都要坚持经济主权原则。

在国内立法实践方面，作者认为，在我国经济特区和沿海开放城市的涉外经济立法中，不应明文规定在任何情况下都不对外资实行征用或国有化。其主要理由是，从外资国有化问题的论战史、中外签订的双边投资保护协定、西方国家对"国有化"的理解及中国的宪法精神和现有政策等方面看，我国涉外经济立法中不适宜、不必要、不应当、不容许作此规定。其结论是，"鉴于东道国在必要时有权依法征收境内外资，并且给予适当补偿，乃是当代国家经济主权权利之一，而且已经成为国际通行的立法惯例，中国不应通过立法自行'弃权'"；"务必留权在手，但决不任意滥用！"[2]

在国际条约实践方面，作者主张，中国在"入世"谈判中应坚持经济主权原则，指出："中国是主权牢牢在握的独立国家，中国人民十分珍惜自己经过长期奋斗得来不易的主权权利……尽管'复关'和加入世贸组织的谈判旷日持久，难关重重，中国坚持经济主权原则，有关加入多边贸易体制的基本立场和方针不变。"[3]

当前，国际投资法发展迅速，其趋向值得密切关注。传统国际投资法本来就是发达国家为保护其海外投资者的产物，带有与生俱来的片面维护资本输出国权益的烙印，其新近发展并未起到平衡发达国家与发展中国家之间和东道国与外国投资者之间的权利和利益关系，而是更加片面强调保护发达国家和外国投资者的权益，进一步限制东道国的主权。通过此类规范的不断强化，发达国家推动投资自由化，以实现其国家利益。近年来，双边投资条约普遍规定接受"解决投资争端国际中心"（ICSID）的管辖，甚至规定投资者可以单方面启动 ICSID 程序。在经济全球化、自由化的背景下，我国的某些条约实践顺应了西方国家主导和推波助澜的所谓"时代潮

---

〔1〕 陈安：《世纪之交在经济主权上的新争议与"攻防战"：综合评析十年来美国单边主义与 WTO 多边主义交锋的三大回合》，载陈安：《陈安论国际经济法学》，第 1 卷第 1 编第 X 部分，复旦大学出版社 2008 年版，第 420 页。

〔2〕 陈安：《我国涉外经济立法中可否规定对外资绝不实行国有化》，载陈安：《陈安论国际经济法学》，第 3 卷第 3 编第 VIII 部分，复旦大学出版社 2008 年版，第 1197—1209 页。

〔3〕 陈安：《论中国在'入世'谈判中应当坚持经济主权原则》，载陈安：《陈安论国际经济法学》，第 1 卷第 1 编第 IX 部分，复旦大学出版社 2008 年版，第 365 页。

流"。针对 20 世纪 90 年代末以来中外双边投资协定"争端解决"条款的新发展,作者明确指出,中外双边投资协定实践中的"逐案审批同意""当地救济优先""东道国法律适用"和"重大安全例外"等四大"安全阀"不宜贸然全面拆除;[1]进而主张,应区分南、北两类国家,实行差别互惠,明文排除最惠国条款对争端程序的普遍适用,切实维护中国的应有权益。[2]

(二) 公平互利原则

公平互利原则是在"公平"这一传统法律概念基础上结合"互利"概念发展起来的国际经济法基本原则,强调实质上的平等,进一步明确了平等互利的含义,是平等互利原则的新发展。

关于公平互利原则,作者重点研究公平互利原则是平等互利原则的发展及公平互利原则的主旨。

1. 公平互利原则是平等互利原则的发展

作者在分析公平互利原则的形成过程中指出,在国际交往实践中,发展中国家认识到,仅仅从或主要从政治角度上强调主权平等原则,往往只能做到形式上的平等,难以实现实质上的平等。在某些场合,发达国家往往以形式上的平等掩盖实质上的不平等。因此,应从经济角度、从实质上重新审视传统意义上的主权平等原则,赋予其新的时代内容,互利原则由此产生。国家之间的关系,只有建立在平等的基础上,才能做到互利;只有真正地实行互利,才算是贯彻了平等的原则,才能实现实质上的平等。[3]

把传统的国际法上分立的平等原则与互利原则结合成调整国际政治、经济关系的一项基本原则,标志着国际法上平等原则的新发展。[4] 作者特别指出中国有关平等互利原则的实践对公平互利原则形成的贡献。在国内法实践方面,中国人民政治协商会议在 1949 年 9 月 29 日通过的《共同纲领》中,明确把平等互利规定为与外国建立外交关系的前提条件及对外经济交往、调整国际经济关系的基本准则。在国际法实践方面,1954 年 4—6 月,中国与印度、缅甸一起,率先把平等互利原则与互相尊重主权和领土完整、互不侵犯、互不干涉内政、和平共处等五项原则作为指导当代国

---

〔1〕　陈安:《中外双边投资协定中的四大"安全阀"不宜贸然拆除—美、加型 BITs 谈判范本关键性"争端解决"条款剖析》,载陈安:《陈安论国际经济法学》,第 3 卷第 3 编第 Ⅴ 部分,复旦大学出版社 2008 年版,第 1079—1108 页。

〔2〕　陈安:《区分两类国家,实行差别互惠:再论 ICSID 体制赋予中国的四大"安全阀"不宜贸然全面拆除》,载陈安:《陈安论国际经济法学》,第 3 卷第 3 编第 Ⅵ 部分,复旦大学出版社 2008 年版,第 1109—1146 页。

〔3〕　陈安:《论国际经济法中的公平互利原则是平等互利原则的重大发展》,载陈安:《陈安论国际经济法学》,第 1 卷第 1 编第 Ⅻ 部分,复旦大学出版社 2008 年版,第 446—447 页。

〔4〕　周鲠生:《国际法》(上册),商务印书馆 1981 年版,第 213 页。

际关系的基本准则,逐渐获得了国际社会的普遍认同。[1]

2. 公平互利原则的主旨

关于公平互利原则的主旨,作者认为:"在国际经济交往中强调公平互利,究其主要宗旨,端在于树立和贯彻新的平等观。对于经济实力相当、实际地位基本平等的同类国家说来,公平互利落实于原有平等关系的维持;对于经济实力悬殊、实际地位不平等的不同类国家说来,公平互利落实于原有形式平等关系或虚假平等关系的纠正以及新的实质平等关系的创设。"[2]

在论证公平互利原则主旨的合理性时,作者进一步指出,"这种新的平等观,是切合客观实际需要的,是科学的,也是符合马克思主义基本观点的。早在百余年前,马克思在剖析平等权利时,就曾经指出:用同一尺度去衡量和要求先天禀赋各异、后天负担不同的劳动者,势必造成各种不平等的弊病,并且断言:'要避免所有这些弊病,权利就不应当是平等的,而应当是不平等的。'马克思的这种精辟见解,对于我们深入理解当代发展中国家提出的关于贯彻公平互利原则、实行非互惠普惠制等正义要求,具有现实的指导意义。"[3]作者形象生动的结论是,对经济实力悬殊的国家,"平等"地用同一尺度去衡量,用同一标准去要求,实行绝对的、无差别的"平等待遇"的实际效果,"有如要求先天不足、大病初愈的弱女与体魄强健、训练有素的壮汉,在同一起跑点上'平等'地赛跑,从而以'平等'的假象掩盖不平等的实质"。[4]

（三）全球合作原则

全球合作原则是 1974 年《建立国际经济新秩序宣言》和《各国经济权利和义务宪章》倡导的一项富有时代特点的国际经济法基本原则。基于南北问题的认识,要实现建立国际经济新秩序的目标,必须进一步强调、坚持和实践全球合作原则。

关于全球合作原则,作者重点论证南北合作是全球合作原则的中心环节和南南联合自强是建立国际经济新秩序的唯一路径。

1. 南北合作是全球合作原则的中心环节

在揭示南北矛盾是当代国际经济关系主要矛盾的基础上,作者指出,南北合作是全球合作原则的中心环节,是国际经济关系上众多弱者与少数强者之间在不同阶段的互相妥协和互相让步;就其内在实质而言,是国际经济关系中剥削者与被剥削

---

〔1〕 陈安:《论国际经济法中的公平互利原则是平等互利原则的重大发展》,载陈安:《陈安论国际经济法学》,第 1 卷第 1 编第 XII 部分,复旦大学出版社 2008 年版,第 447—448 页。
〔2〕 同上书,第 449 页。
〔3〕 同上书,第 449—450 页。
〔4〕 同上书,第 448—449 页。

者、强者与弱者之间的妥协,也是对弱肉强食规则缓慢的逐步否定。[1]

南北合作的依据是发达国家与发展中国家在现实经济生活中存在极其密切的互相依存和互相补益关系。这决定了南北两类国家"合则两利,离则两伤",促使南北两类国家在不同发展阶段的斗争中终究要相互妥协,作出"南北合作"的选择,从而解决各个相应阶段的南北矛盾。

南北合作的阻力来自发达国家,特别是来自第一世界的美国。相对而言,第二世界的政界、法界中,出现了一些能较冷静正视南北互相依存现实的明智人士。

关于南北合作的成效,基于对《洛美协定》和《科托努协定》的研究,作者在肯定南北合作生命力之后,深刻指出,"《洛美协定》式的南北合作,仍然远未能从根本上改变南北双方之间很不平等、很不公平的经济关系";"距离实现彻底公平互利的南北合作从而建立起国际经济新秩序的总目标,还有相当漫长、艰辛的路程"。[2]

2. 南南联合自强是建立国际经济新秩序的唯一路径

在分析南南合作与南北合作的本质区分的基础上,作者指出,南南合作是国际经济关系上众多弱者之间的互济互助,以共同应对或联合反抗来自强者或霸者的弱肉强食。

作者进一步论述南南合作的战略意义,指出:现存的国际经济体制,是在经济实力基础上形成的。要改变它,首先也要靠实力;在经济上过分依赖发达国家,对发展中国家经济发展极为不利。加强南南合作,走弱者联合自强的道路,才是增强自身经济实力的可靠途径;南南合作,把各个分散的、在经济上相对弱小的发展中国家联合起来,凝聚成一股强大的国际力量,可望提高在南北对话中的地位和能力;南南合作是建立在弱者互助互济、公平互利的基础上,是全球合作的新兴模式和强大趋势,本身就是国际经济新秩序的体现。[3]

在专论"南南联合自强五十年的国际经济立法反思:从万隆、多哈、坎昆到香港"(2006 年)中,作者回顾近五十年来南北矛盾与南北合作的史实,总结贯穿全程并将长期存在的发展轨迹,深刻指出,南北矛盾和冲突,南北力量对比上的"南弱北强",势必在今后相当长的历史时期持续存在。鉴此,在南北角力的进程中,南南联合自强者务必树立"持久战"的战略思想,逐步更新国际经济立法、建立国际经济新秩序

---

〔1〕　参见陈安:《全球合作的新兴模式和强大趋势:南南合作与"77 国集团"》,载陈安:《陈安论国际经济法学》,第 1 卷第 1 编第 XIV 部分,复旦大学出版社 2008 年版,第 463—466 页。

〔2〕　参见陈安:《南北合作是解决南北矛盾的最佳选择》,载陈安:《陈安论国际经济法学》,第 1 卷第 1 编第 XIII 部分,复旦大学出版社 2008 年版,第 455—459 页。

〔3〕　参见陈安:《全球合作的新兴模式和强大趋势:南南合作与"77 国集团"》,载陈安:《陈安论国际经济法学》,第 1 卷第 1 编第 XIV 部分,复旦大学出版社 2008 年版,第 466—468 页。

的唯一路径是南南联合自强。[1]

显然，作者关于国际经济法基本原则的论述，以马克思主义为指导，站在发展中国家的立场，有理有据，推陈出新，深刻论证了南北矛盾中形成的"调整国际经济关系的各类法律规范之中的主要精神和指导思想"，是对国际经济法学基本问题特别是南北矛盾发展"6C律"的进一步阐发和深化，均服务于建立国际经济新秩序的目标。经济主权原则强调尊重和维护各国特别是发展中国家的经济主权，反对超级大国推行经济霸权和"淡化"弱国主权的行径，是建立国际经济新秩序的必要基础和前提。公平互利原则旨在确立和贯彻新的平等观，以实质平等取代形式平等，特别是对于经济实力悬殊、实际地位不平等的南北两类国家而言，体现为纠正原有的形式平等关系及创设新的实质平等关系，是建立国际经济新秩序必须遵循的基本准则。全球合作原则旨在促进和调整南北两类国家之间的合作关系和南方国家相互之间合作关系，以期实现各国经济发展和合作共赢的目标，是建立国际经济新秩序必须遵循的路径和规范。可见，上述国际经济法三大基本原则的核心内容表达和凝聚了中国特色国际经济法学的基本立场、法治理念、价值取向和学术追求，奠定了中国特色国际经济法学体系的坚实基础。

四、知识报国，兼济天下，发出中国和南方学者的时代强音

从作者的治学立场、理念、追求及对中国特色国际经济法学的杰出贡献，我们看到了老一辈知识分子的命运是如何与国家的命运紧密相连，更感受到老一辈知识分子"知识报国、兼济天下"的历史责任感、宽广襟怀、坚定的政治立场和鲜明的价值取向。作者强烈的学术使命感、历史与现实结合的研究方法及学术成果"国际化"的不懈努力尤其值得我们学习。

（一）强烈的学术使命感

作者指出，"当今发达国家国际经济法诸多论著的共同基本特点，是重点研究发达国家对外经济交往中产生的法律问题，作出符合发达国家权益的分析和论证。反观中国，作为积弱积贫的发展中国家之一员，这样的研究工作还处在幼弱阶段，远未能适应我国对外交往的迫切需要和对外开放的崭新格局。"[2]作者正是怀着强烈的学术使命感，30多年如一日，身体力行，殚精竭虑，致力于中国特色国际经济法学的创建。

中国国际经济法学主要是在引进和借鉴西方国际经济法学的基础上产生和发

---

[1] 参见陈安：《南南联合自强五十年的国际经济立法反思：从万隆、多哈、坎昆到香港》，载陈安：《陈安论国际经济法学》，第1卷第1编第XV部分，复旦大学出版社2008年版，第479—506页。

[2] 陈安：《〈陈安论国际经济法学〉自序》，载陈安：《陈安论国际经济法学》，第1卷，复旦大学出版社2008年版，第3页。

展起来的,国际经济法学的概念、术语、原则、规则等大多来自西方。汲取和借鉴西方国际经济法学理论,首先要有"扬弃"精神,"取其精华,去其糟粕"。作者之所以能取得独树一帜的国际经济法研究成果,成就中国和发展中国家的"一家之言",最重要的是具有破旧立新的历史责任感、决心和勇气,坚持"扬弃"精神,独立思考,勇于创新,不迷信权威,不盲目附和西方所谓"主流理论"。作者既能深入钻研西方国际经济法学理论,又能摆脱西方学者由立场、视野、目标所决定的不合时宜的法律观念或思维定式,特别是能摆脱阻碍建立国际经济新秩序的西方法律观念的羁绊,为建立国际经济新秩序而创建和发展新的法律概念、观念和理论。

（二）历史与现实结合的研究方法

中国属于发展中的社会主义国家,中国特色国际经济法学的研究服务于建立国际经济新秩序和建立社会主义市场经济体制的目标,这决定了中国国际经济法学界在吸收西方国家有关研究成果的同时,应有符合本国国情和本国目标的研究方法。在种种研究方法中,对创建中国特色国际经济法学尤为重要的当是历史和现实结合的研究方法。

如前所述,作者对南北问题、中国的战略定位和国际经济法基本原则的论述,无不采取历史和现实结合的研究方法。在这方面,我国国际经济法学界老一辈学者的沧桑历练、关注焦点、观察视角、敏感程度及精神境界很值得中青年学者借鉴和学习。老一辈学者曾亲身经历过"三座大山"压迫下的旧社会,对西方列强的本质有深刻的认识和高度的警惕。而中青年学者成长于改革开放的新时代,有更多的机会接受西方的法学教育和理论成果,更容易接受西方主导建构的所谓"主流理论"。对中国特色国际经济法学的一些基本问题,诸如南北矛盾、国家主权等的认识及研究西方理论的"扬弃"精神,中青年学者与老一辈学者相较尚有一定差距。这从一个侧面反映了历史和现实结合研究方法的重要性。我们需要更深入地了解西方国际经济法的渊源、发展及其实质,才能更科学、更全面地探求中国特色国际经济法学的历史使命和发展方向。

（三）学术成果"国际化"的不懈努力

鉴于国际经济法学的学科特色,中国国际经济法学者应积极主动地开展国际学术交流和合作,在国际学术论坛上,对国际经济法学的重要理论和实践问题提出中国学者的见解,表明中国和发展中国家的立场,为世界性国际经济法学的发展和繁荣作出应有的贡献。

作者大学期间专攻法学,修习英语一年,毕业后自学俄语、日语。1981年以"知天命"之年负笈于美国哈佛大学,即与国际学术同行开展平等交流和对话,受到该校东亚法学研究所所长 A. von Mehren 教授、副所长 F. K. Upham 教授的高度评价。[1]

一直以来，作者力倡中国国际经济法学者的学术成果"走出国门"，积极弘扬中华文化，参与国际争鸣，发出"中国之声"。自 1981 年在美国《国际法与比较法学报》首次发表英文论文以来，作者持续发表和出版英文论著，成果丰硕。[2] 特别是，2006—2011 年间，作者在享誉国际经济法学界的《世界投资与贸易学刊》（瑞士日内瓦出版）连续发表 6 篇重要论文，创各国学者在该刊同期发表论文数的最高纪录。[3] 其英文论著立场坚定，论证严谨，特别是具有鲜明的中国特色，因而产生了重要的国际学术影响。发展中国家智库"南方中心"秘书长 Branislav Gosovic 先生认为，作者有关南南联合自强的论述"能给人以清晰鲜明的方针政策性的启示，会使'南方中心'公报的读者们很感兴趣，特别因为这是您从一个正在崛起的举足轻重的大国发出的呐喊！"[4] 更为难得的是，来自发达国家的多边投资担保机构首席法律顾问 L. Weisenfeld 先生和"解决投资争端国际中心"法律顾问 A. Parra 先生等同样对作者的学术主张和水平表示由衷赞赏和信服。[5]

中国特色国际经济法学是世界性国际经济法学的一个重要组成部分。中国特色国际经济法学的发展和繁荣在一定程度上有赖于世界性国际经济法学的发展和繁荣，世界性国际经济法学的发展和繁荣也不能缺少中国特色国际经济法学的参与和奉献。中国特色国际经济法学的使命是，站在中国和广大发展中国家立场，紧密联系中国和国际实践，汲取具有普世价值的国际经济法学精华，维护和发展国际社会普遍认同的国际经济法原则，积极影响和促进国际经济法实践的健康发展。

这是一项长期的、宏大的理论工程，需要几代中国国际经济法学人矢志不移、坚持不懈的努力奋斗。30 多年来，陈安老师等老一辈国际经济法学者筚路蓝缕，为中国特色国际经济法学的创建和发展做出了开拓性的贡献，亦成为后学之师范。近年来，厦门大学国际经济法学术团队中青年教师积极向国外学术刊物投稿，在国际学术界崭露头角，显示出较强的学术发展潜力。自 2002 年以来，厦门大学法学院辩论

---

〔1〕《（美国）哈佛大学法学院斯托利讲座教授、东亚法学研究所所长 A. von Mehren 教授致陈安教授函（1982 年 10 月 25 日）》《（美国）波士顿大学法学院教授、哈佛大学东亚法学研究所前副所长 F. K. Upham 教授致陈安教授函（1982 年 11 月 29 日）》，载陈安：《陈安论国际经济法学》，第 5 卷第 8 编第 III、二（二十六）、（二十五）部分，复旦大学出版社 2008 年版，第 2613—2614 页。

〔2〕陈安老师的主要英文著述，载陈安：《陈安论国际经济法学》，第 4、5 卷第 7 编，复旦大学出版社 2008 年版，第 1725—2513 页。

〔3〕参见康安峰、蒋围：《致力"走出去"：厦门大学国际经济法研究团队科研"国际化"的初步实践》，载《国际经济法学刊》第 18 卷第 2 期，北京大学出版社 2011 年版，第 264—282 页。

〔4〕《南方中心秘书长 Branislav Gosovic 致陈安教授函（2006 年 2 月 1 日）》，载陈安：《陈安论国际经济法学》第 5 卷第 8 编第 III、二（二十二）部分，复旦大学出版社 2008 年版，第 2591—2592 页。

〔5〕《"多边投资担保机构"（MIGA）首席法律顾问 L. Weisenfeld 致陈安教授函（2004 年 5 月 12 日）》《"解决投资争端国际中心"（ICSID）法律顾问 A. Parra 致陈安教授函（1990 年 3 月 22 日，1990 年 8 月 22 日）》，载陈安：《陈安论国际经济法学》第 5 卷第 8 编第 III、二（二十七）、（二十）部分，复旦大学出版社 2008 年版，第 2599—2602 页。

队连续参加 Willem C. Vis 国际商事模拟辩论赛（英文）、Jessup 国际法模拟法庭辩论赛（英文）和国际人道法模拟法庭辩论赛（英文）等国际性专业大赛,形成优良传统,屡获佳绩,如荣获 Jessup 国际法模拟法庭辩论赛"Hardy C. Dillard 最佳书状奖第一名"（2006 年）和"反方诉状第一名"（2011 年）,为我国法学教育赢得了国际声誉,也给国人莫大的启示和鼓舞。需要明确的是,上述辩论赛均是在西方主导下进行的西式"游戏规则"的演练和竞争。鉴此,在研究和掌握这些规则以求"知彼"的同时,更需要独立思考,明确"己方"的立场、信念、追求和使命,力求在"知己知彼"的基础上增强专业能力和创新精神,担负起推动和促进建立国际经济新秩序的历史重任。相比老一辈国际经济法学者和我们这一代"老三届"学者,青年学者和学生后来居上,具有更好的基础、更高的起点、更多的机会及更广阔的发展前景,专心致志,自强不息,在创建和发展中国特色国际经济法学方面当有更大的作为,更大的贡献。

The Notion and Pursuit for International Economic Law
with Chinese Characteristics
—The Academic Initiatives and Achievement of An CHEN
on International Economic Law

Abstract：An CHEN on International Economic Law is the foundation-work for establishing the international economic law with Chinese characteristics. The academic initiatives and achievement of the work are represented mainly by analyzing the development of international economic relations, revealing the source and substance of South-North issue, and clarifying the sovereignty theory under the guidance of Marxism; maintaining the stance of China and developing States, insisting on and developing the "Three World" theory, insisting on the objective of establishing new international economic order and creating the concept of "6C track" on development of South-North contradiction; and expounding economic sovereignty principle, equitable and mutual benefit principle and global cooperation principle. The work fully demonstrates the author's notion and pursuit for establishing international economic law with Chinese characteristics. In particular, the author's strong academic mission, the researching method of combining history with reality and continual efforts for the "internationalization" of his academic fruits are worthy studying.

Key words：South-North contradiction; economic sovereignty; new international economic order

第五节　论中国特色国际经济法学[*]

【摘要】　在探讨国际法学"国家特色"问题的基础上，本文指出，中国国际经济法学研究具有"中国特色"是顺理成章的；尽管具有"国际性"或融合于"国际话语体系"的特征，中国特色国际经济法学的指导思想和理论基础是马克思主义；作为发展中大国，中国奉行独立自主和平等互利原则，坚持建立国际经济新秩序的目标，是建立国际经济新秩序的积极推手和南南联合自强的中流砥柱；面临形形色色西方"新理论"的挑战，中国理应坚持和发展国际社会普遍认同的经济主权、公平互利和合作发展等国际经济法学基本原则；中国特色国际经济法学与世界各国"共同的"国际经济法学的发展相辅相成。

【关键词】　中国特色；国际经济法学；国际经济新秩序；指导思想；基本原则

关于中国特色国际经济法学的一些基本问题，涉及学科建设、治学理念和研究方法，思索再三，略陈管见，希望引起学界进一步关注和讨论。

一、"中国特色国际经济法学"正名

学界普遍认同，国际法学涵盖国际公法学、国际私法学和国际经济法学。[1] 在此，首先讨论国际法学的国家特色问题，如果"中国特色国际法学"这一前提性问题得以明确，"中国特色国际经济法学"的正名问题也就迎刃而解了。

（一）国际法和国际法学的国家特色问题

作为法律部门，顾名思义，国际法为"国家之间"的法律，其"国际性"毋庸置疑。一般认为，不存在中国国际法、美国国际法或法国国际法之分，国际法本应无所谓国家特色或国家属性（country-specific or country oriented）。[2] 进而言之，作为研究国际法发展规律的学科，国际法学可否强调国家特色？各国国际法学是否各具特色？答案似乎也应是否定的。

然而，历史表明，国际法本身自始就具有鲜明的国家类型、国家集团特色或属

　＊　原载《国际经济法学刊》2018 年第 1 期。

　〔1〕　关于国际公法、国际私法、国际经济法之间的关系，参见曾华群：《国际经济法导论（第二版）》，法律出版社 2007 年版，第 38—40 页；曾令良主编：《国际法学》，人民法院出版社、中国社会科学出版社 2003 年版，第 3—4 页。

　〔2〕　See Xue Hanqin, *Chinese Contemporary Perspectives on International Law：History，Culture and International Law*，Martinus Nijhoff Publishers，2012，pp. 52-53.

性。尽管学界对国际法史有不同的解读，[1]一般承认，传统国际法是西方世界的产物，是由西方国家创造并长期主导的。国际法史溯及罗马法的"万民法"(*jus gentium*)。[2] 1648 年终结欧洲新教教徒与天主教教徒之间"三十年战争"的"威斯特伐利亚和约"(Peace of Westphalia)，被视为"近代国际法的源头"。在"威斯特伐利亚体系"(Westphalian system)或"威斯特伐利亚文明"(Westphalian civilization)中，"国际大家庭"(family of nations)的成员限于欧洲基督教国家；调整国家相互之间关系的规则完全由欧洲国家制定，只有欧洲"文明国家"才是国际法的"主体"，而处于殖民地地位的亚、非、拉贫弱民族和处于半封建半殖民地地位的近代中国，则是国际法的"客体"或"准主体"。[3] 所谓"国际习惯"(international custom)也是形成于"文明世界"的"国家实践"和"法律确信"。[4] 晚清学者郑观应目睹列强假"公法"之名恃强凌弱的所作所为，早已深刻指出："公法乃凭虚理，强者可执其法以绳人，弱者必不免隐忍受屈也。"[5]此说入木三分，不仅完全适用于当年，也在一定程度上适用于今日！根据当代国际法，国家不分强弱、大小、贫富，均取得了国际法的"主体"地位，享有法律上(*de jure*)平等的地位，然而，在国际法的创制、适用及解释等，发达国家与发展中国家之间事实上(*de facto*)的不平等是显而易见的。特别表现在，由于传统和现实的原因，国际法的所谓"国际通行规则"(international common rules)通常是由发达国家制定或主导制定的，[6]有些甚至是发达国家国内法的"国际化"。[7] 在国际

---

　　[1]　关于国际法史的代表性简要表述，参见〔英〕M. 阿库斯特：《现代国际法概论》，汪瑄、朱奇武、余叔通、周仁译，中国社会科学出版社 1981 年版，第 14—27 页；〔苏联〕童金主编：《国际法》，邵天任、刘文宗、程远行译，法律出版社 1988 年版，第 11—25 页；邵津主编：《国际法》，北京大学出版社、高等教育出版社 2000 年版，第 3—8 页；〔意〕安东尼奥·卡塞斯：《国际法》，蔡从燕等译，法律出版社 2009 年版，第 29—61 页。See also R. P. Anand (India), *Studies in International Law and History*, *An Asian Perspective*, Martinus Nijhoff Publishers, 2004, pp. xi-xiii, 24-26.

　　[2]　在罗马时代，"市民法"与"万民法"并行不悖。"万民法"意指"各民族共有"的法律，它是在不违反"市民法"古老法律形式的前提下，由罗马裁判官或其他高级长官通过长期的司法实践，吸收其他民族的习惯法，逐渐创制形成的新的法律规范。参见江平、米健：《罗马法基础》，中国政法大学出版社 1987 年版，第 12—13 页。当前，西方学者在研究国际法的新发展中，也采用"新万民法"(new *jus gentium*)的概念。See A. A. Cancado Trindade, *International Law for Humankind*: *Towards a New jus gentium*, Martinus Nijhoff Publishers, 2006.

　　[3]　关于"威斯特伐利亚文明"的简评，参见 David P. Fidler, Revolt Against or From Within the West? TWAIL, the Developing World, and the Future Direction of International Law, *Chinese Journal of International Law*, Vol. 2, No. 1, 2003, pp. 34-39。

　　[4]　See Bin Cheng, *General Principles of Law as Applied by International Courts and Tribunals*, Cambridge University Press, 1994, pp. 11-12.

　　[5]　参见(清)郑观应：《盛世危言·公法》(卷一)，三味堂刊光绪二十四年(1898 年)版，第 42 页。转引自陈安：《论国际经济法的产生和发展》，载陈安：《陈安论国际经济法学》，第 1 卷第 1 编第 III 部分，复旦大学出版社 2008 年版，第 68 页。

　　[6]　关于当前国际经济立法弊端的分析，参见陈安：《论 WTO 体制下的立法、执法、守法与变法》，载陈安主编：《国际经济法学刊》第 17 卷第 4 期，北京大学出版社 2010 年版，第 3—5 页。

　　[7]　例如，世界银行集团多边投资担保机构(Multilateral Investment Guarantee Agency, MIGA)体制源于美国"海外私人投资公司"(Overseas Private Investment Corporation, OPIC)体制。参见陈安主编：《MIGA 与中国》，福建人民出版社 1995 年版，第 3—14 页；GATT/WTO 的主要特点，是根据主要发达国家、尤其是美国的法律和实践模式而形成。发达国家、尤其是美国和欧盟，一直在 GATT/WTO 体系中追求其自身的发展利益和目标，很大程度上已取得成功。参见沓吉拉·劳·达斯(Bhagirath Lal Das)：《WTO 与多边贸易体系之过去、现在与未来》，第三世界网络(TWN)2004 年版，第 16—19 页。

实践中,尽管多边条约或双边条约是以当事国的自愿加入或签订为前提,一些发展中国家迫于作为多边条约主导方或双边条约对方的发达国家的种种现实压力,或别无选择,不得不违心加入或签订相关条约。[1]

相应地,近代以来,作为研究国际法发展规律的学科,国际法学由西方学者创立、发展和传播,由西方学者主导话语权。所谓"国际法之父"、近代国际法学的奠基人是荷兰学者雨果·格老秀斯(Hugo Grotius)。[2] 近现代"国际法学大家"及著名国际法学术论著也大多出自西方国家。对中国和广大发展中国家来说,国际法学是"舶来品",在引进过程中首先需要研究和借鉴西方国际法学的学术成果。特别是,发展中国家的许多国际法学者在西方国家接受系统的法学和国际法学教育,浸润其中,所受的学术影响在所难免。当前,美国主导国际法学"虚理"的所谓"新发展",如"主权淡化"、[3]"先发制人"[4]等,或理论先导实践紧随,或实践先行事后论证,偏离或挑战《联合国宪章》确立的包括国家主权原则等基本国际法规范。国际法学面临"一言堂"或"一家独大"发展的现实危机。显然,尽管没有言明,世上真真切切存在美国特色国际法和美国特色国际法学。[5] 在此情况下,希望有超脱于各国特色的"同一"的、"纯粹"的国际法学,或者,自动放弃或不愿主张本国国际法学的应有特色,显然是天真的,不切实际的。

事实表明,各具特色的各国国际法学是客观存在的。1917年"十月社会主义革命"胜利后,苏联国际法学率先打破了西方国家国际法学的"一统天下",提出了社会主义国际主义、各民族平等与民族自决、和平共处等新原则。[6] 1949年中华人民共和国成立以来,对传统国际法的态度具有批判性反对(critical rejection)和积极建设(positive construction)的明显特征。一方面,我国坚决反对旨在维护殖民主义和帝国主义强权利益、损害绝大多数不发达国家和民族权益的传统国际法,主张列强强

---

〔1〕 See M. Sornarajah, *The International Law on Foreign Investment*, Cambridge University Press, 1996, pp. 227-229.

〔2〕 关于格老秀斯对国际法学的贡献,参见沈宗灵:《格老秀斯的自然法和国际法学说》,载中国国际法学会主办:《中国国际法年刊》(1983),中国对外翻译出版公司1983年版,第54—69页。

〔3〕 关于"主权淡化"论的分析,参见陈安:《世纪之交围绕经济主权的新"攻防战"——从美国的"主权大辩论"及其后续影响看当代"主权淡化"论之不可取》,载陈安主编:《国际经济法论丛》第4卷,法律出版社2001年版,第78—138页。

〔4〕 关于"'预防性'攻击"和"先发制人"战略的违法性之分析,参见梁西:《国际法的危机》,载《法学评论》2004年第1期,第3—9页。

〔5〕 关于"霸权国际法"的分析,参见薛磊:《变动中的国际体系与国际法的发展》,载中国国际法学会主办:《中国国际法年刊》(2006),世界知识出版社2007年版,第222—239页。

〔6〕 参见〔苏联〕童金主编:《国际法》,邵天任、刘文宗、程远行译,法律出版社1988年版,第26—32页。

加于我国的一系列不平等条约无效;[1]另一方面,我国于 1954 年提出了和平共处五项原则,为国际新秩序的创建和国际法的发展作出了积极贡献。[2] 相应地,我国国际法学界也相继提出了"新中国的国际法学""具有中国特色的国际法学"及"有中国特色的国际法学理论"等相关主张。[3] 进而言之,"发展中国家特色国际法学"亦已然存在。战后,广大发展中国家对传统国际法的态度是,既非全盘接受,也非全盘否定。在非殖民化进程中,发展中家的国际法学界结合国际实践,借重联合国等国际体制,批判传统国际法,提出了"民族自决权""自然资源永久主权"及"发展权"等新概念和新原则,以求建立国际新秩序和发展国际法。世纪之交,出现了以"国际法的第三世界进路"(Third World Approaches to International Law,TWAIL)为主题的研究文献,批判性地分析传统国际法以促进形成对发展中家更为公平公正的进路。[4] 也有国际法学者注意比较研究西方学者与第三世界学者对特定国际法问题的不同立场和主张。[5]

应当说明,尽管"各国国际法学各具特色",各国普遍承认,世界上只存在一种国际法体系。[6] 由于国际法学科"国际性"的特征,揭示"各国国际法学各具特色"这一客观存在,并非主张或鼓励各国国际法学界相互对立,分道扬镳,而是期望各国国际法学界在明确"各具特色"的前提下,加强交流互鉴,求同存异,达成共识,逐渐形成国际社会普遍认同的法学理念、概念、原则及规则,从而促进国际法的共同实践和渐进发展,[7]也促进反映国际法共同实践的、各国国际法学界普遍认同的"共同的"国际法学的发展和繁荣。

(二)"中国特色国际经济法学"的求证

作为战后的新兴学科,国际经济法学也是产生于西方国家,其概念、原则、规则

---

〔1〕 关于"不平等条约"概念在我国的提出和使用,参见张建华:《孙中山与中国不平等条约概念的起始》,载《中国国际法年刊》2000/2001 卷,法律出版社 2005 年版,第 273—292 页。

〔2〕 See Xue Hanqin, *Chinese Contemporary Perspectives on International Law:History,Culture and International Law*,Martinus Nijhoff Publishers,2012,pp.57-69.

〔3〕 参见宦乡:《为创建新中国的国际法学而努力》,载中国国际法学会主办:《中国国际法年刊》(1982),中国对外翻译出版公司 1982 年版,第 5 页;潘抱存:《中国国际法理论新探索》,法律出版社 1999 年版,第 4 页;王厚立:《在中国国际法学会"21 世纪初的中国与国际法"研讨会上的讲话》,载中国国际法学会主办:《中国国际法年刊》(2002/2003 卷),法律出版社 2006 年版,第 291—295 页。

〔4〕 See David P. Fidler,Revolt Against or From Within the West? TWAIL,the Developing World,and the Future Direction of International Law,*Chinese Journal of International Law*,Vol.2,No.1,2003,pp.29-76.

〔5〕 See Kalana Senaratne,Internal Self-Determination in International Law:A Critical Third-World Perspective,*Asian Journal of International Law*,Vol.3,Iss.2,2013,pp.305-339.

〔6〕 苏联"十月革命"后,有人曾提出,世界上存在两种国际法体系:一种适用于资本主义国家之间,一种适用于资本主义国家与社会主义国家之间。这种观点很快就放弃了。参见〔英〕M.阿库斯特:《现代国际法概论》,汪瑄、朱奇武、余叔通、周仁译,中国社会科学出版社 1981 年版,第 20—23 页。

〔7〕《联合国宪章》第十三条第一项规定,联合国大会应"发动研究,并作成建议……提倡国际法之逐渐发展与编纂"。可以认为,"促进国际法的共同实践和渐进发展"是各国国际法学界的共同目标和光荣使命。

等大多源自西方国家，[1]长期以来由西方国家主导，也为现行国际经济体制提供了强大的理论支撑。

关于国际经济法的概念，西方学界主要有"狭义说"和"广义说"。"狭义说"认为，国际经济法是国际公法的分支之一，是调整国际公法主体之间，即国家之间、国际组织之间和国家与国际组织之间经济关系的法律规范。国际经济法由于主体、调整对象和渊源与国际公法完全一致，因此属于国际公法的范畴。"广义说"则认为，国际经济法是调整国家之间、国际组织之间、国家与国际组织之间、国家与他国私人之间、国际组织与私人之间以及不同国籍私人之间经济关系的法律规范。由于国际经济法的主体包括国家、国际组织和私人，其渊源包括国际公法规范和国内法规范，已突破传统国际公法体系，成为一个独立的法律部门和法律学科。[2]

自20世纪70年代末以来，中国国际经济法学应改革开放形势发展之需而产生和发展。借鉴西方国际经济法学的研究成果，我国学界也有"狭义说"和"广义说"之区分，"广义说"居于主导地位。[3]由于"中国特色国际法学"可以成立，无论是"狭义说"或"广义说"，研究调整国际经济关系的国际公法规范部分，同样可以具有"中国特色"。在"广义说"中，研究调整国际经济关系的中国国内法规范，本身当然更具有鲜明的"中国特色"。因此，与"中国特色国际法学"的求证同理，"中国特色国际经济法学"是顺理成章、名正言顺的。

事实上，早在1993年中国国际经济法学会年会上，中国社会科学院李泽锐教授和复旦大学董世忠教授就提出了"创建中国特色的国际经济法学派"的建议，得到学会会长陈安教授和学会广大同仁的认同。[4]之后，在学会历届年会上，"中国特色国际经济法学"多次列为重要议题持续予以研讨。

---

〔1〕 关于现行国际经济体制与西方法律文化的联系，参见陈东：《评〈手把手地教导中国：GATT 究竟为何物〉——兼论"基督教治下"的 WTO 法律文化对中国法治的影响》，载陈安主编：《国际经济法学刊》第18卷第3期，北京大学出版社2011年版，第85—131页。

〔2〕 关于国际经济法的概念与特征，参见曾华群：《国际经济法导论（第二版）》，法律出版社2007年版，第18—38页。关于西方国际经济法研究的概况，参见何志鹏：《西方国际经济法研究：重点、方法与立场》，载陈安主编：《国际经济法学刊》第16卷第1期，北京大学出版社2009年版，第183—225页。

〔3〕 在我国，关于国际经济法学的"狭义说"和"广义说"的早期讨论，参见史久镛：《论国际经济法的概念和范围》，载中国国际法学会主办：《中国国际法年刊》(1983)，中国对外翻译出版公司1983年版，第359—372页；姚梅镇：《国际经济法是一个独立的法学部门》，载中国国际法学会主办：《中国国际法年刊》(1983)，中国对外翻译出版公司1983年版，第373—385页；王名扬：《国际经济法是一门独立的学科》，载中国国际法学会主办：《中国国际法年刊》(1983)，中国对外翻译出版公司1983年版，第386—392页；汪瑄：《略论国际经济法》，载中国国际法学会主办：《中国国际法年刊》(1983)，中国对外翻译出版公司1983年版，第393—397页。

〔4〕 参见张永彬：《试论中国特色国际经济法学派的形成及其代表性成果》，载《西南政法大学学报》2012年第2期，第103—104页。

二、中国特色国际经济法学的指导思想

一个学科的产生、形成和发展需要指导思想和理论基础。指导思想和理论基础关乎该学科的目标、使命和特色，更关乎从事该学科研究的学者普遍认同和秉持的立场、原则和方法。在这个意义上，指导思想和理论基础是学科建设的核心和灵魂。

如所周知，中国特色社会主义法治理论是中国特色社会主义理论的重要组成部分之一，其指导思想和理论基础是马克思主义。不言而喻，作为中国特色社会主义法治理论的重要组成部分之一，中国特色国际经济法学尽管具有"国际性"和融合于"国际话语体系"（international discourse system）的特征，其指导思想和理论基础同样是马克思主义。

早在 1982 年，中国国际法学会首任会长宦乡教授就明确要求我国国际法学者"以马克思列宁主义、毛泽东思想为指导，紧密结合国际斗争的现实，作艰苦而富有成效的理论研究，为创建有利世界和平，真正代表世界各国人民利益的新中国的国际法学而坚持不懈地努力。"[1]

我国国际经济法学科奠基人姚梅镇教授、陈安教授的马克思主义修养深厚，一向注重以马克思主义指导国际经济法研究，诚为后学之表率。谨举两例：

一是科学分析国际经济法的调整对象。国际经济关系既是国际经济法借以产生和发展的主要依据，又是国际经济法调整的主要对象。姚梅镇教授在论述国际经济法的产生时，援引马克思《经济学手稿》和马克思、恩格斯《共产党宣言》中有关国际经济关系的论述，指出"在近代条件下，经济问题绝不是一国的现象，必须联系到国际关系上来考察"；国际经济法是反映国际经济关系发展趋势的"上层建筑"。[2]陈安教授以辩证唯物主义和历史唯物主义详细分析国际经济关系发展的三大主要阶段及其特征（即早期的国际经济交往与国际经济关系的初步形成；资本主义世界市场的形成与国际经济关系的重大发展；社会主义国家的出现、众多弱小民族的独立与国际经济关系的本质变化），指出历史唯物主义的基本原理"是对人类社会长期发展进程客观事实的科学总结"，"是对各国社会进行解剖的利器，也是对国际社会实行科学分析的指南"。[3]

---

〔1〕　参见宦乡：《为创建新中国的国际法学而努力》，载中国国际法学会主办：《中国国际法年刊》（1982），中国对外翻译出版公司 1982 年版，第 5 页。

〔2〕　参见姚梅镇：《国际经济法是一个独立的法学部门》，载中国国际法学会主办：《中国国际法年刊》（1983），中国对外翻译出版公司 1983 年版，第 373 页。

〔3〕　参见陈安：《论国际经济关系的历史发展与南北矛盾》，载陈安：《陈安论国际经济法学》，第 1 卷第 1 编第 II 部分，复旦大学出版社 2008 年版，第 40 页。

二是深刻揭示南北问题的根源和实质。姚梅镇教授在论述"国际经济新秩序与国际经济法"时，以列宁《帝国主义是资本主义的最高阶段》有关"垄断"的重要论述为指导，分析南北矛盾斗争的实质，深刻指出："垄断是旧的世界经济体制的本质。在这个体制内，控制与被控制，剥削与被剥削，是发达国家与发展中国家及殖民体制下地区之间最本质的特征。"[1]依据马克思主义经典论述及历史事实，陈安教授以激扬文字历数 15 世纪以来列强在亚、非、美地区推行殖民主义的十大罪恶行径，称为"殖民十恶"（即"欺蒙诈骗，以贱易贵""明火执仗，杀人越货""践踏主权，霸占领土""横征暴敛，榨取脂膏""强制劳役，敲骨吸髓""猎取活人，贩卖奴隶""垄断贸易，单一经济""种毒贩毒，戕民攫利""毁灭文化，精神侵略"和"血腥屠杀，种族灭绝"），进而总结，"漫漫数百年，一部殖民史，就是一部弱肉强食史，也就是欧美列强和全世界众多弱小民族之间的国际经济关系史的主要内容。""15 世纪以来的数百年间，欧洲列强在亚、非、美广大地区实行殖民掠夺的历史，是一部火与剑的历史，也是一部血与泪的历史。"[2]在中外国际经济法学论著中，居于道义制高点，以如此犀利笔触历数殖民之恶，似为仅见。或有学者认为这是政治学或史学的内容。笔者以为，殖民掠夺史在西方国际经济法学论著中讳莫如深，却是中国特色国际经济法学应有的立论之本。正本清源，温故知新。只有回顾殖民掠夺史，才能深刻理解南北问题的根源和实质，认清西方列强罄竹难书的罪恶"发家史"及其对广大发展中国家所欠下的巨大"历史债务"，也才能深刻理解建立国际经济新秩序的正当性、必要性和紧迫性，正确认识社会发展规律和国际经济关系的发展趋向。在法理上，回顾殖民掠夺史，是阐述和论证当代经济主权、公平互利和合作发展等国际经济法基本原则必要的史实依据和理论铺垫。

应当指出，我国国际经济法学界老一辈学者亲历帝国主义、封建主义、官僚资本主义"三座大山"压迫下的旧社会，深有切肤之痛，对西方列强的本质有深入的认识，对马克思主义有坚定的信仰和深刻的理解。他们既重视马克思主义经典原著的钻研，更重视马克思主义基本原理的运用和发展，自觉坚持以马克思主义的立场、观点和方法治学育人。他们的沧桑历练、观察视角、敏感程度及精神境界很值得新一代，特别是中青年学者借鉴和学习。在对外开放、资讯发达的时代，我国新一代学者思想敏锐活跃，努力学习和研究西方学者形形色色的主流"创新"理论或理论工具，这是值得称道的。知己知彼，才能真正开展"有的放矢"的国际交流和学术对话。重要

---

[1] 姚梅镇：《关于国际经济法概念的几个问题》，载姚梅镇：《姚梅镇文集》，武汉大学出版社 2010 年版，第 20—22 页。

[2] 陈安：《论国际经济关系的历史发展与南北矛盾》，载陈安：《陈安论国际经济法学》，第 1 卷第 1 编第 II 部分，复旦大学出版社 2008 年版，第 46—54 页。

的是,对此类"创新"理论,需要独立思考,以马克思主义为指导,以"扬弃"的精神学习和研究,"取其精华,去其糟粕";需要保持清醒的政治头脑,学得进去,跳得出来,增强理论自信,坚守原则立场,不能唯"新"是从,不必附庸西方"风雅",更不能盲目追随西方学术潮流;需要追根溯源,以史为鉴,深入探究此类"创新"理论的"理论与政治'家谱族系'及其历史背景"[1]和思想根源。"南方中心"(South Centre)前秘书长格索维奇(Branislav Gosovic)博士有感于发展中国家某些年轻学者不求甚解,盲目附和西方"创新"理论的现象,曾深刻指出:"殖民时代的史实总被淡忘,似乎与现实不'相关'";"现在(发展中国家)需要完成的使命,便是反击北方国家所操控的全球政策和知识霸权。从某种意义上讲,这需要揭露和解构其历史和知识根源,正是这种历史和知识根源滋养、支撑着北方国家当前的全球架构并使其正当化,助长殖民主义、帝国主义和冷战思维的长期存在,并将其重新包装并适应不断演进的国际环境和时代"。[2] 此说一语中的,振聋发聩。

三、中国特色国际经济法学的立场意识

关于新时期中国在国际经济关系和国际体制中的立场和战略定位,特别是中国在建立国际经济新秩序中的地位与作用,中外学者见仁见智。近年来,随着中国经济的迅速发展和国际影响力的显著提升,某些西方学者热衷于强调中国的"领导作用"和"大国责任",[3]甚至提出"中国威胁"论,[4]其用意发人深思。中国是现存国际经济秩序的受惠者、维护者、改良者、改革者或革命者,众说纷纭。

(一)我国作为"发展中大国"的基本立场

各国国际经济法学者并非居于同一的、纯粹的、超脱的法治立场。由于国家利益、历史传统、意识形态、宗教信仰、文化背景等因素,各国特别是南北两类国家的国际经济法学者各有其不同的基本立场、法治理念、价值取向和学术追求。西方国家国际经济法学者对其立场或直言不讳,或"犹抱琵琶"。在国际经济法学研究中,我

---

〔1〕 参见〔南斯拉夫/塞尔维亚〕布拉尼斯拉夫·格索维奇(Branislav Gosovic):《中国是"威胁"还是"机遇"?评陈安教授驳斥"黄祸"与"中国威胁"谰言的长篇专论——一项研究与解读当代世界政治的重大贡献》,载陈安主编:《国际经济法学刊》第20卷第2期,北京大学出版社2013年版,第51页。

〔2〕 同上书,第50—52页。

〔3〕 参见徐崇利:《现行国际经济秩序的重构与中国的责任》,载陈安主编:《国际经济法学刊》第17卷第2期,北京大学出版社2010年版,第3—4页。

〔4〕 关于"中国威胁"论的历史考察,参见陈安:《"黄祸"论的本源、本质及其最新霸权"变种":"中国威胁"论——中国对外经济交往史的主流及其法理原则的视角》,载《现代法学》2011年第6期。See also An Chen, On the Source, Essence of "Yellow Peril" Doctrine and Its Latest Hegemony "Variant"—the "China Threat" Doctrine: From the Perspective of Historical Mainstream of Sino-Foreign Economic Interactions and Their Inherent Jurisprudential Principles, *The Journal of World Investment & Trade*, Vol. 13, No. 1, 2012.

国学者理应旗帜鲜明地站在中国和发展中国家的立场,坚持和发展"三个世界"理论,坚持建立国际经济新秩序的目标,体现"知识报国,兼济天下"的志向和胸怀。[1]

历史已然成就了中国作为"发展中大国"或"第三世界中坚成员"的地位。作为发展中大国,我国的基本立场理应是,奉行独立自主和平等互利原则,坚持建立国际经济新秩序的战略目标,成为建立国际经济新秩序的积极推手和南南联合自强的中流砥柱。[2]

1. 我国是建立国际经济新秩序的积极推手

作为"发展中大国",我国是现行国际经济秩序的改革者,是建立国际经济新秩序的积极推手和重要实践者。

战后建立的国际经济秩序,即以"国际货币基金组织"(International Monetary Fund,IMF)、"世界银行"(World Bank,WB)和"关税及贸易总协定"(General Agreement on Tariff and Trade,GATT)[其后演变为"世界贸易组织"(World Trade Organization,WTO)]三大支柱作为支撑的"布雷顿森林体制"(Bretton Woods System),是当时西方国家经济实力和权力格局的体现,基本上由西方国家创建、主导及维系,维护和反映了西方国家的既得利益和传统优势地位。其主要构成部分包括:(1) 以不合理、不公平国际分工为基础的资本主义生产体系;(2) 以不平等交换为特征的国际贸易制度;(3) 以垄断为特征的国际货币金融体系;(4) 不平等的国际经济决策制度;(5) 与上述体系或制度相适应的国际法律秩序。[3] 20 世纪 90 年代,美国公然声称其负有"世界领导责任"(responsibility of world leadership),力图以主要由其本国特定利益、重要关切和片面认知决定的"世界领导责任"版本强加于国际社会。[4]

战后 70 多年来,发展中国家的核心诉求是全面改革不公平、不公正的国际经济旧秩序,建立公平公正的国际经济新秩序。发展中国家与发达国家之间的新旧国际

---

〔1〕 关于南北矛盾与新旧国际秩序斗争的精辟分析,参见〔南斯拉夫/塞尔维亚〕布拉尼斯拉夫·格索维奇(Branislav Gosovic):《二十一世纪初联合国将走向何方:改变抑或延续国际旧秩序》,载陈安主编:《国际经济法学刊》第 15 卷第 2 期,北京大学出版社 2008 年版,第 1—14 页。

〔2〕 参见陈安:《三论中国在构建国际经济新秩序中的战略定位:"匹兹堡发轫之路"走向何方》,载《国际经济法学刊》第 16 卷第 4 期,北京大学出版社 2009 年版,第 27—28 页。

〔3〕 参见周晓林:《国际经济新秩序与国际法》,载中国国际法学会主办:《中国国际法年刊》(1983),中国对外翻译出版公司 1983 年版,第 70—76 页。

〔4〕 美国前总统国家安全事务助理安东尼·雷克(Anthony Lake)在 1993 年有关美国外交政策的演讲中声称:"决定美国采取多边或单边行动的唯一首要因素是美国的利益。当多边行动可增进我们的利益时,应采取多边行动。当单边行动符合我们的目的时,则采取单边行动。" See David A. Lake, *Entangling Relations*: *American Foreign Policy in its Century*, Princeton University Press, 1999, p. 199. Quoted from Boutros Boutros Ghali, Branislav Gosovic, *Global Leadership and Global Systemic Issues*: *South*, *North and the United Nations in a 21st Century World*, Transcend University Press Popular, 2011, pp. 8-9.

经济秩序之争此起彼伏,从未止息。20 世纪六七十年代,发展中国家借助联合国体制,努力争取建立国际经济新秩序,取得了重大成果,可称之为新旧国际经济秩序之争的第一个重大回合。经历八九十年代的低潮期之后,发展中国家 2001 年在 WTO 体制中发起的"多哈发展回合",可谓新旧国际经济秩序之争的第二个重大回合,延续至今。[1]

　　鉴于南北矛盾仍然是当前国际经济关系的主要矛盾和国际经济关系发展的重大问题,寻求建立各国普遍认同的公平公正的国际经济秩序不能回避或淡化南北矛盾问题,[2]更不能回避改革国际经济旧秩序、建立国际经济新秩序这一根本性问题。建立国际经济新秩序是广大发展中国家争取国际经济平权地位的共同奋斗目标和战略理念。[3] 在建立国际经济新秩序中,我国理应旗帜鲜明地反对任何国家的所谓"世界领导"作用,旗帜鲜明地支持联合国基于《联合国宪章》发挥积极作用,促进联合国成为多边主义、国际事务民主化与世界人民授权、和平与合作、全球公平与可持续发展的支柱。[4] 2017 年 9 月《金砖国家领导人厦门宣言》明确提出"共同推动建立更加公正、平等、公平、民主和有代表性的国际政治、经济秩序"的目标,[5]并且明确指出联合国在国际秩序的"核心"地位和作用,即:"坚定维护以联合国为核心的公正合理的国际秩序,维护《联合国宪章》的宗旨和原则,尊重国际法,推动国际关系民主化法治化……"[6]

　　作为发展中国家的一员,我国一向积极参与和支持改革国际经济旧秩序、建立国际经济新秩序的斗争。[7] 值得指出的是,改革国际经济旧秩序、建立国际经济新

---

〔1〕 参见陈安、陈辉萍:《中印合作、南南联合自强与国际经济新秩序——聚焦于"多哈回合"中的中印合作》,载陈安主编:《国际经济法学刊》第 13 卷第 4 期,北京大学出版社 2006 年版,第 3 页。

〔2〕 近年有学者认为,国际投资法的范式正在从"南北分野"(north-south divide)向"公私辩论"(private-public debate,即有关东道国与外国投资者之间权益关系的辩论)转变。See Wenhua Shan, Towards a Balanced Liberal Investment Regime: General Report on the Protection of Foreign Investment, *ICSID Review*, *Foreign Investment Law Journal*, Vol. 25, No. 2, 2010, pp. 154-155. 笔者认为,此说值得商榷。问题的关键在于:首先,"南北分野"与"公私辩论"并非同一层级的问题,不存在"转变"或"取代"的问题;其次,"南北分野"政治意涵深刻,触及本质问题,与"国际经济新秩序"密切相关,而"公私辩论"则泛指"南北不分"的一般化现象,与"国际经济新秩序"无直接关涉。

〔3〕 关于国际经济秩序的"新"与"旧"问题及 G20 的发展前景,参见陈安:《三论中国在构建国际经济新秩序中的战略定位:"匹兹堡发轫之路"走向何方》,载陈安主编:《国际经济法学刊》第 16 卷第 4 期,北京大学出版社 2009 年版,第 17—19、27—28 页。

〔4〕 参见〔南斯拉夫/塞尔维亚〕布拉尼斯拉夫•格索维奇(Branislav Gosovic):Whither United Nations at the Start of the 21st Century: An Institution for Changing of Extending the Old Global Order,载陈安主编:《国际经济法学刊》第 15 卷第 2 期,北京大学出版社 2008 年版,第 31—32 页。

〔5〕 参见《金砖国家领导人厦门宣言(全文)》之 2,http://www.gov.cn/xinwen/2017-09/04/content_5222643.htm,2017 年 12 月 16 日访问。

〔6〕 《金砖国家领导人厦门宣言(全文)》之 6,http://www.gov.cn/xinwen/2017-09/04/content_5222643.htm,2017 年 12 月 16 日访问。

〔7〕 关于中国参与建立国际经济新秩序斗争的概况,参见杨泽伟:《新国际经济秩序研究—政治与法律分析》,武汉大学出版社 1998 年版,第 177—187 页。

秩序的路径并不必然意味着对国际经济旧体制的"推倒重来""另起炉灶"，而更为现实可行的路径是"改革国际经济旧体制＋创建国际经济新体制"。两者并行不悖，相辅相成。实行改革开放政策以来，我国积极加入和参与改革现存国际经济体制，同时，不失时机地主持和参与创建国际经济新体制。1980年，我国相继恢复了在IMF和WB的合法席位。近年来，我国积极参与促进国际金融体制的内部改革，其中代表性成果是2006年和2010年IMF和WB先后进行的表决制改革及2015年IMF决定将人民币正式纳入"特别提款权"（SDR）储备货币篮子。[1] 2001年以来，我国的"入世"本身及其全面参与对WTO体制的发展产生了重大影响。我国还积极参与"20国集团"（G20）等国际治理机制的活动。随着全球金融危机的爆发，G20从一个定位模糊的财政部长会议转变为"国际经济合作的重要论坛"。特别是在G20匹兹堡峰会上，各国达成了包括在机构层面和政策层面上改革IMF和WB、完成僵持的WTO多哈谈判的战略决策。[2] 与此同时，我国积极主持和参与创建国际经济新体制，包括：2008年参与主持创建"金砖"（四国）（BRIC）机制、后发展为"金砖"（五国）（BRICS）机制和"金砖＋"合作模式；2013年9、10月，国家主席习近平在访问哈萨克斯坦和印度尼西亚时首次提出的"丝绸之路经济带"（Silk Road Economic Belt）和"21世纪海上丝绸之路"（21st Century Maritime Silk Road）的倡议（"一带一路"倡议，The Belt and Road Initiative）；2013年10月倡议创建、2015年12月正式成立的"亚洲基础设施投资银行"（Asian Infrastructure Investment Bank，AIIB）等，旨在推动建立国际经济新秩序。

2. 我国是南南联合自强的中流砥柱

作为"发展中大国"，中国属于发展中国家大家庭，是与广大发展中国家命运相同、休戚与共、目标一致的同路人，更是南南联合自强的中流砥柱之一。

20世纪50年代以来，随着国际政治经济形势的发展变化，发展中国家在国际场合团结一致，为改革国际经济旧秩序、建立国际经济新秩序进行不懈的斗争，取得了一系列具有历史意义的重大成果。[3] 我国一向积极参与和鼎力支持南南联合自强的行动。特别是实行改革开放政策以来，随着经济实力的逐渐增强，我国在南南联合自强中体现了"发展中大国"的应有担当。国家主席习近平明确指出，"广大发展中国家是我国走和平发展道路的同路人。我国虽然取得巨大发展成就，但仍然是发

〔1〕 贺荣：《论中国司法参与国际经济规则的制定》，载《国际法研究》2016年第1期，第5页。
〔2〕 参见Jeffrey L. Dunoff：《中国在演进的全球秩序中的角色：入世10周年反思》，载陈安主编《国际经济法学刊》第18卷第3期，北京大学出版社2011年版，第3—7，22页。
〔3〕 关于南南联合自强重要成果的简介，参见曾华群《国际经济法导论》（第二版），法律出版社2007年版，第10—18页。

展中国家。要坚持正确义利观,做到义利兼顾,以义为先,切实加强同发展中国家的团结合作,把我国发展与广大发展中国家共同发展紧密联系起来。"[1]值得强调的是,"义利兼顾,以义为先"及"与广大发展中国家共同发展"的理念源于我国"四海一家""兼济天下"的优良传统,[2]迥异于发达国家普遍奉行的"国家利益至上"(supremacy of national interest),鲜明表达了我国作为"发展中大国"的独特品格、博大胸怀和坚定立场。

历史经验表明,新旧国际经济秩序的斗争是长期、艰巨和复杂的,有时甚至是很激烈的。总体上,发展中国家要在联合国大会有关建立国际经济新秩序决议的基础上,在条约实践和国内立法实践中坚持原则,共同奋斗,持之以恒,才可能实现改革国际经济旧秩序、建立国际经济新秩序的长远目标。与此同时,也要讲究策略:一方面,有必要区分调整发展中国家之间经济关系的规范、调整发展中国家与发达国家之间经济关系的规范以及为建立国际经济新秩序而斗争的普遍规范;另一方面,应关注国际经济法在实质和形式上的长期渐进发展,善于积累、巩固和扩大已有的斗争成果。在此长期发展进程中,南南联合自强的"中流砥柱"作用至关重要。在这方面,"金砖"(BRICS)机制是成功的实践,我国当进一步践行"胸怀天下,利己达人"的理念,为南南联合自强和建立国际经济新秩序作出应有贡献。

(二)我国坚持基本立场的原则性与一致性

在国际法律实践中,我国作为"发展中大国"的基本立场是:涉及我国与发达国家之间经济法律关系,应坚持作为"发展中国家"的基本立场,拒绝发达国家基于所谓我国的"领导作用"或"大国责任"而提出的过分要求;涉及我国与其他发展中国家之间经济法律关系,应基于公平互利原则及"义利兼顾,以义为先""共同发展"的理念,给予其他发展中国家力所能及的支持,有时此等支持意味着我国需要承担更大的责任;涉及我国与发达国家、其他发展中国家之间的经济法律关系,考虑到此种情形多出现于创制和维持国际公共产品的国际法律过程中,我国仍可能以负责任的"发展中大国"身份,承担必要的较大责任。[3]

应当进一步指出,我国无论国际经济地位发生怎样的改变,应该有始终如一、坚定的基本立场和原则。以国际投资关系为例,近年来,我国已从净资本输入国转变

---

〔1〕　中共中央宣传部:《习近平总书记系列重要讲话读本》,学习出版社、人民出版社2016年版,第270—271页。

〔2〕　参见陈安:《高举体系变革大纛,发挥旗手引领作用——全球治理:中国的理念与实践轨迹》,载陈安主编:《国际经济法学刊》第23卷第3期,法律出版社2016年版,第1—17页。

〔3〕　参见徐崇利:《现行国际经济秩序的重构与中国的责任》,载陈安主编:《国际经济法学刊》第17卷第2期,北京大学出版社2010年版,第7—11页。

为兼具资本输入国与资本输出国双重身份，将来还可能发展为净资本输出国。无论如何，我国必须始终如一地坚持和强调经济主权、公平互利和合作发展原则，将来不能因为居于净资本输出国地位就片面强调资本输出国和海外投资者的权益，在双边投资条约实践中苛求资本输入国限制其管制外资的主权权力（例如放弃"准入权"条款）。我国一向反对发达国家"以邻为壑""损人利己"，同样，也要引以为戒，严格自律，言行一致。随着我国国际经济地位的改变，对外经济政策可能根据形势的变化而调整，但基本立场和原则要坚定，不因国际经济地位的转变而变化，不因一国之利而无视、影响或损害其他国家的重大关切和重要权益，更不能因一国之利而忽略、漠视甚至放弃建立国际经济新秩序的远大目标和历史使命。我国国际经济法学者进行学术研究应有"发展中大国"学者的"立场"和"责任"意识，政府主管部门在国际经济实践中也应有"发展中大国"的坚定立场和原则。

四、中国特色国际经济法学的基本原则

一般而言，国际经济法的基本原则指国际社会普遍接受的调整国际经济关系的最基本的法律原则。国际经济法学的基本原则，本文指关于国际经济法基本原则的学说。中国特色国际经济法学对国际经济法学的重要贡献，是基于《联合国宪章》和国际社会普遍接受的国际法基本规范，提炼和论证了旨在建立国际经济新秩序的国际经济法三大基本原则，即经济主权原则、公平互利原则和合作发展原则。自 20 世纪 80 年代以来，国际政治经济形势风云变幻，三大基本原则展现其科学的适用性和强大的生命力，也面临严峻的挑战。在理论层面，西方国家智库精心设计和推行的一些理念潜移默化，在不同程度侵蚀或影响了三大基本原则的核心价值，亟须评鉴、澄清或回应。

（一）经济主权原则

如所周知，主权是国际法的基石。当前，为推进经济全球化，西方国家以理论为先导，提出了否定或淡化主权的种种理论。[1] 对于广大发展中国家而言，当前面临的首要任务是坚持和维护《联合国宪章》确立的国家主权原则。[2] 经济主权原则是国家主权原则在经济领域的体现。国家主权意味着对内至高无上，对外独立平等。经济主权原则在对内方面的表现是，根据国际法的"属地管辖"原则，各国对本国境

---

〔1〕 关于西方当代主权观的代表作，可参见 John H. Jackson, *Sovereignty, the WTO, and Changing Fundamentals of International Law*, Cambridge University Press, 2006。

〔2〕 See Boutros Boutros Ghali, Branislav Gosovic, *Global Leadership and Global Systemic Issues: South, North and the United Nations in a 21st Century World*, Transcend University Press, 2011, pp. 24-25.

内自然资源、全部财富和一切经济活动享有完整的、永久的主权。在对外方面的表现是，根据国际法的主权平等原则，各国有权自由选择适合本国国情的经济制度，不受外来干涉；各国无论大小、贫富，在国际经济决策中具有平等的参与和决策权，有权自主确立国际经济关系、签订国际经济条约和参与国际经济组织。经济主权原则强调尊重和维护各国特别是发展中国家的经济主权，反对超级大国推行经济霸权和"淡化"弱国主权的行径，是建立国际经济新秩序的必要基础和前提。[1]

值得警惕的是，近年来，以美国为代表的发达国家以"全球化""自由化""国际治理"为名，行淡化、否定经济主权原则之实。

关于"全球化"（globalization）的涵义见仁见智。国际经济法与全球化的事实和影响密切相关。[2] 我国国际经济法学界曾开展"经济全球化与法律全球化"的讨论，涉及法律全球化的涵义、经济全球化与法律全球化之间的关系、经济全球化与法律全球化对国家主权的影响以及我国应采取的立场等重要问题。[3] 笔者认为，在研究"全球化"理念时，首先，应当注意"全球化"理念的起源和实质。据格索维奇博士考察，"全球化"从未在联合国或任何其他国际机构讨论，也从未寻求发展中国家的意见；"全球化"理念"有如神谕"，不受任何质疑，在世界范围传播、促进及经营；该理念是由与全球权力中心有密切联系的发达国家智库提出的理论建构。[4] 其次，对"全球化"的内涵不能泛化。"全球化"最重要的表现是"经济全球化"，[5]不能轻易推而广之，推及所谓"法律全球化""文化全球化"甚至扩及政治、价值等领域。再次，对"经济全球化"的性质应有适当的解读，称之为"进程"或"趋势"是较为恰当的。马克思主义经典作家对资本主义发展所带来的"一切国家生产和消费的世界性"早有精辟论述，尽管当下"经济全球化"达到了前所未有的程度，也依然属"进程"或"趋势"，不能刻意"提升"为挑战各国经济主权的"全球化体制"。因此，要特别警惕西方国家以"全球化"或"经济全球化"为理论先导或制度工具，借助国际组织、其他国际体制或单边主义措施，淡化或挑战发展中国家的经济主权。最后，对"经济全球化""进程"或"趋势"也应有积极的引领和掌控。"经济全球化"作为世界经济的"进程"或

---

〔1〕 关于经济主权原则的论述，参见曾华群：《国际经济法导论》（第二版），法律出版社 2007 年版，第 217—252 页。

〔2〕 See John H. Jackson, *Sovereignty, the WTO, and Changing Fundamentals of International Law*, Cambridge University Press, 2006, p. 47.

〔3〕 参见"经济全球化与法律全球化"专栏文章，载陈安主编：《国际经济法论丛》第 4 卷，法律出版社 2001 年版，第 1—77 页。

〔4〕 See Branislav Gosovic, *The South Shaping the Global Future, Six Decades of the South-North Development Struggle in the UN*, Transcend University Press, 2014, p. 167.

〔5〕 关于全球化的含义及其对发展中国家的影响，参见张向晨：《发展中国家与 WTO 的政治经济关系》（修订本），法律出版社 2002 年版，第 34—46 页。

"趋势"，显然不应是由美国为代表的西方国家主导的"西方化"甚至"美国化"，而应是《金砖国家领导人厦门宣言》提出的"开放、包容、均衡的经济全球化"。[1] 可见，以金砖国家为代表的发展中国家并未"因人废言"，简单排斥"经济全球化"的概念，而是因势利导，在"国际话语体系"中，还原其应有之义，明确其创新内涵，也申明了发展中国家的立场和主张。

"自由化"（liberalization）也是当下西方国家普遍推崇备至的理念。在国际经济领域，由"贸易自由化"发展到"投资自由化"，再到"金融自由化"，似乎"自由化"是势不可挡的世界潮流。笔者认为，在研究"自由化"理念时，应当注意"自由化"与"开放"的区别。就"自由化"而言，"自由"广受认同和赞赏，关键问题是谁主导"自由化"，谁"化"谁，谁被"化"，如何"化"？事实上，对广大发展中国家而言，在与发达国家的经济交往中，由于实力对比悬殊，"自由化"意味着本国的"被开放"。而"开放"则一般是各国根据本国国情主动为之，开放的范围及进程仍由本国掌握。显然，《金砖国家领导人厦门宣言》提出的"建设开放型世界经济"的主张，[2] 更准确反映了发展中国家不同于西方国家"经济自由化"的立场。近年来，"由外促内倒逼改革"之说在我国时有流行。笔者以为，经历 40 年来的成功实践，改革开放已深入人心，成为我国的基本国策。在此形势下，完全可根据我国国情主动决定进一步开放的范围和进程，大可不必借助外力寻求"被开放"。

"国际治理"（international governance）或"全球治理"（global governance）近年也成为国际经济法的流行语。例如，在国际投资法领域，提出了所谓"外国直接投资的全球治理体系"（the global governance system for FDI）的概念，并指出这一体系主要是由双边投资条约构成的。[3] "国际治理"或"全球治理"概念流行的结果，一是由于悄然取代了"国际经济秩序"，"平息"或"回避"了南北矛盾和新旧国际经济秩序之争；二是由于主张某些国内经济管理事务也属于"国际治理"或"全球治理"的范围，限缩了各国管制本国境内一切经济活动的"政策空间"，因而侵蚀了各国的经济主权。值得注意的是，当前我国和其他发展中国家也采用"全球治理"和"全球经济治

---

〔1〕 参见《金砖国家领导人厦门宣言（全文）》之 6，http://www. gov. cn/xinwen/2017-09/04/content_5222643. htm，2017 年 12 月 16 日访问。党的"十九大"报告提出"推动经济全球化朝着更加开放、包容、普惠、平衡、共赢的方向发展"，进一步指明了我国主张的"经济全球化"的意涵及其发展方向。

〔2〕 参见《金砖国家领导人厦门宣言（全文）》之 3，http://www. gov. cn/xinwen/2017-09/04/content_5222643. htm，2017 年 12 月 16 日访问。

〔3〕 See Axel Berger, China's New Bilateral Investment Treaty Programme: Substance, Rational and Implications for Investment Law Making, *Paper for the American Society of International Law International Economic Law Group（ASIL IELIG）2008 biennial conference "The Politics of International Economic Law: The Next Four Years"*, Washington, D. C., November 14-15, 2008.

理"的概念,并赋予其革新性涵义,[1]主要表现在:一是提出了"共商共建共享的全球治理观",在"治理"中增强"改革"的内涵;[2]二是将"治理"的主要关切严格限定于"国际"层面,避免"全球经济治理"侵蚀各国经济主权;三是揭示"全球经济治理"与"国际经济新秩序"的关系,明确"全球经济治理"是手段,"国际经济新秩序"是目标。例如,《金砖国家领导人厦门宣言》提出,"加强沟通协调,完善经济治理,建立更加公正合理的国际经济秩序。我们将努力提高金砖国家及新兴市场和发展中国家在全球经济治理中的发言权和代表性,推动建设开放、包容、均衡的经济全球化,以促进新兴市场和发展中国家发展,为解决南北发展失衡、促进世界经济增长提供强劲动力。"[3]

在强调经济主权原则的同时,国际社会也要注意防范和抑制经济霸权。个别发达国家凭借其经济和政治优势,在经济主权方面实行双重标准,即淡化他国的经济主权,强化本国的经济霸权,甚至顽固推行其单边主义、保护主义政策,将维护本国利益的所谓"主权"和内国法律凌驾于其参与的条约和国际体制之上。WTO 成立以来,就一再发生以 WTO 为代表的多边主义与美国单边主义之间、规则与强权之间的激烈交锋。[4]

(二)公平互利原则

公平互利原则的基本含义是,所有国家在法律上一律平等,作为国际社会的平等成员有权充分有效地参与国际经济问题的决策过程并公平分享由此产生的利益。该原则的目标是在国际经济关系上实现实质上的主权平等。在该原则中,互利是核心。没有互利就谈不上公平,公平必然要求互利。

公平互利原则是在"公平"这一传统法律概念基础上结合"互利"概念发展起来的国际经济法基本原则,旨在确立和贯彻新的平等观,以实质平等取代形式平等。该原则进一步明确了平等互利的含义,是平等互利原则的新发展。在当前的国际条

---

〔1〕　参见陈安:《高举体系变革大纛,发挥旗手引领作用——全球治理:中国的理念与实践轨迹》,载陈安主编:《国际经济法学刊》第 23 卷第 3 期,法律出版社 2016 年版,第 1—17 页;贺荣:《论中国司法参与国际经济规则的制定》,载《国际法研究》2016 年第 1 期,第 4—5 页。

〔2〕　党的"十九大"报告指出:"中国秉持共商共建共享的全球治理观,倡导国际关系民主化,坚持国家不分大小、强弱、贫富一律平等,支持联合国发挥积极作用,支持扩大发展中国家在国际事务中的代表性和发言权。中国将继续发挥负责任大国作用,积极参与全球治理体系改革和建设,不断贡献中国智慧和力量。"

〔3〕　《金砖国家领导人厦门宣言(全文)》之 6,http://www.gov.cn/xinwen/2017-09/04/content_5222643.htm,2017 年 12 月 16 日访问。

〔4〕　参见陈安:《世纪之交围绕经济主权的新"攻防战"——从美国的"主权大辩论"及其后续影响看当代"主权淡化"论之不可取》,载陈安主编:《国际经济法论丛》第 4 卷,法律出版社 2001 年版,第 78—138 页;陈安:《十年来美国单边主义与 WTO 多边主义交锋的三大回合——"201 条款"争端之法理探源和展望》,载陈安主编:《国际经济法学刊》第 10 卷,北京大学出版社 2004 年版,第 13—36 页。

件下,对于经济实力相当的发达国家之间或发展中国家之间的关系而言,公平互利
原则体现于原有的平等互利关系的维持;而对于经济实力悬殊的发达国家与发展中
国家的关系而言,公平互利原则体现于原有形式上平等关系的纠正和新的实质上平
等关系的创设。为此,发达国家应承担义务,通过采取各种措施,让发展中国家单方
面享有非对等的、非互惠的特惠待遇,以实现实质上的平等,达到真正的公平。[1] 事
实表明,只有对发展中国家和发达国家分别适用不同的法律原则和规则,才能纠正
由国际经济旧秩序造成的不公正状态,缩小两类国家的贫富悬殊现象,实现所有国
家经济上的均衡发展。

由于公平互利原则的提出,就法律上的平等待遇而言,出现了发达国家与发展
中国家之间正式的差别待遇。这种积极的差别待遇作为促进实质平等的工具已从
学术辩论发展为具体的国际义务并产生一定的经济效果。该原则的确立对发展中
国家极为重要。据之,发展中国家第一次被承认处于特殊的地位,应享有特殊的
待遇。

公平互利原则不仅对发展中国家有利,从发达国家本身利益出发,在发达国家
与发展中国家之间建立公平互利关系,有利于发达国家与发展中国家保持长期、稳
定、可持续发展的经济关系,这对于发达国家经济的进一步发展和世界的和平与稳
定,均具有重要的积极意义。[2]

公平互利原则的初步实践,可以 GATT/WTO 体制给予发展中国家的"特殊与
差别待遇"(special and differential treatment,SDT)为例。经过发展中国家的长期
斗争,在 GATT 体制中,SDT 条款逐渐发展起来,确立了"承担义务的非互惠模式"。
主要包括:(1) GATT 第 18 条。该条虽未采用发展中国家的概念,但允许"经济只能
维持低生活水平并处于发展初期阶段的缔约方",在使用贸易措施保护幼稚产业和
使用数量限制以减轻国际收支困难等方面有一定的灵活性;(2) 1966 年生效的
GATT 第 4 部分"贸易和发展"(第 36—38 条)。该部分明确采用了"欠发达缔约方"
(less-developed contracting parties)的概念,涉及 GATT 有关发展中国家的原则和
目标,鼓励发达国家改善其市场准入条件,并表明发展中国家不必对发达国家降低
贸易壁垒的承诺作出互惠承诺;(3) "授权条款"(enabling clause),即 1979 年《关于
发展中国家差别和更优惠待遇、互惠和更充分参与的决定》。允许发达国家给予发
展中国家优惠待遇及发展中国家之间相互给予优惠待遇。据统计,WTO 协定中的

---

〔1〕 参见陈安主编:《国际经济法总论》,法律出版社 1991 年版,第 179 页。
〔2〕 关于公平互利原则的论述,参见曾华群:《国际经济法导论》(第二版),法律出版社 2007 年版,第 252—271
页。

SDT 条款合计有 145 项,分别载于不同的多边货物贸易协定、《服务贸易总协定》《与贸易有关的知识产权协定》《争端解决的规则和程序谅解书》以及许多部长级会议决议。[1] 然而,进一步的分析表明,透过 WTO 体制 SDT 条款大量增加的表象,GATT 体制 SDT 条款的"承担义务的非互惠模式"已悄然改变为"履行义务的非互惠模式",即发展中国家须承担与发达国家同等的实体性义务,只是在履行该义务的程序方面有所区别(如"过渡期"的规定)。[2] 这实际上意味着公平互利原则在 GATT/WTO 体制中实践的倒退。

近年来,SDT 条款也开始渗入国际投资领域。2000 年,联合国贸易和发展会议(United Nations Conference on Trade and Development,UNCTAD)主张,SDT 原则应引入双边投资条约。[3] 2012 年,UNCTAD 发布的"国际投资协定要素:政策选项"(Elements of International Investment Agreements:Policy Options)专门规定了 SDT 条款,旨在从整体结构上纠正传统双边投资条约中"形式平等"掩盖下的"实质不平等"。为达此目标,该条款一方面规定"不对称的责任"(asymmetrical obligations),使较不发达缔约一方承担较轻的责任;另一方面规定"附加工具"(additional tools),促进较发达缔约一方作出积极贡献。[4]

然而,在传统国际实践中,处理国家相互之间的关系,"国家利益至上"说似乎成了"铁律",发达国家普遍认同且付诸实践。美国现政府也直言不讳地宣称其"美国优先"(American first)的国策。这意味着,当美国的国家利益与他国的国家利益或国际社会的利益不发生冲突时,"美国优先"是"不损人"的"自私自利"行为;而当两者发生冲突时,"美国优先"则只能是"有言在先""光明正大"的"损人利己"行为。事实上,在发达国家普遍奉行"国家利益至上"的情况下,发达国家与发展中国家之间的"形式平等"尚且不易,追求两类国家的"实质平等"更是举步维艰。在 WTO 多哈回合中,发达国家对两类国家"形式平等"的顽固坚持及对发展中国家"实质平等"诉求的强烈抵制即为明证。

近年来,随着我国对外投资活动的迅猛发展,我国居于资本输入国与资本输出

---

〔1〕　参见世界贸易组织秘书处编:《乌拉圭回合协议导读》,索必成、胡盈之译,法律出版社 2001 版,第 309—310 页。

〔2〕　参见曾华群:《论"特殊与差别待遇"条款的发展及其法理基础》,载《厦门大学学报》(哲学社会科学版)2003 年第 6 期,第 5—13 页。

〔3〕　See UNCTAD, *International Investment Agreements*:*Flexibility for Development*, UNCTAD Series on Issues in International Investment Agreements, UNCTAD/ITE/18, New York and Geneva, 2000, pp. 29-36.

〔4〕　See UNCTAD, *World Investment Report 2012*, *Towards a New Generation of Investment Policies*, United Nations, 2012, p. 159. 参见曾华群:《论我国"可持续发展导向"双边投资条约的实践》,载《厦门大学学报》(哲学社会科学版)2015 年第 1 期,第 80—89 页。

国"双重地位"。有学者主张，应根据这一变化调整我国的条约实践，以适应我国"身份转变"的需要，维护国家利益。这在一定程度上反映了"国家利益至上"说的影响或困扰。笔者以为，此种"身份转变"本身与立场问题无关，"身份转变"并不当然影响我国国际投资活动的基本立场。作为"负责任的发展中大国"和"第三世界中坚成员"，我国应始终不渝地坚持我国国际投资活动的基本立场，坚持公平互利原则，旗帜鲜明地反对发达国家奉行的"国家利益至上"主张。党的"十七大""十八大""十九大"报告提出的有关"各国人民共同利益""合作共赢""共同维护国际公平正义""秉持正确义利观"及"人类命运共同体"等理念和主张是公平互利原则的重要阐释和发展，[1]为公平互利原则的实践奠定了坚实的理论基础，与发达国家奉行的"国家利益至上"主张泾渭分明，在理论和实践层面均应准确把握。

（三）合作发展原则

合作发展原则（国际合作以谋发展原则）是1974年《建立国际经济新秩序宣言》和《各国经济权利和义务宪章》倡导的一项富有时代特点的国际经济法基本原则。基于南北问题的认识，要实现建立国际经济新秩序的目标，必须进一步强调、坚持和实践合作发展原则。[2]

合作发展原则是发展权（right to development）[3]与国际合作义务相结合而形成的新法律原则。其主要内容是，各国应进行合作，以促进建立公平互利的国际经济关系，并进行符合所有国家特别是发展中国家的需要和利益的国际经济结构改革；所有国家有责任在经济、社会、文化、科学和技术领域内进行合作，以促进全世界，尤其是发展中国家的经济发展和社会进步。就"合作"与"发展"而言，发展是权利、目标，合作是责任、手段。发展中国家的发展权利和国际合作是密切联系的。只有承认发展中国家发展的权利，才能实现真正的国际合作。只有通过国际合作，才能促进和保障所有国家特别是发展中国家的共同发展。应当指出，我国近年倡导的

---

〔1〕 党的"十七大"报告指出："坚持把中国人民利益同各国人民共同利益结合起来，以更加积极的姿态参与国际事务，发挥负责任大国作用"。党的"十八大"报告进一步阐明我国关于国际关系的主张，即："在国际关系中弘扬平等互信、包容互鉴、合作共赢的精神，共同维护国际公平正义……合作共赢，就是要倡导人类命运共同体意识，在追求本国利益时兼顾他国合理关切，在谋求本国发展中促进各国共同发展，建立更加平等均衡的新型全球发展伙伴关系，同舟共济，权责共担，增进人类共同利益。"党的"十九大"报告第十二部分题为"坚持和平发展道路，推动构建人类命运共同体"，指出："中国将高举和平、发展、合作、共赢的旗帜，恪守维护世界和平、促进共同发展的外交政策宗旨，坚定不移在和平共处五项原则基础上发展同各国的友好合作，推动建设相互尊重、公平正义、合作共赢的新型国际关系"；呼吁"各国人民同心协力，构建人类命运共同体，建设持久和平、普遍安全、共同繁荣、开放包容、清洁美丽的世界"。

〔2〕 关于合作发展原则的论述，参见曾华群：《国际经济法导论（第二版）》，法律出版社2007年版，第272—294页。

〔3〕 关于发展权的论述，参见 A. A. Cancado Trindade, *International Law for Humankind：Towards a New jus gentium*, Martinus Nijhoff Publishers, 2006, pp. 401-411.

"共同发展""合作共赢"概念是对合作发展原则的重要贡献。在 2015 年 9 月 26 日
"联合国发展峰会"上,国家主席习近平发表题为《谋共同永续发展,做合作共赢伙
伴》的重要讲话,强调国际社会要以《2015 年后发展议程》为新起点,共同走出一条公
平、开放、全面、创新的发展之路,努力实现各国共同发展。中国将继续秉持"义利相
兼、以义为先"的原则,以落实《2015 年后发展议程》为己任,团结协作,推动全球发展
事业不断向前。[1]《金砖国家领导人厦门宣言》提出的"坚持互利合作,谋求共同发
展",[2]进一步明确和丰富了合作发展原则的基本内涵,也揭示了公平互利原则与合
作发展原则的关联和互动。

一般认为,国际合作是由南北合作和南南合作两个层面构成的。

南北合作指发展中国家与发达国家之间的合作,是实施合作发展原则的中心环
节。在实践中,一些发达国家从未认真遵循合作发展原则,而是消极应对,甚至时有
发生漠视发展权和违反国际合作义务的事例。尽管合作发展原则已确立多年,直至
20 世纪末,发展中国家的整体状况并未改观,许多发展中国家的经济发展仍然停滞
不前,富国与穷国的经济差距仍不断扩大。经济全球化并未缩小发达国家与发展
中国家之间的差距,相反,发达国家对发展中国家的经济援助和技术转让持续减
少,经济发展与环境保护的矛盾、贸易与知识产权保护的关系进一步凸显了南北
矛盾。[3]

南南合作指发展中国家相互之间的经济合作。南南合作是以平等互利为基础,
互相尊重主权、互不干涉内政、不要求任何特权、不附带任何政治条件的国际经济合
作。南南合作的重要政治基础是"尊重各自选择的发展道路,理解和支持彼此利
益"。[4]"互尊互谅、平等相待、团结互助、开放包容、互惠互利的金砖精神"也是南南
合作的精神。[5] 这是一种新型的国际经济关系。因此,南南合作本身是国际经济新
秩序的组成部分。南南合作的产生和发展有着深刻的经济和社会基础,表现在发展
中国家一致要求建立国际经济新秩序,共同面临发展民族经济的历史任务,经济上
存在一定的互补性。应明确的是,南南合作并不是排斥或替代南北合作,也不是发
展中国家的集体自给自足。南南合作的目的,是通过发展中国家的集体力量,主要

---

〔1〕 习近平:《谋共同永续发展,做合作共赢伙伴》,http://news. xinhuanet. com/world/2015-09/27/c_
1116687809. htm,2017 年 12 月 16 日访问。

〔2〕《金砖国家领导人厦门宣言(全文)》之 3,http://www. gov. cn/xinwen/2017-09/04/content_5222643.
htm,2017 年 12 月 16 日访问。

〔3〕 薛捍勤:《新世纪国际法的挑战》,载中国国际法学会主办:《中国国际法年刊》(2002/2003),法律出版社
2006 年版,第 298 页。

〔4〕《金砖国家领导人厦门宣言(全文)》之 3,http://www. gov. cn/xinwen/2017-09/04/content_5222643.
htm,2017 年 12 月 16 日访问。

〔5〕 同上。

依靠自身的努力,建立起发展经济所必需的结构。为了保障共同的利益,发展中国家在南北关系上应协调其政策,采取联合行动,形成一股强大的国际力量以增强同发达国家谈判的能力,争取南北经济关系的改善。可以说,只有开展广泛深入的南南合作,才能出现富有成效的南北对话和合作。我国近年积极推动南南合作事业深化发展。在 2015 年 9 月 26 日由中国和联合国共同举办的"南南合作圆桌会"上,国家主席习近平指出,"南南合作是发展中国家联合自强的伟大创举,是平等互信、互利共赢、团结互助的合作,帮助我们开辟出一条崭新的发展繁荣之路"。基于南南合作的历史经验,他还就新时期南南合作事业提出了探索多元发展道路、促进各国发展战略对接、实现务实发展成效及完善全球发展架构等重要努力方向。[1]

应当指出,长期以来,由于"发展权"和"国际合作责任"尚未完全确立等现实原因,合作发展原则的实践及其实际产生的法律效力和影响不容乐观。

理论上,发展权受到了来自发达国家的严峻挑战。西方学者近年质疑发展权的法律基础,批评发展权概念是多余、含糊的,且具偏向性。他们指出,发展权未对发展中国家施加任何义务,至少应要求发展中国家谨慎诚实地管理来自国际合作机制的利益。他们主张,冷战的结束表明推行多元民主治理(pluralistic democratic governance)的可行性,发展中国家首先要做好其国内的事情。1992 年,西方学者托马斯.福兰克(Thomas Franck)从国际视角阐释"民主治理"的概念。他指出:"新形成中的法律——要求合法统治的民主性——不仅仅是特定国家的法律……也正在成为一体适用的国际法要求,通过全球标准并在区域性组织和国际组织的协助下实施";"发展的国际法已经扩大(如果不是转移)其重心为强调民主治理"。[2] 由此可见,西方学者已巧妙地将其"国际合作以谋发展"的义务改变为发展中国家本身"民主治理"的义务。

当下,"可持续发展"(sustainable development)概念在很大程度上取代了"发展权",广泛应用于国际性政策文件和条约等国际规范。"可持续发展"不同于传统的经济增长和经济发展,是指一种人本主义的经济、社会与环境的持续发展。[3] 尽管

---

〔1〕 陈赟、王丰丰、孟娜:《习近平在南南合作圆桌会上发表讲话》,http://news. xinhuanet. com/world/2015-09/27/c_1116689451. htm,2017 年 12 月 16 日访问。

〔2〕 See Franck. T. , The Emerging Right to a Democratic Governance, 86 *American Journal of International Law*, 1992, p. 47. Quoted from Francis N. N. Botchway, Historical Perspectives of International Economic Law, in Asif H. Qureshi (ed.), *Perspectives in International Economic Law*, Kluwer Law International, 2002, pp. 321-323.

〔3〕 按照世界环境与发展委员会报告《我们共同的未来》的定义,"可持续发展"是,"既满足当代人的需要,又不对后代人满足其需要的能力构成危害的发展"。根据联合国《21 世纪议程》,"可持续发展"的实体内容包括消除贫穷、改变消费形态、人口动态与可持续能力、保护和促进人类健康、促进人类住区的可持续发展、保持和管理资源以促进发展。参见王彦志:《经济全球化、可持续发展与国际投资法第三波》,载陈安主编:《国际经济法学刊》第 13 卷第 3 期,北京大学出版社 2006 年版,第 181—184 页。

字面上"可持续发展"与"发展权"差别不大,甚至前者加上"可持续"的限定词似乎更具科学意义,两者的涵义及核心显然不同。至关重要的是,"发展权"强调的是在国际关系中国家特别是发展中国家的发展权利,是基本人权的重要组成部分,与建立国际经济新秩序密切相关;而"可持续发展"并非重点关注国际关系中国家"可持续发展"的权利,而往往是具体关注各国国内环境、劳工等社会问题及人与自然、现代与后代等更为宽泛、长远的社会问题,要求国家自身承担更多的责任和义务,不涉及新旧国际经济秩序问题。显然,发展中国家提出的"发展权"经过"可持续发展"的微妙改造或替换,其核心价值已然发生了重大改变。有学者指出,国际发展议程的实际终结是以1981年坎昆南北峰会为标志的。该峰会原要考虑由主席布兰特(Willy Brandt)领导的国际发展问题独立委员会提出的《北方 一南方:共存的计划》(North-South:A Programme for Survival),由于两位美国领导人相继拒绝了该报告和整个国际发展议程的建议,也拒绝了参与考虑后续行动,霸权领导的时代开始了。[1]

显然,合作发展原则只有在各国进一步强调和增强其法律效力,认真维护和加强其权威性的情况下,才能有效地调整国际经济关系,服务于建立国际经济新秩序的远大目标。在国际法上,我国一向主张,发展权是普遍的、不可分(inalienable)的权利,是基本人权的组成部分。[2]"中国的发展同世界的发展紧密相关,中国愿同世界各国一道努力,使21世纪真正成为'人人享有发展的世纪'。"[3]鉴于当前"可持续发展"概念的积极意义及其广泛运用,我国在赞同和实践"可持续发展"原则或理念的同时,应继续坚持和实践合作发展原则,积极促进南北合作和南南合作,维护和加强各国特别是发展中国家的发展权,促进各国发展权利和目标的实现。我国2008年以来参与创建和发展的"金砖"(BRICS)机制和"金砖＋"合作模式,2013年提出的"一带一路"倡议,2015年成立的"亚洲基础设施投资银行"等,均是合作发展原则的重要实践。

五、结语

在经济全球化趋势下,国际经济法处于迅速发展之中,各国在国际贸易、国际投

---

〔1〕 参见〔南斯拉夫/塞尔维亚〕布拉尼斯拉夫·格索维奇(Branislav Gosovic):《全球领导与全球系统性问题—21世纪的南方及联合国》,载陈安主编:《国际经济法学刊》第17卷第3期,北京大学出版社2010年版,第13页。

〔2〕 See Xue Hanqin, *Chinese Contemporary Perspectives on International Law:History, Culture and International Law*, Martinus Nijhoff Publishers, 2012, 146-149.

〔3〕《中国国家主席胡锦涛在联合国成立60周年首脑会议发展筹资高级别会议上的讲话—促进普遍发展,实现共同繁荣》(2005年9月14日),载中国国际法学会主办:《中国国际法年刊》(2005),世界知识出版社2007年版,第397页。

资、国际货币金融、国际税务等诸多领域面临挑战和抉择。中国 40 年来改革开放的发展成就和国际经济法实践令世人瞩目。各国特别是发展中国家的国际经济法学者关注中国，对中国国际经济法学界寄予厚望。[1]

中国特色国际经济法学的使命是，站在中国和广大发展中国家立场，以马克思主义为指导思想，紧密联系中国和国际实践，坚持建立国际经济新秩序的目标，汲取国际社会长期积淀的国际经济法学精华，开拓创新，丰富和革新"国际话语体系"，坚定维护和发展国际社会普遍认同的经济主权、公平互利、合作发展等国际经济法学基本原则，为促进国际经济法实践的健康发展，为推动构建"人类命运共同体"作出积极的学术贡献。

诚然，国际经济法学具有"国际性"，融合于"国际话语体系"。各具特色的各国国际经济法学的"求同存异"和"交流互鉴"，汇聚成为"共同的"国际经济法学。中国特色国际经济法学是我国国际经济法学者长期共同努力的集体成果，也是"共同的"国际经济法学的重要组成部分之一。中国特色国际经济法学的发展和繁荣在一定程度上有赖于"共同的"国际经济法学的发展和繁荣，"共同的"国际经济法学的发展和繁荣也不能缺少中国特色国际经济法学的参与和奉献。

创建和发展中国特色国际经济法学，是我国国际经济法学者的光荣使命。这是一项宏大、艰巨、长期的理论工程，需要我国一代又一代国际经济法学者矢志不移、持之以恒的艰苦奋斗。我们应增强使命感，潜心治学，开拓创新，勇于探索国际经济法的发展规律和现实课题。我们应增强"道路自信、理论自信、制度自信、文化自信"，更积极主动地开展国际经济法领域的学术研究、交流和合作，提出国际经济法理论和实践的"中国主张"和"中国方案"，为中国特色国际经济法学和"共同的"国际经济法学的发展和繁荣做出应有的贡献。

On International Economic Law with Chinese Characteristics

Abstract: Based on discussion of issue on "country-specific or country oriented" of international law, the author argues that the concept of international economic law

---

[1] 参见〔南斯拉夫/塞尔维亚〕布拉尼斯拉夫·格索维奇（Branislav Gosovic）:《中国是"威胁"还是"机遇"？评陈安教授驳斥"黄祸"与"中国威胁"谰言的长篇专论——一项研究与解读当代世界政治的重大贡献》，载陈安主编:《国际经济法学刊》第 20 卷第 2 期，北京大学出版社 2013 年版，第 57—60 页；Boutros Boutros Ghali, Branislav Gosovic, *Global Leadership and Global Systemic Issues*: *South*, *North and the United Nations in a 21st Century World*, Transcend University Press Popular, 2011, pp. 85-87.

with Chinese characteristics (IELCC) is undoubtedly logical; being with the feature of "international" or "international discourse system", the guiding ideology and theoretical basis for IELCC are Marxism; being a large developing state, China endorses the principles of "independent" and "equality and mutual benefit", insists on the objective of new international economic order (NIEO), and makes contributions for establishing NIEO and South-South joint self-improvement as a promoter and a mainstay; facing challenges of various Western "new theories", China shall insist and develop the fundamental principles of "economic sovereignty", "equitable and mutual benefit" and "cooperation and development" accepted generally by the international society; and the development of IELCC and the development of "common" international economic law composed by states around the world supplement and promote each other.

Key words: Chinese characteristics; international economic law; new international economic order; guiding ideology; fundamental principles

第二章
国际经济法的基本原则

第一节　外资征收及其补偿标准:历史的分野与现实的挑战 *

【摘要】　　本文从历史和现实角度,分别探讨国有化或征收的概念、征收的合法性问题、征收补偿标准之争及其新发展和中国关于征收及其补偿标准的立场与实践。作者强调,征收是国家经济主权的正当行使,"赫尔"规则的要害是否定发展中国家的征收权,发展中国家特别是我国应当维护征收权和坚持适当补偿原则。

国际投资法中的外资国有化或征收的合法性及其补偿标准问题,长期以来是南北矛盾斗争的焦点之一,也是双边投资条约(bilateral investment treaties,BITs)谈判[1]和多边投资协定谈判的最重要议题之一。其实质是经济主权之争,即发展中国家坚持和维护本国经济主权和发达国家力图削弱和否定发展中国家经济主权的斗争。在经济全球化的趋势下,特别是世界贸易组织(World Trade Organization,WTO)体制不断向包括投资的"与贸易有关"领域扩张的情况下,这一焦点之争的天平,似乎已向发达国家的主张倾斜。在此情况下,发展中国家面临的已不仅是历史上理论和实践分歧的自然延续,而是现实的严峻挑战,即发展中国家是否和能否坚持和维护本国经济主权? 是否和能否坚持有关国有化或征收合法性及其补偿标准的原则立场?

---

* 原载陈安主编:《国际经济法学刊》第 13 卷第 1 期,北京大学出版社 2006 年版。

〔1〕 BITs 的数量近 10 年来急剧增加。20 世纪 90 年代初以前,BITs 发展缓慢。截至 1994 年 9 月,140 个国家签署了 700 多个 BITs;截至 1999 年,160 多个国家签署了 1300 多个 BITs;截至 2002 年,签署了 2181 个 BITs。See W. Michael Reisman & Robert D. Sloane, Indirect Expropriation and Its Valuation in the BIT Generation, *The British Year Book of International Law* (2003), Oxford, 2004, p. 115.

一、国有化或征收的概念及其新发展

（一）国有化或征收的概念

国有化（nationalization）或征收（expropriation）指国家基于公共利益的需要对私人企业全部或部分资产实行征用，收归国家所有。国际法学会在 1952 年会议上采取的定义是，"国有化是通过立法行为和为了公共利益，将某种财产或私有权利转移给国家，目的在于由国家利用或控制它们，或由国家将它们用于新的目的"[1]。典型的征收、国有化或没收通常指东道国政府通过颁布有关法令等方式将外国投资企业的全部或部分资产收归国有。

国有化或征收的具体情况很复杂：或对某一工业部门企业或对个别企业；或对企业全部资产，或对企业部分资产；或有偿，或无偿；或基于经济目的，或基于政治、军事目的；或由于外国投资者或资本输出国与资本输入国的争端产生，或并无此类原因。

与国有化或征收相关的概念是"取得"（taking）。直到第二次世界大战结束，学者通常将所有类型的"取得"（taking）称为"征收"。一些学者区分"征收"与"没收"（confiscations），主张"征收"是伴随支付充分赔偿（adequate indemnity）的"取得"，而"没收"是未予以赔偿的"取得"。其他学者则试图将"没收"专用于对非法行为（如走私）的合法制裁。有学者主张以"取得"作为包括国有化在内的所有此类情形的中性用语。还有学者主张采用"财富剥夺"（wealth deprivation）取代"取得"的概念。第二次世界大战结束之后，许多学者区分"小规模取得"和"大规模取得"两种情形，前者称为"征收"，后者称为"国有化"。[2]

1962 年，在《英国国际法年刊》中，英国学者克里斯蒂（G. C. Christie）在分析两个早期的有关征收的国际案件时指出了两种可能构成间接征收的情况：其一，一国实际干预了财产权，即使该国声称无意为之；其二，即使该国无意干预财产权，但其行动使财产权归于无效。此后，一些国际裁决和评论引用了其结论。国际法庭、法官和学者普遍认为，各国可能以正式法令以外的方式实行征收，经常试图以合法的外衣掩盖其征收行为。因此，越来越多的法庭和仲裁庭认为，征收应以随后产生的效果论，而不是正式的表述。对于作出充分赔偿的国家责任而言，国际法未区分间

---

〔1〕　余劲松：《跨国公司的法律问题研究》，中国政法大学出版社 1989 年版，第 28 页。

〔2〕　See Ignaz Seidl Hohenveldern, *International Economic Law*, 2nd revised edition, Martinus Nijhoff Publishers, 1992, pp. 138-139.

接征收与直接征收。[1]

在 20 世纪 70 年代以来，出现了逐渐征收(creeping expropriation)的概念。逐渐征收原义指东道国政府和外国投资者事先约定，外国投资者在一定年限内，按一定比例分期将其股份逐步转让给东道国政府或国民，使东道方所持股份达到 51％以上，甚至达到全部转让。[2] 然而，西方国家对逐渐征收的认定不限于此。根据经济合作开发组织开发援助委员会(OECD. DAC)投资保证专门委员《关于保护外国人财产的条约》第 3 条的注释，逐渐征收具体指不适当的独断性征税、汇款的限制、禁止解雇、拒绝批准原材料等的进出口。根据美国众议院的资料，逐渐征收是指对外国投资者的歧视待遇、外资政策的改变、强制国产化、借入限制、雇用外国人的限制、强制出口、价格统制等。[3] 逐渐征收的另一典型表述，见于美国海外私人投资公司签发的海外私人投资保险合同。[4] 该合同第 1 条第 13 款所列举的五种情况，虽不一定具备被东道国政府直接接管的条件，但均可被认定为"征收"或"国有化"。其中最经常被引用的逐渐征收，是指东道国政府以任何形式"阻碍海外美资企业对本企业重要财产的使用和处置实行切实有效的控制，阻碍建设或经营该投资项目。"在国际索赔的实践中，美国有关机构又对此项规定作尽量广义的解释。[5] 美国所强调的逐渐征收的含义和据此索赔的法律主张，为发达国家所支持和师法。其共同目的，显然在于尽量扩大对本国国民海外投资法律保护的范围，尽量扩大国际索赔的"法理根据"和求偿权能。作为吸收外资的第三世界国家，对于西方发达国家尽量扩大"征收"或"国有化"一词含义的理论和实践，应有充分的理解和必要的防范。

一般而言，国有化或征收都是由国家采取的将私人财产收归国有的强制措施，具有相同的基本内容和法律性质。因此，这两个概念是可以相互替代的。而逐渐征收则是国有化或征收的表现形式之一，亦属国有化或征收的范畴。国有化或征收尽管基本含义相同，仍有一些细微的区别：首先，征收是传统的法律概念，国家征收权被认为是主权国家所固有的权力，在格老秀斯、普芬道夫等自然法学家的著作中已

〔1〕 See W. Michael Reisman & Robert D. Sloane, Indirect Expropriation and Its Valuation in the BIT Generation, *The British Year Book of International Law*（2003），Oxford，2004，pp. 119-121.

〔2〕 参见《中国大百科全书·法学》，中国大百科全书出版社 1984 年版，第 256 页。

〔3〕 参见樱井雅夫：《国际经济法研究—以海外投资为中心》，1977 年日文版，第 97—98 页。

〔4〕 参见《海外私人投资公司 234KGT12—70 型合同(修订版)》，1982 年英文单行本，第 4 页。

〔5〕 例如，在 1967 年"瓦伦泰因石油化工公司索赔案"中，主要由于东道国政府因美企业有违约行为而取消了一项垄断性的特许合同，导致美资企业产品成本增加，营业利润减少，美国仲裁委员会也认为东道国"阻碍美国资方对本企业重要财产的使用和处置实行切实有效的控制"，由此确认征收或国有化的风险事故已发生，并有权据以实行索赔和国际代位索赔。详见陈安：《从海外私人投资公司的体制和案例看美国对海外投资的法律保护》，载中国国际法学会主编：《中国国际法年刊》(1985)，中国对外翻译出版公司 1985 年版，第 105—107 页。

有述及；[1]而国有化的概念,则是在苏联十月革命后,特别是 20 世纪 60 年代以来,才被广泛应用。其次,实行征收不一定需要颁布专门性的法令,而实行国有化则一般需要颁布专门性的国有化法令。最后,国有化的规模、范围一般比征收较大,并反映国家的社会经济结构的变化。[2]因此,狭义的国有化似可定义为,国家基于公共利益的需要,根据国有化法令,较大规模地对私人企业全部资产实行征用、收归国家所有。[3]

国有化或征收的概念具有重要的实践意义。征收险(risk of expropriation)是各国海外投资保证制度和国际投资条约对国际投资者实行法律保护的政治风险之一。[4] 在汇兑险(currency risk)[5]、征收险、政治暴力险(risk of political violence)[6]和违约险(risk of breach of contract)[7]等四种典型政治风险中,征收险是最常发生的,征收,特别是间接征收也是在国际司法和国际仲裁实践中产生最多争议的概念。[8]

(二) 征收概念的新发展

如前所述,征收、间接征收的概念直接关系到资本输出国海外投资保证制度、多边投资担保机构体制和 BITs 的适用问题。

传统上,在 BITs 的征收条款中,一般都采用"相当于国有化或征收效果的措施"(measures tantamount to nationalization or expropriation)的用语,指东道国政府

---

〔1〕 〔英〕戴维·M. 沃克:《牛津法律大辞典》,光明日报出版社 1989 年中文版,第 286 页。

〔2〕 余劲松:《跨国公司的法律问题研究》,中国政法大学出版社 1989 年版,第 281—282 页。

〔3〕 《中华人民共和国外资企业法》第 5 条、《中华人民共和国中外合资经营企业法》第 2 条第 3 款将国有化或征收分列为两个概念,似应理解为该款对国有化一词作狭义的限定。

〔4〕 一般而言,政治风险是指与东道国政治、社会和法律相关的人为风险。

〔5〕 亦称外汇险,包括货币兑换险和汇出险。这种风险是指东道国通过颁布法律或采取其他措施,禁止或限制外国投资者将其投资本金或收益兑换成可自由使用的货币并转移出东道国境外,致使外国投资者遭受损害。

〔6〕 政治暴力险(risk of political violence),亦称战乱险,包括战争险和内乱险,指外国投资者在东道国的投资因当地发生战争等军事行动或内乱而遭受损害。在 2001 年"9.11 事件"之后,"恐怖主义险"(terrorist cover)的需求急剧增长,已产生了"纯恐怖主义"险("pure terrorist" cover)的需求。一些海外投资保证机构以往将"恐怖主义险"包含在战乱险中,未另收保险费用。"9.11 事件"之后,这些海外投资保证机构或者专门对"恐怖主义险"收取保险费用,或者不再将"恐怖主义险"包含于战乱险。事实上,"9.11 事件"已产生了战乱险的实际涵盖范围以及恐怖主义活动是否能被涵盖于战乱险的问题。目前,所有海外投资保证机构正密切关注保险市场的政治和经济发展。多数此类机构已开始重新审查其保险合同中战乱险的措辞。对潜在的恐怖主义事件的高度关注已影响了战乱险的性质和费用,同时更为注重单独设立"恐怖主义险"。See Vivian Brown, Political Risk Insurance after September 11 and the Argentine Crisis: A Public Provider's Perspective, Theodore H. Moran (ed.), *International Political Risk Management*, *The Brave New World*, *The World Bank Group*, MIGA, p. 20.

〔7〕 指东道国政府对投资者的毁约或违约,一般以无法诉诸东道国司法或仲裁机构解决,或者东道国司法或仲裁机构判决或裁决迟延或不能执行为条件。

〔8〕 国际法院有关国际投资的两个案例,即"巴塞罗纳公司"(the Barcelona Traction)案和"恩古拉电力股份公司"(ELSI)案均涉及征收问题。有关后一案例的评论,参见 F. A. Mann, Foreign Investment in the International Court of Justice: The ELSI Case, *American Journal of International Law*, Vol. 86, No. 1, 1992, pp. 92-102.

在未从法律上取得外国投资者所有权的情况下，采取阻碍或影响外国投资者对其资产行使有效控制权、使用权或处分权的行为，诸如强制国产化、强制股权转让、强制转让经营权、不适当地大幅度提高税率等。此类措施亦称为事实上征收（*de facto* expropriation）、逐渐征收（creeping expropriation）、间接征收（indirect expropriation）或本地化（indigenization or localization）。然而，对特定 BIT 的缔约双方而言，"相当于国有化或征收效果的措施"究何所指？如何认定？则需要进一步解释或澄清。

鉴此，近年发达国家的 BITs 范本对"间接征收"的含义及其认定标准专门作出规定。《加拿大与某国促进和保护投资协定 2004 年范本》（Agreement between Canada and—for the Promotion and Protection of Investments，2004，简称《加拿大 2004 年范本》）可作为典型的例子。该范本第 13 条题为"征收"，第 1 款提及"间接征收"的概念，为求更大的稳定性，附 B.13（1）对"间接征收"的概念作了如下澄清：

> "征收
>
> 缔约双方确认其共识：
>
> （1）间接征收产生于由缔约一方采取具有相当于直接征收后果的未正式转移所有权或未完全没收的一种或一系列措施；
>
> （2）缔约一方采取的一种或一系列措施是否构成间接征收需要个案、基于事实的调查，考虑的因素包括：
>
> （i）该措施或该系列措施的经济影响，虽然仅有缔约一方采取的一种或一系列措施对投资的经济价值具有负面影响之事实不足以确立间接征收已发生；
>
> （ii）该措施或该系列措施对明确、合理的投资预期的干预程度；及
>
> （iii）该措施或该系列措施的特性；
>
> （3）除非在极个别的情况下，例如就其宗旨而言，严格意义上，一种或一系列措施不能被合理地视为已被善意采取和实施，缔约一方旨在和适用于保护合法的公共福利目标如健康、安全和环境的非歧视措施，不构成间接征收。"

上述条款的要点及其意义可简要解读如下：

第一，明确了间接征收产生于东道国的措施。东道国采取的具有相当于直接征收后果的未正式转移外国投资者所有权或未完全没收外国投资的一种或一系列措施，产生了间接征收。在此，何谓"具有相当于直接征收后果"？留下了相当大的解释空间。

　　第二，是否构成间接征收需要个案、基于事实的调查，考虑的因素包括该措施或该系列措施的经济影响、该措施或该系列措施对明确、合理的投资预期的干预程度及该措施或该系列措施的特性。该规定仅仅表明，仅凭该措施或该系列措施对投资的经济价值具有负面影响之事实不足以确立间接征收已发生，但对于其他两个因素的考虑及其标准，即如何判定措施的"干预程度"？如何判定措施的"特性"？未作进一步规定。显然，考虑的三方面因素都是很抽象的。在此情况下，投资者母国主管机构对于判断间接征收是否发生具有很大的自由裁量权。

　　第三，一般而言，缔约一方旨在和适用于保护合法的公共福利目标如健康、安全和环境的非歧视措施，不构成间接征收，但不能被合理地视为已善意采取和实施的此类措施，不在此限。这意味着，即使是基于公共利益的非歧视措施，也可能以"非善意"而归入"间接征收"的范围。[1]

　　除了上述一般性规定，加拿大在 BITs 实践中，进一步将"间接征收"的解释扩及知识产权保护领域。加拿大 2004 年 6 月提出的《某国与加拿大促进和保护投资协定草案》(New text proposed by Canada as of June 2004，Agreement between—and Canada for the Promotion and Protection of Investments，简称《加拿大 2004 年草案》第 5 条第 2 款规定：

　　　　"本条规定不适用于与知识产权有关的授予的强制许可的颁布，或知识产权的撤销、限制或创设，以此种颁布、撤销、限制或创设符合 1994 年 4 月 15 日在马拉喀什签订的世界贸易组织协定为限。"

　　上述条款规定的重要意义首先是，虽然表面上排除了该 BIT 对与知识产权有关的授予的强制许可的颁布或知识产权的撤销、限制或创设的适用，但实际上表明了该协定具有适用的可能性。换言之，缔约方与知识产权有关的授予的强制许可的颁布或知识产权的撤销、限制或创设如不符合《世界贸易组织协定》，特别是《与贸易有关的知识产权协定》(TRIPS)的有关规定，可能被认定为"间接征收"。更值得注意的是，该条款的征收认定与《世界贸易组织协定》相联系，反映了 BITs 实践与 WTO 体制挂钩的新动向。

　　加拿大在 BITs 实践中还直接规定征收条款适用于税务措施。《加拿大 2004 年

---

　　[1]　在 2000 年 8 月 22 日作出裁决的 Metalclad 案例中，墨西哥未曾预料其环境保护措施可被视为根据《北美自由贸易协定》项下的征收。See M. Sornarajah, A Developing Country Perspective of International Economic Law in the Context of Dispute Settlement, in Asif H. Qureshi(ed.), *Perspectives in International Economic Law*, Kluwer Law International，2002，p. 88.

草案》第 5 条第 3 款规定：

> "本条规定适用于税务措施，除非缔约双方的税务当局，在接到质疑税务措施的投资者通知的 6 个月之内，共同判定该措施不是征收。"

上述规定意味着缔约一方的税务措施很可能被认定为"间接征收"，因为在外国投资者指控东道国税务措施构成间接征收的情况下，作为缔约一方的投资者母国税务当局与作为缔约另一方的东道国税务当局在 6 个月时限内共同判定某税务措施不是征收的可能性毕竟是不容乐观的。

从加拿大最新 BITs 实践可以看出，在 BITs 中明确"间接征收"的定义及其认定标准是征收概念的重要发展。其实践意义在于，首先，在实体规则方面，间接征收的认定范围更广，即间接征收产生于一种或一系列措施。而不加限定词的措施，含义是相当广泛的。如所周知，措施包括法律和政策，也包括抽象行政行为和具体行政行为。其次，在程序规则方面，对外国投资者母国认定间接征收的程序和考虑的因素也作了规定，在外国投资者主张东道国间接征收已发生时，外国投资者母国"有法可依"，即根据 BITs 的有关规定，具有判断间接征收的主动权和最后决定权。

二、征收的合法性问题及其新发展

（一）征收的合法性问题

1. 从征收权之争到征收补偿标准之争

关于东道国政府对境内的外国人资产实行国有化或征收的合法性问题，在相当长的历史时期内存在激烈的争论。在殖民主义盛行的年代，按照西方殖民列强的传统观点，亚非拉国家政府对于境内外国投资者的财产，只有保护的义务，没有任何权利。一旦对外资实行征收或国有化，就构成所谓"国际不法行为"，投资者的母国政府就"有权"追究东道国的"国家责任"，甚至可以"护侨"为名兴兵索债。面对这种横暴的武装入侵，东道国"有忍受干涉的法律义务"。[1] 这种观点在西方国际法学界曾长期占统治地位。直至 20 世纪初，南美著名法学家、阿根廷外交部长德拉果率先向这种传统观点挑战，谴责殖民强国向弱国兴兵索债乃是侵略他国领土、干涉他国内政之举，是一种真正的国际违法行为。对于这种来自弱小民族的正义呼声，直至 20 世纪 50 年代，西方国际法学界仍有一些"权威"学者公然表示反对，扬言"德拉果

---

〔1〕 参见劳特派特修订：《奥本海国际法》，上卷，第一分册，商务印书馆 1981 年中译本，第 230—233、235、257页。

主义"是"没有根据的，并且未得到一般的承认"。[1]

随着弱小民族的进一步觉醒，从 20 世纪 30 年代末起，上述根本否认东道国政府有权征收外资的传统观点，因其不符合时代潮流，毕竟难以坚守原来的阵地，不得不开始有所后退。这一迹象较典型地体现于美国对 1937 年 12 月墨西哥征用境内的美资地产和石油企业时所采取的立场。1938 年，美国国务卿赫尔(Cordell Hull)致墨西哥驻美大使纳耶拉的外交照会提出："依据法律和衡平法的一切准则，不论为了何种目的，如果不针对征收提供充分、及时、有效(adequate，prompt，effective)的赔偿，任何政府都无权征收(外国人的)私有财产。"其中，"充分、及时、有效的赔偿"标准就是所谓的"赫尔"规则(Hull formula)，代表了美国对征收及其补偿标准的法律和政策立场。上述措辞尽管十分强硬，在逻辑上却可以推导出这样的结论：如果给予"充分、及时、有效的赔偿"，东道国政府就有权征收境内的外国人私有财产。后来，在《美国涉外法律诠解(第二版)》中更明确地阐述了美国的上述观点，即：国家征收境内的外国人财产，如果不是为了公益目的，或不按上述标准给予赔偿，就是国际法上的不法行为；反之，就不视为国际法上的不法行为。这意味着，在为了公益目的而征收外国私人财产的场合，就此种征收本身而论，并非国际法上的不法行为，只有在征收时不按上述标准给予赔偿，这种"拒赔"才构成国际法上的不法行为，从而引起"国际责任"问题。[2]

20 世纪 60 年代以来，一些西方国际法学者主张，国有化的内国立法，如果在未尊重既得权原则，亦即未给予"及时、充分和完全"(prompt，adequate and full)的情况下剥夺外国人的财产，可以在内国法院提起确认该法无效的诉讼。此类主张得到了 1962 年国际法学会第 50 届大会的支持。[3] 西方学者保罗·科麦斯(Paul E. Comeaux)和斯蒂芬·金舍拉(N. Stephan Kinsella)明确主张，根据国际法，一些征收可视为"合法的"，而另一些征收可视为"违法的"。如果征收是非歧视、为公共目的并伴随全部赔偿，就是"合法的"。[4]

从表面上看，此时国有化或征收的合法性问题争执的焦点，似已转移到赔偿标

〔1〕 参见劳特派特修订：《奥本海国际法》，上卷，第一分册，商务印书馆 1981 年中译本，第 233 页。

〔2〕 对于给予"充分、及时、有效"赔偿的征收是国际法上的不法行为，或是实行征收国主权的正当行使，有许多评论。依"不法行为"论，这种"不法行为"的逻辑结果是实际履行(specific performance)的责任。而在绝大多数情况下，这种"恢复原状"是不现实的。然而，依"主权行使"论，未支付充分赔偿可被视为构成国际法上的"拖欠债务"(delinquency)。See Ignaz Seidl Hohenveldern，*International Economic Law*，2nd revised edition，Martinus Nijhoff Publishers，1992，p. 139.

〔3〕 Wolfgang Friedmann，*The Changing Structure of International Law*，Columbia University Press，1964，pp. 226-227.

〔4〕 Paul E. Comeaux，N. Stephan Kinsella，*Protecting Foreign Investment under International Law*，*Legal Aspects of Political Risk*，Oceana Publications Inc.，1997，p. 5.

准上，实则并不尽然。因为，按照美国所主张的赔偿原则，即所谓"国际法上的公平标准"，往往索价极高，甚至几近敲诈勒索，这样实际上就大大削弱、限制甚至取消了贫弱的发展中国家征收外资的基本权利。美国的这一主张得到西方发达国家（多是原先的殖民强国）的支持。与此相反，鉴于许多外资企业在殖民主义统治时期或在被征收前业已攫取了巨额利润，鉴于本国财力薄弱的现实情况，发展中国家一贯主张在征收时只按照东道国国内法的规定，给予补偿，从而维护本国的政治主权和经济主权。发展中国家学者主张，在评估征收补偿时，应当考虑征收国的支付能力。不容否认的事实是，国家越贫穷，越需要社会改革，而"充分、及时、有效的赔偿"义务将使穷国无法采取任何征收措施。[1] 可见，关于征收补偿标准问题之争，究其实质，依然是发展中国家对外资是否充分享有征收权之争，或者说，它是历史上长期存在的征收权之争的延续。

2. 联大决议确立的征收权和适当补偿原则

1962 年联合国第 17 届大会通过了《关于天然资源之永久主权宣言》（简称《资源宣言》），该宣言规定，"采取国有化、征收或征用措施，应当以公共事业、社会安全或国家利益等理由或原因作为依据"，表明国际社会普遍承认各国有权对外资控制的自然资源及其有关企业实行国有化或征收；但它同时规定，"采取此等措施以行使其主权之国家应依据本国现行法规及国际法，予原主以适当之补偿"。[2] 这种妥协性的措辞，实际上就是上述两种对立主张的简单相加，是非并未判明，分歧并未解决。

在 20 世纪 60、70 年代联合国有关永久主权概念、新国际经济秩序、国家经济权利和义务的辩论中，77 国集团强调国家的征收权。1974 年 12 月联合国第 29 届大会通过的《各国经济权利和义务宪章》（简称《经济宪章》）明文规定，各国有权"把外国资产收归国有、征用或转移所有权"。在对外资实行国有化或征收时，"应由采取此种措施的国家给予适当的赔偿，要考虑到它的有关法律、条例以及该国认为有关的一切情况。因赔偿问题引起的任何争议均应由实行国有化国家的法院依照其国内法加以解决，除非有关各国自由和互相同意根据各国主权平等并依照自由选择方法的原则寻求其他和平解决办法。"[3] 对比《资源宣言》，《经济宪章》不仅重申了"有权征收"的原则，还在征收补偿的法律适用方面，删除了"国际法"等字样。至此，终于在一项具有相当权威性的国际经济法的基本文献中，以毫不含糊的语言，不但肯定了各国可对境内外资实行国有化或征收的主权权利，而且排除了发达国家对发展中

---

〔1〕 See Ignaz Seidl Hohenveldern，*International Economic Law*，2nd revised edition，Martinus Nijhoff Publishers，1992，p. 139.

〔2〕《资源宣言》第 1 节第 4 款。

〔3〕《经济宪章》第 2 条第 2 款第 3 项。

国家施加的所谓征收补偿的"国际法标准"的约束。[1] 这一主张在当时居于主导地位。[2] 其重要意义在于,一是在征收权方面,针对西方国家"不得征收"的原则,明确提出了"有权征收"的原则;二是在征收补偿标准方面,针对西方国家的"赫尔"规则,明确提出了适当补偿原则;三是在有关赔偿问题争议的法律适用和解决方式方面,针对西方国家的依国际法的国际司法或仲裁解决方式,明确提出了依东道国法的国内司法解决方式。

应当指出,《经济宪章》所确立的征收及其补偿标准的原则实际上是重申久已确立的国家主权原则。如所周知,主权是指对内最高、对外独立的权力。根据主权原则的属地最高权(territorial supremacy),各国有权决定其政治、经济、社会和文化制度,对外资实行征收是各国主权的正当行使。《经济宪章》所确立的这一原则得到发展中国家的普遍接受,也得到不同法系国家的普遍认同。[3] 然而,《经济宪章》的上述原则并未被美国等发达国家所接受。1975 年 12 月,即该宪章通过一年之后,美国国务卿基辛格在有关"外国投资与国有化"的声明中仍然宣称,即使是非歧视、基于公益目的而实行的国有化,美国仍具有要求"充分、及时、有效"赔偿的权利。[4]此外,美国还力图通过缔结新型的 BITs,在有关条款中坚持"充分、及时、有效"赔偿的原则,逐一对缔约国对方施以新的国际法约束。[5] 其他发达国家也起而效法。一些西方学者也主张,在 BITs 中规定,在实行国有化的情况下,给予受影响的外国投资者"充分、及时、有效"的赔偿,将消除其疑虑。[6]

由此可见,世界上弱小民族对境内外资实行国有化或征收的合法权利,是经过长期的奋斗才获得国际社会普遍承认和充分肯定的。这是来之不易的主权权利。然而,"树欲静而风不止",以美国为代表的一些发达国家并未接受《经济宪章》的有关规定。迄今为止,征收的合法性问题一直是新旧两种国际经济秩序矛盾斗争的焦点之一。[7]

---

〔1〕 参见陈安主编:《国际投资法》,鹭江出版社 1987 年版,第 88—90 页正文及有关注解。

〔2〕 Paul Peters, Recent Developments in Expropriation Clauses of Asian Investment Treaties, *Asian Yearbook of International Law*, Vol. 5, 1995, p. 71.

〔3〕 伊斯兰法也承认国家的征收权。1981 年独任仲裁员马哈萨尼(Mahmassani)博士在 LIAMCO 案的裁决中指出,*Sharia* 原则本身不禁止征收财产,基本的前提是强制的必要性、取得中的非歧视和支付补偿的责任。*Sharia* 的文义是:"走向胜地之路—遵循以达到《可兰经》制定的目标之权利。"Javaid Rehman, Islamic Perspectives on International Economic Law, Asif H. Qureshi(ed.), *Perspectives in International Economic Law*, Kluwer Law International, 2002.

〔4〕 参见〔日〕樱井雅夫:《国际经济法研究—以海外投资为中心》,1977 年日文版,第 63 页。

〔5〕 陈安:《美国对海外投资的法律保护及典型案例分析》,鹭江出版社 1985 年版,第 12—15 页。

〔6〕 See Ignaz Seidl Hohenveldern, *International Economic Law*, 2nd revised edition, Martinus Nijhoff Publishers, 1992, p. 154.

〔7〕 参见陈安编译:《国际经济法的历史和现状》,法律出版社 1982 年版,第 46—55 页。

（二）征收合法性问题的新发展

20 世纪 90 年代以来,发达国家在多边投资条约和 BITs 实践中,逐渐对国有化或征收的合法性作了类似的规定,形成了背离《经济宪章》有关规定的模式。

在 OECD 成员国谈判起草的《多边投资协定》（草案）（Multilateral Agreement on Investment,MAI）中,关于征收的规定是,缔约国不应采取任何措施直接或间接对位于其领土内的另一缔约国投资者的投资实行征收或国有化,除非:(1) 为了公共利益;(2) 在非歧视待遇基础上;(3) 根据正当法律程序;及(4) 伴随及时、充分和有效的赔偿。[1] 在征收方面,MAI 有许多保护外国投资者的"发明":一是征收条款不仅适用于财产,也适用于契约权利和对协议的任何"违反";二是 MAI 的一般例外条款不适用于征收和补偿;三是征收条款适用于税务措施;四是联邦政府或中央政府应对第二级实体(州或省)或地方政府采取的征收措施负责;最后是投资者与政府之间争端解决机制作为实现由具体征收和补偿待遇保护的外国投资者权利的有效方式。[2]

美国主导的《北美自由贸易区协定》（North American Free Trade Agreement, NAFTA)第 1110 条规定,"除非出于公共目的,以非歧视的方式,经过适当法律程序并符合第 1105 条第 1 款的规定,并支付赔偿,任何缔约方不得直接或间接地征收或采取相当于征收的措施"。而赔偿标准是"毫不迟延、可以完全兑现"并且"相当于被征收投资的公平市场价值"。[3]

在多数 BITs 中,一般列举三至四项征收的前提条件,有些仅列举两项条件,另一些则列举五至六项条件。在 BITs 中列为征收前提条件的依使用的频度为序是:(1) 赔偿;(2) 公共目的;(3) 非歧视;(4) 正当法律程序;(5) 不违反具体承诺(specific undertakings);(6) 全部适用(catch-all);(7) 透明度(clarity);(8) 公平待遇。[4]

《加拿大 2004 年范本》第 13 条第 1 款规定:

"缔约任何一方均不得对涵盖的投资直接实行国有化或征收,或者间接地通过具有相当于国有化或征收效果的措施(以下称为'征收')实行国有化或征

---

[1] 参见陈辉萍:《〈多边投资协议〉谈判回顾与展望》,载陈安主编:《国际经济法论丛》第 2 卷,法律出版社 1999 年版,第 300 页。

[2] See CHEN Huiping, *OECD's Multilateral Agreement on Investment*, *A Chinese Perspective*, Kluwer Law International, 2002, pp. 122-123.

[3] 参见叶兴平:《〈北美自由贸易协定〉的投资规则及其对多边国际投资立法的影响》,载陈安主编:《国际经济法论丛》第 6 卷,法律出版社 2002 年版,第 252—254 页。

[4] See Paul Peters, Recent Developments in Expropriation Clauses of Asian Investment Treaties, *Asian Yearbook of International Law*, Vol. 5, 1995, pp. 56-67.

收,除非出于公共目的,根据正当法律程序,以非歧视的方式并且给予及时、充分和有效的赔偿。"

尽管表述略有不同,《加拿大 2004 年草案》也作了内容相同的规定。[1]

从发达国家关于征收的典型规定可见,首先,发达国家依然把"不得征收"外资作为一般的法律原则。虽然,发达国家并非一般地否定国家对外资的征收权,但对征收权作了严格的限制性前提条件,通常是"为公共利益目的""依照法律程序""非歧视"及"给予及时、充分和有效赔偿"等四项,以是否满足前提条件为依据进一步区分了"合法的征收"和"非法的征收",并主张依国际法和国内法(包括投资者母国和投资东道国的法律)保留对东道国政府征收行为是否合法的裁判权。

其次,发达国家更为强调"赫尔"规则,即"给予及时、充分和有效赔偿"的标准。在上述对征收权的四项前提条件中,"给予及时、充分和有效赔偿"无疑是决定性的。对发展中国家来说,在实行征收时满足为公共利益目的、依照法律程序、非歧视性等三项前提条件是相对容易做到的,而"给予及时、充分和有效赔偿"则难以做到甚至无法做到。因为发展中国家经济能力有限,在实行经济改革目标的大规模征收时,往往无力支付"及时、充分和有效赔偿"。而一旦无力支付,则征收就无法实施。如果强行实施,就将被判定为"非法的征收",须承担国际责任。在此情况下,发展中国家的征收权实际上被彻底否定了。[2]

应当指出,上述发达国家关于征收的典型规定明显违背了《经济宪章》第 2 条第 2 款第 3 项的"有权征收"的规定。根据后者规定,对外资实行征收是国家主权的正当行使,征收权不应由第三方强加任何前提条件,更不能让第三方作出征收属于"合法"或"非法"的裁断。[3] 重要的问题是,发展中国家在实践中,应注意坚持《经济宪章》"有权征收"的原则,防止发达国家利用 BITs 或多边投资体制,以四项前提条件限制甚至否定征收权。

---

〔1〕　该草案第 5 条规定:"缔约任何一方的投资者的投资或收益在缔约另一方领土不得被征收、国有化或被采取具有与征收或国有化相同的措施(以下称为'征收'),除非出于公共目的,根据正当法律程序,以非歧视的方式并且给予及时、充分和有效的赔偿。"

〔2〕　有西方学者指出,应区分两种征收:一是小规模的、只涉及少数人的征收,二是大规模的、长远社会改革进程中的征收。前者不会因征收补偿问题而影响到国家的财政能力;而后一种征收,如按"赫尔"规则要求,东道国可能因征收赔偿数额而对必不可少的征收迟疑不决。See Ignaz Seidl Hohenveldern, *International Economic Law*, 2nd revised edition, Martinus Nijhoff Publishers, 1992, p. 138.

〔3〕　事实上,就上述征收权的四项限定条件来说,征收是否出于公共利益目的,最适格的评判者是实施征收的国家,而不是国际性法庭或仲裁庭。See Ignaz Seidl Hohenveldern, *International Economic Law*, 2nd revised edition, Martinus Nijhoff Publishers, 1992, pp. 137-138.

三、征收补偿标准之争及其新发展

（一）三种理论主张与有关实践

关于国有化或征收的补偿标准，一直是发达国家与发展中国家之间不同观点之源，[1]主要有三种理论主张，以下结合有关实践予以评述。

1. "赫尔"规则

所谓"赫尔"规则，亦即上述美国国务卿赫尔1938年主张的"充分、及时、有效"的赔偿标准。它成为美国有关征收政策的旗帜，并坚持至今。其他一些国家，如英国、澳大利亚、加拿大、丹麦、芬兰和瑞典等也将其作为国际法上的征收最低标准，称为"三重标准"（triple standard）。[2]

从"赫尔"规则本身看，值得注意的是，首先，它虽然没有直接断言征收是非法的，但它将"充分、及时、有效"的赔偿标准作为合法征收的前提条件；其次，"充分、及时、有效"的赔偿标准适用于任何征收行为，尽管当时有所谓"合法征收"和"违法征收"之分；最后，"充分、及时、有效"的赔偿标准的含义是不明确的。

不言而喻，"赫尔"规则代表了海外投资者的利益，得到大多数资本输出国的支持。长期以来，西方国家及某些西方学者坚持主张，根据国际法，实行国有化的国家有义务以"充分、及时、有效"的方式赔偿财产被国有化的外国人。所谓"充分"指赔偿金额应与被征收财产的全部价值（即"公平的市场价值"）相等，并包括直至支付赔偿金时的利息，在某些情况下，甚至包括预期利润；"及时"，指支付赔偿金应"及时"实现，在分期支付的情况下，应支付欠款利息以作为补偿；"有效"，指赔偿金应以允许可盈利再投资（profitable reinvestment）的方式支付，可兑换货币（一般是国际市场上的硬通货）的支付通常是有效的。

何种赔偿是"完全"（full）或"充分"，成为赔偿标准的最重要问题。在美国签订的保护财产的条约中，这两个用语并列使用，互为解释。西方学者主张，"完全"的价值不包含所有人附属于财产的社会情感价值。"完全"的价值在存在市场的情况下，最好就是市场价值，同时应考虑时间因素，即该项征收为公众所知的前一刻的市场价值。换言之，征收意图为公众所知导致的损失亦属赔偿范围。在企业正常运作的情况下，市场价值相当于兴旺企业价值（going concern value），该企业的买主不仅要评

---

[1] Asif H. Qureshi, Perspectives in International Economic Law-An Eclectic Approach to International Economic Engagement, Asif H. Qureshi(ed.), *Perspectives in International Economic Law*, Kluwer Law International, 2002, p. 15.

[2] See Paul Peters, Recent Developments in Expropriation Clauses of Asian Investment Treaties, *Asian Yearbook of International Law*, Vol. 5, 1995, p. 71.

估设备的价值,还要评估使用该设备可创造的价值。因此,对该企业的赔偿不仅包括设施与设备的损失,还包括预期利润的损失。在不存在市场的情况下,评估被征收的财产将更为困难,这通常发生在大规模国有化的场合。[1]

"充分、及时、有效"的赔偿标准的依据之一是"尊重既得权"原则。某些西方学者把尊重既得权作为国际法的基本原则之一。根据这一原则,当某人根据一国国内法取得某种地位或权利时,他人有义务尊重这种既得的地位或权利。有一种观点把尊重既得权原则作为外国财产不受国有化法律影响的依据。据此,损害外国人财产权的征收措施相当于对外国人的侵权行为,该外国人有权要求恢复原状或给予全部的损害赔偿。这种观点实际上否认了国家的征收权,在实践上行不通。因为任何国家、包括发达国家都不会放弃在必要时对私人财产的征收权。以后出现的另一种观点认为,尊重既得权原则体现于对被征收财产的原业主进行赔偿。据此,对外国人财产实行国有化或征收,如果没有伴随全部赔偿或给予相等的新权利,在国际法上就不是合法的。

这一标准的另一依据是"不当得利"(unjust enrichment)原则。根据这一原则,没有合法根据,损害别人的利益而取得不当利益的人,应将取得的不当利益返还受损失的人,或向后者作出赔偿。东道国政府征收外国人的财产,即使尚未从该财产未来可能产生的利润中得益,也已从该财产本身的价值中受惠。因此,东道国对被征收了财产的所有人负有赔偿义务。根据"不当得利"原则,完全未得到赔偿或未得到充分赔偿的所有人,可诉诸取得(较高)赔偿的一般原则。[2]

应当指出,"尊重既得权"原则和"不当得利"原则一般均适用于无法律根据的行为,如果把它们作为补偿标准的依据,就等于把征收这一合法行为视为不合法行为。[3]

在理论上,一些西方学者对"充分、及时、有效"的赔偿标准提出异议。劳特派特(H. O. Lauterpacht)和布朗里(I. Brownlie)区分国家对个别财产的征收和"国家政治制度和经济结构的根本改变或长远社会改革对私人财产造成的大规模干预",认为传统的赔偿标准(即"赫尔"规则)适用于前者,而部分赔偿适用于后者是适当的。

[1] See Ignaz Seidl Hohenveldern, *International Economic Law*, 2nd revised edition, Martinus Nijhoff Publishers,1992,pp. 144-145.

[2] 事实上,"不当得利"的观念也体现在,智利阿连德总统在对美资智利铜矿实行国有化时,提出了从赔偿额中扣除超额利润(excess profits)的权利主张。美国投资者否认其曾取得如同阿连德总统单方面评定的高额利润。虽然阿连德总统从未披露他计算赔偿额的基准,在跨国公司内部将转移定价转变为正常价格的困难可以解释有关赔偿额的分歧。See Ignaz Seidl Hohenveldern, *International Economic Law*, 2nd revised edition, Martinus Nijhoff Publishers,1992,pp. 145-146.

[3] 参见余劲松:《论国际投资法中国有化补偿的根据》,载《中国社会科学》1986年第2期,第56—59页。

沙赫特（O. Schacter）认为，"充分、及时、有效的赔偿"规则从来就不是传统的国际法规则，因此它在所有国有化案件中肯定不具有现代国际法的效力。他指出，对战后国有化案件的国家实践的研究表明，赔偿是部分赔偿并且经常是以不可兑换的货币支付。在进行类似的研究之后，布林（O. E. Bring）认为，传统的"充分、及时、有效"的赔偿标准是过时的，唯一实际上受到国家实践支持的因素是"有效"的赔偿。他主张，从国家实践中无法引申出普遍承认的有关赔偿数额的国际标准或规则，可以引申的是，在考虑一切有关情况后，真诚承担支付赔偿的义务。

发展中国家政府和学者从法理上对"充分、及时、有效"的赔偿标准进行了深入的分析和批判。主要论点是：首先，这一标准不正当地使发展中国家承担法律义务，实际上剥夺了发展中国家采取适当措施以改造其经济结构的能力。因为，发展中国家为确保有效控制其经济和实现其发展目标而实行的国有化，如果由传统的赔偿标准支配，就意味着主要资本输出国对发展中国家进行的基本经济和社会改革可以行使否决权。其次，将蕴含于"充分"的"公平市场价值"概念用于重要的经济改造，包括大规模的土地改革或在自然资源等战略部门实行的国有化，是将传统的商业和财产概念用于非一般商业性买卖场合，显属不当。在自然资源部门的企业，并非经营于传统的市场条件，而是通常取得东道国授予的便利条件、优惠和特权。基于"公平市场价值"的赔偿要求不仅包括了外国投资者的原有投资，而且包括了自然资源本身的价值、特许权或其他有关勘探开发该资源的权利。这种要求无异于要求东道国对本来就归属于它的财产支付赔偿，并且在任何情况下，将产生阻止实行国有化的后果。最后，"及时、有效"的赔偿标准与《国际货币基金组织协定》业已确立的国家管制资金转移的权利不一致，并且将对发展中国家的外汇平衡产生不利的影响。因此，多数发展中国家坚持在一定期间内以债券或其他形式分期支付赔偿的权利。[1]

在国际实践中，至今还找不到按照"充分、及时、有效"标准补偿的案例。据联合国秘书长 1974 年 9 月 20 日向联合国大会提出的报告，从 1960 年至 1974 年中期，62 个国家发生的 875 件国有化或接管事件均未进行"充分、及时、有效"的补偿。联邦德国国际法学者温勒在研究剖析国际法院有关判决后得出的结论是，任何非歧视性征收事件中都不存在要求完全（充分）补偿的国际法院判例。前国际法院院长夏尔·德·威谢也指出，在大规模的国有化案件中，国家实践已经实质性地限制了要求完全、迅速补偿被征收的外国人财产的权利。[2] 1991 年对 51 个发展中国家外国投资

---

〔1〕 Samuel K. B. Asante, International Law and Foreign Investment: A Reappraisal, *International and Comparative Law Quarterly*, Vol. 37, No. 3, 1988, pp. 595-601.

〔2〕 〔美〕奥斯卡·沙赫特：《征用外国人财产的补偿问题》，载《外国法学译丛》1986 年第 1 期，第 2—3 页。

法的研究结果显示,在征收的补偿标准问题上,这些国家尚无规定采用"充分、及时、有效"标准者。[1] 新加坡国立大学学者索那纳吉在实证研究之后也明确指出,不存在支持"完全赔偿"(full compensation)一般规则的条约法和国际实践。[2]

值得注意的是,1995 年西方学者保罗·彼得(Paul Peters)对 282 项 BITs 的研究结果表明,发达国家与发展中国家两类国家对"赫尔"规则的立场并非"泾渭分明",在发达国家中,对"赫尔"规则的立场亦非完全一致。在 BITs 中坚定奉行"赫尔"规则的国家包括美国、英国、澳大利亚、加拿大、丹麦、芬兰和瑞典等。法国在其 BITs 中规定了"及时、充分"的标准,瑞士则在其 BITs 中规定了"充分、有效"的标准。意大利、韩国和土耳其对"赫尔"规则并不推崇。反对"赫尔"规则的国家包括奥地利、德国、荷兰、挪威、西班牙、中国以及广大发展中国家。[3]

在国际仲裁实践中,ICSID 仲裁庭对于所谓东道国"非法"征收外国投资的情形,出现了裁决东道国应支付"全部补偿"的实例。在"阿姆科公司诉印度尼西亚"案的第一次裁决中,仲裁庭认为,印度尼西亚武装力量的协助接管行为和政府吊销投资许可行为剥夺了外国投资者的合同权利,"因此,为了对受到损害的投资者进行国际法所要求的全部、有效的补偿,1980 年 4 月 1 日被占领的企业的净价值必须折算成当日的美元价值","在必要限度内,依此裁定的利息应视为申请方所得补偿的组成部分,以使补偿尽可能接近于国际法规定的全部补偿"。[4] 需要指出的是,征收是主权国家的固有权力,本无所谓"合法""非法"之分。在上述案件中,仲裁庭裁决东道国"非法"征收外国投资,并无法律根据。即使如此,仲裁庭裁决的"全部补偿"由于只是净价值加上利息,也不等同于"赫尔"规则。

总体上,"赫尔"规则尚未在现代国际实践中得到证明。即使是坚持"赫尔"规则的国家,也常常接受"部分补偿"的安排。尽管一些学者极力主张征收补偿的"一揽子协议"(lump-sum agreement)没有背离"赫尔"规则标准,无可否认,此类"一揽子协议"是基于接受"部分补偿"。[5]

2. 不予补偿

苏联、东欧国家和拉美国家一些学者主张,一国在对外国人财产实行国有化或

---

[1]　Antonio R. Parra, Principles Governing Foreign Investment, as Reflected in National Investment Codes, *ICSID Review—Foreign Investment Law Journal*, Vol. 7, 1992, p. 443, table 5.

[2]　M. Sornarajah, *The International Law on Foreign Investment*, Cambridge University Press, 1996, pp. 361-365.

[3]　See Paul Peters, Recent Developments in Expropriation Clauses of Asian Investment Treaties, *Asian Yearbook of International Law*, Vol. 5, 1995, pp. 72-73.

[4]　*ICSID Reports*, Vol. 1, 1993, pp. 499, 504, 506.

[5]　M. Sornarajah, Nationalisation of Foreign Investment, K. C. D. M. Wilde (ed.), *International Transactions, Trade and Investment, Law and Finance*, The Law Book Company Limited, 1993, p. 339.

征收之后，不存在补偿义务。其主要依据之一是国家主权原则。他们认为，由于国际法中并无将外国人财产收归国有必须给予补偿的原则，因此，是否给予补偿，乃是一国主权范围内的事，由国内法决定。另一主要依据是国民待遇原则。据此，如果一国实行国有化时对其本国国民不予补偿，对外国人当然也不例外。此外，在联合国有关"自然资源永久主权"的辩论中，苏联国际法学者还从"不平等条约"的理论出发，主张对外国资本主义势力在殖民主义时代取得的财产权利和其他经济利益，应在不予任何补偿的情况下实施征收。在此，"不平等"（inequality）实际上是"威逼"（duress）的替代词，而"威逼"作为"拒不偿付债款"的理由在西方的理论和实践中已受到普遍承认。[1]

历史上，资产阶级国家和社会主义国家都有征收外国人财产不予补偿的实例。1789 年法国大革命后，法国国民议会曾决定无偿废除封建财产权，其中包括位于法国亚尔萨斯省的德意志皇室亲王的许多小领地，均未予以赔偿。十月革命后，苏联在采取一系列国有化措施时完全拒绝补偿。有关国家在后来同苏联签订的双边条约中，明示或默示地放弃了其赔偿要求。东欧国家在第二次世界大战后实行国有化时亦拒绝补偿。[2]

3. 适当补偿

适当补偿原则在《经济宪章》中获得普遍承认从而得以确立，其主要依据之一是公平互利原则。根据这一原则，在补偿时要考虑东道国和外国投资者双方的情况，兼顾双方利益。一方面，要考虑到东道国实行社会和经济改革的需要、其经济发展水平和财政支付能力。另一方面，也考虑到外国投资者的合法权益遭受损失的各种情况，并予以适当补偿。因为，国有化虽是东道国主权的正当行使，但如果外国投资者因其合法权益得不到法律保护或资产被征收后得不到合理补偿而不来投资，也不利于东道国经济的发展。有些国家在考虑外国投资企业因国有化或征收导致的损失情况时，联系考察其历史情况，从对其补偿的数额中扣除其过去取得的超额利润。例如，智利 1971 年征用美资铜矿企业时，就曾采取这种做法。

适当补偿原则的另一依据是自然资源永久主权原则。根据这一原则，东道国对其境内某项自然资源开发项目实行国有化时，参加开发该自然资源的外国投资者不应对产生于该自然资源的利益主张权利，而只能就其资产考虑补偿。如果强求东道国对外国投资者的预期利益（或所谓"潜在利润"）和其他间接损失作出补偿，这就无

---

〔1〕 Wolfgang Friedmann，*The Changing Structure of International Law*，Columbia University Press，1964，pp. 335-336.

〔2〕 余劲松：《论国际投资法中国有化补偿的根据》，载《中国社会科学》1986 年第 2 期，第 59—61 页。

异于对自然资源永久主权的否定。[1]

适当补偿的标准不仅为广大发展中国家普遍接受,在一些发达国家的仲裁和司法实践中也有所反映。在 1977 年"得克萨科海外石油公司诉利比亚"案的仲裁裁决中,杜普伊教授指出,适当补偿原则是反映"在这个领域内既存的习惯法状态"的"共同法律信念"(*opinio juris communis*)。1981 年美国上诉法院在"班康·纳希奥纳勒"案的判决中也指出,"要求征用国给予'适当补偿'—尽管该用语还缺乏确切定义—将最接近于反映国际法的要求"。[2]

在实践中,适当补偿标准长期以来被各国广泛采用。例如,在 1947—1951 年间,一些国家在就英国索赔而达成的协议中,均规定给予部分补偿:如 1947 年,墨西哥补偿索赔额的 30%;1948 年,波兰、捷克斯洛伐克分别补偿 33%;阿根廷补偿 60%;1949 年,南斯拉夫补偿 50%;1951 年,法国补偿 70%。1954 年,伊朗政府对被其收归国有的英伊石油公司原业主的补偿,只相当于后者索赔额的 10%。印度在 20 世纪 50 年代与外国石油公司签订的在印度建立炼油厂的三个投资协议中,承诺在 25 年内不征收该投资企业,其后的征收将给予"合理补偿"(reasonable compensation)。[3] 20 世纪 60 年代以后,亚非拉国家在实行国有化时都是给予部分补偿,而且补偿的支付也不是"及时"的。[4]

20 世纪 80 年代以来,许多发展中国家外国投资法律政策的目标从限制外资转向鼓励和促进外资。尽管如此,在有关征收补偿标准的国内立法中,广大发展中国家总体上仍坚持适当补偿原则。据 1991 年的调查统计,关于征收的补偿标准和方式,在 51 个被调查的发展中国家中,24 国未作一般性规定,14 国规定了公平合理(fair and equitable)、合理适当(fair and adequate)、合理(fair)、公正(just)或公平(equitable)标准,5 国规定了市场价值(market value)标准,3 国规定了实际价值(actual value)标准,另有 5 国只规定事先补偿的方式,未规定补偿的标准。[5] 上述规定虽然用语和标准不尽相同,但均可视为从本国国情出发,根据"适当补偿"标准而作的。

(二)征收补偿标准之争的新发展

20 世纪七八十年代,适当补偿原则在理论上占主流地位,在实践上亦有不同程度的反映。90 年代以来,随着国际政治、经济形势的发展,一些发展中国家为解决债

---

[1] 余劲松:《论国际投资法中国有化补偿的根据》,载《中国社会科学》1986 年第 2 期,第 66—68 页。

[2] 〔美〕奥斯卡·沙赫特:《征用外国人财产的补偿问题》,载《外国法学译丛》1986 年第 1 期,第 4—5 页。

[3] Wolfgang Friedmann, *The Changing Structure of International Law*, Columbia University Press, 1964, pp. 359-360.

[4] 余劲松:《论国际投资法中国有化补偿的根据》,载《中国社会科学》1986 年第 2 期,第 61 页。

[5] Antonio R. Parra, Principles Governing Foreign Investment, as Reflected in National Investment Codes, *ICSID Review—Foreign Investment Law Journal*, Vol. 7, 1992, pp. 442-444.

务危机或出于吸收外资的实际需要,在 BITs 中,对发达国家作出了不同程度的让步或妥协。在此情势下,"赫尔"规则似乎回潮,俨然成为"时尚"。

1. 体现"赫尔"规则的条约实践

在征收补偿标准方面,出现了一些体现"赫尔"规则的国际条约实践。如1994年《能源宪章条约》第13条规定,除非"伴随支付及时、充分和有效的补偿",缔约国不得对有关投资实行征收或国有化;这种补偿,应相当于估价之日被征收财产的公平市场价值。[1]

如前所述,《加拿大2004年范本》第13条第1款提出"及时、充分和有效"赔偿。第2—4款进一步规定:

> "该赔偿应相当于该被征收投资在征收发生前一刻(征收日)的公平市场价值,并且不得反映因较早时征收意图已为公众所知而产生的任何价值上的改变。估价标准包括兴旺企业价值,财产价值包括有形财产宣称的税收价值,和其他适当的标准以决定公平市场价值。
>
> 赔偿应不迟延地、完全实现和自由转移地作出支付。赔偿应以自由可兑换货币支付,且应包括自征收之日直至支付之日基于正常商业利率的利息。
>
> 受影响的投资者应有权根据实施征收的缔约一方法律,通过该缔约方的司法或其他独立机构,根据本条规定的原则提出其案件及其投资价值评估的重审意见。"

上述条款的要点及其意义可解读如下:

第一,以"及时、充分和有效"作为国有化或征收赔偿的规则。

第二,对"及时、充分和有效"的含义作了明确的规定,即在满足"充分"的条件方面,规定了计算公平市场价值的时间点和估价标准;在满足"及时"的条件方面,规定了"不迟延"的规则,并以赔偿"应包括自征收之日直至支付之日基于正常商业利率的利息"加以约束;在满足"有效"的条件方面,规定了赔偿"完全实现和自由转移地""以自由可兑换货币支付"的规则。

第三,为国际投资者提供了在东道国寻求救济的法律依据,即投资者有权根据东道国法律,通过该国司法或其他独立机构,根据"赫尔"规则提出对征收案件及其投资价值评估的重审意见。其重要意义是为"赫尔"规则在国内层面的适用提供了国际法依据。

---

〔1〕 *ICSID Review—Foreign Investment Law Journal*, Vol. 10, 1995, p. 273.

2. "赫尔"规则的仲裁实践

20 世纪 90 年代以来,从 ICSID 仲裁实践看,几乎所有案件的仲裁庭都主张对被征收的投资进行全部补偿(full compensation)。在"LETCO 诉利比里亚"案中,部分采取现金流量折现法(discounted cash flow,DCF),对申请人丧失的投资和预期利润(foregone future profits)裁付补偿。在"阿姆科诉印尼"案首次仲裁中,仲裁庭认为,印尼应对其违约行为导致的损失进行充分补偿,即补偿申请人的实际损失和所损失的利润。由于剥夺申请人对饭店的管理权实际上导致申请人丧失了一个"兴旺企业",因此仲裁庭采取 DCF 方法来计算补偿额。在该案重新仲裁中,仲裁庭将应予补偿的期限划分为二,分别计算补偿额:第一阶段是自 1980 年接管行为发生至 1989 年重新仲裁,由于有基本的计算参数,如通货膨胀、汇率、税率等可供适用,仲裁庭未按"理智商人所能预期"(the perspective of what the reasonable businessman could foresee)之原理,而是运用上述参数对基期价值进行调整;第二阶段是自 1990 年 1 月 1 日至 1999 年合同约定的终止之日,由于无上述计算参数,仲裁庭采取 DCF 方法来估计该期间的损失并计算补偿额。[1]

3. "赫尔"规则与适当补偿原则的"调和"

如前所述,"赫尔"规则与适当补偿原则分别具有其鲜明的"烙印"(hall-mark)。由于两个规则/原则的表述均不具体,这两种表述已成为区分发达国家与发展中国家不同立场的象征。[2] 从《经济宪章》的立法史看,起草者力图避免使用"根据国际法……适当补偿"的用语,因为该"国际法"的表述自然会被发达国家具体解读为"赫尔"规则。[3] 新加坡学者索那纳吉认为,"赫尔"规则是资本输出国主张的规则,而适当补偿原则是资本输入国主张的原则。[4] 可见,"赫尔"规则与适当补偿原则是迥然不同的、代表不同类型国家利益和立场的规则/原则。然而,近 20 多年来,出现了"调和"两个规则/原则的实践。

1981 年 6 月批准的伊斯兰会议组织《促进、保护和保证伊斯兰会议组织成员国之间投资协定》(简称《伊斯兰会议组织投资协定》)第 10 条第 2 款规定,允许"为公共

---

〔1〕 陈安主编:《国际投资争端仲裁——"解决投资争端国际中心"机制研究》,复旦大学出版社 2001 年版,第 353—354 页。

〔2〕 See Paul Peters, Recent Developments in Expropriation Clauses of Asian Investment Treaties, *Asian Yearbook of International Law*, Vol. 5, 1995, pp. 71-72.

〔3〕 Burns H. Weston, The Charter of Economic Rights and Duties of States and the Deprivation of Foreign-Owned Wealth, in Charlotte Ku & Paul F. Diehl (ed.), *International Law*, *Classic and Cotemporary Readings*, Lynne Rienner Publishers, 1998, p. 527.

〔4〕 关于"赫尔"规则和适当补偿原则的依据和理由,参见 M. Sornarajah, *The International Law on Foreign Investment*, Cambridge University Press, 1996, pp. 357-411.

利益、依据法律、非歧视并依东道国调整征收的法律向投资者及时支付充分和有效的赔偿而实行征收，以该投资者有权在东道国适格法院质疑该征收措施为条件。"值得注意的是，该条款看来是试图调和适当补偿原则和"赫尔"规则，"依东道国调整征收的法律"是适当补偿原则的体现，而"及时支付充分和有效的赔偿"则符合"赫尔"规则的全部要求。[1]

无独有偶。1992年9月25日，世界银行集团发展委员会公布了《外国直接投资待遇指南》（简称《外资指南》）。该指南第4部分第2条规定："对被该国取得的特定投资之补偿，根据以下具体规定，将被视为'适当'（appropriate），如果它是充分、有效和及时的。"该条规定的一大"贡献"首先是"不经意"地混淆了适当补偿原则和"赫尔"规则的界限，即适当补偿原则等于"赫尔"规则，似乎南北国家从来不存在这方面的分歧。

该指南第4部分第3条还规定了"适当"补偿的标准，即："补偿将被视为'适当'，如果它基于该被取得投资在该取得发生前一刻或取得该财产的决定为公众所知前一刻确定的公平市场价值。"第4部分第6条进一步规定了"适当"补偿的不同评估方法：对有关于盈利能力的可靠记录的兴旺企业，采用DEF方法确定其价值；对于明显缺乏盈利能力，不能证明为可持续经营的企业，则以清算价值为基础进行评估；对于其他财产，则采用重置价值法或账面价值法。[2]

应当指出，《伊斯兰会议组织投资协定》与《外资指南》两者具有明显的不同：（1）就适用范围而言，前者限于伊斯兰会议组织成员国之间，而后者力图成为世界各国的共同指南；（2）就法律依据而言，前者强调以内国法为依据，后者则强调以"赫尔"规则为依据。

《外资指南》有关征收补偿的规定反映了发达国家在此问题上采取的"割断历史，混淆文义"的新策略。应强调的是，适当补偿原则与"赫尔"规则之间存在根本的区别。从原则/规则的产生和形成看，适当补偿原则是由联大决议通过、国际社会普遍接受的征收补偿标准，而"赫尔"规则是以美国为代表的发达国家主张的征收补偿标准；从原则/规则的实现目标看，根据适当补偿原则的标准一般是征收国财力所能承担的部分或相应补偿，而"赫尔"规则是严格主张在所有情况下都给予"充分、及时、有效"的补偿；从原则/规则实施的法律后果看，根据适当补偿原则的标准旨在维护国家的征收权，而"赫尔"规则可能损害甚至否定国家的征收权。因此，适当补偿原则绝不能混同于"赫尔"规则。

---

〔1〕 Javaid Rehman, Islamic Perspectives on International Economic Law, in Asif H. Qureshi(ed.), *Perspectives in International Economic Law*, Kluwer Law International, 2002, pp. 251-253.

〔2〕 参见陈安主编：《国际投资争端仲裁——"解决投资争端国际中心"机制研究》，复旦大学出版社2001年版，第357页。

四、中国关于征收及其补偿标准的立场与实践

（一）中国关于征收权的立场与实践

中国是社会主义国家，属于第三世界，在关于国有化或征收权利问题上的基本立场是鲜明的，即始终与广大发展中国家站在一起。

早在 1956 年 8 月 15 日，中国政府在关于苏伊士运河问题的声明中就明确指出："埃及把苏伊士运河公司收归国有，这是埃及为了维护自己的主权和独立而采取的正义行动，不论从法律上或道义上来说，埃及的这一行动是完全正确的。"

1974 年，在联合国第六次特别会议上，邓小平同志代表中国政府庄严指出："我们支持发展中国家对自己自然资源享有和行使永久主权。我们支持发展中国家对一切外国资本特别是'跨国公司'进行控制和管理，直至把它们收归国有。"[1]在联合国贸发会议上，中国代表团也一贯支持发展中国家要求对外国投资进行控制直至国有化的主张。

中国同广大发展中国家既有共同的遭遇和命运，又有自己的国情和特点。在不同的历史时期中，取决于不同的政治经济情况，中国对外国投资的立场和态度亦有显著区别。

建国初期，中国的当务之急是"肃清帝国主义国家在中国的一切特权。"而对帝国主义在华资产实行国有化，则是肃清帝国主义特权的一个重要组成部分。因此，中国政府根据各外国企业和各种外国资产的性质和内容，并根据当时的具体条件，分别发布不同的法令，采取一系列不同的措施和方法，对外资实行国有化，[2]保障了新中国政治的独立和经济的自主发展。

事实表明，1979 年以来，中国坚定不移地实行对外开放政策，利用外资成为加速中国社会主义现代化建设的有效方法之一。为此，中国的政策、法律允许外商投资企业与公有制经济长期并存，对外国投资国有化或征收问题，持十分慎重的态度。

在中国同外国签订的 BITs 中，对征收条件分别作了规定，概括起来，有如下四种表述：

（1）为了安全和公共利益，依照法律程序，所采取的措施是非歧视性的，并给予补偿；

（2）为了法律允许的目的，在非歧视的基础上，根据其法律，并给予补偿；

---

[1]《我国代表团出席联合国有关会议文件集》(1973 年 7 月—1974 年 7 月)，第 11 页。

[2]　西方学者认为中国在历史上曾采取的国有化形式包括公然的(outright)国有化、拒付前中国政府的债务和冻结财产，将来可能因外资政策或对外开放政策的改变、政府更迭等而发生国有化事件。See Jay S. Laifman, Treaties and Nationalization: The People's Republic of China Experience, *Hastings International and Comparative Law Review*, Vol. 11, 1988, pp. 328-332.

（3）为了国家利益的公共目的，给予公平合理的补偿，并在非歧视性的基础上和根据普遍适用的国内法律；

（4）为了公共利益并给予补偿。

应当指出，在国际法上，对外资的征收权是各国经济主权的体现。在 BITs 实践中承诺对征收权施以一定的约束条件（包括征收补偿），是主权国家行使经济主权的自我限制，而不是遵循习惯国际法，更不能理解为满足"合法征收"的前提条件。从中国的 BITs 实践中，约束条件从两项到四项不等，反映了缔约双方的共同意愿，也从一个侧面反映了在这方面并不存在习惯国际法。根据国家主权原则，无论是发达国家还是发展中国家，无论是居于资本输出国还是资本输入国地位，不能以任何方式干涉或否定一国的征收权及其行使。

1986 年 4 月颁行的《中华人民共和国外资企业法》（简称《外资企业法》）第 5 条规定："国家对外资企业不实行国有化或征收；在特殊情况下，根据社会公共利益的需要，对外资企业可以依照法律程序实行征收，并给予相应的补偿。"在 1990 年修正的《中华人民共和国中外合资经营企业法》（简称《中外合资经营企业法》）第 2 条第 3 款又重申了这一立场。这表明，在一般情况下，我国对外国投资不实行国有化或征收，但并未放弃特殊情况下可依法行使的征收权。这里所谓"特殊情况"，主要指发生战争、战争危险或其他紧急状态以及严重自然灾害等不可抗力事故。[1]

《中华人民共和国宪法》（2004 年修正）第 13 条第 3 款规定："国家为了公共利益的需要，可以依照法律规定对公民的私有财产实行征收或者征用并给予补偿。"上述规定虽然仅适用于中国公民，不直接适用于外国人及外国投资，但其原则精神也为处理外资征收及其补偿问题提供了指南。由于对外资实行国民待遇原则是各国的普遍实践，对外资征收及其补偿参照适用上述规定，也是无可厚非的。

上述法律规定与中国参与签订的 BITs 的有关规定大体一致。其重要意义在于，以国内法的形式明确表明了中国对此问题的基本立场，对其所属国同中国签订了 BITs 的外国投资者而言，中国国内法与 BITs 相辅相成，形成了国内法和国际法的双重保护；对其他外国投资者而言，则明确了其投资所能取得的中国国内法保护，增强了其在中国投资的安全感。

中国在新的历史时期中不会、也不必对外国投资实行大规模国有化的主要原因是：首先，在政治上，中国已彻底肃清了帝国主义在中国的一切特权，人民民主专政的政治局面空前巩固，作为一个独立的主权国家，中国在国际社会中已享有应有的

---

〔1〕 正如 1982 年《中华人民共和国对外合作开采海洋石油资源条例》第 26 条所规定的："在战争、战争危险或其他紧急状态下，中国政府有权征购、征用外国合同者所得的和所购买的石油的一部或全部。"

地位,有权利、有能力与其他国家在平等互利基础上进行经济交往。这样就排除了建国初期那种需要对外国投资实行大规模国有化的政治原因。其次,在经济上,中国已确立了社会主义公有制在整个国民经济中的主导地位,独立的、较为完整的社会主义工农业体系业已形成。因此,有选择地吸收外资形成的外商投资经济与个体经济、私营经济等非公有制经济一样,是社会主义市场经济的重要组成部分。只要坚持平等互利原则,依法管制外国投资活动,就不可能发生整个国民经济依附于或受控于外国资本的局面。因此,不存在对外国投资实行大规模国有化或征收的经济原因;再次,发展对外经济交流,吸收外资,不是中国的权宜之计,而是中国为加快社会主义现代化建设而制定的基本国策和长期方针。中国对外国投资实行大规模国有化的可能性微乎其微。然而,如前所述,由于西方国家的"间接征收"概念不断扩大,中国则存在"间接征收"的现实可能性。[1]

（二）中国关于征收补偿标准的立场与实践

在中国同外国签订的 BITs 中,都有关于国有化或征收的补偿标准的规定。关于补偿数额的规定不一,包括:"补偿款额应相当于采取征收、国有化或其他类似措施前一刻投资的价值";"补偿应按措施为公众所知前一刻的投资的市场价值为基础计算";"补偿应相当于被征收投资的适当价值";"补偿应等于投资在征收已为公众所知前一刻的真正价值";"补偿应该使国民和公司处于未被采取征收和国有化或其他类似效果的措施时相同的财政状况"。关于补偿的支付时间和方式,一般都规定不应无故迟延或不适当迟延;并应是可兑换的和可自由转移的。

在中国《外资企业法》第 5 条和《中外合资经营企业法》第 2 条第 3 款规定中,出现了"相应的补偿"这一新的概念。

由此产生的问题是,中国是否事实上已经接受了"赫尔"规则? 或者,中国另立了新的补偿标准?

答案是否定的。应当指出,上述中外投资保护协定和中国外资法中关于国有化或征收补偿的规定,与"赫尔"规则有本质上的区别。首先,中国坚持主张征收有否补偿不能作为征收是否"合法"的尺度,而"赫尔"规则的实质是将国家的征收行为等同于国家不法侵害行为,据此强加给弱小民族和发展中国家无法承受的最高补偿标准,意在否定弱小民族和发展中国家的国有化或征收权力。其次,中国在 BITs 接受

---

〔1〕　例如,在 MIGA 作为斡旋人的"美国海岸公司与江苏省电力管理部门纠纷案"中,根据 MIGA 的观点,江苏省电力管理部门违反与美国海岸公司签订的合同,应被视为一种征收行为。关于该案案情简介,参见〔美〕劳伦·S.威森费尔德:《多边投资担保机构的十五年发展历程》,徐崇利译,载陈安主编:《国际经济法学刊》第 9 卷,北京大学出版社 2004 年版,第 231—237 页。

的补偿标准，即投资的"市场价值""适当价值"或"真正价值"并非当然等同于"充分"的标准。关键的区别是，前者并未明确承诺补偿"预期利润"，也未明确接受评估补偿额的 CEF 方法。再次，"不应无故迟延或不适当迟延"与"应毫不迟延地支付"的用语虽然语义相近，但却有可为和不可为之别，即前者"不应无故"意味着在有原因的情况下，可以迟延，而后者则应无条件地及时支付。

五、结语

自 1978 年实行改革开放政策以来，我国吸收外资取得了举世瞩目的成就，在很大程度上归功于由政治、经济、法律和社会诸多因素构成的良好投资环境。在创设良好投资环境中，我国外商投资法律制度的建立和健全以及国际投资条约实践均发挥了重要的作用。然而，应当指出，我国 BITs 实践对于我国吸收外资的成功并不是决定性的作用，其中征收条款，特别是征收补偿标准的作用更不宜夸大。[1] 20 多年来，在我国参与的 BITs 谈判中，征收条款一向是分歧的焦点之一，适当补偿原则与"赫尔"规则之争从未止息。实际上，在我国的 BITs 实践中，已包含许多对发达国家的妥协，反映了我国对外资实行充分法律保护的立场。在此情况下，某些发达国家"得寸进尺"，要求我国在 BITs 明确接受"赫尔"规则。笔者以为，这已涉及原则的底线问题，我国不能且不必一再妥协。[2] 笔者以为，在决定我国的有关立场时，只有深入了解和记取历史上南北国家在这一问题上的分野，才能深刻认识现实的严峻挑战，坚持我国作为发展中国家应当坚持的基本原则和基本立场。当前，对外资征收及其补偿标准问题，应特别强调以下基本认识：

第一，征收权是国家经济主权的正当行使。根据久已确立的国家主权原则，一国对其境内外资实行征收是其主权在经济领域的正当行使，属于其属地管辖权范围内的事项，不受外国干预。一国对外资的征收权本身不应附加任何条件，除非受其参与缔结的国际条约或其制定的内国法的约束。因此，应强调的是，一国对外资的征收无所谓"合法""非法"之分。当然，各国为创设良好的投资环境，一般不会滥用对外资的征收权，相反，往往通过其参与缔结的国际条约或其制定的内国法对征收

---

〔1〕 事实上，许多外国投资者认为，中国的政治风险水平低于其预期。2000 年以来，MIGA 对华担保项目需求的迅速回落在一定程度上说明了这个问题。参见〔美〕劳伦·S. 威森费尔德：《多边投资担保机构的十五年发展历程》，徐崇利译，载陈安主编：《国际经济法学刊》第 9 卷，北京大学出版社 2004 年版，第 217—218 页。

〔2〕 即使是最近重新谈判的 BITs，由于我国的坚持，缔约对方也未能突破我国坚守的原则底线。例如，《中华人民共和国和德意志联邦共和国关于促进和相互保护投资的协定》第 4 条第 2 款规定："缔约一方投资者在缔约另一方境内的投资不得被直接或间接地征收、国有化或者对其采取具有征收、国有化效果的其他任何措施（以下称'征收'），除非为了公共利益的需要并给予补偿。这种补偿应等于采取征收或征收为公众所知的前一刻被征收投资的价值，以在先者为准。"《中华人民共和国政府和荷兰王国政府关于鼓励和相互保护投资协定》第 5 条也有类似规定。

权作适当限制。而这种限制是各国对其主权权力的自我约束。

第二，"赫尔"规则的要害是否定发展中国家的征收权。根据现代国际法，除自愿承担予以补偿的条约义务之外，征收国并未承担支付征收补偿的国际法律责任，[1]更未承担支付"充分、及时、有效"赔偿的国际法律责任。从"赫尔"规则产生的历史看，该规则显然是作为对抗发展中国家征收权的产物。如前所述，西方国家将"赫尔"规则作为所谓征收赔偿的"传统标准"或"国际法标准"，甚至偷梁换柱，将"赫尔"规则与适当补偿原则混为一谈，其目的在于，将"赫尔"规则作为征收合法性的前提条件，以否定发展中国家，特别是最不发达国家的征收权。由于"赫尔"规则的"漫天要价"，在实践中将严重削弱甚至否定发展中国家，特别是最不发达国家的经济主权。中国亦不例外。值得警惕的是，如果多数发展中国家在 BITs 中接受"赫尔"规则，长此以往，"赫尔"规则可能逐渐形成国际实践，甚至构成习惯国际法。届时，《经济宪章》所确立的征收权和适当补偿原则就可能被严重削弱甚至被具体否定。

第三，发展中国家必须坚持适当补偿原则。首先，应当以历史的眼光，从建立新国际经济秩序(NIEO)的高度，从宏观上、理论上和原则上充分认识这一问题的实质和重要性，洞察西方国家以"赫尔"规则取代适当补偿原则的"良苦用心"。在两军对垒中，一方的任何松懈和动摇，将导致严重的甚至是全面崩溃的后果。

进而言之，应当深刻认识我国坚持适当补偿原则的必要性。一种观点认为，现在发展中国家普遍接受"赫尔"规则，我国不必孤立地"硬扛"不合时宜的原则。诚然，一些发展中国家由于经济实力的制约等原因，在国际实践中不同程度地未能坚持适当补偿原则，甚至接受"赫尔"规则，这不应成为我国也放弃适当补偿原则的适当理由。须知在当前的国际现实中，作为个体，能与发达国家有一定抗衡力量的，只有少数发展中大国。因此，应明确我国作为发展中大国在维护发展中国家整体利益、建立 NIEO 方面所承担的义不容辞的历史责任和国际责任。我国如果以其他发展中国家已接受"赫尔"规则为"先例"而心安理得地援引或遵循，甚至以"赫尔"规则为"时代潮流"而随波逐流，与"负责任的发展中大国"的身份是不相符的。另一种观点认为，我国在国际投资活动中的地位目前已发生了重要的改变，即从净资本输入国向资本输入国和资本输出国双重身份发展，因此，应从资本输出国的角度更多考虑海外投资的保护问题。笔者以为，由于适当补偿原则是联大决议确立的国际社会普遍接受的原则，我国在国际投资中地位的改变与我国是否坚持适当补偿原则的问

---

〔1〕　参见余劲松:《论国际投资法中国有化补偿的根据》,载《中国社会科学》1986 年第 2 期,第 63 页。

题无关。随着对外投资的迅速发展，即使将来我国在国际投资中的地位由资本净输入国发展为资本净输出国，也不能动摇坚持适当补偿原则的立场。

The Expropriations of Foreign Investment and the Standards of Compensation: Historical Division and Practical Challenge

Abstract: From the historical and practical aspects, this article discusses the concept of nationalization or expropriation, the legitimacy of expropriation, the controversies on the standards of compensation and their new developments, as well as China's position and practice on expropriation and the standards of compensation. The author emphasis that the expropriation is the proper exercise of States' economic sovereignty; the crucial point of the Hull formula is to deny the right to expropriation of developing countries; developing countries, especially China should defend the right to expropriation and insist on the principle of appropriate compensation.

第二节　论"特殊与差别待遇"条款的发展及其法理基础[*]

【摘要】　根据 GATT 体制的"特殊与差别待遇"条款（S&D 条款），"承担义务的非互惠模式"逐步发展和确立。而在 WTO 体制中，此种模式被限制、淡化或转化，悄然改变为"履行义务的非互惠模式"。这是值得重视的趋向。由于发达成员与发展中成员经济实力迥异，且这一经济现实在今后相当长的历史时期将继续存在，WTO 体制的 S&D 条款并非权宜之计，也不宜仅表述为 WTO 体制非歧视待遇原则的例外。发展中国家应坚持主张和强调，S&D 条款的法理基础是公平互利原则。

【关键词】　S&D 条款；非互惠；公平互利；新国际经济秩序

2001 年 11 月世界贸易组织（WTO）第四届部长级会议授权贸易与发展委员会对"特殊与差别待遇"条款（"special and differential treatment" provisions，S&D 条款）及其履行情况进行评估，反映了国际社会对此问题的关注。本文认为，首先需要研究的基本问题是，在宏观上如何评价 S&D 条款的发展？S&D 条款的法理基础是什么？这两个问题事关 WTO 体制基础和发展方向，对广大发展中成员尤为重要。

一、S&D 条款的产生和发展述评

（一）GATT 体制 S&D 条款的产生

在国际经济交往中，互惠（reciprocity）可被表述为回报（recompense）、报答（requital）、诚实信用（good faith）等用语。在国际法上，互惠被定义为一国给予对方国及其国民相当于对方国给予该国及其国民相应的待遇。第二次世界大战以后建立的"布雷顿森林体制"以"互惠""非歧视"的自由贸易原则为指导思想。[1] 1947 年《关税及贸易总协定》（GATT）对"互惠"作了较充分的表述，即"互惠互利安排"（reciprocal and mutually advantageous arrangements）。直至 20 世纪 60 年代初，绝大多数的多边或双边经济条约遵循同样的原则和模式。

---

[*]　原载《厦门大学学报》（哲学社会科学版）2003 年第 6 期。

〔1〕　1944 年 7 月 1 日至 22 日，在美国新罕布什尔州召开的有 45 国代表参加的联合国国际货币金融会议（称为"布雷顿森林会议"）上，签订了《国际货币基金协定》和《国际复兴开发银行协定》。1945 年 12 月 27 日，布雷顿森林组织（Bretton Woods organizations）成立，包括国际货币基金组织（IMF）和国际复兴开发银行（IBRD），标志布雷顿森林体制的建立。

20世纪50、60年代，在联合国大会通过的一系列有关建立新国际经济秩序的决议推动下，发展中国家与发达国家之间经济发展水平悬殊产生的矛盾和问题（"南北问题"）逐渐受到国际社会的广泛关注。1964年，联合国贸易和发展会议从国际经济现实出发，对GATT的"互惠原则"以及旧国际经济秩序提出了尖锐的问题：国际贸易法律应具有什么性质？它是否根据世界由基本相似、实力平等和经济发展水平相当的各国组成这一假定，因此，基于互惠和非歧视原则？或者，它应是承认各国经济发展水平和经济社会制度各不相同的法律？

历史和现实表明，对经济发展水平和经济实力悬殊的南北国家适用"互惠"与"非歧视"原则不可避免地产生了对发展中国家的实质性歧视。南北国家之间基于正式的"互惠"关系在殖民主义时代表现为不平等条约，在当代则表现为双边或多边贸易体制下的"平等"的经济交往。不争的事实是，在南北国家之间按照同一"游戏规则"进行"互惠""非歧视"的自由竞争，正如运动场上不分性别、不分级别的竞技，实质上是不公平的。在此种自由竞争中，发达国家可轻易地凭借其经济实力，"合法"地对发展中国家进行经济剥削和掠夺。其结果，两类国家之间的经济差距势必加速扩大，导致富者愈富，贫者愈贫。

显然，发展中国家应当寻求"游戏规则"的变革，即以南北国家之间"不平等"和"非互惠"的正式法律安排纠正南北国家在双边或多边贸易体制中的不公平地位。

经过发展中国家的长期斗争，在GATT体制中，S&D条款逐渐发展和确立起来，主要包括：(1) GATT第18条。该条虽未采用发展中国家的概念，但允许"经济只能维持低生活水平并处于发展初期阶段的缔约方"在使用贸易措施保护幼稚产业和使用数量限制以减轻国际收支困难等方面有一定的灵活性；(2) 1966年7月27日生效的GATT第4部分"贸易和发展"（第36—38条）。该部分明确采用了"欠发达缔约方"（less-developed contracting parties）的概念，涉及GATT有关发展中国家的原则和目标，鼓励发达国家改善其市场准入条件，并表明发展中国家不必对发达国家降低贸易壁垒的承诺作出互惠承诺；(3)"授权条款"（enabling clause），即1979年11月28日《关于发展中国家差别和更优惠待遇、互惠和更充分参与的决定》。允许发达国家给予发展中国家优惠待遇及发展中国家之间相互给予优惠待遇。

S&D条款最早是基于"经济特惠"的概念。经济特惠是基于不同理由的一种特权，其实施可能排除最惠国待遇条款的适用。鉴于在国际关系中尚无习惯法或选择性程序可循，一国给予另一国的经济特惠反映了前者对后者的具体经济政策。在GATT体制中，发展中国家认为，非歧视原则虽然能在消除贸易壁垒方面发挥作用，但它不能为发展中国家提供在国际市场上竞争的平等机会。[1] 因此,发达国家应对发展中国家提供经济特惠待遇。与传统的基于地理、政治等因素的经济特惠待遇不同,对发展中国家提供的经济特惠待遇是以国家的发展程度为根据。这是传统国际法规则的一大突破。根据 S&D 条款,发展中国家在法律上第一次居于特殊的地位,即发达国家应给予发展中国家优惠待遇,但不要求发展中国家提供反向优惠,创设了 GATT 缔约方"承担义务的非互惠模式"。

应当指出,作为纠正南北国家不平衡和不公正关系的工具,GATT 体制 S&D 条款为数甚少,履行艰难,对发展中国家经济发展的作用或影响很有限,但其创立的"承担义务的非互惠模式"毕竟代表了多边贸易体制改革和发展的方向。

（二）WTO 体制 S&D 条款的转变

据统计,WTO 协定中的 S&D 条款合计有 145 项,分别载于不同的多边货物贸易协定、《服务贸易总协定》《与贸易有关的知识产权协定》《争端解决的规则和程序谅解书》以及许多部长级会议决议。根据 WTO 秘书处的分类,S&D 条款有 6 种类型:(1)旨在增加发展中成员贸易机会的规定;(2)要求所有 WTO 成员保障发展中成员利益的规定;(3)承诺、行动的灵活性及政策工具(policy instruments)的应用;(4)过渡期;(5)技术援助;(6)有关最不发达成员的规定。[2] 该秘书处认为,由于发展中国家的普遍参与,乌拉圭回合对发展中国家的长期影响比以往任何多边贸易谈判的结果较大。乌拉圭回合的各项协定和决定包含了许多有利于发展中国家的特殊规定。[3] 这些规定作为一个整体,代表了乌拉圭回合参加方考虑到发展中国家特殊需要所作的努力,还有一些是从 GATT 1947 继承下来的条款。[4]

进一步研究表明,尽管数量上有大幅增加,WTO 体制 S&D 条款的实质已悄然发生了变化。首先表现在,在指导思想上,提出了"鼓励将所有发展中国家融入WTO 正常的法律框架"。[5] 换言之,S&D 条款已被打入"另册",不属"WTO 正常的法律框架"。众所周知,20 世纪 60 年代以来,南北国家经济发展水平的悬殊差距不但没有缩小,反而日益扩大,适用 S&D 条款的基础性前提条件并未发生改变。在

〔1〕　See Janusz Gilas, International Economic Equity, *Polish Yearbook of International Law*, Vol. 14, 1985, pp. 82-83.

〔2〕　WTO, Committee on Trade and Development. Implementation of Special and Differential Treatment Provisions in WTO Agreements and Decisions（WT/COMTD/W/77）, 25 October 2000.

〔3〕　乌拉圭回合协议中有关发展中国家条款的情况概述,参见世界贸易组织秘书处:《乌拉圭回合协议导读》,索必成、胡盈之译,法律出版社 2001 年版,第 309—310 页。

〔4〕　参见世界贸易组织秘书处:《乌拉圭回合协议导读》,索必成、胡盈之译,法律出版社 2001 年版,第 310—311 页。

〔5〕　参见世界贸易组织秘书处:《乌拉圭回合协议导读》,索必成、胡盈之译,法律出版社 2001 年版,第 311 页。

此情况下，主张对南北国家适用统一的"正常的法律框架"，实际上是试图改变或否定 GATT 体制确立的"承担义务的非互惠模式"。

其次，在适用范围上，更为强调区分最不发达（least-developed）成员与发展中成员，[1]尽可能缩小 S&D 条款的适用范围。在 145 项 S&D 条款中，有 22 项仅适用于最不发达成员。[2] 许多 S&D 条款不是自动给予的，必须由发展中成员（包括最不发达成员）提出申请。在某些情况下，还要求对 S&D 待遇的适用范围进行审议，以便"鼓励将所有发展中国家融入 WTO 正常的法律框架"。[3] 实践中，在加入 WTO 的双边谈判中，一些发展中国家被迫接受与其身份不相符合的条件。近年来，关于比较发达的发展中国家是否接受更为完整的 WTO 一般性非歧视原则（即所谓"毕业条款"问题），亦产生激烈的争论。[4]

再次，在给予优惠的内容和性质方面，从 GATT 体制"承担义务的非互惠模式"转变为"履行义务的非互惠模式"。后者如"过渡期"优惠，指在单一的法律制度中，允许发展中成员在承担与发达成员同等义务的情况下，有较长的过渡期履行其义务。显然，在"履行义务的非互惠模式"中，发展中成员并未获得任何实体性权利，较长的过渡期一旦届满，即融入统一的"正常的法律框架"。

复次，对发展中国家特殊困难的关注从经济和市场转移到政治和政府，涉及人权、反腐败等领域。

最后，由于大量避实就虚的"最佳努力条款"，[5]对于发达成员在多大程度上履行"最佳努力条款"，缺乏衡量的尺度和监督的机制。

总之，透过纷繁的表象，可以看出 WTO 体制已从各个方面、各种方式限制、淡化或转化 GATT 体制 S&D 条款的"承担义务的非互惠模式"。这是值得发展中国家关注的趋向。

---

〔1〕《马拉喀什建立世界贸易组织协定》序言强调的宗旨之一是："进一步认识到需要作出积极努力，以保证发展中国家，特别是其中的最不发达国家（the least developed among them），在国际贸易增长中获得与其经济发展需要相当的份额"。

〔2〕 在 WTO 体制中，除 25 个发达成员外，有 120 个发展中成员（包括"转型经济国家"）。最不发达国家由联合国确定并定期审议，目前有 49 个，其中有 30 个是 WTO 成员。它们是：安哥拉、孟加拉、贝宁、布吉纳法索、布隆迪、中非、乍得、刚果、吉布提、冈比亚、几内亚、几内亚比绍、海地、莱索托、马达加斯加、马拉维、马尔代夫、马里、毛里塔尼亚、莫桑比克、缅甸、尼日尔、卢旺达、塞内加尔、塞拉利昂、所罗门群岛、坦桑尼亚、多哥、乌干达和赞比亚。

〔3〕 参见世界贸易组织秘书处：《乌拉圭回合协议导读》，索必成、胡盈之译，法律出版社 2001 年版，第 310—311 页。

〔4〕 参见〔美〕约翰·H. 杰克逊：《世界贸易体制——国际经济关系的法律与政策》，张乃根译，复旦大学出版社 2001 年版，第 350—351 页。

〔5〕 指不具强制力的劝导性、鼓励性 S&D 条款，如"对总体利益的承认"等类别的条款。参见世界贸易组织秘书处：《乌拉圭回合协议导读》，索必成、胡盈之译，法律出版社 2001 年版，第 312—336 页。

（三）S&D 条款转变的主要原因

WTO 体制 S&D 条款之所以发生上述转变，原因是多方面的，择要分析如下：

1. 发达成员拥有 WTO 体制发展方向的主导权

由于 GATT/WTO 体制本质上是谈判机制，发达成员凭借其经济实力和制定、运用"游戏规则"的优势，拥有该体制发展方向的主导权。特别是美国因看重 WTO 强制性执行机制，越来越倚重 WTO，企图主导多边贸易体制，在经济、贸易、金融、科技等领域建立其全球霸主地位。[1] 而发展中成员在多边贸易体制中，不仅在经济实力和制定、运用"游戏规则"等方面处于劣势，而且缺乏专业人员，有时界定自身的利益比捍卫自身的利益更加艰难。[2]

在乌拉圭回合中，发达成员声称，发达成员和发展中成员完成了"总交易"（grand bargain），达成了两类成员利益的"妥协"和"平衡"，即发达成员开放对发展中成员有利的纺织品和农业等领域，同时，作为交易条件，发展中成员在知识产权和服务贸易等新领域作出了承诺。进一步研究表明，发达成员同意降低进口关税，提供传统的市场准入，可能存在某些调整成本，但实际付出甚少。而发展中成员提供新领域的市场准入，实际上远不只是市场准入问题，知识产权和服务贸易等领域的义务涉及国内经济体制的改革，代价甚高。显然，乌拉圭回合仍然是由发达成员主导的，发达成员和发展中成员在乌拉圭回合中的"总交易"并未实现真正的平衡，南北国家的"双赢"局面并未产生。[3]

2. 发展中国家对多边贸易体制的两难选择

乌拉圭回合前后，发展中国家面临更为严峻的形势。发展中国家与多边贸易体制的关系由敌视和冷漠逐渐转为关注和参与。乌拉圭回合的历史表明，大多数发展中国家是为避免处境更为不利而被动参与谈判的。[4] 如上所述，发达国家在多边贸易体制中居于主导地位，在"国家利益至上"的国际经济关系中，发展中国家在参与此种体制、接受种种规则约束的情况下，并不能奢望体制的主导者主动分配其多少权利和利益。然而，更大的问题是，在各国经济相互依存性不断加深，各主要贸易体

---

〔1〕　美国实现其全球经济霸主地位的手段主要是：(1) 在市场开放搞双重标准，一方面，要求别国开放市场，动辄运用 301 条款进行经济制裁，另一方面推行贸易保护主义；(2) 贸易问题政治化。竭力把劳工标准、环境标准和所谓"反腐败"等属于他国主权范围的事项纳入多边贸易体制；(3) 推行金融霸权主义。利用美元的霸权地位，通过影响和操纵汇率、利率等手段，捞取巨大的经济利益，并力图控制国际金融体系改革的主导权；(4) 左右国际经济游戏规则的制定。在国际贸易和金融组织中，按照美国的需要，推进符合其自身利益需要的贸易和投资自由化。参见张向晨：《发展中国家与 WTO 的政治经济关系（修订本）》，法律出版社 2002 年版，第 16、41—42 页。

〔2〕　参见张向晨：《发展中国家与 WTO 的政治经济关系（修订本）》，法律出版社 2002 年版，第 7 页。

〔3〕　印度 WTO 专家巴格拉达先生的比较研究表明，在乌拉圭回合中，发展中国家的承诺超出发达国家的承诺。参见张向晨：《发展中国家与 WTO 的政治经济关系（修订本）》，法律出版社 2002 年版，第 28—30 页。

〔4〕　参见张向晨：《发展中国家与 WTO 的政治经济关系（修订本）》，法律出版社 2002 年版，第 6 页。

普遍成为 WTO 成员的情况下，发展中国家如不参与多边贸易体制，无异于自己选择了"体制外"或"边缘化"的地位，在国际经济交往中势必陷入更为不利的处境。[1] 在此两难的政策选择中，发展中国家在申请加入 WTO 时的谈判能力、签订各多边贸易协定的谈判能力以及必要时退出 WTO 的最后手段，在很大程度上被削弱甚至剥夺了。相应地，在 S&D 条款的制订过程中，发展中国家的影响和作用也相当有限。

3. S&D 条款缺乏基本法律原则的支持

20 世纪 80 年代以来，由于种种原因，主张建立新国际经济秩序的声浪日渐减弱，S&D 条款的法理基础未能得到充分的申明和强调，因此，S&D 条款实践的发展一直未能得到道德规范和法律原则的强有力支持。西方学者一般将 S&D 条款视为 GATT/WTO 规则的例外之一，[2] 对其法理基础和合理性鲜有论及。[3] 在某些发达成员的眼中，S&D 条款成了发达成员对发展中成员的单方面"施舍"，是否"施舍"，如何"施舍"，自然悉听"施主"尊便。某些西方大国总是不失时机地按其最惬意的蓝图来制定国际经济规则，以实现本国利益的最大化。因此，限制、淡化甚至取消 S&D 条款的"承担义务的非互惠模式"，以"履行义务的非互惠模式"装潢门面，当然是其最佳选择。

二、公平互利原则是 S&D 条款的法理基础

在有关 WTO 基本原则的论述中已有涉及 S&D 条款的法理基础。WTO 出版物在论述"鼓励发展与经济改革"原则时涉及 S&D 条款。[4] 我国国际法学界有学者认为 S&D 条款是"优惠待遇原则"的具体体现，并主张该原则"是世界贸易组织法关于发达成员国与发展中成员国之间货物贸易和服务贸易关系的一项基本原则"。[5] 还有学者在"促进发展原则"中论及 S&D 条款。[6] 笔者以为，应当明确主张，S&D 条款的法理基础是国际经济法的公平互利原则。

---

〔1〕 参见张向晨：《发展中国家与 WTO 的政治经济关系（修订本）》，法律出版社 2002 年版，第 1 页。

〔2〕 美国 WTO 专家杰克逊教授将 GATT 第 18 条和第四部分（第 36—38 条）关于发展中国家的各种例外作为"GATT/WTO 中关于义务的法律例外"。〔美〕约翰·H. 杰克逊：《世界贸易体制——国际经济关系的法律与政策》，张乃根译，复旦大学出版社 2001 年版，第 60 页。

〔3〕 西方学者近年还在提问，给予发展中国家特殊待遇有无充足理由，具体而言，有何道德依据？有无实际帮助？参见〔美〕约翰·H. 杰克逊：《世界贸易体制——国际经济关系的法律与政策》，张乃根译，复旦大学出版社 2001 年版，第 350 页。

〔4〕 参见钟兴国、林忠、单文华：《世界贸易组织—国际贸易新体制》，北京大学出版社 1997 年版，第 6—7 页。

〔5〕 参见曾令良：《世界贸易组织法》，武汉大学出版社 1996 年版，第 41—42 页。

〔6〕 参见程宝库：《WTO 与中国的法治建设》天津大学出版社，2003 年版，第 56—58 页。

（一）公平互利原则的涵义

传统伦理学根据亚里士多德的名言"公平即平等"的哲学,承认公平与平等的同一性。[1]

在法律意义上,公平指法律的公正、正当、合理、恰当地适用。[2]

在国际法上,国际法院在 1969 年"北海大陆架"案的判决中指出:"公平作为一个法律概念乃是正义观念的直接反映",是一个"像法律一样能够直接加以适用的一般法律原则"。德·阿契加(De Arechaga)法官在 1982 年国际法院对"突尼斯—利比亚大陆架"案判决的意见中,也从另一个角度明确表达了相同的观点。他认为:"正义的概念不能与公平分开或与之相背离。"由此可见,在国际法上,公平与正义的概念密切相关,并已被承认为可适用的一般法律原则。将公平视为一般法律原则的重要后果是,根据《国际法院规约》第 38 条第 1 款第 3 项规定,公平原则作为"文明各国所公认的一般法律原则",是国际法的渊源之一。

在国际经济关系方面,公平首先意味着超出国际法范围的一系列原则,这些原则包含道德行为规范的意义。其次,公平是适用于国际经济法律制度的最重要的道德规范的总和,调整该制度以确保其内在的道德规范。第三,公平指在适当场合对适当的人适用正确的规则。在上述第一种意义上,公平不属国际经济法的概念。而在第二、三种意义上,公平属国际经济法的概念。从另一角度看,第一、二种意义产生了实质公平(material equity)的概念。在第三种意义中,公平相当于适当(fairness),换言之,公平为国际经济法的适用规定了公正(justification)的要求。

在国际法的发展中,越来越多地适用道德规范。这反映在《国际联盟公约》《联合国宪章》以及作为非殖民化进程成果的联合国大会关于建立新国际经济秩序的一系列规范文件。可以说,不同的历史时期有不同的国际经济公平概念。在自由资本主义时期(1648 年至 1870 年),资本主义国家之间的经济公平基于平等原则。在帝国主义时期(1870 年至 1945 年),歧视原则取代了平等原则,特别是在宗主国与其殖民地之间的关系上。二战后建立的"布雷顿森林体制"确立了"互惠"和"非歧视"原则,在形式上恢复了平等原则。20 世纪 60 年代以来,公平的概念也被引入关于建立新国际经济秩序的联大决议,赋予新的含义。在这些联大决议中,公平的概念几乎与法官的自由裁量权无关,而更多地与政治平等和经济平等相关,特别是与发展中

---

〔1〕　See Janusz Gilas, International Economic Equity, *Polish Yearbook of International Law*, Vol. 14, 1985, p. 79.

〔2〕　参见〔南斯拉夫〕米兰·布拉伊奇:《国际发展法原则》,中国对外翻译出版公司 1989 年版,第 250—252 页。

国家的发展权密切相关。[1]

公平概念与平等原则有密切的联系。虽然公平不等于平等，但平等本身含有公平的趋向，公平深深植根于平等之中。不确保平等原则的实现，就不可能有公平，与此同时，应对平等原则作非形式上的解释。因为在一个由不同经济发展水平的国家组成的国际社会中，公平意味着赋予穷国某些权利，要求富国承担某些义务，而遵守形式上的平等原则本身是不能保证公平的。[2]

20 世纪 60 年代以来的后殖民主义（post-colonialism）时代，自从普惠制被作为国际法原则后，平等原则重新被赋予实质平等（material equality）的意义。[3] 不言而喻，世界各国经济发展水平和经济社会制度各不相同，南北国家的经济发展水平更是相差悬殊。然而，各国无论大小、强弱、富贫，都具有生存权。这是建立新国际经济秩序的基础。在南北国家之间的关系上，公平概念的提出具有特殊的重要意义。当前，发展国际经济关系意味着需要考虑各国在国家财富和满足其生存基本需求的能力方面存在严重的不平等。

在联合国关于建立新国际经济秩序的一系列规范性文件中，确立和重申了公平互利原则。在 1974 年联合国大会通过的《建立新国际经济秩序宣言》中，将"国家待遇公平"作为新国际经济秩序的基础。[4] 在其列举的建立新国际经济秩序的 20 项原则中，有关公平互利的规定包括："国际社会的全体成员在公平待遇的基础上，开展最广泛的合作，这就有可能消除世界上广泛存在的各种差距，保证共同繁荣富强"；"在发展中国家出口的原料、初级产品、制成品和半制成品的价格同其进口的原料、初级产品、制成品、资本货物和设备的价格之间，建立某种公平合理的关系，从而不断改善其不利的贸易条件，并且进一步发展世界经济"；"在国际经济合作的所有可能的领域内，尽可能为发展中国家提供特惠和非互惠待遇"。（第 4 条第 2、10、14 款）

1974 年《各国经济权利和义务宪章》宣布其宗旨是，"促进建立以一切国家待遇公平、主权平等、共同受益和协力合作为基础的新国际经济秩序"，同时明确将"公平互利"作为国际经济关系的基本准则。该宪章在许多条款中提及"公平"或"公平互利"的概念，诸如"公平合理的价格"，"公平合理的国际经济关系"，所有国家"公平分

---

[1] 参见王湘英、胡应志：《国际法上的公平原则及其运用》，载《法学评论》1990 年第 4 期，第 39—42 页。

[2] 参见〔南斯拉夫〕米兰·布拉伊奇：《国际发展法原则》，中国对外翻译出版公司 1989 年版，第 250—252 页。

[3] See Janusz Gilas, International Economic Equity, *Polish Yearbook of International Law*, Vol. 14, 1985, pp. 65-66.

[4] 《建立新国际经济秩序宣言》序言指出，新国际经济秩序"应当建立在一切国家待遇公平、主权平等、互相依存、共同受益以及协力合作的基础之上"。

享"参与国际决策的各种效益,"以公平合理的方式解决一切国家的各种贸易问题",国际贸易"应当根据公平互利和相互给予最惠国待遇的原则"进行,所有国家都有义务"为发展中国家增进公平合理的贸易条件",各国管辖范围以外的海床、洋底、海洋底土资源开发的利益"应当由一切国家公平分享"。(第 6、8、10、14、26、28、29 条)

上述规定构成了公平互利原则的丰富内涵。概括而言,公平互利原则的基本含义是,所有国家在法律上一律平等,作为国际社会的平等成员有权充分有效地参与国际经济问题的决策过程并公平分享由此产生的利益。该原则的目标是在国际经济关系上实现实质上的主权平等。在当前的国际条件下,对于经济实力相当的发达国家之间或发展中国家之间的关系而言,公平互利原则体现于原有的平等互利关系的维持;而对于经济实力悬殊的南北国家的关系而言,公平互利原则体现于原有形式上平等关系的纠正和新的实质上平等关系的创设。为此,发达国家就应承担义务,通过采取各种措施,让发展中国家单方面享有非对等的、非互惠的特惠待遇,以实现实质上的平等,达到真正的公平。[1]

(二)多哈回合以来的公平诉求

多哈回合以来的公平诉求,首先是源于对 WTO 规则的重新审视。发达成员和发展中成员基于不同的立场,对 WTO 规则的关注点亦不相同。主要问题包括:

第一,WTO 规则本身是否对发展中成员构成了歧视?

表面上答案是否定的。不仅如此,WTO 规则还有给予发展中成员特殊照顾和优惠的 S&D 条款。事实上,考虑到适用的对象和实际后果,WTO 规则本身还是可能存在问题的。例如,WTO 规则对发展中成员经常使用的措施(如数量限制),予以严格限制;而对发达成员经常使用的措施(如补贴),则要求宽松。因此,表面上对所有 WTO 成员"一视同仁""宽严相济"的规则,由于事实上"宽""严"规则分别针对不同的潜在对象,构成了对发展中成员的事实上(*de facto*)歧视。

第二个问题是,WTO 规则在多大程度改变了国际经济秩序的不公平? WTO 规则是否能给发展中成员带来一些补偿性优势,以纠正国际经济秩序的不公平?

越来越多的发展中成员认识到,现有 WTO 规则及市场准入的协定,最有利于发达成员,使它们能充分利用其"比较利益"。在多哈回合中,发展中成员明确表明,乌拉圭回合的利益分配是不能接受的。发展中成员期望"发展"成为多哈回合谈判的核心。发展中成员认为它们不必再付出,或者应作出新的平衡,以弥补和纠正乌拉

---

[1] 参见陈安:《国际经济法总论》,法律出版社 1991 年版,第 179 页。

圭回合的不足和不平衡。不仅如此，鉴于乌拉圭回合谈判结果的不平衡，发展中成员也将履行视为纠正乌拉圭回合协定不平衡的方式。而发达成员则反对重新谈判已有协定，主张任何发达成员所作的让步应由发展中成员在谈判中的某些方面作出补偿。

在多哈回合中，发展中成员正在形成特定类型的公平诉求。它们主张，南北国家之间的不平等不是缩小而是增加；即使发展中成员得到某些利益，也不是必然意味着它们得到了公平的份额；由于大量潜在利益来自国际合作，公平的问题集中于这些利益如何分配。它们进一步认为，公平应成为 WTO 体制的核心。有关辩论主题涉及 WTO 决策程序的较封闭性质和边缘化，"与贸易有关的"领域超出 WTO 管辖范围以及决策机制由内国向国际水平的转移等问题。显然，这些问题涉及多边贸易体制的公平问题，表明了发展中成员对 WTO 结构性问题的关切。

（三）公平互利原则应是 S&D 条款的法理基础

多哈回合以来的公平诉求反映了发展中成员在宏观层面上对 WTO 体制的思考，也反映了在 WTO 体制中坚持和实施公平互利原则的重要性和紧迫性。在《多哈宣言》中，各成员方同意所有 S&D 条款应予重审，以利加强此类条款并增强其有效性和可操作性。《多哈宣言》特别授权贸易与发展委员会确认在 S&D 条款中哪些是强制性的，对那些目前尚不具有约束力的 S&D 条款，须考虑使其具有强制性的法律和实践意义。此外，贸易与发展委员会还考虑协助发展中成员，特别是最不发达成员最大限度利用 S&D 条款的方式。在对 WTO 体制 S&D 条款作技术层面努力的同时，应加强有关 S&D 条款法理基础的研究。

公平互利原则作为 S&D 条款法理基础的理由首先是，公平互利原则应成为 WTO 体制的基本原则。半个世纪前，在 GATT 缔约方中，只有 8 个发展中国家，约占当时 23 个缔约方的 1/3。目前，WTO 成员中 5/6 以上来自发展中国家。这一重要的变化不仅表明了 GATT/WTO 体制的变化，也反映了当前国际经济情况与 20 世纪 40 年代的巨大差异。WTO 只有迅速适应这种变化，才能在将来更好地运作。鉴此，WTO 应成为解决南北问题、平衡南北利益的重要场所和机制，而调整南北关系的公平互利原则理应成为 WTO 体制的基本原则。

其次，从公平互利原则发展史看，"为发展中国家提供特惠和非互惠待遇"，一向是公平互利原则的核心内容和重要体现之一。正是基于历史上的"经济特惠"概念和逐渐形成的公平互利原则，产生和发展了 S&D 条款的"承担义务的非互惠模式"。主张公平互利原则是 S&D 条款的法理基础，其实只是对历史和现实的尊重和确认。

最后,实践表明,由于发达成员与发展中成员经济实力的迥异,且这一经济现实在今后相当长的历史时期将继续存在,WTO 体制的 S&D 条款并非权宜之计,也不宜仅仅表述为 WTO 体制非歧视待遇原则的例外,更不能将其排斥于"WTO 正常的法律框架"之外,而应该有坚实的法理基础予以支持。主张 S&D 条款的法理基础是公平互利原则,有利于坚持"承担义务的非互惠模式",促进 S&D 条款的进一步发展,也有利于 WTO 体制在平衡南北国家利益基础上的健康发展。

三、结语

公平互利原则是国际经济法的基本原则,也应成为 WTO 体制的基本原则。多哈回合中提出的公平诉求,反映了国际社会有关 WTO 体制应以公平互利原则为基础的迫切要求。在 WTO 体制中,公平诉求的实现需要坚持和发展 S&D 条款,而 S&D 条款的发展,更需要以公平互利原则为法理基础,坚持和发展"承担义务的非互惠模式"。此外,强调和发展与公平互利原则和新国际经济秩序相关的新法律概念和理论,诸如"国际民主""合作发展""偿还历史债务"等,也有助于促进 S&D 条款的进一步发展。

从根本上说,S&D 条款的发展,取决于广大发展中国家建立新国际经济秩序的战略共识与共同行动。由于国情不同,中国与其他发展中国家可能在国际经济决策和多边贸易谈判中的某些具体利益不尽一致,但基本和长远的利益则是完全一致的。作为 WTO 新成员,中国将致力于加强南南合作和南北对话,在改革和完善 WTO 规则中发挥建设性作用,为建立新国际经济秩序作出应有的贡献。[1]

On the Development and Legal Ground of the "Special and Differential Treatment" Provisions

Abstract:"The model of non-reciprocity on undertaking obligations" had been developed gradually and established in accordance with the "special and differential treatment" provisions (the S&D provisions) in GATT. This model, however, has been limited, dimmed or even transformed under WTO and changed to "the model of

---

〔1〕 Zhang Xiangchen, China's Accession to the WTO and Developing Countries' Participation in Multilateral Trading System, United Nations Conference on Trade and Development, WTO Accessions and Development Policies, United Nations, 2001, pp. 67-68.

non-reciprocity on implementing obligations". This approach is noticeable. As there are big differences of economic powers between developed countries and developing countries, and as the situation will remain long, it is very important for developing countries to insist and emphasis that the legal ground for the S&D provisions is the principle of equal and mutual benefit rather than an expedient measure or an exception of the principle of non-discrimination under WTO.

Key words: S&D provisions; non-reciprocity; equal and mutual benefit; new international economic order

第三节　略论国际经济法的合作发展原则 *

【摘要】 国际经济法的合作发展原则是南北矛盾的产物,解决南北问题是该原则的最主要目标。其主要内容是,各国应进行合作,以促进建立公平互利的国际经济新秩序,促进世界各国,尤其是发展中国家的经济发展和社会进步。就"合作"与"发展"而言,发展是权利、目标,合作是责任、手段。该原则的法律效力依据是,反映国际社会的"法律确信",遵循国家主权平等原则和民主原则,并在实践中不断增强。

【关键词】 南北矛盾;发展权;国际合作;国际经济新秩序;法律效力

国际合作以谋发展,即合作发展原则,符合世界经济发展的总趋势和各国的国家利益,是国际经济法的一项富有时代特点的基本原则。在当前经济全球化的趋势下,发展中国家面临比以往任何时期更严峻的挑战。要实现建立国际经济新秩序的目标,必须进一步强调、坚持和实践合作发展原则。

一、南北问题与合作发展原则

南北问题是国际经济发展的重大问题。在一定意义上,合作发展原则是南北矛盾的产物,解决南北问题是合作发展原则的最主要目标。

早在 1958 年,潘迪特·尼赫鲁就曾指出:"今天世界的重大裂痕,主要不是在共产党国家和反共国家之间,而是在享有高度发达工业经济国家和正在为生存而挣扎的不发达国家之间。"1973 年 9 月,不结盟国家在阿尔及尔举行的第四次会议上,明显把注意力集中于南北问题。它们在估计社会主义与资本主义意识形态对抗的势力、影响及其历史现实性的同时,认为在这条东西之间意识形态裂痕之上,存在一个更为严酷、更为明显的现实情况,即富国与穷国之间,也即南北国家之间的"巨大矛盾"。事实上,当代世界按物质基础被一分为二,不公平的制度造成永久性的不平等划分,使地球的一半可以享受富裕生活,而另一半却连生活必需品也得不到。

事实表明,南北国家之间关系的相互依存性是不对称的。在世界经济体系中,绝大多数发展中国家依然是发达国家的原料产地、销售市场和投资场所,将此表述为"相互依存",虽有互利的一面,但却包含极不平等的性质。"在发展中国家与发达

---

　*　原载《对外经济贸易大学学报》2002 年第 1 期。

国家之间的关系上，是否可以真正地说两者是相互依赖的，是个值得怀疑的问题。至少在某些情况下，还不如说是发展中国家片面地依赖发达国家。"[1]

从根本上说，南北问题虽然更多地以经济形式为特征，但不能不看到，它仍然是国际经济旧秩序的延续和形变。由于发达国家和发展中国家在世界经济力量对比中差距悬殊，发达国家居于明显的优势地位，而发展中国家则处于明显的劣势地位，如固守国际经济旧秩序，任此趋势继续发展，势必富国越来越富，穷国越来越穷。从长远的观点看，不仅阻碍发展中国家的发展，对发达国家的发展也极为不利。因此，南北关系的状况对国际经济和政治形势的发展进程影响重大，未来国际经济和政治形势的根本好转，取决于从根本上改变建立在不公正、不平等的国际经济旧秩序基础上的南北关系。[2]

从国际经济法的角度，要解决南北问题，纠正南北经济差距悬殊和严重失衡，需要建立新的国际规范，借助新的法律概念和原则改革国际经济旧秩序，建立国际经济新秩序。在此时代背景下，经国际社会、特别是发展中国家的共同努力，产生了合作发展原则。

二、合作发展原则的含义

合作发展原则是发展权与国际合作义务相结合而形成的新法律原则。其基本点是，在明确发展中国家的发展权利的前提下，通过要求各国履行国际合作义务来促进所有国家，特别是发展中国家的经济和社会发展。

（一）发展权的概念

发展权是 20 世纪 60 年代以来，发展中国家在争取建立国际经济新秩序的斗争中提出的新的法律概念。

首先，发展权是一项人权。1970 年塞内加尔最高法院院长凯巴·巴耶在斯特拉斯堡人权国际研究所的演说中指出，发展权是一项人权。所有的基本权利和自由必须与生存权、不断提高生活水平的权利联系在一起，即与发展权相联系。发展权是一项人权，因为人类没有发展就不能生存。1977 年，联合国人权与和平司司长卡列尔·瓦萨克将发展权称为人权的第三代。根据其理论，人权的第一代主要指某些政治和公民权利，由于这些权利，国家不得干涉个人的某些自由。第二代人权主要指那些需要国家积极参与实现的社会、经济和文化权利。第三代人权，包括团结的权

---

〔1〕〔南斯拉夫〕米兰·布拉伊奇:《国际发展法原则》,中国对外翻译出版公司 1989 年版,第 317—318 页。
〔2〕参见宦乡:《和平、合作与发展—走向二十一世纪的人类文明》,载《中国国际法年刊》(1985),第 325 页。

利,其中不仅包括发展权,也包括和平权,争取一个健康的、生态平衡的环境权利以及共同享有人类共同遗产的权利。1981 年,联合国人权委员会在纽约举行的关于人权、和平和发展之间关系的讨论会指出,据世界银行的估计,发展中国家大约有 8.5 亿人处于绝对贫困之中,"正是因为发展中国家处于如此严峻的生活条件之中,发展作为一项权利才具有紧迫性"。1986 年,联合国大会(以下简称"联大")通过的《发展权利宣言》明确主张,发展权利是一项不容剥夺的人权。

第二,发展权是一项国家权利。发展权是使人权与各国权利和义务相联系的法律努力,旨在创设个人享有其民事、政治、经济、社会和文化权利的条件,同时,尊重国家主权和国家利益,旨在促使国家通过有关行为责任或效果责任[1]严格遵守其有关人权的承诺。[2] 在联大有关建立国际经济新秩序的一系列决议中,发展权也作为国家权利。1979 年 1 月,联合国人权委员会通过一项决议,重申发展权是一项人权,并指出"发展权利均等;既是国家的权利,也是国家内个人的权利"。

第三,发展权是一项集体人权,是自决权的必然延伸。发展中国家认为,如果将人权仅仅看作公民的政治权利就忽视了经济权利与政治权利之间的直接联系。经济的落后和社会的不发达,影响个人人权的充分实现。集体人权是个人人权的基本前提,是个人人权得以实现的保障。很难设想,一个尚未从殖民统治或外国入侵、占领下解放出来的民族,能切实享有个人的基本人权和自由。因此,发展中国家才将民族自决权作为真正获得个人人权和保障个人人权得以实现的基本前提。

早在 1952 年 12 月联大《关于人民与民族的自决权的决议》中就指出:"人民与民族应享有自决权,然后才能保证充分享有一切基本人权。"1955 年 4 月《亚非会议最后公报》也确认,外国对殖民地人民的征服、统治和剥削"是对基本人权的否定,是对联合国宪章的违反,是对于促进世界和平和合作的一种障碍";并宣布"完全支持联合国宪章中所提出的人民和民族自决的原则,并注意到联合国关于人民和民族自决权利的各项决议,自决是充分享受一切基本人权的先决条件"。1966 年《经济、社会、文化权利国际盟约》第 1 条第 1 款规定:"所有民族均享有自决权,根据此种权利,自由决定其政治地位及自由从事其经济、社会与文化之发展。"这里明确指出了自决权与发展的联系。

---

〔1〕 "行为责任"(obligation of conduct)指实施某种行为的责任,在法律文件上通常表现为一些敦促性用语,如"努力促使""竭尽可能"等。"效果责任"(obligation of result)则指实施某种行为并要求达到某种效果的责任。参见周健:《国际经济法》,远流出版事业股份有限公司 1991 年版,第 25—26 页。

〔2〕 Paul de Waart, The Right to Development: Utopian or Real? Pieter van Dijk (edi), *Restructuring the International Economic Order: The Role of Law and Lawyers*, Kluwer Law and Taxation Publishers, 1987, pp. 100-102.

1985 年,中国代表团在联大全面阐述了对发展权的主张,即:发展权是一项不可剥夺的人权,这项权利是自决权的必然延伸,也是为非殖民化、民族解放、经济独立和发展而斗争所取得的成果。实现发展中国家的发展权将促进发达国家和发展中国家的共同繁荣以及维护世界和平。发展权不应仅仅解释为一项个人的权利。"国家在政治、经济和社会方面的进步能促进个人的发展,而个人的发展反过来又能促进国家的发展。因此,这两个概念是不可分的,更不能认为两者是互不相容的。"[1]

（二）国际合作义务

《联合国宪章》第 1 条第 3 款明确规定,联合国的宗旨之一是"促成国际合作,以解决属于经济、社会、文化及人类福利性质之国际问题,且不分种族、性别、语言或宗教,增进并激励对于全体人类之人权及基本自由之尊重"。该宪章第 9 章规定了各会员国之间进行国际经济和社会合作的目标和义务,即所有会员国为达到经济合作的目的,应承担采取共同及个别行动与联合国合作的法律责任。此外,会员国还必须在极广泛的范围内,通过多边和双边条约来实现这一目标。根据该宪章第 10 章设立的"经济及社会理事会"负责执行第 9 章规定的目标并具体履行该章规定的联合国职责。

1970 年 12 月《关于各国依联合国宪章建立友好关系及合作之国际法原则之宣言》重申了各国的相互合作义务:"各国不问在政治、经济及社会制度上有何差异,均有义务在国际关系之各方面彼此合作";"各国应在经济、社会及文化方面以及在科学与技术方面并为促进国际文化及教育进步,彼此合作。各国应在促进全世界尤其是发展中国家之经济增长方面彼此合作"。

由上述规定可见,作为一项国际法原则,国际合作义务存在于国家之间相互关系的各个领域。

（三）合作发展原则的主要内容

20 世纪 60 年代以来,国际社会普遍认识到,发展是发展中国家和发达国家共同的目标,发展中国家的经济发展问题已成为亟待解决的世界性课题。在各国普遍的关心下,产生了实质性的结果。1964 年成立的"联合国贸易和发展会议"（以下简称"贸发会议"）成为专为促进发展中国家的经济发展而共同商讨国际合作提案,拟订方针政策和进行交涉谈判的场所。贸发会议的设立本身是合作发展原则整个发展过程中关键性的一步。此后,在联合国大会关于建立国际经济新秩序的一系列决议

---

〔1〕 参见〔南斯拉夫〕米兰·布拉伊奇:《国际发展法原则》,中国对外翻译出版公司 1989 年版,第 363—374
页。

中,不断重申合作发展原则。

1974 年 5 月联大通过的《建立新的国际经济秩序宣言》庄严宣告:国际经济新秩序"应当建立在一切国家待遇公平、主权平等、互相依存、共同受益以及协力合作的基础之上,而不问它们的经济制度和社会制度如何"。该宣言进一步指出:"发达国家的利益同发展中国家的利益不能再互相分割开,发达国家的繁荣和发展中国家的发展是紧密地互相关联的,整个国际大家庭的繁荣取决于它的组成部分的繁荣。在发展方面的国际合作是所有国家都应具有的目标和共同责任"。

1974 年 12 月《各国经济权利和义务宪章》将"开展国际合作以促进发展"作为"国际经济关系的基本准则"之一,并且明确规定,"所有国家有责任在经济、社会、文化、科学和技术领域进行合作,以促进全世界,特别是发展中国家的经济发展和社会进步";"国际合作以谋发展是所有国家的一致目标和共同义务,每个国家都应对发展中国家的努力给予合作,提供有利外部条件,给予符合其发展需要和发展目标的积极协助,严格尊重各国主权平等,不附带任何有损于它们主权的条件,以加速其经济和社会发展"。

1986 年《发展权利宣言》指出,人是发展进程的中心主体。发展政策须将人作为发展的主要参与者和受益者;国家负有责任创设有利于实现发展权利的国内和国际条件;国家还在确保发展和排除对发展的障碍方面负有合作义务;国家须基于各国主权平等、独立、互利和合作,促成建立国际经济新秩序并促进人权的尊重和实现。

概括上述规定,合作发展原则的主要内容是,各国应进行合作,以促进建立公平互利的国际经济关系,并进行符合所有国家,特别是发展中国家的需要和利益的国际经济结构改革;所有国家有责任在经济、社会、文化、科学和技术领域内进行合作,以促进全世界,尤其是发展中国家的经济发展和社会进步。就"合作"与"发展"而言,发展是权利、目标,合作是责任、手段。发展中国家的发展权利和国际合作是密切联系的。只有承认发展中国家发展的权利,才能实现真正的国际合作。只有通过国际合作,才能促进和保障所有国家,特别是发展中国家的发展。

三、合作发展原则的法律效力

笔者以为,合作发展原则虽然主要是经过联大决议确立的,[1]其法律效力需要

---

〔1〕　关于联大决议的法律效力问题,见仁见智。参见曾华群:《国际经济法导论》,法律出版社 1999 年版,第135—140 页。

肯定和强调，主要依据如下：

第一，合作发展原则反映了国际社会的法律确信。国际法规则之所以有拘束力，首先是各国认为应当接受其约束，即各国的共同同意是国际法效力的依据。在实质上，特定联大决议是否具有法律效力，归根结底，应看它是否反映了国际社会的法律确信。[1] 确立合作发展原则的联大决议具有明确的造法意向。无可否认，这些决议是国际社会全体或绝大多数成员通过国家的集体行动，表达共同的政治意志和创立新国际法准则的规范性文件，反映了国际社会建立合作发展新秩序的共同法律确信。

第二，合作发展原则的确立遵循了国家主权平等原则和民主原则。联合国作为世界上最有代表性、最具权威的主权国家间的国际组织，在建立国际经济新秩序方面具有不可替代的重要作用。实践表明，确立合作发展原则的联大决议的形成通过了各成员国的充分协商和认真讨论，最后以"一国一票"的议事规则进行表决，以全体一致或压倒性多数通过，严格遵循了国家主权平等原则和处理国际事务的民主原则。[2] 在有关建立国际经济新秩序的国际立法中，只有坚持国家主权平等原则和处理国际事务的民主原则，才能取得成效。对以必要的多数票通过的联大决议，只要投票确实是自由和公正，各国无论投赞成票、弃权票或反对票，均应受该决议的约束。

第三，合作发展原则的法律效力在实践中不断加强。由于国际法律秩序的特点，一个新的行为规范被实际遵守的情况，对其在国际法上的效力也会产生重要的影响。因此，合作发展原则的实施或遵守情况及其对国际实践的影响程度，也是决定其法律效力的重要因素。体现合作发展原则的重要范例是欧共体与非加太国家之间先后签订的四个《洛美协定》。历次新的《洛美协定》都增添了新的内容以适应新的情况。[3] 从法律观点看，非加太—欧共体合作的最重要特征是其条约形式，反映了合作发展原则对国际法的积极影响。

最后应当指出，总体上，合作发展原则实际产生的法律效力和影响不容乐观。南北国家对合作发展原则的解释不一，重视程度各异。在实践中，一些发达国家从

---

〔1〕 D. P. Verma, Rethinking About New International Law-Making Process, *Indian Journal of International Law*, Vol. 29, 1989, p. 46.

〔2〕 根据处理国际事务的民主原则，国际事务只能由各国政府和人民共同商量来办。参见江泽民：《在联合国千年首脑会议上的讲话》，载《人民日报》（网络版）2000 年 9 月 7 日。

〔3〕 Subrata Roy Chowdhury, etc. (edi.), *The Right to Development in International Law*, Martinus Nijhoff Publishers, 1992, pp. 97-98.

未认真遵循这一新原则，而是消极应对，甚至时有发生漠视发展权和违反国际合作义务的事例。尽管合作发展原则已确立多年，直至 20 世纪末，发展中国家的整体状况并未改观，许多发展中国家的经济发展仍然停滞不前，南北经济差距继续扩大。[1] 显然，合作发展原则只有在各国进一步强调和增强其法律效力，认真维护和加强其权威性的情况下，才能有效地调整国际经济关系，服务于建立国际经济新秩序的远大目标。

---

〔1〕 在 20 世纪末，富国与穷国的经济差距仍不断扩大。在 1990—1998 年年人均国民收入呈负增长的 50 个国家中，有 49 个是发展中国家。发展中国家的贫困现象仍然严重存在，10 亿以上的低收入人口每日生活费低于 1 美元。See Development：Human Development and Human Rights Mutually Essential，SUNS（Email Edition），＃ 4698，30 June 2000.

第四节　Balance, Sustainable Development and Integration: Innovative Path for BIT Practice[*]

（平衡、可持续发展与一体化：双边投资条约实践的创新之路）

Abstract: Bilateral investment treaties (BITs) have emerged as one of the most remarkable recent developments in international law and the hot topic of international lawyers. The author indicates that in the history of BIT practice, there is an issue on imbalance and/or un-equality between developed states and developing states due to historical and practical reasons. Under the economic globalization the main clauses of BITs have been further developed to the traditional track elaborately designed by developed states, providing high level substantial and procedural protection and aiming at "liberalization of investment" for the interests of developed states and their overseas investors. For correcting the imbalance and un-equality of traditional BIT practice and reconstructing the international investment order, states and international society have to reach consensus by concepts of "balance", "sustainable development" and "integration", draft new BIT model and conduct new BIT practice.

Bilateral investment treaties (BITs) have emerged as one of the most remarkable recent developments in international law[1] and the hot topic of international lawyers. Currently developed capital-exporting states promote "liberal" BITs by their continuous economic and political priorities. The practice on

---

　　* Balance, Sustainable Development, and Integration: Innovative Path for BIT Practice, *Journal of International Economic Law* (Oxford), ISSN 1369-3034, Vol. 17, No. 2, 2014.

　　The first draft of this article is the text of the author's speech at the Second Symposium on International Investment Agreements/ International Investment Agreements and Investor-State Dispute Settlement at a Crossroads: Identifying Trends, Differences and Common Approaches hosted by OECD and UNCTAD on 14 December 2010. The author extends his gratitude to the invitation by OECD and UNCTAD and the availabilities of related information, reports and researching achievements prepared for the Symposium by the two organizations. This article is one of the achievements of researching project "the Legal Regime for Encouragement and Protection of China's Overseas Investment" [No. 09&ZD032] sponsored by the National Social Science Fund of China.

　　[1] Jason Webb Yackee, Conceptual Difficulties in the Empirical Study of Bilateral Investment Treaties, 33 *Brooklyn J. Int'l L.*, 405 (2008).

"investment liberalization" appears to be the trend of the times and affected greatly BIT practice and other international investment systems. [1] Accordingly most legal scholars from developed capital-exporting states also advocate " investment liberalization" and related international regimes. [2] A commentator indicates that "the traditional conceptual division between capital exporters and capital importers is losing its relevance" and "this traditional configuration is now out of date". [3]

In fact BIT practice is at a crossroads. [4] Since BITs are typically concluded between developed capital-exporting states and developing capital-importing states (North-South BITs), [5] the international society has to revisit the North-South issue reflected in the origin and development of BIT practice, and to recognize the negative impact of unilateral protection and liberalization of investment for capital-exporting states and transnational investors for more than half century. For the healthy and sustainable development of BIT practice as a whole, it is necessary to identify the imbalance elements in traditional BIT practice, to see the evolution of typical imbalanced clauses in BITs under the economic globalization, and to explore the innovative path for future BIT practice.

---

[1] For example, the main novel features of recent BIT practice of OECD member states include: the pursuit of high standards, from the traditional focus of investment protection towards the inclusion of more extensive liberalization disciplines, key investment protections have been redefined, new language has been added to guide the application of the expropriation articles, and investor-state dispute settlement is becoming more widely accepted. OECD Secretariat, Novel Features in OECD Countries' Recent Investment Agreements: An Overview, Document for Symposium Co-organized by ICSID, OECD and UNCTAD on Making the Most of International Invest. , 4-5 (2005).

[2] For the analysis on BIT as instruments of liberalization, see Kenneth J. Vandevelde, Investment Liberalization and Economic Development: the Role of Bilateral Investment Treaties, 36 *Columbia Journal of Transnational Law*, 504-514 (1998).

[3] Angel Gurria, Welcoming Remarks, the Second Symposium on International Investment Agreements/ International Investment Agreements and Investor-State Dispute Settlement at a Crossroads: Identifying Trends, Differences and Common Approaches, OECD Headquarters, 14 December 2010.

[4] In recent years some countries have fundamentally changed their approach towards BITs and denounced some of their treaties. In January 2008, Ecuador declared its intention to cancel several of its BITs (with Cuba, the Dominican Republic, El Salvador, Guatemala, Honduras, Nicaragua, Paraguay, Romania and Uruguay). The Bolivarian Republic of Venezuela has also denounced its BIT with the Netherlands, which will be renegotiated. United Nations Conference on Trade and Development, *World Investment Report 2010*, *Investing in a Low-Carbon Economy*, United Nations, 85-86 (2010).

[5] For the further comments in this regard, see Cai Congyan, China-US BIT Negotiations and the Future of Investment Treaty Regime: A Grand Bilateral Bargain with Multilateral Implications, 12 (2) *Journal of International Economic Law*, 493-495 (2009).

Ⅰ. Imbalance or Un-equality in Traditional BIT Practice

In the history of BIT practice, there is an issue on imbalance and/or un-equality between developed states and developing states due to historical and practical reasons. Today the issue is more serious than ever before.

Ⅰ.1 "Innate Brand" and Continuous Priority for Developed States in BITs

The early mode of BITs may be traced back to friendship, commerce, and navigation treaties (FCNs), the US traditional instrument for dealing with its foreign economic relations. After 1911, US began to add some provisions on overseas investment protection to these treaties. After the World War Ⅱ, since the status of US as a capital-exporting state was promoted remarkably, overseas investment became one of the main vehicles for its international transactions, and FCNs accordingly became the main instruments for performing its oversea investment policy. US conclude a series of 21 FCNs with a wide variety of developed and developing states. The treaties became more concerned with investment-specific needs. A "major purpose" of them was "to protect …… investment abroad".[1] For the emphasis on protection of overseas investment, there are big changes in the whole structure and contents of US FCNs. More than half of the contents in these treaties relates to investment protection. The significance of the treaties for protecting overseas investment is greatly enhanced. The provisions on investment in FCN include mainly the protection for foreigner and their properties, the treatment of foreigners' properties, nationalization or expropriation and standard of compensations etc. It is evident that these provisions refer to the core content of the modern BITs, providing experience of regulating transnational investment relations for the modern BIT practice. Other developed capital-exporting states, like Japan etc. , also take FCN as the main traditional instrument for protecting their overseas investment.[2]

However, the old international legal structure for protecting transnational investment was seriously deficient in several respects. First, applicable international

---

[1] Jason Webb Yackee, Conceptual Difficulties in the Empirical Study of Bilateral Investment Treaties, 33 *Brooklyn J. Int'l L.*, 405 (2008).

[2] For the history of BITs, See Kenneth J. Vandevelde, *U. S. International Investment Agreements*, Oxford University Press, 11-27 (2009); Rudolf Dolzer, Margrete Stevens, *Bilateral Investment Treaties*, Martinus Nijhoff Publishers, 1-11 (1995).

law failed to take account of contemporary investment practices and address important issues of concern to foreign investors. Second, the principles that did exist were often vague and subject to varying interpretations. Third, this existing framework prompted disagreement between industrialized states and newly decolonized developing states. Finally, existing international law offered foreign investors no effective enforcement mechanism to pursue their claims against host states that had injured or seized their investments or refused to respect their contractual obligations. [1] It seems that the main reasons and purposes for changing the traditional international instrument on transnational investment are undoubted all for better protecting foreign investment and foreign investors.

For further serving the policy for protecting their overseas investment, Germany created the first particular treaty on promotion and protection of investment with Pakistan in 1959, taking the investment provisions from FCNs as central contents of these new treaties. [2] The contracting parties to the BITs are typically European states and developing states. Germany and other European states took the lead in this regard. [3] With the decision of US to adopt BIT as an overseas investment protection device in early 1980s the BIT's number started to increase sharply. [4] Gradually BITs are widely accepted by states around the world and have become the most popular form of investment treaty regime. [5]

---

[1] Jeswald W. Salacuse, Nicholas P. Sullivan, Do BITs Really Work?: An Evaluation of Bilateral Investment Treaties and Their Grand Bargain, 46 *Harvard International Law Journal*, 68-69 (2009).

[2] The Treaty between the Federal Republic of Germany and Pakistan for the Promotion and Protection of Investments was concluded in 1959. It contains many substantive provisions that have become common in subsequent BITs. See Andrew Newcombe, Lluis Paradell, Law and Practice of Investment Treaties, Standards of Treatment, *Wolters Kluwer*, 42 (2009); Jason Webb Yackee, Conceptual Difficulties in the Empirical Study of Bilateral Investment Treaties, 33 *Brooklyn J. Int'l L.*, 405 (2008).

[3] Switzerland, France, Italy, United Kingdom, the Netherlands, and Belgium followed Germany's BIT practice in a relatively short time. See Jeswald W. Salacuse, BIT by BIT: The Growth of Bilateral Investment Treaties and Their Impact on Foreign Investment in Developing Countries, 24 *The International Lawyer* 656-657 (1990).

[4] Axel Berger, China's New Bilateral Investment Treaty Programme: Substance, Rational and Implications for Investment Law Making, Paper for the American Society of International Law International Economic Law Group (ASIL IELIG) 2008 biennial conference "The Politics of International Economic Law: The Next Four Years", Washington, D. C., November 14-15, 2008, p. 4.

[5] According to statistics of UNCTAD, there are 3164 international investment agreements (IIAs) by the end of 2011, including 2833 BITs and 331 "other IIAs" (such as free trade agreements, economic partnership agreements). United Nations Conference on Trade and Development, *World Investment Report 2012*, *Towards a New Generation of Investment Policies*, United Nations, 84 (2012). For general picture of BIT practice, see UNCTAD, *Bilateral Investment Treaties 1995-2006: Trends in Investment Rulemaking*, United Nations (2007).

Traditionally most BITs mimic, at least in broad strokes, the Draft International Convention on Investments Abroad (commonly known as the Abs-Shawcross Convention) and OECD 1967 Draft Convention on the Protection of Foreign Property. [1] Due to their common origins, the terms used and subjects covered in different BITs appear remarkably similar over time and across countries. For example, capital-exporting states have long been preoccupied with convincing host states to provide certain generally applicable standards of treatment, like most favored nation (MFN) treatment, national treatment and/or fair and equitable (F & E) treatment, for foreign investors and foreign investment. [2] The provisions on expropriation or nationalization of foreign investment and compensation standards, and investor-state dispute settlement (ISDS) are also major contents in BITs.

Tracing to its source, BITs are essentially created by developed capital-exporting states and definitely served for their foreign policies. It is understandable that due to the "innate brand" there are undue emphasis on powers, rights and interests of developed capital-exporting states and their overseas investors in BITs. The "innate" priority of developed states also reflects the historical weak and passive position of developing states as contracting parties in BITs.

I.2 Un-equal Positions and Bargaining Powers in BIT Negotiation

In theory BIT is a result of bilateral negotiation between contracting states, aiming at providing equal legal protection for both parties. In practice, they are usually agreements between developed capital-exporting states and developing capital-importing states. The rules and standards for investment protection are largely depended on the expectation, positions and bargaining powers of the contracting parties. To some extent the preparation of model BIT reflects the un-equal positions and bargaining powers between developed states and developing states in BIT negotiations.

Developed states devoted considerable time and efforts to the preparation of a

---

[1] For the brief history of the BITs, see Jeswald W. Salacuse, "BIT by BIT: The Growth of Bilateral Investment Treaties and Their Impact on Foreign Investment in Developing Countries", 24 *The International Lawyer* 656-661 (1990).

[2] Jason Webb Yackee, Conceptual Difficulties in the Empirical Study of Bilateral Investment Treaties, 33 *Brooklyn J. Int'l L.*, 415-416 (2008).

model BIT, to serve as a basis of their BIT negotiations. [1] Preparing a model BIT normally involved intensive consultation with relevant government agencies and representative of private sector. In general a model BIT serves several purposes for developed states. First, its preparation is an occasion to study the entire issues of investment protection, to consult with interested governmental and private sector organizations, and to formulate a national position on the issue. Second, a model BIT is considered as an efficient means of communicating to counterpart a concrete idea of the model that the developed state seeks. Thirdly starting all negotiations with the same model is a way to attain the goal of unifying its BITs with various developing states. Finally the model gives developed state a negotiating advantage, since the party who controls the draft usually controls the negotiation. By preparing a model that becomes the basis of discussion, developed state has determined the agenda of BIT negotiation and has established the conceptual framework of BIT. [2]

Most of the developed states use the model as essential means for their BIT practice, [3] and therefore have clear objectives, strong confidence and firm stance in the negotiations. These models have brought satisfactory results for the developed

---

[1] It seems that there are two types of BIT models: one is the European model, the traditional one; the other is the US model, including provisions on some new elements and complicated dispute settlement regime. See the typical European BIT Models: German Model Treaty-2008: Treaty between the Federal Republic of Germany and [……] concerning the Encouragement and Reciprocal Protection of Investments (13 Articles in total); and Draft Agreement between the Government of the Republic of France and the Government of the Republic of [……] on the Reciprocal Promotion and Protection of Investments (2006) (11 Articles in total). There are 37 Articles in the 2012 US Model BIT: Article 1: Definitions; Article 2: Scope and Coverage; Article 3: National Treatment; Article 4: Most-Favored-Nation Treatment; Article 5: Minimum Standard of Treatment; Article 6: Expropriation and Compensation; Article 7: Transfers; Article 8: Performance Requirements; Article 9: Senior Management and Boards of Directors; Article 10: Publication of Laws and Decisions Respecting Investment; Article 11: Transparency; Article 12: Investment and Environment; Article 13: Investment and Labour; Article 14: Non-Conforming Measures; Article 15: Special Formalities and Information Requirements; Article 16: Non-Derogation; Article 17: Denial of Benefits; Article 18: Essential Security; Article 19: Disclosure of Information; Article 20: Financial Services; Article 21: Taxation; Article 22: Entry into force, Duration, and Termination; Article 23: Consultation and Negotiation; Article 24: Submission of a Claim to Arbitration; Article 25: Consent of Each Party to Arbitration; Article 26: Conditions and Limitations on Consent of Each Party; Article 27: Selection of Arbitrators; Article 28: Conduct of the Arbitration; Article 29: Transparency of Arbitral Proceedings; Article 30: Governing Law; Article 31: Interpretation of Annexes; Article 32: Expert Reports; Article 33: Consolidation; Article 34: Awards; Article 35: Annexes and Footnotes; Article 36: Service of Documents; Article 37: State-State Dispute Settlement. The text is divided into three sections: Section A (Article 1 to Article 22), Section B (Article 23 to Article 36) and Section C (Article 37).

[2] Jeswald W. Salacuse, BIT by BIT: The Growth of Bilateral Investment Treaties and Their Impact on Foreign Investment in Developing Countries, 24 *The International Lawyer* 662-663 (1990).

[3] For example, the US, as a new comer of developed states in BIT practice, develops its model BITs in 1983, 1984, 1987, 1991, 1992, 1994, 2004 and 2012 respectively. For the evolution of the US model BITs, see Kenneth J. Vandevelde, *U. S. International Investment Agreements*, Oxford University Press, 91-112 (2009).

states. For example, the 2012 US model BIT follows the approach by the US in its BITs over at least the past decade, indicating the US's continued satisfaction with both its undefeated record as a respondent state in investor-state arbitrations, and the protection its BITs have given to US investors abroad. [1] In BIT negotiations it is very difficult for developing states to change the conditions and terms of a model BIT prepared and insisted on by developed states. [2]

On contrary most of developing states have not prepared model BITs. Accordingly they are in the position of merely accepting or slightly reacting to a model BIT prepared by their counterparts. Only a few developing states have prepared their model BITs. These models are often influenced by the developed states' model BITs due to historical, practical and/or technical elements. Furthermore it is difficult to expect some of the developing states which are signatories to these treaties to have legal departments sophisticated enough to understand the nuances in the variations in the language that is used in these treaties. [3]

It is worth noticing that BIT negotiation may achieve third party-benefit arrangement. It may interfere with investor-state negotiation by granting investors unwaivable protections and safeguards that they might or might not have been able to convince a host state to grant them in direct negotiation. It indicates that the main function of BITs is to limit host state bargaining power from the outset. [4]

It is obvious that the un-equal positions and bargaining powers between developed states and developing states in BIT negotiations have important impact not only on the balance of powers, rights and interests between two contracting parties directly,

[1] Lise Johnson, The 2012 US Model BIT and What the Changes (or Lack Thereof) Suggest about Future Investment Treaties, 8 (2) *Political Risk Insurance Newsletter*, November, 2012.

[2] For example, the unwillingness of the US to compromise rested on several considerations. First, if a potential BIT partner were unwilling to accept the substance of the agreement as proposed, then the US did not regard that country as having the foreign-investment policy that the BITs were intended to reflect. Second, any substantive concession raised the risk that future BIT partners would demand the same concession. Third, to compromise on a longstanding principle even could be counterproductive, resulting in a less favorable situation than if no BIT at all had been concluded. Fourth, if the concession were mistakenly interpreted as clarification of the model BIT rather than a concession, it risked undermining the strength of the BITs already concluded. See Kenneth J. Vandevelde, *U. S. International Investment Agreements*, Oxford University Press, 109 (2009).

[3] M. Sornarajah, *The International Law on Foreign Investment*, 2nd edition, Cambridge University Press, 207-208 (2004).

[4] Jason Webb Yackee, Conceptual Difficulties in the Empirical Study of Bilateral Investment Treaties, 33 *Brooklyn J. Int'l L.*, 458 (2008).

but also on the balance of main objectives and functions of BITs to large extent.

Ⅰ.3 Deviation of Objectives and Functions in BITs

Ⅰ.3.ⅰ Different Motives and Objectives of BITs

The motives and objectives for concluding BITs are different between developed states and developing states due to their different positions and roles in international investment activities.

The movement to conclude BITs is initiated and driven by developed states. Their primary objective is to create clear international legal rules and effective enforcement mechanisms to protect investment by their nationals in the territories of foreign states. The essence of this protection is to defend the investment and the investors from exercises of host states' power with respect to such matters as expropriation, treatment, transfer of currency abroad, and restrictions on operations. These treaty rules and enforcement mechanisms are intended to supplant local legislation and institutions and also to avoid disputes over the content and applicability of customary international law. A secondary objective of developed states is to facilitate the entry of their investments by inducing their counterparts to remove impediments in their regulatory systems. Some developed states, especially US, have sought to encourage or induce investment and market liberalization within their negotiating partners. [1]After the end of cold war, the BIT practice of developed states appears gradually their political purpose. In the eyes of some developed states another purpose of BITs was to counter attacks on the traditional international law of expropriation by developing states in the 1950s through 1970s. A recent purpose of the US BIT program has been to endorse and facilitate trends toward democracy and capitalism in Eastern Europe and the former Soviet Bloc. [2] A BIT can accomplish this by providing protection to US investment and thus encouraging investment in such states, and by providing such states with a framework of the types of protection that must

[1]　The Deputy US Trade Representative stated the US goals in negotiating BITs are to "… (2) encourage adoption in foreign countries of market-oriented domestic policies that treat private investment fairly…". See Jeswald W. Salacuse, Nicholas P. Sullivan, Do BITs Really Work?: An Evaluation of Bilateral Investment Treaties and Their Grand Bargain, 46 *Harvard International Law Journal*, 76 (2005).

[2]　In 2006, Assistant Secretary of State Deniel Sullivan explained in testimony before the Senate Foreign Relations Committee that "one point that I want to emphasize is this idea of our BIT not only as providing protection for U.S. investors, but also as a vehicle to help drive economic reform programs. see Kenneth J. Vandevelde, *U.S. International Investment Agreements*, Oxford University Press, 108 (2009).

be offered to foreign investment in order to attract such investment. [1]

The primary objective pursued by developing states in negotiating BITs is to improve foreign investment climate and encourage foreign investment for the development of national economy. The basic assumption is that a BIT with clear, enforceable rules to protect the foreign investment and foreign investors reduces the risks that the foreign investors would otherwise face. Developing states have sometimes entered into BIT negotiations with the expectation that the capital-exporting state would take affirmative measures to encourage its nationals to invest in the territories of its counterparts of BITs. Capital-exporting states, however, have steadfastly refused to agree to any provision obligating them to encourage their nationals to invest in the foreign state. On the contrary, many BITs have terms that encourage the host state to create favorable investment conditions in its territory. For some developing states, signing a BIT may be a condition to securing other benefits, such as participation in the capital-exporting state's overseas investment guarantee program or obtaining increased political and economic support. [2]Developing states also try to establish the rules for regulating foreign investment and foreign investors by BITs, like the admission clause, which states the screening power of host states on foreign investment at the pre-establishment stage, and the requirements of "the exhaustion of local remedies" in the ISDS clause.

The recent development of BITs indicates that the above different motives and objectives for concluding BITs between developed states and developing states remain almost the same. Furthermore initiated by the strong economic and political power, and benefited by trend of the economic globalization, developed states positively promote their BIT program for achieving and furthering their all objectives of BITs. On the contrary the objective of the developing states for encouraging and regulating foreign investment by BITs is confronted with serious challenges due to current imbalance of economic powers between developed states and developing

---

[1] Paul E. Comeaux, N. Stephan Kinsella, *Protecting Foreign Investment under International Law*, *Legal Aspects of Political Risk*, Oceana Publications Inc., 101-102 and note 9 (1997); Jeswald W. Salacuse, Nicholas P. Sullivan, Do BITs Really Work?: An Evaluation of Bilateral Investment Treaties and Their Grand Bargain, 46 *Harvard International Law Journal*, 75-76 (2005).

[2] Jeswald W. Salacuse, BIT by BIT: The Growth of Bilateral Investment Treaties and Their Impact on Foreign Investment in Developing Countries, 24 *The International Lawyer* 661 (1990).

states. In other words, it is very difficult for developing states to achieve their main objectives of BITs.

Ⅰ.3.ii Deviation of Functions in BITs

It has been said that BITs have two-fold purpose and/or functions: to offer legal protections to foreign investors and their home states with respect to investment in the host states, and to encourage the transnational investment. [1]

In theory the first main function of BITs is the mutual legal protection for transnational investment. It should be further pointed out that although almost all BITs provide the mutual investment protection for investors from two contracting parties, the one-way capital flow between developed states and developing states is very clear. [2] Therefore only investors from home developed states enjoy the investment protection provided by host developing states. [3] It is obvious that the mutual nature of the investment protection in BITs between developed states and developing states is only a formal one. In substance, the high level of the investment protection in BITs provide unilaterally the powers, rights and interests for developed capital-exporting states and their overseas investors, and impose related heavy obligations and duties on developing capital-importing states at the same time. It may be safely concluded that the function for protection of transnational investment in BITs is to serve developed capital-exporting states and their overseas investors unilaterally. For some developed capital-exporting states, the existence of a BIT is a pre-condition for granting investment insurance to their prospective investors. [4]

Furthermore, the legal protection for transnational investment in recent BIT

---

[1] Some say that another purpose of BITs in the eyes of some developed states was to counter attacks on the traditional law of expropriation by developing states in the 1950's through 1970's. See Paul E. Comeaux, N. Stephan Kinsella, *Protecting Foreign Investment under International Law*, *Legal Aspects of Political Risk*, Oceana Publications Inc., 101-102 (1997).

[2] Many developing states, desperately short of capital, would strongly oppose any measure that encouraged their own nationals to invest their capital abroad, rather than at home, therefore the titles of certain BITs refer to "Encouragement and Reciprocal Protection of Investments" rather than the more common designation, "Reciprocal Encouragement and Protection of Investments". See Jeswald W. Salacuse, "BIT by BIT: The Growth of Bilateral Investment Treaties and Their Impact on Foreign Investment in Developing Countries", 24 *The International Lawyer* 662 (1990).

[3] Paul E. Comeaux, N. Stephan Kinsella, *Protecting Foreign Investment under International Law*, *Legal Aspects of Political Risk*, Oceana Publications Inc., 102 (1997).

[4] Rudolf Dolzer, Margrete Stevens, *Bilateral Investment Treaties*, Martinus Nijhoff Publishers, 12-13 (1995).

practice is reaching the highest level in the history. The host states' power on foreign investment admission is transformed gradually to the investors' "establishment rights", the restriction on performance requirements by host states and the host states' obligation on "investment liberalization". The four requirements for expropriation (i. e. for a public purpose, in accordance with due process of law, non-discriminatory and accompanied by compensation) and the Hull formula (i. e. adequate, effective and prompt payment for the properties seized) for the compensation of expropriation are widely applied and strengthened in BITs. There are increasing provisions on giving foreign investors unilateral direct right to initiate arbitral proceedings against host state in International Center for Settlement of Investment Disputes (ICSID). [1] The 2012 US Model BIT has gone on in this road even further. The first category of changes in the new model includes those that add and clarify obligations of host states and are ostensibly designed to make it easier for investors to establish and successfully operate their investments abroad. They consist of new provisions on transparency, performance requirements, and state-owned enterprises (SOEs). These changes appear to reflect concerns raised by the US business interests regarding challenges they have faced when investing abroad. From the host states' perspective, it may, for example, be particularly costly in terms of time and resources for developing states to craft and implement the new expended transparency provisions; and from investors' perspectives, such provisions may greatly increase the ease of doing business in host states. [2] All these new developments further increase the deviation of functions of BITs, putting more undue emphasis on foreign investors and foreign investment while ignoring and crippling the host states' policy objectives for investment promotion and the host states' power on regulating

---

[1] These provisions have caused practical consequence. Over the past ten years, there has been a surge of investor-state arbitrations based on BITs. At least 42 new cases were registered in the first eleven months of 2005. By the end of 2006, the total number of treaty-based arbitrations has risen to 259, 161 of which were brought before the ICSID. See Mary H. Mourra (ed.), *Latin American Investment Treaty Arbitration, the Controversies and Conflicts*, Wolters Kluwer, 17-18 (2009). China became a contracting party of the Washington Convention on 1 July 1992 and accepts the jurisdiction of the ICSID in an increasing number of BITs. The first claim of Chinese investor registered on 12 February 2007, Tza Yap Shum v. Republic of Peru, will be just the beginning of ICSID disputes with Chinese participation. See Monika C. E. Heymann, International Law and the Settlement of Investment Disputes Relating to China, 2008 *Journal of International Economic Law*, 507 (2008).

[2] See Lise Johnson, The 2012 US Model BIT and What the Changes (or Lack Thereof) Suggest about Future Investment Treaties, 8 (2) *Political Risk Insurance Newsletter*, November, 2012.

foreign investment.

The second function of BITs is to promote transnational investment. The function may be considered as common objective and common interest of developed states and developing states. Developed states aim at promoting their overseas investment for strengthening their economic power and competitive abilities in international market, while developing states seek for attracting and receiving foreign investment for their national economic development. In BIT terms, however, the obligation of "investment promotion" is vague. Does it mean that developed capital-exporting states bear the obligation of promoting their private investors to invest in host states, or that developing capital-importing states take the responsibilities of improving their investment climate for promoting foreign investment? In BIT practice, "investment promotion" is definitely not an obligation for developed capital-exporting states, and is actually an obligation of improving investment climate for developing capital-importing states. In fact for developing states to conclude a BIT is also one of the important means for improving their investment climate.

Comparing with protection and promotion of investment, "investment liberalization" is higher objective which developed states pursuit for. In BIT regime, "investment promotion" for host states means that the investment projects approved by them meet the needs of host states' highest interest. "Investment liberalization", as the favorite term for capital-exporting states, means the liberal investment climate created by host states and evaluated by transnational investors. [1] Developed states, which profited from global free trade, controlled sufficient political and economic power to secure their preferred policies regarding liberalization, privatization and foreign investment. They have been able to do so through means of the WTO regime, regional trade agreements (RTAs) and BITs. [2] In the deadlock of negotiations on Multilateral Agreement on Investment (MAI) and investment issues of WTO, developed states pay much attention to the inclusion of investment liberalization clause in BITs and RTAs. Recent BIT practice of the OECD states indicates

---

[1] Jeswald W. Salacuse, Towards a Global Treaty on Foreign Investment: The Search for a Grand Bargain, in Norbert Horn (ed.), *Arbitrating Foreign Investment Disputes*, Kluwer Law International 78-79 (2004).

[2] M. Sornarajah, A Developing Country Perspectives of International Economic Law in the Context of Dispute Settlement, at Asif H. Qureshi (ed.), *Perspectives in International Economic Law*, Kluwer Law International 83 (2002).

that the contents of these BITs are from the traditional focus of investment protection towards the inclusion of more extensive liberalisation disciplines. The rise in standard of foreign investment treatment can largely be attributed to the guarantees in the pre-establishment phase and to new liberalisation commitment. [1] It might be safely concluded that "investment liberalization" further emphasizes the powers, rights and interest of developed states.

According to the logic of some developed states, as the result of limiting the host states powers on foreign investment and providing high level legal protection for foreign investment, the developing states' investment climate has been improved and may attract more foreign investment. This may be considered as a "balance" or "compromise" between the rights and interests between developed capital-exporting states and developing capital-importing states. Ironically for the vast majority of BIT history, there was no statistical or case-study evidence of the effects of the treaties on foreign direct investment (FDI) flows, and only recently have the costs of the treaties—meaning the extent to which a wide variety of host state policies might be successfully challenged before arbitral tribunals—become clear. [2]

II. The Evolution of Typical Imbalanced Clauses in BITs under the Economic Globalization

In recent years, under the economic globalization the main clauses of BITs have been further developed to the traditional track elaborately designed by developed capital-exporting states, ignoring South-North issue in general. The so-called modern or new generation of BITs generally follows the liberal approach for protecting international investment, providing high level substantial and procedural protection for foreign investors [3] and aiming at "liberalization of investment" for the interests of

---

〔1〕 OECD Secretariat, Novel Features in OECD Countries' Recent Investment Agreements: An Overview, Document for Symposium Co-organized by ICSID, OECD and UNCTAD on Making the Most of International Invest, 2005, p. 4.

〔2〕 Jason Webb Yackee, Conceptual Difficulties in the Empirical Study of Bilateral Investment Treaties, 33 *Brooklyn J. Int'l L.*, 459-460 (2008).

〔3〕 Axel Berger, China's New Bilateral Investment Treaty Programme: Substance, Rational and Implications for Investment Law Making, Paper for the American Society of International Law International Economic Law Group (ASIL IELIG) 2008 biennial conference "The Politics of International Economic Law: The Next Four Years", Washington, D. C., November 14-15, 2008.

developed capital-exporting states and their overseas investors. In the main clauses of modern BITs, the adoption, interpretation and related practice of provisions on broad definition of investment, broad definition of investor, right of establishment, extensive application of F & E treatment, extensive adoption of Hull formula, and the direct right for investors in ISDS reflect particularly the general trend, the continuous approach and the firm stance of developed capital-exporting states, and the increasing imbalance and/or un-equality between developed states and developing states in international investment activities.

II.1 Broad Definition of Investment

"Investment" is one of the two most important definitions on the scope of application of rights and obligations under BITs. The definition defines the subject matter jurisdiction or jurisdiction *ratione materiae*[1] and has great implication on the establishment of the jurisdiction of international arbitral tribunals for the investment disputes, and in particular the jurisdiction of ICSID, as it extends to "any dispute arising out of an investment".[2]

BITs usually provide a definition of what constitutes an investment protected by the treaty in their "definition" clause. The definition of investment has been expanded from tangle property to untangle property, from direct investment to indirect investment, from property to right of property,[3] and also from companies to equity or debt interest in companies. Several types of intangible property, including rights under contracts, intellectual property rights, and rights in licenses and permits, are specifically mentioned.[4] The broad definition of "investment" is particularly

[1] Campbell McLachlan QC, Laurence Shore, Matthew Weiniger, *International Investment Arbitration, Substantive Principles*, Oxford University Press, 29 (2007).

[2] Recently one of the most critical questions in BIT cases has been whether rights conferred by contract constitute covered investments. It is possible to identify certain features of an investment on the basis of ICSID and non-ICSID case-law. See OECD, *International Investment Law, Understanding Concepts and Tracking Innovations, Companion Volume to International Investment Perspectives*, OECD, 9, 53-78 (2008).

[3] M. Sornarajah, *The International Law on Foreign Investment*, 2nd edition, Cambridge University Press, 220-224 (2004).

[4] Paul E. Comeaux, N. Stephan Kinsella, *Protecting Foreign Investment under International Law, Legal Aspects of Political Risk*, Oceana Publications Inc., 105 (1997); OECD Secretariat, Novel Features in OECD Countries' Recent Investment Agreements: An Overview, Document for Symposium Co-organised by ICSID, OECD and UNCTAD on Making the Most of International Invest, 2005, p. 5.

drafted by the US and other developed capital-exporting states in their model BITs.[1]

In practice most BITs adopt the broad definition of investment. The "asset based" definition of "investment" prevails. The definition is very broad, typically referring to "every kind of asset", and then adding a specific non-exhaustive list of examples.[2] The new approach is to make the definition more precisely.[3]

China also accepts the broad "asset-based" definition of "investment". Following general practice of most BITs,[4] Article 1. 1 of Agreement between the People's Republic of China and the Federal Republic of Germany on the Encouragement and Reciprocal Protection of Investments (hereinafter China-Germany BIT) provides that:

"the term 'investment' means every kind of asset invested directly or indirectly by investors of one Contracting Party in the territory of the other Contracting Party, and in particular, though not exclusively, includes:

(a) movable and immovable property and other property rights such as mortgages and pledges;

(b) shares, debentures, stock and any other kind of interest in companies;

(c) claims to money or to any performance having an economic value associated with an investment;

(d) intellectual property rights, in particular copyrights, patents and industrial designs, trade-marks, trade-names, technical processes, trade and business secrets, know-how and good-will;

(e) business concessions conferred by law or under contract permitted by law, including concessions to search for, cultivate, extract or exploit natural

---

[1]　See OECD, *International Investment Law*, *Understanding Concepts and Tracking Innovations*, *Companion Volume to International Investment Perspectives*, OECD, 79-82 (2008).

[2]　Andrew Newcombe, Lluis Paradell, *Law and Practice of Investment Treaties*, *Standards of Treatment*, Wolters Kluwer, 65-66 (2009).

[3]　For the definition of investment in BITs, including Model BITs of Canada, France, Germany, UK and US, See OECD, *International Investment Law*, *Understanding Concepts and Tracking Innovations*, *Companion Volume to International Investment Perspectives*, OECD, 79-100 (2008).

[4]　UNCTAD, *Bilateral Investment Treaties 1995-2006*: *Trends in Investment Rulemaking*, United Nations, 8 (2007); Annex1. A1, Definition of Investment in Bilateral Investment Treaties, OECD, *International Investment Law*, *Understanding Concepts and Tracking Innovations*, *Companion Volume to International Investment Perspectives*, OECD, 79-100 (2008).

resources;

any change in the form in which assets are invested does not affect their character as investments······"[1]

In addition to the broad "asset-based" definition, some developed states introduce a tautological or circular definition of "investment". Numerous BITs concluded by US illustrate this approach, such as the BIT with Bahrain (1999). It defines an "investment" as "every kind of investment". Using the tautological or circular definition implies that the contracting parties leave a significant degree of discretion to arbitral tribunals to interpret this concept. [2] It therefore further expands the "asset based" definition of "investment".

A third approach that has emerged to avoid an excessively broad definition of "investment" is a "closed-list" definition. This method differs from the broader "asset-based" definition in that it does not contain a conceptual chapeau to define "investment", but rather consists of an ample, but finite list of tangible and intangible assets to be covered by the BIT. Originally envisaged as an "enterprise-based" definition used in the context of the US-Canada Free Trade Agreement, this approach evolved towards the definition used in Article 1139 of North American Free Trade Agreement (NAFTA). In 1990s this approach began to be also used in BITs. It has been incorporated into the 2004 Canada BIT model. In addition to being finite, the list contains a series of specific clarifications to avoid applying the BIT to certain kinds of assets. [3] It should be pointed out that although this approach does not adopt the traditional open and broad concept of investment, it still contains rather broad content of investment.

A further issue faced in BIT negotiations is whether investments made prior to the treaty will benefit from its provisions. Developing states have sometimes sought to limit a BIT's application to future investment only or at least to those investments

---

[1] For the detailed discussion on China's practice in this regard, see Norah Gallagher, Wenhua Shan, *Chinese Investment Treaties, Policies and Practice*, Oxford University Press, 53-71 (2009).

[2] It provides that: "'investment' of a national or company means every kind of investment owned or controlled directly or indirectly by the national or company, and includes, but it is not limited to, [···]" See UNCTAD, *Bilateral Investment Treaties 1995-2006: Trends in Investment Rulemaking*, United Nations 10 (2007).

[3] See UNCTAD, *Bilateral Investment Treaties 1995-2006: Trends in Investment Rulemaking*, United Nations 8-13 (2007).

made in the relatively recent past. Developed states, on the other hand, have generally sought to protect all investments made by their nationals and companies, regardless of when they were made. [1]

It is evident that the "asset based" definition of "investment", a tautological or circular definition of "investment", and even a "closed-list" definition are all broader definitions of "investment". Accordingly "investment" in BITs covers almost every kind of foreign assets, including tangible properties, intangible properties, and property rights in host state, far beyond the FDI.

For the interest of developed capital-exporting states and overseas investors, the definition of "investment" not only requires a concept ample enough to cover the wide range of forms that investment can take, but also must be flexible enough to apply to new types of investment that might emerge in the future.

It should be further pointed out that the provisions that "a change in the form in which assets are invested does not affect their character as investments" in the broader definition of "investment" have very important practical implications. According to the provisions, the character of investments is "freezed" at the time of making investment. Even the form of the investments changes afterwards, their character as investments is indisputable. The "precaution" provision might prevent or decrease the potential disputes concerning the character of investments.

The developed states traditionally take, develop and insist on the approach of the broad definition while some developing states try to limit their obligation of protecting FDI by narrow definition of investment. [2] The objective behind the broad definition of investment is to ensure that BIT protection could be given to a wide range of activities associated with FDI[3]and the subject matter jurisdiction or jurisdiction *ratione materiae* of BITs. In general it meets and serves for the needs and interests of developed capital-exporting states and their overseas investors and at the same time imposes broad and heavy obligations of protection of developing capital-

---

[1] Jeswald W. Salacuse, Nicholas P. Sullivan, Do BITs Really Work?: An Evaluation of Bilateral Investment Treaties and Their Grand Bargain, 46 *Harvard International Law Journal*, 80-81 (2005).

[2] On the other hand, the "enterprise based" definition of "investment" limits the "investment" to FDI relevant to foreign-invested enterprises. It serves for the developing capital importing states as it limit the scope of investment protected by host states.

[3] M. Sornarajah, *The International Law on Foreign Investment*, second edition, Cambridge University Press, 9 (2004).

importing states in this regard.

Ⅱ.2 Broad Definition of Investors

"Investors" is another most important definition on the scope of application in BITs since the goal of each contracting party is to secure benefits for its own nationals and companies, rather than those of other states. The definition specifically defines the jurisdiction *ratione personae*. The issue is essentially one of determining what link needs to exist between an investor and a contracting party to a BIT in order for the investor to benefit from the treaty's provisions.[1] BITs provide in general that "investors" means "natural persons" or "physical persons" who are nationals of contracting parties[2] and "legal entities" or "companies" incorporated or constituted under the law of contracting parties.

Ⅱ.2.i Natural Persons or Physical Persons

It is a firmly established principle in international law that the nationality of a natural person is determined by the national law of the state whose nationality is claimed. Accordingly, most BITs protect persons who have the nationality of one of the contracting parties. Thus, the typical definition of a national of a party is a natural person recognized by that party's internal law as a national or citizen.[3] However, some BITs introduce alternative criteria such as a requirement of residency or domicile.[4]

---

[1] Jeswald W. Salacuse, Nicholas P. Sullivan, Do BITs Really Work?: An Evaluation of Bilateral Investment Treaties and Their Grand Bargain, 46 *Harvard International Law Journal*, 81 (2005).

[2] Most BITs protect physical persons who have the nationality of one of the contracting parties. Thus the typical definition of a national of a party is a physical person recognized by that party's internal law as a national or citizen. In some cases, the definition of "investor" is even broader to include not only citizens but also individuals, who qualify as permanent residents under domestic law. See UNCTAD, *Bilateral Investment Treaties 1995-2006: Trends in Investment Rulemaking*, United Nations 13 (2007).

[3] UNCTAD, *Bilateral Investment Treaties 1995-2006: Trends in Investment Rulemaking*, United Nations, 13 (2007).

[4] For example, in the Canada-Argentina BIT the term "investor" means "i) any natural person possessing the citizenship of or permanently residing in a contracting party in accordance with its laws". Article 201 of NAFTA provides in part that: "National means a natural person who is a citizen or permanent resident of a party". See OECD, *International Investment Law, Understanding Concepts and Tracking Innovations, Companion Volume to International Investment Perspectives*, OECD, 14 (2008).

Not many BITs address specifically the issue of dual nationalities. [1] The new Canada Model FIPA which replaces the 2004 Model FIPA covers citizens as well as permanent residents of Canada, but it expressly provides that a natural person who is a national of both contracting parties shall be deemed to be exclusively a national of the party of his or her dominant or effective nationality. [2]

In Hong Kong (HK)'s BITs, the provisions for defining "physical persons" as "investors" for HK based on the permanent resident standard are unique due to HK's non-sovereign status and its specific needs for protection to certain people no based on national standard. [3] Traditionally two different approaches have been taken in the drafting of the definition of the term "physical persons". One is to set forth a single definition for applying to both parties. The other is to offer two definitions, one relating to one contracting party, and the other to the second contracting party. [4] It seems that the HK Model BIT creates the third approach. It adopts two standards—permanent resident standard and national standard[5]—for contracting parties: only permanent resident standard for HK; both permanent resident

---

[1] It is indicated that in addition to the issue of dual nationalities, there is another issue on nationality change, concerning the case where an investor changes his nationality after he has already begun to enjoy the protection of a BIT on the basis of his former nationality. In this case, it is doubtful that he would continue to be deemed a national of his formal state for the purpose of the BIT. See Rudolf Dolzer, Margrete Stevens, *Bilateral Investment Treaties*, Martinus Nijhoff Publishers, 34 (1995).

[2] In practice, investment treaty jurisprudence under the ICSID Convention as to the nationality of natural persons is limited to four cases, namely Eudoro A. Olguin v. Republic of Paraguay (ICSID Case No. ARB/98/5), Soufraki v. United Arab Emirates (ICSID Case No. ARB/02/7), Champion Trading v. Egypt (ICSID Case No. ARB/02/9), and Siag and Vecchi v. Egypt (ICSID Case No. ARB/05/15), brought by dual nationals. See OECD, *International Investment Law*, *Understanding Concepts and Tracking Innovations*, *Companion Volume to International Investment Perspectives*, OECD, 14-17 (2008).

[3] According to the Article 1(f)(i) of HK Model BIT, "(i) in respect of either Contracting Party: physical persons who have the right of abode in the area of that Contracting Party……"; "(ii) in respect of [HK's counterpart]: physical persons who are its nationals". For detailed discussion in this regard, see ZENG Huaqun, Initiative and Implications of Hong Kong's Bilateral Investment Treaties, 11 (5) *The Journal of World Investment & Trade*, 675-676 (2010).

[4] Rudolf Dolzer, Margrete Stevens, *Bilateral Investment Treaties*, Martinus Nijhoff Publishers, 31-32 (1995).

[5] There is key difference between "national" and "citizen" in the legal implication in some countries. Under US law, the term "national" is broader than the term "citizen". For example, a native of American Samoa is a national of the US, but not a citizen. See Kenneth J. Vandevelde, *U. S. International Investment Agreements*, Oxford University Press, 144 (2009).

standard and national standard for HK's counterparts. [1]

II. 2. ii Legal Persons

As for legal persons, in BITs they are in general referred as companies. "Company" is defined very broadly, to include any types of legal entities mentioned are corporations, partnerships, joint ventures, sole proprietorships and trusts. [2]

The issues related to the nationality of legal persons can be even more complicated than for natural persons. BITs have essentially relied on three basic criteria to determine the nationality of a "company": (i) the concept of incorporation or constitution; (ii) the concept of the seat; and (iii) the concept of control. [3]Companies today operate in ways that can make it very difficult to determine nationality. It is the general practice in BITs to specifically define the objective criteria which make a legal person a national, or investor, of the party, for the purpose of the BITs. [4]

The definition of a company in BITs in general goes against the traditional notions in international law. [5] Some of the BITs seek to establish alternative tests of corporate nationality for the purpose of investment protection under the treaties. They specify that a company incorporated in one contracting party will be protected by the other party provided that the seat of control of the company is located in the other contracting party or where there is control or a substantial interest in the company by nationals of the other party.

The survey on the BIT practice from 1995 to 2006 by UNCTAD (hereinafter UNCTAD survey) indicates that, concerning the definition of an "investor", various approaches continue to be used to determine the nationality of a legal entity. There

---

[1] In practice only 2 of HK's BITs adopt the provisions on "both permanent resident standard and national/citizen standard for HK's counterparts". Art. 1(f) of HK-Australia BIT provides that: "in respect of Australia: (A) physical persons possessing Australia citizenship or who are permanently residing in Australia in accordance with its law……"Art. 1(2)(b)(i) of HK-New Zealand BIT has similar provisions.

[2] Paul E. Comeaux, N. Stephan Kinsella, *Protecting Foreign Investment under International Law*, *Legal Aspects of Political Risk*, Oceana Publications Inc., 105 (1997).

[3] See Rudolf Dolzer, Margrete Stevens, *Bilateral Investment Treaties*, Martinus Nijhoff Publishers, 35-36 (1995).

[4] See OECD, *International Investment Law*, *Understanding Concepts and Tracking Innovations*, *Companion Volume to International Investment Perspectives*, OECD, 17-18 (2008).

[5] The general rule relating to the diplomatic protection of corporations making investment in foreign countries was stated in the Barcelona Traction Case. According to the International Court of Justice in that case, a corporation has the nationality of the state in which it is incorporated, and only the latter has the right of diplomatic intervention on behalf of the corporation.

has been a tendency in recent BITs to combine the criterion of incorporation with the requirement of also having the seat or the controlling interest in that country. "Control" by an investor of an investment is sometimes explicitly defined; one approach is to understand it as the power to appoint the majority of the board of directors or otherwise to legally direct the operations of the investment. All BITs incorporating the notion of "control" into their definitions refer to "direct" and "indirect" control or ownership. This method highlights an important aspect of BITs—namely, that they protect investments of nationals or companies of a contracting party, no matter how many corporate layers exist between the national or company and the investment. Consequently, more than one home state may exercise diplomatic protection. [1]

As the result of "control" criterion, BITs may cover very wide-ranging of the investors. It is understandable that a multinational company may easily seek for BIT protection for more than one country based on the shareholders' links to their home states. Even for a domestic company own fully by domestic investors, it may become a foreign invested company one day due to control directly or indirectly by foreign investors as second or third corporate layers. It is evident that the broad definition of "investor" for legal persons also meets and serves the needs and interests of developed capital exporting states and their overseas investors as it provides the "BIT protection umbrella" not only for the legal persons based on the concepts of constitution and the seat of contracting parties, but also for the legal persons based on the concept of "control". [2] It is usually very difficult for the developing capital-importing states to predict and find out the "potential" investors who are companies from non-contracting party and may argue that they are "investors" from a counterpart of host state's BIT someday due to "control" criterion. It is really a great and unpredicted challenge for host developing states.

---

[1] UNCTAD, *Bilateral Investment Treaties 1995-2006*: *Trends in Investment Rulemaking*, United Nations, xi, 16-17 (2007).

[2] The only exception for the expending scope of "investors" is that since the objective criteria used may include investors to whom a party would not wish to extend the treaty protection, some BITs themselves include "denial of benefit clauses" allowing exclusion of investors in certain categories. For the definition and relevant practice of "denial of benefit clauses", see OECD, *Investment Law*, *Understanding Concepts and Tracking Innovations*, *Companion Volume to International Investment Perspectives*, OECD, 18, 28-33 (2008).

II. 3 Right of Establishment

Traditionally BITs recognize that foreign investors have no absolute right to entry to host state. On the contrary, it is up to host state to regulate the conditions for admission and only investments which have been properly admitted are entitled to benefit from the provisions of the BIT.[1] In practice foreign investment admission in BITs refers to general provisions on the investment from one contracting party to enter to the other contracting party, reflecting generally the attitude or stance of host states to foreign investment. Two basic models are currently used:

(1) it makes the admission and establishment of foreign investment subject to the laws of host states (called "the admission clause" model), includes several regulations limiting the substantive and procedural protection of foreign investments and thereby preserves the sovereign right of host states to maintain national laws and regulations on the entry and operation of foreign investors in accordance with national development strategies; and

(2) it grants foreign investors a right of establishment, although not in an absolute manner (called "the right of establishment" model). While providing high levels of legal protection for foreign investors, liberal BITs limit host countries' regulatory discretion to restrict national laws and regulations on the entry and operation of foreign investors, particularly multinational enterprises (MNEs). The utilization of liberal BITs tends to lead to a more open and less regulated global investment regime.[2]

According to UNCTAD survey, BITs that "the admission clause" model which leave the contracting parties with discretion concerning the admission and establishment of foreign investors remain dominant. These BITs admit investment of investors from the other contracting party only if such investments conform to the host state's legislation. It allows the host state to apply any admission and screening mechanism for foreign investment that it may have in place and therefore to deter-

---

[1] Rudolf Dolzer, Margrete Stevens, *Bilateral Investment Treaties*, Martinus Nijhoff Publishers, 50 (1995).

[2] Axel Berger, China's New Bilateral Investment Treaty Programme: Substance, Rational and Implications for Investment Law Making, Paper for the American Society of International Law International Economic Law Group (ASIL IELIG) 2008 biennial conference "The Politics of International Economic Law: The Next Four Years", Washington, D. C., November 14-15, 2008.

mine the conditions on which foreign investment will be allowed to enter the country. Another implication of "the admission clause" model is that, regardless of whether the host state maintain any admission and screening mechanism for foreign investment—and unless the BIT states otherwise—there is no obligation on the part of host state to eliminate discriminatory legislation affecting the establishment of foreign investment. [1]

As product of investment liberalization, "the right of establishment" in BITs is becoming more frequent. This right is provided either through the granting of national treatment and MFN treatment or through the latter treatment only. It is subject to exceptions and reservations. These treaties restrict the screening powers of host states in the pre-establishment phase and their sovereignty in regulating the entry of foreign investors, leading to a liberalization of host states' regulatory systems. [2] The use of this approach was traditionally limited to BITs concluded by US and, after the mid-1990s when NAFTA had entered into force, to agreements concluded by Canada. However, during the last 10 years other nations, such as Japan, have also adopted this method. In fact, most developing states currently have to face and accept one of the two models due to the stances of their developed counterparties: one is "the admission clause" model with the European states; the other is "the right of establishment" model with US and Canada etc.

It is indicated that "the admission clause" model is very important for host states since they determine the degree of control that a state party has retained over the conditions on the basis of which investments are allowed into the host states. [3] On contrary, "the right of establishment" model, which restricts or even abolishes the screening power on foreign investment of host states and seeks for the objective of investment liberalization, clear meets and serves the needs and interests of

---

[1] UNCTAD, *Bilateral Investment Treaties 1995-2006: Trends in Investment Rulemaking*, United Nations, xi, 21-22 (2007).

[2] Axel Berger, China's New Bilateral Investment Treaty Programme: Substance, Rational and Implications for Investment Law Making, Paper for the American Society of International Law International Economic Law Group (ASIL IELIG) 2008 biennial conference "The Politics of International Economic Law: The Next Four Years", Washington, D. C., November 14-15, 2008.

[3] Rudolf Dolzer, Margrete Stevens, *Bilateral Investment Treaties*, Martinus Nijhoff Publishers, 51 (1995).

developed capital-exporting states and their overseas investors. [1] It also reflects that the traditional unilateral investment protection has gradually moved to unilateral investment liberalization which is further unilateral benefit to developed capital-exporting states and their overseas investors.

Ⅱ. 4 Extensive Application of Fair and Equitable Treatment

BITs aims at decreasing the political or non-commercial risks[2] by establishing the standards of treatment relating to transnational investments with legal effect. They usually include one or several general principles that, together or individually, are intended to provide overall criteria by which to judge whether the treatment given to an investment and/or investor is satisfactory, and to help interpret and clarify how more specific provisions should be applied in particular situations. These provisions are typical substantive protection for covered investment and investors of BITs. [3]

There are a variety of standards of treatment provided for in BITs. They would usually contain one article on treatment standards but that article would identify several different treatment standards. [4]

There are two broad categories of standards in general practice of BITs. One is absolute treatment standards, including F & E treatment, full protection and security, and the minimum standard of treatment according to customary international law. [5]

---

[1] UNCTAD, *Bilateral Investment Treaties 1995-2006: Trends in Investment Rulemaking*, United Nations, xi, 21-26 (2007).

[2] Typical political risks includes risk of expropriation, currency risk, risk of political violence and breach of contract, for detailed discussion of political risks, see Paul E. Comeaux, N. Stephan Kinsella, *Protecting Foreign Investment under International Law*, *Legal Aspects of Political Risk*, Oceana Publications Inc., 1-22 (1997).

[3] UNCTAD, *Bilateral Investment Treaties 1995-2006: Trends in Investment Rulemaking*, United Nations, 28 (2007); Mary H. Mourra (ed.), *Latin American Investment Treaty Arbitration, the Controversies and Conflicts*, Wolters Kluwer, 169-171 (2009).

[4] US 2004 Model BIT takes a new approach that includes four Articles on investment treatment, namely Article 3: National Treatment, Article 4: Most-Favored-Nation Treatment, Article 5: Minimum Standard of Treatment and Article 8: Performance Requirement. The prohibition on performance requirement attempts to ensure that investments are made in accordance with commercial aims, not a State's promotion of protectionist or other policy goals. See Mary H. Mourra (ed.), Latin American Investment Treaty Arbitration, the Controversies and Conflicts, *Wolters Kluwer*, 170 (2009). US 2012 Model BIT remains the same in this regard.

[5] There are many comments and related practice on these absolute standards, especially on F& E treatment. See Alberto Alvarez-Jimenez, Minimum Standard of Treatment of Aliens, Fair and Equitable Treatment of Foreign Investors, Customary International Law and the Diallo Case before the International Court of Justice, 9 (1) *The Journal of World Investment & Trade*, 51-70 (2008); Mary H. Mourra (ed.), *Latin American Investment Treaty Arbitration, the Controversies and Conflicts*, Wolters Kluwer, 170-171, 188-190 (2009); Paul E. Comeaux, N. Stephan Kinsella, *Protecting Foreign Investment under International Law*, *Legal Aspects of Political Risk*, Oceana Publications Inc., 105-106 (1997).

Absolute treatment means that each party must treat investment from the other party fairly and equitably, and in accordance with international law, regardless of how it investment from its own nationals or from third countries. The second is relative treatment standards, mainly referring to national treatment and MFN treatment. Both impose an obligation to provide "non-discriminatory" treatment. [1]

It is pointed out that though the BITs between developed states and developing states contemplate a two-way flow of investments between contracting parties to the treaties, it is usually only a one-way flow that is contemplated and feasible in reality in the context of disparities of wealth and technology between the two parties. As a result of the "one-way flow", only developed capital-exporting states and their overseas investors gain benefit from the high level of standards on treatment of investment in BITs.

New development on foreign investment treatment is reflected particularly in the extensive adoption and application of F & E treatment in BITs. [2] The origin of F & E treatment clause seems to date back to the treaty practice of US in the period of FCN. Subsequent international model drafts for international investment agreements (IIAs) have continued to rely on the clause. [3] F & E treatment has emerged as perhaps the most important standard of treatment in IIAs. The term F & E treatment has its provenance in post-World War II. F & E treatment clauses appear in most IIAs. Further, even where there is no such express clause in the IIA, the standard is likely to be applicable based on an MFN clause. IIA tribunals have interpreted F & E treatment as providing a wide range of procedural and substantive protections, including the protection of legitimate expectation. Given the breadth of the treatment standard, claims of a breach of F & E treatment can succeed where claims under more specific standards might fail. [4] In current litigation practice, hardly any

---

[1]　Mary H. Mourra (ed.), *Latin American Investment Treaty Arbitration, the Controversies and Conflicts*, Wolters Kluwer, 169-170 (2009).

[2]　For the detailed analysis on F& E treatment clause, see Rudolf Dolzer, Fair and Equitable Treatment: A Key Standard in Investment Treaties, 39 *The International Lawyer*, 87-106 (2005).

[3]　Rudolf Dolzer, Fair and Equitable Treatment: A Key Standard in Investment Treaties, 39 *The International Lawyer*, 89 (2005).

[4]　Andrew Newcombe, Lluis Paradell, *Law and Practice of Investment Treaties, Standards of Treatment*, Wolters Kluwer, 255-298 (2009).

lawsuit based on an IIA is filed without invocation of F & E treatment clause.[1] Nearly all recent BITs require that investments and investors covered under the treaty receive F & E treatment, in spite of the fact that there is no general agreement on the precise meaning of this phrase.[2]

Some debate has taken place over whether reference to F & E treatment is tantamount to the minimum standard required by international law or whether the principle represents an independent, self-contained concept.[3] The issue has great implication for foreign investors and host states, particularly in ISDS.

According to some scholars, the obligation to grant foreign investment F & E treatment is not different from the obligation to treat the investment in accordance with the international minimum standard. The latter, so it is argued, is part of customary international law, which in turn comprises a bundle of international legal principles. In the views of some developed states, there is close links among F & E treatment, full protection and security and international minimum standards. These three treatment standards might be interpreted and supplemented one another.[4]

During the period from 1995 to 2006, the content of F & E treatment standard has been mostly contested in NAFTA's Chapter 11 arbitrations, where arbitral tribunals were called upon in several cases to address the scope and content of NAFTA's Article 1105. Tribunal interpretations varied, which added to the fact that some of the interpretations of this provision were strongly opposed by all contracting parties. This prompted the intervention of NAFTA Free Trade Commission. On 31 July 2001, this commission issued a Note of Interpretation stating that F & E treatment standard as set out in NAFTA's Article 1105 did not entail any treat-

---

[1] Rudolf Dolzer, Fair and Equitable Treatment: A Key Standard in Investment Treaties, 39 *The International Lawyer*, 87 (2005).

[2] According to the UNCTAD survey on 1995-2006 BIT practice, while most BITs include the standard of F& E treatment—sometimes combined with the principle of full protection and security and/or the international minimum standard—only a small fraction of them clarify the meaning of this provision. Different approaches are in use—for example, a statement that F& E treatment does not mean more than what is prescribed by customary international law, a reference to international law, or the linkage of F& E treatment principle to non-discriminatory treatment.

[3] Rudolf Dolzer, Margrete Stevens, *Bilateral Investment Treaties*, Martinus Nijhoff Publishers, 58-59 (1995).

[4] The "full protection and security" standard requires the host state not only not to attack the facilities or personnel of the investor, but to defend the investor or investment against others, including, for instance, rebel force. See Andreas F. Lowenfeld, *International Economic Law*, Second Edition, Oxford University Press, 558-559 (2008).

ment beyond that established by customary international law. [1] Considering the influence of US in the commission, we might see that even US, as the largest developed capital-exporting state in the world, also denies the expending interpretation of F & E treatment.

On contrary some scholars pointed out that the concept of F & E treatment is new territory discovered essentially in the late 1990's. It has been contained in treaties and other documents for some time but has only been applied in arbitral practice recently. [2] The treatment means something different from the international minimum standard[3] and should be given its plain meaning. This results in a case-bycase application of a test based on equity in order to determine whether the standard has been infringed. [4] At a minimum, F & E treatment means no discrimination by nationality or origin, in respect of such matters as access to local courts and administrative bodies, applicable taxes, and administration of governmental regulations. [5] It is a broad, overarching standard that contains various elements of protection, including those elements commonly associated with the minimum standard of treatment, the protection of legitimate expectations, non-discrimination, transparency and protections against bad faith, coercion, threats and harassment. [6] In fact F & E treatment has been applied successfully in a number of contexts.

---

[1] UNCTAD, *Bilateral Investment Treaties 1995-2006: Trends in Investment Rulemaking*, United Nations, 29-30 (2007).

[2] C. H. Schreuer, Investment Arbitration—A Voyage of Discovery, 2 (5) *Transnational Dispute Management*, 9 (2005).

[3] F. A. Mann argues that the introduction of the concept of the "international minimum standard" serves no purpose, and indicates that: "the terms 'fair and equitable treatment' envisage conduct which goes far beyond the minimum standard and afford protection to a greater extent and according to a much more objective standard than any previously employed form of words. A tribunal would not be concerned with a minimum, maximum or average standard. It will have to decide whether in all the circumstances the conduct in issue is fair and equitable or unfair and inequitable. No standard defined by other words is likely to be material. The terms are to be undersood and applied independently and autonomously." See Rudolf Dolzer, Margrete Stevens, *Bilateral Investment Treaties*, Martinus Nijhoff Publishers, 59 (1995).

[4] UNCTAD, *Bilateral Investment Treaties 1995-2006: Trends in Investment Rulemaking*, United Nations, xii, 28-33 (2007).

[5] See Andreas F. Lowenfeld, *International Economic Law*, Second Edition, Oxford University Press, 556-557 (2008).

[6] For detailed analysis of those elements of F & E treatment in practice, see Andrew Newcombe, Lluis Paradell, *Law and Practice of Investment Treaties, Standards of Treatment*, Wolters Kluwer, 279-298 (2009); C. H. Schreuer, Investment Arbitration-A Voyage of Discovery, Transnational Dispute Management, Vol. 2, Issue 5, November 2005, p. 9; Jeswald W. Salacuse, Towards a Global Treaty on Foreign Investment: The Search for a Grand Bargain, in Norbert Horn (ed.), *Arbitrating Foreign Investment Disputes*, Kluwer Law International, 83 (2004).

It is indicated that documents prepared on the multilateral level in the 1970s and 1980s by the developing states, or under their dominant influence, such as Charter of Economic Rights and Duties of States and Asian-African Legal Consultative Committee Revised Draft of Model Agreements for Promotion and Protection of Investments, contains no reference to F & E treatment standard. [1]

Essentially, the purpose of F & E treatment clause as used in BIT practice is to fill gaps which may be left by the more specific standards, in order to obtain the level of investor protection intended by the treaties. Some treaties even directly tie the clause to the fundamental goal of legal stability. [2] It is general accepted that the broad purpose of this clause is to provide a basic and general standard which is detached from the host state's domestic law. All these elements of the "independent clause" explanation on F & E treatment relate to acts of host states and impose heavy obligations and responsibility on host states. It is obvious that according to the "independent clause" explanation, host states have to undertake more obligations and responsibilities than the treatment established by customary international law, which is even unacceptable for the developed capital-exporting states like U. S. etc. in related practice in the position of host state. For the developing capital-importing states, F & E treatment clause with the "independent clause" explanation is new and heavy obligations of investment protection in addition to the traditional national treatment and MFN treatment.

II. 5 Extensive Adoption of Hull Formula

The standard of compensation for expropriation continued to be a source of significant disagreement in the post World War II era. The most important, and historically the most contested requirement, is the standard of compensation. Hull formula, representing the stance of most developed countries, insists that "adequate, effective and prompt payment for the properties seized" are required under international law, while developing countries propose the standard of "appropriate"

---

[1]　Rudolf Dolzer, Fair and Equitable Treatment: A Key Standard in Investment Treaties, 39 *The International Lawyer*, 89 (2005).

[2]　For instance, the US-Argentina BIT of 1991 provides in the preamble that "fair and equitable treatment of investment is desirable in order to maintain a stable framework". See Rudolf Dolzer, Fair and Equitable Treatment: A Key Standard in Investment Treaties, 39 *The International Lawyer*, 90 (2005).

compensation. [1]

The UNCTAD survey indicates that one of the most salient trends among recent BITs is that most BITs include language that has the effect of applying the standard of prompt, adequate and effective compensation, based on the market or genuine value of the expropriated investment. Some BITs between developing countries, like Egypt-Thailand BIT, also have similar compensation provisions. The differences among BITs now focus on the level of specificity with which concrete issues related to compensation are addressed, including applicable interest, currency in which compensation has to be paid, and risk of devaluation, etc. [2] In practice the provisions on compensation for expropriation of BITs typically address four issues: (1) the standard of compensation and valuation methods; (2) the date for determining compensation; (3) convertibility and transferability; and (4) payment of interest. In addition, some BITs have provisions for a right to judicial review of expropriations. [3]

It is noticeable that there is a case of interpreting "appropriate compensation" as "full compensation" in the early 1980s. In the Government of Kuwait v. American Independent Oil Company (AMINOIL), the tribunal applied international law, as chosen by the parties, to resolve the disputes. The tribunal then found that the appropriate level of compensation was "appropriate compensation" for a "lawful expropriation", which was to be determined by an inquiry into all the circumstances surrounding the case. This value, however, was determined by the tribunal to be the depreciated replacement value of the fixed assets and the going concern value of the enterprise, all adjusted with interest and for inflation. [4]

Furthermore case studies indicate that IIA tribunals have separately interpreted

---

[1] For the history and the competing norms on the standards of compensation, see M. Sornarajah, *The International Law on Foreign Investment*, 2nd edition, Cambridge University Press, 435-488 (2004); Paul E. Comeaux, N. Stephan Kinsella, *Protecting Foreign Investment under International Law*, *Legal Aspects of Political Risk*, Oceana Publications Inc., 81-98 (1997); Andrew Newcombe, Lluis Paradell, *Law and Practice of Investment Treaties*, *Standards of Treatment*, Wolters Kluwer, 18, 369 (2009); Mary H. Mourra (ed.), *Latin American Investment Treaty Arbitration*, *the Controversies and Conflicts*, Wolters Kluwer, 23-28 (2009).

[2] UNCTAD, *Bilateral Investment Treaties 1995-2006: Trends in Investment Rulemaking*, United Nations, 48-52 (2007).

[3] Andrew Newcombe, Lluis Paradell, *Law and Practice of Investment Treaties*, *Standards of Treatment*, Wolters Kluwer, 377 (2009).

[4] See Paul E. Comeaux, N. Stephan Kinsella, *Protecting Foreign Investment under International Law*, *Legal Aspects of Political Risk*, Oceana Publications Inc., 70-71 (1997).

the terms of "equivalent to the actual value", "prompt, adequate and effective compensation" (further defined as market value), "fair market value", "just compensation" (further defined as representing genuine value), "actual value" and "value" provided in different BITs, as requiring full compensation—in the sense of the fair market value of the expropriated investment. [1]

It seems that developing states have to face the highest standard of compensation in the history. Considering the expansive and broad definition of indirect expropriation, the issue is more serious than ever before for developing states.

It should be pointed out that the meaning of the standard of "appropriate" compensation is stated clear in the Charter of Economic Rights and Duties of States that "appropriated compensation paid……taking into account the relevant laws and regulations and all circumstance that the state considers pertinent". In the 1970s and 1980s, the standard of "appropriate" compensation prevails in theory and had some reflections in practice. Since 1990s, some developing states have changed their stance on foreign investment policies from regulation to encouragement due to specific needs for settling foreign debt crisis. In these situations, "Hull formula" seems to be popular in BIT practice and ISDS. It is noticeable that OECD Guidelines for Treatment of Foreign Direct Investment (1992) interprets "Hull formula" as "appropriate compensation". Although it is clear not correct explanation of the principle of "appropriate compensation" in the historical and practical aspects, to some extent it reflects the unilateral intention and effort of changing, mixing or replacing the meaning of "appropriate compensation" by some developed states.

II.6 Direct Right for Investors in ISDS

An efficient and comprehensive dispute resolution mechanism is considered as one of the key elements for constituting mutual confidence between contracting parties of the BITs. [2] Therefore dispute resolution mechanisms both for investment disputes and disputes between the contracting parties are main contents of the

---

[1] For the detailed technical issues on the compensation standards of expropriation, see Andrew Newcombe, Lluis Paradell, *Law and Practice of Investment Treaties, Standards of Treatment*, Wolters Kluwer, 384-398 (2009).

[2] Li Shishi, "On Bilateral Investment Agreements concluded by China" (in Chinese), 1990 *the Yearbook of Chinese International Law*, 121-122.

BITs.[1] In the BIT context, ISDS refers to the mechanism for settling a dispute between an investor of one contracting party and the other contracting party concerning an investment of the former in the area of the latter. The special nature of investment dispute is indicated to involve many aspects.[2]

According to the UNCTAD survey, a group of BITs have undertaken to address ISDS in greater detail, providing more guidance to the disputing parties concerning the conduct of arbitration and strengthening the rule orientation of adjudication mechanisms. However, the majority of BITs have continued with the traditional approach of only sketching out the main features of ISDS, relying on specific arbitration convention to regulate the details. Some new BITs have incorporated various innovative provisions directed at fostering several objectives, such as to provide greater predictability, promote judicial economy, ensure consistency of awards and promote the legitimacy of arbitration procedures within civil society.[3]

Many BITs make significant progress in the area of the resolution of investment disputes by specifying arbitration in a neutral forum as the method of resolution of these disputes. In standard international practice, investor-state arbitration is most often conducted under the rules of ICSID.[4] ICSID regime becomes the most popular dispute resolution mechanism provided in BITs. There are several different types of clauses creating different obligations as to such arbitration. At the lowest level, the clauses merely direct the parties to ICSID arbitration as a way of dispute settlement. At the highest level, the clauses entitle the foreign investor to initiate pro-

[1] Andrew Newcombe, Lluis Paradell, *Law and Practice of Investment Treaties, Standards of Treatment*, Wolters Kluwer, 65 (2009).

[2] Typically, it is indicated that: (1) the investment dispute will involve a sovereign as the defendant; (2) the foreign investor will challenge acts and measures taken by the sovereign State or a sub-entity thereof in its sovereign capacity. See United Nations Conference on Trade and Development, *Investor-State Disputes: Prevention and Alternatives to Arbitration*, UNCTAD Series on International Investment Policies for Development, United Nations, 10-12 (2010).

[3] UNCTAD, *Bilateral Investment Treaties 1995-2006: Trends in Investment Rulemaking*, United Nations, xiii (2007).

[4] For the latest development of investor-State arbitration under ICSID regime, see Mary H. Mourra (ed.), *Latin American Investment Treaty Arbitration, the Controversies and Conflicts*, Wolters Kluwer, 163-166 (2009); Andrew Newcombe, Lluis Paradell, *Law and Practice of Investment Treaties, Standards of Treatment*, Wolters Kluwer, 58-59 (2009).

ceedings by himself before an ICSID tribunal.[1]This is a breakthrough in international law in term of individual in international tribunals. Compared to traditional means of enforcing public international law through diplomatic protection granted by the investor's home state, this empowerment of private investor has accurately been described as a "change in paradigm in international investment law." Instead of depending on the discretion of its home state to grant diplomatic protection, these BITs provide the covered investors with a unilateral direct right to initiate arbitral proceedings against the host state which usually gives general and advance consent to ICSID regime.

The chief innovation that the BIT program brought to US foreign investment policy was a provision guaranteeing to an investor the right to arbitrate investment disputes directly with the host state and to obtain judicial enforcement of any resulting award in domestic courts—all without the involvement of the investor's own state in the dispute.[2]The effect of this innovation is to achieve so-called "depoliticization of foreign investment disputes".

It is indicated that BITs between developing states also adopt this approach. The China-Barbados BIT, signed in July 1998, can be described as a watershed as it was the first treaty to offer foreign investors unrestricted access to international arbitration. This pioneering provision on ISDS, which was adopted in 21 later BITs, marked the turning away from the first-generation BIT approach of restricted ISDS.[3]Such provisions on direct right to investors in investment dispute settlement deviate from the rights authorized to host states by international convention, including the right to "consent case by case", the right to require "the exhaustion of local remedies", the right to "apply the host states' laws", and the right to invoke the

---

[1] Until 1993, a majority of capital-importing States had not enter into a strong BIT—which contains dispute settlement provisions that allow foreign investors to initiate binding international arbitration against host State—with a major capital-exporting State. But by the end of the sample (2002), 117 out of the 149 developing countries—seventy-nine percent—had at least one strong BIT in force. See Jason Webb Yackee, Conceptual Difficulties in the Empirical Study of Bilateral Investment Treaties, 33 *Brooklyn J. Int'l L.*, 432-433 (2008).

[2] See Kenneth J. Vandevelde, *U.S. International Investment Agreements*, Oxford University Press, 2009, p. 27.

[3] Axel Berger, China's New Bilateral Investment Treaty Programme: Substance, Rational and Implications for Investment Law Making, Paper for the American Society of International Law International Economic Law Group (ASIL IELIG) 2008 biennial conference "The Politics of International Economic Law: The Next Four Years", Washington, D. C., November 14-15, 2008.

"exception for the state's essential security". [1]

One key concern for developing states is to increase their ability to manage the investor-state disputes effectively. Their vulnerability in this regard is based on their limited technical capacity to handle investment disputes coupled with the increase number of such disputes, the potentially high costs involved of conducting such procedures, and the potential impact of awards on the budgets and a country's reputation as an investment location. At the same time, the proper functioning of the dispute settlement system is dependent on well-informed partners. [2]Therefore technical assistance is necessary required to enable developing states to make effective and efficient use of dispute settlement systems in BITs.

It is suggested that another way of preventing investment disputes from emerging and reaching the international arbitration phase is by enhancing state-state cooperation on relevant matters. To a certain extent, communication and interaction among states on issues related to investment agreements and investment disputes have constituted common practice in the past, offering important lessons when considering approaches to making such practice more formal. [3]One of the practical ways for formalizing the practice is to add clauses on information exchanges and/or state-state joint commissions in BITs.

Ⅱ.7 General Comments

From the survey on the evolution of typical imbalanced clauses in BITs under the economic globalization, we might see clear general picture and the road map of BIT practice from "investment protection" to "stronger investment protection" and "investment liberalization". The traditional imbalance and/or un-equality of powers, rights and obligations between developed capital-exporting states and developing capital-importing states in BITs is firmly maintained and further extended.

---

[1] For the detailed comments on this regard, see An CHEN, Should the Four Great Safeguards in Sino-Foreign BITs Be Hastily Dismantled? Comments on Provisions concerning Dispute Settlement in Model U. S. and Canadian BITs, 7 (6) *The Journal of World Investment & Trade*, 899-933, (2006).

[2] James Zhan, Joerg Weber, etc. , Latest Developments in Investor-State Dispute Settlement, [IIA Monitor No. 4 (2005)], p. 7, Symposium Co-organized by ICSID, OECD and UNCTAD on Making the Most of International Investment Agreements: A Common Agenda, 12 December 2005, Paris.

[3] United Nations Conference on Trade and Development, *Investor-State Disputes: Prevention and Alternatives to Arbitration*, UNCTAD Series on International Investment Policies for Development, United Nations, 93 (2010).

Things will develop in the opposite direction when they become extreme. It is not likely that developed capital-exporting states can lead or drive the BITs at their unilateral will to further realizing the objectives of "stronger investment protection" and "investment liberalization". There are some direct reactions from developing states recently. Latin American States, home of the Calvo Doctrine, shifted their position on BITs and began signing BITs in the late 1980s. Over the past two decades, they have signed more than 500 BITs with countries around the world. [1] However, some Latin American states are reconsidering their new stance of BITs and terminating their BITs due to new situations. [2]

III. Seeking for Innovative Path of BIT Practice

The issue on imbalance and/or un-equality between developed states and developing states in traditional and existing BIT practice might be a common sight for states, peoples and international society to some extent.

For correcting the imbalance and un-equality of BIT practice and reconstructing the international investment order, states and international society have to reach consensus and seek for innovative path of BIT practice. The followings are three preliminary suggestions.

III. 1 Reaching Consensus by Concepts of "Balance", "Sustainable Development" and "Integration"

As a precondition of taking common practical actions, the international society, states and international lawyers should reach consensus based on the concepts of "balance", "sustainable development" and "integration" in seeking innovative path of BIT practice.

The title of World Investment Report (WIR) 2012, *Towards a New Generation*

---

〔1〕 See Mary H. Mourra (ed.), *Latin American Investment Treaty Arbitration*, *the Controversies and Conflicts*, Wolters Kluwer, 1 (2009).

〔2〕 In 2008, Ecuador terminated nine BITs—with Cuba, the Dominican Republic, El Salvador, Guatemala, Honduras, Nicaragua, Paraguay, Romania and Uruguay. Other denounced BITs include those between El Salvador and Nicaragua, and the Netherlands and the Bolivarian Republic of Venezuela. In 2010, Ecuador's Constitutional Court declared arbitration provisions of six more BITs (China, Finland, Germany, the UK, Venezuela and United States) to be inconsistent with the country's Constitution. It is possible that Ecuador will take action to terminate these (and possibly other) BITs. Wolfgang Alschner, Ana Berdajs, Vladyslav Lanovoy and Sergey Ripinsky etc., Denunciation of the ICSID Convention and BITs: Impact on Investor-State Claims, United Nations, UNCTAD, *IIA Issues Note*, No. 1, December 2010, page 1, note 3.

of Investment Policies, is very significant and encouraging for international lawyers in particular. It is the first time for WIR to pay such great attention and emphasis to the level of investment policy-making and policy-makers. Furthermore policy-making in this context includes foreign investment law making in domestic law aspect and investment treaty (mainly BIT) practice in international law aspect. The report states Investment Policy Framework for Sustainable Development (IPFSD). Indeed IPFSD is UNCTAD's great contributions to international governance on international investment. It indicates general direction for the development of investment policy. Among other things, it refers the concepts of "balance", "sustainable development" and "integration" as themes and key considerations of investment policy for international society, particularly investment policy makers.

Ⅲ. 1. i Concept of "Balance"

In BIT context, "balance" might be represented at different levels: First, "balance" might be represented in the relation between contracting parties of BITs and/or between one contracting party and third party, particularly relating to the powers, rights and obligations between/among developed capital-exporting states and developing capital-importing states, and relating to the rights and obligations between public authority and private interest, especially host states and foreign investors, and also between domestic investors and foreign investors. [1]"Balance" is especially needed for the BITs between developed states and developing states. A BIT between two developed states or two developing states with similar economic abilities, both of whose nationals expect to invest in the territory of the other, would be based on the notion of reciprocity and mutual protection. However, this bargain would not seem applicable in the context of a BIT between a developed state and a developing state whose nationals are unlikely to invest abroad. [2] Therefore for adjusting "unilateral benefit" situation, the considerations for "balance" are

---

[1] For example, in April 2011, the Australian Government issued a trade policy statement announcing that it would stop including ISDS clauses in its future IIAs. Explaining this decision, the Government stated that ISDS would give foreign businesses greater legal rights than domestic businesses and would constrain the Government's public policymaking ability (e. g. the adoption and implementation of social, environmental and economic law. See United Nations Conference on Trade and Development, *World Investment Report 2012*, *Towards a New Generation of Investment Policies*, United Nations, 87 (2012).

[2] Jeswald W. Salacuse, Nicholas P. Sullivan, Do BITs Really Work?: An Evaluation of Bilateral Investment Treaties and Their Grand Bargain, 46 *Harvard International Law Journal*, 77 (2005).

needed for two parties of the BITs.

Second, "balance" might be represented in the relation between aims of investment policy, for example, between protection and encouragement, between protection and regulation, and between economy and other public or social purpose of both contracting parties of BITs.

There are some innovative developments in this regards. Among the selected 20 IIAs signed in 2011, there are 17 IIAs with "detailed exceptions from the free-transfer-of-funds obligation, including balance-of-payments difficulties and/or enforcement of national laws", and "omission of the so-called 'umbrella' clause"; 12 IIAs with "fair and equitable treatment standard equated to the minimum standard of treatment of aliens under customary international law". These provisions indicate the "balance" of the rights and obligations between developed states and developing states, and the rights and obligations between host states and foreign investors to some extent. [1]

Ⅲ. 1. ii Concept of "Sustainable Development"

The concept or principle of "sustainable development" is universally accepted as a general rule for economic development and international relationship. It should be also adopted as general rule in BIT practice. In BIT context, the concept of "sustainable development" is definitely a win-win objective for both contracting parties. It meets the need of capital-importing states as it emphasizes the economic and social development of host states. It also benefit for foreign investors as it encourage the healthy investment climate. The concept should not only be applied to the relation of contracting parties of BITs, but also applied to the relation of host states and foreign investors, and also the development of BIT practice as a whole.

According to C. Schreuer, it is possible to identify certain features of an invest-

---

[1] The selected 20 IIAs signed in 2011 include United Republic of Tanzania-Turkey BIT, Nigeria-Turkey BIT, Mexico-Peru FTA, Republic of Korea-Peru FTA, Panama-Peru FTA, Japan-Papua New Guinea BIT, India-Slovenia BIT, India-Nepal BIT, India-Malaysia FTA, India-Lithuania BIT, India-Japan EPA, Guatemala-Peru FTA, Czech Republic-Sri Lanka BIT, Costa Rica-Peru FTA, Colombia-Japan BIT, China-Japan-Republic of Korea TIA, Central America-Mexico FTA, Bosnia and Herzegovina-San Marino BIT, Azerbaijan-Czech Republic BIT, and Australia-New Zealand Investment protocol. See Table III. 3. Examples of sustainable-development-friendly aspects of selected IIAs signed in 2011, United Nations Conference on Trade and Development, *World Investment Report 2012*, *Towards a New Generation of Investment Policies*, United Nations, 90 (2012).

ment under the ICSID Convention on the basis of ICSID case-law. One of the typical features of an investment is that the operation should be significant for the host state's development. The preamble of ICSID Convention speaks of "the need for international cooperation for economic development and the role of private international investment therein". It may be argued that there should be some positive impact on development.[1]The Convention does not define the term investment. It is, however, possible to identify certain typical characteristics of investment under the Convention which have been increasingly used by arbitral tribunals: (i) duration of the project; (ii) regularity of profit and return; (iii) risk for both sides; (iv) a substantial commitment; and (v) the operation should be significant for the host state's development.[2]

There are some important developments of BIT and IIA practice on "sustainable development" in recent years. In fact, more and more BITs include this concept in the preamble.[3] A number of recent developments indicate that sustainable development elements are starting to play a more prominent role in investment policies. Among the selected 20 IIAs signed in 2011, there are 12 IIAs with "references to the protection of health and safety, labour rights, environment or sustainable development in the treaty preamble"; and 11 IIAs with "explicit recognition that parties should not relax health, safety or environmental standards to attract investment".[4] Several of these features are meant to ensure that the treaty does not interfere with, but instead contributes to, countries' sustainable development strategies that focus on inclusive economic growth, policies for industrial development,

---

[1] See OECD, *International Investment Law*, *Understanding Concepts and Tracking Innovations*, *Companion Volume to International Investment Perspectives*, OECD, 61 (2008).

[2] See OECD, *International Investment Law*, *Understanding Concepts and Tracking Innovations*, *Companion Volume to International Investment Perspectives*, OECD, 9 (2008).

[3] The preamble of most BITs states that "the need for international cooperation for economic development and the role of private international investment therein". According to the UNCTAD survey, an increasing number of preambles indicate that BITs do not purport to promote and protect investment at the expense of other key values such as health, safety, labor protection and environment. UNCTAD, *Bilateral Investment Treaties 1995-2006*: *Trends in Investment Rulemaking*, United Nations, 4 (2007).

[4] See Table III. 3. Examples of sustainable-development-friendly aspects of selected IIAs signed in 2011, United Nations Conference on Trade and Development, *World Investment Report 2012*, *Towards a New Generation of Investment Policies*, United Nations, 90 (2012).

and the environmental and social impacts of investment. [1]

Ⅲ. 1. iii Concept of "Integration"

The concept of "integration" is new in BIT context. It serves different purposes, particularly in the substantial and format aspects. First, it means the combination of host states' investment protection and foreign investors' liabilities for correcting the undue emphasis on protection for foreign investors without imposing necessary obligations on them. Second, considering that national and international policies must be considered in an integrated manner, and both need to evolve with a country's changing circumstances, [2] the concept of "integration" refers to the close linkage between BITs or other IIA instruments and national laws.

It is striking to find that, although foreign investors are real beneficiaries of BITs, their misconduct are hardly regulated in BITs. In terms of conduct of transnational corporation, OECD Guidelines on International Investment and Multinational Enterprises (2000 OECD Guidelines) is very close to 1984 Draft UN Code of Conduct on Transnational Corporation. To some extent they represent some general rules for regulating the conduct of foreign investors and may be considered to be included in BITs as an integrated part. [3]

---

〔1〕 In the IIA context, paying due regard to sustainable development implies that a treaty should (i) promote and protect those investments that are conducive to host state development; (ii) provide treatment and protection guarantees to foreign investors without hindering the host state's power to regulate in public interest (e. g. for environmental, public health or safety purposes); (iii) not overexpose a state to costly litigation and the risk of exorbitant financial liabilities; and (iv) stimulate responsible business practices by foreign investors. In addition, a number of other recent developments in investment policymaking indicate increased attention to sustainable development considerations. The typical example is that the U. S. 2012 Model BIT turns the best-endeavor Commitment not to relax domestic environmental and labour laws into a binding obligation. The Secretariat of the Commonwealth, a voluntary association of 54 countries, is preparing a handbook entitled "Integrating Sustainable Development into International Investment Agreement: A Guide for Developing Countries", which is designed to help developing states to negotiate IIAs that better promote sustainable development. For more examples and comments, see United Nations Conference on Trade and Development, *World Investment Report 2012*, *Towards a New Generation of Investment Policies*, United Nations, 89-92 (2012).

〔2〕 United Nations Conference on Trade and Development, *World Investment Report 2012*, *Towards a New Generation of Investment Policies*, United Nations, 161 (2012).

〔3〕 It is suggested that China-US BIT pioneer in regulating conduct of investors by incorporating some rules of 2000 OECD Guidelines or the Draft UN Code of Conduct on Transnational Corporation. Rules on conduct of investors in China US BIT may be designed in four ways: (i) declaratory way. For instance, the preamble of the BIT can provide that investors should contribute to economic, social, and environmental progress in host state; (ii) mandatory way. For instance, the BIT may require that investors carry their business abiding by host state's national laws, regulations, national and international-established practice relating to the protection of consumers, and the preservation of environment, etc.; (iii) prohibited way. For instance, the BIT may require that investors should not engage in any kind of bribery and corruption; and (iv) persuasive way. For instance, the BIT may require that investors shall make full use of local resources and personnel in undertaking substantial research activities. See Cai Congyan, China-US BIT Negotiations and the Future of Investment Treaty Regime: A Grand Bilateral Bargain with Multilateral Implications, 12 (2) *Journal of International Economic Law*, 495-496 (2009).

The concepts of "balance", "sustainable development" and "integration" are interactive and supplementary one another. As the result of emphasis on "balance" and "sustainable development", host states' public authority should be better respected and protected. Therefore, the "integration" for protection and regulation in BITs is logical. To some extent "balance" and "integration" are preconditions for "sustainable development". "Sustainable development" is a useful means and/or mark for "balance" and "integration".

In short, the concepts of "balance", "sustainable development" and "integration" are realization of principle of fair and mutual benefit with universal value. They should become the basic ideas and consensus of developed capital-exporting states and developing capital-importing states in designing and constructing new generation of BITs. All states, especially developing states have to make great efforts to promote and encourage the formation and establishment of the consensus. From the perspective of North-South issue, they are basic concepts for establishing new international investment order. Particularly China and other developing states should consistently insist on the concepts in BIT practice.

Ⅲ. 2 Drafting New BIT Model by States and International Organizations

Based on the concepts of "balance", "sustainable development" and "integration", the new model of BITs should be designed to serve for protection, promotion, and regulation of international investment, so as to realize the balanced powers, rights and interests between developed capital-exporting states and developing capital-importing states, and between host states and foreign investors. To these aims, developing states should enjoy absolute power on investment admission, performance requirement, etc. , and bear the obligations of protection for foreign investment in their territories. Developed states have to take the responsibilities for regulating their overseas investors and preventing host developing states from harm and/or damage caused by negative conducts of foreign investors, especially multinational corporations, while attaining the international legal protection for their overseas investment.

It is reported that in recent years, several states have either created or revised their model BITs (the Russian Federation in 2001 with an amendment in 2002, France in 2006, and Colombia, Mexico, Austria and Germany in 2008). Others are currently in the process of developing a new model BIT (Argentina, the Bolivarian Republic of Venezuela, Ecuador, Morocco, the Plurinational State of Bolivia, South Africa, Turkey, and US), and more states are planning a review process (Thailand and India with model BITs dating from 2002 and 2003, respectively). States usually review their model BITs to (i) establish clearer rules and ensure great precision in treaty-making; (ii) ensure consistency with the public interest and a state's overall economic agenda, including the host states' right to regulate in the public interest; (iii) seek a balance between protecting investors and the host states; and (iv) adjust the model BIT to new developments, such as the interpretations tribunals adopted in ISDS awards, and bring it up to date. [1] It seems that this model BIT practice by developed states and developing states reflects the concepts of "balance", "sustainable development" and "integration" to some extent.

After detailed studies, the WIR 2012's IPFSD provides an expert guidance for investment law and policy, namely the guidance for domestic policy and the reference for negotiations and evaluations of IIAs. Although IPFSD provide an important jurisprudence for future BIT practice, it is only an expert guidance sponsored by an international organization. Elements of International Investment Agreements: Policy Options (Policy Options) in the WIR 2012 is only a list of all the relative policy options of IIAs for "adapt and adopt" by each state, and certainly not a model of IIAs as a base of negotiation with great implication of treaty-making for the contracting parties. It still needs generally accepted guidance and common basis of BIT negotiations for all states, especially for developing states.

There is a precedent of Model BIT drafted by international organization. The Asian-African Legal Consultative Committee (AALCC) published a detailed model treaty with two variants in 1984. [2] It is evident that world-wide international organ-

---

[1] United Nations Conference on Trade and Development, *World Investment Report 2010*, *Investing in a Low-Carbon Economy*, United Nations, 85 (2010).

[2] The AALCC Model Treaty and its two variants are reprinted in 23 ILM 254 (1984). The AALCC prepared three draft model treaties in 1985. The provisions of model A are similar to those found in treaties between capital-importing and capital-exporting countries, with stronger emphasis however on the promotional aspect of the agreement. Model B contains a more restrictive attitude towards the protection of investments on the part of host countries. Model C is similar to model A but its applicability is restricted to specific classes of investments as determined by the host State. Rudolf Dolzer, Margrete Stevens, *Bilateral Investment Treaties*, Martinus Nijhoff Publishers, 5 (1995).

izations, especially UNCTAD and OECD, are more neutral and independent than individual state in preparing a model BIT with equal and balanced consideration for developed capital-exporting states and developing capital-importing states.

It has very important practical implication that international organizations, especially UNCTAD, draft a new model of BIT based on the concepts of "balance", "sustainable development" and "integration". In the content of the new model, developed capital-exporting states and developing capital-importing states have enjoyed equal powers, rights and interests and born equal, corresponding obligations and duties. For the balance of powers, rights and interests between developed states and developing states and between host states and foreign investors, BITs shall have objectives of protection, promotion and regulation for transnational investment. Developing states shall have powers on foreign investment admission, performance requirement, and assume the obligations for protecting foreign investment. Developed states should bear the responsibilities for regulating their overseas investors and investment, promising and protecting developing states from injures and/or damages of negative conducts of foreign investors, especially the multinational corporations. [1]

III. 3 Conducting New BIT Practice between Developing States

The BIT practice based on the concepts of "balance", "sustainable development" and "integration", contains and emphasizes the innovative contents on the "host states' power, rights and interests" and the "home states' and foreign investors' obligations and duties" in BIT practice. In current international regime, it is unrealistic to expect developed states to change their stance by their own and conduct voluntarily the sustainable-friendly BIT practice under the IPFSD in future. In the situation that developed states still insist on their traditional and liberal BIT practice based on their national interests, developing states how to conduct the BIT negotiations between themselves? Do they follow the developed states' model, or seek for a new way to conclude a new type of BIT? It seems that developing states do

---

[1] The obligations of multinational corporations include mainly the obligation not to interfere in domestic politics, obligations relating to human rights, liability for violations of environmental norms, and the obligation to promote economic development. See M. Sornarajah, *The International Law on Foreign Investment*, 2nd edition, Cambridge University Press, 171-181 (2004).

not pay much attention to the importance of creating and developing a new type of BIT from their own practice. Most of these BITs just follow the developed states' model. Some of them even follow the new developments of developed states' model, such as provisions on giving the investors' unilateral direct right to ICSID.

It should be pointed out that South-South cooperation has great implication in establishing new international economic order and new international investment norm. In the negotiation of BITs between two developing states, as equal partners with historical mission, common objectives and values, both contracting parties may constitute new international investment practice and norms in accordance with the principles established in the Charter of Economic Rights and Duties of States, IPFSD, and the innovative elements of Policy Options. The new international investment practice and norms in turn may have certain impacts on BITs between developed states and developing states and the trend of BITs as a whole. China, as the largest developing capital-importing and potential big capital-exporting state, should take more responsibilities and get something accomplished for innovation and development of BITs.

附:南方中心(South Centre)前秘书长格索维奇 (Branislav Gosovic)博士的评语

Dear Professor Huaqun Zeng, dear comrade and brother,

Thank you very much for your message and the enclosed article on BITs. I read it with great interest. I congratulate you on your excellent, scholarly work which should be of great usefulness to developing countries as they struggle with asymmetries and inequities of BITs, and represents an important contribution to the ongoing efforts to modify these instruments rooted in the neo-colonial age.

I have forwarded the article to the South Centre, and will send it to my old time colleagues who are still in UNCTAD. I will also send it to G77 in New York.

As the year of the goat celebrations approach, I am sure you will be going to your home town or village. Enjoy it!

With warm regards, fraternally

Branislav GOSOVIC

11/01/2015 (by email)

第二编
国际投资法的中国特色实践

导　言

本编主要研讨国际投资法领域的中国特色实践问题。国际投资法是调整国际投资活动的国内法规范和国际法规范的总称。在国内法规范层面,1979 年《中外合资经营企业法》是我国实行改革开放政策的重要标志,也是当时计划经济体制中的"飞地法"。相应地,中外合营企业的法律实务成为中国特色国际经济法的早期重要课题。第三章探讨中外合营企业的法律实务,分别探讨股权策略(第一节)、管理权分享(第二节)、管理机构(第三节)、事实控制(第四节)、技术转让(第五节)及合营者之间争端解决(第六节)等专题。第四章进一步探讨外商投资法律向"市场经济型"的发展(第一节)和对外资实行国民待遇原则的法律实践(第二节)等专题。在国际法规范层面,国际投资条约体制是主要规范。第五章探讨多边投资条约谈判前瞻(第一节)、变革期双边投资条约实践(第二节)、"可持续发展的投资政策框架"与我国的对策(第三节)、双边投资条约范本的演进与中国的对策(第四节)和中国与"一带一路"国家间投资条约实践的创新(第五节)等专题,评述我国参与国际投资条约实践的发展历程、基本立场及可能的革新贡献。

作者的主要观点:

(1) 关于中外合营企业的法律实务。合营企业作为自成一类的法律关系和组织,产生和发展于普通法系国家。在中外合营企业的法律实务中,应深入理解和掌握合营企业的法律概念与特征,依法作出有利于合营企业发展和维护合营各方合法权益的合同安排。

(2) 关于外商投资法"市场经济型"发展的重要意义。我国外商投资法的"市场经济型"发展适应了经济转型的新形势,其重要意义是促进和保障了外资的持续发展,对外资待遇产生了重要影响,推动了我国外资法体系的结构性调整,即由相对独立的"单纯"的外资法体系(即"飞地法"体系)转化为由专门性外资法与统一的经济法和民商法构成的"混合法"体系。

(3) 关于创建"共同发展导向"国际投资条约体制。半个多世纪以来,传统国际投资条约体制的路线图从"投资保护导向"发展为"投资自由化导向"，是"事实上资本输出国单方受益"体制。当下，改革传统国际投资条约体制已成国际共识。中国特色国际投资条约理论和实践可能的革新贡献是，创建"共同发展导向"国际投资条约体制。可以预见，在国际社会的共同努力下，经历渐进发展，"共同发展导向"国际投资条约实践必将成为各国普遍认同的、符合各国共同和长远利益的国际投资条约实践发展主流。

第三章
中外合营企业法律实务

第一节　跨国公司参与合资企业的股权策略浅析[*]

20世纪60年代以来,跨国公司越来越多地以合资企业作为其海外直接投资的形式。跨国公司采取不同股权策略的原因和股权比例的意义,是东道国合营者与跨国公司商定合资企业股权比例时首先应明确的问题。

一

各国跨国公司参与国际合资企业的态度不同。一般认为,美国跨国公司多数较不愿参与国际合资企业,尤其不愿居于少数股权者地位;日本跨国公司则较积极参与国际合资企业,也较常居于少数股权者地位;西欧跨国公司的态度介于美、日之间。一些资料也证实了上述观点。据统计,180个美国跨国公司在发展中国家的子公司中总数的46.3%是由母公司拥有全部股权,135个西欧跨国公司的相应数字为18.9%,而日本跨国公司的相应数字为6.1%。美国跨国公司在发展中国家接受少数股权地位的占21.5%,西欧跨国公司的相应数字为42.1%,日本跨国公司的相应数字为74.2%。[1]

应当指出,美、日跨国公司参与海外合资企业的不同态度不宜过分强调。美、日跨国公司在海外合资企业中股权占有情况的区别主要是由于它们进入海外投资市场的历史条件和所提供的技术不同而形成的。在中国这个投资市场向美、日同时开

---

　　[*]　原载《南开经济研究》1990年第5期。
　　〔1〕　See V. V. Ramanadham(ed.), *Joint Ventures and Public Enterprises in Developing Countries*, International Centre for Public Enterprises in Developing Countries, 1980, pp. 74-75.

放并对所引进的技术有同等要求的情况下，两者的区别就不会太大。据日本大和证券《就日中合营事业征询日本企业意识调查总结分析报告》透露，接受调查的 33 家日本企业对希望在中日合资企业中占多少出资比例问题的答复如下：希望占 100％的 3家，占 51％的 10 家，占 50％的 8 家，占 49％以下的 6 家，其他附带各种条件的 6 家。可见，除了附带各种条件的企业外，多数企业希望占 50％以上的出资比例。这与美国跨国公司的一般态度相差不远。

显然，仅根据某国跨国公司对合资企业的一般态度难以更确切地判断该国某跨国公司的股权策略。各跨国公司的股权策略取决于多方面的因素，试析如下：

（一）选择多数股权者地位的原因

从国际实践看，跨国公司在国际合资企业的股权比例安排中寻求多数股权者地位的原因主要是：

（1）协调跨国经营的需要。跨国公司一般实行有计划的全球经营战略，因此，众多子公司和分公司之间的协调对于跨国公司集团通常具有重要的意义。这种协调的需要程度因行业而异。例如，The Unilever 集团主要生产食用油等，产品大部分销往发展中国家，在多数情况下，该集团的子公司和分公司之间没有进行什么交易，因此，在国际合资企业中居于少数股权者地位不致影响该集团跨国经营的协调。而在电子行业的跨国公司中，生产通常是高度专业化，并包含了非常复杂和迅速变化的技术，最终产品销往不同的市场，显然需要较高度的跨国经营协调。

另一方面，由于不同的跨国公司集团具有不同的经营方式，即使同一行业，也可能有不同的跨国经营的协调方式。例如，荷兰菲力浦（Philips）集团认为，在电子行业中，拥有国际合资企业多数股权以便取得表决权优势并非其实现跨国经营协调的必备条件。该集团自信能使当地合营者服从其全球经营战略。而美国国际商务机器公司（IBM）则认为，为了跨国经营的协调，拥有全部股权的子公司是适应其生产要求的最佳方式。[1]

（2）协调跨国销售的需要。在世界各地设立生产性子公司或销售机构的跨国公司集团一般力图避免其子公司或分公司生产或销售的产品之间发生竞争。因此，在许多国际合资企业合同中包含了限制合资企业产品出口以防止此类竞争的条款。跨国公司有时将拥有合资企业多数股权视为签订和保障上述限制出口条款的手段。跨国公司凭借其多数股权者地位，可在上述条款签订后抵制修改。[2]

---

〔1〕 See Wolfgang G. Friedmann, Jean-Pierre Beguin, *Joint International Business Ventures in Developing Countries*, Columbia University Press, 1971, pp. 382-384.

〔2〕 Ibid., p. 370.

（3）保护技术的需要。跨国公司如向其海外合资企业转让母公司特有的、非成熟的、在短期内可能改变的技术，为了保障对其技术的控制，也可能要求拥有多数股权。在一些化学和制药公司中，尤其如此。例如，默克公司（Merck & Co. Inc.）实际上通过拥有多数股权来保护其转让给印度境内合资企业的专利和专有技术[1]。由于保护技术的需要程度不同，同一跨国公司可能根据不同产品所包含的技术而采取不同的股权策略。一些化工、医药公司在设立生产特殊产品（如具有专利权的药品）的国际合资企业中，要求拥有多数股权，而在设立生产一般产品（如塑料等）的国际合资企业中，则接受少数股权者地位。[2]

（4）"转移定价"的需要。跨国公司如在国际合资企业拥有多数股权，就可以通过母公司或其分支机构同该合资企业的交易获取较大利益。例如，跨国公司向该合资企业销售机器、部件、零件或原料时，可以利用其在该合资企业的多数股权者地位定价，取得高额利润。[3] 母公司与其参股的国际合资企业之间的交易比之母公司与其海外独资公司之间的交易表面上更具有"非内部交易"的性质，因此，有利于进行"转移定价"。[4]

（5）归类于子公司的需要。一些发达国家，如美国、英国，将本国公司拥有多数股权的海外合资企业归类于子公司。子公司财产可合并于母公司的资产负债表，其结果将直接影响母公司股票交易信用程度的变化。[5]

（6）筹资的需要。一些外国金融机构或国际金融机构经常以由外国合营者控制国际合资企业的财务和管理作为贷款给该合资企业的条件。例如，美国银行向海外合资企业提供长期贷款的明确要求是，美国合营方应负责该合资企业的日常经营管理。为了确保此类管理权，外国合营者经常需要以拥有多数股权为基础。[6]

（二）接受少数股权者地位的原因

在分析跨国公司在国际合资企业中居于少数股权者地位的原因时，一些西方学者提出了"自愿的（voluntary）少数股权参与"和"强制的（compelled）少数股权参与"的区别。前者是合营各方自愿协商的产物，后者则是东道国法律、政策等强制因素

---

〔1〕 See Wolfgang G. Friedmann, Jean-Pierre Beguin, *Joint International Business Ventures in Developing Countries*, Columbia University Press, 1971, p. 368.

〔2〕 Ibid., p. 267.

〔3〕 Ibid., pp. 369-370.

〔4〕 See Paul W Beamish, The Characteristics of Joint Ventures in Developed and Developing Countries, *Columbia Journal of World Business*, Autumn 1985, pp. 13-14.

〔5〕 See Wolfgang G. Friedmann, Jean-Pierre Beguin, *Joint International Business Ventures in Developing Countries*, Columbia University Press, 1971, p. 381.

〔6〕 Ibid., pp. 381-382.

的后果。实际上,跨国公司居于少数股权者地位的最后抉择通常是多方面因素交互作用的结果,这些因素大致包括:

(1) 东道国法律政策因素。东道国的外资法律政策不同程度地影响了国际合资企业的股权比例安排。一般而言,发展中国家的有关法律政策鼓励或要求外国投资者采取国际合资企业这种投资形式。西方学者有关国际合资企业设立原因的一项抽样调查表明,在发达国家中,17%的国际合资企业是东道国法律政策要求的结果;而在发展中国家中,57%的国际合资企业因东道国法律政策要求而设立。另一项在发展中国家的抽样调查研究也得出了类似结论,即近一半的国际合资企业是东道国法律政策要求的结果。[1] 尽管如此,在发展中国家,有关法律政策"强制"外国合营者居于少数股权者地位的为数不多。

(2) 减少投资风险。在一些发展中国家投资,需要冒一定的非商业性风险,如国有化、外汇管制、税率提高或货币贬值等。因此,一些跨国公司宁愿居于少数股权者地位以图减少此类风险。例如,法国雷诺汽车公司(Renault)是出口型企业,由于在海外经营活动中曾遭受资本和利润转移的风险,对海外投资持消极态度。然而,根据一些国家的有关法律政策,雷诺如要向它们出口机器、汽车部件或其他类型的汽车,必须在它们境内设立国际合资企业。这些国家的法律政策与雷诺力图减少海外投资风险的意愿达成的妥协就是少数股权参与的方式。一些外国投资者认为,居于少数股权者地位有利于其在可预见的风险发生之前退出国际合资企业。[2]

(3) 节省资金和人员。即使是大跨国公司,在资金和管理人员方面也会有一定的限制。因此,一些跨国公司在资金和人员短缺的情况下,愿意在国际合资企业中居于少数股权者地位,并由当地合营者承担主要管理责任。如在美国凯泽铝业化学公司(Kaiser Aluminum & Chemical Corporation)与印度伯拉公司(Birla Corporation)设立的合资企业中,美方以现金和技术投资方式取得26%的股权,同时相信印方合营者能有效管理该企业,只派遣少数美方雇员。[3]

(4) 取得当地企业的"认同"。一些有经验的西方投资者指出,在国际合资企业中居于少数股权者地位具有补偿性利益。作为少数股权者,外国投资者可以避免采用繁琐的"保护少数股权者程序"(procedure of minority protection)的责任,也不会被指责为单方控制了合资企业。外国投资者居于少数股权者地位的重要法律后果

〔1〕 See Paul W Beamish, The Characteristics of Joint Ventures in Developed and Developing Countries, *Columbia Journal of World Business*, Autumn 1985, pp. 13-14.

〔2〕 See Wolfgang G. Friedmann, Jean-Pierre Beguin, *Joint International Business Ventures in Developing Countries*, Columbia University Press,1971, p. 381.

〔3〕 Ibid., pp. 381-382.

还在于,其参与设立和经营的合资企业可归类于"国内企业",因此规避了适用于外资企业的立法和行政措施。美国一些大跨国公司主要基于上述原因,在其海外合资企业中接受少数股权者地位。如美国人造丝公司(the Celanese Corporation of American)和杜邦公司(du Pont)在设立于墨西哥的合资企业中,就只拥有少数股权。[1]

二

根据各国公司法的一般原则,股权是公司管理权的基础,拥有较高的股权比例,一般将在公司的股东大会和董事会中取得较高的代表权和表决权。然而,由于国际合资企业通常是根据合资各方之间的契约性文件(即合资企业合同、协议和章程等)设立的,在不违反东道国有关法律的情况下,也可能有与股权比例不相称的表决权安排。国际合资企业 FRIA 的"十倍表决权的股权"(decuple-vote shares)就是典型一例:FRIA 是 1957 年根据法属几内亚(现几内亚共和国)法律设立的提炼铝土矿的国际合资企业。在设立该企业时,合营各方决定,各方拥有的股权比例应同其购买该企业产品的比例一致。这意味着,法国合营者 Peching 公司和 Ugine 公司总共拥有合资企业的 26.5% 股权。法国合营者认为,尽管合营对方奥林. 马西林公司(Olin Mathieson)拥有近 50% 的合资企业股权,鉴于当地政治条件,它们必须控制 FRIA。为此,该合资企业先将股份分为 A、B 两类,A 类股份各具有一票表决权,B 类股份各具有十票表决权,然后,分配足够的 B 类股份给法国合营者以保证其控制表决权的需要。[2]

其实,即使不作如上特殊安排,按一股一票表决权的一般原则,合营各方对合资企业的管理控制也并非自动地由其拥有的股权比例决定。许多因素可能使合营各方拥有的股权比例同其本应具有的管理控制权分离。

第一,在现代公司中,具有表决权的股份如分散于大量的个人或小团体的股东,大股东不需要拥有多数股权就可实际控制公司的经营。这种情况同样存在于由不同国籍合营者拥有股份的国际合资企业。墨西哥金伯利-克拉克公司(Kimberly-Clark)的股权比例变化及其后果有助于说明这个问题:1962 年以前,美国金伯利-克拉克公司拥有墨西哥金伯利-克拉克公司的全部股权。1962 年,该公司通过墨西哥国家财政部将其 40% 的股份出售给墨西哥公众。1973 年,由于墨西哥外资法律要

---

[1] See Wolfgang G. Friedmann, George Kalmanoff, *Joint International Business Ventures*, Columbia University Press, 1961, pp. 267-268.

[2] Note, International Joint Venture Corporations: Drafting of Control Arrangement, *Duke Law Journal*, Vol. 1963, No. 3, p. 519.

求，在国际合资企业中墨西哥人应拥有多数股权，墨西哥金伯利-克拉克公司允许墨西哥人在该公司的股权比例增至 53％，同时决定将股份分为普通股和记名股。普通股占公司全部股份的 53％，持股人限于墨西哥人。记名股占公司全部股份的 47％，持股人限于外国人（由美国金伯利-克拉克拥有 43％，余下 4％ 由其他外国投资者拥有）。由于墨方拥有的 53％ 股份分散于 1200 多个当地投资者，美方虽然居于少数股权者地位，实际上保持了其在该公司的支配地位。[1]

第二，在国际合资企业中，关键问题不在于合营各方拥有股权的多寡，而在于哪一方实际控制了公司的活动。在一些实例中，当地合营者只充当公司红利的分享者，或者只在形式上定期参加董事会会议，而把实际管理权交给外国合营者。另一方面，外国合营者，特别是跨国公司在居于少数股权者地位的情况下，可能凭借其人员配备、技术或销售等方面的优势，对国际合资企业实行事实控制。[2]

三

综上所述，跨国公司出于协调跨国经营和销售、保护技术、转移定价、归类于子公司以及便利筹资等需要，在国际合资企业中寻求多数股权者地位；而由于希望减少投资风险、节省资金和人员以及取得当地企业的"认同"等，愿意接受少数股权者地位。可见，跨国公司由其生产、销售、技术、资金等因素决定，各有参与国际合资企业的股权策略，需要具体了解和分析，才能恰到好处地作出符合合营各方利益的股权比例安排。与此同时，在国际合资企业的契约性文件中，还须依据合营各方的股权比例作出分享管理权力的规定，以利维护合营各方的应有权益。

---

[1]　See OCEANA，*Multinational Corporations Law*，B13—B32，Case Studies of Joint International Business Ventures，OCEANA，1982，pp. 141-146.

[2]　参见曾华群：《合资企业的事实控制问题》，载《法学研究》1987 年第 2 期。

第二节　中外合营企业管理权分享探讨[*]

合营各方分享管理权,是合资企业的重要特征之一,也是合营各方实现各自目标的基本保障。

在已建立的中外合资企业中,还存在较严重的合资不合营的现象。据1983年初的统计,在27%左右的中外合资企业中,外国投资者没有直接参与管理。合资不合营,不仅可能使已作投资的外国投资者对再投资和技术引进兴味索然,还可能使即将来投资的外国投资者趑趄不前。道理很明白,外国投资者不愿将其资金和技术投入既不能有效参与管理、又要承担风险的企业。另一方面,由中方单独经营也不利于实现合资企业的预期目标,因为在经营(特别是海外经营)方面,没有发挥外方积极作用,不仅难以学到外国先进管理技术,而且不能取得较好的经济效益。因此,管理权分享是否落实,事关合资企业成败,不可等闲视之。

《中华人民共和国中外合资经营企业法》(以下简称《中外合资法》)只对中外合资企业的组织形式、权力和行政机构作一些原则规定,又由于我国至今尚未颁布公司法等专门法规,所以,管理权分享的具体安排需要合营各方自行商定。这种安排不仅要寻求合营各方管理权力合情合理的分配,还要保障具有较高的工作效率。因此,在中外合资企业合同中需要详细规定合营各方如何分享管理权,包括有关董事名额分配、董事会议事规则和总经理副总经理的委任等具体安排。

一、董事名额分配问题

董事会是中外合资企业的最高权力机构,合营各方分享管理权,基本上是通过董事会的工作实现的。董事名额的多寡与是否拥有表决权优势直接关联。因此,董事名额的分配,是合营各方分享管理权具体安排的重要问题。

《中华人民共和国中外合资经营企业法实施条例》(以下简称《实施条例》)第34条规定:"董事名额的分配由合营各方参照出资比例协商确定"。由于是"参照","协商",可以理解为董事名额的分配不一定完全反映出资比例的安排。例如,出资比例50∶50的合资企业(以下简称50∶50合资企业)不一定组成董事名额相等的董事会,出资比例25∶75的合资企业不一定组成董事名额比例为1∶3的董事会。

董事名额的分配应注意保障少数股权者的代表权。即使按照出资比例,少数股

＊　原载《法学评论》1985年第5期。

权者无法派出在董事会的代表（例如少数股权者出资比例为5％，合资企业董事会由3或5人组成），一般也应分配给少数股权者任命董事的名额。由于《中外合资法》没有规定外资比例上限，外国学者估计，中国合营者在居于少数股权地位时，也会像西方合营者在东欧那样要求平等的代表权。事实表明，中国合营者并无此意，而只是要求各方都有一定的代表权。各方代表权不一定相等。一般情况下，多数股权者所分配的董事名额较多，少数股权者较少。

在中外合资企业中，由于有了《实施条例》第36条的规定，合营各方拥有对该条所列重大问题的否决权，管理权分享已得到基本保障。在此情况下，防止产生僵局较为重要，应尽量消除可能导致僵局的因素。因此，董事名额的分配，以不对等为宜，即使50∶50合资企业也应争取如此。如果50∶50合资企业双方不能就名额多寡达成协议，似可采取定期轮换方式。例如，在7人组成的董事会中，第一届董事会甲方委派4人，乙方委派3人；第二届董事会由乙方委派4人，甲方委派3人，如此循环。

董事名额分配之后进一步的问题是由谁担任董事。董事一般由合营各方委派，被委派者可以是该合营方人员，也可以是该合营方之外的其他人员。如南斯拉夫合资企业共同业务机构的南合营者代表包括了银行官员、律师等。在中外合资企业中，由中方委派的董事有的是主管部门负责人，有的是当地政府官员。西方投资者认为，虽然当地政府官员参与合资企业可能给合资企业带来一些好处，如可从政府机构取得所需要的许可证批准等，但"经常发现的缺陷是政府参与者缺乏商业经验"，"政府参与合资企业决策可能具有不利的商业影响，特别是当一般的政府利益与合资企业利益发生冲突时。"笔者以为，合资企业董事会成员主要应由合营各方编制内人员担任，如有必要，也可委派合营方编制外的少数经济、法律专业人员担任董事或无表决权的咨询董事，尽量不委派政府官员为董事。这不仅可以避免外国合营者产生某些疑虑，也有利于管理权在合营各方的实际分享。

二、董事会议事规则的适用问题

董事会议事规则的适用虽属程序问题，但它可能影响董事名额分配所作的分享管理权的安排，并且直接关系到董事会的工作效率。因此，在中外合资企业合同中，不仅要重视董事名额分配，还要重视所适用的议事规则。

同一般公司法的规定一样，中外合资企业董事会的议事规则可分为一致通过、特别多数通过和简单多数通过三种。以下对三种议事规则的适用问题作一评述：

1. 一致通过议事规则的适用

《实施条例》第36条规定，必须适用一致通过议事规则的事项为：（1）合资企业章程的修改；(2) 合资企业的中止、解散；(3) 合资企业注册资本的增加、转让；(4) 合资企业与其他经济组织的合并。显然，这些都是关系合资企业根本性问题的事项。明文规定对这些事项适用一致通过的议事规则，是对少数股权者分享管理权的法律保障。这里有一个潜在的问题不能忽略。《实施条例》第 35 条规定："董事会会议应有三分之二以上董事出席方能举行"。那么，如果合营一方的董事比例小于三分之一（这是很可能的，特别是在合营一方出资比例小于三分之一的情况下），在该方董事因某些特殊情况不能出席董事会会议的情况下，董事会会议仍可通过一致通过的议事规则对上述事项作出决定。这样，未能出席董事会会议的合营者的管理权将化为乌有。因此，一致通过议事规则的适用，需要以合营各方都有代表出席董事会会议为前提。保证这个前提的一种方法是规定确保合营各方都有代表参加董事会会议的法定人数。这可在合资企业合同中具体规定。如南 Semperit-Sava 合资企业共同业务机构由南合营者和奥地利合营者各委派 3 名代表组成。出席该机构会议的法定人数定为 4 人，这就是保证了双方都有代表参加表决。另一种方法是明确规定董事会会议必须有合营各方的代表出席。如中国迅达电梯股份有限公司章程第 8 条第 4 款规定："参加董事会会议的法定人数每次都不得少于五人，或董事亲自参加，或其代理董事或代表参加。在法定人数中应包括副董事长和怡迅公司方面的董事，或分别代表他们的代理董事或代表。"

美国学者贾斯洛指出："十分重要的是，不要在合资企业规定过多的需要一致通过的事项，因为这将会妨碍合资企业的日常经营。"这是经验之谈。在中外合资企业合同中，对于需要适用一致通过议事规则的事项，应严格限制。除了《实施条例》第 36 条规定的事项外，应尽量少规定或不规定适用此议事规则的事项，以利于提高董事会的工作效率。有些中外合资企业合同事无巨细，一概适用一致通过的议事规则，这似不宜效法。

2. 特别多数通过议事规则的适用

适用特别多数通过议事规则的目的之一是给予少数股权者否决权以保障其分享管理权。与适用一致通过的议事规则不同，在适用特别多数通过的议事规则时，少数股权者的一个反对票并不能构成否决权，其几个或一致的反对票才能构成否决权，这种否决权似可称为联合否决权。保障联合否决权的第一种方式是在合资企业合同（或协议、章程）中规定特别多数票为多数股权者总票数加少数股权者一票之和。例如，在董事名额分配为甲方 5 名，乙方 2 名的董事会中，如果适用 2/3 特别多数通过的议事规则，由于乙方的 2 个反对票不能构成否决权，甲方可轻易地以其董事名额优势单方面通过决议；而只有规定多数票为 6 票（即甲方总票数加乙方一票之和），乙方才能拥有联合否决权。保障联合否决权的第二种方式是明确规定特别多数票中必须包括少数股权者的赞成票。如中国迅达电梯股份有限公司章程第 8 条第 7 款 A 项规定："在作出与颁发和修改董事会指示有关的决议和任命合资公司高级负责人员时，须经三分之二多数通过，其中必须包括副董事长或怡迅公司方面的董事（或其代理董事或代表）。"

适用特别多数通过议事规则的目的之二是保障合资企业遵循合营各方多数董事的意志行事。为此，在合资企业合同（或协议、章程）中所规定的特别多数票数，需要超过多数股权者总票数加少数股权者一票之和。例如，在董事名额分配为甲方 5 名、乙方 4 名的董事会中，如果仅仅为了保障联合否决权，规定适用 2/3 特别多数通过的议事规则即可，但是符合 2/3 特别多数通过的要求可能有两种情况：(1)甲方 5 票赞成，乙方 1 票赞成、3 票反对；(2)乙方 4 票赞成，甲方 2 票赞成、3 票反对。显然，在以上情况下，甲、乙方可能被迫去做违背该方多数董事意志的事。而如果规定特别多数票为 7 票，就可保证所通过的事项得到合营各方一半以上的董事赞成。这种旨在保障合资企业按合营各方多数董事意志行事的特别多数，比之旨在保障联合否决权的特别多数要求更高的一致，较容易产生董事会僵局。因此，对适用这种特别多数通过议事规则的事项也应从严掌握。

3. 简单多数通过议事规则的适用

简单多数通过议事规则的适用结果可以较明显地反映合营各方分享管理权的优劣势。在合营各方股权不等因而董事名额分配不等的董事会中，简单多数通过议事规则的适用将使拥有多数股权因而委派多数董事的合营方在表决中占优势。这不足为奇，所有权与管理权结合是合资企业的重要特点之一。由于合资企业的风险一般按出资比例分担，多数股权者在承担较大风险的同时拥有较大管理权力是顺理成章的。中国迅达电梯股份有限公司章程的有关规定比较特殊，值得一提。该章程第 8 条第 7 款 B 项规定："如与其他业务有关的决定，须经简单的多数通过即可，其中必须包括副董事长或怡迅公司方面的董事（或其代理董事或代表）。"由于此项规定，虽然该合资企业中外方出资比例为 75：25，董事名额比例为 6：2，但由于外方拥有否决权，中方全然没有表决优势，如此简单多数通过的议事规则名实不符，似不宜采用。

三、总经理副总经理的委任问题

在合资企业中，合营各方分享管理权不仅表现在决策权的分享，还表现在行政管理权的分享。行政管理权分享方面的主要问题是如何委任合资企业总经理、副总经理。

东欧国家对合资企业总经理有较严格的国籍限制，行政管理权明显"一边倒"。

在南斯拉夫合资企业中,如果是外国投资者与南企业合资的情况,经理必须由南公民担任;如果是与南企业的分部合资,经理是否必须由南公民担任尚不明确,因为外资法对此未作规定。多数观点认为,南劳动法允许外国人担任后一类合资企业的经理,能否担任,取决于合同规定。然而,不同类型的南合资企业合同不论是否包括委任经理的规定,被委任的经理总是南公民。外国投资者一般很重视合资企业的总经理委任问题,认为"合资企业的官员和经理构成了董事会之下重要的第二级管理控制。西方合资者任命某些官员和经理的权力提供了对日常经营的极大控制机会,并且进一步确保合资者期望的实现。"所以,东欧国家有关合资企业总经理国籍的限制性规定,不能不影响到外国投资者的投资决定。

对比东欧国家有关合资企业总经理的法律规定,《中外合资法》这方面比较开放。该法第 6 条第 3 款规定:"正副总经理(或正副厂长)由合营各方分别担任。"《实施条例》第 40 条第 1 款又进一步明确规定:"总经理副总经理由董事会聘请,可以由中国公民担任,也可以由外国公民担任。"这些规定使外国投资者深受鼓舞。美国学者贾斯洛认为,"在这方面,中国显然比东欧自由","西方合营者在此经营水平上可能有效地实行较大控制"。学习外国先进管理技术是我举办合资企业的重要目的之一。然而,学习外国先进管理技术,要以形成新的人际关系为前提。在其位,才能谋其政。要想学会外国先进管理技术,就要舍得让外国合资者担任主要管理职务。因此,《中外合资法》和《实施条例》中有关总经理的开放性规定是正确的,不过,需要防止其他规定起抵消作用。

《实施条例》第 40 条第 3 款的规定可能是一个潜在的抵消因素。该款规定:"总经理处理重要问题时,应同副总经理协商"。这一规定的本意想来是体现行政管理权的分享,但实施结果可能贻误商业时机。总经理负责日常经营,在"重要问题"难以事先限定的情况下,可能事事都要同副总经理协商,而副总经理又常常不止一人,不难想见协商之难。不仅如此,有的中外合资企业合同还把"协商"具体化,规定了"共同签署制",即有关合资企业经营事项的决定应由合资企业总经理、副总经理共同签署才能生效,这无异于再来一次集体表决。

从现有的中外合资企业合同看来,有关总经理副总经理的规定主要有四种安排:(1) 中方担任总经理、外方担任副总经理,如西湖藤器企业有限公司、天津化纤棉制造厂;(2) 外方担任总经理,中方担任副总经理,如天津丽明化妆品合营工业公司、中国东方租赁有限公司;(3) 合营前期由外方担任总经理、中方担任副总经理,之后由中方担任总经理,外方担任副总经理,如上海福克斯波罗有限公司、中国南海贝克钻井有限公司;(4) 中外方轮流执政,如北京吉普汽车有限公司、中国江苏三得利食品有限公司。上述四种安排，哪种为优，不可贸然论定。在外方掌握先进管理技术的情况下，第一种安排可能会限制外方管理才干的发挥，因为外方担任副职毕竟只能起协助作用；第二种安排可能影响中方对先进管理技术的全面掌握，并可能导致外方对合资企业的事实上控制；第三种安排似不利于外方持续地引进先进管理技术，因为管理技术也在不断更新，许多合资企业合营期限长达一二十年，在合营前期过后，由中方长期担任总经理，不利于继续学习外国先进管理技术；第四种安排似可弥补上述各种之不足，既可为中方提供学习外国先进管理技术的榜样和实践机会，又可在实际经营中充分调动合营各方的积极性。这种安排还较充分地体现了合营各方行政管理权的分享。

第三节　合营公司的管理结构：中、美、日有关法律的比较[*]

20 世纪 60 年代以来，合营公司（joint venture corporations）发展成为国际投资活动的重要形式。1979 年《中华人民共和国中外合资经营企业法》（以下简称《中外合资法》）的颁布，正式表明我国也采用这一形式。在设立和经营中外合营公司的实践中，合营各方经常面临管理结构方面的法律问题。本文拟概略比较中、美、日有关合营公司管理结构的法制，冀能有助于理解和解决这类问题。[1]

一、绪论

（一）合营公司的法律概念

合营企业是两个或两个以上的人（自然人或法人）联合其资金、财产、知识、技术、经验、时间或其他资源从事某项商务的契约性组织。合营各方通常分享利益、分担亏损和风险，并对企业具有一定程度的控制。合营企业作为一种商务组织形式，历史已久，而作为一种法律形式，则近代才发展起来。一般认为，美国法院最早提出合营企业的概念。

合营企业的概念被用于表述契约式合营企业和股权式合营企业，亦即合营公司。契约式合营企业是合营者设立的松散组织，未组成新的法人。而合营公司则是由合营者组成的新法人。因此，合营公司可定义为，由两个或两个以上的人（自然人或法人）采取合营企业的安排和公司的组织、管理、经营结构以实现其经济目标的独立法律实体。它结合了公司形式和传统的合营企业关系两方面的优点。

（二）合营公司的法律形式

1. 美国

20 世纪 60 年代以前，美国境内的合营公司大多设立于铁路、建筑和石油等行业，之后，广泛设立于各行各业。例如，1983 年 2 月 17 日，美国通用汽车公司和日本丰田公司签订了为期 12 年的合营公司协议。该公司 1984 年 2 月 22 日于美国加利福尼亚州设立。

虽然，合营公司的概念未见于美国联邦或州法律，一些美国学者指出，美国的合

---

[*]　原载《比较法研究》1989 年第 3—4 期。

[1]　美国、日本分别属于普通法系国家和大陆法系国家，对中国而言，美国和日本都是重要的资本输出国。因此，比较研究中、美.日有关合营公司管理结构的法制，在理论和实践上都具有典型意义。

营公司采取封闭公司(close corporation)的法律形式；[1]合营公司问题大多在概念上与封闭公司相同；在对合营公司的法律分析中，关键是必须明确，不论国际合营公司或国内合营公司，都是封闭公司。

封闭公司通常具有如下多数特征：股东较少；股东互相认识；股东积极参与管理；股东会议取代董事会；股份不能自由转让；股份不能在一般股票市场上买卖。

2. 日本

合营公司通常由一个日本公司和一个外国公司组成，各拥有合营公司的二分之一股份。多数合营公司采取合股公司(joint stock company)的形式，股票公开发行。1938年，日本公司法规定了有限责任公司的法人形式。这种形式与美国的封闭式公司相类。该法有关规定限制股东人数，允许召开非正式会议，限制转让成员资格并简化设立程序、公司结构等。在日本，几乎所有闻名的大公司都是合股公司，而许多小公司是有限责任公司。尽管有限责任公司的形式更适合于合营公司，但在日本却未得普遍采用。令人感兴趣的是，在其他一些大陆法系国家，合营公司也采取合股公司的形式。

3. 中国

合营公司采取有限责任公司的形式。[2]由于公司法尚未颁布，有限责任公司的性质仍待确定。然而，在有关法律中，已有一些关于有限责任公司的规定，包括：合营公司是中国法人；[3]合营各方对合营公司的责任以其出资额为限；[4]合营各方以其出资比例分享利润、分担亏损和风险；[5]合营一方转让股权须经另一方同意；[6]须设立董事会。[7]最近颁布的《中华人民共和国私营企业暂行条例》对有限责任公司作了较具体的规定，可资借鉴。[8]

由上述可见，日本的多数合营公司采取合股公司形式，而美国和中国的合营公司采取类似的公司形式，即封闭公司和有限责任公司。封闭公司和有限责任公司主要的共同特征是：股东较少；股东积极参与管理；限制股权转让；股份不能在一般股

　[1]　关于封闭公司有不同的定义，但一般认为，封闭公司是指股东人数较少、所有权和管理相结合、股份不能在证券市场买卖的公司。参见 Henderson, Contract Problems in U. S. -Japanese Joint Ventures, 39 *Washington Law Review*, p.490, note 52 (1964).
　[2]　《中外合资法》，第4条；《合资法实施条例》，第19条。
　[3]　《合资法实施条例》，第2条。《中华人民共和国民法通则》第37条规定："法人应当具备下列条件：(一) 依法成立；(二) 有必要的财产或者经费；(三) 有自己的名标、组织机构和场所；(四) 能够独立承担民事责任。"
　[4]　《合资法实施条例》，第19条。
　[5]　《中外合资法》，第4条。
　[6]　同上。
　[7]　《中外合资法》，第6条。
　[8]　《中华人民共和国私营企业暂行条例》，第9、14条。

票市场上买卖。虽然合股公司形式和有限责任公司形式都适用于合营公司,一般认为,有限责任公司具有的组织简便灵活、经营节省、商务保密等特征更符合合营公司的需要。

（三）合营公司的法律框架

1. 美国

美国的合营公司由一般公司法、封闭公司法、案例法和契约性文件调整。

1963年以前,美国公司法对公开公司（public corporation）和封闭公司未加区分。1963年,佛罗里达州率先颁布了独立、完整的封闭公司法。1967年,特拉华州和马里兰州也颁布了封闭公司法。1968年和1972年,宾夕法尼亚州和堪萨斯州相继大体采纳了特拉华州封闭公司法的模式。现已有十多个州颁布了此类法律。[1]

美国的合营公司也受判例法调整。在此,合营各方有权改变一般公司的分级管理结构,合营企业协议在公司成立时仍然有效。

主要的契约性文件包括股东协议、公司组织章程和章程（bylaws）。虽然美国各州对股东协议的效力和强制力看法不一,但根据普通法原则,封闭公司一致的股东协议是有效力的。股东通过这类协议规划未来经营,避免潜在问题,并保障少数股股东分享管理权。公司组织章程必须包括某些法定的内容,如公司名称、经营期限、经营目的、筹资、公司住所、首届董事会的组成等。章程是调整公司内部事务的一系列规则,经常被视为公司与成员之间、各成员之间的契约。

2. 日本

《日本民法典》是有关设立和经营合营公司的一般原则之渊源。第一编（第3—20条、第90—137条）有关法律行为和法律能力的规定适用于契约。第三编（第399—696条）包括了有关债的规定,第399—548条是有关契约成立和效力的规定,第549—696条列举十三种契约的类型。

《日本商法典》第三编对商务交往作了详明规定。由于日本公司是商人,根据商法典,商人的所有同其商务有关的交易都是商务交往,不论另一方是否为商人。合营公司的组成、管理、财务和清算均受商法典调整。如商法典未作规定,则适用习惯。如无有关的习惯,则适用民法典。

在契约性文件中,最重要的是合营企业协议。合营企业协议由民法典调整,通常在一些基本方面设定合营各方的权利义务,诸如:合营各方的出资及出资比例、合

---

〔1〕 Hamilton, *The Law of Corporations*, 2nd ed, West Publishing Company, 1987, p. 265. 在大陆法系国家,合股公司和有限责任公司分别由不同的、独立的法律调整,或者至少是由同一法律的不同篇章调整。而在美国,多数给予封闭公司特别待遇的州没有为此颁布独立的法律。

营公司的资金、合营各方委派的董事人数、清算和结业的方式等。在多数情况下，还要签订有关对合营公司的技术援助、专利许可、人员派遣与管理以及产品销售等协议。公司组织章程是合营各方据以实现共同管理的最基本的法律文件之一。它规定了合营公司管理的具体安排，是合营企业协议有关规定的补充。由于它调整股东和合营公司之间的关系，因此，必须谨慎制定以反映股东之间的紧密关系并调和相互冲突的利益。公司组织章程须附属于合营企业协议，合营各方通过合营企业协议采用公司组织章程。虽然日本有关法律未作规定，合营公司的章程也可能附属于合营企业协议，或者，在规定采用章程的单独协议中予以确认。

3. 中 国

调整中外合营公司的法律规范主要是《中外合资法》《中华人民共和国中外合资经营企业法实施条例》（以下简称《合资法实施条例》）和契约性文件。

《中外合资法》规定了设立和经营合营公司的基本框架，不仅是经济措施，而且是政治宣言，即中国实行对外开放政策的标志。另一重要的立法是 1983 年颁布的《合资法实施条例》。该条例规定了设立和经营合营公司的许多细节。这些规定，在一些方面弥补了中国尚无公司法的缺陷。

在三种主要的契约性文件中，合营企业合同最重要，它是合营各方就设立合营公司的相互权利、义务关系达成一致意见而订立的文件。合营公司章程按照合营企业合同规定的原则，规定合营公司的宗旨、组织原则和经营管理方式等事项，是设定合营公司管理结构的重要文件。合营企业协议是合营各方有关设立合营公司的一些要点和原则的协议，可视为导向合营企业合同的重要步骤。合营企业协议如与合营企业合同抵触，以合营企业合同为准。合营企业合同和章程都是必须签订的，而合营企业协议是任择性的。[1]

综上所述，除了契约性文件之外，美国的合营公司受成文法和案例法调整；日本的合营公司主要由成文法调整，在某种程度上亦由习惯调整；而中国的合营公司由成文法调整。这大致反映了普通法系国家、大陆法系国家和社会主义国家法律渊源的一般特征。就调整合营公司的成文法而言，也有区别：在美国是公司法（包括封闭公司法）；在日本是民法典、商法典和公司法；在中国主要是《中外合资法》及其实施条例，这些专门性法规受益于外国的经验，[2]较为具体明确。

在契约性文件中，美国封闭公司一致的股东协议、日本的合营企业协议和中国

---

〔1〕《合资法实施条例》，第 13 条。

〔2〕《中外合资法》的起草者在起草过程中，借鉴罗马尼亚、南斯拉夫、日本和新加坡有关合营企业的法律，分析了吸引外国投资的必要因素，特别是有利于实现中国举办合营企业预期目标的因素。

的合营企业合同分别是在三国境内设立合营公司的最重要的契约性文件,因为合营各方的基本权利义务关系主要是通过上述文件确立的。值得注意的是,在三国的有关实践中,相同名称的契约性文件,并不必然意味着其实际内容的一致。例如,日本的合营企业协议并非等同于中国的合营企业协议,从实际内容看,它更类似于中国的合营企业合同;中国的合营企业合同相当于美国的公司组织章程和股东协议某些内容的结合体。

由于中国尚未颁布公司法,中外合营公司的契约性文件在设立合营公司的管理结构中尤为重要,当具体详明地规定各个细节。此外,由于中国的经济制度不同于美国和日本,在签订中美合营公司或中日合营公司的契约性文件中,合营各方须注意不同经济管理模式的协调。

二、合营公司的权力机构

(一) 美国

由于多数合营公司由一般的公司法调整、有些由封闭公司法具体调整,多数合营公司的权力机构包括股东会议和董事会,有些只设股东会议。以下分述一般的公司法有关股东会议和董事会的规定以及封闭公司法的特殊规定。

1. 股东会议

各州公司法多少都包括了一些有关公司股东会议的一般规定。《标准商务公司法》(修正案)(Revised Model Business Corporation Act)规定,股东会议应"根据章程规定的时间每年举行"。股东年会或特别会议的通知得在会前 60 天至 10 天期间送达。股东年会的主要目的是选举董事,也可讨论决定其他有关事项,不限于通知所规定的内容。股东特别会议是股东年会以外的任何股东会议,可由公司法或公司章程中所规定的人召集。与股东年会不同,股东特别会议考虑的议题限于通知所列明的事项。

2. 董事会

在美国公司中,股份分为两类,两类股份的股东分别选派董事的安排是常见的。这保障了不同股东集团的代表权。董事人数一般须根据公司组织章程或章程规定。只有个人才能担任董事。早先,各州公司法都要求董事会至少由三名董事组成。许多州的公司法还要求董事须具备一定资格,诸如必须是股东或本州居民。现在,许多州的公司法允许董事会由一名或两名董事组成。有关董事资格的法定要求也几乎全取消了。董事会例会可按周、月、季度或任何间隔期召开。通常在股东年会前后召开董事会会议。董事会特别会议是董事会例会以外的任何董事会会议,董事会例会与董事会特别会议的区别之一是前者未经通知可以举行,后者则"至少须在两天前通知会议的时间和地点"。与股东特别会议不同,董事会特别会议可处理任何有关商务,即使有关商务未在通知中列举。

3. 特殊规定

一般的公司法设定了公司中由股东、董事和行政管理人员构成的等级管理制。在封闭公司中,参与者一般承担上述两种或三种职能,并且不注重分级管理的意义。这种实践在一些州得到有关法律的认可。例如,特拉华州封闭公司法允许此类公司的章程规定,公司的业务由股东会议管理,不设董事会。马里兰州封闭公司法也有类似规定。

（二）日本

合营公司的权力机构由股东会议和董事会组成。

1. 股东会议

《日本商法典》规定了股东例会和股东特别会议的主要职能和程序。除了合营企业协议和公司组织章程规定的某些限制外,股东会议拥有合营公司的最终控制权。[1] 股东大会批准资产负债表、损益计算书、商务报告以及有关盈余保留、利润分配的提案;选举董事和法定审计员或审计员;规定董事和审计员的薪金以及审议其他管理事务。股东大会每年至少须在规定的日期召开一次。虽然法律未规定股东大会召开的日期,由于税收申报以股东大会批准的财务报告为基础,并须在财政年度结束后的两个月之内申报,股东大会须在财政年度结束后的两个月之内召开。股东特别会议可能由董事召集,或者经持续六个月拥有全部股份 3% 以上的股东请求而召开。

2. 董事会

日本合股公司的董事会至少须由三名董事组成。董事不必是股东、日本国民或居民。[2] 在日本的主要行业中,董事会的平均人数为 14.4 人,比西方国家的相应数高得多。然而,许多董事职务仅仅是荣誉职务。根据《日本商法典》,累积表决不是强制性的,所有公司都通过章程规定不采用累积表决。因此,拥有少数股股权的股东几乎不可能选举代表其利益的董事。董事任期不得超过两年,但可连选连任。董事会根据商法典、公司组织章程和合营企业协议对合营公司实行全面指导和管理。

---

〔1〕 这也代表了大陆法系国家的趋向。例如,根据法国的有关法律,在多数地区,公司的最高权力属于股东会议。与美国的实践相反,法国公司权力的实质部分特地保留于股东会议,并且不可授予董事会。

〔2〕 虽然日本法律没有关于董事国籍要求的强制性规定,1968 年有关丰田汽车公司的裁决主张,公司章程要求董事具有日本国籍的规定并非违反日本宪法的平等保护条款。

一般而言,董事是公司的雇员,同时也是公司的管理人员。董事中的一人或数人可被任命为董事代表。董事代表有权执行所有有关公司商务的行动。

(三) 中国

中外合营公司的权力机构没有采用股东会议和董事会两级分权的模式。[1] 根据《合资法实施条例》,董事会是合营公司的最高权力机构,决定合营公司的一切重大问题。[2]《合资法实施条例》明确授予董事会聘请高级管理人员的权力,但未规定其他具体的权力。董事由合营各方委派。董事名额的分配由合营各方参照出资比例协商确定。由于《中外合资法》没有规定外方出资比例的上限,也没有规定外方委派董事的最高限,外方可能通过拥有多数股权而取得多数董事职务。董事任期四年。类似于日本的合营公司,中外合营公司的某些董事职务也仅仅是荣誉职务。董事会至少由三名董事组成。[3] 每年至少召开一次董事会会议,由董事长召集和主持。经三分之一以上董事提议,可由董事长召开董事会临时会议。[4]

中外合营公司董事会的重要特征之一是不论合营各方的出资比例如何,董事长由中方委派,副董事长由外方委派。[5] 这一法律规定在国外引起了不同的反应。有的学者认为,由于这一规定,中方增强了对董事会的控制。另一种观点认为,由于董事长在适用一致通过的议事规则中不起决定性作用,这一规定对外方没有什么影响。

(四) 比较分析

由公司形式和有关法律所决定,美国的一些合营公司的权力机构包括股东会议和董事会;另一些合营公司则只设股东会议作为权力机构。日本的合营公司权力机构由股东会议和董事会组成。在股东会议和董事会的分工方面,普通法系国家的公司与大陆法系国家的公司有明显的区别。在普通法系国家的公司中由董事会决定的事项,在大陆法系国家的公司中可能是由股东会议决定。在普通法系国家,公司的法定管理几乎全部授予董事会。董事会在管理决策中起重要作用。而在大陆法系国家,董事会主要管理公司的日常经营活动,股东会议是主要的决策机构。

---

〔1〕 与其他社会主义国家的国际合营公司相比,中外合营公司的权力机构与西方国家较相似。例如,在南斯拉夫,合营公司由南斯拉夫合营者和外国合营者组成的共同业务机构管理。然而,根据工人自治原则,合营公司的最高权力机构是工人委员会。See McMillan & Charles, Joint Ventures in East Europe: A Three-Country Comparison, in Gordon (edit.), *Materials on Comparative Joint International Business Ventures*, p. 445 (1977).

〔2〕《合资法实施条例》,第 33 条。

〔3〕《合资法实施条例》,第 34 条。

〔4〕《合资法实施条例》,第 35 条。

〔5〕《合资法实施条例》,第 34 条。

中外合营公司的权力机构是董事会。这种单一权力机构的方式类似于美国某些合营公司只设股东会议的安排。实际上，中外合营公司董事会的职能类似于美、日境内合营公司的股东会议和董事会，因此，合营各方在公司章程中似应规定较经常性的董事会会议（例如，每季度召开一次）。此外，由于《中外合资法》及其实施条例未规定董事会的具体权力，合营各方在签订合营企业合同时，有必要对此予以明确规定。

国际合营公司的经验表明，股份分类和董事由合营各方分别委派的安排适合于合营公司的实际情况，特别是合营各方不愿严格按出资比例分享公司管理权时，更是如此。这种方式在中、美、日三国都是法律允许的。由于委派各自的董事是合营各方的特权，合营各方须认真考虑董事的选择方式，公司管理的连续性和董事的管理经验都是应予考虑的重要因素。

三、合营公司的议事规则

（一）美国

1. 法定人数

在美国公司中，股东年会或股东特别会议的法定人数为拥有已发行股票的多数股股东，除非公司组织章程或章程另有规定。各州公司法通常规定法定人数的最低限，一般为拥有三分之一已发行股票的股东。各州公司法未规定法定人数的最高限，因此，在公司组织章程或章程中，可能规定法定人数为拥有全部已发行股票的股东。这种规定有时被封闭公司作为策略而采用。

在规模固定的董事会中，法定人数为多数董事组成。在规模不固定（即董事人数可变动）的董事会中，法定人数为会前在职董事的多数。但公司组织章程或章程可允许法定人数为三分之一的董事。一些封闭公司董事会的法定人数由所有董事组成或适用一致通过的议事规则，以此作为控制公司的手段。

2. 一致通过的议事规则

一般的公司法设计了公司管理的民主制，据此，代表多数股权的表决票占优势。这一趋向被视为在决定公司的长期政策中是有效和公平的。然而，封闭公司的股东一般认为他们是合伙人而不是股东伙伴。在一些封闭公司，特别是合营公司中，股东甚至希望所有事项都适用一致通过的议事规则。在这类公司中，可能在股东协议、公司组织章程或章程中包括明示的否决权规定，即规定在股东会议或董事会会议适用一致通过的议事规则。马里兰封闭公司法规定，有关设定或修改重要的结构或管理安排的事项，须经股东一致批准。这些事项包括：修改公司章程以选择或放弃封闭公司的地位;修改有关调整公司事务或股东关系的股东协议;联合、合并、出售、租借或交换所有或实际上所有的公司财产。

实际上,各州公司法都允许股东未经开会而通过一致的书面同意决定公司事务。这种方式特别有利于封闭公司。因为在这类公司中,需要较多适用一致通过的议事规则,以书面同意的方式,可节省正式开会的程序和费用。

3. 特别多数通过的议事规则

在美国公司的组织章程中,经常规定对某些股东审议的事项适用比公司法的要求更高的议事规则,这种实践在许多州的公司法中得到明确认可。此外,一些州的公司法规定,即使在公司组织章程中未予规定,股东会议对于某些重要事项,也须适用特别多数通过的议事规则。同样,根据公司组织章程、章程或股东协议的规定,董事会也可采用特别多数通过的议事规则。

4. 简单多数通过的议事规则

各州公司法大多规定,除非另有规定,股东会议或董事会会议在符合法定人数要求的情况下,对审议的事项适用简单多数通过的议事规则。

（二）日本

1. 法定人数

在日本的合股公司,股东会议的法定人数由拥有多数股票的股东构成。除非另有规定,董事会会议的法定人数由多数董事构成。董事会会议要求董事实际参加,这对于外方董事住在国外的合营公司可能产生问题。解决这一问题的最好方式是设立合营公司的"执行委员会"。董事会将其所有职责(法律规定不得移交者除外)移交给执行委员会。该委员会的程序不受商法典调整,因此,合营各方可灵活规定该委员会行使其职责的方式。

2. 一致通过的议事规则

日本法律没有明示禁止公司决策的否决权。合营企业协议通常规定,董事会对某些重要事项适用一致通过的议事规则。这些重要事项包括:举借大笔款项;批准年度预算和商务计划;分配红利;新项目的开工以及出售公司的重要财产。然而,值得注意的是,日本的权威法律学者认为,一致通过的议事规则是不合法的,因其违背了董事经讨论作出决定的职责。[1]

3. 特别多数通过的议事规则

《日本商法典》第343条的三分之二多数通过的议事规则适用于一些重要的事

---

〔1〕 根据大陆法系的原则,法律学者的观点在法院是有说服力的。

项,包括:修改公司组织章程;转让该商务的全部或重要部分;签订、修改或撤销有关租让该商务全部的契约;取得另一公司的全部商务;以"特别优惠"价格对非股东发行新股票及其他事项。这一规定通常是用以保护少数股权者的利益。对股东的一般决议或选举董事等事项适用的议事规则,宜在公司组织章程中明确规定。同样,有关董事会决议的法定人数和议事规则如规定于公司组织章程,就能被更严格地实施。

4. 简单多数通过的议事规则

除了商法典第 343 条和第 342 条规定的事项之外,商法典第 239 条规定,除非在公司组织章程中另有规定,股东决议经拥有 50% 以上股份的股东的多数通过,即为有效。

（三）中国

1. 法定人数

中外合营公司董事会会议的法定人数为三分之二以上的董事。董事在不能出席董事会会议的情况下可委托他人代表其出席和表决。[1]

2. 一致通过的议事规则

根据《合资法实施条例》的规定,在董事会会议适用一致通过议事规则的事项包括:合营公司章程的修改;合营公司的中止、解散;注册资本的增加、转让;合营企业与其他经济组织的合并。[2] 显然,上述都是关系合营公司结构的重要问题。由于合营各方对这些问题具有否决权,基本上保障了管理权力的分享。不仅如此,在实践中,合营各方还经常在合营公司章程中规定对其他事项也适用一致通过的议事规则,用以保护少数股股权者的权益。

3. 特别多数或简单多数通过的议事规则

除了法定的适用一致通过议事规则的事项之外,其他事项可根据合营各方在合营公司章程中规定的议事规则作出决议。[3] 在实践中,特别多数通过的议事规则、简单多数通过的议事规则都被普遍采用。

（四）比较分析

对合营公司的一些重要事项适用一致通过的议事规则,是中、美、日的普遍实践。必须注意的是,适用一致通过的议事规则要和法定人数的要求相结合,才能实现保护少数股股权者利益的目标。关于法定人数,美、日法律有关多数股东或

---

[1]《合资法实施条例》,第 35 条。
[2]《合资法实施条例》,第 36 条。
[3] 同上。

董事出席的规定和中国法律有关三分之二董事出席的规定都存在潜在的问题。这就是,如果合营一方的股东或董事比例不及二分之一(美、日)或不及三分之一(中国),在该方股东或董事因故不能出席股东会议或董事会会议的情况下,会议仍可照常举行,合营另一方可能适用一致通过的议事规则单方面作出决议。这样,少数股股权者的利益就无法得到保障。因此,适用一致通过的议事规则,需要以合营各方都有代表出席会议为前提。在合营公司的契约性文件中,对此应予明确规定。

另一方面,适用一致通过的议事规则将使参加表决的合营各方所有代表都具有否决权。否决权固然是保障少数股股权者利益的可靠方式,但也是产生僵局的最主要根源。因此,在合营公司的管理决策中如过多适用一致通过的议事规则,将阻碍合营公司的正常经营。为了在保障少数股股权者利益的同时也保障合营公司权力机构的工作效率,必须根据不同的事项适用不同的议事规则。一般而言,适用一致通过或特别多数通过议事规则的范围要严格限制。

在董事会成员较多,特别是外方董事在国外的中外合营公司中,可以考虑设立类似日本合营公司的"执行委员会"或采用美国某些公司管理决策中的书面同意方式。这类措施和方式有利于提高合营公司权力机构的工作效率。

四、合营公司的行政首长

(一) 美国

《标准商务公司法》(修正案)规定,各公司应有据其章程所规定的或由其董事会任命的管理人员。公司管理人员的明示权能来源于各州的商务公司法、公司组织章程、章程以及董事会采纳的公司安排。

美国公司的行政首长是总裁和副总裁。总裁是公司董事会领导下的主要管理人员。他监督和管理公司商务,执行公司的契约、担保证书和其他文件。副总裁在总裁缺席、死亡、不合格、无能力或拒绝履行职责的情况下履行总裁职责。虽然各州公司法对公司总裁、副总裁没有国籍的限制,但根据 1964 年《民事权利法案》第七编的规定,任何有利于外籍管理人员的歧视性雇佣可能被禁止。在美国通用汽车公司和日本丰田公司设立的合营公司中,由丰田公司任命合营公司总裁(最高执行官员和最高管理官员)的安排产生了是否构成歧视性雇佣的问题。[1]

---

〔1〕　美国最高法院在审理 Sumitomo Shoji America Inc. v. Avagliano 一案中认为,独资子公司的国籍取决于公司成立地。美国通用汽车公司与日本丰田汽车公司合资组成的合营公司引起了不同的、与此有关的问题,即如何决定合营公司的国籍。如果该合营公司被视为美国公司,就应受 1964 年《民事权利法案》第七篇要求的约束。如果它被视为日本公司,就受《美日友好通商航海条约》第 8 条第 1 款的调整。该条款给予在美国经营的日本公司雇用其选择的某些日籍人员的权利。

关于公司总裁和其他重要行政官员的任命，一些股东协议包括了任命某些或全部公司管理人员的规定，或者授权某些合营者任命某些管理人员。[1] 此外，公司和某些重要管理人员（不论是否股东）的雇佣合同亦被采用。这类合同如延长期限，须经董事会决议的明确授权。

（二）日本

日本的合营公司也设总裁和副总裁职务。典型的安排是由日方任命总裁，外方任命副总裁。总裁是日方力求取得的职务，鉴于日本境内的合营公司是日本籍公司，这种倾向也许是正当的。然而，由于总裁的主要工作是在中、高级管理人员业已形成的决议上盖章，其实际权能有限。

董事代表和总经理是日本合营公司的重要行政管理职务，一般由日方和外方分别担任。由于合营公司的日常事务通常是由董事代表或总经理管理，分别取得董事代表和总经理的职务使合营各方分享了对合营公司经营的重要控制权。[2]

由于《日本商法典》规定由董事管理公司的事务，并任命董事代表，试图将此实际上的正式任命权由董事转给股东是不合法的。然而，有关任命行政官员和其他重要雇员的股东协议被认为是合营公司中正常的安排。应注意的是，在董事会决定无视这种股东协议而行使其权力的情况下，这种股东协议可能是无效的。

（三）中国

《合资法实施条例》规定，合营公司须建立经营管理机构，设总经理一人，副总经理若干人以负责日常经营管理工作。合营公司的董事可兼任总经理或其他高级管理职务。总经理或副总经理不得兼任其他经济组织的同样职务。总经理、副总经理有营私舞弊或严重失职行为的，经董事会决议可随时解聘。[3]

总经理的主要职责是执行董事会决议；组织领导合营公司的日常经营管理；在董事会授权范围内对外代表合营公司，对内任免下属等。副总经理协助总经理工作。总经理在处理重要问题时，应同副总经理协商。[4] 在实践中，有些合营企业合

---

[1] 然而，这类规定受到批评。批评的主要理由是：(1) 这类规定违背了各州公司法有关董事会管理公司事务的规定；(2) 它违背了多数州公司法有关董事选择公司官员的明文规定；(3) 它使董事忽视其对于公司和其他股东的信托义务；(4) 它对于未参加签订协议的股东是不公平的，或可能对他们产生不利影响。

[2] "董事代表"的概念规定于日本商法典第 261 条和民法典第 54 条。董事代表类似于欧洲的"代理人"（procurator）。他们是经特别任命的公司官员，可以代表公司与第三方签约。他们由董事会决议任命。在日美合营公司中，日方董事代表可能兼任公司总裁，而美方董事代表可能兼任副总裁。有关任命董事代表和董事代表只能由公司总裁和副总裁担任的规定须载公司组织章程。

[3] 《合资法实施条例》，第 40、41 条。

[4] 《合资法实施条例》，第 38、39、40 条。

同或章程还把"协商"具体化，规定了"共同签署制度"，即有关合营公司经营事项的决定应由总经理、副总经理共同签署同意才能生效。

关于总经理、副总经理的任命问题，《中外合资法》规定："正副总经理（或正副厂长）由合营各方分别担任"。[1]《合资法实施条例》又进一步明确规定："总经理副总经理由董事会聘请，可以由中国公民担任，也可以由外国公民担任。"[2]在合营企业合同中，有关总经理副总经理的安排主要有四种：（1）中方担任总经理，外方担任副总经理；（2）外方担任总经理，中方担任副总经理；[3]（3）合营前期由外方担任总经理，中方担任副总经理，之后由中方担任总经理，外方担任副总经理；（4）中外双方定期轮流担任总经理。近年来，还出现了由合营一方单独承担管理责任的实例。在深圳，截至1987年，已有八家合营公司实行由合营一方单独承包经营的管理方式，其中六家由外方承包，两家由中方承包。承包指标主要包括产值、各项税利、固定资产折旧、设备完好率、产品质量、外销指标及债务偿还等。[4] 在天津、厦门和舟山等地的合营公司中，也有此类承包经营的管理方式。[5] 然而，这种方式只是在某些情况下的特殊安排，因为由合营各方共同管理毕竟是合营公司的重要特征之一。

（四）比较分析

合营公司的主要管理人员是权力机构之下的第二级重要管理控制，因此，他们的任命问题非常重要。由于合营各方选派的合营公司主要管理人员经常具有"双重效忠"（即同时对合营公司和其母公司效忠），在合营公司的契约性文件中，应有相应的规定以确保合营公司的行政首长根据合营各方的共同利益、而不是合营一方的利益行事。

虽然美国的合营公司和日本的合营公司都设有总裁职务，但两者权能不同：美国合营公司总裁是主要的执行官员，而日本合营公司总裁的实际权能则比较有限。

在合营公司行政首长的正副职关系方面，看来中国的有关法律和实践试图使合营各方在行政管理方面相互制约。似应注意到，商务活动，特别是国际商务活动，需要讲究效率。为了保障和提高行政管理效率，合营公司行政首长正副职的关系，应是主辅关系，而不是相互牵制的关系。因此，美国公司法中有关总裁权能和总裁与

---

[1] 《中外合资法》，第6条。

[2] 《合资法实施条例》，第40条。

[3] 实践中，中外合营公司较多任命外籍总经理。

[4] 《深圳中外合资企业试行承包经营》，载《人民日报》（海外版）1987年11月10日第3版。

[5] 参见《首开外商承包管理先河》，载《人民日报》（海外版）1988年7月11日第3版；《厦门一合营企业让外商承包经营》，载《人民日报》（海外版），1988年2月6日第3版；《舟洋公司经济效益列同行前茅》，载《人民日报》（海外版），1988年7月21日。

副总裁关系的规定是值得借鉴的。

五、结语

上述比较可列表概括如下：

美、日、中有关合营公司管理结构的法制

比较内容		国别		
		美国	日本	中国
公司形式		封闭公司	合股公司	有限责任公司
法律框架	主要成文法	公司法或封闭公司法	民法典、商法典和公司法	中外合资法及实施条例
	主要契约性文件	股东协议、公司组织章程、章程	合营企业协议、公司组织章程、章程	合营企业协议、合营企业合同、章程
权力机构		股东会议和董事会或股东会议	股东会议和董事会	董事会
议事规则		一致通过、特别多数通过、简单多数通过	一致通过、特别多数通过、简单多数通过	一致通过、特别多数通过、简单多数通过
行政首长		总裁、副总裁	总裁、副总裁、董事代表和总经理	总经理、副总经理

显然，美国、日本、中国有关合营公司管理结构的法律制度有区别，更有类似或相通之处。不仅如此，合营公司的契约性文件也为合营者提供了一定的灵活性。美日合营公司、中美合营公司和中日合营公司的合营各方均可在东道国的有关法律制度框架之内，通过契约性文件设计和商定足以保障各方权益的、高效率的管理结构。

第四节　合资企业的事实控制问题*

合资企业的事实控制（*de facto* control）是目前国内理论界尚未涉及、实践中容易忽略的关系合资企业经营和发展的重要问题

所谓合资企业的事实控制，主要是指由合资企业合同或其他专门合同中非直接与管理权有关的条款（例如技术、销售方面的条款）或由某些优势（例如人员配备、技术、销售等优势）形成的对合资企业经营活动的实际控制。事实上控制的后果往往改变了合资企业合同中有关管理的条款所规定的法定控制（*de jure* control），变管理权分享为一方专权。东欧合资企业的经验表明：西方投资者，特别是跨国公司，在处于少数股权地位情况下，常常通过管理能力、经验的优势和技术优势取得对合资企业的事实上控制。同样，西方投资者也认为，中国合营者可能不愿放弃对合资企业的控制，因此，需要寻求从合同中间接产生的或从合同外产生的控制。[1] 针对这种情况，在签订中外合资企业合同中，我方应未雨绸缪。有些条款是必不可少的，不可疏漏。有些条款必须规定得详细、严谨，不可笼而统之。

西方投资者，特别是跨国公司，对合资企业实行事实上控制的方式错综复杂，本文略述三种较常见的方式，并初步探讨相应的防范措施。

一、人员配备策略产生的事实上控制问题

跨国公司有其人员配备策略，通过人员的选择和使用实现对合资企业的事实上控制。

在居于少数股权地位的情况下，跨国公司往往委派本公司高级管理人员担任合资企业的高级管理职务。如墨西哥与美国等合资的金伯利-克拉克公司，1973 年以后墨美双方的出资比例为 53：43（其他外国投资者拥有 4％的股权），该董事会由 13人组成，墨方委派 10 人，美方委派 3 人。表面看来，上述安排对美方极为不利。但是，由于美方委派的 3 名董事中有 2 名是美方母公司的董事，他们分别担任了该合资企业的董事长兼总经理、副总经理，对企业的实际经营起了重要的支配作用。[2] 发

　＊　原载《法学研究》1987 年第 2 期。

　〔1〕　See Craig A. Jaslow, Practical Considerations in Drafting an Joint Venture Agreement with China, *American Journal of Comparative Law*, Vol. 31, No. 2, 1983, p. 221.

　〔2〕　See OCEANA, *Multinational Corporations Law*, B13-B32, Case Studies of Joint International Business Ventures, OCEANA, 1982, pp. 141-146.

展中国家的经验表明,跨国公司委派的合资企业总经理的长期履历是与母公司联系而不是与合资企业联系,他们管理合资企业主要是为其母公司取得最高水平的利润。[1] 他们的工作同时要对母公司和合资企业负责,这种"双重的效忠"会影响其决定的公正性,特别是在合资企业与其母公司发生利害冲突的场合。[2] 为了防止外方通过人员配备策略可能产生的事实上控制,在中外合资企业合同中,我方对总经理、副总经理的任命、任期和培训我方管理人员的规定应慎重考虑,总经理一般不宜由外方长期担任,对培训我方管理人员的范围、期限等要具体落实。

即使有如上规定,还不能完全防止外方通过人员配备策略可能产生的事实上控制。因为跨国公司可以利用的人员不仅包括总公司所在国国籍人员和第三国人员,还包括了合资企业所在国人员。墨西哥合资企业案例表明,跨国公司可以从本公司人员或当地人员中选择代表其利益的董事。[3] 由于跨国公司派其本公司人员到合资企业任职有费用高昂等难处,越来越倾向于培训东道国人员担任合资企业的重要管理职务。从形式上看,这似与多数发展中国家的有关法律政策不谋而合,其实大相径庭。因为跨国公司对东道国人员的培训重点在于"培养他们克服执行(跨国公司)战略的联系障碍和能力",使其"充分地掌握母公司的观点","与战略执行保持足够的联系"。[4] 对此,我方人员在接受外方提供的培训时应有清醒的认识。在中外合资企业这种特殊的经济形式中,广泛的国际经济联系、包括与外方母公司的交往必不可少,但是,中外合资企业作为中国法人,应保持企业自主权,不能把企业命运委之外方。

二、技术优势形成的事实上控制问题

美国学者弗里德曼和贝吉恩指出:虽然许多外国投资者可能感到表决权和法律上的控制总是联系的,但他们大部分认为,即使居于少数股权地位,他们技术上的优势将是行使最后实际控制合资企业的手段。[5]

〔1〕 See V. V. Ramanadham (ed.), *Joint Ventures and Public Enterprises in Developing Countries*, International Centre for Public Enterprises in Developing Countries, 1980, p. 72.

〔2〕 See Pompiliu Verzariu, Jay A. Burgess, *Joint Venture Agreement in Romania*, East West Trade Bureau of the U. S. Department of Commerce, 1977, p. 31.

〔3〕 See OCEANA, *Multinational Corporations Law*, B33, Comparative Analysis of Case Studies, OCEANA, 1982, p. 44.

〔4〕 John Fayerweather, *International Business Strategy and Administration*, Ballinger Publishing Company, 1982, p. 490.

〔5〕 Wolfgang G. Friedmann, Jean-Pierre Beguin, *Joint International Business Ventures in Developing Countries*, Columbia University Press, 1971, p. 386. Quoted from Lewis D. Solomon, *Multinational Corporations and the Emerging World Order*, Kennikak Press, 1978, p. 109.

在合资企业中,跨国公司如果处于少数股权地位,就可能在许可证协议中通过质量管理、许可证范围的限制等寻求保护母公司在技术方面的利益,也可能在任何技术性服务协议中试图明确规定母公司的作用。在技术变化特别重要的工业部门中,跨国公司可能通过规定由母公司向合资企业转让技术的技术合同对合资企业实行控制。[1] 在合资企业合同中,跨国公司一般都力图最大限度地控制其引进的技术。

举办中外合资企业的主要目的之一是引进外国先进技术。因此,许多中外合资企业或是在合资企业合同中订有技术引进条款,或是另订有技术引进的专门合同。为了防止外方利用技术优势形成对合资企业的事实上控制,在签订有关条款或合同时,需要特别引起注意的几个方面是:

（一）不承担只从外方取得技术的义务

发展中国家合资企业的一些经验证实了不承担这项义务的重要性。在墨美合资的 Industrias Resistol 公司中,董事名额分配为墨方 10 名,美方（蒙森托公司）5 名,美蒙森托公司副总裁和国际分部总经理以及负责设备和计划人员的副总裁都参加该合资企业的董事会,该董事会副董事长实际上也是由蒙森托公司委派。此局面与上述金伯利-克拉克公司例相似,颇有通过此人员配备形成事实上控制之势。其实不然。对该合资企业的研究结论认为,该合资企业在其经营活动中比较独立于美蒙森托公司。这主要是因为该合资企业没有承担只从蒙森托公司取得技术的义务,它向世界各地其他公司,如 British Petrolenm, Uniroyal, ICI 和 Mitsubishi 等公司购买技术。[2] 对印美合资企业的研究也表明,由于印度合营者坚持合资企业可从其他美国公司或欧洲公司取得所需技术的立场,美国合营者控制不了合资企业。[3] 可见,广开技术来源,不承担只从外方取得所需技术的义务,是避免外方以技术垄断地位对合资企业实行事实上控制的有效措施之一。

（二）要求外方承担连续性技术转让的义务

尽管东欧国家合资企业法一般都要求外国合营者引进先进技术,但难以严格实施。匈牙利学者来哈里. 西麦在匈牙利的调查表明,匈合资企业接受的技术都是属于成熟类（即使用 5 年以上的技术）。在罗美合资企业 Control Data 中,美方引进的

---

〔1〕　See Lewis D. Solomon, *Multinational Corporations and the Emerging World Order*, Kennikak Press, 1978, pp. 109-110.

〔2〕　See OCEANA, *Multinational Corporations Law*, B13-B32, Case Studies of Joint International Business Ventures, OCEANA, 1982, pp. 73-86.

〔3〕　John Fayerweather, *International Business Strategy and Administration*, Ballinger Publishing Company, 1982, p. 410.

是其母公司制造最旧型号印刷机的技术。[1] 在由美吉列公司与南商业公司组成的合资企业中，吉列公司 1973 年、1977 年两次引进的生产技术分别是该公司 60 年代早期和晚期采用的技术。在中外合资企业中也不乏其例。因此，在中外合资企业合同中，有必要要求外方承担连续性技术转让的义务。有此规定，即使合营之初外方引进的技术不够先进，我方尚可在合营期间责成外方不断引进其母公司的先进技术。而如果没有此类规定，外方不承担连续性技术转让的责任；何时引进新技术，悉听其便。外方在每次新的技术转让时，都可能附加某些条件以求达到控制合资企业的目的。

（三）承担共同贡献、研究和发展合资企业技术的责任

在合资企业中，合营各方有可能共同贡献、研究和发展合资企业的技术。Bata 工业公司（一家电力设备公司）在一个举办多年的合资企业中进行了最大规模的海外经营活动，该合资企业研究和发展能力得到充分发展。其生产线的重要部分由同母公司生产线甚至母公司的技术无关的项目组成。[2] 墨美合资的 Industrias Resistol 公司也拥有一些专门从事研究和发展的大实验室，有能力发展其本身的多种技术，在技术上不必依赖外国企业，并已对外出售技术。[3]

虽然，在中外合资企业中，我方一般是作为技术输入方，但在有条件的情况下，我方应发挥技术特长，作出实质性的贡献，并在合同中确定合营各方承担共同贡献技术的责任。中外合资企业所应用的技术如果由合营各方贡献的技术混合构成，为合营各方共同掌握，就可以有效地防止外方通过技术优势形成的事实上控制。

在我方暂时不能提供实质性技术贡献的中外合资企业中，应在合资企业合同或有关技术转让的专门合同中争取签订共同研究和发展技术的条款，这是逐步摆脱依赖外国技术的有效措施。但在签订此类条款时，需要认真确定共同研究和发展技术的具体项目。在跨国公司中，研究和发展技术活动一般高度集中于母公司，子公司的研究和发展技术活动受到母公司的高度控制。即使新产品或工艺可能在子公司的实验室发明，也可能要交由母公司安排应用。若干年过后，该技术才可能应用于它的子公司。在由跨国公司子公司和我方组成的合资企业中进行的研究和发展技术活动，也可能发生此类情况。因此，在有关合同条款中，有必要明确规定，合资企

---

[1] See V. V. Ramanadham (ed.), *Joint Ventures and Public Enterprises in Developing Countries*, International Centre for Public Enterprises in Developing Countries, 1980, p. 125.

[2] See Lawrence G. Franko, *Joint Venture Survival in Multinational Corporations*, Praeger Publishers Inc., 1971, pp. 30-31.

[3] See OCEANA, *Multinational Corporations Law*, B13-B32, Case Studies of Joint International Business Ventures, OCEANA, 1982, p. 125.

业的研究和发展技术活动直接为本企业生产服务,以免劳民伤财,到头来为他人作嫁。

（四）制订培训我方技术人员的具体计划

在合资企业合同中,有无培训当地技术人员的条款,在一定程度上决定了合资企业的成败。墨意合资企业 Tubos de Arero 由于实行了培训当地技术人员的计划,对外方的技术依赖程度显著减轻:1975 年底,外方技术人员从 1959 年底的 45 人左右减至 6 人,支付外方的技术使用费也从 1971—1973 年的每年 20 万美元减至 8.4 万美元。[1] 牙买加合资企业 Cadbuny 在外方撤走后,由牙方经营如常;而牙买加的另一合资企业 Ovaltine 在外方决定撤走时,牙方不知所措。之所以有这两种结局,主要是由于前者实行了培训当地技术人员的计划,实行了全面的技术转让,而后者外方的专有技术没有充分转让给牙方。[2]

在中外合资企业合同中,如果没有关于培训我方技术人员的条款,或只是含糊地规定外方负责培训我方技术人员,外方就可能根据其需要,保留某些不向我方人员提供培训的关键技术领域,也可能随心所欲地拖延培训我方技术人员的期限,以便以技术优势实行对合资企业的事实上控制。因此,在中外合资企业合同中,不仅要有培训我方技术人员的条款,还要有培训范围、质量以及我方技术人员取代外方的期限等具体规定。要求外方培训操作技术人员比较容易,但要求外方培训设计人员,特别是机械方面的设计人才可能很困难。如果在有关合同中没有培训设计人员的规定,在合营期间,外方根本不会提供这方面的培训。因此,在合同谈判中,就要力争规定此类条款。否则,技术转让就不是完整的。[3]

三、销售优势形成的事实上控制问题

外国合营者希望控制合资企业销售的动机,除了从定价机会中取得最大可能的利益之外,更重要的是取得对合资企业的事实上控制。美国学者贾斯洛认为:合同中某些规定可能增强事实上控制……例如合资企业的全部产品或绝大部分产品由西方合营者销售。[4] 另两位美国学者为美国海外投资者精心设计的保证控制海外合资企业的五个方案中,有两个是通过控制销售来实现的:一是"合同规定合资企业

---

〔1〕　See OCEANA, *Multinational Corporations Law*, B13-B32, Case Studies of Joint International Business Ventures, OCEANA, 1982, pp. 15-22.

〔2〕　See V. V. Ramanadham (ed.), *Joint Ventures and Public Enterprises in Developing Countries*, International Centre for Public Enterprises in Developing Countries, 1980, p. 72.

〔3〕　参见拉纳·辛格:《技术转让》,载《经济研究参考资料》1980 年第 94 期,第 50 页。

〔4〕　See Craig A. Jaslow, Practical Considerations in Drafting an Joint Venture Agreement with China, *American Journal of Comparative Law*, Vol. 31, No. 2, 1983, p. 221.

所有产品将售给美国控制的销售公司"，二是"给予当地合营者对生产公司的控制以换取销售公司的 51％股权"。

在中外合资企业中，由于我方缺乏国外销售渠道和经验，外方较容易取得外销权。在有关合同条款中，我方丧失外销权有两种情况：第一种是规定外方负责外销，未作期限的规定，也没有我方参与的安排。例如，天津丽明化妆品合营工业公司合同规定，外销由联邦德国威娜公司通过其销售渠道网负责，内销由合资企业负责。[1]第二种是虽有我方参与外销的安排，但外方仍拥有绝对优势。如中国迅达电梯有限公司协议第 6 条第 2 款规定："在本协议有效期再加上延续的五年之内，怡迅公司（即瑞士迅达股份有限公司拥有全部股权的子公司——引者）与迅达公司（即瑞士迅达股份有限公司——引者）将作为合资企业产品出口的唯一代理商。……经过合资公司董事会的一致同意，合资公司可以直接向既无迅达公司也无怡迅公司销售机构的国家出口'产品'。"[2]丧失外销权，我方经济损失自不待言，更重要的是，可能导致外方对合资企业的事实上控制。在合营期间，外方利用外销权，可能根据其母公司的全球性销售计划，从销售安排上反过来影响合资企业的产品、产量，从而影响合资企业的长期经营目标。在合资企业合同濒临期满时，外方凭借外销权，可在是否延长合资企业期限的谈判中占优势地位。因为外方独掌外销权，一旦撤走，外销渠道随之堵塞，合资企业外销产品出路以至企业的继续经营都成大问题。在此情况下，我方即使有种种不愿延长合资企业期限的原因，为求企业生计，也可能挽留外方。由外方独掌外销权的局面不改，我方很难有自主之日。

在另一些中外合资企业合同中，有我方参与外销的安排，大致可分为两种：第一种是多渠道销售。如中国郑州电缆厂深圳联合公司协议规定：产品销售渠道如下："(1) 本公司自销；(2) 中国机械设备进出口公司广东分公司收购外销；(3) 甲方（即深圳机械工业公司——引者）代销内销部分的 50％。"[3]第二种安排是由外方暂时代理，我方有参与权。如中瑞化工有限公司协议书第 6 条第 1 款规定："产品以外销为主，海外之市场销售，暂由中瑞[即中瑞机械工程有限公司（外方）——引者]代理及销售，合营公司有权派人协助工作并在任何适当时期收回代理权，另委代理商或自行销售。"[4]在不同的中外合资企业中，中、外方的销售能力不同，产品销售市场各异，需要根据具体情况研究分析，才可能作出恰当的销售安排。一般说来，我方不宜轻易放弃外销权。如果合营之初，我方参与外销的条件尚不具备，可暂由外方负责

〔1〕 参见《中国经济新闻》1981 年第 42 期，第 13 页。
〔2〕《中国经济新闻》增刊，1980 年 4 月 7 日。
〔3〕《关于在深圳市合资经营"中国郑州电缆厂深圳联合公司"的协议书》（原档摘录，现存厦门大学法律系）。
〔4〕《北京化工厂与中瑞机械工程有限公司合作投资协议书》（原档摘录，现存厦门大学法律系）。

外销,但应争取规定我方参与外销的具体日期。如果日期无法确定,也应有如同上述中瑞化工有限公司协议书有关条款的一般规定。仅有我方参与销售的规定还不够,因为如果没有称职的销售人员,这种参与只能是徒有虚名。因此,在合同中还要争取签订有关培训销售人员的条款,并要明确规定培训的具体标准、期限等。

第五节　中外合资企业的技术转让条款探讨*

中外合资经营企业（以下简称"合资企业"）引进外国技术主要采取两种形式：一是技术资本化形式，即中外合营双方签订合资企业合同有关技术转让条款，允许外国合营者以技术作价投资；另一种是技术转让形式，即合资企业与外国合营者或第三方签订技术转让协议，引进合资企业所需的技术。本文拟初步探讨签订合资企业合同或技术转让协议时中外合营双方比较关注的若干条款。

一、技术的定义与标准

一般说来，"技术"一词用于表述积累的、用于完成某项技术成果的所有手段。在实践中，各国根据是否受成文法保护把技术分为工业产权和专有技术。[1]我国也不例外。

在签订合资企业合同有关条款和技术转让协议中，首先需要明确合资企业引进的工业产权和专有技术的定义。除了一般的定义性规定之外，应在合同、协议的有关条款或附录中说明专利的名称、数量和颁发日期。专利许可证并不等同于专利权。它只是被视为专利权人不诉专利受让人侵权的一种承诺。因此，对专利许可的权限和范围，尤应明确。[2]有关专有技术的定义可能较为困难。技术受方出于使用专有技术的考虑，通常希望较广义的表述，而出于支付使用费的考虑，则可能希望较狭义的表述。[3]而技术供方可能发现，如果定义过广，将无法与其提供的专有技术相符。有关专有技术转让的条款可能包括技术资料、质量控制、原料及来源、操作规程、工艺流程、产品设计、说明书、经验积累以及其他秘密资料等内容。[4]无论采用技术资本化或技术转让形式，技术供方都应提交工业产权或专有技术的有关资料，包括专利证书或商标注册证书的复印件、有效状况及其技术特征、实用价值等有关文件，作为合资企业合同或技术转让协议的附件。[5]

---

* 原载《厦门大学学报》（哲学社会科学版）1990 年第 1 期。

〔1〕 See James Dobkin, Negotiating an International Technology Joint Venture, *Connecticut Journal of International Law*, Vol. 1, 1985, p. 95.

〔2〕 Ibid. , p. 100.

〔3〕 Ibid. , p. 97.

〔4〕 See Charles J. Conroy, Technology Transfer to China: Legal and Practical Considerations, *Stanford Journal of International Law*, Vol. 21, No. 2, p. 560.

〔5〕 参见《中华人民共和国中外合资经营企业法实施条例》（以下简称《实施条例》）第 29、45 条。

关于合资企业引进外国技术的标准,《中华人民共和国中外合资经营企业法》(以下简称《中外合资经营企业法》)第 5 条规定:"外国合营者作为投资的技术和设备,必须确实是适合我国需要的先进技术和设备。如果有意以落后的技术和设备进行欺骗,造成损失的,应赔偿损失。"可见,"先进"和"适用"是合资企业引进外国技术不可或缺的两个标准。先进的技术是指同我国现有技术水平比较,相对先进的技术,并不一定要求世界一流水平。适用性之所以同时强调,是因为技术的应用常有许多限制条件,先进的技术要适合我国的需要和实际接受能力,才能发挥其经济效益。有的外国学者认为,上述法律规定中的"适合""先进"等措辞不严密,可由中方单方面解释;另外,对"有意"欺骗也未作明确定义,可能使外国合营者心存疑惧。[1]实践表明,这些问题可通过签订有关合同、协议条款解决。外国合营者或其他技术供方如果根据实际情况,认为向合资企业提供二、三流技术将比一流技术更适用,可在谈判中明确说明并在有关条款中实事求是地指出所提供技术的先进程度、质量以及提供该技术的适当原因。[2]这样,不仅可以使"先进""适用"的标准具体化,还可以有效地避免"有意"欺骗之嫌。例如,在设立天津奥的斯电梯有限公司的合同谈判中,外国合营者美国奥的斯电梯公司主张先转让较一般的技术给该合资企业,主要理由是,应用该技术生产的产品适合我国现有的制造能力、服务能力和市场需要。在有关合同、协议条款中规定,在合营双方积累经验和增强相互信任感的情况下,美国奥的斯电梯公司将引进较先进的技术,并拟定了持续性技术转让的日程表。该表反映了国内市场需要和经营的可行性比技术的复杂性更为重要。[3]目前,该合资企业通过引进美方技术,已试制出交流双速和交流调速两种新规格的电梯,达到了发达国家 20 世纪 80 年代初的水平。[4]

二、回授条款

国际技术转让中的回授条款是指技术受方允许技术供方取得其改进技术的协议。在签订回授条款中,技术供方可能要求技术受方回授非独占性的、免费的改进技术的许可,由此取得改进技术的应用或分许可等有关权利。多数回授条款还规定

〔1〕　See JoAnne Swindle, The New Legal Framework for Joint Ventures in China: Guidelines for Investors, *Law & Policy in International Business*, Vol. 16, No. 3, 1984, p. 1039.

〔2〕　See Kevin K. Maher, Foreign Investment in The People's Republic of China: Compensation Trade, Joint Ventures, Industrial Property Protection and Dispute Settlement, *Georgia Journal of International and Comparative Law*, Vol. 10, No. 2, p. 248.

〔3〕　See Steven R. Hendryx, Implementation of a Technology Transfer Joint Venture in People's Republic of China: A Management Perspective, *The Columbia Journal of World Business*, Vol. 21, No. 1, 1986, pp. 59-60.

〔4〕　参见《中美在津合资电梯企业经营有方》,载《人民日报》(海外版),1988 年 5 月 10 日第 3 版。

了技术受方向技术供方报告其有关技术改进的程序。[1]

《中华人民共和国中外合资经营企业法实施条例》（以下简称《实施条例》）第 46 条规定，"技术转让协议必须符合以下规定：……订立技术转让协议双方，相互交换改进技术的条件应对等。"《中华人民共和国技术引进合同管理条例》（以下简称《技术引进条例》）第 9 条也有类似规定。这正式表明，我国有条件地接受了技术转让协议中的回授条款，即主张以对等原则订立双向性的回授条款。这符合国际上的一般实践。许多国家、包括一些发达国家都认为，当回授条款在实际上造成了知识和革新的单向流动、由技术供方单方面受益时，就不能接受。典型的回授条款经常同技术供方有关向技术受方提供改进技术的承诺相联系，由此成为技术受方保留取得最新技术渠道的方式。[2] 由于这种改进技术的所有权和转让权是不确定的，在有关条款中，必须对改进技术的使用费作出规定。[3]

有些技术转让协议规定，技术转让双方相互免费回授改进技术。这种规定貌似对等，其实不然。因为在履行技术转让协议期间，很可能出现仅有一方（技术供方或技术受方）作出技术改进或者双方所作的技术改进程度和范围不同的情况，如相互免费回授改进技术，后果很可能显失公平。特别是在外国合营者为技术供方，合资企业为技术受方的情况下，更不宜作此规定。因为合资企业作为技术受方，意味着技术供方向技术受方提供的改进技术是由中外合营双方共同享用和获益的，而技术受方向技术供方提供的改进技术，则由外国合营者单独享用和获益。在此情况下，即使在履行技术转让协议期间，技术转让双方所作的技术改进程度和范围相同，也无法产生公平的后果。[4]

三、保密条款

在国际技术转让中，技术供方为了保障其技术的市场收益，避免第三人使用其技术，一般要求在技术转让协议中签订保密条款。保密条款的核心是技术供方和技术受方承诺不将有关技术公开给第三人，除非该技术另行进入公众领域。在签订技术转让协议中，有关"第三人"的含义曾发生问题。有些技术受方只愿承担"不将专有技术内容以任何形式公开给中国以外的任何第三人"的义务。另一些技术受方虽

〔1〕 See Vincent D. Travaglini, Foreign Licensing and Joint Venture Arrangement, *North Carolina Journal of International Law and Commercial Regulations*, Vol. 4, No. 1, 1978, p. 164.

〔2〕 See Philip J. Wilson, The Legal Structures Governing Technology Transfer and Joint Venture with People's Republic of China, *International Tax and Business Lawyer*, Vol. 3, No. 1, 1985, p. 43.

〔3〕 See Charles J. Conroy, Technology Transfer to China: Legal and Practical Considerations, *Stanford Journal of International Law*, Vol. 21, No. 2, p. 562.

〔4〕 参见郑成思：《国际技术转让法通论》，中国展望出版社 1987 年版，第 81 页。

然接受"第三人"的一般含义并承认中国的其他企业或个人属于"第三人",但不愿将此明示规定于有关条款。[1] 这种情况在一定程度上妨碍了合资企业引进外国技术的工作。现在,有关"第三人"的含义在我国有关法律中已经明确。《中华人民共和国专利法》第12条规定:"……被许可人无权允许合同规定以外的任何单位或者个人实施该专利。"《技术引进条例》第7条也规定:"受方应当按照双方商定的范围和期限,对供方提供的技术中尚未公开的秘密部分,承担保密义务。"显然,我国对合资企业引进的外国技术给予明确的法律保护,有关"第三人"的含义与国际实践一致,技术受方以外的中国企业或个人均属"第三人"。因此,在签订保密条款中,作为技术受方的合资企业可以而且应当承担不将有关技术以任何形式公开给任何第三人(包括其他中国企业或个人)的法律义务。这种规定虽然在一定时期内限制了有关技术的推广应用,但为引进更多的外国先进技术创设了良好的法律环境。而那种"一家引进,百家分享"的引进方式,即使在短期内具有推广应用有关技术的显著效益,但对引进外国先进技术的全局而言,则不能不说是一种竭泽而渔的方式。

保密条款一般还应规定,合营各方的雇员必须履行有关保密义务;除了从事合资企业业务需要,不得使用技术秘密资料等。这类防止合资企业雇员泄密的条款还可进一步详细规定于合资企业与雇员签订的劳动合同。[2]

四、商标条款

合资企业可能选择:(1) 专用于合资企业产品或服务的新商标;(2) 合营一方在相同或类似领域中已享有信誉的商标;(3) 合营各方知名商标的联合。

在第一种情况下,商标权属于合资企业。这种新商标所表示的产品或服务的信誉全凭合资企业自身来建立,与合营各方原有商标的信誉无关。在合资企业提供的产品或服务质量欠佳时,就意味着合资企业的实际损失,甚至可能导致新商标的废弃。[3]

合资企业如选择外国合营者的商标,就产生了商标的转让或许可使用问题。由于商标权不具有跨国效力,根据《中华人民共和国商标法》的有关规定,外国合营者首先需要在我国注册登记拟转让或许可使用的商标。如转让注册商标,转让人和受让人应共同向国家工商行政管理局商标局申请,并经批准。如许可使用商标,则许

---

〔1〕 See Philip J. Wilson, The Legal Structures Governing Technology Transfer and Joint Venture with People's Republic of China, *International Tax and Business Lawyer*, Vol. 3, No. 1, 1985, pp. 41-42.

〔2〕 See James Dobkin, Negotiating an International Technology Joint Venture, *Connecticut Journal of International Law*, Vol. 1, 1985, p. 105.

〔3〕 See Saul Lefkowitz, Double Trademarking—We've Come a Long Way, *The Trademark Reporter*, Vol. 73, No. 1, 1983, pp. 15-16.

可人与被许可人应签订商标使用许可合同,并报商标局备案。[1] 商标的转让和商标的许可使用产生了不同的法律后果:前者,商标权已转移给合资企业;后者,商标权仍保留于外国合营者。在许可使用商标的情况下,如合资企业的产品或服务质量不佳,势必影响到外国合营者商标的信誉。因此,在签订商标条款中,首先应明确商标是转让或许可使用。在许可使用时,为了中外合营双方的共同利益,也为了保障外国合营者商标的信誉,应具体商定有关质量监督和外国合营者提供连续性技术转让的条款。

合资企业如选择合营各方知名商标的联合,可以利用合营各方在相同或类似领域中业已建立的信誉,有助于开辟产品市场或开展服务。这种联合商标是由合营各方共有的。合营各方保留对本方商标的直接控制和监督。[2]

在商标权属于合资企业的情况下,当合资企业的合营期限届满时,将产生商标权的归属问题。在合资企业的清算工作中,对清偿债务后的剩余财产一般按照合营各方的股权比例进行分配。而对于商标权,就不能采取这种分配方式。如果允许合营各方分别取得合资企业的商标权,由于同一商标代表了原合营各方不同的产品或服务,将可能危害消费者的利益,也可能损害该商标的信誉。为了维护消费者的利益和保持商标的统一性,在有关合同、协议条款中,应商定在合资企业的合营期限届满时,由合营一方有偿或无偿取得合资企业的商标权。[3]

五、出口限制条款

在国际技术转让中,技术供方经常要求限制技术受方的产品销售区域。其主要目的是,保证其出售许可证的收益大于因出售许可证而出让给技术受方的市场的收益。技术供方一般保留在技术转让协议期间限制或扩大技术受方的被许可区域等权利,限制或扩大的主要依据是技术受方在被许可区域履行协议的情况以及提供保证金和服务的能力。[4] 技术供方之所以愿意让给技术受方一部分市场,通常是因为它在该区域缺少销售机构、经营能力不足或已不能维持择优价格,试图通过出售许可证来弥补这些缺陷,使专利权获得最大限度的利润。[5]

《实施条例》第46条规定,在技术转让协议中,"除双方另有协议外,技术输出方

〔1〕《中华人民共和国商标法》第25、26条。

〔2〕 See Saul Lefkowitz, Double Trademarking—We've Come a Long Way, *The Trademark Reporter*, Vol. 73, No. 1, 1983, pp. 15-16.

〔3〕 See J. Thomas Mccarthy, Joint Ownership of a Trademark, *The Trademark Reporter*, Vol. 73, No. 1, 1983, p. 6.

〔4〕 See Vincent D. Travaglini, Foreign Licensing and Joint Venture Arrangement, *North Carolina Journal of International Law and Commercial Regulations*, Vol. 4, No. 1, 1978, pp. 161-162.

〔5〕 王静安:《许可证合同》,知识出版社1987年版,第16页。

不得限制技术输入方出口其产品的地区、数量和价格"。《技术引进条例》第 9 条也规定,"未经审批机关特殊批准,合同不得含有下列限制性条款:……不合理地限制受方的销售渠道或出口市场。"显然,根据我国有关法律规定,技术供方一般不得限制技术受方出口其产品。开拓国际市场、扩大出口贸易,不仅是我国举办合资企业的主要目标之一,也是合资企业维持本身外汇平衡以利经营发展的必要措施。因此,在技术转让协议中,合资企业一般不宜接受技术供方对其产品出口的限制。特别是在外国合营者为技术供方的情况下,更不宜接受此类限制。因为,首先,外国合营者作为合资企业的股权所有者,可以从合资企业产品的出口创汇中直接获利;其次,在合资企业产品部分内销的情况下,中国合营者通常提供其内销渠道,外国合营者在持续分享内销收益的同时,理应尽可能向合资企业开放其原有的国外市场。

当然,我国有关法律并非完全禁止出口限制条款。鉴于技术供方或技术本身的某些特殊情况,例如,合资企业引进技术所生产产品的出口的确会严重影响技术供方的利益,或者该产品属进口替代产品,也可以接受对这类产品出口的某些限制。

六、期限与终止条款

《技术引进条例》第 8 条规定:"合同的期限应当同受方掌握引进技术的时间相适应,未经审批机关特殊批准不得超过十年。"在实践中,有关专利许可的许可证协议的期限通常与该专利的期限相同,但也可能商定不同于该专利期限的规定。有关商标许可使用的协议期满时,被许可人不得再使用该商标。但这类协议也可规定,允许在原许可使用期限之后延期,可延至该商标的有效期届满。[1] 多数技术转让协议的期限为 5 至 10 年。在外国合营者为技术供方、合资企业为技术受方的情况下,可以商定比较灵活的期限安排。[2] 例如,天津奥的斯电梯有限公司的合资企业合同期限为 30 年,而技术合作协议期限为 10 年,由于外方将在整个合营期间提供连续性的技术转让,中外合营双方商定,在设立该合资企业 6 年之后,根据"实际上相同"的条件进行有关延长技术合作协议期限的谈判。这为便利连续性的技术转让和保证补偿外方的技术转让提供了达成新协议的基础。[3]

在设立合资企业时,合营各方应认识到,在合资企业不同的发展和经营阶段都

---

〔1〕　See Vincent D. Travaglini, Foreign Licensing and Joint Venture Arrangement, *North Carolina Journal of International Law and Commercial Regulations*, Vol. 4, No. 1, 1978, pp. 161-162.

〔2〕　See Charles J. Conroy, Technology Transfer to China: Legal and Practical Considerations, *Stanford Journal of International Law*, Vol. 21, No. 2, p. 562.

〔3〕　See Steven R. Hendryx, Implementation of a Technology Transfer Joint Venture in People's Republic of China: A Management Perspective, *The Columbia Journal of World Business*, Vol. 21, No. 1, 1986, pp. 59-60.

可能发生企业终止的情况。商定终止条款经常比商定合资企业合同其他条款的总和更为费时耗力。在有关技术转让方面，合营各方至少必须对以下问题达成协议：(1) 合资企业设立时取得的工业产权和专有技术中的哪些权利应转让给原所有人；(2) 在合资企业作为一经济实体继续存在的情况下，合资企业设立时取得的工业产权和专有技术中的哪些权利将在合营各方间交叉许可，或者许可、分许可给该经济实体；(3) 在合资企业经营期间由合营各方共同发展的工业产权和专有技术中的哪些权利将由合资企业许可或分许可给合营各方；(4) 哪一合营方有权进行合资企业有关技术的改进。[1]

---

〔1〕 See James Dobkin，Negotiating an International Technology Joint Venture，*Connecticut Journal of International Law*，Vol. 1，1985，pp. 102-103.

第六节　中外合营者之间争端的解决方式评析*

中外合资企业的实践表明,中外合营者之间有关合资企业合同的解释和履行以及管理决策等方面的分歧和争端在所难免,如能及时、妥善解决,企业可继续经营和发展;如不能解决,则将导致企业经营的严重困难,甚至解散。因此,中外合营者之间争端的解决方式是合资企业合同的重要内容,可能成为决定企业成败的关键因素。[1] 本文拟根据我国有关法律规定和借鉴国外有关实践,对解决中外合营者之间争端的一般方式和特殊方式试作评析。

一

《中华人民共和国中外合资经营企业法》(以下简称《中外合资法》)和《中华人民共和国中外合资经营企业法实施条例》(以下简称《实施条例》)对中外合营者之间争端的解决方式作了原则规定,即合营各方可通过协商、调解、仲裁以至司法解决方式解决争端。

（一）协商与调解方式

《实施条例》第 109 条规定:"合营各方如在解释或履行合营企业协议、合同、章程时发生争议,应尽量通过友好协商或调解解决。"可见,协商与调解方式是中外合营者首先应考虑的解决争端方式。

协商方式是指争端当事人自愿直接磋商解决争端的方式。其主要特点是,一般没有第三人参与,由争端当事人"通过查明事实寻找真理",找出具有法律和合同依据的解决办法。[2] 采取协商方式解决中外合营者之间争端的优点首先是有利于保持和发展合营者之间的友好合作关系,因为这种方式属企业内部的"友好讨论"或"友好谈判",不伤感情;其次,这种方式无成规可循,比较灵活,简便易行。只要合营一方提出协商愿望,另一方表示同意,即可进行,可以通过函电磋商,亦可进行面对面的谈判。在争端当事人双方诚心实意的努力下,可望通过这种方式圆满解决争

---

* 原载《厦门大学学报》(哲学社会科学版)1992 年第 1 期。

〔1〕 See Thomas J. Kalitgaad, People's Republic of China Joint Venture Dispute Resolution Procedures, *UCLA Pacific Basin Law Journal*, Vol. 1, No. 1, 1982, p. 5.

〔2〕 See Steven N. Robinson, George R. A. Doumar, "It is Better to Enter a Tiger's Mouth than a Court of Law" or Dispute Resolution Alternatives in US-China Trade, *Dickinson Journal of International Law*, Vol. 5, No. 2, 1987, p. 263.

端。厦门有关部门的调查表明，厦门的中外合资经营企业合营者之间的争端大部分是通过协商解决的。[1] 然而，这种方式的缺点也是明显的：由于协商是在争端当事人之间进行，没有外部干预，当事人能否达成协议，达成的协议能否执行，全靠当事人的诚实信用，不具备任何强制性保证；此外，协商解决通常需要花费较长的时间。

调解方式是指争端当事人自愿在调解人协助下解决争端的方式。调解人的主要职责是查清有关事实情况并提交当事人各方，促使当事人各方达成协议，无权作出具有法律约束力的裁决。近年来，调解方式已成为解决国际经济争端的重要方式之一。[2] 一些常设仲裁机构，如解决投资争端国际中心、国际商会仲裁院、苏黎世商会仲裁院和捷克斯洛伐克、匈牙利、南斯拉夫等国商会仲裁机构以及格丁尼亚海事与内河航行仲裁院、太平洋工业产权协会等，都制定了调解规则或在仲裁规则中作出有关调解的规定。另一些常设仲裁机构，如美国仲裁协会、瑞典斯德哥尔摩商会仲裁院、伦敦仲裁院、苏联工商会对外贸易仲裁委员会等，虽然在其仲裁规则中对调解未作规定，但在实践中也支持调解工作。调解方式的优点除了有利于保持当事人之间的友好合作关系外，还表现在，同协商方式比较，由于有调解人的积极参与，即较客观地调查事实真相并提出建设性的和解建议，可望较快、较公正地解决争端；同司法和仲裁解决方式比较，程序较为简便灵活，解决争端较迅速，费用较低。

《中外合资法》第 14 条规定："合营各方发生纠纷，董事会不能协商解决时，由中国仲裁机构进行调解或仲裁，也可由合营各方协议在其他仲裁机构仲裁。"《实施条例》第 109 条对进行调解的机构未作规定。由于上述规定未明示排除在外国仲裁机构调解的可能性，可以理解为中外合营者可以选择由外国仲裁机构或其他机构调解解决争端。在实践中，有的中外合资企业合营各方在协商解决争端不成之后，通过请中国地方政府主管部门出面调解，妥善解决了争端。

近年来，中国仲裁机构创造了与外国仲裁机构联合调解的方式，引起了各国的普遍注意。有的外国学者甚至认为，虽然目前采用这种方式的实例很少，但在不久的将来，这种方式将比仲裁方式更为重要。[3] 这种方式一般是，由争端当事人双方各选择一名调解人，两名调解人在调查研究、分析争端事实和性质的基础上向争端当事人双方提出不具约束力的和解建议，并附具和解条件及理由。当事人双方如接

---

〔1〕 参见廖延豹主编：《常见涉外经济合同的签订和履行》，鹭江出版社 1989 年版，第 94 页。

〔2〕 See Terrance W. Conley, Paul W. Beamish, Joint Ventures in China: Legal Implications, *The Business Quarterly*, Vol. 51, No. 3, 1986, p. 42.

〔3〕 See Steven N. Robinson, George R. A. Doumar, "It is Better to Enter a Tiger's Mouth than a Court of Law" or Dispute Resolution Alternatives in US-China Trade, *Dickinson Journal of International Law*, Vol. 5, No. 2, 1987, p. 263.

受和解建议,达成和解协议,调解人将予以确认,并作成调解书,由当事人双方自动执行。目前我国已同美国、法国和意大利等国签订了有关仲裁机构联合调解的协议。

(二) 仲裁方式

除了以上援引的《中外合资法》第 14 条规定外,《实施条例》第 110 条进一步明确规定:"合营各方根据有关仲裁的书面协议,提请仲裁。可以在中国国际贸易促进委员会对外经济贸易仲裁委员会仲裁,按该会的仲裁程序规则进行。如当事各方同意,也可以在被诉一方所在国或第三国的仲裁机构仲裁,按该机构的仲裁程序规则进行。"

根据以上规定,仲裁协议中有关仲裁机构、仲裁程序规则可由合营各方选择;另者,关于仲裁适用的实体法,未作明确规定,这是合营各方在签订仲裁协议时需要解决的两个主要问题。

1. 仲裁机构和仲裁程序规则的选择

国际经济仲裁实践表明,仲裁机构和仲裁程序规则的选择将极大地影响合营各方在解决争端过程中的程序性权利,由于仲裁程序规则调整仲裁员的选择、法律适用以及仲裁裁决的执行,将对仲裁结果产生一定的影响。[1]

在许多国家,仲裁程序是由仲裁地国家的仲裁程序规则调整的。这是基于"管辖权理论"(jurisdictional theory)。该理论"承认国家控制和调整在其管辖权范围之内进行的所有仲裁的权力"。中国向来遵循这一国际经济仲裁惯例。过去,为了确保中国仲裁程序规则的适用,多数中国企业签订的国际经济贸易合同都规定了在中国仲裁的条款。另一选择是规定在被诉方所在国进行仲裁。由于中方极少主动申请仲裁,在多数仲裁案件中,中方居于被诉方地位,因此,仲裁仍在中国进行。[2]

国际经济争端在第三国仲裁机构根据其仲裁规则解决是普遍接受的国际惯例。这被视为有助于保证争端当事人之间的平等。在东欧国家的国际合营企业实践中也有先例。[3] 我国实行对外开放政策以来,随着国际经济交往的进一步发展,已从一般坚持在中国仲裁的立场转变为接受在第三国仲裁。《中外合资法》第 14 条和《实施条例》第 110 条的规定反映了这一转变。在实践中,一些中外合资企业合同已订有

---

〔1〕　See Thomas J. Kalitgaad, People's Republic of China Joint Venture Dispute Resolution Procedures, *UCLA Pacific Basin Law Journal*, Vol. 1, No. 1, 1982, p. 11.

〔2〕　See Mary Celeste Doty, An Evaluation of the People's Republic of China's Participation in International Commercial Arbitration: Pragmatic Prospectus, *California Western International Law Journal*, Vol. 12, No. 1, 1982, pp. 134-135.

〔3〕　See Miodrag Sukijasovic, *Yugoslav Foreign Investment Legislation at Work: Experiences So Far*, Belgrade, 1970, pp. 147-151.

在第三国仲裁的条款。如中国南海贝克钻井有限公司合同、天津奥的斯电梯有限公司合同等。[1]

尽管第三国仲裁机构一般能以较超然的姿态解决争端，但选择第三国仲裁机构并不一定是最佳选择。仲裁机构的选择取决于当事人的便利、所在地法律、仲裁协议条款等多方面因素。由于实际需要，仲裁地首先应是便利的。如果当事人、证人和有关专家等容易出庭，对争端的及时、公正解决将大有裨益。如果特定工厂是争端的标的，并且有必要经过调查解决争端，就应考虑选择邻近该工厂的仲裁机构。[2]鉴于中外合资企业设立地、主要经营地都在我国，在中国国际经济贸易仲裁委员会（以下简称中国仲裁委员会）按其仲裁规则进行仲裁，对于调查、取证、当事人出庭等无疑是最便利的。中国仲裁委员会成立30多年来，以事实为根据，以法律为准绳，尊重当事人的合同规定，参照国际惯例，公正合理地解决了许多国际经济贸易争端，有效地维护了中外当事人的合法权益，在国内外赢得了信誉。特别是该会仲裁员名册中的仲裁员由中国贸促会从国际经济贸易、科学技术和法律等方面具有专门知识和实际经验的中外人士中聘任，更从组织上保障了仲裁的公正性。因此，合营各方在签订中外合资企业合同仲裁条款或独立的仲裁协议时，中国仲裁委员会似应作为优先考虑的选择对象。

中国香港地区目前正在发展成为东方的国际经济贸易仲裁中心，并获得了中国内地和西方国家的赞成和支持。[3] 1985 年成立的香港国际仲裁中心明确表明受理中外合资企业合营者之间的争端案件。[4] 将中国香港地区作为仲裁地，特别有利于中外合营者之间争端的解决：首先，在地理上是很便利的；其次，在很大程度上消除了中外双方的语言障碍。因此，在外国合营者坚持要在第三国仲裁，而中国合营者主张在中国仲裁的情况下，商定在中国香港地区仲裁，不失为一种可取的折中方案。

2. 法律适用问题

仲裁协议中的法律适用条款经常是国际经济合同的"热点"（boilerplate）部分。当仲裁条款和法律适用条款一起规定于国际经济合同时，选择的法律制度将适用于争端的实质问题。在争端当事人未规定适用于其争端的实体法的情况下，将由仲裁

---

〔1〕 参见《中国经济新闻》1983 年第 11 期，第 17 页；《中国经济新闻》1982 年第 25 期，第 13 页。

〔2〕 See Michael A. Hertzberg, Brian E. McGill, Conflict Resolution, *The North Carolina Journal of International Law and Commercial Regulation*, Vol. 6, No. 1, 1980, p. 290.

〔3〕 See Mary Celeste Doty, An Evaluation of the People's Republic of China's Participation in International Commercial Arbitration: Pragmatic Prospectus, *California Western International Law Journal*, Vol. 12, No. 1, 1982, p. 139.

〔4〕 See Charles J. Conroy, *Legal Aspects of Doing Business with Hong Kong*, Practising Law Institute, 1986, pp. 198-199, 247.

庭选择实体法。仲裁庭可能通过有关国家的冲突法或各国普遍接受的冲突法规则选择实体法。

《中外合资法》第2条第2款规定:"合营企业的一切活动应遵守中华人民共和国法律、法令和有关条例规定。"这一规定产生了在中外合资企业合同仲裁条款或仲裁协议中是否需要预先确定实体法的问题。外国学者对此见解不一。一种观点认为,如果争端解决程序、特别是仲裁程序被视为合资企业的"活动",即使在仲裁条款或协议中未确定实体法,也应适用中国法律,因为中国法律已有明文规定。另一方面,由于中外合资企业设立于中国,中国法优先是合乎逻辑的。另一种观点则主张需要由合营各方预先确定实体法。其主要理由是,即使《中外合资法》第2条第2款的规定适用于争端解决程序,仍然存在确定实体法的问题:其一,在中国法律未作规定的情况下,如何选择实体法;其二,根据"合营企业的一切活动"一词的推论,如果合资企业在第三国进行销售等活动,在没有法律适用条款的情况下,什么法律优先是不清楚的;[1]其三,即使合资企业的"一切活动"均在中国境内进行,所谓"活动"是指合资企业与其他在中国境内的第三人(自然人、法人或中国政府)之间的活动,抑或包括产生于合营者之间的争端,尚存疑义。

在1985年《中华人民共和国涉外经济合同法》颁布之后,上述问题已基本明确,即"在中华人民共和国境内履行的中外合资经营企业合同……适用中华人民共和国法律";中国法律未作规定的,可以适用国际惯例;中国缔结或参加的有关国际条约同中国法律有不同规定的,适用该国际条约的规定,但中国声明保留的条款除外。[2]因此,在仲裁协议中,合营各方不得有相反的规定。至于部分条款(例如外销条款)需要在中国境外履行的中外合资企业合同如何解决法律适用问题,则是值得进一步探讨的。

(三)司法解决方式

由于中外合资企业合营各方之间的争端实际上是不同国家私人之间的争端,牵涉到司法管辖权的问题。行使司法管辖权是行使国家主权的具体表现。此外,确定司法管辖权是受理特定案件、进行诉讼的前提,并往往同法律适用问题密切相关,从而直接影响案件的审理结果。

《实施条例》第111条规定:"如合营各方之间没有仲裁的书面协议,发生争议的

---

〔1〕　See Pat Chew-LaFitte, The Resolution of Transnational Commercial Disputes in the People's Republic of China: A Guide for U.S. Practitioners, *The Yale Journal of World Public Order*, Vol. 8, No. 2, 1982, pp. 257-258.

〔2〕　《中华人民共和国涉外经济合同法》第5条、第6条。

任何一方都可以依法向中国人民法院起诉。"关于外国合营者能否在外国法院提起对中国合营者的诉讼，未作明文规定。

国际上主要的涉外经济管辖权制度包括属地管辖权制度，即以当事人（主要是被告）的住所地、居所地或事物的存在地、事情的发生地等"地域"因素为行使管辖权依据的制度；(2) 属人管辖权制度，即以当事人的国籍为行使管辖权依据的制度；(3) 普通法管辖权制度，即以"实际控制"为行使管辖权依据的制度。[1] 无论实行上述哪一种管辖权制度，外国法院都可能对中外合资企业合营者之间的争端主张管辖权。在实行属地管辖权制度的国家，即使在中国合营者作为被告的情况下，也可能以事物的存在地或事情发生地等"地域"因素作为行使管辖权的依据。在实行属人管辖权制度的国家，可能以外国合营者的国籍作为行使管辖权的依据。在实行普通法管辖权制度的国家，更可基于对中国合营者或其财产的"实际控制"行使管辖权。美国学者克利特加德主张，美国联邦法院或州法院如对中国合营者或其财产取得管辖权，外国合营者就可在美国提起对中国合营者的诉讼。[2] 这是一个值得注意的问题。为了避免在外国法院进行有关中外合营者之间争端的诉讼，根据《中华人民共和国民事诉讼法》第 246 条规定，中外合营者似应在合资企业合同中明确规定合营各方接受中国人民法院对此类争端的专属管辖。

二

除了上述一般解决方式之外，在国际实践中还形成了一些解决合营者之间争端的特殊方式，可资借鉴。

（一）僵局解决方式

合资企业董事会陷入僵局（deadlock）是合营者之间争端的表现形式之一。所谓董事会僵局是指在董事会会议中，合营各方对需要表决通过的事项发生分歧，适用议事规则无效、僵持不下的局面。在合营双方股权比例对等因而董事名额相等、给予少数股权者否决权以及滥用一致通过或特别多数通过议事规则等情况下，特别容易产生僵局。

概括各国的有关实践，主要有以下几种僵局解决方式：

1. 授权机动董事（the swing man）解决的方式

合资企业合同可规定，合营双方董事名额相等，由一个双方都接受的、独立于双

---

〔1〕 详见董立坤、卢绳祖：《涉外经济贸易的诉讼与仲裁》，同济大学出版社 1988 年版，第 13—15 页。

〔2〕 See Thomas J. Kalitgaad, People's Republic of China Joint Venture Dispute Resolution Procedures, *UCLA Pacific Basin Law Journal*, Vol. 1, No. 1, 1982, p. 34.

方的个人担任有决定权的董事,在僵局产生时由其投决定票,但这种方式的缺陷是:(1)如果该机动董事是积极主动者,他就可能在合营双方尚未充分协商、取得一致的解决办法之前赞成某一方的主张,结果对另一方产生不利的影响。为避免这种情况,虽然也可在合同中规定机动董事只能在严重僵局的情况下参加表决,但这种规定可能由于含糊不清而难以实施;(2)一般说来,机动董事将由东道国公民担任。这样,其公正性亦难保障;[1](3)合资企业的决定权和经营资料须提交第三方。[2] 南斯拉夫 Beogradski graficki zavod 合资企业合同的有关规定基本上属于这种方式。该合同虽然规定共同业务机构(类似董事会的机构)由三人组成,但实际上只由合营双方各委派一人组成,没有第三人(共同业务机构主席)。该合同规定,如果合营双方委派的两人在第一次会议上就某事项无法达成协议,该事项得在下次会议作进一步研究,直至达成新的合意。如果不能达成,才选出第三人作为决定者。[3] 这种对机动董事虚位以待的安排基本上克服了这种方式的第一个缺陷。

2. 授权董事长和其他人员解决的方式

合资企业合同规定授权董事长解决僵局可以有两种方式:(1)当董事会僵局影响合资企业继续有利的经营时,董事长拥有决定权;(2)董事长在合营各方估计可能产生冲突的某些领域中拥有广泛权力,并且,只有董事会的表决通过才能改变这一权限。

此外,合资企业合同还可规定,在董事会陷于僵局时,副董事长、销售经理、生产经理等分别在不同领域中拥有某种权力。[4] 在任何情况下,合营各方应事先考虑解决特别麻烦的问题,诸如,规定当有关专利权、商标权等方面的争端发生并且董事会陷入僵局时,自动地由某一合营方处理。如有必要,合营各方同意的技术专家应被指定为解决技术方面争端的决定者。[5]

3. 授权合营各方负责人解决的方式

合资企业合同可规定,当董事会对某事项无法表决通过、陷入僵局时,可将该事项提交合营各方的负责人解决。合营各方负责人之间解决不成才提交仲裁。南斯

　〔1〕　See Miodrag Sukijasovic, *Yugoslav Foreign Investment Legislation at Work: Experiences So Far*, Belgrade, 1970, pp. 147-151.

　〔2〕　See Wolfgang G. Friedmann, Jean-Pierre Beguin, *Joint International Business Ventures in Developing Countries*, Columbia University Press, 1971, pp. 376-377.

　〔3〕　See Miodrag Sukijasovic, *Yugoslav Foreign Investment Legislation at Work: Experiences So Far*, Belgrade, 1970, p. 142.

　〔4〕　Ibid., pp. 408-409.

　〔5〕　See David I. Salem, The Joint Venture Law in the People's Republic of China: Business and Legal Perspectives, *The International Trade Law Journal*, Vol. 7, No. 1, 1981-1982, p. 110.

拉夫 Crvenazastava，Elektrosrbija 和 Cinkana 合资企业合同都有此类规定。[1]

4. 授权第三人解决的方式

这种方式与授权机动董事解决的方式类似,主要区别是该第三人并未在合资企业中任职。例如,根据 1965 年 1 月 17 日合资企业协议,由 Nioc 为一方,Agip, Philips 和印度石油与天然气委员会为另一方组成了对等型合资企业"伊朗国际海洋石油公司"(Iminoco)。该公司章程规定,合营双方将相当于公司资本 1% 的股票存入指定的瑞士银行。根据有关授权委托,在该公司股东会议陷入僵局时,由该瑞士银行介入解决。类似的方式也规定于国际合资企业 Sirip 的章程。这类安排产生的结果是,企业经营管理权专属地由合营者各方掌握,一旦发生僵局,即由第三人介入。[2]

在现有的中外合资企业合同中,一般未规定董事会僵局的解决方式。在实践中,中外合资企业董事会僵局一旦产生,常因无章可循而旷日持久,难以解决,以致严重影响了企业的生存和发展。因此,合营各方在签订合资企业合同时,似应根据实际情况和需要,参考国际实践,预先规定可望及时解决僵局的方式。

(二) 买或卖安排(buy-or-sell arrangement)

合营各方如果因企业经营情况或目标的变化、个人之间的矛盾等而对企业的重大问题产生严重分歧,在不愿诉诸其他解决争端方式的情况下,就可能采取买或卖安排,即由合营一方以公平价格购买合营另一方的全部股份从而接管企业的经营,这是一种避免企业解散的最后解决方式。

在美国,最常采用的买或卖安排是允许合营一方先定该方拟出售其股份或拟购买合营另一方股份的价格。在此基础上,合营另一方应决定愿意以该价格买或卖,或者定一较高的价格(根据一定的比例,例如 10%),将买或卖的决定权留给合营对方。为了保护愿意购买股份但在短期内筹资有困难的合营者,也为了防止买或卖安排被利用作为"吓人战术"(a surprise tactic),允许购买方在一定期限内依合理的条件支付价款。

在法国,虽然没有成文法或判例直接涉及买或卖安排的合法性问题,原则上,这种安排是得到认可的。由股东给予第三人以固定价格购买其股权的选择构成了无可置疑的合法要约。股东以固定或确定的价格回赎的条款亦不存在问题。由买主定价的出售股份协议和由卖主定价的购买股份协议显然都是不可实行的。买或卖

---

[1] See Miodrag Sukijasovic, *Yugoslav Foreign Investment Legislation at Work: Experiences So Far*, Belgrade, 1970, pp. 137-138.

[2] See Wolfgang G. Friedmann, Jean-Pierre Beguin, *Joint International Business Ventures in Developing Countries*, Columbia University Press, 1971, pp. 376-377.

安排是一种相互性的选择方式,即由一方定价,另一方根据该价格决定买或卖。这种方式不是取决于单方面的意志,可能产生公平合理的价格。买或卖安排是否可订入法国公司章程,因此由公司直接执行,而不是通过诉诸司法程序执行,尚存疑问。公司章程规定允许股东或公司以合理价格取得另一股东拟转让给第三方的股权,这在法国法中是明显合法的。如果价格的确定被视为公平,这种先买权方式和买或卖安排的重要区别是,后者是在选择者作出决定时才发生股权转让,而不是可预期的转让,因此,股东实际上可能是被迫出售其股份。由于出售股份的选择和购买股份的安排可以由股东合法地规定于合同,这两者一起载入公司章程以利解决僵局在原则上是允许的。[1]

在中外合资企业中,由于有关法律允许合营者之间的股权转让,合营各方亦可考虑以买或卖安排作为解决它们之间争端的最后方式。值得注意的是,这种"一刀两断"的方式通常引起企业性质的变化。例如,在一家国有企业与一家外国公司设立的中外合资企业中,如由前者购买后者的全部股权,该企业将转变为国有企业,而由后者购买前者的全部股权,则转变为外资企业。显然,采用这种解决方式须经过政府主管机构审批后才能生效。而在多边中外合资企业中,一方出售其全部股权可能就不会引起企业性质的变化。

---

〔1〕　See PH. John Kozyris, Equal Joint-Venture Corporations in France: Problems and Resolution of Deadlocks, *American Journal of Comparative Law*, Vol. 17, No. 4, 1969, pp. 524-526.

第一节　Chinese Foreign Investment Laws: Recent Developments towards a Market Economy[*]

（中国外资法：迈向市场经济的新发展）

Abstract: Since 1993, Chinese foreign investment laws (CFILs) have been moving towards the common principles of foreign investment laws in market economies. This article (1) summaries four features of the common principles; (2) surveys four aspects of recent developments of CFILs toward these principles, namely, expanding the economic sectors for foreign direct investment (FDI), allowing multiple forms or types of FDI, granting national treatment to FDI step by step, and pursuing transparency of CFILs; and (3) comments on the significance of recent developments of CFILs. The author points out that recent developments of CFILs toward common approach have brought great positive impacts on FDI to China, treatment of FDI in China and structural adjustment of CFILs.

I . Introduction

1. The Common Approach of Foreign Investment Laws of Market Economies

Although foreign investment laws of the market economies (hereinafter MEs)

---

　* *Chinese Foreign Investment Laws: Recent Developments towards a Market Economy*, East Asian Institute Contemporary China Series No. 23，World Scientific and Singapore University Press，ISBN981-02-4224-7（pbk），1999.

are different in terms of the form or content, there are some common characteristics comparing with that of central planned economies (hereinafter CPEs).

The first common feature is the open attitude towards the admission of foreign direct investment (hereinafter FDI). Under the international law, the opening of domestic market for FDI is a matter completely within the sovereignty of each State. In CPEs, key industries are generally prohibited or under restriction to FDI. However, MEs advocate a liberal investment policy and provide rather free investment admission for FDI.

The second is the multiple FDI vehicles. In CPEs, the FDI vehicles, namely the forms or types of FDI are very limited for the purpose of securing national interests and national economy. For example, in the early 1980's, the only or major FDI vehicle in China or the former Soviet Union and other east Europe countries, was joint venture. In comparison, there is no such a limitation in MEs. Foreign investors may select their favourite FDI vehicles.

The third is to grant the national treatment to FDI. In typical CPEs, "nationals" or economic entities are instruments for implementing the national plan. It seems the pre-condition for granting the national treatment to FDI is a domestic market with independent actors. Therefore, there is no such pre-condition in CPEs. In MEs, domestic markets are well established and the equality of actors (including nationals and foreigners) in domestic markets is emphasised, so the principle of national treatment is generally observed.

The fourth is the transparency of foreign investment laws (hereinafter FILs). In CPEs, the FDI is governed not only by laws, but also by policies, including some internal documents. Foreign investors can not well predict the future of their investments as they are not privileged to such information. In MEs, the transparency is another important feature of FILs. Foreign investors are clearly informed of all laws and regulations relating to their investments.

The above-mentioned common approach of FILs in MEs has been further endorsed by the basic principles of the World Trade Organisation (hereinafter WTO). It is generally accepted that trade liberalisation, non-discrimination and transparency are the three basic principles of WTO. Free FDI admission and multiple FDI vehicles in fact reflect the principle of trade liberalisation. The national treatment for FDI is exactly one of the two major aspects of the principle of non-discrimination of WTO. Finally, the transparency of FIL embodies the principle of transparency of WTO.

The current world economy is basically based on market economy. Most of the CPEs have moved toward market economic system since late 1980's. In this sense, the approach of FILs in MEs represents the common trend of FILs around the world.

2. The Turning Point of Chinese Foreign Investment Laws

The Chinese foreign investment laws (hereinafter CFILs), namely the laws and regulations governing FDI in China[1], have contributed significantly to China's success in FDI. CFILs have developed rapidly in last two decades. From 1979 to 1992, China was in the transition period from "central planned economy" to "market economy under the guidance of central planning", accordingly, the system of CFILs in that period was an "enclave" system to some extent separating from general legal system in China. Since the establishment of the goal of market economy by the Chinese Constitution (1993 amended),[2] and 14th Congress of Chinese Communist Party (CCP),[3] CFILs have been moving toward common approach of FILs in MEs, namely expanding FDI admissions, taking multiple FDI vehicles, performing national treatment and pursuing transparency.

Ⅱ. Expanding FDI Admissions

1. New Developments on FDI Admissions

There is no provision on sectors prohibited or restricted to FDI in China-foreign Joint Venture Laws. Instead the Regulations for the Implementation of the Law of the People's Republic of China on Chinese-foreign Equity Joint Ventures provides

---

[1] CFILs in general include the laws promulgated by National People's Congress and its Standing Committee, and the national regulations enacted by the State Council and other central governmental departments, as well as the local regulations enacted by local People's Congresses and local governments. In broad sense, CFILs may also cover the multilateral and bilateral investment treaties in which China has engaged.

[2] Art. 7, PRC, Constitution.

[3] See The CCP Decision on Some Questions of Establishing Socialist Market Economic System, *People's Daily*, 7 Nov 1993, p. 1.

guidance for investment sectors with respect to FDI. [1] On the other hand, according to the Detailed Rules for the Implementation of the Law of the People's Republic of China on Wholly Foreign-owned Enterprises in China (hereinafter Detailed Rules of WFOEL), the establishment of a wholly foreign-owned enterprise (hereinafter WFOE) is prohibited or restricted in some lines of business. [2] In practice, there are few examples that foreign investors establish China-foreign joint ventures in the above prohibited sectors specified in the Detailed Rules of WFOEL.

The new attitude of Chinese government to FDI admissions to the Chinese market was described in the Provisional Regulations on Foreign Investment Guidelines (hereinafter the Guidelines) and the Catalogue of Industries for Guiding Overseas Investment published in 1995. [3] The Guidelines provide the principles of the industrial policy for FDI. In general, potential foreign investors will be encouraged to invest in agriculture facilities, environmental protection industries, and exported industries so as to increase the proportion of foreign capital in these sectors. The Catalogue is renewable and may be readjusted when necessary according to the country's economic development status.

The new Catalogue of Industries for Guiding Overseas Investment (hereinafter the new Catalogue), which became effective on 1 January 1998, is an effort to broaden opportunities and to provide greater market access for foreign investors. It is also aimed at increasing and expanding FDI in China. It expands the list of indus-

---

[1] According to Art. 3 of Regulations for the Implementation of the Law of the People's Republic of China on China-foreign Joint Ventures, the principal sectors in which the establishment of joint ventures is permitted are: (1) Energy resources development, and the construction materials, chemical and metallurgical industries; (2) the machine-building, instrument and meter industries, and offshore oil-mining equipment manufacturing; (3) electronic industry, computer industry and communication equipment manufacturing; (4) light industries, and the textile, food, pharmaceutical, medical apparatus and instruments and packaging industries; (5) agriculture, animal husbandry and aquiculture; and (6) tourism and service trades.

[2] According to the Art. 4 & 5, Detailed Rules of WFOEL, the establishment of a wholly foreign-owned enterprise (WFOE) is prohibited in the following lines of business: (1) news, publication, broadcast, television, firm; (2) domestic commence, foreign trade, insurance; (3) posts and telecommunications; (4) any others prohibited by provisions of Chinese government. The establishment of a WFOE is restricted in the following lines of business: (1) public utilities; (2) communications and transportation; (3) real estate; (4) trust investment; (5) lease.

[3] The Guidelines and the Catalogue were published and made effective by the State Planning Commission, together with the State Economic and Trade Commission and the Ministry of Foreign Trade and Economic Co-operation on June 20, 1995.

tries and project sectors, which are encouraged for FDI.[1] From the Catalogue it seems that almost all the economic sectors, including some key sectors, were open to FDI in varying degrees. There are still a few or some industries prohibited or restricted to FDI. However, it should be noted that continued prohibition or restriction to FDI does not necessary means a discriminatory policy. As FDI is private in nature, the prohibition or restriction in the same industries may be also applicable to Chinese private investors.

There are also some specific regulations for further opening of Chinese domestic market for FDI. For example, there are regulations on finance, insurance, foreign trade, domestic commence, infrastructure and public utilities. This also reflects the fact that in the background of proposed reform of Chinese investment and financing system,[2] the provisions on FDI admission in CFILs have basically transferred from the type of CPEs to that of MEs.

2. Opening of the Key Industries

The industrial sectors, such as finance, insurance, foreign trade, domestic commence, infrastructure and public utilities are generally considered as key sectors relating to national economy and the people's livelihood. Even MEs take cautious attitude to open these key sectors to FDI. Since 1993 China has promulgated a series of regulations for opening these key sectors, seeking for maximising the space within the existing framework of CFILs.

(1) Finance and Insurance

According to the Detailed Rule of WFOEL, insurance is one of the prohibited sectors for WFOE.[3]

---

[1] Additional entries appear in the new Catalogue under the following industry and product categories: environmental protection (in relation to agriculture, forestry, animal husbandry and fishery), transport, postal and telecommunication industries, coal industry, power industry, petroleum, petrochemical and chemical industries, mechanical industry, electronic industry, medical and pharmaceutical industries, medical apparatus and equipment, newly emerged industries (emphasising environmental protection) and service industries (emphasising high technology and the development of new products). See Sally A Harpole, Recent Policy and Law Developments Favour Foreign Investment, 7 *China Law News*, pp. 1-3 (1998).

[2] China's reform of investment and financing system has been underway. Currently, an industry entry policy for both domestic and foreign investors is being formulated. The basic principles are: except for naturally monopoly sectors, all industries will expand their opening to private, collective and foreign capital. Even for naturally monopoly items, Sino-foreign joint investment and co-operation will be permitted. See Han Guojian, Investment System Reform Getting Underway, *Beijing Review*, 41 (35), p. 15 (1998).

[3] Art. 4, Detailed Rules of WFOEL.

For the opening of finance and insurance sectors, the Chinese government is currently in the experimental stage, attempting to establish an effective monitoring and controlling regime from the beginning. The founding and service of foreign-funded financial institutions are regulated by the Provisions of the PRC on the Management of Foreign-Funded Financial Institutions promulgated by the State Council on 1 April 1994. By the end of 1997, China had approved the establishments of 162 foreign-funded financial institutions engaged in business operations. [1]

The government of China now permits foreign insurance companies to set up businesses in Shanghai and Guangzhou. This kind of businesses are required to follow the Insurance Law of PRC (1995) and the Provisional Management Methods for Foreign-Funded Insurance Institutions in Shanghai issued in 1992. By April of 1998, Shanghai and Guangzhou had approved 11 foreign-funded insurance businesses, including 10 branches of foreign insurance companies and one China-foreign jointly funded insurance company. In addition, 100-strong insurance companies and re-insurance insurance institutions from scores of countries and regions have opened more than 180 representative offices and liaison offices in China. [2]

In the new Catalogue, banks, financial companies, trust investment companies and insurance companies belong to Restricted (II) category. There is no provision for "off limits to solely foreign-funded enterprises" on the establishment of insurance companies in the new Catalogue, which is inconsistent with the provisions of the Detailed Rules of the WFOEL.

(2) Foreign Trade

Foreign trade was one of the most prominent State monopoly sectors in Chinese central planning economic system. Detailed Rules of WFOEL prohibit foreign investors to establish a WFOE in this sector. [3]

Since 1990 foreign investors have been permitted to conduct foreign trade and set up corresponding enterprises in the 15 free trade zones approved by the central government to handle entrepot trade, import raw materials and parts for the produc-

---

〔1〕　They include 142 foreign branch bank, five exclusively foreign-funded banks, seven Sino-foreign jointly funded banks, one Sino-foreign investment bank, and seven exclusively foreign-funded and Sino-foreign jointly funded financial companies. See Liu Guangxi, Progress in Opening Up Service Sector, *Beijing Review*, 41 (36), p. 17 (1998).

〔2〕　See Liu Guangxi, Progress in Opening Up Service Sector, *Beijing Review*, 41 (36), p. 17 (1998).

〔3〕　Art. 4, Detailed Rules of WFOEL.

tion of enterprises located in these zones and export their products. [1]

On 6 December 1995, the State Council authorised multinational trading firms to set up EJVs in Shanghai on an experimental basis. [2] In early 1996, an "experimental" foreign trade joint venture law was implemented in Pudong, the new industrial-business section of Shanghai. Under the "experimental" law, foreign investors were permitted to set up China-foreign foreign trade EJVs. [3] The Experimental Policy on China-foreign Foreign Trading Equity Joint Ventures was issued by Ministry of Foreign Trade and Economic Co-operation (hereinafter MOFTEC) on 30 September 1996, which specifies the requirements for the Chinese and foreign parties involved as the promoters in such ventures as well as those for companies themselves. [4] This practice is an indication of Chinese government's prudent attitude in opening this field for foreign investors. [5]

In the new Catalogue, foreign trade belongs to Restricted (Ⅱ) category. [6]

---

[1] These zones are Futian and Shatoujiao in Shenzhen, Shantou, Guangzhou and Zhuhai in Guangdong, Xiamen and Fuzhou in Fujian, Dalian in Liaoning, Tianjin, Qingdao in Shandong, Zhangjiagang in Jiangsu, Ningbo in Zhejiang, Waigaoqiao in Shanghai, and Haikou and Yangpu in Hainan.

[2] See Trading Firms allowed, *China Joint Venturer*, 1 (5), p. 3 (1996); Liu Ping: Regulations on Foreign-funded Insurance Institutions Soon on Place, 39 *China Economic News*, p. 3 (1998).

[3] The early birds-Mannesman Demag of Germany, Mitsubishi of Japan and Daewoo of Korea-have been allowed to set up the first foreign trade EJVs in Pudong, Shanghai. See Foreign Trade Joint Ventures Are Now Permitted, *China Joint Venturer*, 1 (9), p. 2 (1996).

[4] According to Art. 4 of the Experimental Policy on China-foreign Foreign Trading Equity Joint Ventures, the requirements to foreign promoters of a China-foreign foreign trading equity joint venture include: (1)the turnover of the year before application in excess of US＄5000 million; (2) average volume of trade with China in three years before application in excess of US＄30 million; (3) having set up a representative office or invested more than US ＄30 million in China before application. There are some other requirements for the Chinese promoters of such ventures. As for the ventures themselves, according to art. 3 of the Experimental Policy, they are limited liability companies; the proportion of investment contributed by the foreign investors shall not be less than 25％ and not more than 49％ of the registered capital of the companies; the legal representatives of the companies shall be appointed by Chinese side.

[5] There are 5 Sino-foreign trading equity joint venture companies have been approved by the central government by Oct 1998. Three of them are located in Shanghai, two located in ShenZhen. The Chinese parties have controlling stake in these companies. See Approval to Trading Firm JVs, 8 *China Economic Review*, p. 12 (Oct, 1998). In 1997, Pudong approved the founding of two foreign trade joint ventures—Dong Ling Trade Co. Ltd. Funded by Chinese, Japanese and American businesses and the Sino-ROK (Republic of Korea) Shanghai Lansheng-Daewoo Co. Ltd. See Liu Guangxi, Progress in Opening Up Service Sector, *Beijing Review*, 41 (36), p. 16 (1998).

[6] The "restricted" category in the new catalogue is subdivided into category (Ⅰ) and category (Ⅱ) activities. The latter is more restricted and has more strict approval procedures which require approval by the relevant industrial department under the State Council and filing with the State Planning Commission even if the investment is less than US＄ 30 million. Category (Ⅰ) of "restricted" activities are also given more leeway if the enterprise export more than 70％ of its production or is based in China's interior provinces. The provisions "not permitted for wholly foreign-owned enterprises" or "state assets shall form the majority stake" are also included in some cases.

The document also provides that in the case of setting up China-foreign foreign trade joint venture, Chinese participant should command the majority of stakes. It is reported that China will expand the experimental ranges of foreign trade. [1]

(3) Domestic Commence

Domestic commence is also one of the sectors in which foreign investors are prohibited to set up a WFOE according to the Detailed Rules of WFOEL. [2]

China-foreign retail joint ventures are required to follow the Opinions on the Issues Concerning the Utilisation of Foreign Capital in the Retail Sector promulgated by the State Council. At present, China does not allow the establishment of exclusively foreign-funded retail or wholesale enterprises, and China-foreign jointly funded wholesale enterprises. [3]

In Catalogue 1998, it was made explicit that domestic commence belongs to Restricted (II); a WFOE is not allowed in this sector. In case of setting China-foreign joint ventures in this sector, Chinese partner shall command the majority of stakes.

(4) Infrastructure and Public Utilities

Considering that infrastructure and public utilities are the typical economic sector relating to national economy and people's livelihood, as well as public authorities of government, Detailed Rules of WFOEL classifies public utilities as Restricted category. [4]

In recent years the Chinese government permits and encourages foreign investors to construct and operate transportation infrastructure facilities, encourages China-foreign joint investment in the construction and operation of public wharves and berths, and also encourages China-foreign joint investment or solely foreign investment in the construction of highways, independent bridges and tunnels. China also allows foreign investors to construct civil airports (with the exception of those for joint civil and military use), and flight areas, including runways, taxi ranks and

---

[1] See Xun Guangxiang, Concrete Measures on Improving Foreign Fund Utilisation Work and Readjustment of the Mid-west Policy, *China Foreign Investment*, No. 11, 1998, p. 5.

[2] Art. 4, Detailed Rules of WFOEL.

[3] See Liu Guangxi, Progress in Opening Up Service Sector, *Beijing Review*, 41 (36), p. 18 (1998).

[4] Art. 5, Detailed Rules of WFOEL.

parking aprons. [1]One of the specific laws involving the field of infrastructure and public utilities is the Several Provisions on Establishment of Construction Enterprises with Foreign Investment issued in 1995. [2]The Provisions apply to China-foreign equity joint ventures or co-operative joint ventures, which involve civil engineering designs, pipe line and equipment installations, and building decoration and renovation projects. The establishment of construction WFOEs is still closed for the time being.

The PRC Electric Power Law was adopted on 28 December 1995 and became effective on 1 April 1996, containing stipulations on the construction of power facilities, and the management and supervision of power generation and power consumption. It facilitates both domestic and foreign economic entities and individuals to invest in the establishment of power generating companies, and stipulates the principle that whoever invests in the power sector, he shall receive the benefit from the industry. [3]

It is worth noting that the new Catalogue makes different provisions based on different project of infrastructure and public utilities, some belong to Prohibited category while some belong to Restricted (Ⅱ) or even Encouraged categories. Projects prohibited to FDI include construction and management of electric networks and construction and management of urban water supply and drainage, gas and heat supply networks. Projects restricted to FDI include construction and operation of trunk railways (with the Chinese side commanding the majority of stakes). Projects encouraged FDI include construction and operation of branch railways, local railway lines and their bridges, tunnels and ferrying facilities (WFOEs being not allowed), production and operation of urban underground trains and light rails (with the Chinese side commanding the majority of stakes), construction and operation of roads, independent bridges and tunnels, construction and operation of port public utilities (with the Chinese side commanding the majority of stakes), construction and operation of civilian airports (with the Chinese side commanding the majority of

---

[1] See Liu Guangxi, Progress in Opening Up Service Sector, *Beijing Review*, 41 (36), p. 18 (1998).

[2] The Provisions were promulgated by the Ministry of Construction and MOFTEC on 18 September 1995 and took effect on that date.

[3] Art. 3, PRC, Electric Power Law. For the whole picture of foreign participation in China's power industry, see John Wong and Wong Chee Kong, China's Power Sector: Recent Changes and Scope for Foreign Participation, *EAI Background Brief*, No. 23, November 10, 1998.

stakes).

Ⅲ. Taking Multiple FDI Vehicles

1. New Developments of Traditional FDI Vehicles

Before 1993, the typical FDI vehicles provided by CFILs in China were equity joint ventures (hereinafter EJVs), co-operative joint ventures (hereinafter CJVs) and wholly foreign-owned enterprises (hereinafter WFOEs).

The proportional contributions between Chinese and foreign participants in EJVs have been changing gradually. Before 1990's, a foreign majority stakes in EJV was rare and difficult to obtain. In recent years, many new EJVs have had controlling foreign stakes. Existing EJVs have also undergone changes to meet the demands of foreign investors for controlling stakes. [1]

There have been few regulations concerning CJVs for a long time. The legal relations between the Chinese and foreign partners in CJVs were negotiated and established between the partners themselves, which was attractive for the foreign investors who favoured this type of FDI vehicle. However, CJVs have lost some of their appeal partially due to the introduction of the Detailed Rules for Implementation of the Law of People's Republic of China on China-foreign Co-operative Joint Venture Law in September 1995, which limit the contractual rights of potential parties of CJV. Far fewer new CJVs have been established since then. Moreover, in some cases, investors are changing their FDI vehicle from an existing CJV to an EJV. [2]

More significantly, the preferred FDI vehicle has shifted from EJVs to WFOEs. 1997 was the first time that WFOE became the preferred FDI vehicle. For new FIEs in 1997, 45.2% was WFOEs, 43.5% was EJVs and 11.3% was CJVs. [3]

These changes provide more room and more freedom for foreign investors to select preferred FDI vehicles in China. Moreover, the fact that WFOE became the preferred FDI vehicle and foreign investors took the controlling interests in existing EJVs also reflected the open and flexible attitudes of Chinese authorities in the

---

[1] See A Second Bite at the Cherry: Issues in Restructuring JVs, *China Joint Venturer*, 1 (1), pp. 8-12 (1995).

[2] See "Where's My Equity?" Cooperative Joint Ventures Change into Equity Joint Ventures, *China Joint Venturer*, 1 (8), pp. 6-9 (1996).

[3] See Francis Bassolino, China Opens Its Doors, *China Economic Review*, 8 (10), p. 32 (1998).

procedure of approving FDI.

2. Developing New FDI Vehicles

After 1993, China introduced a series of regulations on FDI vehicles, permitting and encouraging foreign investor to take new FDI vehicles, such as Companies Limited by Shares, Holding Companies, Merger and Acquisition, as well as Building-Operation-Transfer.

(1) Companies Limited by Shares

Provisions relating to FDI in Chinese companies limited by shares can be initially found in local legislation, notably the Guangdong Provincial Regulations on Foreign Related Companies in the Special Economic Zones in 1985. There were some national regulations dealing with the issuing and trading of shares of companies in early 1990s[1]. Although the Chinese Company Law provided for the establishment of companies limited by shares,[2] it did not specifically address the possibility of FDI in this type of company. On 10 January 1995 the Tentative Provisions of Certain Questions on Establishment of Foreign Investment Companies Limited by Shares was issued by MOFTEC (hereinafter Provisions on Companies Limited by Shares) which repeated the provisions of Company Law, but also took into account the special features of FDI. As a result of these Provisions, foreign investors may establish their investment enterprises in the form of companies limited by shares; and existing FIEs may also re-organise themselves into the new form.

However, there is legal conflict in this new development. According to Article 4 of China-foreign JVL, an EJV shall take the form of a limited liability company. However, Provisions of Companies Limited by Shares allowed not only a new EJV to take the form of a company limited by shares, but also an existing EJV to transfer its form from a limited liability company to a company limited by shares. From the viewpoint of hierarchy of legal effect, as the former is a law approved by the National

---

[1] For example, Tentative Regulations on the Administration of the Issuing and Trading of Shares, by the State Council on 22 April 1993; Special Provisions on Companies limited by Shares Issuing Shares and Seeking a Listing Outside China, by the State Council on 4 August 1994.

[2] The Company Law of PRC was promulgated on 29 December 1993 and made effective on 1 July 1994. According to the PRC Company Law, the company limited by shares, which is open to foreign investment could change the whole nature of JV restructuring in China. Many of difficulties of restructuring encountered in changing JV contracts and seeking fresh approvals would be bypassed in a structure where a foreign investor could increase its stake by buying additional shares. See Companies Limited By Shares: A New Option, *China Joint Venturer*, 1 (1), p. 11 (1995).

People's Congress and the latter is regulations issued by the State Council, the former might prevail over the latter. If we consider the latter as the detailed rule for implementing Company Law of PRC, then the China-foreign JVL and Company Law conflict each other at the same level.

（2）Holding Companies

Since 1993 it has become possible for foreign investors to set up a holding company in China. By the end of 1994 more than 50 holding companies were approved by MOFTEC. On 4 April 1995 MOFTEC published the Tentative Provisions on Establishment of Companies with an Investment Nature by Foreign Investors (hereinafter the Provisions on Investment Companies), which stipulates that a holding company can take the form of either a WFOE or an EJV and list types of services which a holding company may provide. [1] This new FDI vehicle is especially important for foreign investors who seek to enhance management of multiple investment in China. They can procure machinery, equipment, raw materials and spare parts for their subsidiaries, provide assistance in balancing foreign exchange and labour matters within their group, and provide financial support and help with loans and guarantees. There are intangible benefits of having a holding company. It is widely accepted that a holding company may play a flagship role for its groups in China. [2]

According to the Provisions on Investment Companies, a holding company may establish an EJV on its own or with other foreign investors. Such an enterprise in which the ratio of foreign exchange-investment in total registered capital is more than 25% is treated as foreign investment enterprise. This provision is in conflict with provisions of China-foreign JVL. Firstly, As the holding company established by the Provisions on Investment Companies is a domestic legal person under the Chinese law,

---

[1] It seems that China wants to limit holding companies to multinational corporations, stipulating that parent companies must have assets in excess of US$ 400 million. They must have invested US$ 10 million in China already, inject a further US$ 30 million to set up the holding company and have three or more project approvals pending. "Problems Concerning the 'Establishment of Companies With an Investment Nature by Foreign Investors Tentative Provisions' Explanation" was promulgated by MOFTEC on 16 February 1996, which clarifies issues set out in the Provisions, covering the increase of registered capital after the establishment, detailing capital contribution and business scope, outlining the requirements for establishing branches and provision of a warranty on capital contribution and technology transfer by such companies.

[2] Holding Companies: Unfolding the New MOFTEC Rules, *China Joint Venturer*, 1 (1), p. 6 (1995).

it is not accord with the definition of "foreign investor" in China-foreign JVL. [1] Secondly, in case of setting up a subsidiary in the form of an EJV, even the proportion of China-foreign contributions is 10:90 and ratio of foreign exchange-investment in total registered capital reaches 25%, the new EJV still can not meet the minimum requirement on foreign investment rate in China-foreign JVL. [2]

(3) Merger and Acquisition

In recent years, "merger" and "acquisition" [3](hereinafter M & A) have become one of the most important FDI vehicles around the world. FDI may take one of the two forms: (1) new establishment; (2) M & A. However, foreign investors in China are only able to take the first form according to Chinese basic foreign investment enterprise laws. [4] Until a few years ago, EJVs were almost without exception formed by new establishment. With the Circular on Examination and Approval of Projects Utilising Foreign Investment for the Reformation of Existing Enterprises issued by the State Economic and Trade Commission in 1995, forming a foreign investment enterprise (hereinafter FIE)[5] by acquiring a Chinese investment enterprise (hereinafter CIE)[6] as a whole, not only its assets, entered as a more standard option. The practice that has developed recently is for the foreign investors to buy a part of State-owned enterprises (hereinafter SOEs) followed by setting up an EJV with Chinese partner. [7]

---

[1] According to Art. 1 of the China-foreign JVL, the term "foreign joint venturers" refers to " foreign companies, enterprises, other economic organisations or individuals".

[2] According to Art. 4 of the China-foreign JVL, the proportion of the investment contributed by the foreign joint venturer (s) shall generally not be less than 25% of the registered capital of a joint venture.

[3] "Merger" and "acquisition" are distinct concepts. "Merger" is a term used of companies and similar bodies rather than of assets or liabilities. The effect of a merger is that two formerly separate companies become a single indistinguishable whole, and the former owners of two separate companies become the proportionate owners of the single merged company. In an acquisition, ownership passes from one person to another.

[4] These laws refer to Sino-foreign Equity Joint Venture Law, 1979; Sino-foreign Co-operative Joint Venture Law, 1988 and Foreign Enterprises Law, 1986.

[5] FIEs in China refer to China-foreign Equity Joint Ventures, China-foreign Co-operative Joint ventures and Wholly Foreign-owned Enterprises. FIEs are main forms or types of FDI in China. FDI may also be performed by other vehicles such as M & A, BOT etc.

[6] CIE in this paper refers to State-owned enterprise, collective-owned enterprise and town-village owned enterprise and other enterprises invested by Chinese individuals or entities.

[7] SOEs in China are undergoing a rapid structural change. The massive restructure of SOEs has become possible only after the 15th Communist Party Congress held in September 1997, at which the Party announced that in order to revitalise the SOEs, diversified ownership thereof would be allowed. It is described as "diversification of public ownership", a phrase that is used to circumvent the political and ideological obstacles to reform of SOEs. The measures introduced at the Congress for restructuring SOEs include "reorganisation, joint operation, merger, lease, management contract, joint stock companies, and sell-out". This reform demonstrates great potential for foreign investors. There are more than 480,000 small and medium size SOEs, accounting for 96% of total SOEs in China. Under the policy of "grabbing big and releasing small", the reform of large amount of such SOEs provide many opportunities of M & A by foreign investment. See Meng Xiangang, Reform of State-owned Enterprises and Opportunities of Foreign Investment, *China Foreign Investment*, No. 10, 1998, p. 23.

Foreign investors looking to expand business in China are also increasingly examining the possibility of acquiring an existing FIE. Acquiring existing SOEs or FIEs can hasten the speed of market entry, bypass many of the troublesome teething problems associated with establishing a new FIE in China. There are some general and special laws and regulations governing main aspects of M & A in China. [1]

(4) Building-Operation-Transfer

Building-Operation-Transfer (hereinafter BOT)[2] has emerged as a new FDI vehicle in China. One of the major differences between BOT and other FDI vehicles is the government's involvement. [3] The Chinese government is allowed to make certain undertakings by law, including the government guarantee for related government acts, the permission to allow future reasonable increase of charges for facility use. The extension of concession period may also be allowed if a project company were to suffer serious economic losses as a result of changes of State policies. The government may also guarantee the conversion and repatriation of foreign exchange required for repaying principal and interests on loans as well as profits. The new model incorporates several new features, which will significantly change the current Chinese legal framework on FDI. Most importantly, all BOT projects, regardless of size, will have required approvals from the State Planning Commission. The present legal framework directly governing BOT investment in China consists of two simple

---

[1] The key legislation on M & A in China include Administration of State Asset Valuation Procedures, 1991; PRC, Company Law, 1994; MOFTEC, Certain Questions on the Establishment of Foreign Investment Company limited by Shares Tentative Provisions; PRC, Sino-foreign Cooprative Joint Venture Law Implementing Rules, 1995; State Administration of Registration of Foreign Investment Enterprises as Company Shareholders or Sponsors Several Provisions, 1995; State Administration of Taxation, Income Tax Treatment of Reorganisation of Equity and Asset Transfer Tentative Provisions, 1997; MOFTEC and SAIC, Changes in Equity Interest of Investors in Foreign Investment Enterprises Several provisions,1997; the State Administration of Taxation, Income Tax Treatment of Reorganisations of Foreign Investment Enterprises Such as Mergers, Splits, Reorganisation of Equity and Asset Transfer Tentative Provisions on 28 April 1997.

[2] BOT, as a FDI vehicle, especially in infrastructure sector, is getting popular in recent years. In legal aspect, BOT involves a set of contract relations. It generally embraces the concession agreement whereby host government empowered certain public or administrative power to foreign investors. Foreign investors establish a project company by themselves or with local investors. The project company is responsible for the investment, financing, construction, operation and maintenance of the project. Although the project facilities are to be transferred to host government without compensation upon expiration of the concession period, the project company is granted ownership rights over these facilities during the concession period.

[3] There are some comments on the nature of government guarantee in the BOT project, see Mu Yaping and Zhao Kang, The Problems on BOT and Chinese BOT legislation, *Legal Studies*, No. 2, 1998, pp. 79-80.

circulars at present. [1] A special law on BOT, though announced as being drafted in 1995, has not been promulgated. Therefore, the existing CFILs serve as regulatory means on many key aspects of BOT projects. In addition, general laws and regulations not specifically enacted for FDI also play important roles in structuring specific aspects of BOT projects. These include the 1997 Highway Law, the 1997 Pricing Law and the 1995 Secured Interests law. [2]

Ⅳ. Granting National Treatment

Requirement for national treatment of FDI and FIEs is one of prominent issues in various China-involved multilateral trades and finance negotiations, including negotiation on membership in the WTO. At the same time, as the result of economic reform, CIEs, particularly the SOEs which lose their priorities on supply and sale through previous central planning channels, have demanded the treatment equal to FIEs.

In the policy statement aspect, at the end of 1993 China declared that it would create the conditions in which to apply national treatment to FIEs step by step. [3] This can be considered as the key point or basis of the recent adjustment of CFILs. In September 1997, President Jiang Zhemin in his speech in 15th Congress of CCP emphasised to protect the rights and benefits of FIEs and to apply the national treatment to them.

From the legal aspect, it is rather clear that China has promoted to provide national treatment for FDI and FIEs by two approaches: one is to level the playing field for CIEs and FIEs with regard to enterprise income tax rates, tariff exemptions

---

[1] Namely Circular on Several Questions concerning the Use of BOT as a Form to Attract Foreign Investment issued by MOFTEC (the MOFTEC Circular) in January 1995, and Circular on Several Issues concerning the Examination, Approval and Administration of Experimental Foreign-invested Concession Projects (issued jointly by the State Planning Commission, the Ministry of Power Industry and the Ministry of Communications (the SPC Circular) on 21 August 1995. According to the MOFTEC Circular, foreign investors may establish a BOT project company by the form of an EJV, CJV or WFOE. The examination and approval project proposals, feasibility studies, project contracts and articles of association are all subject to the existing foreign investment examination and approval processes. The two Circulars have made some breakthrough on CFIL. For example, the SPC Circular uses the term "foreign invested concession project".

[2] See Jianfu CHEN, BOT as a New Form of Investment in China, 14 *China Law News*, pp. 1-2 (1998).

[3] See the Chinese Communist Party Decisions on Some Questions of Establishing a Socialist Market Economic System, *People's Daily*, November 7, 1993, p. 1.

and other preferential policies;[1] the other is to unify Chinese economic and commercial laws, aiming at establishing a unified legal framework for performing equal treatment for both domestic and foreign investors.

1. Levelling the Playing Field

(1) Reform of Income Tax System

With the aim of establishing a unified tax system, under which FIEs and CIEs would enjoy uniform tax treatment, the Chinese government instituted dramatic reforms in taxation of CIEs with the promulgation of uniform enterprise income tax rates in 1994. The unified enterprises income tax rates resulted in no change in income tax rates for FIEs (remain as 33％), but brought significantly lower income tax rate for CIEs which was reduced from 55％ to 33％.

While the general policy of uniformity in taxation continues to be focused, significant forms of preferential tax treatment for FIEs remain in effect. The two-year tax holiday and three year 50％ tax reduction which are enjoyed by most FIEs, and the reduced levels of foreign enterprise income tax offered within the special economic zones, in most case at the 15％ level, will not change in the near future. This is consistent with the Chinese government's policy to create a fair and equal tax environment, while assuring continuity and a level of stability for foreign investors.

However, eventual changes of tax structure over the long term may occur. This is consistent with certain policies of Chinese Ninth Five-year Plan and Long-range Objectives, aiming at gradually eliminating tax exemptions and deductions solely available to foreign or foreign-related entities by the year 2010.[2]

(2) Elimination of Preferential Tariffs

Historically, FIEs were exempted from paying customs duties on capital imports while CIEs enjoyed no similar advantage. The regulations were justified not only to encourage FDI, but also to encourage the importation of advanced technology machinery and equipment. The elimination of the preferential tariffs for most FIEs was announced at the end of 1995 which became effective on 1 April 1996 for the

---

[1] See Dong Dong Zhang, Negotiating for a Liberal Economic Regime: the Case of Japanese FDI in China, *The Pacific Review*, 11 (1) p. 70 (1998).

[2] See Sally A. Harpole, Policy Trends in Taxation of Foreign-invested Enterprises, 2 *China Law News*, pp. 1-5 (1997).

purpose of creating a more level playing field for FIEs and CIEs. To lessen the negative influence of the change for FIEs, a new policy took place at about the same time as the establishment of lower customs tariffs in many product categories for both FIEs and CIEs.

As this marked the removal of a very significant incentive for foreign investors, FIEs that were established before the effective date of the new policy were allowed a period ranging from one to two years within which they could import capital items under the previous preferential policy. Two extensions of the time frame for the previous preference were announced after the original promulgation date in order to address various special concerns and policy interests related to large-scale investment projects, investment involving advanced technology and investment in certain industry sectors. The time extensions and further refinements in the implementation of this major change in customs policy are understandable, given the fact that an important foreign investment incentive had been removed and numerous practical and policy considerations required special measures. [1]

According to the Circular on the Adjustment of Tax Policies on Imported Equipment (1997), since January 1998, only foreign investment projects listed in the "encouraged" or "restricted category (II)" of Catalogue of Industries for Guiding Overseas Investment (revised in December 1997) shall enjoy the import duty exemption. At the same time, domestic investment projects met the requirement of the Catalogue of Major Industries, Products and Technologies Encouraged for Development in China (approved by the State Council on 29 December 1997) will also enjoy the same import duty exemption as above-mentioned foreign investment projects.

2. Unification of Economic and Commercial Laws

China economic and commercial laws have entered into an important stage since early 1990's. One of the main characteristics in these developments is the unification trend. It means that the Chinese new economic and commercial laws have emerged to have jurisdiction on both domestic economic relations and foreign economic relations. This clear reflects a legislative trend on granting national treatment for FDI and foreign investors.

---

[1] See Sally A. Harpole, Policy Trends in Taxation of Foreign-invested Enterprises, 2 *China Law News*, pp. 1-5 (1997).

(1) Business Organisation Laws

China had no formal company code before 1994 although many companies existed for a long period of time. The Company Law of the PRC (1994) may be considered as the first unified commercial law in China.

According to article 75 of the Company Law, in setting up a company limited by shares, there should be at least five promoters with over half of them living within China. This provision explicitly recognises the principle of national treatment for promoters of company limited by shares. It means that the foreigners (individuals or legal persons) without domiciles in China may become promoters of company limited by shares in the same position as Chinese.

The Company Law also contains provisions on its relation with the foreign investment enterprise laws. It applies to FIEs if the foreign investment enterprise laws have no specific provisions. [1] For example, the provisions on qualifications of directors, the prohibition of competitive positions of directors and managers and the compensation duty of enterprise leaders related to violation of law etc., are applicable to FIEs. [2]

The Partnership Law of the PRC was enacted on 23 February 1997 and became effective on 1 August 1997. As CJVs and WFOEs may take the form of partnership, the law is also applicable to FDI in China.

These two basic unified business organisation laws for all practical purposes have filled the gaps of Chinese business organisation laws. There are other specific regulations on business organisation which are also applicable to both CIEs and FIEs, such as the Tentative Regulations on Registration of Company Registered Capital (1996) etc. [3]

---

[1]　Art. 18, Company Law.

[2]　Arts. 57, 61 and 63, Company Law.

[3]　The PRC, Tentative Regulations on Registration of Company Registered Capital became effective on 1 March 1996. They clarify the procedures for registering a company's capital, and apply to both CIEs and FIEs. The law is only applicable to FIEs where it does not come into conflict with FIE laws. One major difference between the FIEs and CIEs is that FIEs can get a business licence before any capital is contributed, while CIEs have to show that they have contributed capital before they get business licence. See Registered Capital Laws Don't Rock the Boat, *China Joint Venturer*, 1 (8), p. 2, 1996. The Provisions on Registration and Control of Legal Representatives of Enterprise Legal Person promulgated by the National Industrial and Commercial Administration on Aril 7, 1998 are also applicable to CIEs and FIEs.

（2）Securities Law

Eight years after establishment of Chinese securities market, the Securities Law of the PRC was approved by the Standing Committee of National People's Congress on 29 December 1998 and took effect on 1 July 1999. The law is applicable to the issuing and trading of securities in China. Since foreign investors may establish their ventures in the form of the companies limited by shares or conduct their investment activities by merger or acquisition, they may involve the issuing and trading of securities and shall equally observe the provisions of Securities Law as domestic investors.

（3）Contract Laws

For a long period of time in the past, Chinese contract system included four main legislation: the General Principles of Civil Law provides the basic principles in the contract laws; the Economic Contract Law, the Foreign Economic Law governed the domestic economic contract and foreign economic contract relations respectively while the Technology Contract Law and the Administrative Regulation on Technology Transfer Contracts dealt with contract relating technology transactions. In addition there are some contract provisions in Chinese laws on trademark, patent, copyright, guarantee, railroad, marine and civil aviation etc.

Based upon the researches of the laws, concepts and theory on contract of market economic countries, the Contract Law of the PRC (effective on 1 October 1999) is consistent with the common contract principles and standards of the market economic countries. [1] One of the underlying principles in the new law is the principle of uniformity, comprising the goal of achieving the unity of domestic and foreign contract laws. [2] The new law will replace the Economic Contract Law, the Foreign Economic Law and the Technology Contract Law. It is expected that after taking effective of the law, a more modern, comprehensive and complete contract law than ever before will govern FDI activities in China.

---

[1] For example, the principle of freedom of contract, etc., see Ping Jiang, Drafting the Uniform Contract Law in China, 10 *Columbia Journal of Asian Law*, pp. 248-250 (1996).

[2] See Ping Jiang, Drafting the Uniform Contract Law in China, 10 *Columbia Journal of Asian Law*, pp. 245-248 (1996). On the detailed drafting process, see Renzi, Liang Huixing: The Drafting and Proving of Chinese Unified Contract Law, *Chinese Lawyer*, No. 1, 1998, pp. 65-68.

（4）Arbitration Law

In the procedure law aspect, Arbitration Law of the PRC (effective on 1 September 1995) also reflects the objective of a unified approach. According to Article 66 of the Arbitration Law, foreign arbitration commissions may be organised by Chinese International Commercial Association.[1] The provision does not exclude the jurisdiction of other arbitration institutions, mainly local arbitration commissions on foreign arbitration cases. The Circular on Some Questions for Performing Arbitration Law of PRC by Office of the State Council (1996) affirms the jurisdiction of the local arbitration commissions in this regard. Item 3 of the Circular states that the main functions of the local arbitration commissions are to accept domestic arbitration cases. Whereas the parties to foreign-related arbitration case voluntarily select arbitration by a local arbitration commission, such commission may accept the case.

V. Pursuing Transparency

Since 1995, China has made great effort to make CFILs more transparent. The following three aspects of CFILs may indicate the new developments.

1. The Industrial Sectors Open to FDI

Before 1995, there were broad provisions on foreign investment industrial sectors in the main foreign enterprise laws. The Provisional Regulations on Foreign Investment Guidelines (hereinafter the Guidelines) and the Catalogue of Industries for Guiding Overseas Investment (hereinafter the Catalogue) enacted in 1995 are the first formal legislation to establish the legal basis upon which certain industries and projects are encouraged, restricted, permitted or prohibited to FDI.[2]

The Guidelines and the Catalogue showed that China was moving away from a policy of FDI incentive on the basis of geographical location (e. g. special economic

---

[1] The established foreign arbitration commission organised by the China Chamber of International Commerce is China International Economic and Trade Arbitration Commission (CIETAC). The Arbitration Rules for CIETAC were first adopted in September 1988 and were revised in September 1995. On May 6, 1998 the China Chamber of International Commerce revised them again, effective on May 10,1998. The new rules list five types of dispute under CIETC jurisdiction, which specifically include disputes between two FIEs or between any FIE and a Chinese-funded legal person. Additionally, the list includes disputes arising from project financing, invitation for tender, bidding, construction and other activities conducted by Chinese legal persons which use capital, technology or services originating from foreign countries, in addition to Hong Kong, Macao and Taiwan.

[2] Projects that endanger State security, infringe on public interests, pollute the environment and damage the ecological balance should be strictly prohibited.

zones) to one based on industrial sectors. More significantly this is also an important step towards a greater transparency of CFILs, as it makes the project evaluation process more transparent to foreign investors and also narrows the scope of bargaining between Chinese government and foreign investors.[1] In addition, some of the industrial sectors and local authorities also provide further detailed rules or guidance for foreign investors.[2]

2. The Examination and Approval of FDI

The Opinion on Directing of the Examination and Approval of Foreign Investment Enterprises was issued by MOFTEC on 5 November 1996. It is an attempt to integrate the policy and practice on the approval of FDI in specific industries and sectors, as well as approval of specific types of FDI vehicles. The Opinion is divided into three parts, specifying the policies, principles and procedures for approval of: (1) FDI in specific industries; (2) certain special categories of FDI, such as companies limited by shares, or holding companies; and (3) the expansion of the registered capital of existing FIEs. Foreign investors are likely to find it helpful to have this working document that may be referred to in discussing the procedures to be followed.[3]

Moreover, governments at all levels are required to enhance work efficiency and provide high-quality, standard and streamlined service to foreign investors. During the process to broaden the reform of investment and financial systems, governments should further improve examination and approval methods for FDI and simplify relevant procedures.[4]

3. The Assignment of Shareholders' Rights in FIEs

The assignment of shareholders' rights in FIEs is a very important issue as it

---

[1] See Guidelines to Put Squeeze on Locally Approved Investment, *China Joint Venturer* 1 (1), p. 2 (1995).

[2] For example, Further Strengthening the Administration of the Telecommunications Market Notice issued by the Department of Telecommunications, Administration of the Ministry of Posts and Telecommunications on June 1, 1995, provides more detailed rules about the regulation of FDI in this key sector. Shenzhen SEZ provides foreign investment industrial guidance and catalogue for foreign investors.

[3] See Lucille A. Barale, MOFTEC Opinion Adds New Restrictions as Investment Terms Toughen, *Chinese Joint Venturer*, 2 (10), pp. 14-19 (1997).

[4] See Further Expanding Opening & Utilisation of Foreign Capital, 41 *Beijing Review*, p. 14 (Sep 14-20, 1998).

amounts to a reorganisation of the enterprise. [1] The Certain Regulations on Changes to Shareholders' Rights in Foreign Investment Enterprises (hereinafter the Regulations) were promulgated by the MOFTEC and the State Administration for Industry and Commerce on 28 May 1997 which became effective on the same day. It is the first law of this kind that regulates changes to shareholders with the aim of eliminating confusion and strengthening supervision in this area. [2] It also reflects the new levels attained in the Chinese legal system in formulating effective laws.

In formulating in detail the principal categories of changes to shareholders' rights and corresponding procedural formalities, the Regulations ensure that assignments of changes to shareholders' rights are transparent and are standardised. Seven principal categories of changes to shareholders' rights are listed and each of these is dealt with separately in terms of what documents are to be submitted for the approval of that category of changes to shareholders' rights.

In addition, different approval authorities apply for different categories. The time limits for an assignment of shareholders' rights apply in three different stages. Failure to effect such alteration of registration will subject to penalty. All relevant penalties are clearly set out in the Regulations, thus providing both applicant and approval authorities with certainty. [3]

Ⅵ. Significance of the Recent Developments of CFILs

The recent developments of Chinese foreign investment laws (CFILs) towards common approach of foreign investment laws in market economies have brought great impacts on FDI to China, the treatment of FDI in China and structural adjustment of CFILs.

1. Promoting and Guaranteeing the Continual Developments of FDI in China

Since 1993 China has for six consecutive years remained the second largest

---

[1] In absence of effective controls, parties may circumvent laws and regulations to achieve illegal ends. This issue has been neglected for some time in contrast to the attention that has been given to the approval procedures for establishing FIEs.

[2] The Regulations lay down clear rules to follow in pledge of equity interests of FIEs, and have significant legal and practical implications for FIEs attempting to alter the equity stakes of their respective partners. With the promulgation of the Regulations, efficient supervision procedures are set up to control the assignment of shareholders' rights in FIEs and to assist the smooth and healthy development of FIEs in China. See Nan Wang, Wave of JV Restructuring Prompts Ruling on Changes in Equity Stake, *China Joint Venturer*, 3 (1), p. 1 (1997).

[3] See Wei Jiaju, Foreign Investment Enterprises: Assigning Interests, 5 *China Law News*, pp. 1-5 (1997).

recipient country of FDI next only to U. S. By the end of 1998, China had approved 324,000 foreign-invested projects. These projects have a combined contractual FDI of US $ 572.5 billion, of which US $ 267.4 billion has already been invested. [1]It is generally accepted that CFILs have made great contributions to encourage the developments of FDI in China. The recent developments of CFILs toward common approaches of FILs in MECs played an important role for promoting and guaranteeing the continual developments of FDI in China.

Firstly, the recent developments of CFILs have further improved the foreign investment climate in China. Before 1993 the developments of FDI was to some extent restricted by the framework of CFILs with some CPECs' characteristics. The recent developments of CFILs have affirmed the open attitude to FDI admissions, the multiple FDI vehicles and the national treatment for FDI, which meet the needs of further reform and wider-opening to the outside world. It also helped to speed up the transition from central planning economy to market economy, and therefore facilitates the continual development of FDI in China.

Secondly, the new developments of CFILs have encouraged the diversification of FDI resources. In last two decades, most of China's FDI were not from foreign countries, but from the special regions of China proper—Hong Kong, Macao and Taiwan;[2] and the major foreign investors are ethnic Chinese around the world, especially those from Southeast Asia. [3]The initiatives of investments in China by the investors from the special regions and overseas Chinese are related not only to economic concerns, but also to social and culture factors. Probably as one of the results from Asian financial crisis, China's new policies on FDI is to absorb FDI through multiple channels. Continued efforts have been made to absorb FDI from

---

〔1〕 China news: Foreign Investments in China Increasing Again, *Mingbao*, electronic version, 27 Jan. 1999.

〔2〕 This characteristic of China's FDI is recognised by international economic organisations as the figures of China's FDI produced by Chinese government are accepted by them. See Xinfa Lin and Ayo Eso, General Concept of FDI and China's FDI, *China Report* 34 (1), pp. 20-21 (1998).

〔3〕 Top ten investors in China in the period 1979-1994 are Hong Kong & Macao, Taiwan, U. S. , Japan, Singapore, UK, South Korea, Thailand, Germany and Canada. China's FDI from U. S. and E. U. account relative low proportion comparing with the global investment amount from U. S. and E. U. For example, in 1996 China's FDIs from U. S. and E. U. only account 4.6% and 2.6% of total amount of FDIs from U. S. and E. U. See Xia youfu, Li Xin, Studies on China's Absorbing Foreign Direct Investment in the Asian Financial Crisis, *China Foreign Investment*, No. 9, 1998, p. 29; John WONG, Southeast Asian Ethnic Chinese Investing in China, *EAI Working Paper*, No. 15 (1998).

Hong Kong, Macao and Taiwan, as well as Southeast Asian countries. Meanwhile, emphasis has been put on expanding investment from North America, EU, Japan and other developed countries. [1] To help accomplish this aim, China has to further adjust its legal systems to cater to the US and EU. [2] The new developments of CFILs have provided new investment opportunities and better legal environment for Western investors, so the FDI from West have been increased steadily.

Thirdly, the recent developments of CFILs have encouraged to raise the quality of FDI in China. In the wake of rapid economic growth and the increase in FDI, China has moved to emphasise "quality" instead of "quantity" of FDI projects. High requirements for FDI showed in the CFILs and the actual increase in intensive competition may encourage foreign investors to bring more advanced management and technology to their enterprises, especially in East China. Generally large companies, particularly multinational companies may gain more advantages by their superiority in technology and marketing. Small and medium size companies have to seek a place in the sun by selecting their investment industries and business locations correctly. As the result of the mutual function of large companies and small and medium size companies, the level of the quality of FDI as a whole in China may take a new step forward.

2. Exerting a Great Influence on the Treatment of FDI and Foreign Investors in China

As a result of China's granting national treatment to FDI and foreign investors step by step, foreign investors may enjoy the same rights and opportunities as domestic investors. They may reduce or avoid the political risks in their investment in China (such as expropriation or nationalisation, etc.). Their legitimate rights and interests may be more effectively protected by Chinese laws. It is doubtless that the new developments of CFILs towards national treatment principle have further improved the treatment of FDI and foreign investors in a long run.

At the same time, with the performance of national treatment and the application of unified economic and commercial laws, foreign investors have to accept the

---

[1] See Further Expending Opening & Utilisation of Foreign Capital, *Beijing Review*, 41 (37), p. 13 (1998).

[2] See Francis Bassolino, China Opens Its Doors, *China Economic Review*, 8 (10), p. 29 (1998).

fact that they would eventually be treated in the same way as their Chinese counterparts. A foreign investor has to compete with domestic investors and other foreign investors in a level playing field. Until recently, FDI and foreign investors in China have enjoyed the "superior-national treatment" and "inferior-national treatment" at the same time. However, as a whole, the benefits gained by foreign investors from the "superior-national treatment" may exceed their losses caused by the "inferior-national treatment". In other words, FDI and foreign investors may lose their interests due to the performance of national treatment. This change has had different impacts on different foreign investors in China. In general, those sought low production costs were negatively affected, as the removal of preferential treatments increased their operational cost. Other companies, especially large ones, which were engaged in high-technology or high value-added production and wanted to tap into the Chinese domestic market, continued to invest and gain profit in China. [1] In this new business environment, foreign investors have to adjust their investment and business activities in China to balance their gains and losses.

3. Encouraging a Structural Adjustment for the System of CFILs

Since 1979 China has set up the two-tiered economic legal system, namely applying different economic legal systems to FIEs and CIEs. Before 1993, as the FDI vehicles are mainly EJV, CJV and WFOE, the China-foreign EJVL, the China-foreign CJVL and FWOEL have constituted the basic framework of CFILs, supplemented by a series of specific regulations concerning the approval, registration, land use, taxation, finance and accountancy, labour, export and import, etc. It seems that from 1979 to 1993, CFILs are "pure" special legal system separated from other domestic economic legal systems.

The developments of CFILs towards common approach of FILs in MECs have encouraged great changes in the two-tiered economic legal system in China. At the same time, in the process of these new developments, some problems have emerged, such as legislation lagging behind practice, some conflicts and overlapping of provisions from different legal sources, especially from the specific foreign investment laws and the unified economic and commercial laws. Therefore, the new develop-

---

[1] See Dong Dong Zhang, Negotiating for a Liberal Economic Regime: the Case of Japanese FDI in China, *The Pacific Review*, 11 (1) p. 71 (1998).

ments of CFILs themselves have asked for recommendation of structural adjustment of CFILs.

As far as the system of CFILs is concerned, in the process of new developments, CFILs have showed new "mixed" characteristic. They include not only specific foreign investment laws, but also unified economic and commercial laws. The former is a major part of CFILs while latter is supplementary to them. [1] However, the latter has become a very important source of CFILs applicable to FDI and FIEs. Moreover, in the concurrent development of specific foreign investment laws and unified economic and commercial laws, unified economic and commercial laws will take the place of the specific foreign investment laws step by step. This process has been guided and promoted by unification trend of economic and commercial laws, and by the legislative direction of granting national treatment to FDI and FIEs. Then, unified economic and commercial laws may not completely take the place of the specific foreign investment laws because of the specific features of FDI activities. In other words, the two-tiered economic legal system may be getting blunted and will not become a single system in the near future.

As far as the structure of the specific foreign investment laws is concerned, it is necessary to co-ordinate or remove the conflict or overlapping norms in the specific foreign investment laws and unified economic and commercial laws. It is suggested that the better way is to combine the basic contents of specific foreign investment laws (namely the China-foreign Equity Joint Venture Law, the China-foreign Cooperative Joint Venture Law and Wholly-foreign-owned Enterprises Law) as a unified foreign investment code. At the same time, it may still be necessary to put into effect certain specific foreign investment laws so as to regulate the new emerging forms of FDI activities. However, Chinese main efforts for absorbing FDI are not to be accomplished by granting more investment incentives, but by creating a equal investment environment for foreign and domestic investors. Therefore, the specific

---

〔1〕　Even very recently, China has still promulgated some laws and regulations particularly applying to FDI and FIEs. For examples, CJV regulations, liquidation regulations for FIEs and The State Administration of Taxation, Issues Concerning the Tax Treatment of Rent Income Obtained from Leasing of Houses and Buildings in PRC by Foreign Enterprises Circular, issued on 20 November 1996 and retrospective to 1 October 1996, Implementation of Joint Annual Audits of Foreign Investment Enterprises Circular issued on 26 December 1996 and Implementation of Joint Annual Audits of Foreign Investment Enterprises Supplementary Circular issued on 3 January 1997.

foreign investment laws will be expected to decrease.

Hopefully，when Chinese market economic system is fully established and the unified economic and commercial laws are further improved and put into place，the system of CFILs will be composed of the unified specific foreign investment laws and the unified economic and commercial laws. The latter will play more important role than that of former. This change will have great positive impact on FDI and FIEs in China.

第二节 我国对外资实行国民待遇原则的法律实践 *

【摘要】 对外资实行国民待遇,一般指东道国给予外资以同内资同等的待遇,其内涵需要进一步廓清。自 1993 年以来,我国有关外商投资的法律实践表明,我国已从"整平游戏场地"与"经济法和民商法的统一化"两个方面逐步对外资实行国民待遇原则。这一法律实践的重要意义首先是对在华外资待遇产生了重要影响,其次是推动了我国外资法体系的结构性调整,即由相对独立的"单纯"的外资法体系转化为由专门性外资法与统一的经济法和民商法构成的"混合法"体系。

【关键词】 国民待遇;整平游戏场地;经济法和民商法的统一化;外资法体系

近年来,关于对在华外国投资者和外国投资(以下统称"外资")实行国民待遇原则的理论探讨,见仁见智。[1] 本文拟在分析对外资实行国民待遇的涵义的基础上,简略概括 1993 年以来我国在国内法层面上逐步对外资实行国民待遇原则的主要发展,并初步探讨其对在华外资待遇及我国外资法体系的影响。

一

对外资实行国民待遇,通常指东道国给予外资以同内国投资者和内国投资(以下统称"内资")同等的待遇。

关于国民待遇的概念,有学者认为,相对于"泛提的国民待遇"(或称"全面的国民待遇"),适应我国经济体制转轨时期特定的经济条件,我国目前对外资实行的是"特定国民待遇标准"。其特征首先是过渡性,即实行于转轨时期,随着市场经济体制的最终确立,将转变为"泛提国民待遇";其次,表现在国内法和国际法实践中,不能笼统、全面承诺实行国民待遇,只能采取列举方式规定实行国民待遇的范围、领域,而"泛提国民待遇"则相反,列举不实行国民待遇的范围、领域作为例外;最后,由于采取列举式,具有透明度和可塑性。

有学者进一步提出"国际通用的国民待遇"和"非国际通用的国民待遇"的概念。前者指按照国际公认的标准,东道国实行的国民待遇已达到作为一项外资待遇"原

---

* 原载《厦门大学学报》(哲学社会科学版)2001 年第 4 期。

〔1〕 有关外资国民待遇的近期研究成果,参见徐崇利:《试论我国对外资实行国民待遇标准的问题》;单文华:《外资国民待遇基本理论问题研究》,载《国际经济法论丛》第 1 卷,1998 年,第 175—201、240—267 页;张庆麟:《论当代国际投资法中的国民待遇》,载《珞珈法学论坛》第 1 卷,2000 年,第 178—190 页。

则或标准"的程度。后者指东道国只在特定领域给予外资以不低于内资的待遇,即东道国在相当程度上仍对外资实行差别待遇。按照公认的标准,在此情况下,国民待遇尚未发育成为一项外资待遇"原则或标准"。[1]

实行国民待遇原则需要明确的重要问题之一是国民待遇与优惠待遇的关系。有学者认为,综观各国外资立法和双边投资条约的规定,国民待遇的定义有两种表述:一是指东道国给予外资的待遇应不低于(no less favorable than)其给予内资的待遇。按此定义,从法律上看,国民待遇与东道国对外资实行高于内资的优惠待遇是兼容的;第二种表述是指东道国给予外资的待遇应等同于(as the same favorable as)其给予内资的待遇。据此,国民待遇与优惠待遇则是不兼容的。[2] 这一问题与我国实行国民待遇的国内法取向密切相关。如所周知,由于经济体制等方面的原因,我国改革开放以来,长期对外资同时实行优于内资的待遇(即所谓"超国民待遇")和低于内资的待遇(即所谓"次国民待遇")。在我国对外资实行国民待遇时,是给予外资不低于内资的待遇,即取消"次国民待遇",保留"超国民待遇"? 还是既取消"次国民待遇",也取消"超国民待遇"?

本文以为,在讨论对外资实行国民待遇的概念时,需要明确:第一,国民待遇原则是基于人人平等的人文思想,[3]是要实现不分内外国人,一视同仁的目标;第二,从历史上看,国民待遇原则是一柄双刃剑,既反对对外国投资者实行歧视待遇,也反对外国投资者享有特权;第三,国民待遇原则本质上是以本国国民为参照标准的法律概念,不存在国际通用或公认的标准;第四,对作为国民待遇参照标准的"本国国民"不能笼统而论,应作具体分析,外国投资者属私人投资者,其待遇只能与内国私人投资者同等,而不能与国有投资者同等。[4] 最后,严格地说,国民待遇应是指东道国给予外资以同内资同等的待遇,虽然国民待遇与优惠待遇可能兼容或并存,但国民待遇本身并不包含优惠待遇。此外,由于对外资实行太多的优惠待遇势必产生外资与内资的悬殊待遇,致使国民待遇形同虚设,在这个意义上,两种待遇的关系是此长彼消,甚至是相互排斥的。

---

〔1〕 徐崇利:《试论我国对外资实行国民待遇标准的问题》,载陈安主编:《国际经济法论丛》(第1卷),法律出版社1998年版,第180页。

〔2〕 同上书,第183—187页。

〔3〕 张庆麟:《论当代国际投资法中的国民待遇》,载武汉大学法学院主办:《珞珈法学论坛》(第1卷),武汉大学出版社2000年版,第178—180页。

〔4〕 一些双边投资条约规定,东道国只对"任何类似的企业"(如1969年挪威与印度尼西亚协定第3条)实行国民待遇,或只承诺对外国投资者实行与本国私人投资者相同的待遇,但仍保留给予本国国有企业以特权的权力(如1977年前联邦德国与马里协定附件)。参见徐崇利:《试论我国对外资实行国民待遇标准的问题》,载陈安主编:《国际经济法论丛》(第1卷),法律出版社1998年版,第177页。

二

在理论上,对我国目前是否已对外资实行国民待遇原则,尚有不同理解。从法律实践角度看,自1993年我国宪法和中共中央确立社会主义市场经济体制目标以来,[1]我国已逐步对外资实行国民待遇原则:一方面是"整平游戏场地"(leveling the playing field),即通过税制改革和投资优惠改革等给予外商投资企业和内资企业同等的待遇;[2]另一方面是制定统一的经济法和民商法,旨在建立为外商投资企业和内资企业提供同等待遇的统一的法律框架。

(一)"整平游戏场地"

长期以来,外商投资企业在我国享有内资企业所不能享有的税收减免和进出口权等优惠待遇,即享有"超国民待遇";另一方面,外商投资企业在投资行业、信贷支持和生产经营环节等方面也无法享有与内资企业同等的待遇,即得接受"次国民待遇"。对"整平游戏场地"的一般解释是,如果外商投资企业不再接受低于内资企业的"次国民待遇",它们也不应再享有高于内资企业的"超国民待遇"。这也是对实行国民待遇原则的一般理解。[3]1993年以来,我国以法律和政策"整平游戏场地"的努力可概括为如下四方面:

1. 税制改革

为了建立外商投资企业和内资企业享有同等税收待遇的统一的所得税制,1993年国务院发布了《中华人民共和国企业所得税暂行条例》,对内资企业(包括国有企业、集体企业、私营企业、联营企业、股份制企业以及有生产、经营所得和其他所得的其他组织)规定了统一的企业所得税率。该税率不适用于外商投资企业。外商投资企业的所得税率虽未发生变化,但内资企业的税率则从55%调为33%,与外商投资企业的所得税率(包括地方所得税率)一致。

1993年《全国人大常委会关于外商投资企业和外国企业适用增值税、消费税、营业税等税收暂行规定》明确指出,其目的在于"统一税制,公平税负,改善我国的投资环境,适应建立和发展社会主义市场经济的需要"。根据该规定,外商投资企业自1994年1月1日起适用国务院发布的增值税暂行条例、消费税暂行条例和营业税暂

---

[1] 《中华人民共和国宪法修正案》(1993年3月29日第八届全国人民代表大会第一次会议通过)第7条;《中共中央关于建立社会主义市场经济体制若干问题的决定》,载《人民日报》1993年11月7日第1版。

[2] Dong Dong Zhang, Negotiating for a Liberal Economic Regime: The Case of Japanese FDI in China, *The Pacific Review*, Vol. 11, No. 1, 1998, p. 70.

[3] Bruce McLaughlin, China's WTO Entry Could Threaten FIE Market Share, *China Joint Venturer*, Vol. 9, No. 1, 1996, p. 4.

行条例。

在对外资新开放的金融和保险业，也反映了"统一税制，公平税负"的目标。根据1997年《国务院关于调整金融保险业税收政策有关问题的通知》[国发（1997）5号]，金融、保险企业的所得税税率一律调整为33％，金融保险业营业税税率由5％提高为8％，对1997年1月1日后在经济特区以外设立的外商投资的金融、保险企业和外国金融、保险企业一律执行8％的营业税税率。

虽然税制统一化的总政策尚在进行之中，但对外商投资企业的税收优惠仍然有效。这些优惠包括外商投资企业的"超税负返还"[1]、"两免三减"所得税优惠和设立于经济特区的外商投资企业可享有15％所得税率等。[2]这种方式表明我国现行政策是，创设公平的税收环境，同时保持对外商投资企业税收优惠的持续性和稳定性。然而，长远看来，对外商投资企业单方面的税收优惠终将改变。

2. 关税优惠调整

过去，外商投资企业享有其所需的资本性货物进口的免除关税待遇，而内资企业未享有此种待遇。这一规定的合理性一是鼓励外资，二是鼓励先进机器设备的进口。1995年颁发的《国务院关于改革和调整进口税收政策的通知》[国发（1995）34号]旨在"按照社会主义市场经济体制的要求和国际通行规则，建立统一、规范、公平、合理的进口税收政策"，为外商投资企业和内资企业创设公平的竞争环境。根据该通知，自1996年4月1日起，对新批准设立的外商投资企业投资总额内进口的设备和原材料，一律按法定税率征收关税和进口环节税。由于这一转变意味着取消对外国投资者的此项重要关税优惠，在新政策实施之前设立的外商投资企业可以在一至两年内依然享有原先的资本性货物进口的免税待遇。在上述通知之后，外商投资企业可继续享受关税优惠的期限又作两次延长，表明了我国对大型投资项目的特别关注和政策支持。[3]

1998年1月以来，我国对一些外商投资项目继续适用资本性货物进口的免税待遇。根据《国务院关于调整进口设备税收政策的通知》[国发（1997）37号]，符合1998年《外商投资产业指导目录》鼓励类或限制乙类并转让技术的外商投资项目，在投资总额内进口的自用设备，除《外商投资项目不予免税的进口商品目录》所列商品外，可享受免除关税和进口环节增值税的待遇。尤其具有重要意义的是，该通知同时规定，对符合《当前国家重点鼓励发展的产业、产品和技术目录》的国内投资项目给予

---

〔1〕《全国人大常委会关于外商投资企业和外国企业适用增值税、消费税、营业税等税收暂行规定》。

〔2〕《中华人民共和国外商投资企业和外国企业所得税法》第7、8条。

〔3〕 Sally A Harpole, Policy Trends in Taxation of Foreign-invested Enterprises, *China Law News*, Vol. 2, 1997, pp. 1-5.

同上述外商投资项目相同的免税待遇。这从一个侧面反映了我国"整平游戏场地"的努力。

3. 专门性外资法的"国民待遇"规定

在消除外商投资企业和内资企业之间原有差别待遇的同时,我国注意尽可能在新的专门性外资法中体现国民待遇原则,避免产生新的差别待遇。

1994 年国务院发布的《中华人民共和国外资金融机构管理条例》未规定外商独资设立的或中外合资设立的银行或财务公司可享有外商投资企业法所规定的地位及享有的权利。这是一个重要的发展,表明我国对外商投资的金融机构已不再实行"超国民待遇"原则。[1] 另一方面,1996 年中国人民银行颁布的《上海浦东外资金融机构经营人民币业务试点暂行管理办法》批准在上海浦东的 9 家外资银行经营人民币业务及其后扩大试点范围,预示着在华外资金融机构将来在经营范围方面可能逐渐享有与我国其他金融机构同等的机会和待遇。

1996 年外经贸部发布的《关于设立中外合资对外贸易公司试点暂行办法》也采取相同的原则。其中明确规定,中外合资外贸公司在申请许可证、配额招标、外汇、融资、税收和出口退税等方面均享有与国内其他外贸公司,特别是国有外贸公司同等的待遇,而不像生产领域的外商投资企业一样享有"超国民待遇"。

4. 外商投资企业法的重要修改

2000 年 10 月 31 日,第九届全国人大常委会第十八次会议通过了《全国人民代表大会常务委员会关于修改〈中华人民共和国中外合作经营企业法〉的决定》和《全国人大常委会关于修改〈中华人民共和国外资企业法〉的决定》。2001 年 3 月 15 日,第九届全国人大四次会议又通过了《全国人民代表大会关于修改〈中华人民共和国中外合资经营企业法〉的决定》。这些修改主要是适应我国加入 WTO 的需要,使我国外资法基本符合 WTO 体制的规则,同时也反映了我国对外资实行国民待遇原则的最新发展。修改内容主要是:

(1) 关于外汇平衡条款。删除《中华人民共和国中外合作经营企业法》(以下简称《中外合作经营企业法》)第 20 条和《中华人民共和国外资企业法》(以下简称《外资企业法》)第 18 条第 3 款关于外商投资企业应自行解决外汇收支平衡问题的要求。[2] 修改的主要原因是,1994 年我国外汇管理体制实行了人民币经常项目下有条件可兑换。1996 年我国取消了所有经常性国际支付和转移的限制,正式宣布接受

---

[1]　江平:《我国进一步吸引外资的新法律举措》,载《东亚论文》1997 年第 4 期,第 9 页。

[2]　《中外合资经营企业法》没有关于外汇平衡的明确规定,相关内容规定于《中外合资经营企业法实施条例》第 75 条,国务院目前正进行相应的修改。

《国际货币基金组织协定》第 8 条的义务，实现人民币经常项目可兑换。1997 年修正的《中华人民共和国外汇管理条例》第 5 条明确规定："国家对经常性国际收支和转移不予限制"。显然，在内资企业已适用上述新规定的情况下，外资法中有关外商投资企业自行解决外汇收支平衡的原有规定已构成了"次国民待遇"，不符合对外资实行国民待遇的原则。

（2）关于"尽先在我国购买"的内容。删除《中外合作经营企业法》第 19 条关于"尽先在我国购买"的内容，修改为："合作企业可以在经批准的经营范围内，进口本企业需要的物资，出口本企业生产的产品。合作企业在经营范围内所需的原材料、燃料等物资，按照公平、合理的原则，可以在国内市场或者在国际市场购买。"《外资企业法》第 15 条和《中华人民共和国中外合资经营企业法》（以下简称《中外合资经营企业法》）第 9 条第 2 款也作类似的修改。这是因为，"尽先在我国购买"的要求，是专门针对外商投资企业的，可能被视为与国际通行规则不符的"当地成分"的投资措施。不仅如此，依照国际通行规则和市场经济规律，在一般情况下，外商投资企业与内资企业一样，应享有根据国内外市场情况进行采购和销售的自主权。

（3）关于"出口实绩要求"条款。修改《外资企业法》第 3 条第 1 款关于设立外资企业的条件，将"必须采用先进的技术和设备，或者产品全部出口或者大部分出口"修改为"必须有利于我国国民经济的发展。国家鼓励举办产品出口或者技术先进的外资企业"。这是因为，原规定专门适用于外资企业，属于《与贸易有关的投资措施协议》（TRIMs）禁止的"出口实绩要求"，也不符合市场经济体制的原则和国民待遇原则。在市场经济条件下，无论是内资企业或外商投资企业，都应能根据国内外市场情况自主决定企业产品的销售。

（4）关于"企业生产计划备案"条款。删除《外资企业法》第 11 条第 1 款和《中外合资经营企业法》第 9 条第 1 款关于企业生产计划备案的规定。其主要原因是，我国目前已逐步建立社会主义市场经济体制，企业享有充分的经营自主权，逐步成为真正的市场竞争主体。政府管理经济主要是通过经济、金融、法律等宏观调控手段。在对内资企业已不再要求生产计划备案的情况下，如对外商投资企业仍有此要求，将被视为"次国民待遇"。[1]

（二）经济法和民商法的统一化

1993 年以来，我国经济法和民商法进入了一个重要的发展时期，其重要特点是形成了统一化趋向，即经济法和民商法不仅调整国内经济关系，也调整涉外经济关

---

〔1〕 王新：《外商投资企业法律修改探源》，载《国际经贸消息》2001 年 3 月 12 日。

系。这明确反映了我国对外资实行国民待遇原则的立法导向。以下,以同外商投资关系最为密切的公司法、证券法、合同法和仲裁法的新发展为例,说明这一新趋向。

1. 公司法

虽然我国的内资公司早已有之,外商投资公司自 1979 年以来也迅速发展,但在 1994 年之前尚无正式的《公司法》予以规范。《中华人民共和国公司法》(以下简称《公司法》)颁布于 1993 年 12 月 29 日,1994 年 7 月 1 日生效。该法适用于在我国设立的股份有限公司和有限责任公司,包括内资公司和外商投资公司,首开民商法统一化的先河。

《公司法》第 75 条规定:"设立股份有限公司,应当有五人以上为发起人,其中须有过半数的发起人在我国境内有住所。"该规定明确承认股份有限公司发起人的国民待遇原则,即在我国没有住所的外国人(包括自然人和法人)可成为我国股份有限公司的发起人。[1]

《公司法》对该法与外商投资企业法的关系也作了明确的规定。根据该法第 18 条,在外商投资企业法未作规定的情况下,该法也适用于外商投资的有限责任公司。例如,董事的资格、董事和经理的竞业禁止、企业领导人因违法给企业带来严重损失的赔偿责任等规定,均适用于外商投资企业。学说上进一步认为,中外合资企业的合营各方在《中外合资经营企业法》和《公司法》有不同规定的情况下,可能依一定的程序自由选择适用的法律。例如中外合资企业组织机构的设置,既可依《中外合资经营企业法》设立董事会和总经理,也可依《公司法》设立股东会、董事会、总经理和监事会。[2]

1995 年《国务院关于股份有限公司境内上市外资股的规定》明确表明是根据《公司法》制定的,并规定境内上市外资股投资人限于外国的自然人、法人和其他组织;我国香港、澳门、台湾地区的自然人、法人和其他组织;定居在国外的我国公民和国务院证券委员会规定的境内上市外资股其他投资人。该规定还进一步体现了"同股同权"的公司法原则,即"持有同一种类股份的境内上市外资股股东与内资股股东,依照《公司法》享有同等权利和履行同等义务。"据之,不问投资来源于国内或国外,不问投资者来自国内或国外,同股同权。

1996 年《中华人民共和国公司注册资本登记暂行规定》明确规定了公司资本登记的程序。该法适用于外商投资企业和内资企业,但在适用于外商投资企业的情况下,以不同外商投资企业法冲突为前提。在这方面,外商投资企业与内资企业的主

---

〔1〕　江平:《我国进一步吸引外资的新法律举措》,载《东亚论文》1997 年第 4 期,第 1 页。
〔2〕　杨忠孝:《"合资企业如何适用公司法"研讨会综述》,载《法学》1998 年第 9 期,第 63—64 页。

要区别之一是，外商投资企业可在缴资之前取得商业许可证，而内资企业须表明其缴资后方能取得商业许可证。

2. 证券法

在我国证券市场建立 8 年之后，《中华人民共和国证券法》（以下简称《证券法》）于 1998 年 12 月 29 日由全国人大常委会通过，1999 年 7 月 1 日生效，适用于我国境内的所有证券发行和交易活动。由于外商投资企业可以采取股份有限公司的形式设立，另一方面，外国投资者可以通过并购形式进行其直接投资活动，必然涉及股票发行和交易活动。因此，外国投资者在设立股份有限公司或进行并购活动时应遵守《证券法》的有关规定。外商投资股份有限公司在股票发行和交易活动中，享有与内资股份有限公司同等的待遇。

3. 合同法

在 1999 年 10 月 1 日之前，我国涉及外商投资的合同制度包括了 5 项主要法律：1986 年《中华人民共和国民法通则》规定了合同法的基本原则；1981 年《中华人民共和国经济合同法》（以下简称《经济合同法》，1993 年修正）和 1985 年《中华人民共和国涉外经济合同法》（以下简称《涉外经济合同法》）分别调整国内经济合同关系和涉外经济合同关系；而 1987 年《中华人民共和国技术合同法》（以下简称《技术合同法》）和 1985 年《中华人民共和国技术引进合同管理条例》（以下简称《技术引进合同管理条例》）分别调整涉及技术交易的国内合同关系和涉外合同关系。此外，在涉及商标、专利、版权、担保等我国法律规定中，也有一些关于合同的规定。中外投资者设立中外合资企业或中外合作企业的合同属涉外经济合同，由《涉外经济合同法》调整。外商投资企业之间或外商投资企业与内资企业之间的合同属国内经济合同，由《经济合同法》调整。在外商投资企业设立或经营中所需签署的技术转让合同则视技术供方是否外国人（包括法人和自然人）而适用《技术引进合同管理条例》或《技术合同法》。

基于对市场经济国家合同法律和理论的研究，1999 年 3 月 15 日颁布的《中华人民共和国合同法》在很大程度上采纳了市场经济国家共同的合同原则和标准。该法的重要原则之一是统一性，包含了建立统一合同制度的目标。[1] 该法第 2 条规定："本法所称合同是平等主体的公民、法人、其他组织之间设立、变更、终止民事权利义务关系的协议。"该法自 1999 年 10 月 1 日起施行，《经济合同法》《涉外经济合同法》和《技术合同法》同时废止。上述规定明确表明了该法适用于国内合同关系和涉外

---

[1] Ping Jiang, Drafting the Uniform Contract Law in China, *Columbia Journal of Asian Law*, Vol. 10, 1996, pp. 245-248.

合同关系,包括中外合资企业或中外合作企业中外方之间、外商投资企业之间以及外商投资企业与其他合同主体之间的合同关系。

4. 仲裁法

在程序法领域,1995 年 9 月 1 日施行的《中华人民共和国仲裁法》(以下简称《仲裁法》)也反映了民商法的统一化趋势。

《仲裁法》的重要贡献之一是组建符合国际通行的仲裁制度的常设国内仲裁机构,并赋予一定的涉外案件管辖权。根据《仲裁法》第 79 条规定,该法施行前在直辖市和省、自治区人民政府所在地的市设立的仲裁机构应依照该法的有关规定重新组建。关于新组建的仲裁委员会对涉外案件的管辖问题,该法未作明文规定。该法第 66 条规定,涉外仲裁机构可以由中国国际商会组织设立,同时并未排除地方设立受理涉外案件的仲裁委员会的可能性。

1996 年《国务院办公厅关于贯彻实施〈仲裁法〉需要明确的几个问题的通知》[国办发(1996)22 号]第 3 条规定:"涉外仲裁案件的当事人自愿选择新组建的仲裁委员会仲裁的,新组建的仲裁委员会可以受理。"这一规定的直接后果是,各地仲裁委员会在当事人自愿选择的情况下,有权受理中外投资争议。这是有关仲裁解决中外投资争议的法制的一个重要发展。原来,在我国只有中国国际经济贸易仲裁委员会有权仲裁解决中外合营者之间的投资争议。《仲裁法》的上述规定改变了这种"单一"仲裁机构的局面,有利于仲裁机构之间形成竞争的态势,以确保仲裁的独立和公正。

三

1993 年以来我国逐步对外资实行国民待遇原则的法律实践,对于当前在华外资待遇和我国外资法体系的结构性调整均具有重要的意义。

(一) 对在华外资待遇产生了重要的影响

作为对外资实行国民待遇原则的结果,外资与内资享有同等的待遇,不仅可以同内资在"整平的游戏场地"中平等竞技,而且可以最大限度地避免或减少投资政治风险(主要包括征收风险、汇兑风险和战乱风险等),其合法权益将受到更为充分有效的法律保护。毫无疑问,长远看来,我国对外资实行国民待遇原则将有利于进一步改善在华外资待遇。

与此同时,作为逐步实行国民待遇原则的结果,随着外商投资优惠的逐步取消,经济法和民商法对外商投资企业和内资企业的统一适用,外国投资者最终将与内国的竞争者居于同等的地位。长期以来,外资在我国虽然同时享有"超国民待遇"和接受"次国民待遇",但总体上说,享有"超国民待遇"所得到的利益远大于因接受"次国民待遇"而遭受的损失。换言之，对外资而言，从眼前利益看，实行国民待遇原则可能产生得不偿失的后果。

我国目前依法逐步对外资实行国民待遇原则，已对不同的外国投资者产生了不同的实际影响。一般而言，那些采用一般技术、寻求低生产成本的外国投资者面临比以往较不利的经营环境。因为，取消原有专门给予外资的优惠待遇将直接增加其经营成本，"整平游戏场地"的种种努力势必提高内资企业的竞争地位和能力。而采用高新技术、从事高增值生产和希望拓展我国市场的外国投资者则可继续保持其优势地位并取得预期的回报。[1] 在这种新的经营环境中，外国投资者需要调整其在华投资战略和经营活动以重新平衡其利弊得失。

（二）推动了我国外资法体系的结构性调整

1979 年以来，我国在经济法律体制上实行"双轨制"，即对外商投资企业和内资企业分别适用不同的法律制度。在 1993 年以前，由于我国利用外资的主要形式是中外合资企业、中外合作企业和外资企业，1979 年《中外合资经营企业法》、1988 年《中外合作经营企业法》和 1986 年《外资企业法》三部外商投资企业基本法律及其实施条例或施行细则以及一系列配套的涉及外商投资企业的审批、登记、土地、税收、财务会计、劳务、金融和进出口等方面的单行法规，共同构成了以"企业为本位"的外资法体系的基本框架。外资法不仅是经济行政法，也是企业组织法。显然，该时期的外资法是区别于国内其他经济法律制度的相对独立的较"单纯"的特别法律制度。这种立法模式在当时具有针对性强、便于贯彻实施的优点，也适应了当时我国民商法尚不发达，特别是《公司法》尚未颁布的实际情况和现实需要。

随着国内经济体制改革的深入发展，特别是 1993 年确立建立社会主义市场经济体制目标以来，这种立法模式已不能适应形势发展的需要。首先，市场经济要求各民事主体处于平等的竞争地位，因此，经济、民商立法应统一适用于各市场主体，既适用于内资企业，也适用于外商投资企业，只有这样，才能确保各市场主体处于平等的竞争地位；其次，市场经济要求参与商品交换的市场主体均遵守平等、自愿、等价有偿以及诚实信用的原则，与市场主体的性质无关，因此，内资企业和外商投资企业适用不同的法律，显然与市场经济的这种基本要求相悖。

我国逐步对外资实行国民待遇原则的法律实践促使我国经济法律体制的"双轨制"发生了重要的变化。特别是，由于统一的经济法和民商法的发展，出现了有关调整外资活动的不同法律渊源，即专门性的外资法与统一的经济法和民商法之间的重

---

〔1〕 Dong Dong Zhang，Negotiating for a Liberal Economic Regime：The Case of Japanese FDI in China，*The Pacific Review*，Vol. 11，No. 1，1998，pp. 70-71.

叠或冲突等问题。因此,该实践的发展本身提出了对我国外资法体系进行结构性调整的迫切要求。

当前,在逐步对外资实行国民待遇原则的法律实践的推动下,我国外资法体系已在一定程度上凸显出其新的"混合型"的体系特征,即包容了专门性的外资法与统一的经济法和民商法,前者为主,后者为辅。统一的经济法和民商法成为外资法不可或缺的组成部分,适用于外资和外商投资企业。不仅如此,在专门性的外资法与经济法和民商法并行发展的过程中,由于经济法和民商法的统一化趋向与对外资实行国民待遇原则的立法导向,经济法和民商法将越来越多地取代专门性的外资法而适用于外资和外商投资企业。然而,取决于外资活动本身的特殊性及我国经济法和民商法的发展程度,在今后一段时期,经济法和民商法尚不能完全取代专门性的外资法。[1] 换言之,我国经济法律的"双轨制"虽然可能逐渐淡化,但不能彻底"合二而一",专门性的外资法仍然有其存在的合理性和必要性。

就专门性外资法的结构而言,在逐步对外资实行国民待遇原则的新形势下,当务之急是按市场经济体制发展的需要与经济法和民商法统一化的实际发展情况,全面修订专门性的外资法,删除或协调与统一的经济法和民商法重叠或冲突的规范,把专门性外资法的基本组成部分,即《中外合资经营企业法》《中外合作企业经营法》和《外资企业法》重构为统一的外商投资法,[2] 同时辅之以少数必要的专门性外资单行法规。市场经济强调公平竞争。尽管我国今后还可能继续颁布专门性外资单行法规,但在战略上,我国今后吸引外资的工作重点,不再是对外资给予更多的优惠待遇,而是给予国民待遇,从而创设一个更为优良、公平的投资环境。相应地,专门性外资单行法规将是有限的,逐渐减少的。

不难预见,在我国社会主义市场经济制度完全确立,我国统一的经济法和民商法进一步发展和完善的条件下,我国外资法体系将由调整外商投资的统一的外商投资法与统一的经济法和民商法构成。前者主要调整外资准入活动,后者则主要调整外资营运活动。在此法律框架下,外资在营运活动中,将享有全面、充分的国民待遇。

---

[1] 例如,在 1999 年 8 月 30 日第九届全国人大常委会第十一次会议通过、自 2000 年 1 月 1 日起施行的《中华人民共和国个人独资企业法》明确规定,"外商独资企业不适用本法"。

[2] 参见罗明达、李抉:《进一步完善外商投资法律环境的思考》,载《法学评论》,1990 年第 2 期,第 4 页;谢庄、吕国平:《我国应制定外国投资法》,载《现代法学》1992 年第 1 期,第 58—61 页;陆泽峰:《论中国外资立法的改革和重构》,载《法学评论》1996 年第 5 期,第 72 页;夏友富、李昕:《亚洲金融危机中我国吸收外商直接投资研究》,载《我国外资》1998 年第 9 期,第 30 页。

Chinese Legislation on National Treatment Principle
Applied to Foreign Investment

Abstract: In general, national treatment principle applied to foreign investment refers to that the host country grants the same treatment to both domestic and foreign investments. The contents of the concept, however, needed to be further clarified. Since 1993, Chinese legislation on foreign investment has showed that China has granted national treatment principles to foreign investment gradually in the way of "leveling the playing field" and "unification of economic, civil and commercial laws". This legislation has exerted great influence on the foreign investment in China and encouraged structural adjustment to the system of Chinese foreign investment laws. The relatively "pure" system of specific foreign investment laws has changed to the "mixed" system consisting of specific foreign investment laws and unified economic, civil and commercial laws.

Key words: national treatment; leveling the playing field; unification of economic, civil and commercial laws; system of foreign investment laws

国际投资条约变革的中国主张

第一节　多边投资协定谈判前瞻[*]

【摘要】　制定一个具有普遍约束力的综合性、实体性的多边投资协定（MAI），是国际社会，特别是发达国家长期追求而迄今未能实现的目标。在探讨 MAI"适当谈判场所"的选择问题之后，作者指出，主张 MAI 谈判不能纳入 WTO 体制，具有充分的法律依据；无论 MAI 的谈判场所如何选择，MAI 谈判应有发达国家和发展中国家的普遍认同和参与；MAI 谈判注重平衡资本输出国与资本输入国的权益，是 MAI 取得成效的基本要素。

　　制定一个具有普遍约束力的综合性、实体性的多边投资协定（Multilateral Agreement on Investment，MAI），是国际社会，尤其是发达国家自 1948 年《国际贸易组织宪章》（即《哈瓦那宪章》）以来长期努力而迄今未能实现的目标。[1] 在乌拉圭回合中，通过"与贸易有关"领域的扩展，世界贸易组织（World Trade Organization，WTO）体制已涵盖了投资议题。当前，多数发达国家力图进一步将 MAI 谈判纳入 WTO 体制。MAI 的"适当谈判场所"如何选择？将 MAI 谈判纳入 WTO 体制的法律依据何在？MAI 谈判取得成效的基本要素是什么？这些是值得我国国际经济法学界认真思考和研究的重要问题。

---

　　*　原载陈安主编：《国际经济法学刊》第 17 卷第 3 期，北京大学出版社 2010 年版。

　　本文为国家社科基金重大项目"促进与保护我国海外投资的法律体制研究"（项目批准号：09&ZD032）（2009—2012）的研究成果之一。

　　〔1〕　关于制定实体性多边投资协定的早期努力，参见陈安主编：《国际投资法》，鹭江出版社 1988 年版，第 21—28 页。

一、MAI"适当谈判场所"的选择问题

在一定意义上，MAI 难产的重要原因之一是国际社会对 MAI 的"适当谈判场所"迄今未能达成共识。半个多世纪以来，从联合国贸易和发展会议（United Nations Conference on Trade and Development，UNCTAD）、经济合作与发展组织（Organization for Economic Cooperation and Development，OECD）到 WTO，都不同程度地作出了有关制定国际投资实体规则的努力，也留下了发展中国家与发达国家有关 MAI"适当谈判场所"分歧的记录。[1]

（一）UNCTAD

20 世纪 50、60 年代以来，联合国大会是建立国际经济新秩序、发展国际经济法基本原则的策源地，通过了《各国经济权利与义务宪章》等一系列有关建立国际经济新秩序的决议，确立了国际投资法的基本原则和重要规范。

作为联合国负责贸易和发展问题的专门机构，UNCTAD 长期致力于促进对发展中国家的技术援助和能力建设（capacity building），开展了有关研究国际投资协定的计划。该组织还是联合国研讨贸易、金融、技术、投资和可持续发展等相互联系问题的中心。它通过综合的方式，即结合研究和政策分析、技术援助、能力建设以及"形成共识"（consensus-building）等活动开展工作。1996 年，UNCTAD 在南非米德兰会议上决定专门研究投资问题，拟制定一个多边投资法律框架，以帮助发展中国家以最佳地位参与国际上有关外国直接投资的讨论和谈判。2005 年，UNCTAD 起草有关发展的第二代国际投资政策的研究报告，包括有关区域一体化协定投资专章和新一代双边投资条约（bilateral investment treaties，BITs）的报告。[2] UNCTAD 投资与企业司（Division on Investment and Enterprise，DIAE）具体负责国际投资协定领域的研究和政策分析。有关国际投资条约的近期研究成果《1990 年代中期的双边投资条约》和《1995—2006 年双边投资条约：投资规则制定的趋向》，[3]对 BITs 实践的发展作了系统深入的实证分析，为较全面认识 BITs 的现状及发展趋向提供了重要的参考。

---

〔1〕 参见张庆麟、彭忠波：《晚近多边投资规则谈判的新动向——兼论我国多边投资谈判策略的选择》，载陈安主编：《国际经济法学刊》第 12 卷第 3 期，北京大学出版社 2005 年版，第 117—120 页。

〔2〕 See Annex：United Nations Conference for Trade and Development，for Symposium Co-organised by ICSID, OECD and UNCTAD on Making the Most of International Investment Agreements：A Common Agenda，12 December 2005，Paris.

〔3〕 两份重要研究文献的英文题目分别为：United Nations Conference for Trade and Development，*Bilateral Investment Treaties in the Mid-1990s*，United Nations，1998；United Nations Conference for Trade and Development，*Bilateral Investment Treaties 1995-2006：Trends in Investment Rulemaking*，United Nations，2007.

联合国成员国的普遍性、构成状况及"一国一票"的表决制度,决定了发展中国家和发达国家在选择联合国作为 MAI 谈判场所的不同立场。发展中国家极力倡导在联合国系统内,特别是 UNCTAD 进行 MAI 谈判,而发达国家则坚决反对,并否定联合国大会有关建立国际经济新秩序的一系列决议的法律效力。[1] 鉴于发展中国家和发达国家的对立立场,加之当前 UNCTAD 本身有关国际投资协定的立场,[2] UNCTAD 显然不是 MAI 谈判场所的现实选择。

（二）OECD

OECD 自成立以来,一直是研讨国际投资协定的中心。20 世纪 60 年代初期,《OECD 关于外国财产保护的公约》（草案）为各国的 BITs 谈判提供了一个基础。在 80 年代,它报告了 OECD 成员有关国际投资协定主要特征的立场。在国际投资协定领域,OECD 的优势之一是通过健全的委员会"审查与平衡"（checks and balance）程序开展高质量的分析工作。为增进各国政府与国际投资者对国际投资协定的共同理解,OECD 投资委员会参与讨论由国际投资协定产生的问题,包括不同国际投资协定之间的关系、关键条款（如公平公正待遇、间接征收、管理权利和最惠国待遇）的解释以及有关国家与他国投资者之间仲裁制度本身的问题。2005 年 6 月,OECD 投资委员会发布了有关支持在国际投资仲裁中增加透明度的报告。[3]

1995 年至 1998 年间,OECD 有关 MAI 的谈判是发达国家创设全球性投资实体规则的重要尝试。之前,发达国家试图将 MAI 谈判纳入关税及贸易总协定（General Agreement on Tariffs and Trade,GATT）体制,因遭到发展中国家的普遍反对而转为选择 OECD。OECD 成员国设计了导向全球性投资实体规则的两个阶段性程序:第一阶段是在 OECD 的 25 个成员国范围内谈判商签全球性投资条约,预期大多数成员国具有共同的投资利益,较容易达成协议;第二阶段是在该条约制定后,促使非 OECD 成员国参加。[4] 以发达国家为主组成的 OECD,素有"富人俱乐部"之称。其有关 MAI 的谈判反映了追求高标准的投资保护和投资自由化的政策目标,片面考虑和强调跨国公司的利益。由于其成员国有关"区域一体化例外"和"文化产业保护

〔1〕　参见张庆麟、彭忠波:《晚近多边投资规则谈判的新动向——兼论我国多边投资谈判策略的选择》,载陈安主编:《国际经济法学刊》第 12 卷第 3 期,北京大学出版社 2005 年版,第 118 页。

〔2〕　UNCTAD 投资与企业司詹晓宁司长在 2010 年国际投资协定研讨会（中国厦门,2010 年 9 月 8 日）上表示,UNCTAD 本身无意推动 MAI 的签订,是否签订 MAI,应由各国政府决定。

〔3〕　See Annex: Organisation for Economic Co-operation and Development, for Symposium Co-organised by ICSID, OECD and UNCTAD on Making the Most of International Investment Agreements: A Common Agenda, 12 December 2005, Paris.

〔4〕　See Jeswald W. Salacuse, Towards a Global Treaty on Foreign Investment: The Search for a Grand Bargain, in Norbert Horn (ed.), *Arbitrating Foreign Investment Disputes*, Kluwer Law International, 2004, p. 81.

例外"等议题的严重分歧,加之非政府组织的强烈反对,[1]1998年12月,在巴黎召开的OECD非正式会议决定终止该谈判。

尽管OECD有意在适当时机重启MAI谈判,实践已经表明,在OECD成员国内部进行MAI谈判,然后推及非OECD成员国,是广大发展中国家所不能接受的。有学者深刻地指出,鉴于MAI是世界性的,对许多非OECD成员国具有重要的潜在影响,OECD作为该条约的谈判场所是错误的。[2]

（三）GATT/WTO

长期以来,发达国家试图将投资议题纳入GATT/WTO体制。在1982年GATT部长级会议上,美国作为主要倡议者,首次提出了将投资议题纳入GATT体制的建议。由于欧共体成员和发展中国家反对,该提议被取消。在乌拉圭回合中,在美国等发达国家的强力推动下,产生了《与贸易有关的投资措施协定》(Agreement on Trade-Related Investment Measures,TRIMs协定)。1996年,在WTO新加坡部长级会议上,各成员同意考虑投资、竞争政策、政府采购透明度及贸易便利化等议题(统称为"新加坡议题")。在该会议上达成的决议是,WTO应研究贸易与投资之间的关系,并成立了"贸易与投资关系工作组",开展专门研究。OECD的MAI谈判失败后,随之产生了WTO能否接此重任的问题。日本和欧共体极力推动在1999年召开的WTO西雅图部长级会议上启动MAI议题的谈判。这一企图因受到一些发展中国家代表团和非政府组织的反对而偃旗息鼓。2001年召开的WTO多哈部长级会议仍未达成明确启动多边投资规则框架谈判的最后决议,只是提及正式决议留待坎昆部长级会议决定。在2003年召开的WTO坎昆部长级会议上,多数发展中国家表示还未做好MAI议题谈判的准备。[3] 由于各成员在农产品议题和新加坡议题的

---

[1] 在谈判过程中,主要来自发达国家的NGOs结成了广泛的同盟,对MAI谈判的程序和内容均提出了批评。1997年,NGOs取得了MAI草案。当发现MAI谈判者已同商务利益团体协商,但未与市民社会的其他成员协商时,NGOs通过网络发动了世界性的有效抗议活动。它们指出,该谈判程序是有缺陷的,由于OECD秘密进行谈判,牺牲了市民社会其他成分(如工会、环境保护者和人权组织等)的利益,维护和促进了商人利益。反全球化力量迅即参与抗议活动,认为MAI是以本地利益团体及其利益为代价促进全球化的工具。See Jeswald W. Salacuse, Towards a Global Treaty on Foreign Investment: The Search for a Grand Bargain, in Norbert Horn (ed.), *Arbitrating Foreign Investment Disputes*, Kluwer Law International, 2004, pp. 83-85; M. Sornarajah, *The International Law on Foreign Investment*, 2nd edition, Cambridge University Press, 2004, pp. 3-4, 79-80.

[2] See Jeswald W. Salacuse, Towards a Global Treaty on Foreign Investment: The Search for a Grand Bargain, in Norbert Horn (ed.), *Arbitrating Foreign Investment Disputes*, Kluwer Law International, 2004, pp. 83-85; M. Sornarajah, *The International Law on Foreign Investment*, 2nd edition, Cambridge University Press, 2004, p. 83.

[3] 参见冯军:《从多哈回合议程谈中国多边投资框架谈判立场》,载陈安主编:《国际经济法学刊》第10卷,北京大学出版社2004年版,第315—316页。

尖锐矛盾无法调和,坎昆会议重蹈西雅图会议无果而终之覆辙。[1] 2005 年,在
WTO 香港部长级会议上,投资议题仍未能取得进展。[2]

　　值得注意的是,发达国家在 WTO 体制中提出投资议题,只是"投石问路",其更
重要的目标是将 MAI 纳入 WTO 体制。早在 OECD 的 MAI 谈判期间,就有学者主
张,MAI 最后文本形成后,应由 WTO 接管,即实施所谓"将 MAI 纳入 WTO 的战
略"。[3] 1998 年,时值 MAI 谈判陷入困境,法国政府委托进行的一项有关 MAI 的研
究结果认为,OECD 不是 MAI 的适当谈判场所,不能在已有基础上继续该谈判。法
国总理进一步指出,MAI 的适当谈判场所不是 OECD,而"很自然地是 WTO"。[4]
面临大多数发展中国家反对的情况,一些主要发达国家提出了表面看来较为弹性的
两项建议:一是将 MAI 定位为"复边协定"(Plurilateral Agreement)。[5] 依此定位,
对 WTO 投资议题谈判感兴趣的 WTO 成员可启动并持续进行 MAI 谈判,达成协议
后,由希望成为 MAI 当事方的 WTO 成员签署并加入。这样,未参与谈判的其他成
员不会受到损害,因为它们可自主决定选择保留在 MAI 之外,甚至是 MAI 谈判之
外;二是 MAI 采用 WTO 体制下《服务贸易总协定》(General Agreement on Trade in
Service,GATS)"积极清单"(positive list)的承诺方式。该方式意味着,MAI 的约束
力不会自动延伸到缔约国所有行业和所有投资领域。相反,各缔约国可规定承担义
务的行业和承担义务的种类。[6]

　　应当指出,GATT/WTO 体制是发达国家主导的体制。在对 GATT/WTO 体制

---

〔1〕 参见周汉民、邱一川:《坎昆峰会述评与 WTO 多哈回合展望》,载陈安主编:《国际经济法学刊》第 11 卷,北
京大学出版社 2004 年版,第 128—133 页。See M. Sornarajah, *The International Law on Foreign Investment*, 2nd
edition, Cambridge University Press, 2004, p. 88. 事实上,WTO 成员之间有关投资议题是否纳入多哈回合议程是
该回合谈判中断的重要因素之一。在 2003 年 WTO 部长会议上,欧共体贸易代表同意在多哈回合议程中取消投资
议题,美国随后也支持这一决定。参见 Andrew Newcombe, Lluis Paradell, *Law and Practice of Investment Treaties, Standards of Treatment*, Wolters Kluwer, 2009, pp. 55-56.

〔2〕 See Doha Work Programme, *Ministerial Declaration*, Adopted on 18 December 2005(WT/MIN(05)/
DEC)[Z]. 22 December 2005.

〔3〕 See M. Sornarajah, *The International Law on Foreign Investment*, 2nd edition, Cambridge University
Press, 2004, p. 291.

〔4〕 See Jeswald W. Salacuse, Towards a Global Treaty on Foreign Investment: The Search for a Grand Bargain, in Norbert Horn(ed.), *Arbitrating Foreign Investment Disputes*, Kluwer Law International, 2004, pp. 83-
85; M. Sornarajah, *The International Law on Foreign Investment*, 2nd edition, Cambridge University Press, 2004,
p. 84.

〔5〕 《WTO 协定》包含两类附件:第一类为多边贸易协定(Multilateral Trade Agreements),对此类协定,各国
或具有单独关税区地位的地区在加入 WTO 时应采取一次性一揽子接受的方式,不得对任何协定或条款采取选择加
入或保留。第二类为复边贸易协定(Plurilateral Trade Agreement),对此类协定,仍允许各国或具有单独关税区地位
的地区在加入 WTO 时选择加入。因此,此类协定只约束选择加入特定协定的成员,对未加入的成员不产生任何权
利和义务。

〔6〕 参见〔印〕哈吉拉·劳·达斯:《WTO 与多边贸易体系之过去、现在与未来》,第三世界网络(TWN),2004
年,第 94—95 页。

作历史考察之后，印度 WTO 专家哈吉拉·劳·达斯先生指出，发达国家，尤其是美国和欧共体一直在 GATT/WTO 体制中追求其自身的发展利益和目标，在很大程度上已获得了成功。历史表明，GATT 体制是由发达国家主导和创建的，[1]发达国家无论何时意识到某些对其有重要利益的议题，都会将其纳入 GATT/WTO 谈判议程。因此，GATT/WTO 体制一直以来几乎都承载着发达国家的利益主题，而 GATT/WTO 法的主要特点是依据主要发达国家，尤其是美国的法律和惯例模式而形成。[2]将 MAI 纳入 WTO 体制，同样反映了发达国家的利益。其主要目的是，通过 WTO 的贸易自由化机制扩大投资的自由化，确保其海外投资者能在发展中国家自由进入和经营，从而消除或削弱发展中国家调整外资准入和外资经营的权力。如果在 WTO 体制中形成 MAI，其义务将如同 WTO 其他协定一样约束各成员。对发展中国家而言，这是十分困难的局面，意味着发展中国家将丧失其在发展过程中调整投资政策的所有灵活性。此外，将 MAI 纳入 WTO 体制所产生的严重后果之一是，使发展中国家因投资问题而面临交叉报复的风险。[3]

事实上，即使实施发达国家提出的上述两项弹性建议，也无法减轻对发展中国家的事实上的约束和压力。在 MAI 以"复边协定"形式存在于 WTO 体制的情况下，随着缔约方的增多，游离于 MAI 之外的发展中国家将被迫参加或被边缘化。GATS 的经验还表明，"积极清单"方式在向发展中国家提供保护方面也有明显的局限性。在 GATS 及其下属具体行业，如金融服务和电信服务的谈判中，发展中国家面临着将更多领域和更多措施纳入条约约束的巨大压力。由于 MAI 的总体目标是确保发展中国家的外国投资者能相对自由地投资经营，发展中国家自然有理由担心"积极清单"方式不可能对其提供保护，也会担心在国际投资领域将面临需要作出高度承诺的压力。此外，发展中国家在已作承诺的领域中不可能重新采用某些限制性的投资措施。在经济发展过程中，发展中国家需要审时度势，制定、修改或撤销某些不合时宜的外资政策和措施，而这种灵活性将在已作承诺的领域中丧失殆尽。在 OECD 主导的 MAI 谈判期间，由印度领导的发展中国家反对 MAI 和旨在创设保护外资和

---

〔1〕 关于美国在创建 GATT 中的作用，参见 Ronald A. Brand, *Fundamentals of International Business Transactions*, Kluwer Law International, 2000, pp. 277-281。

〔2〕 参见〔印〕哈吉拉·劳·达斯：《WTO 与多边贸易体系之过去、现在与未来》，第三世界网络（TWN），2004 年，第 16—19 页。

〔3〕 根据《关于争端解决规则与程序的谅解》第 22 条第 3 款："在考虑中止哪些减让或其他义务时，起诉方应适用下列原则和程序：(a) 总的原则是，起诉方应首先寻求对与专家组或上诉机构认定有违反义务或其他造成利益损失或减损情形的部门相同的部门中止减让或其他义务；(b) 如该方认为对相同部门中止减让或其他义务不可行或无效，则可寻求中止对同一协定项下的其他部门的减让或其他义务；(c) 如该方认为对同一协定项下的其他部门中止减让或其他义务不可行或无效，且情况足够严重，则可寻求中止另一适用协定项下的减让或其他义务……"

促进投资自由化的新国际法规则的任何企图,认为 MAI 是对发展中国家主权和经济独立的威胁。[1]

(四) 何去何从

各国对 MAI 谈判场所的选择,取决于各国自身谈判目标的选择和国家整体利益的考虑。根据国际经济法的公平互利原则,MAI 的"适当谈判场所"应能保障发展中国家和发达国家的平等参与权,特别是保障发展中国家在谈判中的话语权,同时,应能保障谈判参与的广泛性、充分性和公开性。然而,严峻的现实是,经济全球化是发达国家主导和推动的,MAI"适当谈判场所"的选择,发达国家也力图掌控主导权。[2]

如前所述,关于 UNCTAD 能否成为 MAI 谈判场所问题,发展中国家与发达国家两军对垒,无法达成共识。而 OECD 主导的 MAI 谈判已尝败绩,在主客观条件未发生根本变化的情况下,以 OECD 为谈判场所"卷土重来"绝非明智之举。当前,由于发达国家极力主张在 WTO 体制下启动 MAI 谈判,发展中国家面临的 MAI"适当谈判场所"问题实际上已归结为,是否接受或能否拒绝将 MAI 谈判纳入 WTO 体制的问题。

二、MAI 谈判纳入 WTO 体制的法律依据问题

有西方学者在预见 MAI 谈判的前景时指出,MAI 或类似的条约,最终将在WTO 伞之下占有一席之地;如果在 WTO 受阻,则会在其他现有的或未来新设立的体制结构中达成。[3] 还有西方学者更为乐观地预测,很有可能,甚至可以肯定,有关投资议题的谈判最终将在 WTO 体制中完成。[4] 也有中国学者认为,"中国应该积极参与多边投资框架的谈判,以争取在 WTO 框架下建立一个较为公平、兼顾发达和发展成员方利益的多边投资框架";[5] "西方国家所主导的多元化谈判格局,决定了

---

〔1〕　See Jeswald W. Salacuse, Towards a Global Treaty on Foreign Investment: The Search for a Grand Bargain, in Norbert Horn (ed.), *Arbitrating Foreign Investment Disputes*, Kluwer Law International, 2004, pp. 83-85; M. Sornarajah, *The International Law on Foreign Investment*, 2nd edition, Cambridge University Press, 2004, p. 83.

〔2〕　参见张庆麟、彭忠波:《晚近多边投资规则谈判的新动向——兼论我国多边投资谈判策略的选择》,陈安主编:《国际经济法学刊》第 12 卷第 3 期,北京大学出版社 2005 年版,第 116—117 页。

〔3〕　See John H. Jackson, *Sovereignty, the WTO and Changing Fundamentals of International Law*, Cambridge University Press, 2006, p. 243.

〔4〕　Edward Kwakwa, Institutional Perspectives of International Economic Law, in Asif H. Qureshi (ed.), *Perspectives in International Economic Law*, Kluwer Law International, 2002, p. 58.

〔5〕　参见冯军:《从多哈回合议程谈中国多边投资框架谈判立场》,载陈安主编:《国际经济法学刊》第 10 卷,北京大学出版社 2004 年版,第 316 页。

中国在选择谈判场所时，仍要坚持'两条腿'走路，积极参与各种场所的投资规则谈判"。[1] 笔者以为，上述观点均忽略了将 MAI 谈判纳入 WTO 体制的法律依据问题，这实际上是一个前提性的关键问题。从法律层面看，主张 MAI 谈判不能纳入 WTO 体制，具有充分的法律依据。

（一）WTO 体制与国际投资法是分立的法律体制

虽然，试图调整国际投资的努力可追溯到 1947 年 GATT 成立之初和流产的国际贸易组织（International Trade Organization，ITO），GATT 作为《哈瓦那宪章》和 ITO 的遗产继承人，显然与国际投资无关，或者更准确地说，GATT 的管辖范围并未扩及东道国对外资准入和外资经营所规定的条件。国际贸易与国际投资的分立，对脆弱的 GATT 是有益的。历史上，在东方国家与西方国家之间、南方国家与北方国家之间许多最基本的争议问题，诸如东道国对外国投资者的责任、征收的法律后果、国际经济新秩序以及起草《跨国公司行为守则》等，GATT 均置身事外。这些问题曾在联合国大会及其下属机构、世界银行、国际货币基金组织以及旨在签订友好通商航海条约和 BITs 的双边谈判中辩论，但从未发生于 GATT。[2]

就国际经济法体系而言，WTO 法属国际贸易法，而国际贸易法与国际投资法分立，同样作为国际经济法的重要分支。两者虽然不是泾渭分明，但具有基本的分界，互不隶属。

由于发达国家的强力推动，随着 WTO 体制"与贸易有关"领域的不断扩展，投资已成为 WTO 多边贸易谈判的议题之一，WTO 法与国际投资法的涵盖内容也出现了一定程度的重叠或交叉，如与贸易有关的投资措施（trade-related investment measures，TRIMs）、与投资有关的贸易措施（investment-related trade measures，IRTMs）等。[3] 然而，TRIMs 毕竟属于"与贸易有关"的领域，而 IRTMs 则仍然是贸易措施。尽管涵盖"与贸易有关"的领域，WTO 体制性质上毕竟是多边贸易体制。WTO 法与国际投资法的涵盖内容出现的此类重叠或交叉，并不能改变国际贸易法

---

[1] 参见张庆麟、彭忠波：《晚近多边投资规则谈判的新动向——兼论我国多边投资谈判策略的选择》，陈安主编：《国际经济法学刊》第 12 卷第 3 期，北京大学出版社 2005 年版，第 126—127 页。

[2] See Andreas F. Lowenfeld, *International Economic Law*, Oxford University Press, 2002, p. 94.

[3] IRTMs 指影响外国直接投资的数量、部门构成及地理分布的较为一般性的贸易政策措施。与 TRIMs 比较，它们通常不涉及具体的贸易或外国直接投资交易。IRTMs 对直接的贸易流动具有第一层次的影响，同时，对随贸易流动之后产生的外国直接投资具有第二层次的影响，影响潜在投资者的决策，而外国直接投资的变化对未来有关的贸易流向又具有重要的第三层次的影响。根据 UNCTAD 的研究，IRTMs 大致可分为市场准入限制、市场准入发展优惠、出口鼓励措施和出口限制措施等四大类。目前，对于 IRTMs，主要由 GATT/WTO 有关 RTAs、原产地规则、国家技术标准、受限产业部门的贸易安排等规范调整。参见余劲松主编：《国际经济交往法律问题研究》，人民法院出版社 2002 年版，第 22—37 页。

（含 WTO 法）与国际投资法两种分立体制的基本分野。[1]

诚然,在当代世界,贸易与投资联系密切,甚至密不可分,一些涉及投资的多边经济协定,如《北美自由贸易协定》(North American Free Trade Agreement,NAF-TA)和《能源宪章条约》等都是在多边贸易谈判中产生的。其原因是,在多边经济谈判中将贸易与投资问题相联系,提供了支撑条约谈判的宽广的交易基础,这是单纯的多边投资谈判无法企及的谈判方式。这是基于贸易的投资谈判方式。特别是,发展中国家为增加其在发达国家市场的贸易量,将导致它们对外资采取更自由的保护性政策。不仅如此,从谈判理论的观点看,在多边谈判中涉及的问题越多,当事方就可能设计越多的协调点(trade-offs)。而当事方拥有越多的协调点,就越可能发现达成协议的基础。[2] 然而,尽管发达国家一再强调 MAI 对于促进国际贸易的重要性,在 WTO 体制中是否需要 MAI,尚未达成共识。[3] 更重要的是,WTO 体制对其本身的范围和职能已有明确的法律界定,并未涵盖 MAI。

（二）WTO 体制是调整国际贸易关系的法律体制

针对 WTO“与贸易有关”领域不断扩张的趋势,有学者尖锐地指出,如果将特定问题纳入 WTO 体制的唯一标准是该问题影响了贸易,那么实际上任何问题都可能纳入,因此,认定这些问题的重要原则是,WTO 涵盖的领域是与 GATT 一样限于贸易问题,或者,WTO 是不同于 GATT 的涵盖贸易以外领域的国际组织。[4]另有学者指出,尽管有“将 MAI 纳入 WTO 体制”的提议,“很难想象 MAI 如何与 WTO 相融合。WTO 并没有处理诸如投资者设立权(right of establishment)等事项的职能”。[5]

笔者以为,能否在 WTO 体制中启动 MAI 谈判的基本问题在于,该谈判有否 WTO 法上的根据。

《马拉喀什建立世界贸易组织协定》(以下简称《WTO 协定》)第 2 条题为“WTO

---

〔1〕 关于 WTO 体制与国际投资法之间关系的进一步评论,参见曾华群:《论 WTO 体制与国际投资法的关系》,《厦门大学学报》(哲学社会科学版)2007 年第 6 期,第 105—113 页。

〔2〕 See Jeswald W. Salacuse, Towards a Global Treaty on Foreign Investment: The Search for a Grand Bargain, in Norbert Horn (ed.), *Arbitrating Foreign Investment Disputes*, Kluwer Law International, 2004, pp. 83-85; M. Sornarajah, *The International Law on Foreign Investment*, 2nd edition, Cambridge University Press, 2004, p. 87.

〔3〕 See Yong-Shik Lee, *Reclaiming Development in the World Trading System*, Cambridge University Press, 2006, p. 122.

〔4〕 See Edward Kwakwa, Institutional Perspectives of International Economic Law, in Asif H. Qureshi (ed.), *Perspectives in International Economic Law*, Kluwer Law International, 2002, p. 49.

〔5〕 See M. Sornarajah, *The International Law on Foreign Investment*, 2nd edition, Cambridge University Press, 2004, note 47.

的范围"，第 1 款明确规定："WTO 在与本协定附件所含协定和相关法律文件有关的事项方面，为处理其成员间的贸易关系提供共同的组织机构。"该基本规定表明，WTO 的管辖范围是"其成员间的贸易关系"。显然，WTO 是调整其成员间贸易关系的国际组织，而不是富有夸张意味的所谓"经济联合国"。[1]

《WTO 协定》第 3 条进一步规定了 WTO 的职能，指出 WTO"应为其成员间就多边贸易关系进行的谈判提供场所"。关于未来的谈判议题和协定，"WTO 还可按部长级会议可能作出的决定，为其成员间的多边贸易关系的进一步谈判提供场所，并提供实施此类谈判结果的体制"。显然，无论是当前或未来的谈判议题，都必须在"多边贸易关系"的涵盖范围之内。由于 MAI 并非"多边贸易关系"的一部分，MAI 谈判显然不属 WTO 的职能范围。尽管 TRIMs 协定第 9 条规定，WTO 货物贸易理事会"应考虑本协定是否应补充有关投资政策和竞争政策的规定"，但该条款也无法支持在 WTO 体制中启动 MAI 谈判的主张。就前述发达国家"将 MAI 定位为复边协定"的弹性建议而言，由于货物贸易理事会是 WTO 体系的一个正式多边机构，在任何情况下，该机构的审查对象都不可能是"复边协定"。此外，该条款仅仅授权理事会"考虑"，该用语明显不能解读为授权启动 WTO 体制中的 MAI 谈判。[2]

（三）WTO 体制的投资议题不能等同于 MAI

乌拉圭回合的成果涉及投资的规范包括 TRIMs 协定，GATS 和《与贸易有关的知识产权协定》（Agreement on Trade-Related Aspects of Intellectual Property Rights，TRIPS 协定）。其中，TRIMs 协定最为典型，而 GATS 和 TRIPS 协定只是内容上有涉及投资。[3]就 TRIMs 协定而言，顾名思义，是规范"与贸易有关的投资措施"的协定，不是一个有关投资的综合性多边法律框架，比之 OECD 主导的 MAI 和各国普遍接受的 BITs，其适用范围极为有限，只能视为朝向有关投资的多边管制框架迈出的一小步。[4]

WTO 成员同意多哈回合有关贸易与投资关系的讨论集中于澄清范围与定义、透明度、非歧视、基于 GATS 型"积极清单"的设立前承诺、发展的规定、例外与收支

---

[1] 有学者指出，把 WTO 称为"经济联合国"在法律上有误导作用。参见张玉卿：《善用 WTO 规则》，载陈安主编：《国际经济法学刊》第 10 卷，北京大学出版社 2004 年版，第 8 页。

[2] 参见〔印〕哈吉拉·劳·达斯：《WTO 与多边贸易体系之过去、现在与未来》，第三世界网络（TWN），2004 年，第 94 页。

[3] GATS 中主要是"商业存在"作为服务提供方式，本身也是一种投资方式。而 TRIPS 协定通过对"与贸易有关的知识产权"的保护而与国际投资密切相关。关于 WTO 体系投资规则的概述，参见叶兴平：《WTO 体系内制定投资规则的努力》，载《现代法学》2004 年第 1 期，第 149—157 页。

[4] See Yong-Shik Lee, *Reclaiming Development in the World Trading System*, Cambridge University Press, 2006, pp. 116-117.

平衡的保障以及协商与成员之间争端的解决。在该框架中没有 BITs 等传统国际投资条约包含的重要问题,如给予外国投资者的保护性待遇、货币转移、针对征收的保护以及外国投资者与东道国之间争端的解决。《多哈部长级会议宣言》未规定传统国际投资条约有关投资保护、促进和自由化的宗旨,而是强调其他新目标,即"任何框架应以平衡的方式反映母国和东道国利益,并适当考虑东道国政府的发展政策和目标以及它们为公共利益的管制权利"。上述新目标涉及的三个因素值得注意:一是促进的利益限于国家利益,而未提及私人投资者的利益;二是适当考虑的国家利益主要是东道国的利益,而不是投资者母国的利益;三是坚持"管制权利"意味着界定外资财产权利与东道国管制外资的权利是多哈回合有关谈判的争议焦点。[1]

显然,目前 WTO 体制的投资议题仍然限于"与贸易有关"的领域,不能等同于 BITs 等传统国际投资条约或 MAI,两者不能混淆。需要特别引起警惕的是,在 WTO 体制中,发达国家看来是采取"步步为营"和"得陇望蜀"的策略,从投资议题的谈判谈起,一俟时机成熟即转为 MAI 谈判。

应当强调的是,从法律的角度,只有在《WTO 协定》有关 WTO 范围和职能的规定作出修改、明确涵盖了国际投资关系之后,在 WTO 体制中启动 MAI 谈判才具有基本的法律依据。

三、MAI 谈判取得成效的基本要素

应当进一步强调,比确定 MAI 的"适当谈判场所"更为重要的甚至是决定 MAI 能否取得成效的基本要素是,MAI 谈判应有发展中国家与发达国家的普遍认同和参与,应真正平衡发展中国家与发达国家的权益。

（一）MAI 谈判应有发展中国家与发达国家的普遍认同和参与

历史经验反复表明,无论 MAI 的"适当谈判场所"如何选择,由于 MAI 将适用于发展中国家和发达国家,MAI 谈判首先需要发展中国家和发达国家的普遍认同和参与。

迄今为止,全球性多边投资条约的重要成果是 1965 年《解决国家与他国国民间投资争端公约》（Convention on the Settlement of Investment Disputes between States and Nationals of other States）和 1985 年《多边投资担保机构公约》（Conven-

---

〔1〕 See Jeswald W. Salacuse, Towards a Global Treaty on Foreign Investment: The Search for a Grand Bargain, in Norbert Horn (ed.), *Arbitrating Foreign Investment Disputes*, Kluwer Law International, 2004, pp. 83-85; M. Sornarajah, *The International Law on Foreign Investment*, 2nd edition, Cambridge University Press, 2004, p. 86.

tion Establishing the Multilateral Investment Guarantee Agency，简称 MIGA 公约）。在展望 MAI 谈判前景时，回顾 MIGA 公约的立法史是有借鉴意义的。[1] 在 1962 年 3 月发表的《国际复兴开发银行：多边投资担保——职员报告》（IBRD，Multilateral Investment Insurance，A Staff Report）中，曾提出有关多边投资担保机构成员国的三种不同的方案：(1) 所有资本输入国与资本输出国；(2) 创设该多边投资担保制度的所有资本输出国；(3) 创设该多边投资担保制度的部分资本输出国。经过长期的分析研究，特别是将有关方案提供给国际复兴开发银行各成员国，广泛征求意见，最终确定了国际复兴开发银行所有成员国和瑞士均可成为多边投资担保机构（the Multilateral Investment Guarantee Agency，MIGA）的成员国，即包括了资本输入国与资本输出国。[2] 然而，国际复兴开发银行成员国没有参加 MIGA 的义务。MIGA 公约认识到资本输出国与资本输入国参与的重要性，特别反映于该公约第 61 条第 2 款和第 39 条的规定。[3] 由于发展中国家和发达国家较普遍了解和参与 MIGA 公约的起草过程，并在公约中注意体现两类国家权益的维护和平衡，该公约为两类国家普遍认同和接受。截至 2010 年 8 月，该公约已有 175 个成员国。

令人遗憾的是，时隔 10 年，1995 年 OECD 主导的 MAI 谈判采取了与 MIGA 公约相反的封闭模式，即在 OECD 成员国（主要是资本输出国）内部进行。旨在提供程序性投资保护的 MIGA 公约尚且注意到资本输入国与资本输出国的普遍参与，而旨在提供实体性和程序性投资保护的 MAI 却采取资本输出国单方面"闭门造车"的模式，这不能不说是历史的倒退。在一定意义上，这一先天性缺陷注定了 MAI 失败的命运。在 MAI 谈判期间，发展中国家已质疑 OECD 作为 MAI 谈判场所的合法性，指出它未能提供发展中国家充分参与谈判的机会。美国著名国际经济法学家杰克逊在分析 MAI 谈判的失败原因时也指出，MAI 谈判缺乏绝大多数发展中国家的有效参与，而这种参与对 MAI 的成效至关重要。[4]

应当明确，发展中国家和发达国家的普遍认同和参与 MAI 谈判，实际上是平衡发展中国家和发达国家权益的组织保障。

---

[1] 关于 MIGA 公约的立法史，参见陈安主编：《国际投资法》，鹭江出版社 1988 年版，第 28—40 页。

[2] MIGA 公约第 4 条第 1 款。

[3] 根据 MIGA 公约第 61 条第 2 款，公约生效的条件之一是 5 个以上发达国家和 15 个以上发展中国家批准公约。MIGA 公约第 39 条为平衡发达国家与发展中国家之间的表决权作了技术性安排，以反映两类国家在 MIGA 的平等利益。关于 MIGA 投票权制度的分析，参见陈安主编、徐崇利副主编：《MIGA 与中国——多边投资担保机构述评》，福建人民出版社 1995 年版，第 153—165 页。

[4] See John H. Jackson, *Sovereignty, the WTO and Changing Fundamentals of International Law*, Cambridge University Press, 2006, p. 242.

（二）MAI 谈判应真正平衡发展中国家与发达国家的权益

经济全球化的重要特征之一是,作为可获得的投资和金融资产竞争集中的结果,各国特别是发展中国家可选择的范围日益缩小。另一个重要特征是,各国不同程度地受外部力量驱动作出其经济决策。得益于全球自由贸易的发达国家,控制了充足的政治和经济力量以确保推行其有关自由化、私有化和外国投资的政策。它们通过创设 WTO 等国际组织及其体制和有关投资的双边或区域性条约来达到其目的。[1]

追根溯源,国际投资条约是发达国家创造并服务于其对外经济政策的工具。从传统的友好通商航海条约到 1959 年以来蓬勃发展的 BITs,[2]从《1959 年海外投资国际公约草案》(the 1959 Draft International Convention on Investments Abroad)到 OECD 的 MAI,无不打上发达国家片面强调投资保护的深刻烙印。发达国家的这一"先天烙印"也是其"先天优势",反映了历史上发展中国家在国际投资条约谈判中的被动的弱者地位。

就缔约方而言,MAI 与 BITs 一样,可分为资本输出国和资本输入国。所不同者,前者是多方资本输出国和多方资本输入国的组合,而后者是一方资本输出国和一方资本输入国的组合。

一般而言,BIT 定义为两个国家之间签订的一国同意对另一国的投资者和投资提供保护的协定。[3] 典型的 BITs 是发达的资本输出国与发展中的资本输入国之间的条约。半个多世纪以来,多数 BITs 效仿《1959 年海外投资国际公约草案》和 OECD《1967 年外国资产保护公约草案》(1967 Draft Convention on the Protection of Foreign Property)。[4]由于来源相同,不同国家和时期的 BITs 所用的术语和涵盖的事项明显相似。[5]新加坡国立大学国际投资法学家索那纳亚教授深刻地指出,虽然

---

〔1〕　See M. Sornarajah, A Developing Country Perspective of International Economic Law in the Context of Dispute Settlement, in Asif H. Qureshi (ed.), *Perspectives in International Economic Law*, Kluwer Law International, 2002, p. 83.

〔2〕　根据 UNCTAD 的统计,截至 2009 年底,各国共签订了 2750 项 BITs。See United Nations Conference on Trade and Development, *World Investment Report 2010*, p. 81. 20 世纪 80 年代末期,一向奉行卡尔沃主义的拉丁美洲国家改变其有关 BITs 的立场,近 20 年来共签订了 500 多项 BITs。See Mary H. Mourra (ed.), *Latin American Investment Treaty Arbitration, the Controversies and Conflicts*, Wolters Kluwer, 2009, p. 1.

〔3〕　See Paul E. Comeaux, N. Stephan Kinsella, *Protecting Foreign Investment under International Law, Legal Aspects of Political Risk*, Oceana Publications Inc., 101 and note 7 (1997).

〔4〕　关于 BITs 的简史,参见 Jeswald W. Salacuse, "BIT by BIT: The Growth of Bilateral Investment Treaties and Their Impact on Foreign Investment in Developing Countries", *The International Lawyer*, Vol. 24, 1990, pp. 656-661.

〔5〕　See Jason Webb Yackee, "Conceptual Difficulties in the Empirical Study of Bilateral Investment Treaties", *Brooklyn J. Int'l L*, Vol. 33, 2008, pp. 415-416.

BITs 设计为缔约双方的双向投资，实际考虑的只是单向投资。在缔约双方资金和技术差距悬殊的情况下，这是显而易见的。因此，声称作为条约基础的"双向流动"是冠冕堂皇的虚构，缺乏充分的对价(*quid pro quo*)。这种不平等的条约产生一些耐人寻味的问题，诸如：参与签订 BITs 的发展中国家是否拥有能充分理解条约用语的细微差别的法律专家？ BITs 的签订能否产生资本输出国的资本流向资本输入国的实际效果？此类协定未包含资本输出国保证此种资本流动的明确责任，而资本输入国为得到此种"预期的外资流动"必须先让渡其主权，平等何在？ 尽管存在此种不平等，BITs 表面上是合法的，签订此种条约的国家被推定为愿意受其约束。除非有胁迫的证据（如以提供援助、贷款或贸易优惠为签约的条件），应认为 BITs 是基于自愿的基础达成的。[1]当前，OECD 国家参与 BITs 和 RTAs 实践的重心已从传统的投资保护转向更广泛的自由化规则。外资待遇标准更为侧重投资准入阶段的保护和新的自由化承诺。[2]东道国投资促进政策中的外资审批权力逐渐演变为承认"设立权"、禁止"履行要求"和投资自由化义务，征收的四项前提条件（即出于公共利益、非歧视、正当法律程序和给予赔偿）和征收赔偿的"赫尔"规则（即给予充分、及时、有效赔偿）得以强化适用以及"外国投资者诉诸国际仲裁的单边启动模式"等，[3]进一步加剧了 BITs 主要功能的偏向性，即更侧重于对外国投资和外国投资者的保护，而相应削弱了东道国管制外资的权力，同时，基本上忽略了东道国投资促进和管理的政策目标。

以往 MAI 的内容设计，并未脱离传统 BITs 的窠臼，甚至是 BITs 的"升级版"。实际上，OECD 的 MAI 在很多方面与 NAFTA 的投资条款相似，而 NAFTA 的投资条款则基于美国的 BIT 范本。[4] 其目标是为外国投资者提供比 BITs 更高水平的保护。显然，索那纳亚教授上述有关 BITs 资本输出国与资本输入国之间不平等关系的精辟分析，同样适用于 MAI。

从发展的观点看，MAI 将扩大东道国的义务，进一步限制发展中国家采取外资

---

〔1〕 See M. Sornarajah, *The International Law on Foreign Investment*, 2nd edition, Cambridge University Press, 2004, pp. 207-208.

〔2〕 See OECD Secretariat, Novel Features in OECD Countries' Recent Investment Agreements: An Overview, Document for Symposium Co-organised by ICSID, OECD and UNCTAD on Making the Most of International Invest, 12 December 2005, Paris, p. 4.

〔3〕 直到 1993 年，大多数资本输入国尚未与主要资本输出国签署含有"外国投资者诉诸国际仲裁的单边启动模式"的 BITs。2002 年的抽样调查表明，149 个发展中国家中有 117 个国家至少签署一个此类条约。See Jason Webb Yackee, "Conceptual Difficulties in the Empirical Study of Bilateral Investment Treaties", *Brooklyn J. Int'l L*, Vol. 33, 2008, pp. 432-433.

〔4〕 See M. Sornarajah, *The International Law on Foreign Investment*, 2nd edition, Cambridge University Press, 2004, pp. 291-292.

措施以促进国内产业和促进发展,并不符合发展中国家的发展利益。一种观点认为,MAI 将为外国投资者提供制度性保障,由此有助于吸引外资进入发展中国家。事实上,各个发展中国家也可通过制定既符合其发展利益,又保护外国投资者的国内法提供此种制度性保障。这种做法比之对具有不同发展需求的各个发展中国家施加一系列多边条约义务更为有效。[1] 另一种观点声称,MAI 将促进对发展中国家的外资流动。实践表明,外资流动在很大程度上取决于东道国的经济、政治和社会环境,而不是取决于东道国是否在外资准入和经营上采取更为开放的政策。

按发达国家的逻辑,限制东道国自主选择投资政策和措施,对外国投资提供高水平的法律保护,"自然而然"带来了外资输入东道国的后果,这就是"平衡资本输出国与资本输入国之间的权益"。[2] 在传统 MAI 的内容设计中,资本输入国自主选择外资政策和措施的权力和权利受到限制,同时承担了保护外资的义务;而资本输出国的权力和权利未受任何限制,其跨国投资者的权利受到高水平的国际法保护,资本输出国及其跨国投资者均未承担任何义务。这显然片面维护了资本输出国的权益。需要明确的是,所谓"平衡资本输出国与资本输入国之间的权益",意味着在MAI 的内容设计中,资本输出国与资本输入国都要享有权力和权利,并承担相应的义务,真正平衡资本输出国与资本输入国之间的权益以及东道国与外国投资者之间的权益。只有资本输出国与资本输入国达成这样的共识,才有可能达成两类国家普遍接受的新型 MAI。

作为平衡发展中国家与发达国家的权益的具体体现,新型 MAI 应具有保护、促进跨国投资与管制跨国投资者行为的双重目标。早在 20 世纪 70 年代初,国际社会进行了国际投资立法另一方面的多边努力。该努力的重心是管制外国投资者,特别是跨国公司的不良行为。多年来,一些国际组织,包括 UNCTAD、OECD、国际商会和国际劳工组织等先后起草有关管制跨国公司行为的一些方面(包括竞争、税务、雇佣关系、技术转让、贿赂、信息及披露等)的规则。然而,这方面努力所取得的进展甚微。值得注意的是,一直以来,保护国际投资和促进投资自由化的努力与管制跨国投资者行为的努力分别在不同的场所进行。两种努力各行其道,均未能构建起达到

---

〔1〕 See Yong-Shik Lee, *Reclaiming Development in the World Trading System*, Cambridge University Press, 2006, pp. 122-123.

〔2〕 具有讽刺意味的是,在 BITs 历史的大部分时期,没有任何统计的或个案研究的证据证明 BITs 对 FDI 流量的作用,只是最近签署 BITs 的代价——意味着东道国的各项政策在仲裁庭面前可被成功地挑战——变得明朗化了。See Jason Webb Yackee, "Conceptual Difficulties in the Empirical Study of Bilateral Investment Treaties", *Brooklyn J. Int'l L*, Vol. 33, 2008, pp. 459-460.

其目标所需要的多边法律框架。从国际现实出发，也许两种努力应合并进行。[1] 发达国家和发展中国家应争取共同建立一个新型的 MAI 谈判平台。在新型 MAI 的设计中，应体现"平衡发展中国家与发达国家的权益"的革新意识，发展中国家应具有加入 MAI 的自由选择权和自主决定外资准入领域、外资履行要求的权力，并承担保护跨国投资的义务；而发达国家则在取得海外投资的国际法律保护的同时，须承担监管本国海外投资的责任，承诺和保护发展中国家免受外国投资者，特别是跨国公司负面行为方式的损害。[2]

四、结语

历史表明，制定一个具有普遍约束力的 MAI 绝非易事。首先，MAI 的"适当谈判场所"迄今难以确定，MAI 纳入 WTO 体制明显缺乏法律依据，如何纳入现有或未来的相关体制，依然是关山重重，云遮雾绕；其次，MAI 谈判应有发达国家和发展中国家的普遍认同和参与，MAI 谈判应注重平衡资本输出国与资本输入国的权益，当是 MAI 取得成效的基本要素，而国际社会对此尚未达成必要的共识。

当前，国际投资条约的"自由化"发展趋向值得关注。作为 MAI 模本的 BITs 片面维护资本输出国和跨国投资者权益的"先天不足"，在长达 50 年的"后天"不仅未得到应有的纠正，反而被不断强化和扩张，发展中国家的谈判地位和能力进一步被削弱，发展中国家基于国家主权原则的权力和利益进一步被剥夺。此种发达国家与发展中国家之间权益严重失衡的条约实践，严重背离了普遍认同的国际法的主权原则和公平原则，实际上，也不利于国际投资条约实践本身的健康和可持续发展。

笔者以为，国际社会应充分认识 BITs 实践片面维护资本输出国和跨国投资者权益的危害性，在相关国际实践中纠正此种"失衡"现象。面对"经济全球化""投资自由化"的所谓"时代潮流"，发展中国家比以往任何时期更需要联合自强，确立和维护共同的价值取向和基本立场，首先在相互之间的 BITs 实践中创立平衡资本输出国与资本输入国之间权益的新型 BITs，进而形成普遍接受的国际实践和国际投资新规范，为创立新型 MAI 的主要规范奠定必要的国际实践基础。

---

〔1〕 See Jeswald W. Salacuse，Towards a Global Treaty on Foreign Investment：The Search for a Grand Bargain，in Norbert Horn（ed.），*Arbitrating Foreign Investment Disputes*，Kluwer Law International，2004，pp. 83-85；M. Sornarajah，*The International Law on Foreign Investment*，2nd edition，Cambridge University Press，2004，pp. 87-88.

〔2〕 跨国公司的此类负面行为方式包括对东道国政治的干预、违反人权标准、违反环境规范等。See M. Sornarajah，*The International Law on Foreign Investment*，2nd edition，Cambridge University Press，2004，pp. 171-181.

Prospect of Negotiation for Multilateral Agreement on Investment

Abstract: Making a comprehensive and substantial multilateral agreement on investment（MAI）with general binding force is an objective which international society，especially developed states pursue for the long period of time. After discussing the issue on "proper forum" for MAI negotiation，the author points out that there are strong legal grounds for the argument that MAI negotiation cannot be integrated into WTO regime. The essential elements for a successful MAI negotiation are general recognition and participation of both developed states and developing states，and the balanced rights and interests between developed states and developing states.

第二节　变革期双边投资条约实践述评[*]

【摘要】 在评述变革期双边投资条约（BIT）实践的主要特征和 BITs 主要条款的发展之后，作者主张，为维护经济主权，发展中国家在 BIT 实践中，对 BIT 主要功能的偏向性、发达国家与发展中国家签订 BIT 的不同动机、发达国家与发展中国家之间 BIT 当事方的不平等、发达国家与发展中国家在 BIT 中权益的不平衡以及发展中国家相互之间的 BIT 实践对 BIT 总体发展趋势的意义等问题应有进一步的思考和把握。

早在 200 多年前，就有涉及国际投资保护的双边条约。[1] 自 1959 年联邦德国与巴基斯坦签订第一个专门性的双边投资条约（BIT）以来，BIT 成为 20 世纪下半期涉及外国投资待遇的首要条约，为各国所普遍接受；而其内容和形式几乎一成不变。近 20 年来，随着国际投资活动的深入发展和南北矛盾的不断演化，BIT 实践不仅呈现加速发展态势，其内容和形式也发生了一些值得关注的变革。种种迹象表明，BIT 实践已进入重要的变革期。本文将联系中国的实践，在简要评述变革期 BITs 实践的主要特征、BIT 主要条款的发展之后，提出值得进一步思考和研究的相关问题。

一、变革期 BITs 实践的主要特征

概括而言，变革期 BIT 实践的主要特征表现在其数量的迅速增长、内容的创新和缔约方的变化等三个方面。

（一）BITs 数量的迅速增长

就数量增长速度而言，BIT 经历了由缓慢增长到迅速增长的不同发展阶段。

自 20 世纪 50 年代末至 60 年代，各国共签订了 65 个 BITs，70 年代则签订了 86 个。显然，各国签订 BIT 的进展迟缓。其基本困难在于：（1）发达国家与发展中国家经济利益与政治观点的分歧；（2）一些国家政府不愿将有关本国经济政策的事务置于国际法的管辖范围之内；（3）一些资本输入国愿意对某项或某些投资实行保护，而不愿意对任何投资实行保护。这些因素，在不同程度上阻碍或制约了这类条约的

---

　　* 原载陈安主编：《国际经济法学刊》第 14 卷第 3 期，北京大学出版社 2007 年版。

　　〔1〕 1788 年美国与法国签订的友好通商航海条约包含了有关外国投资待遇的规定。See UNCTAD, *Bilateral Investment Treaties 1995-2006*: *Trends in Investment Rulemaking*, United Nations, 2007, p. 2.

发展。

　　20世纪80年代以来,发展中国家普遍采取对外国投资开放的态度,在对外国投资实行必要管制的同时,注意通过法律手段促进和保护外国投资。而发达国家则一向重视对其海外私人投资的法律保护问题。由于发展中国家与发达国家在保护国际投资方面有共同的利益,BIT作为保护国际投资的重要方式之一,逐渐为国际社会普遍接受。有学者认为,20世纪80、90年代,许多发展中国家和社会主义国家认识到,基于市场原则的自由体制和国际争端解决机制是比《各国经济权利和义务宪章》中确立的原则更好的促进投资方式。[1] 联合国贸易和发展会议(UNCTAD)的研究报告指出,外国投资者与东道国之间投资争端的大量增加也是BIT数量迅速增长的原因之一。在1995年只有6个此类案件,2005年底则增至226个。[2]

　　20世纪80年代以来,BIT数量急剧增长:80年代各国共签订211个BITs;[3]至1994年,140个国家签订了700多个BITs;至1999年,160多个国家签订了1300多个BITs;到2002年则增至2181个。[4] 仅2001年,97个国家签订了158个BITs,创造了自1959年以来BIT年度签订数的最高纪录。这一努力的结果是形成了日益紧密的覆盖170个国家的BIT网络。[5] 截至2005年7月,作为全球化进程的主角,经济合作与发展组织(OECD)国家与约140个非OECD国家共签订了1240个BITs和36个包含投资内容的贸易协定。值得注意的是,在OECD国家,与传统上占主导地位的BIT比较,包含投资内容的贸易协定显示了后来居上的发展势头。[6] 就世界范围而言,情况也是如此。截至2005年底,各国共签订约2500个BITs。然而,自2001年以来,每年签订BIT的数量呈现持续下降的趋势。2005年,各国签订了70个新的BITs。而包含投资规定的自由贸易协定和其他经济合作条约发展迅速,在1996年只有80个此类条约,而到2005年底则增至232个。[7]

---

　　〔1〕 See Paul Peters, Recent Developments in Expropriation Clauses of Asian Investment Treaties, *Asian Yearbook of International Law*, Vol. 5, 1995, p. 46.

　　〔2〕 See UNCTAD, *Bilateral Investment Treaties 1995-2006*: *Trends in Investment Rulemaking*, United Nations, 2007, p. 1.

　　〔3〕 Antonio R. Parra, ICSID and Bilateral Investment Treaties, *ICSID News*, Vol. 17, No. 1, 2000.

　　〔4〕 W. Michael Reisman & Robert D. Sloane, Indirect Expropriation and Its Valuation in the BIT Generation, *The British Year Book of International Law* (2003), Oxford, 2004, p. 115.

　　〔5〕 See Jeswald W. Salacuse, Nicholas P. Sullivan, Do BITs Really Work? An Evaluation of Bilateral Investment Treaties and Their Grand Bargain, *Harvard International Law Journal*, Vol. 46, 2005, p. 75.

　　〔6〕 See OECD Secretariat, *Novel Features in OECD Countries' Recent Investment Agreements*: *An Overview*, Document for Symposium Co-organized by ICSID, OECD and UNCTAD on Making the Most of International Invest, p. 2.

　　〔7〕 See UNCTAD, *Bilateral Investment Treaties 1995-2006*: *Trends in Investment Rulemaking*, United Nations, 2007, p. 1.

20 世纪 80 年代以来，中国积极参与商签双边投资条约。截至 2006 年 2 月，中国已同美国、加拿大分别签订了投资保证协议，同德国等 110 个国家签订了 BITs。[1]

（二）BIT 内容的创新

自 1959 年以来，除了在 20 世纪 60 年代增加有关国民待遇和外国投资者与东道国争端解决方式的规定之外，BIT 具有较统一的内容，没有显著的变化。20 世纪 90 年代中期以来，贸易协定中的投资保护条款和根据外国投资者与东道国争端解决条款提交仲裁的案件增多，带来了 BIT 实践的一些创新，BIT 之间的差异更明显了。[2] 这些创新性内容主要包括：

1. 序言的内容。在投资争端增多的背景下，关于 BIT 序言的谈判越来越受到缔约双方的重视。在 1995—2006 年的 BIT 实践中，序言的新内容大致可分为两种类型：其一是强调促进缔约双方经济合作和相互投资的优良环境的重要性，同时认识到此类投资可为东道国带来繁荣；其二是明确规定，投资促进和保护的目标需要尊重其他重要的公共政策目标。此类目标包括健康、安全、环境和消费者的保护，或者国际承认的劳工权利的维护等。[3]

2. 公共利益保障条款。OECD 国家更多关注公共利益的保障，特别是政府设定的特定目标，如健康、安全、环境和国际承认的劳工标准。OECD 国家还提及 BIT 方面的某些一般例外，如税收，基本安全，人类、动物或植物生命或健康的保护，可用竭的自然资源的保护，金融部门或文化部门的审慎措施等方面的例外。[4] 有的国家提出了"不降低标准条款"（"no lowing of standards" clause），即缔约方不应通过降低环保/劳工要求吸引外资，不应通过偏离或豁免环保/劳工要求吸引外资。

3. 竞争政策。受 WTO 体制力图纳入竞争政策的影响，有的国家主张将与竞争政策有关的内容纳入 BITs。例如规定：在设定可能影响另一缔约方投资者利益的行政垄断之前，需事先通知另一缔约方；缔约方应保证行使一定政府权力的垄断企业和国有企业遵守 BITs 的规定等。

4. 透明度问题。新近签订的含有投资自由化内容的 BITs，规定了缔约双方公布有关投资的法律和决定的义务。此外，美国 2004 年 BIT 范本和加拿大 2004 年

---

〔1〕 据商务部条法司提供的资料。

〔2〕 See UNCTAD, *Bilateral Investment Treaties 1995-2006*: *Trends in Investment Rulemaking*, United Nations, 2007, p. 1.

〔3〕 Ibid., pp. xii, 3-4.

〔4〕 See OECD Secretariat, *Novel Features in OECD Countries' Recent Investment Agreements*: *An Overview*, Document for Symposium Co-organized by ICSID, OECD and UNCTAD on Making the Most of International Invest, p. 4.

BIT 范本还包含促进透明度的制度性程序,如向有关投资者提供合理机会以便其参与商讨有关投资的制度改变以及从联系点取得有关 BIT 涵盖事项的信息。[1] 某些国家还提出了旨在增加投资争端仲裁透明度的建议,如仲裁文件(包括仲裁裁决)对外公开、允许任何非当事方向仲裁庭提交意见、仲裁过程对外公开以及非当事缔约方参与仲裁程序等。

此外,在 BITs 的传统条款中,相关概念、标准和规则等也出现了一些新因素。

(三)BITs 缔约方的变化

BITs 缔约方的变化主要反映在缔约主体和缔约双方的组合情况两个方面。

1992 年 11 月 19 日,《香港政府与荷兰王国政府关于鼓励投资和保护投资协定》在香港正式签署,1993 年 9 月 1 日正式生效,开了由非主权实体参与签订 BITs 的先河。其后,截至 2006 年 5 月 10 日,中国香港地区与澳大利亚等签订的 14 个 BITs 亦相继生效。[2]

最初的 BITs 主要是在发达国家与发展中国家之间签订的,现在,发达国家与社会主义国家之间、发展中国家相互之间、发展中国家与社会主义国家之间都签订了此类协定。[3] 在新兴工业化发展中国家中,由于劳工费用逐渐增高,需要将劳动密集型的产业重新安排到初级经济体(less sophisticated economies)。初级经济体生产的产品有权享受普惠制的优惠待遇这一因素,也促进了这种重新安排。此类发展中国家相互之间的 BITs 包括新加坡—斯里兰卡 BIT,泰国—孟加拉国 BIT 等。[4] 这种现象表明,一些发展中国家和社会主义国家也在某些领域和某种程度上,开始转变成为资本输出国。早在 1980 年就有学者认为,这种资本输出国多元化的倾向将会

---

〔1〕 See OECD Secretariat, *Novel Features in OECD Countries' Recent Investment Agreements: An Overview*, Document for Symposium Co-organized by ICSID, OECD and UNCTAD on Making the Most of International Invest, p. 5.

〔2〕 中国香港地区与外国间投资协定无须立法实施,惯常做法是在缔约双方政府确认协定生效后,在《香港政府宪报》(第 5 号特别副刊)(*Special Supplement No. 5 to the Hong Kong Government Gazette*,简称"宪报")上刊登。已生效的中国香港地区与外国间投资协定的缔约对方、协定生效日期及协定刊载处分别是:荷兰(1.9.1993),宪报,134,no. 50(1992):E25—E53;澳大利亚(15.10.1993),135,no. 37(1993):E103—E123;丹麦(4.3.1994),136,no. 6(1994):E19—E48;瑞典(26.6.1994),136,no. 23(1994):E51—E78;瑞士(22.10.1994),136,no. 48(1994):E85—E116;新西兰(5.8.1995),137,no. 34(1995):E95—E115;法国(30.5.1997),2,no. 26(1998):E215—E240;日本(18.6.1997),2,no. 26(1998):E241—E281;韩国(30.7.1997),2,no. 26(1998):E283—E316;奥地利(1.10.1997),2,no. 26(1998):E317—E351;意大利(2.2.1998),2,no. 6(1998):E3—E35;德国(19.2.1998),2,no. 10(1998):E39—E66;英国(12.4.1999),3,no. 15(1999):E391—E414;比利时—卢森堡(18.6.2001),5,no. 25(2001):E175—E222;泰国(12.4.2006),10,no. 18(2006):E31—E40,at www. justice. gov. hk/choice. htm/27/02/2007,June 1,2007.

〔3〕 See UNCTAD,*World Investment Report 1996*,p. 147.

〔4〕 See M. Sornarajah,*The International Law on Foreign Investment*,Cambridge University Press,1996,p. 17,note 55.

使南北之间有关国际投资问题的矛盾趋于缓和；同时，对于进一步增强国际投资的法律保护，也许是一种可喜的征象。[1] 在 1995—2006 年的 BITs 实践中，发展中国家相互之间的 BITs 获得了显著的发展，由 161 个发展为 644 个，在一定程度上反映了一些发展中国家成为资本输出国后积极签订 BITs 的立场。[2]

二、变革期 BITs 主要条款的发展

从法律角度看，世界各国签订的 BITs 的结构和内容十分相似。一般包括适用范围、投资准入、外资待遇、征收及补偿标准、投资财产的转移以及争端的解决等关键条款。[3] 变革期，这些主要条款的内容和形式各有不同程度的发展。

（一）适用范围

形式上，BITs 的适用范围一般分别由适用的地域范围、"投资""投资者"的定义以及涵盖投资的时间界限等条款确定。在新近签订的一些 BITs 中，缔约方往往在单一条款中明确规定适用范围的不同方面。[4]

1. 适用的地域范围

关于协定适用的地域范围，BITs 一般规定适用于缔约一方投资者在缔约另一方领土内所进行的投资活动和投资项目。

BITs 适用的地域范围取决于"领土"（territory）的定义。定义该用语的目的不是为了划定缔约双方的领土，而是基于投资保护的目的，特别是规定，为特定 BIT 的目的，在缔约方领海范围之外海域的投资视为在缔约方领土范围之内。典型的"领土"定义包括缔约方根据国际法行使主权权利或管辖的海域，一般包含大陆架和专属经济区。一些 BITs 对"领土"的定义更为复杂。此类定义不仅是为了明确领海之外的管辖范围，还对空间、人造岛屿、大陆架上的装置和建筑物等作出规定。[5]

此外，由于缔约国历史、政治等因素，某些 BITs 适用的地域范围有时不完全等同于缔约国一方或双方的领土范围，应予明确规定。例如，中英 BIT 规定，在协定签字时或其后任何时候，缔约双方可互换照会同意将协定的规定延伸适用于由英国政

---

〔1〕 参见〔日〕横川新：《论国外投资与双边条约》，载于日本国际问题研究所《国际问题》杂志，1980 年 3 月号；中译文见陈安编译：《国际经济立法的历史和现状》，法律出版社 1982 年版，第 143—144 页。

〔2〕 See UNCTAD, *Bilateral Investment Treaties 1995-2006：Trends in Investment Rulemaking*，United Nations，2007，p. 1.

〔3〕 See Marco Bronckers and Reinhard Quick（ed.），*New Directions in International Economic Law*，Kluwer Law International，2000，pp. 392-393.

〔4〕 如 2001 年澳大利亚与乌拉圭的 BIT 第 2 条"协定的适用"。See UNCTAD, *Bilateral Investment Treaties 1995-2006：Trends in Investment Rulemaking*，United Nations，2007，pp. 5-6.

〔5〕 See UNCTAD, *Bilateral Investment Treaties 1995-2006：Trends in Investment Rulemaking*，United Nations，2007，pp. 17-19.

府负责国际关系的领土。

中国实行"一国两制"方针,香港特别行政区与澳门特别行政区享有一定的对外缔约权,并且已有以其自身名义对外签订 BITs 的实践。与此同时,中国与外国之间签订的 BITs(中外 BITs)一般规定,适用的地域范围包括中国的全部领土,当然包括香港特别行政区与澳门特别行政区,由此产生了中外 BITs 对香港特别行政区、澳门特别行政区的适用问题。这一问题可能存在以下三种情况:

(1) 在中国内地和香港特别行政区或澳门特别行政区分别与特定外国签订有 BIT 的情况下,对香港特别行政区或澳门特别行政区而言,香港特别行政区或澳门特别行政区与该外国签订的 BIT 优先适用;

(2) 在中国内地与特定外国签订有 BIT 而香港特别行政区或澳门特别行政区与该外国尚未签订 BIT 的情况下,根据《香港特别行政区基本法》和《澳门特别行政区基本法》(统称"基本法")的有关规定,如无相反规定,在征询香港特别行政区政府或澳门特别行政区政府的意见后,中国内地与该外国签订的 BIT 可适用于香港特别行政区或澳门特别行政区;

(3) 在中国内地与特定外国尚未签订 BIT 而香港特别行政区或澳门特别行政区与该外国已签订 BIT 的情况下,根据基本法的有关规定,香港特别行政区或澳门特别行政区与该外国签订的 BIT 适用于香港特别行政区或澳门特别行政区。

2. "投资""投资者"的定义

BITs 的保护对象一般通过"投资""投资者"的定义予以限定。

(1) 投资的定义

① "基于资产"的投资定义

传统 BITs 的投资定义采用以经东道国政府批准为限定条件的"基于资产"(asset-based)的投资定义方式,并附有所包括资产类型的列举性清单。多数 BITs 规定了尽可能广泛的投资定义。

许多早期 BITs 的缔约方认为,外国人的无形财产是其所属国法律的产物,不是国际法保护的财产。因此,对知识产权,如专利、版权和专有技术等经常在国际投资活动中涉及的无形财产的保护,以东道国法律承认为限。随着国际投资的发展,越来越多的 BITs 缔约方认识到,无形财产权是投资保护的中心。

特许协议作为矿产资源部门外国投资的主要形式,产生了无形的契约权利。对该契约权利的保护经过一系列国际仲裁案得以确立。许多外国投资合同的新形式涉及无形财产的转让。在许可证协议(licensing agreements)、管理合同(management contracts)和咨询合同(consultancy contracts)中也包含了无形财产的标的。因此，在 BITs 中，外国投资保护不仅包括对投资者有形财产的保护，也包括对其带入投资企业的无形财产的保护。在一些情况下，无形财产比有形财产更为重要。BITs通常规定了受协定保护的无形财产的类型。此外，作为对实际上拒绝股东保护的"巴塞罗纳机车案"的回应，BITs 开始将公司的股份定义为"投资"。[1]

宽泛的基于资产的定义已成为当前 BITs 的普遍规范。新的趋向是更为准确地作出基于资产的"投资"定义。2001 年 11 月 26 日签订、同年 12 月 1 日生效的新中国—荷兰 BIT（简称"新中荷 BIT"）可作为基于资产的投资定义的典型。该协定第 1条第 1 款规定："'投资'一词系指缔约一方投资者在缔约另一方领土内所投入的各种资产，特别是，包括但不限于：（1）动产、不动产以及其他财产权利如抵押权、质押权；（2）公司股份、债券、股票和任何其他形式的参股；（3）金钱请求权或其他具有经济价值的与投资有关行为的请求权；（4）知识产权，特别是著作权、专利权、商标权、商号、工艺流程、专有技术和商誉；（5）法律或法律允许依合同授予的商业特许权，包括勘探、开采、提炼或开发自然资源的特许权。"

② "基于企业"（enterprise-based）的投资定义

BITs"投资"定义的另一新发展表现在，有的国家采取"基于企业"的投资定义方式。例如，墨西哥 BIT 范本规定："'投资'一词指：（a）企业；（b）企业股票；（c）企业债券，其条件是该企业是投资者的附属机构或该债券最初到期日为 3 年以上，但不包括缔约方或国有企业的债券，无论其最初到期日如何；（d）对企业的贷款，其条件是该企业是投资者的附属机构或该债券最初到期日为 3 年以上，但不包括对缔约方或国有企业的贷款，无论其最初到期日如何；（e）使所有人能分享企业收益的企业股权；（f）使所有人能分享企业终止时不属第（c）或（d）项的债务担保或贷款的资产；（g）用于经济利益或其他商业目的的或为此预期而取得的不动产或其他财产，有形或无形的资产；（h）在缔约一方领土的资本承诺或其他资源对该领土经济活动产生的利益，如根据（i）涉及在该缔约方领土的投资者资产投入的合同，或（ii）酬金实质上取决于企业的生产、收入或利润的合同。"

③ "完全清单"（closed-list）的投资定义

"完全清单"的投资定义旨在避免对"投资"作出过于宽泛的定义。与宽泛的"基于资产"的投资定义不同，它没有包含定义"投资"的一般性概念，而是由该条约涵盖的有形财产和无形财产的完全清单构成。该方式原先是设计为 NAFTA 文本采用

〔1〕 See M. Sornarajah, A Developing Country Perspectives of International Economic Law in the Context of Dispute Settlement, in Asif H. Qureshi(ed.), *Perspectives in International Economic Law*, Kluwer Law International, 2002, p. 105.

的"基于企业"的投资定义,之后发展为 NAFTA 第 1139 条采用的定义。近几年的 BITs 实践也开始采用该方式,如加拿大 2004 年 BIT 范本。[1]

④ 循环的(circular)投资定义

在美国 2004 年 BIT 范本中,采取了循环的投资定义,即"投资"指"投资者直接或间接拥有或控制的具有投资特征的任何财产,包括如同资本或其他资源的承诺、收益或利润的预期,或风险的承担等。投资可采取的形式包括:(1) 企业;(2) 企业的股份和其他股权参与形式;(3) 债券和其他债权文件及贷款;(4) 期货、选择权和其他衍生物;(5) 交钥匙、建设、管理、生产、特许、收益分享及其他类似合同;(6) 知识产权;(7) 根据可适用的内国法授予的许可证、授权、允许及类似的权利;及(8) 其他有形或无形财产、动产或不动产以及相关财产权利,包括出租权、抵押权、质押权及保证。"[2]

尽管"投资"的定义通常是广泛而详细的,许多 BITs 规定了对投资的限制,如通常规定仅对经缔约方批准的投资进行保护。这一规定的实施后果是在东道国产生了两种类型的投资,即经批准的投资和未经批准的投资。对前者适用 BITs 机制的特别保护,对后者则适用一般国际法的投资保护原则。对两类投资的区分本身也反映了 BITs 的"特别法"性质。[3]

(2) 投资者的定义

所谓"投资者",一般指具有缔约国国籍的自然人和法人。问题在于,特定投资者需要与缔约方具有何种联系以证明其应受特定 BIT 的保护。这通常取决于该投资者是自然人还是法人。因此,BITs 对两类投资者分别作出规定。

对于自然人,绝大多数 BITs 保护具有缔约一方国籍的人。因此,缔约一方国民的典型定义是指由缔约一方国内法承认为国民或公民的自然人。[4]

对于法人,在 BITs 中一般称为"公司"(company),其定义也是很广泛的,通常包括各种法律实体,其中列举了公司、合伙、合营企业、独家业主(sole proprietorships)

---

〔1〕　See UNCTAD, *Bilateral Investment Treaties 1995-2006: Trends in Investment Rulemaking*, United Nations, 2007, pp. 10-11.

〔2〕　Paul E. Comeaux, N. Stephan Kinsella, *Protecting Foreign Investment under International Law*, *Legal Aspects of Political Risk*, Oceana Publications Inc., 1997, p. 105; OECD Secretariat, *Novel Features in OECD Countries' Recent Investment Agreements*: *An Overview*, Document for Symposium Co-organized by ICSID, OECD and UNCTAD on Making the Most of International Invest, p. 5.

〔3〕　See M. Sornarajah, A Developing Country Perspectives of International Economic Law in the Context of Dispute Settlement, in Asif H. Qureshi(ed.), *Perspectives in International Economic Law*, Kluwer Law International, 2002, pp. 240-245.

〔4〕　See UNCTAD, *Bilateral Investment Treaties 1995-2006: Trends in Investment Rulemaking*, United Nations, 2007, p. 13.

和托拉斯等。[1]"公司"的定义不同于国际法中的传统概念。国际法院在"巴塞罗纳机车案"中，表明了对在海外投资的公司实行外交保护的"设立地规则"。一些 BITs 试图确立符合其保护外资宗旨的有关公司国籍的其他检验方式。如规定，在缔约一方设立的公司，如果其控制住所（seat of control）位于缔约另一方，或者其控制或重要股权（substantial interests）是由缔约另一方国民所拥有，可受到缔约另一方的保护。依此规定，跨国公司拥有全部或多数股权的、设立于东道国的公司可以受到保护。然而，对跨国公司拥有少数股权的、设立于东道国的公司的保护，仍然存在问题。因此，在 BITs 中，将股权列为"投资"的类型，可作为对此种情况保护的方式。[2]

新中荷 BIT 第 1 条第 2 款规定："投资者"是指："（一）依照缔约一方法律拥有缔约一方国籍的自然人；（二）按照缔约一方的法律法规设立和组成，在该缔约方领土内具有住所的任何经济实体，包括公司、社团、合伙和其他组织，不论其是否以营利为目的，其责任是否为有限。"新中—荷 BIT 议定书进一步规定，"'投资'一词包括由缔约一方投资者拥有或控制的第三国法人在缔约另一方领土内依照后者的法律法规已经进行的投资。只有当投资被缔约另一方征收之后该第三国无权或放弃其赔偿请求权的情况下，本协定相关条款方为适用"。这实际上表明了缔约双方有条件地接受了法人国籍认定的"资本控制规则"。

关于"投资者"的定义，在 1995—2006 年的 BITs 实践中，确定法律实体的国籍仍然采用不同的方式。在近年签订的 BITs 中，出现了结合设立地标准和"控制利益"（controlling interest）标准的趋向。一些 BITs 对某项投资中投资者的"控制"作了定义。其中一类是将"控制"（control）理解为任命董事会多数成员的权力或合法管理该项投资的经营活动。[3]

3. 适用的期间

在 BITs 谈判中，涉及适用期间的主要有两个问题：一是特定 BIT 是否适用于该协定生效之前所作的投资；二是该协定适用期限的确定，即其存续期间和终止。

关于第一个问题，主要有两种规定：一是不论投资项目发生于协定生效之前或生效之后，凡经东道国政府批准者，均属协定的适用范围。如新中荷 BIT 第 12 条规定，"本协定同样适用于在其生效之前，缔约一方投资者依照缔约另一方在其进行投

---

〔1〕 See Paul E. Comeaux, N. Stephan Kinsella, *Protecting Foreign Investment under International Law*, *Legal Aspects of Political Risk*, Oceana Publications Inc. , 1997, p. 105.

〔2〕 See M. Sornarajah, A Developing Country Perspectives of International Economic Law in the Context of Dispute Settlement, in Asif H. Qureshi(ed.),*Perspectives in International Economic Law*, Kluwer Law International, 2002, pp. 245-249.

〔3〕 See UNCTAD, *Bilateral Investment Treaties 1995-2006*: *Trends in Investment Rulemaking*, United Nations, 2007, pp. xi, 16-17.

资时有效的法律法规,在缔约另一方的领土内进行的投资";二是明确规定可适用协定的投资的时间界限。如 1983 年中国—德国 BIT 第 9 条规定,1979 年 7 月 1 日之后进行的投资属协定的适用范围。[1] 对 1995—2006 年 BITs 实践的研究表明,主流的规定是,对特定 BIT 生效之前和生效之后的投资均予以保护,同时也规定,不适用于该 BIT 生效之前已产生或已解决的投资争端或权利请求。[2]

关于 BITs 适用期限的确定,与其他国际条约不同,BITs 通常规定一个最低限度的固定期限。其合理性在于,为缔约双方的投资者提供适用于其投资的国际法制的高度稳定性和可预见性,由此确立有利于其经营商务的稳定环境。在 1995—2006 年 BITs 实践中,主流的规定是 BITs 的最初期限为 10 年或 15 年。也有一些 BITs 规定协定持续有效,直至缔约一方通知缔约对方其终止该协定的意愿。在 BITs 的最初期限届满时,希望延期的缔约双方一般采取两种方式:一是规定协定延长一个固定期限(通常是 10 年)继续有效;二是规定协定持续有效,以缔约各方保留事先书面通知终止协定的权利为限。在这方面,1985—1995 年签订的 BITs 和 1995—2006 年签订的 BITs 出现了由第一种方式占优势向第二种方式占优势的转变。无论协定期限如何规定,大多数 BITs 规定,在协定期限届满后,由该协定涵盖的投资还将在一个具体期限内受到保护。这同样是为了向缔约双方投资者提供适用于其投资的可预见的法律环境。[3]

(二)投资准入

BITs 中所谓投资准入,指缔约双方有关允许对方投资进入本国境内的一般规定,通常表明了东道国政府对外来投资的态度或立场。

所有 BITs 都作了有关投资准入的规定。一些 BITs,包括美国签订的所有 BITs,要求在投资准入阶段实行有条件的国民待遇,即除保留某些部门,如民用航空、电讯和金融机构作为例外,其他领域对外资自由开放。未包含在投资准入阶段实行国民待遇的 BITs 通常规定,缔约各方允许缔约对方的投资依前者的法律、法规和规章进入前者境内。外国学者穆罕默德·I. 阿里对世界各国、包括几乎所有发达国家和 90 个发展中国家签订的 335 个 BITs 作了概括和分析,提供了有关国家实践的总轮廓。其 1991 年完成的专题研究(以下简称"阿里专题研究")表明,在其研究的

---

〔1〕 该协定已被 2003 年 12 月 1 日签订的《中华人民共和国和德意志联邦共和国关于促进和相互保护投资的协定》取代。后者第 11 条规定:"本协定应适用于缔约任何一方投资者在缔约另一方境内依照缔约另一方法律法规于本协定生效前或生效后作出的投资。"

〔2〕 See UNCTAD, *Bilateral Investment Treaties 1995-2006*:*Trends in Investment Rulemaking*,United Nations,2007,pp. 16-17.

〔3〕 Ibid.,pp. 19-21.

335 个 BITs 中,126 个协定(其中德国参与签订的占 1/3 以上)规定了缔约双方鼓励促进和创设良好的外国投资环境的一般责任,并且规定缔约双方须根据其法律接受外国投资。54 个协定也包含上述一般责任的规定,并规定缔约双方须根据其法律、法规或行政惯例接受外国投资。在另外 59 个协定(其中 42 个英国参与、7 个荷兰参与、3 个比利时参与签订)中,此类责任表述为根据缔约双方法律授权行使的权利接受外国投资。在 9 个协定中,此类责任减弱了,即规定缔约双方应根据其法律和法规努力接受(endeavor to admit)外国投资。由于此类责任产生于缔约双方的自由谈判,缔约双方仍保留对其本国经济政策的决策权,15 个协定明确表明缔约双方保留上述决策权。另有 14 个协定规定,缔约双方应根据国民待遇或最惠国待遇接受外国投资。[1]

在 1995—2006 年的 BITs 实践中,由缔约双方决定外国投资者的"准入和设立"(admission and establishment)仍居主流地位。此类 BITs 规定,缔约对方投资者的投资只有在符合东道国立法的情况下,才能被批准。这就是所谓的"准入条款"(admission clause)。它允许东道国实施对外国投资的准入和审查机制,由此确定外国投资准入的条件。"准入条款"的另一种表现方式是,除非 BIT 另有规定,无论东道国是否建立外国投资的准入和审查机制,对东道国而言,不存在"禁止有关影响外国投资设立的歧视性立法"之义务。

与此同时,BITs 中含有"设立权"(right of establishment)规定的越来越多。所谓"设立权"是通过在外国投资设立阶段和设立之后给予其国民待遇和最惠国待遇,或者通过给予其最惠国待遇而确立,并附有例外和保留。这意味着,缔约一方投资者在缔约对方境内将享有不低于缔约对方本国投资者和其他任何第三国投资者的待遇。此类条约旨在促进投资自由化。传统上,采用此类条款的限于美国,20 世纪 90 年代中期 NAFTA 生效后,加拿大也采用,随后日本等国亦步亦趋。其结果是,一些发展中国家视缔约对方不同,接受了两种不同的 BIT 模式:一是主要与欧洲国家之间 BITs 的"准入条款"模式;二是主要与美国、加拿大之间 BITs 的"设立权"模式。[2]

近 10 年来,越来越多的 BITs,特别是美国新近签订的 BITs,开始引入在 WTO体制内发展起来的国际投资法的新因素,即禁止或部分禁止"履行要求"。此类禁止由于扩及与服务有关的"履行要求",已超越了 WTO 体制《与贸易有关的投资措施协

---

〔1〕 See Mohamed I. Khalil, Treatment of Foreign Investment in Bilateral Investment Treaties, *ICSID Review-Foreign Investment Law Journal*, Vol. 7, 1992, p. 350.

〔2〕 See UNCTAD, *Bilateral Investment Treaties 1995-2006*; *Trends in Investment Rulemaking*, United Nations, 2007, pp. xi, 21-26.

定》的义务。例如,美国新近签订的 BITs 规定,任何缔约方不得规定以下 6 种履行
要求作为协定涵盖投资的新设、取得、扩大或经营的条件:(1) 当地成分达到一定水
平或比例,或者给予国内成分或资源的服务产品优惠待遇;(2) 限制与特定生产数
量、出口或外汇收益相关的进口;(3) 出口一定水平或比例的产品或服务;(4) 限制
在缔约方领土与特定生产数量或价值、出口或外汇收益相关的销售;(5) 在缔约方领
土向本国公司转移技术;(6) 在缔约方领土开展一定类型、水平或比例的研究与开发
活动。[1]

(三) 外资待遇

外资待遇指东道国给予外国投资者的投资和与投资有关的活动的待遇。所谓
"与投资有关的活动",包括投资企业及其分支机构等的组织、控制、经营和安排,有
关契约的签订和履行,各种有关权利的取得、行使、保护和处置以及资金的借贷、股
权的购买和转让等。在 BITs 中,外国投资的待遇标准一般可分为两大类:一是相对
待遇标准,指缔约方给予来自缔约对方的投资与其本国国民和第三国国民同等的待
遇标准,即国民待遇和最惠国待遇标准;二是绝对待遇标准,指缔约方根据国际法公
平与公正地对待来自缔约对方的投资,无论其对来自本国国民和第三国国民的投资
待遇如何,即公平与公正待遇标准。[2] 有学者将外国投资的待遇标准进一步细分为
6 个组成部分,包括:(1) 公平与公正待遇;(2) 充分保护与保障条款;(3) 不合理或
歧视性措施的防范保护;(4) 不低于国际法给予的待遇;(5) 履行对投资者和投资所
作义务的要求;(6) 国民待遇或/和最惠国待遇。[3]

1. 国民待遇

给予外国投资和外国投资者国民待遇标准是 BITs 的主要内容之一。典型的规
定是,东道国给予外国投资者不低于东道国给予其本国投资者的待遇。

传统上,在有关外国人损害的国家责任问题上,分歧甚大。许多拉丁美洲国家
和资本输入国主张适用外国人待遇的内国标准(the national standard of treatment
of aliens)。《经济宪章》第 2 条第 2 款第 C 项也支持国民待遇原则。然而,鉴于国民
待遇可能低于"国际最低标准"(an international minimum standard),资本输出国向
来主张,应给予外国人国际最低标准。当前,由于各国可能对其国民保留一些经济
部门或特权,享有国民待遇也有其利益。给予外国人国民待遇意味着外国人有权享

---

〔1〕　See Andreas F. Lowenfeld, *International Economic Law*, Oxford University Press, 2002, p. 474.

〔2〕　See Paul E. Comeaux, N. Stephan Kinsella, *Protecting Foreign Investment under International Law*, *Legal Aspects of Political Risk*, Oceana Publications Inc., 1997, pp. 105-106.

〔3〕　See Jeswald W. Salacuse, Nicholas P. Sullivan, Do BITs Really Work? An Evaluation of Bilateral Investment Treaties and Their Grand Bargain, *Harvard International Law Journal*, Vol. 46, 2005, p. 83.

有与内国国民同等的待遇。因此，发达国家倾向于支持国民待遇标准，主张东道国如未能给予外国投资者国民待遇就产生了歧视，由此需要承担国际责任。

给予外国投资国民待遇，对外国投资者而言，也许是可以达到的最佳情况，意味着该国对本国国民与外国人一视同仁，如对外国人有歧视，即产生国际责任。根据国民待遇原则可以主张，履行要求，如出口配额或当地购买要求，至少在外资准入之后，不能施加于外国投资者。它还表明，给予本国国民与外国人差别待遇所依据的经济上的合法理由不能作为该歧视待遇的正当理由。

对欧洲国家而言，这一规定数十年保持不变。而美国参与的 BITs 则规定，在"同类情况"(a like situation)存在时，适用国民待遇条款。美国近年的相关实践又将"同类情况"改为"同类情势"(like circumstances)，这表明美国政府甚至考虑到这两个用语的细微差别。从美国的观点看，适用国民待遇条款是一个具体的事实，首先需要决定，外国投资者与内国投资者是否同处于一个可比较的环境，即所谓"同类情况"或"同类情势"；其次需要决定，给予外国投资者的待遇是否至少不低于给予内国投资者的待遇。NAFTA 的案例也涉及该问题，且牵涉 WTO 体制中"同类产品"用语的相关性及 WTO 争端解决机构解释的适用问题。[1] 由于"同类情势"概念的引入，仲裁庭在判断特定措施是否违反国民待遇标准时，采用了"两个步骤"的分析方法：第一，查证在本国投资和本国投资者与外国投资和外国投资者之间的待遇是否事实上存在不同；第二，如果发现不同的待遇，仲裁庭需要处理两者是否居于"同类情势"的问题。这种裁断需要采取个案基础上的事实分析。[2]

当前，在给予外国投资国民待遇方面，重要的是需要区分外资准入和外资经营两个阶段。在 1995—2006 年的 BITs 实践中，绝大多数 BITs 规定在设立后阶段(post-establishment phase)即外资经营阶段给予外国投资国民待遇。属于此类的一些 BITs 还进一步规定，依据东道国国内法给予外国投资国民待遇。一些 BITs 明确规定，给予外国投资和外国投资者不低于本国投资和本国投资者的待遇的义务限于两者居于"同类情势"。这意味着，给予外国投资和外国投资者不同于实际上居于不同情势的本国投资和本国投资者的待遇，并不违反国民待遇标准。

自 1986 年起，中国已由不采纳国民待遇标准的立场转为有条件地给予外国投资国民待遇。目前，国民待遇标准也成为中国采纳的外国投资待遇标准之一。具体而

---

〔1〕 Rudolf Dolzer, Main Substantive Issues Arising from Investment Disputes, National Treatment: New Developments, Paper for Symposium Co-organized by ICSID, OECD and UNCTAD on Making the Most of International Investment Agreements:A Common Agenda, 12 December 2005, Paris.

〔2〕 See UNCTAD, *Bilateral Investment Treaties 1995-2006*: *Trends in Investment Rulemaking*, United Nations, 2007, pp. xii, 36.

言,中国在签订的 BITs 中,承诺"依据国内的法律法规"给予缔约对方投资者已作出的投资国民待遇。该表述用简单的方式全面排除中国目前未能给予外资国民待遇的领域和相关措施。[1] 此外,将适用范围限于"投资者已作出的投资",意味着国民待遇标准仅在外资经营阶段中适用。

近来,在 BITs 谈判中,有的国家提出,中国所谓"依据国内的法律法规给予外国投资国民待遇"弹性过大,无法预见的因素过多,难以接受。有的国家提出,如中国不能给予无条件的国民待遇,应明确列举不能给予国民待遇的具体领域和具体措施(即国民待遇例外清单)。针对缔约对方的上述要求,中国需要抓紧研究的问题包括:对原有"依据国内的法律法规给予外国投资国民待遇"的规定,能否取消"依据国内的法律法规"的限制词;如不能,采用国民待遇例外清单的可行性;或采用"承诺不增加现有不符合国民待遇原则的措施"(即"冻结条款")加"列出实行国民待遇的具体领域和具体措施清单"(即国民待遇清单)的可行性。

2. 最惠国待遇

在 BITs 规定最惠国待遇条款,意味着东道国对来自缔约对方的投资者和投资给予不低于任何其他国家的投资者和投资所享有的待遇。其后果是允许外国投资者享有东道国作为缔约方的 BITs 所规定的最高待遇标准。[2]

在 1995—2006 年的 BITs 实践中,所有 BITs 均规定了最惠国待遇标准。在多数情况下,适用该标准的例外包括根据避免双重征税条约和区域经济一体化协定而取得的特权。[3] 2003 年中国—德国 BIT 也遵循此类实践。其第 3 条第 4 款规定,公平与公正的待遇、国民待遇和最惠国待遇"不应解释为缔约一方有义务将由下列原因产生的待遇、优惠或特权给予缔约另一方投资者:(一)任何现存或将来的关税同盟、自由贸易区、经济联盟以及共同市场的成员;(二)任何双重征税协定或其他有关税收问题的协定。"

多数 BITs 同时规定了国民待遇和最惠国待遇。据阿里专题研究报告,在 335 个 BITs 中,196 个协定规定东道国给予外国投资的待遇应不低于给予本国投资者或给予任何第三国投资者的待遇,以两者较优者为准。许多协定同时规定上述两种或两种以上的待遇标准。101 个协定只规定最惠国待遇标准。9 个协定只规定国民待

〔1〕　参见赵健:《论中外双边投资保护协定关于待遇标准的规定》,载《法学研究》1992 年第 6 期,第 84—85 页。

〔2〕　See Jeswald W. Salacuse, Nicholas P. Sullivan, Do BITs Really Work? An Evaluation of Bilateral Investment Treaties and Their Grand Bargain, *Harvard International Law Journal*, Vol. 46, 2005, p. 85.

〔3〕　See UNCTAD, *Bilateral Investment Treaties 1995-2006*: *Trends in Investment Rulemaking*, United Nations, 2007, pp. xii, 39-43.

遇标准。[1] 在同时规定国民待遇和最惠国待遇的情况下，缔约各方的国民可主张两者中更为优惠的待遇标准。由于国民待遇看来是当前最为优惠的待遇，缔约各方实施最惠国待遇的后果可能使其国民享有国民待遇。例如，新中荷 BIT 规定了国民待遇和最惠国待遇，即"缔约一方给予缔约另一方投资者的投资和与该投资有关的活动的待遇不应低于其给予本国或任何第三国投资者的投资和与该投资有关的活动的待遇"[2]。该协定还进一步规定了"从优适用"原则，即"如果缔约任何一方的法律或现行国际法的义务或缔约双方除本协定外的约定中含有赋予缔约另一方投资者比本协定更优惠的待遇的一般或具体规定，则该规定应在其更优惠的程度上优于本协定而适用"[3]。

尽管在最近一些国际投资仲裁案的裁决中，对最惠国待遇条款适用范围的见解不一，BITs 实践还未试图进一步明确规定该范围。墨菲兹尼诉西班牙案（Maffezini v. the Kingdom of Spain Case）引发了有关最惠国待遇标准适用范围的争论，特别是 BITs 的最惠国待遇条款是仅适用于实体性义务，或者也适用于争端解决程序。当前，在国际仲裁实践中对该条款的重要分析侧重于主张该条款适用于有关实体性权利。该案表明了在 BITs 中清楚确定最惠国待遇条款适用范围的重要性。一些国家为此在 BITs 谈判中修改其最惠国待遇条款的文本。这也导致了 BITs 如何处理最惠国待遇条款例外的问题。[4]

3. 公平与公正待遇

"公平与公正待遇"条款独立于最惠国待遇条款和国民待遇条款的原因是，即使在未规定非歧视待遇条款的情况下，也明确表明适用于外国投资待遇的最低国际行为标准。[5] 该用语是含糊的，可能有多种解释。它如果符合"公平"要求并平等地适用于外国投资者，可能不同于国民待遇。给予外国投资"公平与公正待遇"至少意味着，在有关诉诸当地法院和行政机构、适用的税收和政府规章的管理等方面，不因国籍或投资来源而有所区别。[6] 据阿里专题研究报告，在 335 个 BITs 中，有 300 多个

---

[1] See Mohamed I. Khalil, Treatment of Foreign Investment in Bilateral Investment Treaties, *ICSID Review-Foreign Investment Law Journal*, Vol. 7, 1992, p. 351.

[2] 新中荷 BIT 第 3 条第 1、3 款。

[3] 新中荷 BIT 第 3 条第 5 款。

[4] See UNCTAD, *Bilateral Investment Treaties 1995-2006: Trends in Investment Rulemaking*, United Nations, 2007, pp. xii, 39-43.

[5] 关于国际投资协定中公平与公正待遇的系统论述，参见陈辉萍、黄玉梅：《国际投资协定中公正与公平待遇标准的新发展》，载陈安主编：《国际经济法学刊》第 13 卷第 3 期，北京大学出版社 2006 年版，第 1—29 页。

[6] See Andreas F. Lowenfeld, *International Economic Law*, Oxford University Press, 2002, p. 474.

协定规定东道国应给予外国投资"公平与公正待遇"。[1]

在 1995—2006 年的 BITs 实践中,绝大多数包含了"公平与公正待遇"标准的规定。一些 BITs 还将该标准结合"充分保护与保障"(full protection and security)原则和"国际最低标准"(international minimum standards)。然而,很少有 BITs 对"公平与公正待遇"的含义作出清晰的界定。BITs 采用不同的解释方法,例如,称"公平与公正待遇"标准并不意味着高于习惯国际法规范,或称该标准为国际法的参考(reference),或将该标准与非歧视待遇联系。

理论上,一些学者主张,给予外国投资"公平与公正待遇"的义务与给予外国投资"国际最低标准"待遇的义务并无区别。他们认为,"国际最低标准"是习惯国际法的组成部分,包含"公平与公正待遇"等许多国际法律原则。另一些学者主张,"公平与公正待遇"蕴含不同于"国际最低标准"的含义。因此,"公平与公正待遇"的用语应给予清晰的含义,应基于衡平检验方式个案适用以确定是否违反该标准。[2]

美国 BIT 范本规定,缔约一方应给予来自缔约对方的投资"公平与公正待遇和充分保护与保障(full protection and security),且应在任何情况下给予不低于国际法所要求的待遇"。该规定意味着,依据国际法已有要求,即使不存在 BIT,也要以"国际最低标准"待遇约束缔约各方。[3] 加拿大 2004 年 BIT 范本也规定,根据"公平与公正待遇"给予的保护不超出"依习惯国际法的外国人最低待遇标准"。可见,在发达国家看来,"公平与公正待遇"与"国际最低待遇标准""充分保护与保障"密切联系,互为解释,相互补充。[4] ICSID 用于解释 BITs 这方面规定的两个案例表明,这一标准并未使东道国对产生于投资的所有损害负责。因此,虽然东道国不是保护人,如果它在保护外资免受损害方面未能显示"应有的勤勉"(due diligence),就必须负责任。ICSID 仲裁庭将"应有的勤勉"定义为"在类似情况下,可预期的行政良好的政府所能采取的合理防范措施"。因此,东道国未能采取合理措施保护投资免受来自强盗或警察和安全官员的威胁,可能要承担依 BIT 赔偿受损害投资者的责任。[5]

〔1〕　See Mohamed I. Khalil, Treatment of Foreign Investment in Bilateral Investment Treaties, *ICSID Review-Foreign Investment Law Journal*, Vol. 7, 1992, p. 351.

〔2〕　See UNCTAD, *Bilateral Investment Treaties 1995-2006: Trends in Investment Rulemaking*, United Nations, 2007, pp. xii, 28-33.

〔3〕　See Paul E. Comeaux, N. Stephan Kinsella, *Protecting Foreign Investment under International Law, Legal Aspects of Political Risk*, Oceana Publications Inc. , 1997, p. 106.

〔4〕　所谓"充分保护与保障"标准要求东道国政府不仅不能损害外国投资者的设备和员工,还需要在一些紧急情况(如叛乱等)下,保护外国投资和外国投资者免受其他人的损害。See Andreas F. Lowenfeld, *International Economic Law*, Oxford University Press, 2002, p. 476.

〔5〕　See Jeswald W. Salacuse, Nicholas P. Sullivan, Do BITs Really Work? An Evaluation of Bilateral Investment Treaties and Their Grand Bargain, *Harvard International Law Journal*, Vol. 46, 2005, p. 83.

在 NAFTA 多个投资仲裁案中,仲裁庭需要对 NAFTA 第 1105 条("公平与公正待遇")的范围和内容作出解释。此类解释见仁见智,包含一些受到 NAFTA 全体缔约方强烈反对的解释,直接导致 NAFTA 自由贸易委员会的干预。2001 年 7 月 31 日,该委员会颁布了关于解释的通知,指出"公平与公正待遇"并未要求缔约方承担超出习惯国际法所确立的任何待遇标准。[1]

中国参与签订的 BITs 一般规定,外国投资享受"公平与公正待遇"。鉴于"国际最低待遇标准"的实践和法理缺陷,中国未接受该用语。[2]

(四) 征收及补偿标准

尽管措辞和强调的重心不同,在所有 BITs 中实际上可找到有关征收的基本规则的共同点,即:(1) 东道国有权在某些情势下征收外国投资;(2) 应当支付补偿;(3) 如果因有关补偿发生争端,可诉诸独立的仲裁。[3] 在 BITs 中,征收条款一般涉及征收的定义、征收的条件及补偿标准。[4] 以下简介有关新发展。

1. 间接征收的定义

传统上,在 BITs 的征收条款中,一般都采用"相当于国有化或征收效果的措施"(measures tantamount to nationalization or expropriation)的用语,指东道国政府在未从法律上取得外国投资者所有权的情况下,采取阻碍或影响外国投资者对其资产行使有效控制权、使用权或处分权的行为,诸如强制国产化、强制股权转让、强制转让经营权、不适当地大幅度提高税率等。此类措施亦称为事实上征收(*de facto* expropriation)、逐渐征收(creeping expropriation)、间接征收(indirect expropriation)或本地化(indigenization or localization)。然而,对特定 BIT 的缔约双方而言,"相当于国有化或征收效果的措施"究竟何所指? 如何认定? 则需要进一步解释或澄清。

鉴于此,近年发达国家的 BITs 范本对"间接征收"的含义及其认定标准专门作出规定。加拿大 2004 年 BIT 范本可作为典型的例子。该范本第 13 条题为"征收",第 1 款提及"间接征收"的概念,为求更大的稳定性,附 B.13(1)对"间接征收"的概念作了如下澄清:

---

〔1〕 See UNCTAD, *Bilateral Investment Treaties 1995-2006*: *Trends in Investment Rulemaking*, United Nations, 2007, pp. 29-30.

〔2〕 关于"国际最低待遇标准"的评论,参见姚梅镇著:《国际投资法》,武汉大学出版社 1985 年版,第 302—306 页。

〔3〕 See Paul Peters, Recent Developments in Expropriation Clauses of Asian Investment Treaties, *Asian Yearbook of International Law*, Vol. 5, 1995, p. 97.

〔4〕 关于征收及其补偿标准的较详细评述,参见曾华群:《外资征收及其补偿标准:历史的分野与现实的挑战》,载陈安主编:《国际经济法学刊》第 13 卷第 1 期,北京大学出版社 2006 年版,第 38—69 页。

　　"征收

　　缔约双方确认其共识：

　　（1）间接征收产生于由缔约一方采取具有相当于直接征收后果的未正式转移所有权或未完全没收的一种或一系列措施；

　　（2）缔约一方采取的一种或一系列措施是否构成间接征收需要通过个案、基于事实的调查认定，考虑的因素包括：

　　（i）该措施或该系列措施的经济影响，虽然仅有缔约一方采取的一种或一系列措施对投资的经济价值具有负面影响之事实不足以确立间接征收已发生；

　　（ii）该措施或该系列措施对明确、合理的投资预期的干预程度；及

　　（iii）该措施或该系列措施的特性；

　　（3）除非在极个别的情况下，例如就其宗旨而言，严格意义上，一种或一系列措施不能被合理地视为已被善意采取和实施，缔约一方旨在和适用于保护合法的公共福利目标如健康、安全和环境的非歧视措施，不构成间接征收。"

　　上述条款的要点及其意义可简要解读如下：

　　第一，明确了间接征收产生于东道国的措施。东道国采取的具有相当于直接征收后果的未正式转移外国投资者所有权或未完全没收外国投资的一种或一系列措施，产生了间接征收。在此，何谓"具有相当于直接征收后果"并不明确，留下了相当大的解释空间。

　　第二，是否构成间接征收需要通过个案、基于事实的调查认定，考虑的因素包括该措施或该系列措施的经济影响、该措施或该系列措施对明确、合理的投资预期的干预程度及该措施或该系列措施的特性。该规定仅仅表明，仅凭该措施或该系列措施对投资的经济价值具有负面影响之事实不足以确立间接征收已发生，但对于其他两个因素的考虑及其标准，即如何判定措施的"干预程度"，如何判定措施的"特性"，未作进一步规定。显然，考虑的三方面因素都是很抽象的。在此情况下，投资者母国主管机构对于判断间接征收是否发生具有很大的自由裁量权。

　　第三，一般而言，缔约一方旨在和适用于保护合法的公共福利目标如健康、安全和环境的非歧视措施，不构成间接征收，但不能被合理地视为已善意采取和实施的此类措施，不在此限。这意味着，即使是基于公共利益的非歧视措施，也可能以"非善意"而归入"间接征收"的范围。[1]

---

　　〔1〕　在 2000 年 8 月 22 日作出裁决的 Metalclad 案例中，墨西哥未曾预料其环境保护措施可被视为 NAFTA 项下的征收。See M. Sornarajah, A Developing Country Perspectives of International Economic Law in the Context of Dispute Settlement, in Asif H. Qureshi(ed.), *Perspectives in International Economic Law*, Kluwer Law International, 2002, p. 88.

2. 征收的条件

在阿里专题研究考察的 335 个 BITs 中,关于征收的条件,有 309 个 BITs 规定以"为了公共利益"作为实行任何征收措施的条件,139 个 BITs 还要求"非歧视",37 个 BITs 则进一步要求"非歧视和不得违反不征收的具体承诺",只有 24 个 BITs 未明示规定以"为了公共利益"作为征收条件,而规定了"非歧视和不得违反不征收的具体承诺"。仅有 2 个 BITs 未明示规定有关征收的条件,只要求作出征收的补偿。关于补偿标准的规定亦各不相同。一些 BITs 规定了公正(just)、完全(full)、合理(reasonable)或公平与公正(fair and equitable)的补偿标准。多数 BITs 从投资价值的角度规定补偿标准,分别规定"以征收之日的价值"(92 个 BITs)、"公平价值"(3 个 BITs)、"真正价值"(70 个 BITs)或"市场价值"(83 个 BITs)作为补偿标准。335 个 BITs 均规定征收补偿数额应不迟延地转移或不得不适当迟延地转移。同时,相当数量的 BITs 允许在有效转移中适当迟延。124 个 BITs 规定,在迟延的情况下,东道国应按一般商业利率支付利息。9 个 BITs 则规定上述利率由缔约双方商定。[1]

20 世纪 90 年代以来,发达国家在 BITs 实践中,一般列举三至四项征收的前提条件,有些仅列举两项条件,另一些则列举五至六项条件。依使用的频率,列为征收前提条件的包括:(1) 赔偿;(2) 公共目的;(3) 非歧视;(4) 正当法律程序;(5) 不违反具体承诺;(6) 全部适用(catch-all);(7) 透明度;(8) 公平待遇。[2] 一些国家,主要是资本输出国主张,根据习惯国际法,国家允许征收外国投资需要符合四项条件,即:(1) 公共目的;(2) 基于非歧视;(3) 根据正当法律程序;(4) 支付及时、充分、有效的赔偿。对 1995 年以来签订的 BITs 的一项研究表明,绝大多数包含了上述四项条件。[3]

从发达国家关于征收的典型规定可见,首先,发达国家依然把"不得征收"外资作为一般的法律原则。虽然发达国家并非一般地否定国家对外资的征收权,但对征收权作了严格的限制性前提条件,以是否满足前提条件为依据进一步区分了"合法的征收"和"非法的征收",并主张依国际法和国内法(包括投资者母国和投资东道国的法律)保留对东道国政府征收行为是否合法的裁判权。其次,发达国家更为强调"赫尔"规则,即"给予及时、充分和有效赔偿"的标准。在上述对征收权的四项前提

---

〔1〕 See Mohamed I. Khalil, Treatment of Foreign Investment in Bilateral Investment Treaties, *ICSID Review-Foreign Investment Law Journal*, Vol. 7, 1992, pp. 374-375.

〔2〕 See Paul Peters, Recent Developments in Expropriation Clauses of Asian Investment Treaties, *Asian Yearbook of International Law*, Vol. 5, 1995, pp. 56-67.

〔3〕 See UNCTAD, *Bilateral Investment Treaties 1995-2006: Trends in Investment Rulemaking*, United Nations, 2007, p. 47.

条件中，"给予及时、充分和有效赔偿"无疑是决定性的。对发展中国家来说，在实行征收时满足为公共利益目的、依照法律程序、非歧视性等三项前提条件是相对容易做到的，而"给予及时、充分和有效赔偿"则难以做到，甚至无法做到。因为发展中国家经济能力有限，在为实行经济改革目标进行大规模征收时，往往无力支付"及时、充分和有效赔偿"。而一旦无力支付，则征收就无法实施。如果强行实施，就将被判定为"非法的征收"，须承担国际责任。在此情况下，发展中国家的征收权实际上被彻底否定了。[1]

3. 征收的补偿标准

20 世纪 70—80 年代，适当补偿原则在理论上占主流地位，在实践上亦有不同程度的反映。90 年代以来，随着国际政治、经济形势的发展，一些发展中国家为解决债务危机或出于吸收外资的实际需要，在 BITs 中，对发达国家作出了不同程度的让步或妥协。在此情势下，"赫尔"规则似乎回潮，俨然成为"时尚"。

在征收补偿标准方面，出现了一些体现"赫尔"规则的条约实践。如加拿大 2004 年 BIT 范本第 13 条第 1 款规定了"及时、充分和有效"的赔偿。对 1995—2006 年 BITs 实践的研究表明，一个重要趋向是多数 BITs 采用了具有适用"及时、充分和有效"赔偿标准效果的用语。一些发展中国家相互之间的 BITs，如埃及与泰国之间 BIT、文莱与韩国之间 BIT 也有类似的实践。[2]

（五）投资财产的转移

外国投资者在海外投资的主要目标是获取利润并汇回其母国。因此，保护外资原本和利润的汇出权成为 BITs 的目标之一。

BITs 一般规定，缔约一方应保证缔约另一方的投资者自由转移其投资原本、收益以及与投资有关的款项。美国 BIT 范本规定，缔约各方应允许"所有有关涵盖投资的转移自由地和不得迟延地进出其领土"，并允许投资者"以自由的可用货币按转移当日通行的市场汇率"兑换其货币。所谓"与投资有关的转移"，分为两类：一是投资者正常经营过程中所发生的转移，二是缔约一方因违法向投资者支付的赔偿。[3]

在阿里专题研究考察的 335 个 BITs 中，均规定投资收益须不迟延地转移。然

---

〔1〕 有西方学者指出，应区分两种征收：一是小规模的、只涉及少数人的征收，二是大规模的、长远社会改革进程中的征收。前者不会因征收补偿问题而影响到国家的财政能力；而后一种征收，如按"赫尔"规则要求，东道国可能因征收赔偿数额过高而对必不可少的征收迟疑不决。See Ignaz Seidl Hohenveldern, *International Economic Law*, 2nd revised edition, Martinus Nijhoff Publishers, 1992, p. 138.

〔2〕 See UNCTAD, *Bilateral Investment Treaties 1995-2006：Trends in Investment Rulemaking*, United Nations, 2007, p. 48.

〔3〕 See Paul E. Comeaux, N. Stephan Kinsella, *Protecting Foreign Investment under International Law, Legal Aspects of Political Risk*, Oceana Publications Inc., 1997, pp. 107-108.

而,考虑到许多发展中国家因其国际收支状况而难以承受大量外币及时转移,60 多个 BITs 规定可分期转移投资收益,22 个 BITs 规定可迟延转移投资原本。1/5 左右的 BITs 允许大量资金的转移(如投资企业清算时投资原本的汇回等)以分期支付的方式进行,期限为 3—5 年。195 个 BITs 规定了外汇汇率。其中,131 个 BITs 规定按照官方或市场汇率,64 个 BITs 规定应遵守 IMF 的外汇规则。许多 BITs 还保证外国投资企业中外国员工工资适当部分的转移。多数 BITs 规定,外国投资者可自由转移其因战争、武装冲突、革命、内乱或国家紧急状态等遭受损失所得的补偿。[1]

许多 BITs 规定了汇出权的绝对保护。这是不现实的,在缔约一方发生因外汇短缺而需要采取外汇管制的情况下,将产生问题。英国参与签订的 BITs 通常规定了汇出权在"特殊的经济或金融情势下"将予以限制。在另一些英国签订的 BITs 中,规定了在外汇困难情况下,投资者每年可汇出利润的百分比要求(一般是 20%)。对征收补偿额的汇出问题,通常在 BITs 中专门作出规定。[2]

在 1995—2006 年的 BITs 实践中,绝大多数 BITs 规定了资产转移条款。此条款给予外国投资者不迟延地转移与投资有关的资金、以规定的汇率使用特定货币的权利。在该条款是否涵盖资金的汇出和汇入,是否任何种类的转移均予以保护或限于明示列举者,该转移权利是否需要根据国内法行使等方面,规定各不相同。相当多数的 BITs 包含了例外规定,主要是确保遵守特定法律(例如有关破产的法律)和保障东道国适当执行其金融货币政策。多数 BITs 未包含处理收支平衡危机的例外条款。[3]

尽管措辞不同,中外 BITs 均对投资收益的自由转移提供了保障。此类措辞有"允许""保证""保障""许可"等。同时还增加了"不得无故迟延""不得作不当限制"和"在不歧视的基础上"等条件。大多数协定规定,可自由汇出的利润包括投资收益,支付与投资有关贷款的资金、补充资金,缔约另一方国民作为雇员的工资收入,部分或全部清算投资的费用、特许费、征收补偿费。

（六）投资争端的解决

BITs 区分缔约国双方关于 BITs 的解释和适用问题的争端和缔约国一方与缔约国另一方国民之间的投资争端,分别规定适用不同的争端解决方式。

---

[1] See Mohamed I. Khalil, Treatment of Foreign Investment in Bilateral Investment Treaties, *ICSID Review-Foreign Investment Law Journal*, Vol. 7, 1992, pp. 360-361.

[2] See M. Sornarajah, A Developing Country Perspectives of International Economic Law in the Context of Dispute Settlement, in Asif H. Qureshi(ed.), *Perspectives in International Economic Law*, Kluwer Law International, 2002, pp. 252-253.

[3] See UNCTAD, *Bilateral Investment Treaties 1995-2006: Trends in Investment Rulemaking*, United Nations, 2007, p. xii.

对于缔约国双方关于协定的解释和适用的争端，一般先应采取协商解决的方式，如果在规定时限内未能解决，可根据缔约国任何一方的请求，将争端提交特设（ad hoc）国际仲裁庭解决。[1] 新中德 BIT 第 8 条规定："一、缔约双方对本协定的解释或适用所产生的争议，应尽可能通过外交途径协商解决。二、如果争议在六个月内未能协商解决，根据缔约任何一方的要求，可将争议提交专设仲裁庭解决。"该条第 3—7 款详细规定了特设仲裁庭的组成、仲裁程序及仲裁费用等，还特别规定了法律适用问题，即"仲裁庭应按照本协定以及缔约双方都承认的国际法的原则作出裁决"。

对于缔约国一方与缔约国另一方投资者之间的投资争端，首先通过友好协商解决，如果在确定时间内不能解决，可以诉诸当地行政或司法程序。中国与丹麦、荷兰、法国、比利时—卢森堡、挪威、澳大利亚等国的 BITs 都规定了诉诸当地救济的程序。对此类争端中涉及征收的补偿金额者，除适用上述解决方式外，也可选择将争端提交特设国际仲裁庭解决。新中荷 BIT 规定了选择性的解决方式：(1) 尽可能由争端各当事方友好解决；(2) 投资者可决定将争端提交有管辖权的国内法院；(3) 如自提交友好解决之日起 6 个月内未能解决，缔约各方无条件同意应有关投资者要求将争端提交 ICSID 或依照《联合国国际贸易法委员会仲裁规则》建立的特设仲裁庭解决。[2]

许多 BITs 规定在中立的仲裁机构仲裁，作为解决缔约国一方与缔约国另一方投资者之间投资争端的方式，这方面有显著的进展。关于此类争端的仲裁解决条款，有多种类型，产生了不同的责任。在最低层面上，有关条款只是指示缔约各方将仲裁作为此类争端的解决方式，此类规定仅仅表述仲裁作为此类争端的解决方式，对缔约各方未产生强制性的提交仲裁的责任。在最高层面上，一些 BITs 规定，外国投资者可向 ICSID 提交仲裁申请。此类条款赋予外国投资者直接诉诸中立的国际仲裁庭以解决其与东道国之间的投资争端。[3] 可以认为，让外国投资者自己处理与东道国之间的投资争端，有助于此类争端的"非政治化"，因为此类争端未演变为投

---

〔1〕　参见李适时：《论中国签订的双边投资保护协定》，载于《中国国际法年刊》(1990)，第 121—122 页。

〔2〕　新中荷 BIT 第 10 条。

〔3〕　阿里专题研究报告指出，几乎所有考察的协定均规定了解决投资争端的仲裁条款。其中，212 个协定规定了 ICSID 条款，或将 ICSID 仲裁作为解决投资争端的唯一方式，或作为方式之一。See Mohamed I. Khalil, Treatment of Foreign Investment in Bilateral Investment Treaties, *ICSID Review-Foreign Investment Law Journal*, Vol. 7，1992，pp. 382-383.

资者母国与东道国之间的争端。[1]

值得注意的是，当前，越来越多的 BITs 通过允许外国投资者单方面诉诸国际仲裁机制而给予外国投资高水平的具有强制力的保护标准。一些拉丁美洲国家放弃了长期坚持的卡尔沃主义，允许此类新标准规定于其缔结的 BITs 中。一种观点认为，它们以前坚持的新国际秩序原则已是"明日黄花"。自 AAPL v. Sri Lanka 案开始，不断积累的许多案例表明，BITs 的有关规定创设了外国投资者单方面诉诸国际仲裁的权利。因此，尽管在外国投资者签订的合同中实际上没有仲裁条款，BITs 的有关规定可被援引解释为东道国政府对外国投资者诉诸国际仲裁的事先同意。在依此方式确立管辖权的仲裁庭的裁决中，对这种"推定同意"（construction of consent）的理论难题未作阐述。此类问题包括"未用尽当地救济原则"是否可成为此种管辖权的障碍，在签订 BITs 时不在缔约方考虑之列的投资者可否援引东道国政府的"事先同意"等。[2]

在 1995—2006 年的 BITs 实践中，一些 BITs 详细规定了缔约国一方与缔约国另一方投资者之间解决投资争端的程序，为争端双方提供了有关仲裁活动的更多规则，增强了审理机制的规则取向。然而，多数 BITs 继续采用传统的方式，即规定解决外国投资者与东道国争端的主要方面，细节问题由具体的仲裁公约予以规范。此外，一些新的 BITs 纳入了不同的创新性规定，旨在促进一些目标的实现，此类目标包括提供更明显的可预见性，促进司法经济，确保裁决的一致性以及促进仲裁程序在市民社会中的合法性等。[3]

三、变革期 BITs 实践引发的思考

如前所述，变革期 BITs 主要条款的内容有了许多重要的发展，在相当程度上影响了 BITs 实践的总体发展趋势，似乎 BITs 实践的发展已进入发达国家依其传统主张精心设计的运行轨道。笔者以为，为维护经济主权，发展中国家在 BITs 实践中，不仅需要关注具体条款的谈判，对以下问题似应有进一步的思考和把握。

（一）BITs 主要功能的偏向性

一般认为，BITs 具有双重功能：一是为外国投资者提供在东道国投资的法律保

---

〔1〕 See M. Sornarajah, A Developing Country Perspectives of International Economic Law in the Context of Dispute Settlement, in Asif H. Qureshi(ed.), *Perspectives in International Economic Law*, Kluwer Law International, 2002, pp. 265-266.

〔2〕 Ibid., pp. 90-91, 106-107.

〔3〕 See UNCTAD, *Bilateral Investment Treaties 1995-2006: Trends in Investment Rulemaking*, United Nations, 2007, p. xii.

护;另一是促进投资的跨国流动。[1] 有学者从自由经济理论出发,进一步分析 BITs 在促进投资自由化和经济发展双重目标上的功能。[2] 在经济全球化趋势下,BITs 的功能主要表现在:

第一,保护跨国投资。主要通过创设有关跨国投资的法律制度保护外国投资和外国投资者。例如,给予缔约国对方投资者以国民待遇或最惠国待遇,规定征收或国有化的条件和补偿标准等,从而创设了良好的投资环境;为缔约国双方的国民或企业预先规定建立投资关系所应遵循的法律规范,避免或减少了法律障碍,促使当事人较顺利地达成投资协议;规定解决投资争端的程序,包括谈判、协商、调解、仲裁以至司法解决等方式,便于及时、妥善地解决投资争端。

第二,促进跨国投资与投资自由化。必须指出,投资促进是发展中国家的基本目标,投资与市场自由化是发达国家的附属目标,两者是分立和不同的。在 BITs 体制内,对东道国而言,投资促进意味着吸收东道国批准的投资项目符合其最高利益;而投资自由化,作为资本输出国青睐的用语,一般指创设由投资者依其利益作出评估的投资环境。[3] 受益于全球自由贸易的发达国家,目前控制了充分的政治和经济权力,正通过 WTO 体制、区域贸易协定(RTAs)和 BITs 保障其惬意的有关自由化、私有化和外国投资的政策。[4]

由上可见,BITs 的所谓双重功能其实都侧重于对外国投资和外国投资者的保护。值得注意的是,发达国家一直致力于利用条约推进投资自由化,特别是在《多边投资协定》(MAI)谈判搁浅和 WTO 投资议题谈判进展缓慢的情况下,更加重视在 BITs 和 RTAs 纳入投资自由化条款。当前,OECD 国家参与 BITs 和 RTAs 实践的重心已从传统的投资保护转向更广泛的自由化规则。外资待遇标准更为侧重投资准入阶段的保护和新的自由化承诺。[5] 在变革期 BITs 实践中,东道国投资促进政策中的外资审批权力逐渐演变为承认"设立权"、禁止"履行要求"和投资自由化义务,征收的四项前提条件和征收赔偿的"赫尔"规则得以强化适用等,进一步加剧了

---

〔1〕 See Paul E. Comeaux, N. Stephan Kinsella, *Protecting Foreign Investment under International Law*, *Legal Aspects of Political Risk*, Oceana Publications Inc., 1997, p. 101.

〔2〕 Kenneth J. Vandevelde, Investment Liberalization and Economic Development: The Role of Bilateral Investment Treaties, *Columbia Journal of Transnational Law*, Vol. 36, 1998, pp. 503-504.

〔3〕 See Jeswald W. Salacuse, Nicholas P. Sullivan, Do BITs Really Work? An Evaluation of Bilateral Investment Treaties and Their Grand Bargain, *Harvard International Law Journal*, Vol. 46, 2005, pp. 78-79.

〔4〕 See M. Sornarajah, A Developing Country Perspectives of International Economic Law in the Context of Dispute Settlement, in Asif H. Qureshi(ed.), *Perspectives in International Economic Law*, Kluwer Law International, 2002, p. 83.

〔5〕 OECD Secretariat, *Novel Features in OECD Countries' Recent Investment Agreements: An Overview*, Document for Symposium Co-organized by ICSID, OECD and UNCTAD on Making the Most of International Invest, p. 4.

BITs 主要功能的偏向性，即更侧重于对外国投资和外国投资者的保护，而基本上忽略了东道国投资促进和管理的政策目标。

（二）发达国家与发展中国家签订 BITs 的不同动机

传统上，取决于在国际投资活动中的不同地位和角色，发达国家与发展中国家签订 BITs 的动机明显不同：发达国家主要是为了扩大本国私人资本输出以获取海外高额利润，增强国际竞争能力，因此，试图通过 BITs 的有关条款来确保其海外投资的安全和既得利益；而发展中国家则主要是为了创设较好的投资环境，以利于吸收和利用外国投资发展本国经济，因此，在对境内外国投资实行保护的同时，希望通过 BITs 的有关条款规定本国对境内外国投资实行管制的权力和外国投资者必须遵守东道国法律等义务。两种动机的重大差异决定了在有关 BITs 的内容和实施方面，发达国家与发展中国家之间一直存在尖锐的斗争：在内容方面，发达国家力图主要规定投资者的权利和资本输入国的义务，发展中国家则主张确立资本输入国对外国投资实行管制的权力；在实施方面，发展中国家主张有关条约的解释和适用的争端，应根据条约的规定通过谈判、仲裁或司法解决，而某些发达国家则习惯于依仗其政治经济实力，通过国内立法，逼迫发展中国家接受其意志。[1]

冷战结束以来，发达国家参与 BITs 的实践也日渐显现其政治目的。在一些发达国家看来，BITs 的另一目的是对 20 世纪 50 至 70 年代期间发展中国家有关征收的传统国际法的反击。[2] 有西方学者指出，美国的 BITs 计划支持东欧国家和苏联集团走向民主和资本主义发展的进程。BITs 可通过在这些国家中提供对美资的保护以促进投资，同时，通过向这些国家提供外资保护的法律框架以吸引投资。[3]

变革期的 BITs 实践表明，发达国家与发展中国家参与 BITs 实践的不同动机依然如故。值得注意的是，发达国家得益于经济全球化的"天时"，在经济和政治双重动机的驱使下，更为积极地推行其 BITs 计划，实现其参与 BITs 实践的种种目标。在此情况下，发展中国家力图通过 BITs 加强对外国投资的管制权力将面临更严峻的挑战。换言之，发展中国家参与 BITs 实践的预期目标更加难以实现。

（三）发达国家与发展中国家之间 BITs 当事方的不平等

应当指出，发达的资本输出国与发展中的资本输入国之间 BITs 是不平等当事方之间的条约。虽然 BITs 适用于缔约双方的双向投资，但实际考虑的只是单向投

---

[1] 例如，1962 年，以巴西征收美国企业为起因，美国通过了"希肯卢珀修正案"，其中规定，如果采取国有化措施的国家对被征收的美国人资产不按美国所理解的"国际法标准"赔偿，美国就断绝对该国的援助。

[2] See Paul E. Comeaux, N. Stephan Kinsella, *Protecting Foreign Investment under International Law, Legal Aspects of Political Risk*, Oceana Publications Inc., 1997, p. 101.

[3] Ibid., pp. 101-102, note 9.

资。在缔约双方资金和技术差距悬殊的情况下,这是显而易见的。因此,声称作为条约基础的"双向流动"是冠冕堂皇的虚构,缺乏充分的对价。这种不平等当事方之间的条约产生一些耐人寻味的问题,诸如:参与签订 BITs 的发展中国家是否拥有能充分理解条约用语的细微差别的法律专家? BITs 的签订能否实际产生资本输出国的资本流向资本输入国的效果? 此类协定未包含资本输出国保证此种外资流动的明确责任,而资本输入国为得到此种"预期的外资流动"必须先让渡其主权,平等何在? 尽管存在此种不平等,BITs 表面上是合法的,签订此种条约的国家被推定为愿意受其约束。除非有胁迫的证据(如以提供援助、贷款或贸易优惠为签约的条件),应认为 BITs 是基于自愿的基础达成的。[1]

变革期的 BITs 实践表明,无论是 BITs 新议题的提出,还是传统条款的革新,主导和推动的力量均来自发达国家。在 BITs 谈判中,凭借经济实力和谈判人才等方面的明显优势,某些发达国家以其 BIT 范本为谈判基础,"一言九鼎",而发展中国家一般处于被动接受的地位,甚至是落入发达国家精心设计的圈套。相应地,BITs 发展的趋势是,越来越重视和加强对外国投资和外国投资者的保护,如"设立权"模式、"赫尔"规则的采用等。显然,BITs 谈判当事方地位和能力的不平等直接影响了BITs 的权益平衡问题。

(四) 发达国家与发展中国家在 BITs 中权益的不平衡

虽然几乎所有 BITs 都规定了相互性的投资待遇,由于多数发达国家与发展中国家之间的 BITs 是由发达国家启动的,两类国家之间的投资关系基本上是单向性的,哪一缔约方投资者需要来自哪一缔约方的保护昭然若揭。[2] 可见,投资待遇的相互性只是表面的、形式上的。实质上,投资待遇越高,意味着赋予资本输出国及其跨国投资者越大的权益,对资本输入国则施加更繁重的义务。

按发达国家的逻辑,限制东道国自主选择投资政策和措施,对外国投资提供高水平的法律保护,"自然而然"带来了外资输入东道国的后果,这就是"平衡资本输出国与资本输入国之间的权益"。在传统 BITs 的内容设计中,资本输入国自主选择外资政策和措施的权力和权利受到限制,同时承担了保护外资的义务;而资本输出国的权力和权利未受任何限制,其跨国投资者的权利受到高水平的国际法保护,资本

---

〔1〕　See M. Sornarajah, A Developing Country Perspectives of International Economic Law in the Context of Dispute Settlement, in Asif H. Qureshi(ed.), *Perspectives in International Economic Law*, Kluwer Law International, 2002, pp. 227-229.

〔2〕　See Paul E. Comeaux, N. Stephan Kinsella, *Protecting Foreign Investment under International Law*, *Legal Aspects of Political Risk*, Oceana Publications Inc., 1997, p. 102.

输出国及其跨国投资者均未承担任何义务。这实际上是片面维护了资本输出国的权益。需要明确的是，所谓"平衡资本输出国与资本输入国之间的权益"，意味着在 BITs 内容设计中，资本输出国与资本输入国都要享有权力和权利，并承担相应的义务，真正平衡资本输出国与资本输入国之间的权益以及东道国与外国投资者之间的权益。

作为平衡发展中国家与发达国家的权益的具体体现，BITs 应具有保护、促进跨国投资与管制跨国投资者行为的双重目标。早在 20 世纪 70 年代初，国际社会进行了国际投资立法另一方面的多边努力。该努力的重心是管制外国投资者，特别是跨国公司的不良行为。多年来，一些国际组织，包括 UNCTAD、OECD、国际商会和国际劳工组织等先后起草了有关管制跨国公司行为（包括竞争、税务、雇佣关系、技术转让、贿赂、信息及披露等）的规则。然而，这方面努力所取得的进展甚微。应当指出，一直以来，保护国际投资和促进投资自由化的努力与管制跨国投资者行为的努力分别在不同的场所进行。两种努力各行其道，均未能构建起达到其目标所需要的多边法律框架。从国际现实出发，也许两种努力应合并进行。[1] 在 BITs 的设计中，发展中国家应具有自主决定外资准入领域、外资履行要求的权力，并承担保护跨国投资的义务；而发达国家则须承担监管本国海外投资的责任，承诺和保护发展中国家免受外国投资者，特别是跨国公司负面行为方式的损害。

（五）发展中国家相互之间 BITs 实践对 BITs 的发展趋势具有重要意义

关于 BITs 的国际法效力，学界见解不同。一些发达国家制订了有关 BIT 谈判的计划，通常以 BIT 范本作为与发展中国家谈判的依据，范本的许多条款基于习惯国际法的规则。[2] 有学者主张，BITs 将导向习惯国际法的产生。另有学者主张，BITs 在创立国际投资法律规则方面具有一定的价值。[3] 还有学者指出，考虑到 BITs 的网络已覆盖各大陆和第一世界、第二世界和第三世界国家，可以认为，作为整体的 BITs 是习惯国际法的证据，即使在特定条约中对某些情况或争议点未明确规定，BITs 也是可以适用的。一些学者强烈反对这一结论，主张 BITs 仅仅是缔约双方之间的特别法。其主要理由是，要产生或证明习惯法，各国不仅需要遵循一定的实

---

〔1〕 See Jeswald W. Salacuse, Nicholas P. Sullivan, Do BITs Really Work? An Evaluation of Bilateral Investment Treaties and Their Grand Bargain, *Harvard International Law Journal*, Vol. 46, 2005, pp. 87-88.

〔2〕 See Paul E. Comeaux, N. Stephan Kinsella, *Protecting Foreign Investment under International Law, Legal Aspects of Political Risk*, Oceana Publications Inc., 1997, pp. 102-103.

〔3〕 See M. Sornarajah, A Developing Country Perspectives of International Economic Law in the Context of Dispute Settlement, in Asif H. Qureshi(ed.), *Perspectives in International Economic Law*, Kluwer Law International, 2002, pp. 73-74.

践,还需要具有法律确信。[1] 无论如何,可以肯定的是,BITs 在不同程度上促进或影响了有关国际投资的国际法规范的形成和发展。

如前所述,就缔约双方的组合而言,BITs 可分为发达国家与发展中国家之间的BITs、发达国家相互之间的 BITs 和发展中国家相互之间的 BITs。其中,发达国家与发展中国家之间的 BITs、发达国家相互之间的 BITs 在很大程度上是由发达国家主导的。变革期 BITs 实践表明,发达国家站在资本输出国的立场,极力强化对跨国投资的国际法保护,弱化东道国管制外国投资的权力。在当前的国际体制下,期望发达国家自觉改弦更张,主动平衡发达国家与发展中国家之间的权益,显然是不现实的。在发达国家企图以其 BIT 范本"一统天下"的情势下,发展中国家相互之间的BITs 实践如何发展,关系重大。是屈从于发达国家主导的 BITs 实践之"大势",还是另辟蹊径,在创立和发展新型 BITs 方面有所作为,是值得认真思考的重大理论和现实问题。笔者以为,在此类 BITs 实践中,发展中国家作为平等的缔约双方,具有建立国际经济新秩序的共同历史使命和奋斗目标,可根据《各国经济权利和义务宪章》确立的经济主权原则、公平互利原则和合作发展原则,在强调"发展"宗旨、维护东道国经济主权、平衡资本输入国与资本输出国的权益等方面形成和发展新的法律概念、规则和标准,逐渐形成新型 BITs 的普遍实践,进而影响发达国家与发展中国家之间 BITs 的实践以及 BITs 的总体发展趋势。

Bilateral Investment Treaty Practice in the Changing Period

Abstracts: After exploring the main features of bilateral investment treaty (BIT) practice and development of BITs' main provisions in the changing period, the author points out that the developing countries should further consider and grasp some important issues, such as the deviation of main functions of BITs, the different motives of developed countries and developing countries for concluding BITs, the unequal status of parties to BITs between developed countries and developing countries, the imbalance of rights and interests of parties to BITs between developed countries and developing countries, and the significance of BITs practice between developing countries to the general trend of the development of BITs.

---

[1] See Andreas F. Lowenfeld, *International Economic Law*, Oxford University Press, 2002, pp. 486-488.

第三节 "可持续发展的投资政策框架"与我国的对策[*]

【摘要】 联合国贸易和发展会议（UNCTAD）制定的"可持续发展的投资政策框架"（IPFSD）产生的主要背景是传统国际投资政策本身面临严峻的挑战和南北国家的国际投资地位发生了显著变化。IPFSD 的主要创新表现在从"偏重保护外资权益"到"促进东道国可持续发展"，从"偏重保护外资"到"平衡当事双方权利义务"，保护外资和管制外资从"各行其道"到"一体化"三个方面。我国的立场和对策应当是促进形成共识，支持 UNCTAD 制定"可持续发展友好型"BIT 范本；建立和健全基于 IPFSD 的我国海外投资法律制度；及时制定我国"可持续发展友好型"BIT 范本，积极开展相关实践。

【关键词】 "可持续发展的投资政策框架"；国际投资政策；可持续发展；一体化

联合国贸易和发展会议（UNCTAD）《2012 年世界投资报告》题为"迈向新一代投资政策"，制定了"可持续发展的投资政策框架"（Investment Policy Framework for Sustainable Development，IPFSD），表明国际社会对国际投资政策的"共同路径"取得了初步共识，也在一定程度上反映了国际投资政策的最新发展趋向。在"新一代投资政策"语境中，"投资政策"包括国内法方面的外国投资立法和国际法方面的国际投资条约实践。我国作为发展中大国，且具有资本输入国和资本输出国双重身份，亟须在分析 IPFSD 产生背景的基础上，重视其主要创新因素，并确立相应的立场和对策。

一、"可持续发展的投资政策框架"的产生背景

IPFSD 是国际投资政策经历长期发展、面临重大转折点的产物。其产生的主要背景是传统国际投资政策本身面临严峻的挑战，南北国家的国际投资地位发生显著变化，引发了国际社会调整国际投资秩序的动机和需求。

（一）传统国际投资政策面临严峻挑战

追根溯源，传统国际投资政策是由发达的资本输出国创造并服务于其对外经济政策的。因此，以促进和保护海外投资作为其主旨，自始片面强调资本输出国及其

———————————
* 原载《厦门大学学报》（哲学社会科学版）2013 年第 6 期。
基金项目：国家社科基金重大项目"促进与保护我国海外投资的法律体制研究"（09&ZD032）。

海外投资者的权益当属顺理成章,也是其先天的、不可磨灭的深刻烙印。长期以来,在发达国家的主导下,传统国际投资政策片面强调对外资和外国投资者的保护和优惠,这实际上也是取决于南北国家的实力。就各国普遍采用的双边投资条约(bilateral investment treaties,BITs)而言,理论上,BITs 是国家之间双边谈判的结果,旨在为缔约双方提供同等的法律保护。事实上,它们常常是作为资本输出国的发达国家与作为资本输入国的发展中国家之间的协定。特定 BIT 所规定的投资保护规则和标准,是缔约双方的期望与它们各自的谈判地位、谈判实力交互作用的结果。当前,BITs 发展的趋势是,越来越重视和加强对外资和外国投资者的保护,如"设立权"(right of establishment)模式、外国投资者单方诉诸国际仲裁的权利等。历史表明,肇始于 20 世纪 50 年代末期的 BITs 实践片面维护资本输出国和外国投资者权益的"先天不足",在长达 50 多年的"后天"不仅未得到应有的纠正,反而被发达国家不断强化和扩张。[1]

　　此种"失衡"的传统国际投资政策,由于严重背离了国际社会普遍认同的经济主权、公平互利和合作发展原则,已面临严峻挑战,甚至面临合法性或正当性危机。2011 年 4 月,澳大利亚颁布一项贸易政策声明,宣称其在将来签订的国际投资协定(international investment agreements,IIAs)[2]中,不再接受"投资者与国家之间争端解决"(investor-State dispute settlement,ISDS)条款。其原因是,该条款给予外国企业高于本国企业的法律权利,且限制了政府的公共决策能力(如社会、环境和经济法律的制定与履行)。[3] 近年来,更有来自发展中国家的激烈反应。例如,"卡尔沃主义"的故乡拉美国家,在 20 世纪 80 年代末转变其抵制 IIAs 的立场,近 20 年来同世界各国签订了 500 多项 BITs。然而,鉴于 IIAs"自由化"发展削弱国家经济主权的新情势,一些拉美国家不得不重新考虑其有关 IIAs 的立场甚至终止或退出 IIAs。[4]

---

　　〔1〕　参见曾华群:《论双边投资条约实践的"失衡"与革新》,载《江西社会科学》2010 年第 6 期。

　　〔2〕　所谓"国际投资协定"(IIAs),一般指国际投资法的主要国际法规范,包括双边投资协定(BITs),三方投资协定(triangle investment agreements,TIAs),区域性投资协定,含有投资规范的自由贸易协定(free trade agreements,FTAs)、区域贸易协定(regional trade agreements,RTAs)或经济合作伙伴协定(economic partnership agreements,EPAs)及《解决国家与他国国民间投资争端公约》(1965)、《多边投资担保机构公约》(1985)等世界性多边投资协定。

　　〔3〕　See UNCTAD, *World Investment Report 2012*, *Towards a New Generation of Investment Policies*, United Nations, 2012, p. 87.

　　〔4〕　2008 年,厄瓜多尔终止了与古巴、多米尼加、萨尔瓦多、危地马拉、洪都拉斯、尼加拉瓜、巴拉圭、罗马尼亚和乌拉圭等国签订的 9 项 BITs。其他宣布终止的 BITs 包括萨尔瓦多与尼加拉瓜、荷兰与委内瑞拉之间的 BITs。玻利维亚退出 ICSID 公约的通知于 2007 年 5 月 2 日提交 ICSID,2010 年 11 月 3 日生效。厄瓜多尔退出 ICSID 公约的通知于 2009 年 7 月 6 日提交 ICSID,2010 年 1 月 7 日生效。See Wolfgang Alschner, Ana Berdajs, Vladyslav Lanovoy and Sergey Ripinsky etc., Denunciation of the ICSID Convention and BITs: Impact on Investor-State Claims, United Nations, UNCTAD, *IIA Issues Note*, No. 1, December 2010, page 1, note 2, 3. 2011 年 6 月,玻利维亚宣布退出其与美国签订的 BIT。2012 年 1 月,委内瑞拉向 ICSID 提交退出 ICSID 公约的通知。See UNCTAD, *World Investment Report 2012*, *Towards a New Generation of Investment Policies*, United Nations, 87 (2012).

（二）南北国家的国际投资地位发生显著变化

长期以来,传统国际投资政策主要调整从发达国家流向发展中国家的投资。发达国家是资本输出国,广大发展中国家一般居于资本输入国地位。典型的 ISDS,通常指来自发达国家的外国投资者与作为东道国的发展中国家之间的投资争端解决。随着国际投资活动的发展,发达国家相互之间、发展中国家相互之间的投资也成为国际投资政策的调整对象。特别是一些发展中国家（主要是发展中大国）在继续吸收外资的同时,逐渐向发达国家投资,在一定程度上改变了发达国家与发展中国家之间的单向投资关系。近年的经济危机已凸显出经济重心由发达国家向新兴市场国家的转移,进一步加强了这一发展趋势。此外,无论在发达国家还是发展中国家,经济危机都导致政府加强其在经济发展中的作用。因此,东道国公共利益与外国投资者私人经济利益之间的矛盾冲突在所难免。在此新形势下,越来越多的发达国家也面临作为东道国的一系列涉及外资和外国投资者的政策和实务问题,甚至成为 ISDS 的当事国,被诉诸"解决投资争端国际中心"（International Centre for Settlement of Investment Disputes, ICSID）等国际投资仲裁机制。国际投资地位的改变促使发达国家反思传统国际投资政策及本国的相关立场。事实上,发达国家和一些发展中国家同样兼具资本输出国和资本输入国地位,此种"一身二任"或"身份混同",客观上有利于两类国家分别"换位思考",较全面、公正审视传统国际投资政策。在宏观层面,两类国家居于相同的立场和角度,有利于达成有关"可持续发展"和"平衡资本输出国与资本输入国权益"等共识。在实践层面,同样作为东道国,同样基于维护国内投资政策和公共利益的目的,两类国家对国际投资政策的解释、实施及发展趋向具有一定程度的共同语言和共同立场。

二、"可持续发展的投资政策框架"的主要创新

IPFSD 由"可持续发展投资决策的核心原则"（Core Principles for Investment Policymaking for Sustainable Development,简称"核心原则"）、"各国投资政策指南"（National Investment Policy Guidelines,简称"各国指南"）和"国际投资协定要素:政策选项"（Elements of International Investment Agreements: Policy Options,简称"协定要素"）三部分构成。其中,"核心原则"是"各国指南"和"协定要素"的设计标准（design criteria）,也是 IPFSD 的法理基础。总体上,IPFSD 的主要创新表现在从"偏重保护外资权益"到"促进东道国可持续发展",从"偏重保护外资"到"平衡当事双方权利义务",保护外资和管制外资从"各行其道"到"一体化"三个方面。

（一）从"偏重保护外资权益"到"促进东道国可持续发展"

传统国际投资政策偏重保护外资和外国投资者权益，未顾及东道国的经济发展，更遑论关注东道国的"可持续发展"。

近年来，"可持续发展"概念或原则被国际社会普遍接受为经济社会发展和国际关系的一般原则[1]，也成为国际投资政策的一般原则。在国际投资政策语境中，"可持续发展"可作为国际投资活动当事各方的"共赢"目标。由于它强调东道国的经济和社会发展，符合资本输入国的基本需要。由于它促进东道国形成健康的投资环境，也符合资本输出国和外国投资者的重要利益。该概念或原则不仅适用于资本输出国与资本输入国之间的关系，也适用于东道国与外国投资者之间的关系。

在传统国际投资政策中，虽未见"可持续发展"的概念，但在某些 IIAs 中仍可发现"投资"与"发展"的关联。例如，《解决国家与他国国民间投资争端公约》（ICSID 公约）序言提及"考虑到经济发展的国际合作之需要与国际私人投资在其中的作用"，可理解为"投资"对"发展"应具有某些积极影响。该公约虽未对"投资"作出定义，但可以确定，"投资"的某些典型特征已为 ICSID 仲裁庭越来越多地适用，即：(1) 项目的持续时间；(2) 利润和收益的经常性；(3) 对双方的风险；(4) 实质性承诺；(5) 对东道国发展应具有重要意义。[2] 近年来，IIAs 有关"可持续发展"的实践已有一些重要的发展。越来越多的 BITs 在序言中表明，BITs 不会为了促进和保护投资而以其他重要价值，如健康、安全、劳工保护和环境为代价。[3] 在 2011 年签订的 20 项 IIAs 中[4]，有 12 项含有"在条约序言中提及健康与安全、劳工权、环境保护或可持续发展"；11 项"明确承认双方不应为吸引投资而放宽健康、安全或环境标准"。[5] 上述规定意味着确保 IIAs 不致干扰缔约国的可持续发展战略，而是应对该战略作出贡献。

---

〔1〕 关于"可持续发展"原则的系统论述，参见〔荷兰〕尼科·斯赫雷弗：《可持续发展在国际法中的演进：起源、涵义及地位》，汪习根、黄海滨译，社会科学文献出版社 2010 年版。

〔2〕 See OECD, International Investment Law, Understanding Concepts and Tracking Innovations, Companion Volume to International Investment Perspectives，OECD，Vol. 61，No. 9，2008.

〔3〕 See UNCTAD, Bilateral Investment Treaties 1995-2006：Trends in Investment Rulemaking，United Nations，4 (2007).

〔4〕 遴选作为研究对象的 2011 年 20 项 IIAs 包括：坦桑尼亚—土耳其 BIT、尼日利亚—土耳其 BIT、墨西哥—秘鲁 FTA、韩国—秘鲁 FTA、巴拿马—秘鲁 FTA、日本—巴布新几内亚 BIT、印度—斯洛文尼亚 BIT、印度—尼泊尔 BIT、印度—马来西亚 FTA、印度—立陶宛 BIT、印度—日本 EPA、危地马拉—秘鲁 FTA、捷克—斯里兰卡 BIT、哥斯达黎加—秘鲁 FTA、哥伦比亚—日本 BIT、中国—日本—韩国 TIA、中美洲—墨西哥 FTA、波斯尼亚与黑塞哥维那—圣马力诺 BIT、阿塞拜疆—捷克 BIT 和澳大利亚—新西兰投资议定书。See UNCTAD, World Investment Report 2012，Towards a New Generation of Investment Policies，United Nations，90 (2012).

〔5〕 表 III. 3. 遴选的 2011 年 IIAs 的"可持续发展友好型"特征示范，载于 UNCTAD, World Investment Report 2012，Towards a New Generation of Investment Policies，United Nations，90 (2012)。

IPFSD 提出的"可持续发展"主要涵盖环境、社会发展、企业社会责任等内容，强调外国投资应纳入东道国的可持续发展战略，倡导各国签订"可持续发展友好型"（sustainable-development-friendly）IIAs。

IPFSD 核心原则（1）题为"为可持续发展的投资"，明确表明投资决策的首要目标是促进包容性增长（inclusive growth）和可持续发展的投资。核心原则（9）"投资促进与便利"，规定投资促进与便利政策应符合可持续发展目标，且设计为尽量减少有害投资竞争的风险。

"各国指南"从三方面强调"可持续发展"：一是投资政策融入国家发展战略。制订符合生产性能力建设（productive capacity building）的优先战略投资和投资政策，包括人力资源发展、基础设施、技术传播、企业发展的政策及敏感产业保护的投资政策等。二是投资政策结合于可持续发展目标。除了体现"平衡"的"具体投资政策和法规的设计"及"旨在最大限度减少投资潜在负面影响"等规定外，还体现为：（1）促进负责任投资（responsible investment）的政策，保证投资符合国际核心标准；（2）投资促进和优惠政策，促进包容性与可持续发展；（3）土地取得的政策，结合"负责任的农业投资原则"制定相关政策。三是确保投资政策的相关性和有效性。主要包括公共治理和制度能力建设，政策有效性和具体措施有效性的评估，涉及量化投资的影响指标等。[1]

"协定要素"将"核心原则"转化为一些提供给 IIAs 决策者的选项，并分析各选项对可持续发展的意义。

首先，调整 IIAs 现有通行规定，通过保障东道国政策空间和限制国家责任条款，使其体现为"可持续发展友好型"。相关选项包括：（1）澄清定义方面，在"征收条款"中规定，追求公共政策目标的非歧视性善意管制不构成间接征收；在"公平公正待遇条款"中，包含政府责任的穷尽清单；（2）投资条件/限制方面，在"范围与定义条款"中规定，要求适格投资符合某些具体特征，如对东道国发展的积极影响；（3）保留/确定（carve-outs）方面，对国民待遇、最惠国待遇或设立前责任的特定国家保留，确定可实施的政策措施（如补贴）、政策区域（如少数民族、土著团体政策）或部门（如社会服务）；（4）涵盖/例外的排除方面，在"范围与定义条款"中，从涵盖范围中排除证券、短期或风险投资；旨在追求合法公共政策目标的国内管制措施的一般例外；（5）省略公平公正待遇条款、保护伞条款。

其次，在以可持续发展为目标的规定中，增加新的或更强有力的条款，以平衡投

---

〔1〕 See UNCTAD，*World Investment Report 2012*，*Towards a New Generation of Investment Policies*，United Nations，2012，p. xxvii.

资者的权利和责任,促进负责任的投资及增强母国的支持。主要表现在:(1) 投资者责任,要求投资者在投资准入和经营阶段遵守东道国法律,促进投资者遵守普遍原则或适用的企业社会责任标准;(2) 具有可持续发展意义的制度建设,据之国家当事方可进行合作,例如审查 IIA 的功能或 IIA 条款的解释,要求当事方合作以促进投资者遵守适用的企业社会责任标准;(3) 促进负责任投资的母国措施,促进对"可持续发展友好型"海外投资提供优惠,投资者遵守适用的企业社会责任标准可作为附加条件。

更具有创新意义的是,引入 GATT/WTO 体制的"特殊与差别待遇"(special and differential treatment,SDT)条款,作为发展水平悬殊的 IIAs 缔约方,特别是缔约一方是最不发达国家的选项,其效力及于现有规定和新规定,使较不发达缔约方的责任水平适合其发展水平。主要内容包括:(1) 较低水平的责任,涵盖较少经济活动的设立前承诺;(2) 责任/承诺的"专注发展例外"(development-focused exceptions),保留或确定具敏感性的有关发展的领域、问题或措施;(3) 最佳努力的承诺(best-endeavour commitments),规定有关公平公正待遇、国民待遇的承诺为最佳努力承诺,不具有法律约束力;(4) 不同的履约时间表,即承担分阶段(phase-in)履约责任,包括设立前、国民待遇、最惠国待遇、履行要求、资金转移及透明度等责任。[1]

(二) 从"偏重保护外资"到"平衡当事双方权利义务"

如前所述,传统国际投资政策与生俱来的典型特征是"偏重保护外资"。在 IIAs 实践中,长期存在发达国家与发展中国家之间在谈判地位与能力、谈判目标与效果、权力与利益等方面的不平等或不平衡现象。近年来,此种不平等或不平衡现象呈现强化和扩张之势。就各国外资法律政策而言,20 世纪 80 年代以来,为吸引和竞争外资,发展中国家的外资法律政策也普遍偏重对外资和外国投资者的保护和优惠,缺乏或放松对外资必要的管制或制约。

在 IIAs 语境中,"平衡"(balance)的概念可体现于不同的层面:首先,"平衡"可体现于缔约双方之间或缔约一方与第三方之间的关系,包括发达资本输出国与发展中资本输入国之间的权力、权利和责任关系,公共机构与私人利益之间,特别是东道国与外国投资者之间的权利与责任关系。"平衡"特别需要适用于发达国家与发展中国家之间的关系。经济实力相当的两个发达国家之间或两个发展中国家之间的任何一方投资者到对方投资,可基于互惠和相互保护的概念和原则。然而,此种概念和原则看来不能适用于经济发展水平悬殊的发达国家与发展中国家之间的 IIAs,因

---

〔1〕 See UNCTAD, *World Investment Report 2012*, *Towards a New Generation of Investment Policies*, United Nations,2012,p. 141.

为发展中国家的国民一般不具有进行相对应海外投资的能力。[1] 因此，为调整单方受益的情况，缔约双方需要有"平衡"的考虑。其次，"平衡"也可体现于投资政策目标之间的关系，如保护外资与促进外资的关系、保护外资与管制外资的关系以及缔约双方经济目标与其他公共或社会目标之间的关系。

近年来，IIA 实践在这方面已有一些创新性发展。在 2011 年签订的 20 项 IIAs 中，有 17 项规定了"资金自由转移责任的详细例外，包括国际收支平衡困难和/或本国法的实施"，"不规定所谓'保护伞'条款"；12 项规定"公平公正待遇标准相当于习惯国际法的外国人最低待遇标准"。[2] 此类规定在不同程度上反映了资本输出国与资本输入国之间、东道国与外国投资者之间权利和责任关系的"平衡"。

IPFSD 直接表达"平衡"概念的是核心原则(5)"平衡权利与义务"，规定投资政策应基于整体发展利益，平衡国家与投资者的权利与义务。鉴于在经济全球化、投资自由化趋势下，东道国管制外资的主权权力面临严峻挑战，IPFSD 在核心原则(6)"管制权利"(right to regulate)中，难能可贵地重申和强调了东道国对外资的管制权利，规定基于国际承诺，为了公共利益，各国拥有确立外资准入和经营条件且尽量减轻其潜在负面影响的主权权利。笔者以为，在肯定该原则的积极意义时，应当特别注意"基于国际承诺"和"为了公共利益"两个限定条件。核心原则(3)、(7)、(8)则分别规定了东道国对外资的法治、开放、保护及待遇的责任，以作为对东道国"管制权利"的"平衡"或"制衡"。核心原则(3)"公共治理与体制"，规定投资政策应发展为涵盖所有利益相关方且融入基于法治的制度框架。该制度框架遵循高标准的公共治理并为投资者确保可预见性、有效性及透明程序。核心原则(7)"开放投资"，规定依据各国发展战略，投资政策应确立开放、稳定和可预见的投资准入条件。核心原则(8)"投资保护与待遇"，规定投资政策应对现有投资者提供充分保护，现有投资者的待遇应是非歧视的。

在"各国指南"中，"平衡"作为投资政策结合于可持续发展目标的工具或体现，如具体投资政策和法规的设计，不仅规定投资的设立与经营、投资待遇与保护及投资促进与便利，也规定投资者的责任；又如，制定旨在最大限度减少投资潜在负面影响的具体指南，如处理逃税、防范反竞争行为、保障核心劳工标准及处理和改善环境影响等。"各国指南"还特别指出，要通过投资促进可持续发展和包容性增长，要最大限度地发挥投资的积极影响和最大限度地消除投资的消极影响，均需要平衡投资

---

〔1〕 See Jeswald W. Salacuse, Nicholas P. Sullivan, Do BITs Really Work?: An Evaluation of Bilateral Investment Treaties and Their Grand Bargain, 46 *Harvard International Law Journal*, p. 77 (2005).

〔2〕 表 III.3. 遴选的 2011 年 IIAs 的"可持续发展友好型"特征示范，载于 UNCTAD, *World Investment Report 2012*, *Towards a New Generation of Investment Policies*, United Nations, 90 (2012).

促进与投资管制。[1]

实际上,前述"协定要素"体现可持续发展目标的条款同样体现了"平衡"的概念。这也从一个侧面表明,"可持续发展"与"平衡"是相辅相成的。在一定意义上,"可持续发展"是目标,"平衡"是实现"可持续发展"目标的主要手段或路径。在此需要特别强调的是,"协定要素"率先主张在 IIAs 引入 SDT 条款,具有十分重要而深远的意义:首先,以南北问题为视角,关注和强调与发达国家经济发展水平悬殊的发展中国家,特别是最不发达国家的可持续发展问题;同时,不仅关注形式公平问题,而且关注实质公平问题,即在承认缔约双方经济发展水平不同的基础上,通过不对称的责任分配以实现实质公平。[2] 这正是 IPFSD 核心原则(5)"平衡"的要义,更是公平互利原则的实践。

(三)保护外资和管制外资从"各行其道"到"一体化"

传统上,一般而言,保护外资和管制外资的两种努力"各行其道"。保护外资的法律,无论国内立法或国际条约,均属"硬法",具有法律约束力。而管制外资的国际规范,则大多流于或属于"软法",成效甚微。如 20 世纪 70—90 年代起草及谈判的《联合国跨国公司行为守则》(草案)因长期未能达成共识,终遭放弃。而 2000 年《OECD 关于国际投资与跨国企业指南》也只是调整外国投资者行为的劝导性或自律性规范。

在国际投资政策语境,"一体化"(integration)的概念是全新的。它服务于不同的目的,特别是在实质和形式方面。首先,它意味着东道国投资保护与外国投资者责任的结合,以纠正片面强调对外国投资者的保护而未对其施加必要的责任;其次,鉴于涉及外资的国内政策与国际政策应整体考虑,两者需要根据国家形势的变化而协调发展,[3]"一体化"的概念强调 IIAs 与国内法之间的紧密联系;再次,鉴于国内外资政策与其他经济和社会政策密切相关,"一体化"的概念要求国内外资政策应融入国家的可持续发展战略;最后,在立法技术层面,"一体化"的概念意味着国际投资政策文件的结构性革新,即在 IIAs 与国内立法中包含保护外资和管制外资的规范,特别是同时规定东道国与外国投资者的权利和责任。

IPFSD 强调保护外资和管制外资的同等重要性及"投资者责任",力图在国内立法和国际条约实践中一体化推进建构保护外资和管制外资的法律体制。

---

〔1〕 See UNCTAD, *World Investment Report 2012*, *Towards a New Generation of Investment Policies*, United Nations, 2012, pp. 116-118.

〔2〕 Ibid., p. 159.

〔3〕 Ibid., p. 161.

核心原则（2）"政策一致性"（coherence），规定外资政策应基于国家的整体发展战略。所有影响外资的政策在国内和国际层面应是连续和协调一致的。

在"各国指南"中，强调外资政策应作为国家发展战略的组成部分。[1] 其主要内容包括：（1）在外资与可持续发展战略方面，外资应结合于国家的可持续发展战略，使外资对生产性能力建设和国际竞争的贡献最大化；（2）在外资管制和促进方面，设计具体的外资政策，涉及外资的设立与经营、外资的待遇与保护、投资者的责任及促进与便利；（3）在有关外资的政策领域方面，确保与其他政策领域包括贸易、税务、知识产权、竞争、劳工市场管理、土地的取得、公司责任与治理、环境保护、基础设施及公共—私人关系等政策的一致性；（4）在外资政策的有效性方面，建立实施外资政策的有效的公共机构，评估外资政策的有效性，从反馈中汲取用于新一轮决策的经验。[2]

IIAs 是各国投资决策的组成部分，可能支持投资促进目标，也可能限制投资和发展决策。作为促进投资的工具，IIAs 通过对外国投资者提供有关投资保护、东道国政策框架的稳定性、透明度及可预见性的附加保障补充了东道国的法规。在限制投资和发展决策方面，IIAs 可能限制发展中国家发展战略的制定，或阻碍包括可持续发展目标的决策等。鉴此，"协定要素"要求明确 IIAs 在国家发展战略和投资政策的地位和作用，保障 IIAs 与其他经济政策（如贸易、产业、技术、基础设施或旨在建立生产性能力和加强国家竞争力的企业政策）和其他非经济政策（如环境、社会、健康或文化政策）的协调一致。[3]

"协定要素"的结构和内容充分体现了"一体化"的概念。"协定要素"分为"设立后"（post-establishment）、"设立前"（pre-establishment）和"特殊与差别待遇"（SDT）三个部分。其中，在"设立后"部分中，"与其他协定的关系"（第 8 条）和"不降低标准条款"（第 9 条）及"投资促进"（第 10 条）分别涉及 BIT 与其他相关国际法、国内法规范的协调一致关系。

在保护外资和管制外资方面，长期以来，由于 IIAs 的缔约主体是国家，绝大多数 IIAs 仅规定国家的保护外资责任，而未规定外国投资者的义务或责任。外国投资者虽是 IIAs 的真正和最终受益者，其不当行为却无从或难以由 IIAs 调整。"协定要素"明确增加了"投资者义务与责任"（第 7 条）的规定。[4] 在 IIAs 中，可要求外国投

---

〔1〕 See UNCTAD, *World Investment Report 2012*, *Towards a New Generation of Investment Policies*, United Nations, 2012, p. 111.

〔2〕 Ibid., pp. 120-121.

〔3〕 Ibid., p. 133.

〔4〕 Ibid., pp. 143-159.

资者在投资和经营期间甚至经营期间之后(如环境清洁期间)遵守东道国有关投资的国内法,以该法律符合东道国国际责任、包括该 IIA 规定的责任为限。此类外国投资者责任的规定还可作为 ISDS 程序规定的基础,即在外国投资者未遵守东道国国内法的情况下,东道国可在 ISDS 程序中对该外国投资者提起反诉。此外,IIAs 还可规定普遍承认的国际准则(如《联合国商务与人权指南》)。此类规定不仅有助于平衡国家承诺与投资者的责任,还可支持正在形成为国际投资政策重要特征的企业社会责任准则的传播。[1]

三、我国的立场与对策

IPFSD 旨在建构资本输入国与资本输出国"可持续发展""和谐共赢"的新国际投资秩序,符合我国和广大发展中国家的共同目标和长远利益,为我国和广大发展中国家提供了重要的法理基础和实践契机。我国作为发展中大国,在基于 IPFSD 的国家实践和国际实践中任重道远,大有可为。

(一)促进形成共识,支持 UNCTAD 制定"可持续发展友好型"BIT 范本

如前所述,"可持续发展""平衡"和"一体化"是 IPFSD 的主要贡献和创新。UNCTAD 制定了 IPFSD,并不意味着国际社会对"可持续发展""平衡"和"一体化"已然达成共识。我国国际法学界、政府主管部门在国际论坛和国际实践中,应通过各种努力,促进各国真正达成此项共识。我国兼具资本输入国和资本输出国双重身份,促进国际社会达成此项共识,不仅符合国际社会普遍认同的经济主权、公平互利和合作发展原则,也符合我国的国家利益。从解决"南北问题"的高度看,"可持续发展""平衡"和"一体化"是改革旧国际投资秩序、构建新国际投资秩序的基本理念,我国作为发展中大国,应始终坚持和积极实践。

UNCTAD 的 IPFSD 虽然为国际投资决策实践提供了重要的法理基础,毕竟只是国际组织主持制定的"专家指南"。而 UNCTAD 提出的"协定要素",则只是汇集 IIAs 各种政策选项供各国"各取所需"(adapt and adopt)的"菜单",而不是作为谈判基础和具有指导意义的 IIA 范本。比之各个国家,UNCTAD 显然更具中立和独立性,更有可能对资本输入国与资本输出国之间的权利义务给予平衡的考虑。鉴此,建议我国政府主管部门和国际法学界积极参与 UNCTAD 建立的网上 IPFSD(即互动式论坛)及其他相关国际论坛和国际活动,促进和支持 UNCTAD 效法"联合国税收协定范本"的相关实践,在 IPFSD 的基础上,制定"可持续发展友好型"BIT 范本,

---

[1] 参见 UNCTAD, *World Investment Report 2012*, *Towards a New Generation of Investment Policies*, United Nations,2012,pp. 135-136.

供各国参考采用，以引领 BITs 的发展方向，逐渐形成新的国际通行规则。

（二）建立和健全基于 IPFSD 的我国海外投资法律制度

自 20 世纪 80 年代以来，经济合作与发展组织（OECD）国家开始注重对其海外投资和海外投资者的责任，结合传统的海外投资保证制度，制定一些政策措施或计划，以促进"负责任的投资"。[1] 为适应实施"走出去"战略的需要，我国相继建立了有关管理和保护海外投资的法律制度。由于 IPFSD 强调"可持续发展""平衡"及"一体化"，意味着我国相关法律制度也面临新的挑战，需要进行适时的调整、健全和完善。事实表明，近年来，我国海外投资企业不仅因利比亚战乱等突发性政治风险而损失惨重，也面临东道国基于公共利益而采取征收等措施的政治风险。显然，国际投资政策发展的新趋向和严峻的客观现实均要求我国在建立和健全海外投资法律制度中，需要有包含"可持续发展""平衡"及"一体化"概念的新视角和新规范。同时，我国还应重视鼓励和支持海外投资企业实施严格的企业社会责任标准，进行负责任的投资，为东道国的"可持续发展"作出积极贡献，从而达到有效防范政治风险、与东道国和谐共赢的目标。

（三）及时制定我国"可持续发展友好型"BIT 范本，积极开展相关实践

BIT 范本可分为欧洲范本和美国范本。欧洲范本是传统范本，条文简明，与投资密切相关，主要涉及定义、准入、待遇、征收、转移、代位、争端解决等传统 IIAs 的主要问题及协定的适用、生效等条约法的一般问题。美国范本 2004 年之前大体遵循欧洲范本模式，之后自成一体。美国 2004 年范本内容宽泛繁杂，不仅在"片面保护外资和外国投资者权益"等传统特征方面进一步升级和强化，还增加了履行要求、透明度、投资与环境、投资与劳工、根本安全、金融服务、税务等新内容及详细复杂的 ISDS 程序。[2] 美国 2012 年范本在此基础上又有新的发展，主要表现在增加新的透明度要

---

[1] See Riva Krut and Ashley Moretz，Home Country Measures for Encouraging Sustainable FDI，Occasional Paper No. 8，Report as part of UNCTAD/CBS Project：Cross Border Environmental Management in Transnational Corporations，CBS，November 1999.

[2] 美国 1977 年启动"BIT 计划"（bilateral investment treaty program），先后制定了 1983 年、1984 年、1987年、1991 年、1992 年、1994 年、2004 年和 2012 年范本。在"BIT 计划"历史上，2004 年范本无论形式和实体内容，都有很大改变，篇幅增为三倍以上。See Kenneth J. Vandevelde，U. S. International Investment Agreement，Oxford University Press，99-107（2009）.该范本分为 A，B，C 三节，共有 37 个条款。第 A 节包括第 1 条至第 22 条，分别是定义、范围、国民待遇、最惠国待遇、最低待遇标准、征收与赔偿、转移、履行要求、高级管理层与董事会、关于投资的法律决定的公布、透明度、投资与环境、投资与劳工、不符措施（Non-Conforming Measures）、特殊程序与信息要求、非减损（Non-Derogation）、拒绝授惠（Denial of Benefits）、根本安全（Essential Security）、信息披露、金融服务、税务、生效：期限与终止等条款。第 B 节包括第 23 条至第 36 条，细化了缔约一方与缔约另一方投资者之间争端的解决方式，分别对磋商与谈判、仲裁请求的提起、各当事方对仲裁的同意、各当事方同意的条件与限制、仲裁员的选定、仲裁的进行、仲裁程序的透明度、准据法、附录解释、专家报告、合并、裁决、附录与脚注、文件服务等作了专款规定。第 C 节第 37 条则专门规定了缔约双方之间争端的解决。

求和扩大劳工和环境保护范围等方面。

毋庸讳言，长期以来，我国 BIT 范本主要借鉴欧洲范本。从形式、内容甚至用语上看，中国系列的 BITs 和德国系列的 BITs 实际上并无显著或本质的区别。作为发展中大国，居于最大的资本输入国和潜在的资本输出大国双重地位，我国具有"平衡南北权益"的内在动因和客观需求。当前，在调整或重构国际投资秩序的新形势下，需要认真总结我国 30 多年来的 BIT 实践经验，深入研究相关国际实践和案例，遵循 IPFSD 的"核心原则"，参考"协定要素"，特别是选择采用其中的创新要素，及时制定我国"可持续发展友好型"BIT 范本，作为与外国商签或修订 BITs 的政策宣示、重要基础和基本准则。在商签或修订中外 BITs 时，可以合理主张，我国"可持续发展友好型"BIT 范本汲取了 IPFSD 的原则和创新要素，代表了新一代国际投资政策的发展趋向。

"可持续发展友好型"BIT 实践的典型特征，是摆脱欧洲范本和美国范本的窠臼，增加了"东道国可持续发展"和"投资者责任"等创新要素，以平衡资本输入国与资本输出国之间、东道国与外国投资者之间的权利义务。在发达国家基于国家利益考虑而固守"传统"的情势下，发展中国家相互之间的 BIT 实践如何发展，至关重要。我国与其他发展中国家作为平等的缔约双方，具有建立新国际经济秩序的共同历史使命和奋斗目标，可遵循 IPFSD 的原则和创新要素，逐渐形成"可持续发展友好型"BIT 的普遍实践，进而影响发达国家与发展中国家之间的 BIT 实践及国际投资政策的总体发展趋势。

Investment Policy Framework for Sustainable Development and China's Countermeasures

Abstract: The background of Investment Policy Framework for Sustainable Development (IPFSD) formulated by UNCTAD are that traditional international investment policy itself faces challenges and the international investment status of South States and North States have greatly changed. The initiatives of IPFSD are realized on three aspects: from "undue protection of rights and interest of foreign investment" to "promotion of sustainable development of host States"; from "undue protection of foreign investment" to "balance of rights and obligations of two parties involved"; and "protection of foreign investment" and "regulation of foreign investment" from "going its own way separately" to "integration". It is suggested that China should promote inter-national consensus on the concepts of "sustainable development", "balance" and "integration" and support UNCTAD to work out a "sustainable development friendly" (SDF) model BIT, set up and improve its legal system for overseas investment based on IPFSD, and also made its SDF model BIT and conduct related practice positively.

Key words: IPFSD; international investment policy; sustainable development; integration

第四节　论双边投资条约范本的演进与中国的对策[*]

【摘要】　在双边投资条约(BIT)实践中,作为缔约各方政策宣示、谈判基础和基本准则的 BIT 范本不断发展,其作用和影响日益彰显。BIT 范本源于发达国家的实践,服务于保护其海外投资的政策目标,其发展趋向长期以来是由发达国家主导和影响的。在经济全球化背景下,BIT 范本及其实践呈现出"自由化"和"可持续发展"两种发展趋向。作为负责任的发展中大国,我国应在总结分析 BIT 范本发展趋向和相关实践的基础上,从解决南北问题的高度,坚持国际经济法基本原则,审慎决定我国新 BIT 范本的目标和模式,以利于制定具有中国特色的"可持续发展导向"BIT 范本,指导和规范我国的实践。

【关键词】　BIT 范本　投资自由化　可持续发展

在经济全球化趋势下,双边投资条约(bilateral investment treaty,BIT)实践已成为国际法最显著的新发展之一。[1] 截至 2016 年 4 月,世界各国共签订了 2953 个此类条约。[2] 在长期的 BIT 实践中,作为缔约各方政策宣示、谈判基础和基本准则的 BIT 范本不断发展,其作用和影响日益彰显。当下,在"改革以 BITs 为主体的国际投资条约体制"渐成国际共识的背景下,各国新修订的 BIT 范本更成为其有关参与此项改革的立场和实践的重要标志。[3] 鉴此,本文在概述 BIT 实践及其范本缘起与特征的基础上,评析 BIT 范本的类型及其发展趋向,进而探讨我国新 BIT 范本的目标和模式选择问题。

一、BIT 实践及其范本的缘起与特征

BIT 范本是顺应 BIT 实践之需要而产生和发展的。探讨 BIT 范本的演进,首先

[*]　原载《国际法研究》2016 年第 4 期。

本文为国家社科基金重大项目"促进与保护我国海外投资的法律体制研究"(项目批准号:09&ZD032)(2009-2012)的研究成果之一。

〔1〕 See Jason Webb Yackee, Conceptual Difficulties in the Empirical Study of Bilateral Investment Treaties, *Brooklyn J. Int'l L.*, Vol. 33, 2008, p. 405.

〔2〕 See UNCTAD, *World Investment Report 2016*, *Investor Nationality*:*Policy Challenges*, United Nations, 2016, p. 101.

〔3〕 关于改革国际投资条约体制的最新进展,参见 UNCTAD, *World Investment Report 2016*, *Investor Nationality*:*Policy Challenges*, United Nations, 2016, pp. 110-112.

需要追溯和探究 BIT 实践及其范本的起源与基本特征。

（一）BIT 实践及其范本缘起

双边商务条约实践已有数百年历史。早期，此类条约旨在促进贸易，而不是投资。一般认为，BITs 的早期形式可溯及“友好通商航海条约”（friendship，commerce，and navigation treaties，FCN），[1]即美国调整其对外经济关系的传统国际法律文件。此类条约虽然旨在促进贸易和航运，但也时常包含关于缔约一方国民在缔约对方拥有财产或经营商务能力的规定。1911 年以后，美国开始在其参与缔结的此类条约中增加有关保障私人企业商务活动的规定。第二次世界大战后，美国作为资本输出国的地位日益提高，海外投资成为美国对外经济交往的主要形式之一。相应地，签订旨在保护美国海外投资的双边条约，成为美国实行对外经济政策的主要措施之一。为了适应以投资为重点的需要，美国参与缔结的友好通商航海条约的结构和内容发生了重大变化，有关保护国际投资的内容约占二分之一。此类条约对保护国际投资的重要性增强了，其有关国际投资的规定主要包括外国国民及其财产的保护、外国人财产的待遇、国有化或征收及其补偿标准等。显然，此类规定已涉及其后产生的 BITs 的核心内容，为后者提供了具体调整国际投资关系的经验。[2]

当时，在国际投资日益成为重要国际经济活动的形势下，寻求国际法保护的外国投资者只能借助由分散的条约规定、尚有争议的少数国际习惯及一般法律原则构成的调整国际投资的临时性国际法律规则。此种规则存在诸多严重缺陷，包括：（1）未能考虑国际投资实践的需求及处理外国投资者关切的重要问题，例如，此种规则实际上未涉及外国投资者从东道国转移其资金的权利；（2）通常是含糊的，可以有多种解释，例如，尽管存在有关“对外资国有化支付赔偿”的国际习惯，但缺乏计算赔偿额的明确规则；（3）缺乏对外国投资者提供有效的执行机制，以支持其针对东道国损害或占有其投资或者拒绝履行契约责任的权利请求。[3]

鉴于上述缺陷，自 1959 年以来，联邦德国等欧洲国家以友好通商航海条约中有关促进和保护国际投资的事项为中心内容，同作为资本输入国的发展中国家签订专门性的“相互促进和保护投资协定”（Agreement concerning Reciprocal Encourage-

---

[1] 早在 1956 年，“友好通商航海条约”就被美国学者称为“促进和保护外国投资的条约”。See Herman Walker，Jr.，Treaties for the Encouragement and Protection of Foreign Investment：Present United States Practice，*The American Journal of Comparative Law*，Vol. 5，No. 2，1956，pp. 229-247.

[2] See Jeswald W. Salacuse，Nicholas P. Sullivan，Do BITs Really Work？：An Evaluation of Bilateral Investment Treaties and Their Grand Bargain，*Harvard International Law Journal*，Vol. 46，No. 1，2005，pp. 71-73.

[3] Ibid.，pp. 68-69.

ment and Protection of Investments），即现代 BITs。[1] 历经半个多世纪，多数 BITs 模仿或至少广泛照搬 1959 年《海外投资国际公约草案》（Draft International Convention on Investments Abroad）和 1967 年经济合作开发组织（OECD）《保护外国财产的公约草案》（Draft Convention on the Protection of Foreign Property）的主要条款。由于来源相同，不同 BITs 的主题、结构和用语，在不同的时期、不同的国家实践仍显得非常相似。[2] 典型 BIT 的缔约方为一方为欧洲国家，另一方为发展中国家。[3] 20 世纪 80 年代初，美国决定采用 BIT 作为保护其海外投资的工具之后，此类条约更为迅速发展，[4] 逐渐为世界各国普遍接受，成为国际投资条约体制中最为重要的形式。

在 BIT 实践中，发达国家往往花费大量的时间和精力起草 BIT 范本（model），作为与各个发展中国家谈判的基础。[5] 在起草 BIT 范本中，发达国家通常需要向各种组织、包括相关政府机构和私人团体咨商。一般而言，范本的主要功能是：第一，其起草过程是各国研究海外投资保护问题的重要机会，通过与相关政府机构和私人团体咨商，可形成国家政策立场，亦有助于保障本国立法机构认可和批准政府签订的特定 BIT；第二，由于发达国家计划与众多发展中国家商签 BITs，其范本可向相关缔约方传达其所寻求的具体谈判目标；第三，发达国家期望在同众多发展中国家商签 BITs 时保持其政策立场的相对一致性，以范本为基础开展 BIT 谈判是达此目标的有效方式；第四，由于范本在手，不必为各项 BIT 谈判逐一准备条约草案，明显加速了谈判进程；第五，通过提供作为谈判基础的范本，发达国家事实上确立了 BIT 谈判的基本框架，也掌控了谈判的发展进程；最后，范本有利于发达国家坚持和强化其既有立场和优势。在 BIT 谈判中，发达国家通常声称其范本中的规则是适用于各国的"国际通行规则"，而不是专门适用于特定谈判对方的规则，亦时常凭借其范本，以某

---

〔1〕 1959 年，联邦德国与巴基斯坦签订了第一个"关于促进和保护投资的条约"。该条约包含了许多实体性规定，为其后 BITs 所效法。See Andrew Newcombe, Lluis Paradell, *Law and Practice of Investment Treaties, Standards of Treatment*, Wolters Kluwer, 2009, p. 42.

〔2〕 Jason Webb Yackee, Conceptual Difficulties in the Empirical Study of Bilateral Investment Treaties, *Brooklyn J. Int'l L.*, Vol. 33, 2008, pp. 415-416.

〔3〕 瑞士、法国、意大利、英国、荷兰和比利时等欧洲国家紧随联邦德国 BIT 实践，与发展中国家签订 BITs。See Jeswald W. Salacuse, BIT by BIT: The Growth of Bilateral Investment Treaties and Their Impact on Foreign Investment in Developing Countries, *The International Lawyer*, Vol. 24, 1990, pp. 656-657.

〔4〕 Axel Berger, China's New Bilateral Investment Treaty Programme: Substance, Rational and Implications for Investment Law Making, Paper for the American Society of International Law International Economic Law Group (ASIL IELIG) 2008 biennial conference "The Politics of International Economic Law: The Next Four Years", Washington, D. C., November 14-15, 2008.

〔5〕 例如，美国作为发达国家在 BIT 实践方面的后来者，其 BIT 范本历经 1983、1984、1987、1991、1992、1994、2004、2012 年 8 次修订。关于美国 BIT 范本的演进，参见 Kenneth J. Vandevelde, *U. S. International Investment Agreements*, Oxford University Press, 2009, pp. 91-112。

种让步未曾给予其他国家为由,拒绝作出违背其范本规则的妥协。[1]

(二) BIT 范本的基本特征

如前所述,BIT 范本是发达国家在 BIT 实践中创造的,其发展趋向基本上也是由发达国家主导的。概括而言,BIT 范本的基本特征主要表现在:

第一,先天的"资本输出国烙印"。追根溯源,BIT 范本由欧美发达资本输出国精心设计并作为其对外政策的组成部分,旨在维护资本输出国的权益及解决其海外投资者关切的重要问题。因此,以"促进和保护海外投资"作为其主旨,片面强调资本输出国及其海外投资者的权益顺理成章,也是其先天的、不可磨灭的烙印。对发达国家而言,传统 BIT 范本为其带来了"与生俱来"的优势,也为 BIT 范本的进一步发展提供了基本模式。长期以来,由于发展水平和实力对比的悬殊及与所谓"国际通行规则""接轨"的现实需要,发展中国家的 BIT 范本一般是在发达国家 BIT 范本的基础上修订的,在结构、内容、用语甚至目标上与发达国家的范本亦步亦趋,并无实质性的区别。

第二,偏重"保护投资"的功能。理论上,BITs 是缔约国之间双边谈判的结果,旨在为缔约双方提供同等的法律保护。事实上,它们常常是作为资本输出国的发达国家与作为资本输入国的发展中国家之间的协定。BIT 范本在其名称和序言中往往声称其具有"保护投资"和"促进投资"双重功能,"保护投资"显然有利于资本输出国及其海外投资者,"促进投资"似乎较有利于资本输入国。值得注意的是,在 BIT 语境中,"促进投资"的用语是含糊的。"促进投资"是指"促进对外投资",还是"促进外来投资",抑或两者兼而有之? 可以明确的是,"促进投资"并不一定意味着缔约双方相互的"促进对外投资"。许多发展中国家因缺乏资金而反对本国投资者对外投资,其参与签订的 BITs 称为"促进和相互保护投资"(the encouragement and reciprocal protection of investment),而不是更为普遍采用的"相互促进和保护投资"(the reciprocal encouragement and protection of investment)。[2] 由于"促进投资"用语的含糊,"促进投资"的责任也是含糊的。它意味着发达国家承担促进其投资者对外投资的责任,抑或发展中国家承担改善其投资环境以吸引外资的责任? 实践表明,BIT 范本向来偏重于资本输入国"保护投资"的功能,基本忽略资本输出国"促进对外投资"的功能。主要表现在,对资本输入国而言,"保护投资"是具有法律约束力的条约责

---

〔1〕 Jeswald W. Salacuse, BIT by BIT: The Growth of Bilateral Investment Treaties and Their Impact on Foreign Investment in Developing Countries, *The International Lawyer*, Vol. 24, 1990, pp. 662-663; Kenneth J. Vandevelde, *U.S. International Investment Agreement*, Oxford University Press, 2009, p. 91.

〔2〕 Jeswald W. Salacuse, BIT by BIT: The Growth of Bilateral Investment Treaties and Their Impact on Foreign Investment in Developing Countries, *The International Lawyer*, Vol. 24, 1990, p. 662.

任；而对资本输出国而言，"促进对外投资"通常只是其促进海外投资的"最佳努力"（best-endeavour）宣示，而非具有法律约束力的条约责任。"促进投资"的条约责任通常落实在资本输入国创设优良投资环境以"促进外来投资"和实现"投资自由化"等方面，而基本忽略了资本输入国"促进外来投资"以利本国发展的政策目标。[1]

第三，单方的规范或指导意义。顾名思义，BIT 范本具有示范、规范或指导的意义，不是特定 BIT 谈判的文本（text）或草案（draft）。BIT 范本是一国有关国际投资政策和立场的反映，是其 BIT 谈判最高期望和最高目标的宣示。由于它来源于本国既有条约实践，试图为本国未来的条约实践提供指南或参考，具有单方的规范或指导意义。不言而喻，在缔约双方各有其 BIT 范本的情况下，缔约各方的范本只是规范其本身的范本，而不是规范缔约对方的范本。即使在缔约一方有范本、缔约另一方没有范本的情况下，该范本仍然是"一家之言"，是规范该缔约一方本身的范本，绝非规范缔约双方的具有"普适性"的"国际通行规则"。在 BIT 谈判实践中，美国等发达国家，往往声称其范本代表所谓"国际通行规则"的新发展，且倚仗其实力，对缔约对方施压，以便各个击破，实现其基于"美国利益至上"理念的既定政策目标。在中美 BIT 谈判中，美国清楚表明其立场，声称"美国将以美国 BIT 范本为基础进行谈判，该范本反映了高水平的投资者保护"。[2] 因此，缔约各方切忌将缔约对方的范本盲目接受为"反映 BIT 最新发展趋势的经典"，甚至奉为"放之四海而皆准"的圭臬。缔约各方的范本均为基于本国国情参与制定国际投资规则的谈判文件，独立自主，各具特色，本无优劣、高下或主次之分，既不能妄自尊大，也不必妄自菲薄。缔约各方的范本作为具有单方规范或指导意义的谈判文件，不能强求作为特定 BIT 谈判的基础，更不能强迫缔约对方接受。

第四，与谈判实力相辅相成。诚然，特定 BIT 所规定的保护投资规则和标准，是缔约双方的期望与它们各自的谈判地位、谈判实力交互作用的结果。BIT 范本从一个侧面反映了南北国家在 BIT 谈判中悬殊的地位和能力。在 BIT 实践中，发达国家通常有范本可依，成竹在胸，主导和掌控谈判的发展进程，加之实力雄厚，可强势推行其既定政策目标。而发展中国家大多没有 BIT 范本，只能被动应对，甚至盲目接受发达国家范本的严苛条款。少数发展中国家即使备有 BIT 范本，由于历史和现实

---

〔1〕　关于发达资本输出国与发展中资本输入国之间 BIT 传统实践的不平衡或不平等，参见 Zeng Huaqun, Balance, Sustainable Development, and Integration: Innovative Path for BIT Practice, 17（2）*Journal of International Economic Law*（2014）, pp. 300-308。

〔2〕　See US Fact Sheet of the Fourth Cabinet-Level Meeting of the US-China Strategic Economic Dialogue, in Kong Qingjiang, US-China Bilateral Investment Treaty Negotiations, *EAI Background Brief No. 507*, 25 February 2010, p. 5.

的种种因素,往往也未能摆脱发达国家 BIT 范本的深刻影响,[1]且未必拥有能充分理解条约用语细微差别的法律专家。[2] 一些缺乏谈判能力和法律专家的发展中国家,不得不迁就或迎合发达国家不断发展变化的 BIT 范本。[3] 在经济发展水平悬殊的发达国家与发展中国家之间,缔约双方分别作为谈判基础的两个范本所起的作用如何,实际上是双方博弈的结果。首先,重要的前提是,双方范本是否真正反映了各自不同的利益诉求。从当前情况看,由于具有“资本输出国烙印”的发达国家范本对发展中国家范本的深刻影响早已潜移默化,后者往往未能反映发展中国家居于资本输入国立场的基本利益诉求。因此,即使以两个范本为谈判基础的博弈,也不是简单“一对一”的条款比对或增减就可达到双方权益的平衡。就两个范本的相同或类似条款规定而言,双方在谈判中的“一拍即合”并不必然意味着“双赢”,而很可能是缔约一方的“单赢”。例如,有利于发达国家的外资征收赔偿的“充分、及时、有效”规则(即“赫尔”规则)早已“暗度陈仓”,被一些发展中国家的范本所采纳。就两个范本的不同条款规定而言,缔约一方以放弃 A 条款作为缔约另一方放弃 B 条款的条件,也并不必然意味着双方实现了“互有对等或适当让步”的妥协。A 条款与 B 条款分别对缔约各方的重要意义和法律后果决定了是妥协或“单赢”。例如,缔约一方以放弃“公平与公正待遇”(fair and equitable treatment)条款作为缔约另一方放弃“准入”(admission)条款的条件,[4]并不必然意味着缔约双方的妥协。在缔约一方的投资向缔约另一方单向流动的情况下,缔约另一方“准入”条款的重要意义和法律后果远高于缔约一方的“公平与公正待遇”条款。因为,“准入”条款的放弃意味着“投资自由化”,东道国实质上放弃了外资审批权,权力、权利及利益关系重大;而“公平与公正待遇”条款的放弃,则尚有无须明文规定的“习惯国际法”作为替代,在未对“公平与公正待遇”条款作“独立、自给自足(self-contained)条款”解释的情况下,并未产生实

---

　　[1] 例如,斯里兰卡 BIT 范本共 13 条,依次为定义、投资的促进与保护、最惠国待遇、例外、损失的赔偿、征收、投资的汇回、缔约一方与缔约另一方投资者间投资争端的解决、缔约方之间的争端、代位、生效、协定的适用、期限与终止等条款,与德国等发达国家 BIT 范本的基本结构和内容大体一致。See Campbell McLachlan QC, Laurence Shore, and Matthew Weiniger, *International Investment Arbitration*, *Substantive Principles*, Appendix 9, Oxford University Press, 2007, pp. 427-431.

　　[2] See M. Sornarajah, *The International Law on Foreign Investment*, 2nd edition, Cambridge University Press, 2004, pp. 207-208.

　　[3] 参见詹晓宁等:《国际投资协定:趋势和主要特征》,载陈安主编:《国际经济法学刊》第 14 卷第 1 期,北京大学出版社 2007 年版,第 126—127 页。

　　[4] 所谓“准入”条款,指缔约双方允许对方投资进入本国境内的一般规定,通常表明了东道国对外资的态度或立场。据之,东道国可根据国家发展战略,实施有关外资准入和经营的国内法律和政策。See Axel Berger, China's New Bilateral Investment Treaty Programme: Substance, Rational and Implications for Investment Law Making, Paper for the American Society of International Law International Economic Law Group (ASIL IELG) 2008 biennial conference "The Politics of International Economic Law: The Next Four Years", Washington, D. C., November 14-15, 2008.

质性的法律后果。[1]

在 BIT 谈判实践中,美国通常固守其范本条款。其不愿妥协的主要原因:一是如果谈判对方不愿接受其范本的实质部分,美国就认为该国不具有其范本所期望的外资政策;二是任何实质性妥协都可能导致将来的 BIT 谈判对方提出相同的要求;三是对已确立的原则作出妥协的后果可能适得其反,产生比之未签订 BIT 更为不利的情况;四是如果某妥协被错误解读为对其范本的澄清,而不是妥协,将可能导致削弱其已有 BITs 的效力。[2] 美国对其范本的功效亦自我欣赏,称其 2012 年范本遵循美国长期的 BIT 实践,将继续保障其在投资争端中作为被诉国的"不败纪录",也将为其海外投资者提供有效的 BIT 保护。[3]

显然,作为发展中国家,对发达国家主导的 BIT 范本的上述基本特征应有清晰、深刻的认识,对特定缔约对方的范本应有充分、深入的研究,特别需要研究各个概念和条款的来龙去脉、法理依据、相关典型案例以至相关经济社会背景等。同时,应密切关注 BIT 范本的发展趋向,基于本国国情制定具有本国特色的 BIT 范本,在相关概念和条款中主张和维护本国政策和权益,切实反映本国的政策目标和利益诉求。

二、BIT 范本的类型及其发展趋向

发达国家的 BIT 范本大致可分为欧洲模式和美国模式两类。欧洲模式以德国范本为代表,瑞士、法国、英国、荷兰等欧洲国家普遍效法该模式。美国模式源于欧洲模式,自 2004 年以来自成一体,以美国范本为代表,加拿大等国采用或接受该模式。联合国贸易和发展会议(UNCTAD,简称"贸发会议")2012 年发布的"国际投资协定要素:政策选项"(Elements of International Investment Agreements: Policy Options,简称"协定要素")[4]虽是政策选项,不是范本,但源自各国 BIT 范本及其实践,兼容并蓄,既包含传统 BITs 的基本结构和主要条款,又提出重要的创新条款,与

---

[1] See Rudolf Dolzer, Fair and Equitable Treatment: A Key Standard in Investment Treaties, 39 *The International Lawyer* (2005), pp. 87-106.

[2] See Kenneth J. Vandevelde, *U. S. International Investment Agreements*, Oxford University Press, 2009, p. 109.

[3] See Lise Johnson, The 2012 US Model BIT and What the Changes (or Lack Thereof) Suggest about Future Investment Treaties, 8 (2) *Political Risk Insurance Newsletter*, November, 2012.

[4] UNCTAD《2012 年世界投资报告:迈向新一代投资政策》制定了"可持续发展的投资政策框架"(Investment Policy Framework for Sustainable Development, IPFSD),由"可持续发展投资决策的核心原则"(Core Principles for Investment Policymaking for Sustainable Development)、"各国投资政策指南"(National Investment Policy Guidelines)和"国际投资协定要素:政策选项"三部分构成。"协定要素"全文载于:UNCTAD, *World Investment Report 2012, Towards a New Generation of Investment Policies*, United Nations, 2012, pp. 143-159. 关于 IPFSD 的评论,参见曾华群:《"可持续发展的投资政策框架"与我国的对策》,载《厦门大学学报》(哲学社会科学版)2013 年第 6 期,第 59—67 页。

德国范本和美国范本具有一定的可比性。[1] 以下简略比较德国范本、美国范本和"协定要素"的形式和内容，以期探讨和揭示 BIT 范本的类型及其发展趋向。

（一）BIT 范本的类型

1. "超稳定状态"的德国范本

《德国 2008 年条约范本：德意志联邦共和国与某国关于促进和相互保护投资的条约》（German Model Treaty-2008：Treaty between the Federal Republic of Germany and［…］concerning the Encouragement and Reciprocal Protection of Investments)（简称"德国范本"）可作为欧洲模式的典型。该范本合计 13 个条款。分别是定义、准入与投资保护、国民待遇与最惠国待遇、征收情况下的赔偿、自由转移、代位、其他规定、适用范围、缔约国间争端的解决、缔约国一方与缔约国另一方投资者间争端的解决、缔约国间的关系、登记条款、生效，期限与终止通知等条款。显然，德国范本的条文简约，直接规范国际投资活动，涉及国际投资的主要问题及条约法的一般问题。其中，"准入"条款是唯一体现尊重和维护东道国主权的条款，也是资本输入国在 BITs 中承诺给予外资待遇和保护的唯一回报。

对比欧洲各国的 BIT 实践，可知以德国范本为典型代表的欧洲模式历经半个多世纪，保持"超稳定状态"。欧洲各国分别与广大发展中国家签订了 BITs。截至 2016 年 6 月，德国已签订 135 个 BITs，签约数位居全球第一。[2] 有学者指出，欧洲模式较为成功的原因主要是，欧洲国家在有关当地货币汇兑、履行要求[3]及征收等事项的保障方面，比美国的相关要求较为宽松。此外，欧洲国家与其前殖民地之间的特殊历史联系也可能影响一些新独立国家的 BIT 实践，后者可能认为与其前宗主国签订 BIT 会更有利些。[4] 笔者以为，从技术层面看，欧洲模式的条文简约及其"超稳定状态"，也是促成其 BIT 谈判成功的重要因素之一。

值得关注的是，自 2009 年 12 月《里斯本条约》（Lisbon Treaty）生效后，欧盟决定

---

　　[1] "协定要素"的"政策选项"以国际投资协定（international investment agreements，IIAs）主要条款为序，列举从"最有利于投资者"（the most investor-friendly）或"最高保护"（most protective）到为国家提供较高灵活性的各种选项。See UNCTAD, *World Investment Report 2012*，*Towards a New Generation of Investment Policies*，United Nations，2012，p. 144.

　　[2] http://investmentpolicyhub. unctad. org/IIA/（last visited June 23，2016).

　　[3] 所谓"履行要求"（performance requirements），广义上指东道国对外国投资经营实施的管制措施，一般是要求外国投资者作出投资时履行某些相关要求（如当地成分、出口业绩、当地员工雇佣等），作为批准该投资或该投资享有优惠待遇的前提条件。此类管制措施旨在保障外国投资经营有利于东道国的发展目标，通常是利用外资增加当地就业、取得新技术及促进贸易平衡等。See Kenneth J. Vandevelde，*U. S. International Investment Agreement*，Oxford University Press，2009，p. 387.

　　[4] Jeswald W. Salacuse，BIT by BIT：The Growth of Bilateral Investment Treaties and Their Impact on Foreign Investment in Developing Countries，*The International Lawyer*，Vol. 24，1990，p. 657.

以其名义与第三国签订 BITs,取代之前欧盟各成员国分别与第三国签订的 1300 多个 BITs。[1] 目前,欧盟以其名义与加拿大等国之间包含投资规范的区域贸易协定(regional trade agreements,RTAs)谈判和与新加坡之间的 BIT 谈判正在进行。[2] 作为谈判基础的"欧盟 BIT 范本",亦即名副其实的"欧洲模式"如何协调制定和发展,必将对世界各国 BIT 范本及其实践的发展趋向产生重大而深远的影响。

2."自由化导向"的美国范本

在 BIT 实践及制定范本方面,比之欧洲国家,美国是后来者。美国 1977 年启动"BIT 计划"(bilateral investment treaty program),第一步是制定用于谈判的《美国政府与某国政府关于促进和相互保护投资的条约范本》(Treaty between the Government of the United States of America and Government of [Country] Concerning the Encouragement and Reciprocal Protection of Investment)。

1982 年,美国制定其第一个 BIT 范本。该范本包含 13 个条款。其中,5 个条款属实体性规范,涉及投资待遇(第 2 条)、征收赔偿(第 3 条)、战乱导致损害的赔偿(第 4 条)、转移(第 5 条)和税务(第 11 条)。三个条款涉及争端解决措施,包括协商、投资者与国家间仲裁及缔约双方间仲裁(第 6—8 条)。两个条款确定某些权力、权利和责任不属于条约适用的范围(第 9、10 条)。余下三个条款涉及条约的适用范围:一是对某些用语作出定义(第 1 条),二是对缔约方的次级政治机构(political subdivisions)适用该条约(第 12 条),三是规定条约的生效、有效期及终止(第 13 条)。由此可见,早期美国 BIT 范本比之德国范本,除不采用"准入"和"代位"条款、增加"税务"条款外,在形式和内容方面大同小异。

美国 BIT 范本历经 1983、1984、1987、1991、1992、1994、2004、2012 年 8 次修订。[3] 1983 年范本保持 1982 年范本的条款结构,修订了部分条款内容。1984 年范本包含 12 个条款,合并征收条款和战乱条款,对范本用语作了较大修改。1987、1991、1992 年范本是为处理 BIT 谈判产生的具体问题而个别修改的结果。1992 年12 月《北美自由贸易协定》(North American Free Trade Agreement,NAFTA)的签署,促使美国考虑进一步修改其 BIT 范本内容。1994 年范本是对原范本进行整体综合审查的成果,包含 16 个条款。在美国 BIT 计划历史上,2004 年范本是实行最广泛

---

[1]　UNCTAD, *World Investment Report 2011*, *Non-Equity Modes of International Production and Development*, United Nations, 2011, p. 100.

[2]　UNCTAD, *World Investment Report 2013*: *Global Value Chains*: *Investment and Trade for Development*, United Nations, 2013, p. 104.

[3]　美国 1982、1983、1984、1987、1991、1992、1994、2004 年范本均收录于 Kenneth J. Vandevelde, *U.S. International Investment Agreement*, Oxford University Press, 2009, pp. 769-852。

修改的成果，在形式和内容方面均有许多重要改变，篇幅骤增为三倍。[1] 2012 年范本在保持原范本基本结构的基础上，对一些条款的内容作了修改或补充，特别表现在增加新的透明度要求和扩大劳工和环境保护范围等方面。

美国 2012 年范本（简称"美国范本"）分为三节，共有 37 个条款。第 A 节包括第 1 条至第 22 条，分别是定义、范围、国民待遇、最惠国待遇、最低待遇标准、征收与赔偿、转移、履行要求、高级管理层与董事会、关于投资的法律决定的公布、透明度、投资与环境、投资与劳工、不符措施、[2]特殊程序与信息要求、非减损、[3]拒绝授惠[4]、根本安全、[5]信息披露、金融服务、税务及生效：期限与终止等条款。第 B 节包括第 23 条至第 36 条，细化了"投资者与国家间争端解决程序"（investor-State dispute settlement，ISDS）的规定，分别对磋商与谈判、仲裁请求的提起、各当事方对仲裁的同意、各当事方同意的条件与限制、仲裁员的选定、仲裁的进行、仲裁程序的透明度、准据法、附录解释、专家报告、合并、裁决、附录与脚注、文件服务等作了专门条款规定。第 C 节第 37 条则专门规定了缔约双方之间争端的解决。

概括而言，美国范本内容的新发展主要表现在传统条款的发展、"投资自由化"条款及"与投资有关的"条款三个方面。

在传统条款的发展方面，美国范本对资本输出国及其海外投资者特别关切的概念或条款进一步澄清和细化规定，力图解决以往相关条文的不确定性，为外资和外国投资者提供更为充分的国际法保护，主要表现在：(1) 对"投资"和"投资者"作了更明确的定义；[6](2) 将投资待遇条款"一分为三"，分为"国民待遇""最惠国待遇"和

---

〔1〕 Kenneth J. Vandevelde, *U. S. International Investment Agreement*, Oxford University Press, 2009, pp. 99-107.

〔2〕 所谓"不符措施"（Non-Conforming Measures），是美国 2004 年 BIT 范本第 14 条的名称。该条款允许缔约各方在 BIT 附录中具体规定其现有不符"履行要求"规定的措施和将来有权采取不符"履行要求"规定的措施的特定部门。该条款规定了不符国民待遇、最惠国待遇和雇佣规定的措施。See Kenneth J. Vandevelde, *U. S. International Investment Agreement*, p. 395. 相关研究表明，美国等声称对外资实行"准入前"国民待遇的国家，毫无例外地在 BITs 中附加了"不符措施"和/或"保留和例外"（reservations and exceptions）条款，以维护其国家利益和经济安全。此类"准入前"国民待遇加"不符措施"和/或"保留和例外"的安排，在很多情况下成为"口惠而实不至"的法律策略。

〔3〕 所谓"非减损"（Non-Derogation），是美国 2012 年 BIT 范本第 16 条的名称，旨在明确 BIT 不减损缔约各方投资者或涵盖投资基于缔约方法律法规、行政实践或程序、行政或司法裁决、缔约方的国际法律责任或承诺享有的更为优惠的待遇。

〔4〕 由于采用客观的"投资者"标准可能涵盖缔约方不愿给予 BIT 保护的投资者，一些 BITs 规定了"拒绝授惠"（Denial of Benefits）条款，允许缔约方对虽设立于该方、但与该方缺乏充分联系的投资者不适用 BIT 保护。关于"拒绝授惠"条款的定义和实践，参见 OECD, *International Investment Law*, *Understanding Concepts and Tracking Innovations*, *Companion Volume to International Investment Perspectives*, OECD, 2008, pp. 9, 28-33。

〔5〕 所谓"根本安全"（Essential Security），是美国 2012 年 BIT 范本第 18 条的名称，旨在明确 BIT 不得被解释为要求缔约方披露其认为违反其根本安全利益的信息，也不得被解释为不允许缔约方采取其认为必要的措施，以履行维护或恢复国际和平或安全或保护其本身根本安全利益的责任。

〔6〕 美国 2012 年 BIT 范本第 1 条。

"最低待遇标准"三个条款;并进一步澄清和完善投资待遇条款,包括国民待遇和最惠国待遇的不符措施,将"公平与公正待遇"和"充分保护和保障"(full protection and security)明示归类于习惯国际法等规定;[1](3)通过增加确立判断"间接征收"规则的新附录,澄清了征收条款;[2](4)细化"投资者与国家间争端解决程序"的规定,对投资者权利请求的提出、缔约双方在该程序的参与、透明度、加速程序、合并仲裁、救济方式等作了具体规定。[3]此类规定虽源自传统条款,但其专业化和精致化的规定在很大程度上决定了"投资者与国家间争端解决程序"的条约"法定模式"和"司法化",从而弱化、排斥甚至否定了其他投资争端解决方式。

在"投资自由化"条款方面,美国范本增加履行要求、高级管理层与董事会、关于投资的法律决定的公布、透明度、不符措施、特殊程序与信息要求、信息披露等条款,特别表现在:(1)禁止履行要求的范围进一步扩大。该范本禁止履行要求的规定适用于任何投资,不限于涵盖投资。某些作为接受利益条件的履行要求亦属禁止之列;[4](2)规定透明度和正当程序,如要求缔约各方指定有关涵盖投资事务的联系点,要求缔约各方答复对方提出的有关影响 BIT 实施的实际措施或拟议措施,在某措施适用于特定人的情况下,后者应得到通知并有提出答辩、要求司法审查或行政复议的机会等。[5]此类规定反映了美国作为资本输出大国对 BIT 目标和功效的新追求。

在"与投资有关"条款方面,美国范本增加投资与环境、投资与劳工、金融服务、税务等条款。[6]特别是,要求缔约方尽最大努力保障其"不为吸引外资而放松环境措施和保护某些国际承认的劳工权利的措施"。

值得注意的是,美国范本未规定欧洲模式中唯一体现东道国主权的"准入"条款,以要求东道国给予外国投资者"设立权"取代。[7]美国范本在国民待遇、最惠国待遇及履行要求[8]等三个条款中均采用"设立"(establishment)的概念,与"取得"(acquisition)、"扩大"(expansion)、"管理"(management)、"行为"(conduct)、"经营"(operation)、"出售"(sale)或其他投资的处置方式并列,表明其实施"设立权"模式,

---

〔1〕　美国 2012 年 BIT 范本第 3—5 条。

〔2〕　美国 2012 年 BIT 范本第 6 条及附录 A,B。

〔3〕　美国 2012 年 BIT 范本第 B 节第 23—36 条。

〔4〕　美国 2012 年 BIT 范本第 8 条。

〔5〕　美国 2012 年 BIT 范本第 11 条。

〔6〕　美国 2012 年 BIT 范本第 12 条、第 13 条、第 20 条、第 21 条。

〔7〕　所谓"设立权"(right of establishment),是通过在外资设立阶段和设立之后给予外国投资者国民待遇和最惠国待遇,或者仅给予最惠国待遇(亦称"设立前国民待遇和最惠国待遇"或"设立前最惠国待遇")而确立,并附有例外和保留。

〔8〕　美国 2012 年范本第 8 条。

即"设立前国民待遇和最惠国待遇"的立场。[1] 由于国民待遇适用于"设立前"，意味着缔约一方投资者享有与缔约对方投资者同等的"设立权"，亦即要求东道国采取对国内投资者和外国投资者一视同仁的"投资自由化"政策。此类"设立权"条款旨在限制东道国在外资设立阶段的审查权力和管制外资准入的主权权力，导致东道国外资法律制度的自由化。[2] 此类条款的创设和推行，反映了美国对"片面保护外资和外国投资者"的传统 BIT 立场的坚持和发展。

显然，"自由化导向"的美国范本是在保持传统 BIT 范本基本特征的基础上，强化"保护投资"功能的"升级版"和推进"投资自由化"的"更新版"。其主要目标是给予投资者更充分的投资保障和自由，同时，进一步限缩东道国的主权权力和政策空间。

3. "可持续发展导向"的"协定要素"

首先，需要明确的是，贸发会议提出的"协定要素"是汇集国际投资协定各种政策选项（policy options）供各国"各取所需"（adapt and adopt）的"菜单"，而不是作为谈判基础和具有单方规范或指导意义的 BIT 范本。由于"协定要素"主要来源于各国 BIT 实践，在一定意义上是集各国 BIT 实践之大成，提供了 BIT 结构、用语和内容的重要汇集、选项或参照。更为可贵的是，"协定要素"倡导各国签订"可持续发展导向"（sustainable-development-friendly）BITs，提出了"投资者义务与责任""母国措施"[3]及"特殊与差别待遇"（special and differential treatment，SDT）等创新因素，在很大程度上反映了 BIT 范本的创新理念和发展趋向。

"协定要素"分为"设立后"（post-establishment）、"设立前"（pre-establishment）和"特殊与差别待遇"三个部分。

"设立后"部分在传统欧洲模式的基础上有所创新，是"协定要素"的最主要部分，共有 12 条，依次为序言、条约范围、准入、待遇与保护标准、公共政策例外、争端解决、投资者义务与责任、与其他协定的关系、不降低标准条款、投资促进、制度建设及

---

〔1〕 美国 2012 年范本第 3 条、第 4 条、第 8 条。

〔2〕 See Axel Berger, China's New Bilateral Investment Treaty Programme: Substance, Rational and Implications for Investment Law Making, Paper for the American Society of International Law International Economic Law Group (ASIL IELIG) 2008 biennial conference "The Politics of International Economic Law: The Next Four Years", Washington, D. C., November 14-15, 2008.

〔3〕 广义上，"母国措施"（home country measures）指投资者母国基于合作发展原则，为促进、保护和规范其海外投资和海外投资者而制定或采取的国内措施和国际措施。一些资本输出国初步意识到规范其海外投资者在东道国经营活动的责任，且付诸行动。有学者指出，"可持续的投资"的成就是母国政府、东道国政府、母国私人、东道国私人、环境组织及公民等行为者的共同责任。因此，母国政府和母国私人应采取和接受必要的措施或规范。See Riva Krut and Ashley Moretz, Home Country Measures for Encouraging Sustainable FDI, Occasional Paper No. 8, Report as part of UNCTAD/CBS Project: Cross Border Environmental Management in Transnational Corporations, CBS, November 1999, pp. 1-2.

最后条款。其中,序言、条约范围、准入、待遇与保护标准、争端解决、与其他协定的关系及最后条款等 7 个条款与德国范本类似。而公共政策例外、投资者义务与责任、不降低标准条款、投资促进及制度建设等 5 个条款则具有明显的创新因素。

在"设立前"部分,涉及"设立前责任"(pre-establishment obligations),包含了"设立权"、限制"设立权"及保留"准入权"的不同选项。[1]

在"特殊与差别待遇"部分,共有 2 个条款,分别题为"不对称的责任"(asymmetrical obligations)和"附加工具"(additional tools)。[2] 该部分作为经济发展水平不同的发达国家与发展中国家之间 BITs 的选项,突出反映了发达国家与发展中国家之间 BITs 的结构性创新。

总体上,"协定要素"的主要特色表现在,力图通过调整 BIT 传统条款和增加创新条款,保障东道国的主权权力和政策空间,限制东道国的责任条款,同时,要求外国投资者及其母国承担必要的义务与责任,由此构建"可持续发展导向"BITs。

在调整传统条款方面,主要包括:(1)"投资"的涵盖范围不包括证券、短期或风险投资,要求符合"对东道国发展的积极影响"等具体特征;[3](2)对国民待遇、最惠国待遇或设立前责任的特定国家保留,确定可实施的政策措施(如补贴)、政策区域(如少数民族、土著团体政策)或部门(如社会服务);[4](3)"征收条款"规定,追求公共政策目标的非歧视性善意管制不构成间接征收;[5](4)不采用"公平与公正待遇"条款、"保护伞"条款。[6] 此类规定旨在纠正传统条款中资本输出国与资本输入国之间、外国投资者与东道国之间权益的不平衡。

---

〔1〕"协定要素"第 B 部分第 1 条。*See UNCTAD*,*World Investment Report 2012*,*Towards a New Generation of Investment Policies*,pp. 157-158.

〔2〕"协定要素"第 C 部分第 12 条。*See UNCTAD*,*World Investment Report 2012*,*Towards a New Generation of Investment Policies*,p. 159.

〔3〕"协定要素"第 A 部分第 2.1 条。*See UNCTAD*,*World Investment Report 2012*,*Towards a New Generation of Investment Policies*,p. 144.

〔4〕"协定要素"第 A 部分第 2.3 条,第 B 部分第 1 条。See UNCTAD, *World Investment Report 2012*,*Towards a New Generation of Investment Policies*,pp. 145,157-158.

〔5〕"协定要素"第 A 部分第 4.5 条。See UNCTAD, *World Investment Report 2012*,*Towards a New Generation of Investment Policies*,p. 148.

〔6〕"协定要素"第 A 部分第 4.3、4.10 条。See UNCTAD, *World Investment Report 2012*,*Towards a New Generation of Investment Policies*,pp. 147,150. 作为单独的投资保护条款,"保护伞条款"(umbrella clause)可溯及 1956—1959 年《阿部—相互保护海外私人财产权利国际公约草案》(Abs Draft International Convention for the Mutual Protection of Private Property Rights in Foreign Countries)第 4 条。该条款规定:"根据政府间协定、其他协定或缔约一方行政法规承诺给予非国民高于国民的待遇,包括最惠国待遇,此种承诺(promises)应优先适用。"1959 年《阿部—绍克拉斯—外国投资公约草案》第 2 条将该条款修改为:"缔约各方应在任何时候保证遵守其已作出的与缔约对方国民投资有关的任何承诺(undertakings)。"其后,1959 年德国—巴基斯坦 BIT 第 7 条规定:"缔约各方应遵守其已承担的与缔约对方国民或公司投资有关的任何其他责任(obligation)。" See OECD Secretariat, Improving the System of Investor-State Dispute Settlement:An Overview, Document for Symposium Co-organized by ICSID, OECD and UNCTAD on Making the Most of International Invest. (2005),p. 31.

在增加创新条款方面，主要是：(1)"投资者的义务与责任"条款，要求投资者在投资准入和经营阶段遵守东道国法律，促进投资者遵守企业社会责任（corporate social responsibilities，CSR）的普遍原则或可适用的企业社会责任标准；[1] (2)"母国措施"条款，主要体现在"投资促进"和"制度建设"条款，特别是要求投资者母国制订促进"负责任的投资"（responsible investment）的措施；[2] (3)"特殊与差别待遇"条款，作为发展水平悬殊的 BIT 缔约方，特别是缔约一方是最不发达国家的选项，其效力适用于现有和新的规定，使较不发达缔约方的责任水平适合其发展水平。[3] 此类创新条款旨在从整体结构层面纠正传统 BITs 中资本输出国与资本输入国之间、外国投资者与东道国之间权益的不平衡。

（二）BIT 范本的发展趋向

在一定意义上，BIT 范本最突出的问题分别是目标和模式问题。目标问题关系范本的指导思想和价值取向，模式问题关系范本的基本结构和主要条款。两者的新发展可反映出 BIT 范本整体的发展趋向。

1. BIT 范本目标的新发展

"保护投资"是以德国范本为代表的传统 BIT 范本及其实践确立的明确目标。在德国范本基础上发展起来的美国范本在强化"保护投资"的同时，提出了"自由化"的新目标，反映了传统 BIT 范本及其实践的新发展。2004 年以来，美国范本的形式和内容均发生了显著的变化和发展。美国范本坚持和发展传统国际投资政策，"片面保护外资和外国投资者"的传统立场、基调和路线始终不渝，且逐步升级。其发展历程可大致概括为：从"传统的保护投资"发展为"更高水平的保护投资"，进而确立和追求"投资自由化"的新目标。其新增加的"投资自由化"条款集中反映了美国作为资本输出大国对 BIT 目标和功效的新追求。

而"协定要素"则在汇集和借鉴传统 BIT 范本及其实践各种"要素"的基础上，提出了"可持续发展"的创新性目标，力图通过调整"资本输入国与资本输出国之间权益不平衡"（简称"南北权益不平衡"）的传统条款和增加"平衡资本输入国与资本输出国之间权益"（简称"平衡南北权益"）的创新条款，纠正传统 BITs 中资本输出国与资本输入国之间、外国投资者与东道国之间权益的不平衡，为缔约双方提供公平的

〔1〕 "协定要素"第 A 部分第 7 条。See UNCTAD, *World Investment Report 2012*, *Towards a New Generation of Investment Policies*, p. 154.

〔2〕 "协定要素"第 A 部分第 10、11 条。See UNCTAD, *World Investment Report 2012*, *Towards a New Generation of Investment Policies*, pp. 155-156.

〔3〕 "协定要素"第 C 部分第 12 条。See UNCTAD, *World Investment Report 2012*, *Towards a New Generation of Investment Policies*, p. 159.

法律基础和规则,也反映了国际社会为改革和重构国际投资条约体制所需要的"平衡""可持续发展"和"一体化"等创新理念和共识。[1]概括而言,"协定要素"对 BIT 目标取向的创新意义主要表现在:

第一,主张 BITs 由"片面保护外资"发展为"平衡当事双方权利义务和多元目标"。在传统 BIT 实践中,长期存在发达国家与发展中国家之间在谈判地位与能力、谈判目标与效果、权力与利益等方面的不平等或不平衡现象。"协定要素"强调资本输出国与资本输入国之间权利义务、东道国与外国投资者之间权利义务的平衡;同时,也主张 BIT 多元目标相互之间的平衡,包括保护外资与管制外资之间的平衡、经济与其他公共利益之间的平衡。

第二,主张 BITs 由"片面保护外国投资者权益"发展为"促进东道国可持续发展"。传统 BITs 片面保护外国投资者权益,未顾及东道国的经济发展,更遑论关注东道国的"可持续发展"。"协定要素"提出的"可持续发展"主要涵盖环境、社会发展、企业社会责任等内容,强调外资应纳入东道国的可持续发展战略,倡导各国签订"可持续发展导向"BITs。

第三,主张 BITs"一体化"推进保护外资和管制外资的两种功能。在传统国际立法中,保护外资和管制外资的两种努力"各行其道"。保护外资的 BITs 属于"硬法",具有法律强制力。而管制外资的国际规范,则大多属于"软法",成效甚微。"协定要素"强调保护外资和管制外资的同等重要性,提出在 BITs 中纳入"投资者义务与责任"等创新条款,力图在 BIT 实践中"一体化"推进保护外资和管制外资的两种功能。

"自由化导向"的美国范本和"可持续发展导向"的"协定要素"反映了当前 BIT 范本的两种不同发展趋向。何者能代表世界各国普遍认同的、符合世界各国长远利益的 BIT 范本的发展趋向,取决于世界各国的共识和实践。客观上,美国范本代表发达国家普遍的利益诉求,源于 BIT 传统实践,凭借发达国家的经济实力,在经济全球化的背景下强势推行,惯性相助,明显居于优势地位。而"协定要素"代表广大发展中国家的利益诉求,脱胎于 BIT 传统实践,力图变革创新,其"可持续发展导向"BITs 的创新理念和规范尚属催生或新生期,亟须各国,特别是发展中国家达成共识和付诸实践。

2. BIT 范本模式的新发展

如前所述,BIT 范本是欧美发达国家在 BIT 实践中创造的,带有先天的"资本输

---

〔1〕　关于"协定要素"体现的"平衡""可持续发展"和"一体化"等创新理念,参见 Zeng Huaqun, Balance, Sustainable Development, and Integration: Innovative Path for BIT Practice, 17(2) *Journal of International Economic Law* (2014), pp. 323-329。

出国烙印"。美国范本是在德国范本的基础上发展起来的。在这个意义上,德国范本和美国范本实质上是一脉相承的,均可作为传统 BIT 范本的典型。以德国范本为代表的欧洲模式长期保持"超稳定"的基本结构和主要条款,美国 2004 年之前的范本也与欧洲模式大体保持一致。显然,2004 年之前,欧洲模式在世界各国 BIT 范本及其实践中居于主导和主流地位。美国 2004 年范本在形式和内容方面作了大幅修改,由简入繁,才出现了迥异于欧洲模式的"自由化导向"的美国模式。严格意义上,2004 年之后,BIT 范本才有欧洲模式和美国模式的明确区分,出现了欧洲模式和美国模式并行不悖的局面。当前,需要明确的是,在欧洲模式保持"超稳定状态"的情况下,尽管美国模式颇有"后来居上"之势,尚不能轻易断言美国模式代表了 BIT 范本的发展趋势,更不能轻易断言美国模式取代欧洲模式的地位,成为当前"引领"世界各国 BIT 实践的"放之四海而皆准"的"国际通行规则"。

"协定要素"产生于 2012 年,由于源自各国 BIT 范本及其实践,包括德国范本的主要规定和美国范本的部分规定,形式上与德国范本和美国范本也具有一定程度的关联性。值得注意的是,"协定要素"未采纳美国范本中的投资与环境、投资与劳工、非减损、拒绝授惠、金融服务、税务等条款,增加了公共政策例外、投资者义务与责任、不降低标准条款、投资促进、制度建设及特殊与差别待遇等创新条款,形成了独特的"可持续发展导向"模式。显然,"协定要素"是传统 BIT 模式的创新性发展,既包含经调整的传统条款,又提出了重要的创新条款,由此改变了传统 BIT 范本"片面保护外资和外国投资者"的基本结构。

欧洲模式、美国模式和"协定要素"模式三者孰优孰劣,尚待各国审慎选择并付诸实践。假以时日,才可望逐渐形成各国普遍认同的 BIT 模式的总体发展趋向。当然,在选择和推行 BIT 模式的国际实践中,缔约各方的立场、实力及参与程度必将产生相当重要甚至决定性的作用。不难预料,在中美 BIT、欧美 BIT 及中欧 BIT 谈判中,采用何种模式,对缔约各方都是重要的选择和严峻的考验,对 BIT 模式的总体发展趋向,对国际投资领域"国际通行规则"的形成与确立,也必将产生重大而深远的影响。

三、我国新 BIT 范本的目标和模式选择

作为实行改革开放政策的重要标志,自 1982 年 3 月与瑞典签订第一个中外 BIT 以来,我国积极参与 BIT 实践,后来居上,迄今已签订 129 个 BITs,签约数名列全球

次席。[1] 在实施"走出去"战略的新形势下,我国海外投资事业迅速发展,亟须进一步参与改革和重构以 BITs 为主体的国际投资条约体制。作为兼有资本输入国和资本输出国双重地位的发展中大国,我国参与改革和重构国际投资条约体制的基本立场不仅事关国家权益,对国际投资条约体制的发展和新国际经济秩序的建立也具有十分重要的意义。当前,BIT 范本及其实践的发展处于十字路口,各国面临挑战或抉择。我国应在总结分析中外 BIT 范本发展趋向和相关实践的基础上,[2] 从解决南北问题的高度,坚持经济主权、公平互利和合作发展三大国际经济法基本原则,审慎决定我国新 BIT 范本的目标和模式,以利于及时制定新范本,指导和规范我国的实践。

（一）我国新 BIT 范本的目标选择

如前所述,长期以来,"保护投资"是以德国范本为代表的传统 BIT 范本及其实践确立的明确目标。在德国范本基础上发展起来的美国范本在强化"保护投资"目标的同时,提出了"自由化"的新目标,反映了传统 BIT 范本及其实践的新发展。当前,以美国范本为代表的"自由化导向"和以"协定要素"为代表的"可持续发展导向"可分别作为各国 BIT 范本及其实践的目标选项。

显而易见,在存在资本输出国与资本输入国之分的情况下,"自由化导向"BITs 是缔约一方受益、缔约另一方受限的安排。20 世纪 90 年代以来,BIT 范本及其实践出现了许多重要的新发展,总体上是忽略或淡化南北问题、特别是资本输出国与资本输入国的区分,强调"投资自由化"。[3] 在多边投资协定（Multilateral Agreement on Investment,MAI）谈判搁浅和 WTO 投资议题谈判举步维艰的情况下,发达国家更加重视在 BITs 和 RTAs 中纳入"投资自由化"条款。[4] 发达国家凭借其经济和政治优势促进"自由化导向"BITs,通常要求东道国遵循国际投资保护的"自由取向"

---

〔1〕 http://investmentpolicyhub. unctad. org/IIA/(last visited June 23，2016).

〔2〕 关于我国 BIT 实践的总结分析,参见李玲:《中国双边投资保护协定缔约实践和面临的挑战》,载陈安主编:《国际经济法学刊》第 17 卷第 4 期,北京大学出版社 2010 年版,第 114—126 页。

〔3〕 关于 BIT 作为自由化工具的评论,参见 Kenneth J. Vandevelde, Investment Liberalization and Economic Development：the Role of Bilateral Investment Treaties, 36 *Columbia Journal of Transnational Law* (1998)，pp. 504-514. 有西方学者指出,"传统概念上对资本输出国与资本输入国的区分正失去其意义","此种传统结构已经过时"。See Angel Gurria, Welcoming Remarks, the Second Symposium on International Investment Agreements/International Investment Agreements and Investor-State Dispute Settlement at a Crossroads：Identifying Trends, Differences and Common Approaches, OECD Headquarters，14 December 2010.

〔4〕 近年来,"自由化"导向的美国范本影响逐渐蔓延。OECD 成员国参与 BIT 和 RTA 实践的重心已从传统的"投资保护"转向"投资自由化"。其新近 BIT 实践的主要特征包括：(1) 高标准的追求,即从传统的关注"投资保护"发展为包含更广泛的自由化规则；(2) 重新定义关键的"投资保护",增加指导适用征收条款的新措词；(3) 越来越广泛地接受"投资者与国家间争端解决程序"等。See OECD Secretariat, Novel Features in OECD Countries' Recent Investment Agreements：An Overview, Document for Symposium Co-organized by ICSID, OECD and UNCTAD on Making the Most of International Invest (2005)，pp. 4-5.

(liberal approach)，注重为外国投资者提供高水平的实体性和程序性保护，[1]外资待遇标准更为侧重投资设立前的保护和新的自由化承诺。[2]

实践表明，对待"投资自由化"议题，取决于缔约双方的组合情况，不同的 BITs 之间存在明显差别。总体而言，与发展中国家相互之间签订的 BITs 相比，发达国家与发展中国家之间签订的 BITs 更倾向于规定"投资自由化"的内容。[3] 不言而喻，此类"投资自由化"规定的结果通常是，发达国家投资者单向自由投资于发展中国家，而发展中国家投资者一般尚未具备反向投资的能力。

随着我国改革开放不断深化、综合国力逐渐增强及实施"走出去"战略，我国兼具资本输入国和资本输出国身份，"自由化导向"BIT 是否自然而然地成为我国 BIT 实践的目标选项呢？

笔者认为，"投资自由化"不属 BITs 的涵盖内容，也不是 BITs 的必要条款，更不是 BITs 的主要目标。"投资自由化"的实质是限缩东道国管理外资的主权权力和政策空间，偏重和强化资本输出国及其海外投资者的权益。鉴此，基于经济主权原则和公平互利原则，在经济实力悬殊的发达国家与发展中国家之间，由于属单向投资关系，一般不能在 BITs 中采用显失公平的"投资自由化"条款；在经济实力相当的发达国家相互之间或发展中国家相互之间，虽属双向投资关系，由于涉及限制缔约各方管理外资的主权权力和政策空间，是否将 BITs"保护投资"的目标升格为"投资自由化"，是否在 BITs 中采用"投资自由化"条款，也应取决于缔约双方的共同意愿。事实上，尽管表面推崇"投资自由化"，发达国家相互之间通常也不愿意签订"自由化导向"BITs，相互不愿意洞开国门，使本国企业面临来自缔约对方投资者的竞争压力。[4] 显然，我国新 BIT 范本不应以"投资自由化"为目标选项。在 BIT 实践中，我国应根据缔约双方的国情和经济实力对比情况，审慎应对缔约对方提出的"投资自由化"条款。[5]

---

〔1〕 See Axel Berger, China's New Bilateral Investment Treaty Programme: Substance, Rational and Implications for Investment Law Making, Paper for the American Society of International Law International Economic Law Group(ASIL IELIG) 2008 biennial conference "The Politics of International Economic Law: The Next Four Years", Washington, D. C., November 14-15, 2008.

〔2〕 See OECD Secretariat, Novel Features in OECD Countries' Recent Investment Agreements: An Overview, Document for Symposium Co-organized by ICSID, OECD and UNCTAD on Making the Most of International Invest (2005), p. 4.

〔3〕 参见詹晓宁等：《国际投资协定：趋势和主要特征》，载陈安主编：《国际经济法学刊》第 14 卷第 1 期，北京大学出版社 2007 年版，第 121 页。

〔4〕 Jeswald W. Salacuse, Nicholas P. Sullivan, Do BITs Really Work?: An Evaluation of Bilateral Investment Treaties and Their Grand Bargain, *Harvard International Law Journal*, Vol. 46, No. 1, 2005, p. 78.

〔5〕 在中美 BIT 谈判中，美国依据其范本，提出给予投资者"设立前国民待遇"等"自由化"要求，中美双方重申，在经济不稳定的时刻，进行的中美 BIT 谈判将为履行 2009 年 G-20 高峰会议有关"开放性全球经济"(open global economy)的承诺作出贡献。有学者指出，中美 BIT 谈判如按美国范本处理美国提出的问题，将成为最自由化的 BIT。See Kong Qingjiang, US-China Bilateral Investment Treaty Negotiations, *EAI Background Brief* No. 507, 25 February 2010, pp. 5, 9-10.

近年来,发展中国家长期主张的"发展权"(right to development)概念在很大程度上已为"可持续发展"概念所取代,"可持续发展"原则被各国普遍接受为经济发展和国际关系的一般原则。[1] 越来越多的 BITs 在序言中包括了"可持续发展"原则。总体上,"可持续发展"导向 BIT,应体现为"平衡南北权益"的实践。资本输出国与资本输入国均需要享有权力和权利,并承担相应的责任和义务,真正平衡资本输出国与资本输入国之间的权益及东道国与外国投资者之间的权益。具体而言,BITs 应具有保护、促进跨国投资与管制外国投资者行为的双重目标和功能。在 BIT 范本的内容设计中,应强化或增加有关东道国管制外资权力和投资者母国促进、管制海外投资活动的条款,即东道国应具有自主决定外资准入领域、外资履行要求等管制外资的权力,并承担保护跨国投资的义务;而投资者母国则须承担监管本国海外投资的责任,承诺和保护东道国免受外国投资者,特别是跨国公司负面行为方式的损害。[2]

我国新 BIT 范本理应顺势而为,以"可持续发展"为目标选项。在国际投资政策语境中,"可持续发展"可作为 BIT 缔约各方的"共赢"目标。由于它强调东道国经济和社会的发展,符合资本输入国的基本需要。由于它促进东道国创设健康的投资环境,也符合资本输出国及其海外投资者的重要利益。在我国新 BIT 范本及其实践中,"可持续发展"目标的确立,旨在从实质内容和结构形式上纠正传统 BITs 中资本输出国与资本输入国之间权益、东道国与外国投资者之间权益的不平等或不平衡。

(二)我国新 BIT 范本的模式选择

一般认为,BITs 是调整国际私人投资关系的兼有实体性和程序性规范的专题性协定。BIT 实践及其范本经历 50 多年的发展,已形成了体现于欧洲模式和美国模式(简称"欧美模式")的"共同语言"和各国普遍认同的"国际通行规则"。制定我国新 BIT 范本,并非要求完全脱离或排斥欧美模式和传统 BIT 实践,"另起炉灶",而是需要坚持国际经济法基本原则,以"扬弃"精神借鉴欧美模式传统条款的合理成分,重视采纳"协定要素"的创新因素,推陈出新。

1. 欧美模式传统条款的"扬弃"

毋庸讳言,长期以来,我国 BIT 范本主要借鉴以德国范本为代表的欧洲模式。实践表明,从形式、内容甚至用语上看,中国系列的 BITs 和德国系列的 BITs 并无实

---

〔1〕 关于"可持续发展"原则的系统论述,参见〔荷兰〕尼科·斯赫雷弗:《可持续发展在国际法中的演进:起源、涵义及地位》,汪习根、黄海滨译,北京:社会科学文献出版社 2008 年版。

〔2〕 跨国公司的此类负面行为方式包括对东道国政治的干预、违反人权标准、违反环境规范等。See M. Sornarajah, *The International Law on Foreign Investment*, Cambridge University Press, 2nd edition, 2004, pp. 171-181.

质上的区别。[1] 德国范本中的定义、准入与投资保护、国民待遇与最惠国待遇、征收情况下的赔偿、自由转移、代位、其他规定、适用范围、缔约国间争端的解决、缔约国一方与缔约国另一方投资者间争端的解决、缔约国间的关系、登记条款、生效，期限与终止通知等条款涉及促进和保护国际投资的主要问题和条约法的一般问题，均为BITs 的必要条款。美国范本第 A 节的定义、范围、国民待遇、最惠国待遇、最低待遇标准、征收与赔偿、转移及生效；期限与终止等 8 个条款及第 C 节第 37 条缔约双方之间争端解决条款，亦遵循欧洲模式的传统条款。这些传统条款的形式，值得我国在制定新 BIT 范本中继续借鉴。

美国范本第 A 节的另 14 个条款属于新增条款。其中，履行要求、高级管理层与董事会、不符措施等属"投资自由化"条款；关于投资的法律决定的公布、透明度、特殊程序与信息要求和信息披露等属"透明度"条款，与"投资自由化、便利化"密切相关；投资与环境、投资与劳工、金融服务、税务属"与投资有关"条款；非减损、拒绝授惠及根本安全则分别是传统 BITs 中序言、适用范围及例外条款的深化或扩大化。一般而言，"投资自由化"条款涉及国家主权，往往限缩发展中国家管制外资的主权权力和政策空间。"与投资有关"条款则不断扩张 BITs 的适用范围，使 BITs 的谈判、签订和履行趋向复杂化，背离了 BITs 作为专题性协定的初衷和特质。[2] 美国范本第 B 节第 23 条至第 36 条有关"投资者与国家间争端解决程序"的规定，细化了投资争端的解决方式，是其最大特色，同时，也明显影响了 BITs 实体性与程序性规范的均衡和 BITs 中各种争端解决方式的均衡。对美国范本的上述新发展，我国在制订新 BIT 范本中应审慎评估，一般不予采纳。

应当指出，借鉴欧美模式的上述传统条款，绝非生搬硬套，"照单全收"，而是需要深入分析德国范本与美国范本的异同及各传统条款的来源、涵义及效果，以"扬弃"精神择善而从。谨以"准入""公平与公正待遇"及征收条款为例，进一步说明我国的应有立场和实践。

"准入"条款是德国范本和传统 BIT 实践中唯一体现维护东道国主权的条款，迄今仍为欧洲发达国家和广大发展中国家普遍采用。而"设立权"模式是美国为代表

---

[1] 西方学者有关中国 BIT 实践发展的评论，参见 Monika C. E. Heymann, International Law and the Settlement of Investment Disputes relating to China, *Journal of International Economic Law*，Vol. 11, No. 3, 2008, pp. 507-526。

[2] 应当明确，经济议题与社会、政治等议题相关，投资议题与贸易、税务等议题相关，专题性的 BIT 不可能、也不适合解决所有相关问题。当前，"与投资有关"的议题主要包括"投资与环境""投资与劳工"等，也涉及金融、税务、人权等，在形式上，也从序言的一般性宣示发展为专门条款规定。显然，如任凭 BIT 中"与投资有关"的议题自由发展，BIT 将逐渐发展成为综合性的领域宽泛的"超投资""超经济"的条约。一旦"与投资有关"的内容"尾大不掉"，将导致 BIT 偏离投资主题的严重后果。

的少数发达国家旨在推动"投资自由化"的新模式。值得重视的是,2012年,贸发会议制定的"可持续发展的投资政策框架"(IPFSD)重申和强调了《各国经济权利和义务宪章》(简称《经济宪章》)确立的东道国对外资的管制权利,规定基于国际承诺,为了公共利益,各国拥有确立外资准入和经营条件且尽量减轻其潜在负面影响的主权权利。[1] 我国作为发展中国家,一向倡导和坚持经济主权原则,在新BIT范本中,理应继续坚持德国范本"准入"条款的实践,同时,不采用美国范本的"设立权"模式和"禁止履行要求"等条款,以维护和保障管制外资进入的主权权力和必要的政策空间。

"公平与公正待遇"条款的广泛采用是外资待遇条款的新发展。理论上,"公平与公正待遇"是相当于习惯国际法要求的"国际最低标准",抑或代表独立、自给自足的概念,即"独立条款"解释,见仁见智。[2] 由于"独立条款"解释的所有要素均与东道国行为有关,东道国显然需要承担高于"国际最低标准"的外资保护责任。应当指出,"公平与公正待遇"条款并非BITs不可或缺的条款。传统上,发展中国家起草或主导的国际规范性文件通常不予采用。[3] 一些发达国家即使采用该条款,也不接受"独立条款"解释。鉴于"公平与公正待遇"条款因涵义不明,在实践中容易产生争议甚至滥用等情况,我国新BIT范本可考虑不予采用,以利维护和保障给予外资待遇的主权权力和可控性。

在近年BIT范本及其实践中,征收的前提条件仍然是征收条款的核心问题。发达国家得陇望蜀,步步为营,不断强化和细化征收的限制性前提条件,意在进一步剥夺或限缩东道国征收和管制外资的主权权力和政策空间,与《经济宪章》确立的"有权征收"原则背道而驰,[4] 渐行渐远。首先,发达国家坚持把"不得征收"外资作为一

---

〔1〕　此为"可持续发展投资决策的核心原则"之(6)"管制权利"(right to regulate)的表述。See UNCTAD, *World Investment Report 2012*, *Towards a New Generation of Investment Policies*, pp.106-110. 笔者以为,在肯定该原则的积极意义时,应当特别注意其"基于国际承诺"和"为了公共利益"两个限定条件。

〔2〕　有学者主张,给予外资"公平与公正待遇"的义务与给予外资"国际最低标准"待遇的义务并无区别,"国际最低标准"是习惯国际法的组成部分,包含"公平与公正待遇"等一系列国际法律原则。另有学者主张,"公平与公正待遇"蕴含不同于"国际最低标准"的含义,应作"独立条款"解释,依衡平检验方式个案适用以确定是否违反该标准。See Rudolf Dolzer, Margrete Stevens, *Bilateral Investment Treaties*, Martinus Nijhoff Publishers, 1995, pp.58-59; UNCTAD, *Bilateral Investment Treaties 1995-2006*: *Trends in Investment Rulemaking*, United Nations, 2007, pp.28-33.

〔3〕　在20世纪70、80年代由发展中国家起草或主导的国际规范性文件,如联合国《各国经济权利和义务宪章》、亚非法律咨商委员会《促进和保护投资协定范本修正案》(Revised Draft of Model Agreements for Promotion and Protection of Investments),均未提及"公平与公正待遇"标准。See Rudolf Dolzer, Fair and Equitable Treatment: A Key Standard in Investment Treaties, *The International Lawyer*, Vol.39, 2005, p.89.

〔4〕　《各国经济权利和义务宪章》第2条第2款规定:"各国有权:……(e)将外国财产的所有权收归国有、征收或转移,在收归国有、征收或转移时,应由采取此种措施的国家给予适当补偿(appropriate compensation),要考虑到它的有关法律和规章以及该国认为有关的一切情况……"

般法律原则,与"有权征收"原则相悖。虽然,发达国家并非完全否定国家对外资的征收权,但对征收权作了严格的限制性前提条件,进而以是否满足前提条件为据区分"合法征收"与"非法征收",并主张依国际法和国内法(包括投资者母国和东道国的法律)保留对东道国政府征收行为是否合法的裁判权。其次,发达国家更为强调适用"及时、充分和有效的赔偿"规则(即"赫尔"规则),与《经济宪章》确立的"适当补偿"原则相悖,可能产生实质否定发展中国家征收权的严重后果。[1] 鉴此,我国新BIT范本及其实践理应坚持《经济宪章》确立的各国对外资的"征收权"和"适当补偿"原则。

2. "协定要素"创新因素的采纳

"协定要素"在调整BIT传统条款的同时,提出了公共政策例外、投资者义务与责任、不降低标准条款、投资促进、制度建设及特殊与差别待遇等创新条款,反映了国际社会创造"可持续发展导向"BIT模式的努力。我国新BIT范本应重视采纳"协定要素"的创新因素,进一步丰富其内容,并勇于实践。谨以"投资者义务与责任""投资促进""制度建设"及"特殊与差别待遇"条款为例,进一步说明我国的应有立场和实践。

"投资者义务与责任"条款是"协定要素"基于经济主权原则和公平互利原则的重要创新。"协定要素"提出,在BIT实践中,以"可持续发展"为目标,增加"投资者义务与责任"条款,以平衡外国投资者的权利和责任,促进"负责任的投资"。具体表现在:要求外国投资者在投资准入和经营阶段遵守东道国法律,促进外国投资者遵守普遍承认的劳工和人权标准,促进外国投资者遵守可适用的企业社会责任标准。[2] 应当指出,该条款内容尚属原则性规定,主要强调外国投资者本应在东道国承担的基本法律义务与责任。尽管如此,在BIT范本及其实践中,此类规范从无到有,仍具有重要的创新意义。鉴于该条款是平衡东道国与外国投资者之间权益及平衡外国投资者本身权利与义务的重要体现,是对传统国际投资条约体制的重要突破,我国新BIT范本理应率先采纳该条款,并积极付诸实践。

"协定要素"以"可持续发展"为目标,在"投资促进"和"制度建设"条款中规定了"母国措施"内容。主要表现在:制定促进海外投资,特别是"最有利于国家发展战略的投资"条款;建立缔约各方开展合作的制度框架,促进履行BITs以利最大限度发挥其对可持续发展的贡献。上述规定的重要创新是基于合作发展原则,强调资本输

---

〔1〕 参见曾华群:《变革期双边投资条约实践述评》,载陈安主编:《国际经济法学刊》第14卷第3期,北京大学出版社2007年版,第23页。

〔2〕 See UNCTAD, *World Investment Report 2012*, *Towards a New Generation of Investment Policies*, p. 154.

出国与资本输入国之间的"国际合作"义务,将"母国措施"作为资本输出国有关"投资促进"和"制度建设"的条约义务。鉴于"母国措施"是 BITs 平衡资本输出国与资本输入国之间权益的重要体现,我国新 BIT 范本理应率先采纳"协定要素"涉及"母国措施"的规定,进一步丰富其内容,并积极付诸实践。

"特殊与差别待遇"条款是"协定要素"基于公平互利原则和合作发展原则的重要创新。在 GATT/WTO 体制中,"特殊与差别待遇"条款早已确立。2000 年,贸发会议主张,"特殊与差别待遇"原则应引入 BITs。[1]"协定要素"以南北问题为视角,规定了"特殊与差别待遇"条款,旨在从整体结构上纠正传统 BITs"形式平等"掩盖下的"实质不平等"。为达此目标,该条款一方面规定"不对称的责任",使较不发达缔约一方承担较轻的责任;另一方面规定"附加工具",促进较发达缔约一方作出积极贡献。[2]我国新 BIT 范本应积极采纳该条款,根据缔约双方经济发展水平等具体情况,予以适用,以实现和保障缔约双方的实质公平和可持续发展。作为发展中国家,我国在与发达国家商签 BITs 时,可主张采纳和适用"特殊与差别待遇"条款,我国作为较不发达缔约一方,承担相对较轻的责任。作为负责任的发展中大国,我国在与经济发展水平不同的其他发展中国家,特别是最不发达国家商签 BITs 时,应主动采纳和适用"特殊与差别待遇"条款,我国作为较发达缔约一方,承担相对较重的责任。[3]

总之,我国新 BIT 范本模式应继续借鉴欧洲模式,专注于投资问题,形式力求简约;同时,以"扬弃"精神借鉴欧美模式的传统条款,重视采纳"协定要素"的创新条款,形成符合国际经济法基本原则、具有鲜明中国特色的"可持续发展导向"BIT 范本。应当指出,"协定要素"是倡导制定"可持续发展导向"BIT 范本的国际性重要文件。基于"协定要素"的创新因素,我国新 BIT 范本可望开创"可持续发展导向"BIT 范本之先河,为世界各国 BIT 范本和国际投资条约体制的发展和创新作出应有的贡献。

四、结语

BIT 范本及其实践历经半个多世纪的发展,在以德国范本为代表的欧洲模式保

---

[1] See UNCTAD, *International Investment Agreements: Flexibility for Development*, *UNCTAD Series on Issues in International Investment Agreements* (UNCTAD/ITE/18, New York and Geneva, 2000), pp. 29-36.

[2] See UNCTAD, *World Investment Report 2012*, *Towards a New Generation of Investment Policies*, p. 159.

[3] 参见曾华群:《论我国"可持续发展导向"双边投资条约的实践》,载《厦门大学学报》(哲学社会科学版) 2015 年第 1 期,第 80—89 页。

持"超稳定状态"的情况下，出现了"自由化导向"的美国范本和"可持续发展导向"的"协定要素"，分别代表当前 BIT 范本的两种发展趋向。美国范本是传统 BIT 模式的"升级版"和"更新版"，体现于强化"片面保护外资"和追求"投资自由化"新目标。而"协定要素"是传统 BIT 模式的创新性发展，体现于调整"南北权益不平衡"的传统条款和增加"平衡南北权益"的创新条款，追求世界各国长远利益和人类共同福祉的"可持续发展"新目标，在很大程度上反映了国际社会改革和重构国际投资条约体制的创新理念、共识、诉求和初步成就。

值此国际投资条约体制发展的关键时刻，发达国家理应反思和调整其传统的"利己"立场和模式，改弦更张，以适应"南北合作共赢"的时代发展之需。而发展中国家则更需要及时改变和扭转其以往在国际投资条约实践的被动姿态和弱势地位，为 BIT 范本及其实践的改革和创新而积极作为。

居于最大的资本输入国和新兴的资本输出大国双重地位，我国具有"平衡南北权益"的内在动因和客观需求。作为发展中大国，我国应有"负责任的发展中大国"的意识和立场，应有改革旧国际经济秩序、构建新国际经济秩序的使命感和责任感，应有积极主动参与制定、影响及引领国际投资条约体制总体发展趋向的自信和作为。在国际投资条约体制面临改革和重构的新形势下，我国需要认真总结中外 BIT 实践经验，深入研究相关国际实践和典型案例，遵循经济主权、公平互利和合作发展原则，经由欧美模式传统条款的"扬弃"和"协定要素"创新因素的采纳，及时制定具有中国特色的"可持续发展导向"BIT 范本，作为与外国商签或修订 BITs 的政策宣示、谈判基础和基本准则，也借以表明我国参与改革和重构国际投资条约体制的立场和实践。在商签或修订中外 BITs 时，以我国新 BIT 范本作为谈判基础之一，可以合理主张，我国新 BIT 范本汲取了"协定要素"的创新因素，寻求缔约双方权益的平衡和共赢，代表了新一代国际投资政策的发展趋向。从现实考虑，在发达国家基于国家利益考虑而固守传统 BIT 模式的情势下，我国与其他发展中国家作为平等的缔约双方，具有建立新国际经济秩序的共同历史使命和奋斗目标，可率先开展"可持续发展导向"BIT 实践，逐渐形成为"国际通行规则"，进而影响发达国家与发展中国家之间的 BIT 实践及国际投资条约体制的总体发展趋势。

On the Evolution of Bilateral Investment Treaty Models and China's Response

Abstract: In the bilateral investment treaty (BIT) practice, the BIT models, as policy statement, negotiating basis and basic norms, are developing continuously.

Their roles and influence are increasingly demonstrated. The BIT models are originated from developed states' practice, serving for the policy goal for protecting their overseas investment. The trend of the BIT models is dominated and influenced by the developed states for a long time. Under the economic globalization, there are "liberalization" approach and "sustainable development" approach in the development of BIT models and related practice. As a responsible large developing state, basing on the analysis of the trend of BIT models and related practice and aiming at dealing with the North-South issues, China should insist on the fundamental principles of international economic law, determine deliberately the objective and pattern of China's BIT model, for formulating the "sustainable-development-friendly" BIT model with Chinese characteristics, and guiding and regulating China's BIT practice.

Key words: bilateral investment treaty models; investment liberalization; sustainable development

第五节　共同发展：中国与"一带一路"
国家间投资条约实践的创新[*]

【摘要】　在简述"一带一路"国际合作法制背景的基础上，本文探讨中国与"一带一路"国家之间 BIT 实践目标、模式和内容的创新问题。本文认为，"投资保护—投资自由化"是传统 BIT 实践目标的演进轨迹，"可持续发展"是 BIT 实践目标的新倡议，而"共同发展"可作为中国与"一带一路"国家之间 BIT 实践的创新目标；在传统 BIT 实践模式基础上，中国与"一带一路"国家可借鉴和汲取"可持续发展导向"BIT 实践模式的创新因素，通过 BIT 结构和条款的革新和改造，创造"共同发展导向"BIT 实践模式；在既有 BIT"国际话语体系"内，中国与"一带一路"国家可通过"共同发展"条款的引入、传统条款的"扬弃"和创新条款的采纳，实现对传统 BIT 实践内容的改革，形成服务于"共同发展导向"BIT 实践的内容。

【关键词】　共同发展；"一带一路"；双边投资条约；目标创新；模式创新；内容创新

经历 40 年来的改革开放，中国已发展成为世界上重要的资本输入国与资本输出国。"一带一路"倡议更为中国与"一带一路"国家之间的合作提供了新的发展机遇。本文在简述"一带一路"国际合作法制背景的基础上，初步探讨中国与"一带一路"国家之间双边投资条约（bilateral investment treaty，BIT）实践目标、模式和内容的创新。

一、"一带一路"国际合作的法制背景

在法言法。"一带一路"倡议需要法律的调整和保障，才能顺利推进。鉴此，本文首先简述"一带一路"倡议的法律意涵、"一带一路"国际合作法律框架的特征及"一带一路"国际法制的创新实践，为进一步探讨中国与"一带一路"国家之间 BIT 实践的创新提供时代和法制背景。

（一）"一带一路"倡议的法律意涵

基于悠远的中外交往历史，2013 年，国家主席习近平在访问哈萨克斯坦和印度

---

[*]　原载《国际经济法学刊》2019 年第 1 期。

尼西亚时首次提出了"丝绸之路经济带"(Silk Road Economic Belt)和"21 世纪海上丝绸之路"(21st Century Maritime Silk Road)的倡议(简称为"一带一路"倡议)。该倡议旨在进一步促进中国与"一带一路"沿线国家和区域间基于历史精神和国家、人民共同意愿的经济联系和合作,寻求与各国和区域的经济发展目标或发展规划的契合和协调。历史上的"丝路精神"可概括为和平合作、开放包容、互鉴互学及互利共赢。该倡议的目标是创建政治互信、经济一体化及文化包容的利益、命运和责任共享的共同体,是构建人类命运共同体的伟大实践。

在法律意义上,"一带一路"倡议可视为中国向世界各国发出的一个开放的"要约",寻求一个或数个合作伙伴的"承诺",以便构成双边或多边的国际合作体制。历史上,"一带"是通过中亚、西亚陆路连接中国与欧洲,"一路"是海路连接中国与东南亚、非洲和欧洲。当下,"一带一路"已超越了地理的意义,实际上并无确定的地理界限。由于它是国际合作的倡议,对"一带一路"沿线国家和所有国家开放。2017 年 5 月 14 日,在北京召开"'一带一路'国际合作高峰论坛",100 多个国家和国际组织领导人出席,反响热烈。[1] 2018 年 7 月 2—3 日,在北京召开"'一带一路'法治合作国际论坛",标志"一带一路"国际合作进入了"法治化"的新阶段。[2]

(二)"一带一路"国际合作法律框架的特征

"一带一路"倡议的任务主要包括"政策沟通,设施联通,贸易畅通,资金融通,民心相通"。在法律层面,主要关注广义的政策(policy),包括国内政策法律和国际法制。2018 年 7 月 3 日发表的《"一带一路"法治合作国际论坛共同主席声明》强调指出:"国际法治是捍卫国家主权、维护世界和平、促进共同发展的重要制度保障,反映了各国对主权平等、和平包容、合作共赢、公正高效等理念和价值的普遍追求。良好的国际法治环境是'一带一路'建设顺利推进的必要前提"。[3]

"一带一路"国际合作法律框架的特征首先是国际法制与国内法制的密切结合。不言而喻,由于"一带一路"国际合作主要通过市场运作,需要国际法制和国内法制(包括东道国法制、母国法制)的促进、调整和保障。对各个具体合作项目而言,相关国际法制和国内法制构成了一般的法制环境或基础,而特定项目合同则是项目具体实施的法律根据和保障。就形式而言,"一带一路"国际合作法律框架的组成部分包

---

〔1〕 参见《"一带一路"国际合作高峰论坛,2017》,at http://www.mofcom.gov.cn/article/zt_ydyl/ 2018 年 9 月 27 日。

〔2〕 参见许军珂:《推进"一带一路"法治合作恰逢其时》,at http://finance.sina.com.cn/roll/2018-07-05/doc-ihevauxk7692189.shtml, 2018 年 9 月 27 日。

〔3〕 参见《"一带一路"法治合作国际论坛共同主席声明》第 4 段,at https://baijiahao.baidu.com/s? id=1604967553984053495&wfr=spider&for=pc, 2018 年 10 月 2 日。

括"一带一路"国家参与的多边经济体制、缔结的区域贸易协定（regional trade agreements，RTAs）和双边经贸条约、国家与外国私人之间签订的"特许协议"[1]以及不同国籍私人之间签订的合同等。上述国际法制与国内法制密切联系，相辅相成。

"一带一路"国际合作法律框架的另一特征是既有法制与创新法制的长期共存和相互融通。总体上，尽管"一带一路"国际合作是区别于传统国际合作的新事物，由于"实践先行，法律滞后"的规律，其法律框架首先是由"一带一路"国家既有国际法制和既有国内法制（统称为"既有法制"）构成的。在此基础上，需要根据新形势发展和新合作形式的需要创新法制，进行"既有法制的改革创新"和"创建新型法制"。从现实情况出发，现阶段当以"既有法制的改革创新"为主。随着"一带一路"国际合作的深入开展，"创建新型法制"将逐渐居于重要地位。长远看来，在"一带一路"国际合作的法律框架中，既有法制与创新法制势必长期共存，且显现"相互包容，相互促进"的发展趋向。

（三）"一带一路"国际法制的创新实践

"一带一路"国际合作具有两个重要涵义：一是通过相互合作促进共同发展，是"区域合作"和"南南合作"的新领域和新方式；二是通过利用有利于其发展的全球各地资源和要素促进"一带一路"国家的发展。[2]"一带一路"国际合作虽是市场运作，但各国政府积极参与其中，发挥重要的引领、促进和保障作用，国际法制尤为重要。

在国际法层面，"一带一路"国际合作的法律框架包括多边经济体制、RTAs及双边经贸条约。

多边经济体制可进一步分为传统国际经济体制和新国际经济体制两种类型。传统国际经济体制，即以"国际货币基金组织"（International Monetary Fund，IMF）、"世界银行"（World Bank，WB）和"关税及贸易总协定"（General Agreement on Tariff and Trade，GATT）〔其后演变为"世界贸易组织"（World Trade Organization，WTO）〕三大支柱作为支撑的"布雷顿森林体制"（Bretton Woods System），是当时西方国家经济实力和权力格局的体现，基本上由西方国家创建、主导及维系，维护和反映了西方国家的既得利益和传统优势地位。中国和绝大多数"一带一路"国家均为该体制成员，有必要共同推进改革，更公正有效地运用既有体制和规范调整相互间

---

〔1〕 特许协议（concession agreement），又称经济发展协议（economic development agreement），是东道国政府与外国投资者签订的规定前者将其拥有和行使的特定权力和权利授予后者的协议。典型的特许协议一般是为开发自然资源而签订的。在其他投资领域，包括铁路、电讯、发电、不动产开发以及石油产品销售，也常采用特许协议形式。参见曾华群：《国际经济法导论》（第二版），法律出版社 2007 年版，第 210-213 页。

〔2〕 See Jun He, "One Belt, One Road": China's New Strategy and Its Impact on FDI, in Julien Chaisse, Tomoko Ishikawa, Sufian Jusoh (ed.), *Asia's Changing International Investment Regime*, *Sustainability*, *Regionalization*, *and Arbitration*, Springer, 2017, pp.167-168.

的关系。以 WTO 为例,中国与绝大多数"一带一路"国家作为 WTO 成员,需要遵守 WTO 规则,也负有改革重任。与此同时,近年在发展中国家的共同努力下,新创建 的国际经济体制方兴未艾。例如,中国参与创建的亚洲基础设施投资银行(Asian Infrastructure Investment Bank,AIIB)、新丝路基金(New Silk Road Fund,NSRF) 及金砖国家新开发银行(BRICS New Development Bank)已相继成立,创立了新规范 和新体制。

在传统 RTAs 中,欧洲联盟(简称"欧盟")和东南亚国家联盟(简称"东盟")最具 典型意义。近年来,中国和"一带一路"国家积极参与 RTA 实践。迄今,中国已先后 与东盟、澳大利亚、智利、哥斯达黎加、韩国、新西兰、新加坡、冰岛、巴基斯坦、秘鲁、 瑞士、挪威等签订 RTAs。中国还参与创建新型合作发展组织或机制,如上海合作组 织(SCO)和金砖国家(BRICS)机制等。

双边经贸条约是"一带一路"国际合作最重要、最直接的国际法制。谨以 BITs 为例。中国已同绝大多数"一带一路"国家签署 BITs。中国作为兼具重要资本输入 国和资本输出国地位的发展中国家,与"一带一路"国家共同创建新的国际投资规 范,正当其时。应当指出,在"一带一路"国际合作中,BITs 具有特别重要的意义,主 要表现在:(1)国际投资是"一带一路"国际合作的重要内容,相应地,调整国际投资 的法制居于重要地位,而 BITs 是调整国际投资关系的最主要的国际法规范;(2)基 础设施建设是"一带一路"国际合作的重要内容,关系国计民生,东道国须担负和行 使重要的管治职能,而外国投资者因此类项目投资巨大、回收期长而倍感"风险", BITs 是确立双方权利义务关系、维护双方合法权益的重要国际法保障;(3)一般认 为,BITs 是东道国具有良好投资环境的标志之一,与东道国的投资法律和投资者母 国的海外投资保证制度一起,构成了对外国投资和外国投资者的国内法和国际法双 重保护;(4)当前,国际投资法制面临变革,由于中国与绝大多数"一带一路"国家同 属发展中国家和新兴经济体,具有共同的发展目标和历史使命,中国与"一带一路" 国家在修订已有 BITs 或新签 BITs 时,可进行"既有法制的改革创新",共同开展有 关 BIT 实践目标、模式和内容的创新。

二、中国与"一带一路"国家间 BIT 实践目标的创新

在一定意义上,BIT 实践的首要问题是目标或宗旨问题,一般表述于 BITs 的序 言并体现于其具体条款,关系 BITs 的模式和内容的指导思想和价值取向,实质上决 定了 BITs 缔约双方权利义务关系的基本格局和 BITs 本身的实际功效。传统 BIT 实践目标经历了"投资保护—投资自由化"的演进,近年出现了"可持续发展"(sustainable development）BIT 实践目标的新倡议，在此基础上，笔者主张，以"共同发展"（common development）作为中国与"一带一路"国家之间 BIT 实践目标的创新。

（一）"投资保护—投资自由化"：传统 BIT 实践目标的演进

在 BIT 实践中，作为缔约各方政策宣示、谈判基础和基本准则的 BIT 范本不断发展，其作用和影响日益彰显，实际上集中反映了 BIT 实践的目标取向。[1] 长期以来，"投资保护"是以德国 BIT 范本为代表的传统 BIT 范本及其实践确立的明确目标。在德国范本基础上发展起来的美国范本在强化"投资保护"目标的同时，提出了"投资自由化"的新目标，反映了传统 BIT 范本及其实践的传承和发展。

1. 德国式"投资保护导向"（investment protection oriented）BITs

历史表明，BITs 是发达国家在其海外投资实践中创造的，带有先天的"资本输出国烙印"。一般认为，BITs 的早期形式可溯及"友好通商航海条约"（friendship, commerce, and navigation treaties, FCN）。[2] 1959 年以来，联邦德国等欧洲国家以 FCN 中有关促进和保护国际投资的事项为中心内容，同作为资本输入国的发展中国家签订专门性的"相互促进和保护投资协定"（Agreement concerning Reciprocal Encouragement and Protection of Investments），即现代 BITs。[3] 历经半个多世纪，多数 BITs 模仿或至少广泛照搬 1959 年《海外投资国际公约草案》（Draft International Convention on Investments Abroad）和 1967 年经济合作开发组织（OECD）《保护外国财产的公约草案》（Draft Convention on the Protection of Foreign Property）的主要条款。由于来源相同，不同 BITs 的主题、结构和用语，在不同的时期、不同的国家实践仍显得非常相似。[4] 典型 BITs 的缔约方为一方为欧洲国家，另一方为发展中国家。[5] 20 世纪 80 年代初，美国决定采用 BIT 作为保护其海外投资的工具之后，

---

〔1〕 关于 BIT 实践及其范本的缘起与特征，参见曾华群：《论双边投资条约范本的演进与中国的对策》，载《国际法研究》2016 年第 4 期，第 60—65 页。

〔2〕 早在 1956 年，FCN 就被美国学者称为"促进和保护外国投资的条约"。See Herman Walker, Jr., Treaties for the Encouragement and Protection of Foreign Investment: Present United States Practice, *The American Journal of Comparative Law*, Vol. 5, No. 2, 1956, pp. 229-247.

〔3〕 1959 年，联邦德国与巴基斯坦签订了第一个"关于促进和保护投资的条约"。该条约包含了许多实体性规定，为其后 BITs 所效法。See Andrew Newcombe, Lluis Paradell, *Law and Practice of Investment Treaties, Standards of Treatment*, Wolters Kluwer, 2009, p. 42.

〔4〕 See Jason Webb Yackee, Conceptual Difficulties in the Empirical Study of Bilateral Investment Treaties, *Brooklyn Journal of International Law*, Vol. 33, 2008, pp. 415-416.

〔5〕 瑞士、法国、意大利、英国、荷兰和比利时等欧洲国家紧随联邦德国 BIT 实践，与发展中国家签订 BITs。See Jeswald W. Salacuse, 'BIT by BIT: The Growth of Bilateral Investment Treaties and Their Impact on Foreign Investment in Developing Countries', *The International Lawyer*, Vol. 24, 1990, pp. 656-657.

BITs 更为迅速发展。[1] BITs 逐渐为世界各国普遍接受,成为国际投资条约体制中最为重要的形式。

　　理论上,BITs 是缔约国之间双边谈判的结果,旨在为缔约双方提供同等的法律保护。事实上,它们常常是作为资本输出国的发达国家与作为资本输入国的发展中国家之间的协定。BITs 在其名称和序言中往往声称其具有"投资保护"和"促进投资"双重功能,"投资保护"显然有利于资本输出国及其海外投资者,"促进投资"似乎较有利于资本输入国。值得注意的是,在 BIT 语境中,"促进投资"的用语是含糊的。"促进投资"是指"促进对外投资","促进外来投资",抑或两者兼而有之? 可以明确的是,"促进投资"并不一定意味着缔约双方相互的"促进对外投资"。许多发展中国家因缺乏资金而反对本国投资者对外投资,其参与签订的 BITs 称为"促进和相互保护投资"(the encouragement and reciprocal protection of investment),而不是更为普遍采用的"相互促进和保护投资"(the reciprocal encouragement and protection of investment)。[2] 由于"促进投资"用语的含糊,"促进投资"的责任也是含糊的。它意味着发达国家承担促进其投资者对外投资的责任,抑或发展中国家承担改善其投资环境以吸引外资的责任? 事实表明,BIT 实践向来偏重资本输入国"投资保护"的功能,基本忽略资本输出国"促进对外投资"的功能。主要表现在,对资本输入国而言,"投资保护"是具有法律约束力的条约责任,而对资本输出国而言,"促进对外投资"通常只是其促进海外投资的"最佳努力"(best-endeavour)宣示,而非具有法律约束力的条约责任。"促进投资"的条约责任通常落实在资本输入国创设优良投资环境以"促进外来投资"和实现"投资自由化"等方面,而基本忽略了资本输入国"促进外来投资"以利本国发展的政策目标。[3]

　　由此可见,尽管法律形式是缔约双方"双向""对等"的权利义务关系,德国式"投资保护导向"BIT 实践自始带有实质上"片面保护外资和外国投资者"和"服务于资本输出国及其海外投资者单方权益"的鲜明特征,可称为"事实上(de facto)资本输出国单方受益体制"。

---

〔1〕　See Axel Berger, China's New Bilateral Investment Treaty Programme: Substance, Rational and Implications for Investment Law Making, Paper for the American Society of International Law International Economic Law Group (ASIL IELIG) 2008 biennial conference "The Politics of International Economic Law: The Next Four Years", Washington, D. C., November 14-15, 2008.

〔2〕　See Jeswald W. Salacuse, 'BIT by BIT: The Growth of Bilateral Investment Treaties and Their Impact on Foreign Investment in Developing Countries', *The International Lawyer*, Vol. 24, 1990, p. 662.

〔3〕　关于发达资本输出国与发展中资本输入国之间 BIT 传统实践的不平衡或不平等,参见 Zeng Huaqun, Balance, Sustainable Development, and Integration: Innovative Path for BIT Practice, *Journal of International Economic Law*, Vol. 17, No. 2, 2014, pp. 300-308。

2. 美国式"投资自由化导向"(investment liberalization oriented)BITs

20 世纪 90 年代以来,BIT 范本及其实践出现了许多重要的新发展,总体上是忽略或淡化南北问题,特别是资本输出国与资本输入国的区分,强调"投资自由化"。[1]在多边投资协定(Multilateral Agreement on Investment,MAI)谈判搁浅和 WTO 投资议题谈判举步维艰的情况下,发达国家更加重视在 BITs 和 RTAs 中纳入"投资自由化"条款。发达国家凭借其经济和政治优势促进"投资自由化导向"BITs,通常要求东道国遵循国际投资保护的"自由取向"(liberal approach),注重为外国投资者提供高水平的实体性和程序性保护,[2]外资待遇标准更为侧重投资设立前的保护和新的自由化承诺。[3]

在 BIT 实践及制定范本方面,比之欧洲国家,美国是后来者。美国 1977 年启动"BIT 计划"(bilateral investment treaty program),第一步是制定用于谈判的《美国政府与某国政府关于促进和相互保护投资的条约范本》(Treaty between the Government of the United States of America and Government of [Country] Concerning the Encouragement and Reciprocal Protection of Investment)。1982 年,美国制定其第一个 BIT 范本,之后历经 1983、1984、1987、1991、1992、1994、2004、2012 年 8 次修订。[4]美国范本坚持和发展传统国际投资政策,"片面保护外资和外国投资者"的传统立场、基调和路线始终不渝,且逐步升级。其发展历程可大致概括为:从传统的"投资保护"发展为"更高水平的投资保护",进而确立追求"投资自由化"的新目标。其新增加的"投资自由化"目标和条款集中反映了美国作为资本输出大国对 BIT 实践目标和功效的新追求。近年来,"自由化"导向的美国范本影响逐渐蔓延。OECD 成员国参与 BIT 和 RTA 实践的重心已从传统的"投资保护"转向"投资自由化"。其新近 BIT 实践的主要特征包括:(1) 高标准的追求,即从传统的关注"投资保护"发展

---

〔1〕 关于 BIT 作为自由化工具的评论,参见 Kenneth J. Vandevelde, Investment Liberalization and Economic Development: the Role of Bilateral Investment Treaties, *Columbia Journal of Transnational Law*, Vol. 36, 1998, pp. 504-514。有西方学者指出,"传统概念上对资本输出国与资本输入国的区分正失去其意义","此种传统结构已经过时"。See Angel Gurria, Welcoming Remarks, the Second Symposium on International Investment Agreements/ International Investment Agreements and Investor-State Dispute Settlement at a Crossroads: Identifying Trends, Differences and Common Approaches, OECD Headquarters, 14 December 2010.

〔2〕 See Axel Berger, China's New Bilateral Investment Treaty Programme: Substance, Rational and Implications for Investment Law Making, Paper for the American Society of International Law International Economic Law Group (ASIL IELIG) 2008 biennial conference "The Politics of International Economic Law: The Next Four Years", Washington, D. C., November 14-15, 2008.

〔3〕 See OECD Secretariat, Novel Features in OECD Countries' Recent Investment Agreements: An Overview, Document for Symposium Co-organized by ICSID, OECD and UNCTAD on Making the Most of International Invest, 2005, p. 4.

〔4〕 美国 1982、1983、1984、1987、1991、1992、1994、2004 年范本均收录于:Kenneth J. Vandevelde, *U. S. International Investment Agreement*, Oxford University Press, 2009, pp. 769-852。

为包含更广泛的自由化规则;(2) 重新定义关键的"投资保护",增加指导适用征收条款的新措辞;(3) 越来越广泛地接受"投资者与国家之间争端解决程序"(investor-State dispute settlement,ISDS)等。[1]

实践表明,对待"投资自由化"议题,取决于缔约双方的组合情况,不同的 BITs 之间存在明显差别。总体而言,与发展中国家相互之间签订的 BITs 相比,发达国家与发展中国家之间签订的 BITs 更倾向于规定"投资自由化"的内容。[2] 此类"投资自由化"规定的结果通常是,发达国家投资者单向自由投资于发展中国家,而发展中国家投资者一般尚未具备反向投资的能力。

应当指出,"投资自由化"不属传统 BITs 的涵盖内容,也不是 BITs 的必要条款,更不是 BIT 实践的主要目标。"投资自由化"的实质是限缩东道国管理外资的主权权力和政策空间,进一步偏重和强化资本输出国及其海外投资者的权益。鉴此,基于经济主权原则和公平互利原则,在经济实力悬殊的发达国家与发展中国家之间,由于属单向投资关系,一般不能在 BITs 中采用显失公平的"投资自由化"条款;在经济实力相当的发达国家相互之间或发展中国家相互之间,虽属双向投资关系,由于涉及限制缔约各方管理外资的主权权力和政策空间,是否将 BITs"投资保护"的目标升级为"投资自由化",是否在 BITs 中采用"投资自由化"条款,也应取决于缔约双方的共同意愿。事实上,尽管表面推崇"投资自由化",发达国家相互之间通常也不愿意签订"投资自由化导向"BITs,相互不愿意洞开国门,使本国企业面临来自缔约对方投资者的竞争压力。[3]

总之,美国范本是在德国范本的基础上发展起来的。在这个意义上,美国范本和德国范本实质上是一脉相承的,均可作为传统 BIT 范本的典型。在存在资本输出国与资本输入国之分、国际投资单向流动的情况下,与"投资保护导向"BITs 相同,"投资自由化导向"BITs 是缔约一方受益、缔约另一方受限的安排。不难看出,"投资自由化导向"BITs 进一步强化了传统 BIT 实践实质上"片面保护外资和外国投资者"和"服务于资本输出国及其海外投资者单方权益"的鲜明特征,是"事实上资本输出国单方受益体制"的"升级版"。

---

〔1〕 OECD Secretariat,Novel Features in OECD Countries' Recent Investment Agreements:An Overview,Document for Symposium Co-organized by ICSID,OECD and UNCTAD on Making the Most of International Invest,2005,pp. 4-5.

〔2〕 参见詹晓宁等:《国际投资协定:趋势和主要特征》,载陈安主编:《国际经济法学刊》第 14 卷第 1 期,北京大学出版社 2007 年版,第 121 页。

〔3〕 See Jeswald W. Salacuse,Nicholas P. Sullivan,Do BITs Really Work?:An Evaluation of Bilateral Investment Treaties and Their Grand Bargain,*Havard International Law Journal*,Vol. 46,No. 1,2005,p. 78.

（二）"可持续发展"：BIT 实践目标的新倡议

世纪之交，"国际投资条约体制的发展处于十字路口，变革势在必行"已成国际社会共识。[1] 在"改革以 BITs 为主体的国际投资条约体制"渐成主流共识的背景下，各国新修订的 BIT 范本更成为其有关参与此项改革的立场和实践的重要标志。[2]

在此新形势下，经长期关注和系统深入研究，联合国贸易和发展会议（UNCTAD）2012 年发布了"国际投资协定要素：政策选项"（Elements of International Investment Agreements：Policy Options，简称"协定要素"）。[3] 首先需要明确的是，UNCTAD 提出的"协定要素"是汇集国际投资协定（international investment agreements，IIAs）[4] 各种政策选项（policy options）供各国"各取所需"（adapt and adopt）的"菜单"，而不是作为谈判基础和具有单方规范或指导意义的 BIT 范本。

"协定要素"在汇集和借鉴传统 BIT 范本及其实践各种"要素"的基础上，提出了"可持续发展"的创新性目标，力图通过调整"资本输入国与资本输出国之间权益不平衡"（简称"南北权益不平衡"）的传统条款和增加"平衡资本输入国与资本输出国之间权益"（简称"平衡南北权益"）的创新条款，纠正传统 BIT 实践中资本输出国与资本输入国之间、外国投资者与东道国之间权益的不平衡，为缔约双方提供公平的法律基础和规则，也反映了国际社会为改革和重构国际投资条约体制所需要的"平

---

〔1〕 例如，2010 年 12 月 14 日，OECD 和 UNCTAD 联合主办的第二届国际投资协定研讨会题为"处于十字路口的国际投资协定与投资者—国家争端解决程序：探寻趋势、分歧与共同进路"（International Investment Agreements and Investor-State Dispute Settlement at a Crossroads：Identifying Trends, Differences and Common Approaches）。

〔2〕 关于改革国际投资条约体制的最新进展，参见 UNCTAD, *World Investment Report 2016*, *Investor Nationality：Policy Challenges*, pp. 110-112。

〔3〕 UNCTAD《2012 年世界投资报告：迈向新一代投资政策》制定了"可持续发展的投资政策框架"（Investment Policy Framework for Sustainable Development，IPFSD），由"可持续发展投资决策的核心原则""各国投资政策指南"和"国际投资协定要素：政策选项"三部分构成。其"国际投资协定要素：政策选项"以国际投资协定（international investment agreements，IIAs）主要条款为序，列举从"最有利于投资者"（the most investor-friendly）或"最高保护"（most protective）到为国家提供较高灵活性的各种选项。"协定要素"全文载于 UNCTAD, *World Investment Report 2012*, *Towards a New Generation of Investment Policies*, United Nations, 2012, pp. 143-159。关于 IPFSD 的简评，参见曾华群：《"可持续发展的投资政策框架"与我国的对策》，载《厦门大学学报》（哲学社会科学版）2013 年第 6 期，第 59—67 页。

〔4〕 所谓"国际投资协定"（IIAs），一般指国际投资法的主要国际法规范，包括双边投资协定（BITs）、三方投资协定（triangle investment agreements，TIAs）、区域性投资协定，含有投资规范的自由贸易协定（free trade agreements，FTAs）、区域贸易协定（regional trade agreements，RTAs）或经济合作伙伴协定（economic partnership agreements，EPAs）及《解决国家与他国国民间投资争端公约》（1965）、《多边投资担保机构公约》（1985）等世界性多边投资协定。

衡""可持续发展"和"一体化"等创新理念和共识。[1]

就 BIT 目标取向而言,UNCTAD 在"协定要素"中提出的"可持续发展导向"(sustainable development oriented)BIT 倡议具有重要的创新意义,主要表现在:

第一,主张 BIT 实践由"片面保护外资"发展为"平衡当事双方权利义务和多元目标"。在传统 BIT 实践中,长期存在发达国家与发展中国家之间在谈判地位与能力、谈判目标与效果、权力与利益等方面的不平等或不平衡现象。"协定要素"强调资本输出国与资本输入国之间权利义务、东道国与外国投资者之间权利义务的平衡;同时,也主张 BIT 多元目标相互之间的平衡,包括保护外资与管制外资之间的平衡、经济与其他公共利益之间的平衡。

第二,主张 BIT 实践由"片面保护外国投资者权益"发展为"促进东道国可持续发展"。传统 BITs 片面保护外国投资者权益,未顾及东道国的经济发展,更遑论关注东道国的"可持续发展"。"协定要素"提出的"可持续发展"主要涵盖环境、社会发展、企业社会责任等内容,强调外资应纳入东道国的可持续发展战略,倡导各国签订"可持续发展导向"BITs。

第三,主张 BIT 实践"一体化"推进保护外资和管制外资的两种功能。在传统国际立法中,保护外资和管制外资的两种努力"各行其道"。保护外资的 BITs 属于"硬法",具有法律强制力。而管制外资的国际规范,则大多属于"软法",成效甚微。"协定要素"强调保护外资和管制外资的同等重要性,提出在 BITs 中纳入"投资者义务与责任"等创新条款,力图在 BIT 实践中"一体化"推进保护外资和管制外资的两种功能。

近年来,"可持续发展"原则被各国普遍接受为经济发展和国际关系的一般原则。[2]越来越多的 BITs 在序言中包括了"可持续发展"原则。总体上,"可持续发展"导向 BITs 应体现为"平衡南北权益"的实践。资本输出国与资本输入国均需要享有权力和权利,并承担相应的责任和义务,真正平衡资本输出国与资本输入国之间的权益及东道国与外国投资者之间的权益。具体而言,BITs 应具有保护、促进跨国投资与管制外国投资者行为的双重目标和功能。在 BIT 范本的内容设计中,应强化或增加有关东道国管制外资权力和投资者母国促进、管制海外投资活动的条款,即东道国应具有自主决定外资准入领域、外资履行要求等管制外资的权力,并承担

---

[1]　关于"协定要素"体现的"平衡""可持续发展"和"一体化"等创新理念,参见 Zeng Huaqun, Balance, Sustainable Development, and Integration: Innovative Path for BIT Practice, *Journal of International Economic Law*, Vol. 17, No. 2, 2014, pp. 323-329。

[2]　关于"可持续发展"在国际法中的基础,参见〔荷〕尼科·斯赫雷弗:《可持续发展在国际法中的演进:起源、涵义及地位》,汪习根、黄海滨译,社会科学文献出版社 2008 年版,第 78—139 页。

保护跨国投资的义务；而投资者母国则须承担监管本国海外投资的责任，承诺和保护东道国免受外国投资者，特别是跨国公司负面行为方式的损害。[1]

在国际投资政策语境中，"可持续发展"可作为 BIT 缔约各方的"共赢"目标。由于它强调东道国经济和社会的发展，符合资本输入国的基本需要。由于它促进东道国创设健康的投资环境，也符合资本输出国及其海外投资者的重要利益。"可持续发展"目标的确立，旨在从实质内容和结构形式上纠正传统 BIT 实践中资本输出国与资本输入国之间权益、东道国与外国投资者之间权益的不平等或不平衡。显然，"可持续发展"导向 BIT 倡议对传统 BIT 实践的革故鼎新，既包含经调整的传统条款，又提出了重要的创新条款，力图改变传统 BIT 范本"片面保护外资和外国投资者"的基本结构，这是对传统 BIT 实践模式和内容的重大突破，对传统 BIT 实践目标也产生了重要影响。

与此同时，为求 BIT 实践的进一步创新，有必要反思"可持续发展"的概念及其特征。"可持续发展"的经典定义是："满足当代的需要，且不危及后代满足其需要的能力的发展。"[2]学界主张，该概念经历在国际法中的演进，其七项要素包括"可持续利用自然资源，健全的宏观经济发展，环境保护，时间要素：暂时性、长久性与及时性，公众参与和人权，善治，一体化与相互联系"。[3] 显然，"可持续发展"是内涵极为丰富的多元概念，以其作为 BIT 实践的新目标，虽容易获得普遍赞同，但其宽泛、"跨界"、模糊的特征，客观上殊难成为引领 BIT 实践的"指南"。事实上，传统"投资保护导向"BITs 和"投资自由化导向"BITs 均有具体明确的"目标"和"诉求"。以"可持续发展"概念作为 BIT 实践的新目标，与传统 BIT 实践"事实上资本输出国单方受益体制"的区别不甚明晰，是否真正脱离传统模式的窠臼，是否能引领 BIT 实践走向革新之路，是值得进一步探究的。

（三）"共同发展"：BIT 实践目标的创新

笔者主张，借鉴"可持续发展导向"BIT 的新倡议，在中国与"一带一路"国家之间 BIT 实践中，需要坚持改革国际经济旧秩序和创建国际经济新秩序的目标，遵循经济主权、公平互利、合作发展三大国际经济法基本原则，重申和发展"发展权"的概念，将"可持续发展导向"BITs 改进和提升为"共同发展导向"（common development ori-

---

[1]　跨国公司的此类负面行为方式包括对东道国政治的干预、违反人权标准、违反环境规范等。See M. Sornarajah, *The International Law on Foreign Investment*, Cambridge University Press, 1994, pp. 171-181.

[2]　World Commission on Environment and Development, *Our Common Future*, Oxford University Press, 1987, p. 43. 转引自〔荷〕尼科·斯赫雷弗：《可持续发展在国际法中的演进：起源、涵义及地位》，汪习根、黄海滨译，社会科学文献出版社 2008 年版，第 1 页。

[3]　同上书，第 185—196 页。

ented)BITs。

1. "共同发展"概念的涵义

如所周知,和平与发展是战后世界各国人民和国际社会长期认同和追求的两大主题。"发展""发展观""发展权"(the right to development)"可持续发展"和"共同发展"等概念如何区分,有何特定意涵,相互关系如何,值得深思。[1]

1.1. "共同发展"与"发展权"

首先必须明确,"共同发展"是基于"发展权"概念和发展权原则衍生和演进的概念。

"发展权"是 20 世纪 70 年代以来,发展中国家在争取建立国际经济新秩序的斗争中提出的新法律概念。1972 年,塞内加尔最高法院院长凯巴·巴耶(Keba M'baye)在斯特拉斯堡国际人权研究所的演讲中第一次提出了"发展权"的理论,提及发达国家协助发展中国家提高其经济福利水平的义务。其结论是,"发展权"是一项人权,因为人类没有发展就不能生存;人的所有基本权利和自由必须与生存权、不断提高生活水平的权利联系在一起,即与"发展权"相联系。随后,发展权原则由联合国大会(简称"联大")通过一系列决议确立。[2] 1986 年,联大通过了《发展权利宣言》,146 个国家投了赞成票。[3]

发展中国家普遍主张,"发展权"是一项不可剥夺的人权,这项权利是自决权的必然延伸,也是为非殖民化、民族解放、经济独立和发展而斗争所取得的成果。实现发展中国家的"发展权"将促进发达国家和发展中国家的共同繁荣以及维护世界和平。[4] 实际上,"发展权"概念自始就是发展中国家的"共同发展权"(common right to development),发展权的目标是"发达国家和发展中国家的共同繁荣",已蕴含发达国家和发展中国家共享"共同发展"成果的目标。

20 世纪 70 年代,联大通过了一系列有关建立国际经济新秩序的决议,进一步促进了"共同发展"概念的形成。1974 年联大先后通过的《建立国际经济新秩序宣言》和《各国经济权利和义务宪章》(简称《经济宪章》)序言指出,国际经济新秩序的基础是"一切国家待遇公平、主权平等、互相依存、共同受益和协力合作"。显然,上述两

---

[1]　关于"发展观"和"发展权"的论述,参见朱炎生:《发展观的变迁与发展权实现机制的转变》,载陈安主编:《国际经济法学刊》第 13 卷第 4 期,北京大学出版社 2006 年版,第 105—117 页。

[2]　这些联合国大会决议包括:UN Doc. A/C. 3/34/SR. 24-30, 33-38, 41. UN Doc. E/CN. 4/SR. 1389, 1392-8 (1977) GA Res. 174, 35 UNGAOR (1980). See Francis N. N. Botchway, Historical Perspectives of International Economic Law, in Asif H. Qureshi(ed.), *Perspectives in International Economic Law*, Kluwer Law International, 2002, p. 321, note 66.

[3]　美国是唯一对该宣言投反对票的国家,另有其他 8 个发达国家投弃权票。

[4]　关于"发展权"的概念,参见曾华群:《国际经济法导论》(第二版),法律出版社 2007 年版,第 272—274 页。

个建立国际经济新秩序的纲领性文件中提出的"一切国家""互相依存""共同受益"和"协力合作"的概念,蕴含和深化了"共同发展"概念的内涵。特别是强调,"互相依存""共同受益"和"协力合作"是建立国际经济新秩序基础的核心要素,尤具深刻意涵。

1.2. "共同发展"与"可持续发展"

就调整国际投资关系的 BIT 实践而言,尽管"可持续发展"和"共同发展"均关注"发展",两者存在实质上十分重要的区别。

首先,"共同发展"的概念强调"共同""相互""双向"的重要性,涉及 BIT 缔约双方(特别是资本输出国为一方,资本输入国为另一方)的共同目标、共同意愿、共同愿景、共同努力、共同贡献及共同成就等,与传统 BITs 的"事实上资本输出国单方受益体制"截然相反,是从"单方受益"向"双方共同发展"的根本转变。当然,"可持续发展"目标关注缔约双方之间权益和重要关切的平衡,比之传统 BITs 的"事实上资本输出国单方受益体制"已有重大革新。"共同发展"比之"可持续发展"的先进之处是,缔约双方同舟共济,同创共同事业,谋求"共同发展"目标,体现了更宽广的胸怀和更高的境界。

其次,"共同发展"的概念因基于"发展权"的概念而包含了"共同发展权"的重要涵义。近年来,"可持续发展"概念在很大程度上取代了"发展权",广泛应用于国际性政策文件和条约等国际规范。"可持续发展"不同于传统的经济增长和经济发展,是指一种人本主义的经济、社会与环境的持续发展。[1] 尽管字面上"可持续发展"与"发展权"差别不大,甚至前者加上"可持续"的限定词似乎更具科学意义,两者的涵义及核心显然不同。至关重要的是,"发展权"强调的是在国际关系中国家,特别是发展中国家的发展权利,是基本人权的重要组成部分,与建立国际经济新秩序密切相关;而"可持续发展"并非重点关注国际关系中国家"可持续发展"的权利,而往往是具体关注各国国内环境、劳工等社会问题及人与自然、现代与后代等更为宽泛、长远的社会问题,要求国家自身承担更多的责任和义务,且不直接涉及新旧国际经济秩序问题。显然,发展中国家提出的"发展权"经过"可持续发展"的微妙改造或替换,其核心价值已然发生了重大改变。[2] 应当强调,"共同发展"的概念包含各国为

---

〔1〕 根据联合国《21 世纪议程》,"可持续发展"的实体内容包括消除贫穷、改变消费形态、人口动态与可持续能力、保护和促进人类健康、促进人类住区的可持续发展、保持和管理资源以促进发展。参见王彦志:《经济全球化、可持续发展与国际投资法第三波》,载陈安主编:《国际经济法学刊》第 13 卷第 3 期,北京大学出版社 2006 年版,第 181—184 页。

〔2〕 印度著名国际法学家安南(R. P. Anand)在考察"可持续发展"概念和《里约环境与发展会议》文件后,认为该会议未取得实质性进展,并在分析南北问题的基础上,提出了"进展为了谁,导向何处"(Progress Towards What and Progress for Whom)的严重质疑。See R. P. Anand, *Studies in International Law and History*, *An Asian Perspective*, Martinus Nijhoff Publishers, 2004, pp. 245-273.

实现其"共同目标"的"共同发展权",与建立国际经济新秩序密切相关,因而对于缔约各方,特别是发展中国家的 BIT 实践是非常重要的。

再次,"共同发展导向"BIT 实践是国际经济法三大基本原则之一"合作发展(即国际合作以谋发展)"原则的重要实践。由于具有"共同发展"的目标和权利,"共同发展"的概念直接关系各国的"国际合作责任"。因为,缔约各方一旦确立了"共同发展"的目标和权利,也相应承担了"国际合作责任"。如果明确规定于 BITs,"国际合作"就成为现实的条约责任,需要规定合作的具体措施。而严格意义上,"可持续发展"原则并非关注国家之间的"合作发展",而是更为关注国家本身的责任,与"国际合作责任"之间的关系并非紧密关涉。

最后,"共同发展"的概念与"创建人类命运共同体"的概念密切相关,是创建人类命运共同体实践的核心理念之一。登高望远,为了共同的美好未来,缔约双方理应通过国际合作,共同发展。而"可持续发展"则强调"可持续"而非"共同",与"创建人类命运共同体"的概念并未密切契合。

2. 中国对"共同发展"概念的贡献

"共同发展"的概念深植于中国传统文化。中国传统文化的"整体观","上善若水"的包容思想及"四海一家""大同社会"的美好愿景,不仅是"互融共赢"的思想内核,[1]也是"共同发展"概念的原始根基。

"共同发展"的概念也深植于中国和印度 1954 年倡导的和平共处五项原则。该原则不仅包括了和平原则,也包括了发展原则。中国在平等互利基础上努力促进世界经济的共同发展。[2]

作为国家大政方针的中国共产党的"十七大""十八大""十九大"报告不断丰富和深化"共同发展"的概念。

党的"十七大"报告指出:"坚持把中国人民利益同各国人民共同利益结合起来,以更加积极的姿态参与国际事务,发挥负责任大国作用"。在此,强调了"把中国人民利益同各国人民共同利益结合起来",阐释了《建立国际经济新秩序宣言》和《经济宪章》中"共同受益"概念的内涵。

党的"十八大"报告进一步阐明我国关于国际关系的主张,即:"在国际关系中弘扬平等互信、包容互鉴、合作共赢的精神……合作共赢,就是要倡导人类命运共同体意识,在追求本国利益时兼顾他国合理关切,在谋求本国发展中促进各国共同发展,

---

〔1〕　参见李万强、潘俊武:《"一带一路"倡议:"东方"国际法的理念与实践》,载《国际经济法学刊》2018 年第 1 期,第 29 页。

〔2〕　See Wen Jiabao, Carrying forward the Five Principles of Peaceful Coexistence in the Promotion of Peace and Development, *Chinese Journal of International Law*, Vol. 3, No. 2, 2004, pp. 363-368.

建立更加平等均衡的新型全球发展伙伴关系，同舟共济，权责共担，增进人类共同利益。"这里，在解释"合作共赢"概念时，进一步阐明"本国利益"与"他国合理关切"之间的关系和"本国发展"与"各国共同发展"之间的关系。同时，也指明了"共同发展"的要素或基础是"建立更加平等均衡的新型全球发展伙伴关系，同舟共济，权责共担"。

党的"十九大"报告第十二部分题为"坚持和平发展道路，推动构建人类命运共同体"，指出"中国将高举和平、发展、合作、共赢的旗帜，恪守维护世界和平、促进共同发展的外交政策宗旨，坚定不移在和平共处五项原则基础上发展同各国的友好合作，推动建设相互尊重、公平正义、合作共赢的新型国际关系"；呼吁"各国人民同心协力，构建人类命运共同体，建设持久和平、普遍安全、共同繁荣、开放包容、清洁美丽的世界"。值得注意的是，在此，中国明确将"促进共同发展"作为"外交政策宗旨"，同时，进一步重申和强化了"共同发展""共同繁荣"和"构建人类命运共同体"的理念。

国家主席习近平曾深刻论述"共同发展"的内涵，指出："'穷则独善其身，达则兼善天下。'这是中华民族始终崇尚的品德和胸怀。""中国将始终做全球发展的贡献者，坚定走共同发展道路"，"实现共同发展"。[1] 在 2015 年 9 月 26 日"联合国发展峰会"上，习近平主席发表题为《谋共同永续发展，做合作共赢伙伴》的重要讲话，强调国际社会要以《2015 年后发展议程》为新起点，共同走出一条公平、开放、全面、创新的发展之路，努力实现各国共同发展；"公平、开放、全面、创新的发展之路"的目标是"发展机会更加均等""发展成果惠及各方""发展基础更加坚实"和"发展潜力充分释放"，[2]进一步深刻揭示了"共同发展"的意涵和要素。

实际上，"共同发展"也是中国和广大发展中国家的共同愿景。《金砖国家领导人厦门宣言》明确提出"坚持互利合作，谋求共同发展"。[3]

3. "共同发展导向"BIT 实践的意涵

综上所述，"共同发展"是基于"发展权"而衍生和演进的重要概念，是在建立国际经济新秩序进程中逐渐形成和发展的，中国和广大发展中国家为"共同发展"概念的形成和发展作出了重要贡献。"共同发展"的主要涵义是：在各国相互依存的现实情况下，各国的发展与他国的发展密切相关，在追求本国发展的同时，需要关注他国

---

〔1〕 参见中共中央宣传部：《习近平总书记系列重要讲话读本》，学习出版社、人民出版社 2016 年版，第 15—17 页。

〔2〕 参见《习近平在联合国发展峰会上的讲话（全文）》，http://news. xinhuanet. com/world/2015-09/27/c_ 1116687809. htm，2017 年 10 月 16 日访问。

〔3〕 参见《金砖国家领导人厦门宣言（全文）》之 3，http://www. gov. cn/xinwen/2017-09/04/content_ 5222643. htm，2017 年 10 月 15 日访问。

的发展和重要关切,谋求国际社会的公平、开放、全面、创新的发展。

事实上,UNCTAD 已有"以发展为导向"BIT 实践的倡议。IIAs 服务于发展,向来是 UNCTAD 在该领域的工作核心,涉及两方面的问题:一是确保发展问题在国际投资法中能够获得充分考虑;二是使发展中国家具有实施 IIAs 的能力,使其通过此类协定吸引外资并从中获益。[1] UNCTAD 发布的《2003 年世界投资报告—促进发展的外国直接投资政策:各国与国际的视角》(World Investment Report 2003,FDI Policies for Development:National and International Perspective),将"发展"明确作为"外资政策"的目标,引发了"发展中国家如何通过 BIT 实践促进发展"的关注和讨论。有学者提出了"以发展为导向"BIT 实践的新思路,其含义一是发展中国家基于实现其发展目标进行 BIT 实践,二是发展中国家根据其所处发展阶段进行 BIT 实践。[2]

与上述"以发展为导向"BIT 实践比较而言,"共同发展导向"BIT 实践更为强调缔约各方的"共同发展",同时,不仅包括发展中国家的"共同发展",也包括发展中国家和发达国家的"共同发展"。显然,以"共同发展"作为 BIT 实践的目标,是对传统 BITs 的"事实上资本输出国单方受益体制"的根本性纠正和结构性变革,对"可持续发展"或"发展"的 BIT 目标而言,也是重要的提升和超越。

三、中国与"一带一路"国家间 BIT 实践模式的创新

在国际投资法语境中,BIT 实践模式指为达到 BIT 目标而采取的条约方式或类型,通常由 BITs 的基本结构和主要条款构成。BIT 实践模式集中体现于各国的 BIT 范本(model),也体现于特定国家 BIT 实践所形成的 BIT 系列,如德国 BIT 系列,美国 BIT 系列等。中国与"一带一路"国家在传统 BIT 实践模式基础上,可借鉴和汲取"可持续发展导向"BITs 的创新因素,通过 BIT 结构和条款的革新和改造,创造"共同发展导向"BIT 实践模式。

(一)BIT 实践模式的发展

发达国家的 BIT 范本大致可分为欧洲模式和美国模式两类。欧洲模式以德国范本为代表,瑞士、法国、英国、荷兰等欧洲国家普遍效法该模式。美国模式源于欧洲模式,自 2004 年以来自成一体,以美国范本为代表,加拿大等国采用或接受该模

---

[1] 参见詹晓宁:《国际投资协定应服务于发展》,载陈安主编:《国际经济法学刊》第 13 卷第 2 期,北京大学出版社 2006 年版,第 26 页。

[2] 参见蔡从燕:《国际投资结构变迁与发展中国家双边投资条约实践的发展—双边投资条约实践的新思维》,载陈安主编:《国际经济法学刊》第 14 卷第 3 期,北京大学出版社 2007 年版,第 51—54 页。

式。2012 年 UNCTAD 发布的"协定要素"虽是政策选项，不是范本，但源自各国 BIT 范本及其实践，兼容并蓄，既包含传统 BITs 的基本结构和主要条款，又提出重要的创新条款，与德国范本和美国范本具有一定的可比性。以下简略比较德国范本、美国范本和"协定要素"模式的结构和条款，以期进一步探讨"共同发展导向"BIT 模式的发展趋向。

1. 德国范本

《德国 2008 年条约范本：德意志联邦共和国与某国关于促进和相互保护投资的条约范本》（German Model Treaty-2008：Treaty between the Federal Republic of Germany and [……] concerning the Encouragement and Reciprocal Protection of Investments，简称"德国范本"）可作为欧洲模式的典型。该范本合计 13 个条款。分别是定义、准入与投资保护、国民待遇与最惠国待遇、征收情况下的赔偿、自由转移、代位、其他规定、适用范围、缔约国之间争端的解决、缔约国一方与缔约国另一方投资者之间争端的解决、缔约国之间的关系、登记条款、生效，期限与终止通知等条款。显然，德国范本的条文简约，直接规范国际投资活动，涉及国际投资的主要问题及条约法的一般问题。其中，"准入"条款是唯一体现尊重和维护东道国主权的条款，也是资本输入国在 BITs 中承诺给予外资待遇和保护的唯一回报。[1]

对比欧洲各国的 BIT 实践，可知以德国范本为典型代表的欧洲模式历经半个多世纪，保持"超稳定状态"。欧洲各国分别与广大发展中国家签订了 BITs。截至 2018 年 10 月，德国已签订 132 个 BITs，签约数位居全球第一。[2] 有学者指出，欧洲模式较为成功的原因主要是，欧洲国家在有关当地货币汇兑、履行要求[3] 及征收等事项的保障方面，比美国的相关要求较为宽松。此外，欧洲国家与其前殖民地之间的特殊历史联系也可能影响一些新独立国家的 BIT 实践，后者可能认为与其前宗主

---

〔1〕 所谓"准入"条款（admission clause），指缔约双方有关允许对方投资进入本国境内的一般规定，通常表明了东道国对外资的态度或立场。据之，东道国可根据国家发展战略，实施有关外资准入和经营的国内法律和政策。See Axel Berger, 'China's New Bilateral Investment Treaty Programme: Substance, Rational and Implications for Investment Law Making', Paper for the American Society of International Law International Economic Law Group (ASIL IELIG) 2008 biennial conference "The Politics of International Economic Law: The Next Four Years", Washington, D. C., November 14-15, 2008.

〔2〕 http://investmentpolicyhub.unctad.org/IIA/，2018 年 10 月 6 日。

〔3〕 所谓"履行要求"（performance requirements），广义上指东道国对外国投资经营实施的管制措施，一般是要求外国投资者作出投资时履行某些相关要求（如当地成分、出口业绩、当地员工雇佣等），作为批准该投资或该投资享有优惠待遇的前提条件。此类管制措施旨在保障外国投资经营有利于东道国的发展目标，通常是利用外资增加当地就业、取得新技术及促进贸易平衡等。See Kenneth J. Vandevelde, U. S. International Investment Agreement, Oxford University Press, 2009, p. 387.

国签订 BITs 会更有利些。[1] 笔者以为，从技术层面看，欧洲模式的条文简约及其"超稳定状态"，也是促成其 BIT 谈判成功的重要因素之一。

值得关注的是，自 2009 年 12 月《里斯本条约》(the Lisbon Treaty)生效后，欧盟决定以其名义与第三国签订 BITs，取代之前欧盟各成员国分别与第三国签订的 1300 多个 BITs。[2] 目前，欧盟以其名义与加拿大等国之间包含投资规范的 RTA 谈判和与新加坡之间的 BIT 谈判正在进行。[3] 作为谈判基础的"欧盟 BIT 范本"，亦即名副其实的"欧洲模式"如何协调制定和发展，必将对世界各国 BIT 范本及其实践的发展趋向产生重大而深远的影响。

2. 美国范本

1982 年，作为其"BIT 计划"的最初成果，美国制定其第一个 BIT 范本。该范本包含 13 个条款。其中，五个条款属实体性规范，涉及投资待遇(第 2 条)、征收赔偿(第 3 条)、战乱导致损害的赔偿(第 4 条)、转移(第 5 条)和税务(第 11 条)。三个条款涉及争端解决措施，包括协商、投资者与国家之间仲裁及缔约双方之间仲裁(第 6—8 条)。两个条款确定某些权力、权利和责任不属于条约适用的范围(第 9、10 条)。余下三个条款涉及条约的适用范围：一是对某些用语作出定义(第 1 条)，二是对缔约方的次级政治机构(political subdivisions)适用该条约(第 12 条)，三是规定条约的生效、有效期及终止(第 13 条)。由此可见，早期美国 BIT 范本比之德国范本，除不采用"准入"和"代位"条款、增加"税务"条款外，在形式和内容方面大同小异。

在美国 BIT 范本 1983、1984、1987、1991、1992、1994、2004 和 2012 年八次修订中，修订缘起、内容及幅度各不相同。1983 年范本保持 1982 年范本的条款结构，修订了部分条款内容。1984 年范本包含 12 个条款，合并征收条款和战乱条款，对范本用语作了较大修改。1987、1991、1992 年范本是为处理 BIT 谈判产生的具体问题而个别修改的结果。1992 年 12 月《北美自由贸易协定》(North American Free Trade Agreement，NAFTA)的签署，促使美国考虑进一步修改其 BIT 范本内容。1994 年范本是对原范本进行整体综合审查的成果，包含 16 个条款。在美国 BIT 计划历史上，2004 年范本是实行最广泛修改的成果，在形式和内容方面均有许多重要改变，篇

---

〔1〕　See Jeswald W. Salacuse, Nicholas P. Sullivan, Do BITs Really Work?: An Evaluation of Bilateral Investment Treaties and Their Grand Bargain, *Havard International Law Journal*, Vol. 46, No. 1, 2005, p. 657.

〔2〕　UNCTAD, *World Investment Report 2011*, *Non-Equity Modes of International Production and Development* (United Nations, 2011), p. 100.

〔3〕　UNCTAD, *World Investment Report 2013*, *Global Value Chains*: *Investment and Trade for Development* (United Nations, 2013), p. 104.

幅骤增为三倍。[1] 2012 年范本在保持原范本基本结构的基础上，对一些条款的内容作了修改或补充，特别表现在增加新的透明度要求和扩大劳工和环境保护范围等方面。

美国 2012 年范本分为三节，共有 37 个条款。第 A 节包括第 1 条至第 22 条，分别是定义、范围、国民待遇、最惠国待遇、最低待遇标准、征收与赔偿、转移、履行要求、高级管理层与董事会、关于投资的法律决定的公布、透明度、投资与环境、投资与劳工、不符措施、[2]特殊程序与信息要求、非减损、[3]拒绝授惠[4]、根本安全、[5]信息披露、金融服务、税务及生效：期限与终止等条款。第 B 节包括第 23 条至第 36 条，细化了 ISDS 规定，分别对磋商与谈判、仲裁请求的提起、各当事方对仲裁的同意、各当事方同意的条件与限制、仲裁员的选定、仲裁的进行、仲裁程序的透明度、准据法、附录解释、专家报告、合并、裁决、附录与脚注、文件服务等作了专门条款规定。第 C 节第 37 条则专门规定了缔约双方之间争端的解决。

概括而言，美国 2012 年范本内容的新发展主要表现在传统条款的发展、"投资自由化"条款及"与投资有关的"条款三个方面。

在传统条款的发展方面，美国 2012 年范本对资本输出国及其海外投资者特别关切的概念或条款进一步澄清和细化规定，力图解决以往相关条文的不确定性，为外资和外国投资者提供更为充分的国际法保护，主要表现在：(1) 对"投资"和"投资者"作了更明确的定义；[6](2) 将"国民待遇与最惠国待遇"条款"一分为三"，分为"国民待遇""最惠国待遇"和"最低待遇标准"三个条款；并进一步澄清和完善投资待遇条

---

[1] See Kenneth J. Vandevelde, *U. S. International Investment Agreement*, Oxford University Press, 2009, pp. 99-107.

[2] 所谓"不符措施"(Non-Conforming Measures)，是美国 2004 年 BIT 范本第 14 条的名称。该条款允许缔约各方在 BIT 附录中具体规定其现有不符"履行要求"规定的措施和将来有权采取不符"履行要求"规定的措施的特定部门。该条款规定了不符国民待遇、最惠国待遇和雇佣规定的措施。See Kenneth J. Vandevelde, *U. S. International Investment Agreement*, Oxford University Press, 2009, p. 395. 相关研究表明，美国等声称对外资实行"准入前"国民待遇的国家，毫无例外地在 BITs 中附加了"不符措施"和/或"保留和例外"(reservations and exceptions) 条款，以维护其国家利益和经济安全。此类"准入前"国民待遇加"不符措施"和/或"保留和例外"的安排，在很多情况下成为"口惠而实不至"的法律策略。

[3] 所谓"非减损"(Non-Derogation)，是美国 2012 年 BIT 范本第 16 条的名称，旨在明确 BIT 不减损缔约各方投资者或涵盖投资基于缔约方法律法规、行政实践或程序、行政或司法裁决、缔约方的国际法律责任或承诺享有的更为优惠的待遇。

[4] 由于采用客观的"投资者"标准可能涵盖缔约方不愿给予 BIT 保护的投资者，一些 BITs 规定了"拒绝授惠"(Denial of Benefits) 条款，允许缔约方对虽设立于该方、但与该方缺乏充分联系的投资者不适用 BIT 保护。关于"拒绝授惠"条款的定义和实践，参见 OECD, *International Investment Law*, *Understanding Concepts and Tracking Innovations*, *Companion Volume to International Investment Perspectives*, (OECD, 2008) pp. 9, 28-33。

[5] 所谓"根本安全"(Essential Security)，是美国 2012 年 BIT 范本第 18 条的名称，旨在明确 BIT 不得被解释为要求缔约方披露其认为违反其根本安全利益的信息，也不得被解释为不允许缔约方采取其认为必要的措施，以履行维护或恢复国际和平或安全或保护其本身根本安全利益的责任。

[6] 美国 2012 年 BIT 范本第 1 条。

款,包括国民待遇和最惠国待遇的不符措施,将"公平与公正待遇"(fair and equitable treatment,FET)和"充分保护和保障"(full protection and security)明示归类于习惯国际法等规定;[1](3) 通过增加确立判断"间接征收"规则的新附录,澄清了征收条款;[2](4) 细化 ISDS 的规定,对投资者权利请求的提出、缔约双方在该程序的参与、透明度、加速程序、合并仲裁、救济方式等作了具体规定。[3] 此类规定虽源自传统条款,但其专业化和精致化的规定在很大程度上决定了 ISDS 的条约"法定模式"和"司法化",从而弱化、排斥甚至否定了其他投资争端解决方式。

在"投资自由化"条款方面,美国 2012 年范本增加履行要求、高级管理层与董事会、关于投资的法律决定的公布、透明度、不符措施、特殊程序与信息要求、信息披露等条款,特别表现在:(1) 禁止履行要求的范围进一步扩大,即禁止履行要求的规定适用于任何投资,不限于涵盖投资,某些作为接受利益条件的履行要求亦属禁止之列;[4](2) 规定透明度和正当程序,如要求缔约各方指定有关涵盖投资事务的联系点,要求缔约各方答复对方提出的有关影响 BIT 实施的实际措施或拟议措施,在某措施适用于特定人的情况下,后者应得到通知并有提出答辩、要求司法审查或行政复议的机会等。[5] 此类规定反映了美国作为资本输出大国对 BIT 目标和功效的新追求。

在"与投资有关"条款方面,美国 2012 年范本增加投资与环境、投资与劳工、金融服务、税务等条款。[6] 特别是,要求缔约方尽最大努力保障其"不为吸引外资而放松环境措施和保护某些国际承认的劳工权利的措施"。

值得注意的是,美国 2012 年范本未规定欧洲模式中唯一体现东道国主权的"准入"条款,以要求东道国给予外国投资者"设立权"取代。[7] 此类"设立权"条款旨在限制东道国在设立阶段的审查权力和管制外资准入的主权权力,导致东道国外资法律制度的自由化。[8] 此类条款的创设和推行,反映了美国对"片面保护外资和外国

---

〔1〕　美国 2012 年 BIT 范本第 3、4、5 条。

〔2〕　美国 2012 年 BIT 范本第 6 条及附录 A,B。

〔3〕　美国 2012 年 BIT 范本第 B 节第 23—36 条。

〔4〕　美国 2012 年 BIT 范本第 8 条。

〔5〕　美国 2012 年 BIT 范本第 11 条。

〔6〕　美国 2012 年 BIT 范本第 12、13、20、21 条。

〔7〕　所谓"设立权"(right of establishment)是通过在外资设立阶段和设立之后给予外国投资者国民待遇和最惠国待遇,或者仅给予最惠国待遇而确立(亦称"设立前国民待遇和最惠国待遇"或"设立前最惠国待遇"),并附有例外和保留。

〔8〕　See Axel Berger, China's New Bilateral Investment Treaty Programme: Substance, Rational and Implications for Investment Law Making, Paper for the American Society of International Law International Economic Law Group (ASIL IELIG) 2008 biennial conference "The Politics of International Economic Law: The Next Four Years", Washington, D. C. , November 14-15, 2008.

投资者"的传统 BIT 立场的坚持和发展。

显然，"自由化导向"的美国 2012 年范本是在保持传统 BIT 范本基本特征的基础上，强化"投资保护"功能并进而推进"投资自由化"。其主要目标是给予投资者更充分的投资保障和自由，同时，进一步限缩东道国的主权权力和政策空间。

3. "协定要素"模式

"协定要素"模式既包括德国范本的主要规定和美国范本的部分规定，又提出重要的创新条款，代表 BIT 范本及其实践"可持续发展导向"（sustainable development oriented）的新发展。[1]

由于"协定要素"模式主要来源于各国 BIT 实践，在一定意义上是集各国 BIT 实践之大成，提供了 BIT 结构、用语和内容的重要汇集、选项或参照。更为可贵的是，"协定要素"倡导各国签订"可持续发展导向"BIT，提出了"投资者义务与责任""母国措施"[2]及"特殊与差别待遇"（special and differential treatment，SDT）等创新因素，在很大程度上反映了 BIT 实践模式的创新理念和发展趋向。

"协定要素"模式分为"设立后"（Post-establishment）、"设立前"（Pre-establishment）和 SDT 三个部分。

"设立后"部分在传统欧洲模式的基础上有所创新，是"协定要素"模式的最主要部分，共有 12 条，依次为序言、条约范围、准入、待遇与保护标准、公共政策例外、争端解决、投资者义务与责任、与其他协定的关系、不降低标准条款、投资促进、制度建设及最后条款。其中，序言、条约范围、准入、待遇与保护标准、争端解决、与其他协定的关系及最后条款等 7 个条款与德国范本类似。而公共政策例外、投资者义务与责任、不降低标准条款、投资促进及制度建设等 5 个条款则具有明显的创新因素。

在"设立前"部分，涉及"设立前责任"（pre-establishment obligations），包含了"设立权"、限制"设立权"及保留"准入权"的不同选项。[3]

在 SDT 部分，共有 2 个条款，分别题为"不对称的责任"（asymmetrical obligations）和"附加工具"（additional tools）。[4] 该部分作为经济发展水平不同的发达国

---

〔1〕 关于国际投资法发展的政策选项，参见〔美〕Karl P. Sauvant：《演进中的国际投资法律与政策体制：未来路向》，载陈安主编《国际经济法学刊》第 23 卷第 2 期，法律出版社 2016 年版，第 102—113 页。

〔2〕 广义上，"母国措施"（home country measures）指投资者母国基于合作发展原则，为促进、保护和规范其海外投资和海外投资者而制订或采取的国内措施和国际措施。See Riva Krut and Ashley Moretz, Home Country Measures for Encouraging Sustainable FDI, Occasional Paper No. 8, Report as part of UNCTAD/CBS Project：Cross Border Environmental Management in Transnational Corporations，CBS，November 1999，pp. 1-2.

〔3〕 "协定要素"第 B 部分第 1 条。UNCTAD，*World Investment Report 2012*，*Towards a New Generation of Investment Policies*，United Nations，2012，pp. 157-158.

〔4〕 "协定要素"第 C 部分第 1、2 条。UNCTAD，*World Investment Report 2012*，*Towards a New Generation of Investment Policies*，United Nations，2012，p. 159.

家与发展中国家之间 BITs 的选项,突出反映了发达国家与发展中国家之间 BITs 的结构性创新。

总体上,"协定要素"模式的主要特色表现在,力图通过调整 BIT 传统条款和增加创新条款,保障东道国的主权权力和政策空间,限制东道国的责任条款,同时,要求外国投资者及其母国承担必要的义务与责任,由此构建"可持续发展导向"BIT 实践模式。

在调整传统条款方面,主要包括:(1)"投资"的涵盖范围不包括证券、短期或风险投资,要求符合"对东道国发展的积极影响"等具体特征;[1](2)对国民待遇、最惠国待遇或设立前责任的特定国家保留,确定可实施的政策措施(如补贴)、政策区域(如少数民族、土著团体政策)或部门(如社会服务);[2](3)"征收条款"规定,追求公共政策目标的非歧视性善意管制不构成间接征收;[3](4)不采用 FET 条款、"保护伞"条款。[4] 此类规定旨在纠正传统条款中资本输出国与资本输入国之间、外国投资者与东道国之间权益的不平衡。

在增加创新条款方面,主要是:(1)"投资者的义务与责任"条款,要求投资者在投资准入和经营阶段遵守东道国法律,促进投资者遵守企业社会责任的普遍原则或可适用的企业社会责任标准;[5](2)"母国措施"条款,主要体现在"投资促进"和"制度建设"条款,特别是要求投资者母国制定促进"负责任的投资"(responsible investment)的措施;[6](3)SDT 条款,作为发展水平悬殊的 BIT 缔约方,特别是缔约一方是最不发达国家的选项,其效力适用于现有和新的规定,使较不发达缔约方的责任

---

〔1〕 "协定要素"第 A 部分第 2.1 条。UNCTAD, *World Investment Report 2012*, *Towards a New Generation of Investment Policies*, United Nations, 2012, p. 144.

〔2〕 "协定要素"第 A 部分第 2.3 条,第 B 部分第 1 条。UNCTAD, *World Investment Report 2012*, *Towards a New Generation of Investment Policies*, United Nations, 2012, pp. 145, 157-158.

〔3〕 "协定要素"第 A 部分第 4.5 条。UNCTAD, *World Investment Report 2012*, *Towards a New Generation of Investment Policies*, United Nations, 2012, p. 148.

〔4〕 "协定要素"第 A 部分第 4.3、4.10 条。UNCTAD, *World Investment Report 2012*, *Towards a New Generation of Investment Policies*, United Nations, 2012, pp. 147, 150. 作为单独的投资保护条款,"保护伞条款"(umbrella clause)可溯及 1956—1959 年《阿部—相互保护海外私人财产权利国际公约草案》(Abs Draft International Convention for the Mutual Protection of Private Property Rights in Foreign Countries)第 4 条。该条款规定:"根据政府间协定、其他协定或缔约一方行政法规承诺给予非国民高于国民的待遇,包括最惠国待遇,此种承诺(promises)应优先适用。"1959 年《阿部—绍克拉斯—外国投资公约草案》第 2 条将该条款修改为:"缔约各方应在任何时候保证遵守其已作出的与缔约对方国民投资有关的任何承诺(undertakings)。"其后,1959 年德国—巴基斯坦 BIT 第 7 条规定:"缔约各方应遵守其已承担的与缔约对方国民或公司投资有关的任何其他责任(obligation)。"See OECD Secretariat, Improving the System of Investor-State Dispute Settlement: An Overview, Document for Symposium Co-organized by ICSID, OECD and UNCTAD on Making the Most of International Invest, 2005, p. 31.

〔5〕 "协定要素"第 A 部分第 7 条。UNCTAD, *World Investment Report 2012*, *Towards a New Generation of Investment Policies*, United Nations, 2012, p. 154.

〔6〕 "协定要素"第 A 部分第 10、11 条。UNCTAD, *World Investment Report 2012*, *Towards a New Generation of Investment Policies*, United Nations, 2012, pp. 155-156.

水平适合其发展水平。[1] 此类创新条款旨在从整体结构层面纠正传统 BITs 中资本输出国与资本输入国之间、外国投资者与东道国之间权益的不平衡。

4. 小结

如前所述，BIT 范本是欧美发达国家在 BIT 实践中创造的，带有先天的"资本输出国烙印"。美国范本是在德国范本的基础上发展起来的。在这个意义上，德国范本和美国范本实质上是一脉相承的，均可作为传统 BIT 范本的典型。以德国范本为代表的欧洲模式长期保持"超稳定"的基本结构和主要条款，美国 2004 年之前的范本也与欧洲模式大体保持一致。显然，2004 年之前，欧洲模式在世界各国 BIT 范本及其实践中居于主导和主流地位。美国 2004 年范本在形式和内容方面作了大幅修改，由简入繁，才出现了迥异于欧洲模式的"投资自由化导向"的美国模式。严格意义上，2004 年之后，BIT 范本才有欧洲模式和美国模式的明确区分，出现了欧洲模式和美国模式并行不悖的局面。当前，需要明确的是，在欧洲模式保持"超稳定状态"的情况下，尽管美国模式颇有"后来居上"之势，尚不能轻易断言美国模式代表了 BIT 范本的发展趋势，更不能轻易断言美国模式取代欧洲模式的地位，成为当前"引领"世界各国 BIT 实践的"放之四海而皆准"的"国际通行规则"。应当指出，欧洲模式和美国模式同属传统模式，发展趋向是一致的。追求高标准一贯是 OECD 投资政策对话背后的主要驱动力。调查表明，OECD 国家正在对 BITs 进行革新，包括制定更广泛的自由化规则、实体和程序条款更为明确的适用范围及用于澄清缔约方意图的解释性注释。[2] 可见，总体上，发达国家对 BITs 进行的所谓"革新"，并未脱离其单方面"投资保护""投资自由化"的窠臼，而是在传统"投资保护""投资自由化"的基础上，追求更高的标准和更精致的技术规范。

"协定要素"模式产生于 2012 年，由于源自各国 BIT 范本及其实践，包括德国范本的主要规定和美国范本的部分规定，形式上与德国范本和美国范本也具有一定程度的关联性。值得注意的是，"协定要素"模式未采纳美国范本中的投资与环境、投资与劳工、非减损、拒绝授惠、金融服务、税务等条款，增加了公共政策例外、投资者义务与责任、不降低标准条款、投资促进、制度建设及 SDT 等创新条款，形成了独特的"可持续发展导向"模式。显然，"协定要素"模式是传统 BIT 实践模式的创新性发展，既包含经调整的传统条款，又提出了重要的创新条款，由此改变了传统 BIT 实践模式"片面保护外资和外国投资者"的基本结构，为传统模式的革新完成了"量的积

---

〔1〕 "协定要素"第 C 部分第 1、2 条。UNCTAD，*World Investment Report 2012*，*Towards a New Generation of Investment Policies*，United Nations，2012，p. 159.

〔2〕 参见〔美〕理查德·赫克林格：《充分利用国际投资协定》，载陈安主编：《国际经济法学刊》第 13 卷第 2 期，北京大学出版社 2006 年版，第 20 页。

累"。然而,由于其调整的传统条款和提出的创新条款均是"选择性"的,加之诸多革新之"目"缺乏统领全局的革新之"纲"(涵义宽泛的"可持续发展"概念显然不能担此重任),因此,仅凭"协定要素"模式体现的"可持续发展导向"模式,尚不能完成传统BIT 实践模式革新的"质的飞跃"。在"一带一路"国际合作中,中国与"一带一路"国家可在"协定要素"模式倡导的"可持续发展导向"BIT 实践模式的基础上,寻求"共同发展导向"BIT 实践模式的创新。

(二)比较与借鉴

总体上,由于部分来源相同及相互影响,德国范本、美国范本及"协定要素"模式的条款形式和内容方面尽管各具特色,亦有共通之处。兹列表简要比较三者,并揭示"共同发展导向"BIT 实践模式拟采用的主要条款。

德国范本、美国范本、"协定要素"模式及"共同发展"模式的条款一览表[1]

德国范本	美国范本	"协定要素"模式	三者简要比较	"共同发展"模式
序言	序言	序言(第1条)	三者均有规定。	序言
定义(第1条)	定义(第1条)	投资定义(第2.1条);投资者定义(第2.2条)	三者均有规定。	定义
准入与投资保护(第2条)	/	准入(第3条)	德国范本与"协定要素"规定。	准入
国民待遇与最惠国待遇(第3条)	国民待遇、最惠国待遇、最低待遇标准(第3、4、5条)	待遇与保护标准(第4条)	三者均有规定,美国范本与"协定要素"详细。	待遇标准
征收情况下的赔偿(第4条)	征收与赔偿(第6条)	征收(第4.5条)	三者均有规定,美国范本最为严格。	征收与补偿
自由转移(第5条)	转移(第7条)	资金的转移(第4.7条)	三者均有规定。	资金的转移
代位(第6条)	/	/	德国范本规定。	/
其他规定(第7条)	/	与其他协定的关系(第8条)	德国范本与"协定要素"规定。	与其他协定的关系
适用范围(第8条)	范围(第2条)	条约范围(第2.3、2.4条)	三者均有规定。	适用范围
缔约国间争端的解决(第9条)	缔约国间争端的解决(第C节第37条)	国家间争端的解决(第6.1条)	三者均有规定。	缔约国间争端的解决

〔1〕 资料来源:German Model Treaty-2008:Treaty between the Federal Republic of Germany and〔……〕concerning the Encouragement and Reciprocal Protection of Investments;Treaty between the Government of the United States of America and Government of〔Country〕Concerning the Encouragement and Reciprocal Protection of Investment,2012;and Elements of International Investment Agreements:Policy Options,in UNCTAD, *World Investment Report 2012*, *Towards a New Generation of Investment Policies*,United Nations,2012,pp.143-159.

（续表）

德国范本	美国范本	"协定要素"模式	三者简要比较	"共同发展"模式
缔约国一方与缔约国另一方投资者间争端的解决（第10条）	缔约国一方与缔约国另一方投资者间争端的解决（第B节第23—36条）	投资者与国家间争端的解决（第6.2—4条）	三者均有规定，美国范本最为详细。	缔约国一方与缔约国另一方投资者间争端的解决
缔约国间的关系（第11条）	/	/	德国范本规定。	/
登记条款（第12条）	/	/	德国范本规定。	/
生效，期限与终止通知等条款（第13条）	生效：期限与终止（第22条）	最后条款（第12条）	三者均有规定。	生效，期限与终止通知等条款
/	履行要求（第8条）	履行要求（第4.9条）	美国范本与"协定要素"规定。	/
/	高级管理层与董事会（第9条）	员工（第4.11条）	美国范本与"协定要素"规定。	/
/	关于投资的法律决定的公布（第10条）	透明度（第4.8条）	美国范本与"协定要素"规定。	/
/	透明度（第11条）	透明度（第4.8条）	美国范本与"协定要素"规定。	/
/	投资与环境（第12条）	/	美国范本规定。	/
/	投资与劳工（第13条）	/	美国范本规定。	/
/	不符措施（第14条）	/	美国范本规定。	/
/	特殊程序与信息要求（第15条）	透明度（第4.8条）	美国范本与"协定要素"规定。	/
/	非减损（第16条）	/	美国范本规定。	/
/	拒绝授惠（第17条）	/	美国范本规定。	/
/	根本安全（第18条）	公共政策例外（第5条）	美国范本与"协定要素"规定。	/
/	信息披露（第19条）	透明度（第4.8条）	美国范本与"协定要素"规定。	/
/	金融服务（第20条）	/	美国范本规定。	/
/	税务（第21条）	/	美国范本规定。	/
/	/	公共政策例外（第5条）	"协定要素"规定。	公共利益保障
/	/	投资者义务与责任（第7条）	"协定要素"规定。	投资者义务与责任

（续表）

德国范本	美国范本	"协定要素"模式	三者简要比较	"共同发展"模式
/	/	不降低标准条款（第9条）	"协定要素"规定。	不降低标准条款
/	/	投资促进（第10条）	"协定要素"规定。	投资促进
/	/	制度建设（第11条）	"协定要素"规定。	制度建设
/	国民待遇、最惠国待遇、履行要求（第3、4、8条）	设立前（第B部分）	美国范本与"协定要素"规定。	/
/	/	特殊与差别待遇（第C部分）	"协定要素"规定。	特殊与差别待遇
/	/	/		共同发展

（三）"共同发展导向"BIT 实践模式的基本结构与主要条款

考虑到中国与大多数"一带一路"国家已签订了 BITs，从现实出发，中国与"一带一路"国家之间的"共同发展导向"BIT 实践模式并非对传统 BIT 实践模式"全盘否定"，"另起炉灶"，而是在新签订或修订 BITs 的实践中，在既有 BIT"国际话语体系"（international discourse system）中，求同存异，开拓创新。

中国与"一带一路"国家在新签订或修订 BITs 的实践中，首先需要商定"共同发展导向"BITs 的基本结构与主要条款。概括而言，大致包括如下三方面条款：

一是制定富有创新性的"共同发展"条款。在"共同发展导向"BITs 中，需要明确规定缔约双方"共同发展"的意愿和措施。首先在序言中，明确申明"共同发展"的目标和宗旨。同时，可考虑订立专门的"共同发展"条款。

二是保留经调整或"扬弃"的德国模式传统条款，主要包括序言、定义、准入、待遇标准、征收与补偿、资金的转移、与其他协定的关系、适用范围、缔约国之间争端的解决、缔约国一方与缔约国另一方投资者之间争端的解决、生效，期限与终止通知等条款。

三是采纳"协定要素"体现的创新条款，实现结构性调整。包括公共利益保障、投资者义务与责任、不降低标准条款、投资促进、制度建设、SDT 等条款。

总体上，由"共同发展"条款＋调整的传统条款＋采纳的创新条款，已大致构建了"共同发展导向"BITs 的基本框架。在三个组成部分中，应明确"共同发展"条款是"点睛之笔"，是进一步增加和完善相关条款的"指南"和"圭臬"。就 BIT 实践模式发展而言，"共同发展导向"BIT 实践模式最具革新性意义，实现了"由量变到质变"的飞跃，意味着传统 BITs 的"事实上资本输出国单方受益体制"的终结和"资本输出国与资本输入国双方受益体制"的开端。

为了促进"共同发展导向"BIT 实践模式的形成，中国和"一带一路"国家分别制订或修改各自的 BIT 范本，是很有意义的工作，通过结构和条款的革新和改造，成为"共同发展导向"的新模式。进而言之，中国和"一带一路"国家在实践中不断总结和积累经验，在适当时机形成供各国选择适用的"共同发展导向"BIT 范本，[1]将更为有效地服务于实践。

四、中国与"一带一路"国家间 BIT 实践内容的创新

毋庸讳言，传统 BIT 实践的模式和内容经过长期的发展，已形成"国际话语体系"，受到各国普遍认同。中国与"一带一路"国家之间 BIT 实践内容的创新是在确立"共同发展导向"BIT 实践目标和模式的基础上，通过"共同发展"条款的引入、传统条款的"扬弃"和创新条款的采纳，实现对传统 BIT 整体内容的改革和创新，形成服务于"共同发展导向"BITs 的实体性和程序性内容。

（一）"共同发展"序言与条款

在中国与"一带一路"国家之间"共同发展导向"BITs 中，可在序言明确申明缔约双方"共同发展"的缔约宗旨和目标，作为双方的政策宣示，也作为相关条款履行和解释的重要依据。

"共同发展"条款或系列条款是"共同发展导向"BITs 的必要内容，体现双方"同舟共济"的精神，包括共同发展机构和共同发展措施两个主要方面。

在共同发展机构方面，双方建立投资合作机构，由主管国际投资事务的双方政府部门组成，定期或不定期召开会议。其主要功能包括：

（1）评估 BIT 的履行及双方投资法律政策的实施情况；

（2）投资政策协调和投资问题研讨，及时研究解决双方在投资领域的"重要关切"问题。在这方面，已有重要的实践。例如，挪威 2007 年 BIT 范本规定，设立由双方代表组成的相关共同委员会讨论关于公司社会责任、保护环境、公共健康和安全、可持续发展目标、反腐败、就业和人权等问题；[2]

（3）评估重大投资项目的进展情况；

（4）投资争端的预防和协商解决，防患于未然，或在投资争端发生之初争取协商解决。

---

〔1〕 例如，亚非法律咨商委员会曾制定《促进和保护投资协定范本修正案》（Revised Draft of Model Agreements for Promotion and Protection of Investments）。See Rudolf Dolzer，Fair and Equitable Treatment：A Key Standard in Investment Treaties，*The International Lawyer*，Vol. 39，2005，p. 89.

〔2〕 Norway 2007 Model BIT，Article 23(3)(viii). 转引自韩秀丽：《中国海外投资地环境保护》，载陈安主编：《国际经济法学刊》第 17 卷第 3 期，北京大学出版社 2010 年版，第 160—161 页。

在共同发展措施方面，双方可商定促进经济和社会发展的具体措施，包括：

（1）双方定期或不定期组织投资促进活动，为双方投资者搭建合作交流平台；

（2）双方就对方重大投资项目纳入本国经济社会发展规划而开展磋商；

（3）双方就促进海外投资者投资于对方等事宜开展磋商。

（二）传统条款的"扬弃"

所谓 BIT 传统条款，指自 1959 年以来，以德国 BIT 范本及其实践为代表的欧洲模式的主要条款。以美国 BIT 范本及其实践为代表的美国模式是欧洲模式的"升级版"，体现于强化"片面保护投资"和追求"投资自由化"的新目标。客观上，BIT 实践及其范本经历长期的发展，已形成了体现于欧洲模式和美国模式（简称"欧美模式"）的"共同语言"和各国普遍认同的"国际通行规则"。鉴此，中国与"一带一路"国家 BIT 实践内容的创新，基于"共同发展"目标，需要参考欧美模式的合理成分，以"扬弃"原则择善而从，推陈出新。关于 BIT 传统条款的取舍和调整问题，谨以最具争议性的"准入"、FET、征收及 ISDS 条款为例。

1."准入"条款

所谓"准入"条款，指缔约双方有关允许对方投资进入本国境内的一般规定，通常表明了东道国对外资的态度或立场。据之，东道国可根据国家发展战略，实施有关外资准入和经营的国内法律和政策。"准入"条款是德国 BIT 范本和传统 BIT 实践中唯一体现尊重和维护东道国主权的条款，也是资本输入国在 BITs 中承诺给予外资待遇和国际法保护的唯一回报。实践表明，各国，特别是发展中国家需要保留足够的外资政策空间，在不减损 BIT 有效性的同时促进本国经济的发展。[1] 显然，在 BIT 实践中，"准入"条款是实施东道国外资政策以实现其发展目标的重要保障，也是缔约双方尊重对方管制外资权力和"重要关切"、实现"共同发展"目标的重要保障。

与"准入"条款模式相对立的是"设立权"（right of establishment）模式。"设立权"概念来源于美国现代 FCN 的实践，即规定缔约一方国民在缔约对方设立商务企业的权利。[2] 美国 2012 年范本在"国民待遇""最惠国待遇"及"履行要求"[3]等三个条款中均采用"设立"（establishment）的概念，与"取得"（acquisition）、"扩大"（expansion）、"管理"（management）、"行为"（conduct）、"经营"（operation）、"出售"（sale）或

---

〔1〕　参见詹晓宁：《国际投资规则的制定：晚近趋势及对发展的影响》，载陈安主编：《国际经济法学刊》第 13 卷第 2 期，北京大学出版社 2006 年版，第 48 页。

〔2〕　See Kenneth J. Vandevelde, *U. S. International Investment Agreement*, Oxford University Press, 2009, pp. 236-237.

〔3〕　美国 2012 年范本第 8 条。

其他投资的处置方式并列,表明其实施"设立权"模式,即"国民待遇、最惠国待遇适用于设立"的立场。[1] 由于国民待遇适用于"设立",意味着缔约一方投资者享有与缔约对方投资者同等的"设立权",亦即东道国采取了对国内投资者和外国投资者一视同仁的"投资自由化"政策。1994 年 1 月 NAFTA 生效之后,加拿大在 BIT 实践中也采用"设立权"模式,日本等国亦随后效法。其产生的后果是,一些发展中国家取决于缔约对方的立场,在实践中采取了两种 BIT 模式:(1) 在与欧洲国家签订的BITs 中,继续沿袭"准入"条款模式;(2) 在与美国、加拿大等国签订的 BITs 中,不得不接受"设立权"模式。[2] 两者的重大区别在于,在采用"准入"条款模式的情况下,东道国拥有对外资进入的甄别和审查权,保持管制外资的主权权力和必要的政策空间;而在采用"设立权"模式的情况下,东道国由于承担"投资自由化"义务,放弃了对外资进入的甄别和审查权,基本上放弃了管制外资的主权权力和必要的政策空间。

根据经济主权原则,各国拥有管制外资的主权权力。UNCTAD"可持续发展的投资政策框架"(IPFSD)在"核心原则"中,重申和强调了各国对外资的管制权利(right to regulate),明确规定,各国基于国际承诺和为了公共利益,拥有确立外资准入和经营条件且尽量减轻其潜在负面影响的主权权利。[3] 中国与大多数"一带一路"国家作为发展中国家和新兴经济体,在"共同发展导向"BIT 实践中,理应坚持"准入"条款的实践,同时,不采用或接受"禁止履行要求"条款,以保持管制外资的主权权力和必要的政策空间。事实上,"准入"条款是长期以来绝大多数国家、包括广大发展中国家和多数发达国家的共同立场和普遍实践。当前"准入"条款受到以美国2012 年范本为代表的"设立权"模式及相关实践的严峻挑战。各国,特别是居于资本输入国地位的广大发展中国家,对坚持"准入"条款的必要性、法律意义和现实功效,需要有深刻的认识和客观的评估,更需要有坚定的立场和实践。

2. FET 条款

FET 是 20 世纪 90 年代后期才引起关注的新课题。该概念虽存在于条约和其他文件多年,近年才被运用于仲裁实践。[4] FET 条款的广泛采用反映了 BITs 外资待遇条款的新发展。

---

[1] 美国 2012 年范本第 3、4、8 条。

[2] UNCTAD, *Bilateral Investment Treaties 1995-2006*:*Trends in Investment Rulemaking*, United Nations,2007, pp. xi, 21-26.

[3] UNCTAD, *World Investment Report 2012*, *Towards a New Generation of Investment Policies*, United Nations,2012, p. 109.

[4] See C. H. Schreuer, Investment Arbitration—A Voyage of Discovery, *Transnational Dispute Management*, Vol. 2, No. 5, 2005, p. 9.

FET 条款可溯及美国现代 FCN 实践。[1] 其后,IIAs 的国际性范本草案持续采用该条款。[2] 战后,FET 逐渐成为 IIAs 中最重要的待遇标准。多数 IIAs 规定了 FET 条款。不仅如此,即使某项 BIT 未作明示规定,基于最惠国待遇条款,也可能通过援引其他 BIT 而适用 FET 标准。国际仲裁实践表明,FET 条款提供了广泛的程序性和实体性保护,包括合法预期(legitimate expectation)的保护。由于 FET 覆盖宽泛,以其他具体待遇标准为据未能获胜的诉求,以 FET 标准为据则可胜诉。[3] 在近年投资争端解决程序中,外国投资者一般都会援引 FET 条款。[4]

FET 条款独立于非歧视待遇条款(即最惠国待遇条款和国民待遇条款)的主要原因是,即使在 IIAs 未规定非歧视待遇条款的情况下,也明确表明适用于外资待遇的"国际最低标准"(international minimum standards)。非歧视待遇属相对待遇标准,而 FET 则属绝对待遇标准。FET 是含糊的,可能有多种解释。理论上,FET 是相当于习惯国际法要求的"国际最低标准",抑或代表独立、自给自足(self-contained)的概念,即"独立条款"解释,见仁见智。[5] 一些学者主张,给予外资 FET 的义务与给予外资"国际最低标准"待遇的义务并无区别,"国际最低标准"是习惯国际法的组成部分,包含 FET 等一系列国际法律原则。另一些学者则主张,FET 蕴含不同于"国际最低标准"的含义,应作"独立条款"解释,依衡平检验方式个案适用以确定是否违反该标准。[6] FET 指超越"国际最低标准"的行为、给予更高水平的保护及依据更为客观的标准。仲裁庭关注的不是国际最低、最高或平均标准,而是需要决定在所有情势下,该行为是否公平公正。因此,该用语应独立自主地理解和适用。[7] FET 至少意味着,在诉诸当地法院和行政机构、适用的税收及政府管制的实施等方

---

〔1〕 美国现代 FCNs 包括一些规定给予"涵盖投资"(covered investment)绝对待遇标准的条款,以便在缺乏具体规定的情况下,为外资和外国投资者提供更高水平的保护。各条约用语不同,1951 年开始出现了一致的实践。1956 年后,"FET"的用语有时取代了"公平待遇"(equitable treatment)。See Kenneth J. Vandevelde, *U. S. International Investment Agreement*, Oxford University Press, 2009, pp. 234-235.

〔2〕 See Rudolf Dolzer, Fair and Equitable Treatment: A Key Standard in Investment Treaties, *The International Lawyer*, Vol. 39, 2005, p. 89.

〔3〕 See Andrew Newcombe, Lluis Paradell, *Law and Practice of Investment Treaties*, *Standards of Treatment*, Wolters Kluwer, 2009, pp. 255-298.

〔4〕 See Rudolf Dolzer, Fair and Equitable Treatment: A Key Standard in Investment Treaties, *The International Lawyer*, Vol. 39, 2005, p. 87.

〔5〕 See Rudolf Dolzer, Margrete Stevens, *Bilateral Investment Treaties*, Martinus Nijhoff Publishers, 1995, pp. 58-59.

〔6〕 UNCTAD, *Bilateral Investment Treaties 1995-2006: Trends in Investment Rulemaking*, United Nations, 2007, pp. xii, 28-33.

〔7〕 See Rudolf Dolzer, Margrete Stevens, *Bilateral Investment Treaties*, Martinus Nijhoff Publishers, 1995, p. 59.

面,无论投资者国籍或投资来源,均一视同仁。[1] FET 是宽泛的标准,包含保护的各种因素,包括与"国际最低标准"联系的共同因素、合法预期的保护、非歧视、透明度和针对恶意(bad faith)、胁迫(coercion)、威胁(threats)和骚扰(harassment)的保护。[2]

在近年的 BIT 实践中,绝大多数包含了 FET 标准的规定。然而,很少 BITs 对 FET 的含义作出清晰的界定。BITs 采用不同的解释方法,例如,称 FET 标准并不意味着高于习惯国际法规范,或称该标准为国际法的佐证(reference),或将该标准与非歧视待遇标准相联系。[3] 美国 2012 年 BIT 范本第 5 条规定,缔约各方应根据习惯国际法给予涵盖投资待遇,包括 FET 和"充分保护与保障",[4] 且进一步明确规定,FET 和"充分保护与保障"的概念不超过"国际最低标准",也未增加实体权利。在一些发达国家看来,FET 与"国际最低标准""充分保护与保障"密切联系,互为解释,相互补充。

在 ISDS 中,FET 条款对外国投资者和东道国的诉求及争端处理结果尤具重要的现实意义。[5] "解决投资争端国际中心"(ICSID)和 NAFTA 仲裁庭有关 FET 解释的实践,进一步引起了对是否及如何适用该条款的广泛关注。ICSID 用于解释 BITs 的 FET 条款的两个案例表明,FET 标准并未要求东道国对影响外资的所有损害负责,但东道国如在保护外资免受损害方面未能显示"应有的勤勉"(due diligence),就必须承担责任。ICSID 仲裁庭将"应有的勤勉"定义为"在类似情况下,可预期的行政良好的政府所能采取的合理防范措施"。[6] 在 NAFTA 多个投资仲裁案中,各仲裁庭对 NAFTA 第 1105 条(涉及 FET)范围和内容的解释迥然不同,其中包含 NAFTA 全体缔约方强烈反对的解释,直接导致了 NAFTA 自由贸易委员会的干

---

[1] See Andreas F. Lowenfeld, *International Economic Law*, 2nd ed, Oxford University Press, 2008, pp. 556-557.

[2] 关于实践中 FET 要素的详细分析,参见 Andrew Newcombe, Lluis Paradell, *Law and Practice of Investment Treaties*, *Standards of Treatment*, Wolters Kluwer, 2009, pp. 279-298; C. H. Schreuer, Investment Arbitration—A Voyage of Discovery, *Transnational Dispute Management*, Vol. 2, No. 5, 2005, p. 9; Jeswald W. Salacuse, Towards a Global Treaty on Foreign Investment: The Search for a Grand Bargain, in Norbert Horn (ed.), *Arbitrating Foreign Investment Disputes*, Kluwer Law International, 2004, p. 83。

[3] UNCTAD, *Bilateral Investment Treaties 1995-2006*: *Trends in Investment Rulemaking*, United Nations, 2007, pp. 28-33.

[4] 所谓"充分保护与保障"标准要求东道国政府不仅不能损害外国投资者的设备和员工,还需要在一些紧急情况(如叛乱等)下,保护外资和外国投资者免受其他人的损害。See Andreas F. Lowenfeld, *International Economic Law*, 2nd ed, Oxford University Press, 2008, pp. 558-559.

[5] 在实践中,基于 BITs 的诉讼均援引 FET 条款。See Rudolf Dolzer, Fair and Equitable Treatment: A Key Standard in Investment Treaties, *The International Lawyer*, Vol. 39, 2005, p. 87.

[6] Jeswald W. Salacuse, Towards a Global Treaty on Foreign Investment: The Search for a Grand Bargain, in Norbert Horn (ed.), *Arbitrating Foreign Investment Disputes*, Kluwer Law International, 2004, p. 83.

预。2001 年 7 月 31 日，该委员会颁布了关于解释 FET 的通知，明确反对"独立条款"解释，指出 FET 并未要求缔约方承担超出习惯国际法所确立的任何待遇标准。[1]

实质上，BIT 实践中适用 FET 条款的目的是弥补其他具体待遇标准的缺失，以期达到条约设定的保护投资者的水平。一些 BITs 甚至直接将 FET 条款与法律稳定性的基本目标相联系。[2] 一般认为，FET 条款的明显目的是，规定超脱于东道国国内法的基本的一般标准。由于"独立条款"解释的所有要素均与东道国行为有关，进一步加重了东道国的责任。显然，根据"独立条款"解释，东道国须承担比习惯国际法确立的"国际最低标准"更高水平的外资保护责任。

应当明确，FET 条款并非 BITs 不可或缺的条款。"协定要素"在调整 BIT 传统条款方面的选项之一是，不采用 FET 条款。[3] 传统上，发展中国家在国际规范性文件中也不采用 FET 条款。在 20 世纪 70、80 年代由发展中国家起草或主导的国际规范性文件，如联合国《经济宪章》、亚非法律咨商委员会《促进和保护投资协定范本修正案》(Revised Draft of Model Agreements for Promotion and Protection of Investments)，均未提及 FET 标准。[4] 事实上，一些发达国家即使采用 FET 条款，也不接受"独立条款"解释。例如，美国 2012 年范本的上述规定，也竭力避免增加外国投资者的实体权利。鉴于 FET 条款因涵义不明在实践中容易产生争议甚至滥用等情况，且可能对东道国施加过重的保护外资责任，中国与"一带一路"国家在"共同发展导向"BIT 实践中，可考虑不采用该条款。如确因需要而采用 FET 条款，应对其涵义作出明确规定，以避免法庭或仲裁庭作出基于"独立条款"的扩大化解释。

3. 征收条款

长期以来，对外资的征收权及赔偿标准问题是国际投资法理论和实践的热点问题，也是南北矛盾的最集中体现。[5] "协定要素"指出，IIAs 的征收条款并非剥夺国家征收私人财产的权利，而是保护投资者免遭专断的、无赔偿的征收，建立对外资包

〔1〕 UNCTAD, *Bilateral Investment Treaties 1995-2006*: *Trends in Investment Rulemaking*, United Nations, 2007, pp. 29-30.

〔2〕 例如，1991 年美国—阿根廷 BIT 序言规定，"希望通过 FET 保障稳定的框架"。See Rudolf Dolzer, Fair and Equitable Treatment: A Key Standard in Investment Treaties, *The International Lawyer*, Vol. 39, 2005, p. 90.

〔3〕 "协定要素"第 A 部分第 4.3.4 条。UNCTAD, *World Investment Report 2012*, *Towards a New Generation of Investment Policies*, United Nations, 2012, p. 147.

〔4〕 See Rudolf Dolzer, Fair and Equitable Treatment: A Key Standard in Investment Treaties, *The International Lawyer*, Vol. 39, 2005, p. 89.

〔5〕 参见曾华群：《外资征收及其补偿标准：历史的分野与现实的挑战》，载陈安主编：《国际经济法学刊》第 13 卷第 1 期，北京大学出版社 2006 年版，第 38—69 页。

容的、具有稳定和可预见性的法律框架。[1] 在近年 BIT 范本及实践中，征收的前提条件仍然是征收条款的核心问题。

在传统 BIT 实践中，依使用的频率，在 BITs 中列举的征收前提条件包括：（1）赔偿；（2）公共目的；（3）非歧视；（4）正当法律程序；（5）不违反具体承诺（specific undertakings）；（6）全部适用（catch-all）；（7）透明度（clarity）；（8）公平待遇。就特定 BIT 而言，缔约双方一般列举三至四项征收的前提条件，少则仅列举两项，多则列举五至六项。[2] 近年来，发达国家在 BIT 范本及其实践中，主张根据习惯国际法，国家不得征收外资，除非：（1）为公共目的；（2）基于非歧视；（3）根据正当法律程序；（4）给予及时、充分、有效的赔偿（即"赫尔"规则）。[3] 美国 2012 年范本第 6 条"征收与赔偿"规定，征收的前提条件是：（1）为了公共目的；（2）以非歧视的方式；（3）给予及时、充分和有效的支付；及（4）根据法律的正当程序和第 5 条"最低待遇标准"第 1—3 款的规定。显然，美国 2012 年范本的相关规定更为严苛，特别表现在将"赫尔"规则和"最低待遇标准"同时列为征收的前提条件，且详细规定于征收条款。

《经济宪章》第 2 条第 2 款规定："各国有权：……（e）将外国财产的所有权收归国有、征收或转移，在收归国有、征收或转移时，应由采取此种措施的国家给予适当补偿（appropriate compensation），要考虑到它的有关法律和规章以及该国认为有关的一切情况……"长期以来，发达国家得陇望蜀，步步为营，不断强化和细化征收的限制性前提条件，意在进一步剥夺或限缩东道国征收和管制外资的主权权力和政策空间。这与《经济宪章》的上述规定背道而驰，渐行渐远。首先，发达国家坚持把"不得征收"外资作为一般的法律原则，与上述"有权征收"的规定相悖。虽然，发达国家并非一般地否定国家对外资的征收权，但对征收权作了严格的限制性前提条件，进而以是否满足前提条件为据区分"合法征收"与"非法征收"，并主张依国际法和国内法（包括投资者母国和东道国的法律）保留对东道国政府征收行为是否合法的裁判权。其次，发达国家更为强调适用"赫尔"规则，与上述"适当补偿"的规定相悖。在发达国家普遍主张的征收四项前提条件中，"赫尔"规则无疑是决定性的。对发展中国家而言，在实行征收时要符合为公共利益目的、依照法律程序、非歧视性等三项前提条件相对可行，而要符合"赫尔"规则的赔偿标准则难以甚至无法企及。因为发展

---

〔1〕 UNCTAD，*World Investment Report 2012*，*Towards a New Generation of Investment Policies*，United Nations，2012，p. 148.

〔2〕 See Paul Peters，Recent Developments in Expropriation Clauses of Asian Investment Treaties，*Asian Yearbook of International Law*，Vol. 5，1995，pp. 56-67.

〔3〕 对 1995 年以来签订的 BITs 的一项研究反映了有关征收条件的高度一致，绝大多数包含了上述四项条件。UNCTAD，*Bilateral Investment Treaties 1995-2006：Trends in Investment Rulemaking*，United Nations，2007，p. 47.

中国家受限于经济实力,在实行征收,特别是实行以经济结构改革为目标的大规模征收时,往往无力支付"及时、充分和有效的赔偿"。而一旦无力支付,则征收就无法实施。如果强行实施,就将被判定为"非法征收",必须承担国际责任。在此情况下,发展中国家的征收权实际上被彻底否定了。

"协定要素"规定,征收须符合公共目的、非歧视、正当程序及支付赔偿等四项前提条件。[1] 比较而言,"协定要素"的"支付赔偿"规定与美国 2012 年范本有关"给予及时、充分和有效的支付"规定的重大区别在于,前者未涉及赔偿标准问题,而后者则明确规定了依照"赫尔"规则的赔偿标准。

鉴于传统 BITs 的征收条款对征收的前提条件作了严格限定,特别是以"赫尔"规则作为征收的前提条件,实质上剥夺了广大发展中国家对外资的征收权,中国与"一带一路"国家之间的 BIT 实践应坚持《经济宪章》确立的经济主权原则,特别是各国对外资的"征收权"和"适当补偿"原则。当前,传统 BITs 征收条款对外资"征收权"的否定式表述(即"不得征收……除非")已司空见惯,从传统 BITs 保护外资的首要目标和功能看,似乎也在情理之中。然而,应当指出,此种否定式表述附加"赫尔"规则由于片面强调资本输出国和外国投资者的权益,忽视甚至否定资本输入国的主权权力,明显有违《经济宪章》关于"有权征收"和"适当补偿"的规定。鉴此,在中国与"一带一路"国家之间的"共同发展导向"BIT 实践中,可考虑在缔约双方达成共识的情况下,以肯定式表述缔约各方对外资的"征收权"和"适当补偿"原则。实际上,在 BIT 范本及其实践中,以肯定式表述的缔约各方"有权征收"外资取代否定式表述的缔约各方"不得征收"外资,仅是重申各国普遍承认的关于国家"征收权"的传统法律原则。事实上,基于"共同发展"的目标,缔约各方相互尊重征收权,行使征收权亦慎之又慎。在"共同发展"条款中,还可具体规定"征收"发生时缔约双方政府之间的联络和协助等事项。

4. ISDS 条款

外国投资者与东道国之间的投资争端,是典型的国际投资争端。主要由《解决国家与他国国民间投资争端公约》(简称"ICSID 公约")和 BITs 确立的 ISDS 机制,赋予外国投资者在国际性程序的"出诉权",被视为传统国际法发展的一大创新。其受到国际社会,特别是发达国家肯定的主要缘由:一是避免了投资者母国行使"外交保护权"甚至"举兵索债"而导致的国家之间冲突;二是作为私人的外国投资者在国际性程序具有"出诉权"地位,与东道国具有平等的法律地位,其投资权益受到了充

---

〔1〕 "协定要素"第 A 部分第 4.5 条。UNCTAD, *World Investment Report 2012*, *Towards a New Generation of Investment Policies*, United Nations, 2012, p. 148.

分的国际法保护。

近年来，ISDS 体制已面临来自发达国家和发展中国家的严峻挑战，甚至面临合法性或正当性危机。2011 年 4 月，澳大利亚颁布一项贸易政策声明，宣称其在将来签订的 IIAs 中，不再接受 ISDS 条款。其原因是，该条款给予外国企业高于本国企业的法律权利，且限制了政府的公共决策能力（如社会、环境和经济法律的制定与履行）。[1] 近年来，更有来自发展中国家的激烈反应。例如，"卡尔沃主义"的故乡拉美国家，在 20 世纪 80 年代末转变其抵制 IIAs 的立场，近 20 年来同世界各国签订了 500 多项 BITs。[2] 然而，鉴于 IIAs"自由化"发展，特别是 ISDS 条款削弱国家经济主权的新情势，一些拉美国家不得不重新考虑其有关 IIAs 的立场甚至终止 BITs 和退出 ICSID。[3] 厄瓜多尔、委内瑞拉和尼加拉瓜等拉美国家还通过终止其签署的 BITs 达到摆脱 ICSID 管辖权的目的。这些重要举措被称为"卡尔沃主义"的复兴。[4]

当前，国际社会对 ISDS 改革已成共识，并付诸实践。最为激进的改革方案分别来自美国和欧盟。ICSID 最重大且具争议性的改革是投资仲裁上诉机构的创设问题。2002 年，美国国会通过的《国际贸易促进授权法案》第一次出现了建立投资仲裁上诉机制的提法，并在美国与智利、新加坡、摩洛哥、乌拉圭、秘鲁等国签订的自由贸易协定和 BITs 中体现了这一改革设想。[5] 另一重大改革是欧盟的常设投资法院机制（investment court system）提案及实践。2015 年 11 月 12 日，欧盟委员会公布《跨大西洋贸易与投资伙伴协定》（简称《TTIP 协定》）投资章节建议案，规定了常设投资法院机制的机构设置和运作模式，将被用于欧美之间的《TTIP 协定》谈判。加拿大

---

〔1〕 UNCTAD, *World Investment Report 2012*, *Towards a New Generation of Investment Policies*, United Nations, 2012, p. 87.

〔2〕 See Mary H. Mourra（ed.）, *Latin American Investment Treaty Arbitration*, *the Controversies and Conflicts*, Wolters Kluwer, 2009, p. 1.

〔3〕 2008 年，厄瓜多尔终止了与古巴、多米尼加、萨尔瓦多、危地马拉、洪都拉斯、尼加拉瓜、巴拉圭、罗马尼亚和乌拉圭等国签订的 9 项 BITs。其他宣布终止的 BITs 包括萨尔瓦多与尼加拉瓜、荷兰与委内瑞拉之间的 BITs。玻利维亚退出 ICSID 公约的通知于 2007 年 5 月 2 日提交 ICSID，2010 年 11 月 3 日生效。厄瓜多尔退出 ICSID 公约的通知于 2009 年 7 月 6 日提交 ICSID，2010 年 1 月 7 日生效。See Wolfgang Alschner, Ana Berdajs, Vladyslav Lanovoy and Sergey Ripinsky etc., Denunciation of the ICSID Convention and BITs: Impact on Investor-State Claims, United Nations, UNCTAD, *IIA Issues Note*, No. 1, December 2010, p. 1, notes 2, 3. 2011 年 6 月，玻利维亚宣布退出其与美国签订的 BIT。2012 年 1 月，委内瑞拉向 ICSID 提交退出 ICSID 公约的通知。UNCTAD, *World Investment Report 2012*, *Towards a New Generation of Investment Policies*, United Nations, 2012, p. 87.

〔4〕 参见 Silvia Karina Fiezzoni:《论拉美国家对 ICSID 的挑战》，载陈安主编:《国际经济法学刊》第 18 卷第 3 期，北京大学出版社 2011 年版，第 222—238 页。

〔5〕 参见崔悦:《国际投资仲裁上诉机制初探》，载陈安主编:《国际经济法学刊》第 20 卷第 1 期，北京大学出版社 2013 年版，第 119—138 页。

和越南同意在其与欧盟缔结的自由贸易协定中接受欧盟提出的常设投资法院机制。[1]

在 ISDS 方面,中国与"一带一路"国家之间的"共同发展导向"BIT 实践具有新的投资争端解决共识、立场和基础。其主要创新可表现在:

(1) 创建投资争端预防机制,防患于未然;

(2) 采用"用尽当地救济"(exhaustion of local remedies)规则。[2] 例如,印度 2016 年 BIT 范本规定,外国投资者首先将投资争端诉诸国内法院,自投资者知悉该争端措施之日起至少 5 年期间寻求用尽当地救济。如外国投资者表明,不存在可获得的对该措施能合理提供的当地法律救济,则不在此限;[3]

(3) 采用多元化投资争端解决方式。注重利用缔约方的国际性调解和仲裁机构或中国和"一带一路"国家等"第三方"国际性调解和仲裁机构,打破 ICSID 的"市场支配"(market dominance)地位。[4] ICSID 作为投资争端的解决方式之一,而不是唯一的解决方式。同时,应重视利用 ICSID 的调解功能。

(三) 创新条款的采纳

"协定要素"是 BIT 模式的创新性发展,集中体现于调整"南北权益失衡"的传统条款和增加"平衡南北权益"的新规范,追求世界各国的长远利益、共同福祉和"可持续发展"的新目标,在很大程度上反映了国际社会重构国际投资条约体制的创新理念、共识、诉求和初步成就。在中国与"一带一路"国家之间"共同发展导向"BIT 实践中,就 BIT 创新条款的采纳而言,"公共利益保障""投资者义务与责任""母国措施"和 SDT 等条款尤为重要。

---

〔1〕 参见杨帆:《试析投资者—国家争端解决机制当代改革的欧盟模式——以欧盟 TTIP 建议案中常设投资法院机制为例》,载陈安主编:《国际经济法学刊》第 23 卷第 3 期,法律出版社 2016 年版,第 99—126 页。

〔2〕 该规则指当外国人与东道国政府或私人发生争议时,应诉诸东道国的行政或司法机构按东道国的程序法和实体法予以解决;在未用尽东道国法律对其仍然适用的所有救济手段之前,不得寻求国际程序解决,该外国人的母国政府也不能对其行使外交保护权。该规则是确立已久的习惯国际法规则,得到各国实践、国际判例和国际组织的普遍认同。然而,在 BIT 实践中,绝大多数未明确规定此项原则,引发了是否"默示放弃"此项原则的问题。关于"用尽当地救济"规则的涵义及在 BIT 实践适用情况的较系统论述,参见石静遐:《用尽当地规则与国际投资争议的解决》,载陈安主编:《国际经济法论丛》第 2 卷,法律出版社 1999 年版,第 309—328 页。

〔3〕 See Prabhash Ranjan, Investment Protection and Host State's Right to Regulate in the Indian Model Bilateral Investment Treaty: Lessons for Asian Countries, in Julien Chaisse, Tomoko Ishikawa, Sufian Jusoh (ed.), *Asia's Changing International Investment Regime, Sustainability, Regionalization, and Arbitration*, Springer, 2017, pp. 63-64.

〔4〕 See Andrea K. Bjorklund and Bryan H. Druzin, Breaking the Market Dominance of ICSID? An Assessment of the Likelihood of Institutional Competition, Especially from Asia, in the Near Future, in Julien Chaisse, Tomoko Ishikawa, Sufian Jusoh (ed.), *Asia's Changing International Investment Regime, Sustainability, Regionalization, and Arbitration*, Springer, 2017, pp. 243-260.

1. "公共利益保障"条款

在 IIAs 传统实践中，极少规定"公共政策例外"（public policy exceptions）条款。近年来，越来越多的 BITs 通过采用"一般例外"（general exceptions）条款重申国家在公共利益领域的管制权利。"协定要素"的"公共政策例外"条款规定，允许在具体、例外的情况下，采取与 IIAs 不符的公共政策措施。其主要问题在于，"一般例外"条款的适用范围及是否"自裁决"（self-judging）性质。在 BIT 实践中，有的将"一般例外"条款的适用范围严格限于"国家安全措施和/或有关维护国际和平与安全的措施"，有的将"一般例外"条款的适用范围扩及旨在维护合法公共政策目标的国内管制措施，诸如保护人权，保护公共健康，维护环境，保护公共道德或公共秩序保留等。[1]

根据经济主权原则，各国对其公共利益领域拥有完全的管制权力。而在传统 BIT 实践中，由于以"投资保护""投资自由化"为目标，东道国的"公共利益"管制权力未受到应有的关注和尊重，对东道国"公共利益保障"原来未作任何规定。之后在实践中，出现了因外国投资导致"公共利益"严重受损而无从救济的情况。即使新近发展的"一般例外"条款，也是作为"例外"规定的，且留下了解释难题。

在 BITs 中明确规定"公共利益保障"条款，当是"共同发展导向"BITs 的重要特征。"公共利益"指属于社会的好处。在法律语境中，公共利益理论的基本观念是法律应当反映"公益"，代表全体人民，或者"最大多数人民的最大利益"。公共利益应当代表社会大众的利益，国家利益在形式和内容上都应当包含公共利益。在国际投资法中，公共利益主要体现在环境、公共健康、人权与安全等方面。[2]

近年来，"可持续投资""包容性投资""东道国社会公共利益优于私人投资者利益"已渐成国际投资法领域的流行语。涉及"公共利益"的投资争端，特别是征收案例，"公共利益保障"条款日益为缔约双方政府所关注。在中国与"一带一路"国家之间"共同发展导向"BIT 实践中，"公共利益保障"符合缔约双方的"共同诉求"，理应作为重要条款。这绝不是简单的在私人投资者利益、国家利益与社会公共利益之间寻求平衡的问题，而是社会公共利益在国际投资法律体制，特别是在 BITs 中的定位问题。[3]

---

［1］ UNCTAD, *World Investment Report 2012*, *Towards a New Generation of Investment Policies*, United Nations, 2012, p. 151.

［2］ 参见李武健：《论投资条约中的公共利益》，载陈安主编：《国际经济法学刊》第 17 卷第 4 期，北京大学出版社 2010 年版，第 128—130 页。

［3］ 同上书，第 127—140 页。

2. "投资者义务与责任"条款

"投资者义务与责任"条款是"协定要素"基于经济主权原则和公平互利原则的重要创新,对中国与"一带一路"国家之间"共同发展导向"BIT实践具有十分重要的意义。

传统上,由于BITs的缔约主体一般是国家,绝大多数BITs仅规定东道国保护外资的义务或责任,而全然未规定外国投资者的义务或责任。外国投资者虽是BITs的真正和最终受益者,享有BITs提供的有关其投资的待遇、诉权等法律保障,其在东道国境内有关投资和经营的不当行为却无从或难以由BITs调整。

一般认为,条约是规范和调整条约主体的,由于外国投资者不是BITs的主体,因而不能承担BITs课以的义务。这是值得进一步推敲的。根据普遍认同的"权利义务对等原则",由于BITs赋予外国投资者各种权利,同样可课以外国投资者相应的义务。有学者指出,鉴于外国投资者经由BITs取得了ICSID的"出诉权",已具有国际法意义上的法律人格,可在BITs中直接为其规定国际法上的义务。换言之,以外国投资者的义务平衡其享有的权利。[1]

早在20世纪70年代初,国际社会进行了国际投资立法另一方面的多边努力,重心是管制外国投资者,特别是跨国公司的不良行为。多年来,UNCTAD、经济合作开发组织(OECD)、国际商会和国际劳工组织等曾先后起草和制定有关管制跨国公司行为(包括竞争、税务、雇佣关系、技术转让、贿赂、信息及披露等)的规则。然而,这方面努力的进展和实效甚微。应当指出,一直以来,保护国际投资和促进投资自由化的努力与管制跨国投资者行为的努力在不同的场所分别进行。两种努力各行其道,互不交集,均未能构建起达到其目标所需的法律框架。从国际现实出发,也许两种努力应合并进行。[2] 1984年《联合国跨国公司行为守则》(草案)和2011年《OECD跨国企业指南》内容相近,在一定程度上反映了规制外国投资者的一般规则,可视为国际社会制定"投资者义务与责任"规范的初步尝试。

"协定要素"提出,在IIA实践中,以"可持续发展"为目标,增加"投资者义务与责任"条款,以平衡外国投资者的权利和责任,促进"负责任的投资"。具体表现在:(1)要求外国投资者在投资准入和经营阶段遵守东道国法律,制定针对"不遵从"(non-compliance)行为的处罚措施,包括:拒绝对违反东道国法律所作的投资予以条约保护,拒绝对违反反映国际法律责任(例如,为履行有关劳工标准、反腐败、环境等

---

〔1〕 参见李武健:《论投资条约中的公共利益》,载陈安主编:《国际经济法学刊》第17卷第4期,北京大学出版社2010年版,第160页。

〔2〕 Jeswald W. Salacuse, Towards a Global Treaty on Foreign Investment: The Search for a Grand Bargain, in Norbert Horn (ed.), *Arbitrating Foreign Investment Disputes*, Kluwer Law International, 2004, pp. 87-88.

条约义务）的东道国法律所经营的投资予以条约保护，规定在因外国投资者违反东道国法律而引起的 ISDS 中，东道国有权对该外国投资者提起反诉；（2）促进外国投资者遵守普遍承认的标准，如《国际劳工组织关于跨国企业和社会政策的三方原则宣言》和《联合国商务与人权指导原则》，且履行有关经济发展、社会和环境风险的企业适当谨慎（corporate due diligence），规定法庭或仲裁庭在解释和适用条约保护（如 FET 条款）或决定给予投资者赔偿数额时将考虑有关投资者"不遵从"行为的情况；（3）促进外国投资者遵守可适用的企业社会责任（corporate social responsibilities，CSR）标准，可提供 CSR 标准清单或规定 CSR 标准的内容，规定法庭或仲裁庭在解释和适用条约保护（如 FET 条款）或决定给予投资者赔偿数额时将考虑有关投资者"不遵守"（non-observance）行为的情况；（4）要求缔约各方之间在促进遵守可适用的 CSR 标准方面的合作；（5）促进母国以投资者在社会和环境方面的可持续行为作为给予海外投资促进优惠的条件。[1] 应当指出，上述"投资者义务与责任"条款内容尚属原则性规定，主要强调外国投资者遵守东道国法律和普遍承认的 CSR 标准的一般义务与责任，是外国投资者本应在东道国承担的基本法律义务与责任。尽管如此，在 BITs 中，此类规范从无到有，仍具有重要的创新和实践意义。

关于 BIT 规制外国投资者的具体形式和内容，有学者建议，可尝试以不同方式制定规制外国投资者行为的规则：（1）宣示性方式，如 BIT 序言可规定，投资者应对东道国经济、社会和环境的进步作出贡献；（2）强制性方式，如 BIT 可规定，外国投资者经营活动应遵守东道国法律法规、有关消费者保护和环境保护等国内、国际惯例等；（3）禁止性方式，如 BIT 可要求外国投资者不得进行任何形式的贿赂；及（4）劝导性方式，如 BIT 可要求外国投资者在进行实质性研究活动时，应充分利用本地资源和员工。[2]

鉴于"投资者义务与责任"条款是平衡东道国与外国投资者之间权益及外国投资者本身权利与义务的重要体现，是国际投资条约体制的重要突破，中国与"一带一路"国家之间的"共同发展导向"BIT 实践理应率先采纳该条款，并丰富和强化相关规范。

3. "母国措施"条款

"母国措施"条款也是"协定要素"的重要创新。广义上，"母国措施"指投资者母

---

[1] UNCTAD, *World Investment Report 2012*, *Towards a New Generation of Investment Policies*, United Nations, 2012, p. 154.

[2] See Cai Congyan, China-US BIT Negotiations and the Future of Investment Treaty Regime: A Grand Bilateral Bargain with Multilateral Implications, *Journal of International Economic Law*, Vol. 12, No. 2, 2009, pp. 502-504.

国基于合作发展原则,为促进、保护和规范其海外投资和海外投资者而制定或采取的国内措施和国际措施。"母国措施"条款关注东道国的权益和"重要关切",服务于"共同发展"目标,理应采纳为中国与"一带一路"国家之间"共同发展导向"BITs 的重要条款。

传统上,BIT 范本及实践赋予投资者母国"代位权"等权利,未施加任何责任。据此,投资者母国在拥有和行使保护其海外投资者权利的同时,未承担促进或规范其投资者海外投资活动的责任。投资者母国为其海外投资和海外投资者提供法律保护,促进或规范其投资者海外投资活动仅出于维护本国权益的考虑,未顾及东道国的权益。[1]

自 20 世纪 80 年代以来,OECD 国家如美国、英国、德国、丹麦、挪威、新西兰、瑞士和加拿大等,开始关注对其海外投资者在东道国的环境保护、人权、商业行为、雇员权利及健康与安全等方面的责任,结合传统的海外投资保证制度或对外援助制度,制定了相关政策措施或项目计划,以促进对外"负责任的投资"和"可持续的投资"(sustainable investment)。1999 年 1 月,OECD 环境政策委员会和国际投资与跨国企业委员会在海牙召开"外国直接投资与环境大会",建议投资者母国制定指导其投资者在本国和国际经营活动的环境标准。这表明,一些资本输出国初步意识到规范其海外投资者在东道国经营活动的责任,且付诸行动。有学者指出,"可持续的投资"的成就是母国政府、东道国政府、母国私人、东道国私人、环境组织及公民等行为者的共同责任。因此,母国政府和母国私人应采取和接受必要的措施或规范。[2]

"协定要素"以"可持续发展"为目标,在"投资促进"和"制度建设"条款中,规定了"母国措施"的内容。主要表现在:(1) 投资促进方面,制定促进海外投资,特别是"最有利于国家发展战略的投资"条款。可能的机制包括:鼓励母国提供投资保证等海外投资优惠,以具有促进可持续发展效应的投资或投资者遵守普遍原则和可适用的 CSR 标准为条件;组织共同的投资促进活动,如展览、会议、专题研讨及延伸项目;交流有关投资机会的信息;保证投资促进机构经常性的咨商;通过建立 IIAs 机构加强促进投资活动;(2) 制度建设方面,建立缔约各方开展合作的制度框架,促进履行 IIAs 以利最大限度发挥其对可持续发展的贡献,包括:颁布 IIAs 条款的解释;审查 IIA 的功效;商定条款的修改和通过再谈判,促使 IIAs 更为适应缔约各方的可持续

---

〔1〕 关于投资者母国促进和规范其海外投资的动机分析,参见 M. Sornarajah, *The International Law on Foreign Investment*, Cambridge University Press, 1994, pp. 65-67。

〔2〕 See Riva Krut and Ashley Moretz, Home Country Measures for Encouraging Sustainable FDI, Occasional Paper No. 8, Report as Part of UNCTAD/CBS Project: Cross Border Environmental Management in Transnational Corporations, CBS, November 1999, pp. 1-2.

发展政策；组织和审查投资促进活动，包括投资促进机构参与的投资机会信息交流、组织投资促进的专题研讨等；讨论 IIAs 的履行，包括有关具体瓶颈、非正式壁垒、繁文缛节及投资争端解决等问题；定期审查缔约各方遵守"不降低标准"（not lowering of standards）条款的情况；对发展中缔约方提供技术援助，使其参与 IIAs 的制度化后续安排；确认和更新 CSR 标准并组织促进遵守 CSR 标准的活动。[1]

"母国措施"条款是 BITs 平衡资本输出国与资本输入国之间权益的重要体现。发达国家已有国内法实践。"协定要素"的创新之处是基于合作发展原则，强调资本输出国与资本输入国之间的"国际合作"义务，将"母国措施"作为资本输出国有关"投资促进"和"制度建设"的条约义务。中国与"一带一路"国家之间"共同发展导向"BIT 实践理应率先采纳"母国措施"条款，进一步丰富其内容。实际上，"协定要素"提倡的"投资促进"和"制度建设"条款，如由 BIT 缔约双方共同商定，共同承担相关条约义务，也可作为"共同发展"条款或系列条款的重要内容。

4. SDT 条款

SDT 条款是"协定要素"基于公平互利原则和合作发展原则的重要创新，理应成为中国与"一带一路"国家之间"共同发展导向"BITs 的必要条款。

在 GATT/WTO 体制中，SDT 条款早已确立。2000 年，UNCTAD 主张，SDT 原则应引入 IIAs。[2]"协定要素"规定了 SDT 条款，作为发展水平悬殊的 IIAs 缔约各方，特别是缔约一方属最不发达国家的选项。其效力及于现有规定和新规定，使较不发达缔约方承担的责任水平适合其发展水平。为达此目标，SDT 条款涉及"减负"和"增压"两方面的规范。在"减负"方面，规定"不对称的责任"，使较不发达缔约一方承担较轻的责任。主要内容包括：（1）延期履行义务。为较不发达缔约一方规定延期履行 IIA 义务的时间表，即承担分阶段（phase-in）履约义务，可适用于设立前义务、国民待遇、资金转移、履行要求、透明度及投资争端解决等方面；（2）降低规范强度。允许较不发达缔约一方以最佳努力承诺（best-endeavour commitments）取代具有法律约束力的义务，可适用于设立前义务、国民待遇、履行要求及透明度等方面；（3）保留。包括一般义务的国家特定保留，例如确定敏感部门、政策领域或具体规模的企业等保留，可适用于设立前义务、国民待遇、最惠国待遇、履行要求、透明度及雇用员工等方面；（4）"发展导向"（development-friendly）解释。基于缔约各方不同发展水平的考虑解释投资保护标准，可适用于 FET、充分保护与保障及给予赔偿

---

〔1〕 UNCTAD, *World Investment Report 2012*, *Towards a New Generation of Investment Policies*, United Nations, 2012, pp. 155-156.

〔2〕 UNCTAD, *International Investment Agreements*: *Flexibility for Development*, UNCTAD Series on Issues in International Investment Agreements, UNCTAD/ITE/18, New York and Geneva, 2000, pp. 29-36.

的数额等方面。在"增压"方面,规定"附加工具",促进较发达缔约一方作出积极贡献。主要内容包括:(1)技术援助。承担提供履行 IIA 义务和促进投资的技术援助的义务;(2)投资促进。为海外投资提供投资优惠,如投资保证。[1]

需要特别强调的是,"协定要素"主张在 IIAs 引入 SDT 条款,具有十分重要而深远的意义:首先,以南北问题为视角,从发达国家与发展中国家发展水平不同的基本现实出发,关注和强调与发达国家经济发展水平悬殊的发展中国家,特别是最不发达国家的可持续发展问题;其次,不仅关注形式公平问题,而且关注和力图实现实质公平问题,即在承认特定缔约双方经济发展水平不同的基础上,通过不对称的责任分配以实现实质公平;最后,不对称的责任分配意味着较发达缔约一方承担相对较重的责任,较不发达缔约一方承担相对较轻的责任,确保缔约各方承担与其能力及发展战略目标相符合的责任,量力而行,实际上也有助于保障 IIAs 的顺利履行及其目标的实现。

中国与"一带一路"国家之间"共同发展导向"BIT 实践应积极采纳 SDT 条款,根据缔约双方经济发展水平等具体情况,予以适用,以实现和保障缔约双方的实质公平和共同发展。作为负责任的发展中大国,中国在与经济发展水平不同的其他发展中国家,特别是最不发达国家商签或修订 BITs 时,应主动采纳和适用 SDT 条款,中国作为较发达缔约一方,承担相对较重的责任。事实上,这种责任分担安排也反映了中国"以义为先""扶困济危"的气度,体现了缔约双方谋求"共同发展"的共同意愿和务实态度。

五、结语

"一带一路"国际合作是新型的国际合作,BIT 实践创新在"一带一路"国际合作"法治化"进程中具有重要而深远的意义。

当下,BIT 实践的发展处于十字路口,何去何从,取决于世界各国的共识和实践。历经 60 年的 BIT 实践亟须改革创新,已成为国际共识。然而,BIT 实践的实质性改革创新绝非易事。客观上,"投资保护导向"和"投资自由化导向"BIT 实践,沿袭历史传统,代表发达国家普遍的利益诉求,凭借发达国家的经济实力,以"投资自由化"和"法律技术精细化"作为"改革"幌子,在经济全球化的背景下强势推行,惯性相助,仍然居于明显优势地位。而 UNCTAD 提出的"可持续发展导向"BIT 实践新倡议,脱胎于 BIT 传统实践,代表广大发展中国家的利益诉求,力图变革创新,其创新理念和

---

〔1〕　UNCTAD, *World Investment Report 2012*, *Towards a New Generation of Investment Policies*, United Nations, 2012, p. 159.

规范尚属新生期,亟须各国特别是广大发展中国家充分重视,努力达成共识并积极付诸实践。在理论和实践层面,涵义宽泛、多元的"可持续发展"概念作为 BIT 实践发展的"指南"是否适当,值得反思。

作为负责任的发展中大国,中国理应有改革国际经济旧秩序、构建国际经济新秩序的使命感和责任感。中国与"一带一路"国家理应有积极主动参与制定、影响或引领国际投资条约体制总体发展趋向的自信和作为。当前,中国与"一带一路"国家之间 BIT 实践正是中国和"一带一路"国家对既有国际投资条约体制进行改革创新的"用武之地"和重要契机。

中国与"一带一路"国家之间"共同发展导向"BIT 实践是"既有法制的改革创新",可分为三个层面:一是目标层面。以"共同发展"作为创新目标,是对传统 BIT 实践"事实上资本输出国单方受益体制"的根本性纠正和结构性变革,也是对"可持续发展导向"BIT 实践新倡议的提升和超越;二是模式层面。在传统 BIT 实践模式基础上,可借鉴和汲取"可持续发展导向"BIT 实践模式的创新因素,通过 BIT 结构和条款的革新和改造,创造新型的"共同发展导向"BIT 实践模式;三是内容层面。在既有 BIT"国际话语体系"内,基于"共同发展导向"BIT 实践目标和模式,通过"共同发展"条款的引入、传统条款的"扬弃"和创新条款的采纳,可实现对传统 BIT 整体内容的改革和创新,形成"共同发展导向"BITs 的实体性和程序性内容。

中国与"一带一路"国家之间"共同发展导向"BIT 实践由中国倡议和践行,是中国"促进共同发展"的外交政策宗旨在国际投资领域的重要体现,也是中国和"一带一路"国家对国际投资条约体制改革创新的共同贡献。可以预见,"共同发展导向"BIT 实践由于符合历史发展规律和世界各国人民的共同意愿,在国际社会的共同努力下,经历渐进发展,必将成为各国普遍认同的、符合各国共同和长远利益的 BIT 实践发展主流。

Common Development: The Initiative on the Bilateral Investment Treaty Practice between China and "One Belt One Road" States

Abstract: Based on the introduction to the legal background on the international cooperation of the "One Belt One Road", the author studies the issues on initiative for purposes, models and contents of bilateral investment treaty (BIT) practice between China and the "One Belt One Road" States. The author indicates that "investment protection—investment liberalization" is the evolution path of traditional purposes of BIT practice, the "sustainable development" is a new suggestion for the purpose of BIT practice, and the "common development" shall be the initiative for the purpose of BIT practice between China and the "One Belt One Road" States; on the traditional model of BIT practice, China and the "One Belt One Road" States shall learn from innovative elements of "sustainable development oriented" BIT model, create the "common development oriented" BIT model by innovation and reconstruction on the structure and articles of BITs; in the existing "international discourse system", China and the "One Belt One Road" States shall make innovation on the contents of traditional BIT practice by introduction of "common development" provisions, develop-discard of traditional provisions and adoption of innovative provisions, and constitute the new contents for serving the "common development oriented" BIT practice.

Key words: common development; "One Belt One Road"; bilateral investment treaty; initiative on purpose; initiative on model; initiative on contents

Exploring International Economic Law

with Chinese Characteristics *Volume II*

中国特色国际经济法学探索

下册

曾华群◎著

北京大学出版社
PEKING UNIVERSITY PRESS

下　册

第三编

国际贸易法的中国特色实践

第四编

香港涉外经济法律实践

第五编
中国特色国际经济法学科的创建

附　编

惠风和畅　家国情感

第三编

国际贸易法的中国特色实践

导 言 ⚖

　　本编主要研讨国际贸易法领域的中国特色实践问题。当下,WTO 体制与区域贸易协定(RTA)体制并行发展,是国际贸易法发展的重要特征。中国在这方面的特色实践,首先表现在 WTO 体制"一个中国,四个 WTO 席位"(简称"一国四席")的实践。第六章探讨 WTO 体制"一国四席"的法律依据、相互关系和重要意义(第一、二节)。其次,表现在由"一国四席"衍生的中国 RTA 实践。第七章探讨"一国四席"相互之间 RTA 实践的法律思考(第一节)、内地与香港更紧密经贸关系的安排(CEPA)的性质(第二节)及《海峡两岸经济合作框架协定》(ECFA)的实践(第三、四节)等专题。在国际贸易法领域的双边层面,中国与欧盟之间、中国与东盟之间经贸法律关系具有特别重要的意义。第八章在探讨欧共体明示与隐含缔约能力(第一节)的基础上,重点探讨构建调整中国—欧盟经济关系的双边法律新框架(第二、三节),继而探讨 WTO 规则与中国—东盟自由贸易区的发展(第四、五节),也作为中国与国际组织之间 RTA 实践的典例。

　　作者的主要观点:

　　(1) 关于 WTO 体制"一国四席"的形成原因及其重要意义。WTO 体制"一国四席"实践,是中国对 WTO 成员制度发展的重要贡献。"一国四席"的形成,是由《WTO 协定》的有关规定、中国独特的历史发展进程和"一国两制"的政策取向所决定的。"一国四席"的重要意义是,反映了国际法的新发展,强化了国际社会对"一个中国"原则的共识,并为两岸四地相互之间建立更紧密的经贸关系提供了新契机。

　　(2) 关于中国国内 RTA 实践的性质与特征。中国国内 RTA 实践,是中国对 RTA 体制发展的重要创新。作为同一主权国家的不同关税区和 WTO 的不同成员,内地与香港、澳门分别签订的 CEPAs 和两岸签订的 ECFA 既是符合GATT 第24 条的 WTO 成员之间的协定,实质上又不是国际条约,而是部分内容受 WTO 规则规范和调整的一国国内的区域经济一体化安排。

　　(3) 关于构建中国—欧盟双边经济法律新框架。历史表明,影响中欧经济关系及有关法律安排的政治问题主要是人权和港澳自治权问题。为构建中欧双边经济法律新框架，在宏观决策方面，需要严格区分政治问题与经济问题，尽快签订新的中欧贸易与经济合作协定；在具体规范方面，需要理解和分清欧盟及其成员国的缔约能力，协调和并行发展不同层面的中欧双边经济法律规范。

（4）关于中国—东盟自由贸易区法制的发展。《中国—东盟全面经济合作框架协定》是中国与东盟之间经济合作发展的重要里程碑，不仅为中国与东盟之间的全面经济合作提供了基本的法律框架，也为建立中国—东盟自由贸易区打下了坚实的法律基础。值得关注的是，该协定也是一个符合 WTO 规则且部分内容受 WTO 规则调整的 RTA，反映了 WTO 体制与 RTA 体制在推动经济自由化进程中的兼容性和互补性。

第一节　略论 WTO 体制的"一国四席"*

【摘要】　根据 WTO 体制有关成员资格的规定,中国香港地区、澳门地区、中国和中国台湾地区相继加入 WTO,形成了"一国四席"的局面。"一国四席"之间的关系既是 WTO 体制平等成员之间的关系,也是一国不同关税区之间的关系。"一国四席"的重要意义是反映了国际法的新发展,强化了国际社会对"一个中国"原则的共识,并为两岸四地相互之间建立更紧密的经贸关系提供了新契机。

【关键词】　WTO 体制;"一国四席";主权国家;单独关税区

2001 年 12 月 11 日和 2002 年 1 月 1 日,中国与"台湾、澎湖、金门、马祖单独关税区"(以下简称"中国台北")[1]先后成为世界贸易组织(WTO)正式成员后,连同于1995 年 1 月 1 日分别成为 WTO 创始成员的中国香港和中国澳门,在 WTO 体制中出现了前所未有的"一国四席"局面。本文对 WTO 体制"一国四席"的法律依据及其形成、平等成员关系以及重要意义作初步探讨。

一、"一国四席"的法律依据及其形成

WTO 体制中"一国四席"的形成,是由 1995 年《建立世界贸易组织协定》(以下简称《WTO 协定》)有关成员资格的规定、中国独特的历史发展进程和"一国两制"的

---

*　原载《厦门大学学报》(哲学社会科学版)2002 年第 5 期。
〔1〕　英文为 the Separate Customs Territory of Taiwan, Penghu, Kinmen and Matsu(Chinese Taipei)。对 Chinese Taipei,中国大陆地区一般译为"中国台北"或"中国台湾",中国台湾地区一般译为"中华台北"。

政策取向所决定的。

（一）《WTO 协定》有关成员资格的规定

根据 1947 年《关税及贸易总协定》(GATT 1947)第 26、32、33 条规定，主权国家并不是 GATT 缔约方资格的必要条件。任何实体，不论是否主权国家，只要构成一个关税区，均可按一定程序成为 GATT 的缔约方；相反，即使是一个独立的主权国家，如未形成关税区，也不可能成为 GATT 的缔约方。

《WTO 协定》第 11 条第 1 款规定了创始成员(original members)的资格，即："本协定生效之日的 GATT 1947 缔约方和欧洲共同体，如接受本协定和多边贸易协定，并将减让和承诺表附于 GATT 1994，将具体承诺减让表附于 GATS，应成为 WTO 的创始成员。"根据部长级会议《关于世界贸易组织协定的接受与加入的决议》规定，所有符合创始成员条件者须在《WTO 协定》生效后两年之内批准。截至 1997 年 3 月 27 日，131 个 GATT 缔约方均成为 WTO 成员。[1]

《WTO 协定》第 12 条第 1 款规定了纳入成员(members by accession)的资格和程序："任何国家或在处理其对外商业关系及本协定和多边贸易协定规定的其他事务中享有充分自治权的单独关税区(separate tariff territory)，可按它与 WTO 议定的条件加入本协定。此加入适用于本协定及所附多边贸易协定。"可见，该协定承袭 GATT 的传统，继续采用"单独关税区"的概念。[2] 为了将"单独关税区"的法律概念纳入整个 WTO 多边贸易规则中，《WTO 协定》的"解释性说明"特别指出，"本协定和多边贸易协定中使用的'country or countries'应理解为包括任何 WTO 单独关税区成员。对于 WTO 单独关税区成员，除非另有规定，如本协定和多边贸易协定中用'national'一词表述，该表述也应理解为是指单独关税区"。[3]

由于 WTO 成员资格向主权国家和非主权的单独关税区开放，一个主权国家与隶属于该主权国家的一个或数个单独关税区分别加入 WTO，或者在一个主权国家未加入 WTO 的情况下，隶属于该主权国家的数个单独关税区分别加入 WTO，都可能形成 WTO 体制的"一国多席"局面。

（二）WTO 体制"一国四席"的形成

以下简要评述中国大陆、中国香港、中国澳门和中国台北加入 WTO 的历程及各

〔1〕 See John Croome, *Guide to Uruguay Agreements*, Kluwer Law International, 1999, p. 12, note 43.

〔2〕 这一概念可溯及战后的特定情况，即存在宗主国与附属领土，而适用于附属领土的关税制度可能与宗主国不同。在 GATT 体制中，"单独关税区"最初是指适用不同于宗主国的关税制度的附属领土。由于近 40 多年来国际政治经济形势的发展和深刻演变，在 WTO 体制中，"单独关税区"具有更准确的经济和法律内涵，一般与殖民主义制度无关。

〔3〕 参见赵维田：《世贸组织(WTO)的法律制度》，吉林人民出版社 2000 年版，第 42—44 页。

自的法律依据。

1. 中国的 WTO 成员资格

中国是 GATT 的创始缔约方之一。1950 年 3 月,非法占据中国席位的台湾当局宣布退出 GATT。中国于 1986 年 7 月正式向 GATT 提出要求恢复中国在 GATT 的合法席位(即"复关")的申请。然而,由于少数西方大国的阻挠和中国经济体制融入 WTO 体制本身的实际困难等种种因素,中国与美国、欧共体等主要贸易伙伴的双边谈判旷日持久,"复关"终未成就。1995 年 11 月,应中国政府要求,GATT 中国"复关"工作组更名为 WTO 中国"入世"工作组。中国在"入世"谈判中坚持的三原则是:(1) 权利与义务对等原则;(2) 以发展中国家身份加入原则;(3) 以乌拉圭回合协议为基础,承担与其经济发展水平相一致的义务。经过历时 15 年艰苦曲折的谈判,2001 年 11 月 9 日,多哈 WTO 部长级会议全体会议以协商一致的方式通过中国的"入世"申请;11 月 11 日,中国通知 WTO,中国全国人大常委会已完成有关批准中国"入世"的程序;12 月 11 日,中国成为 WTO 第 143 个正式成员。必须强调的是,中国是根据《WTO 协定》第 12 条规定,以中华人民共和国的名义,即以主权国家的资格"入世"。同时,中国是以发展中国家的身份"入世",作出与发展中国家身份相适应的国际承诺。

2. 中国香港的 GATT 单独缔约方和 WTO 成员资格

1984 年《中英关于香港问题的联合声明》(以下简称《中英联合声明》)签署后,如何在 1997 年 7 月 1 日之后保持香港在 GATT 中的地位,成为中英双方关注并致力解决的重要国际法问题之一。从 GATT 有关条款看,1997 年 7 月 1 日后保持香港在 GATT 中的地位,有两种选择:

(1) 中国"复关"后适用 GATT 于香港。根据 GATT 第 26 条第 5 款第 1 项规定,凡接受该协定的各政府系为其本土及由该政府负国际责任的其他领土而接受。显然,如果中国政府决定通过这一方式使 GATT 在 1997 年 7 月 1 日后适用于香港特别行政区(以下简称"香港特区"),就意味着中国必须在 1997 年 7 月 1 日之前"复关",并在对香港恢复行使主权时,声明 GATT 适用于香港特区。在法律程序上,这一方式比较复杂。特别是,尽管中国当时已正式向 GATT 提出"复关"申请,但同GATT 各缔约方的有关谈判尚需时日,而对香港工商界而言,明确香港回归后在GATT 的地位则刻不容缓。[1]

(2) 香港成为单独缔约方。GATT 第 26 条第 5 款第 3 项规定:"原由一缔约方

---

[1] 参见程翔、刘敏仪:《香港的关贸地位问题》,载《香港文汇报》1985 年 12 月 4 日。

代表其接受本协定的任何单独关税区，如拥有或取得处理对外商务关系和本协定规定的其他事项方面的充分自治权，经由对其负责的缔约方发表声明确认上述事实，应视为本协定的一个缔约方"。该条款旨在使某缔约方的单独关税区，在 GATT 适用的意义上，能与该缔约方分开而被视为单独缔约方。

中英两国政府通过中英联合联络小组研究，决定采取上述第二种方式。其主要优点是：首先，在中国尚未"复关"的情况下，可确保香港在 GATT 中的地位。其次，不需要同其他缔约方重新谈判。1961 年 GATT 的一个工作组报告指出，根据 GATT 第 26 条第 5 款第 3 项，单独关税区成为缔约方的条件将与原由负责其国际关系的缔约方代表它接受 GATT 时的条件相同。由于 1948 年英国作为创始缔约方使 GATT 无条件适用于香港，香港按上述条款成为缔约方，仍继续行使其原有权利，承担其原有义务。最后，所需履行的手续简单。只要英国作为负责香港对外关系的缔约方向 GATT 声明，香港已具备在处理其对外商务关系和 GATT 规定的其他事项的充分自治权，而香港本身又表示愿意成为缔约方，香港自声明之日即被视为缔约方。

1986 年 4 月 23 日，英国声明并通知 GATT 总干事，香港在处理其对外商务关系和 GATT 规定的其他事项中具有充分的自治权。根据 GATT 第 26 条第 5 款第 3 项规定，并根据香港的意愿，香港将被视为缔约方，自本声明之日起生效。中国同时发表相应的声明，确认香港的 GATT 缔约方地位。

《WTO 协定》生效后，根据该协定第 11 条规定，香港基于其本身的权利，即 GATT 缔约方的地位，于 1995 年 1 月 1 日成为 WTO 的创始成员。值得注意的是，由于 1986 年 4 月 23 日香港根据 GATT 第 26 条第 5 款第 3 项成为单独缔约方的原有权利和义务不变，它不是以发展中成员的身份成为 WTO 的创始成员。

就法律依据而言，香港之所以能成为 WTO 成员，首先是由于香港作为在对外商务关系活动中具有充分自治权的单独关税区，本身符合 WTO 成员的条件。其次，是基于 1984 年《中英联合声明》第 3(6)、(10)条和附件 1 第 6 节的规定，即"香港特别行政区将保持自由港和独立关税地区的地位"；"可以'中国香港'的名义单独地同各国、各地区及有关国际组织保持和发展经济、文化关系，并签订有关协议"；"可参加关税和贸易总协定"。1990 年《香港特别行政区基本法》第 116、151、152 条进一步重申和明确了上述规定。

1997 年 7 月 1 日中国对香港恢复行使主权后，香港在 WTO 中更名为"中国香港"（Hong Kong，China）。

3. 中国澳门的 GATT 单独缔约方和 WTO 成员资格

澳门遵循香港模式成为 GATT 单独缔约方。根据 1987 年 4 月 13 日签订的《中葡关于澳门问题的联合声明》第 2(7)条和附件 1 第 10 节的规定，"澳门特别行政区可以'中国澳门'的名义单独同各国、各地区及有关国际组织保持和发展经济、文化关系，并签订有关协定"；"作为自由港和单独关税地区"，"继续参加关税和贸易总协定"。1993 年《澳门特别行政区基本法》第 112、136—138 条进一步予以重申。

1991 年 1 月，中、葡两国政府同时向 GATT 秘书处递交声明。葡萄牙政府的声明指出，澳门自 1991 年 1 月 11 日起成为 GATT 的单独缔约方。中国政府的声明则宣布，自 1999 年 12 月 20 日起，澳门特别行政区可以"中国澳门"的名义继续作为 GATT 的单独缔约方。

《WTO 协定》生效后，澳门基于其本身的权利成为 WTO 的创始成员。与香港一样，澳门也不是以发展中成员的身份成为 WTO 的创始成员。1999 年 12 月 20 日中国对澳门恢复行使主权后，澳门在 WTO 中更名为"中国澳门"（Macao，China）。

4. 中国台北的 WTO 成员资格

在 1992 年 9 月 29 日至 10 月 1 日的 GATT 代表理事会会议上，成立了 GATT 工作组，审议中国台北根据 GATT 1947 第 33 条申请加入的条件。工作组先后于 1992 年 11 月 6 日，1993 年 4 月 15 日、6 月 28 日、10 月 12 日，1994 年 5 月 17 日、7 月 26 日、12 月 21 日召开会议。

《WTO 协定》生效后，在中国台北的请求下，根据总理事会 1995 年 1 月 31 日决议，该工作组转变为 WTO 工作组，根据《WTO 协定》第 12 条审查中国台北的"入世"申请，于 1997 年 2 月 28 日、1998 年 5 月 8 日、1999 年 5 月 12 日和 2001 年 9 月 18 日举行会议进行审议。2001 年 9 月 18 日，WTO 完成了中国台北"入世"条件的谈判，11 月 11 日，紧接中国"入世"签署仪式之后，WTO 部长级会议对中国台北的成员资格也给予正式批准。中国台北于 2002 年 1 月 1 日成为 WTO 第 144 个正式成员。

值得注意的是，中国台北申请加入 GATT 和申请加入 WTO 的法律根据存在重要的区别。前者的依据是 GATT 1947 第 33 条。该条规定："不属本协定缔约方的政府，或代表在处理其对外商务关系和本协定规定的其他事项方面拥有充分自治权的单独关税区的政府，可代表该政府本身或代表该关税区，按该政府与缔约方全体议定的条件加入本协定……"从 GATT 的立法背景看，上述"代表……单独关税区的政府"一般指代表单独关税区的原宗主国政府。[1] 而从文义上解释，"代表……单独关税区的政府"除代表单独关税区的原宗主国政府外，也可以指代表单独关税区的本级政府本身。由于中国台北并不符合上述原宗主国政府的资格条件，GATT 工作

---

〔1〕 有学者基于这一理解认为，"台湾根据总协定第 33 条提出以'单独关税领土'加入总协定，在国际法上是非法之举。"参见曾令良：《世界贸易组织法》，武汉大学出版社 1996 年版，第 68—71 页。

组只有在认定中国台北是指代表单独关税区的本级政府本身的前提下，才具备受理其申请和进行有关审议工作的法律依据。

中国台北申请加入 WTO 的依据是《WTO 协定》第 12 条。根据该条第 1 款规定，申请者是"任何国家或在处理其对外商务关系及本协定和多边贸易协定规定的其他事务中享有充分自治权的单独关税区"。显然，该规定避免了上述 GATT 第 33 条中"代表……单独关税区的政府"可能导致的解释歧义，明确表明，在 WTO 体制中，以单独关税区身份申请加入者只能是单独关税区本身，不存在由其他任何代表者代为申请的法律依据。

客观事实表明，中国台北从申请加入 GATT 至转为申请加入 WTO 的全过程，一直是明确以"台湾、澎湖、金门、马祖单独关税区"的身份，也只有以此身份，才有法律上的依据。由于《WTO 协定》第 12 条的"国家"与"单独关税区"是并列的两个主体概念，排除了"单独关税区"等于"国家"的可能性。在 WTO 体制中，"单独关税区"可以是隶属于一个主权国家的区域性实体（如中国香港、中国澳门），但不可能是一个独立的、不归属于任何主权国家的区域性实体。由于国际社会普遍承认"一个中国"原则，在法律和事实上，"台湾、澎湖、金门、马祖单独关税区"与中国香港、中国澳门一样同属于中国，是不言而喻的。

二、"一国四席"的平等成员关系及其特殊性

在 WTO 体制中，中国、中国香港、中国澳门、中国台北相互之间的关系首先是平等成员之间的关系，表现在分别具有平等的代表权、平等的参与权和决策权、独立的申诉权和责任承担制度以及平等参与区域经济一体化的权利等，与此同时，由于同属一个主权国家，也是一国不同关税区之间的关系。

（一）平等、独立的代表权

WTO 常设机构有部长级会议、总理事会、分理事会、委员会和秘书处等。《WTO 协定》第 4.1、4.2 条规定，部长级会议由所有成员的代表组成，应履行 WTO 职能并为此采取必要的行动，在成员的请求下，有权按《WTO 协定》和有关多边贸易协定中关于决策的具体要求，对任何多边贸易协定项下的所有事项作出决定。总理事会也是由所有成员的代表组成，在部长级会议休会期间，行使部长级会议的职能。据之，中国、中国香港、中国澳门、中国台北的代表分别参加部长级会议和总理事会。在 WTO 部长级会议、总理事会中，中国、中国香港、中国澳门、中国台北的代表分别代表中国大陆、香港特区、澳门特区、台湾地区的经济利益，互不统属。

此外，由于 WTO 分理事会和委员会的成员资格也对所有 WTO 成员开放，中

国、中国香港、中国澳门、中国台北还可分别参加货物贸易理事会、服务贸易理事会、与贸易有关的知识产权理事会、贸易与发展委员会、国际收支限制委员会以及预算、财务与行政委员会等。

实践表明，作为 WTO 的创始成员，中国香港单独向 WTO 各机构选派代表，得到其他 WTO 成员的信任和支持。2001 年 2 月，香港驻 WTO 的常任代表 Stuart Harbinson 先生以其个人身份当选为 WTO 总理事会 2001 年度主席。香港代表还经常被任命为 WTO 分理事会、委员会、专家组的主席或副主席。[1]

（二）平等、独立的参与权和决策权

在 WTO 体制中，各成员尽管承担的义务不尽一致，对 WTO 规则的制定和多边贸易谈判享有平等、独立的参与权和决策权。

香港通过贸易工业署和香港驻日内瓦经济贸易办事处，积极参与 WTO 各委员会的工作，参加监督或评价 WTO 的实际运作和其他成员履行其承诺的各种讨论。在参与 WTO 的各项活动时，香港享有独立的发言权，可根据其本身的利益作出独立的决策。在 WTO 有关基础电讯和金融服务的谈判中，香港发挥了积极的作用。在 1996 年 12 月、1998 年 5 月、1999 年 11 月至 12 月分别于新加坡、日内瓦和西雅图召开的 WTO 第一、二、三届部长级会议上，香港均积极、建设性地参与有关活动。[2]

事实上，中国大陆与香港特区、澳门特区和台湾地区在经济发展水平、经济制度、法律制度和社会制度等方面存在明显不同，特别是，中国大陆坚持以发展中成员身份“入世”，在多边贸易体制中相应作出不同于中国香港、澳门和台湾地区的承诺。因此，在参与多边贸易谈判和 WTO 决策的某些场合，中国与中国香港、中国澳门和中国台北发出不同的声音，采取不同的立场是正常的。

应当指出，平等、独立的 WTO 成员地位并不意味着各成员立场的必然不同。相反，在 WTO 体制中，所有成员为实现 WTO 宗旨，经常通过协调立场，达成共识。WTO 成员之间可能为了共同的经济利益而采取一致立场，并利用 WTO 各种机制争取合法权益。中国、中国香港、中国澳门和中国台北属于同一主权国家，基于国家利益原则和共同的经济利益，更可能通过协调，在参与多边经贸谈判和 WTO 决策中采取共同的立场。[3] 同时，中国香港和中国澳门作为 WTO 创始成员和中国的特别行政区，今后在提供 GATT 和 WTO 经验和作为连接中国内地与世界市场的“桥梁”

---

〔1〕　See Hong Kong's Participation in the World Trade Organization. https://www.tid.gov.hk/english/ito/wto/index.html, visited on 2020-12-3.

〔2〕　Ibid.

〔3〕　See Cyril C. K. Chow and Michael C. M. Kwan, Hong Kong's Role in APEC under "One Country-Two Systems", *Policy Bulletin*, No. 3, January 1998, p. 10.

等方面将继续发挥积极作用。两岸关系目前虽因台湾当局的现行政策而无法处于良好的互动关系，两岸"入世"也为双方的沟通和交流带来了新契机。

（三）独立的申诉权和责任承担制度

根据《关于争端解决规则与程序的谅解书》（以下简称《谅解书》）第1条规定，该《谅解书》的规则和程序应适用于该《谅解书》附录1所列各项协定的磋商和争端解决规定所提出的争端和各成员之间有关它们在《WTO协定》和该《谅解书》规定下的权利和义务的磋商和争端解决。显然，在上述适用范围的争端解决方面，分别作为WTO成员的中国、中国香港、中国澳门和中国台北各自拥有独立的申诉权，并实施独立的责任承担制度。中国香港、中国澳门或中国台北如发现其权利遭受WTO其他成员损害，可按《谅解书》规定的程序提出申诉，而不必通过中国；反之，如果其他国家发现中国香港、中国澳门或中国台北有违反其WTO义务的行为，也不必向中国追究责任，而应直接对中国香港、中国澳门或中国台北提出申诉。在WTO体制下，中国与中国香港、中国澳门和中国台北之间在上述适用范围的争端，也属WTO不同成员之间的争端，可通过WTO争端解决程序解决。

在实践中，由于中国香港长期实行开放的贸易政策，未曾成为WTO争端解决程序的被诉方。根据《谅解书》第10.2条规定，WTO成员可作为第三方，即在特定WTO争端解决程序中，除争端当事人以外，对专家组审理的问题具有实质性利益关系的任何WTO成员。迄今，香港成为三个WTO案件中的第三方。这三个案件分别是"虾—海龟案"（The Shrimp-Turtle case）[1]、"土耳其数量限制案"[The Turkey Quantitative Restrictions（Quota）case][2]和"美国301条款案"（The US Section 301 case）[3]。前两个案子诉诸上诉机构。在三个案子中，香港都向专家组提交书面陈述。对诉诸上诉机构的事项，香港也提交了书面陈述。[4]

由于同属一个主权国家，中国与中国香港、中国澳门和中国台北之间经贸关系中不属WTO体制调整的方面，即有关成员方不受WTO规则约束和未在多边经贸

---

[1] 该案涉及美国采取的禁止从一些WTO成员进口虾的某些措施，旨在保护濒危动物海龟。香港关注的主要问题是，这些措施的实施是否符合WTO有关禁止专断的、歧视性的进口限制的原则。

[2] 该案涉及WTO成员土耳其对纺织品进口采取的限制措施。土耳其主张，该限制措施是其履行加入关税联盟或自由贸易区的责任所必需。这意味着在市场准入方面，非关税联盟或自由贸易区成员的WTO成员，一旦加入关税联盟或自由贸易区，将导致对其他WTO成员更不利的后果。这一原则性问题促使香港作为第三方参与该程序。

[3] 在该案中，香港关注的问题是，对WTO成员具有约束力的WTO争端解决机制与WTO成员美国国内法（《1974年美国贸易法》）规定的单边制裁方式之间的关系。涉及此类国内立法是否符合《WTO协定》，以及可否在WTO争端解决程序中对此类国内立法提起申诉等问题。

[4] See David Little, WTO Dispute Settlement: A Hong Kong Perspective, speech on Inter-Pacific Bar Association Conference "WTO Dispute Resolution System: Does It Work?", May 2000.

谈判中作出承诺的方面,以及由此类经贸关系中产生的中国与中国香港、中国澳门和中国台北之间的经贸争端,属于国内管辖事项,当然不属于 WTO 规则的调整对象和 WTO 争端解决机制的管辖范围。最后,即使是属于 WTO 体制调整的中国与中国香港、中国澳门和中国台北之间经贸关系产生的争端,虽属 WTO 成员之间的争端,也并不当然要诉诸 WTO 争端解决机构解决。因为此类争端同时也属特殊的国内经贸争端,可通过国内解决方式,更多地采用协商、谈判和磋商等双边解决方式。

（四）平等参与区域经济一体化的权利

关税同盟和自由贸易区是经济合作方式,一般属于区域性经济联盟或经济一体化安排。其法律模式主要包括欧盟模式、北美自由贸易区模式和东南亚国家联盟模式等。

GATT 允许其成员建立关税同盟和自由贸易区。WTO 沿用 GATT 的惯例,允许成员之间关税同盟和自由贸易区的存在。

GATT 第 24 条第 8 款分别为关税同盟和自由贸易区作了明确的定义。据之,关税同盟"应理解为一个单一关税领土取代两个或两个以上的关税领土",以便"对于同盟成员领土之间的实质上所有贸易或至少对于产生于此类领土产品的实质上所有贸易,取消关税和其他限制性贸易法规（如必要,第 11、12、13、14、15 条和第 20 条允许的关税和其他限制性贸易法规除外)","同盟各成员对同盟以外领土的贸易实施实质相同的关税或其他贸易法规";自由贸易区"应理解为在两个或两个以上的关税领土组成的一个关税领土中,对成员领土之间实质上所有有关产自此类领土产品的贸易取消关税和其他限制性贸易法规（如必要,第 11、12、13、14、15 条和第 20 条允许的关税和其他限制性贸易法规除外)"。由此可见,两者的关键区别在于,关税同盟成员对同盟以外领土的贸易须实施实质相同的关税或其他贸易法规,而自由贸易区成员则无此要求。显然,前者的经济一体化程度更高。

根据 GATT 第 24 条第 4、5 款规定,各成员认识到通过自愿签署此类协定以发展缔约方之间的更紧密的经济一体化和增加贸易自由的需要;并认识到 GATT 的规定不得阻止在缔约方领土之间形成关税同盟或自由贸易区,或阻止通过形成关税同盟或自由贸易区所必需的临时协定;此类临时协定应包括在一合理持续时间内形成此种关税同盟或自由贸易区的计划和时间表。[1] 有学者将这种导向关税同盟或自由贸易区的临时协定称为区域经济一体化的一种形式或一种层次。[2]

实际上,关税同盟、自由贸易区和导向关税同盟或自由贸易区的临时协定是区

---

〔1〕《关于解释 1994 年关税与贸易总协定第 24 条的谅解》规定,上述"合理持续时间"一般不超过 10 年。

〔2〕参见赵维田:《世贸组织（WTO）的法律制度》,吉林人民出版社 2000 年版,第 84—85 页。

域经济一体化安排的不同层次和类型。关税同盟是区域经济一体化的最高层次，自由贸易区次之，而导向关税同盟或自由贸易区的临时协定是区域经济一体化的初级层次或阶段。

中国与中国香港、中国澳门和中国台北作为 WTO 体制下的平等成员，在适当时机，可以根据 GATT 第 24 条建立关税同盟或自由贸易区，或者商谈形成关税同盟或自由贸易区所必需的临时协定。考虑到中国实行"一国两制"，中国大陆、中国香港、中国澳门和中国台北之间政治、经济和法律制度的不同以及经济发展的不平衡，选择自由贸易区模式更适合中国国情。在建立自由贸易区之前，首先是商谈形成自由贸易区所必需的临时协定。值得注意的是，欧盟、北美自由贸易区和东南亚国家联盟都是由两个以上主权国家组成的，是区域性国际组织。而同为 WTO 成员的中国、中国香港、中国澳门和中国台北则同属一个主权国家。如中国、中国香港、中国澳门和中国台北签署导向自由贸易区的临时协定，在 GATT 和 WTO 体制下的关税同盟或自由贸易区安排中，也是一个创举。其实质是一国的经济一体化安排，而不是区域性国际组织的经济一体化安排。

在 WTO 体制下，两岸四地建立自由贸易区的重要意义首先是解决 WTO 非歧视原则的适用的特殊问题，为中国大陆对港澳台实行更为优惠的法律和政策措施提供必要的法律基础。

应当明确的是，中国与中国香港、中国澳门和中国台北以 WTO 成员地位谈判建立自由贸易区，是 WTO 成员之间经贸层面的谈判，各方均以 WTO 成员身份，谈判的法律基础是 WTO 协定。两岸在 WTO 体制下开展建立自由贸易区的谈判本身是向国际社会宣告，中国经济一体化已经启动，向和平统一的方向迈出了重要一步。建立中国、中国香港、中国澳门和中国台北自由贸易区的重要的历史性意义在于建立两岸经济合作的新机制，以经济合作交流和经济一体化促进祖国统一大业的实现。

三、"一国四席"的重要意义

从国际和国内两个层面看，WTO 体制"一国四席"的实现具有重要的理论和现实意义。在实践中需要准确把握，因势利导，以维护国家主权和国家最高利益。

（一）"一国四席"反映了国际法的新发展

传统国际法认为，主权是缔约权的唯一依据，即只有主权国家才是条约的缔结主体。在不断发展的现代国际实践中，由非主权实体参与缔结国际条约并非罕见。一些实例表明，国际条约的缔结主体除主权国家外，还有国际组织、联邦制国家的成员、交战团体、享有自治权的殖民地和区域性非主权实体。上述非主权实体的缔约权分别来源于国际组织的基本文件、国家宪法、条约法和国际习惯法等。[1] 相应地,一些非主权实体通过缔结国际条约成为国际组织的成员。应强调的是,非主权实体通过缔结条约或参加国际组织并不能改变其法律地位。

　　传统上,国际组织一般指两个或两个以上主权国家政府为了实现共同的目标,通过一定的协议形式建立的具有常设机构和相应职能的组织。[2] 随着国际实践的发展,一些国际组织的成员已不限于主权国家。目前,从成员资格看,国际组织可大致区分为仅由主权国家组成的国际组织和由主权国家、非主权实体组成的国际组织两种类型。WTO 不是仅由主权国家组成的国际组织,其成员包括国家、国际组织和单独关税区。其在成员资格方面的创新在于,无论是主权国家或单独关税区,作为WTO 成员的地位是平等的。中国在 WTO 体制的"一国四席"实际上与早年在国际奥林匹克委员会中首创的"中国奥林匹克委员会"与"中国台北奥林匹克委员会"模式以及后来在"亚洲开发银行"和"亚太经济合作组织"的类似安排是一致的,反映了国际法特别是国际组织法的新发展。

　　(二)"一国四席"可强化国际社会对"一个中国"原则的共识

　　在法律上,中国是以主权国家的资格"入世",而中国香港、中国澳门和中国台北是以单独关税区的资格"入世"。由于中国实行"一国两制",香港、澳门在回归后继续保持其在 WTO 中的成员地位,不受中国"入世"的影响。以"一国两制"方针实现祖国统一大业后,台湾也将遵循香港、澳门模式,继续保持其在 WTO 中的成员地位。鉴此,中国与中国香港、中国澳门和中国台北之间的关系可视为中国主体与三个单独关税区之间的关系。

　　另外,从中国长达 15 年的"复关"和"入世"谈判过程、坚持的立场以及所作的承诺看,事实上,作为 WTO 成员的中国目前是指中国大陆。相对于中国香港、中国澳门和中国台北三个单独关税区,中国大陆本身也是一个关税区。在这个意义上,同样作为 WTO 成员,中国大陆与中国香港、中国澳门和中国台北之间的关系,也可视为中国各关税区相互之间的关系。值得密切关注和始终坚持的是,由于中国台北是以单独关税区身份"入世",其名称和地位在"入世"后绝不容许有任何改变。在其提供给 WTO 及其成员的所有文件中,必须明确冠以 the Separate Customs Territory of Taiwan, Penghu, Kinmen and Matsu (Chinese Taibei),如为中文,则为"台湾、澎湖、金门、马祖单独关税区"或简称"中国台北"。WTO 体制的"一国四席"由于首先

---

〔1〕　参见李浩培:《条约法概论》,法律出版社 1988 年版,第 240 页。
〔2〕　参见梁西:《国际组织法》,武汉大学出版社 1993 年版,第 1—5 页。

是"一个国家"，这一法律定位本身必将进一步明确反映和强化 WTO 全体成员和国际社会对"一个中国"原则的共识。

（三）"一国四席"可为两岸四地之间建立更紧密的经贸关系提供新契机

WTO 体制下中国、中国香港、中国澳门与中国台北之间的成员关系，为两岸四地之间建立更紧密的经贸关系提供了新契机。

目前，中国台湾地区以"单独关税区"身份作为 WTO 成员的法律地位已经明确，并为 WTO 本身及其全体成员（包括中国、中国香港和中国澳门）所承认和接受。在当前错综复杂的两岸关系中，这一新的定位为两岸四地相互之间以 WTO 成员身份开展经贸层面的谈判奠定了新的法律基础，提供了一个新的现实选择。应当明确的是，中国、中国香港、中国澳门与中国台北相互之间的关系具有双重性质。从国际层面看，是 WTO 这一国际经济组织的平等成员之间的关系。而从国内层面看，由于同属一个主权国家，又是中国不同关税区之间的关系。在经济全球化的背景下，为在两岸四地之间建立更紧密的经贸关系以谋共同发展，可根据国家主权原则和现实情况，以更富有远见和更灵活务实的态度，以 WTO 体制"一国四席"的法律定位，适时启动两岸四地之间属 WTO 协定调整范围的经贸活动的沟通和谈判。

On the "One Country, Four Seats" of WTO Framework

Abstract: Hong Kong region, Macao region, China and Taiwan region have entered into World Trade Organization (WTO) one after another in accordance with the WTO provisions on membership. The situation of "one country, four seats" in WTO has emerged. The relations among "four seats in one country" are not only the relations of equal members within WTO framework, but also the relations of different customs regions within a sovereign State. The signification of "one country, four seats" is to reflect the latest development of international law, strengthen the consensus of "one China" principle in international society, and provide new opportunity for mainland China, Hong Kong, Macao and Taiwan to establish more close economic and trade relations among themselves.

Key words: WTO framework; "one country, four seats"; sovereign State; separate customs territory

第二节 "One China Four WTO Memberships": Legal Grounds, Relations and Significance[*]
("一个中国,四个 WTO 席位":法律依据,相互关系与重要意义)

Abstract: Hong Kong region, Macao region, China and Taiwan region became WTO members one after another in accordance with the WTO relevant provisions. The situation of "one China, four WTO memberships" in the WTO regime has emerged. The relations among the four members are not only the relations of equal members within the WTO regime, but also the relations of different customs regions within a sovereign State. The main features of the relations among the four members include equal representation and participation in the WTO institutions and decision-making, separate claim and liabilities systems as well as equal participation in RTAs. The significance of "one China four WTO memberships" is to reflect the latest development of international law, to strengthen the consensus of the one-China principle in international society, and to provide new opportunities for four members to establish closer economic relations.

Key words: WTO regime; membership; sovereign State; separate customs territory

On 11 December 2001 and 1 January, 2002, China and the Separate Customs Territory of Taiwan, Penghu, Kinmen and Matsu (referred to as "Chinese Taipei") became members of the World Trade Organization (hereinafter WTO) one after another, and together with Hong Kong and Macao, the two WTO original members on 1 January 1995, the situation of "One China four WTO memberships" in the WTO regime has emerged. It is not only the new phenomenon in the history of the WTO, but also the most important issue of China's accession to the WTO. What are the legal grounds for "one China four WTO memberships"? What are the relations

---

    * "One China Four WTO Memberships": Legal Grounds, Relations and Significance, *The Journal of World Investment & Trade*, ISSN 1660-7112, Vol. 8, No. 5, 2007.

among the four WTO members? What is the significance of the unique situation? The paper will discuss these questions.

I. Legal Grounds and Formation of "One China Four WTO Memberships"

The formation of "one China four WTO memberships" is the product of provisions of Marrakesh Agreement Establishing the World Trade Organization (hereinafter WTO Agreement), the unique development of Chinese history and the successful practice of China's policy of "one country two systems".

1. Provisions on membership in WTO Agreement

According to Articles 26, 32, 33 of the General Agreement on Tariffs and Trade (hereinafter GATT), sovereignty is not a precondition of a GATT contracting party. Any entity, being a separate customs territory (hereinafter SCT), may become a contracting party, if it meet certain conditions by related procedures. On contrary, even a sovereign State, if not a SCT, cannot become a contracting party.

WTO Agreement follows the modes of the GATT on a contracting party in general and narrows the GATT procedures for membership to two modes, namely the original members and the members by accession. [1]

According to Article 11 of WTO Agreement, the original membership is conferred on any GATT contracting party and the European Communities (hereinafter the EC) that accepted both Uruguay Round treaties and negotiated schedules of concessions for goods and services. [2] For the members by accession, Article 12 of WTO Agreement reads as: "Any State or separate customs territory possessing full autonomy in the conduct of its external commercial relations and of the other matters provided for in this Agreement and the Multilateral Trade Agreements annexed thereto." For this mode, practice considerably embellishes the procedure, so that

---

[1] The GATT had several different modes for accepting a contracting party status, including the provision that allowed colonial mother countries to "sponsor" GATT status for a colonial entity with independent customs territory status. See John H. Jackson, *Sovereignty, the WTO and Changing Fundamentals of International Law*, Cambridge University Press, 2006, p. 108.

[2] Article 11 of WTO Agreement provides that "The contracting parties to GATT 1947 as of the date of entry into force of this Agreement, and the European Communities, which accept this Agreement and the Multilateral Trade Agreements and for which Schedules of Specific Commitment and annexed to GATT 1994 and for which Schedules of Specific Commitment and annexed to GATS shall become original Member of the WTO."

sometimes the accession process is very arduous.[1]

There are some other provisions relating to membership in WTO Agreement. The main characteristics on WTO membership might be summarized as follows:

First, as to the name of participants of the organization, different from a "contracting party" in the GATT, the WTO uses a "member" instead. It is important mark that the WTO has become a *de jure* international organization from the GATT, a *de facto* international organization.

Second, the EC becomes a formal member of the WTO from its position of a *de facto* contracting party in the GATT. It is noticeable that the EC is currently the only WTO member from international organizations. For the long period of time, the EC was a *de facto* contracting party while its member States were *de jure* contracting parties in the GATT. According to Article 11 of WTO Agreement, the EC takes up the new position of a *de jure* and original member in the WTO.

Third, it seems that the WTO follows the tradition of the GATT, continues to adopt the concept of a SCT. In order to use the legal concept of a SCT to the whole multilateral trade rules, the explanatory note of WTO Agreement particularly indicates: "the terms 'country or countries' as used in this Agreement and the Multilateral Trade Agreements are to be understood to include any SCT member of the WTO. In the case of a SCT member of the WTO, where an expression in this Agreement and the Multilateral Trade Agreements is qualified by the term 'national', and such expression shall be read as pertaining to that customs territory, unless otherwise specified."[2]

Four, the developing country members,[3] especially the least-developed country (hereinafter LDC)[4] members may be granted extensive special and differential

---

[1] John H. Jackson, *Sovereignty, the WTO and Changing Fundamentals of International Law*, Cambridge University Press, 2006, p. 109.

[2] ZHAO Weitian, *Legal Systems of the WTO* (in Chinese), Jilin People's Press, 2000, pp. 42-44.

[3] Although the term "developing" is generally used as opposed to "developed", which represents the status of an industrialized economy generating high levels of income, there is no clear definition of "developing" status that is universally applicable. In the WTO, a developing status is self-declared, and there is no clear cut-off standard. See Yong-Shik Lee, *Reclaiming Development in the World Trading System*, Cambridge University Press, 2006, pp. 3-4, footnote 11.

[4] The WTO recognized the LDCs as designated by the United Nations (UN) based on multiple criteria such as a low-income criterion (under $ 750 for inclusion, above $ 900 for graduation), a human resource weakness criterion, and an economic vulnerability criterion. Fifty LDCs are on the UN list. See Yong-Shik Lee, *Reclaiming Development in the World Trading System*, Cambridge University Press, 2006, p. 26, footnote 94.

treatment.

Five, as the WTO membership is open to sovereign States and non-sovereign SCTs, a sovereign State and one or more of its SCT(s) enter into the WTO separately, or even two or more SCTs of a sovereign State enter into the WTO when the sovereign State does not do so, the situation of "one State several memberships" in the WTO regime may occurs. On contrary, if several sovereign States constitute a SCT, they may become a WTO member, namely "several States one membership" in the WTO regime. The good example in this regards is the EC's status in the GATT and the WTO. [1]

Finally, as a WTO member, a sovereign State, the EC, or a SCT, enjoys equal legal standing or position in the WTO.

2. The formation of "one China four WTO memberships"

2.1 China's WTO membership

China was one of the original contracting parties of the GATT in 1947. The Taiwan authorities in the name of "the Republic of China" withdrew from the GATT in 1950. The People's Republic of China (hereinafter the PRC or China) made an application for resuming its position of the GATT in 1986. However, it was really a hard work for China due to the passive attitude of Western powers and the China's then non-market economic system, China's application for resuming its position of the GATT failed. In November 1995, required by Chinese government, China GATT working party changed its name as China WTO accession working party. China's three principles for WTO accession negotiation are: (1) to equalize and balance China's rights and obligations; (2) to insist on its status as a developing country; (3) to undertake the obligations based on the Uruguay Round agreements.

In fact, there are some special difficulties for China's accession to the GATT/WTO: first, as China then performed the non-market economic system while the GATT/WTO is based on the market economic system as a whole, it is difficult for China to adapt to the international market-orientated organization; second, as China is the largest developing country with increasing economic power, it is difficult for it

---

[1] In history 15 member States of the EC, as a separate unified customs territory, become one *de facto* contracting party in the GATT and one *de jure* member in the WTO on 1 January 1995. Currently 27 member States of the EC become one *de jure* member in the WTO.

to insist on its status as a developing country; third, as China is one of a few Communist countries in the world, there are some political and ideological considerations by Western countries.

On 11 November 2001, Doha WTO ministerial conference adopted the China's application of WTO accession by consensus. China notified the WTO that it had ratified its membership and became WTO's 143rd member on 11 December 2001.

It should be emphasized that China as a sovereign State entered into the WTO in the name of the PRC according to Article 12 of WTO Agreement. The history of China's accession to the WTO shows that the process is very arduous, requiring fifteen years. Over 500 questions were tabled for China at the working party stage. [1] China made its commitments as a developing country in general with some high-level commitments in particular. [2]

2.2 Hong Kong's GATT and WTO membership

After effective of the Joint Declaration of the Government of United Kingdom of Great Britain and Northern Ireland and the Government of People's Republic of China on the Question of Hong Kong (hereinafter UK-PRC JD), [3] how to remain the position of Hong Kong in the GATT after 1 July 1997, is one of the key international legal issues for China and UK. There are two solutions considering the relevant provisions of the GATT:

First, the GATT would be applied to Hong Kong after China resumes its contracting party position in the GATT. According to the provision of Article 26 (5) (a) of the GATT, "each government accepting this Agreement does so in respect of its metropolitan territory and of the other territories for which it has international responsibility…" It is clear that if China decides to apply the GATT to Hong Kong Special Administrative Region (hereinafter HKSAR) after 1 July 1997 by this way,

---

〔1〕 John H. Jackson, *Sovereignty, the WTO and Changing Fundamentals of International Law*, Cambridge University Press, 2006, p. 109.

〔2〕 The high-level commitments or so-called "Articles disadvantageous to China" in the legal documents of China's accession to the WTO are the articles of non-market economy, transitional product-specific safeguard measures, special safeguard measures on textiles and transitional trade policy review mechanism. See GAO Yongfu, Commentaries on Some Articles Disadvantageous to China in the Legal Documents of China's Accession to the WTO (in Chinese), *Journal of International Economic Law*, Vol. 11, 2004, pp. 46-81.

〔3〕 UK-PRC JD was formally signed on 19 December 1984 and came into force on 27 May 1985. The agreement was reprinted in *ILM*, Vol. 23, 1984, pp. 1371-1380.

it has to resume its GATT contracting party position before that date and makes a declaration on the application as it resumes exercising its sovereignty over Hong Kong. This way is rather complicated in legal procedure. In particular, though China sent its application for resuming its GATT contracting party position in July 1986, it is very difficult to predict when to conclude the long negotiations due to China's unique situations and the strict requirements from the GATT and Western powers. For Hong Kong's industries and commercial circle, it is very urgent for clarifying the position of Hong Kong in the GATT after 1 July 1997. [1]

Second, Hong Kong becomes a separate contracting party of the GATT. According to Article 26 (5) (c) of the GATT: "If any of the customs territories, in respect of which a contracting party accepted this Agreement, possesses or acquires full autonomy in the conduct of its external commercial relations and other matter provided for in this Agreement, such territory shall, upon sponsorship through a declaration by the responsible contracting party establishing the above-mentioned fact, be deemed to be a contracting party. " The purpose of this article is to make a customs territory within a contracting party become a SCT in the sense of application of the GATT.

After studies by the Sino-British Joint Liaison Group, China and UK governments decided to choose the second solution, which was terminated "sponsorship" procedure of the UK. [2] The main advantages for Hong Kong are multiple: first, it may keep the Hong Kong's position in the GATT before China's resuming its GATT contracting party position; second, it is not necessary for Hong Kong to negotiate with other contracting parties since it remains same rights and obligations as those of UK; thirdly, the "sponsorship" procedure is simpler, which only needs a UK's declaration.

Hong Kong became a separate contracting party of the GATT through the UK's declaration on 23 April 1986. China made a declaration on the same day to allow Hong Kong to keep that position in the GATT after 1 July 1997. Since that date Hong Kong has maintained its open trade policies and fulfilled its obligations in the

---

〔1〕 CHENG Xiang, LIU Minyi, The Status of Hong Kong in the GATT (in Chinese), *Wen Hui Bao* (HK), 4 December 1985.

〔2〕 John H. Jackson, *Sovereignty, the WTO and Changing Fundamentals of International Law*, Cambridge University Press, 2006, p. 109.

GATT/WTO regime. [1]

After effective of WTO Agreement, Hong Kong became an original WTO member based on its own rights of a GATT contracting party, in accordance with Article 11 of that Agreement. It is noticeable that the rights and obligations of Hong Kong as a SCT remain unchanged, so Hong Kong does not become an original WTO member in the status of a developing member.

There are twofold legal bases for Hong Kong. One is that Hong Kong is a SCT, meeting the requirements of WTO membership by itself. The other basis is that HKSAR shall maintain the positions of free port and separate customs region based on UK-PRC JD. [2] According to the provisions of UK-PRC JD and the Basic Law of the Hong Kong Special Administrative Region of the People's Republic of China (hereinafter HKSAR BL) promulgated on 4 April 1990, HKSAR may on its own, using the name "Hong Kong, China", maintain and develop relations and conclude and implement agreements with foreign States and regions and relevant international organizations in the appropriate fields, including the economic, trade etc. [3]

On 1 July 1997 when China resumed exercising its sovereignty over Hong Kong, Hong Kong changed its name as "Hong Kong, China" in the WTO regime.

2.3 Macao's GATT and WTO membership

According to the Joint Declaration of the Government of Portugal Republic and the Government of People's Republic of China on the Question of Macao (hereinafter PR-PRC JD) signed on 13 April 1987, Macao Special Administrative Region (hereinafter Macao SAR) may on its own, using the name "Macao, China", maintain and develop relations and conclude and implement agreements with foreign States and

---

[1]　The WTO conducted a comprehensive review of Hong Kong's trade policies and practices on December 7 and 8, 1998, in Geneva. The review was the first since the establishment of the WTO in 1995 and since Hong Kong's reunification with the PRC. It covered a full range of Hong Kong's trade policies and practices, including goods, services and intellectual property rights, as well as the trade and economic situation in Hong Kong. The members of the WTO Trade Policy Review Body commended on Hong Kong's maintaining open trade and investment regime after 1997, despite the Asian crisis. The members also expressed confidence that with these policies, Hong Kong's economy would soon resume strong and sustained economic growth. They believed that Hong Kong is one of the most open economies in the world. See WTO Members Commend Hong Kong for Its Free Trade Stance, *HK Files*, February 1999 Issue, p. 3.

[2]　Arts. 3 (6), (10) and Sec. Ⅵ of Annex Ⅰ of UK-PRC JD.

[3]　Arts. 3, 9, 10, UK-PRC JD; Sec. Ⅺ of Annex Ⅰ of UK-PRC JD; Art. 151, HKSAR BL.

regions and relevant international organizations in the appropriate fields, including the economic, culture etc. As a free port and a SCT, Macao may continue to participate in the GATT. [1] There are the same provisions in the Basic Law of the Macao Special Administrative Region of the People's Republic of China (hereinafter Macao BL). [2]

Macao follows the Hong Kong mode to be a separate contracting party in accordance with Article 26 (5) (c) of the GATT. In January 1991, Portuguese government and Chinese government submitted their declarations to secretariat of the GATT at the same time. The declaration of Portuguese government pointed out that Macao would be a separate contracting party of the GATT since 11 January 1991. The declaration of Chinese government stated that Macao SAR would remain the position of a separate contracting party of the GATT in the name of "Macao, China" after 20 December 1999 when China resumes exercising its sovereignty over Macao.

After effective of WTO Agreement, Macao also became an original WTO member based on its own rights of a contracting party of the GATT in accordance with Article 11 of the Agreement. The same as Hong Kong, Macao also does not become an original WTO member in the status of a developing member. On 20 December 1999, Macao changed its name as "Macao, China" in the WTO regime.

2.4 Chinese Taipei's WTO membership

At its meeting on 29 September-1 October 1992, the GATT Council of Representatives established a working party, as reflected in the respective Minutes (document C/M/259), to examine the application of Chinese Taipei to accede to the GATT under Article 33 of that Agreement, and to submit to the Council recommendations which may include a Draft Protocol of Accession. The membership of the working party was open to all contracting parties wishing to serve on it. Following the request of Chinese Taipei, circulated in document WT/ACC/TPKM/1, and pursuant to the decision of the General Council of 31 January 1995, the GATT working party was transformed into a WTO working party to negotiate the terms of accession

---

[1] Art. 2(7)and Sec. X of Annex I of PR-PRC JD.
[2] Arts. 112, 136-138, Macao SAR BL.

of Chinese Taipei to WTO Agreement under Article 12 of that Agreement.[1]

After China's signing ceremony, WTO ministers formally approved the membership of Chinese Taipei. Chinese Taipei became WTO 144th member on 1 January 2002.

It is noticeable that the legal basis of Chinese Taipei's application for a contracting party position of the GATT is different from its application for a membership of the WTO. The former is Article 33 of the GATT, which stipulates that: "A government not party to this Agreement, or a government acting on behalf of a separate customs territory possessing full autonomy in the conduct of its external commercial relations and of the other matters provided for in this Agreement, may accede to this Agreement, on its own behalf or on behalf of that territory, on terms to be agreed between such government and the CONTRACTING PARTIES." From the legislative history of the GATT, the above mentioned "a government acting on behalf of a separate customs territory" generally refers to the government of original metropolitan State acting on behalf of a SCT.[2] From the original meaning of the text, the term "a government acting on behalf of a separate customs territory" might also refer to a government of the SCT itself. As Chinese Taipei is not a government of original metropolitan State acting on behalf of a SCT, only the GATT working party identifies that Chinese Taipei is the government of the SCT itself, it has the legal ground for receiving and reviewing Chinese Taipei's accession application to the GATT.

The legal ground for Chinese Taipei to apply for WTO membership is Article 12.1 of WTO Agreement. According to the provision, applicant is "Any State or separate customs territory possessing full autonomy in the conduct of its external commercial relations and of the other matters provided for in this Agreement and the Multilateral Trade Agreements". It is very clear that a State and a SCT are two separate concepts in Article 12.1 of WTO Agreement. It means that a SCT is not a

[1] The working party met on 6 November 1992, 15 April 1993, 28 June 1993, 12 October 1993, 17 May 1994, 26 July 1994, 21 December 1994, 28 February 1997, 8 May 1998, 12 May 1999, and 18 September 2001 under the Chairmanship of H. E. Mr. M. Morland (United Kingdom). The terms of reference and the membership of the working party are set out in document WT/ACC/TPKM/6/Rev. 6.

[2] A commenter points out that according to international law it is illegal that the Taiwan authorities apply for the accession to the GATT as a SCT based on Article 33 of the GATT. See ZENG Lingliang, *Law of the World Trade Organization* (in Chinese), Wuhan University Press, 1996, pp. 68-71.

State, and precludes the possibility that a SCT is equal to a State. The provision avoids the ambiguity and explanative differences on terms of "a government acting on behalf of a separate customs territory…" in Article 33 of the GATT. It is obvious that an entity in the status of a SCT is the SCT itself. There is no any legal ground for a government to represent any other entity in the WTO regime.

It is evident that the Taiwan authorities always use the name of "the Separate Customs Territory of Taiwan, Penghu, Kinmen and Matsu (Chinese Taipei)" in the whole process of its accession application to the GATT and the WTO. Professor John H. Jackson points out that Chinese Taipei took the same type of membership as Hong Kong, "Which carefully crafted its application for GATT (and then WTO) status as such independent customs territory".[1] Chinese Taipei should only use this name and in a SCT status after it becomes a WTO member, otherwise it will lose its legal ground in the WTO regime. In practice, a SCT generally is a regional entity within a sovereign State, such as "Hong Kong, China" and "Macao, China". As the one-China principle is well recognized by the international society, it is self-evident that "Hong Kong, China", "Macao, China" and Chinese Taipei all belong to China in factual and legal basis.

In summary, China, "Hong Kong, China", "Macao, China" and Chinese Taipei are equal WTO members. The key difference among the four WTO memberships is very clear that China in the name of the PRC, is a sovereign State while "Hong Kong, China", "Macao, China" and Chinese Taipei are all SCTs under the WTO regime.

II. Relations among the Four WTO Members

The main features of the relations among China, "Hong Kong, China", "Macao, China" and Chinese Taipei include equal representation and participation in the WTO institutions and decision-making, separate claim and liabilities systems as well as equal participation in regional trade agreements (hereinafter RTAs).

1. Equal representation and participation in WTO institutions

1.1 Equal representation in WTO institutions

The main institutions of the WTO include the Ministerial Conference, the

---

[1] See John H. Jackson, *Sovereignty, the WTO and Changing Fundamentals of International Law*, Cambridge University Press, 2006, p. 109.

General Council, Councils, Committees and Secretariat etc. According to Articles 4. 1, 4. 2 of WTO Agreement, the Ministerial Conference is composed of representatives of all WTO members. It shall carry out the functions of the WTO and take actions necessary to this effect. It shall have the authority to take decisions on all matters under any of the Multilateral Trade Agreement in accordance with the related procedures. The General Council is also composed of representatives of all WTO members. In the intervals between two Ministerial Conferences, its functions shall be conducted by the General Council. According to these provisions, China, "Hong Kong, China", "Macao, China" and Chinese Taipei have separately sent their representatives to and participate in the Ministerial Conference and General Council. In the Ministerial Conference and General Council, the said four members represent economic interests of Chinese mainland, Hong Kong, Macao and Taiwan separately.

In addition, as the membership of WTO councils and committees are also open to all WTO members, China, "Hong Kong, China", "Macao, China" and Chinese Taipei have also participated in the Council for Trade in Goods, the Council for Trade in Services, the Council for Trade-related Aspects of Intellectual Property Rights, the Committee on Trade and Development, the Committee on Balance-of-Payments Restrictions, and the Committee on Budget, Finance and Administration separately.

Hong Kong has been in the forefront of multilateral trade liberalization efforts since the GATT days. Through the Trade and Industry Department and the Hong Kong Economic and Trade Office in Geneva, Hong Kong participates actively in various WTO committees to seek to ensure the effective operation of the WTO and the faithful implementation of commitments by other WTO members. Existing practice shows that Hong Kong's representatives are trusted and supported by other WTO members. In February 2001, Mr. Stuart Harbinson, the first permanent representative of Hong Kong to the WTO, was elected as 2001 Chairman of General Council of the WTO on his own. The representatives of "Hong Kong, China" are often appointed as chair or vice chair of the Councils, Committees and panels. Mr. Joshua Law, the Permanent Representative of Hong Kong to the WTO served as the

Chairman of the Committee on Budget, Finance and Administration for the year 2003.[1]

There are some differences among the delegations in Geneva from China, "Hong Kong, China", "Macao, China" and Chinese Taipei due to their different legal status. For example, the titles of the heads of the four delegations are different. For China, as a sovereign State, the title of her head of delegation is ambassador. For "Hong Kong, China", "Macao, China" and Chinese Taipei, the title of their heads of delegations are representatives due to their non-sovereignty status.

1.2 Equal participation in the decision-making of WTO

Though the members' obligations under the WTO might be different, all members enjoy equal rights to participate in the multilateral trade negotiations (hereinafter MTNs) and the decision-making of the WTO in legal sense.

In fact, there are big differences of the development level, economic systems, legal systems and social systems among China, "Hong Kong, China", "Macao, China" and Chinese Taipei. In particular, China insisted on its status of a developing country in negotiation for accession to the WTO, and made different commitments from those of Hong Kong, Macao and Taiwan. It is understandable that the four WTO members have different standings and voices in the MTNs and decision-making of the WTO.

It should be pointed out that the equal membership does not necessarily mean the different positions of members in the MTNs and the decision-making of the WTO. On contrary, all WTO members often conciliate their positions and reach the consensus in the MTNs and the decision-making for pursuing the objectives and purposes of the WTO. At the same time, WTO members in groups may take a common standing for their common economic interests and seek for legitimate rights and interests by every rule and the mechanism of the WTO.

As Chinese mainland, "Hong Kong, China", "Macao, China" and Chinese Taipei belong to a sovereign State, it is easier for them to conciliate and take the common standings in the MTNs and the decision-making of the WTO in theory. Moreover, as original WTO members and China's Special Administrative Regions,

---

[1] Hong Kong's Participation in the World Trade Organization. http://www.info.gov.hk/info/wto.htm

"Hong Kong, China", "Macao, China" have played important role in providing their rich GATT/WTO experience and bridging the Chinese mainland's market and international market. [1]

2. Separate claim and liabilities systems

2.1 Four members' disputes with a third member

According to Article 1 of Understanding on Rules and Procedures Governing the Settlement of Disputes (hereinafter DSU), the rules and procedures provided in DSU shall be applied to the disputes brought pursuant to the consultation and disputes settlement provisions of the agreements listed in Appendix 1 to DSU. It is obvious that as equal WTO members, China, "Hong Kong, China", "Macao, China" and Chinese Taipei make their separate claims and fulfill their liabilities system. If "Hong Kong, China", "Macao, China" or Chinese Taipei considers that its rights and interests have been injured by a third member, it will resort to the disputes settlement mechanism (hereinafter DSM) of the WTO without through the PRC. [2] If a third member considers that its rights and interests have been injured by "Hong Kong, China", "Macao, China" or Chinese Taipei, it will resort to the DSM of the WTO without through the PRC. Similarly the WTO cases involving China as a complainant or a respondent are totally unrelated to "Hong Kong, China", "Macao, China" or Chinese Taipei in legal sense. [3]

In practice, as Hong Kong performs strictly the traditional free trade policy for the long time, it is never claimed by other members in the DSM of WTO. Hong Kong has been a third party in three famous WTO cases. [4] The three cases are the Shrimp-Turtle case, the Turkey Quantitative Restrictions (Quota) case and the US Section 301 case. The former two cases were resorted to the Appellate Body (here-

---

[1] Cyril C. K. Chow and Michael C. M. Kwan, Hong Kong's Role in APEC under "One Country-Two Systems", *Policy Bulletin*, No. 3, January 1998, p. 10.

[2] There are 2 cases involving Chinese Taipei as a complainant, ie., Definitive Safeguard Measure on Imports of Certain Steel Products (DS274) (Chinese Taipei etc. v. United States), and Antidumping Measures on Certain Products from the Separate Customs Territory of Taiwan, Penghu, Kinmen and Matsu (DS 318) (Chinese Taipei v. India). Chinese Taipei as a third party also involves 34 cases. www.wto.org/19/08/2007

[3] There are 71 cases involving China, 1 case as a complainant, 9 cases as a respondent, and 61 cases as a third party. www.wto.org/19/08/2007.

[4] According to Article 10.2 of DSU, WTO member may be a third party in the WTO dispute settlement regime, namely besides the parties to a dispute, any other members "having a substantial interest in a matter before a panel and having notified its interest to the DSB".

inafter AB) of the WTO. In the three cases, Hong Kong all sent its written statement to the panel. For the former two cases, Hong Kong also refers its written
statement to AB. [1]

2.2 Different disputes among the four members: WTO-related or not

As a WTO member, it only bears obligations within the ambit of the WTO. It
is very important therefore to distinguish the concepts of "within the ambit of the
WTO" and "beyond the ambit of the WTO" for a WTO member. "Within the ambit
of the WTO" it is undoubted that all members have to observe WTO rules and fulfill
their commitments to the WTO seriously. At the same time, as the duties and obligations of WTO members are limited to their commitments to the WTO, members
may regulate their trade relations "beyond the ambit of the WTO" by non-WTO
rules, including RTAs, bilateral treaties or even domestic laws.

Accordingly, we should further distinguish the concepts of "the WTO-related
disputes" from "the non-WTO-related disputes" between or among WTO members.

"The WTO-related disputes" refer to the disputes between or among WTO
members on the rights and obligations under WTO agreements. This type of
disputes between or among China, "Hong Kong, China", "Macao, China" and Chinese Taipei are the disputes between or among WTO members and may be subject to
the DSM of the WTO. However since these disputes are also the special domestic
disputes, they are not necessarily resorted to the DSM of the WTO. They might be
resorted to domestic and flexible resolutions, such as consultation, negotiation,
arbitration and lawsuits etc.

"The non-WTO-related disputes" mean the disputes between or among WTO
members unrelated to the rights and obligations under WTO agreements. Certainly
they are not subject to the DSM of the WTO. As China, "Hong Kong, China",
"Macao, China" and Chinese Taipei belong to a same sovereign State, "the
non-WTO-related disputes" between or among the four members are internal and
domestic disputes rather than "the WTO-related disputes" between or among WTO
members. Therefore they are subject to domestic jurisdiction and domestic resolutions rather than the DSM of the WTO.

---

[1] David Little, *WTO Dispute Settlement: A Hong Kong Perspective*, speech on Inter-Pacific Bar Association Conference "WTO Dispute Resolution System: Does It Work?" May 2000.

3. Equal participation in RTAs

3.1 WTO Rules on RTAs

The non-discrimination principle, one of basic principles of the WTO, stipulates that trade among WTO members should be conducted without any discrimination, requiring all members to extend the most-favored nation treatment and national treatment to other members, except in certain circumstances detailed otherwise in the GATT/WTO.

To establish a RTA among some WTO members is likely conflict with the non-discrimination principle as the treatment for members (including WTO members) of the RTA might be more favorable than that of outsiders (including WTO members). Therefore WTO members who wish to establish a RTA have to seek for exceptions of the non-discrimination principle, so as to avoid violation of this principle.[1]

As the provisions of the GATT "shall not prevent, as between the territories of contracting parties, the formation of a customs union or of a free-trade area or the adoption of an interim agreement necessary for the formation of a customs union or a free-trade area",[2] a customs union (hereinafter CU) and a free trade area (hereinafter FTA), the typical modes of RTAs, become exceptions of the non-discrimination principle with certain conditions. Following the GATT practice, the WTO allows the existence of its members' CUs and FTAs with some detailed rules. The key provisions on RTAs in the GATT/WTO regime are as follows:

3.1.1 Article 24 of the GATT and Understanding on Article 24

Article 24 (8) of the GATT makes clear definitions for a CU and a FTA.[3] It

---

[1] RTAs include important economic entities, such as the EU, and they have significant effects on international trade because 90 percent of WTO members have signed at least one or more RTAs. See Yong-Shik Lee, *Reclaiming Development in the World Trading System*, Cambridge University Press, 2006, p. 141.

[2] Article 24 (5) of the GATT.

[3] According to the provisions, "A customs union shall be understood to mean the substitution of a single customs territory for two or more customs territories, so that (i) duties and other restrictive regulations of commerce (except, where necessary, those permitted under Articles XI, XII, XIII, XIV, XV and XX) are eliminated with respect to substantially all the trade between the constituent territories of the union or at least with respect to substantially all the trade in products originating in such territories", and "substantially the same duties and other regulations of commerce are applied by each of the members of the union to the trade of territories not included in the union". "A free-trade area shall be understood to mean a group of two or more customs territories in which the duties and other restrictive regulations of commerce (except, where necessary, those permitted under Articles XI, XII, XIII, XIV, XV and XX) are eliminated on substantially all the trade between the constituent territories in products originating in such territories".

seems that the key difference between these two is that members of a CU have to apply substantially the same duties and restrictive regulations to the trade of territories not included in the union while these requirements are not applicable for members of a FTA. In fact, a CU, a FTA and an interim agreement necessary for the formation of a CU or a FTA are different types or levels of RTAs. Among them, a CU is at the top level, a FTA is at the second place, and an interim agreement necessary for the formation of a CU or a FTA is at the primary stage of RTAs.

The Understanding on the Interpretation of Article 24 of the General Agreement on Tariffs and Trade 1994 (hereinafter the Understanding on Article 24) was formulated as part of Final Act of the Uruguay Round. Two major principles on RTAs are laid down in the Understanding: one is that a RTA must cover substantially all trade; the other is that other countries must not be worse off as a result of a RTA.[1] The Understanding clarifies some rules of Article 24 of the GATT. However, it has not resolved the more difficult issues, and it was hoped that further clarification would come from the Committee on Regional Trade Agreements (CRTA)[2] which also has in its mandate the responsibility "to consider the systemic implications of such agreements and regional initiatives for multilateral trading system and the relationship between them, and make appropriate recommendations to the General Council".[3]

3. 1. 2 Article 5 of the GATS

The provisions of Article 5 of the General Agreement on Trade in Services (hereinafter GATS) comfort with the principles of Article 24 of the GATT. It adopts the concept of "economic integration", and provides that "this Agreement

---

[1] The "substantially all trade" requirement ensures that a RTA is not abused as a cover for narrow sectoral discriminatory arrangement. The same requirement is also laid down in the Article 5 of the GATS which requires a "substantially sectoral coverage" in services. Unfortunately there is not agreement on the meaning of these wordings among WTO members, and in fact some RTAs omit from their coverage major and sensitive sectors such as agriculture and textile. The "not worse off" requirement is to ensure that not-participating members are not harmed by the RTAs. See Qingjiang KONG, China's WTO Accession and the ASEAN-China Free Trade Area: the Perspective of a Chinese Lawyer, *Journal of International Economic Law*, Vol. 7, No. 4, 2004, pp. 811-812.

[2] The CRTA was established in February 1996. The mandate of the Committee is to carry out the examination of agreements referred to it by the Council for Trade in Goods, the Council for Trade in Services and the Committee on Trade and Development. The CRTA is also charged to make recommendations on the reporting requirements for each type of agreement and to develop procedures to facilitate and improve the examination process.

[3] Jo-Ann Crawford and Sam Laird, Regional Trade Agreements and the WTO, http://www.tradeobservatory.org/library/12/23/2003.

shall not prevent any of its members from being a party to or entering into an agreement liberalizing trade in services between or among the parties to such an agreement" provided that such an agreement meet certain conditions. WTO Rules on RTAs in the field of trade in goods therefore extend to the field of trade in service.

Most recently these have attempted to identify the issues arising from the interpretation and application of individual provisions of Article 5 of the GATS and the possible linkages between Article 5 of the GATS and Article 24 of the GATT, particularly in regard to the scope of "substantial sectoral coverage" and "substantial all discrimination". [1]

3.1.3 The Enabling Clause

The GATT contracting parties adopted a decision in 1979, allowing derogations to the most-favored nation treatment in favor of the developing countries in trade in goods. This includes differential and more favorable treatment, reciprocity and fuller participation of developing countries, and provisions related to the establishment of preferential trade agreements among the developing countries, granting the possibilities of not meeting the substantially-all-trade requirements. [2]

3.2 RTAs between or among the four members and third parties

As equal WTO members, China, "Hong Kong, China", "Macao, China" and Chinese Taipei may separately establish a CU or FTA or negotiate and conclude an agreement necessary for establishing a CU or FTA with a third party in accordance with Article 24 of the GATT, Understanding on Article 24 and Article 5 of the GATS. As a developing member, China may separately establish a RTA with a third developing party or third developing parties in accordance with the Enabling Clause.

The Framework Agreement on Comprehensive Economic Co-operation between the Association of Southeast Asian Nations and the People's Republic of China

---

[1] Jo-Ann Crawford and Sam Laird, Regional Trade Agreements and the WTO, http://www.tradeobservatory.org/library/12/23/2003.

[2] Sung-Hoon Park, The Current Status and Future Prospects of Regionalism and Multilateralism in the World Economy: A Case Study of Economic Relations Between EU and APEC in the WTO Era, pp. 4-5, http://www.ecsanet.org/conferences/ecsaworld3/park.htm/12/23/2003

(hereinafter FACEC) was concluded on 4 November 2002 and ratified on 1 July 2003. [1] This is China's first RTA practice after its accession to the WTO. The Parties agree to negotiate expeditiously in order to establish an ASEAN-China FTA within 10 years[2] and pave the way towards closer cooperation in the elimination of tariffs and non-tariffs barriers on trade in goods and services, create an open and competitive investment regime and encourage the simplification and standardization of customs procedures. [3] It is very important to clarify and emphasize that China in FACEC context is only referred to Chinese mainland, not including "Hong Kong, China", "Macao, China" and Chinese Taipei. [4]

In recent years the Taiwan authorities try to conclude FTA agreements with other countries like US, Japan, Singapore, New Zealand and Central American countries etc. in the name of "Taiwan" instead of its formal name of "the Separate Customs Territory of Taiwan, Penghu, Kinmen and Matsu (Chinese Taipei)" in the WTO[5] and also proposed establishing a FTA agreement with the 10-member ASEAN nations. [6] It reflects the "creeping independence" or "*de facto* independence" policy of the Taiwan authorities. It should be emphasized that since 1949, China's position has been that any State or international organization, which wishes to deal with China, should recognize the government of the PRC as the sole legitimate government of China and Taiwan as an inalienable part of China. This one-China principle has been generally accepted and recognized by international society. As Chinese Taipei accedes to the WTO in the Status of a SCT, the WTO membership does not bring any substantial change to its legal personality. WTO Mem-

---

[1] The extracts of the Agreement are available at *China: An International Journal*, Vol. 1, No. 1, pp. 170-178. For the brief history of FACEC, see Qingjiang KONG, China's WTO Accession and the ASEAN-China Free Trade Area: The Perspective of a Chinese Lawyer, *Journal of International Economic Law*, Vol. 7, No. 4, 2004, pp. 802-803.

[2] Article 2 of FACEC.

[3] ASEAN Secretariat, News Release, 30 October 2002, ASEAN-China Free Trade Area Negotiations to Start Next Year, http://www. aseansec. org/13125. htm.

[4] For general comment on the relations between WTO rules and FACEC, see ZENG Huaqun, WTO Rules and China-ASEAN FTA Agreement, in John WONG, ZOU Keyuan and ZENG Huaqun (eds.), *China-ASEAN Relations: Economic and Legal Dimensions*, World Scientific Publishing Co. Pte. Ltd. , 2006, pp. 93-109.

[5] ZHU Lei, How Taiwan Concludes "Free Trade Agreements" (in Chinese), *Kai Fang Chao*, 2002 (7), pp. 24-25.

[6] On 12 November 2002, Taiwan "Economic Minister" LIN Yifu made the suggestion in Malaysia. Yow Cheun Hoe, China-ASEAN Relations in 2002: Chronology of Events, *China: An International Journal*, Vol. 1, No. 1, 2003, p. 168.

bers shall adhere to the one-China principle consistently and shall not set up any FTA with Chinese Taipei in the name of "Taiwan" or any other name different from its formal name of "the Separate Customs Territory of Taiwan, Penghu, Kinmen and Matsu (Chinese Taipei)" in the WTO.

3.3 CEPAs or other ECR among the four WTO members

As equal WTO members, China, "Hong Kong, China", "Macao, China" and Chinese Taipei may also establish a CU or a FTA between or among them. The significance of a CU or a FTA between or among the four members under the WTO regime is to deal with the special problems on the application of WTO non-discrimination principle, setting up a necessary legal basis for closer economic relations between or among the four regions within a sovereign State. The potential Closer Economic Partnership Arrangement (hereinafter CEPA) or other Economic Cooperation Regime (hereinafter ECR) among China, "Hong Kong, China", "Macao, China" and Chinese Taipei leading to so-called "great China FTA" might provide new opportunities for further economic cooperation and integration among the four WTO members. [1]

Considering China's "one country two systems" policy and big differences among the four members in political, economic and legal systems and development levels, to establish a FTA, rather than a CU, is more suitable for them. This arrangement may also have impact on other WTO Members. In fact, both of the CEPA between Chinese mainland and Hong Kong and the CEPA between Chinese mainland and Macao came into effect from 1 January 2004.

There is big divergence on the nature of a CEPA. Some scholars consider it as international treaty or semi-international treaty since it is regulated by international law, while others deem it as domestic legal arrangement since it is a legal document concluded by two parties from a same sovereign State. [2] From further studies on

[1] There are many comments on RTAs among the four members, for examples, ZENG Lingliang, The Legal Position and Development Trend of Regional Trade Arrangement under WTO Regime—Several Legal Issues Concerning Establishing A Free Trade Area among the Mainland, Taiwan, Hong Kong and Macao (in Chinese); WANG Guiguo and LIANG Meifen, An Analysis of the Proposition of Establishing Free Trade Area between Hong Kong and the Mainland (in Chinese), *Journal of International Economic Law*, Vol. 7, 2003, pp. 1-16, 69-83.

[2] ZHU Zhaomin, The Legal Basis and Framework for Closer Economic and Trade Cooperation among China's Separate Customs Territories after Its Accession to WTO (in Chinese), *Journal of International Economic Law*, Vol. 7, 2003, pp. 17-36.

the issue, we found some features of the CEPA between Chinese mainland and Hong Kong: (1) the subjects of the CEPA have dual status, ie., the mainland customs territory and Hong Kong SCT in the domestic regime and two members in the WTO regime; (2) the objects of the CEPA also have dual nature, ie., the economic relationships between the two customs territories in a same sovereign State and the trade relationships between the two WTO members; (3) the legal grounds for the CEPA involve relevant provisions in Chinese domestic laws and the WTO rules on RTAs. Therefore we might conclude that the CEPA between Chinese mainland and Hong Kong, in the status of the two customs territories in a sovereign State and in the status of the two WTO members, is an agreement between the two WTO members in conformity with Article 24 of the GATT, Understanding on Article 24 and Article 5 of the GATS,[1] but essentially not a treaty.[2] It is a domestic legal arrangement for a RTA with its partial contents regulated by the WTO rules.[3]

III. Significance of "One China Four WTO Memberships"

At the international and domestic levels, the formation of "one China four WTO memberships" has great implications both in theoretical and practical sense. The significance of this unique situation is to reflect the latest development of international law, to strengthen the consensus of the one-China principle in international society, and to provide new opportunities for four members to establish closer economic relations.

---

[1] In fact, both of the CEPA between Chinese mainland and Hong Kong and the CEPA between Chinese mainland and Macao as FTAs are reported to the CRTA of the WTO for examination (WT/REG162, WT/REG162 S/C/N/264 and WT/REG163, WT/REG163 S/C/N/265) on 12 January 2004.

[2] Article 2 of the Vienna Convention on the Law of Treaties of 1969 defines a "treaty" as "an international agreement concluded between states in written form and governed by international law, whether embodied in a single instrument or in two or more related instruments and whatever its particular designation". Article 2.1 (a) of the Vienna Convention on the Law of Treaties between States and International Organizations or between International Organizations of 1986 modifies the above definition by recognizing that "treaty" also includes international agreement "between one or more states and one or more international organizations; or between international organizations". As the CEPA between Chinese mainland and Hong Kong does not meet the basic requirement of "between states", "between a state and an international organization" or "between international organizations", it can not be regarded as a treaty essentially.

[3] ZENG Huaqun, On the Nature of CEPA between Chinese Mainland and Hong Kong (in Chinese), *Xiamen University Journal* (*Arts & Social Sciences*), No 5, 2002, pp. 5-14.

1. To reflect the latest development of international law

1. 1 First practice on "one State several memberships" in WTO

According to traditional international law, only sovereignty can be a subject or party of international treaties. However, following modern international practice, there are some non-sovereign entities participating in international treaties, such as international organizations, members of federal States, belligerent and regional entities. The legal grounds of the treaty-making power of these entities come separately from basic agreements of the international organizations, constitutional laws, laws of treaties and customary international law. [1] Accordingly some non-sovereign entities become members of international organizations. It is worthy noticing that non-sovereign entities can not change their legal status by concluding international treaties or being members of international organizations. [2]

Traditionally an international organization refers to an organization which is established by two or more than two sovereign States, aiming to realize common objectives and purposes and having some permanent organs by an agreement. [3] According to the new development of international practice, the membership of an international organization is not always limited to sovereign States. Currently there are two types of international organizations in terms of membership. One is that their membership is still only limited to sovereign States. The other is that their membership is open to sovereign States and non-sovereign entities. The WTO is the latter. Its members include sovereign States and non-sovereign entities, such as SCTs and the EC. The WTO members are equal whatever sovereign States and non-sovereign entities. In fact, "one China four WTO memberships" is not a total new mode. It takes the mode of International Olympic Committee mode in which Chinese Olympic Committee and Chinese Taipei Olympic Committee served as National O-

---

[1] LI Haopei, *On Laws of Treaties* (in Chinese), Law Press, 1988, p. 240.

[2] For example, Hong Kong has on its own concluded many international treaties and become members of many international organizations since 1986. This important international practice can not change Hong Kong's legal status as a non-sovereign entity. See ZENG Huaqun, Hong Kong's Autonomy: Concept, Developments and Characteristics, *China: An International Journal*, Vol. 1, No. 2, 2003, pp. 313-325.

[3] LIANG Xi, *International Institutional Law* (in Chinese), Wuhan University Press, 1993, pp. 1-5.

lympic Committees (NOCs) under the International Olympic Committee (IOC). [1] Also the mode is the same as the arrangements in Asia Development Bank (ADB) [2] and Asia Pacific Economic Cooperation Conference (APEC). [3] The mode is new for the WTO in terms of the first and only practice on "one State several memberships", reflecting the new development of international law and especially international institutional law in this important universal organization.

1.2 Precedents for domestic RTAs governed by WTO rules

It is worth noticing that the EC, North American Free Trade Agreement (NAFTA) and ASEAN are all international economic regional organization consisting of more than two sovereign States. If China, "Hong Kong, China", "Macao, China" and Chinese Taipei negotiate and conclude an agreement for establishing a RTA between or among them, the arrangement is a new creature in the history of the RTAs. It is a RTA within a sovereign State rather than a RTA of a regional international organization. Furthermore, as all parties to the arrangement belong to a sovereign State, it is a domestic legal arrangement subject to Article 24 of the GATT rather than an international treaty. Therefore we might conclude that since one State may have several WTO memberships, there are possibilities, feasibilities and practice of domestic RTAs governed by WTO rules. "One China four WTO memberships" and the CEPAs between Chinese mainland and Hong Kong, Macao are valuable precedents on this regards.

2. To strengthen the consensus of the one-China principle in international society

In legal sense, China entered into the WTO in the status of a sovereign State,

---

[1] Chinese Olympic Committee created in 1910, representing the Olympic movement of Chinese mainland. Chinese Taipei Olympic Committee created in 1960, representing the Olympic movement of Chinese Taipei. There are currently 205 NOCs. Although most NOCs are from nations, the IOC also recognizes independent territories, commonwealths, protectorates, and geographical areas. www. olympic. org/19/08/2007.

[2] ADB is a multilateral development financial institution owned by 67 members, 48 from the region and 19 from other parts of the globe. Taipei, China was a founding member of ADB in 1966. People's Republic of China has been a member of ADB in 1986. The term "country", as used in ADB's context, refers to a member of ADB. It does not imply any view on ADB's part as to sovereignty or independent status. www. adb. org/19/08/2007 For the history of the ADB's arrangement and the passive position of the Taiwan authorities, see ZHAO Guocai, On the Membership of the People's Republic of China in Asia Development Bank (in Chinese), *Chinese Yearbook of International Law and International Affairs*, Vol. 1, 1985-1986, pp. 36-55.

[3] By 18 August 2007, APEC has 21 economies. People's Republic of China, Hong Kong, China and Chinese Taipei became APEC members on 12-14 November 1991. www. apec. org/18/08/2007.

while "Hong Kong, China", "Macao, China" and Chinese Taipei in the status of the SCTs. As China performs the policy of "one country two systems", "Hong Kong, China" and "Macao, China" remain their WTO member positions without any negative impact by China's WTO accession. After China's reunification, certainly Chinese Taipei will follow the mode of "Hong Kong, China" and "Macao, China" and maintain its SCT position in the WTO regime.

From the fifteen years negotiation process and its positions and commitments, in fact, as a WTO member, China refers to Chinese mainland. Comparing with "Hong Kong, China" and "Macao, China" and Chinese Taipei, the Chinese mainland is also a customs region. In this sense, the relations among China, "Hong Kong, China", "Macao, China" and Chinese Taipei are also the relations among the four customs regions in China.

It should be stressed that Chinese Taipei entered into the WTO in the status of a SCT, its name and status can not be changed after its WTO accession. In all of its documents referred to the WTO institutions and members, the formal name of "the Separate Customs Territory of Taiwan, Penghu, Kinmen and Matsu (Chinese Taipei)" should be clear indicated. Therefore the legal situation of "one China four WTO memberships" further reflects that the one-China principle is well recognized by WTO members and international society.

The Taiwan authorities stressed that it would conclude a FTA rather than a CEPA under the WTO regime with Chinese mainland. It seems that the two concepts of a FTA and a CEPA are attached misleading political sense, such as a FTA having international implication while a CEPA using only for the Special Administrative Regions of the PRC. [1] From legal point of view, there is not any substantial difference between a FTA and a CEPA since they are all modes of RTAs without any international or domestic implication. If we clarify and recognize that there are two types of RTAs, namely domestic RTAs and international RTAs, we might find that regardless of the modes and names of RTAs, domestic RTAs are RTAs between or among members from a sovereign State while international RTAs are RTAs between or among members from different sovereign States or internation-

[1] ZHAO Hongjing, Cross-Strait Economic Cooperation Issues from Aspect of Regional Economic Integration, II (in Chinese), *Xinyong Hezuo*, October 2005, pp. 27-32.

al organizations. Therefore it makes not any legal implication for the Taiwan authorities to insist on its position for concluding a FTA rather than a CEPA with Chinese
mainland. Furthermore a FTA, a CEPA or any other mode of a RTA between Chinese mainland and Chinese Taipei makes not difference in legal nature from the CE-
PAs between Chinese mainland and Hong Kong, Macao. In this sense any mode and
name of a RTA between Chinese mainland and Chinese Taipei will enhance the consensus of the one-China principle in international society since it is a formal and legal
arrangement accepted by cross-Straits authorities and recognized by international society.

3. To provide new opportunities for the four members to establish closer
economic relations

The WTO member relations among China, "Hong Kong, China", "Macao,
China" and Chinese Taipei provide the great potential for establishing closer economic relations among them. The successful performance of the CEPAs between
Chinese mainland and Hong Kong, Macao since 1 January 2004 has demonstrated
that the CEPAs are mutually beneficial to the two parties. The only issue in this
regard is the possibility and feasibility of the formal legal arrangement for establishing closer cross-Straits economic relation.

Currently the legal status of Chinese Taipei as a SCT and a WTO member is
clarified and recognized by the WTO and all its other members, including China,
"Hong Kong, China" and "Macao, China". Considering the complicated cross-
Straits relations, the new position of equal WTO members of Chinese mainland and
Chinese Taipei provides a new legal basis and practical alternative for negotiating the
cross-Straits economic relations. If Chinese mainland and Chinese Taipei successfully initiate the negotiation, it is a great step for the great undertaking of China's
peaceful reunification.

It is reported that according to the official and civil investigations in Taiwan,
the policy of "one country two systems" in economic aspect is more acceptable than
that policy in political aspect for the people in Taiwan. [1] The CEPAs between

---

[1] "One Country Two Systems" in Economic Aspect Is More Acceptable and It Is Hard to Reach a Compromise in Political Aspect (in Chinese), *United Daily* (Lian He Bao), 18 July 2001, p. 15.

Chinese mainland and Hong Kong, Macao are very attractive for every circle in Taiwan. [1] The Taiwan media stresses that the CEPAs marks the beginning and development of the "Great China Economic Circle" under the one-China principle. As the Taiwan authorities refused to accept the one-China principle, the consultation and negotiation between Chinese mainland and Taiwan are still in deadlock. Therefore, Taiwan would be out of integration of the "Great China Economic Circle" and the economy of Taiwan would gradually go into marginalization. [2] Some politicians in Taiwan also delivered important and valuable suggestions on the cross-Straits relations. Mr. Vincent SIEW, the former Vice Chairman of Kuomintang (hereinafter KMT), pointed out that it is a feasible and peaceable means for mainland and Taiwan to reach gradually political integration by economic integration. [3] He also created a new concept of the Closer Economic Operation Framework (hereinafter CEOF) for substituting the contentious concepts of a FTA and a CEPA. In Mr. SIEW's opinions, there are three stages for promoting the development of the Cross-Straits Common Market (hereinafter CSCM): in first stage, the main task is to promote the normalization of the cross-Straits relations; in second stage, to promote the harmonization of the economic systems across the Straits; in third stage, to promote the integration of the cross-Straits economy in all aspects, and to realize the objectives of the CSCM. [4] Mr. James SOONG, Chairman of People First Party (hereinafter PFP), indicated that mainland and Taiwan might learn from the experience of the EC, starting from economic conformity, to social cooperation and finally reaching political integration. [5] On 29 April 2005, Communist Party of China (hereinafter CPC) General Secretary HU Jintao and KMT Chairman LIEN Chan met in Beijing and issued a joint communiqué. According to the joint communiqué, the two parties agreed to strengthen cross-Straits economic and trade exchanges including

---

[1] See LUO Changfa, Significance of FTA Agreement to the relations between Taiwan and Mainland, Hong Kong (in Chinese), at ZHANG Xianchu (ed.), *WTO Rules and Legal Relations on Economic and Trade among Four Regions across Taiwan Straits*, the Commercial Press (Hong Kong), Ltd., 2003, pp. 40-63.

[2] Every Circle in Taiwan Pays Attention to the CEPA between Hong Kong and Mainland (in Chinese), *Fujian Daily*, 2 July 2003, p. 6.

[3] The Foundation for Cross-Straits Common Market Prepared by Vincent SIEW Setting Up (in Chinese), *China Times* (Zhongguo Shibao), 27 March 2001, p. 1.

[4] Three Stages for Promoting the Cross-Straits Common Market, Establishing the Closer Economic Operation Framework (in Chinese), *Central Daily* (Zhongyang Ribao), 11 May, 2005, p. 3.

[5] James SOONG: Three Stages for Dealing with the Cross-Straits Issues (in Chinese), *United Daily* (Lian He Bao), 4 January 2001, p. 4.

the establishment of the CSCM. [1] On 12 May 2005, CPC General Secretary HU Jintao and PFP Chairman James SOONG, also met in Beijing and agreed to exchange views on establishing a long-term and stable regime for trade facilitation and liberalization across the Straits (ie., cross-Straits FTA) after resuming the cross-Straits consultation. [2] Recent development of the cross-Straits relations demonstrates that there are consensus at party-to-party level and practical possibilities for Chinese mainland and Chinese Taipei to negotiate a cross-Straits legal arrangement for economic cooperation. [3] Under the globalization, Chinese mainland and Chinese Taipei might initiate the negotiation leading to a cross-Straits legal arrangement for closer economic cooperation and integration in accordance with the WTO rules, and with more farseeing and more flexible attitude.

---

[1] XING Zhigang, CPC, KMT Leaders Vow to End Hostility across the Straits, *China Daily*, 30 April 2005, p. 1.

[2] Point 4, The Joint Communiqué of Communist Party of China General Secretary HU Jintao and People First Party Chairman James SOONG on 12 May 2005 (in Chinese), *People's Daily*, 13 May 2005, p. 1.

[3] Unfortunately the Taiwan authorities run into the opposite direction due to their "creeping independence" policy. For example, the Taiwan authorities encouraged Solomon Islands etc. to present a letter for the inclusion of the so-called "Taiwan's entry into the United Nations" issue on the agenda of the 62nd UN General Assembly to President Haya Rashed al Khalifa of the 61st UN General Assembly on 14 August 2007. See Taiwan's UN Move "Doomed to Failure", *China Daily*, 17 August 2007, p. 3.

第七章
国内区域贸易协定

第一节　两岸四地建立更紧密经贸关系的法律思考[*]

2001 年 12 月 11 日和 2002 年 1 月 1 日,中国与"台湾、澎湖、金门、马祖单独关税区"(简称"中国台北")[1]先后成为 WTO 正式成员,[2]连同于 1995 年 1 月 1 日分别成为 WTO 创始成员的中国香港和中国澳门,在 WTO 体制中出现了前所未有的"一国四席"局面。由于同属一个主权国家,中国大陆、香港、澳门、台湾(以下简称"两岸四地")之间的经贸关系是一国国内不同关税区之间的经贸关系。同时,由于 WTO体制"一国四席"的新定位,两岸四地之间的经贸关系又是 WTO 平等成员之间的经贸关系。两岸四地之间建立更紧密经贸关系,虽然是一国国内不同关税区之间的经贸安排,但由于这种"更紧密经贸关系"客观上是与其他 WTO 成员比较而言的,必须符合 WTO 规则,不可能游离于 WTO 体制之外。[3]鉴此,本文在论述 WTO 体制"一国四席"的形成及其影响的基础上,对两岸四地建立更紧密经贸关系的法律模式及法律特征作一初步探讨。

一、"一国四席":两岸四地的新定位

WTO 体制中"一国四席"的形成,是由《WTO 协定》有关成员资格的规定、中国独特的历史发展进程和"一国两制"的政策取向所决定的。"一国四席"的重要意义

---

[*]　原载陈安主编:《国际经济法论丛》第 7 卷,法律出版社 2003 年版。

[1]　英文为 the Separate Customs Territory of Taiwan, Penghu, Kinmen and Matsu(Chinese Taibei)。对 Chinese Taipei,中国大陆一般译为"中国台北"或"中国台湾",中国台湾地区一般译为"中华台北"。

[2]　http://www-svca.wto-ministerial.org/english/thewto_e/minist_e/min01_e/min01_11nov_e.htm

[3]　这在中国《加入议定书》已有明确的承诺。该文件第 4 条规定:"自加入时起,中国应取消与第三国和单独关税区之间的、与《WTO 协定》不符的所有特殊贸易安排,包括易货贸易安排,或使其符合《WTO 协定》。"

首先是确立了两岸四地新的法律地位，这是建立两岸四地更紧密经贸关系必须面对的前提性、基础性问题。

（一）《WTO 协定》关于成员资格的规定

根据 1947 年《关税及贸易总协定》（GATT 1947）第 26、32、33 条规定，主权国家并不是 GATT 缔约方资格的必要条件。任何实体，不论是否主权国家，只要构成一个关税区，均可按一定程序成为 GATT 的缔约方；相反，即使是一个独立的主权国家，如未形成一个关税区，也不可能成为 GATT 的缔约方。GATT 有关条文均把关税区作为成员资格的先决条件。

《建立世界贸易组织协定》（以下简称《WTO 协定》）沿袭了 GATT 1947 有关成员资格的规定。第 11 条第 1 款规定了创始成员（original members）的资格，即："本协定生效之日的 GATT 1947 缔约方和欧洲共同体，如接受本协定和多边贸易协定，并将减让和承诺表附于 GATT 1994，将具体承诺减让表附于 GATS，应成为 WTO 的创始成员。"[1]

《WTO 协定》第 12 条第 1 款规定了纳入成员（members by accession）的资格和程序："任何国家或在处理其对外商业关系及本协定和多边贸易协定规定的其他事务中享有充分自治权的单独关税区（separate tariff territory），可按它与 WTO 议定的条件加入本协定。此加入适用于本协定及所附多边贸易协定。"

显然，WTO 体制有关成员的规定是 GATT 体制有关缔约方规定的继承和发展。其特征主要表现在：

第一，从成员名称上看，与 GATT 的缔约方（contracting party）不同，WTO 的成员称为成员（member），是 WTO 从 GATT 这一事实上（de facto）国际经济组织演变为法律上（de jure）国际经济组织的重要标志之一。

第二，在 GATT 体制中发展为事实上缔约方的欧共体成为 WTO 的正式创始成员。

第三，成员分为主权国家和"单独关税区"两类。承袭 GATT 的传统，《WTO 协定》继续采用"单独关税区"的概念。这一概念可溯及战后的特定情况，即存在宗主国与附属领土，而适用于附属领土的关税制度可能与宗主国不同。在 GATT 体制中，"单独关税区"最初是指适用不同于宗主国的关税制度的附属领土。由于近 40 多年来国际政治经济形势的发展和深刻演变，在 WTO 体制中，"单独关税区"具有更准

---

〔1〕 根据部长级会议《关于世界贸易组织协定的接受与加入的决议》规定，所有符合创始成员条件者须在《WTO 协定》生效后两年之内批准。截至 1997 年 3 月 27 日，131 个 GATT 缔约方均成为 WTO 成员。See John Croome, *Guide to the Uruguay Round Agreements*, Kluwer Law International, 1999, p. 12, note 43.

确的法律和经济内涵,一般与殖民主义制度无关。由于采用这一概念,中国香港和中国澳门以中华人民共和国的特别行政区和单独关税区的身份,分别继续作为WTO 的创始成员。[1] 为了将"单独关税区"的法律概念纳入整个 WTO 多边贸易规则中,《WTO 协定》的"解释性说明"特别指出,"本协定和多边贸易协定中使用的'country or countries'应理解为包括任何 WTO 单独关税区成员。对于 WTO 单独关税区成员,除非另有规定,如本协定和多边贸易协定中用'national'一词表述,该表述也应理解为是指单独关税区"[2]。

第四,发展中成员(developing country member),特别是最不发达成员(least-developed country member)享有比在 GATT 体制下更多的特殊待遇。[3]

第五,WTO 的创始成员与纳入成员的权利义务并无区分。

最后,作为 WTO 的成员,无论是国家、国际组织,还是单独关税区,在 WTO 体制中的法律地位是平等的。

在上述主要特征中,可以看出存在"一国多席"的可能性。由于 WTO 成员资格向主权国家和非主权的单独关税区开放,一个主权国家与隶属于该主权国家的一个或一个以上单独关税区分别加入 WTO,或者在一个主权国家未加入 WTO 的情况下,隶属于该主权国家的二个或二个以上单独关税区分别加入 WTO,都可能形成WTO 体制的"一国多席"局面。而在"一国多席"中,也可能有创始成员与纳入成员、发展中成员与其他成员的不同组合。

(二)"一国四席"的形成及其法律依据

WTO 体制的"一国四席"是历史发展和现实选择的产物,且具有国际法和国内法的依据。

1. 中国的 GATT 创始缔约方和 WTO 纳入成员资格

中国是 GATT 的创始缔约方之一。1950 年 3 月,非法占据中国席位的台湾当局宣布退出 GATT。中国政府于 1986 年 7 月正式向 GATT 提出要求恢复中国在GATT 的合法席位(即"复关")的申请,并提出"复关"三原则:(1) 采取恢复合法席位方式;(2) 力争以关税减让作为承诺条件;(3) 坚持以发展中国家的地位进行谈判,并承担与我国经济贸易水平相适应的义务。然而,由于少数西方大国的阻挠和中国

---

[1] http://www.wto.org/english/thewto_e/whatis_e/eol/e/wto02/wto2_11.htm#note1

[2] 赵维田:《世界贸易组织(WTO)的法律制度》,吉林人民出版社,2000 年,第 42—44 页。

[3] 在《农产品协议》《纺织品与服装协议》《贸易技术壁垒协议》《与贸易有关的投资措施协议》《反倾销协议》《许可证协议》《补贴与反补贴协议》《保障措施协议》和《服务贸易总协定》等均规定了发展中成员特别是最不发达成员不同于一般成员的责任、不同的调整规则、技术援助以及较长的过渡期等。See John Croome, *Guide to the Uruguay Round Agreements*, Kluwer Law International, 1999, pp.223-246. 参见徐兆宏:《世界贸易组织机制运行论》,上海财经大学出版社,1999 年,第 305—308 页。

经济体制融入 GATT 体制本身的实际困难等种种因素，中国与美国、欧共体等主要贸易伙伴的双边谈判旷日持久，"复关"终未成就。

1995 年 11 月，应中国政府要求，GATT 中国"复关"工作组更名为 WTO 中国"入世"工作组。中国在"入世"谈判中坚持的三原则是：(1) 权利与义务对等原则；(2) 以发展中国家身份加入原则；(3) 以乌拉圭回合协议为基础，承担与其经济发展水平相一致的义务。

经过历时 15 年艰苦曲折的谈判，2001 年 11 月 9 日，多哈 WTO 部长级会议全体会议以协商一致的方式通过中国的"入世"申请；11 月 11 日，中国通知 WTO，中国人大常委会已完成有关批准中国"入世"的程序；12 月 11 日，中国成为 WTO 第 143 个正式成员。必须强调的是，中国是以中华人民共和国的名义，即以主权国家的资格"入世"。同时，中国是以发展中国家的身份"入世"，作出与发展中国家身份相适应的国际承诺。

2. 香港的 GATT 单独缔约方和 WTO 创始成员资格

1984 年《中华人民共和国政府和大不列颠及北爱尔兰联合王国政府关于香港问题的联合声明》（以下简称《中英联合声明》）签署后，如何在 1997 年 7 月 1 日之后保持香港在 GATT 中的地位，成为中英双方关注并致力解决的重要国际法问题之一。从 GATT 有关条款看，1997 年 7 月 1 日后保持香港在 GATT 中的地位，有两种选择：

（1）中国"复关"后适用 GATT 于香港。根据 GATT 第 26 条第 5 款第 1 项规定，凡接受该协定的各政府系为其本土及由该政府负国际责任的其他领土而接受。显然，如果中国政府决定通过这一方式使 GATT 在 1997 年 7 月 1 日后适用于香港特别行政区（以下简称"香港特区"），就意味着中国必须在 1997 年 7 月 1 日之前"复关"，并在中国对香港恢复行使主权时，声明 GATT 适用于香港特区。按此方式，中国在 GATT 中的全部权利和义务原则上同样适用于香港。如果中国主张香港在 GATT 的原有权利不因中国代表香港而发生任何变化，从法律上说，经其他缔约方同意，中国可事先在"复关"议定书中说明。可见，在法律程序上，这一方式比较复杂。特别是，尽管中国当时已正式向 GATT 提出"复关"申请，但由于中国社会经济制度与 1947 年时的旧中国迥然有别，中国同 GATT 各缔约方的有关谈判尚需时日，而对香港工商界而言，明确香港回归后在 GATT 的地位则刻不容缓。[1]

（2）香港成为单独缔约方。GATT 第 26 条第 5 款第 3 项规定："原由一缔约方

---

〔1〕 参见程翔、刘敏仪：《香港的关贸地位问题》，载《香港文汇报》1985 年 12 月 4 日。

代表其接受本协定的任何单独关税区,如拥有或取得处理对外商务关系和本协定规定的其他事项方面的充分自治权,经由对其负责的缔约方发表声明确认上述事实,应视为本协定的一个缔约方"。该条款旨在使某缔约方的单独关税区,在 GATT 适用的意义上,能与该缔约方分开而被视为单独缔约方。[1]

中英两国政府通过中英联合联络小组研究,决定采取上述第二种方式。其主要优点是:首先,在中国尚未"复关"的情况下,可确保香港在 GATT 中的地位。其次,不需要同其他缔约方重新谈判。1961 年 GATT 的一个工作组报告指出,根据 GATT 第 26 条第 5 款第 3 项,单独关税区成为缔约方的条件将与原由负责其国际关系的缔约方代表它接受 GATT 时的条件相同。由于 1948 年英国作为创始缔约方使 GATT 无条件适用于香港,香港按上述条款成为缔约方,仍继续行使其原有权利,承担其原有义务。最后,所需履行的手续简单。只要英国作为负责香港对外关系的缔约方向 GATT 声明,香港已具备在处理其对外商务关系和 GATT 规定的其他事项的充分自治权,而香港本身又表示愿意成为缔约方,香港自声明之日即被视为缔约方。

1986 年 4 月 23 日,英国声明并通知 GATT 总干事,香港在处理其对外商务关系和 GATT 规定的其他事项中具有充分的自治权。根据 GATT 第 26 条第 5 款第 3 项规定,并根据香港的意愿,香港将被视为缔约方,自本声明之日起生效。中国同时发表相应的声明,确认香港的 GATT 缔约方地位。从法律程序上说,只有英国的声明使香港取得了 GATT 的缔约方地位,中国的声明只是表明中国对上述事实的认可,其意义是向 GATT 各缔约方表明,香港是中国领土的一部分,并承诺 1997 年 7 月 1 日后中国对香港恢复行使主权将不影响香港继续其在 GATT 的缔约方地位。上述声明发表之后,香港成为 GATT 的第 91 个缔约方。香港在 GATT 中已正式与英国分离,香港派驻 GATT 的代表不再隶属于英国代表团,其驻 GATT 的办事处已改为"香港政府经济贸易事务处"。在处理其对外商务关系和事务及履行 GATT 的各项义务方面,香港享有完全的自治权。[2]

《WTO 协定》生效后,根据该协定第 11 条规定,香港基于其本身的权利,即 GATT 缔约方的地位,于 1995 年 1 月 1 日成为 WTO 的创始成员。值得注意的是,由于 1986 年 4 月 23 日香港根据 GATT 第 26 条第 5 款第 3 项成为单独缔约方的原有权利和义务不变,它不是以发展中成员的身份成为 WTO 的创始成员。

[1]　在 GATT 历史上,许多获得独立的国家在殖民地时期就根据 GATT 第 26 条第 5 款第 3 项的规定被视为缔约方,并在独立时不需重新谈判条件而自动继承其 GATT 缔约方的地位。1950 年印度尼西亚是第一个通过此方式成为 GATT 缔约方的国家,其后又有 30 多个国家相继效法。
[2]　参见曹建明主编:《关税与贸易总协定》,法律出版社 1994 年版,第 297—299 页。

　　就法律依据而言，香港之所以能成为 WTO 成员，首先是由于香港作为在对外商务关系活动中具有完全自治权的单独关税区，本身符合 WTO 成员的条件。其次是基于 1984 年《中英联合声明》的规定，即"香港特别行政区将保持自由港和独立关税地区的地位"；"可以'中国香港'的名义单独地同各国、各地区及有关国际组织保持和发展经济、文化关系，并签订有关协议"；"可参加关税和贸易总协定"。[1] 1990 年《中华人民共和国香港特别行政区基本法》进一步重申和明确了上述规定。[2] 由此可见，香港的 WTO 成员资格具有国际法和国内法的双重依据，也是"一国两制"政策的产物。

　　1997 年 7 月 1 日中国对香港恢复行使主权后，香港在 WTO 中正式更名为"中国香港"（Hong Kong，China）。

　　3. 澳门的 GATT 单独缔约方和 WTO 创始成员资格

　　澳门遵循香港模式成为 GATT 单独缔约方。根据 1987 年 4 月 13 日签订的《中华人民共和国政府和葡萄牙共和国政府关于澳门问题的联合声明》，"澳门特别行政区可以'中国澳门'的名义单独同各国、各地区及有关国际组织保持和发展经济、文化关系，并签订有关协定"；"作为自由港和单独关税地区"，"继续参加关税和贸易总协定"。[3] 1991 年 1 月，中、葡两国政府同时向 GATT 秘书处递交声明。葡萄牙政府的声明指出，澳门自 1991 年 1 月 11 日起成为 GATT 的单独缔约方。中国政府的声明则宣布，自 1999 年 12 月 20 日起，澳门特别行政区可以"中国澳门"的名义继续作为 GATT 的单独缔约方。

　　1995 年 1 月 1 日《WTO 协定》生效后，澳门基于其本身的权利成为 WTO 的创始成员。与香港一样，澳门也不是以发展中成员的身份成为 WTO 的创始成员。

　　1999 年 12 月 20 日中国对澳门恢复行使主权后，澳门在 WTO 中正式更名为"中国澳门"（Macao，China）。

　　4. 中国台北的 WTO 纳入成员资格

　　在 1992 年 9 月 29 日至 10 月 1 日的 GATT 代表理事会会议上，成立了 GATT 工作组，审议中国台北根据 GATT1947 第 33 条申请加入的条件。工作组先后于 1992 年 11 月 6 日，1993 年 4 月 15 日、6 月 28 日、10 月 12 日，1994 年 5 月 17 日、7 月 26 日、12 月 21 日召开会议。

---

〔1〕《中英联合声明》第 3(6)、(10) 条、附件 1 第 6 节。
〔2〕《香港特别行政区基本法》第 116、151、152 条。
〔3〕《中葡关于澳门问题的联合声明》第 2(7) 条、附件 1 第 10 节。1993 年《中华人民共和国澳门特别行政区基本法》第 112、136—138 条进一步重申了上述规定。

《WTO 协定》生效后,在中国台北的请求下,[1]根据总理事会 1995 年 1 月 31 日决议,该工作组转变为 WTO 工作组,根据《WTO 协定》第 12 条审查中国台北的"入世"申请,于 1997 年 2 月 28 日、1998 年 5 月 8 日、1999 年 5 月 12 日和 2001 年 9 月 18 日举行会议进行审议。2001 年 9 月 18 日,WTO 完成了中国台北"入世"条件的谈判,[2]11 月 11 日,紧接中国"入世"签署仪式之后,WTO 部长级会议对中国台北的成员资格也给予正式批准。中国台北于 2002 年 1 月 1 日成为 WTO 第 144 个正式成员。[3]

应当指出,中国台北申请加入 GATT 和申请加入 WTO 的法律根据存在重要的区别。前者的依据是 GATT1947 第 33 条。该条规定:"不属本协定缔约方的政府,或代表在处理其对外商务关系和本协定规定的其他事项方面拥有完全自治权的单独关税区的政府,可代表该政府本身或代表该关税区,按该政府与缔约方全体议定的条件加入本协定。缔约方全体在本款下的决定应以三分之二多数作出。"从 GATT 的立法背景看,上述"代表……单独关税区的政府"一般指代表单独关税区的原宗主国政府。[4]而从文义上解释,"代表……单独关税区的政府"除代表单独关税区的原宗主国政府外,也可以指代表单独关税区的本级政府本身。由于中国台北并不符合上述原宗主国政府的资格条件,GATT 工作组只有在认定中国台北是指代表单独关税区的本级政府本身的前提下,才具备受理其申请和进行有关审议工作的法律依据。

中国台北申请加入 WTO 的依据是《WTO 协定》第 12 条。根据该条第 1 款规定,申请者是"任何国家或在处理其对外商务关系及本协定和多边贸易协定规定的其他事务中享有充分自治权的单独关税区"。显然,该规定避免了上述 GATT 第 33 条中"代表……单独关税区的政府"可能导致的解释歧义,明确表明,在 WTO 体制中,以单独关税区身份申请加入者只能是单独关税区本身,不存在由其他任何代表者代为申请的法律依据。

客观事实表明,中国台北从申请加入 GATT 至转为申请加入 WTO 的全过程,均只能是以单独关税区本身的身份,才有法律上的依据。由于《WTO 协定》第 12 条的"国家"与"单独关税区"是并列的两个主体概念,排除了"单独关税区"等于"国家"的可能性。在 WTO 体制中,"单独关税区"可以是隶属于一个主权国家的区域性实

---

〔1〕　文件号 WT/ACC/TPKM/1。

〔2〕　http://www.wto.org/english/news_e/pres01_e/pr244_e.htm

〔3〕　http://www-svca.wto-ministerial.org/english/thewto_e/minist_e/min01_e/min01_11nov_e.htm

〔4〕　有学者基于这一理解认为,"台湾根据总协定第 33 条提出以'单独关税领土'加入总协定,在国际法上是非法之举。"参见曾令良:《世界贸易组织法》,武汉大学出版社 1996 年版,第 68—71 页。

体（如中国香港、中国澳门），但不可能是一个独立的、不归属于任何主权国家的区域性实体。由于国际社会普遍承认"一个中国原则"，在法律和事实上，中国台北与中国香港、中国澳门一样同属于中国，是不言而喻的。

值得注意的是，台湾当局利用加入 WTO 这个所谓"经济联合国"之机，企图拓展所谓"国际生存空间"。为了克服中国台北"入世"的政治敏感性，需要明确坚持的立场和主张主要是：第一，从成员资格看，国际组织可大致区分为仅由主权国家组成的国际组织和由主权国家、非主权实体组成的国际组织两种类型。WTO 不是仅由主权国家组成的国际组织，其成员包括国家、国际组织和单独关税区。中国台北与中国香港、中国澳门一样，是以单独关税区身份成为 WTO 成员的。这实际上与早年在国际奥林匹克委员会中首创的"中国奥林匹克委员会"与"中国台北奥林匹克委员会"模式以及后来在"亚洲开发银行"和"亚太经济合作组织"的类似安排是一致的。无论在法律或事实上，中国台北的"入世"在拓展所谓"国际生存空间"方面并未取得任何形式上或实质性的进展或突破。第二，WTO 是国际经济组织。虽然经济问题与政治问题时有交织，但 WTO 体制和规则的调整对象和适用范围的经济性质还是明确的。当然，对台湾当局利用 WTO 机制将两岸经贸问题"政治化""国际化"的可能及动向须保持应有的警惕。第三，总体上，中国以主权国家资格"入世"，而中国台北与中国香港、中国澳门虽然在取得 WTO 成员资格的时间、依据和方式各不相同，但法律地位完全一致，均是明确以单独关税区身份"入世"，这一客观事实本身已明确反映和更加强化了 WTO 全体成员和国际社会对"一个中国原则"的共识。在实践中，值得密切关注和始终坚持的是，由于中国台北是以单独关税区身份"入世"，其名称和地位在"入世"后绝不容许有任何改变。在其提供给 WTO 及其成员的所有文件中，必须明确冠于 the Separate Customs Territory of Taiwan, Penghu, Kinmen and Matsu (Chinese Taibei)，如为中文，则为"台湾、澎湖、金门、马祖单独关税区"或简称"中国台北"。

WTO 体制"一国四席"的新定位对两岸关系可能发生的突破性发展具有十分重要的意义。长期以来，由于种种原因，两岸的谈判地位问题，特别是中国台湾地区的法律定位成为阻碍两岸关系发展的一大难题。由于中国大陆对"入世"谈判涉及的中国台湾地区"入世"问题采取灵活务实的态度，允许中国台北在中国"入世"后，以单独关税区的身份"入世"。目前，中国台北以"单独关税区"身份作为 WTO 成员的法律地位已经在 WTO 层面上确立，并为 WTO 本身及其全体成员（包括中国、中国香港和中国澳门）所承认和接受。这一新的定位为两岸四地以 WTO 成员身份开展属于 WTO 规则调整范围的经贸关系的谈判奠定了明确的法律基础。

（三）非歧视原则的适用

作为 WTO 体制"一国四席"的法律后果，两岸四地相互之间的经贸关系，两岸四地分别与其他 WTO 成员之间的经贸关系，均须一体适用非歧视原则。这对两岸四地建立更紧密经贸关系的法律模式的选择将产生重要影响。

非歧视原则源于各国主权一律平等的国际法原则，是 WTO 最基本的原则之一，主要由无条件的最惠国待遇原则和国民待遇原则体现。

联合国国际法委员会 1978 年《最惠国条款最后草案》第 5 条对"最惠国待遇"所作的定义是，"给惠国给予受惠国或者与该（受惠）国有确定关系的人或物的优惠，不低于该给惠国给予第三国或者与该第三国有同样关系的人或物的待遇。"第二次世界大战后，GATT 第一次把传统的双边最惠国待遇条款纳入多边贸易体制。最惠国待遇原则主要通过 GATT 第 1 条的最惠国待遇条款体现，即规定任何缔约方对来自或运往其他国家的任何产品所给予的利益、优待、特权或豁免，应当无条件地给予其他缔约方。该条款旨在保证，GATT 所有缔约方的产品作为外国产品，能受到同一缔约方的平等对待。

尽管有支持最惠国待遇原则的政策和法律义务，人们仍普遍认为，在国际贸易中显然有许多偏离最惠国待遇原则的情况。估计国际贸易流动中约有 25％ 是依据偏离最惠国待遇原则的歧视性制度。[1] 出于对现实的接受或妥协，GATT 明文规定的最惠国待遇原则的例外包括祖父条款（第 1 条）、反倾销和反补贴税（第 6 条）、为保障国际收支而实施的限制（第 12 条）、一般例外（第 20 条）、安全例外（第 21 条）和普惠制（第 4 部分）等。隐含的例外有关税联盟和自由贸易区（第 24 条）。此外，在程序上允许援引作例外处理的，有免除义务（第 25 条第 5 款）、按议定条件加入（第 33 条）和一国得不同意对加入国适用总协定（第 35 条）。[2]

作为无条件的最惠国待遇条款的补充，GATT 第 3 条国民待遇条款进一步规定，在征收国内税和有关国内销售、购买、运输、分配所适用的法令法规方面，各缔约方对来自其他缔约方的产品和本国（或本地）产品应一视同仁，由此保证所有缔约方的产品在同一缔约方本国（或本地）市场享有与该方本国（或本地）产品同等的待遇。[3]显然，该规则背后的重要政策是防止利用国内税与管制政策作为保护主义措施。这种措施将使关税约束失去应有作用。应当指出，该义务适用于所有产品，而不只是

---

〔1〕　转引自〔美〕约翰·H.杰克逊：《世界贸易体制——国际经济关系的法律与政策》，张乃根译，复旦大学出版社 2001 年版，第 183 页。

〔2〕　参见赵维田：《世贸组织（WTO）的法律制度》，吉林人民出版社 2000 年版，第 81 页。

〔3〕　参见冯晴：《中国与关贸总协定》，载《北京大学学报》（哲社版）1992 年第 6 期，第 16—17 页。

受约束的产品。因此,该规则有助于实现减少对进口的限制这一基本目标。[1]

对国民待遇原则的适用也有一些例外规定,如 GATT 的"国内税与国内规章的例外"(第 3 条)、"一般例外"(第 20 条)和"安全例外"(第 21 条)等。

非歧视原则原来只适用于货物贸易领域,"乌拉圭回合"的结果使非歧视原则的适用范围进一步扩大,不仅进一步规定于货物贸易领域的《保障措施协定》[第 2(2)条]、《装运前检验协定》(第 2 条)和《技术性贸易壁垒协定》(第 2、5 条),还规定于货物贸易以外新领域的《服务贸易总协定》(第 2、17 条)、《与贸易有关的投资措施协议》(第 2 条)和《与贸易有关的知识产权协定》(第 3、4 条)等。

在未适用非歧视原则例外规定的情况下,作为 WTO 的成员,两岸四地同样需要严格遵循非歧视原则。其后果首先是,根据最惠国待遇原则,两岸四地在 WTO 规则调整范围内相互给予的待遇,应无条件地给予其他成员。

其次,两岸四地相互之间不能对对方的中国国民、产品或服务等适用完全的、不附加例外规定的国民待遇。在国际法上,国民待遇的原义指条约的缔约国一方在本国领域内对缔约国另一方的自然人、法人、商船或产品等给予与本国的自然人、法人、商船或产品等相同的权利或待遇。可见,国民待遇的最关键因素是国籍或国别。据之,由于中国大陆和中国香港、中国澳门、中国台北同属一个主权国家,相互理应对对方的中国国民、产品或服务等适用完全的、不附加例外规定的国民待遇。然而,从 WTO 有关规定看,由于明确规定《WTO 协定》及多边贸易协定中的"country or countries"应理解为包括 WTO 的单独关税区成员方,同属一个主权国家的中国大陆和中国香港、中国澳门、中国台北相互之间的关系与同其他 WTO 成员之间的关系未加区分。换言之,在当前 WTO 体制下,中国大陆和中国香港、中国澳门、中国台北相互对对方的中国国民、产品或服务等适用完全的、不附加例外规定的国民待遇尚无明确的法律根据。

二、自由贸易区:两岸四地更紧密经贸关系的法律模式

在 WTO 体制下,部分成员之间建立更紧密经贸关系与各成员之间一般适用非歧视原则是相互抵触的。该部分成员需要寻求适用非歧视原则的例外,才可能建立符合 WTO 规则的更紧密经贸关系。作为 WTO 成员的中国、中国香港、中国澳门、中国台北尽管同属一个主权国家,在建立更紧密经贸关系的安排中,亦应循此通例,选择符合 WTO 规则和中国国情的法律模式。

---

〔1〕 参见〔美〕约翰·H.杰克逊:《世界贸易体制——国际经济关系的法律与政策》,张乃根译,复旦大学出版社 2001 年版,第 237 页。

（一）区域经济一体化例外

在经济全球化的背景下，以 WTO 规则为主导的多边贸易体制与区域经济一体化体制并行不悖，对各国经济的发展产生了重要的影响。

在历史上，GATT 允许关税同盟和自由贸易区[1]的例外起初是为了迁就英国对其殖民地和英联邦国家的所谓"帝国特惠制"（imperial preferential sysytem）安排。[2] 后来则是考虑到欧洲联盟和北美自由贸易区等区域性国际组织的存在现实和特殊需要。[3] WTO 沿用 GATT 的惯例，允许成员之间关税同盟和自由贸易区的存在。

关税同盟和自由贸易区是区域性经济合作方式，一般属于区域性经济联盟或经济一体化安排。[4] GATT 第 24 条第 8 款分别为关税同盟和自由贸易区作了明确的定义。据之，关税同盟"应理解为一个单一关税领土取代两个或两个以上的关税领土"，以便"对于同盟成员领土之间的实质上所有贸易或至少对于产生于此类领土产品的实质上所有贸易，取消关税和其他限制性贸易法规（如必要，第 11、12、13、14、15 条和第 20 条允许的关税和其他限制性贸易法规除外）"，"同盟各成员对同盟以外领土的贸易实施实质相同的关税或其他贸易法规"；自由贸易区"应理解为在两个或两个以上的关税领土组成的一个关税领土中，对成员领土之间实质上所有有关产自此类领土产品的贸易取消关税和其他限制性贸易法规（如必要，第 11、12、13、14、15 条和第 20 条允许的关税和其他限制性贸易法规除外）"。由此可见，关税同盟与自由贸易区的区别在于：前者对内没有关税，对外有统一的关税制度和关税税境；后者各成员对区内成员的产品取消关税，对区外仍各自保留自己的关税制度和关税税境。显然，前者的经济一体化程度更高。

根据 GATT 第 24 条第 4、5 款规定，各成员认识到通过自愿签署此类协定以发展缔约方之间的更紧密的经济一体化和增加贸易自由的需要；并认识到 GATT 的规定不得阻止在缔约方领土之间形成关税同盟或自由贸易区，或阻止通过形成关税同

---

〔1〕 自由贸易区（Free Trade Area or Free Trade Zone）的概念用于两种场合：（1）区域经济一体化的一种类型。其法律模式主要包括欧盟模式、北美自由贸易区模式和东南亚国家联盟模式等；（2）国内经济性特区。传统的自由贸易区一般有自由港（free port）和中转贸易区（transit zone）两种类型，后来发展为出口加工区（export processing zone）、经济特区（special economic zone）等。可见，自由贸易区并非国际法的专属概念。自由贸易区作为区域经济一体化的一种类型，从发展和动态的角度看，又可能是区域经济一体化进程的一个特定阶段。从国际实践看，区域经济一体化安排包括优惠贸易安排、以导向自由贸易区为目标的临时协议、自由贸易区、关税同盟、共同市场和经济货币联盟。

〔2〕 参见赵维田：《世贸组织（WTO）的法律制度》，吉林人民出版社 2000 年版，第 83 页。

〔3〕 参见朱兆敏：《论入世背景下两岸四地经济一体化的法律问题》，载《中国"入世"后海峡两岸经贸法律新问题研讨会论文集》，2001 年，第 23 页。

〔4〕 参见莫世健：《论世贸组织内的大中国自由贸易区法律框架》，载《中国"入世"后海峡两岸经贸法律新问题研讨会论文集》，2001 年，第 9—14 页。

盟或自由贸易区所必需的临时协定；此类临时协定应包括在一合理持续时间内形成此种关税同盟或自由贸易区的计划和时间表。[1] 有学者将这种导向关税同盟或自由贸易区的临时协定称为区域经济一体化的一种形式或一种层次。[2]

实际上，关税同盟、自由贸易区和导向关税同盟或自由贸易区的临时协定是区域经济一体化安排的不同层次和类型。三者比较，关税同盟是区域经济一体化的最高层次，自由贸易区次之，而导向关税同盟或自由贸易区的临时协定是区域经济一体化的初级层次或阶段。

应当进一步指出，关税同盟和自由贸易区例外的适用受到某些重要限制。首先，在理论上，限于"实质上所有"涉及的贸易都实现自由化的关税同盟或自由贸易区；其次，就关税同盟而言，要求受惠集团针对第三方的"外部"贸易的共同关税安排，"总体上"的限制应少于关税同盟成立前关税的"总负担"和管制。然而，这些法律观念难以适用，在 GATT 内引起了许多争议。此外，GATT 允许缔约方之间签订在"合理时间"建立关税同盟或自由贸易区的临时协定，何谓"合理时间"也不得而知。[3] 《关于解释 1994 年关税与贸易总协定第 24 条的谅解》（以下简称《第 24 条谅解》）对关税同盟和自由贸易区协定予以肯定，[4] 并在一定程度上细化了 GATT 第24 条的规定。

为确保 WTO 成员间的区域经济一体化安排能成为多边贸易体制的补充而不是威胁或损害，GATT 第 24 条和《第 24 条谅解》规定了建立关税同盟、自由贸易区和签订导向关税同盟、自由贸易区的临时协定的原则和规则，主要是：

（1）以促进贸易自由为目标，而不是增加其他成员与此类领土之间的贸易壁垒。[5]

（2）不得对其他成员产生负面影响，即不论是关税同盟、自由贸易区或导向关税同盟、自由贸易区的临时协定的成员，不得对其他成员实施高于或严于形成关税同盟、自由贸易区或临时协定之前的关税和贸易管制，[6] 并且明确规定了评估关税同

---

[1] 《关于解释 1994 年关税与贸易总协定第 24 条的谅解》规定，上述"合理持续时间"一般不超过 10 年。

[2] 参见赵维田：《世贸组织（WTO）的法律制度》，吉林人民出版社 2000 年版，第 84—85 页。

[3] 参见〔美〕约翰·H. 杰克逊：《世界贸易体制——国际经济关系的法律与政策》，张乃根译，复旦大学出版社 2001 年版，第 186—187 页。

[4] 《第 24 条谅解》认为"此类协定参加方的经济更紧密的一体化可对世界贸易的扩大作出贡献"，鼓励将"成员领土之间关税和其他限制性商业法规的取消延伸至所有贸易"，并且"重申此类协定的目的应为便利成员领土之间的贸易，而非提高其他成员与此类领土之间的贸易壁垒；在此类协定形成或扩大时，参加方应在最大限度内避免对其他成员的贸易造成不利影响"。

[5] GATT1947 第 24 条第 4 款。

[6] GATT1947 第 24 条第 5 款(a),(b)。

盟形成前后适用的关税和其他贸易法规的总体影响的方法。[1]

（3）任何导向关税同盟或自由贸易区的临时协定应包括在一合理持续时间内形成关税同盟或自由贸易区的计划和时间表。[2]"合理持续时间"一般不超过 10 年。[3]

（4）必须提供必要的有关信息。[4]应由一工作组按照 GATT1994 的有关规定和《第 24 条谅解》第 1 款的规定进行审议，并将审议结果报告货物贸易理事会。[5]

（5）对于在实施 GATT 第 24 条关于关税同盟、自由贸易区或导致关税同盟或自由贸易区形成的临时协定的过程中产生的任何事项，可诉诸 WTO 争端解决程序。[6]

（二）两岸四地更紧密经贸关系的法律模式选择

两岸四地之间建立更紧密的经贸关系，意味着分别作为 WTO 成员的中国、中国香港、中国澳门、中国台北相互之间的关系应不同于其他一般的 WTO 成员关系。具体而言，一是中国、中国香港、中国澳门、中国台北之间相互给予的某些特殊待遇应能避免其他 WTO 成员援引为例，根据最惠国待遇原则要求享有同等待遇；二是中国、中国香港、中国澳门、中国台北应能相互给予对方的中国国民、产品或服务等以完全的国民待遇，同时又能避免其他 WTO 成员援引为例，根据国民待遇原则要求享有同等待遇。为达到这一目标，只有两个解决途径：一是修改 WTO 规则，规定"一国多席"情况下适用非歧视原则的例外，即规定"同一主权国家的例外"；二是根据 GATT 第 24 条建立关税同盟或自由贸易区，或者签订形成关税同盟或自由贸易区所必需的临时协定。

在法律上，由于修改 WTO 规则，规定"同一主权国家的例外"前景尚难预期，而两岸四地之间建立更紧密经贸关系则时不我待，实际上，第二种途径已成为两岸四地之间建立更紧密经贸关系的现实选择。考虑到中国实行"一国两制"，两岸四地之间政治、经济和法律制度的不同以及经济发展的不平衡，选择自由贸易区模式更适合中国国情。[7] 在 2001 年 11 月第五次东盟与中国领导人会议上，朱镕基总理正式提出了建立中国—东盟自由贸易区的计划。有关专家论证将在 10 年内建成该自由

〔1〕《第 24 条谅解》第 2 款。

〔2〕 GATT1947 第 24 条第 5 款（c）。

〔3〕《第 24 条谅解》第 3 款。

〔4〕 GATT1947 第 24 条第 7 款。

〔5〕《第 24 条谅解》第 7 款。

〔6〕《第 24 条谅解》第 12 款。在"香蕉案"中，这一问题显得很突出。谈判代表期望加强"香蕉案"的两个专家组报告中的观点，即第 24 条可以引用，尽管有的学者认为第 24 条有一些单独的、可适用某些争端的程序。参见〔美〕约翰·H. 杰克逊：《世界贸易体制——国际经济关系的法律与政策》，张乃根译，复旦大学出版社 2001 年版，第 187 页。

〔7〕 朱兆敏：《论入世背景下两岸四地经济一体化的法律问题》，载《中国"入世"后海峡两岸经贸法律新问题研讨会论文集》，2001 年，第 24—25 页。

贸易区。[1] 一个逻辑的结论是，在中国—东盟自由贸易区建成之前，中国内地与中国香港、中国澳门之间或中国大陆与中国香港、中国澳门、中国台湾地区之间建立自由贸易区势在必行。在建立自由贸易区之前，首先是签订形成自由贸易区所必需的临时协定。该临时协定的主要内容须符合 GATT 第 24 条和《第 24 条谅解》的规定。[2]

（三）建立两岸四地自由贸易区的基本步骤

现实问题是，建立两岸四地自由贸易区是一步到位或分两步走？即由中国、中国香港、中国澳门和中国台北一起谈判，或由中国、中国香港和中国澳门先谈，进而再同中国台北谈？这在很大程度上取决于台湾当局的两岸政策取向和实际行动。

台湾当局在 2001 年初提出"统合"的概念，原则上以两岸加入 WTO 的时程作为推动广义"三通"和两岸政策开放的时间点，[3] 希望两岸在 WTO 共同规范下，开展更为广泛的经贸往来与合作。[4] 在 2001 年 3 月 18 日国民党政策研究基金会举行的修订《两岸人民关系条例》座谈会上，前"陆委会"副主委高孔廉指出，由于全球化趋势和两岸即将"入世"的新形势，《两岸人民关系条例》中采取的"原则禁止，例外准许"的立法原则，有必要转变为"原则准许，例外禁止"。[5] 2001 年 3 月 26 日国民党副主席、前"行政院长"萧万长在"两岸共同市场基金会"成立会上指出，两岸藉由经济统合逐步走向政治统合，是一条最可行的和平途径。[6] 亲民党主席宋楚瑜认为可以参考欧盟整合经验，以"三阶段论"处理两岸问题，即从"经济整合"出发，到"社会互动"，最后达到"政治统合"。[7] 民进党大陆事务部主任颜建发也呼吁两岸应先避开政治问题，直接切入经贸谈判。[8] 2001 年 11 月 7 日，台湾地区行政管理机构通过《落实大陆投资"积极开放，有效管理"执行计划》。[9] 台湾媒体也主张，"有关部门宜规划在两岸加入 WTO 后，展开于 WTO 架构下建立两岸直接经贸管道。"[10] 据报道，

---

〔1〕 http://www.xjbs.com.cn/news/xwmb/gn.htm11-08,2001

〔2〕 值得注意的是，实践中的关税同盟或自由贸易区是否 GATT 第 24 条意义上的关税同盟或自由贸易区，常常没有得出结论。法律问题常常被忽视或无结论地搁置，或根据豁免条款予以豁免。虽有大量的关税同盟或自由贸易区协议被 GATT 审议，但极少获得批准。参见郭寿康、韩立余：《国际贸易法》，中国人民大学出版社，2000 年，第 199 页。

〔3〕 参见《蔡英文：两岸政策不会倒退》，载《经济日报》2001 年 7 月 28 日第 7 版。

〔4〕 参见《检讨戒急用忍，列大陆政策重点》，载《联合报》2001 年 2 月 3 日第 4 版。

〔5〕 参见《两岸人民关系条例拟朝更开放修订》，载《经济日报》2001 年 3 月 19 日第 11 版。

〔6〕 参见《萧万长筹组两岸共同市场基金会成立》，载《中国时报》2001 年 3 月 27 日第 1 版。

〔7〕 参见《宋楚瑜：三阶段处理两岸问题》，载《联合报》2001 年 1 月 4 日第 4 版。

〔8〕 参见《颜建发：两岸关系解套应从经贸着手》，载《联合报》2001 年 1 月 21 日第 13 版。

〔9〕 参见《落实大陆投资"积极开放，有效管理"政策说明》，载《两岸经贸》第 119 期，2001 年 11 月号，第 6—11 页。

〔10〕《积极面对实力上升中的中国大陆经济》，载《经济日报》2001 年 7 月 19 日第 2 版。

台湾的官方调查和民间调查显示,当前对台湾民众而言,"一国两制"在经济层面呈现较高的支持率,而政治层面则不易接受。[1]

上述种种迹象表明,在 WTO 框架下,两岸以 WTO 平等成员身份谈判建立两岸自由贸易区存在可能性。在此应当指出,台湾方面提出的所谓"参考欧盟整合经验处理两岸关系"论混淆了两类不同性质的关系,因为欧盟整合的对象是各个主权国家,而处理两岸关系则纯属一国内政。但是,这一以经济入手的"三阶段论"则与中国大陆长期坚持的"以经济文化交流促进实现祖国和平统一"的政策不谋而合,可因势利导。需要明确的是,中国、中国香港、中国澳门和中国台北以 WTO 成员地位谈判建立自由贸易区,是 WTO 成员之间经贸层面的谈判,与两岸政治谈判迥然有别。两岸在 WTO 体制下开展建立自由贸易区的谈判,并不意味着中国大陆在两岸政治谈判中一向坚持"一个中国原则"的立场有任何松动。相反,这一谈判本身是向国际社会宣告,中国经济一体化已经启动,向和平统一的方向迈出了重要一步。实际上,两岸建立自由贸易区的谈判毕竟不可能取代政治层面的谈判。对台湾当局而言,"一个中国原则"终究是回避不了的。

在台湾当局积极回应的情况下,中国、中国香港、中国澳门和中国台北可共同举行有关签订旨在建立两岸自由贸易区的临时协定的谈判。由于两岸四地同时参加,更加凸显了"一国两制"的特色,即实行社会主义制度的中国大陆与实行资本主义制度的香港、澳门和台湾一起商谈,可能创造更理性、务实的谈判氛围。

在台湾当局消极回应的情况下,可考虑先在中国、中国香港、中国澳门之间谈。由于不存在政治层面上的问题,三方有关签订旨在建立自由贸易区的临时协定的谈判可望较顺利进行。事实上,"一国两制"在香港、澳门的成功实施对台湾具有十分重要的影响和示范作用。在经济持续发展的形势下,中国内地与香港、澳门旨在建立更紧密经贸关系的谈判本身将引起台湾产业界和广大民众的极大关注,也势必对台湾当局的有关决策构成巨大的压力。

三、两岸四地自由贸易区临时协定的法律特征

传统国际法认为,主权是缔约权的唯一依据,即只有主权国家才是条约的缔结主体。在不断发展的现代国际实践中,由非主权实体参与缔结国际条约并非罕见。一些实例表明,国际条约的缔结主体除主权国家外,还有国际组织、联邦制国家的成员、交战团体、享有自治权的殖民地和区域性非主权实体。上述非主权实体的缔约权分别来

---

[1]　参见《一国两制经济面较能接受,政治面不易妥协》,载《联合报》2001 年 7 月 18 日第 15 版。

源于国际组织的基本文件、国家宪法、条约法和国际习惯法等。[1] 相应地，一些非主权实体通过缔结国际条约成为国际组织的成员。应强调的是，非主权实体，如中国香港、中国澳门和中国台北参与缔结条约或参加国际组织并不能改变其法律地位。[2]

在法律上，中国是以主权国家的资格"入世"，而中国香港、中国澳门和中国台北是以单独关税区的资格"入世"。作为 WTO 成员，同属一主权国家的国家主体（中国）与非主权实体（中国香港、中国澳门和中国台北）之间签订的形成自由贸易区所必需的临时协定既是符合 GATT 第 24 条的成员之间的协定，实际上又不是国际条约，而是受国际条约规范和调整的一国国内的法律安排。

值得注意的是，符合 GATT 第 24 条的 WTO 成员之间的关税联盟和自由贸易区安排一般都是由两个以上主权国家组成的，属区域性国际组织的经济一体化安排。而同为 WTO 成员的中国、中国香港、中国澳门和中国台北签署的导向自由贸易区的临时协定，在 GATT 和 WTO 体制下的关税同盟或自由贸易区安排中，是一个创举。其实质是一国国内的经济一体化安排，而不是区域性国际组织的经济一体化安排。

---

〔1〕 参见李浩培：《条约法概论》，法律出版社，1988 年，第 240 页。

〔2〕 香港过渡期以来以其名义单独签订一系列双边协定和加入一些国际组织，并未改变其区域性实体的法律地位。参见曾华群：《香港特别行政区高度自治权刍议——对外事务实践的视角》，载《比较法研究》2002 年第 1 期，第 75—91 页。

第二节　论内地与香港 CEPA 之性质[*]

　　【摘要】　本文认为,《内地与香港关于建立更紧密经贸关系的安排》(CEPA)的主体具有双重身份,即在国内体制中,分别是内地关税区与香港单独关税区,而在 WTO 体制中,则分别是 WTO 正式成员;CEPA 的调整对象也具有双重性,即调整一国国内不同关税区之间的经济关系和 WTO 不同成员之间的贸易关系;CEPA 的法律基础主要涉及国内法、国际法有关香港高度自治权的规定与 WTO 区域经济一体化例外规则。作为一主权国家的两个关税区和 WTO 的两个成员,内地与香港签订的 CEPA 既是符合 GATT 第 24 条的 WTO 成员之间的协定,实质上又不是国际条约,而是部分内容受 WTO 规则规范和调整的一国国内的区域经济一体化安排。

　　【关键词】　CEPA;区域经济一体化;WTO 规则

　　近年来,关于两岸四地经济一体化模式的性质、内容及其发展等问题,学界见仁见智。[1] 2003 年 6 月 29 日,中华人民共和国商务部安民副部长与香港特别行政区(以下简称"香港特区")财政司梁锦松司长共同签署了《内地与香港关于建立更紧密经贸关系的安排》(以下简称 CEPA)[2]文本及有关磋商纪要,2004 年 1 月 1 日正式实施,为两岸四地经济一体化模式提供了一个现实的范例。本文从 CEPA 的主体、调整对象及法律基础三个方面对 CEPA 的性质作一初步评论。

一、CEPA 的主体

　　法律文件的主体,即法律文件的制定或缔结主体和履行主体,是判断该法律文件性质的重要标准之一。同样,CEPA 的主体,是考察 CEPA 性质的首要问题。

　　(一)CEPA 的主体是一国国内的两个关税区

　　从 CEPA 文本本身看,正如其名称所指出的,CEPA 的主体一方是内地,代表内地签署者是中华人民共和国商务部副部长,另一方是香港,代表香港签署者是香港特区财政司司长。

---

　　* 原载《厦门大学学报》(哲学社会科学版)2004 年第 6 期。
　　[1] 参见"两岸四地经贸合作的法律问题"专栏文章,载陈安主编:《国际经济法论丛》第 7 卷,法律出版社 2003 年版,第 1—172 页。
　　[2]《内地与香港关于建立更紧密经贸关系的安排》为中文本,"更紧密经贸关系的安排"英文为 Closer Economic Partnership Arrangement,简称 CEPA。在本文中,除另有说明,CEPA 指《内地与香港关于建立更紧密经贸关系的安排》。

CEPA 明确指出，"内地系指中华人民共和国的全部关税领土"。[1] 这里需要强调的是"内地"作为 CEPA 的主体一方的整体性。[2] 所谓"中华人民共和国的全部关税领土"是指"内地全部关税领土"，不包括香港特区关税领土、澳门特别行政区关税领土及台湾、澎湖、金门、马祖单独关税区（简称"中国台北"）[3]。

CEPA 名称的选择经历了谨慎的演变过程，最终是避免使用"自由贸易区"（Free Trade Areas，FTAs）和"协定"（agreement）的概念。[4] 传统上，"自由贸易区"一般用于两个或两个以上国家建立的区域性国际组织的经济一体化安排。[5] 而在国际法上，"协定"一般用于两个或两个以上国家签订的国际法律文件。为避免误解，内地与香港已有的双边法律文件有意采用"安排"（arrangement）用语，由双方代表签署，之后由双方通过颁布适用于本区域的法律文件实施。[6] 1999 年 6 月 21 日，最高人民法院与香港特区政府签署《关于内地与香港特别行政区相互执行仲裁裁决的安排》首创该模式。该安排详细规定了两地法院受理和执行对方仲裁裁决的具体程序，然后由两地分别通过发布司法解释和修改香港《仲裁条例》予以执行。[7] CEPA签署之后，商务部、财政部、工商行政管理总局、建设部、文化部、海关总署等单独或联合颁布了履行 CEPA 的一系列国内行政规章，[8] 表明亦遵循此模式。

---

〔1〕 参见《内地与香港关于建立更紧密经贸关系的安排》，注 1。

〔2〕 在讨论建立内地与香港之间自由贸易区或更紧密经贸关系时，内地方面曾有种种方案，包括"粤港自由贸易区方案""深港自由贸易区方案"等。参见张宪初：《香港内地更紧密经贸关系安排的法律基础和难点》，载张宪初主编：《世贸规则与两岸四地经贸法律关系》，商务印书馆 2003 年版，第 103 页。

〔3〕 英文为 the Separate Customs Territory of Taiwan，Penghu，Kinmen 和 Matsu（Chinese Taipei）。对于 Chinese Taipei，中国台湾地区学者一般译为"中华台北"。

〔4〕 参见张宪初：《香港内地更紧密经贸关系安排的法律基础和难点》，载张宪初：《世贸规则与两岸四地经贸法律关系》，商务印书馆 2003 年版，第 87—90 页。

〔5〕 有学者指出，无论是一般国际法，还是 WTO 法律，并未规定自由贸易区只能在主权国家之间建立，两岸四地建立的自由贸易区关系可考虑直述其名。参见曾令良：《论 WTO 体制下区域贸易安排的法律地位与发展趋势——兼论中国两岸四地建立自由贸易区的几个法律问题》，《国际经济法论丛》第 7 卷，法律出版社 2003 年版，第 13—14 页。

〔6〕 See Kong Qingjiang，Closer Economic Partnership Agreement between China and Hong Kong，*China—An International Journal*，Vol. 1，No. 1，2003，pp. 134-135.

〔7〕 2000 年 1 月 13 日颁布的香港特区《仲裁（修订）条例》采用了"内地"和"内地裁决"的概念，增加了第 IIIA 部"内地裁决的强制执行"，明确规定了对内地裁决的强制执行问题。2000 年 1 月 24 日，内地最高人民法院以法释（2000）3 号司法解释公布《安排》，自 2000 年 2 月 1 日实施。参见高莎薇：《内地与香港特别行政区相互执行对方仲裁裁决有章可循》，载《中国法律》1999 年 10 月号，第 18—20 页。

〔8〕 在这些国内行政规章中，有的采用专门性行政规章。例如：《〈港、澳、台地区会计师事务所来内地临时执行审计业务的暂行规定〉补充规定》（财政部 2003 年 11 月 26 日印发，自 2004 年 1 月 1 日起施行）《中华人民共和国海关关于执行〈内地与香港关于建立更紧密经贸关系的安排〉项下〈关于货物贸易的原产地规则〉的规定》（署务会 2003 年 12 月 24 日审议通过，自 2004 年 1 月 1 日起施行）。有的采用涉外经济法的"补充规定"或"附件"形式。例如：《关于〈外籍中国注册会计师注册审批暂行办法〉的补充规定》（财政部 2003 年 11 月 27 日印发，自 2004 年 1 月 1 日起施行）；《〈关于设立中外合资对外贸易公司暂行办法〉补充规定》（商务部 2003 年 12 月 7 日颁布，自 2004 年 1 月 1 日起施行）；《中外合作音像制品分销企业管理办法》（文化部、商务部 2003 年 12 月 8 日发布，自 2004 年 1 月 1 日起施行）；《〈外商投资城市规划服务企业管理规定〉的补充规定》（建设部第 24 次常务会议和商务部部务会议 2003 年 12 月 9 日审议通过，自 2004 年 1 月 1 日起施行）；《〈外商投资建设工程设计企业管理规定〉的补充规定》（建设部第 24 次常务会议和商务部部务会议 2003 年 12 月 9 日审议通过，自 2004 年 1 月 1 日起施行）；《关于〈外商投资道路运输业管理规定〉的补充规定》（交通部、商务部 2003 年 12 月 31 日颁布，自 2004 年 1 月 1 日起施行）；《外商投资广告企业管理规定》（国家工商行政管理总局、商务部 2004 年 3 月 2 日公布生效）；《外商投资商业领域管理办法》（商务部 2004 年 4 月 16 日颁布，自 2004 年 6 月 1 日起施行）。

CEPA 签署方的名称同样反映了起草者力求将该法律文件区别于"协定"的匠心。在内地方面,签署方是"中华人民共和国商务部副部长",而不是"中华人民共和国";在香港方面,签署方是"中华人民共和国香港特别行政区财政司司长",而不是香港在 WTO 中的正式名称"中国香港"(Hong Kong, China)。显然,CEPA 签署方的名称更为直观地反映 CEPA 是一国不同行政机构代表不同关税区签署的文件。

笔者以为,考察 CEPA 性质的关键问题并不在于"自由贸易区"或"更紧密经贸关系""协定"或"安排"用语的选择,[1]而是在于,根据"条约是国家间所缔结而以国际法为准之国际书面协定"这一最基本的定义,[2]同一主权国家内的两个行政机构签订的文件,无论如何均不具有"国际"或"国家间"(inter-nations)因素,因而也就根本谈不上是国际条约或准国际条约。

需要进一步指出,香港的缔约主体资格与 CEPA 的性质无关。传统国际法认为,主权是缔约权的唯一依据,即只有主权国家才是条约的缔结主体。在不断发展的现代国际实践中,由非主权实体参与缔结国际条约并非罕见。一些实例表明,国际条约的缔结主体除主权国家外,还有国际组织、联邦制国家的成员、交战团体、享有自治权的殖民地和区域性非主权实体。上述非主权实体的缔约权分别来源于国际组织的基本文件、国家宪法、条约法和国际习惯法等。[3] 值得注意的是,尽管缔约主体范围有了明显扩大,国际条约仍必须具有"国际"因素,必须是由不同主权国家之间、隶属于不同主权国家的非主权实体之间或一主权国家与另一主权国家的非主权实体之间缔结的协定。换言之,隶属于同一主权国家的非主权实体之间或一主权国家与隶属于该主权国家的非主权实体之间的协定无论如何不能成其为国际条约。对于香港而言,作为中国的非主权实体,它与外国之间或与外国非主权实体之间缔结的协定属于国际条约,而它与中国国家主体之间或中国其他非主权实体之间缔结的协定则不属国际条约,而是一国国内的区际协定。

(二) CEPA 的主体同时也是 WTO 体制下的两个正式成员

尽管 CEPA 的主体在形式上不同于 WTO 体制下的"中华人民共和国"和"中国香港"两个正式成员,由于"内地系指中华人民共和国的全部关税领土",而香港则指香港特区,CEPA 的主体双方实际上代表的也是 WTO 体制下的两个正式成员。因

---

〔1〕　实际上,"更紧密经贸关系""安排"也用于国际条约,如澳大利亚与新西兰之间的区域经济一体化协定称为"更紧密经贸关系协定"(Closer Economic Relations Agreement),2004 年 1 月 1 日正式实施的《中国与巴基斯坦优惠贸易安排》也采用"安排"这一用语。

〔2〕　1969 年《维也纳条约法公约》第 2 条第 1 款(甲)项规定:"称'条约'者,谓国家间所缔结而以国际法为准之国际书面协定,不论其载于一项单独文书或两项以上相互有关之文书内,亦不论其特定名称为何"。

〔3〕　参见李浩培:《条约法概论》,法律出版社 1988 年版,第 240 页。

此，进一步的问题是，由于 WTO 是国际组织，其成员之间的协定是否当然是国际协定？

答案是否定的。可从以下三方面分析：

第一，WTO 的成员资格是以关税区、而不是以主权国家为适格条件。根据 1947 年《关税及贸易总协定》（GATT1947）第 26、32、33 条规定，主权国家并不是 GATT 缔约方资格的必要条件。任何实体，不论是否主权国家，只要构成一个关税区，均可按一定程序成为 GATT 的缔约方；相反，即使是一个独立的主权国家，如未形成一个关税区，也不可能成为 GATT 的缔约方。GATT 有关条文均把关税区作为成员资格的先决条件。《建立世界贸易组织协定》（以下简称《WTO 协定》）沿袭了 GATT1947 有关成员资格的规定。第 11 条第 1 款规定了创始成员（original members）的资格，即："本协定生效之日的 GATT1947 缔约方和欧洲共同体，如接受本协定和多边贸易协定，并将减让和承诺表附于 GATT1994，将具体承诺减让表附于 GATS，应成为 WTO 的创始成员。"[1]第 12 条第 1 款规定了纳入成员（members by accession）的资格和程序："任何国家或在处理其对外商业关系及本协定和多边贸易协定规定的其他事务中享有充分自治权的单独关税区（separate customs territory），可按它与 WTO 议定的条件加入本协定。此加入适用于本协定及所附多边贸易协定。"可见，WTO 成员资格的特征之一是继续采用"单独关税区"的概念。这一概念可溯及战后的特定情况，即存在宗主国与附属领土，而适用于附属领土的关税制度可能与宗主国不同。在 GATT 体制中，"单独关税区"最初是指适用不同于宗主国的关税制度的附属领土。由于战后以来国际政治经济形势的发展和深刻演变，在 WTO 体制中，"单独关税区"具有更准确的法律和经济内涵，一般与殖民主义制度无关。[2]

第二，以关税区为 WTO 成员的适格条件产生了"一国多席"。由于 WTO 成员资格向主权国家和非主权的单独关税区开放，一个主权国家与隶属于该主权国家的一个或数个单独关税区分别加入 WTO，或者在一个主权国家未加入 WTO 的情况下，隶属于该主权国家的数个单独关税区分别加入 WTO，都可能形成 WTO 体制的"一国多席"局面。2001 年 12 月 11 日和 2002 年 1 月 1 日，中华人民共和国与中国台

---

　　〔1〕　根据部长级会议《关于世界贸易组织协定的接受与加入的决议》规定，所有符合创始成员条件者须在《WTO 协定》生效后两年之内批准。截至 1997 年 3 月 27 日，131 个 GATT 缔约方均成为 WTO 成员。See John Croome, *Guide to the Uruguay Round Agreements*, Kluwer Law International, 1999, p. 12, note 43.
　　〔2〕　为了将"单独关税区"的法律概念纳入整个 WTO 多边贸易规则中，《WTO 协定》的"解释性说明"特别指出，"本协定和多边贸易协定中使用的'country or countries'应理解为包括任何 WTO 单独关税区成员。对于 WTO 单独关税区成员，除非另有规定，如本协定和多边贸易协定中用'national'一词表述，该表述也应理解为是指单独关税区。"参见赵维田：《世贸组织（WTO）的法律制度》，吉林人民出版社 2000 年版，第 42—44 页。

北先后成为 WTO 正式成员,连同于 1995 年 1 月 1 日分别成为 WTO 创始成员的香港和澳门,在 WTO 体制中出现了前所未有的"一国四席"局面。[1]

第三,WTO 体制的"一国多席"意味着 WTO 成员之间协定并不当然是国际条约。由于 WTO 体制"一国多席"的存在,WTO 成员之间的协定依其主体不同可分为两类:第一类是不同主权国家成员之间、一主权国家成员与隶属另一主权国家的单独关税区成员之间或隶属不同主权国家的单独关税区成员之间的协定,属国际条约;第二类是一主权国家成员与隶属于该主权国家的一个或一个以上单独关税区成员之间的协定或同属一主权国家的两个或两个以上单独关税区成员之间的协定,由于缺乏"国际"因素,显然不属国际条约。CEPA 属于第二类。

二、CEPA 的调整对象

法律文件的调整对象,也是判断该法律文件性质的重要标准。CEPA 的调整对象是内地与香港之间的经济关系。由于主体的双重身份,CEPA 的调整对象也具有双重性。

（一）CEPA 调整一国国内不同关税区之间的经济关系

CEPA 所调整的一国国内不同关税区之间的经济关系,实际上是一国国内的区域经济一体化安排。

为明确 CEPA 调整对象这一层面的特点,首先,需要区分 WTO 规则的调整对象与区域经济一体化规则的调整对象。两者绝非一致或重合。其主要原因如下:一是从体制上看,WTO 体制与区域经济一体化体制是并行发展的,两者并无相互隶属的关系。二是从调整对象看,WTO 是贸易组织,调整其成员之间的贸易关系,而区域经济一体化组织调整成员之间包含贸易的经济关系。虽然乌拉圭回合之后,WTO 规则调整的领域不断扩大,但毕竟无法涵盖成员之间的所有经济关系。实际上,区域经济一体化安排往往超出 WTO 规则调整的范围。[2] 三是从成员看,区域经济一体化组织成员不一定是 WTO 成员,两者并无存在作为前提的成员关系。[3] 四是从历史上看,许多区域经济一体化组织先于 GATT/WTO 而存在。GATT/WTO 有关区域经济一体化安排的规则,在很大程度上,是对既有现实的承认或妥协。可见,对WTO 成员来说,区域经济一体化安排并非必须根据 WTO 规则签订,也并非局限于

---

〔1〕　参见曾华群:《略论 WTO 体制的"一国四席"》,载《厦门大学学报(哲社版)》2002 年第 5 期,第 5—14 页。

〔2〕　如欧洲联盟(EU)向经济和货币联盟的发展,东南亚国家联盟(ASEAN)、北美自由贸易区(NAFTA)制定的投资规范等。

〔3〕　如申请加入国际复兴开发银行者须以具备国际货币基金组织成员资格为前提条件。

WTO 规则的调整范围，而是其相关内容应符合 WTO 规则。

其次，需要区分传统区域经济一体化规则的调整对象与 CEPA 的调整对象。传统区域经济一体化规则是调整同一区域两个或两个以上主权国家之间的经济关系，而 CEPA 则调整一国国内不同关税区之间的经济关系。由于调整对象不同，前者主要适用或涉及国际法，而后者则主要适用或涉及国内法。

最后，需要区分 WTO 规则调整范围"之内"与调整范围"之外"。毋庸质疑，在 WTO 规则调整范围之内，各成员应严格遵循规则，履行承诺。另外，由于各成员的履约责任以其承担的 WTO 义务为限，在 WTO 规则调整范围之外，各成员可通过双边或区域性多边安排，调整相互之间的经济关系。内地与香港之间经济关系中不属 WTO 规则调整者，是纯粹的一国国内不同关税区之间的经济关系，可不受 WTO 规则或其他国际法规范的约束。作为新型的一国国内的区域经济一体化安排，CEPA 所调整的内地与香港之间的经济关系完全可以超出 WTO 规则调整的范围。实际上，CEPA 第五章"贸易投资便利化"已超出 WTO 规则调整的范围。这种安排并不是为了摆脱 WTO 规则的调整，而是区域经济一体化安排的通常实践。

（二）CEPA 调整 WTO 不同成员之间的贸易关系

由于中华人民共和国与中国香港双方分别是 WTO 正式成员，CEPA 调整的对象同时是 WTO 两个成员之间的贸易关系。需要明确的是，CEPA 调整的 WTO 两个成员之间的贸易关系须以 WTO 规则调整的范围为限。

在 WTO 体制下，中华人民共和国与中国香港之间的贸易关系，从法律和事实两个方面看，具有不同的意义。在法律上，中华人民共和国是根据《WTO 协定》第 12 条规定，以主权国家的资格成为 WTO 纳入成员，而中国香港是以单独关税区的资格成为 WTO 创始成员。鉴此，同样作为 WTO 成员，中华人民共和国与中国香港之间的贸易关系应视为中国国家主体与单独关税区之间的贸易关系。另外，从中国长达 15 年的"复关"和"入世"谈判过程、坚持的立场以及所作的承诺看，事实上，作为 WTO 成员的中华人民共和国目前是指内地，不包括单独关税区。相对于香港单独关税区，内地本身也是一个关税区。在这个意义上，同样作为 WTO 成员，中华人民共和国与中国香港之间的贸易关系，也可视为中国两个不同关税区相互之间的贸易关系。

强调 CEPA 调整 WTO 两个成员之间的贸易关系，其重要意义首先在于，就整体而言，CEPA 不仅受中国法律的规范和调整，也受 WTO 规则规范和调整。这意味着 CEPA 的规定不可违反 WTO 规则，CEPA 中涉及 WTO 规则的概念、条款（如"关税配额""保障措施""原产地规则"等）的解释和适用可能有赖于 WTO 规则的解释和有关实践。其次,在 WTO 体制下,同样作为 WTO 成员,中华人民共和国与中国香港之间的法律关系是平等的。这意味着涉及 WTO 规则的 CEPA 条款的谈判、起草、修订和发展,需要双方通过平等协商达成。最后,同样作为 WTO 成员,中华人民共和国、中国香港与其他成员之间的法律关系也是平等的。在 CEPA 的签订和履行中,内地和香港无论单独或共同违反 WTO 规则,WTO 其他成员均可通过 WTO 贸易审查机制或争端解决机制追究违反方的法律责任。

三、CEPA 的法律基础

法律文件的法律基础,即法律文件赖以形成的法律根据,也是判断该法律文件性质的重要尺度。关于 CEPA 的法律基础,需要重点解决的问题是:在国内法和国际法层面,作为 CEPA 主体的香港特区具有何种特殊法律地位?在国际法层面,CEPA 有关区域经济一体化的内容是否符合 WTO 规则?

(一)关于香港特区高度自治权的法律规定

CEPA 第 2 条明确规定,"遵循'一国两制'的方针"是其达成、实施与修正应遵照的原则。该规定揭示了香港特区享有特殊法律地位的政策和法律依据。

《中华人民共和国宪法》(以下简称《宪法》)第 31 条规定:"国家在必要时得设立特别行政区。在特别行政区内实行的制度按照具体情况由全国人民代表大会以法律规定。"《宪法》作为国家的根本大法,是中国国际条约实践和国内立法的基础和根据。

在国际条约实践方面,中国以《宪法》第 31 条为依据,谈判和签署了《中英关于香港问题的联合声明》(以下简称《联合声明》),决定设立香港特区,并作出一系列关于香港特区高度自治权的政策声明和国际承诺。[1]关于香港特区与中央人民政府之间的关系,《联合声明》确立的原则是,外交事务和国防属于中央人民政府的权力范围,同时,授权香港特区在某些领域从事对外事务。因此,"外交事务"与"对外事务"的区别值得注意。前者主要指涉及国家主权的政治事务,后者主要指经济和文化等领域的事务。[2]香港特区自治权的各个主要方面分别由《联合声明》附件一《中华人民共和国对香港的基本方针政策的具体说明》第三节(法院与司法)、第六节(经济与商业事务)、第八节(航运)、第九节(民用航空)、第十一节(对外关系)和第十四节(旅行

---

　〔1〕　参见《中英关于香港问题的联合声明》,第 3 条第 1 款,附件一第 1 条。

　〔2〕　See Yash Ghai, *Hong Kong's New Constitutional Order*, *The Resumption of Chinese Sovereign and the Basic Law*, Hong Kong University Press, 1997, p. 433.

与移民事务）等确立与调整。[1] 此外，附件一第二节规定，1997 年之后香港原有法律基本不变，所谓"原有法律"也包含了涉及国际实践的法律制度。

在国内立法方面，1990 年 4 月 4 日颁布的《中华人民共和国香港特别行政区基本法》（以下简称《基本法》）在序言中重申了设立香港特区的宪法根据，并进一步对香港特区享有的自治权范围作了具体明确的规定。

显然，《联合声明》和《基本法》赋予香港特区高度的自治权。特别是，这种自治权由《联合声明》和《基本法》分别在国际法和国内法层面上承诺和确立，属于法律上（de jure）自治权。中央人民政府实际保留的"仅仅是特别行政区因其不是国家而不能以'中国香港'名义进行的跨国或对外关系的那部分权力"。[2] 然而，应当指出，无论香港特区的高度自治权范围如何广泛，均来自中央人民政府的授权，真正的主权和最终权力仍保留在中央人民政府。[3]

香港特区之所以能成为 WTO 成员，首先是由于香港特区作为在对外商务关系活动中具有完全自治权的单独关税区，本身符合 WTO 成员的条件。其次是基于《联合声明》附件一第六、十一节的规定，即"香港特别行政区将保持自由港地位"，"可参加关税和贸易总协定"；"可以'中国香港'的名义，在经济、贸易、金融、航运、通讯、旅游、文化、体育等单独地同世界各国、各地区及有关国际组织保持和发展关系，并签订和履行有关协议"。《基本法》第 116、151、152 条进一步重申和明确了上述规定。

由此可见，根据"一国两制"方针，香港特区享有高度自治权，在中国宪政体系中具有特殊的法律地位，同时，也具有作为 WTO 成员的必要条件和法律依据。显然，香港特区作为 CEPA 的主体一方，无论是作为国内体制下与内地关税区对应的单独关税区，还是作为 WTO 体制下的两个成员之一，均具有充分的国内法和国际法依据。

（二）WTO 区域经济一体化例外规则

CEPA 第 2 条明确规定，其达成、实施与修正应遵照的另一原则是"符合世界贸易组织的规则"。

内地与香港之间建立更紧密经贸关系，虽然是一个主权国家不同关税区之间的经贸安排，但由于这种"更紧密经贸关系"客观上是与其他 WTO 成员比较而言的，必

---

[1] See Albert H. Y. Chen, The Relationship Between the Central Government and the SAR, in Peter Wesley-Smith & Albert H. Y. Chen (eds.), *The Basic Law and Hong Kong's Future*, Butterworths, 1988, pp. 114-115.

[2] See Roda Mushkat, The Transition from British to Chinese Rule in Hong Kong: A Discussion of Salient International Legal Issues, *Denver Journal of International Law & Policy*, Vol. 14, 1986, p. 188.

[3] See Marius Olivier, Hong Kong: An Exercise in Autonomy, *South African Yearbook of International Law*, Vol. 18, 1992-93, pp. 87-88.

须符合 WTO 规则,不可能游离于 WTO 体制之外。这在中国《加入议定书》已有明确的承诺。该文件第 4 条规定:"自加入时起,中国应取消与第三国和单独关税区之间的、与《WTO 协定》不符的所有特殊贸易安排,包括易货贸易安排,或使其符合《WTO 协定》。"

在 WTO 体制下,某些成员之间建立更紧密经贸关系与成员之间非歧视待遇原则的一般实施是抵触的。因此,有关成员需要寻求适用非歧视待遇原则的例外,才可能建立符合 WTO 规则的相互间的更紧密经贸关系。内地与香港尽管同属一个主权国家,作为 WTO 成员,在建立双方更紧密经贸关系的安排中,亦应循此通例。

由于 GATT 的规定"不得阻止在缔约方领土之间形成关税同盟或自由贸易区,或阻止通过形成关税同盟和自由贸易区所必需的临时协定",区域经济一体化安排的主要形式关税同盟和自由贸易区被视为适用非歧视原则的一个例外。该例外的适用必须符合两个基本条件:一是对组成地区之间的"实质上所有贸易"取消贸易限制;二是关税同盟或自由贸易区的关税率不得高于组成之前各组成地区适用的平均水平。[1] 乌拉圭回合进一步发展了 GATT 的区域经济一体化规则。《服务贸易总协定》(General Agreement on Trade in Services,GATS)第 5 条规定与 GATT 第 24 条规定的原则基本一致,采用"经济一体化"概念,明确规定,"本协定不得阻止任何成员参加或达成在参加方之间实现服务贸易自由化的协定"。据此,WTO 体制允许的区域经济一体化安排涵盖的领域扩及服务贸易。《关于解释 1994 年关税与贸易总协定第 24 条的谅解》(以下简称《第 24 条谅解》)对关税同盟和自由贸易区协定予以肯定。[2]

根据 GATT 第 24 条第 8 款,关税同盟与自由贸易区两者的关键区别在于,关税同盟成员对同盟以外领土的贸易须实施实质相同的关税或其他贸易法规,而自由贸易区成员则无此要求。显然,前者的经济一体化程度更高。此外,根据 GATT 第 24 条第 4、5 款规定,允许各成员之间签订形成关税同盟或自由贸易区所必需的临时协定。实际上,关税同盟、自由贸易区和导向关税同盟或自由贸易区的临时协定是区域经济一体化安排的不同层次和类型。关税同盟是区域经济一体化安排的最高层次,自由贸易区次之,而导向关税同盟或自由贸易区的临时协定是区域经济一体化

---

〔1〕　See Michael J. Trebilcock & Robert Howse, *The Regulation of International Trade*, 2nd edition, Routledge, 1999, pp. 115-116.

〔2〕　《第 24 条谅解》认为"此类协定参加方的经济更紧密的一体化可对世界贸易的扩大作出贡献",鼓励将"成员领土之间关税和其他限制性商业法规的取消延伸至所有贸易",并且"重申此类协定的目的应为便利成员领土之间的贸易,而非提高其他成员与此类领土之间的贸易壁垒;在此类协定形成或扩大时,参加方应在最大限度内避免对其他成员的贸易造成不利影响"。

安排的初级层次或阶段。

为确保 WTO 成员间的区域经济一体化安排能成为多边贸易体制的补充而不是威胁或损害，根据 GATT 第 24 条和《第 24 条谅解》的规定，建立关税同盟、自由贸易区和签订导向关税同盟、自由贸易区的临时协定必须遵循的原则和规则主要是：

(1) 以促进贸易自由为目标，而不是增加其他成员与此类领土之间的贸易壁垒（GATT1947 第 24 条第 4 款）；

(2) 不得对其他成员产生负面影响，即不论是关税同盟、自由贸易区或导向关税同盟、自由贸易区的临时协定的成员，不得对其他成员实施高于或严于形成关税同盟、自由贸易区或临时协定之前的关税和贸易管制[GATT1947 第 24 条第 5 款(a)，(b)]，并且明确规定了评估关税同盟形成前后适用的关税和其他贸易法规的总体影响的方法（《第 24 条谅解》第 2 款）；

(3) 任何导向关税同盟或自由贸易区的临时协定应包括在一合理持续时间内形成关税同盟或自由贸易区的计划和时间表[GATT1947 第 24 条第 5 款(c)]。"合理持续时间"一般不超过 10 年（《第 24 条谅解》第 3 款）；

(4) 必须提供必要的有关信息（GATT1947 第 24 条第 7 款）。应由一工作组按照 GATT1994 的有关规定和《第 24 条谅解》第 1 款的规定进行审议，并将审议结果报告货物贸易理事会（《第 24 条谅解》第 7 款）；

(5) 对于在实施 GATT 第 24 条关于关税同盟、自由贸易区或导向关税同盟或自由贸易区的临时协定的过程中产生的任何事项，可诉诸 WTO 争端解决程序（《第 24 条谅解》第 12 款）。

实践表明，尽管仍存在某些缺失，WTO 对区域经济一体化安排的事前审查、事后监督和争端解决机制已实际运作。[1]

CEPA 第 1 条明确规定其目标是，通过采取"逐步减少或取消双方之间实质上所有货物贸易的关税和非关税壁垒"，"逐步实现服务贸易的自由化，减少或取消双方之间实质上所有歧视性措施"，"促进贸易投资便利化"等措施，加强内地与香港之间贸易和投资合作，促进双方的共同发展。CEPA 还包括双方对货物贸易和服务贸易自由化的具体承诺。其 6 个附件分别是内地对原产香港的进口货物实行零关税安排、适用于 CEPA 的原产地规则、原产地证签发程序和合作监管机制、内地与香港相互开放服务贸易领域的具体承诺、"服务提供者"定义及相关规定、贸易投资便利化措施。从 CEPA 的签订背景、主要内容和发展趋向看，基本符合 GATT 第 24 条、

---

〔1〕 参见钟立国：《WTO 对区域贸易协定的规制及其完善》，载《法学家》2003 年第 4 期。

GATS 第 5 条和《第 24 条谅解》的规定，可视为内地与香港形成自由贸易区所必需的临时协定。换言之，GATT 第 24 条、GATS 第 5 条和《第 24 条谅解》的规定是 CEPA 得以产生和发展的 WTO 规则基础。

四、结语

综上所述，CEPA 的主体具有双重身份，即在国内体制中，分别是内地关税区与香港单独关税区，而在 WTO 体制中，则分别是 WTO 正式成员。CEPA 的调整对象也具有双重性，即调整一国国内不同关税区之间的经济关系和 WTO 不同成员之间的贸易关系。CEPA 的法律基础主要涉及国内法、国际法有关香港特区高度自治权的规定与 WTO 区域经济一体化例外规则。主体、调整对象和法律基础的双重性决定了 CEPA 的双重性质。作为一主权国家的两个关税区和 WTO 的两个正式成员，内地与香港签订的 CEPA 既是符合 GATT 第 24 条的 WTO 成员之间的协定，实质上又不是国际条约，而是部分内容受 WTO 规则规范和调整的一国国内的特殊法律安排，即中华人民共和国内地关税区与中华人民共和国单独关税区[1]之间的区域经济一体化安排。

在认清 CEPA 性质的基础上，笔者以为，在实践中需要进一步明确：

第一，CEPA 是区域经济一体化中自成一类的新模式，将发展成为两岸四地区域经济一体化的重要模式。[2]由于一个主权国家成员与属于该主权国家的单独关税区成员之间在 WTO 框架下建立更紧密经贸关系安排是史无前例的，CEPA 本身的内容、发展趋向及其与 WTO 规则之间的关系必然具有独创性，亟须内地和香港的政府主管机构、经贸实务界、学术界进一步加强沟通和合作，在实践中不断研究、开拓和创新。

第二，鉴于 CEPA 调整对象的双重性，应当强调"WTO 规则调整范围内外有别"的概念。在 WTO 规则调整范围之内，CEPA 的相关规定应符合 WTO 规则，特别是非歧视原则，不能因主体、调整对象和法律基础的双重性而主张其特殊性。而在 WTO 规则调整范围之外，CEPA 则不受 WTO 规则约束，内地与香港双方完全可依据主权原则和"一国两制"方针，考虑国家的整体利益，作出有利于一方或双方发展的法律安排。在这方面，可自主拓展的空间很大，特别是投资自由化、争端解决机制

---

〔1〕《中华人民共和国对外贸易法》（2004 年修订）明确采用"中华人民共和国的单独关税区"的概念。该法第 69 条规定："中华人民共和国的单独关税区不适用本法。"

〔2〕 2004 年 1 月 1 日，《内地与澳门特别行政区关于建立更紧密经贸关系安排》也正式实施。台湾各界亦高度关注内地与香港、澳门之间的区域经济一体化安排。参见罗昌发：《自由贸易区协定对台湾与大陆、香港关系之意涵》，载张宪初主编：《世贸规则与两岸四地经贸法律关系》，商务印书馆 2003 年版，第 40—63 页。

等安排。就此意义而言，CEPA 是部分内容受 WTO 规则规范和调整的一国国内的区域经济一体化安排。

第三，鉴于 CEPA 是自成一类的国内特殊法律安排，为履行 CEPA 的配套立法、文告或其他细节安排应自成体系。由于 CEPA 不是国际条约，履行 CEPA 的配套立法、文告不宜与履行国际条约的配套立法、文告混淆。[1] 由于香港、澳门分别于 1997 年和 1999 年回归祖国，为履行 CEPA 的配套立法似应单独立法，不宜以涉外经济法的"补充规定"或"附件"形式实施。由于内地与香港、澳门之间 CEPA 自 2004 年 1 月 1 日起生效，而内地与台湾之间迄今尚未启动 CEPA 谈判，因此，为履行 CEPA 的配套立法的调整范围目前应限于内地与香港、澳门之间的经济关系。[2]

On the Nature of CEPA between Mainland of China and Hong Kong

Abstract：The subjects of Closer Economic Partnership Arrangement between Mainland of China and Hong Kong（CEPA）have dual status，ie the mainland customs territory and Hong Kong separate customs territory in the domestic regime and two full members in the WTO regime. The objects of the CEPA also have dual nature，ie the economic relationships between the two customs territories in the same country and the trade relationships between the two WTO members. The legal grounds for the CEPA involve relevant provisions in Chinese domestic laws，international laws，and the WTO rules on regional economic integration exceptions. The CEPA concluded by mainland of China and Hong Kong in the status of the two customs territories in a sovereignty State and the two WTO members，is an agreement between the two WTO members in conformity with article 24 of GATT but essentially not a treaty. It is an arrangement for domestic regional economic integration with its partial contents regulated by the WTO rules.

Key words：CEPA，regional economic integration，WTO rules

---

[1] 2003 年 12 月 29 日发布的中华人民共和国海关总署公告（2003 年第 78 号）将内地与香港 CEPA、内地与澳门 CEPA 同《中国—东盟全面经济合作框架协议》《中泰蔬菜水果协议》《中国向老挝、柬埔寨、缅甸提供特殊优惠关税待遇的换文》等相提并论，似不妥。
[2] 例如，根据《外商投资商业领域管理办法》第 25 条，为履行内地与香港、澳门之间 CEPA，香港、澳门商业服务提供者享有优于台湾商业服务提供者的待遇。

第三节 ECFA：“两岸特色”的区域贸易协定实践 *

【摘要】《海峡两岸经济合作框架协定》（ECFA）是区域贸易协定（regional trade agreement，RTA）实践和两岸经济合作机制的重要发展。ECFA 在名称、主体、调整对象、基本原则、执行机制等方面显示鲜明的“两岸特色”，不仅不同于一般的主权国家之间的 RTA 实践，也不同于中国 RTA 实践特殊形式中的内地与香港、澳门之间的 CEPAs。ECFA 对实现两岸经济合作关系的正常化、法制化具有重要的里程碑意义，其对中国台北 RTA 实践发展可能具有的法律意义也值得关注和研讨。

【关键词】 ECFA；区域贸易协定；两岸经济合作

《海峡两岸经济合作框架协定》（The Economic Cooperation Framework Agreement，ECFA）2010 年 6 月 29 日由两岸双方签署，同年 9 月 12 日生效。ECFA 是区域贸易协定（regional trade agreement，RTA）实践和两岸经济合作机制的重要发展。本文在简述中国 RTA 实践特殊形式的基础上，以《内地与香港关于建立更紧密经贸关系的安排》（以下简称 CEPA）[1]为主要参照，对 ECFA 的主要特色及其法律意义作一初步探讨。

一、中国 RTA 实践的特殊形式

中国 RTA 实践的特殊形式是由中国在世界贸易组织（WTO）体制“一国四席”的特殊地位所决定的。

根据 1947 年《关税和贸易总协定》（GATT 1947）第 26、32、33 条规定，主权国家并不是 GATT 缔约方资格的必要条件。任何实体，不论是否主权国家，只要构成一个关税区，均可按一定程序成为 GATT 的缔约方；相反，即使是一个独立的主权国家，如未形成一个关税区，也不可能成为 GATT 的缔约方。《建立世界贸易组织协

* 原载《厦门大学学报》（哲学社会科学版）2011 年第 4 期。
基金项目：司法部 2009 年度国家法治与法学理论研究重点课题“两岸经济合作框架协议研究”（09SFB1008）。

[1] 2003 年 6 月 29 日签署、2004 年 1 月 1 日生效的《内地与香港关于建立更紧密经贸关系的安排》为中文本，“更紧密经贸关系的安排”英文为 Closer Economic Partnership Arrangement，简称 CEPA。在本文中，除另有说明，CEPA 指《内地与香港关于建立更紧密经贸关系的安排》。

定》(以下简称《WTO 协定》)沿袭了 GATT 1947 有关成员资格的规定,[1]其主要特征之一是继续采用"单独关税区"的概念,由此,WTO 成员可区分为主权国家成员和单独关税区成员。

由于 WTO 成员资格向主权国家和非主权的单独关税区开放,就可能形成 WTO 体制的"一国多席"局面。形成的主要情况是:一个主权国家与隶属于该主权国家的一个或数个单独关税区分别加入 WTO,或者在一个主权国家未加入 WTO 的情况下,隶属于该主权国家的数个单独关税区分别加入 WTO。1995 年 1 月 1 日,香港和澳门根据《WTO 协定》第 11 条第 1 款分别成为 WTO 创始成员,2001 年 12 月 11 日和 2002 年 1 月 1 日,中华人民共和国与"台湾、澎湖、金门、马祖单独关税区"(简称"中国台北")[the Separate Customs Territory of Taiwan, Penghu, Kinmen and Matsu(Chinese Taipei)]根据《WTO 协定》第 12 条第 1 款先后成为 WTO 纳入成员后,在 WTO 体制中出现了前所未有的"一国四席"局面。这不仅首开 WTO 体制"一国多席"之先河,也是中国加入 WTO 的重要特征。应当明确,中华人民共和国、香港、澳门和中国台北虽然同为 WTO 体制下的平等成员,其根本区别在于,中华人民共和国是以主权国家的资格加入 WTO,而香港、澳门和中国台北则是以单独关税区的身份成为 WTO 成员。[2]

根据 GATT 第 24 条规定,WTO 成员相互之间可建立关税同盟或自由贸易区,或者商谈形成关税同盟或自由贸易区所必需的临时协定(可统称为 RTAs)。WTO 体制有关成员资格的规定和"一国多席"的现实意味着 WTO 成员之间的 RTAs 并不当然是国际条约。依其主体组合情况的不同,WTO 成员之间的 RTAs 可分为两类:第一类是国际 RTAs,包括不同主权国家成员之间、一主权国家成员与隶属另一主权国家的单独关税区成员之间或隶属不同主权国家的单独关税区成员之间的协议,由于符合"国家间所缔结而以国际法为准之国际书面协定"的必要条件,[3]属国际条约,如中华人民共和国与新加坡、巴基斯坦、新西兰、智利、秘鲁和哥斯达黎加等签订

---

〔1〕《WTO 协定》第 11 条第 1 款规定了创始成员的资格,即:"本协定生效之日的 GATT 1947 缔约方和欧洲共同体,如接受本协定和多边贸易协定,并将减让和承诺表附于 GATT 1994,将具体承诺减让表附于 GATS,应成为 WTO 的创始成员。"第 12 条第 1 款规定了纳入成员的资格和程序:"任何国家或在处理其对外商业关系及本协定和多边贸易协定规定的其他事务中享有充分自治权的单独关税区(separate customs territory),可按它与 WTO 议定的条件加入本协定。此加入适用于本协定及所附多边贸易协定。"

〔2〕 参见曾华群:《略论 WTO 体制的"一国四席"》,载《厦门大学学报》(哲社版)2002 年第 5 期,第 5—14 页。

〔3〕 1969 年《维也纳条约法公约》第 2 条第 1 款(甲)项规定:"称'条约'者,谓国家间所缔结而以国际法为准之国际书面协定,不论其载于一项单独文书或两项以上相互有关之文书内,亦不论其特定名称为何。"

的 RTAs；[1] 第二类是国内 RTAs，即以"一国多席"为前提，是同一主权国家的 WTO 成员之间的 RTAs，包括一主权国家成员与隶属于该主权国家的一个或一个以上单独关税区成员之间的协议或同属一主权国家的两个或两个以上单独关税区成员之间的协议，如内地与香港 CEPA、内地与澳门 CEPA 和 ECFA。这类 RTAs 既是符合 GATT 第 24 条的 WTO 成员之间的协议，但实质上因不符合"国家间所缔结……之国际书面协定"的必要条件，不属国际条约，而是部分内容受 WTO 规则规范和调整的一国国内的经济一体化安排。[2] 迄今为止，中国是 WTO 体制中唯一实践"一国多席"的国家，也是唯一实践国内 RTAs 的国家。在这个意义上，国内 RTAs 可视为中国 RTA 实践的特殊形式。

二、ECFA 的主要特征

ECFA 在名称、主体、调整对象、基本原则、执行机制等方面显示鲜明的"两岸特色"，不仅不同于一般的主权国家之间的 RTA 实践，也不同于中国 RTA 实践特殊形式中的内地与香港、澳门之间的 CEPAs。

（一）名称

传统上，"自由贸易区"（Free Trade Areas，FTAs）一般用于两个或两个以上国家建立的区域性经济一体化安排。在国际法上，"协议"（agreement）一般用于两个或两个以上国家签订的国际法律文件。经历谨慎的推敲和选择，CEPA 名称最终是避免使用"自由贸易区"，采用"建立更紧密经贸关系"，并以"安排"（arrangement）取代"协议"。[3] 1997 年以来，内地与香港之间的双边法律文件有意采用"安排"用语，由双方代表签署，之后由双方通过颁布适用于本区域的法律文件实施。[4] CEPA 亦循此例。

由于两岸关系的复杂性，比之 CEPA，ECFA 的名称经历了长期的酝酿和审慎的选择。早在 20 世纪 90 年代初，两岸学者分别提出了有关两岸经济合作制度的构想

---

〔1〕 目前，中华人民共和国正与五大洲的 28 个国家和地区建设 15 个自由贸易区。已生效的 10 项 RTAs 包括中华人民共和国与东盟、新加坡、巴基斯坦、新西兰、智利、秘鲁和哥斯达黎加之间 RTAs，内地与香港 CEPA、内地与澳门 CEPA 和 ECFA。正在商建的自由贸易区有 5 个，分别是中华人民共和国与海湾合作委员会、澳大利亚、挪威、瑞士、冰岛自由贸易区。同时，中华人民共和国已完成与印度的区域贸易安排联合研究，与韩国结束了自由贸易区联合研究，正在开展中日韩自由贸易区官产学联合研究。此外，中华人民共和国还加入了《亚太贸易协定》。http://fta.mofcom.gov.cn16/06/2011

〔2〕 参见曾华群：《论内地与香港 CEPA 之性质》，载《厦门大学学报》（哲社版）2004 年第 6 期，第 36 页。

〔3〕 张宪初：《香港内地更紧密经贸关系安排的法律基础和难点》，载张宪初主编：《世贸规则与两岸四地经贸法律关系》，商务印书馆 2003 年版，第 87—90 页。

〔4〕 Kong Qingjiang, Closer Economic Partnership Agreement between China and Hong Kong, 1 (1) *China: An International Journal*, 134-135 (2003).

和建议。世纪之交，虽然政治因素的干扰时有发生，以两岸相继加入 WTO 为契机，两岸经贸关系有了一定的发展。在两岸政党层面，有关建立两岸经济合作机制的共识逐渐形成。[1] 2008 年 5 月，国民党重新执政，两岸关系进入了新的历史发展时期。同年 12 月，两岸空运、海运直航和直接通邮同步实施，"海峡两岸综合性经济合作协议"（Comprehensive Economic Cooperation Agreement，CECA）逐渐成为台湾当局的议题，亦得到大陆方面的积极回应。[2]

英文缩写 CEPA 与 CECA，仅是一字之差。在台湾，CEPA 被附加的政治符号是，由于内地与香港、澳门采用 CEPA，意味着是中央政府与特别行政区之间的关系。台湾如接受 CEPA，将被"港澳化"。两岸经济合作机制名称最后由 CECA 确定为"全民共识度较高"的"海峡两岸经济合作框架协议"（ECFA）。[3] 台湾当局对 ECFA 的定位是，"不采港澳模式，也非一般的'自由贸易协定'（FTA），而是属于两岸特殊性质的经济合作协议"。[4]

ECFA 名称的特色在于：第一，比较 CEPA 名称中的"内地与香港"和"内地与澳门"，ECFA 采用两岸多年接受的"两岸"，避免了协议主体名称的潜在争议；第二，比较 CEPA 名称中的"安排"（arrangement），ECFA 采用了 CEPA 避而不用的"协议"（agreement），迎合了台湾方面"与大陆签订经济合作协议"的政治考虑和基本立场。此外，ECFA 中的"框架协议"（framework agreement）更为准确地表明了该基础性、结构性法律文件的性质和内容。ECFA 名称的确定，反映了两岸特别是大陆方面避免形式问题争议的积极态度，也反映了两岸决策者务实创新的政治智慧。

（二）主体

从 CEPA 文本本身看，正如其名称所指出的，CEPA 的主体一方是内地，另一方是香港。CEPA 签署方的名称同样反映了起草者力求将该法律文件区别于"协议"的匠心。在内地方面，签署方是"中华人民共和国商务部副部长"，而不是"中华人民共和国"；在香港方面，签署方是"中华人民共和国香港特别行政区财政司司长"，而不

---

〔1〕 Zeng Huaqun, "One China, Four WTO Memberships"：Legal Grounds, Relations and Significance, 8 (5) *The Journal of World Investment & Trade*，689-690 (2007).

〔2〕 2008 年 12 月 31 日，胡锦涛总书记在"纪念《告台湾同胞书》30 周年座谈会"上，明确提及促进两岸签订 CECA。2009 年 3 月 5 日，温家宝总理在《政府工作报告》中表示，将推动签订 CECA，逐步建立具有两岸特色的经济合作机制。

〔3〕 2009 年 3 月 6 日，财团法人海峡交流基金会江丙坤董事长表示，第三次江陈会高层对话中将针对 ECFA 交换意见，若取得对方同意，再讨论是否纳入第四次江陈会协商议题。至于名称从 CECA 改为 ECFA，江先生指出，名称不重要，重要的是内容。架构该怎么建构，得待主管机关决定，并通过海基会与海峡两岸关系协会协商后才能决定。参见《江丙坤：ECFA 纳江陈会议题》，载《澳门日报》2009 年 3 月 7 日第 A9 版。

〔4〕 中国台湾地区经济事务主管部门：《推动两岸经济合作架构协议之可能内容》，2009 年 4 月 7 日，发布于中国台湾地区经济事务主管部门网站。

是香港在 WTO 中的正式名称"中国香港"（Hong Kong, China）。显然,CEPA 签署方的名称更为直观地反映 CEPA 是一国不同行政机构代表不同关税区签署的文件。

ECFA 与 CEPA 的主体同样是一国国内的两个关税区,不同之处在于,ECFA 的主体是统一前的一国国内的两个关税区。台湾地区学者曾建议,两岸在 WTO 体制下签署 FTA,可直接使用其 WTO 成员名称,以避免双方在名称问题上的争议。如按此方式,ECFA 的签署方当为中华人民共和国与台澎金马单独关税区（中国台北）。这是两岸均可接受的选择,在国际上也能得到普遍认同。然而,如进一步参照 CEPA 的签署方模式,则可能面临官方机构名称及层级对等的问题。

实际上,ECFA 由两岸的受权机构,即大陆方面的海峡两岸关系协会和台湾方面的财团法人海峡交流基金会负责商谈,主体和签署方顺理成章地安排为海峡两岸关系协会会长和财团法人海峡交流基金会董事长,避免了官方机构名称及层级对等的难题。

尽管 ECFA 的主体在形式上不同于 WTO 体制下的中华人民共和国和中国台北两个正式成员,由于海峡两岸关系协会和财团法人海峡交流基金会分别取得中华人民共和国和中国台北的正式授权,"两岸"实质上指中华人民共和国和中国台北,ECFA 的主体双方代表的也是 WTO 体制下的两个正式成员。在两岸按 GATT 第 24 条第 7 款第（a）项规定,向 WTO 提交 ECFA、履行通知义务时,对 WTO 区域贸易协定委员会而言,比之 CEPA 模式,ECFA 的主体和签署方名称可能更为陌生。在 WTO 历史上,ECFA 是第一例由 WTO 成员授权的、以完全不同于该成员正式名称的受权机构名义签署的 RTA,也是第一例由非官方机构代表签署的 RTA。

（三）调整对象

CEPA 的调整对象是内地与香港之间的经济关系。由于主体的双重身份,CEPA 的调整对象也具有双重性:一是双方同属一国,是统一的一国国内不同关税地区之间的经贸关系;二是双方分别是 WTO 成员,也是 WTO 成员间的贸易关系。与 CEPA 的不同点在于,ECFA 调整对象是统一前的一国国内不同关税区之间的经济关系。与 CEPA 的相同点在于,ECFA 也同时调整 WTO 成员之间的贸易关系。

为明确 ECFA 调整对象这一层面的特点,需要区分 WTO 规则"调整范围之内"与"调整范围之外"。在 WTO 规则调整范围之内,各成员应严格遵循规则,履行承诺。在 WTO 规则调整范围之外,各成员则可通过 RTA 或其他双边协议,调整相互之间的经济关系。两岸经济关系中不属 WTO 规则调整者,是统一前的一国国内不同关税区之间的经济关系,可不受 WTO 规则或其他国际法规范的约束。作为两岸经济合作的框架性协议,ECFA 的内容涵盖了两岸主要经济活动,包括货物贸易、服务贸易、投资和其他经济活动。与传统 RTA 比较，ECFA 对投资尤其重视。在 ECFA"目标"中，明确指出"加强和增进双方之间的经济、贸易和投资合作"；"促进双方货物和服务贸易进一步自由化，逐步建立公平、透明、便利的投资及其保障机制"。在"合作措施"中，明确指出"提供投资保护，促进双向投资"；"促进贸易投资便利化和产业交流与合作"。第二章题为"贸易与投资"，两者置于同等、并列的地位。第 5 条为投资条款，专门规定了有关商签投资协议的时限和内容。此外，在"经济合作"事项中，"金融合作""海关合作""电子商务合作""产业和项目合作"及"中小企业合作"等明显属于"WTO 规则调整范围之外"的事项，反映了两岸寻求建立更广泛、更紧密经济合作关系的意向。ECFA 有关争端解决和机构安排等规定也超出了 WTO 规则调整的范围。

由于中华人民共和国与中国台北分别是 WTO 正式成员，两岸贸易关系不可能游离于 WTO 体制之外，ECFA 调整的对象也包括 WTO 两个成员之间的贸易关系。之所以强调 ECFA 调整 WTO 两个成员之间的贸易关系，其重要意义首先在于，就整体而言，ECFA 的商谈、签订和实施，不仅受两岸法律的规范和调整，也受 WTO 规则的规范和调整。如 ECFA 第 3 条规定，两岸货物贸易协议磋商内容包括"非关税措施，包括但不限于技术性贸易壁垒（TBT）、卫生与植物卫生措施（SPS）"，"贸易救济措施，包括世界贸易组织《关于实施 1994 年关税与贸易总协定第六条的协定》《补贴与反补贴措施协定》《保障措施协定》规定的措施及适用于双方之间货物贸易的双方保障措施"。这意味着 ECFA 的相关规定及将来签订的附属协议不可违反 WTO 规则，ECFA 中涉及 WTO 规则的概念的解释和适用可能有赖于 WTO 规则的解释和有关实践。其次，在 WTO 体制下，同样作为 WTO 成员，中华人民共和国与中国台北之间的法律关系是平等的。这意味着涉及 WTO 规则的 ECFA 条款的商谈、签订、实施及修订，需要双方通过平等协商达成。最后，同样作为 WTO 成员，中华人民共和国、中国台北与其他 WTO 成员之间的法律关系也是平等的。在 ECFA 的签订和实施中，两岸无论单独或共同违反 WTO 规则，WTO 其他成员均可通过 WTO 贸易审查机制或争端解决机制追究违反方的法律责任。

（四）基本原则

CEPA 实施及修订的原则为：（1）遵循"一国两制"的方针；（2）符合 WTO 的规则；（3）顺应双方产业结构调整和升级的需要，促进稳定和可持续发展；（4）实现互惠互利、优势互补、共同繁荣；（5）先易后难，逐步推进。

ECFA 确立的两项基本原则分别是"平等互惠、循序渐进"和"符合 WTO 规则"，实际上涵盖了上述 CEPA 第（2）至（5）项原则的内容。

1. 平等互惠、循序渐进

ECFA 序言明确指出："海峡两岸关系协会与财团法人海峡交流基金会遵循平等互惠、循序渐进的原则……"所谓"平等互惠、循序渐进"，实际上是上述 CEPA 原则第(3)、(4)、(5)项的概括。在 ECFA 的"目标"中也体现了该原则，即："一、加强和增进双方之间的经济、贸易和投资合作。二、促进双方货物和服务贸易进一步自由化，逐步建立公平、透明、便利的投资及其保障机制。三、扩大经济合作领域，建立合作机制。"

在台湾当局主张的 ECFA 指导原则中，"对等原则"主要是出于政治上的考虑，强调"不会出现一国两制"；"由易到难"的含义是"以点带面，分阶段、分步骤推进；正常化与双边合作同时进行"。[1]

应当指出，"两岸关系特殊、经济体量悬殊"的现实是商谈 ECFA 所必须面对的，特别是"两岸关系特殊"更是理解 ECFA 区别于其他 RTAs 特别是国家之间 RTAs 的关键点。在此情况下，平等互惠原则的适用需要有更长远的目标和更宏观的视野。因此，平等互惠不应简单理解为开放领域或优惠项目的具体对等、对应或相当。[2]

ECFA 的附件包括"货物贸易早期收获产品清单及降税安排""适用于货物贸易早期收获产品的临时原产地规则""适用于货物贸易早期收获产品的双方保障措施""服务贸易早期收获部门及开放措施"和"适用于服务贸易早期收获部门及开放措施的服务提供者定义"，涉及"货物贸易早期收获产品"和"服务贸易早期收获部门"的具体安排，以此为示范，揭示了 ECFA 的效益前景和发展方向，也是"平等互惠、循序渐进"原则的具体体现。

2. 符合 WTO 规则

由于中华人民共和国和中国台北同为 WTO 成员，在商谈、签订和实施 ECFA 中，应遵守 WTO 规则，分别履行 WTO 项下的承诺和责任。ECFA 序言明确指出："双方同意，本着世界贸易组织（WTO）基本原则，考虑双方的经济条件，逐步减少或消除彼此间的贸易和投资障碍，创造公平的贸易与投资环境……"

在"合作措施"中进一步体现了这一原则："双方同意，考虑双方的经济条件，采取包括但不限于以下措施，加强海峡两岸的经济交流与合作：一、逐步减少或消除双方之间实质多数货物贸易的关税和非关税壁垒。二、逐步减少或消除双方之间涵盖

---

〔1〕　中国台湾地区经济事务主管部门：《推动两岸经济合作架构协议之可能内容》，2009 年 4 月 7 日，发布于中国台湾地区经济事务主管部门网站。

〔2〕　例如，根据 ECFA 第 7 条及附件一，在货物贸易方面，大陆将对 539 项原产于台湾的产品实施降税，台湾将对 267 项原产于大陆的产品实施降税。

众多部门的服务贸易限制性措施。三、提供投资保护，促进双向投资。四、促进贸易投资便利化和产业交流与合作。"

以上第一、二项措施明显涵盖于 WTO 规则"调整范围之内"。ECFA 的其他规定，如投资条款和经济合作条款，在不同程度上也与 WTO 规则相关。ECFA 第 9 条题为"例外"，明确规定："本协议的任何规定不得解释为妨碍一方采取或维持与世界贸易组织规定相一致的例外措施。"该条款特别强调了 ECFA 的"任何规定"不得影响两岸"符合 WTO 规则"的例外措施。ECFA 第 7 条第 2 款涉及"货物贸易早期收获计划的实施"，规定"双方应按照附件一列明的早期收获产品及降税安排实施降税；但双方各自对其他所有世界贸易组织成员普遍适用的非临时性进口关税税率较低时，则适用该税率"。该条款旨在强调双方遵守 WTO 非歧视待遇原则，明确规定，两岸如各自对其他 WTO 成员采用优于 ECFA 的关税税率，应同等适用于对方。

（五）执行机制

对于国家之间或地区之间稳定、持续的经济合作而言，执行机制安排是非常重要的。建立具有强制力的执行机制以推进两岸经济合作进一步发展是 ECFA 的重要成就。

与 CEPA 比较而言，ECFA 建立了具有较强执行力、强制力的执行机制。

根据 ECFA 第 11 条规定，双方成立"两岸经济合作委员会"。该委员会由双方指定的代表组成，负责处理与本协议相关的事宜，包括但不限于："（一）完成为落实本协议目标所必需的磋商；（二）监督并评估本协议的执行；（三）解释本协议的规定；（四）通报重要经贸信息；（五）根据本协议第十条规定，解决任何关于本协议解释、实施和适用的争端。"

成立两岸经济合作委员会及推动双方经贸社团互设办事机构，是两岸经贸关系走向机制化、制度化的重要标志。[1] 值得注意的是，根据 ECFA 第 10 条的规定，双方应不迟于本协议生效后六个月内就建立适当的争端解决程序展开磋商，并尽速达成协议，以解决任何关于本协议解释、实施和适用的争端。在上述争端解决协议生效前，任何关于本协议解释、实施和适用的争端，应由双方通过协商解决，或由两岸经济合作委员会以适当方式加以解决。

不难预见，一俟建立自成体系的 ECFA 争端解决程序，两岸间经济争端、包括贸易争端将主要提交 ECFA 的争端解决机构，而不是 WTO。鉴于内地与香港、澳门CEPAs 均未建立争端解决机制，ECFA 争端解决机制是一国国内 RTA 的重大创新。

---

〔1〕 李浩培：《条约法概论》，法律出版社 1988 年版，第 240 页。

三、ECFA 的法律意义

不言而喻，ECFA 对实现两岸经济合作关系正常化、法制化具有重要的里程碑意义。ECFA 对中国台北 RTA 实践发展可能具有的法律意义也值得关注和研讨。

（一）两岸经济合作的法律框架

建立两岸经济合作的法律框架是 ECFA 的基本目标和重大成就。正如其名称所指出的，ECFA 是两岸经济合作的框架协议，是一个统领其涵盖的专题性协议群的基础性、纲领性法律文件。

长期以来，即使在两岸分别加入 WTO 之后，由于政治因素，两岸经济关系未能实现正常化。就贸易而言，目前，两岸货物贸易、服务贸易的开放程度实际上尚未能达到 WTO 规则的一般要求。两岸作为 WTO 成员，在给予对方和其他 WTO 成员的待遇方面，尚未能实施 WTO 体制的非歧视待遇原则。ECFA 的实施不仅可望逐步消除两岸贸易的壁垒，基于区域经济一体化安排，也可能相互给予优于其他 WTO 成员的待遇。在投资领域，由于台湾当局实施限制大陆对台投资的政策，两岸投资关系总体上是台湾对大陆投资的单向流动关系。ECFA 第 5 条明确规定，投资保障协议包括"建立投资保障机制、提高投资相关规定的透明度、逐步减少双方相互投资的限制、促进投资便利化"等事项，旨在确立保护和促进两岸相互投资的基本规范。[1] 协议生效后，可望促进两岸投资关系由单向流动向双向流动的转变。据悉，双方就商签两岸投资保障协议具体事宜进行了多轮磋商，进展总体顺利，在大部分问题上已达成一致意见。[2]

ECFA 规定了两岸投资保障协议、争端解决协议、货物贸易协议和服务贸易协议的基本内容和启动商谈程序的时限。根据相关时间表，在 ECFA 生效半年之内，两岸将分别启动商谈上述协议。可以预期，上述协议相继签订生效后，将成为两岸经济合作机制的重要支柱，可望进一步推进两岸经济合作关系的正常化和法制化。

（二）对中国台北 RTA 实践发展的可能影响

台湾当局将 ECFA 视为"舒缓参与区域合作瓶颈""改善推动""与其他国家洽签双边自由贸易协定之利基，参与区域经贸整合"的关键一步。[3] 财团法人海峡交流基金会江丙坤董事长指出，ECFA 的签署，"不但是两岸经贸关系史上的重要里程碑，

---

〔1〕《国台办：两岸投资保护和促进相互投资相辅相成》，https://news.qq.com/a/20101215/001258.htm。

〔2〕《两岸投资保障协议磋商进展顺利》，http://www.taiwan.cn/jl/jm/jm/201106/t20110616_1889811.htm。

〔3〕中国台湾地区经济事务主管部门：《推动两岸经济合作架构协议之可能内容》，2009 年 4 月 7 日，发布于中国台湾地区经济事务主管部门网站。

也是两岸各自面向区域经济整合和全球化发展趋势下，极为关键的一大步"。[1]

ECFA 的签订是否意味着台湾 RTA 实践的重大"突破"，即由于与大陆签订了 RTA，实现了经济关系正常化，可进而寻求与接受"一个中国"原则的其他 WTO 成员签订 RTA？WTO 成员相关立场的新动向可以新加坡为例。新加坡的新近立场是，"如果台湾与中国大陆能在自由贸易协定方面取得进展，两岸关系得以改善，而且只要经济事务不被政治化，新台之间将有许多增进经济合作的可能性"。[2] 2010年 8 月 5 日，驻新加坡台北代表处和新加坡驻台北商务办事处发布新闻稿称，台澎金马单独关税区与新加坡均为 WTO 成员，双方同意开展对经济合作协议可行性的探讨，并将在同年稍后会商相关事宜。

大陆方面对此新闻及时回应。国务院台湾事务办公室发言人应询表示，关于新加坡与台澎金马单独关税区将探讨商签经济协议的可行性，相信新加坡会继续奉行"一个中国"政策，并据此妥善处理与台湾的经贸关系。同时，希望台湾方面切实维护两岸业已形成的共同政治基础，维护两岸关系和平发展大局。外交部发言人就此答记者问时指出，我们对于外国和台湾开展经贸往来的立场是一贯的，也是明确的。希望有关国家继续恪守"一个中国"原则，审慎处理有关事宜。[3]

根据传统国际法规则，主权国家是条约的唯一主体。在不断发展的现代国际实践中，由非主权实体参与缔结国际条约并非罕见。国际组织、联邦制国家的成员、交战团体和享有自治权的区域性实体等非主权实体也可能成为条约的主体。上述非主权实体的缔约权分别来源于国际组织的基本文件、国家宪法、条约法和国际习惯法等。[4] 区域性实体成为条约主体的必要前提是，该实体取得主权国家的缔约授权和国际承认。[5] 台湾当局能否以 ECFA 为"先例"，以"中国台北"名义与外国签订 RTA？笔者认为，答案是否定的。应当明确，GATT 第 24 条是区域经济一体化例外条款，并非授权 WTO 成员签订 RTAs 的条款。由于中国台北是以单独关税区的身份加入 WTO，其 WTO 成员地位并未改变其法律地位，因而与缔约权问题并无关联。

---

〔1〕 《江丙坤：签署 ECFA 是两岸经贸关系史上重要里程碑》，http://tga. mofcom. gov. cn/article/zt_lhst/subjectgg/201007/20100707005099. shtml。

〔2〕 《蔡宏明：经贸全方位，先定两岸框架协议》，载《联合报》2008 年 5 月 12 日。

〔3〕 《新加坡与台湾方面将探讨商签经济协议可行性》，载《厦门日报》2010 年 8 月 6 日。

〔4〕 李浩培：《条约法概论》，法律出版社 1988 年版，第 240 页。

〔5〕 例如，《中华人民共和国香港特别行政区基本法》第 151 条规定："香港特别行政区可在经济、贸易、金融、航运、通讯、旅游、文化、体育等领域以'中国香港'的名义，单独地同世界各国、各地区及有关国际组织保持和发展关系，签订和履行有关协议"。经此授权，1997 年以来，香港特别行政区以"中国香港"名义，与外国签订了一系列双边协议，且获得国际社会的广泛承认。See Zeng Huaqun, Unprecedented International Status: Theoretical and Practical Aspects of the HKSAR's External Autonomy, 9 (3) *The Journal of World Investment & Trade*, Vol. 9, 283-287 (2008)。

同理,由于 ECFA 是中国 RTA 实践的特殊形式,是一国国内经济一体化安排,不属国际条约,中国台北作为 ECFA 的主体地位无从构成其作为条约主体的"先例"。遵循普遍接受的国际法规则和国际实践,中国台北要成为条约的主体,同样需要具备"取得主权国家的缔约授权和国际承认"的必要前提条件。显然,中国台北如果要与外国签订 RTA,首先需要取得主权国家的缔约授权。在国际社会普遍接受"一个中国"原则的情况下,中国台北能否及如何取得"一个中国"的缔约授权,对两岸决策者和国际法学者都是值得审慎研究的重大法律问题。

ECFA: Regional Trade Agreement Practice with "Cross-Strait Characteristics"

Abstract: The Economic Cooperation Framework Agreement across the Taiwan Strait (ECFA) is important development of the practice of regional trade agreements (RTAs) and the regime of economic cooperation across the Strait. ECFA shows its clear "cross-Strait characteristics" in the aspects of its title, subject, object, basic principles, and enforcement mechanism, etc. , not only different from the general practice of RTAs between or among sovereign States, but also from the special form of China's RTA practice, namely Closer Economic Partnership Arrangements between Mainland and Hong Kong or Macao. ECFA is a milestone in realizing the normalization and legalization for the economic cooperation relations across the Strait. Its possible legal implication for Chinese Taipei's RTA practice is worth considering and researching.

Key words: ECFA;RTA;economic cooperation across the Strait

第四节　Characteristics and Implications of ECFA[*]
（ECFA 的特征与意涵）

The Economic Cooperation Framework Agreement across the Taiwan Strait (ECFA) was signed on 29 June 2010 and entered into force on 12 September 2010. ECFA is important development of China's regional trade agreement (RTA) practice and economic cooperation regime across the Taiwan Strait (the Strait). Comparing with the Closer Economic Partnership Arrangement between Mainland China and Hong Kong (CEPA) and Hong Kong Special Administrative Region (HKSAR)'s external autonomy to some extent, this paper will briefly discuss the main characteristics and international implications of ECFA.

I. Introduction

For better understanding the characteristics and implications of ECFA, we have to learn the China's special memberships in WTO regime, and the unique form of China's RTA practice.

1. "One China four WTO memberships"

On 11 December 2001 and 1 January, 2002, China and the Separate Customs Territory of Taiwan, Penghu, Kinmen and Matsu (referred to as "Chinese Taipei") became members of the World Trade Organization (WTO) one after another, and together with Hong Kong and Macao, the two WTO original members on 1 January 1995, the situation of "one China four WTO memberships" in the WTO regime has emerged. It is not only the new phenomenon in the history of the WTO, but also the most important issue of China's accession to the WTO.

The formation of "one China four WTO memberships" is the product of provi-

---

　*　Characteristics and Implications of ECFA, *Korean Journal of International Economic Law*, ISSN 2005-9949, Vol. 8, No. 2, 2010.

　This paper is the text of the author's speech at Korea-China Symposium on "Korea-China FTA—Seeking Ways to Reduce Trade Barriers for the Special Partnership" hosted by Korea Society of International Economic Law and Chinese Society of International Economic Law on 20 August 2010 and is one of the achievements of researching project "On the Economic Cooperation Framework Agreement across the Taiwan Strait" [No. 09SFB1008] sponsored by the Ministry of Justice, P. R. China.

sions of Marrakesh Agreement Establishing the World Trade Organization (herein-after WTO Agreement), the unique development of Chinese history and the success-ful practice of China's policy of "one country two systems". The main features of the relations among China, "Hong Kong, China", "Macao, China" and Chinese Taipei include equal representation and participation in the WTO institutions and decision-making, separate claim and liabilities systems as well as equal participation in RTAs. [1]

2. Unique form of China's RTA practice

2.1 RTAs between or among the "four WTO members"

As equal WTO members, China, "Hong Kong, China", "Macao, China" and Chinese Taipei may establish RTAs between or among them. The significance of RTAs between or among the four members under the WTO regime is to deal with the special problems on the application of WTO non-discrimination principle, setting up a necessary legal basis for closer economic relations between or among the four regions within a sovereign State. The potential RTAs among China, "Hong Kong, China", "Macao, China" and Chinese Taipei leading to so-called "great China FTA" might provide new opportunities for further economic cooperation and integration among the four WTO members. [2]

Furthermore it is very important in legal sense that the legal status of Chinese Taipei as a SCT and a WTO member is clarified and recognized by the WTO and all its other members, including China, "Hong Kong, China" and "Macao, China". Considering the complicated cross-Strait relations, the new position of equal WTO members of Chinese mainland and Chinese Taipei provides a new legal basis and practical alternative for negotiating the cross-Strait economic relations.

Considering the situation of "one China four WTO memberships", RTAs between or among mainland China and "Hong Kong, China", "Macao, China" and Chinese Taipei might be considered as unique form of China's RTA practice. In fact

---

[1] For the detailed comments on this issue, see ZENG Huaqun, "'One China, Four WTO Memberships': Legal Grounds, Relations and Significance", 8 (5) *The Journal of World Investment & Trade*, 671-690 (2007).

[2] There are many comments on RTAs among the four members, for examples, ZENG Lingliang, "The Legal Position and Development Trend of Regional Trade Arrangement under WTO Regime—Several Legal Issues concerning Establishing a Free Trade Area among the Mainland, Taiwan, Hong Kong and Macao" (in Chinese); WANG Guiguo and LIANG Meifen, "An Analysis of the Proposition of Establishing a Free Trade Area between Hong Kong and the Mainland" (in Chinese), 7 *Journal of International Economic Law* 1-16, 69-83 (2003).

CEPAs between mainland China and Hong Kong, Macao respectively came into effect from 1 January 2004. ECFA is the latest development of unique form of China's RTA practice. It is more difficult and complicated than CEPAs due to political reasons mainly for a long period of time.

2.2 Nature of RTAs between or among the "four WTO members"

The multilateral RTAs, like the European Communities (EC), North American Free Trade Agreement (NAFTA) and Association of South East Asian Nations (ASEAN) are all international economic regional organization consisting of more than two sovereign States. The bilateral RTAs usually are concluded by two sovereign States. RTA between or among mainland China, "Hong Kong, China", "Macao, China" and Chinese Taipei is a new creature in the history of the RTAs. It is a RTA within a sovereign State rather than a RTA of a regional international organization or of two or more sovereign States. Therefore we might safely conclude that since one State may have several WTO memberships, there are possibilities, feasibilities and practice of internal RTAs governed by WTO rules. CEPAs and ECFA are valuable precedents in this regard.

There is big divergence on the nature of CEPA between mainland China and Hong Kong or Macao. Some scholars consider it as international treaty or semi-international treaty since it is regulated by international law, while others deem it as domestic legal arrangement since it is a legal document concluded by two parties from a same sovereign State. [1] From further studies on the issue, we found some features of CEPA: (1) the subjects of CEPA have dual status, i. e., the mainland customs territory and Hong Kong SCT or Macao SCT in the domestic regime and two members in the WTO regime; (2) the objects of CEPA also have dual nature, i. e., the economic relationships between the two customs territories in a same sovereign State and the trade relationships between the two WTO members; (3) the legal grounds for CEPA involve relevant provisions in Chinese domestic laws and the WTO rules on RTAs. Therefore we might conclude that CEPA, considering its contracting parties in the status of the two customs territories in a sovereign State and in

---

[1] ZHU Zhaomin, "The Legal Basis and Framework for Closer Economic and Trade Cooperation among China's Separate Customs Territories after Its Accession to WTO" (in Chinese), 7 *Journal of International Economic Law* 17-36 (2003).

the status of the two WTO members, is an agreement between the two WTO members in conformity with Article 24 of the GATT, Understanding on Article 24 and Article 5 of the General Agreement on Trade in Service (GATS),[1] but essentially not a treaty.[2] It is a domestic legal arrangement for a RTA with its partial contents regulated by the WTO rules.[3] It follows that ECFA is also a domestic legal arrangement for a RTA due to the same status of its contracting parties as that in CEPA.

II. Name and Mode

The WTO member relations among China, "Hong Kong, China", "Macao, China" and Chinese Taipei provide the great potential for establishing closer economic relations among them. The successful performance of the CEPAs between mainland China and Hong Kong, Macao has demonstrated that the CEPAs are mutually beneficial to the two parties since 1 January 2004.

In earlier 2000s it was reported that according to the official and civil investigations in Taiwan, the policy of "one country two systems" in economic aspect was more acceptable than the policy in political aspect for the people in Taiwan.[4] CEPAs between mainland China and Hong Kong, Macao were very attractive for every circle in Taiwan.[5] The Taiwan media stressed that CEPAs marked the beginning

---

[1] In fact, CEPAs between mainland China and Hong Kong, Macao as FTAs are reported to the Committee on Regional Trade Agreement of WTO for examination (WT/REG162, WT/REG162 S/C/N/264 and WT/REG163, WT/REG163 S/C/N/265) on 12 January 2004.

[2] Article 2 of the Vienna Convention on the Law of Treaties of 1969 defines a "treaty" as "an international agreement concluded between States in written form and governed by international law, whether embodied in a single instrument or in two or more related instruments and whatever its particular designation". Article 2. 1 (a) of the Vienna Convention on the Law of Treaties between States and International Organizations or between International Organizations of 1986 modifies the above definition by recognizing that "treaty" also includes international agreement "between one or more States and one or more international organizations; or between international organizations". As the CEPA between mainland China and Hong Kong does not meet the basic requirement of "between States", "between a State and an international organization" or "between international organizations", it can not be regarded as a treaty essentially.

[3] See ZENG Huaqun, "On the Nature of CEPA between Mainland China and Hong Kong" (in Chinese), 5 *Xiamen University Journal (Arts & Social Sciences)* 5-14 (2002).

[4] "'One Country Two Systems' in Economic Aspect Is More Acceptable and It Is Hard to Reach a Compromise in Political Aspect" (in Chinese), *United Daily* (Lian He Bao), 18 July 2001, p. 15.

[5] See LUO Changfa, "Significance of FTA Agreement to the Relations between Taiwan and Mainland, Hong Kong" (in Chinese), at ZHANG Xianchu (ed.), *WTO Rules and Legal Relations on Economic and Trade among Four Regions across Taiwan Strait*, the Commercial Press (Hong Kong), Ltd., 40-63 (2003).

and development of the "Great China Economic Circle" under the one-China principle. As the Taiwan authorities refused to accept the one-China principle, the consultation and negotiation across the Strait were still in deadlock then. Therefore, Taiwan would be out of integration of the "Great China Economic Circle" and the economy of Taiwan would gradually go into marginalization.[1]

Some politicians in Taiwan also delivered important and valuable suggestions on the cross-Strait relations. Mr. James SOONG, Chairman of People First Party (PFP), indicated that mainland and Taiwan might learn from the experience of the EC, starting from economic conformity, to social cooperation and finally reaching political integration.[2] Mr. Vincent SIEW, the former Vice Chairman of Kuomintang (KMT), pointed out that it is a feasible and peaceable means for mainland and Taiwan to reach gradually political integration by economic integration.[3] He also created a new concept of the Closer Economic Operation Framework (CEOF) for substituting the contentious concepts of a FTA and a CEPA. In Mr. SIEW's opinions, there are three stages for promoting the development of the Cross-Strait Common Market (CSCM): in first stage, the main task is to promote the normalization of the cross-Strait relations; second, to promote the harmonization of the economic systems across the Strait; and third, to promote the integration of the cross-Strait economy in all aspects, and to realize the objectives of the CSCM.[4]

There is a remarkable progress in this regard by the Party-to-Party meeting across the Strait in 2005. On 29 April 2005, Communist Party of China (CPC) General Secretary HU Jintao and KMT Chairman LIEN Chan met in Beijing and issued a joint communiqué. According to the joint communiqué, the two parties agreed to strengthen cross-Strait economic and trade exchanges, including the establishment of the CSCM.[5] On 12 May 2005, CPC General Secretary HU Jintao and

---

[1] "Every Circle in Taiwan Pays Attention to the CEPA between Hong Kong and Mainland" (in Chinese), *Fujian Daily*, 2 July 2003, p. 6.

[2] "James SOONG: Three Stages for Dealing with the Cross-Strait Issues" (in Chinese), *United Daily* (Lian He Bao), 4 January 2001, p. 4.

[3] "The Foundation for Cross-Strait Common Market Prepared by Vincent SIEW Setting Up" (in Chinese), *China Times* (Zhongguo Shibao), 27 March 2001, p. 1.

[4] "Three Stages for Promoting the Cross-Strait Common Market, Establishing the Closer Economic Operation Framework" (in Chinese), *Central Daily* (Zhongyang Ribao), 11 May, 2005, p. 3.

[5] XING Zhigang, "CPC, KMT Leaders Vow to End Hostility across the Strait", *China Daily*, 30 April 2005, p. 1.

PFP Chairman James SOONG, also met in Beijing and agreed to exchange views on establishing a long-term and stable regime for trade facilitation and liberalization across the Strait (i. e., cross-Strait FTA) after resuming the cross-Strait consultation. [1] Rapid development of the cross-Strait relations in 2005 indicates that there are consensus at the Party-to-Party level and practical possibilities for mainland China and Chinese Taipei to negotiate a cross-Strait legal arrangement for economic cooperation.

In May 2008, KMT regained the power in Taiwan, the cross Strait relation has developed smoothly since then. After realizing the "three communications" (post, trade and transportations across the Strait) on 15 December 2008, the Comprehensive Economic Cooperation Agreement across the Taiwan Strait (CECA) became an important topic in Taiwan.

In the long time consideration, discussion and debates in political, academic circles and civil society of Taiwan, the RTA across the Strait is finally named as "Economic Cooperation Framework Agreement across the Taiwan Strait" (ECFA) in earlier March, 2009. Mr. Chiang Ping-kun, the Chairman of Straits Exchange Foundation (SEF), pointed out that the content of ECFA is more important than its name. The structure of ECFA would be consulted and decided by the meeting of SEF and the Association for Relations across the Taiwan Strait (ARATS). [2]

The main differences between the name of CEPA and that of ECFA are as follows:

(1) comparing with terms "Mainland and Hong Kong or Macao" in CEPA, "across the Taiwan Strait" in ECFA has been fully accepted by the two contracting parties for decades, avoiding potential dispute on the names of the instrument and reflecting the political wisdom of the two parties; and

(2) comparing with term "arrangement" in CEPA, "agreement" in ECFA is more adaptable to political consideration and stance of Taiwan authorities for "concluding a FTA with mainland China". In addition, the term "framework agreement" in ECFA is more precise to indicate the nature and contents of this structural and

---

[1] Point 4, The Joint Communiqué of Communist Party of China General Secretary HU Jintao and People First Party Chairman James SOONG on 12 May 2005 (in Chinese), *People's Daily*, 13 May 2005, p. 1.

[2] "Chiang Ping-kun: ECFA listed in Schedule of Chiang-Chen Meeting" (in Chinese), *Macau Daily*, 7 March 2009, p. A9.

fundamental instrument.

As for the names of contracting parties of ECFA, the two parties use the names of organs authorized by mainland China and Chinese Taipei, namely the ARATS for mainland China and the SEF for Chinese Taipei instead of their official names under WTO regime. To the Committee on Regional Trade Agreement (CRTA) of WTO, the names of contracting parties in ECFA are stranger than that in CEPA.[1] It is the only case in WTO history that two WTO members submit their RTA to CRTA by authorized organs, using the total different names from their official names in WTO. It is also the first case in RTA history that the RTA is concluded by authorized organs rather than authorities themselves.

III. Basic Principles

Principles for fulfilling and revising CEPA are: (1) following the policy of "one country two systems"; (2) conforming to WTO rules; (3) adapting the needs for adjustment and promotion of mutual industrial structures, promoting stable and sustainable development; (4) realizing mutual benefits, supplement of superiority and common prosperity; and (5) easy first and making progress step by step. To some extent most of the principles of CEPA are also adaptable to ECFA due to the same objectives and purposes of the two instruments.

According to the text the basic principles of ECFA are: (1) equal and mutual benefits, making progress step by step; and (2) conforming to WTO rules.

1. Equal and mutual benefits, making progress step by step

The preamble of ECFA states that the two contracting parties "observe the principle of equal and mutual benefits, making progress step by step..." In fact, the so called "the principle of equal and mutual benefits, making progress step by step" is the summary of the above principles (3), (4) and (5) in CEPA.

The objectives of ECFA also embody this basic principle:

"1. enhancing and promoting the economic, trade and investment cooperation across the Strait;

---

[1] The names of contracting parties in CEPA are the Ministry of Commerce of PRC for mainland China and Financial Department of HKSAR for Hong Kong.

　　2. promoting further liberalization of trade in goods and service, and setting up gradually an equal, transparent, and efficient investment regime and its guarantee regime;

　　3. expanding the fields of economic cooperation, and setting up a cooperation regime. "

For Chinese Taipei, the equal principle is especially considered from political aspect. It should be pointed out that "the specialty of the cross-Strait relations" is the key to understand the difference between ECFA and other general RTAs. In this sense, the application of the principle of equal and mutual benefits does not mean the balanced arrangements in specific sectors or projects one by one. It might be considered with a wide field of vision and long term perspective. [1]

　　2. Conforming to WTO rules

As China and Chinese Taipei are separate WTO members, they have to comply with WTO rules when they negotiate and conclude ECFA, fulfilling their relevant commitments and obligations of WTO. Trade relations between them cannot be out of WTO regime.

The preamble of ECFA states that "the two contracting parties agree to decrease or abolish the barrier of trade and investment and to create a fair and equitable environment for trade and investment based on basic principles of WTO and considering the situations of both parties…"

There are some other provisions on WTO rules in ECFA. For examples, as for contents of negotiation on Agreement on Trade in Goods across the Strait, it refers to Agreement on Technical Barriers to Trade (TBT), Agreement on the Application of Sanitary and Phytosanitary Measures (SPS), and measures of trade remedies under WTO regime, including Agreement on Implementation of Article VI of General Agreement on Tariffs and Trade 1994, Agreement on Subsidies and Countervailing Measures, and Agreement on Safeguards, etc. [2] According to the Application

---

　　[1] For example, according to Article 7 of ECFA and Annex 1, in the aspect of trade in goods, mainland China should reduce the tariffs for 539 items of products originated from Taiwan, while Taiwan should only reduce the tariffs for 267 items of products originated from mainland China.

　　[2] Art. 3, ECFA.

of Agreement on Safeguards to Earlier Harvest of Trade in Goods across the Strait, [1] if there is not rule provided in the Annex, Agreement on Safeguards under WTO regime applies with some limitations or conditions.

Clauses on Investment[2] and Economic cooperation[3] in ECFA are also relevant to WTO rules to some extent.

However it should be further pointed out that as a WTO member, it only bears obligations within the ambit of WTO. [4] To a member of WTO, it is very important to distinguish the concept of "within the ambit of WTO" and "beyond the ambit of WTO". Within the ambit of WTO it is undoubted that all members have to observe WTO rules and fulfill their commitments to WTO seriously. At the same time, as all the duties and obligations of all WTO members are limited to their commitments to WTO, beyond the ambit of WTO, members may regulate their economic relations through bilateral agreement or RTAs. Since the investment and other economic matters across the Strait are "beyond the ambit of WTO", they are subject to ECFA and other cross-Strait bilateral agreements rather than WTO rules.

Ⅳ. Institutional Arrangements

Institutional regime is very important for stable and consistent economic cooperation among or between States and/or regions. Indeed setting up an institutional

---

[1]　Annex 3 to ECFA.

[2]　Art. 5, ECFA.

[3]　Art. 6, ECFA.

[4]　It seems that for a WTO member who is at the same time a member of RTA, the key issue is to identify the relationship between RTAs and WTO rules. The objects of WTO rules and RTAs are different. They are not identical or overlapped. The main reasons are that first, WTO systems and RTA systems have been developing concurrently and have not been subordinate to each other. Second, WTO is a trade organization, regulating the trade relations among its members, and a RTA is an economic integration arrangement, regulating the economic (including trade) relations among its parties. Although the fields governed by WTO rules have been extended greatly after Uruguay Round, WTO rules certainly cannot cover all economic sectors of its members. In fact, the fields governed by RTAs might be wider than those governed by WTO rules. Third, even in the same fields covered by WTO rules and RTAs, due to inherent defects of a multilateral framework, the WTO rules could not replace RTAs. Fourth, a membership of WTO is not a prerequisite for parties to a RTA. Some parties of a RTA who are not WTO members have not any obligations to WTO. Finally, many RTAs have been established before GATT or WTO. To some extent, the rules on RTAs of GATT/WTO are recognition or compromise to the reality of existing RTAs. Therefore a RTA concluded by WTO members is not necessarily required to be consistent fully with WTO rules or only limited in the fields governed by WTO rules. The only requirement for WTO members is that those subject to WTO rules in a RTA shall be consistent with WTO rules. In other words, when a WTO member engages in a RTA, it should fulfil its WTO obligations.

regime with stronger binding force for further economic cooperation across the Strait is a remarkable achievement of ECFA. There are three important aspects in the institutional arrangements under ECFA.

1. Scope of economic cooperation with emphasis on investment

ECFA is a comprehensive economic cooperation agreement. The content of ECFA substantially covers all the main economic activities (i. e. trade in goods and service, investment, and other economic cooperation) across the Strait. Comparing with a traditional RTA, there is great emphasis on investment in ECFA.

The objectives of ECFA include enhancing and promoting the economic, trade and investment cooperation across the Strait; and promoting further liberalization of trade in goods and service, and setting up gradually an equal, transparent, and efficient investment regime and its guarantee regime. [1]

Among the cooperation measures of ECFA, there are indications on providing investment protection, promoting mutual investment; and promoting efficient of trade and investment, and industry exchanges and cooperation. [2]

Chapter 2 of ECFA titled as "trade and investment" clearly indicates that the contracting parties put the trade and investment in equal position.

Furthermore the Article 5 of ECFA is an "investment clause", dealing exclusively with the investment matter. It provides that the items of future investment agreement across the Strait include: (1) to set up investment guarantee regime; (2) to improve the transparency of investment regulations; (3) to decrease the restrictions on mutual investment; and (4) to promote the efficient of investment.

For the long period of time, the economic relation across the Strait is abnormal due to political reasons even after China and Chinese Taipei's accession to WTO. In particular, the investment relation across the Strait is one-way movement only from Taiwan to mainland due to prohibition by Taiwan authorities. By above-mentioned provisions, ECFA will greatly promote comprehensive economic cooperation across the Strait, and especially change the investment relation across the Strait from one-way to two-way movement.

---

[1] Art. 1, ECFA.
[2] Art. 2, ECFA.

2. Group of topic-oriented agreements with timetable

As its name indicates, ECFA is a framework agreement for economic cooperation across the Strait, serving as a fundamental instrument for other topic-oriented agreements within its domain.

According to relevant schedule, the two parties of ECFA will negotiate agreements on investment guarantee, dispute settlement, trade in goods, and trade in service respectively within half a year after taking effect of ECFA. Among the four items, investment guarantee is listed in the schedule of sixth Chen-Jiang Meeting[1] held in the end of this year. The negotiation for trade in goods and trade in service will be held within three months after taking effect of ECFA.

3. Enforcement mechanism with strong binding force

Comparing with CEPA, ECFA sets up an enforcement mechanism with stronger binding force, and especially provides time limit for negotiation on setting up a proper proceedings for cross-Strait dispute resolutions. According to Article 11 of ECFA, the two parties set up the Committee on Economic Cooperation across the Strait (hereinafter the Committee).

The Committee is composed of representatives from both sides, dealing with related matters of ECFA, including but not limit to: (1) conciliation for completing objectives of the Agreement; (2) supervising and evaluating the enforcement of the Agreement; (3) explaining the provisions of the Agreement; (4) reporting important information on economic and trade; and (5) settling the disputes on explanation, enforcement and application of the Agreement.

The two parties of ECFA should conduct the conciliation and conclude an agreement as soon as possible for setting up proceedings for settling the disputes on explanation, enforcement and application of the Agreement within six months after taking effect of the Agreement. Before the establishment of the dispute settlement proceedings, the said disputes will be settled by the Committee.[2]

Setting up the Committee is an important landmark of realization of the regime

---

[1] The Chen-Jiang Meeting refers to the Cross-Strait Meeting led by Mr. Chen Yunlin, the President of ARATS (mainland China) and Mr. Chiang Ping-kun, the Chairman of SEF (Taiwan).

[2] Art. 10.1, ECFA.

of economic and trade relations across the Strait. [1] It seems that after establishment of the dispute settlement proceedings across the Strait, the economic disputes, including the trade disputes across the Strait, will be submitted to the dispute settlement body by ECFA, rather than dispute settlement mechanism of WTO. This is great initiative of an internal RTA practice in this regard.

Ⅴ. International Implications

ECFA is considered by Taiwan authorities as key step for its further RTA practice with foreign States. Mr. Chiang Ping-kun, the head of SEF, pointed out that ECFA is not only an important milestone in the history of economic and trade relations across the Strait, but also a key step of both contracting parties of ECFA for dealing with relevant matters under the regional economic integration and globalization. [2]

According to Xinhua News Agency, Press Release from Taipei Representative Agency in Singapore and Singapore Commerce Office in Taipei on 5 August 2010, states that Chinese Taipei and Singapore, being WTO members, agree to conduct a research on the feasibilities for concluding an economic cooperation agreement and will discuss the issue late this year. [3] It might indicate a possible breakthrough for Chinese Taipei's RTA practice with foreign States. However the treaty-making power of Chinese Taipei is still the foremost crucial issue.

1. Treaty-making power of non-sovereign entities: experience of HKSAR

According to traditional international law, only sovereign States may be contracting parties of treaties. In the development of modern international practice, more and more non-sovereign entities have become the contracting parties of treaties. In addition to sovereign States, international organizations, member States of federal States, belligerent, and regional entities with high autonomy, etc., have become the new comer for negotiating and concluding treaties. The legal grounds for

---

[1] "Experts: 'ECFA Has the Same Objectives and Approach as CEPA'", *Wen Hui Bao* (*Hong Kong*), 30 June 2010.

[2] "Chiang Ping-kun: 'Signing ECFA Is an Important Milestone for Economic and Trade Relations across the Taiwan Strait'", www. chinataiwan. org, 2010-07-05.

[3] "Singapore and Taiwan Will Explore the Feasibility for Concluding Economic Agreement", *Xiamen Daily*, 6 August 2010, p. 18.

these non-sovereign entities are different. The source of their treaty-making power comes from basic instruments for international organizations, from federal constitutions for member States of federal States, from customary international law for belligerent, and from authorization by sovereign States for regional entities. [1]

The HKSAR is granted general authority to conclude bilateral treaties with foreign States and other regions in the appropriate fields by provisions of Sino-British Joint Declaration on the Question of Hong Kong (hereinafter the JD)[2] and the Basic Law of Hong Kong Special Administrative Region of the People's Republic of China (hereinafter the BL). The HKSAR may on its own, using the name "Hong Kong, China", maintain and develop relations and conclude and implement agreements with foreign States and regions and relevant international organizations in the appropriate fields, including the economic, trade, financial and monetary, shipping, communications, tourism, cultural and sports fields. [3] Although this kind of formulation has not yet acquired popular usage in international law, its form clearly constituted Hong Kong as an entity with the capacity to enter into bilateral treaties within the specified fields. [4]

Furthermore the treaty-making power of HKSAR is based on the HKSAR's external autonomy. It is indicated that the HKSAR's external autonomy does not solely depend on the unilateral desire of Hong Kong, China or the UK—it also depends on whether other States are willing to recognize this status. [5] Actually the HKSAR's external autonomy could become meaningless if few States and international organizations were interested in developing and maintaining separate relations with it. According to principle of international law, unlike States and international organizations, which are regarded as the normal types of international legal persons

---

[1] See Haopei LI, *On the Laws of Treaties* (in Chinese), Law Press, 240 (1988).

[2] Joint Declaration of Government of United Kingdom of Great Britain and Northern Ireland and the People's Republic of China on the Question of Hong Kong was formally signed on 19 December 1984 and came into force on 27 May 1985. The agreement was reprinted in 23 *ILM* 1371-1380 (1984).

[3] Art. 3, 9, 10, the JD; Section XI of Annex I of the JD; Art. 151, the BL. The key to the scope of HK's treaty-making power is the concept of "appropriate fields". The term itself is not defined, and it is necessary to examine all the provisions of the BL to determine in what areas Hong Kong may have capacity for external relations. See Yash Ghai, *Hong Kong's New Constitutional Order*, *The Resumption of Chinese Sovereignty and the Basic Law*, Hong Kong University Press, 435-436 (1997).

[4] See Anthony Neoh, "Hong Kong's Future: The View of a Hong Kong Lawyer", 22 *Cal. W. Int'l L. J.* 351-352 (1992).

[5] Albert H. Y. Chen, "Some Reflections on Hong Kong's Autonomy", 24 *HKLJ*, 179-180 (1994).

and can acquire their international personalities by meeting fixed conditions, the HKSAR's external autonomy and international legal status relies on not only China's authorization but also the recognition and acceptance of other existing international persons.[1]

2. Challenge for Chinese Taipei's RTAs with foreign States

May Chinese Taipei take ECFA as a precedent for concluding RTAs with foreign States? This is a very important and sensitive issue for international lawyers.

Two legal points should be clarified before touching the core issue:

First, Chinese Taipei's WTO membership is irrelevant to the issue on its treaty-making power. According to Article 12 of WTO Agreement, WTO members include sovereign States and SCTs.[2] Since Chinese Taipei enters into the WTO in the status of a SCT, its status of non-sovereign entity remains unchanged.[3]

Second, ECFA is an internal RTA concluded by the two parties from a same sovereign State, not a treaty. Therefore Chinese Taipei's position as a contracting party of ECFA is also irrelevant to the issue on its treaty-making power. There is sharp difference in nature between an internal RTA and an international RTA. A qualified contracting party of an internal RTA may be not qualified as a contracting party of an international RTA due to not meeting the certain requirements of international law.

It is evident that Chinese Taipei should follow modern international law on treaty-making power of non-sovereign entities in its RTA practice with foreign States. According to modern international law and practice, the treaty-making power of a non-sovereign entity relies on not only sovereign State's authorization but also the recognition and acceptance of other existing international persons.[4] HKSAR is

---

〔1〕 Xiaobing XU, George D. Wilson, "The Hong Kong Special Administrative Region as a Model of Regional External Autonomy", 32 *Case W. Res. J. Int'l L.*, 31 (2000).

〔2〕 Article 12 of WTO Agreement provides that: "Any State or separate customs territory possessing full autonomy in the conduct of its external commercial relations and of the other matters provided for in this Agreement and the Multilateral Trade Agreements may accede to this Agreement, on terms to be agreed between it and the WTO. Such accession shall apply to this Agreement and the Multilateral Trade Agreements annexed thereto."

〔3〕 For the comments on treaty-making power of Hong Kong, see ZENG Huaqun, "Unprecedented International Status: Theoretical and Practical Aspects of the HKSAR's External Autonomy", 9 (3) *The Journal of World Investment & Trade*, 283-287 (2008).

〔4〕 See Xiaobing XU, George D. Wilson, "The Hong Kong Special Administrative Region as a Model of Regional External Autonomy", 32 *Case W. Res. J. Int'l L.*, 31 (2000).

good example in this regard. HKSAR has been authorized treaty-making power by central government of PRC and widely recognized by international society. For Chinese Taipei, to meet the first prerequisite of sovereign State's authorization for its treaty-making power is a great challenge due to the present political situation across the Strait. The solution should be sought for by common efforts across the Strait for achieving consensus, cooperation, and legal initiative.

The legal situation of "one China four WTO memberships", indicating clearly the SCT status of Chinese Taipei, further reflects that the one-China principle is well recognized by all WTO members and international society. Therefore Chinese Taipei and its potential counterparts should follow the one-China principle in their RTA practice.

第一节　欧共体明示与隐含缔约权力浅析[＊]

【摘要】　本文根据《罗马条约》的有关规定,结合欧洲法院有关判例和意见,初步分析欧共体明示缔约权力与隐含缔约权力的内涵。作者指出,在明示缔约权力方面,《罗马条约》已有"共同商业政策"等明示规定,其含义通过欧洲法院的实践进一步丰富和发展;隐含缔约权力是欧共体对外缔约的另一重要法律基础,是其缔约权力的重要组成部分;平行发展原则派生于欧共体的隐含缔约权力原则,对欧共体对外缔约活动的发展起了重要的推动作用。

【关键词】　明示缔约权力;隐含缔约权力;平行发展原则

在中国与欧洲联盟(the European Union,EU,以下简称"欧盟")经济关系的发展中,需要签订中国与欧洲共同体(the European Communities, EC,以下简称"欧共体")之间的双边经济条约。[1]鉴于欧共体法律体系庞大复杂,在中国与欧共体谈判

　＊　原载《厦门大学学报》(哲学社会科学版)2000年第1期。

　〔1〕　关于欧盟的法律人格问题,目前学者之间和欧盟成员国之间均存在分歧。有学者认为,根据国际法院的"功能主义检验方式",欧盟可具有法律人格。另有学者指出,基于如下原因,欧盟不具有法律人格:(1) 在《欧盟条约》中,没有如《罗马条约》第210条的明示规定;(2) 期望欧盟可行使的对外权力事实上已由欧共体行使。在"共同外交与防务"等新领域,《欧盟条约》未授权给欧盟;(3) 在《欧盟条约》谈判期间,欧共体成员国明确的意愿是不赋予欧盟法律人格。

　多数欧共体成员国认为,赋予欧盟国际法律人格有利于欧盟在有关共同外交和防务、司法与内务等对外领域签订国际条约。它们认为,欧盟未成为法律实体是导致混乱的根源,并且将削弱其对外作用。另一些成员国认为,创设欧盟的国际法律人格将导致与其成员国法律权利混淆的危险。荷兰政府坚决主张欧盟不能具有法律人格。英国的观点是,欧盟不具有国际法律人格。See Dominic McGoldrick, *International Relations Law of the European Union*, Longman, pp. 36-39 (1997)。

　关于这一问题的讨论,可进一步参阅 Jan Klabbers, Presumptive Personality: The European Union in International Law, in Martti Koskenniemi(ed.), *International Law Aspects of the European Union*, Kluwer Law Internationnal, pp. 231-253 (1998); Ramses A. Wessel, The International Legal Status of the European Union, 2 *European Foreign Affairs Review*, pp109-129 (1997); Constantine A. Stephanou, The Legal Nature of the European Union, in Nicholas Emiliou and David O'Keeffe (ed.), *Legal Aspects of Integration in the European Union*, Kluwer Law International, pp. 171-185 (1997)。鉴于欧盟的国际法律人格尚未确立,首先应当指出,是欧共体具有缔约权力,而不是欧盟。

签订双边经济条约时,应对欧共体的缔约权力有较明确、深入的认识和理解。本文拟根据《建立欧洲经济共同体条约》(the Treaty Establishing European Economic Community,以下简称《罗马条约》)的有关规定,结合欧洲法院的有关判例和意见,对欧共体缔约权力问题的一个层面,即明示与隐含缔约权力的内涵作一初步分析。[1]

一、明示缔约权力原则与隐含缔约权力原则

《罗马条约》第 210 条清楚而准确地规定,欧共体"具有法律人格"。这是主张国际法上的人格,而不是在各成员国中的法律人格。因为第 211 条明确规定了欧共体在各成员国中"享有法人的最广泛的法律能力"。根据国际法的一般原则,国际组织的国际法律人格未包含一般的缔约权力。其缔约权力可依"授权"(empowerment)和"专业"(speciality)原则从其宗旨和职能推断。[2] 由于欧共体是一体化程度最高的国际组织,其缔约权力更显得复杂。在欧共体对外关系发展过程中,出现了先后占主导地位的明示缔约权力原则和隐含缔约权力原则。

（一）明示缔约权力原则(Doctrine of Explicit power)

《罗马条约》第 228 条明确规定了欧共体的缔约权力,即欧共体可同其他国家或国际组织签订"建立含有相互权利和责任、共同行动和特别程序的联系"协定。问题在于,欧共体的缔约权力是否限于《罗马条约》明示规定的范围。

在欧共体成立初期,明示缔约权力原则居主导地位。该原则主张,由于《罗马条约》第 228 条规定欧共体谈判由"(罗马)条约规定由其签订"的协定,欧共体的缔约权力限于《罗马条约》明示规定者。该条约采取列举权力的模式,分配具体权力给欧共体,未分配的权力仍保留于成员国。[3] 这一解释通过将《罗马条约》第 228 条与《欧洲原子能共同体条约》第 101 条明确的用语比较而得到加强。根据后者的有关规定,欧洲原子能共同体的缔约权力是很广泛的。

为了在欧共体各机构之间建立一种平衡关系,《罗马条约》第 228 条规定,在该条约规定由欧共体签订国际协定时,应由欧共体执行委员会(以下简称"执委会")进行谈判,由欧共体部长理事会(以下简称"理事会")签订此种协定。在《罗马条约》规

---

〔1〕 关于欧共体缔约权力的另一重要层面是欧共体的专属权力(exclusive power)和共享权力(shared power)问题,涉及缔约主体和条约责任归属问题。限于篇幅,笔者拟另文探讨。

〔2〕 See Constantine A. Stephanou, The Legal Nature of the European Union, in Nicholas Emiliou and David O'Keeffe (ed.), *Legal Aspects of Integration in the European Union*, Kluwer Law International, pp. 181-182 (1997).

〔3〕 See Moshe Kaniel, *The Exclusive Treaty-Making Power of the European Community: Up to the Period of the Single European Act*, Kluwer Law International, p. 38 (1996).

定的情况下,还须经向欧洲议会咨询的程序。自《欧洲联盟条约》(the Treaty on the European Union)生效之后,理事会被授权在特别多数通过（qualified majority）的情况下进行对外签约活动。但是,在签订《罗马条约》第 238 条规定的联系协定和涉及特定领域(即需要适用一致通过程序的内部规则的领域)的协定时,理事会在对外签约之前,需要适用一致通过的程序。[1]

在 1985 年《单一欧洲法令》(the Single European Act)中也体现了欧共体在特定领域明示规定缔约权力的趋向。该法令对《罗马条约》增加了两个条款,确立了有关技术研究与发展、环境方面的权力。根据新增的条款,即第 130M 条[2]和 103R 条,欧共体在上述两个领域的合作协定应根据《罗马条约》第 228 条谈判和签署。[3]

（二）隐含缔约权力原则(Doctrine of Implicit Power)

持隐含缔约权力原则者反对援引《罗马条约》第 228 条作为论证明示缔约权力的法律依据。他们认为,第 228 条不能视为规定欧共体的实体性缔约权力,而只能视为规定谈判签约程序之前的最初步骤。换言之,欧共体的缔约权力可以是明示的,也可以是隐含的。在确定欧共体是否具有签订特定国际协定的权力时,应考虑《罗马条约》的整个体制。欧共体的缔约权力不仅产生于《罗马条约》的明示授予,也同样来自该条约的其他规定以及由欧共体机构通过的、在这些条约规定框架之内的措施。有的学者还认为,《罗马条约》第 235 条可作为隐含缔约权力的法律基础。[4]

实践中,欧洲法院在"欧洲路运协定"(ERTA)案等判例一致支持和进一步确立了隐含缔约权力原则。[5] 因此,该原则目前已取代明示缔约原则居于主导地位。

二、欧洲法院有关明示缔约权力的意见

一般认为,欧共体两项最重要的明示缔约权力体现于根据《罗马条约》第 113 条和第 238 条分别签订商务协定和联系协定的权力。鉴于第 238 条在实践中未产生重

---

〔1〕　See Nicholas Emiliou and David O'Keeffe (eds.), *The European Union and World Trade Law: After the GATT Uruguay Round*, John Wiley & Sons Ltd., p. 41 (1996).

〔2〕　《罗马条约》第 130N 条由《欧盟条约》修改为第 130M 条。

〔3〕　See Moshe Kaniel, *The Exclusive Treaty-Making Power of the European Community: Up to the Period of the Single European Act*, Kluwer Law International, pp. 28-29 (1996).

〔4〕　《罗马条约》第 235 条规定:"在共同市场的运作过程中,如果本共同体之行为的确为实现本共同体宗旨之一所必要,而且本条约尚未规定必要之权力,理事会根据执委会的提案,并与大会协商后,应以全体一致的方式采取适当措施。"从字面上看,该规定未明确提及欧共体的对外关系措施,但从欧共体的实践看,该规定的"行为"和"措施"可以是欧共体内部事项,也可以是涉外事项。参见曾令良:《欧洲共同体与现代国际法》,武汉大学出版社 1992 年版,第 59—61 页。

〔5〕　See Moshe Kaniel, *The Exclusive Treaty-Making Power of the European Community: Up to the Period of the Single European Act*, Kluwer Law International, pp. 29-30 (1996).

要分歧，[1]以下评述欧洲法院有关第113条涵义的意见。

"对第三国建立共同关税和共同商业政策"，是欧共体为实现其宗旨而确立的重要原则。[2]《罗马条约》第113条是欧共体共同商业政策的主要条款。该条未包含共同商业政策的定义，但规定了未穷尽的统一原则，即"特别是有关税率的变化，关税和贸易协定的签订，统一自由化措施的达成，出口政策和在倾销和津贴情况下的贸易保护措施"。

在程序方面，执委会应向理事会提出实施共同商业政策的各种建议。[3]当需要与第三国签订协定时，执委会应向理事会提出建议，后者应授权前者进行必要的谈判。[4]如谈判成功，则由理事会代表欧共体签订协定。[5]

关于共同商业政策的范围，欧共体各主要机构意见不尽一致。理事会认为，仅有贸易的数额或流动属于共同商业政策的范围。然而，执委会在许多场合主张，理事会这一评价是针对调整国际贸易措施的基本特征而作出的。法院虽未表明明确的立场，但其判例对共同商业政策范围的进一步具体化作出了贡献。

法院的出发点是共同商业政策概念无论适用于成员国或欧共体的国际行动的场合，内容是相同的。因此，对适用于欧共体场合的共同商业政策概念作狭义解释，并无明显的理由。相反，关税联盟的适当职能使第113条的广义解释和欧共体机构据之拥有权力的广义解释成为合理的，即"使其通过独立采取的措施和通过协议充分地控制对外贸易"。

根据这一逻辑，法院认为，第112条涉及的对向第三国出口的援助和有关出口信贷的措施，必然属于第113(1)条的"出口政策"范围。第113(1)条规定的统一原则范围还包括"无论税务或商务领域，影响与第三国贸易的各国不同的限制措施。"法院还认为，不能将第113条解释为，共同商业政策只是对传统对外贸易有效工具的利用，而排除更为发达的国际贸易机制，例如，与联合国有关新国际经济秩序的发展相关的国际商品协定。否则，共同商业政策"将注定随时间的推移而归于无效。虽然可以认为，在条约起草时，贸易自由化是主导的理念，无论如何，条约不会阻碍欧共体发展旨在调整特定产品的世界市场、而不仅仅是贸易自由化的商业政策"。

---

　　[1]　该条款主要是为当时在欧洲经济合作组织中谈判建立欧洲自由贸易区而订立的，虽然未能如愿，但成为后来欧共体与有关第三国建立特殊关系的重要法律根据。从实践看，联系协定的主要对象国包括欧共体成员国之外的其他欧洲国家、与欧共体成员国有历史联系（殖民地与宗主国关系等）和地中海沿岸国家。参见曾令良：《欧洲共同体与现代国际法》，武汉大学出版社1992年版，第57页。

　　[2]　《罗马条约》第3条。

　　[3]　《罗马条约》第113(2)条。

　　[4]　《罗马条约》第113(3)条。

　　[5]　《罗马条约》第114条。

不仅如此,根据法院的观点,欧共体对发展中国家的普遍关税优惠"反映了国际贸易关系的新概念,其中,发展旨在发挥重要作用"。因此,欧共体适用于普遍关税优惠制度的规则属于共同商业政策的范围,无须《罗马条约》第113条之外的其他法律根据。

在法院第1/78号意见中,涉及欧共体签订由联合国主持的国际橡胶协定的权力。法院发现没有理由因该协定对某些部门的经济政策可能产生影响,或者因建立产品库存具有政治意义,而将该协定排除于共同商业政策范围之外。从该意见中可见,对协定的表述"应在考虑其基本宗旨的基础上,而不是在附属性的各个条款的基础上评估"。[1]

法院在第1/94号意见中对共同商业政策的概念作了进一步解释。该意见涉及欧共体签署关贸总协定乌拉圭回合协定(包括《建立世界贸易组织协定》、《多边货物贸易协定》、《服务贸易总协定》和《与贸易有关的知识产权协定》等)的权能。执委会要求法院根据《罗马条约》第228(6)条提供意见。该意见主要集中于欧共体是否具有签订这些协定的专属权力。

法院认为,根据《罗马条约》第113条,欧共体具有签订多边货物贸易协定的专属管辖权。这些权力包括贸易的技术壁垒协议并扩及农产品以及由《欧洲原子能共同体条约》和《欧洲煤钢共同体条约》所包括的产品的关税规则。

对于《服务贸易总协定》,法院裁定,签订该协定的权力应由欧共体及其成员国分享。法院认为,共同商业政策的概念应予以广义的、非限制的解释,服务可属于《罗马条约》第113条的范围。然而,法院也指出,在《服务贸易总协定》规定的提供服务的四种模式中,只有跨国提供服务"不容置疑地包含于条约意义上的共同商业政策"。其他三种服务模式由于包含了自然人和法人的流动,由《罗马条约》确立共同商业政策以外的其他宗旨所涵盖,因此不属于第113条的范围。

对《与知识产权有关的贸易协定》,法院认为,除了欧共体有关禁止伪造品自由流转的措施外,知识产权不属于《罗马条约》第113条的范围。虽然知识产权与货物贸易之间存在联系,例如知识产权拥有者可防止第三人从事某些交易行为,但这种联系不能构成将知识产权归属于第113条范围的适当理由,因为知识产权并非具体地与国际贸易相关;它们影响国内贸易与影响国际贸易相同。因此,签订《与知识产权有关的贸易协定》的权力应由欧共体及其成员国分享。[2]

---

〔1〕 该意见发表于 M. van Empel, H. G. Schermers, E. L. M. Volker, J. A. Winter (eds.), *Leading Cases on the Law of the European Communities*, Kluwer Law and Taxation Publishers, pp. 690-695 (1990)。

〔2〕 See Nicholas Emiliou and David O'Keeffe (eds.), *The European Union and World Trade Law: After the GATT Uruguay Round*, John Wiley & Sons Ltd., pp. 31-38 (1996).

三、欧洲法院有关隐含缔约权力的判例

由于隐含缔约权力原则主要是在欧洲法院判例中发展，以下选择两个典型案例进一步说明。

（一）欧洲路运协定案（ERTA Case）

1962年，在联合国欧洲经济委员会主持下，欧共体当时的五个成员国与另一欧洲国家签订了有关从事国际运输的汽车司机工作的协定。1967年，在欧洲运输部长执委会（the European Commission of Transport Ministers）的主持下，开始展开修改该协定的谈判。在谈判期间，1969年，欧共体理事会颁布了内部层面上的有关该事项的法规。

1970年，欧共体理事会决定了欧共体六个成员国在欧洲路运协定会议上的共同谈判立场，并形成决议。随后，在欧洲路运协定会议上欧共体六个成员国签署了该协定。然而，在该协定签署之前，欧共体执委会根据《罗马条约》第173条，要求欧洲法院裁决该领域属于欧共体的管辖权，只有欧共体——而不是其成员国——可签署该协定，相应地，欧共体理事会1970年关于共同谈判立场的决议和由成员国与第三国签订的该协定应属无效。

作为原则问题，法院必须决定，在交通运输领域进行谈判和签订国际条约的权力是属于欧共体或其成员国。法院认为，《罗马条约》对该事项未作明示规定，因此有必要遵循有关与第三国签订协议的欧共体法一般方式。欧共体的缔约权力可来自《罗马条约》的一般体制（scheme），与来自明示的规定相同。该权力也可来自欧共体机构采取的行为，特别是为履行《罗马条约》规定的政策而颁布规则和法规。《罗马条约》第210条规定，欧共体具有法律人格，这意味着在对外关系中，欧共体拥有在《罗马条约》第一部分确立的宗旨框架中，与非成员国签订协议的能力。

在实施《罗马条约》的规定时，可能区分在内部层面采取的措施和在对外层面上建立的关系。根据《罗马条约》第3(e)条，在运输领域采取共同政策明示表述为宗旨之一。按该条约第5条规定，成员国应采取所有适当措施以确保履行产生于该条约的责任或产生于欧共体机构采取的行为的责任，并且应避免采取任何可能阻碍该条约宗旨实现的行为。法院认为，上述两条款共同导向的结论是，一旦欧共体规定了为实现《罗马条约》宗旨的规则，成员国就不得采取任何可能阻碍此类规则或修改其范围的行为。换言之，构成此类规则的基础的权力专属于欧共体。

法院进而提及《罗马条约》第74、75条。第74条规定，《罗马条约》宗旨必须根据共同政策在属于运输领域的各个方面实现。第75(1)条指示理事会颁布共同规则和

其他适当的规定以履行第 75 条。第 75(1)(a)条明示规定此类共同规则应适用于来往或途径成员国领土的国际运输。因此,欧共体的权力也扩及来源于使其与第三国签订协定成为必要的国际法之关系。

就本案事实而言,理事会第 543/69 号法规涉及欧洲路运协定会议主题的领域。其结果是,虽未明示表述,欧共体在有关欧洲路运协定享有专属权力。成员国不享有在此领域的权力(包括平行权力)。因为,成员国如享有此项权力,将与共同市场的统一和欧共体法的统一适用不相符合。

法院最后判决,虽然原则上欧共体在此领域享有专属权力,鉴于该案的特殊情况,包括第一个协定是在过渡期间签订、执委会未根据第 75 条和 116 条提出共同政策或根据第 228 条提出有关谈判的议案等,法院最后确认了欧共体理事会决议和由成员国签订的协议的有效性。[1]

欧洲路运协定案的判决具有很重要的意义。首先,在该案中,法院第一次明确判决欧共体具有隐含缔约权力。它指出,根据普遍接受的国际法规则,欧共体的缔约权力可来自《罗马条约》的一般体制,不限于该条约中明示规定者。其次,法院认为,在实施《罗马条约》的规定时,不可能区分欧共体在内部层面上采取的措施和在对外层面上建立的关系。不仅如此,法院将欧共体的对内权力和对外权力紧密联系起来,指出欧共体的对外权力是其对内权力的自然延伸。因此,欧共体在其有权作出有约束力的内部规则的所有领域中,有权与第三国签订条约。[2]

(二)克雷默案(Kramer Case)

这是在荷兰法院提起的对荷兰渔民克雷默等的刑事诉讼。原告指控被告违反了荷兰根据《东北大西洋渔业公约》(以下简称《渔业公约》)[3]的有关规定颁布的规则。被告律师辩称,由于欧共体在该领域具有专属权力,荷兰政府无权在此领域颁布规则。根据《罗马条约》第 177 条,该问题提交欧洲法院,请求作出欧共体在该领域是否具有专属权力的裁决。1970 年,欧共体理事会通过的第 2141/70 号和第 2142/70 号法规涉及此领域。

法院首先重申在欧洲路运协定案的判决,即根据《罗马条约》第 210 条,欧共体有权签订有关《罗马条约》第一部分为达其宗旨而列举的任何事项的国际协定。《罗马

---

〔1〕 See Moshe Kaniel, *The Exclusive Treaty-Making Power of the European Community*: *Up to the Period of the Single European Act*, Kluwer Law International, pp. 31-33 (1996).

〔2〕 See Henry G. Schermers, The Internal Effect of Community Treaty-Making, in David O'Keeffe and Henry G. Schermers (eds.), *Essays in European Law and Integration*, Kluwer Law and Taxation Publishers, p. 169 (1982).

〔3〕 1959 年由欧共体一些成员国,苏联和波兰签订该公约。

条约》第四部分(始于第 210 条)补充第一部分。在决定欧共体是否在特定领域具有缔约能力,有必要考察欧共体法的整个体制。此种权力可产生于明示的规定,也可通过隐含的方式。

接着,法院考察欧共体在渔业领域的权力。在农业领域的共同政策是《罗马条约》第 3(d)条列举的宗旨之一。由第 38(3)条和《罗马条约》附录可见,渔业显然属于农业。《罗马条约》第 39—46 条涉及农业领域:在第 39 条统一政策的因素包括确保产品的发展与提供;根据第 40 条,应建立农业生产者的共同组织;第 43 条规定,欧盟理事会有权在农业领域颁布法规、指令和决定。理事会据此颁布第 2141/70 号和第 2142/70 号法规。同样,欧共体根据《加入条约》(the Accession Treaty)第 102 条,应作出有关渔业条件的规定,以保护海洋生物资源。

法院认为,在内部层面上,欧共体显然具有采取保护资源的任何措施的权力,包括确定各成员国之间的份额。达成有效的保护资源的唯一方式是对有关国家,包括成员国施加有约束力的制度。在此情况下,欧共体在内部层面上授予其机构的权力,也延伸为欧共体在该领域签订国际协定的权力。

最后,法院需要解决的问题是决定欧共体是否已实际采取和承担了源于《渔业公约》的职能和责任。法院认为:首先,《渔业公约》签订于欧共体颁布有关法规之前,修改一协定应由该协定的缔约方进行谈判;其次,从《罗马条约》条款的用语明显可见,它们只授权欧共体机构采取如同其成员国在《渔业公约》框架内承担和实际履行的措施,而欧共体尚未行使此种权力。

法院的结论是,由于欧共体尚未充分行使其在渔业领域的职能与权力,成员国在本案诉讼期间,享有和承担《渔业公约》的有关权力和责任。然而,法院强调两个重要的观点:其一,根据《加入条约》第 102 条,成员国的权力是暂时的;其二,根据《罗马条约》第 5、116 条有关需要采取措施和协调产生于该条约的共同政策的规定,成员国在所有有关《渔业公约》的谈判中应受到欧共体责任的约束。因此,成员国不能承担可能阻碍欧共体依《加入条约》第 102 条履行其职能的新责任。一旦欧共体机构制定为履行此职能所需的程序,成员国应确保欧共体是《渔业公约》和其他同类协定的当事方。

法院在克雷默案中进一步发展了欧洲路运协定案确立的原则。在克雷默案中,法院认为,欧共体缔约权力不仅规定于《罗马条约》第 113 条的明示规定,也隐含于该条约的其他条款、《加入条约》的有关规定以及欧共体机构在上述规定框架中采取的措施。[1]比较克雷默案和欧洲路运协定案，就欧共体在特定领域缔约权力的基本条件而言，前者更为自由。在欧洲路运协定案判决中，前提是，有关规则必须由欧共体在对外层面上实际行使，即使只是平行的权力。在克雷默案中，法院判决，即使有关规则未实际行使，只要存在可据以行使的有关规则，例如该案的第 2141/70 号和第 2142/70 号规则，欧共体在该领域的缔约权力就已确立，虽然该权力不是专属性的。[2]

值得注意的是，上述两个判例确立了由欧共体隐含缔约权力原则派生的一项重要司法原则，即"平行发展原则"（the principle of parallel development），亦称"平行主义原则"（the doctrine of "parallelism"）。其含义是，允许欧共体的对外事务权能扩大为超出《罗马条约》明示规定以符合其对内部事务的日益增加的权能。[3]简言之，欧共体对内、对外的权力具有并行发展的性质。[4]欧洲路运协定案之后，一些欧共体成员国在理事会上反对某些内部措施，其理由是这些措施的通过将提高欧共体在相同事务方面的缔约能力。[5] 这从一个侧面反映了"平行主义原则"已为欧共体成员国和理事会肯定和接受。

四、结语

欧共体与第三国签订的条约在欧共体法律体系中的最高性得到其成员国的普遍承认。欧共体成员国不得与第三国签订任何与欧共体所承担的责任相冲突的条约。[6] 在这个意义上，中国与欧共体之间的双边经济条约安排对于发展中国与欧盟及其成员国之间的经济关系具有框架性、建设性和规范化的重要作用。

当前，调整中国与欧盟之间经济关系的总体性法律框架仍然是 1985 年《欧洲共同体与中华人民共和国之间贸易与经济合作协定》（the Trade and Economic Cooperation Agreement between the European Community and the People's Republic of China）。近 15 年来，中国的经济体制结构发生了重要转变，经济发展取得了举世瞩

---

〔1〕 See T. C. Hartley, *The Foundations of European Community Law*, Oxford University Press, p. 11 (1998).

〔2〕 See Moshe Kaniel, *The Exclusive Treaty-Making Power of the European Community: Up to the Period of the Single European Act*, Kluwer Law International, pp. 33-36 (1996).

〔3〕 See Ilona Cheyne, International Agreements and the European Community Legal System, 19 *European Law Review*, p. 583 (1994).

〔4〕 参见曾令良:《欧洲共同体与现代国际法》,武汉大学出版社 1992 年版,第 63 页。

〔5〕 See Nicholas Emiliou and David O'Keeffe (eds.), *The European Union and World Trade Law: After the GATT Uruguay Round*, John Wiley & Sons Ltd., pp. 40-41 (1996).

〔6〕 See Anne Peters, The Position of International Law within the European Community Legal Order, 40 *German Yearbook of International Law*, pp. 38-40 (1997).

目的成就,而欧共体的一体化发展迅速,在经济和政治方面均达到了新的水平。中欧经济和政治关系的发展也相应进入了建立"全面伙伴关系"的新阶段。在此形势下,签订更符合当前实际需要的新的中欧贸易与经济合作协定势在必行。另外,根据欧盟执委会 1998 年《关于建立与中国的全面伙伴关系》,中欧经贸对话将通过在特定领域,如海上运输,航空运输,原子能贸易与安全保障,科学与技术等领域签订双边条约予以加强。[1]

在同欧共体谈判和签订新的中欧贸易与经济合作协定和其他双边经济条约时,应对欧共体的缔约权力有深入的理解和全面的认识。首先,在明示缔约权力方面,《罗马条约》已有共同商业政策等明示规定,法院判例表明,共同商业政策概念是动态的概念。[2] 其含义并非一成不变,随着时间的推移和情势的变化,将通过欧洲法院的判例和意见进一步丰富和发展。

其次,隐含缔约权力是欧共体开展对外交往与合作的另一重要依据。自 70 年代以来,欧洲法院的判例确立和发展了欧共体隐含缔约权力原则。实践表明,隐含缔约权力为欧共体对外缔约提供了更为广泛、灵活的法律基础,是欧共体缔约权力的重要组成部分。然而,应指出的是,隐含缔约权力产生了法律的不确定。适用隐含缔约权力和适用《罗马条约》第 235 条之间的区分经常是模糊不清的。[3]

欧洲法院在其涉及欧共体隐含缔约权力的判例中,确立了欧共体对内管辖权与对外关系权平行发展的原则。可以说,平行发展原则派生于欧共体的隐含缔约权力原则。该原则的深刻含义在于,欧共体的缔约权力并不限于《罗马条约》的明示规定,欧共体在任何领域的内部权能均蕴藏着相应的对外缔约权力。这一原则对欧共体对外缔约活动的发展起了重要的推动作用。[4] 鉴此,作为欧共体的重要经济伙伴,中国对欧共体缔约权力及其内部权能的发展,均应予以持续的关注。

On EC's Explicit and Implicit Treaty Making Powers

Abstract: In the development of EC's foreign relations, the explicit and the implicit treaty making powers have been prevailed one after another. As for the explicit

---

〔1〕 See Communication from the Commission, Building a Comprehensive Partnership with China, *COM* (1998) 181 final, pp. 16-17.

〔2〕 See Nicholas Emiliou and David O'Keeffe (eds.), *The European Union and World Trade Law after the GATT Uruguay Round*, John Wiley & Sons Ltd., pp. 31, 35 (1996).

〔3〕 See Moshe Kaniel, *The Exclusive Treaty-Making Power of the European Community: Up to the Period of the Single European Act*, Kluwer Law International, pp. 41-42 (1996).

〔4〕 参见曾令良:《欧洲共同体与现代国际法》,武汉大学出版社 1992 年版,第 65 页。

treaty making power，there are provisions on the term "common commercial policy" in the Treaty of Rome. The meaning of the term has been further developed and enriched by the practice of European Court of Justice. The implicit treaty making power is another important legal basis for EC to conclude international treaties and is an important component of EC's treaty making power. The principle of parallel development is derived from the implicit treaty making power doctrine which has greatly promoted EC's international treaty practice.

Key words：explicit treaty making power，implicit treaty making power，principle of parallel development

第二节　调整中欧经济关系的双边法律框架初探*

【摘要】 1949 年以来的中欧经济关系及有关法律安排的发展可大致分为开创、法律化和促进三个主要阶段。影响中欧经济关系及有关法律安排的政治问题主要是人权和港澳自治权问题。在经济全球化的背景下，为构建中欧双边经济法律新框架，需要严格区分政治问题与经济问题，尽快签订新的中欧贸易与经济合作协定，协调和并行发展各层面的中欧双边经济法律规范。

【关键词】 中欧经济关系；人权；自治权；法律框架

1993 年以来，中国确立了建立社会主义市场经济体制的目标，由计划经济体制朝市场经济体制转变，逐渐成为与国际市场接轨的主要贸易国家之一。另外，欧洲联盟的建立进一步促进了该组织经济一体化的发展。上述新发展凸显了中欧经济关系的重要性，同时提出了进一步构建有关双边法律框架的要求。本文在概述和分析中欧经济关系及有关法律安排的发展、相关政治问题的基础上，初步探讨构建中欧双边法律新框架所涉及的重要问题。

一、中欧经济关系及有关法律安排的发展

中国与欧洲的经济关系历史悠久。1949 年以来，中欧经济关系及有关法律安排的发展可大致分为以下三个主要阶段。

（一）开创阶段（1949—1974）

在 20 世纪 50、60 年代，从中国的角度看，存在两个重要的三角关系。第一个是中国、西欧和美国之间的关系。50 年代初期，美国视中国为敌国，对中国实行经济封锁。与此相反，西欧国家采取较现实的态度，对华贸易仍然继续。第二个三角关系是中国、西欧和苏联之间的关系。1958 年欧共体成立时，苏联和绝大多数东欧国家拒绝承认。而中国奉行独立自主的外交政策，基于"三个世界"的理论，积极发展与欧共体的经济关系。中国支持欧洲一体化的努力，视欧共体为重要的经济伙伴和维持世界稳定的重要因素。[1]

---

* 原载《欧洲》2001 年第 4 期。

〔1〕 See Christopher Piening, *Global Europe：The European Union in World Affairs*, Lynne Rienner Publishers, p. 155 (1997).

改善中国与欧共体双边关系的真正契机是 70 年代初。1971 年 10 月中国恢复在联合国的合法席位。一些欧共体成员国在 70 年代初相继同中国建立外交关系,如意大利(1970 年)、比利时(1971 年)、联邦德国(1972 年)和卢森堡(1972 年)。另外,由于 1973 年英国、爱尔兰和丹麦的加入,欧共体成为最重要的国际经济组织。这些新发展提供了中国与欧共体之间贸易和经济关系进一步发展的基础,实际上排除了建立双方外交关系的障碍。

（二）法律化阶段（1975—1989）

1975 年以来,中欧经济关系的发展进入了主要由法律调整的新阶段,双边法律框架在中国与欧共体之间和中国与欧共体成员国之间两个层面上逐步建立。

1. 中国与欧共体之间的经济条约

1975 年中国与欧共体建立外交关系后,中欧贸易与经济关系发展迅速。1978 年 4 月 3 日,中欧签署了《欧洲经济共同体与中华人民共和国之间贸易协定》(以下简称《1978 年协定》),成为调整中欧贸易关系的总体性法律框架。

最惠国待遇条款是中欧贸易关系的基石。中国在欧共体对外经济关系中的地位一般是与非联系的发展中国家(non-associated developing countries)相同,严格遵守最惠国待遇原则。《1978 年协定》的最惠国待遇条款附带的限制是,该待遇不适用于欧共体给予关税联盟或自由贸易区其他成员、邻国的待遇,或欧共体履行国际商品协定义务所采取的措施。由于该条款比《关税及贸易总协定》的最惠国待遇条款限制更严,比较欧共体其他贸易伙伴,中国居于较为不利的地位。[1] 此外,该协定还包括保障条款、价格条款和贸易平衡等主要条款。

80 年代初,中欧之间在直接投资、贷款和经济援助等领域的经济合作持续增长,《1978 年协定》显然未能适应实际需要,1985 年 5 月 23 日,中欧双方签署了《欧洲共同体与中华人民共和国之间贸易与经济合作协定》(以下简称《1985 年协定》)。该协定的创新主要表现在拓宽了中欧经济合作的领域,包括在工业和矿业、农业、科学技术、能源、交通通讯、环境保护以及在第三国的合作。该协定具体提及一些合作的方式,如合营企业、技术转让、组织讲座和专题研讨会等,以达到双方工业与经济合作的目标。该协定还包含投资条款,规定双方在现有法律、规章和政策框架内,通过基于平等互利原则的双边安排,进一步促进和鼓励相互投资。[2]

---

〔1〕　See Hu Yuanxiang, *Legal and Policy Issues of the Trade and Economic Relations between China and the EEC*, *A Comparative Study*, Kluwer Law and Taxation Publishers, pp. 57-59 (1991).

〔2〕　《1985 年协定》第 10—12 条。

2. 中国与欧共体成员国之间的经济条约

《1985 年协定》规定，欧共体及其采取的任何行动，不影响欧共体成员国在经济合作领域与中国进行双边活动的权力，也不影响欧共体成员国在适当的情况下与中国签订新的合作协定的权力。[1] 中国与欧共体成员国之间的双边投资协定是中国自 80 年代以来与发达国家签署的第一批此类协定，[2]也是中欧经济合作历史发展的延续。这些协定主要调整欧洲在中国的直接投资，也在一定程度上调整中国在欧洲的直接投资。

令人遗憾的是，中欧经济合作不断发展的良好势头在 1989 年"政治风波"后受阻。欧共体以所谓人权问题在 1989 年 6 月 4 日至 1990 年 10 月 22 日对中国实行贸易制裁，中欧经济关系的发展暂时中断、倒退，双方蒙受了重大的损失。

（三）促进阶段（1991—现在）

90 年代以来，欧共体采取多种促进形式，包括颁布一系列有关中欧经济关系的通告（communications）、中欧高层互访及签订双边经济条约等，促进了中欧经济关系的持续发展。

1. 关于中欧经济关系的通告

在战略层面，欧盟 1995 年最重要的发展是加强与中国的联系。1995 年 7 月，欧盟执委会通过了《关于中欧关系长期政策的通告》。该文件规定了欧盟对华长期政策的原则，并要求提高欧盟在中国的形象地位。通告还提及欧盟支持中国加入 WTO 的立场，但附有人权和贸易政策方面的条件。1995 年 12 月，欧盟理事会通过该通告。[3] 1997 年 6 月，欧洲议会通过了《〈关于中欧关系长期政策的通告〉的决议》。

1998 年 3 月 25 日，执委会颁布了《关于与中国建立全面伙伴关系的通告》。该通告的主要内容包括：促使中国进一步参与国际社会；支持中国向基于法治和尊重人权的开放性社会过渡；使中国经济进一步结合于世界经济；促进欧洲基金进一步发展；提高欧盟在中国的形象地位。该通告指出，欧盟的贸易政策应该以促进对华投资、与中国的商务和工业合作的全面战略为后盾，以利加强欧洲在中国市场的地位。欧盟应制定战略，主要集中于电讯、能源、环境技术和服务、交通和金融服务等

---

〔1〕 See Nicholas Emiliou and David O'Keeffe (eds.), *The European Union and World Trade Law: After the GATT Uruguay Round*, John Wiley & Sons Ltd., p. 366 (1996).

〔2〕 See Margrete Stevens and Ruvan de Alwis, References on Bilateral Investment Treaties，7(1)*ICSID Review*, *Foreign Investment Law Journal*, p. 256 (1992).

〔3〕 See *The European Union* 1995，*Annual Review of Activities*，Blackwell Publishers，p. 78 (1996).

具有明显优势的行业。[1] 2000 年 9 月 8 日,执委会通过了《关于实施 1998 年〈关于与中国建立全面伙伴关系的通告〉的报告》。该文件肯定了欧共体与中国在经济、发展合作和对话各领域的活动和进展,强调了中欧有关区域安全、经济与贸易问题和人权对话的发展,并且决定进一步扩大这些对话领域的范围,包括非法移民、毒品走私、洗钱和集团犯罪等。[2]

2. 高层访问与中欧高峰会议

1998 年 10 月 29 日至 11 月 3 日,欧盟执委会主席桑特先生对中国进行正式访问,签署了《航天电讯领域工业合作谅解备忘录》、《中国与欧盟之间法律与司法合作计划财务协定》和《中国与欧盟之间关于欧盟支持中国加入 WTO 的框架计划的财务协定》等三个法律文件。[3]

1998 年 4 月 2 日,第一次中欧高峰会议(China-EU summit meetings)在伦敦举行并通过联合声明。双方强调,改善中欧之间的对话与合作不仅符合双方的利益,而且符合世界和平、稳定与发展的利益。中欧双方同意通过每年举行的其他高级会晤,保持高级别交流的势头。[4] 第二、三次中欧高峰会议分别于 1999 年 12 月和 2000 年 10 月在北京举行。中欧高峰会议为双方最高领导层提供了及时就中欧全面关系交换意见的场所。[5]

3. 2000 年中国与欧共体贸易协定

2000 年 5 月 19 日,中国与欧共体贸易协定在北京签订。这标志着中欧经济关系的重要发展。该协定与 1999 年签署的中国与美国贸易协定一起,实际上铺平了中国"入世"的道路。[6]

从上述中欧经济关系发展的三个阶段可以看出,中欧经济关系 50 多年来稳步发展。除 1989 年 6 月至 1990 年 10 月的短暂期间外,西欧国家和欧共体基本上未将政治因素与其对华经济关系相联系。因此,中欧经济关系不断发展,双方也从这种稳定的关系中持续受益。

二、影响中欧经济关系及有关法律安排的主要政治问题

近 10 多年来,虽然中欧经济关系不断发展是主流,但也存在若隐若现的干扰或

---

〔1〕 See Communication from the Commission, Building a Comprehensive Partnership with China, *COM* (1998) 181 final, pp. 16-17.

〔2〕 http://europa. eu. int/comm/external_relations/china/intro/index. htm/15/03/01

〔3〕 See Sino-EU Ties Emphasized, 41 (46), *Beijing Review*, p. 4 (1998).

〔4〕 See European Commission, *Bulletin of the European Union*, 4-1998, p. 64.

〔5〕 http://europa. eu. int/comm/external_relations/china/intro/index. htm/15/03/01

〔6〕 Ibid.

影响主流的政治问题。

（一）人权问题

1989 年以后，人权成为中欧经济关系的一个重要问题。在 1995 年《关于中欧关系长期政策的通告》中，欧盟执委会对中国的人权问题提出了三方面的对策（a three-pronged approach）：一是支持开放和自由化的中国社会生活的各个方面，以此促进基于法治的市民社会的发展；二是在同中国的双边对话中继续提出人权问题；三是在多边场合、如联合国，促使国际社会参与人权对话。[1]

1997 年 6 月 12 日欧洲议会通过的《〈关于中欧关系长期政策的通告〉的决议》，是欧盟关于中国人权问题的代表作。该文件涉及在中国废除死刑、释放政治犯、撤销不符合法治国家目标的法律以及所谓"西藏自治"等问题。[2]全国人大常委会授权外事委员会及时发表严正声明，强烈谴责该决议对中国内部事务的干预。

在 1998 年 3 月《关于与中国建立全面伙伴关系的通告》中，欧盟对中国人权方面的进展予以较积极的评价。在该文件中，欧盟承认在过去 20 年中，中国人权问题得到改善。经济改革带来了教育、就业、住房、旅行和社会生活其他领域的更多自由。中国已通过了一些新的保护公民权利的民事和刑事法律，同时签署了一些重要的有关国际条约，包括决定签署《经济、社会和文化权利公约》。中国还开始了在地方层面的选举程序。欧盟表示相信，中欧以坦诚、公开和相互尊重的态度，通过各种场合的对话，将能够消除有关分歧。[3]

1999 年 2 月 10 日，欧洲议会通过决议支持 1998 年《关于与中国建立全面伙伴关系的通告》。该决议还要求中国尊重人权、推进政治改革，呼吁西方国家禁止与中国进行军火贸易，并且建议欧盟在新的中欧贸易与经济合作协定中增加人权条款。[4]

（二）港澳自治权问题

欧盟成员国英国和葡萄牙分别长期统治香港和澳门，构成了该两国、欧盟与港澳地区之间的历史联系。这种联系使欧盟特别关注中国对港澳恢复行使主权的有关安排。英、葡两国都从中国寻求保证，港澳地区人民享有的自由、人权和民事权利在港澳分别于 1997 年和 1999 年回归中国时不受影响。经济原因对欧盟更为重要，

---

〔1〕 See Christopher Piening, *Global Europe：The European Union in World Affairs*, Lynne Rienner Publishers, p. 157 (1997).

〔2〕 See European Commission, *Bulletin of the European Union*, 6-1997, pp. 118-119.

〔3〕 See Communication from the Commission, Building a Comprehensive Partnership with China, *COM* (1998) 181 final, pp. 9-11.

〔4〕 mingbao. com/newspaper/990211/cac1. htm

回归后的港澳继续与欧盟保持密切的经济关系是非常重要的。以香港为例,香港是欧盟第十一大贸易伙伴。中国承诺香港在回归后继续保持其经济和贸易政策并保持其在 WTO 的成员地位。香港也是欧盟成员国的主要投资地,有 40 家欧盟银行和 45 家欧盟保险公司在香港获准经营。约 40,000 名欧盟公民是香港居民。不仅如此,香港和澳门在促进欧盟与中国大陆地区之间经济交往方面也发挥了重要的桥梁作用。[1]

在《〈关于中欧关系长期政策的通告〉的决议》中,欧洲议会认为,香港和澳门的将来以及保持其政治、社会和经济自由对欧盟至关重要,决定监督有关情况的发展并谴责解散香港经选举产生的立法会。[2] 1997 年 4 月 10 日,议会通过《关于香港情况的决议》,要求香港主权的转移应严格按照《中英联合声明》和《基本法》规定的原则,还要求理事会制定有关发展欧盟与香港关系的政策,要求执委会提交有关香港政治、经济和人权状况等的年度报告。议会还决定通过派遣调查团等方式,监督香港特别行政区局势的发展。[3]

1997 年 4 月 23 日,执委会向理事会和议会提交了题为《关于欧盟与 1997 年以后的香港的通告》。在该文件中,执委会在强调香港与欧洲之间关系的重要性和分析香港作为中国特别行政区的未来发展之后,提出了加强欧盟与香港之间关系的战略。有关建议包括:直接与香港特别行政区政府交往,并保持经常性的密切联系;出于贸易政策的考虑,继续将香港视为独立的实体和 WTO 体制内的重要伙伴;与国际社会共同努力,监督香港的局势并尊重给予特别行政区居民的权利,出版关于欧盟与香港之间关系等各方面情况的年度报告;继续允许香港政府本身列于共同签证清单(the common visa list);探寻适当方式,将香港与欧盟之间贸易、投资和合作关系置于更为永久的立场并且发展积极的合作。[4]

三、关于构建中欧双边经济法律新框架的思考

在 21 世纪到来之际,经济全球化趋向为中欧经济关系的进一步发展带来了新的机遇和挑战。如何以史为鉴,抓住机遇,将中欧经济关系继续推向前进,是中欧双方面临的重要问题。中国"入世"后,中欧经济关系将属于 WTO 法律体制调整的范围,将发生双方同受 WTO 多边法律体制规制的实质性重大变化。与此同时,调整中欧

---

〔1〕 Communication from the Commission, A Long Term Policy for China-Europe Relations, *COM* (1995) 279 final, pp. 6-7.

〔2〕 European Commission, *Bulletin of the European Union*, 6-1997, pp. 118-119.

〔3〕 European Commission, *Bulletin of the European Union*, 4-1997, p. 89.

〔4〕 Ibid., pp. 88-89.

经济关系的双边法律框架也将继续存在和发展。笔者以为，在考虑构建中欧双边经济法律新框架时，需要明确以下重要问题：

（一）严格区分政治问题与经济问题

政治问题完全不应该成为影响或阻碍中欧经济关系发展的绊脚石。就人权问题而言，中国在人权方面已采取了签署《经济、社会和文化权利国际公约》和《公民权利和政治权利国际公约》等重要步骤。中国尊重人权的普遍性原则，重视人民的生存权和发展权。应当指出，由于不同国家有不同的国情、经济发展水平、文化背景和价值取向，对人权问题有不同看法是正常的。从中欧经济关系的历史看，将人权问题与经济问题联系在一起，或者，将人权问题作为发展中欧经济关系的前提既无必要，也不明智。当前，中国已向全世界开放，一个或少数国家或国际组织要对中国实行经济封锁是徒劳的。如果前者对其与中国的经贸交往设置前提条件（如所谓人权问题），只能是作茧自缚，自己放弃从中国市场获益的机会。中国将从其他国家找到可替代的商业机会。因此，从现实的角度看，如果欧盟将人权问题与对华经贸交往相联系，只能是有利于第三方，对中国可能造成一定程度的影响，而欧盟本身将成为最大的输家。进而言之，对欧盟而言，提及诸如在中国废除死刑、"西藏自治"等所谓人权问题并无法律上的根据。根据国家主权原则，此类事项纯属中国内部事务。

欧盟及其成员国英、葡等国对港澳自治权问题的特别关注，反映了前者力图维护其在港澳地区的既有和潜在利益。港澳回归以来的事实表明，"一国两制"已成功实施，港澳特别行政区依法享有高度自治权。在此必须强调，从法律角度看，中国是通过签订《中英联合声明》和《中葡联合声明》对英、葡两国作出法律承诺并承担国际责任，而不是对欧盟本身或其他欧盟成员国。

半个多世纪以来的中欧经济关系史表明，中欧经济关系在不受政治因素影响的情况下，就能健康发展，双方受益；反之，就遭遇挫折，双方受损。因此，应严格区分政治问题和经济问题，政治问题不应导入中欧双边经济法律新框架。

（二）签订新的中欧贸易与经济合作协定势在必行

欧共体与第三国签订的条约在欧共体法律体系中的最高性得到其成员国的普遍承认。欧共体成员国不得与第三国签订任何与欧共体所承担的责任相冲突的条约。[1] 在这个意义上，中国与欧共体之间的经济条约对于发展中国与欧盟及其成员

---

〔1〕 Anne Peters, The Position of International Law within the European Community Legal Order, 40 *German Yearbook of International Law*, pp. 38-40 (1997).

国之间的经济关系具有建设性和框架性的重要作用。

当前，调整中国与欧盟之间经济关系的总体性法律框架仍然是《1985 年协定》。16 年来，中国的经济体制结构发生了重要转变，经济发展取得了举世瞩目的成就，而欧共体的一体化进程发展迅速，在经济和政治方面均达到了新的水平。中欧经济和政治关系的发展也相应进入了建立"全面伙伴关系"的新阶段。反观《1985 年协定》的内容，在合作领域与形式、最惠国待遇、市场准入、价格和支付等方面的规定已显得滞后，不能有效地发挥调整、规范中欧经济关系的积极作用。此外，为建立中欧的"全面伙伴关系"，也急需在经济领域有新的内容更为丰富的框架性法律安排。显然，在此新形势下，签订更为符合双方实际需要的新的中欧贸易与经济合作协定势在必行，且日益凸显其紧迫性。

（三）中欧双边经济法律框架各层面的规范应并行发展

如前所述，当前调整中欧经济关系的双边法律框架主要由中国与欧共体之间的经济条约和中国与欧共体成员国之间的经济条约两个层面构成。

随着欧盟一体化进程的不断发展，中国与欧共体之间的经济条约将在中欧双边经济法律框架中居于越来越重要的地位。根据《关于与中国建立全面伙伴关系的通告》，中欧经贸对话将通过在特定领域，如海上运输、航空运输、原子能贸易与安全保障、科学与技术等领域签订双边条约予以加强。[1]

中国与欧共体之间的经济条约一般只能以欧共体在特定领域具有专属缔约权且各成员国在该领域的权利义务已协调一致为前提，不可能取代中国与欧共体成员国之间的经济条约。以双边投资条约为例，欧共体本身为了寻求效率和标准的投资保护制度，防止其成员国在这方面差别过大，也许更希望在欧共体层面上与第三国签订双边投资协定。然而，由于此类协定需要为所有成员国创设具体的权利义务，目前尚难达此目标。[2] 中国与欧共体各成员国之间的双边条约主要包括经济与技术合作协定、避免双重征税协定以及相互促进和保护投资协定等。

由于欧共体及其成员国"共有权能"的存在，在中欧经济关系进一步深入发展的形势下，中欧双边经济法律框架还可能包含以中国为缔约一方、欧共体及其成员国为另一缔约方的经济条约，即所谓"混合条约"（mixed treaties）。

---

〔1〕　Communication from the Commission, Building a Comprehensive Partnership with China, *COM* (1998) 181 final, pp. 16-17.

〔2〕　Hu Yuanxiang, *Legal and Policy Issues of Trade and Economic Relations between China and EEC: A Comparative Study*, Kluwer Law and Taxation Publishers, p. 181 (1991).

总之,中欧双边经济法律新框架可能包含三个层面,即中国与欧共体之间层面、中国与欧共体成员国层面和中国与欧共体及其成员国层面。三个层面的规范应是相辅相成,协调发展。

On the Bilateral Legal Framework Governing China-EU Economic Relations

Abstract：The main developments of China-Europe economic relations and the legal arrangements concerned since 1949 may be roughly divided into the initial stage，legalization stage and promotion stage. The major political issues affecting China-EU economic relations and the legal arrangements concerned are human rights，autonomy of Hong Kong and Macao. In the setting of economic globalization，China and EU shall distinguish strictly political issues from economic matters，conclude a new China-EC trade and economic cooperation agreement as soon as possible and equally develop various tiers of China-EU bilateral legal norms for establishing a new bilateral legal framework of China-EU economic relations.

Key words：China-EU economic relation；human rights；autonomy；legal framework

第三节　Promoting a New Bilateral Legal Framework for China-EU Economic Relations[*]
（构建调整中国—欧盟经济关系的双边法律新框架）

Abstract：Aiming at promoting a new bilateral legal framework for China-EU economic relations without political interference，this paper first surveys the developments of China-Europe economic relations and the relevant legal arrangements since 1949；second，it deals with political issues affecting China-EU economic relations；and third，it discusses basic legal considerations in signing China-EC economic treaties for the Chinese side. The author points out that the China-EC Economic Cooperation Agreement in 1985 has proved insufficient for practical needs and a substitutive agreement should be promoted in the new era.

China's economy has developed dramatically since 1978 when it began the open-door policy. It has gradually become a major trading nation thanks to the economic reform that has transformed it from a centrally planned economy to a market-oriented one. This process has turned China into one of the major economic entities on the world stage. China's accession to the World Trade Organization (hereinafter the "WTO") on December 11, 2001 has greatly integrated China into the world market and the multilateral trade systems.

On the other side，the European integration has reached a high level in both economic and political aspects since the 1980's. Profound changes have been taking place in Europe. The single European market has boosted cross-boarder business，creating economies of scale and increasing Europe's competitiveness and leverage in the world market. The establishment of the European Union (hereinafter the

---

[*]　Promoting a New Bilateral Legal Framework for China-EU Economic Relations，*Chinese Journal of International Law*，ISSN 1540-1650，Vol. 3，No. 1，2004.

"EU")[1] has further encouraged the organization to develop from an economic entity to a political entity. The prospect and process of the EU's enlargement[2] have great impact on its further integration and external relations.

These new developments of both sides further emphasize the significance of China-EU economic relations to the world and invite the reconstruction of the legal arrangement concerned in the new era. Aiming at promoting a new bilateral legal framework for China-EU economic relations without political interference, this paper first surveys the developments of China-Europe economic relations and the relevant legal arrangements since 1949; second, it deals with existing or potential political issues affecting China-EU economic relations and the legal arrangements; and third, it discusses basic legal considerations in signing China-EC economic treaties.

I. Survey of the Developments of China-Europe Economic Relations and the Relevant Legal Arrangements

The main developments of China-Europe economic relations and the legal arrangements concerned since 1949 may be roughly divided into three stages. These will be described below one by one.

I. A Initial Stage (1949—1974)

In the 1950's and 1960's, there were two important triangular economic relations from the Chinese point of view. The first triangle was among China, Western Europe and the United States (hereinafter the "US"). In the early 1950's, the US considered China an enemy, imposing embargo on the latter. Alternatively, Western Europe took a practical attitude toward China. Trade between China and Western Europe continued. China negotiated trade arrangements with commercial delegations from the United Kingdom (hereinafter the "UK"), France, Denmark, etc. In the

---

[1] The terms the European Community (the EC) and the European Union (the EU) in this paper refer to the economic and political entity which was born as the European Economic Community (or Common Market) through the Treaty Establishing the European Economic Community in 1957 and subsequently evolved first into the European Community and finally to the European Union through the Treaty on European Union in 1991 (the Maastricht Treaty of 1991). The treaties of Amsterdam in 1997 and of Nice in 2001 include changes across a wide range of areas relevant to the working of the EU institutions.

[2] On 1 May 2004, Cyprus, Czech Republic, Estonia, Hungary, Latvia, Lithuania, Malta, Poland, Slovakia, Slovenia became new Member States of the EU.

early 1960's, China purchased a number of industrial plants from the EC Member States.

The second triangle consisted of China, Western Europe and the former Soviet Union. When the EC was established in 1 January 1958, the Soviet Union and most Eastern European countries refused to recognize it. Conversely, China developed positively close ties with the EC in the 1970's. China's leaders lent their specific support to European integration efforts, viewing the EC as a useful economic partner, a factor for stability, and an irritant for the Soviet Union. [1]

In fact, China's attitude toward the EC then was based on the Three Worlds Theory: the EC belonged to the Second World. In order to fight against the two superpowers, China had to develop good relations with the EC and form a Common Front with Second World and Third World countries.

A series of important changes concerning China-EC relations occurred during the 1970's. First, China resumed her seat in the United Nations in October 1971. Second, China established diplomatic relations with a number of the EC Member States, notably Italy (November 1970), Belgium (October 1971), Federal Republic of Germany (October 1972), and Luxembourg (November 1972). [2] Third, the EC had emerged as one of the most important international economic entities, following the accession of the UK, Ireland and Denmark on 1 January 1973. These moves provided the basis for further development of China-EC economic relations, and effectively removed the obstacles in establishing formal diplomatic relations between the two parties.

However, at this stage, the scope of China-EC economic co-operation was limited to trade, and the volume of trade between the two sides did not increase substantially. This may be, to a large extent, due to the Chinese domestic situations in that period when China had experienced so many influential political events or movements, particularly the Cultural Revolution (1966—76).

I . B Legalization Stage (1975—1989)

At this stage, China-EC economic relations were mainly governed by law. A

［1］　Christopher Piening, *Global Europe: The European Union in World Affairs*, Lynne Rienner Publishers (1997), 155.

［2］　Nicholas Emiliou and David O'Keeffe (eds.), *The European Union and World Trade Law: After the GATT Uruguay Round*, John Wiley & Sons Ltd. (1996), 364.

bilateral legal framework was established not only at the China-EC Member State level, but also at the China-EC level. A two-tiered legal framework has emerged since then. The main legal developments in this period of time were as follows:

I.B.i China-EC Trade Agreement (1978)

At the end of 1974, trade agreements between the EC Member States and various so-called "state-trading countries" were due to expire. The EC Member States were preparing to conclude new trade agreements. At that time, the EC and China expressed the wish to conclude a trade agreement at the EC level.

In May 1975, Sir Christopher Soames, the then vice-president of the European Commission,[1] visited Beijing. This visit established a basis for China-EC diplomatic relations. On 16 September 1975, China and the EC established their diplomatic relations. This was the first important step in the establishment of a bilateral legal framework for China-EC economic relations.

In 1978, the "four modernizations" programme in China focused on science, technology, industry, agriculture and defense. The programme greatly encouraged China to strengthen and legalize her relations with the EC. As a result of the mutual wishes and efforts by the two sides, the Trade Agreement between the European Economic Community and the People's Republic of China was concluded on 3 April 1978 (hereinafter the "1978 Agreement").

The 1978 Agreement was the first trade agreement concluded by the EC with a state-trading country. It provided a general legal framework for China-EC trade relations. Council Regulation 3421/83 laid down certain detailed rules for the implementation of the 1978 Agreement.

The EC's trade with non-associated countries has been based on the most-favored-nation (hereinafter "MFN") principle. The position of China within the EC's external commercial relations has generally been placed in line with the non-as-

---

[1] The Commission is one of the EC's five institutions. It then consisted of 20 Commissioners independent of EC Member States. The Commission makes proposals for European legislation and action, and oversees the implementation of common policies.

sociated developing countries, and firmly adhered to the MFN principle. [1] The 1978 Agreement contained a MFN clause with some limitations, and did not apply to treatment accorded to other members of customs unions or free trade areas, to neighboring countries, or to measures taken to meet obligations under international commodity agreements. As the clause was more restrictive than the MFN clause in the GATT, it placed China in a relatively disadvantageous position compared to most of the EC trading partners. [2]

I. B. ii China-EC Economic Cooperation Agreement (1985)

As China adopted the open-door policy and promulgated the Sino-foreign Joint Venture Law in 1979, in the period from 1979 to 1983, investments in and loans to China from EC Member States totaled US $ 1,603 million (or 7. 4 percent of the total amount of foreign capital utilized by China during that period), of which US $ 718 million was direct investment, while US $ 885 million was in the form of loans. [3] Economic assistance was also given by the EC to China, mainly in the fields of agriculture and energy. This assistance totaled 16 million ECUs by the end of 1983.

Against the background of increasing China-EC economic cooperation, the 1978 Agreement eventually proved to be an insufficient framework, which led to the conclusion of the Trade and Economic Cooperation Agreement between the European Community and the People's Republic of China on 23 May 1985 (hereinafter "1985 Agreement").

The 1985 Agreement, taking the place of the 1978 Agreement, comprised

---

〔1〕 The trade relations between the EC and developing countries in Latin America and Asia have been based on the MFN principle. This approach was confirmed by the conclusion of trade or co-operation agreements with those countries containing a MFN clause. The conclusion of MFN agreements seemed to have served two objectives of the EC: first, the EC will not be discriminated against in trade with these countries; second, the EC's predominant interests in the countries with which the EC has concluded preferential agreements will be safeguarded.

〔2〕 There are two aspects included in the MFN clause of the GATT, but not included in the same clause in the 1978 China-EC Agreement:

(1) regulations concerning payments, including allocation of foreign currency and transfer of such payment; and

(2) regulations affecting the sale, purchase, transport, distribution, and use of goods and services in the internal market.

See Hu Yuanxiang, *Legal and Policy Issues of the Trade and Economic Relations between China and the EEC: A Comparative Study*, Kluwer Law and Taxation Publishers, (1991), 57-59.

〔3〕 European Parliament Working Document A2-74/85, 3 July 1985, 10.

clauses on MFN, safeguard,[1] price and balance of trade in virtually the same terms as those in the 1978 Agreement and also added new provisions. As the 1985 Agreement, complemented in 1994 and 2002 by exchanges of letters establishing a broad China-EU political dialogue, is still the pillar of the existing bilateral legal framework for China-EU economic relations, its main provisions are briefly discussed as follows:

(1) *Industries and Cooperation Forms*

The 1985 Agreement was broader in scope than the 1978 Agreement. In addition to dealing with trade, it was designed to facilitate economic cooperation between the EC and China in all spheres subject to common accord, and in particular: industry and mining; agriculture, including agro-industry; science and technology; energy; transport and communications; environmental protection; and cooperation in third countries.[2]

The Agreement also referred to numerous methods and forms of cooperation—such as joint ventures, transfer of technology, organisation of seminars and symposia, etc.—for attaining the objectives of industrial and technological co-operation between the two sides.[3] However, these measures were stated in general terms, and the elaboration of specific schemes was left to the parties.

In particular, the Agreement included an investment clause. It laid down specific provisions urging the two parties to promote and encourage their mutually beneficial investment within their respective laws, rules and policies through bilateral arrangements based on the principles of equity and reciprocity by the two parties.[4]

(2) *MFN Principle*

Article 3.1 of the 1985 Agreement accords to both parties MFN treatment, which applies to various aspects concerning customs duties and charges, etc. with

---

[1] Safeguard clause refers to provision on safeguard of trade balance in bilateral trade agreement, such as the Article 4 of the 1985 Agreement.

[2] 1985 Agreement, art. 10.

[3] 1985 Agreement, art. 11.

[4] 1985 Agreement, art. 12. See Nicholas Emiliou and David O'Keeffe (eds.), *The European Union and World Trade Law: After the GATT Uruguay Round*, John Wiley & Sons Ltd. (1996), 366; Hu Yuanxiang, *Legal and Policy Issues of Trade and Economic Relations between China and EEC: A Comparative Study*, Kluwer Law and Taxation Publishers (1991), 181.

same the limitations as those provided in the 1978 Agreement. [1]

The intention of this article is to impose on each party an obligation not to practice discrimination. Of course, the European Court of Justice (hereinafter the "Court") may have to develop a proper interpretation of the definition of the MFN clause. [2]

It should be pointed out that the MFN treatment does not grant China the same treatment as that of the most important trade partners of the EC. The EC has maintained preferential trade policy with the Member States of European Free Trade Association (EFTA) on the basis of the free trade agreements. The EC has also offered non-reciprocal preferences both on tariffs and quantities to the African-Caribbean-Pacific (ACP) countries under the four Lome Conventions (signed in 1975, 1980, 1985 and 1989) and the Cotonou Agreement. [3] In addition, the EC's preferential treatment is accorded to Mediterranean countries under the Cooperation Agreements inspired by the EC's global policy toward the region. [4]

(3) Access to the Markets

According to Article 5, China will give favourable consideration to imports from the EC. To this end, the competent Chinese authorities will ensure that the EC exporters have the possibility of participating fully in opportunities for trade with China. On the other hand, the EC will strive for an increasing liberalisation of im-

---

[1] According to art. 3.1, the two Contracting Parties shall accord each other most-favored-nation treatment in all matters regarding:

• customs duties and charges of all kinds applied to the import, export, re-export, or transit of products, including the procedures for the collection of such duties or charges;

• regulations, procedures and formalities concerning customs clearance, transit, warehousing and transshipment of products imported or exported;

• taxes and other internal charges levied directly or indirectly on products or services imported or exported;

• administrative formalities for the issue of import or export licenses.

[2] Hu Yuanxiang, *Legal and Policy Issues of Trade and Economic Relations between China and EEC: A Comparative Study*, Kluwer Law and Taxation Publishers (1991), 53.

[3] Lome IV embraced systematic economic, financial and social co-operation in favor of ACP countries. For the main content and analyses of the Lome IV, see Subrata Roy Chowdhury, Erik M. G. Denters and Paul J. I. M. de Waart (eds.), *The Right to Development in International Law*, Martinus Nijhoff Publishers (1992), 98-110. The Lome Convention was replaced by the Cotonou Agreement, a New Partnership Agreement between the European Union (EU) and its associated States from Africa, the Caribbean and the Pacific (ACP) signed on 23 June 2000. See The Cotonou Agreement and the Challenges of Making the New EU-ACP Trade Regime WTO Compatible, 35 *Journal of World Trade* (2001), 123-144.

[4] Hu Yuanxiang, *Legal and Policy Issues of Trade and Economic Relations between China and EEC: A Comparative Study*, Kluwer Law and Taxation Publishers (1991), 54-57.

ports from China. To this end, it will endeavour progressively to introduce measures extending the list of products for which imports from China have been liberalised and to increase the amounts of quotas.

Based on this article, it seems that China has taken more responsibilities for opening its market to the EC. Moreover, the terms "give favourable consideration" and "strive for" in this article are flexible and can't impose definite legal obligations on the parties concerned.

(4) *Consultation and Visit*

The two parties shall exchange information on any problems that may arise with regard to their trade and shall maintain friendly consultations, with the intention of promoting trade and for the purpose of seeking mutually satisfactory solutions to those problems. Both parties also take further responsibilities that no action is taken before consultations are held. [1] The EC Council Regulation 3421/83 transferred the obligation of consultation into an obligation of the EC law. [2] This arrangement shows that the EC assume the obligation of consultation both at the international law level and at the EC law level. Moreover, as China and the EC are members of the WTO, the consultation commitments by both sides are further affirmed by their obligations under Article 4 of Understanding on Rules and Procedures Governing the Settlement of Disputes.

Article 5. 2 provides an exception where either party may take protective measures, but must endeavour as far as possible to hold friendly consultations before doing so. Therefore, this paragraph can't in itself produce direct effect. A question exists in the interpretation of the so-called "exceptional case". [3]

The two parties also undertake to promote visits by persons, groups and delegations from economic, trade and industrial circles, to facilitate industrial and tech-

---

[1] 1985 Agreement, art. 5.1.

[2] According to art. 189 of the EC Treaty, an EC Council Regulation is essentially legislative (normative). It lays down general rules which are binding both at the Community level and at the national level. See T. C. Hartley, *The Foundations of European Community Law*, Oxford University Press (1998), 99.

[3] If the protective measure is taken in a justified "exceptional case", then Article 5. 2 shall apply and the consultation requirement cannot be invoked to defend the individuals. On the other hand, if the protective measure cannot be justified to have been taken in "an exceptional case", Article 5. 1 shall apply, in which case the consultation obligation is compulsory and can be relied on before the national courts. See Hu Yuanxiang, *Legal and Policy Issues of Trade and Economic Relations between China and EEC: A Comparative Study*, Kluwer Law and Taxation Publishers (1991), 54.

nical exchanges and contracts connected with trade, and to foster the organisation of fairs and exhibitions by both sides and the relevant provision of services.

(5) *Price*

Trade in goods and the provision of services between the two parties shall be effected at market-related prices and rates.

The price clause is not precise as to what particular "market" should be followed. Before 1998, China was classified as a non-market economy by the EC. The market-related prices are difficult to assess. In practice, as the EC anti-dumping regulations provide detailed rules and criteria for market prices, the EC companies and individuals concerned can rely on the EC anti-dumping regulations in anti-dumping proceedings. [1] Therefore, the "market-related prices" requirement in the 1985 Agreement has hardly any direct effect in these cases. Recognising that the process of reform in China has fundamentally altered their economies, the Council Regulation (EC) No. 905/98 removes China from the list of countries to which non-market economic treatment applies. It will allow the Commission to use domestic price information in anti-dumping investigations of producers that can demonstrate that they comply with market economy conditions. Investigations will be conducted on a case-by-case basis. [2]

As a result of China's economic reform, more and more Chinese products have been based on market prices since the 1990's, which makes this article more applicable and enforceable to the Chinese side.

(6) *Payment*

Payment for transactions shall be made, in accordance with their respective existing laws and regulations, in currencies of the EC Member States, RMB or any convertible currency accepted by the two parties concerned in the transaction.

The launching of the Euro in January 1999 changed the payments of most of the

---

[1] Hu Yuanxiang, *Legal and Policy Issues of Trade and Economic Relations between China and EEC: A Comparative Study*, Kluwer Law and Taxation Publishers (1991), 54.

[2] The Regulation, amending Council Regulation (EC) No 384/96 on protection against dumped imports from countries not members of the EC, was adopted on 27 April 1998 and entered into force on 1 July 1998. See europa. eu. int/abc/doc/off/bull/en/9804/p103018. htm.

EC Member States in international transactions.[1] They shall pay in Euros instead of their national currencies in their trade with China. At the same time, China may accept Euro as a stable reserve currency. Therefore, some arrangements on Euro payment should be considered in a new China-EC economic agreement.

(7) Joint Committee

Under the agreement, China and the EC set up a Joint Committee comprised of representatives from both sides. The tasks of the Joint Committee are to: monitor and examine the functioning of this Agreement and review various co-operation schemes implemented; examine any questions that may arise in the implementation of this agreement; examine problems that could hinder the development of commercial and economic co-operation between the two parties; examine means and new opportunities of developing commercial and economic co-operation; and, make recommendations that may help in attaining the objectives of this agreement, in the areas of common interest.[2]

I. B. iii China-EC Member States Bilateral Economic Treaties

It should be emphasized, however, that the divisions of the competences over external economic relations between the EC and its Member States are not absolutely clear. While the EC has the exclusive power to conclude trade or trade-related agreements with non-Member States, the Member States have the power to conclude such agreements as bilateral investment treaties (hereinafter the "BITs") and tax treaties with non-Member States. The 1985 Agreement also provided that the EC, and any action taken by it, shall in no way affect the powers of any of the EC Member States to undertake bilateral activities with China in the field of economic co-operation and to conclude, where appropriate, new economic co-operation agreements with China (art. 14).[3]

In the late 1950's, the first BIT was concluded, aiming at promotion and protection of transnational investment. The parties to the BITs are sovereign states,

---

[1] The Euro was introduced in eleven countries in 1999 in no-cash form (as bank money). Greece joined the regime in 2001. In January 2002, Euro banknotes and coins began circulating. As national banknotes and coins were withdrawn from circulation, the Euro became the sole legal tender from March 2002 on. Among the fifteen old Member States, three EC Member States (UK, Sweden and Denmark) still stay outside as the "pre-Ins".

[2] 1985 Agreement, art. 15.

[3] Nicholas Emiliou and David O'Keeffe (eds.), *The European Union and World Trade Law: After the GATT Uruguay Round*, John Wiley & Sons Ltd. (1996), 366.

typically the European countries and developing countries. Germany and Switzerland took the lead in this regard. The BITs between China and the EC Member States are the first group of any such agreements that China ever concluded with developed countries since the early 1980's. The emergence of such agreements echoes the historical development of economic co-operation between China and the EC. Some of the agreements were concluded and entered into force before the 1985 Agreement. The BITs between China and the EC Member States regulate European direct investment in China and, to a lesser degree, Chinese direct investment in Europe. [1]

As the BITs were concluded between China and the EC Member States, interference from the EC was avoided. This approach conforms to the provisions of the 1985 Agreement. The EC itself probably favored an EC agreement in this field for the purpose of seeking an efficient and standard investment protection regime and preventing its Member States from departing too far from their partners in the EC. However, as the agreement must be specific enough to create concrete rights and obligations for all the Member States, it is difficult to achieve at the moment. [2]

China-EC economic co-operation has increased since 1985, mainly in the areas of agriculture, energy, science and technology, and personnel training. This process was interrupted only by the immediate post-Tiananmen Square period of the EC trade sanctions between 4 June 1989 and 22 October 1990.

Ⅰ.C Promotion Stage (1991-present)

Two years after resuming China-EC relations, China officially adopted the market economy system and formulated its market-oriented policy. The great implica-

---

[1] China has concluded BITs with 14 EC Member States: Sweden (29 March 1982, Signature; 29 March 1982, Entry into Force); Germany (7 October 1983; 18 March 1985); France (30 May 1984; 15 March 1985); BeLux-Union (4 June 1984; 5 October 1986); Finland (4 September 1984; 26 January 1986); Italy (28 January 1985; 28 August 1987); Denmark (29 April 1985; 29 April 1985); Netherlands (17 June 1985; 1 February 1987); Austria (12 September 1985; 11 October 1986); United Kingdom (15 May 1986; 15 May 1986); Portugal (3 February 1992, Signature); Spain (6 February 1992; 1 May 1993) and Greece (25 June 1992; 21 December 1993). See Margrete Stevens and Ruvan de Alwis, References on Bilateral Investment Treaties, 7 (1) *ICSID Review*, *Foreign Investment Law Journal* (1992), 256 and ICSID Website: www. worldbank. org/icsid/treaties/china. htm. Only Ireland has not signed a BIT with China but it is in negotiation. See Wenhua Shan, Towards a New Legal Framework for EU-China Investment Relations, 34 *Journal of World Trade* (2000), 155.

[2] Hu Yuanxiang, *Legal and Policy Issues of Trade and Economic Relations between China and EEC: A Comparative Study*, Kluwer Law and Taxation Publishers (1991), 181. Recently, it has been argued that a BIT between the EC and China might be considered as a new legal framework for China-EU investment relations at this stage. See Wenhua Shan, Towards a New Legal Framework for EU-China Investment Relations, 34 *Journal of World Trade* (2000), 174-178.

tion in this regard is that China and the EU have a common ground in terms of an economic system for further developing their relations to some extent.

Some of the EU's China-related policy documents were released during the last decade. It is worth noticing that the following EU Communications are basically the policy statements within the EU, providing some guidance for its Member States but not having legal force. In addition, the recent meetings and visits of Chinese leaders and EU leaders have also made important contributions to the improvement and promotion of China-EU economic relations.

I.C.i A Long-term Policy for China-Europe Relations (1995)

On 13 July 1994 the European Commission issued a Communication entitled "Towards a New Asian Strategy" to the Council. [1] It concluded that the EU should give Asia a higher priority, place greater emphasis on pro-active economic co-operation, and help countries such as China—which are moving from state-controlled to market-oriented economies—to integrate into the market-based world trading system.

Performing on this new Asian strategy, the European Commission adopted a new Communication on "A Long-term Policy for China-Europe Relations" in July 1995. This strategy paper set out the principles of the EU policy and called for raising the EU's profile in the Chinese setting. Amongst other things, the Communication made reference to China's campaign for membership of the WTO. The EU's posture was more relaxed than that of the US, although it was clear that EU support for the Chinese did not come without qualifications, particularly in the areas of human rights and trade policies. The European Council adopted the Communication in December 1995. [2]

I.C.ii Building a Comprehensive Partnership with China (1998)

The European Commission policy paper on "Building a Comprehensive Partnership with China" was issued on 25 March 1998. The main contents of the Communication included goals to engage China further in international community; to support China's transition to an open society based on the rule of law and respect for human rights; to integrate China further in the world economy; to make Europe's funding

---

[1] Commission of the European Communities, Towards a New Asia Strategy, (Communication from the Commission to the Council), COM (94) 314 Final, Brussels, 13 July 1994.

[2] The European Union 1995, Annual Review of Activities, Blackwell Publishers (1996), 78.

go further;[1] and to raise the profile of the EU in China.

The Communication pointed out that the Asian financial crisis, which had reduced foreign direct investment in China, made it all the more important for China to attract investment from its other partners, especially Europe and the US. The EU trade policy must be backed by a comprehensive strategy to promote investment, as well as business and industrial co-operation with China, so as to strengthen the European presence in the Chinese market. The EU should launch such a strategy, focusing primarily on industrial sectors such as telecommunications, energy, environmental technology and services, transport and financial services in which Europe has a clear competitive advantage. There are some investment programmes to encourage the EC's investment in China.[2]

As evidence of the Communication, Mr. Jacques Santer was sent on an official visit to China from 29 October to 3 November 1998. He was the first European Commission President to visit China in 12 years. Three legal documents were signed in this visit: the Memorandum of Understanding on Industrial Co-operation in the Field of Aeronautics and Telecommunications; the Financing Agreement on China-EU Legal and Judicial Co-operation Programme; and the Financing Agreement on the China-EU Framework Program for the EU Support to China's Accession to the WTO.[3]

On 15 May 2001 the EU Commission adopted a communication entitled "EU Strategy towards China: Implementation of the 1998 Communication and Future Steps for a more Effective EU Policy". The aim of the Communication was to fine-tune, and not to re-define, the strategy set out in the 1998 Communication.[4] A new policy paper of EU Commission entitled "A Maturing Partnership: Shared Interests and Challenges in EU-China Relations" was endorsed by the EU on 13

---

〔1〕 This idea encourages consideration of all possible avenues for improving the efficiency of EC's funding. See Communication from the Commission, Building a Comprehensive Partnership with China, *COM* (1998) 181 final, 22-24.

〔2〕 E. g. , the European Community Investment Partner (ECIP) programme, which aims at supporting the creation of joint ventures between European and Chinese companies in China; and the Asia-Invest program, which aims at helping European small and medium-sized enterprises identify potential partners in China. Communication from the Commission, Building a Comprehensive Partnership with China, *COM* (1998) 181 final, 16-17.

〔3〕 Sino-EU Ties Emphasized, 41 (46) *Beijing Review* (1998), 4.

〔4〕 See www. europa. eu. int/comm/external_relations/china/intro/index. htm.

October 2003. The aim of this document was to update the strategy set out in 2001 and in the 1998 Communication.[1]

I.C.iii China-EU Summits since 1998

The first China-EU summit, at the Heads of Government level, brought together Chinese Prime Minister Mr. Zhu Rongji, the UK Prime Minister Mr. Blair, and President of the European Council, Mr. Santer and Sir Leon Brittan in London on 2 April 1998. The summit adopted a joint communiqué in which the two sides stressed the need to improve dialogue and co-operation between them, not only in their own interests, but also in the interests of peace, stability and development in the world. The Chinese Prime Minister welcomed the Commission's Communication on "Building a Comprehensive Partnership with China", and the two parties expressed the hope that they could build a stable and lasting partnership in the 21st century and stressed that a strong economic and trade link constituted an important basis for the continuous development of their ties. They also reaffirmed their commitment to China's rapid accession to the WTO and their desire to co-operate to advance the accession negotiations. China also expressed its support for launching the Euro. The EU welcomed the progress made in China with respect to human rights and agreed with China's firm stance vis-à-vis the Asian financial crisis, where China was determined not to devalue its currency but instead tried to adhere to the economic and financial reforms already under way.[2]

The second and third China-EU summits were held in Beijing in December 1999 and October 2000.[3] The fourth EU-China summit, the most successful to date, was held in Brussels on 5 September 2001. Premier Zhu Rongji, Prime Minister Guy Verhofstadt of Belgium—in his capacity as President of the European Council—and the President of European Commission Romano Prodi attended the Summit. The summit agreed on a Joint Press Statement for the first time, which, taking its cue from the Commission's 2001 Communication, outlined the areas, ways and means of widening and broadening EU-China relations through increased exchanges, stepped-up dialogue and greater co-operation and co-ordination across the board.

---

[1] See europa. eu. int/comm/external_relations/china/intro/index. htm/23/12/03.

[2] European Commission, Bulletin of the European Union, 4-1998, 64.

[3] See europa. eu. int/comm/external_relations/china/intro/index. htm/15/03/01.

The fifth summit was held in Copenhagen in September 2002. [1] The sixth summit took place in Beijing on 30 October 2003.

These summits have provided a forum for top leaders of China and the EU to regularly exchange their views and opinions on China-EU comprehensive relations.

Ⅰ. C. iv China-EU Agreement on China's Accession to the WTO (2000) and afterwards

The China-EU Agreement on China's Accession to the WTO was concluded in Beijing on May 19, 2000, which marked an important development in China-EU economic relations. [2] The Agreement, along with the China-US Agreement signed in 1999, paved the way for China's accession to the WTO. [3] On 9 November 2001, Doha WTO ministerial conference adopted China's application of the WTO accession by consensus. China notified the WTO that it ratified its membership and became a full member, the WTO's 143rd, on 11 December 2001. [4]

After China's accession to the WTO, China-EU economic relations have been subject to the multilateral trade systems of the organization to some extent, which is a substantial change for both parties. [5] China might be more competitive in the world market as it has gained more trade opportunities and improved its trade relations with other WTO members (including the US, Canada, Japan and Southeast Asia countries) based on WTO rules. China also started a process for multilateral regional economic integration. The main achievements in this regard are the Framework Agreement on Comprehensive Economic Cooperation between the Association of Southeast Asian Nations and the People's Republic of China on 4 November 2002[6] and the Closer Economic Partnership Arrangements (the CEPAs) between

---

[1] See europa. eu. int/comm/external_relations/china/intro/index. htm.

[2] For a brief introduction of the agreement, see The Sino-EU Agreement on China's Accession to the WTO: Results of the Bilateral Negotiations, see www. ecd. org. cn/en/eu_china_wto/wto7. htm.

[3] See europa. eu. int/comm/external_relations/china/intro/index. htm/15/03/01.

[4] On 1 January, 2002, the Separate Customs Territory of Taiwan, Penghu, Kinmen and Matsu (Chinese Taipei) became a member of WTO, as did Hong Kong and Macao, the two original members on 1 January 1995. One China, four WTO memberships emerged, which is the new phenomenon in GATT/WTO history. See ZENG Huaqun, One Country, Four Seats under WTO Regime, 5 *Xiamen University Journal* (2002), 5-14 (in Chinese).

[5] For the EU, Council Regulation (EC) No 3286/94 of 22 December 1994 laying down Community procedures in the field of the common commercial policy in order to ensure the exercise of the Community's rights under international trade rules, in particular those established under the auspices of the WTO.

[6] Extracts of the Agreement are published in 1 (1) *China: An International Journal* (2003), 170-178.

Mainland China and the HKSAR, the Macao SAR in 2003.[1] On the other hand, the EU's further enlargement has had great impact on its external relations. It might reconsider its relations with China in light of the upcoming enlargement.

As the multilateral trade systems and regional economic integration arrangements do not cover every field and every subject matter in China-EC economic transactions and can not substitute for the bilateral treaties, the bilateral legal framework for China-EU economic relations will retain its function and might play more important role along with the development of further economic exchanges and greater cooperation between the two parties. Furthermore, China needs to make more concrete bilateral agreements with the EC and other WTO members under the WTO rules. It is expected that more and more bilateral arrangements will be made by the parties. According to EU Commission's Communication on "Building a Comprehensive Partnership with China", the EU-China trade dialogue could be further strengthened through the conclusion of specific bilateral agreements in areas of particular interest, such as maritime transport, air transport, nuclear trade and safety, customs, and science and technology.[2]

I.D Summary

From the above-mentioned three stages of the development of China-Europe economic relations, we see clearly that economic relations between China and Europe have developed steadily in the last half century. The significance of the development from the initial stage to the legalisation stage was to legalise the said relations, which provided both parties a bilateral legal framework for their economic relations. China-EU economic relations today have entered into a new era in which both parties are eager to develop their relations constructively and to consider their economic relations at a strategic level, which in turn will further the improvement and reconstruction of the bilateral legal framework for their economic relations.

We have to bear in mind two key points after recalling this history. First, even as early as the 1950s, China has had an internal motive and impetus for developing

---

[1] The CEPAs between Mainland China and HKSAR, Macao SAR have been concluded on 29 June 2003 and 17 October 2003 respectively and all initiated since 1 January 2004. See www.mofcom.gov.cn/table/hk-main.pdf, www.mofcom.gov.cn/article/200310/20031000136512_1.xml.

[2] Communication from the Commission, Building a Comprehensive Partnership with China, *COM* (1998) 181 final, 16-17.

and promoting its economic relations with the rest of the world. More importantly, as the results of learning from both positive and negative experience of about 30 years, China has taken two revolutionary steps in the last quarter of the 20th century: it has applied the open door policy since 1978 and worked with a market-oriented economic system since 1993. As far as China-EC economic relations are concerned, the former has provided broader fields and more opportunities of economic cooperation for companies and businessmen from the EC. The latter not only provides the same economic system as the EC Member States for Chinese companies and businessmen, but also greatly improves the business environment for the EC's traders and investors. The two breakthroughs in Chinese decision-making have great positive impact on China-EC economic relations in the long run. Secondly, it is obvious that at the former two stages, as the Western European countries did not link political issues to economic relations with China, the economic relations between the two sides grew closer, and both sides gained benefits from the stable relations.

II. Major Political Issues Affecting China-EU Economic Relations and the Legal Arrangements Concerned

Although China-EU economic relations have developed rapidly, the two parties still confront a political issue from time to time, especially since 1989 and during the promotion stage. The major existing issues—political or politics-related—affecting China-EU economic relations and the legal arrangements concerned are human rights, autonomy of Hong Kong and Macao, as well as the Taiwan issue. [1]

II. A Human Rights

Human rights have become the central issue to China-EU economic relations since 1989.

In the 1995 Communication on China Policy, the European Commission proposed a three-pronged approach to the issue: first, it supported efforts to open up and liberalize all aspects of Chinese life (thus encouraging the development of a civil society based on the rule of law); second, it promoted the continuance of a bilateral dialogue with China to raise human rights issues; and third, it recognized the influence of the interna-

---

[1] There are also some economic issues affecting China-EC relations. Among them, antidumping may be the hottest one.

tional community in the dialogue through multilateral fora like the United Nations. [1]

The European Parliament[2] Resolution on the Commission Communication on a Long-term Policy for China-Europe Relations was adopted on 12 June 1997, and was a typical EU document on human rights in China. It recommended that the biannual dialogue between China and the EU on human rights be maintained and called on Chinese authorities to abolish the death penalty, to release political prisoners and to repeal laws in general that were incompatible with the development of a State genuinely governed by the rule of law. Condemning China's occupation of Tibet, it further called on the Chinese government to resume negotiations with the Dalai Lama on the basis of recognition of the people of Tibet's right to self-government. [3]

China made a quick response to the Parliament Resolution. On 13 June 1997, the Committee on Foreign Affairs authorized by the Standing Committee of National People's Congress of the PRC published a solemn statement on this Parliament resolution, condemning strongly its interference with China's internal affairs.

In the 1998 Communication on Building a Comprehensive Partnership with China, the EU's attitude toward China's human rights issues was more positive. In the document, the EU acknowledged that the situation of human rights in China has improved over the last twenty years. Economic reform has introduced greater freedom of choice in education, employment, housing, travel and other areas of social activity. China has passed new civil and criminal laws to protect citizens' rights and has signed several key instruments bringing the country closer to international norms, including its decision to sign the International Covenant on Economic, Social and Cultural Rights. It has also taken steps to develop the electoral process at the local level, allowing villagers to designate their local authorities. The EU believes in

---

[1] Christopher Piening, *Global Europe: The European Union in World Affairs*, Lynne Rienner Publishers (1997), 157.

[2] The European Parliament has been a direct elected institution of EC since 1979. The Parliament helps to draft, amend and adopt European laws and budget, as well as making policy proposals. Since 1957, the Parliament's powers have gradually grown, and particular since the signature of the Single European Act (1986) and of the Treaty on European Union (1992). The parliament is fully involved in adopting Community legislation and the EC budget. It also supervises the activities of the Commission and the Council of EC. The members of the Parliament represent the interests of the citizen, through the Committee on Petitions, and by appointing the European Ombudsman. It also takes a keen interest in the defence of human rights. See *The European Parliament*, Office for Official Publications of the European Communities (1997), 4, 7.

[3] European Commission, *Bulletin of the European Union*, 6-1997, 118-119.

the merits of dialogue, in all appropriate fora, over confrontation; the EU and China should therefore tackle their differences in a frank, open and respectful manner. The Commission also promoted human rights in China through open debate and co-operation. [1]

On 10 February 1999 the European Parliament adopted a decision to support the 1998 Commission Communication on Building a Comprehensive Partnership with China. The decision requested China to respect human rights and suggested that EU introduce an article on human rights to the new trade and economic co-operation treaty between China and the EU. Moreover, the decision encouraged China to implement political reforms and appealed to Western countries to abolish any arms trading with China. [2]

As a matter of fact, China has taken important steps to improve human rights and to establish the rule of law in the country in recent years. It signed the International Covenant on Economic, Social and Cultural Rights and the International Covenant on Civil and Political Rights on 27 October 1997 and 5 October 1998 respectively. [3] From the Chinese point of view, any and all suggestions for improving human rights in China are welcome. However, learning from the history of China-Europe economic relations, we may find that it is not necessary to link human rights and trade together or to consider human rights as a precondition of China-EU economic relations. As human rights issues will remain problematic due to the different situations and different value approaches in different societies, it is unwise to politicize the issues or to introduce an article on human rights in the new China-EC trade and economic co-operation agreement. Furthermore, there is no legal ground for the EU to raise the so-called human rights issues, such as the death penalty, [4] Tibet's self-government, etc., which are essentially China's internal affairs except for any international commitments they may involve.

Today, as China is open to the whole world, it is impossible for one or a few

---

[1] Communication from the Commission, Building a Comprehensive Partnership with China, *COM* (1998) 181 final, 9-11.

[2] www. mingbao. com/newspaper/990211/cac1. htm.

[3] For a general picture and the process of China human rights, www. humanrights. cn/china/rqlc/menu. htm.

[4] According to art. 6 of International Covenant on Civil and Political Rights, the death penalty is not prohibited but the article has imposed some limitations.

countries or entities to impose an embargo on China. If one country or entity set pre-requests or pre-conditions (such as the human rights issue) for its trade with China, it may hinder or even block its way to gain benefits from China. China may easily find alternative business opportunities from other countries. A Chinese idiom states that when a snipe and clam grapple, the fisherman profits. From a practical and economic point of view, the results of the EU's current position on Chinese human rights might not be good for the EU and China, but good for third parties.

Ⅱ. B Autonomy of Hong Kong and Macao

Related to the human rights problem is the autonomy of Hong Kong (hereinafter "HK") and Macao. Two of the EU Member States—the UK and Portugal—ruled people of HK and Macao for many generations. This is an important historical tie among the two countries, Europe and the two regions, inevitably meaning that the EU has taken a particular interest in the arrangements for China's resumption of the exercise of the sovereignty over the two regions.

Both of the former colonial powers have sought guarantees from China that the human and civic rights enjoyed by the populations of the two regions would remain unaffected by China's commencement of sovereignty on 1 July 1997 and 20 December 1999 respectively.

Instead of political reasons, economic reasons are more important to the EU. HK and Macao's continued close relations with the EU are essential to the EU. In the mid-1990's, HK is the EU's eleventh largest trading partner. Five of the EU Member States enjoy bilateral trade with HK of over 2 billion ECUs. HK is also a key destination for investment from across the EU Member States, with 40 EU banks and 45 insurance companies licensed in HK. Some 40,000 EU citizens are residents of HK. Moreover, both HK and Macao serve as gateways to other regions of China, and can act as key facilitators for increased European trade and investment with China. [1]

The EU Parliament adopted a Resolution on the Situation in HK on 10 April 1997, which showed the EU's concern for the autonomy of HK after 1997. In this document, the Parliament called for the transfer of sovereignty of HK to take place

---

[1] Communication from the Commission, A Long Term Policy for China-Europe Relations, Commission of the European Communities, Brussels, 05.07. 1995 *COM* (95) 279 final, 6-7.

in full accordance with the principles set out in the Joint Declaration of the Government of United Kingdom of Great Britain and Northern Ireland and the Government of People's Republic of China on the Question of Hong Kong (hereinafter "Sino-British Joint Declaration")[1] and the Basic Law of Hong Kong Special Administration Region of People's Republic of China (hereinafter the "Basic Law"). [2] It called on the Council to establish how it intended to develop relations with HK and on the Commission to present an annual report covering political, economic and human rights in Hong Kong Special Administrative Region (hereinafter "HKSAR"). The parliament also resolved to monitor the situation in HKSAR, notably by sending a fact-finding mission. [3]

Following the Parliament Resolution, a Commission Communication to the Council and Parliament entitled "The European Union and Hong Kong: Beyond 1997" was adopted on 23 April 1997. In this document, the Commission, after underlining the importance of ties between HK and Europe and analyzing HK's future as a SAR within the PRC, outlines a strategy for strengthening relations between the EU and HK. Proposals include: dealing directly and maintaining regular and close contacts with the government of HKSAR; continuing to treat HK as an independent entity for trade policy purposes and an important partner within the WTO; monitoring the situation in HK and respect for the rights granted to its citizens under the SAR, working with the international community and publishing an annual report on all aspects of relations between the EU and HK; continuing to assess the HK government on its own merits for the purposes of the common visa list; exploring ways of putting trade, investment and co-operation relations between HK and the EU on a more permanent footing; and developing active co-operation with HK as an Asian hub. [4]

In early 1999, the EU Parliament adopted a Decision which reaffirmed the democratic development in HKSAR and hoped that Macao would become a demo-

---

[1] The Joint Declaration was formally signed on 19 December 1984 and came into force on 27 May 1985. The agreement was reprinted in 23 *ILM* (1984), 1371-1380.

[2] The Basic Law was promulgated on 4 April 1990.

[3] European Commission, *Bulletin of the European Union*, 4-1997, 89.

[4] European Commission, *Bulletin of the European Union*, 4-1997, 88-89.

cratic and prosperous society after it is returned to China. [1]

In the period of colonialism, colonialist power ruled the colonial people arbitrarily. So did the colonialist powers in the *de facto* colonies HK and Macao respectively. It is very unusual and interesting that former colonizers paid much attention to human rights of the two regions, even after they withdrew from the two regions. The new phenomenon might reflect, first, the profound changes of the political situation in the world; second, the Western countries' sympathetic concern on the future of people in the two regions; and last and most importantly, the Western countries' own existing interests and potential in the two regions. It should be emphasized that from the legal point of view, China has not had any commitment concerning HK or Macao with the EU. Instead, China has signed the Joint Declarations with the UK and Portugal and bears international obligations to the two countries, not to the EU itself or any other EU Member States.

HK's experience in the period of transition and after 1997 shows that the concepts of "one country, two systems" and "high autonomy" have been implemented successfully. HK has maintained its own economic and trade policy and kept its membership in the WTO. [2] The HK's practice on international treaties has demonstrated convincingly its high autonomy. The Agreement between the Government of Hong Kong and the Government of Kingdom of Netherlands on Promotion and Protection of Mutual Investment was signed on 19 November 1992 and effective on 1 September 1993. [3] By 21 May 2003, HK had concluded BITs with 15 countries. 10 of them are the EU Member States, [4] namely in addition to the Netherlands, Denmark (effective on 4 March 1994), [5] Sweden (26 June 1994), [6] France (30

---

[1] www. mingbao. com/newspaper/990211/cac1. htm

[2] On 23 April 1986, HK became a full member of GATT through the UK's Statement. China made a Statement on the same day to allow HK to keep that position in GATT beyond 1 July 1997. HK became an original member of WTO on 1 January 1995 according to article 11 of WTO Agreement and changed its name to "Hong Kong, China" on 1 July 1997. Following the HK's model, Macao became a full member of GATT through Portugal's and China's Statements on 11 January 1991, then became an original member of WTO on 1 January 1995 and changed its name to "Macao, China" on 20 December 1999.

[3] Texts published in *Special Supplement No. 5 to the Hong Kong Government Gazette* (*SS No. 5 HKGG*) (1992), E27-53.

[4] www. justice. gov. hk/table1_e. htm14/01/2004

[5] Texts published in 136 (6) *SS No. 5 HKGG* (1994), E19-E48.

[6] Texts published in 136 (6) *SS No. 5 HKGG* (1994), E51-E78.

May 1997), [1] Austria(1 October 1997), [2] Italy (2 February 1998), [3] Germany (19 February 1998), [4] the UK (12 April 1999)[5] and Belgium-Luxembourg (18 June 2001). [6] By 11 November 2003, HK had signed 55 air service agreements and air services transit agreements (hereinafter "air agreements"), 49 of them being effective. [7] The air agreements between HK and the EU Member States, including Netherlands (effective on 26 June 1987), [8] France (10 May 1991), [9] Germany (23 June 1997), [10] UK (25 July 1997), [11] Italy (19 January 1998), [12] Austria (1 December 1998), [13] Sweden (14 March 2000), [14] Denmark (14 March 2000)[15], Finland (1 April 2000)[16] and Belgium (1 July 2003)[17] came into force one after another. HK's air agreements with the other 2 EC Member States, Greece and Luxembourg, have been signed respectively but have not yet come into force. [18]

Currently, the HKSAR has plans to extend the network of bilateral economic treaties with more countries and will examine new multilateral treaties that may be relevant to the HKSAR. These multifarious external legal relations helped to strengthen HKSAR's external autonomy and international status. [19] The latest developments of CEPAs between Mainland China and HKSAR, Macao SAR have further confirmed and guaranteed the autonomy of these two regions as separate

---

[1]　Texts published in 2 (26) SS No. 5 HKGG (1998), E215-E240.

[2]　Texts published in 2 (26) SS No. 5 HKGG (1998), E317-E351.

[3]　Texts published in 2 (6) SS No. 5 HKGG (1998), E3-E35.

[4]　Texts published in 2 (10) SS No. 5 HKGG (1998), E39-E66.

[5]　Texts published in 3 (15) SS No. 5 HKGG (1999), E391-E414.

[6]　Texts published in 5 (25) SS No. 5 HKGG (2001), E175-E222.

[7]　www. justice. gov. hk/table1_e. htm14/01/2004

[8]　Texts published in 129 (26) SS No. 5 HKGG (1987), E 201-E233; Amendment to the Agreement of 17. 9. 86, published in 139 (2) SS No. 5 HKGG (1997), E 3-E30.

[9]　Texts published in 132 (36) SS No. 5 HKGG (1990), E 153-E202.

[10]　Texts published in 137 (19) SS No. 5 HKGG (1995), E27-E92. Amendment to the Air Service Agreement of 5. 5. 1995, published in 139 (21) SS No. 5 HKGG (1997), E 483-E500.

[11]　Texts published in 1 (6) SS No. 5 HKGG (1997), E47-E88.

[12]　Texts published in 138 (45) SS No. 5 HKGG (1996), E377-E429.

[13]　Texts published in 3 (11) SS No. 5 HKGG (1999), E183-E245.

[14]　Texts published in 5 (9) SS No. 5 HKGG (2001), E87-E125.

[15]　Texts published in 5 (7) SS No. 5 HKGG (2001), E3-E41.

[16]　Texts published in 4 (36) SS No. 5 HKGG (2000), E1175-E1210.

[17]　Texts published in 2 (49) SS No. 5 HKGG (2000), E553-E594.

[18]　www. justice. gov. hk/table1_e. htm14/01/2004

[19]　Elsie Leung, The Rule of Law and Its Operation in Hong Kong after Reunification, 6 Policy Bulletin (1998), 9-10.

customary territories in the WTO regime.[1]

It seems that the autonomy of HKSAR and Macao SAR has been fully protected by Chinese laws and international treaties.[2] The realization of "one country, two systems" and "high autonomy" in these two regions indicates that the autonomy of Hong Kong and Macao might no longer be a political issue affecting China-EU economic relations.

Ⅱ. C The Taiwan Issue

The status of Taiwan, comparatively speaking, is an old issue in China-EC relations. It may be traced back to early 1970 when China and the EC began to negotiate the establishment of official relations between the two parties. The main point of contention in the negotiation was the status of Taiwan.

Since 1949, China's position has been that any State or international organization which wishes to deal with China should recognize the government of PRC as the sole legitimate government of China and Taiwan as an inalienable part of China. When the EC and China decided to establish official relations, this was the first issue that had to be dealt with. The EC delegation initially gave an informal assurance that the EC considered the Beijing government to be the only government of China, and that it had no relation with Taiwan. However, China insisted that the EC formally and publicly declare its support to China's above-mentioned contention. Skillfully the EC delegation refused to make such a declaration on the legal ground that it had no legal mandate to make any declaration that involved States. Sir Christopher Soames, the then vice-president of the European Commission, further explained that such matters as the recognition of States did not come within the responsibility of the EC. A compromise was finally reached when Sir Christopher Soames publicly stated that the EC had no official relations, nor did it have any agreement, with Taiwan, and that this was in conformity with the position taken by all the Member States.[3]

---

[1] For the further comment on the issue, see KONG Qingjiang, Closer Economic Partnership Agreement between China and Hong Kong, 1 (1) *China: An International Journal* (2003), 133-143.

[2] For the general comment on the autonomy of HK, See ZENG Huaqun, On the Autonomy of Hong Kong Special Administrative Region: External Aspects, 1 *Journal of Comparative Law* (2002) (in Chinese), 75-91; ZENG Huaqun, Hong Kong's Autonomy: Concept, Developments and Characteristics, 1 (2) *China: An International Journal* (2003), 313-325.

[3] 18 (2) *Beijing Review* (1985), 5 and *EC Bull*. 5-1975 point 1.2.04.

For a long time, the EU and its Member States have never recognized the Taipei regime and maintain no Commission office there. Ostensibly, the EU supports the "One China" principle, while seeking to maintain cordial, if informal, relations with the island.

However, there have been some unfavorable events relating to the status of Taiwan. For example, on 22 May 1997, the Committee on Foreign Affairs, Security and Defense Policy of European Parliament invited Zhang Xiaoyan to visit the European Parliament in the name of "governmental member of Republic of China". The Committee on Foreign Affairs of National People's Congress of PRC issued a solemn statement the following day, strongly protesting against the invitation. [1]

It is worth noting that the attitudes of some members in the European Parliament are different from that of the EU as a whole or any individual Member State. The European Parliament, many of whose members have been intensively lobbied by the Taipei authorities, has already called for Taiwan to be admitted to various UN agencies. So far, the EU and its Member States have resisted such calls. [2]

Recently the EU recognized Taiwan as a separate customs territory in the WTO context. Given Taiwan's economic importance as the EU's 11th largest trading partner and the world's 14th largest trading entity in 1999, the EU endeavors to develop economic and trade relations with the island. EU industry in Taiwan is represented by the European Council of Trade and Industry in Taipei (ECCT) which helps to promote commercial relations and identify obstacles in bilateral trade and investment. [3] On 1 January 2002, Taiwan became a member of the WTO in the name of "the Separate Customs Territory of Taiwan, Penghu, Kinmen and Matsu (Chinese Taipei)", which provided a legal ground for the EU-Chinese Taipei trade relations, the same as the EU-Hong Kong, China trade relations and the EU-Macao, China

---

[1] Committee on Foreign Affairs of National People's Congress of PRC's Solemn Statement on the Invitation to Zhang Xiaoyan to visit European Parliament by Committee on Foreign Affairs, Security and Defence Policy of European Parliament (23 May, 1997).

[2] Christopher Piening, *Global Europe: The European Union in World Affairs*, Lynne Rienner Publishers (1997), 158.

[3] See www. europa. eu. int/comm/external_relations/china/intro/index. htm.

trade relations. [1] As for settlement of the Taiwan issue, the EU calls for the peace-ful resolution of differences between Taiwan and mainland China. [2]

It should be pointed out that the "One China" principle has been generally accepted and recognized by the international society, including the US, the EU and all the EU Member States. The Taiwan issue therefore is completely an internal af-fair of China and will be settled by the Chinese themselves. There is no legal ground for any foreign country or entity to engage in the Taiwan issue in accordance with in-ternational law or international practice. [3] As for the means of resolution for the Taiwan issue, peaceful resolution is undoubtedly a priority and the best choice for mainland China, simply because the people across the Taiwan Strait are Chinese and the land is part of China. However, peaceful resolution definitely is not the only choice because of the complicated local and international elements involved.

Ⅲ. Basic Legal Considerations in Signing China-EC Economic Treaties

Due to the complex legal framework of the EU[4] and the characteristics of the EC's bilateral treaties with non Member States, when China is going to enter a bilateral treaty with the EC, it may have to consider the following three basic and important issues: the EC's treaty-making power; the responsibility of the EC mixed

---

[1] For the members by accession, Article 12 of the WTO Agreement read as: "Any State or separate cus-toms territory possessing full autonomy in the conduct of its external commercial relations and of the other matters provided for in this Agreement and the Multilateral Trade Agreements may accede to this Agreement, on terms to be agreed between it and the WTO. Such accession shall apply to this Agreement and the Multilateral Trade Agreements annexed thereto. " It seems that the WTO follows the tradition of GATT, continuing to adopt the concept of separate customs territories (SCTs). In order to use the legal concept of SCTs in context with the whole multilateral trade rules, the explanatory note of the WTO Agreement particularly indicates: "the terms 'country or countries' as used in this Agreement and the Multilateral Trade Agreements are to be understood to include any SCT member of the WTO. In the case of a SCT member of the WTO, where an expression in this Agreement and the Multilateral Trade Agreements is qualified by the term 'national', such expression shall be read as pertaining to that customs territory, unless otherwise specified. "

[2] On 20 July 1999, the EU Presidency made a statement, on behalf of the Union, supporting the "One China" principle, underlining the need to resolve the question of Taiwan peacefully through constructive dialogue, and urging both sides to avoid taking steps or making statements that increase tension (www. europa. eu. int/comm/exter-nal_relations/china/intro/index. htm).

[3] However, it is worth noticing that there are some comments on the topic in Western countries from time to time. Most recently, Jonathan I. Charney and J. R. V. Prescott, Resolving Cross-Strait Relations between China and Taiwan, 94 *AJIL* (2000), 452-477.

[4] It is pointed out that the EC law is a "new legal order" that is distinct from international law. See Anne Peters, The Position of International Law within the European Community Legal Order, 40 *German Yearbook of In-ternational Law* (1997), 10.

treaties; and the direct effect of EC treaties, which are very distinct from ordinary bilateral treaties.

III. A EC's Treaty-making Power

According to Article 210 of the Treaty of Rome (hereinafter the "Treaty"), the EC is endowed with international personality. According to the general rule of international law, international personality of an international organization does not imply a general treaty-making power. The treaty-making power of international organizations may be deduced from their functions and purposes, in accordance with the principles of "empowerment" and "specialty". [1] Due to the highest integration of the EC among international organizations, the treaty-making power of the EC is far more complicated than that of other international organizations.

First of all, it is worth mentioning here that the EC, not the EU, has treaty-making power. As the result of the Treaty on European Union (also known as the Maastricht Treaty), which came into force on 1 November 1993, a number of changes have occurred. [2] However, there is no provision on the EU's legal personality under the Maastricht Treaty. As the EU's new functions include common foreign and security policy and co-operation in justice and home affairs, it is controversial whether the EU may represent all of its Member States in these two vital and sensitive fields. [3] Some comments and court decisions clearly indicate that the EU

---

[1] Constantine A. Stephanou, The Legal Nature of the European Union, in Nicholas Emiliou and David O'Keeffe (eds.), *Legal Aspects of Integration in the European Union*, Kluwer Law International (1997), 181-182.

[2] These changes include mainly:

• the Member States of the three European Communities, the EEC, the European Coal and Steel Community and the European Atomic Energy Community, are now members of the EU;

• all nationals of these Member States are citizens of the EU;

• the EU is based on a combination of the provisions of three existing treaties (each of which has been slightly amended by the new Treaty of the EU) and new provisions set out in the Treaty on EU which provide the basis for a common foreign and security policy and for co-operation in justice and home affairs between the Member States and the EU;

• one of the major changes to the EEC Treaty was the addition of a section on a common economic and monetary policy;

• The EEC Treaty is now called the EC Treaty.

See Lesley Ainsworth, EEC, EC, EU or EEA? All You Ever Wanted to Know about Abbreviations Starting with E- But Were Afraid to Ask, *Lawyers' Europe*, Summer 1994, p. 2.

[3] For further discussion on the EU constitutional order, see Youri Devuyst, The European Union's Constitutional Order? Between Community Method and *ad hoc* Compromise, 18 *Berkeley J. Int'l L.* (2000), 1-52.

does not have international personality or is not a subject of international law. [1]

Secondly, it seems clear that we must distinguish between the EC's bilateral treaties made with non-Member States and those made with Member States. The Member States are supposed to know all the internal rules of the EC. An EC treaty with one or more Member States will be illegal if it breaches any article of the EC treaties or any other rule of law based on it. The situation is different with respect to treaties with non-Member States. Non-Member States cannot be expected to know the extent of the competence of the EC. As a general rule, whenever the EC concludes a treaty, non-Member States may presume that it is competent to do so. If the EC acted beyond its powers, it will nonetheless be bound unless it or its Member States can prove both its lack of competence and its manifest character. The latter will be especially difficult because of the complicated nature of the EC law. [2] Before entering into a bilateral economic treaty with the EC, we should better understand the developments, characteristics and doctrines of the EC's treaty-making power.

Ⅲ. A. i EC's Explicit and Implicit Treaty-making Powers

The question of the EC's explicit and implicit treaty-making powers refer to the limits of the EC's competence to make treaties. This is also described as the "existence" question, which asks: according to what legal rationale, and in what circumstances, or otherwise is the EC to act internationally, in the absence of express authorization under the Treaty?[3] The key issue therefore is whether the EC has unwritten powers to make treaties. [4] The history of the EC shows that the extent to which the EC can participate in the field of international relations depends first upon its capacity to enter into international agreements as provided in the Treaty, and second upon whether the EC in a given case has the authority is a matter which

---

[1] See Anne Peters, The Position of International Law within the European Community Legal Order, 40 German Yearbook of International Law (1997) 10, n3. For further discussion on the issue of the international legal personality of the EC and the EU, see Dominic McGoldrick, *International Relations law of the European Union*, Longman (1997), 26-39; Jan Klabbers, Presumptive Personality: The European Union in International Law, in M. Koskenniemi (eds.), *International Law Aspects of the European Union*, Kluwer Law International (1998), 231-253.

[2] Henry G. Schermers, The Internal Effect of Community Treaty-Making, in David O'Keeffe and Henry G. Schermers (ed.), *Essays in European Law and Integration*, Kluwer Law and Taxation Publishers (1982), 173.

[3] Alan Dashwood, Implied External Competence of the EC, in M. Koskenniemi (ed.), *International Law Aspects of the European Union*, Kluwer Law International (1998), 113.

[4] For further discussing the issue, see Meinhard Hilf, Unwritten EC Authority in Foreign Trade Law, 2 *European Foreign Affairs Review* (1997), 437-454.

is to be established by the European Court of Justice (hereinafter the "Court").

Ⅲ. A. i. 1 Doctrine of Explicit Power

The advocates of the doctrine of explicit power dominated the scene during the initial period following the founding of the EC. Its supporters relied principally on the first part of Article 228 of the Treaty, which states: "Where this treaty provides for the conclusion of agreements...." In other words, the treaty-making power exists only as expressly provided in the Treaty.

Two of the most significant express treaty-making powers relate to: (1) commercial agreements under Article 113 of the Treaty;[1] and (2) association agreements under Article 238.

The tendency towards explicitly mentioning the EC's treaty-making power in specific fields was embodied in the Single European Act. The Act adds two articles to the Treaty, establishing powers in respect to technological research and development and the environment. According to the newly added articles, namely Article 130N and 103R, the arrangements for the EC's co-operation in these two fields shall be negotiated and concluded in accordance with Article 228.[2]

Ⅲ. A. i. 2 Doctrine of Implicit Power

The advocates of the doctrine of implicit power rejected the inference from Article 228, arguing that the article does not purport to concern the EC's treaty-making power substantively, but rather to lay down the procedure of negotiations and preliminary steps preceding the conclusion of treaties. In other words, the EC's treaty-making power may be either explicit or implicit. The doctrine of implicit power is a purely judicial construction. Its broad lines were developed by the Court in a

---

[1] Article 113 does not contain a definition of commercial policy but provides a non-exhaustive list of uniform principles on which it is to be based: "particularly in regard to changes in tariff rates, the conclusion of tariff and trade agreements, the achievement of uniformity in measures of liberalization, export policy and measures to protect trade such as those to be taken in case of dumping and subsidies." It is generally accepted that the common commercial policy embraces all measures (autonomous or conventional) which serve to regulate economic relations with third countries and concern the free movement of goods and related traffic in services and payments. Classification of agreements as commercial policy agreements should depend therefore on their essential objective and not on what is also covered by them as subsidiary or ancillary matters. Moreover, the Court's case law makes it clear that the concept of commercial policy is a dynamic one. See Nicholas Emiliou and David O'Keeffe (eds.), *The European Union and World Trade Law: After the GATT Uruguay Round*, John Wiley & Sons Ltd. (1996), 31-32, 35.

[2] Moshe Kaniel, *The Exclusive Treaty-Making Power of the European Community: Up to the Period of the Single European Act*, Kluwer Law International (1996), 28-29.

rather small number of leading cases in the 1970s. [1] The Court, in the *ERTA* case, [2] unequivocally endorsed and further established the doctrine of implicit power. [3]

In the *ERTA* case, the Court first concluded that, according to generally accepted rule of international law, the EC's power may also be inferred from the general "scheme" of the Treaty, no less than from an explicit provision therein. Article 210 of the Treaty provides that the EC has legal personality, and this means that in external relations, the EC enjoys the capacity to enter into agreements with non-Member States within the framework of the objectives defined in Part I of the Treaty. Secondly, the Court considered that when applying the provisions of the Treaty, it is impossible to distinguish between the EC measures taken at the internal level and relations at the external level. Furthermore, the Court strongly linked the external to the internal competence. In its decision, the external powers are held to be the natural extension of the internal ones. Therefore, the EC is competent to enter into international obligations in all fields where it is competent to make binding rules internally. [4]

The *Kramer* case[5] has further developed the principle established in the *ERTA* case. In the *Kramer* case, the Court held that the EC's treaty-making power arose not only from an express conferment by the Treaty (e. g. Article 113) but might equally flow implicitly from other provisions of the Treaty, the Act of Accession and the measures adopted within the framework of those provisions by the EC

---

[1] Alan Dashwood, Implied External Competence of the EC, in M. Koskenniemi (ed.), *International Law Aspects of the European Union*, Kluwer Law International (1998), 113.

[2] The judgment is commonly referred to by the acronym "ERTA", which stands for the agreement in question, the European Road Transport Agreement. For a brief analysis on the case, see Moshe Kaniel, *The Exclusive Treaty-Making Power of the European Community: Up to the Period of the Single European Act*, Kluwer Law International (1996), 31-33.

[3] Moshe Kaniel, *The Exclusive Treaty-Making Power of the European Community: Up to the Period of the Single European Act*, Kluwer Law International (1996), 29-30.

[4] Henry G. Schermers, The Internal Effect of Community Treaty-Making, in David O'Keeffe and Henry G. Schermers (eds.), *Essays in European Law and Integration*, Kluwer Law and Taxation Publishers (1982), 169.

[5] Case 3/76 Officier van Justitie v. Cornelis Kramer and Others (1976) 2 *C. M. L. R.* 440. For a brief analysis on the case, see Moshe Kaniel, *The Exclusive Treaty-Making Power of the European Community: Up to the Period of the Single European Act*, Kluwer Law International (1996), 33-36.

institutions. [1] Compared with the *ERTA* case, the *Kramer* case is more liberal in regard to the fundamental condition for conferring treaty-making power upon the EC in a particular field. According to the *ERTA* judgment, there is a preliminary requirement that the rules must actually be applied by the EC at the external level, even if only as a power parallel to that of its members. In the *Kramer* case, the court ruled that even if the rules were not actually applied, the mere provision of a framework within which those rules can be exercised—such as the promulgation of Regulations 2141/70 and 2142/70 in the case—gives the EC external power in that field, although the power is not exclusive.

The analysis of the *Rhine* opinion[2] leads to the conclusion that it also substantially widened the doctrine of implicit power. Whereas the *ERTA* case speaks of creation of power when measures are attained by "common policy", the *Rhine* opinion uses instead the term "objective", which is wider and more comprehensive. The term "common policy" refers to instances where rules already exist in a given field. The term "objective" is more abstract. It is clear that "objectives" provided in articles 2 and 3 of the Treaty are more generalized and wider. Therefore the *Rhine* opinion represents a fundamental transformation of the "implicit power" into "potential power". [3]

The development in jurisprudence of the Court in the above three cases may be summarized as follows: the EC's competence under the Treaties to lay down legally binding measures comprises internal action (regulations, directives and decisions) and external action. The latter, however, is subject to the condition that the exter-

[1] The EU has five institutes—the Commission, the Council, the European Parliament, the Court of Justice, and the Court of Auditors. The first three are political institutions and play different roles in decision-making and law-making in the EU. See T. C. Hartley, *The Foundations of European Community Law*, Oxford University Press (1998), 11.

[2] Opinion 1/76 Re the Draft Agreement Establishing an European Laying-Up Fund for Inland Waterway Vessels (1997) 2 *C. M. L. R.* 279. For a brief analysis on the case, see Moshe Kaniel, *The Exclusive Treaty-Making Power of the European Community: Up to the Period of the Single European Act*, Kluwer Law International (1996), 36-40.

[3] See Moshe Kaniel, *The Exclusive Treaty-Making Power of the European Community: Up to the Period of the Single European Act*, Kluwer Law International (1996), 39.

nal measure is necessary to achieve one of the objectives of the Treaty. [1] Some authors describe the doctrine of implicit power as the doctrine of "parallelism" and point out that the doctrine allows EC competence in external affairs to expand beyond those expressed in the Treaty in order to match its increasing competence over internal affairs. [2]

III. A. ii EC's Exclusive and Shared Treaty-making Powers

The question of the EC's exclusive and shared treaty-making powers refers to the division of EC's competence to make treaties. This is also described as the "exclusivity" question, which asks: What are the factors that may render this exclusive?[3] In other words, is that competence to be attributed to the EC or to its Member States or can it be shared by the EC and its Member States?

III. A. ii. 1 The Notion of Exclusive Power

The notion of the exclusive EC competence is a creation of the Court. [4] As early as the *Simmenthal* case, [5] the Court stressed that the supremacy of the EC legal order required not only that Member States give preference to the EC law over conflicting national law, but also that they abstain from adopting legal norms which are incompatible with the EC law. Moreover, the Member States could not copy provisions of an EC Regulation into national legal provisions as this might detract from the authority of the EC law, creating confusion as to the source of the obligations and the date of their entry into force. The same considerations also apply to external relations. The EC legal order requires not only the supremacy of the EC acts, but also the exclusive powers for conclusion of treaties, as uncertainty may arise in

---

[1] For further discussion on this topic, see Nicholas Emiliou and David O'Keeffe (eds.), *The European Union and World Trade Law: After the GATT Uruguay Round*, John Wiley & Sons Ltd. (1996), 31-45; ZENG Huaqun, On the Explicit Contracting Power and Implicit Contracting Power of EC, 1 *Xiamen University Journal* (2000) (in Chinese), 74-82.

[2] Ilona Cheyne, International Agreements and the European Community Legal System, 19 *European LR* (1994), 583; Nicholas Emiliou and David O'Keeffe (eds.), *The European Union and World Trade Law: After the GATT Uruguay Round*, John Wiley & Sons Ltd. (1996), 38-41.

[3] Alan Dashwood, Implied External Competence of the EC, in M. Koskenniemi (ed.), *International Law Aspects of the European Union*, Kluwer Law International (1998), 113-114.

[4] Nanette A. Neuwahl, Shared Powers or Combined Incompetence? More on Mixity, 33 *Common Market Law Review* (1996), 669-670.

[5] The *Simmenthal* case, Case 106/77, (1978) ECR 629, for the key points of the case, see T. C. Hartley, *The Foundations of European Community Law*, Oxford University Press (1998), 218-219.

their absence.[1] In certain fields, the Member States have transferred the treaty-making power exclusively to the EC.

For a non-Member State, like China, in cases in which there is an apparent overlap between the EC's and its Member States' powers, the primary problem is to establish whether a given matter comes under the jurisdiction of the EC, and if so, whether the competence of the EC is exclusive.[2] If the jurisdiction of the EC is not exclusive, the more complicated issue of "shared powers" or "shared competence" follows.

III. A. ii. 2 The Notion of Shared Powers

The doctrine of exclusivity does not meet the practical needs and is not sufficient in itself to regulate joint participation of the EC and its Member States in international treaties (hereinafter the "EC mixed treaties"). This is where the notion of "shared powers" comes in. By contrast to the concept "exclusivity", the notion of "shared competence" in the Court's case law clearly applies to the negotiation, conclusion, application and implementation of mixed treaties. The notion of "shared competence" serves to stress that the entire life of mixed treaties is the joint affair of the EC and its Member States.[3] More importantly, the existence of "shared powers" gives rise to mutual obligations between the EC and its Member States. This is very important, because in areas ultimately within the national sovereign powers, there is little room for the Court single-handedly to impose hard obligations on Member States.[4]

In opinion 1/94, the Court ruled that, while including some areas of the exclusive EC competence, the WTO also embraces areas in which the EC and its Member States have concurrent competence, and that in these areas there is an "obligation to co-operate [that] flows from the requirement of unity in the international represen-

---

[1] In Member States, such as the Netherlands, international treaties override statutes, and later treaties "trump" earlier ones, so that in the absence of exclusivity the priority of the EC law and the EC treaties would not be guaranteed in courts or in practice.

[2] Nicholas Emiliou and David O'Keeffe (eds.), *The European Union and World Trade Law: After the GATT Uruguay Round*, *John* Wiley & Sons Ltd. (1996), 41.

[3] "Shared competences" is further divided into "coexistent competences" and "concurrent competences". See Allan Rosas, Mixed Union-Mixed Agreement, in M. Koskenniemi (ed.), *International Law Aspects of the European Union*, Kluwer Law International (1998), 125-148.

[4] Nanette A. Neuwahl, Shared Powers or Combined Incompetence? More on Mixity, 33 *Common Market Law Review* (1996), 676-678.

tation of the Community. "[1] The Court concluded that the EC would acquire exclusive external powers whenever: a) it included in international legislative Acts certain provisions relating to the treatment of nationals of non-Member States; b) expressly conferred on its institutions powers to negotiate with non-Member States; or c) where the EC had achieved complete harmonization of the rules governing access to a self-employed activity. As harmonization was not yet complete in all these fields, the Court held that the power to conclude the General Agreement on Trade in Services ("GATS") was shared between the EC and its Member States.

With regard to the Agreement on Trade-Related Aspects of Intellectual Property Rights ("TRIPS"), the Court, following the same line of reasoning, ruled that the power to conclude the agreement was shared between the EC and its Member States, as the harmonization of the different regimes of intellectual property rights was only partial or, in some fields, completely non-existent. [2]

In general, one can conclude that China-EC bilateral economic treaties are not under the exclusive power of the EC. According to Article 14 of the 1985 Agreement, without prejudice to the relevant provisions of the Treaties establishing the EC, the Agreement and any action taken hereunder shall in no way affect the powers of any of the EC Member States to undertake bilateral activities with China in the field of economic co-operation and conclude, where appropriate, new economic co-operation agreements with China.

It seems that in the fields of trade and economic co-operation, the EC prefers a two-tiered system, namely, to conclude a bilateral treaty between the EC and China and a bilateral treaty between an EC Member State and China, instead of a mixed treaty to which EC and its Member States are one contracting party and China is the other. This is a good arrangement for China, considering the clear responsibilities of the two contracting parties in accordance with traditional international treaty practice. However, China may be confronted by the mixed bilateral or multilateral treaties with the EC in the near future as China-EU economic relations have further developed and China has engaged further in the world market, especially within the

---

[1] Opinion 1/94 Agreement establishing the World Trade Organisation, 15 November 1994, para 108 (English transcript).

[2] Nicholas Emiliou and David O'Keeffe (eds.), *The European Union and World Trade Law: After the GATT Uruguay Round*, John Wiley & Sons Ltd. (1996), 39-40.

WTO regime since 11 December 2001. [1]

Ⅲ. B The Responsibilities of EC Mixed Treaties

As far as the bilateral legal framework for China-EU economic relations is concerned, more complicated is the issue of international responsibilities of the EC mixed treaties due to the unique constitutional order of the EC. [2] This may be a potential problem for China.

The legal and practical problems relating to the EC mixed treaty can be roughly divided into two groups: (1) problems relating to the very existence and scope of treaty rights and obligations; and (2) problems relating to the application and interpretation of such rights and obligations. [3] The legal engagement becomes important only when one of the parties is no longer interested in performing the engagement. Then, the legal obligation to do so must compel the party to continue applying the treaty. Though the EC may bear joint or separate responsibility with its Member States, it may well be that the EC's mixed treaty proves to be insufficient in the responsibility-undertaking. This kind of treaty leads to a number of problems under international law because it may not be clear whether the EC or its Member States are liable. Thus, the counterpart of the treaty with the EC and its Member States may find it difficult to enforce the mixed treaty. Equally, the EC and its Member States might shift the burden of the treaty from one to the other, which would increase the uncertainty to the counterpart. The EC mixed treaty is a problem shifter. Its effect is that both the EC and its Member States are competent to enter into the same treaty and that the solutions to the problems of division of competence and division of liability among the EC and its Member States are postponed until the ap-

---

〔1〕 For example, the proposed BIT between China and EC will be a mixed treaty rather than a sole treaty at this stage. See Wenhua Shan, Towards a New Legal Framework for the EU-China Investment Relations, 34 *Journal of World Trade* (2000), 175.

〔2〕 For discussion on EC's constitutional order, see Alan Dashwood, States in the European Union, 23 *European LR* (1998), 201-216; Daniel Bethlehem, International Law, European Community Law, National Law: Three Systems in Search of a Framework, in M. Koskenniemi (ed.), *International Law Aspects of the European Union*, Kluwer Law International (1998), 169-196.

〔3〕 Allan Rosas, Mixed Union-Mixed Agreement, in M. Koskenniemi (ed.), *International Law Aspects of the European Union*, Kluwer Law International (1998), 133.

plication of the treaty.[1]

The EC's mixed treaties also invite questions as to the responsibilities of Member States towards each other for the fulfillment of the treaty. In the cases of parallel competence, it is clear that such responsibility exists. If competence is shared, and especially in the case of a predominantly bilateral treaty involving concurrent competence, it is doubtful whether the Member States are, under public international law, responsible *inter se*.

Furthermore, as Member States are responsible for implementing a mixed treaty, they have to deal with questions on the methods of national implementation. These questions become especially relevant in the following two cases: (1) Member States hold that they have exclusive or reserved national competence in the specified fields covered by a mixed treaty, in which case this part of the mixed-treaty arguably does not become part of EC law; also (2) Member States, such as the UK and Nordic countries, follow a dualist system with respect to the status of international treaties in domestic law; therefore, a mixed treaty has no legal effect before it becomes part of domestic law through constitutional procedure. One can also envisage other problems of a constitutional nature, such as the question whether binding decisions of a joint body established under a mixed-treaty belong to the area of national competence and thus would entail a new transfer of powers from the national to the international level.[2]

There were some responsibility-division arrangements in the EC's multilateral mixed treaties. For instance, the Food and Agriculture Organization (hereinafter "FAO") Charter obliged the EC to make a declaration regarding power sharing between itself and the Member States in the area of FAO responsibility. Moreover, a special declaration to the same effect is required for each item included in the agenda of the organization's meetings.[3] This might also be a practical way for third parties to enter a bilateral mixed treaty with the EC and its Member States.

---

[1] Henry G. Schermers, The Internal Effect of Community Treaty-Making, in David O'Keeffe and Henry G. Schermers (eds.), *Essays in European Law and Integration*, Kluwer Law and Taxation Publishers (1982), 170.

[2] Allan Rosas, Mix Union-Mixed Agreement, in Martti Koskenniemi (ed.), *International Law Aspects of the European Union*, Kluwer Law International (1998), 142-143.

[3] For analysis of the FAO example, see Nanette A. Neuwahl, Shared Powers or Combined Incompetence? More on Mixity, 33 *Common Market Law Review* (1996), 680-683.

On the other hand, Marrakesh Agreement establishing the World Trade Organization does not lay down obligations to that effect, leaving the issue unresolved. Third parties cannot expect to be briefed on the EC power-sharing arrangements before each meeting of the WTO institutions, nor can they be expected to rely on the findings of Opinion 1/94 of the Court. Under the negotiating arrangements adopted by the Council, the Commission acts as the spokesman for the EC and its Member States, undertaking commitments on their behalf, in their respective fields of competence. In view of these arrangements and the need to ensure legal certainty to third parties, the EC and its Member States may be held jointly and severally responsible for any breach of the WTO Agreement and its annexes. [1] As the EC is a formal member of the WTO and an independent party of the WTO dispute settlement regime, the responsibility-division arrangements are very important for the other WTO members, including China. However, it is an unfortunate fact that the EC work in the external field is riddled with disagreement between the Commission and the Member States on the division and exercise of competences.

When China begins to negotiate a bilateral economic treaty with the EC, it is wise first for China to establish whether the potential treaty will be mixed in nature or not. If it will be a mixed treaty, considering the special legal consequences of the potential treaty, the necessary responsibility-division arrangements among the EC and its Member States might be one of subject-matters in negotiation for the sake of effective implementation of the treaty.

Ⅲ.C The Direct Effect of EC's Treaties

The problem of direct effect of international treaties concluded by the EC in the EC laws and the laws of the EC Member State suffers from a considerable degree of confusion. [2] According to Anne Peters, "direct effect" may be defined as follows:

---

〔1〕 In Opinion 1/94, the Court held that the Community had exclusive competence under Article 113 of EC Treaty to conclude the Multilateral Agreement on Trade in Goods. However, the competence to conclude the General Agreement on Trade in Services (GATS) and the Agreement on Trade-Related Aspects of Intellectual Property Rights (TRIPs) is "shared" between the EC and the Member States. See Nanette A. Neuwahl, Shared Powers or Combined Incompetence? More on Mixity, 33 *Common Market Law Review* (1996), 667-669.

〔2〕 A principal source of confusion is the absence of generally acknowledged definitions. Authors use a variety of terms and define those terms differently, often with subtle distinctions. Some distinguish "direct effect" from "direct applicability". Some speak of enforceability or invocation. Many use "self-executing" synonymously. See Anne Peters, The Position of International Law within the European Community Legal Order, 40 *German Yearbook of International Law* (1997), 42-43.

A provision in an international treaty has direct effect whenever courts are entitled and bound to apply the rule without having to wait for any executive legislation. This is the case when two conditions are fulfilled: the Contracting Parties must have intended the rule to be applicable by the judiciary, and the rule must be, by its contents, suited to give rise to concrete legal consequences. In the purely domestic context, the fulfillment of these conditions makes national laws "justifiable". [1]

According to the Treaty, the treaties concluded by the EC pursuant to the procedures laid down in Article 228. 1 shall be binding on the institutions of the EC and on the Member States. The Court has held that the treaties concluded by the EC with non-Member States form an integral part of the EC legal system and thus have legal binding force as EC law. Moreover, as implied by paragraph 2 of Article 228 of the Treaty, the EC's treaties shall have primacy over the EC secondary legislation and the acts of the Member States.

In practice, the Court ensures, indirectly, that the international rights of non-Member States are protected in their dealings with the EC. The effect of direct applicability within the EC legal system is that international treaty takes priority over EC secondary legislation and other EC acts. International treaties may be implemented directly, by incorporating the wording of the treaty or its provisions into the secondary legislation, or indirectly, by indicating (typically in the preamble) that it is the purpose of the legislation to put the treaty or its provisions into effect. [2]

According to these principles, the China-EC economic treaties must also be legally binding on the EC institutions and the Member States by virtue of the EC legal order. The rights created and obligations imposed by the treaty must therefore be carried out within the EC. Theoretically, this means that the China-EC economic treaties can also be relied upon to challenge the acts of the EC institutions and the acts of the Member States through direct and indirect actions if the latter are not compatible with the provisions of the treaties. [3]

---

[1] Anne Peters, The Position of International Law within the European Community Legal Order, 40 *German Yearbook of International Law* (1997), 42-44.

[2] Ilona Cheyne, International Agreements and the European Community Legal System, 19 *European Law Review* (1994), 585-587.

[3] Hu Yuanxiang, *Legal and Policy Issues of the Trade and Economic Relations between China and the EEC: A Comparative Study*, Kluwer Law and Taxation Publishers (1991), 48.

In addition, the EC constitutes a new legal order in international law where the subjects of the law are not just Member States but also the people of those States. It is clear that the Member States have tacitly accepted that the EC law is unique and that unlike international law, it can confer rights directly on individuals which they can rely on in their national court. [1] It follows that as part of the EC law, China-EC economic treaties may be referred to by individuals of the EC Member State in their national courts.

IV. Conclusions

The historical development of China-Europe economic relations shows that in general, China has developed good relations with Western Europe for the last half century. This reality also strongly convinces us that the more deeply involved the EU becomes, through a combination of co-operation and support for Chinese economic development, the steadier and less accident-prone the relations will be. The good relations between China and the EU are based on the internationally-recognized principle of equity and reciprocity and on the common interests of the peoples of both sides. We have to cherish the good relations and make common efforts to promote and legalize the relations further in the 21st century.

Although political issues and economic relations are inter-related, [2] the existing or potential political or politics-related issues affecting China-EU economic relations and the legal arrangements concerned, such as human rights, autonomy of HK and Macao, and Taiwan issue, are basically China's internal affairs. Such issues are somewhat the legacy of Cold War and originated from the conflicting ideologies. According to the well-recognized rule of international law, "non-interference in each other's internal affairs", China has not intervened in any internal affairs of the EU or its Member States. In return, the EU and its Member States have to make its policies and legal regime for China-EU economic relations under the same rule.

---

[1] Imelda Maher, Community Law in the National Legal Order: A Systems Analysis, 36 (2) *Journal of Common Market Studies* (1998), 242.

[2] Some commentaries argue that international trade and international human rights can and must be coexist. For example, S. Zia-Zarifi, Protection without Protectionism, Linking a Multilateral Investment Treaty and Human Rights, in E. C. Nieuwenhuys and M. M. T. A. Brus (eds.), *Multilateral Regulation of Investment*, E. M. Meijers Institute and Kluwer Law International (2001), 101.

It has been asserted that law has been one of the most important factors in the Pacific economic boom. Law, legal processes and legal culture will play an important role in future relations between China and the EU. [1] Considering the rapid developments in China and the EU and in their mutual relations, the current bilateral legal framework for China-EU economic relations established by the 1985 Agreement has definitely proved insufficient for practical needs. Therefore, a new bilateral legal framework for China-EU economic relations without political interference should be promoted and reconstructed urgently. In the new framework, the two-tiered system would still be adaptable for both sides. In concluding bilateral treaties with the EC, China has to fully learn and understand the EC treaty-making power, the division of treaty-making power between the EC and its Member States, and the direct effect of the EC treaties. Particularly, when China has to sign mixed treaties with the EC and its Member States, it should recognize the legal consequences of the treaties and make the necessary responsibility-division arrangements.

---

〔1〕 Nicholas Emiliou and David O'Keeffe (eds.), *The European Union and World Trade Law after the GATT Uruguay Round*, John Wiley & Sons Ltd. (1996), 363-364.

第四节 WTO 规则与中国—东盟自由贸易区的发展 *

【摘要】《东南亚国家联盟与中华人民共和国全面经济合作框架协定》是中国与东盟之间经济合作发展的重要里程碑,不仅为中国与东盟之间的全面经济合作提供了基本的法律框架,也为建立中国—东盟自由贸易区打下了坚实的法律基础。另外,该协定是一个符合 WTO 规则且部分内容受 WTO 规则调整的区域贸易协定。在一定程度上,WTO 规则为该协定和中国—东盟自由贸易区的发展提供了重要的国际法律基础。

【关键词】 区域贸易协定;WTO 规则;自由贸易区

《东南亚国家联盟与中华人民共和国全面经济合作框架协定》(Framework Agreement on Comprehensive Economic Co-operation between the Association of Southeast Asian Nations and the People's Republic of China,FACEC)2002 年 11 月 4 日正式签署,2003 年 7 月 1 日生效。缔约双方同意尽快开展旨在 10 年内建成中国—东盟自由贸易区的谈判。该协定属于区域贸易协定(Regional Trade Agreements,RTAs),是中国参与 RTAs 的重要实践。由于中国是 WTO 成员,谈判时东盟方的 7 个成员也是 WTO 成员,该协定调整和规范缔约双方之间货物贸易、服务贸易和投资自由化等重要问题,与 WTO 规则调整和规范对象重合,缔约方不可避免地面临该协定涉及的 WTO 规则和义务的履行问题。本文探讨 FACEC 缔约方的法律特征、FACEC 缔约方的 WTO 责任以及 FACEC 与 WTO 规则的联系,在此基础上,试图揭示 WTO 规则与中国—东盟自由贸易区发展之间的关系。

一、FACEC 缔约方的法律特征

考虑到东盟本身作为一个国际组织的特殊性以及中国在 WTO 体制中的特殊性,FACEC 缔约方的法律特征是值得探讨的首要问题。

根据国际法的一般原则,条约只对条约的缔约方发生效力。就 FACEC 而言,重要的问题在于,FACEC 的缔约方究何所指? 在其缔结和履行 FACEC 时,为何和如何与 WTO 规则相关?

---

* 原载《厦门大学学报》(哲学社会科学版)2005 年第 6 期。

显而易见，FACEC 缔约双方在 WTO 体制中的地位是不同的。中国是 WTO 的正式成员，而东盟本身不是。就东盟本身而言，它未承担任何遵守 WTO 规则的责任。[1] 进言之，东盟的国际法律人格及其缔约能力是一个有争议的问题。有学者指出，由于东盟不具有国际法律人格，也不具有缔约能力，FACEC 是东盟 10 成员与中国之间的多边协定。[2] 笔者以为，尽管 FACEC 可视为由 11 个缔约当事方（contracting parties）缔结的多边协定，但"10＋1"的表述更为准确地反映了 FACEC 缔约方的现实，即东盟 10 成员为集合的缔约一方（collective contracting side），中国为缔约另一方。以下分述 FACEC 缔约双方的特殊性。

（一）一个东盟，两组成员

根据 FACEC 规定的两种标准，东盟成员作出两种区分：一是以 WTO 成员资格为标准，区分为 WTO 成员和非 WTO 成员；二是以经济发展水平为标准，区分为"东盟 6 成员"和"新东盟成员"。

1. WTO 成员与非 WTO 成员

首先，在 FACEC 中，区分了东盟成员中的 WTO 成员与非 WTO 成员。签订 FACEC 时，在东盟 10 个成员中，有 7 个是 WTO 成员，3 个是非 WTO 成员。7 个 WTO 成员分别是文莱、印度尼西亚、马来西亚、缅甸、菲律宾、新加坡和泰国。显然，它们在参与 RTAs 之同时需要履行对 WTO 的承诺。当时 3 个非 WTO 成员是柬埔寨、老挝和越南。2004 年 10 月 13 日，柬埔寨成为东盟成员中的第 8 个 WTO 成员。越南和老挝目前是 WTO 的观察员并都处于申请加入 WTO 的程序。越南在加入程序中进展显著，[3] 而老挝的进展则较为缓慢。[4] 对它们而言，在法律上，除非另有约定，并未对 WTO 承担任何责任。然而，由于它们已是申请加入 WTO 的当事方，是 WTO 责任的潜在承担者，即一旦加入 WTO，就必须承担 WTO 的有关责任。

---

〔1〕 尽管对东盟的国际法律主体地位见仁见智，在东盟 10 个成员均加入 WTO 后，随着东盟一体化进程的发展，东盟也有可能发展成为 WTO 的事实上（de facto）成员，甚至成为法律上（de jure）成员。这方面，欧共体在 GATT/WTO 体制中地位的发展是一先例。

〔2〕 See Jiangyu Wang, Two International Legal Issues in the China-ASEAN Free Trade Agreement, Paper for Symposium on "China's Relations with ASEAN: New Dimensions", 3-4 Dec. 2004, Singapore, pp. 9-19.

〔3〕 1995 年 1 月 31 日，"越南加入工作组"成立，双边性市场准入联系启动。该工作组讨论的项目包括：农业、关税制度、进口许可、国民待遇、实施卫生与植物卫生措施（SPS）、技术性贸易壁垒（TBT）、国营贸易、贸易权和与贸易有关的知识产权（TRIPS）。2003 年 5 月 12 日，该工作组召开第六次会议，同年 12 月 12 日召开第七次会议。2004 年 6 月 15 日，与越南商谈有关成员资格一揽子安排的 63 个 WTO 成员，称赞该东南亚国家已显著改善其有关货物和服务的市场准入要约及其适用 WTO 协定的计划。2004 年 11 月，发布了该工作组报告草案，该报告是概括工作组讨论内容的详细文件。目前，基于货物和服务的修订要约（revised offers）之双边性市场准入谈判继续进行。该工作组第九次会议于 2004 年 12 月召开。http://www.wto.org/english/thewto_e/acc_e/a1_vietnam_e.htm2005/07/27

〔4〕 1998 年 2 月 19 日，"老挝人民民主共和国加入工作组"成立。2001 年 3 月发布对外贸易体制备忘录，2003 年 10 月答复 WTO 成员所提出的问题。2004 年 10 月 28 日，该工作组召开第一次会议。http://www.wto.org/english/thewto_e/acc_e/a1_laos_e.htm/2005/07/27

在 FACEC 中,对 WTO 成员与非 WTO 成员区别对待的条款例如,第 3 条(b)规定:"'适用的最惠国关税率'包括配额关税率,对东盟成员(2003 年 7 月 1 日之前是 WTO 成员)和中国,指 2003 年 7 月 1 日各自适用的税率,对东盟成员(2003 年 7 月 1 日之前不是 WTO 成员),指 2003 年 7 月 1 日适用于中国的税率。"值得注意的是,对 2003 年 7 月 1 日之前不是 WTO 成员的东盟成员而言,其 2003 年 7 月 1 日适用于中国的税率实际上并非多边性的"最惠国关税率",因为它们未受 WTO 协定约束。该规定的结果是,东盟成员中的 WTO 成员,享有 RTAs 带来的"最惠国关税率"利益,实际上也是它们作为 WTO 成员,依非歧视待遇原则本可享有的利益。而东盟成员中的非 WTO 成员,则享有与 WTO 成员相同的利益,因为中国须根据 WTO 规则给予东盟全体成员、包括其中的非 WTO 成员"最惠国关税率"。换言之,中国实际上是单方面给予东盟成员中的非 WTO 成员以关税减让。[1]

2. "东盟 6 成员"和"新东盟成员"

由东南亚地区全部 10 个国家组成的"大东盟"标志着区域一体化在东南亚地区的重要发展。与此同时,东盟 10 成员中也出现了发达成员和欠发达成员的区分。[2]所谓"东盟 6 成员"指文莱、印度尼西亚、马来西亚、菲律宾、新加坡和泰国等 6 个经济相对发达的东盟创始成员。"新东盟成员"则指柬埔寨、老挝、缅甸和越南等 4 个经济相对欠发达的国家。在"新东盟成员"中,柬埔寨、老挝和缅甸等 3 个国家列于 48 个最不发达国家的名单。在 FACEC 履行中,"新东盟成员"享有特殊、差别和灵活待遇。例如,《农业合作谅解备忘录》单独签署,该文件特别有利于"新东盟成员"。

鉴于"东盟 6 成员"和"新东盟成员"经济发展水平的不同,中国与两类成员之间实现贸易自由化的进程也应有所区别。事实上,FACEC 明确规定了中国与两类成员建立货物自由贸易区的不同时间表,即中国与"东盟 6 成员"在 2010 年之前建成,与"新东盟成员"则在 2015 年之前建成。[3]

(二)一个中国,四个 WTO 成员

应当明确,作为 FACEC 的缔约一方,中国指中国内地,不包括香港特别行政区、

---

〔1〕 See Qingjiang Kong, China's WTO Accession and the ASEAN China Free Trade Area: The Perspective of a Chinese Lawyer, *Journal of International Economic Law*, Vol. 7, No. 4, 2004, p. 817.

〔2〕 参见陈宁:《大东盟的形成及今后面临的问题》,载《东南亚研究》1998 年第 3 期,第 22—24 页。

〔3〕 该协定谈判的时间表是:

(1) 在货物贸易领域,有关关税减让的谈判始于 2003 年初,2004 年 6 月 30 日完成以便在 2010 年之前建立中国与东盟 6 成员之间的货物自由贸易区,在 2015 年之前建立中国与东盟新成员之间的货物自由贸易区;

(2) 在服务贸易和投资领域,有关谈判始于 2003 年,根据商定的时间表尽快完成;

(3) 在其他合作领域,缔约方应继续建设已有的项目和开发新项目并为各项目的履行尽快签订协定。

See Briefing Paper on the Establishment of the ASEAN-China Free Trade Area (FTA) 18 February 2003, http://www. tariffcommission. gov. ph/briefing_paper_fta. htm12/23/2003.

澳门特别行政区和台湾地区。

2001 年 12 月 11 日和 2002 年 1 月 1 日，中国与"台湾、澎湖、金门、马祖单独关税区"（简称"中国台北"）[1]先后成为 WTO 正式成员后，连同于 1995 年 1 月 1 日分别成为 WTO 创始成员的香港和澳门，在 WTO 体制中出现了前所未有的"一国四席"局面。[2]

对东盟及其成员而言，"一国四席"具有重要的意义。作为 WTO 体制的平等成员，中国、中国香港和中国澳门可单独与东盟和/或其一个或一个以上成员谈判和签订关税同盟、自由贸易区或导向关税同盟和自由贸易区的协定。

值得注意的是，近年来，台湾当局宣称不考虑采取"中国台北"的名称，而直接以"台湾"的名义，与外国或地区签署所谓"自由贸易协定"，企图以此凸显其国际政治或法律地位，继续推进其渐进式"台独"分裂活动。从政治、经济等因素考虑，台湾当局锁定的签约对象有美国、日本、新加坡、新西兰和中美洲国家，[3]也曾在马来西亚提出与东盟签订"自由贸易协定"的建议。[4] 应当强调，自 1949 年以来，中国长期坚持的立场是，任何与中国交往的国家或国际组织应当承认，中华人民共和国政府是代表中国的唯一合法政府，台湾是中国不可分割的一部分。这个"一个中国"原则已为国际社会普遍接受。因此，台湾问题完全是中国内政，将由中国人自己解决。根据国际法，任何国家、国际组织或其他实体都不能干涉中国的内政。[5] 中国台北的 WTO 成员地位并未给台湾带来任何国际法律地位的变化。东盟及其成员应继续坚持"一个中国"原则，不能与台湾建立任何正式关系。

与此同时，中国、中国香港、中国澳门和/或中国台北（两岸四地）可考虑建立关税同盟或自由贸易区，以解决 WTO 非歧视待遇原则适用的特殊问题，并为建立两岸四地间更紧密经贸关系打下必要的法律基础。考虑到中国实行"一国两制"政策，两岸四地之间政治、经济和法律制度的不同以及经济发展的不平衡，选择自由贸易区模式更适合中国国情。[6] 在建立两岸四地自由贸易区之前，首先是签订形成自由贸

---

〔1〕 英文为 the Separate Customs Territory of Taiwan, Penghu, Kinmen and Matsu（Chinese Taipei）。对 Chinese Taipei，中国大陆地区一般译为"中国台北"或"中国台湾"，中国台湾地区一般译为"中华台北"。

〔2〕 参见曾华群：《略论 WTO 体制的"一国四席"》，载《厦门大学学报（哲社版）》2002 年第 5 期，第 5—14 页。

〔3〕 参见朱磊：《看台湾如何签订"自由贸易协定"》，载《开放潮》2002 年第 7 期，第 24—25 页。

〔4〕 2002 年 11 月 12 日，中国台湾地区经济事务主管部门负责人林义夫提出与东盟签订"自由贸易协定"的建议。See Yow Cheun Hoe, China-ASEAN Relations in 2002: Chronology of Events, *China: An International Journal*, Vol. 1, No. 1, 2003, p. 168.

〔5〕 然而，值得注意的是，在西方国家，不时有对此问题发表评论者，如 Jonathan I. Charney and J. R. V. Prescott, Resolving Cross-Strait Relations Between China and Taiwan, *A. J. Int'l L.*, Vol. 94, 2000, pp. 452-477.

〔6〕 参见朱兆敏：《论"入世"后中国各单独关税区间建立紧密经贸合作关系的法律基础和框架》，载陈安主编：《国际经济法论丛》第 7 卷，法律出版社 2003 年版，第 26—28 页。

易区所必需的临时协定。该临时协定的主要内容须符合 GATT 第 24 条和《关于解释 1994 年关税与贸易总协定第 24 条的谅解》(以下简称《第 24 条谅解》)的规定。[1] 2003 年 6 月 29 日,中华人民共和国商务部安民副部长与香港特别行政区财政司梁锦松司长共同签署了《内地与香港关于建立更紧密经贸关系的安排》[2]文本及有关磋商纪要,2004 年 1 月 1 日正式实施。《内地与澳门特别行政区关于建立更紧密经贸关系的安排》签署于 2003 年 10 月 17 日,2004 年 1 月 1 日亦正式实施。内地与香港、澳门更紧密经贸关系安排的顺利实施以及两岸四地将来可能建立的自由贸易区为 FACEC 和中国—东盟自由贸易区的进一步发展提供了机遇。

二、FACEC 缔约方的 WTO 责任

由于 FACEC 属于 RTAs,为确认 FACEC 缔约方的 WTO 责任,首先需要了解 WTO 有关 RTAs 的规则和 RTAs 与 WTO 规则的区别。

(一) WTO 有关 RTAs 的规则

WTO 基本原则之一非歧视待遇原则要求 WTO 成员之间的贸易应在非歧视的基础上进行,即各成员对其他成员实行"最惠国待遇"和"国民待遇",除非在 GATT/WTO 中另有规定。

在 WTO 体制下,某些成员之间建立有别于其他成员的 RTAs 与非歧视待遇原则的一般实施是抵触的。因此,有关成员需要寻求适用 WTO 体制非歧视待遇原则的例外,才可能建立符合 WTO 规则的 RTAs。

由于 GATT 的规定"不得阻止在缔约方领土之间形成关税同盟或自由贸易区,或阻止通过形成关税同盟和自由贸易区所必需的临时协定",RTAs 的主要形式关税同盟和自由贸易区被视为适用非歧视待遇原则的一个例外。乌拉圭回合进一步发展了 GATT 的 RTAs 规则。GATT/WTO 关于 RTAs 的规则可概要如下:

1. GATT 第 24 条及《第 24 条谅解》

根据 GATT 第 24 条第 8 款,关税同盟与自由贸易区两者的关键区别在于,关税同盟成员对同盟以外领土的贸易须实施实质相同的关税或其他贸易法规,而自由贸易区成员则无此要求。显然,前者的经济一体化程度更高。此外,根据 GATT 第 24

---

[1] 值得注意的是,实践中的关税同盟或自由贸易区是否 GATT 第 24 条意义上的关税同盟或自由贸易区,常常未能得出结论。法律问题常常被忽视或无结论地搁置,或根据豁免条款予以豁免。虽有大量的关税同盟或自由贸易区协议被 GATT 审议,但极少获得批准。参见郭寿康、韩立余:《国际贸易法》,中国人民大学出版社 2000 年版,第 199 页。

[2] 《内地与香港关于建立更紧密经贸关系的安排》为中文本,"更紧密经贸关系的安排"英文为 Closer Economic Partnership Arrangement,简称 CEPA。

条第 4、5 款规定,允许各成员之间签订形成关税同盟或自由贸易区所必需的临时协定。实际上,关税同盟、自由贸易区和导向关税同盟或自由贸易区的临时协定是RTAs 的不同层次和类型。关税同盟是 RTAs 的最高层次,自由贸易区次之,而导向关税同盟或自由贸易区的临时协定是 RTAs 的初级层次或阶段。[1]

《第 24 条谅解》对关税同盟和自由贸易区协定予以肯定。[2] 该谅解澄清了GATT 第 24 条的一些规则。然而,该谅解未能解决更为困难的问题。进一步的澄清有待"区域贸易协定委员会"(the Committee on Regional Trade Agreements,CRTA)[3]作出。该委员会的职责包括"考虑此类协定和区域行动对多边贸易体制的制度性意义和两者之间的关系,并向总理事会提出适当建议"。[4] 其主要职能是监督 RTAs 的运作,特别是关注 RTAs 符合 WTO 规则的方式。[5]

为确保 WTO 成员间的 RTAs 能成为多边贸易体制的补充而不是威胁或损害,根据 GATT 第 24 条和《第 24 条谅解》的规定,建立关税同盟、自由贸易区和签订导向关税同盟、自由贸易区的临时协定必须遵循的两大原则一是"涵盖实质上所有贸易"的要求,即应对关税同盟成员领土之间的实质上所有贸易或至少对产于此类领土产品的实质上所有贸易,对自由贸易区成员领土之间的产于此类领土产品的实质上所有贸易,取消关税和其他限制性贸易法规[GATT 第 24 条第 8 款(a)(b)];二是"不得对其他成员产生负面影响"的要求,即不论是关税同盟、自由贸易区或导向关税同盟、自由贸易区的临时协定的成员,不得对其他成员实施高于或严于形成关税同盟、自由贸易区或临时协定之前的关税和贸易管制[GATT 1947 第 24 条第 5 款(a)、(b)],并且明确规定了评估关税同盟形成前后适用的关税和其他贸易法规的总体影响的方法(《第 24 条谅解》第 2 款)。[6]

---

〔1〕 赵维田:《世贸组织(WTO)的法律制度》,吉林人民出版社 2000 年版,第 84—85 页。

〔2〕 《第 24 条谅解》认为"此类协定参加方的经济更紧密的一体化可对世界贸易的扩大作出贡献",鼓励将"成员领土之间关税和其他限制性商业法规的取消延伸至所有贸易",并且"重申此类协定的目的应为便利成员领土之间的贸易,而非提高其他成员与此类领土之间的贸易壁垒;在此类协定形成或扩大时,参加方应在最大限度内避免对其他成员的贸易造成不利影响"。

〔3〕 1996 年 2 月,区域贸易协定委员会成立。该委员会的职责是审查货物贸易委员会、服务贸易委员会和贸易与发展委员会提交的协定。该委员会还负责就各类协定的报告要求提出建议,并发展旨在便利和改善此种审查制度的程序。

〔4〕 Jo-Ann Crawford & Sam Laird, Regional Trade Agreements and the WTO, http://www. tradeobservatory. org/library12/23/2003.

〔5〕 Sung-Hoon Park, The Current Status and Future Prospects of Regionalism and Multilateralism in the World Economy: A Case Study of Economic Relations Between EU and APEC in the WTO Era, http://www. ecsanet. org/conferences/ecsaworld3/park. html12/23/2003.

〔6〕 Michael J. Trebilcock & Robert Howse, *The Regulation of International Trade*, 2nd ed., Routledge, 1999, pp. 115-116.

2. GATS 第 5 条

《服务贸易总协定》(General Agreement on Trade in Services，GATS)第 5 条规定与 GATT 第 24 条规定的原则基本一致，采用了"经济一体化"的概念，明确规定，"本协定不得阻止任何成员参加或达成在参加方之间实现服务贸易自由化的协定"，以后者符合某些条件为限。据此，WTO 体制允许的 RTAs 的涵盖领域已扩及服务贸易。

3. "授权条款"(The Enabling Clause)

1979 年，GATT 缔约方通过了《关于发展中国家差别、更优惠、互惠和较全面参与的决定》。该决定通称为"授权条款"，允许发达国家给予发展中国家差别、更优惠待遇，并允许发展中国家之间建立的 RTAs 免除 GATT 第 1 条"最惠国待遇"的适用。"授权条款"虽未直接规定 RTAs，但包括了发展中国家的特殊与差别待遇、互惠和充分参与，涉及发展中国家之间的优惠贸易协定，给予不必符合上述"实质上所有贸易"要求的可能性。

从 FACEC 的内容可见，FACEC 是导向自由贸易区所需要的临时协定，符合 GATT 第 24 条、《第 24 条谅解》以及 GATS 第 5 条的规定。由于中国与东盟各成员均为发展中国家，"授权条款"也适用于 FACEC。

(二) RTAs 与 WTO 规则的区别

即使是 WTO 成员，它也只是在 WTO 调整范围内承担其责任。显然，当某 WTO 成员同时也是某 RTAs 成员时，关键的问题是，RTAs 与 WTO 规则之间的关系如何？

笔者以为，首先，需要区分 WTO 规则的调整对象与 RTAs 的调整对象。两者绝非一致或重合。其主要原因如下：一是从体制上看，WTO 体制与 RTAs 是并行发展的，两者并无相互隶属的关系。二是从调整对象看，WTO 是贸易组织，调整其成员之间的贸易关系，而 RTAs 组织调整成员之间包含贸易的经济关系。虽然乌拉圭回合之后，WTO 规则调整的领域不断扩大，但毕竟无法涵盖成员之间的所有经济关系。实际上，RTAs 往往超出 WTO 规则调整的范围。[1] 三是从成员看，RTAs 组织成员不一定是 WTO 成员，两者并无存在作为前提的成员关系。[2] 四是从历史上看，许多 RTAs 组织先于 GATT/WTO 而存在。GATT/WTO 有关 RTAs 的规则，在很大程度上，是对既有现实的承认或妥协。可见，对 WTO 成员而言，RTAs 并非

---

〔1〕 如欧洲联盟(EU)向经济和货币联盟的发展，东南亚国家联盟(ASEAN)、北美自由贸易区(NAFTA)制定的投资规范等。

〔2〕 如申请加入国际复兴开发银行者须以具备国际货币基金组织成员资格为前提条件。

必须根据 WTO 规则签订，也并非局限于 WTO 规则的调整范围，而是要求其相关内容符合 WTO 规则。[1] 换言之，WTO 成员在参与 RTAs 时，应履行其 WTO 责任。其次，对 WTO 成员而言，需要区分"WTO 调整范围之内"和"WTO 调整范围之外"的概念。毋庸质疑，在 WTO 规则调整范围之内，各成员应严格遵循规则，履行承诺。另外，由于各成员的履约责任以其承担的 WTO 义务为限，在 WTO 规则调整范围之外，各成员可根据一般国际法，通过双边安排或 RTAs 调整相互之间的经济关系。

应当指出，FACEC 并未排斥其他法律安排。《修改中国—东盟框架协定议定书》第 12A 条题为"本协定之外之协定"，规定："本协定并未防止或禁止任何东盟成员与中国和/或其他东盟成员签订有关货物贸易、服务贸易、投资和/或本协定调整范围之外经济合作其他领域的双边或多边协定。"该规定表明，FACEC 并非封闭式协定。它为中国与东盟成员之间经济关系的发展提供了灵活的方式，中国与东盟一成员或数成员之间可能存在调整经济关系的多重国际法律安排。

（三）FACEC 缔约方在 WTO 体制中的责任

WTO 关于 RTAs 的矫正规则是，WTO 如认为某 RTA 不符合 WTO 有关规定，有关 WTO 成员应在 CRTA 的建议下修改该 RTA。如有关 WTO 成员拒不修改该 RTA，就不能继续维持该 RTA 或使之生效。如有关成员拒不履行 CRTA 的建议，则该 RTA 的任何条款可能被诉诸 WTO 争端解决程序。

虽然目前东盟本身及其两个成员不是 WTO 成员，但中国和东盟的 8 个成员作为 WTO 成员，需要严格履行 WTO 责任，包括参与 RTAs 所应承担的 WTO 责任。考虑到东盟本身随着其区域一体化进程的发展可能成为事实上的 WTO 成员，目前东盟成员中的两个非 WTO 成员在不久的将来也可能成为 WTO 成员，FACEC 缔约双方在签订、履行该协定以及将来商订进一步的自由贸易区协定时，肯定不会忽视 WTO 规则和责任。

三、FACEC 与 WTO 规则的联系

由于 FACEC 签署于 WTO 协定生效之后，当时中国和东盟的 7 个成员是 WTO 成员，该协定的一些条款直接或间接涉及 WTO 规则。这是 RTAs 发展的新情况，表明 FACEC 缔约方遵循 WTO 规则的共识。以同 WTO 原则的联系为标准，FACEC

---

〔1〕 事实上，RTAs 完全符合 GATT 规定者甚为罕见。截至 1994 年底，在 GATT 实施的 46 年中，根据 GATT 第 24 条规定报告的共有 98 个 RTAs，多数分别由各工作组审查。然而，对这些 RTAs 与 GATT 规定的相符性达成共识的仅有捷克—斯洛伐克关税同盟一例。See Jo-Ann Crawford & Sam Laird, Regional Trade Agreements and the WTO, http://www.tradeobservatory.org/library12/23/2003.

的条款可分为两类。

（一）涉及 WTO 规则的条款

在 FACEC 中，许多条款受 WTO 规则调整，涉及 GATT 的传统领域，如货物贸易，或涉及乌拉圭回合的新领域，如服务贸易、与贸易有关的知识产权等。

FACEC 第 2 条题为"全面经济合作的措施"，规定相关措施包括："（1）逐渐取消实质上所有货物贸易的关税和非关税壁垒；（2）逐渐实现涵盖众多服务部门的服务贸易自由化。"上述规定实际上与 GATT 第 24(8)(b)条和 GATS 第 5(1)条的规定相类。有的用语甚至完全一致，如"实质上所有贸易""涵盖众多服务部门"。

FACEC 第 6(3)(d)条题为"WTO 规定的适用"，明确规定："调整承诺的修改、保障行动、紧急措施和其他贸易救济措施，包括反倾销和反补贴措施的 WTO 规定，应适用于早期收获方案[1]实行期间涵盖的产品，并且在这些规则不完善的情况下，由缔约方根据本协定第 3(8)条谈判达成的有关规则取代之。"该规定明确反映了 FACEC 将某些 WTO 规则作为缔约双方直接适用的第一选择。

FACEC 中有的条款还直接援引 WTO 的具体规则，如第 3 条题为"货物贸易"，援引 GATT 第 24 条的 RTAs 例外，即"除非，在必要时，WTO 关贸总协定第 24(8)(b)条所允许的情况"。

FACEC 的一些条款甚至不顾东盟本身及其两个成员不是 WTO 成员的实际情况，要求缔约方履行 WTO 有关 RTAs 的要求。第 3(6)条规定："缔约方根据本条款和本协定第 6 条所作的承诺应履行有关对成员方之间实质上所有贸易减免关税的 WTO 要求。"

不仅如此，FACEC 缔约方还同意根据 WTO 有关规则谈判建立中国—东盟自由贸易区。第 3(8)(d)(f)(g)(h)条规定，缔约方之间有关建立涵盖货物贸易的中国—东盟自由贸易区的谈判应包括，但不限于：（1）基于 GATT 第 28 条的货物贸易协议项下一缔约方的承诺之修改；（2）基于 GATT 原则的保障，包括，但不限于下列因素：透明度，涵盖范围，采取行动的客观标准，包括严重损害或严重损害威胁的概念和临时性质；（3）基于已有 GATT 规则的有关补贴和反倾销措施的规则；和（4）基于已有 WTO 和其他有关规则，促进和提升与贸易有关的知识产权的有效、平等保护。

在服务贸易领域，FACEC 第 4(a)条规定："逐渐取消缔约方之间实质上的所有

---

[1] 所谓"早期收获方案"（Early Harvest Programme）或"早期收获一揽子交易"（Early Harvest Package），是在 2002 年 9 月中国与东盟经济部长会议上原则商定并纳入 FACEC，涉及对一些货物（主要是农产品）关税的迅速减让，自 FACEC 生效第二年 7 月 1 日起三年内生效。See Qingjiang Kong, China's WTO Accession and the ASEAN-China Free Trade Area: The Perspective of a Chinese Lawyer, *Journal of International Economic Law*, Vol. 7, No. 4, 2004, p. 815.

歧视和/或禁止缔约方之间有关服务贸易的新的或更多的歧视性措施,除非是 WTO 服务贸易总协定(GATS)第 5(1)(b)条所允许的措施。"

值得注意的是,FACEC 缔约方看来希望比它们对 WTO 的承诺走得更远。例如,第 4 条明确规定了对 GATS 承诺的超越,即:(1) 在东盟成员和中国根据 GATS 所作承诺之外,在服务贸易自由化的深度和广度的加深和扩大[FACEC 第 4(b)条];和(2) 促进缔约方之间服务的合作以改善效率和竞争以及使缔约方各服务提供者的服务提供和分布多样化[FACEC 第 4(c)条]。

从上述规定中可以肯定,FACEC 的一些条款与 WTO 规则之间存在紧密的联系。在一定程度上,FACEC 的一些条款是以 WTO 规则作为依据、基础或补充。

（二）WTO 规则调整范围以外的条款

当前 RTAs 的重要特征是,与早期 RTAs 相比,它们具有广泛的涵盖范围,许多 RTAs 已超越了传统的关税减让实践,包括服务、投资、知识产权、技术壁垒、争端解决、超国家的制度安排等。[1]

FACEC 亦属新型 RTAs,其规定不仅超越了传统的关税减让实践,也超出了 WTO 的涵盖范围。

FACEC 第 1 条规定的宗旨是:(1) 加强和促进缔约方之间的经济、贸易和投资合作;(2) 逐步促进货物贸易和服务贸易的自由化,并创设透明、自由和便利的投资体制;(3) 开辟新领域和发展缔约方之间的更紧密经济合作的适当措施。

由上述宗旨可见,"投资合作""投资体制"表明了投资在 FACEC 中的重要性。FACEC 第 5 条进一步专门规定投资体制、投资合作与投资保护事项。[2] "新领域"则意味着传统货物贸易和投资以外的领域。FACEC 缔约方采取谈判建立自由贸易区的渐进方式,即:全面的,但简易优先,贸易优先,随后是服务和投资。不仅如此,它们的目标并非限于自由贸易区,而是在全面经济合作基础上的更紧密伙伴关系。至于合作领域或"新领域",FACEC 的五个优先合作部门是农业、信息通信技术、人力资源发展、投资和湄公河盆地开发。其他领域包括银行、金融、旅游、工业合作、交通、知识产权、中小企业、环境、生物技术、渔业、矿业、能源和准区域发展。

FACEC 规定的全面经济合作措施也反映出其合作领域超越了 WTO 的涵盖范围。此类措施包括:(1) 建立一个便利和促进在中国—东盟自由贸易区内投资的开

---

〔1〕 See Jo-Ann Crawford & Sam Laird, Regional Trade Agreements and the WTO, http://www.tradeobservatory.org/library12/23/2003.

〔2〕 FACEC 第 5 条题为"投资",规定:"为促进投资和创设一个自由、便利、透明和竞争的投资体制,缔约方同意:(a)参与谈判以逐渐使投资体制自由化;(b)加强投资合作,便利投资和改善投资规则和法规的透明度;和(c)提供投资保护。"

放和竞争的投资体制[FACEC 第 2(c)条];(2)建立有效的贸易与投资的便利措施,包括但不限于通关程序的简化和相互承认安排的发展[FACEC 第 2(f)条];(3)扩大缔约双方相互商定的经济合作领域,并制订行动计划和规划以履行商定的合作部门/领域的合作[FACEC 第 2(g)条]。更为重要的是,所谓"新领域"是开放性的,可由中国和东盟谈判商定。

由上述可见,FACEC 的涵盖范围甚为广泛,而且是开放性的。笔者以为,为达到全面经济合作和经济一体化的目标,FACEC 缔约各方经过持续的谈判,在不违反WTO 义务的前提下,可进一步发展传统领域和"新领域"的经济合作。

四、结语

FACEC 是中国与东盟之间经济合作发展的重要里程碑。它不仅为中国与东盟之间的全面经济合作提供了基本的法律框架,[1]也为建立中国—东盟自由贸易区打下了坚实的法律基础。它还制定了建立中国—东盟自由贸易区应遵循的互利、谅解和团结原则。

另外,FACEC 是一个符合 WTO 规则且部分内容与 WTO 规则密切联系的RTAs。在一定程度上,WTO 规则为 FACEC 和中国—东盟自由贸易区的发展提供了重要的国际法律基础和国际通行规则。可以预期,在越南、老挝加入 WTO 之后,WTO 规则在这方面的作用将更为凸显。尽管学界有关 RTAs 对多边贸易体制的影响评价不一,[2]WTO 规则与 FACEC 之间相辅相成的密切关系,从一个侧面反映了以 WTO 为代表的多边贸易体制与 RTAs 在推动经济自由化进程中的兼容性和互补性。

最后应当指出,尽管发展水平有所不同,中国和东盟 10 个成员均属发展中国家,因此,FACEC 是缔约双方期望"双赢"的"南南合作"安排。缔约双方的共同目标首先是通过 RTAs 促进本区域的经济发展。不仅如此,中国—东盟自由贸易区的建立也将成为一个区域问题的讲坛或谈判场所,有助于一些普遍关注的区域性重要问题、包括南海开发问题等的妥善解决。

---

〔1〕 2004 年 11 月,在老挝万象召开的第十次东盟峰会上,根据 FACEC,东盟 10 国和中国的经贸部长签署了《东南亚国家联盟与中华人民共和国全面经济合作框架协定之货物贸易协定》和《东南亚国家联盟与中华人民共和国全面经济合作框架协定之争端解决机制协定》。

〔2〕 See Jo-Ann Crawford & Sam Laird, Regional Trade Agreements and the WTO, http://www.tradeobservatory.org/library12/23/2003.

WTO Rules and the Development of FTA Agreement
between China and ASEAN

Abstract：Framework Agreement on Comprehensive Economic Co-operation between the Association of Southeast Asian Nations and the People's Republic of China (FACEC) is an important milestone for development of China-ASEAN economic cooperation. It provides not only a basic legal framework for comprehensive economic co-operation between China and ASEAN，but also a firm groundwork for establishment of China-ASEAN free trade area (FTA). At the same time FACEC is a WTO rules-consistent regional trade agreement with its partial contents regulated by WTO rules. To some extent WTO rules provide the international legal basis for the development of FACEC and China-ASEAN FTA process.

Key words：regional trade agreement；WTO rules；free trade area

第五节 WTO Rules and the Development of FTA Agreement between China and ASEAN[*]
（WTO 规则与中国—东盟自由贸易区的发展）

Framework Agreement on Comprehensive Economic Co-operation between the Association of Southeast Asian Nations and the People's Republic of China (FACEC) was concluded on 4 Nov. 2002 and entered into force on 1 Jul. 2003.[1] The Agreement would lead to the creation of China-ASEAN Free Trade Area (FTA) within ten years[2] and pave the way towards closer cooperation in the elimination of tariffs and non-tariff barriers on trade in goods and service, create an open and competitive investment regime and encourage the simplification and standardization of customs procedures.[3] As the People's Republic of China (China) and seven out of the ten Member States of the Association of Southeast Asian Nations (ASEAN) were full members of World Trade Organization (WTO) at that time, and the provisions of FACEC involve liberalization of trade in goods and trade in service as well as investment, the same subjects as those regulated by WTO rules among the parties, the parties to FACEC have to deal with the issues on application

---

[*] WTO Rules and the Development of China-ASEAN FTA Agreement, in John Wong, Zou Keyuan, Zeng Huaqun (eds.), *China-ASEAN Relations: Economic and Legal Dimensions*, World Scientific Publishing Co. Pte, Ltd, ISBN 981-256-657-0, 2006.

[1] The Framework Agreement on Comprehensive Economic Cooperation between the Association of Southeast Asian Nations and the People's Republic of China. The extracts of the Agreement are available at *China: An International Journal*, Vol. 1, No. 1, pp. 170-178. For the brief history towards FACEC, see Kong Qingjiang, China's WTO Accession and the ASEAN China Free Trade Area: the Perspective of a Chinese Lawyer, *Journal of International Economic Law*, 7 (4), pp. 802-803 (2004).

[2] The timeframes of the negotiations on the Agreement are:

(1) for trade in goods, negotiations on the Agreement for tariff reduction/elimination shall commence in early 2003 and concluded by 30 June 2004 in order to establish the FTA for trade in goods by 2010 for China and ASEAN6 and by 2015 for newer ASEAN Member States;

(2) for trade in services and investments, negotiations shall commence in 2003 and concluded expeditiously as possible in accordance to the timeframes to be agreed;

(3) for other areas of cooperation, the parties shall continue to build on existing programs, develop new programs and conclude agreements expeditiously for each implementation.

See Briefing Paper on the Establishment of the ASEAN-China Free Trade Area (FTA) 18 February 2003, http://www. tariffcommission. gov. ph/briefing_paper_fta. htm12/23/2003.

[3] ASEAN Secretariat, News Release, 30 Oct., 2002 ASEAN-China Free Trade Area Negotiations to Start Next Year, http://www. aseansec. org/13125. htm.

of WTO rules in the Agreement. This paper deals with the issues on characteristics of the parties to FACEC, the WTO responsibilities of parties to FACEC and provisions of FACEC within or beyond WTO regime, and then tries to explore and indicate the relationship between WTO rules and the development of FTA agreement between China and ASEAN.

Ⅰ. Parties to FACEC: Facts and Differences

According to general principle of international law, parties to a treaty are only bound by the treaty they have entered into. Then in the context of FACEC the important questions are that why and how the parties to FACEC relate to WTO rules? Do they bear any WTO obligations when they conclude and/or implement FACEC?

It is clear that the legal status of the two parties to FACEC is different in WTO regime. China is a WTO full member while ASEAN itself is not. For ASEAN itself, it therefore currently bears not any obligation to observe WTO rules in general. [1] Considering the complex of ASEAN as an international economic organization and the unique position of China in the WTO regime, the characteristics of the two parties to FACEC are the first and most important issues for this study. The characteristics of the two parties to FACEC might be summarized as follows.

1. One ASEAN, Two Groups of Member States

For ASEAN Member States, they are divided into two groups by two criteria provided in the text of FACEC: one group are WTO members and non-WTO members by the criterion of WTO membership and the other are "ASEAN6" and the newer ASEAN Member States by the criterion of level of development to large extent.

1.1 WTO Members and Non-WTO Members

First, we shall distinguish between the WTO members of ASEAN Member States and non-WTO members of ASEAN Member States in the context of FACEC. Among ten of ASEAN Member States, seven out of them were WTO members and three were not at the point of concluding FACEC. The seven WTO members were

---

[1] It is possible that ASEAN become a *de facto* or even a *de jure* member of WTO after all its ten Member States enter into WTO. EC is a pioneer in this regard in GATT/WTO regime.

Brunei, Indonesia, Malaysia, Myanmar, Philippines, Singapore and Thailand. Obviously they have their commitment to WTO though the ASEAN itself bears not any obligation to WTO.

The three non-WTO members were Cambodia, Laos and Viet Nam. Cambodia became the eighth WTO member among Member States of ASEAN on 13 Oct. 2004.[1] Both of Viet Nam and Laos are currently the observers of WTO and are also in the process of accession to WTO. Viet Nam has made great achievements in the process[2] while Laos's process is relatively slow.[3] For them currently there are no any obligations and responsibilities of WTO except those they commit to. However as they are applying countries for accession to WTO, they have potential obligations and responsibilities to WTO.

In FACEC there are different provisions for WTO members and non-WTO members of ASEAN Member States.

According to Article 3 (b) of FACEC, "applied MFN tariff rates" shall: "(i) in the case of ASEAN Member States (which are WTO members as of 1 Jul. 2003) and China, refer to their respective applied rates as of 1 Jul. 2003; and (ii) in the case of ASEAN Member States (which are non-WTO members as of 1 Jul. 2003), refer to the rates as applied to China as of 1 Jul. 2003.[4] It is noticeable that for the ASEAN Member States (which are non-WTO members as of 1 Jul. 2003), the rates as applied to China as of 1 Jul. 2003 are not multilateral "MFN tariff rates" since they are not bound by WTO treaties.

The results of the above provisions are that for WTO members in ASEAN, they enjoy the benefits from the RTA; for non-WTO members in ASEAN, they also

---

[1]　http://www.wto.org/english/thewto_e/countries_e/cambodia_e.htm2004/10/19

[2]　The Working Party on the accession of Viet Nam was established on 31 January 1995. Bilateral market access contacts have been initiated. Topics under discussion in the Working Party include: agriculture, the customs system, import licensing, national treatment, SPS and TBT, State trading, trading rights and TRIPS. The sixth meeting of the Working Party took place on 12 May 2003, and the seventh meeting is held on 12, December 2003. The 63 WTO members negotiating a membership package with Viet Nam praised the Southeast Asian country on 15 June 2004 for considerably improving its market access offers for goods and services, and its programme for applying WTO agreements. http://www.wto.org/english/thewto_e/acc_e/a1_vietnam_e.htm2004/10/19

[3]　The Lao People's Democratic Republic's Working Party was established on 19 February 1998. The Memorandum on the Foreign Trade Regime was circulated in March 2001 and replies to questions from Members in October 2003. The Working Party has not yet met. http://www.wto.org/english/thewto_e/acc_e/a1_laos_e.htm2004/10/19

[4]　There is a same provision in Art. 6 Early Harvest of FACEC.

enjoy the treatment of WTO members, as China shall accord MFN treatment consistent with WTO rules and disciplines to them. [1]

1.2 "ASEAN6" and the Newer ASEAN Member States

The formation of "Great ASEAN" marked the important development of the RTA in the region. At the same time the ASEAN members are divided into developed members and less developed members. [2] "ASEAN6" refers to the six original ASEAN Member States like Brunei, Indonesia, Malaysia, Philippines, Singapore and Thailand. The newer ASEAN Member States refer to the four less developed ASEAN Member States like Cambodia, Laos, Myanmar and Viet Nam. [3] Three of the four newer ASEAN Member States, namely Cambodia, Laos and Myanmar, are on the list of 48 least developed countries. [4] The latter will be offered special and differential treatment and flexibility in implementation of FACEC. [5] The memorandum of understanding on agricultural cooperation was signed separately. It will especially helpful to the newer ASEAN Member States.

There are different requirement for "ASEAN6" and the newer ASEAN Member States. Considering the internal differences, liberalization will be done by different tracks and different timetables. In fact, FACEC will serve as the fulcrum for establishing China-ASEAN FTA by 2010 for China and "ASEAN6", and by 2015 for China and the four newer ASEAN Member States. [6]

It should be further pointed out that the ambiguous legal personality[7] and

---

[1] Article 9 of FACEC.

[2] For the formation of Great ASEAN and its related impacts, see Chen Ning, The Formation of Great ASEAN and the Problems Confronting us in the Future (in Chinese), *Southeast Asian Studies*, No. 3, pp. 22-24 (1998).

[3] Briefing Paper on the Establishment of the ASEAN-China Free Trade Area (FTA) 18 February 2003, http://www. tariffcommission. gov. ph/briefing_paper_fta. htm12/23/2003.

[4] http://www. wto. org/english/thewto_e/whatis_e/tif_e/org7_e. htm2004/10/19

[5] ASEAN Secretariat, News Release, 30 Oct. , 2002 ASEAN-China Free Trade Area Negotiations to Start Next Year, http://www. aseansec. org/13125. htm.

[6] Article 3(4) (a) of FACEC deals with the "Normal Track" and stipulates that products listed in the Normal Track by a party on its own accord shall have their respective applied MFN tariff rates gradually reduced or eliminated in accordance with specified schedules and rates (to be mutually agreed by the Parties) over a period from 1 Jan. 2005 to 2010 for ASEAN6 and China, and in the case of the newer ASEAN Member States, the period shall be from 1 Jan. 2005 to 2015 with higher starting tariff rates and different staging.

[7] Some scholars challenged the legal personality and treaty-making power of ASEAN and concluded that FACEC is a multilateral treaty among 11 countries rather than a bilateral treaty between China and ASEAN. See Wang JiangYu, Two International Legal Issues in the China-ASEAN Free Trade Agreement, Paper for Symposium on "China's Relations with ASEAN: New Dimensions", 3-4, December 2004.

division of two-group members of ASEAN do not refuse the bilateral nature of FACEC. In fact, as the treaty deal with the comprehensive economic co-operation between ASEAN and China, it is clear that one contracting party is China, the other parties are ASEAN 10 members as a whole. However, the fact that all the names of ASEAN 10 members and China appear in FACEC as the contracting parties except ASEAN, and the provision that "the Parties undertake to complete their internal procedures for the entry into force of this Agreement"[1]indicate that the legal obligations of complying with the treaty may be born by ASEAN up to 10 members collectively or an member individually.[2]

2. One China, Four WTO Memberships

In general China's membership in WTO has greatly extended the horizon of China's regional economic co-operation and brought ASEAN members together within the multilateral trading system.[3]

It is very important to clarify and emphasize that China in FACEC context is only referred to Chinese mainland, not including Hong Kong Special Administrative Region, Macao Special Administrative Region and Chinese Taipei.

On 11 December 2001 and 1 January 2002, China and Separate Customs Territory of Taiwan, Penghu, Kinmen and Matsu (Chinese Taipei) became members of WTO one after another, and together with Hong Kong and Macao, the two original WTO members on 1 January 1995, "one China, four WTO memberships" has emerged, which is the new phenomenon in the General Agreement on Tariffs and Trade (GATT)/WTO history.[4]

To ASEAN and its Member States, "one China, four WTO memberships" have great significance. As equal members under WTO regime, China, Hong Kong, China and Macao, China may separately establish a customs union (CU) or FTA or negotiate and conclude an agreement necessary for establishing a CU of FTA with ASEAN and/or one or more than one of its Member States in accordance with

---

[1] Article 16 of FACEC.

[2] This is a new form of bilateral treaty, better than EU's mixed treaty.

[3] See Kong Qingjiang, China's WTO Accession and the ASEAN-China Free Trade Area: the Perspective of a Chinese Lawyer, *Journal of International Economic Law*, 7(4), p. 810 (2004).

[4] Zeng Huaqun, On the One Country Four Memberships in WTO Regime (in Chinese), *Xiamen University Journal*, 2002 (5), pp. 5-14.

Article 24 of GATT.

Recently the authorities of Taiwan try to conclude FTA agreements with other countries like US, Japan, Singapore, New Zealand and Central American countries etc. in the name of "Taiwan" instead of its formal name of "Separate Customs Territory of Taiwan, Penghu, Kinmen and Matsu (Chinese Taipei)" in WTO,[1]and also proposed establishing a Free Trade Agreement with the 10-member ASEAN nations.[2]It reflects the "creeping independence" or "*de facto* independence" policy of Taiwan authorities. It should be emphasized that since 1949, China's position has been that any State or international organization, which wishes to deal with China, should recognize the government of PRC as the sole legitimate government of China and Taiwan as an inalienable part of China. This "one China" principle has been generally accepted and recognized by international society. The Taiwan issue therefore is completely an internal affair of China and will be settled by Chinese themselves. There is no legal ground for any foreign country, international organization or other entity to engage in the Taiwan issue in accordance with international law or international practice.[3] The WTO membership of Chinese Taipei does not bring any change of legal status of Taiwan. The ASEAN and its Member States shall adhere to the "one China" principle consistently and shall not set up any official relations with Taiwan.

At the same time, China, Hong Kong, China, Macao, China and/or Chinese Taipei may also establish a CU or FTA mutually, tripartitely or quadrilaterally. The significance of a CU or FTA among China, HK, China, Macao, China and/or Chinese Taipei under WTO regime is to deal with the special problems on the application of WTO non-discrimination principle, setting up a necessary legal basis for closer economic relations among the four regions. Considering China's "one country two systems" policy, there are big differences among China, Hong Kong, China, Macao, China or Chinese Taipei in political, economic and legal systems and the eco-

---

[1] Zhu Lei, How Taiwan Concludes "Free Trade Agreements", *Kai Fang Chao*, 2002 (7), pp. 24-25.

[2] On 12 November 2002, Taiwan "economic minister" Lin Yifu made the suggestion in Malaysia. Yow Cheun Hoe, China-ASEAN Relations in 2002: Chronology of Events, *China: An International Journal*, 1 (1), p. 168 (2003).

[3] However, it is worth noticing that there are some comments on the topic in Western countries from time to time. Most recently, Jonathan I. Charney and J. R. V. Prescott, Resolving Cross-Strait Relations between China and Taiwan, 94 *A. J. Int'l L.*, 452-477 (2000).

nomic level, to establish a FTA, rather than a CU, is more suitable for them. Before setting up a FTA, they have to negotiate and conclude an agreement necessary for establishing a FTA. This arrangement may also have impact on ASEAN and its Member States. In fact, both of the Closer Economic Partnership Arrangements (CEPAs) between Chinese mainland and Hong Kong and between Chinese mainland and Macao came into effect from 1 January 2004. The potential CEPAs among the Chinese mainland, Hong Kong, Macao and even Chinese Taipei leading to so call "great China FTA" certainly provide opportunities for further expansion of FACEC. It is probably logic that the great China FTA will be established before the completion of China-ASEAN FTA.

Ⅱ. WTO Responsibilities of Parties to FACEC

For identifying the WTO responsibilities of parties to FACEC, we shall first study WTO rules on RTAs and the differences between RTAs and WTO rules.

1. WTO Rules on RTAs

The non-discrimination principle, one of basic principles of WTO, stipulates that trade among WTO members should be conducted without any discrimination, requiring all members to extend the "most-favored nation (MFN)" treatment and "national treatment" to other members, except in certain circumstances detailed otherwise in GATT/WTO.

To establish a RTA among some WTO members is likely conflict with the non-discrimination principle of WTO as the treatment for members (including WTO members) of the RTA might be more favorable than that of outsiders (including WTO members). Therefore WTO members who wish to establish a RTA have to seek for exceptions of the non-discrimination principle, so as to avoid violation of this principle.

As the provisions of GATT "shall not prevent, as between the territories of contracting parties, the formation of a customs union or of a free-trade area or the adoption of an interim agreement necessary for the formation of a customs union or a free-trade area", [1] a CU and a FTA, the typical models of RTAs, become excep-

---

[1] Article 24 (5) of GATT.

tions of the non-discrimination principle with certain conditions. Following the GATT practice, WTO allows the existence of its members' CU and FTA with some detailed rules. The key provisions on RTAs in GATT/WTO regime are as follows:

1.1 Article 24 of GATT and Understanding on Article 24

Article 24 (8) of GATT makes clear definitions for a CU and a FTA.[1] It seems that the key difference between these two is that members of a CU have to apply substantially the same duties and restrictive regulations to the trade of territories not included in the union while these requirements are not applicable for members of a FTA. In fact, a CU, a FTA and an interim agreement necessary for the formation of a CU or a FTA[2] are different types or levels of RTAs. Among them, a CU is at the top level, a FTA is at the second place, and an interim agreement necessary for the formation of a CU or a FTA is at the primary stage of RTAs.

The Understanding on the Interpretation of Article 24 of the General Agreement on Tariffs and Trade 1994 (Understanding on Article 24) was formulated as part of Final Act of the Uruguay Round. It clarifies some rules of Article 24 of GATT. However, the Understanding has not resolved the more difficult issues, and it was hoped that further clarification would come from the Committee on Regional Trade Agreements (CRTA)[3] which also has in its mandate the responsibility "to consider the systemic implications of such agreements and regional initiatives for multilateral trading system and the relationship between them, and make

---

[1] According to the provisions, "A customs union shall be understood to mean the substitution of a single customs territory for two or more customs territories, so that (i) duties and other restrictive regulations of commerce (except, where necessary, those permitted under Articles XI, XII, XIII, XIV, XV and XX) are eliminated with respect to substantially all the trade between the constituent territories of the union or at least with respect to substantially all the trade in products originating in such territories", and "substantially the same duties and other regulations of commence are applied by each of the members of the union to the trade of territories not included in the union". "A free-trade area shall be understood to mean a group of two or more customs territories in which the duties and other restrictive regulations of commence (except, where necessary, those permitted under Articles XI, XII, XIII, XIV, XV and XX) are eliminated on substantially all the trade between the constituent territories in products originating in such territories".

[2] A comment indicates that the interim agreement is a form or a level for RTA. See Zhao Weitian, *The Legal Systems of WTO* (in Chinese), Jilin People Press, 2000, pp. 84-85.

[3] The CRTA was established in February 1996. The mandate of the Committee is to carry out the examination of agreements referred to it by the Council for Trade in Goods, the Council for Trade in Services and the Committee on Trade and Development. The CRTA is also charged to make recommendations on the reporting requirements for each type of agreement and to develop procedures to facilitate and improve the examination process.

appropriate recommendations to the General Council". [1]

To RTAs two major principles are laid down in Understanding on the Article 24: one is that a RTA must cover substantially all trade; the other is that other countries must not be worse off as a result of a RTA. [2] In addition, according to the Article 24 and Understanding on the Article 24, the principles and rules on a FTA and/or an interim agreement necessary for the formation of a FTA are mainly as follows:

(1) The purpose of a FTA should be to facilitate trade between the constituent territories and not to raise barriers to the trade of other contracting parties with such territories. [3]

(2) The duties and other regulations of commerce maintained in each of the constituent territories and applicable at the formation of such FTA, or the adoption of such interim agreement to the trade of contracting parties not included in such area or not parties to such agreement, shall not be higher or more restrictive than the corresponding duties and other regulations of commerce existing in the same constituent territories prior to the formation of the FTA, or interim agreement as the case may be. [4]

(3) Any interim agreement leading to the formation of a FTA shall include a plan and schedule for the formation of such a FTA within a reasonable length of time. [5] The "reasonable length of time" should exceed 10 years only in exceptional case. [6]

(4) Any contracting party deciding to enter into a FTA or an interim agreement leading to the formation of a FTA shall promptly notify the CONTRACTING PAR-

---

[1]　Jo-Ann Crawford and Sam Laird, Regional Trade Agreements and the WTO, http://www. tradeobservatory. org/library12/23/2003.

[2]　The "substantially all trade" requirement ensures that a RTA is not abused as a cover for narrow sectoral discriminatory arrangement. The same requirement is also laid down in the Article 5 of GATS which requires a "substantially sectoral coverage" in services. Unfortunately there is not agreement on the meaning of these wordings among WTO members, and in fact some RTAs omit from their coverage major and sensitive sectors such as agriculture and textile. The "not worse off" requirement is to ensure that not-participating members are not harmed by the RTAs. See Qingjiang Kong, China's WTO Accession and the ASEAN China Free Trade Area: the Perspective of a Chinese Lawyer, *Journal of International Economic Law*, 7(4), pp. 811-812 (2004).

[3]　Art. 24 (4) of GATT.

[4]　24(5) (b) of GATT.

[5]　24(5) (c) of GATT.

[6]　Para. 3 of Understanding on Article 24.

TIES and make available to them such information regarding the proposed FTA as will enable them to make such reports and recommendations to contracting parties as they may deem appropriate. [1] All such notifications shall be examined by a working party in the light of the relevant provisions of GATT and of paragraph 1 of Understanding on Article 24 and submit a report to the Council for Trade in Goods on its findings in this regard. [2]

(5) The provisions of Articles 22 and 23 of GATT as elaborated and applied by the Dispute Settlement Understanding may be invoked with respect to any matters arising from the application of those provisions of Article 24 relating to FTAs or interim agreements leading to the formation of a FTA. [3]

The relevant practice shows that the systems of pre-examine, supervisions and the dispute settlement on RTAs have been established and operated properly though there are still some defects. [4]

1. 2 Article 5 of GATS

The provisions of Article 5 of General Agreement on Trade in Services (GATS) comfort with the principles of Article 24 of GATT. It adopts the concept of "economic integration", and provides that "this Agreement shall not prevent any of its members from being a party to or entering into an agreement liberalizing trade in services between or among the parties to such an agreement" provided that such an agreement meet certain conditions. WTO Rules on RTAs in the field of trade in goods therefore extend to the field of trade in service.

Most recently these have attempted to identify the issues arising from the interpretation and application of individual provisions of Article 5 of GATS and the possible linkages between the Article 5 of GATS and the Article 24 of GATT, particularly in regard to the scope of "substantial sectoral coverage" and "substantial all discrimination". [5]

---

[1] 24(7) (a) of GATT.

[2] Para. 7 of Understanding on Article 24.

[3] Para. 12 of Understanding on Article 24.

[4] Zhong Liguo, On the Regulation of WTO on the Regional Trade Agreements on its Completion (in Chinese), *Jurists' Review*, No. 4, 2003, pp. 156-157.

[5] Jo-Ann Crawford and Sam Laird, Regional Trade Agreements and the WTO, http://www. tradeobservatory. org/library12/23/2003.

1. 3 The Enabling Clause

The GATT contracting parties adopted a decision in 1979, allowing derogations to the most-favored nation treatment in favor of developing countries in trade in goods. This includes differential and more favorable treatment, reciprocity and fuller participation of developing countries, and provisions related to the establishment of preferential trade agreements among developing countries, granting the possibilities of not meeting the substantially-all-trade requirements. [1]

From the contents of FACEC it is obvious that FACEC in nature is an interim agreement necessary for the formation of a FTA and meets the requirement of Article 24 of GATT, Understanding on Article 24 and Article 5 of GATS. As China and Member States of ASEAN are all developing countries, the enabling clause is also applicable to them.

2. WTO Rules versus RTAs

Even as a WTO member, it only bears obligations within the ambit of WTO. It seems that for a WTO member who is at the same time a member of RTA, the key questions are: What are the WTO members' obligations within the ambit of WTO? What is the relationship between RTAs and WTO rules?

The objects of WTO rules and RTAs are different. They are not identical or overlapped. The main reasons are that first, WTO systems and RTA systems have been developing concurrently and have not been subordinate to each other. Second, WTO is a trade organization, regulating the trade relations among its members, and a RTA is an economic integration arrangement, regulating the economic (including trade) relations among its parties. Although the fields governed by WTO rules have been extended greatly after Uruguay Round, WTO rules certainly cannot cover all economic sectors of its members. In fact, the fields governed by RTAs might be wider than those governed by WTO rules. [2] Third, even in the same fields covered

---

[1] Sung-Hoon Park, The Current Status and Future Prospects of Regionalism and Multilateralism in the World Economy: A Case Study of Economic Relations Between EU and APEC in the WTO Era, pp. 4-5, http://www. ecsanet. org/conferences/ecsaworld3/park. html 12/23/2003.

[2] For example, the development of EU from FTA to the Union of Economic and Currency, the investment rules made by ASEAN, NAFTA, etc.

by WTO rules and RTAs, due to inherent defects of a multilateral framework,[1] the WTO rules could not replace RTAs. Fourth, a membership of WTO is not a prerequisite for parties to a RTA.[2]Some parties of a RTA who are not WTO members have not any obligations to WTO. Finally, many RTAs have been established before GATT or WTO. To some extent, the rules on RTAs of GATT/WTO are recognition or compromise to the reality of existing RTAs. Therefore a RTA concluded by WTO members is not necessarily required to be consistent fully with WTO rules or only limited in the fields governed by WTO rules. The only requirement for WTO members is that those subject to WTO rules in a RTA shall be consistent with WTO rules.[3] In other words, when a WTO member engages in a RTA, it should fulfill its WTO obligations.

To a member of WTO, it is very important to distinguish the concept of "within the ambit of WTO" and "beyond the ambit of WTO". Within the ambit of WTO it is undoubted that all members have to observe WTO rules and fulfill their commitments to WTO seriously. At the same time, as all the duties and obligations of all WTO members are limited to their commitments to WTO, beyond the ambit of WTO, members may regulate their trade relations through bilateral or RTAs in accordance with general international law.

There is some other legal regime for FACEC. Article 12A of Protocol to Amend FACEC, titled as "Agreements Outside this Agreement" provides: "Nothing in this Agreement shall prevent or prohibit any individual ASEAN Member State from entering into any bilateral or pluralateral agreement with China and/or the rest of the ASEAN Member States relating to trade in goods, trade in services, investment, and/or other areas of economic co-operation outside the ambit of this Agreement.

---

〔1〕 WTO rules are inherently deficient. For example, the consensus system on which WTO is based has shortcomings so that many issues end up without any measurable results. In contrast, countries in a region generally have more commonality so they are more likely to diffuse differences and reach RTAs. See Qingjiang Kong, China's WTO Accession and the ASEAN-China Free Trade Area: the Perspective of a Chinese Lawyer, *Journal of International Economic Law*, 7(4), p. 804 (2004).

〔2〕 For example, the membership of International Monetary Fund is the prerequisite of applying for a membership of International Bank for Reconstruction and Development.

〔3〕 In fact, the full conformity of RTAs with GATT provisions is rare. In the 46 years of GATT up to the end of 1994, a total of 98 RTAs had been notified under Article 24 of GATT, most of which were examined in individual working parties. But, consensus on the conformity of these RTAs with GATT provisions was reached in only one case: the Czech-Slovak customs union. Jo-Ann Crawford and Sam Laird, Regional Trade Agreements and the WTO, http://www. tradeobservatory. org/library12/23/2003.

The provisions of this Agreement shall not apply to any such bilateral or plurilateral agreement. " The provision shows there might be overlap international relations between an ASEAN Member State and China or among some of ASEAN Member States and China. FACEC is not a closed agreement as it provides more flexible way for China-ASEAN Member States relations.

3. Responsibilities of Parties to FACEC under WTO Regime

The general WTO rules on RTAs is that where the WTO deems a RAT to be inconsistent with WTO provisions, the WTO members concerned shall modify it with a recommendation by CRTA. If they are not prepared to modify it they "shall not maintain or put into force" such an agreement. If the WTO members concerned fail to implement the recommendation, any provision in a RTA is likely to be subject to WTO dispute settlement procedures. Each member undertakes to accord sympathetic consideration to and to afford adequate opportunity for consultation on the RTA disputes before panel procedure. [1] As a matter of fact, the WTO Dispute Settlement Body (DSB) once faulted Turkey's move to impose quotas on non-EU textile imports as part of a customs union agreement with EU. [2] When the DSB has ruled that a provision of GATT has not been observed, the responsible member shall take such reasonable measures as may be available to it to ensure its observance. Failure to do that the provisions relating to compensation and suspension of concessions or other obligations would apply. [3]

Although ASEAN itself and two ASEAN Member States are currently not WTO members, China and eight out of ten ASEAN Member States are WTO members. It is reasonably safe for WTO members to formulate a RTA in accordance with WTO rules. [4] Considering ASEAN itself might become a *de facto* WTO member through its further integration and the two non-WTO members of ASEAN Member States might become WTO members in the near future, the two parties to FACEC definitely can not ignore WTO rules when they conclude, implement FACEC and

---

[1] Para. 15 of Understanding on Article 24.

[2] See Qingjiang Kong, China's WTO Accession and the ASEAN-China Free Trade Area: the Perspective of a Chinese Lawyer, *Journal of International Economic Law*, 7(4), p. 813 and note 28 (2004).

[3] Para. 14 of Understanding on Article 24.

[4] Kong Oingjiang, Closer Economic Partnership Agreement between China and Hong Kong, *China: An International Journal*, Vol. 1, No. 1, pp. 136-137 (2003).

negotiate the further FTA agreement in the future.

III. WTO Rules in FACEC: Within Coverage or Beyond

As China and eight Member States of ASEAN are WTO members and they concluded FACEC after WTO agreements, some articles of FACEC refer directly or indirectly to WTO rules. This is unique in the history of RTAs, indicating the consensus of the WTO members in FACEC to observe WTO rules.

There are two categories of provisions in FACEC by criteria of relationship to WTO rules:

1. Provisions Related to WTO Rules

In FACEC, there are some articles related to WTO rules, dealing with the traditional fields of GATT, namely the trade in goods, and the new fields of Uruguay Round, including trade in service, and trade-related intellectual property rights (TRIPS) etc.

Article 2 of FACEC deals with the measures for comprehensive economic co-operation. It states that the measures include (a) progressive elimination of tariffs and non-tariff barriers in substantially all trade in goods; (b) progressive liberalization of trade in services with substantial sectoral coverage. The provisions are similar to the provisions of Article 24 (8) (b) of GATT and Article 5 (1) of GATS. Some terms like "in substantially all trade in goods", "trade in services with substantial sectoral coverage" are even exactly the same as those in WTO rules. [1]

Article 6(3) (d) of FACEC titled as "Application of WTO provisions" clear indicates the general application of WTO rules, providing that WTO rules governing modification of commitments, safeguard actions, emergency measures and other trade remedies, including anti-dumping and subsidies and countervailing measures, shall, in the interim, be applicable to the products covered under the Early Harvest Program. [2]

---

[1] For the discussion of the coverage of RTAs, see Jo-Ann Crawford and Sam Laird, Regional Trade Agreements and the WTO, http://www.tradeobservatory.org/library12/23/2003.

[2] The "Early Harvest" program involves the quick reduction of tariffs on a number of goods that will take effect within a targeted date of three years from July 1 next year when the Agreement comes into force. ASEAN Secretariat, News Release, 30 Oct., 2002 ASEAN-China Free Trade Area Negotiations to Start Next Year, http://www.aseansec.org/13125.htm; Qingjiang Kong, China's WTO Accession and the ASEAN-China Free Trade Area: the Perspective of a Chinese Lawyer, *Journal of International Economic Law*, 7 (4), p. 815 (2004).

Furthermore some provisions of FACEC refer directly to the specific WTO rules. For example the Article 3 titled as "Trade in Goods" refers to the exception for RTAs in Article 24 of GATT: "except, where necessary, those permitted under Article XXIV (8) (b) of the WTO General Agreement on Tariffs and Trade".

Some provisions even require the parties to FACEC to fulfill the requirements of WTO rules on RTAs in spite of non-WTO member positions of ASEAN and its three Member States at that time. Article 3 (6) of FACEC states that the commitments undertaken by the parties under this Article and Article 6 of this Agreement shall fulfill the WTO requirements to eliminate tariffs on substantially all the trade between the parties.

Moreover, the parties to FACEC also agree to conduct their negotiation to establish the ASEAN-China FTA in accordance with WTO rules concerned. According to Article 3 (8) of FACEC, the negotiations between the Parties to establish the ASEAN-China FTA covering trade in goods shall also include, but not be limited to the following, *inter se*: (1) modification of a Party's commitments under the agreement on trade in goods based on Article 28 of the GATT;[1] (2) safeguards based on the GATT principles, including, but not limited to the following elements: transparency, coverage, objective criteria for action, including the concept of serious injury or threat thereof, and temporary nature;[2] (3) disciplines on subsidies and countervailing measures and anti-dumping measures based on the existing GATT disciplines;[3] and (4) facilitation and promotion of effective and adequate protection of trade-related aspects of intellectual property rights based on existing WTO, World Intellectual Property Organization (WIPO) and other relevant disciplines. [4]

As to the field of trade in services, Article 4 (a) of FACEC provides that progressive elimination of substantially all discrimination between or among the Parties and/or prohibition of new or more discriminatory measures with respect to trade in services between the Parties, except for measures permitted under Article 5(1) (b) of the GATS.

---

[1] Art. 3 (8) (d) of FACEC.
[2] Art. 3 (8) (f) of FACEC.
[3] Art. 3 (8) (g) of FACEC.
[4] Art. 3 (8) (h) of FACEC.

From the above-mentioned provisions of FACEC it is safe to conclude that there is a close link and relationship between some provisions of FACEC and WTO rules. To certain extent some provisions of FACEC are based on or governed by WTO rules.

2. Provisions beyond the Coverage of WTO Rules

The important features of modern RTAs are that they have more extensive product coverage than in earlier agreements and many go beyond the traditional tariff-cutting exercises. They now may cover services, investment, intellectual property, technical barriers to trade, dispute settlement, super-national institutional arrangements etc. [1] There are some provisions beyond the coverage of WTO rules in FACEC.

The objectives of FACEC are: (1) strengthen and enhance economic, trade and investment co-operation between the Parties; (2) progressively liberalize and promote trade in goods and services as well as create a transparent, liberal and facilitative investment regime; (3) explore new areas and develop appropriate measures for closer economic co-operation between the Parties. [2]

It is noticeable from the above provisions that firstly, "investment co-operation" and "investment regime" show the importance of investment in FACEC. [3] Article 5 of FACEC further deals with solely the investment[4]. Secondly, "new areas" means the areas in addition to the traditional trade in goods and investment. The parties to FACEC adopt a gradual approach in the negotiation for the FTA: comprehensive, but easy first, trade goods first, service and investment later. Moreover they aim at not just a FTA, but a closer partnership based on comprehensive cooper-

---

[1] Jo-Ann Crawford and Sam Laird, Regional Trade Agreements and the WTO, http://www. tradeobservatory. org/library12/23/2003.

[2] Art. 1 of FACEC.

[3] On March 20, 2004, Swiss President Joesph Deiss concluded an official visit to Thailand after launching an ASEAN-China Investment Fund aiming at financing small-and medium-sized enterprises in Southeast Asia and China with 125 million US dollars. Switzerland was one of the initial investors in the 125 million US dollars fund, along with the Asian Development Bank, French financial development institution Proparco, the Japan Asia Investment Co and the United Overseas Bank of Singapore. See ASEAN/China investment fund launched, http://news3. xinhuanet. com/english/2004-03/20/content_1376020. htm.

[4] It provides that: To promote investments and to create a liberal, facilitative, transparent and competitive investment regime, the Parties agree to: (a) enter into negotiations in order to progressively liberalize the investment regime; (b) strengthen co-operation in investment, facilitate investment and improve transparency of investment rules and regulations; and (c) provide for the protection of investments.

ation. As for areas of cooperation or "new areas", five priority sectors for cooperation in FACEC are agriculture, information and communications technology, human resources development, investment, and Mekong River basin development. Also other areas include banking, finance, tourism, industrial co-operation, transport, IPR, SMEs, environment, biotechnology, fishery, forestry, mining, energy and sub-regional development.

The measures for comprehensive economic co-operation provided in FACEC also indicate the areas beyond the coverage of WTO rules. The measures include: (1) establishment of an open and competitive investment regime that facilitates and promotes investment within the ASEAN-China FTA;[1] (2) establishment of effective trade and investment facilitation measures, including, but not limited to, simplification of customs procedures and development of mutual recognition arrangements;[2] (3) expansion of economic co-operation in areas as may be mutually agreed between the Parties and formulation of action plans and programs in order to implement the agreed sectors/areas of co-operation. [3] Again "new areas" are open to negotiation and might be agreed between ASEAN and China.

Even in the fields within the coverage of WTO rules, it seems that the parties to FACEC wish to go further than their commitments in WTO regime. For example, Article 4 of FACEC deals with trade in services, providing that: (1) expansion in the depth and scope of liberalization of trade in service beyond those undertaken by ASEAN Member States and China under the GATS;[4] and (2) enhanced co-operation in services between the Parties in order to improve efficiency and competitiveness, as well as to diversify the supply and distribution of services of the respective service suppliers of the Parties. [5]

In sum, the parties to FACEC might develop traditional areas and "new areas" for economic cooperation and integration to meet their needs in substantial aspect and the regional dispute settlement regime in procedural aspect.

---

〔1〕　Art. 2 (c) of FACEC.
〔2〕　Art. 2 (f) of FACEC.
〔3〕　Art. 2 (g) of FACEC.
〔4〕　Art. 4 (b) of FACEC.
〔5〕　Art. 4 (c) of FACEC.

IV. Conclusions

FACEC is a milestone for development of China-ASEAN comprehensive economic cooperation and groundwork for establishment of China-ASEAN FTA. It has both economic and political significances. [1] It also sets up important principles for China-ASEAN FTA process, which are mutual benefit, compromise, and consolidation.

At the same time FACEC is a RTA with its partial contents regulated by WTO rules. WTO rules provide the legal basis for and have close link to the development of FACEC and China-ASEAN FTA process. After the two non-WTO members in ASEAN complete their accession to WTO, WTO rules might be more applicable in general. Though there are different and even opposite views on the influence of RTAs to multilateral trade systems, [2] the close link between WTO rules and FACEC indicates the possible complementarities between WTO and RTAs in the road to economic liberalization.

It should be further pointed out that ASEAN is composed of ten developing countries, and China is also a developing country, FACEC therefore is an arrangement of South-South cooperation with win-win wishes. As developing countries, China and ASEAN Member States share much in common in the history, economic development, international participation, etc. The common goal of the parties to FACEC is to facilitate the economic development through regional economic integration. Moreover the establishment of China-ASEAN FTA may provide a forum for regional issues, including the development of South China Sea etc.

---

[1]   The future of China-ASEAN FTA is encouraging. ASEAN is currently China's fifth largest trade partner, and China the sixth of ASEAN. The planned China-ASEAN FTA is projected to boost Chinese and ASEAN exports by 50 percent while adding one percent growth of ASEAN's GDP and 0.3 percent of China's economy. The decision to set up China-ASEAN FTA is a demonstration of the Chinese and ASEAN leaders' commitment to "enhancing friendship and co-operation in a face of economic globalization". See Qingjiang Kong, China's WTO Accession and the ASEAN-China Free Trade Area: the Perspective of a Chinese Lawyer, *Journal of International Economic Law*, 7 (4), pp. 805-806 (2004).

[2]   Jo-Ann Crawford and Sam Laird, Regional Trade Agreements and the WTO, http://www.tradeobservatory.org/library12/23/2003.

第四编

香港涉外经济法律实践

导　言

本编主要研讨中国实行"一国两制"国策衍生的香港涉外经济法律实践问题,亦为西方国家特别关注的国际经济法领域的中国特色实践问题。第九章探讨香港特区高度自治权在对外事务领域的实践及其基本特征(第一、二节)。第十章专门研讨香港双边投资条约实践问题,概括分析香港双边投资条约(BIT)实践的创新与意涵(第一、二节),进而研讨其特殊条约适用问题,提出中国系列 BITs 与中国香港系列 BITs 的适用原则(第三节)。

作者的主要观点:

(1) 关于香港特区对外事务领域的自治权问题。根据《中英联合声明》和《基本法》的规定,香港特区对外事务领域的自治权体现于一定条件下的单独缔约权、参加国际会议和国际组织的权利、适用国际协定的特别安排等。其特征主要表现在授权性质、双重法律依据和国际保障等方面。同时应当强调,香港特区的自治权地位问题本质上属中国内政。因此,外国的法律和国际组织的文件单方面制定的涉及香港特区自治权地位的规定缺乏国际法依据,违背了"互不干涉内政"的国际法原则。

(2) 关于香港 BIT 实践对国际法的重要贡献。香港 BIT 实践对国际法特别是国际投资法和国际条约法作出了重要贡献。从总体上看,过渡期香港 BIT 实践创造了在特殊历史条件下条约实践的新模式,它简化甚至避免了条约继承或续订的复杂问题;在 BIT 历史上,香港与荷兰 BIT 是第一例由非主权实体与主权国家签订的此类协定,是 BITs 缔约主体方面的重大突破;一些新的法律概念、原则和新的程序安排由香港 BITs 的缔约双方共同创造或接受,构成新的国际实践,也提出了国际法研究的新课题。

(3) 关于建构中国系列 BITs 与中国香港系列 BITs 相互衔接的适用机制。香港 BIT 实践衍生了国际法实践史无前例的"特殊条约适用"问题,需要在理论和实践层面上予以探讨和解决。在中国系列 BITs 与中国香港系列 BITs 长期并存的情况下，亟须确立和遵循"香港 BIT 实践重点发展""中国香港系列 BITs 优先适用"及"中国系列 BITs 明确适用安排"三项原则，建构中国系列 BITs 与中国香港系列 BITs 密切衔接、相辅相成的适用机制。

第一节　香港特别行政区高度自治权刍议
——对外事务实践的视角*

编者按： 香港回归后，作为中国的一个特别行政区将如何与中央政府或国家同时参与世界性的贸易活动，它在政治、法律和经济制度上的相对自主，势必引发一系列区域和国际上的法律问题。中国入世之后，这个问题显得更加迫切和紧要。此处所发曾华群教授文章在探讨自治权发展的基础上，概述香港过渡期以来根据《中英联合声明》和《基本法》有关规定在单独缔约权、参加国际会议和国际组织的权利、适用国际协定的特别安排等方面的初步实践，并分析了香港特别行政区高度自治权的授权性质、法律根据和国际保障等基本特征。资料充分，线索清晰。该文为我们了解香港特区在国际贸易领域既有的法律地位和状况提供了法律制度和法律技术上的诠释，这对于学界和有关部门今后思考如何维护和调整国家与特区之间、国家和特区与世界其他国家和地区之间的贸易关系显然是有帮助的。

根据 1984 年《中华人民共和国政府和大不列颠及北爱尔兰联合王国政府关于香港问题的联合声明》（以下简称《联合声明》）和 1990 年《中华人民共和国香港特别行政区基本法》（以下简称《基本法》）的有关规定，1997 年 7 月 1 日中国对香港恢复行使主权后，香港特别行政区（以下简称"香港特区"）享有高度自治权。1997 年前后，

---

* 原载《比较法研究》2002 年第 1 期。

关于在香港特区实行"一国两制,高度自治"的可能性,海内外学者或肯定[1],或质疑[2]。一般承认,从《联合声明》和《基本法》的有关规定看,香港特区在处理内部事务和对外事务方面均被授予高度自治权。问题在于,自治权究何所指? 对比其他自治实体,香港特区高度自治权有何基本特征? 实证研究能否表明香港特区在对外事务方面具有高度自治权?[3] 本文从理论和实践两方面对此作一初步探讨。

一、香港自治权的发展

(一) 自治权的涵义

自治权(autonomy)一词的语义解释是指在未受外来影响或干预的情况下自主作出决定的权力和能力。[4] 进一步研究表明,该词曾在不同历史时期、不同场合使用,涵义不尽相同。

首先,自治权是一历史概念。自治权概念最早出现于希腊习惯法,比主权概念更为古老。自治权的概念原先是作为对相对独立的城邦的承认。自然权利及社会契约理论将其由团体的转变为个体的概念,而民族主义再将其转变为团体的概念。[5]

其次,自治权也可作为用于国内场合的政治或法律概念。在现代政治学中,该概念指在一个主权国家内政府权力分配的特定模式。[6] 自治权的关键属性是第二

〔1〕 一些学者根据中国在遵守国际条约方面的良好记录判断中国会严格履行《联合声明》的责任和义务。See Deborah L. Bayles, The Reunification of China: An Examination of the Legal Systems of the People's Republic of China, Hong Kong and Taiwan, 19 *Den. J. Int'l. L. & Pol'y*, p. 463 (1991); Roda Mushkat, The Transition from British to Chinese Rule in Hong Kong: A Discussion of Salient International Legal Issues, 14 *Den. J. Int'l L. & Pol'y*, p. 193 (1986). 一些肯定的评论的依据是,保留香港的资本主义制度,对中国具有重要的外交、经济和军事意义。See Christian C. Day, The Recovery of Hong Kong by the People's Republic of China—A Fifty Years Experiment in Capitalism and Freedom, 11 *Syr. J. Int'l L. & Com.*, pp. 643-649 (1989); Johnson C. Ng, Hong Kong after 1997: An Experimental Governmental Practising Capitalism within a Socialist Sovereign, 10 *N. Y. L. Sch. J. Int'l L.*, pp. 92-93 (1989).

〔2〕 See David A. Jones, Jr., A leg to Stand on? Post-1997 Hong Kong Courts as a Constraint on PRC Abridgement of Individual Rights and Local Autonomy, 12 *Yale J. Int'l L.*, p. 292 (1987); David M. Corwin, China's Choices: The 1984 Sino-British Joint Declaration and Its Aftermath, 19 *L. & Pol. in Int'l Bus.*, pp. 518-519, 526-528 (1987); Eric Johnson, Hong Kong after 1997: A Free City?, 40 *German Yearbook of International Law*, p. 404 (1997); Hong Kong One Year after the Handover, *Inside China Mainland*, September 1998, pp. 19-23.

〔3〕 See Marius Olivier, Hong Kong: An Exercise in Autonomy, 18 *South African Yearbook of Int'l L.*, pp. 61-62 (1992-93).

〔4〕 See Anthony Neoh, Hong Kong's Future: The View of a Hong Kong Lawyer, 22 *Cal. W. Int'l L. J.*, pp. 332-333 (1992).

〔5〕 See Sanford Lakoff, Between Either/Or and More or Less: Sovereignty versus Autonomy under Federalism, 24 *The Journal of Federalism*, p. 76 (1994).

〔6〕 See Albert H. Y. Chen, Some Reflections on Hong Kong's Autonomy, 24 *HKLJ*, p. 174 (1994).

级实体(the secondary entity)在其权利能力范围内不受中央政府或联邦政府干预，特别是该自治安排的主要目标是保持该实体独特的文化、宗教、种族、经济和其他认同(identities)。同样，自治权的程度也可通过第二级实体受中央政府或联邦政府控制的程度来衡量。在国家实践中，西班牙在恢复民主制度后，重新组成为"自治权的国家"(the state of the autonomies)。根据 1978 年《西班牙宪法》，西班牙现由主要负责经济和国防事务的国家政府和 17 个自治实体组成。在政制良好的国家，如加拿大、法国和英国等，代表语言、文化或区域的团体也提出了自治的要求。此类自治实体不具有任何国际因素，由本国法律确立和规范。[1]

最后，自治权也可用于国际场合。在国际场合，自治权难以定义，因为根据国际法而存在的这种地位有种种形式，如领土(区域性)实体、具有公民资格或不具有公民资格的自由联盟、保护国等，各具不同程度的自治权。[2] 此类自治实体可能具有多种国际因素。由国际条约产生的自治实体可拥有某种国际保证，中央政府与自治实体之间的关系受到国际监督，这意味着中央政府不具有单方面改变这种关系性质的权力。

1980 年国际法程序问题研究所(Procedural Aspects of International Law Institute，PAIL)为美国国务院进行了一项有关自治实体的综合性研究。该项研究报告将自治实体分为四类：

(1) 联邦制国家的成员国，它们平等地联合成为一个国家；

(2) 国际领土，基于政治考虑，它们在国际监督下产生；

(3) 联系国，它们属较新近产生的领土单位，结成主要国与次要国关系(a primary state-secondary state relationship)；

(4) 混合类(miscellaneous category)，即上述各种类型的混合。[3]

事实上，由于对自治实体广泛的、不同程度的承认和有关自治权的安排迥然不同，已不可能作出适用于各种自治权的定义。鉴此，对自治权进行综合研究的各国学者，试图确定作为充分自治和自行管辖(full autonomous and self-governing)的实

---

〔1〕　See Ruth Lapidoth，Autonomy and Sovereignty—Are They Mutually Exclusive?，in Amos Shapira，Mala Tabory(ed.)，*New Political Entities in Public and Private International Law：With Special Reference to the Palestinian Entity*，Kluwer Law International，p. 5 (1999).

〔2〕　关于自治权概念的详细讨论，参见 Brian Z. Tamanaha，Post-1997 Hong Kong：A Comparative Study of the Meaning of "High Degree of Autonomy" with a Specific Look at the Commonwealth of the Nothern Mariana Islands，5 *China Law Reporter*，pp. 164-168 (1989)。

〔3〕　See Brian Z. Tamanaha，Post-1997 Hong Kong：A Comparative Study of the Meaning of "High Degree of Autonomy" with a Specific Look at the Commonwealth of the Nothern Mariana Islands，5 *China Law Reporter*，p. 166 (1989).

体所需要拥有的最低限度的政府权力。他们普遍认为,此类政府权力包括由本地选举产生的能对本地事务独立决策的立法机构、本地选择的负责行政管理和执行本地法令的行政长官、独立的本地司法权以及一定程度的对外交往权。

自治实体在对外事务中享有的自治权,特别表现于参加国际组织和缔结或适用国际条约等方面的自治权。自治实体对外事务方面的自治权是主权国家加强自治实体国际地位的战略设计的重要组成部分。广义上,自治实体的对外事务包括对外国或国际组织的事务和对本国其他地区的事务。

西方学者赫斯特·汉纳(Hurst Hannum)在对一些自治实体,包括欧洲国家(西班牙、英国和北欧国家)、亚非独立的多元种族国家(印度、斯里兰卡和苏丹)、非国家社会(Kurds)、土著民族(Saamis,Miskitos)的自治实体和中国香港特区进行比较研究之后指出,虽然自治实体各有特色,能保持其自治权地位的基本因素包括:语言、教育、进入政府公共服务和社会服务的渠道、土地与自然资源以及本地政府的结构。[1] 陈弘毅教授则认为,构建自治权模式的重要问题是:(1)本地政府组成的方式;(2)中央政府与本地政府之间在立法、行政和司法方面权力的分配;(3)错误纠正与争端解决机制。[2] 值得注意的是,在上述列举的基本因素和重要问题均未包括自治实体在对外事务方面的自治权。

由此可见,自治实体并不必然具有在对外事务方面的自治权。换言之,具有对外事务自治权的自治实体可能从一个侧面表明它具有较高度的自治权。

(二)香港自治权的发展

20 世纪下半叶,香港经历了从事实上(de facto)自治权向法律上(de jure)自治权的重要历史转变和发展。

在漫长的英占时期,香港作为英国事实上的海外属土,在法律上不具有自治权。在对外交往权方面,香港的对外联系由英国牢牢控制。[3] 然而,随着香港工商业的发展和国际地位的不断提高,英国逐步在事实上承认和允许香港在国际场合具有一定程度的自治权。[4] 这种情况在 1973 年 1 月 1 日英国加入欧共体后更为明显。在

---

[1] See Hurst Hannum, *Autonomy, Sovereignty, and Self-Determination, The Accommodation of Conflicting Rights*, Revised Edition, The University of Pennsylvania Press, p. 458 (1996).

[2] See Brian Z. Tamanaha, Post-1997 Hong Kong: A Comparative Study of the Meaning of "High Degree of Autonomy" with a Specific Look at the Commonwealth of the Nothern Mariana Islands, 5 *China Law Reporter*, p. 166 (1989).

[3] 关于英国对其属土管辖权力的评论,参见 Kenneth Roberts-Wray, *Commonwealth and Colonial Law*, Stevens & Sons, pp. 138-246 (1966).

[4] See Marius Olivier, Hong Kong: An Exercise in Autonomy, 18 *South African Yearbook of Int'l L.*, pp. 67-68 (1992-93).

过渡期(自 1984 年 12 月至 1996 年 6 月),香港已成为一些多边或双边条约的缔约方和许多国际性或区域性组织的正式成员或准成员。例如,在经贸领域,香港已成为关税及贸易总协定(GATT)、多边纤维协定(MFA)、亚洲生产力组织(APO)和亚洲开发银行(ADB)的正式成员。香港也是联合国亚洲太平洋地区经济及社会委员会(ESCAP)、亚洲太平洋电讯组织(APT)和世界气象组织(WMO)等的准成员。[1] 事实表明,当时香港的对外交往能力已逐渐为国际社会广泛接受。

一般认为,在英占时期后期,香港在对外事务方面享有事实上自治权,在其相应的国际权利、义务和能力范围内具有国际法律人格。然而,应当明确,香港的这种国际地位和人格是通过英国逐项具体授权而形成和确立的。[2] 总体上说,直至 1997 年 6 月 30 日以前,香港仍不是具有正式或法律上自治权(formal or *de jure* autonomy)的实体。

英占时期后期香港对外事务方面的事实上自治权在《联合声明》第 3 条中国对香港的基本方针的声明中得到确认、促进和法律化。《联合声明》确立的原则是,外交事务和国防属于中央人民政府的权力范围,同时,授权香港特区在某些领域从事对外事务。因此,"外交事务"与"对外事务"的区别值得注意。前者主要指涉及国家主权的政治事务,后者主要指经济和文化等领域的事务。[3] 根据《联合声明》的规定,香港特区的高度自治权在对外事务方面主要表现在一定的单独缔约权、参加国际会议和国际组织的权利和适用国际协定的特别安排等。

香港特区高度自治权的各个主要方面分别由《联合声明》附件一《中华人民共和国对香港的基本方针政策的具体说明》第三节(法院与司法)、第六节(经济与商业事务)、第八节(航运)、第九节(民用航空)、第十一节(对外关系)和第十四节(旅行与移民事务)等确立与调整。[4] 此外,附件一第二节规定,1997 年之后香港原有法律基本不变,所谓"原有法律"也包含了涉及国际实践的法律制度。

1990 年 4 月 4 日颁布的《基本法》重申和细化了《联合声明》中有关香港特区高度自治权的规定。

---

〔1〕　关于香港对外关系概况,参见简家聪:《香港对外关系简介》,载港人协会编:《香港法律 18 讲》,商务印书馆香港分馆 1987 年版,第 445-469 页。

〔2〕　See Marius Olivier, Hong Kong: An Exercise in Autonomy, 18 *South African Yearbook of Int'l L.*, pp. 70-71 (1992-93).

〔3〕　See Yash Ghai, *Hong Kong's New Constitutional Order*, *The Resumption of Chinese Sovereign and the Basic Law*, Hong Kong University Press, p. 433 (1997).

〔4〕　See Albert H. Y. Chen, The Relationship Between the Central Government and the SAR, in Peter Wesley-Smith, Albert H. Y. Chen(eds.), *The Basic Law and Hong Kong's Future*, Butterworths, pp. 114-115 (1988).

显然，《联合声明》和《基本法》赋予香港特区高度的自治权。特别是，这种自治权由《联合声明》和《基本法》分别在国际法和国内法层面上承诺和确立，属于法律上自治权。

二、香港基于高度自治权的对外事务实践

如前所述，是否享有对外事务方面的自治权，可作为衡量自治实体是否具有高度自治权的尺度之一。海内外国际法学者更为关注的是，过渡期以来香港基于高度自治权在对外事务方面的实践。主要原因是，这些实践不仅是中国履行其国际承诺的重要标志，也反映了国际法的最新发展。

过渡期，在中英联合联络小组主持下，保持和发展香港对外关系的工作已经开展。[1] 当时香港的国际实践不仅依据其事实上的自治权，而且受到《联合声明》和《基本法》有关规定精神的重要调整或影响。该时期的国际实践有助于阐释《联合声明》和《基本法》有关香港特区高度自治权的规定，也是中国履行其国际承诺的佐证。在此基础上，1997 年 7 月 1 日以后，香港特区严格遵照《联合声明》和《基本法》的有关规定，高度自治权对外事务方面的实践有了长足的发展。鉴于香港在过渡期与回归之后两个时期对外事务方面的发展密切相关，兹分单独缔约权、参加国际会议和国际组织的权利以及适用国际协定的特别安排三个主要方面概述如下：

（一）单独缔约权

《联合声明》附件一第 11 条第 1 款和《基本法》第 151 条明确规定，香港特区可以"中国香港"的名义，在经济、贸易、金融、航运、通讯、旅游、文化和体育等有关领域单独地同世界各国、各地区及有关国际组织保持和发展关系，并签订和履行有关协定。

上述授权方式虽然尚未成为国际法中的普遍实践，但它明确确立了香港特区在规定领域中单独签订双边条约的能力。理解香港特区缔约权范围的关键是"有关领域"概念的界定。该条款本身未作定义，因此只能从《联合声明》和《基本法》全部相关条款中寻求答案。[2] 1985 年以来，香港已进行了一系列以香港名义单独与外国签订双边协定的实践，在民航关系和国际投资关系领域成效尤为显著。

1. 香港与外国之间的民航协定

作为国际贸易和金融中心，香港的经济前途首先在很大程度上取决于是否拥有

---

〔1〕 根据《联合声明》第 4 条规定，在过渡期，英国政府负责香港的行政管理，以维护和保持其经济繁荣和社会稳定，中国政府对此予以合作。《联合声明》附件二第 4、5 条进一步规定了中英两国政府通过中英 联合联络小组在国际关系领域的合作。

〔2〕 See Yash Ghai, *Hong Kong's New Constitutional Order*, *The Resumption of Chinese Sovereign and the Basic Law*, Hong Kong University Press, pp. 435-436 (1997).

自由航空港。[1]

　　传统上,关于主权国家之间相互交换商业性航空权利的双边民航协定是国际法的重要渊源。在英占时期,香港由于被视为英国境内的始发站或目的站,其对外民航关系由英国同有关国家的双边民航协定(以下简称"英外民航协定")调整。1986年以前,英国在谈判、签署或适用与香港有关的双边民航协定时,在香港没有特别程序可循。实践中,在谈判之前或谈判期间,英国有时会征询香港本地国际性航空公司的意见,并且一般会邀请香港政府代表参与谈判。[2]截至1987年,计有23个适用于香港的英外民航协定和另一些非正式安排。[3] 1997年7月1日中国对香港恢复行使主权后,英外民航协定中的涉港部分即自动失效。由于民航业尤其需要准确、详明的法律安排,香港的对外民航关系的重新安排就成为过渡期英国和香港政府最紧迫和重要的法律工作。

　　解决方案是,香港以其名义同外国谈判和签署新的独立于英国的双边民航协定。在此之前,首先需要通过香港本地立法改变香港与英国之间的民航关系。1985年2月1日,香港政府颁布了《一九四九年民用航空法·一九八五年空运(航空服务领牌)(修订)规例》[Civil Aviation Act 1949, Air Transport. (Licensing of Air Services)(Amendment) Regulations 1985]。[4]据之,香港政府拥有签发有关航空服务的营业许可证的充分权力。这表明,香港与英国及其他外国的民航关系已不再隶属于英国。这是香港单独同外国签订民航协定的必要前提。

　　1986年9月17日《香港政府和荷兰王国政府关于航班的协定》在海牙签署,1987年6月26日生效。[5]这是双边民航协定历史上第一项由非主权实体和主权国家签订的协定,是双边民航协定发展的一大突破。[6]随后,在过渡期,香港与下列19

---

〔1〕　See Susan L. Karamanian, Legal Aspects of the Sino-British Draft Agreement on the Future of Hong Kong, 20 *Texas Int'l L. J.*, p. 177(1985).

〔2〕　See Gary N. Heilbronn, The Changing Face of Hong Kong's International Air Transport Relations, 20 *Case W. Res. J. Int'l L.*, pp. 202-203(1988).

〔3〕　截至1987年,英国与下列国家签订的双边民航协定延伸适用于香港:澳大利亚、缅甸、加拿大、锡兰、法国、德国、印度、印度尼西亚、意大利、日本、肯尼亚、韩国、科威特、黎巴嫩、马来西亚、新西兰、菲律宾、葡萄牙、新加坡、南非、瑞士、泰国和美国。See Gary N. Heilbronn, Hong Kong's First Bilateral Air Service Agreement: A Milestone in Air Law and an Exercise in Limited Sovereignty, 18 *HKLJ*, pp. 64-65, note 2; 219, note 133 (1988).

〔4〕　详见《香港政府宪报》(第2号特别副刊),1985年,第B44-B46页。

〔5〕　协定文本载于《香港政府宪报》(第5号特别副刊)(*Special Supplement No. 5 to Gazette*),第129卷第26期,第E201—E233页。《1986年9月17日协定的修正案》(Amendment to the Agreement of 17.9.86),载《香港政府宪报》(第5号特别副刊),第139卷第2期,第E3—E30页。

〔6〕　See Gary N. Heilbronn, Hong Kong's First Bilateral Air Service Agreement: A Milestone in Air Law and an Exercise in Limited Sovereignty, 18 *HKLJ*, pp. 64-65,75 (1988).

个国家签订的民航协定相继生效：加拿大(1988 年 6 月 24 日)[1]、文莱(1989 年 1 月 9 日)[2]、新西兰(1991 年 2 月 22 日)[3]、马来西亚(1991 年 3 月 4 日)[4]、法国(1991 年 5 月 10 日)[5]瑞士(1993 年 2 月 1 日)[6]、斯里兰卡(1993 年 2 月 24 日)[7]、澳大利亚(1993 年 9 月 15 日)[8]、巴西(1994 年 3 月 16 日)[9]、新加坡(1996 年 4 月 30 日)[10]、韩国(1996 年 7 月 9 日)[11]、印度(1996 年 10 月 10 日)[12]、美国(1997 年 4 月 7 日)[13]、缅甸(1997 年 6 月 11 日)[14]、泰国(1997 年 6 月 12 日)[15]、日本(1997 年 6 月 18 日)[16]、德国(1997 年 6 月 23 日)[17]、菲律宾(1997 年 6 月 26 日)[18]和印度尼西亚(1997 年 6 月 27 日)[19]。

1997 年 7 月 25 日，香港特区与英国签订了民航协定。[20] 这是香港特区根据《联合声明》《基本法》的有关规定和中国外交部长授权函，以"中国香港"名义单独与外国签订双边条约的第一例，缔约对方为英国，具有重要的历史意义。随后，香港特区继续积极与外国商签双边民航协定。截至 2001 年 5 月 10 日，香港特区与英国(1997 年 7 月 25 日)、意大利(1998 年 1 月 19 日)[21]、巴基斯坦(1998 年 2 月 17 日)[22]、巴林(1998 年 3 月 3 日)[23]、阿联酋(1998 年 4 月 29 日)[24]、马尔代夫(1998 年 5 月 18

---

[1] 《香港政府宪报》(第 5 号特别副刊)，第 130 卷第 45 期，第 E171—E218 页；《1988 年 6 月 24 日航空服务协定修正案》(Amendment to the Air Services Agreement of 24.6.1988)，载同上刊，第 138 卷第 36 期，第 E357—E374 页。

[2] 《香港政府宪报》(第 5 号特别副刊)，第 131 卷第 4 期，第 E3—E46 页。

[3] 《香港政府宪报》(第 5 号特别副刊)，第 133 卷第 9 期，第 E3—E34 页；《1991 年 2 月 22 日协定修正案》(Amendment to the Agreement of 22.2.91)，载同上刊，第 138 卷第 34 期，第 E341—E354 页。

[4] 《香港政府宪报》(第 5 号特别副刊)，第 133 卷第 10 期，第 E37—E88 页。

[5] 《香港政府宪报》(第 5 号特别副刊)，第 132 卷第 36 期，第 E153—E202 页。

[6] 《香港政府宪报》(第 5 号特别副刊)，第 130 卷第 6 期，第 E5—E38 页。

[7] 《香港政府宪报》(第 5 号特别副刊)，第 135 卷第 8 期，第 E3—E64 页。

[8] 《香港政府宪报》(第 5 号特别副刊)，第 135 卷第 37 期，第 E67—E102 页。

[9] 《香港政府宪报》(第 5 号特别副刊)，第 133 卷第 38 期，第 E215—E265 页。

[10] 《香港政府宪报》(第 5 号特别副刊)，第 138 卷第 20 期，第 E155—E189 页。

[11] 《香港政府宪报》(第 5 号特别副刊)，第 138 卷第 2 期，第 E97—E153 页。

[12] 《香港政府宪报》(第 5 号特别副刊)，第 138 卷第 45 期，第 E431—E477 页。

[13] 《香港政府宪报》(第 5 号特别副刊)，第 139 卷第 18 期，第 E211—E250 页。

[14] 《香港政府宪报》(第 5 号特别副刊)，第 139 卷第 13 期，第 E123—E151 页。

[15] 《香港政府宪报》(第 5 号特别副刊)，第 139 卷第 15 期，第 E155—E208 页。

[16] 《香港政府宪报》(第 5 号特别副刊)，第 139 卷第 12 期，第 E69—E119 页。

[17] 《香港政府宪报》(第 5 号特别副刊)，第 137 卷第 19 期，第 E27—E92 页；《1995 年 5 月 5 日航空服务协定修正案》(Amendment to the Air Services Agreement of 5.5.1995)，载同上刊，第 139 卷第 21 期，第 E483—E500 页。

[18] 《香港政府宪报》(第 5 号特别副刊)，第 139 卷第 23 期，第 E503—E537 页。

[19] 《香港政府宪报》(第 5 号特别副刊)，第 139 卷第 24 期，第 E541—E575 页。

[20] 《香港政府宪报》(第 5 号特别副刊)，第 1 卷第 6 期，第 E47—E88 页。

[21] 《香港政府宪报》(第 5 号特别副刊)，第 138 卷第 45 期，第 E377—E429 页。

[22] 《香港政府宪报》(第 5 号特别副刊)，第 2 卷第 12 期，第 E69—E105 页。

[23] 《香港政府宪报》(第 5 号特别副刊)，第 2 卷第 17 期，第 E109—E172 页。

[24] 《香港政府宪报》(第 5 号特别副刊)，第 3 卷第 3 期，第 E3—E68 页。

日)[1]、毛里求斯(1998 年 7 月 3 日)[2]、以色列(1998 年 9 月 8 日)[3]、尼泊尔(1998
年 10 月 29 日)[4]、奥地利(1998 年 12 月 1 日)[5]、阿曼(1999 年 3 月 26 日)[6]、吉尔
吉斯(1999 年 7 月 15 日)[7]、越南(1999 年 9 月 10 日)[8]、白俄罗斯(1999 年 12 月 3
日)[9]、柬埔寨(2000 年 1 月 17 日)[10]、瑞典(2000 年 3 月 14 日)[11]、丹麦(2000 年 3
月 14 日)[12]、南非(2000 年 3 月 18 日)[13]、芬兰(2000 年 4 月 1 日)[14]、蒙古(2000 年
5 月 4 日)[15]、挪威(2000 年 6 月 2 日)[16]、立陶宛(2000 年 7 月 7 日)[17]和孟加拉国
(2000 年 10 月 24 日)等 23 个国家签署的民航协定也先后生效。

目前,香港与外国签订并生效的民航协定已达 43 个。其中,为取代原在香港适
用的英国与外国民航协定或安排而签署的有 23 个,另有 20 个则反映了香港单独与
外国建立的全新的民航关系。这一实践充分表明了香港过渡期以来力图保持并发
展其对外民航关系的积极姿态。

2. 香港与外国之间的投资协定

双边投资条约一般指缔约国之间确定有关跨国投资的权利义务关系的协议,主
要有"友好通商航海条约""美国式投资保证协议"以及"德国式促进和保护投资协
定"(以下简称"双边投资协定")三种形式。其中,旨在促进和保护跨国投资的、兼有
实体性和程序性规定的双边投资协定产生于 50 年代后期,为各国广泛接受,逐渐发
展成为双边投资条约的最普遍形式。双边投资协定的缔约方均为主权国家。典型
的是一方为欧洲国家,另一方为发展中国家。德国和瑞士在这方面居领先地位。英
国自 1974 年起参与双边投资协定的谈判。[18]正如对外民航关系,在英占时期,香港

---

〔1〕《香港政府宪报》(第 5 号特别副刊),第 2 卷第 23 期,第 E191—E211 页。
〔2〕《香港政府宪报》(第 5 号特别副刊),第 3 卷第 9 期,第 E111—E146 页。
〔3〕《香港政府宪报》(第 5 号特别副刊),第 2 卷第 44 期,第 E449—E512 页。
〔4〕《香港政府宪报》(第 5 号特别副刊),第 3 卷第 9 期,第 E147—E180 页。
〔5〕《香港政府宪报》(第 5 号特别副刊),第 3 卷第 11 期,第 E183—E245 页。
〔6〕《香港政府宪报》(第 5 号特别副刊),第 3 卷第 12 期,第 E249—E318 页。
〔7〕《香港政府宪报》(第 5 号特别副刊),第 3 卷第 31 期,第 E527—E575 页。
〔8〕《香港政府宪报》(第 5 号特别副刊),第 4 卷第 50 期,第 E1255—E1293 页。
〔9〕《香港政府宪报》(第 5 号特别副刊),第 4 卷第 8 期,第 E3—E34 页。
〔10〕《香港政府宪报》(第 5 号特别副刊),第 4 卷第 52 期,第 E1297—E1371 页。
〔11〕《香港政府宪报》(第 5 号特别副刊),第 5 卷第 9 期,第 E87—E125 页。
〔12〕《香港政府宪报》(第 5 号特别副刊),第 5 卷第 7 期,第 E3—E41 页。
〔13〕《香港政府宪报》(第 5 号特别副刊),第 4 卷第 37 期,第 E1213—E1252 页。
〔14〕《香港政府宪报》(第 5 号特别副刊),第 4 卷第 36 期,第 E1175—E1210 页。
〔15〕《香港政府宪报》(第 5 号特别副刊),第 4 卷第 35 期,第 E1121—E1172 页。
〔16〕《香港政府宪报》(第 5 号特别副刊),第 5 卷第 8 期,第 E45—E83 页。
〔17〕《香港政府宪报》(第 5 号特别副刊),第 2 卷第 29 期,第 E355—E387 页。
〔18〕关于英国双边投资条约实践情况,参见 Eileen Denza, Shelagh Brooks, Investment Protection Treaties:
United Kingdom Experience, 36 *Int'l & Com. L. Q.*, pp. 908-923 (1987)。

的对外投资关系也是由英国与外国的双边投资协定（以下简称"英外投资协定"）调整。英国通过"领土延伸"的换文将一些英外投资协定延伸适用于香港。[1]此类协定在香港的法律效力也仅延续至1997年6月30日。为了保持和发展香港的对外投资关系，香港面临两种选择：一是中国签订的双边投资协定的适用范围在1997年7月1日后扩及香港，二是香港以其名义单独同外国签订双边投资协定。香港选择后者。鉴于香港与中国内地之间经济和法律制度的重大差异以及在国际投资活动中的不同地位，[2]这一选择将更能适应香港的实际需要，并且更有效地服务于促进和保护香港对外投资和外来投资的目标。

　　1992年11月19日，《香港政府与荷兰王国政府关于鼓励投资和保护投资协定》在香港正式签署，1993年9月1日正式生效，[3]首开由非主权实体签订双边投资协定的先河。其后，香港与澳大利亚（1993年10月15日）[4]、丹麦（1994年3月4日）[5]、瑞典（1994年6月26日）[6]、瑞士（1994年10月22日）[7]、新西兰（1995年8月5日）[8]、法国（1997年5月30日）[9]、日本（1997年6月18日）[10]、韩国（1997年7月30日）[11]、奥地利（1997年10月1日）[12]、德国（1998年2月19日）[13]、意大利（1998年2月2日）[14]、英国（1999年4月12日）[15]以及比利时—卢森堡（2001

---

〔1〕　英国参与缔结的双边投资条约通常在定义条款中对领土作定义，该条款进一步提及关于领土延伸的单独规定。例如，英国与斯里兰卡投资协定第1条规定：

　　　"（e）'领土'指

　　　（i）对于英国：大不列颠和北爱尔兰以及本协定根据第11条规定延伸适用的任何领土；……"

　　第11条规定：

　　　"在本协定批准时，或其后任何时间，经缔约双方以换文形式同意，本协定的规定可延伸适用于英国政府负责其国际关系的领土。"

　　然而，应注意的是，此类延伸适用的换文生效的时间迟于协定本身。例如，英国与约旦投资协定于1980年生效，而有关延伸适用该协定于香港的换文延至1984年5月14日生效。有关延伸适用英国与斯里兰卡投资协定于香港的换文则在协定生效后的一个月生效。See Rudolf Dolzer, Margrete Stevens, *Bilateral Investment Treaties*, Martinus Nijhoff Publishers, pp. 42-43(1995).

〔2〕　在国际投资活动中，香港属资本输出地区，而中国大陆属资本输入地区。

〔3〕　《香港政府宪报》（第5号特别副刊），第134卷第50期，第E25—E53页。

〔4〕　《香港政府宪报》（第5号特别副刊），第135卷第37期，第E103—E123页。

〔5〕　《香港政府宪报》（第5号特别副刊），第136卷第6期，第E19—E48页。

〔6〕　《香港政府宪报》（第5号特别副刊），第136卷第23期，第E51—E78页。

〔7〕　《香港政府宪报》（第5号特别副刊），第136卷第48期，第E85—E116页。

〔8〕　《香港政府宪报》（第5号特别副刊），第137卷第34期，第E95—E115页。

〔9〕　《香港政府宪报》（第5号特别副刊），第2卷第26期，第E215—E240页。

〔10〕　《香港政府宪报》（第5号特别副刊），第2卷第26期，第E241—E281页。

〔11〕　《香港政府宪报》（第5号特别副刊），第2卷第26期，第E283—E316页。

〔12〕　《香港政府宪报》（第5号特别副刊），第2卷第26期，第E317—E351页。

〔13〕　《香港政府宪报》（第5号特别副刊），第2卷第10期，第E39—E66页。

〔14〕　《香港政府宪报》（第5号特别副刊），第2卷第6期，第E3—E35页。

〔15〕　《香港政府宪报》（第5号特别副刊），第3卷第15期，第E391—E414页。

年)[1]等 14 国签订的 13 个双边投资协定相继生效。

涉及香港特区单独缔约权的第一个问题是,过渡期香港单独与外国签订的双边协定在 1997 年 7 月 1 日之后的适用问题及其与香港特区签订的同类协定的关系问题。过渡期香港单独与外国签订的双边条约,原则上成为香港特区单独缔约实践中遵循的先例。[2]其理由首先是,这些条约的效力已跨越 1997 年 7 月 1 日持续有效;[3]其次,这些条约基于《联合声明》的有关规定以及香港的实际情况,其实体性规定不同于中国签订的有关双边条约,因此为香港特区的双边条约实践积累了宝贵经验。在程序性方面,这些条约也为香港特区提供了重要的参考性模式。

第二个问题是单独缔约的授权程序问题。《联合声明》附件一第 11 条第 1 款和《基本法》第 151 条规定尚不清楚的是,香港特区在从事单独缔约活动中,是否必须逐项事先与中央人民政府协商并在缔约之前取得中央人民政府批准。如果这种逐项的事先协商和批准不是必要的,香港特区就具有在这些领域中处理对外事务的决策性自治权。[4]

1997 年 7 月 7 日,中国外交部驻香港特区特派员公署特派员向香港特区行政长官转交了中国外交部长的一封授权函。该授权函通知,中央人民政府已授权香港特区在航班过境、促进和保护投资、移交逃犯、移交被判刑人和刑事司法协助等五个领域与有关国家就双边协定展开谈判。[5]从 1997 年 7 月 1 日至 1999 年 7 月 1 日,中央人民政府根据《基本法》向香港特区政府颁发了 130 项授权文件,授权其与有关国家谈判和签署涉及上述五个领域的双边协定,还一次性授权香港特区政府与其他国家(未建交国除外)谈判互免签证协议或作出行政安排;审核了香港特区政府需报请中央人民政府核准的 45 个双边协议草签文本;[6]并向联合国和国际民航组织登记了香港特区与英国、以色列等 12 个国家签署的双边民航协定。[7]从上述实践看,除谈判互免签证协议或作出行政安排采取"一次性授权"形式外,香港特区与外国签订双边协定一般采取逐项授权的形式。

---

〔1〕《香港政府宪报》(第 5 号特别副刊),第 5 卷第 25 期。

〔2〕 See Gary N. Heilbronn, Hong Kong's First Bilateral Air Service Agreement: A Milestone in Air Law and an Exercise in Limited Sovereignty, 18 *HKLJ*, pp. 64-65 (1988).

〔3〕香港双边民航协定没有确定的期限规定,此类协定为其本身的终止所规定的原因为单方解约。在香港双边投资协定中,详细规定了协定的有效期限。例如,香港与荷兰投资协定和香港与瑞士投资协定有效期为 15 年,其后在不须言明的情况下延长 10 年,缔约各方有权在当时有效期限届满之前至少 12 个月通知对方终止协定。可见,这些协定的期限可以跨越 1997 年 7 月 1 日,对 1997 年 7 月 1 日以后也未作特别的期限安排。这从一个侧面反映了缔约对方当时相信香港将平稳向香港特区过渡,1997 年 7 月 1 日后香港的国际地位将保持不变。

〔4〕 See Albert H. Y. Chen, Some Reflections on Hong Kong's Autonomy, 24 *HKLJ*, p. 177 (1994).

〔5〕参见《外交部驻港特派员马毓真拜会董建华》,载《厦门日报》1997 年 7 月 8 日第 3 版。

〔6〕 http://www.fmcoprc.gov.hk/fmco-p4/fmco-p4-bl.htm/08/08/2001

〔7〕 http://www.fmprc.gov.cn/chn/2400.html/08/08/2001

（二）参加国际会议和国际组织的权利

根据《联合声明》附件一第 11 条第 1 款和《基本法》第 152 条规定，对以国家为单位参加的、同香港特区有关的、适当领域的国际组织和国际会议，香港特区政府可派遣代表作为中国代表团的成员或以中央人民政府和上述有关国际组织或国际会议允许的身份参加，并以"中国香港"的名义发表意见。香港特区可以"中国香港"的名义参加不以国家为单位参加的国际组织和国际会议。对中国已参加而香港也以某种形式参加了的国际组织，中央人民政府将采取必要措施使香港特区以适当形式继续保持在这些组织中的地位。对中国尚未参加而香港已以某种形式参加的国际组织，中央人民政府将根据需要使香港特区以适当形式继续参加这些组织。

自 1985 年起，中英双方就香港与有关国际组织的关系问题进行了多次磋商，并就香港特区继续参加 34 个政府间国际组织的活动问题达成了共识。1997 年 6 月，中国外交部明确表示，自 1997 年 7 月 1 日起，香港特区可以中国政府代表团成员身份参加国际民航组织、国际货币基金组织等 19 个政府间国际组织的活动和出席有关会议，还可以成员、联系成员等身份，以"中国香港"名义参加亚洲开发银行、国际海事组织等 15 个政府间国际组织的活动。上述有关安排符合《联合声明》和《基本法》的有关规定以及有关国际组织的章程，也符合香港的区域性实体地位和实际需要。中国外交部已先后向 34 个国际组织采取外交行动，递交照会，说明香港特区与这些国际组织的关系以及参加其有关活动的方式。[1]

这方面最典型的范例是，香港通过中英两国政府的分别声明，成为关税及贸易总协定（GATT）的正式成员。1986 年 4 月 23 日，英国声明并通知 GATT 总干事，香港在处理其对外商务关系和 GATT 规定的其他事项中具有充分的自治权。根据 GATT 第 26 条第 5 款第 3 项规定，并根据香港的意愿，香港将被视为缔约方，自本声明之日起生效。中国同时发表相应的声明，确认香港的 GATT 缔约方地位。从法律程序上说，只有英国的声明使香港取得了 GATT 的缔约方地位，中国的声明只是表明中国对上述事实的认可，其意义是向 GATT 各缔约方表明，香港是中国领土的一部分，并承诺 1997 年 7 月 1 日后中国对香港恢复行使主权将不影响香港继续其在 GATT 的缔约方地位。

1995 年 1 月 1 日《世界贸易组织协定》生效，世界贸易组织取代 GATT。根据该协定的有关规定，香港基于其本身的权利，即 GATT 缔约方的地位，于 1995 年成为

---

[1] 《就香港特区继续参加国际组织活动外交部发言人发表谈话》，载《人民日报》1997 年 6 月 25 日第 4 版。

WTO 的创始成员,并于 1997 年 7 月 1 日起更名为"中国香港"。[1] 就国际法而言,香港可以成为 WTO 成员首先是由于 WTO 的成员资格不限于国家。香港作为在对外商务关系活动中具有完全自治权的单独关税区,本身符合 WTO 成员的条件。其次,是基于《中英联合声明》和《基本法》的规定。《基本法》第 116 条进一步明确规定,香港特区是"单独的关税地区",可以"中国香港"的名义参加《关税和贸易总协定》。

在实践中,作为 WTO 的创始成员,香港向 WTO 各机构选派代表,香港代表还经常被任命为 WTO 分理事会、委员会、专家组的主席或副主席。2001 年 2 月,香港驻 WTO 的常任代表 Stuart Harbinson 先生以其个人身份被选为 WTO 总理事会2001 年度主席。香港通过贸易工业署和香港驻日内瓦经济贸易办事处,积极参与WTO 各委员会的工作,参加监督或评价 WTO 的实际运作和其他成员履行其承诺的各种讨论。在参与 WTO 的各项活动时,香港享有独立的发言权,可根据其本身的利益作出独立的决策。在 WTO 有关基础电讯和金融服务的谈判中,香港发挥了积极的作用。在 1996 年 12 月、1998 年 5 月、1999 年 11 月至 12 月分别于新加坡、日内瓦和西雅图召开的 WTO 第一、二、三届部长级会议上,香港均积极、建设性地参与有关活动。在贸易争端解决方面,香港独立行使其权利和义务。迄今,香港根据《关于争端解决规则和程序谅解书》第 10.2 条规定,成为三个 WTO 案件中的第三方。[2]这三个案件分别是"虾—海龟案"(The Shrimp-Turtle case)[3]、"土耳其数量限制案"[The Turkey Quantitative Restrictions (Quota) case][4] 和"美国 301 条款案"(The US Section 301 case)[5]。前两个案子诉诸上诉机构。在三个案子中,香港都向专家组提交书面陈述。对诉诸上诉机构的事项,香港也提交了书面陈述。[6]

---

〔1〕 值得注意的是,单独关税区成为 GATT 缔约方的条件,将与原由负责其国际关系的缔约方代表其接受GATT 时的条件相同。1948 年英国作为创始缔约方使 GATT 无条件适用于香港,1986 年香港根据 GATT 第 26 条第 5 款第 3 项成为单独缔约方,仍继续行使其原有权利,承担其原有义务。显然,香港不是以发展中成员的身份成为WTO 的创始成员。

〔2〕 即在特定 WTO 争端解决程序中,除争端当事人以外,对专家组审理的问题具有实质性利益关系的任何WTO 成员。

〔3〕 该案涉及美国采取的禁止从一些 WTO 成员进口虾的某些措施,旨在保护濒危动物海龟。香港关注的主要问题是,这些措施的实施是否符合 WTO 有关禁止专断的、歧视性的进口限制的原则。

〔4〕 该案涉及 WTO 成员土耳其对纺织品进口采取的限制措施。土耳其主张,该限制措施是其履行加入关税联盟或自由贸易区的责任所必需。这意味着在市场准入方面,非关税联盟或自由贸易区成员的 WTO 成员,一旦加入关税联盟或自由贸易区,将导致对其他 WTO 成员更不利的后果。这一原则性问题促使香港作为第三方参与该程序。

〔5〕 在该案中,香港关注的问题是,对 WTO 成员具有约束力的 WTO 争端解决机制与 WTO 成员美国国内法(《1974 年美国贸易法》)规定的单边制裁方式之间的关系。涉及此类国内立法是否符合《WTO 协定》,以及可否在WTO 争端解决程序中对此类国内立法提起申诉等问题。

〔6〕 David Little (Law Office, Department of Justice, Hong Kong), WTO Dispute Settlement: A Hong Kong Perspective, speech on Inter-Pacific Bar Association Conference "WTO Dispute Resolution System: Does It Work?", May, 2000.

1998 年 12 月，WTO 贸易政策检查组对香港特区的贸易政策和实践，包括货物、服务、工业产权以及香港的贸易和经济情况作了综合性检查。检查组称赞香港特区在 1997 年 7 月 1 日后，保持其开放的贸易和投资制度，并相信香港特区经济会很快摆脱亚洲金融危机的影响，恢复强劲和持续发展的势头，继续保持其世界上最开放经济体之一的地位。[1]

另一典型例子是中国香港特区与中国在亚太经济合作组织（Asia Pacific Economic Cooperation Conference，APEC）的成员资格。1991 年，中国与香港地区、台湾地区同时加入该组织。自 1997 年 7 月 1 日起，香港在该组织中正式更名为"中国香港"。在"一国两制"方针下，中国与中国香港可以继续代表各自的经济利益，不必以同一个声音发言。另外，基于"一国"的概念，中国香港可通过对 APEC 问题的研究和分析，帮助中国熟悉 APEC 的计划和参与 APEC 的活动。中国香港与东南亚国家联盟成员国多边的政府和商业联系可作为中国与这些国家非正式政府和商业联系的良好基础。[2]

据统计，1997 年 7 月 1 日至 1999 年 7 月 1 日，中央人民政府协助香港特区政府官员、包括外籍人员以中国政府代表团成员的资格出席国际会议 120 多次；授权香港特区政府自行签发单独参加国际会议的全权证书；以中央人民政府名义为香港特区政府申办亚洲电信展和国际药物规管会议，协助香港特区政府主办其他政府间国际会议 10 次；同意香港特区加入两个国际组织以及同意国际组织在香港设立两个办事处；协助香港特区政府制定《联合国制裁法》并立法执行联合国安理会通过的 17 项制裁决议。[3]

（三）适用国际协定的特别安排

根据 1969 年《维也纳条约法公约》第 29 条确立的规则，条约是否适用于各缔约国的全部领土，可由各缔约国依据意思自治原则协商确定，但如无明示或默示的相反意思，应认为条约适用于各缔约国的全部领土。[4]

《联合声明》附件一第 11 条第 2 款和《基本法》第 153 条规定，中国缔结的国际协定，中央人民政府可根据香港特区的情况和需要，在征询香港特区的意见后，决定是否适用于该地区；中国尚未参加但已适用于中国香港的国际协定仍可继续适用。中央人民政府根据需要授权或协助香港特区政府作出适当安排，使其他有关国际协议

---

[1]　WTO Members Commend Hong Kong for Its Free Trade Stance，*HK Files*，February 1999 Issue，p. 3.

[2]　See Cyril C. K. Chow, Michael C. M. Kwan, Hong Kong's Role in APEC under "One Country-Two Systems"，*Policy Bulletin*，No. 3，January 1998，p. 10.

[3]　http://www.fmcoprc.gov.hk/fmco-p4/fmco-p4-bl.htm/08/08/2001

[4]　中国于 1997 年 5 月 9 日加入《维也纳条约法公约》。

适用于香港特区。

上述规定显然排除了将中国缔结的所有国际条约不加分析地适用于香港特区的可能性,表明了中国采取的有选择、有条件适用的立场。这是因为考虑到,由于香港特区的历史和现状,特别是香港特区与中国内地社会经济和法律制度的重大差异,中央人民政府缔结的条约不一定能完全适用于香港。为了遵循和体现"一国两制"和香港特区高度自治的原则,中央人民政府庄严承诺,在决定特定国际条约是否适用于香港特区时,需要从实体上考察,以该条约符合香港特区的情况和需要为依据;在程序上,需要征询香港特区的意见。此外,对于中国尚未参加但已适用于中国香港的国际协定的继续适用问题,中国也持积极支持的态度。

1997 年 6 月 20 日,中国常驻联合国代表向联合国秘书长递交外交照会,全面阐述了中国政府关于香港特区适用国际条约的原则立场。照会的两个附件列明了自 1997 年 7 月 1 日起适用于香港特区的 214 项国际条约。照会特别提到,《公民权利和政治权利国际公约》和《经济、社会与文化权利的国际公约》适用于香港的规定,自 1997 年 7 月 1 日起继续有效。照会指出,未列入照会附件的、中国是当事方或将成为当事方的其他条约,如决定将继续适用于香港特区,中国政府将另行办理有关手续。对属于外交、国防类或根据条约的性质和规定必须适用于国家全部领土的条约,中国政府无须办理有关手续。[1]

1997 年 7 月 1 日以来,中国政府根据《联合声明》和《基本法》的规定,在国际公约适用于香港方面主要做了如下工作:

第一,处理香港回归前后国际公约适用于香港的遗留或后续问题。一方面是就中国未参加的公约适用于香港问题继续做缔约各方的工作,争取其支持和理解。例如,与香港特区联合组团参加经合组织核能署组织的磋商会,就《关于核能方面第三方责任公约》适用于香港问题直接与有关方面对话;就《修正 1971 年设立国际油污损害赔偿基金公约的 1992 年议定书》适用于香港问题出具书面文件,在该公约大会上散发;就《保护迁徙野生动物公约》保存机关提出的某些问题作出答复。目前,这些问题已基本圆满解决。另一方面是处理中国已参加的公约适用于香港的问题,如《关于禁止发展、生产、储存及使用化学武器以及销毁此类武器的公约》和《国际商标注册马德里议定书》等在港立法履约问题等。

第二,就中国拟参加的公约是否适用于香港征求香港特区意见,根据香港的情况和实际需要,就公约适用于香港问题作出特殊安排,并在参加制定新公约大会(如

---

〔1〕 王子珍:《就香港特别行政区适用的国际条约中国向联合国递交照会》,载《人民日报》(海外版)1997 年 6 月 23 日第 6 版。

《扣船公约》）时，为公约适用于香港提供法律意见，对公约作出适当修正以符合香港的特殊情况。从 1997 年 7 月 1 日至 1999 年底，除继续适用于香港的 214 项国际公约外，又有《维也纳条约法公约》等 8 个外交、国防类国际公约和《准予就业最低年龄公约》（即 138 号劳工公约）等 4 个非外交、国防类国际公约适用于香港特区；同时，《修正 1971 年设立国际油污损害赔偿基金公约的 1992 年议定书》仅适用于香港特区；在加入《国际植物新品种保护公约》时声明该公约暂不适用于香港特区。

第三，中央人民政府作为香港特区履行国际公约产生的权利与义务的承担者，继续为香港特区履行中国已参加或未参加的劳工公约、麻醉品公约以及人权公约等向公约保存机关递交报告、转发数据与资料，安排香港特区代表参加中国代表团出席公约机构对有关香港特区提交报告的审议会议。

第四，就香港特区提出的有关公约适用方面的问题作出研究和答复，如《联合国粮农组织公约》适用于香港等。[1]

值得注意的是，自 1997 年 7 月 1 日起，虽然同一国际条约适用于香港，就香港的对外关系而言，适用该条约的法律根据与法律后果发生了根本性变化。以 1958 年《承认与执行外国仲裁裁决公约》（以下简称《公约》）为例。1977 年，作为英国加入并决定延伸适用的结果，《公约》适用于香港。中国在 1987 年 4 月加入《公约》。其后至 1997 年 7 月 1 日之前，在香港作出的仲裁裁决可在约 90 个《公约》缔约国（包括中国）申请承认和执行。反之亦然。自 1997 年 7 月 1 日之后，由于香港特区适用《公约》的根据是基于中国的《公约》缔约国地位，中国内地与香港特区之间已不能相互承认和执行对方的仲裁裁决。在 1998 年 1 月香港法院审理的 Ng Fung Hong Ltd v. ABC 案中，法院接受的观点是，自 1997 年 7 月 1 日起，香港特区与中国内地已经不再是《公约》中相互独立的一方。[2] 而在 1997 年 10 月和 1998 年 1 月审理的 Hebei Import & Export Corporation v. Polytek Engineering Co Ltd 案中，香港法院认为，由于中国内地和香港特区是两个不同的法域，按《公约》的精神，1997 年 7 月 1 日之后中国内地的仲裁裁决在香港不能被视为"本地裁决"，《公约》仍适用于此类裁决。[3] 虽然这一意见同样注意到 1997 年 7 月 1 日之后在香港适用《公约》的法律根据的变化，但同时强调实行"一国两制"和香港特区的高度自治权。由于《公约》明文规定适用于缔约国之间（不包括同一缔约国不同法域之间）的仲裁裁决，此意见尚欠法律依据。

1999 年 6 月 21 日，中国内地和香港特区代表签署了《内地与香港特别行政区相

〔1〕 http://www.fmprc.gov.cn/chn/2400.html/08/08/2001
〔2〕 《香港判例报告与概要》（*Hong Kong Law Reports & Digest*），Vol. 1，pp. 155-157 (1998).
〔3〕 《香港判例报告与概要》（*Hong Kong Law Reports & Digest*），Vol. 1，pp. 287-303 (1998).

互执行仲裁裁决的安排》的备忘录。《安排》详细规定了两地法院受理和执行对方仲裁裁决的具体程序，将在两地通过发布司法解释和修改香港《仲裁条例》予以执行。[1] 2000 年 1 月 13 日，香港特区正式公布《2000 年仲裁（修订）条例》，废除旧《仲裁条例》中与《基本法》抵触的定义和内容，增加"内地"（the Mainland）、"内地裁决"（Mainland award）等概念，明确"内地裁决"不是"公约裁决"，确保了内地与香港仲裁裁决的相互执行，并体现了"一国两制"框架下两地仲裁制度的协调与合作。[2]

三、香港特区高度自治权的基本特征

香港特区基于高度自治权的对外事务实践从一个侧面表明，中国严格履行《联合声明》中的国际承诺，香港特区在法律上和事实上均享有高度自治权。与此同时，需要进一步指出，对比国外其他区域性自治实体，香港特区享有的高度自治权具有以下基本特征：

（一）香港特区高度自治权的授权性质

《基本法》第 12 条规定："香港特别行政区是中华人民共和国的一个享有高度自治权的地方行政区域，直辖于中央人民政府。"该规定明确了香港特区的法律地位，是理解香港特区高度自治权性质的关键。

中国是单一制国家，香港特区是中国不可分割的部分，是中央人民政府直辖的地方行政区域。这决定了香港特区的自治权只能是全国人大和中央人民政府授予的。而在联邦制国家中，其成员享有的自治权则是联邦政府与其成员分权的结果。

授权与分权是两个不同的概念，表达两种不同的权力关系。其主要区别在于：首先，授权是权力主体将原属于它的权力授予被授权者，被授权者的权力范围以授予的权力为限，未授予的权力仍保留于权力主体。而分权是两个或两个以上权力主体分割权力，除明确划分归属各权力主体的权力外，需要解决"剩余权力"（residual power）的归属问题。其次，在授权的情况下，权力主体对被授权者有监督权，而在分权的情况下，各权力主体独自行使其权力，各权力主体之间的争端由独立的第三方解决。

掌握授权与分权的区别，对于正确认识香港特区高度自治权，正确处理中央人民政府与香港特区之间的关系，至关重要。首先，由于在授权的情况下，并未产生"剩余权力"的问题，香港特区高度自治权以全国人大明示授予的为限，未明示授予的保留于中央人民政府。其次，由于中央人民政府对香港特区在其授权范围内行使

---

〔1〕　参见高莎薇：《内地与香港特别行政区相互执行对方仲裁裁决有章可循》，载《中国法律》1999 年 10 月号，第 18—20 页。

〔2〕　参见黎晓光：《香港〈2000 年仲裁（修订）条例〉评述》，载《仲裁与法律》2000 年第 2 期，第 52—55 页。

权力拥有监督权,在这个意义上,中央人民政府与香港特区并非平等的权力主体,两者之间的争端不能诉诸第三方解决。[1]

值得注意的是,授权与分权的区别与自治权的程度,并无必然联系。具体说来,联邦制国家的第二级实体所拥有的自治权程度,不一定高于单一制国家的第二级实体。无论是联邦制国家的第二级实体或是单一制国家的第二级实体,自治权程度的高低,取决于相关法律的规定。

必须指出,在强调《联合声明》《基本法》有关香港特区高度自治权的规定时,中国对香港恢复行使主权和《联合声明》《基本法》的相关规定也应予以同等重视。授予香港特区高度自治权应在中国对香港恢复行使主权的历史背景下考察。中国对香港恢复行使主权主要体现于外交权和国防权的行使。原则上,中央人民政府负责管理与香港特区有关的外交事务,香港特区对外交、国防等国家行为无管辖权。外交事务行为是主权权力的最显著象征,与国际经济交往行为比较,从实践观点看,前者具有更重要的意义。另外,《基本法》授权香港特区依照该法自行处理有关对外事务,具有范围广泛的高度自治权,中央人民政府实际保留的"仅仅是特别行政区因其不是国家而不能以'中国香港'名义进行的跨国或对外关系的那部分权力"。[2]然而,无论香港特区的高度自治权范围如何广泛,均来自中央人民政府的授权。香港特区在国际法律关系中的权利能力和行为能力是由中央人民政府授予的,因此是有限的、相对的。虽然中央人民政府将其对外交往的诸多权力授予香港特区行使,但真正的主权和最终权力仍保留在中央人民政府。[3]

(二) 香港特区高度自治权的法律根据

如上所述,在国际实践中,有的自治实体,如所谓"国际领土"的地位及其自治权是由国际条约确立的。[4]鉴此,有的西方学者主张,香港特区也是国际条约的产物,香港特区高度自治权不是特定国家根据国内法的授权;《联合声明》创设和保障了香

---

〔1〕 参见王叔文主编:《香港特别行政区基本法导论》,中共中央党校出版社 1990 年版,第 83—90 页。

〔2〕 See Roda Mushkat, The Transition from British to Chinese Rule in Hong Kong: A Discussion of Salient International Legal Issues, 14 *Den. J. Int'l L. & Pol'y*, p. 188 (1986).

〔3〕 See Marius Olivier, Hong Kong: An Exercise in Autonomy, 18 *South African Yearbook of Int'l L.*, pp. 61-62, 81-82, 87-88 (1992-93).

〔4〕 例如,根据《但泽自由条约》(Free Treaty of Danzig),但泽(Danzig)在 1920—1939 年被视为由国际法原则和规则调整的享有法律人格的自由城市。See Roda Mushkat, Hong Kong as an International Legal Person, 6 *Emory International Law Review*, pp. 109-110 (1992).

港的特殊地位,并保留了香港的自治权利。[1] 有的西方学者主张,香港特区类似欧洲中世纪具有经济、政治和法律独立性的"自由城市"(free cities)。[2] 此类观点显然是错误和片面的,因为它不适当地夸大了《联合声明》的作用,而忽略了《联合声明》有关规定的法律根源。

诚然,由于香港特区高度自治权的法律依据包括了国内法和国际法,香港特区可归属于混合类自治实体。然而,在双重法律依据中,有主从之分,层次之分。应当明确,香港特区高度自治权的法律根据首先是 1982 年《中华人民共和国宪法》(以下简称《宪法》)。《宪法》第 31 条规定:"国家在必要时得设立特别行政区。在特别行政区内实行的制度按照具体情况由全国人民代表大会以法律规定。"

《宪法》作为国家的根本大法,是中国国际条约实践和国内立法的基础和根据。

在国际条约实践中,中国以《宪法》第 31 条为依据,谈判和签署了《联合声明》,决定设立香港特区。《联合声明》第 3 条第 1 款明确指出,"为了维护国家的统一和领土完整,并考虑到香港的历史和现实情况,中华人民共和国决定在对香港恢复行使主权时,根据中华人民共和国宪法第 31 条的规定,设立香港特别行政区"。《联合声明》的一系列关于香港特区高度自治权的规定均为中国基于《宪法》第 31 条所作的政策声明和国际承诺。[3]

在国内立法方面,《基本法》在序言中重申了设立香港特区的《宪法》根据,[4]并进一步对香港特区享有的自治权范围作了具体明确的规定。

显然,香港特区是《宪法》的产物,[5]同时也由《联合声明》予以确认和保障。在理解香港特区高度自治权时,特别需要认识《宪法》作为决定性的第一级法律根据或法律根源的重要作用。《联合声明》有关规定尽管也可援引为香港特区高度自治权的法律根据,但毕竟是属于第二级的,并且明确属于"中国对香港的基本方针政策"的声明内容。如果将《联合声明》有关规定作为香港特区高度自治权的唯一根据,并

---

〔1〕　See Roda Mushkat, Hong Kong as an International Legal Person, 6 *Emory International Law Review*, p. 110 (1992); Brian Z. Tamanaha, Post-1997 Hong Kong: A Comparative Study of the Meaning of "High Degree of Autonomy" with a Specific Look at the Commonwealth of the Nothern Mariana Islands, 5 *China Law Reporter*, p. 168 (1989).

〔2〕　See Eric Johnson, Hong Kong after 1997: A Free City?, 40 *German Yearbook of International Law*, pp. 402-404. (1997).

〔3〕　参见《联合声明》第 3 条第 1 款和《联合声明》附件 1 第 1 条。

〔4〕　《基本法》序言指出:"为了维护国家的统一和领土完整,保持香港的繁荣和稳定,并考虑到香港的历史和现实情况,国家决定,在对香港恢复行使主权时,根据中华人民共和国宪法第三十一条的规定,设立香港特别行政区,并按照'一个国家,两种制度'的方针,不在香港实行社会主义制度和政策。"

〔5〕　See Albert H. Y. Chen, Further Aspects of the Autonomy of Hong Kong under the PRC Constitution, 14 *HKLJ*, p. 343 (1984).

据此强调香港特区的"国际化"，将香港特区混同于所谓"国际领土"或"自由城市"，[1]实属牵强附会，是违背客观现实的。

应当指出，享有高度自治权的香港特区与享有自治权的所谓"国际领土"或"自由城市"有本质的区别：前者是直辖于中国中央人民政府的地方行政区域，是主权国家宪政体制中不可分割的组成部分，其权利和义务主要由中国国内法确立和调整；而后者则是在特定历史条件下，主权归属或国内法地位尚未确定的区域实体，其权利和义务主要由国际条约确立和调整。

（三）香港特区高度自治权的国际保障

香港特区高度自治权不仅取决于香港、中国或英国的单方面愿望，也取决于其他国家是否承认这种地位。[2]

过渡期香港双边条约的实践，由于众多主权国家的积极参与，已为国际社会，特别是那些对同非主权实体签订双边条约持犹豫观望立场的国家起了示范作用，必将在很大程度上为香港特区铺平双边条约谈判的道路。[3]另外，由于过渡期以来香港根据《联合声明》和《基本法》有关规定精神签订和加入的双边和多边条约与众多国家相联系，香港特区的高度自治权已得到国际社会的普遍接受并将受到持续性的国际监督。香港特区计划进一步扩大其双边和多边条约关系。随着时间的推移和香港特区对外交往实践的进一步发展，由香港特区参与的双边和多边条约构成的国际法网络一旦形成，香港特区的高度自治权地位将受到国内法和国际法的充分保障。

20 世纪 90 年代以来，美国和欧盟相继颁布了涉及香港特区自治权地位的法律和决议。1992 年，美国出于某些法律和政治目的的需要，颁布了《美国—香港政策法》。虽然在该法中有关香港自治权的规定未超出《联合声明》和《基本法》的范围，但它规定了制裁性条款。[4]1997 年 4 月 10 日，欧洲议会通过了有关香港情况的决

---

〔1〕 See Roda Mushkat, Hong Kong as an International Legal Person, 6 *Emory International Law Review*, pp. 109-111(1992).

〔2〕 See Albert H. Y. Chen, Some Reflections on Hong Kong's Autonomy, 24 *HKLJ*, pp. 179-180 (1994).

〔3〕 See Gary N. Heilbronn, The Changing Face of Hong Kong's International Air Transport Relations, 20 *Case W. Res. J. Int'l L.*, p. 223 (1988).

〔4〕 此类制裁性条款如，美国总统如果判定香港未达到充分的自治程度，致使美国根据特别法或有关法律规定对香港适用不同于中国大陆的待遇成为不适当，他可中止有关美国法律对香港的适用。此外，该法还规定，在 1993—2000 年期间，美国政府要向国会报告涉及美国利益的香港情况，包括香港民主制度的发展等。See Yash Ghai, *Hong Kong's New Constitutional Order*, *The Resumption of Chinese Sovereign and the Basic Law*, Hong Kong University Press, pp. 459-461 (1997).

议,表明了欧盟对香港 1997 年 7 月 1 日以后的关注。[1] 1997 年 4 月 23 日,欧盟委员会向欧盟理事会和欧洲议会提交一份题为《欧盟与香港:1997 年之后》的通告(Communication),概括了加强欧盟与香港之间关系的战略。[2]

应当指出,从法律观点看,就香港特区高度自治权问题,中国通过《联合声明》对英国作了国际法上的承诺,然而,中国未对美国、欧盟或国际社会整体作出同样法律性质的承诺。香港特区的自治权本质上属中国内政。因此,外国的法律和国际组织的文件单方面制定的涉及香港特区自治权地位的规定缺乏法律根据,违背了"互不干涉内政"的国际法原则。

四、结语

中国香港特区享有范围广泛的法律上的高度自治权,这是英占时期的香港所无法比拟的。香港特区高度自治权的法律设计独具一格,也与国内场合或国际场合的其他自治实体迥然有别。应当明确,香港特区的高度自治权是全国人大和中央人民政府根据《宪法》第 31 条规定,通过《联合声明》和《基本法》授予和确立的,具有国内法和国际法的双重保障。在此双重法律结构中,《宪法》是第一级法律根据或法律根源;《联合声明》和《基本法》是根据《宪法》第 31 条签订和制定的,属第二级法律根据。在这个意义上,香港特区高度自治权的决定性法律基础是中国国内法。

在过渡期,遵循《联合声明》和《基本法》的有关规定精神,在对外事务方面,香港已有许多体现高度自治权的成功实践,为香港特区提供了宝贵的经验和模式。1997 年 7 月 1 日以来,中国中央人民政府严格履行在《联合声明》中的国际承诺和《基本法》的有关规定,香港特区高度自治权的实际行使有了良好的开端,受到国际社会的普遍理解、接受和支持。事实表明,香港特区的高度自治权已通过香港过渡期以来签订和加入的双边和多边国际条约以及加入国际组织等国际实践不断得到加强和保障。

---

〔1〕　在该文件中,欧洲议会要求香港的"主权移交"严格按照《联合声明》和《基本法》的规定进行。它还要求欧盟理事会制订发展欧盟与香港之间关系的计划,要求欧盟委员会提交有关香港特区政治、经济和人权问题的年度报告。欧洲议会还决定关注香港特区的情况,特别是通过派遣考察团来达此目的。See European Commission, *Bulletin of the European Union*, 4-1997, p. 89.

〔2〕　该文件内容包括,与香港特区政府直接进行和保持经常性的紧密联系,继续将香港视为贸易政策意义的独立实体和世贸组织中的重要伙伴,关注香港的情况和尊重香港特区授予其居民的权利,与国际社会一起工作,发表有关欧盟与香港之间各方面关系的年度报告,继续让香港政府以其本身的名义参与共同签证名单,探讨建立香港与欧盟之间更长期性的贸易、投资和合作关系的途径以及发展以香港作为亚洲中心的积极合作。See European Commission, *Bulletin of the European Union*, 4-1997, pp. 88-89.

第二节 Unprecedented International Status: Theoretical and Practical Aspects of the HKSAR's External Autonomy[*]
（史无前例的国际地位：香港特别行政区对外自治权的理论与实践）

According to the Sino-British Joint Declaration on the Question of Hong Kong (hereinafter the JD),[1] after 1 July 1997, the Hong Kong Special Administrative Region (hereinafter the HKSAR) shall enjoy a high degree of autonomy and retain its capitalist system and own institutions, including the pre-existing legal system and independent judicial authority for a period of 50 years. Would the concept of "one country two systems" be realized in the HKSAR? What is the meaning of the phrase "high degree of autonomy" in the context of the HKSAR? Could the HKSAR retain its pre-existing international status after 1997? There are many comments before and after 1997. Some are affirmative[2] while some are doubtful.[3] The question is what extent an empirical inquiry lends support to this claim of a high degree of autonomy.[4] In addition to the HKSAR's internal autonomy, international lawyers

---

[*] Unprecedented International Status: Theoretical and Practical Aspects of the HKSAR's External Autonomy, *The Journal of World Investment & Trade*, ISSN 1660-7112, Vol. 9, No. 3, 2008.

[1] Joint Declaration of the Government of the United Kingdom of Great Britain and Northern Ireland and the Government of the People's Republic of China on the Question of Hong Kong was formally signed on 19 December 1984 and came into force on 27 May 1985. The agreement was reprinted in 23 *ILM* 1371-1380 (1984).

[2] See Jack Chan, "Hong Kong's Role after 1997", 12 *Loy. L. A. Int'l & Com L. J.*, 58-60 (1989). Some observers made their affirmative comments based on that China has good records in observing international treaties. See Deborah L. Bayles, "The Reunification of China: An Examination of the Legal Systems of the People's Republic of China, Hong Kong and Taiwan", 19 *Den. J. Int'l. L. & Pol'y.* 463 (1991); Roda Mushkat, "The Transition from British to Chinese Rule in Hong Kong: A Discussion of Salient International Legal Issues", 14 *Den. J. Int'l L. & Pol'y*, 193 (1986). Some comments based on that there are strong diplomatic, economic and military reasons for China to preserve the basic capitalistic structure of Hong Kong. See Christian C. Day, "The Recovery of Hong Kong by the People's Republic of China-A fifty years Experiment in Capitalism and Freedom", 11 *Syr. J. Int'l L. & Com.* 643-649 (1989); Johnson C. Ng, "Hong Kong after 1997: An Experimental Governmental Practising Capitalism within a Socialist Sovereign", 10 *N. Y. L. Sch. J. Int'l L.* 92-93 (1989).

[3] See David A. Jones, Jr., "A Leg to Stand on? Post-1997 Hong Kong Courts as a Constraint on PRC Abridgement of Individual Rights and Local Autonomy", 12 *Yale J. Int'l L.* 292 (1987); David M. Corwin, "China's Choices: The 1984 Sino-British Joint Declaration and Its Aftermath", 19 *L. & Pol. in Int'l Bus.* 518-519, 526-528 (1987); Eric Johnson, "Hong Kong after 1997: A Free City?" 40 *German Yearbook of International Law*, 404 (1997); "Hong Kong One Year after the Handover", *Inside China Mainland*, September 1998, 19-23.

[4] Marius Olivier, "Hong Kong: An Exercise in Autonomy", 18 *South African Yearbook of Int'l L.* 62 (1992-93).

are more interested in the HKSAR's external autonomy. Based on the Hong Kong's relevant practice since 1984, this paper discusses the HKSAR's external autonomy in both theoretical and practical aspects.

Ⅰ. Concept of the HKSAR's External Autonomy

1. Definition of Autonomy

A plain language interpretation of the term "autonomy" suggests the ability to make decisions independent of any external influence. [1] When we further study the concept, we might find out the concept is far more complex than that we image. Various scholars used this term with different, though related, meaning in different contexts.

First, autonomy is a historical concept. The concept of autonomy (or *autonomia* in the original Greek usage) is even older than that of sovereignty. The ancient ideal of autonomy (*autonomia*) began as recognition of the relative independence of one *poli* from another. It was initially transformed from natural rights/social contract theory from a corporate to an individual ideal, but nationalism has again made it a corporate ideal as well. [2]

Second, it might be used as a political and legal concept in a domestic context. As used in modern political science, the concept refers to a particular mode of distribution of governmental power within a sovereign state. [3] Autonomous areas are regions of a sovereign state, which have been granted separate powers of internal administration to whatever degree, without being detached from the state of which they are a part. [4] These autonomous entities do not have any international element and are established solely on the basis of internal constitutional acts (for example,

---

[1] Anthony Neoh, "Hong Kong's Future: The View of a Hong Kong Lawyer", 22 *Cal. W. Int'l L. J.* 332-333 (1992).

[2] See Sanford Lakoff, "Between Either/or and More or Less: Sovereignty versus Autonomy under Federalism", 24 *The Journal of Federalism*, 76 (1994).

[3] Albert H. Y. Chen, "Some Reflections on Hong Kong's Autonomy", 24 *HKLJ*, 174 (1994).

[4] J. Crawford, The Creation of States in International Law, Clarendon Press 211-212 (1979), See Brian Z. Tamanaha, "Post-1997 Hong Kong: A Comparative Study of the Meaning of 'High Degree of Autonomy'—with a Specific Look at the Commonwealth of the Northern Mariana Islands", 5 *China Law Reporter*, 164 (1989).

the Faroe Islands, Greenland, and the provinces of Spain).[1]

Third, it might be used as a legal concept in international context. In this context, autonomy is difficult to define since there exists under international law a whole continuum of such statuses, ranging from territorial, to free association with citizenship or without citizenship, to protectorates, each with lesser or greater amounts of autonomy.[2] This category of autonomy may have several types of international elements.[3] Autonomous regions created by treaties consequently enjoy an internationally sanctioned assurance of their viability of enforcement, which varies greatly. At the very least, the fact that the relation comes under international purview implies that the central government of a state does not have an unfettered right to unilaterally alter the nature of the relationship.[4]

A comprehensive survey of autonomous entities was conducted in 1980 for the United States Department of State by the Procedural Aspects of International Law Institute (PAIL). The PAIL Report divided these entities into four categories:

(1) federal states, which are equal entities jointed in a union;

(2) international territories, which are entities created under international supervision in response to political considerations;

(3) associated states, which are relatively recent territories, having entered

---

[1] Ruth Lapidoth, "Autonomy and Sovereignty—Are They Mutually Exclusive?" in Amos Shapira and Mala Tabory (eds.), *New Political Entities in Public and Private International Law: With Special Reference to the Palestinian Entity*, Kluwer Law International, 5 (1999).

[2] For more detailed discussion on the concept of autonomy, see Brian Z. Tamanaha, "Post-1997 Hong Kong: A Comparative Study of the Meaning of 'High Degree of Autonomy' with a Specific Look at the Commonwealth of the Northern Mariana Islands", 5 *China Law Reporter*, 164-168 (1989).

[3] These types include:

(1) It may have been established in pursuance of a resolution of an international institution; for example, the autonomy in Eritrea, 1952-62, was established following a UN General Assembly resolution;

(2) An international treaty may have been involved in its establishment; for example, the 1924 Paris Convention concerning the Memel Territory;

(3) Autonomy may include an international machinery of supervision (such as the right that existed in Aland to appeal to the League of Nations), or a machinery for dispute resolution (such as the jurisdiction that Permanent Court of International Justice had with regard to Memel);

(4) The autonomous community may have an ethnic affinity with foreign country.

Ruth Lapidoth, "Autonomy and Sovereignty—Are They Mutually Exclusive?" in Amos Shapira and Mala Tabory (eds.), *New Political Entities in Public and Private International Law: With Special Reference to the Palestinian Entity*, Kluwer Law International, 5 (1999).

[4] Brian Z. Tamanaha, "Post-1997 Hong Kong: A Comparative Study of the Meaning of 'High Degree of Autonomy' with a Specific Look at the Commonwealth of the Northern Mariana Islands", 5 *China Law Reporter*, 166 (1989).

into a primary state-secondary state relationship;

（4）miscellaneous category, which encompasses several idiosyncratic situations.[1]

Research evidence suggests that there is no universally accepted model for autonomy. Accordingly there is no universally accepted definition of autonomy. Also there is no common criterion for all categories of autonomous entities. For judging degree of an autonomous entity, one should first identify the category to which the entity belongs. Much attention should be paid to differences between an autonomous entity created in domestic context and that created in international context. Then further studies on autonomous degree of the entity in comparison with other autonomous entities in the same category may be possible and meaningful.

2. Meaning of External Autonomy

Autonomy might be divided into internal autonomy and external autonomy. External autonomy means autonomy on external affairs. For an autonomous entity, the term "external affairs" in general refers to the relations between the autonomous entity and foreign countries and/or international organizations. In broad sense, it may also include the relations between the autonomous entity and other entities within the same sovereign state.

After comparative studies on many autonomous entities, include Hong Kong, Punjab (India), the Kurds etc. , Hurst Hannum concludes that while each situation is unique, the conflicts in which autonomy is viewed by one party as essential to the guarantee of its survival concern some or all of the following basic issues: language; education; access to governmental civil service, including police and security force, and social services; land and natural resources; and representative local government structures.[2] It is worth noticing that certain power on external affairs is not included in the list of essential issues.

The said PAIL Report examined the allocation of power between the primary

---

[1] Brian Z. Tamanaha, "Post-1997 Hong Kong: A Comparative Study of the Meaning of 'High Degree of Autonomy'—with a Specific Look at the Commonwealth of the Northern Mariana Islands", 5 *China Law Reporter*, 166 (1989).

[2] Hurst Hannum, *Autonomy, Sovereignty, and Self-Determination*, *The Accommodation of Conflicting Rights*, Revised Edition, The University of Pennsylvania Press, 458 (1996).

state and secondary state in relation to executive, legislative, and judicial authorities,[1] which in its views are key elements of autonomy.

After theoretical research on the concept of autonomy, Professor Albert H. Y. Chen suggested that the following issues are particularly important on the construction of the models of autonomy:

(1) method by which the local government is to be form;

(2) division of powers, in the legislative, executive, and judicial sphere, between the central government and the local government;

(3) mechanisms for rectification of errors and resolution of disputes. [2]

Again certain power on external affairs is not included in the list of essential issues or key elements of autonomy. It seems that autonomous entities do not necessarily enjoy the power on external affairs. In other words, an autonomous entity with external autonomy to large extent demonstrates that it enjoy relatively high degree of autonomy.

3. Developments of Hong Kong's External Autonomy

Hong Kong's external autonomy gradually evolved from its British-influenced international character. [3] As an autonomous regional entity, Hong Kong had enjoyed external autonomy since late 1960s when it achieved its economic miracle. It had experienced great change from *de facto* external autonomy to *de jure* external autonomy in the transition period (from 19 December 1984 to 30 June 1997). In that period and thereafter Hong Kong's practice of external autonomy convincingly indicates that the HKSAR enjoys high degree of *de jure* autonomy.

3.1 Hong Kong's de facto External Autonomy

Before 1 July 1997, Hong Kong, as a British *de facto* dependent territory, its internal affairs were completely controlled by the Governor of Hong Kong, who was

---

[1] Brian Z. Tamanaha, "Post-1997 Hong Kong: A Comparative Study of the Meaning of 'High Degree of Autonomy'—with a Specific Look at the Commonwealth of the Northern Mariana Islands", 5 *China Law Reporter*, 166 (1989).

[2] Albert H. Y. Chen, "The Relationship Between the Central Government and the SAR", in Peter Wesley-Smith and Albert H. Y. Chen (eds.), *The Basic Law and Hong Kong's Future*, Butterworths, 110 (1988).

[3] Xiaobing Xu, George D. Wilson, "The Hong Kong Special Administrative Region as a Model of Regional External Autonomy", 32 *Case W. Res. J. Int'l L.*, 3 (2000).

the representative of the Queen of the United Kingdom (the UK).[1] Its external links, both as a matter and as a proposition of law, were largely controlled by the UK authorities. At the same time, the commercial and industrial prominence of Hong Kong has given it a considerable of autonomy in international contexts.[2] This position has been strongly enhanced since 1 January 1973 when the UK became a member of the European Community and lost its independent status to some extent in international context.

Gradually HK has become a party to a number of multilateral and bilateral treaties and an associate member or a full member of various international and regional organizations. These organizations include: the General Agreements on Tariffs and Trade (GATT); United Nation Conference on Trade and Development (UNCTAD); United Nations Economic and Social Commission for Asia and the Pacific (ESCAP); the Organization for Economic Cooperation and Development (OECD); the Asian Productivity Organization (APO); Asian Development Bank (ADB); Asia-Pacific Telecommunity (APT); and World Meteorological Organization (WMO), etc.[3]

In fact, Hong Kong's competence to function internationally was widely recognized by the international community. However, it should be noticed that in the period of British rule, Hong Kong enjoyed *de facto* external autonomy and was an international legal person to the extent of its corresponding international rights, obligations and competencies. This international status and personality were established by the UK's leave and license on case-by-case basis.[4]

3.2　*Hong Kong's de jure External Autonomy*

Hong Kong's pre-existing *de facto* external autonomy under British rule has been reaffirmed, promoted and formalized in the JD. The guiding principle emerging

---

[1]　For general discussion on UK's authorities over its dependent territories, See Kenneth Roberts-Wray, *Commonwealth and Colonial Law*, Stevens & Sons, 138-246 (1966).

[2]　Marius Olivier, "Hong Kong: An Exercise in Autonomy", 18 *South African Yearbook of Int'l L.* 67-68 (1992-93).

[3]　For general discussion on Hong Kong's foreign relations under British rule, see Jian Jiachong, "Introduction to the Foreign Relations of Hong Kong" (Xianggang Duiwai Guanxi Jianjie)", in Hong Kong People's Association (ed.), 18 *Topics on Hong Kong Law* (Xianggang Falu Shiba Jiang), 445-469 (1987).

[4]　Marius Olivier, "Hong Kong: An Exercise in Autonomy", 18 *South African Yearbook of Int'l L.* 70-71 (1992-93).

from the provisions of the JD is that foreign affairs and defense are matters within the Central People's Government（hereinafter the CPG）'s sphere of competence. However, authorization to conduct certain external affairs independently and to maintain public order in the region is also provided for the HKSAR. [1]A distinction is implied between "foreign affairs" (wai jiao shi wu), which are quintessentially matters of state and international diplomacy, and "external affairs" (dui wai shi wu), which appear to be concerned with economic and cultural matters. The former expression is used when referring to responsibilities of the CPG and the latter when referring to the powers of the HKSAR. [2] In broad sense, for the HKSAR, external affairs may also include relations between the HKSAR and other regions of China, including Mainland China, Macao and Taiwan.

According to the provisions of the JD, the HKSAR's autonomy not only include "executive, legislative and independent judicial powers", [3] but also extend to some external affairs such as the establishment of "mutually beneficial economic relations with the UK and other countries", [4] the maintenance and development of economic and cultural relations and the conclusion of relevant agreements with other countries and international organizations, using the name of "Hong Kong, China", [5] and the issue of travel documents for entry into and exit from Hong Kong. [6]

The HKSAR's external autonomy is provided in detail by Annex I of the JD. The HKSAR's powers over external affairs are conferred and regulated by relevant provisions in sections III (courts and the judiciary), VI (economic and commercial matters), VIII (shipping), IX (civil aviation), XI (external relations) and XIV (travel and immigration matters) thereof. [7] Moreover, section II of Annex I provides for the maintenance after 1997 of Hong Kong's pre-existing laws which would include the frameworks of the legal systems for international practice.

---

[1] Marius Olivier, "Hong Kong: An Exercise in Autonomy", 18 *South African Yearbook of Int'l L.* 79-80 (1992-93).

[2] Yash Ghai, *Hong Kong's New Constitutional Order*, *The Resumption of Chinese Sovereign and the Basic Law*, Hong Kong University Press, 433 (1997)

[3] 3 (2), JD.

[4] 3 (9), JD.

[5] 3 (10), JD.

[6] 3 (10), JD.

[7] Albert H. Y. Chen, "The Relationship Between the Central Government and the SAR", in Peter Wesley-Smith and Albert H. Y. Chen (eds.), *The Basic Law and Hong Kong's Future*, Butterworths, 114-115 (1988).

In the Basic Law of the Hong Kong Special Administrative Region of the People's Republic of China (hereinafter the BL) promulgated on 4 April 1990, there are same provisions on the HKSAR's external autonomy as those in the JD, even using the same terms. Some of these provisions in the BL go into detail.

It is evident that the HKSAR is accorded a high degree of external autonomy, which is more extensive than that in the period of British rule. Furthermore the HKSAR enjoys probably the most extensive external autonomy that has ever existed in an autonomous region in the world, historical or current. Most commentators generally agree that the HKSAR enjoys a high degree of external autonomy that far outstrips the powers granted to other subnational entities in other states. [1] It should be indicated further that the HKSAR's external autonomy has been formally entrusted by the JD at international level and by the BL at Chinese domestic law level, which is *de jure* or formal external autonomy.

II. Practice of Hong Kong's External Autonomy

Hong Kong's *de jure* external autonomy had been put into practice under the auspices of the Joint Liaison Group (the JLG)[2] during the transition period. After 1 July 1997, the practice of the HKSAR's external autonomy has developed continuously. The developments of following four aspects are only examples of Hong Kong's practice in this regard.

1. *Special Positions in International Organizations and Conferences*

1.1 *Legal Provisions*

According to provisions of the JD and the BL, representatives of the HKSAR government may participate, as members of Chinese Delegation, in international organizations or conferences limited to states which affect the HKSAR, or may attend in such other capacity as may be permitted by the CPG and the international organization or conference concerned, and may express their views, using the name of

---

　　[1]　Xiaobing Xu, George D. Wilson, "The Hong Kong Special Administrative Region as a Model of Regional External Autonomy", 32 *Case W. Res. J. Int'l L.*, 6 (2000).

　　[2]　Prior to 1 July 1997, the JLG reached an agreement on the HKSAR's continued participation in over 20 international organizations, and the continued application to the HKSAR of about 200 multilateral treaties in areas such as international arbitration, civil aviation, merchant shipping, private international law and customs cooperation. See Elsie Leung, The Rule of Law and Its Operation in Hong Kong after Reunification, 6 *Policy Bulletin* 9 (1998).

"Hong Kong, China". The HKSAR may participate independently in international organizations and conferences not limited to states, under the name "Hong Kong, China".[1]

1.2 Relevant Practice

Traditionally an international organization refers to an organization which is established by two or more than two sovereign states, aiming to realize common objectives and purposes and having some permanent organs by an agreement.[2] According to the new development of international practice, the membership of an international organization is not always limited to sovereign states. Currently there are two types of international organizations in terms of membership. One is that their membership is still only limited to sovereign states. The other is that their membership is open to sovereign states and non-sovereign entities.

As the HKSAR does not qualify to be a full member for the organizations limited to sovereign states, representative of the HKSAR participate in these organisations as members of delegations of the PRC in general or in such other capacity as may be permitted by the CPG and the international organization concerned. The examples of "such other capacity" are that the HKSAR participates as an Associate Members in Asia-Pacific Telecommunity (APT), Economic and Social Commission for Asia and the Pacific of the United Nations (ESCAP), Heads of National Drug Law Enforcement Agencies, Asia and Pacific (HONLEA, Asia and Pacific), International Maritime Organization (IMO) and World Tourism Organization.[3] It has been argued that Hong Kong should be able to accede to multilateral treaties and participate in international organizations independently even though the parties and members of these treaties and organizations are limited to sovereign states. We find this argument unpersuasive since it lacks obviously any ground in international law.[4]

As to the international organization not limited to sovereign states, HK might participate as full member in accordance with the relevant provisions of those organi-

---

[1] Art 11 (1), Annex I, JD; Art. 152, BL.

[2] Liang Xi, *International Institutional Law* (in Chinese), Wuhan University Press, 1-5 (1993).

[3] www.cmab.gov.hk/23/04/2008

[4] Xiaobing Xu, George D. Wilson, "The Hong Kong Special Administrative Region as a Model of Regional External Autonomy", 32 *Case W. Res. J. Int'l L.*, 7 (2000).

zations. The first example is the Hong Kong's full membership in GATT/WTO regime. [1]Hong Kong became a separate contracting party of the GATT through the UK's declaration on 23 April 1986. China made a declaration on the same day to allow Hong Kong to keep that position in the GATT after 1 July 1997. Since that date Hong Kong has maintained its open trade policies and fulfilled its obligations in the GATT/WTO regime. [2] After effective of WTO Agreement，Hong Kong became an original WTO full member based on its own rights of a GATT contracting party，in accordance with Article 11 of that Agreement. [3] Through the Trade and Industry Department and the Hong Kong Economic and Trade Office in Geneva，Hong Kong participates actively in various WTO committees to seek to ensure the effective operation of the WTO and the faithful implementation of commitments by other WTO members. Existing practice shows that Hong Kong's representatives are trusted and supported by other WTO members. In February 2001，Mr. Stuart Harbinson，the first permanent representative of Hong Kong to the WTO，was elected as 2001 Chairman of General Council of the WTO on his own. The representatives of "Hong Kong，China" are often appointed as chair or vice chair of the Councils，Committees and panels. Mr. Joshua Law，the Permanent Representative of Hong Kong to the WTO served as the Chairman of the Committee on Budget，Finance and Administration for the year 2003. [4]

Another example is the membership of Hong Kong in Asia Pacific Economic Cooperation Conference (APEC). Starting on 1 July 1997，Hong Kong has formally

[1] For the brief history and legal grounds of Hong Kong's GATT/WTO membership，see Zeng Huaqun，"'One China Four WTO Memberships'：Legal Grounds，Relations and Significance"，8 (5) *The Journal of World Investment & Trade*，674-675 (2007).

[2] The WTO conducted a comprehensive review of Hong Kong's trade policies and practices on December 7 and 8，1998，in Geneva. The review was the first since the establishment of the WTO in 1995 and since Hong Kong's reunification with the PRC. It covered a full range of Hong Kong's trade policies and practices，including goods，services and intellectual property rights，as well as the trade and economic situation in Hong Kong. The members of the WTO Trade Policy Review Body commended on Hong Kong's maintaining open trade and investment regime after 1997，despite the Asian crisis. The members also expressed confidence that with these policies，Hong Kong's economy would soon resume strong and sustained economic growth. They believed that Hong Kong is one of the most open economies in the world. See WTO Members Commend Hong Kong for Its Free Trade Stance，*HK Files*，February 1999 Issue，3.

[3] Article 11 of WTO Agreement provides that "The contracting parties to GATT 1947 as of the date of entry into force of this Agreement，and the European Communities，which accept this Agreement and the Multilateral Trade Agreements and for which Schedules of Specific Commitment and annexed to GATT 1994 and for which Schedules of Specific Commitment and annexed to GATS shall become original Member of the WTO."

[4] Hong Kong's Participation in the World Trade Organization. http://www.info.gov.hk/info/wto.htm

changed its name to "Hong Kong, China" in APEC. "Hong Kong, China", Chinese Taipei and China became three independent members of APEC from a sovereign state. [1]Under the concept of "one country two systems", "Hong Kong, China", Chinese Taipei and China need not speak in one voice. APEC acts by consensus, not by vote. "Hong Kong, China", Chinese Taipei and China could continue to speak for their respective economic interests. On the other hand, under the one-country thinking, "Hong Kong, China" could help China get better familiarized in APEC agenda and involved in APEC activities by better research and analysis of APEC issues. Hong Kong's multilateral government and business linkage with Association of Southeast Asian Nations (ASEAN) countries could be good basis for informal linkages with businesses as well as governments then. [2]

In late June 1997 the Foreign Ministry of China declared that the HKSAR might participate in or attend activities or conferences of 19 international organizations, including International Monetary Fund (IMF), International Civil Aviation Organization as member of Chinese delegation. The HKSAR may also take part in the activities of 15 international organizations, including Asia Development Bank, International Maritime Organization, as full member or associate member in the name of "Hong Kong, China". The arrangements were made under the relevant provisions of the JD and the BL and also met requirements of basic documents of the international organizations. [3]

2. Treaty-making Power on Its Own

2.1 Legal Provisions

According to provisions of the JD and the BL, the HKSAR is granted general authority to conclude bilateral treaties with foreign countries and other regions in the appropriate fields. The HKSAR may on its own, using the name "Hong Kong, China", maintain and develop relations and conclude and implement agreements with foreign states and regions and relevant international organizations in the appropriate fields, including the economic, trade, financial and monetary, shipping, communi-

---

〔1〕 By 18 August 2007, APEC has 21 economies. People's Republic of China, Hong Kong and Chinese Taipei became APEC members on 12-14 November 1991. www. apec. org/18/08/2007

〔2〕 Cyril C. K. Chow and Michael C. M. Kwan, "Hong Kong's Role in APEC under 'One Country-Two Systems'", *Policy Bulletin*, No. 3, January 1998, 10.

〔3〕 *People's Daily*, 25 June 1997, 3.

cations, tourism, cultural and sports fields. [1] Although this kind of formulation has not yet acquired popular usage in international law, its form clearly constituted Hong Kong as an entity with the capacity to enter into bilateral treaties within the specified fields. [2]

The key to the scope of HK's treaty-making power is the concept of "appropriate fields". The term itself is not defined, and it is necessary to examine all the provisions of the BL to determine in what areas Hong Kong may have capacity for external relations. [3] What is not clear is whether the HKSAR must consult the CPG beforehand and obtain its approval before signing the agreement concerned. [4]

On 7 July 1997, the specially appointed officer of China's Foreign Ministry to HKSAR sent an authorized letter to Chief Executive of the HKSAR. Through the letter the CPG has granted the HKSAR to conduct negotiation on bilateral agreements with foreign countries in the fields of civil aviation, protection and promotion of investment, surrender of fugitive offenders, surrender of convicts, and criminal judicial assistance. [5]

2.2 Relevant Practice

Since the transition period, Hong Kong has the powers on negotiating bilateral agreements with foreign countries in economic fields with authorization on case-by-case basis. In fact, Hong Kong's bilateral treaties with foreign countries have demonstrated the most remarkable achievements in practice of its external autonomy.

2.2.1 Bilateral Air Service Treaties

As an international trade and financial center, Hong Kong's commercial future firstly depends, to large extent, on the existence of an airport that is freely accessible to foreigners. [6]

---

[1] Art. 3, 9, 10, JD; Section XI of Annex I of the JD; Art. 151, BL.

[2] See Anthony Neoh, "Hong Kong's Future: The View of a Hong Kong Lawyer", 22 *Cal. W. Int'l L. J.* 351-352 (1992).

[3] Yash Ghai, *Hong Kong's New Constitutional Order*, *The Resumption of Chinese Sovereignty and the Basic Law*, Hong Kong University Press, 435-436 (1997).

[4] Albert H. Y. Chen, "Some Reflections on Hong Kong's Autonomy", 24 *HKLJ*, 177 (1994).

[5] Xiamen Daily, 8 July 1997, 3.

[6] Susan L. Karamanian, "Legal Aspects of the Sino-British Draft Agreement on the Future of Hong Kong", 20 *Texas Int'l L. J.* 177 (1985).

Traditionally on the international level, bilateral air services treaties (hereinafter BATs) on exchanging commercial traffic right between sovereign states are an important source of public international law. In the period of British rule, Hong Kong had always been treated as a point of origin or destination within the UK. Its international air transport relations were regulated by the UK's BATs with other countries. Prior to 1986, no special procedure was followed in Hong Kong when the UK negotiated, entered into, applied or gave legal effect to any of these treaties. In practice, some consultations with Hong Kong local international air carriers occurred prior to and during negotiations and Hong Kong government representatives were usually invited to attend negotiations of these treaties.[1] By 1987 there are two dozen of these treaties[2] and more informal arrangements. The legal effect of these treaties in Hong Kong only continue until 30 June 1997 as the result of the UK's ceasing its international responsibilities for Hong Kong.

Since the air service industry badly needed the preciseness and legality, the rearrangement of Hong Kong's international air transport relations was the most urgent and important legal work for the UK and Hong Kong authorities before 1997. The solution was that Hong Kong in its name negotiates and concludes new independent BATs with foreign countries and other regions.

The first one is the Agreement between the Government of Hong Kong and the Government of Kingdom of Netherlands concerning Air Services signed on 17 September 1986 and entered into force on 26 June 1987.[3]

On 25 July 1997, The BAT between the HKSAR and the UK came into force.[4] The agreement has vital historical significance since it is the first HKSAR's bilateral treaty authorized by Chinese Foreign Ministry on the name of "Hong Kong, China" in accordance with the relevant provisions of the JD and the BL. It has great

---

[1] Gary N. Heilbronn, "The Changing Face of Hong Kong's International Air Transport Relations", 20 *Case W. Res. J. Int'l L.*, 202-203 (1988).

[2] By 1987 UK's BATs with the following States were in force in respect of Hong Kong: Australia, Burma, Canada, Ceylon, France, Germany, India, Indonesia, Italy, Japan, Kenya, Korea, Kuwait, Lebanon, Malaysia, New Zealand, Philippines, Portugal, Singapore, South Africa, Switzerland, Thailand and USA. See Gary N. Heilbronn, "Hong Kong's First Bilateral Air Services Agreement: A Milestone in Air Law and an Exercise in Limited Sovereignty", 18 *HKLJ* 64-65, note 2 (1988).

[3] Texts published in *Special Supplement No. 5 to the Hong Kong Government Gazette*, E203 (1987).

[4] *Xiamen Daily*, 26 July 1997, 3.

historical and legal implication as the counterpart of the treaty is the UK.

As at 17 April 2008, 54 BATs between HKSAR and foreign countries came into force. [1] 20 BATs out of them are concluded for substituting the former applicable UK's BATs with other countries. The rest of 34 BATs indicates Hong Kong's new established international air service relations with foreign countries. This important practice demonstrates the HKSAR's positive attitude to maintain and develop its international air service relations with the rest of the world.

2.2.2 Bilateral Investment Treaties

In late 1950's, the first bilateral investment treaty (hereinafter BIT) was concluded aiming at promotion and protection of international investment. The parties to the BITs are sovereign states, typically European countries and developing coun-

---

[1] The counterparts, the dates of entry into force and the texts available of the agreements are: Netherlands (26.6.1987) *Special Supplement No.5 to the Hong Kong Government Gazette*, 129, no. 26 (1987): E201-E233, Amendment, 139, no. 2 (1997): E3-E30; Canada (24.6.1988), Ibid, 130, no.45 (1988): E171-E218, Amendment, 138, no. 36 (1996): E357-E374; Brunei (9.1.1989) 131, no. 4 (1989): E3-E46; New Zealand (22.2. 1991), 133, no. 9 (1991): E3-E34, Amendment, 138, no. 34 (1996): E341-E354; Malaysia (4.3.1991) 133, no. 10 (1991): E37-E88; France (10.5.1991), 132, no. 36 (1990): E153-E203; Switzerland (1.2.1993), 130, no. 6 (1988): E5-E38; Sri Lanka (24.2.1993), 135, no. 8 (1993): E3-E64; Australia (15.3.1993) 135, no. 37 (1993): E67-E102; Brazil (16.3.1994) 133, no. 38 (1991): E215-E265; Korea (9.7.1996), 138, no. 20 (1996): E97-E153; Singapore (30.4.1996), 138, no. 20 (1996): E155-E189; India (10.10.1996), 138, no. 45 (1996): E431-E477; US (7.4.1997), 139, no. 18 (1997): E211-E250; Myanmar (11-6-1997), 139, no. 13 (1997): E123-E151; Thailand (12.6.1997), 139, no. 15 (1997): E155-E208; Japan (18.6.1997), 139, no. 12 (1997): E69-E119; Germany (23.6.1997), 137, no. 19 (1995): E27-E92, Amendment, 139, no. 21 (1997): E483-E500; Philippines (26.6.1997), 139, no. 23 (1997): E503-E537; Indonesia (27.6.1997), 139, no. 24 (1997): E541-E575; UK(25. 7.1997), 1, no. 6 (1997): E47-E88; Italy (19.1.1998), 138, no. 45 (1996): E377-E429; Pakistan (17.2.1998), 2, no. 12 (1998): E69-E105; Bahrain (3.3.1998), 2, no. 17 (1998): E109-E172; United Arab Emirates (29.4. 1998), 3, no. 3 (1999): E3-E68; Maldives (18.5.1998), 2, no. 23 (1998): E191-E211; Mauritius (3.7.1998), 3, no. 9 (1999): E111-E146; Israel (8.9.1998), 2, no. 44 (1998): E449-E512; Nepal (29.10.1998), 3, no. 9 (1999): E147-E180; Austria (1.12.1998), 3, no. 11 (1999): E183-E245; Oman (26.3.1999), 3, no. 12 (1999): E249-E318; Kyrgyz (15.7.1999), 3, no. 31 (1999): E527-E575; Vietnam (10.9.1999), 4, no. 50 (2000): E1255-E1293; Belarus (3.12.1999), 4, no. 8 (2000): E3-E34; Cambodia (17.1.2000), 4, no. 52 (2000): E1297-E1371; Denmark (14.3.2000), 5, no. 7 (2001): E3-E41; Sweden (14.3.2000), 5, no. 9 (2001): E87-E125; South Africa (18.3.2000), 4, no. 37 (2000): E1213-E1252; Finland (1.4.2000), 4, no. 36 (2000): E1175-E1210; Mongolia (24.5.2000), 4, no. 35 (2000): E1121-E1172; Norway (2.6.2000), 5, no. 8 (2001): E45-E83; Lithuania (7.7.2000), 2, no. 29 (1998): E355-E387; Bangladesh (24.10.2000), 5, no. 27 (2001): E225-E264; Turkey (20.4.2001), 1, no. 43 (1997): E391-E446; Hungary (19.11.2001), 5, no. 38 (2001): E573-E611; Ukraine (31.1.2002), 6, no. 10 (2002): E3-E45; Czech Republic (26.4.2002), 6, no. 23 (2002): E49-E87; Belgium (1.7.2003), 2, no. 49 (1998): E553-E594; Croatia (30.1.2003), 8, no. 35 (2004): E15-E68; Luxembourg (6.6.2003), 3, no. 3 (1999): E69-E106; Kenya (21.5.2004), not yet gazetted; Jordan (28.8.2004), not yet gazetted; Iceland (29.10.2004), not yet gazetted; Saudi Arabia (27.06.2006), 12, no. 13 (2008): E35-E70. By 17 April 2008, Hong Kong has signed BATs (but have not yet come into force) with Ethiopia, Estonia, Greece, Kazakhstan, Kuwait, Mexico, Papua New Guinea, Qatar and Russia. www.legislation.gov.hk/22/04/2008

tries. Germany and Switzerland took the lead in this regard. [1]

The UK embarked on the negotiation of BITs in 1974. In the period of British rule, Hong Kong's international investment relations also were conducted within the framework of the UK's BITs. [2] The UK had covered Hong Kong under a number of its BITs by way of territorial extension in exchange of notes. [3] The legal effect of these UK's BITs in Hong Kong also only continued until 30 June 1997.

In order to maintain and develop Hong Kong's international investment relations after 1997, Hong Kong had two choices in the transition period: one was that Hong Kong negotiate and conclude BITs in its name with foreign countries, and the other was that Hong Kong's international investment relations were covered by the framework of Chinese BITs. [4] Hong Kong chose the first one. Considering the different economic and legal systems as well as different status in the international investment context between Hong Kong and Mainland China, the choice may better meet the specific needs of Hong Kong and serve the purpose of promoting and protecting international investment for Hong Kong.

On 19 November 1992, Agreement between Government of Hong Kong and Government of Kingdom of Netherlands on Promotion and protection of Mutual

---

[1] By the end of 2005, there are almost 2500 BITs. United Nations Conference on Trade and Development, *Bilateral Investment Treaties 1995-2006: Trends in Investment Rulemaking*, United Nations, 1 (2007).

[2] For general picture of UK's BITs practice, see Eileen Denza & Shelagh Brooks, "Investment Protection Treaties: United Kingdom Experience", 36 *Int'l & Com. L. Q.*, 908-923 (1987).

[3] The UK's BITs generally define territory in the "definitions" clause which in turn refers to a separate provision on territorial extension. For example, UK-Sri Lanka BIT (1980) which provides in Article 1 that:

"(e) 'territory' means:

(i) in respect of the United Kingdom: Great Britain and Northern Ireland and any territory to which this Agreement is extended in accordance with the provisions of Article 11;"

Article 11 provides that:

"At the time of ratification of this Agreement, or at any time thereafter, the provisions of this Agreement may be extended to such territories for whose international relations the Government of the United Kingdom are responsible as may be agreed between the Contracting Parties in exchange of notes."

However it is noticeable that such exchange of notes may take place later than effective of the Agreement. For example, Exchange of Notes between the UK and Sri Lanka Concerning the Extension to Hong Kong of the Agreement for the Promotion and Protection of Investments took place one month after the Agreement had entered into force in 1980.

See Rudolf Dolzer, Margrete Stevens, *Bilateral Investment Treaties*, Martinus Nijhoff, 42-43 and footnotes 124-126 (1995).

[4] China has participated actively in negotiating BITs with foreign countries since earlier 1980's and currently there are 121 China-foreign BITs.

Investment was signed and entered into force on 1 September 1993. [1] Thereafter, Hong Kong has concluded 14 BITs in its name with 15 foreign countries [2]

2.2.3 Bilateral Taxation Treaties

Typical bilateral taxation treaties (hereinafter BTTs) are agreements between sovereign states on avoiding double income taxation and cooperation in international taxation affairs.

Hong Kong historically has been a separate tariff region with free port and low taxation policies. Hong Kong entered an agreement on avoiding double income taxation on international shipping with the US on 1 August 1989, [3] which may be regarded as the preliminary practice of Hong Kong in BTT field. The HKSAR's practice in this field has made great progress since 2001. By 6 November 2007, the HKSAR concluded other 9 BTTs in its name with foreign countries. [4]

There are currently 79 bilateral agreements between the HKSAR and foreign states in air services (54), investment promotion (15) and taxation (10) fields. The

[1]　Texts published in *Special Supplement No. 5 to the Hong Kong Government Gazette*, E27-53 (1992).

[2]　The counterparts, the dates of entry into force and the texts available of the agreements are: Netherlands (1.9.1993), *Special Supplement No. 5 to the Hong Kong Government Gazette*, 134, no. 50 (1992): E25-E53; Australia (15.10.1993), Ibid, 135, no. 37 (1993): E103-E123; Denmark (4.3.1994),136, no. 6 (1994): E19-E48; Sweden (26.6.1994), 136, no. 23 (1994): E51-E78; Switzerland (22.10.1994), 136, no. 48 (1994): E85-E116; New Zealand (5.8.1995), 137, no. 34 (1995): E95-E115; France (30.5.1997), 2, no. 26 (1998): E215-E240; Japan (18.6.1997), 2, no. 26 (1998): E241-E281; Korea (30.7.1997), 2, no. 26 (1998): E283-E316; Austria (1.10.1997), 2, no. 26 (1998): E317-E351; Italy (2.2.1998), 2, no. 6 (1998): E3-E35; Germany (19.2.1998), 2, no. 10 (1998): E39-E66; UK (12.4.1999), 3, no. 15 (1999): E391-E414; Belgium and Luxembourg (18.6.2001), 5, no. 25 (2001): E175-E222; Thailand (12.4.2006), 10, no. 18 (2006): E41-E65.

[3]　See Double Taxation Relief (Income from Shipping Operations) (United States of America) Order, 1989.

[4]　The counterparts, the dates of entry into force and the texts available of the agreements are: US (16.8.1989), Double Taxation Relief (Income from Shipping Operations) (United States of America) Order: *Ca112, laws of Hong Kong*; UK (3.5.2001), Specification of Arrangements (Government of the United Kingdom of Great Britain and Northern Ireland) (Avoidance of Double Taxation on Shipping Income) Order: *Ca112, laws of Hong Kong*; Netherlands (17.10.2001), Specification of Arrangements (Government of the Kingdom of Netherlands) (Avoidance of Double Taxation on Shipping Income) Order: *Ca112, laws of Hong Kong*; Belgium (7.10.2004), Specification of Arrangements (Government of the Kingdom of Belgium) (Avoidance of Double Taxation on Income and Capital and Prevention of Fiscal Evasion) Order: *Ca112, laws of Hong Kong*; Singapore (30.12.2004), Specification of Arrangements (Government of the Republic of Singapore) (Avoidance of Double Taxation on Income from Shipping or Aircraft Operations) Order: *Ca112, laws of Hong Kong*; Norway (11.1.2005), Specification of Arrangements (Government of the Kingdom of Norway) (Avoidance of Double Taxation on Income from Shipping Operation) Order: *Ca112, laws of Hong Kong*; Germany (17.1.2005), Specification of Arrangements (Government of the Federal Republic of Germany) (Avoidance of Double Taxation on Shipping Income) Order: *Ca112, laws of Hong Kong*; Sri Lanka (30.3.2005), Specification of Arrangements (Government of the Socialist Republic of Sri Lanka) (Avoidance of Double Taxation on Income from Shipping and Aircraft Transport) Order: *Ca112, laws of Hong Kong*; Thailand (7.12.2005) Specification of Arrangements (Government of the Kingdom of Thailand) (Avoidance of Double Taxation on Income and Prevention of Fiscal Evasion) Order: *Ca 112 Laws of Hong Kong*; Denmark (16.12.2005) Specification of Arrangements (Government of the Kingdom of Denmark) (Avoidance of Double Taxation on Income from Shipping Operation) Order: *Ca 112 Laws of Hong Kong*. HKSAR has signed a BTT (but has not yet come into force) with Luxemburg. Besides the Hong Kong's BTTs, a number of Hong Kong's BATs also contain provisions on avoidance of double taxation in respect of air services income. www.legislation.gov.hk/22/04/2008

international practice sets the good examples for the international community and smoothes the way for negotiations by the HKSAR with states more likely to hesitate before entering into bilateral treaties with non-sovereign entity. [1] It should be noticed that before the JD there is no any precedent of Hong Kong's bilateral treaties in above three fields. As a non-sovereign entity, Hong Kong has entered into so many bilateral treaties in its name with foreign countries in such a short period of time, which is definitely the only case in the history of bilateral treaties.

3. Special Arrangements for Applying Treaties

3.1 Legal Provisions

The general principles of treaty law established by Article 29 of the Vienna Convention on Treaties is that in ordinary circumstances a treaty signed by a state would be binding on it in relation to all its territory.

According to the provisions of the JD and the BL, the Chinese government will decide, in accordance with the circumstances and needs of the HKSAR, and seeking the views of the HKSAR government, whether to apply to Hong Kong treaties to which China is or becomes a party; treaties to which China is not a party but which are implemented in Hong Kong shall continue to be implemented in the latter. China is to "take the necessary steps" to ensure that Hong Kong retains its status "in an appropriate capacity" in international organizations of which China is a member and in which Hong Kong now participates. [2]

3.2 Relevant Practice

On 20 June 1997, China's representative to United Nations (UN) presented a diplomatic note to UN Secretary-General, stating China's position on treaties applying to the HKSAR. Two annexes of the note list 214 treaties applying to the HKSAR since 1 July 1997. In particular, the note referred to the provisions of two human rights Conventions shall have been valid since 1 July 1997. The note also points out that for other treaties not listing in the list of which China is a party or potential party, China shall fulfill the formality if she decides to apply them to the HKSAR. For the treaties dealing with foreign affairs and defense affairs or other

---

[1] Gary N. Heilbronn, "The Changing Face of Hong Kong's International Air Transport Relations", 20 *Case W. Res. J. Int'l L.*, 223 (1988).

[2] Art. 11 (2), Annex I; Art. 153, BL.

treaties applying to whole territories up to their nature, China shall apply them to the HKSAR without formalities. [1]

Currently some 200 multilateral treaties are applicable to the HKSAR, more than 70 of which do not apply to the Mainland China. This shows the unique position of Hong Kong as a highly autonomous special administrative region of the PRC. [2]It is worth noting that the legal grounds and consequences of treaties applying to the HKSAR in terms of Hong Kong's external relations have changed since 1 July 1997. The 1958 New York Convention on the Recognition and Enforcement of Foreign Arbitral Award is a good example. This Convention was extended to Hong Kong in 1977, two years after the UK's accession. Before 1997, arbitral awards made in Hong Kong were enforceable in some 90 Conventional countries, including China, which acceded to the Convention in April 1987. Also arbitral awards made in Mainland China were enforceable in Hong Kong. After 1 July 1997, arbitral awards made in the HKSAR or Mainland China are not enforceable in Mainland China or the HKSAR respectively. In *Ng Fung Hong Ltd v. ABC* Case held on 15 and 19 January 1998, the Hong Kong court accepted the opinion that since 1 July 1997, Hong Kong and Mainland China have ceased to be separate parties to New York Convention vis-à-vis each other. [3] However, In *Hebei Import & Export Corporation v. Polytek Engineering Co Ltd* case, the Hong Kong court held that due to "one country two systems" it could be strongly argued that a PRC award made after 1 July 1997 would not be considered a "domestic award" in Hong Kong and that the New York Convention should apply to such awards. [4]

4. Relations with Other Regions in China

Due to the unique development of Chinese history and the adoption of China's policy of "one country two systems", the HKSAR's external autonomy in broad sense may cover the relations between the HKSAR and other regions of China, including Mainland China, Macao and Taiwan, in addition to foreign countries and international organizations.

---

[1]　*People's Daily* (overseas version), 23 June, 1997, 6.

[2]　www. cmab. gov. hk/22/04/2008

[3]　1 *Hong Kong Law Reports & Digest*, 1998, 155-157.

[4]　1 *Hong Kong Law Reports & Digest*, 1998, 287-303.

4.1 Relations with Mainland China

An important aspect of the HKSAR's external autonomy can be seen in the relations between the HKSAR and the Mainland China.

Since 1 July 1997, the HKSAR has stepped up its efforts to foster closer legal, economic and administrative cooperation with Mainland China, covering a wide range of areas such as civil aviation, trade and investment, taxation, environment, shipping, mutual legal assistance, etc. The followings are some examples.

In civil aviation area, there are 2 memorandums, 4 arrangements between the Mainland China and the HKSAR. Among them the basic and comprehensive one titled as Air Services Arrangement between the Mainland and the Hong Kong Special Administrative Region was signed in Beijing on 2 February 2000. [1] These arrangements demonstrate that the HKSAR has set up bilateral air service relations with Mainland China.

In taxation area, the tax authorities of Mainland China and the HKSAR signed a memorandum entitled Arrangement on Avoidance of Double Taxation on Incomes between Mainland China and the HKSAR in early March 1998. The memorandum states that the tax authorities of each side offer tax exemptions to transport incomes of ships, planes and vehicles from their own localities. Tax exemption is also granted to certain residents of the other side. These arrangements came into effect after 1 April 1998 in Hong Kong and after 1 July 1998 in Mainland China. [2] The new development in this area is that the arrangement between the Mainland China and the HKSAR for the Avoidance of Double Taxation and Fiscal Evasion with Respect to Taxes on Income, signed in Hong Kong on 21 August 2006.

---

[1] Other 5 documents in civil aviation area are: Memorandum of Understanding of Flight Inspection Services at Hong Kong International Airport, signed in Beijing on 1 April 1999; Memorandum of Understanding on Long-Term Technical Cooperation in Aviation Weather Services between the Air Traffic Management Bureau of the General Administration of Civil Aviation of China and the Hong Kong Observatory, signed in Hong Kong on 21 April 1999; Arrangement between the General Administration of Civil Aviation of China and the Civil Aviation Department of the government of the Hong Kong Special Administrative Region in Relation to the Delineation of the Sanya Flight Information Region (Area of Responsibility) and the Hong Kong Flight Information Region, signed in Beijing on 11 January 2001; Cooperation Arrangement on Aircraft Accident Investigation and Search and Rescue, signed in Beijing on 7 April 2004; and Cooperation Arrangement on Mutual Acceptance of Approval of Aircraft Maintenance Organisations between General Administration of Civil Aviation of China, Civil Aviation Department, Hong Kong, China and Civil Aviation Authority, Macao, China, signed in Beijing on 2 June 2006.

[2] Zhong Huayan, "Avoidance of Double Taxation in Inland China and Hong Kong", *China Economic News* (No. 10) 16th March 1998, 2.

In mutual legal assistance area, the Arrangement for the Mutual Service of Judicial Documents in Civil and Commercial Proceedings between the Mainland and Hong Kong Courts was signed in Shenzhen on 14 January 1999. According to the Arrangement, the Courts in the Mainland China and the HKSAR may entrust to each other the service of judicial documents in civil and commercial proceedings. Requests for service of judicial documents shall be made through the various Higher People's Courts in the Mainland China and the High Court of the HKSAR. The Supreme People's Court may make direct requests to the High Court of the HKSAR for service of judicial documents. [1] The following is the Arrangement concerning Mutual Enforcement of Arbitral Awards between the Mainland and the Hong Kong Special Administrative Region, signed in Shenzhen on 21 June 1999. The latest and most important achievement in this regard is the Arrangement on Recognition and Enforcement of Judgments in Civil and Commercial Matters by the Courts of the Mainland and of the Hong Kong Special Administrative Region Pursuant to Choice of Court Agreements between Parties concerned, signed in Hong Kong on 14 July 2006, dealing with the mutual recognition and enforcement of court judgments in the specified cases. [2]

In the trade and investment areas, Mainland and Hong Kong Closer Economic Partnership Arrangement (hereinafter CEPA) is a great achievement. As equal WTO members, "Hong Kong, China" and China may establish a customs union (CU) or a free trade area (FTA) between them. The significance of a CU or a FTA between the two members under the WTO regime is to deal with the special problems on the application of WTO non-discrimination principle, setting up a necessary legal basis for closer economic relations between the two regions within a sovereign state. [3] Considering China's "one country two systems" policy and big differences between the two members in political, economic and legal systems and development levels, to establish a

---

[1] Art. 1, 2 of the Arrangement.

[2] The Arrangement will be implemented after the passage of the relevant legislation and on a date to be announced. www. legislation. gov. hk/intracountry/eng/index. htm/30/04/2008

[3] The potential Closer Economic Partnership Arrangement (hereinafter CEPA) or other Economic Cooperation Regime (hereinafter ECR) among China, "Hong Kong, China", "Macao, China" and Chinese Taipei leading to so-called "great China FTA" might provide new opportunities for further economic cooperation and integration among the four WTO members. There are many comments on RTAs among the four members, for examples, ZENG Lingliang, The Legal Position and Development Trend of Regional Trade Arrangement under WTO Regime—Several Legal Issues Concerning Establishing a Free Trade Area among the Mainland, Taiwan, Hong Kong and Macao (in Chinese); WANG Guiguo and LIANG Meifen, An Analysis of the Proposition of Establishing Free Trade Area between Hong Kong and the Mainland (in Chinese), 7 *Journal of International Economic Law*, 1-16, 69-83 (2003).

FTA, rather than a CU, is more suitable for them. The main text and six annexes of CEPA was signed in Hong Kong on 29 June 2003 and 29 September 2003 respectively and came into effect from 1 January 2004, following the 4 supplements to CEPA during 2004 to 2007.[1]

4.2 Relations with Macao

The relation between the HKSAR and the Macao Special Administrative Region (hereinafter the Macao SAR) is unique and unprecedented since it is a relation between two special administrative regions in a sovereign state and two full members in the WTO regime. There are currently some bilateral arrangements between the two parties.

In civil aviation area, the Air Services Arrangement between the Hong Kong Special Administrative Region and the Macao Special Administrative Region was signed in Hong Kong on 13 October 2003. The new development is the Cooperation Arrangement on Mutual Acceptance of Approval of Aircraft Maintenance Organisations between General Administration of Civil Aviation of China, Civil Aviation Department, Hong Kong, China and Civil Aviation Authority, Macao, China, signed in Beijing on 2 June 2006. It is noticeable that in the arrangement the three parties-Mainland, Hong Kong and Macao-in a sovereign state are involved.

In financial cooperation area, the Memorandum of Understanding on Mutual Assistance and Information Exchange between the Monetary Authority of Macao, China and the Insurance Authority of Hong Kong, China was signed in Macao on 9 November 2001. This arrangement might be the first step for economic cooperation between the two parties.

In mutual legal assistance area, the Cooperative Arrangement between Correctional Services Department of the Hong Kong Special Administrative Region and the Macao Prison of the Macao Special Administrative Region was signed in Macao on 29 March 2006, which might be seen as the preliminary result of the two parties in this area.

4.3 Relations with Taiwan

It is doubtless that for the HKSAR the relations between the HKSAR and Taiwan are more complicated and sensitive than those between the HKSAR and Mainland China or between the HKSAR and the Macao SAR.

---

[1] www. legislation. gov. hk/intracountry/eng/index. htm/30/04/2008

Ting lei Miao v. Chen Li Hung & Another Case，a commercial dispute heard by Hong Kong High Court on 9-11 April and 27 June 1997 may illustrated the Hong Kong's judicial view on relation between Hong Kong and Taiwan before and after 1997.

In this case，two preliminary issues have to be tried first：(1) Whether in all the circumstances of the case，the High Court should recognize and give effect to the bankruptcy order of Taipei District Court；(2) Whether in all the circumstances of the case，the High Court should recognize that order of Taipei District Court as having effect over the assets of plaintiff situated in Hong Kong.

Determining the two issues in the negative，Hong Kong High Court held some important points as follows：

(1) The UK did not recognize Taiwan as an independent state. The governmental act of an unrecognized state could not be recognized by the court；

(2) The change of sovereignty of Hong Kong on 1 July 1997 would not cause any material change in respect of recognition of the acts or steps taken by Taiwanese authorities since the stance of the UK was the same as that of the PRC；

(3) There was no legal basis for the courts in HK，which operated differently from their counterparts in the PRC and on well-established common law principles，to follow an alleged practice of the PRC regarding the acceptance and/or recognition of Taiwanese governmental acts in relation to private matters，whether before or after the change of sovereignty. [1]

The HKSAR has had extensive commercial relations and exchange of some forms of representation with Taiwan. [2] As two full members of WTO since 1 January 2002，it is estimated that there is great potential for them to set up and develop closer relations.

III. Basic Characteristics of the HKSAR's External Autonomy

In comparison with other autonomous entities，the basic characteristics of the HKSAR's external autonomy may be summarised as authorisation nature，double legal grounds and international guarantee.

---

〔1〕 *Hong Kong Law Reports & Digest*, 1997, 841-856.

〔2〕 Yash Ghai, *Hong Kong's New Constitutional Order*, *The Resumption of Chinese Sovereign and the Basic Law*, Hong Kong University Press，452 (1997).

1. Authorisation Nature

Article 12 of the BL provides that "Hong Kong Special Administrative Region shall be a local administrative region of People's Republic of China, which shall enjoy a high degree of autonomy and come directly under the Central People's Government." The provision clarifies the legal status of the HKSAR, which is a key to understand the nature of the HKSAR's external autonomy.

China is a unitary country. The HKSAR is an integrated part of China and a local administrative region directly under the CPG. It is obvious that the HKSAR's autonomy is granted by the CPG. The exercise of government authorities partly accrues to the HKSAR, but the true sovereign and final authorities remain in China itself. At this point the HKSAR is different from a member state in a federation. In federal countries, autonomy of member states is the result of division of powers.

"Authorisation" and "division of powers" are two different concepts, indicating two different relations and different legal consequences.

First, the difference may be presented by analysing the delegation of governmental power from historical and logical points of views. "Authorisation" refers an authorising entity grants its own powers to an authorised entity. The scope of latter's power is limited by authorised powers and the former remain all the powers except those authorised. The PRC therefore control the so-called "residual" powers for determining authority not expressly granted in the BL. Any vesting of residual powers in the HKSAR would be inconsistent with the HKSAR's status as a local "administrative region", as well as with the unitary nature of the Chinese state.[1] On the contrary, "division of powers" refers to the division of powers between two or more than two authorities. In this case, further problems that "who possesses residuary powers" should be dealt with.[2]

Second, the HKSAR's autonomy rest upon authorisation by the CPG, however wide those powers may be and irrespective of the fact that in the JD the PRC has undertaken to grant such powers. Therefore, the CPG is at the dominant position in

---

[1] Wu Jianfan, "Several Issues Concerning the Relationship between the Central government of the People's Republic of China and the Hong Kong Special Administrative Region", 2 *Journal of Chinese Law*, 65, 74 (1988).

[2] For further discussion on the Concepts "division of powers", "residual powers", See Albert H. Y. Chen, The Relationship between the Central Government and the SAR, in Peter Wesley-Smith and Albert H. Y. Chen (eds.), *The Basic Law and Hong Kong's Future*, Butterworths, 110-112 (1988).

relations between itself and the HKSAR. Although the HKSAR's external autonomy has so far received strong backing from the PRC, the sovereign status of China vis-a-vis the autonomous, regional status of the HKSAR ultimately defines and determines the future of the HKSAR's external autonomy. [1]There is not third party who has a power to deal with disputes between the CPG and the HKSAR. On the contrary, disputes between federal government and its member states shall be settled by a third party (such as Constitutional Court).

It should be pointed out that the degree of autonomy depends primarily on the range of subject matters the governing power over which is assigned to the autonomous entity, and not on whether the arrangement is federal or not. It is possible that an autonomous entity in a unitary state exercise a degree of autonomy higher than that of a member state of a federation. [2] The case of HKSAR has set a typical example in this regard.

2. Double Legal Grounds

In international practice, legal status and autonomy of a few regional entities, such as so-called internationalised territories were established by treaties. [3]Some Western scholars argued that the JD creates an objective international entity whose rights and responsibilities are governed by treaty, and contended that the HKSAR derives its validity from the international legal order and it is subject to international law which determines its status and regulates its relations with other international entities. It is thereby concluded that as a "creature of international law", the HKSAR's existence or its "right to life" ought to be internationally guaranteed and the "peoplehood" of its inhabitants respected. [4] This conclusion is somewhat misleading as it exaggerated the role of the JD and ignored the origin and sources of

---

〔1〕 Xiaobing Xu, George D. Wilson, "The Hong Kong Special Administrative Region as a Model of Regional External Autonomy", 32 *Case W. Res. J. Int'l L.*, 18 (2000).

〔2〕 Albert H. Y. Chen, The Relationship between the Central Government and the SAR, in Peter Wesley-Smith and Albert H. Y. Chen (eds.), *The Basic Law and Hong Kong's Future*, Butterworths, 112 (1988).

〔3〕 E. g. In 1920-1939 Danzig was considered as free city with a legal personality and regulated by international principles and rules according to Free Treaty of Danzig. See Roda Mushkat, "Hong Kong as an International Legal Person", 6 *Emory International Law Review*, 109-110 (1992).

〔4〕 Roda Mushkat, "Hong Kong as an International Legal Person", 6 *Emory International Law Review* 110, 169 (1992); Brian Z. Tamanaha, "Post-1997 Hong Kong: A Comparative Study of the Meaning of 'High Degree of Autonomy'—with a Specific Look at the Commonwealth of the Northern Mariana Islands", 5 *China Law Reporter*, 168 (1989).

relevant provisions of the JD.

As a basic law of China, the PRC Constitution is the legal sources and foundation for Chinese treaty practice and domestic legislation.

It is worth noting that the original legal basis of the HKSAR's external autonomy is Chinese Constitution. [1] Article 31 of the Constitution is the constitutional embodiment of the Concept of "one country two systems". It provides that "the State may establish special administrative region when necessary. The systems to be instituted in special administrative regions shall be prescribed by laws enacted by the National People's Congress in the light of the specific conditions". China's international promise on the HKSAR's high autonomy in the JD is based on this article. [2] In this sense, the HKSAR is a creature of Chinese domestic law and reaffirmed and guaranteed by international law.

As far as the double legal grounds of the HKSAR' autonomy, it is very important to pay attention to the role of Chinese Constitution as first legal sources and legal foundation. The provisions on the HKSAR's autonomy in the JD are also very important as they may be referred as legal ground of the HKSAR's autonomy. However, they are at the secondary level in terms of legal sources. It is unrealistic to consider relevant provisions of the JD as only legal ground of the HKSAR's autonomy and therefore to claim the HKSAR as a so called "internationalised territory".

Furthermore there is big difference between the HKSAR and an internationalised territory in the nature of their legal status: the HKSAR is a local administrative entity under the CPG within Chinese constitutional system while an internationalised territory is an entity without clear domestic legal status due to specific historical and/or political circumstances. The rights and obligations of such entity are established and regulated by a treaty or treaties.

Finally, we should pay more attention to the historical context of China's arrangement on the HKSAR autonomy. When the HKSAR's high external autono-

---

[1] Wang Hanbin, who was then the Secretary-General of the Standing Committee of the National People's Congress as well as the Chairman of the Commission on Legal affairs of the NPC, explained that Article 31 is contained in the chapter on "general principles". All such general principles are fundamental and stable state policies. This article is also applicable to Macao Special Administrative region and other future special administrative regions in China. See Albert H. Y. Chen, "Further Aspects of the Autonomy of Hong Kong under the PRC Constitution", 14 (3) *HKLJ*, 342-343 (1984).

[2] See Art. 3 (1) of the JD and Section I of Annex I of the JD.

my and related provisions in the JD and the BL are emphasized, the background and prerequisite that China resume to exercise sovereignty over Hong Kong and related provisions in the JD and the BL shall be paid equal attention.[1] The grant of external autonomy to the HKSAR must be seen against the backdrop of the UK's transfer of and the China's resumption of exercising the sovereign power.

3. International Guarantee

The HKSAR's external autonomy does not solely depend on the unilateral desire of Hong Kong, China or the UK—it also depends on whether other countries are willing to recognise this status.[2] Actually the HKSAR's external autonomy could become meaningless if few states and international organizations were interested in developing and maintaining separate relations with it. According to principle of international law, unlike states and international organizations, which are regarded as the normal types of international legal persons and can acquire their international personalities by meeting fixed conditions, the HKSAR's external autonomy and international legal status relies not only China's authorization but also on the recognition and acceptance of other existing international persons.[3]

The guarantee for the HKSAR's external autonomy by international law has great significance for international community, especially the Western countries. From the points of view of the constitutional theorist, the autonomy of an autonomous entity in a unitary state is less securely guaranteed or entrenched than the autonomy of member state in a federation since the former is not directly protected by the constitution.[4] Anthony Neoh further points out: "the Chinese Constitution itself has undergone many revisions since 1954, underlining the ease with which bas-

---

[1] The preamble of the BL points out that "upholding national unity and territorial integrity, maintaining the prosperity and stability of Hong Kong, and taking account of history and realities, the People's Republic of China has decided that upon China's resumption of the exercise of sovereignty over Hong Kong, a Hong Kong Special Administrative Region will be established in accordance with the provisions of Article 31 of the Constitution of the People's Republic of China......"

[2] See Albert H. Y. Chen, "Some Reflections on Hong Kong's Autonomy", 24 *HKLJ*, 179-180 (1994).

[3] See Xiaobing Xu, George D. Wilson, "The Hong Kong Special Administrative Region as a Model of Regional External Autonomy", 32 *Case W. Res. J. Int'l L.*, 31 (2000).

[4] See Albert H. Y. Chen, "The Relationship between the Central Government and the SAR", in Peter Wesley-Smith and Albert H. Y. Chen (eds.), *The Basic Law and Hong Kong's Future*, Butterworths, 112 (1988).

ic legal norms can be changed within the PRC. "[1]

Considering that the recognition and support of the international community would play an important role in determining the degree of the HKSAR's external autonomy, both the PRC and the UK actively and successfully sought out such recognition and support on behalf of Hong Kong in regard to Hong Kong's international rights and obligations during the transition period. [2] Since 1 July 1997, the HKSAR has extended the network of bilateral agreements to cover relations in broad areas with many countries and will examine new multilateral treaties that may be relevant to the HKSAR. These multifarious external legal relations have helped to strengthen the HKSAR's international status. [3] Since the HKSAR's bilateral and multilateral treaties link to many foreign countries, its external autonomy is subject to continual international oversight, which in turn will enhance this status. Once international network of the HKSAR constituted by its bilateral and multilateral treaties has been well set up, the HKSAR's external autonomy will be fully guaranteed by international law.

Experience shows that the international community pay much attention to the HKSAR's external autonomy. It is understandable that the Western countries intend not only to recognize and guarantee the HKSAR's external autonomy, but also to promote and protect their own existing and future interests in Hong Kong.

Some commentators points out that the international community, via its power of recognition and support, can exercise some "constitutive" effect on the HKSAR's autonomous status as a non-sovereign international actor, or it can deny or cut down that recognition and support and thereby undermine the HKSAR's external autonomy. [4] Before 1 July 1997, the US and the EU issued Act and Resolution on status of the HKSAR respectively. In 1992, at the instigation of a few members of the US Congress who were encouraged by some of the groups in Hong Kong, the United States-

---

[1] Anthony Neoh, "Hong Kong's Future: The View of a Hong Kong Lawyer", 22 *Cal. W. Int'l L. J.* 332-333 (1992).

[2] See Xiaobing Xu, George D. Wilson, "The Hong Kong Special Administrative Region as a Model of Regional External Autonomy", 32 *Case W. Res. J. Int'l L.*, 34 (2000).

[3] See Elsie Leung, "The Rule of Law and Its Operation in Hong Kong after Reunification", 6 *Policy Bulletin* 9-10 (1998).

[4] See Xiaobing Xu, George D. Wilson, "The Hong Kong Special Administrative Region as a Model of Regional External Autonomy", 32 *Case W. Res. J. Int'l L.*, 32 (2000).

Hong Kong Policy Act was enacted. The Act seeks to achieve various purposes，some strictly legal and others more political. In all these respects on the HKSAR's external autonomy，the Act does little more than state what is already explicit or implicit in the JD and the BL. However，it has two provisions，which may be seen in the nature of "sanctions". [1]

The EU Parliament adopted a Resolution on the Situation in Hong Kong on 10 April 1997，which showed the EU's concern for the autonomy of Hong Kong after 1997. [2] Following the Resolution，a Commission Communication to the Council and Parliament entitled "The European Union and Hong Kong: Beyond 1997" was adopted on 23 April 1997. In this document，the Commission，after underlining the importance of ties between Hong Kong and Europe and analysing Hong Kong's future as a special administrative region within the PRC，outlines a strategy for strengthening relations between the EU and Hong Kong. [3]

Behind Hong Kong's unprecedented external autonomy lies unprecedented international recognition which might create "constitutive" effect or even pressure on Hong Kong's external autonomy and China's policy on it. It should be emphasised that from international legal point of view，China has not had any international commitment on the HKSAR's external autonomy with the US or the EU. Instead，China has signed the JD with the UK and bears the international obligations to the

[1]　One provision is that the President of US may suspend the application of US laws to Hong Kong if the President "determines" that Hong Kong is not sufficiently autonomous to justify treatment under particular law of US，or any provisions thereof，different from that accorded the PRC. The second provisions is for reporting by the US government to the Congress，at specified period from 1993 to 2000，"on conditions of interest to the United States"，including the development of democratic institutions in Hong Kong (sec. 301)，and it is therefore clearly connected with the transitional period. See Yash Ghai，*Hong Kong's New Constitutional Order*，*The Resumption of Chinese Sovereign and the Basic Law*，Hong Kong University Press，459-461 (1997).

[2]　In this document，the Parliament called for the transfer of sovereignty of Hong Kong to take place in full accordance with the principles set out in the JD and the BL. It called on the Council to establish how it intended to develop relations with Hong Kong and on the Commission to present an annual report covering political，economic and human rights in HKSAR. The parliament also resolved to monitor the situation in HKSAR，notably by sending a fact-finding mission. European Commission，*Bulletin of the European Union*，4-1997，89.

[3]　Proposals include dealing directly and maintaining regular and close contacts with the government of HKSAR；continuing to treat Hong Kong as an independent entity for trade policy purposes and an important partner within the WTO；monitoring the situation in Hong Kong and respecting for the rights granted to its citizens under the SAR，working with international community and publishing an annual report on all aspects of relations between EU and Hong Kong；continuing to assess the Hong Kong government on its own merits for the purposes of the common visa list；exploring ways of putting trade，investment and co-operation relations between Hong Kong and EU on a more permanent footing and developing active co-operation with Hong Kong as an Asian hub. European Commission，*Bulletin of the European Union*，4-1997，88-89.

UK, not to the US or the EU. The HKSAR external autonomy may be further enhanced and guaranteed by treaties, not by domestic laws of foreign countries or documents of international organisations. The HKSAR's autonomy essentially belongs to Chinese internal affairs. China has not undertaken general obligation on the HKSAR's autonomy to international community. Therefore, the countries and/or international organisations without treaty arrangement with China or the HKSAR should observe strictly the general accepted principle of international law "non-interference in each other's internal affairs" in their relations with the HKSAR.

Ⅳ. Conclusions

In sum, the HKSAR's external autonomy has great significance both on theoretical and practical aspects.

The HKSAR's external autonomy established by the JD and the BL develops a new component of autonomy and thereby strengthens and enriches the content of theory of autonomy. The HKSAR's *de jure* external autonomy is the legalization of the concept of "one country two systems" in the international scene. Furthermore the HKSAR's external autonomy is really "high degree", higher than any member state in a federation and any other autonomous entity in the world. In this sense, it sets a unique model of external autonomy for autonomous entities.

The successful practice of the HKSAR's external autonomy demonstrates convincingly that the HKSAR enjoys and develops its unprecedented international status. By the network of bilateral and multilateral treaties, the HKSAR retains and develops its pre-existing international status after 1997. In fact, the practice of the HKSAR's external autonomy has made great contributions to the development of international law.

The characteristics of the HKSAR's external autonomy include authorization nature, double legal grounds and international guarantee. By the authorization of the CPG, the HKSAR has enjoyed and developed its unprecedented international status in accordance with the JD and the BL since 1997. Though international recognition and support is vital important for the HKSAR's external autonomy, any exaggeration or interference to the HKSAR's external autonomy does not help to either justify or define the HKSAR's international personality.

第十章
香港双边投资条约实践

第一节　论香港双边投资条约实践[*]

【摘要】　本文在简述中国香港地区双边投资条约(bilateral investment treaty, BIT)实践沿革的基础上,较细致分析其适用范围、投资待遇、"剥夺"及赔偿标准、争端的解决等主要条款,进而探讨香港缔约权的授权性质及其国际承认的依据问题,以及香港 BIT 实践衍生的条约适用问题。本文指出,香港 BIT 实践遵循了传统模式,因其非主权实体地位,亦具有一些重要特征;香港 BITs 的授权规定进一步明确表明了香港缔约权的授权性质,缔约对方和国际社会承认香港缔约主体地位的决定性法律依据是中国宪法;香港 BIT 实践衍生的条约适用已然成为现实问题,需要认真加以防范。

《中华人民共和国政府和大不列颠及北爱尔兰联合王国政府关于香港问题的联合声明》(简称《中英联合声明》)附件一第 11 条第 1 款和《中华人民共和国香港特别行政区基本法》(简称《基本法》)第 151 条明确规定,香港特别行政区(简称"香港特区")可以"中国香港"的名义,在经济、贸易、金融、航运、通讯、旅游、文化和体育等有关领域单独地同世界各国、各地区及有关国际组织保持和发展关系,并签订和履行有关协议。上述授权方式虽然尚未成为国际法中的普遍实践,但它明确确立了香港

---

　* 原载《国际经济法学刊》第 19 卷第 3 期,北京大学出版社 2012 年版。
　本文为国家社科基金重大项目"促进与保护我国海外投资的法律体制研究"(项目批准号:09&ZD032)(2009—2012)的阶段性研究成果之一。

特区在规定领域中单独签订双边条约的能力。[1] 本文在简述香港双边投资条约(bilateral investment treaty，BIT)实践沿革的基础上，对其主要条款、法律依据及其衍生的条约适用问题作一初步探讨。

一、香港双边投资条约实践的沿革

20 世纪 50 年代后期，联邦德国与巴基斯坦签订了第一个旨在促进和保护跨国投资的 BIT。传统上，BITs 的缔约方均为主权国家。典型的是一方为欧洲国家，另一方为发展中国家。德国和瑞士在这方面居领先地位。历经半个多世纪，多数 BITs 都模仿或至少广泛地照搬 1959 年《海外投资国际公约草案》(Draft International Convention on Investments Abroad)和经济合作与开发组织(OECD)于 1967 年颁布的《保护外国财产的公约草案》(Draft Convention on the Protection of Foreign Property)。[2] 由于来源相同，不同 BITs 的主题、结构和用语，在不同的时期、不同的国家实践仍显得非常相似。[3] 近年来，BITs 为各国广泛接受，已然成为国际投资条约体制的最普遍形式[4]，也是国际法最显著的新发展之一。[5]

英国自 1974 年起参与签订 BITs 的谈判。[6] 在英国管治时期，香港的对外投资关系是由英国与有关国家之间的 BITs(简称"英外 BITs")调整。英国通过"领土延伸"的换文将一些英外 BITs 延伸适用于香港。此类协定在香港的法律效力仅延续至 1997 年 6 月 30 日。在过渡期，为了保持和发展香港的对外投资关系，香港面临两种选择：一是香港以其名义单独同外国签订 BITs，二是中国签订的 BITs 的适用范围在 1997 年 7 月 1 日后扩及香港。香港选择前者。鉴于香港与中国内地之间经济和法律

---

〔1〕 Yash Ghai, *Hong Kong's New Constitutional Order*，*The Resumption of Chinese Sovereignty and the Basic Law*，Hong Kong University Press, 1997, pp. 435-436; Anthony Neoh, Hong Kong's Future: The View of a Hong Kong Lawyer, *Cal. W. Int'l L. J.*，Vol. 22，1992，pp. 351-352.

〔2〕 关于 BITs 的历史，参见 Jeswald W. Salacuse, BIT by BIT: The Growth of Bilateral Investment Treaties and Their Impact on Foreign Investment in Developing Countries, *The International Lawyer*，Vol. 24，1990，pp. 656-661.

〔3〕 See Jason Webb Yackee, Conceptual Difficulties in the Empirical Study of Bilateral Investment Treaties, *Brooklyn J. Int'l L.* Vol. 33，2008，pp. 415-416.

〔4〕 See Michael R. Reading, The Bilateral Investment Treaty in ASEAN: A Comparative Analysis, *Duke Law Journal*，Vol. 42，1992，p. 682. 关于 BIT 实践概况及典型条文分析，参见 United Nations Conference on Trade and Development, *Bilateral Investment Treaties 1995-2006: Trends in Investment Rulemaking*，United Nations，2007. 拉丁美洲国家在 20 世纪 80 年代后期转变其有关 BITs 的传统立场，开始签订 BITs，近 20 年来已签订 500 多个 BITs. See Mary H. Mourra (ed.), *Latin American Investment Treaty Arbitration: The Controversies and Conflicts*，Wolters Kluwer, 2008, p. 1.

〔5〕 Jason Webb Yackee, Conceptual Difficulties in the Empirical Study of Bilateral Investment Treaties, *Brooklyn J. Int'l L.* Vol. 33，2008，p. 405.

〔6〕 关于英国 BIT 实践概况，参见 Eileen Denza, Shelagh Brooks, Investment Protection Treaties: United Kingdom Experience, *Int'l & Com. L. Q.*，Vol. 36，1987，pp. 908-923.

制度的重大差异以及在国际投资活动中的不同角色和地位,这一选择显然更能适应香港的实际需要,并且更能有效地服务于促进和保护香港对外投资和外来投资的目标。

香港以其名义同外国签订双边经济协定的实践肇始于过渡期(1984 年 12 月—1997 年 6 月)。当时,在中英联合联络小组主持下,作为保持和发展香港对外关系的重要工作之一,香港开始在民航、投资和税务等经济领域以其名义单独与外国签订双边协定。[1] 1992 年 11 月 19 日,《香港政府与荷兰王国政府关于鼓励投资和保护投资协定》在香港正式签署,1993 年 9 月 1 日正式生效,首开由非主权实体参与签订BITs 的先河。[2] 在香港 BIT 实践中,香港—荷兰 BIT 作为第一个"先例",影响深远,成为 "事实上范本"(de facto model)。香港 BIT 实践的"法律上范本"(de jure model),即"香港政府与……政府关于促进和保护投资的协定范本"发表于 1995 年。[3] 它遵循了 BITs 的传统结构和一般规则,[4] 为香港 BIT 实践的发展发挥了重要作用。

截至 2011 年 6 月 14 日,香港以其名义与 18 个国家签订了 17 个 BITs,其中 15个正式生效。[5] 值得注意的是,与香港签订 BITs 的缔约对方除泰国外,均为发达国家。[6] 香港成功的 BIT 实践不仅显示了其对外自治权方面的突出成就,[7] 也反映了国际法特别是国际投资法发展的重要突破与创新。

---

〔1〕 参见曾华群:《过渡期香港双边条约实践初探》,载《国际经济法论丛》第 1 卷,法律出版社 1998 年版,第486—510 页。

〔2〕 该文本发表于 *Special Supplement No. 5 to the Hong Kong Government Gazette*,E27-53 (1992)。

〔3〕 香港 BIT 范本发表于 Rudolf Dolzer, Margrete Stevens, *Bilateral Investment Treaties*,Martinus Nijhoff Publishers,1995,pp. 200-208。

〔4〕 BIT 范本有两种类型:一是欧洲范本,是传统型;二是美国范本,包括一些新条款和复杂的争端解决程序。香港 BIT 共有 11 个条款,分别是:第 1 条,定义;第 2 条,投资和收益的促进和保护;第 3 条,投资待遇;第 4 条,损失的赔偿;第 5 条,征收;第 6 条,投资和收益的转移;第 7 条,例外;第 8 条,投资争端的解决;第 9 条,缔约方之间的争端;第 10 条,生效;第 11 条,期限与终止。显然,香港 BIT 范本遵循欧洲范本。参见典型的欧洲范本:德国 2008 条约范本:德意志联邦共和国与[某国]关于鼓励和相互保护投资的条约(总计 13 个条款);法兰西共和国政府与[某]共和国政府关于相互促进和保护投资的协定草案(2006)(总计 11 个条款)。

〔5〕 香港 BITs 无须立法实施,惯常做法是在缔约双方政府确认协定生效后,在《香港政府宪报》(第 5 号特别副刊)上刊登。香港 BITs 的缔约对方、生效日期及协定出处分别是:荷兰 (1993.9.1.),*Special Supplement No. 5 to the Hong Kong Government Gazette*,134,no. 50 (1992):E25-E53;澳大利亚 (1993.10.15.),Ibid.,135,no. 37 (1993):E103-E123;丹麦 (1994.3.4.),136,no. 6 (1994):E19-E48;瑞典 (1994.6.26.),136,no. 23 (1994):E51-E78;瑞士 (1994.10.22.),136,no. 48 (1994):E85-E116;新西兰 (1995.8.5.),137,no. 34 (1995):E95-E115;法国 (1997.5.30.),2,no. 26 (1998):E215-E240;日本 (1997.6.18.),2,no. 26 (1998):E241-E281;韩国 (1997.7.30.),2,no. 26 (1998):E283-E316;奥地利 (1997.10.1.),2,no. 26 (1998):E317-E351;意大利 (1998.2.2.),2,no. 6 (1998):E3-E35;德国 (1998.2.19.),2,no. 10 (1998):E39-E66;英国 (1999.4.12.),3,no. 15 (1999):E391-E414;比利时与卢森堡 (2001.6.18.),5,no. 25 (2001):E175-E222;泰国 (2006.4.12.),10,no. 18 (2006):E41-E65。截至 2011 年 6 月 14 日,香港特区与芬兰、科威特也签署了 BITs,尚未生效。

〔6〕 在 16 个香港 BITs 的缔约对方中,15 个是经济合作开发组织(OECD)的成员国,只有 1 个是发展中国家。

〔7〕 关于香港对外自治权实践的概况,参见 Zeng Huaqun, Unprecedented International Status:Theoretical and Practical Aspects of the HKSAR's External Autonomy, *The Journal of World Investment & Trade*,Vol. 9,No. 3,2008,pp. 275-297。

二、香港双边投资条约的主要条款

一般而言,香港的 BIT 实践遵循了传统模式,因其非主权实体地位,也具有一些重要特征,主要体现于适用范围、投资待遇、"剥夺"及赔偿标准、争端的解决等条款。[1]

(一) 适用范围

广义上,BITs 的适用范围主要指适用的地域、期限和对象,一般由协定的定义、期限等条款确定,对协定的效力具有重要意义。[2] BITs 定义条款的目的是确定协定的适用对象及其范围。典型的 BITs 保护缔约一方投资者在缔约另一方境内的投资。因此,BITs 的适用范围取决于某些关键术语,特别是"投资"和"投资者"的定义。[3] 定义条款通常还对缔约双方的"领土"(territory)概念作出定义,使缔约一方"投资者"在缔约另一方"领土"之内的"投资"得以保护。[4] 此外,BITs 的期限和终止条款也确定了协定适用的时限。

一般而言,香港遵循 BITs 有关适用范围的普遍实践,同时,由于其非主权实体地位,也有一些特殊的规定,尤其在"投资者""地域范围"等方面。

1. 投资

在 BITs 定义条款中,典型的"投资"定义是涵盖"各种资产",且附有未穷尽的资产清单。[5] 美国等资本输出国的 BITs 范本特别青睐宽泛的"投资"定义,旨在确保其 BITs 能保护与其海外投资相关的各种活动。[6]

遵循 BITs 的普遍实践,[7] 香港 BIT 范本第 1(e) 条规定:

> "投资"是指"所有直接或间接持有或投资的资产,特别是,但不限于:
>
> (i) 动产、不动产和任何其他财产权利,如抵押权、留置权、质权或用益权;
>
> (ii) 公司的股份、股票和债券,及在公司的任何其他形式参与;

---

[1] 关于香港 BITs 特征的分析,参见 Zeng Huaqun, Initiative and Implications of Hong Kong's Bilateral Investment Treaties, *The Journal of World Investment & Trade*, Vol. 11, 2010, pp. 669-696。

[2] Michael R. Reading, The Bilateral Investment Treaty in ASEAN: A Comparative Analysis, *Duke Law Journal*, Vol. 42, 1992, p. 695.

[3] United Nations Conference on Trade and Development, *Bilateral Investment Treaties 1995-2006: Trends in Investment Rulemaking*, United Nations, 2007, p. 7.

[4] See Andrew Newcombe, Lluis Paradell, *Law and Practice of Investment Treaties*, *Standards of Treatment*, Wolters Kluwer, 2009, p. 65.

[5] Ibid., pp. 65-66.

[6] See M. Sornarajah, *The International Law on Foreign Investment*, 2nd ed., Cambridge University Press, 2004, p. 9.

[7] See United Nations Conference on Trade and Development, *Bilateral Investment Treaties 1995-2006: Trends in Investment Rulemaking*, United Nations, 2007, p. 8.

(iii) 对金钱请求权或依据合同具有商务价值的履行请求权；

(iv) 知识产权和商誉；

(v) 依据法律或通过合同赋予的经营特许权，包括勘探、耕作、提炼或开发自然资源的特许权。

所投资产形式的变化，不影响其作为投资的性质"。

香港 BIT 实践一般遵循上述规定，采用"基于资产"的宽泛"投资"定义，有的略作修改或补充，[1]其涵盖范围显然超出了"外国直接投资"。[2]

必须指出，所谓"所投资产形式的变化，不影响其作为投资的性质"的规定，具有重要的现实意义。根据该规定，投资的性质"冻结"于投资者作出投资之际，以后即使资产形式发生变化，其作为投资的性质仍无可争议。该规定未雨绸缪，有效避免或减少了潜在的有关投资性质的争端。

2. 投资者

BITs 通常规定，"投资者"指缔约双方的具有国民身份的自然人[3]和依据缔约双方法律设立的公司。香港 BITs 有关"公司"作为"投资者"的定义遵循 BIT 的普遍实践，[4]而由于香港的非主权实体地位及其保护特定人群的需要，有关自然人作为"投资者"的定义则具有明显特征，即以居民资格取代国民资格。

传统上，在"自然人"的定义上一般采取两种方式：一是采取单一定义，适用于缔约双方；二是采取两种定义，分别适用于缔约双方。[5]香港 BIT 范本采取第三种方式。根据该范本的规定，"投资者"指："(i) 对于缔约各方：在该缔约方领域具有居留权的自然人……(ii) 对于【香港的缔约对方】：具有国民身份的自然人"。[6]可见，香

〔1〕　参见香港—荷兰 BIT 第1(3)条；香港—澳大利亚 BIT 第1(e)条；香港—丹麦 BIT 第1(3)条；香港—瑞典 BIT 第1(3)条；香港—瑞士 BIT 第1(5)条；香港—新西兰 BIT 第1.5条；香港—法国 BIT 第1(2)条；香港—日本 BIT 第1.3条；香港—韩国 BIT 第1(4)条；香港—奥地利 BIT 第1(c)条；香港—意大利 BIT 第1(5)条；香港—德国 BIT 第1(2)条；香港—英国 BIT 第1(e)条；香港—比利时与卢森堡 BIT 第1(4)条；香港—泰国 BIT 第1(3)条。香港—韩国 BIT 第1(4)(f)条增加了投资的一种类型，规定："在缔约一方境内，根据其法律法规，租赁协议项下的货物由承租人处理者"。

〔2〕　除了"基于资产"的定义，在 BIT 实践中，还有"投资"的重复或循环定义(tautological or circular definition)、完整清单(closed-list definition)等。See United Nations Conference on Trade and Development, *Bilateral Investment Treaties 1995-2006：Trends in Investment Rulemaking*, United Nations, 8-13 (2007).

〔3〕　绝大多数 BITs 保护具有缔约一方国籍的自然人。因此，缔约一方国民的典型定义是，根据该缔约方国内法承认为国民或公民的自然人。在一些情况下，"投资者"的定义更为宽泛，不仅包括公民，也包括根据内国法作为永久居民的自然人。See United Nations Conference on Trade and Development, *Bilateral Investment Treaties 1995-2006：Trends in Investment Rulemaking*, United Nations, 2007, p.13.

〔4〕　BITs 通常依据三个基本标准决定"公司"的国籍：(1) 设立地标准；(2) 住所地标准；(3) 控制标准。See Rudolf Dolzer, Margrete Stevens, *Bilateral Investment Treaties*, Martinus Nijhoff Publishers, 1995, pp.35-36.

〔5〕　Ibid., pp.31-32.

〔6〕　香港 BIT 范本第1(f)(i)条。

港 BIT 范本采取永久居民和国民两种标准[1]，对香港仅适用永久居民标准，对香港的缔约对方则适用永久居民和国民两种标准。[2]

香港—荷兰 BIT 规定，"投资者指：(i) 对于香港：在该领域具有居留权的自然人……(ii) 对于荷兰王国：具有国民身份的自然人"。[3] 如此规定已成为香港 BITs 的普遍实践。[4] 此类规定与香港 BIT 范本的区别在于，对香港的缔约对方仅适用国民标准。

显然，由于其非主权实体地位，香港不能采用国民标准定义作为"投资者"的"自然人"。其原因在于，除了 1997 年 6 月 30 日之前香港居民复杂的国籍问题外，即使在中国对香港恢复行使主权的 1997 年 7 月 1 日之后，香港 BITs 的保护范围也不能涵盖不具有香港永久居留权的中国国民，包括中国内地、澳门地区和台湾地区的中国国民。而香港 BITs 的保护范围则可能涵盖具有香港永久居留权的外国国民。

然而，对作为"投资者"的"自然人"适用不同的定义标准，可能产生"双重 BIT 保护"问题。作为适用永久居民标准的后果，寻求香港 BITs 保护的香港永久居民可能是具有香港永久居留权的外国人，包括香港 BITs 缔约对方的国民。在此情况下，具有香港永久居民和香港 BITs 缔约对方国民双重身份的自然人，可按其意愿寻求或挑选来自香港或缔约对方的保护。香港 BITs 缔约双方则不得不面临此种棘手的"投资者认同"问题。

为解决这一问题，香港—英国 BIT 第 1(f)(i) 条明确规定，"投资者"指：对于香港："具有香港特别行政区永久居留权且非英国国民的自然人"；对于英国："英国国民且不具有香港特别行政区永久居留权的自然人"。该规定试图澄清和解决"投资者认同"问题，却产生了"BIT 保护真空"的新问题。显然，"具有香港特别行政区永久居留权的英国国民"无法从香港—英国 BIT 的缔约任何一方寻求保护。

---

[1] 在一些国家中，国民(national)和"公民"(citizen)在法律意义上存在重要区别。根据美国法，"国民"的用语比"公民"更为宽泛。例如，美国萨摩 (American Samoa) 土著是美国国民，但不是美国公民。See Kenneth J. Vandevelde, *U. S. International Investment Agreements*, Oxford University Press, 2009, p. 144.

[2] 实践中，只有 2 个香港 BITs 采用"永久居民标准和国民/公民标准均适用于缔约对方"的规定。香港—澳大利亚 BIT 第 1(f) 条规定："投资者"指"在澳大利亚方面：(A)根据澳大利亚法律具有澳大利亚公民身份或永久居留于澳大利亚的自然人……"香港—新西兰 BIT 第 1(2)(b)(i) 条也有类似规定。

[3] 香港—荷兰 BIT 第 1(2) 条。

[4] 香港—丹麦 BIT 第 1(2) 条；香港—瑞典 BIT 第 1(2) 条；香港—瑞士 BIT 第 1(2) 条；香港—法国 BIT 第 1(3)条；香港—日本 BIT 第 1.4 条；香港—韩国 BIT 第 1(5)条；香港—奥地利 BIT 第 1(d)条；香港—意大利 BIT 第 1(6)条；香港—德国 BIT 第 1(4)条；香港—英国 BIT 第 1(f)条；香港—比利时与卢森堡 BIT 第 1(5)条；香港—泰国 BIT 第 1(4)条。

3. 地域范围

在 BITs 实践中,有关地域范围的规定一般采用"领土"(territory)的概念。BITs 适用的地域范围取决于"领土"的定义。定义该用语的目的并非划定缔约双方的领土范围。其重要意义在于,为 BITs 保护投资的目的,将位于缔约方领海之外海域的投资,视为位于缔约方"领土"之内。[1]

值得注意的是,在香港 BITs 中,采用"地区"(area)而不是"领土"的概念。根据香港 BIT 范本第 1(a)(i)条规定,所谓"地区",在香港方面,包括香港岛、九龙和新界;[2]在香港的缔约对方方面,系指包括该主权国家的全部领土,包括特定海域。[3] 以"地区"概念取代"领土",在 BIT 历史上是第一次,也是由香港的非主权实体地位所决定的。"领土"通常用于表述主权国家的地域范围。[4]"地区"的涵义更广,可用于表述非主权实体和主权国家的地域范围。鉴于香港的非主权实体地位,"地区"的概念比之"领土",更能准确表述香港的地域范围。

4. 适用期限

有关适用期限问题,在 BITs 谈判中产生了两个主要问题:一是协定是否适用于原有投资;二是协定适用的期限与终止问题。[5]

4.1 适用于原有投资问题

根据《维也纳条约法公约》,条约通常不具有追溯力。[6] 因此,来自条约的权利和义务仅适用于该条约生效之后,且适用于该条约生效之后发生的行为或事实。BITs 是否在生效后适用于已有的投资,在 BITs 实践中有如下选择:

(1)规定保护将来的投资和已有的投资,但不适用于在 BITs 生效之前产生或处理的任何与投资有关的争端或请求权;

(2)规定仅保护将来的投资;

---

〔1〕 United Nations Conference on Trade and Development,*Bilateral Investment Treaties 1995-2006:Trends in Investment Rulemaking*,United Nations,2007,p.17.

〔2〕 香港 BIT 范本第 1(a)(i)条。这是所有香港 BITs 的实践。

〔3〕 例如,香港—荷兰 BIT 第 1.1 条规定:"在荷兰王国方面,指荷兰王国的领土,包括与该领土海岸相邻的海域,及荷兰王国根据国际法行使主权权利或管辖权的海域。"

〔4〕 对"领土"的一般定义是:"属特定政府管辖权内的地域;该地球表面部分由一国专属占有和控制。"See Bryan A. Garner,*Black's Law Dictionary*,8th ed.,Thomson Press,2004,p.1512.

〔5〕 United Nations Conference on Trade and Development,*Bilateral Investment Treaties 1995-2006:Trends in Investment Rulemaking*,United Nations,2007,p.19.

〔6〕 《维也纳条约法公约》第 28 条规定:"除条约表示不同意思,或另经确定外,关于条约对一当事国生效之日以前所发生之任何行为或事实或已不存在之任何情势,条约之规定不对该当事国发生拘束力。"

（3）对此不作规定。[1]

根据香港 BIT 范本第 1(e)条，"'投资'的用语包括所有投资，不论是在本协定生效日期之前或之后作出"。该条款由所有香港 BITs 一体遵循。[2] 看来，香港 BITs 对此采取最为开放的态度，即明确表明保护将来的投资和已有的投资，同时也不排除在"BITs 生效之前产生或处理的任何与投资有关的争端或请求权"。

4.2　期限与终止问题

与其他国际条约不同，BITs 通常规定其特定的生效期限，旨在为缔约双方投资者提供适用于其投资的国际法制的高度确定性和可预见性。在 BITs 实践中，一般规定 10 年期限，也有规定更长的期限，如 15 年。其他则规定，BITs 持续有效，直至缔约一方通知缔约另一方其终止的意愿。[3]

根据香港 BIT 范本第 11 条：

> 本协定将持续有效直至缔约任何一方给予缔约另一方书面终止通知之日起 12 个月届满。

从上述可见，香港 BIT 范本未规定确定的期限，终止协定的方式是单方面提出书面终止通知。

香港—荷兰 BIT 第 13.1 条采取另一种模式，规定：

> 本协定在十五年内保持有效。除非缔约任何一方在本协定有效期届满之日最少十二个月前给予终止协定通知，本协定在不须言明的情况下每十年延长一次。缔约各方保留在本协定有效期届满之日最少十二个月前基于通知的终止协定权利。[4]

该模式成为香港 BIT 实践的普遍形式。（参见表 1）

---

〔1〕 United Nations Conference on Trade and Development，*Bilateral Investment Treaties 1995-2006*：*Trends in Investment Rulemaking*，United Nations，2007，p. 20.

〔2〕 香港 BIT 范本。参见香港—荷兰 BIT 第 9 条；香港—澳大利亚 BIT 第 1(e)条；香港—丹麦 BIT 第 12(1)条；香港—瑞典 BIT 第 11 条；香港—瑞士 BIT 第 9 条；香港—新西兰 BIT 第 2.2 条；香港—法国 BIT 第 12 条；香港—日本 BIT 第 10 条；香港—韩国 BIT 第 12 条；香港—奥地利 BIT 第 11 条；香港—意大利 BIT 第 9 条；香港—德国 BIT 第 9 条；香港—英国 BIT 第 1(e)条；香港—比利时与卢森堡 BIT 第 11 条；香港—泰国 BIT 第 1(3)条。

〔3〕 United Nations Conference on Trade and Development，*Bilateral Investment Treaties 1995-2006*：*Trends in Investment Rulemaking*，United Nations，2007，p. 20.

〔4〕 香港—荷兰 BIT 第 13.1 条。

表 1　香港 BITs 有关期限与终止的规定[1]

BITs 缔约双方	生效日期(年、月、日)	期限（年）	延长期(年)
香港—荷兰	1993.9.1	15	10
香港—澳大利亚	1993.10.15	15	未确定
香港—丹麦	1994.3.4	15	未确定
香港—瑞典	1994.6.26	15	未确定
香港—瑞士	1994.10.22	15	10
香港—新西兰	1995.8.5	15	未确定
香港—法国	1997.5.30	20	10
香港—日本	1997.6.18	15	未确定
香港—韩国	1997.7.30	15	未确定
香港—奥地利	1997.10.1	15	未确定
香港—意大利	1998.2.2	15	10
香港—德国	1998.2.19	15	未确定
香港—英国	1999.4.12	15	未确定
香港—比利时与卢森堡	2001.6.18	15	10
香港—泰国	2006.4.12	15	未确定

　　值得注意的是,所有香港 BITs 都规定了较长的适用期限(15 年或以上),并附加延长的适用期限。在过渡期生效的香港 BITs 中,有关期限和终止条款的重要意义在于,明确表明了该协定将跨越 1997 年 7 月 1 日而持续有效。此类规定也表明,香港 BITs 的缔约对方确信,香港的国际地位在 1997 年 7 月 1 日之后将保持不变。

　　(二) 投资待遇

　　BITs 主要通过确立具有法律效力的投资待遇标准来减少跨国投资的非商业性风险。[2] 它们通常包括一项或多项待遇标准,以供评判东道国给予外国投资和外国投资者待遇的总体标准是否令人满意,且有助于解释和澄清更为具体的规定如何适用于特定情况。此类规定对 BITs 涵盖的投资和投资者是典型的实体性保护。[3]

　　1. 投资待遇标准的类型

　　BITs 规定的投资待遇标准有多种形式,通常是签订一个投资待遇标准条款,在

　　〔1〕 参见香港—荷兰 BIT 第 13 条;香港—澳大利亚 BIT 第 14 条;香港—丹麦 BIT 第 14 条;香港—瑞典 BIT 第 13 条;香港—瑞士 BIT 第 14 条;香港—新西兰 BIT 第 13 条;香港—法国 BIT 第 14 条;香港—日本 BIT 第 15 条;香港—韩国 BIT 第 14 条;香港—奥地利 BIT 第 13 条;香港—意大利 BIT 第 13 条;香港—德国 BIT 第 13 条;香港—英国 BIT 第 15 条;香港—比利时与卢森堡 BIT 第 13 条;香港—泰国 BIT 第 12 条。

　　〔2〕 Michael R. Reading, The Bilateral Investment Treaty in ASEAN: A Comparative Analysis, *Duke Law Journal*, Vol. 42, 1992, p. 684.

　　〔3〕 United Nations Conference on Trade and Development, *Bilateral Investment Treaties 1995-2006: Trends in Investment Rulemaking*, United Nations, 2007, p. 28; Mary H. Mourra(ed.), *Latin American Investment Treaty Arbitration, the Controversies and Conflicts*, Wolters Kluwer, 2008, pp. 169-171.

该条款中确立不同的待遇标准。[1] 在 BITs 实践中，有两类待遇标准：一是绝对待遇标准，包括公平与公正待遇、充分保护与保障、根据习惯国际法的最低待遇等；[2] 二是相对待遇标准，主要指国民待遇和最惠国待遇。两者均产生了基于"非歧视"待遇的责任。[3]

国民待遇是 BIT 实践普遍支持的最重要的投资保证之一。[4] 在 BITs 中，它意味着缔约一方给予缔约另一方投资者不低于给予其本国投资者投资的待遇。该标准是个"空壳"（an empty shell），可容纳有关给予某些人或某些事项待遇的内容。该标准的效果是在相关市场中为外国投资者创设与本国投资者的平等游戏场地（a level playing field）。[5] 该法律分析涉及东道国给予本国投资与外国投资之间或本国投资者与外国投资者之间待遇的比较。[6]

与国民待遇相同，最惠国待遇也是相对标准。最惠国待遇意味着缔约一方的投资或投资者有权享有缔约另一方给予的、不低于其给予任何第三国的投资或投资者的待遇。该标准确保 BITs 缔约各方的投资或投资者分别取得东道国给予任何第三国的投资或投资者的最佳待遇。因此，最惠国待遇标准至少在原则上，确立了受 BITs 保护的所有外国投资或外国投资者之间的平等游戏场地。[7] 最惠国待遇的责任要求，国家的行为应该对不同国家类似情况的人、实体、货物、服务或投资一视同仁。[8] 近年来，国际投资仲裁庭对最惠国待遇条款的解释已引起了广泛的关注。[9]

---

〔1〕 M. Sornarajah, *The International Law on Foreign Investment*, 2nd ed., Cambridge University Press, 2004, p. 233.

〔2〕 关于绝对待遇标准特别是公平与公正待遇标准，近年来有许多相关实践和评论。See Alberto Alvarez-Jimenez, Minimum Standard of Treatment of Aliens, Fair and Equitable Treatment of Foreign Investors, Customary International Law and the Diallo Case before the International Court of Justice, *The Journal of World Investment & Trade*, Vol. 9, No. 1, 2008, pp. 51-70; Mary H. Mourra(ed.), *Latin American Investment Treaty Arbitration*, *the Controversies and Conflicts*, Wolters Kluwer, 2008, pp. 170, 171, 188-190.

〔3〕 Mary H. Mourra(ed.), *Latin American Investment Treaty Arbitration*, *the Controversies and Conflicts*, Wolters Kluwer, 2008, pp. 169-170.

〔4〕 Stephan W. Schill, Tearing Down the Great Wall: the New Generation Investment Treaties of the People's Republic of China, *Cardozo J. Int'l & Comp. L.*, Vol. 15, 2007, p. 94.

〔5〕 United Nations Conference on Trade and Development, *Bilateral Investment Treaties 1995-2006：Trends in Investment Rulemaking*, United Nations, 2007, p. 33.

〔6〕 Andrew Newcombe, Lluis Paradell, *Law and Practice of Investment Treaties*, *Standards of Treatment*, Wolters Kluwer, 2009, pp. 148-149.

〔7〕 United Nations Conference on Trade and Development, *Bilateral Investment Treaties 1995-2006：Trends in Investment Rulemaking*, United Nations, 2007, p. 38.

〔8〕 Andrew Newcombe, Lluis Paradell, *Law and Practice of Investment Treaties*, *Standards of Treatment*, Wolters Kluwer, 2009, p. 193.

〔9〕 关于本专题的详细评论，参见 Okezie Chukwumerije, Interpreting Most-Favoured-Nation Clauses in Investment Treaty Arbitrations, *The Journal of World Investment & Trade*, Vol. 8, No. 5, 2007, pp. 597-646; Mary H. Mourra(ed.), *Latin American Investment Treaty Arbitration*, *the Controversies and Conflicts*, Wolters Kluwer, 2008, pp. 187-188。

应当指出,虽然 BITs 设计为缔约双方投资的双向流动,但在缔约双方财富和技术实力悬殊的情况下,投资实际上通常是单向流动的。[1] 作为单向流动的结果,只有资本输出国及其海外投资者从 BITs 规定的高水平投资待遇标准获益。然而,由于香港是发达地区,其多数缔约对方是发达国家,当可实现缔约双方投资的双向流动。因此,香港 BITs 规定的投资待遇标准可望给缔约双方带来相互的利益。

2. 香港 BITs 有关投资待遇的模式

香港 BITs 有关投资待遇的条款有两种模式:香港 BIT 范本模式和香港—荷兰 BIT 模式。

2.1　香港 BIT 范本模式

香港 BIT 范本第 3 条规定:

> (1) 缔约一方在其境内给予来自缔约另一方投资者的投资或收益的待遇,不得低于前者给予其本国投资者或任何其他国家投资者的投资或收益的待遇。
>
> (2) 缔约一方在其境内给予来自缔约另一方投资者在管理、维持、使用、享有或处置其投资的待遇不得低于前者给予其本国投资者或任何其他国家投资者的待遇。

看来,香港 BIT 范本模式有关投资待遇的规定采取了合并国民待遇和最惠国待遇的形式。9 个香港 BITs 遵循此种模式,并略作修改和补充。[2]

虽然几乎所有 BITs 都有明示的国民待遇责任,各国民待遇条款之间却明显不同。[3] 香港 BIT 范本和绝大多数香港 BITs 的国民待遇条款表明,该责任与最惠国待遇规定于同一条款,适用于投资者和投资,且规定了其适用的活动类型。它们没有明示的比较条件,如"在类似情况下"(in like circumstances)。此外,除了香港—新西兰 BIT,该条款未明示规定依据内国法。[4]

---

〔1〕 M. Sornarajah, *The International Law on Foreign Investment*, 2nd ed., Cambridge University Press, 2004, p. 207.

〔2〕 香港—澳大利亚 BIT 第 3(1)(2)条;香港—丹麦 BIT 第 3 条;香港—瑞典 BIT 第 3 条;香港—新西兰 BIT 第 4 条;香港—韩国 BIT 第 3 条;香港—奥地利 BIT 第 3 条;香港—德国 BIT 第 3(1)(2)条;香港—比利时与卢森堡 BIT 第 3 条;香港—泰国 BIT 第 3 条。细微的修改和补充例如:香港—澳大利亚 BIT 第 3 条涉及"雇佣"问题;香港—韩国 BIT 第 3 条和香港—泰国 BIT 第 3 条规定:"公平与公正及不低于……"

〔3〕 BITs 的国民待遇的不同种类(variations)包括:该责任是否:(1) 明示规定依据内国法;(2) 与最惠国待遇规定于同一条款;(3) 适用于投资者和投资;(4) 规定其适用的活动类型;(5) 包含明示的比较条件,如"在类似情况下"。See Andrew Newcombe, Lluis Paradell, *Law and Practice of Investment Treaties*, *Standards of Treatment*, Wolters Kluwer, 2009, p. 156.

〔4〕 香港—新西兰 BIT 第 4 条规定,对来自缔约另一方的投资和投资者实行国民待遇应"依据其法律法规"。

2.2. 香港—荷兰 BIT 模式

香港—荷兰 BIT 第 3 条规定：

（1）缔约各方投资者的投资和收益应始终得到公平与公正待遇。缔约一方不得以任何形式通过不合理或歧视性措施损害其境内来自缔约另一方投资者对其投资的管理、维持、使用、享有或处置。

（2）缔约一方在其境内给予来自缔约另一方投资者的投资或收益的待遇，不得低于前者给予其本国投资者或任何其他国家投资者的投资或收益的待遇，以更有利于相关投资者为准。

（3）缔约一方在其境内给予来自缔约另一方投资者在管理、维持、使用、享有或处置其投资的待遇不得低于前者给予其本国投资者或任何其他国家投资者的待遇，以更有利于相关投资者为准。

（4）缔约一方在其境内给予此等投资和收益的充分实质保护和保障水平，在任何情况下均不得低于前者给予其本国投资者或任何其他国家投资者的投资和收益的水平，以更有利于相关投资者为准。

（5）缔约一方得遵守其签署的有关缔约另一方投资者投资的合同责任。

可见，香港—荷兰 BIT 结合了绝对标准和相对标准。首先，在原则上规定，缔约各方投资者的投资和收益，应始终受到公平与公正的待遇。虽然公平与公正待遇的涵义富有争议，缔约任何一方的责任是：不得以不合理或歧视性的措施，损害缔约另一方投资者在其境内对其投资的管理、维持、使用、享有或处置。其次，该协定具体规定了投资待遇的主要方面，并采用"以更有利于相关投资者为准"的原则，包括：(1) 投资或收益的待遇；(2) 在管理、维持、使用、享有或处置其投资的待遇；(3) 给予此种投资或收益的充分实质保护和保障；(4) 投资因战乱而遭受损失之有关恢复、赔偿、补偿或其他解决办法的待遇。[1]在这方面，3 个香港 BITs 在一定程度上采用香港—荷兰 BIT 模式，特别是采用"以更有利于相关投资者为准"的原则。[2]

在有关投资待遇的 BITs 实践中，对于缔约一方投资者的投资和收益，缔约另一方通常在其境内给予国民待遇和最惠国待遇。在两种待遇同时实行的情况下，存在两种待遇的关系问题。一般而言，国民待遇优于最惠国待遇。但在实践中，有的国家为吸收和利用外国投资，通过签订条约或国内立法，在某些方面给予外国投资者优于本国国民的待遇，导致最惠国待遇优于国民待遇。值得注意的是，香港 BITs 采

---

[1] 香港—荷兰 BIT 第 4 条。
[2] 香港—瑞士 BIT 第 3(1)(2)(3)条；香港—法国 BIT 第 4(1)(2)条；香港—意大利 BIT 第 3(1)(2)条。

用上述国民待遇和最惠国待遇双重标准,同时规定"以更有利于相关投资者为准",指明了两者的关系,表明了其维护投资者权益的政策取向。

3. 投资待遇的例外

香港 BIT 范本第 7 条规定:"本协定有关缔约一方给予不低于缔约另一方投资者或任何其他国家投资者的待遇之规定,不得解释为缔约一方应给予缔约另一方投资者来自全部或主要与税务有关的任何国际协议或安排,或全部或主要与税务有关的任何本地法例的任何待遇、特惠或特权的利益。"由此可见,投资待遇的例外仅有税务。在香港 BIT 实践中,只有香港—韩国 BIT 遵循此规定。[1]

香港—荷兰 BIT 第 7 条对投资待遇标准的适用范围作了明确限制,即"在不损害第 3 条第 1 款的情况下,由于下列原因而取得的任何待遇、特惠或特权的利益,不属适用上述待遇标准之列:(1) 全部或主要与税务有关的任何国际协议或安排,或全部或主要与税务有关的任何本地法例;(2) 参与任何现有或将来的关税同盟、经济同盟或类似的国际协议;或(3) 与任何其他国家的互惠安排"。多数香港 BITs 遵循这一模式,规定了投资待遇的税务、区域贸易协定和互惠安排例外。

在香港 BIT 实践中,还有其他例外,诸如"促进奥地利与其邻国之间边境交通的法规不得援引作为本协定最惠国待遇的基础"[2],"根据泰国法律给予特定人或公司'优先人'地位。"[3]

(三)"剥夺"及赔偿标准

自 20 世纪 30 年代以来,东道国对外资实行国有化或征收的合法性及赔偿标准是国际法理论和实践中最具争议的问题。因此,有关国有化或征收的保护及赔偿标准是 BITs 的重要条款。香港 BITs 的相关规定遵循发达国家的传统实践,同时,具有某些技术层面的发展。

1. "剥夺"的前提条件

征收或国有化是跨国投资活动中的非商业风险之一。为防止或减少此种风险,BITs 一般规定了实施征收或国有化应具备的为了公共目的、依正当法律程序、非歧视及给予赔偿等四项前提条件。[4]一般而言,香港 BITs 遵循这一传统实践。

---

[1] 香港—韩国 BIT 第 4 条。

[2] 香港—奥地利 BIT 第 4(2)条。

[3] 香港—泰国 BIT 第 7(c)条。

[4] See Andrew Newcombe, Lluis Paradell, *Law and Practice of Investment Treaties*, *Standards of Treatment*, Wolters Kluwer, 2009, p. 369. 关于征收外国资产的详细分析,参见 M. Sornarajah, *The International Law on Foreign Investment*, 2nd ed., Cambridge University Press, 2004, pp. 344-401; Paul E. Comeaux, N. Stephan Kinsella, *Protecting Foreign Investment under International Law*, *Legal Aspects of Political Risk*, Oceana Publications Inc., 1997, pp. 57-81。

根据香港 BIT 范本第 5(1)条：

> 除非依法，为了与其国内需要相关的公共目的并给予赔偿，缔约一方投资者的投资在缔约另一方境内不得被剥夺或被实施具有此等剥夺后果的措施……

在实践中，4 个香港 BITs 规定了"剥夺"应具备的依法、为了与该缔约方国内需要相关的公共目的及给予赔偿等三项前提条件。[1] 此规定与香港 BIT 范本的规定相同。

除了上述三项剥夺的前提条件外，香港—荷兰 BIT 第 5(1)条增加了"基于非歧视"的前提条件。此种"四项前提条件"的规定由 11 个香港 BITs 所遵循。[2]

值得注意的是，虽然相关条款标题仍保留"征收"（expropriation）的用语，香港 BITs 缔约方在相关条文中审慎采用"剥夺"（deprive）的概念，而未采用征收或国有化的概念。取决于香港的非主权实体地位，香港 BITs 显然不能采用国有化的概念。而就"剥夺"和征收两个概念而言，前者的含义比后者更广。"财产的剥夺"可包括以下情况：政府未取得特定财产的所有权，也未占有、取得控制或使用该财产，但政府行为已造成对享有该财产的严重干预、导致该财产价值的大幅度降低或既有财产权利的破坏或消灭。[3] 因此，香港 BITs 采用"剥夺"的概念，不仅迎合了其非主权实体的特征，还在这方面为投资者提供了较充分的法律保护。

2. "剥夺"的赔偿标准

历史上，坚持依据国际法给予"充分、及时、有效"赔偿的"赫尔规则"代表了绝大多数发达国家的立场，而发展中国家则主张"适当补偿"原则。[4]

实践中，BITs 有关征收的赔偿规定通常涉及赔偿的标准及评估方式、决定赔偿的日期、兑换与转移及利息的支付等四个问题。此外，一些 BITs 还规定了对征收提

---

[1] 香港—奥地利 BIT 第 6(1)条；香港—德国 BIT 第 4(2)条；香港—比利时与卢森堡 BIT 第 5(1)条；香港—泰国 BIT 第 5(1)条。

[2] 香港—荷兰 BIT 第 5(1)条；香港—澳大利亚 BIT 第 6(1)条；香港—丹麦 BIT 第 5(1)条；香港—瑞典 BIT 第 5(1)条；香港—瑞士 BIT 第 5(1)条；香港—新西兰 BIT 第 6.1 条；香港—法国 BIT 第 5(1)条；香港—日本 BIT 第 5.1条；香港—韩国 BIT 第 6(1)条；香港—意大利 BIT 第 5(1)条；香港—英国 BIT 第 5(1)条。

[3] See Albert H. Y. Chen, The Basic Law and the Protection of Property Rights, *Hong Kong Law Journal*, Vol. 23, No. 1, 1993, p. 60.

[4] 关于征收赔偿标准争议的历史，参见 M. Sornarajah, *The International Law on Foreign Investment*, 2nd ed., Cambridge University Press, 2004, pp. 435-488; Paul E. Comeaux, N. Stephan Kinsella, *Protecting Foreign Investment under International Law*, *Legal Aspects of Political Risk*, Oceana Publications Inc., 1997, pp. 81-98; Andrew Newcombe, Lluis Paradell, *Law and Practice of Investment Treaties*, *Standards of Treatment*, Wolters Kluwer, 2009, p. 369; Mary H. Mourra(ed.), *Latin American Investment Treaty Arbitration*, *the Controversies and Conflicts*, Wolters Kluwer, 2008, pp. 23-28。

起司法审查的权利。[1]

关于"剥夺"的赔偿,香港 BIT 范本第 5(1)条规定:

此种赔偿应相当于该项投资被剥夺前一刻或即将进行的剥夺已为公众所知前一刻(以较早者为准)的真实价值,应包括直至支付日按正常商业利率计算的利息,应不迟延地支付,应有效兑换和自由汇出。受影响的投资者有权根据实施该项剥夺的缔约方法律,将该项剥夺的相关投资者情形和该投资的价值诉诸该缔约方司法机构或其他独立机构,请求根据本款规定的原则审查。

实践中,香港 BITs 一般遵循上述有关"剥夺"的赔偿标准。[2] 4 个香港 BITs 进一步涉及赔偿的评估问题,规定:"在赔偿价值未能顺利确定的情况下,赔偿额应考虑投资原本、折旧、已回收的资本、重置价值、现行汇率趋向和其他相关因素,根据普遍认可的评估原则和公平原则确定。"[3]

香港—丹麦 BIT 第 5(1)条还规定了"不适当迟延"的限度,指出"在任何情况下,均不得延长 3 个月的期限"。虽然香港—法国 BIT 以"给予适当赔偿"(against appropriate compensation)作为"剥夺"的四项前提条件之一,该协定第 5(1)条规定,"赔偿……应不迟延地作出"。该规定比其他香港 BITs 更为严格。

香港—泰国 BIT 第 5(1)条还涉及赔偿的准据法,其中规定,赔偿标准"依照本条第 2 款规定",即:"在缔约一方征收仅由不动产构成的投资时,应适用本条第 1 款规定,除非在该财产真实价值确定之时,应适用实行征收该不动产的缔约方的法律和政策"。

香港 BIT 范本第 5(2)条规定:"缔约一方对在其境内任何地方依照有效法律设立或组建的并由缔约另一方投资者持有股份的公司的资产进行征收时,应保证适用本条第一款的规定,从而保护拥有此种股份的缔约另一方投资者就其投资得到第一款所指的补偿。"在实践中,香港 BITs 遵循保障国际合营公司外国股东的

---

〔1〕　Andrew Newcombe, Lluis Paradell, *Law and Practice of Investment Treaties*, *Standards of Treatment*, Wolters Kluwer, 2009, p.377.

〔2〕　香港 BIT 范本第 5(1)条;香港—荷兰 BIT 第 5(1)条;香港—澳大利亚 BIT 第 6(1)条;香港—丹麦 BIT 第 5(1)条;香港—瑞典 BIT 第 5(1)条;香港—瑞士 BIT 第 5(1)条;香港—新西兰 BIT 第 6.1 条;香港—法国 BIT 第 5(1)条;香港—日本 BIT 第 5.1 条;香港—韩国 BIT 第 6(1)条;香港—奥地利 BIT 第 6(1)条;香港—意大利 BIT 第 5(1)条;香港—德国 BIT 第 4(2)条;香港—英国 BIT 第 5(1)条;香港—比利时与卢森堡 BIT 第 5(1)条;香港—泰国 BIT 第 5(1)条。

〔3〕　香港—澳大利亚 BIT 第 6(1)条;香港—新西兰 BIT 第 6.1 条;香港—意大利 BIT 第 5(1)条;香港—比利时与卢森堡 BIT 第 5(1)条。

赔偿原则。[1] 众所周知，国际合营公司是国际投资的重要形式，尽管少数 BITs 在投资定义等规定中略有涉及，但对此类公司外资股份的征收问题作出如此专门性规定，香港 BITs 堪称典范。

（四）争端的解决

高效、全面的争端处理机制常常是构成相互信任气氛的重要因素之一。[2] 因此投资争端和缔约双方之间争端的解决机制是 BITs 的重要内容。[3] 近年来，由 1965 年《解决国家与他国国民间投资争端公约》（简称 1965 年《华盛顿公约》）建立的"解决投资争端国际中心"（International Centre for Settlement of Investment Disputes, ICSID）机制成为 BITs 中最普遍采用的争端解决机制。在这方面，香港 BITs 的明显特征是未采用 ICSID 机制，同时也有一些技术性规定。

1. 投资争端

就 BITs 而言，投资争端指缔约一方投资者与缔约另一方有关前者在后者境内投资的争端。一些 BITs 的缺陷在于，它们创设的有关投资事故的救济是通过追究政府责任的曲折程序（tortuous processes）来实现，而不是外国投资者本身可利用的直接救济。[4] 近年来，许多 BITs 在投资争端解决方面取得了重要的进展，即通过规定将投资争端提交中立的国际仲裁庭解决。采取国际仲裁解决投资争端方式的条款有多种层次。在最低程度，此类条款仅指导当事方以仲裁作为争端解决方式。在最高程度，此类条款使外国投资者有权由其本身直接诉诸 ICSID 仲裁庭。[5]

私人本身直接诉诸国际仲裁庭，是国际法发展的重大突破。比较由母国通过外交保护实施国际公法的传统方式，外国投资者的此种诉权可确切地称为"国际投资法范式的变化"。取代依母国基于自由裁量权提供外交保护，多数 BITs 规定了投资者针对东道国诉诸 ICSID 仲裁程序的单方面权利，而东道国对 ICSID 机制通常给予一般和事先的同意。在国际实践中，外国投资者与东道国之间的仲裁经常依 ICSID

---

〔1〕香港—荷兰 BIT 第 5(2)条；香港—澳大利亚 BIT 第 6(2)条；香港—丹麦 BIT 第 5(2)条；香港—瑞典 BIT 第 5(2)条；香港—瑞士 BIT 第 5(2)条；香港—新西兰 BIT 第 6.2条；香港—法国 BIT 第 5(2)条；香港—日本 BIT 第 5.3 条；香港—韩国 BIT 第 6(3)条；香港—奥地利 BIT 第 6(3)条；香港—意大利 BIT 第 5(3)条；香港—德国 BIT 第 4 (3)条；香港—英国 BIT 第 5(2)条；香港—比利时与卢森堡 BIT 第 5(2)条；香港—泰国 BIT 第 5(3)条。

〔2〕李适时：《论中国签订的双边投资保护协定》，载《中国国际法年刊》(1990)，第 121—122 页。

〔3〕See Andrew Newcombe, Lluis Paradell, *Law and Practice of Investment Treaties*, *Standards of Treatment*, Wolters Kluwer, 2009, p.65.

〔4〕See M. Sornarajah, *The International Law on Foreign Investment*, 2nd ed., Cambridge University Press, 2004, pp.303-304.

〔5〕Ibid., pp.249-250. 直至 1993 年，大多数资本输入国未与主要的资本输出国签署强力的 BIT（a strong BIT），即包含允许外国投资者针对东道国直接诉诸国际仲裁的争端解决条款。据 2002 年的一项研究结果，在 149 个发展中国家中，已有 117 个国家（占 79%）至少签署了一项此类协定。See Jason Webb Yackee, Conceptual Difficulties in the Empirical Study of Bilateral Investment Treaties, *Brooklyn J. Int'l L.* Vol.33, 2008, pp.432-433.

规则进行。[1]

根据香港 BIT 范本第 8 条,投资争端的解决程序是:

(1) 由当事双方友好解决;

(2) 如未能友好解决,应在提出权利请求的书面通知之六个月后,按照争端双方同意的程序解决;或者

(3) 如在该六个月期间内未能就此种程序达成协议,则在有关投资者请求下,依照当时有效的联合国国际贸易法委员会仲裁规则将争端提交仲裁。缔约双方可以书面同意修订这些规则。

香港 BITs 通常遵循上述程序。[2] 实践中,也有一些修改或补充,例如强调投资者提起仲裁的权利[3]和缩短友好解决的时限。[4] 一些香港 BITs 还指出仲裁的性质及仲裁裁决的效力。[5]

应当指出,香港 BITs 未规定缔约一方投资者与缔约另一方之间的争端由 ICSID 管辖,因此,由香港 BITs 涵盖的投资者不具有直接诉诸 ICSID 的权利。究其原因,首先是受到香港非主权实体地位的制约,香港不是 1965 年《华盛顿公约》的缔约方,香港政府本身未经该公约特定缔约方指定和同意,不能作为 ICSID 主持的调解或仲裁程序的当事人;其次,由于香港 BITs 中的投资者在香港方面包括了在香港享有居留权的外籍人士,此类投资者中不具有该公约缔约国国籍者也不能作为 ICSID 主持的调解或仲裁程序的当事人。在此情况下,对香港 BITs 缔约双方而言,投资争端的解决机制仍然是谈判的议题。这一实践的重要启示是,"由外国投资者本身直接诉诸 ICSID 或其他国际法庭"的规定,并非 BITs 中投资争端解决的唯一选项。

2. 缔约方之间的争端

就 BITs 而言,缔约方之间的争端指缔约方有关条约解释和履行的争端。

---

〔1〕 Stephan W. Schill, Tearing Down the Great Wall: the New Generation Investment Treaties of the People's Republic of China, *Cardozo J. Int'l & Comp. L.*, Vol. 15, 2007, pp. 87-88. 关于 ICSID 机制下投资者与国家间仲裁的最新发展,参见 Mary H. Mourra(ed.), *Latin American Investment Treaty Arbitration, the Controversies and Conflicts*, Wolters Kluwer, 2008, pp. 163-166; Andrew Newcombe, Lluis Paradell, *Law and Practice of Investment Treaties, Standards of Treatment*, Wolters Kluwer, 2009, pp. 58-59.

〔2〕 香港—荷兰 BIT 第 10 条;香港—澳大利亚 BIT 第 10 条;香港—丹麦 BIT 第 9 条;香港—瑞典 BIT 第 9 条;香港—瑞士 BIT 第 11 条;香港—新西兰 BIT 第 9 条;香港—法国 BIT 第 9 条;香港—日本 BIT 第 9.2 条;香港—韩国 BIT 第 9(3)条;香港—奥地利 BIT 第 9 条;香港—意大利 BIT 第 10 条;香港—德国 BIT 第 10 条;香港—英国 BIT 第 8 条;香港—比利时与卢森堡 BIT 第 9 条;香港—泰国 BIT 第 8 条。

〔3〕 香港—荷兰 BIT 第 10 条规定:"如在该六个月期间内未能就此种程序达成协议,则在有关投资者请求下,将该争端提交仲裁⋯⋯"香港—瑞士 BIT 第 11 条 和香港—日本 BIT 第 9.2 条也有类似规定。

〔4〕 香港—澳大利亚 BIT 第 10 条规定:"如未能友好解决,应在提出权利请求的书面通知之三个月后,按照争端双方同意的程序解决。"香港—英国 BIT 第 8 条也有类似规定。

〔5〕 香港—韩国 BIT 第 9(4)条规定:"仲裁裁决对争端当事方具有最终效力。缔约各方应确保根据其相关法律法规承认和执行仲裁裁决。"香港—德国 BIT 第 10 条规定:"仲裁裁决对争端当事方具有最终效力,应根据其相关国内法予以执行。"

根据香港 BIT 范本第 9 条的规定，缔约双方有关协定的解释或适用的争端的解决程序是：

（1）尝试以谈判方式解决；

（2）如果未能以谈判方式解决，可将争端提交双方同意的人或机构，或应依缔约任何一方的要求提交由三名仲裁人组成的仲裁庭裁决。

该条款有关特设仲裁庭的设立、审理以及裁决等规定，大体与 BITs 的一般实践相同，但具有如下特点：

（1）强调国际法院院长的私人身份。在缔约各方或两名仲裁人未能在规定的期限内指派仲裁人或第三名仲裁人的情况下，缔约任何一方可以请求国际法院院长以私人及个人身份在 30 天内作出必要的指派。[1] 所谓"以私人及个人身份"的规定也同香港的非主权实体地位有关。如所周知，根据《国际法院规约》，国际法院的适格当事人限于国家。[2] 在国际仲裁实践中，由国际法院院长指派仲裁人，一般也限于争端当事人均为国家的场合。香港 BITs 特别强调国际法院院长"以私人及个人身份"指派，正是为了避免发生有关国际法院院长指派资格的歧见。[3]

（2）规定了明确的仲裁时间表（见表 2）。此规定旨在防止特设仲裁庭因无现成的仲裁规则可循而久拖不决。主要表现在：第一，其他 BITs 未试图如此具体地规定进行仲裁程序的时限；第二，无论相关争端的复杂程度，该程序从组成仲裁庭至作出裁决的时限为四个半月。[4]

（3）仲裁庭须以尊重法律的基础作出裁决。所谓法律，当理解为包括国际法和国内法。此规定意在限制仲裁人的自由裁量权，反对仲裁人以公平正义原则作出裁决。

（4）仲裁庭作出裁决前，可在任何程序阶段向缔约双方建议和解。这种仲裁与调解相结合的方式，反映了国际仲裁实践的发展趋向。

（5）缔约双方可在接到裁决后 15 日内提出有关澄清该项裁决的要求，仲裁庭应在该要求提出后 15 日内作出澄清。此规定表明，仲裁裁决一般不必附具理由，但应当事人要求，仲裁庭应在规定期限内澄清其裁决。

---

〔1〕 与此类规定不同的是香港—法国 BIT 第 11(2)(b)条，规定："如未能在上述规定的期限内作出指派，缔约任何一方可以请求国际商会会长以私人及个人身份在 30 天内作出必要的指派。"

〔2〕 根据《国际法院规约》第 34(1)条："在法院得为诉讼当事国者，限于国家。"

〔3〕 在其他 BIT 范本中，未见"以私人及个人身份"(in a personal and individual capacity)的用语。例如，在德国 2008 约范本第 9(4)条规定："……如未能达成其他相关协议，缔约任何一方可以请求国际法院院长作出必要的指派。"

〔4〕 See Rudolf Dolzer, Margrete Stevens, *Bilateral Investment Treaties*, Martinus Nijhoff Publishers, 1995, p. 127.

表 2　香港 BITs 中有关缔约方之间争端解决时限的主要规定　　　（单位：日）

香港的缔约对方	由当事方指定仲裁员	由仲裁员指定第三仲裁员	由国际法院院长/国际商会会长指定第三仲裁员*	提交仲裁申请书	提交答辩书	开庭审理	颁发书面裁决	提出澄清请求	澄清答复
【范本】	30	60	30	45	60	30	30	15	15
荷兰	60	60	30	45	60	30	30	15	15
澳大利亚	30	60	30	45	60	30	30	15	15
丹麦	30	60	30	45	60	30	/	15	15
瑞典	30	60	30	45	60	30	30	15	15
瑞士	60	60	30	60	60	30	30	30	30
新西兰	60	60	30	45	60	30	30	15	15
法国	30	60	30*	/	/	/	/	/	/
日本	30	60	30	/	/	/	60	/	/
韩国	30	60	30	45	60	30	15	15	15
奥地利	30	60	30	45	60	30	30	15	15
意大利	60	60	30	45	60	30	30	15	15
德国	30	60	30	/	/	/	/	/	/
英国	30	60	30	45	60	30	30	15	15
比利时与卢森堡	30	60	30	45	60	30	30	15	15
泰国	30	60	30	45	60	30	30	15	15

　　香港 BIT 实践原则上遵循香港 BIT 范本的上述主要规定。[1] 然而，也有一些不同于香港 BIT 范本的规定，如准据法、[2] 继任仲裁员的进一步规定、[3] 费用的分担、[4] 裁决的基础[5] 及"不能由缔约双方视为在该争端保持中立的国家之国民"的进一步规定。[6]

---

　　[1]　香港—荷兰 BIT 第 11 条；香港—澳大利亚 BIT 第 10 条；香港—丹麦 BIT 第 10 条；香港—瑞典 BIT 第 10 条；香港—瑞士 BIT 第 12 条；香港—新西兰 BIT 第 10 条；香港—法国 BIT 第 11 条；香港—日本 BIT 第 11 条；香港—韩国 BIT 第 10 条；香港—奥地利 BIT 第 10 条；香港—意大利 BIT 第 11 条；香港—德国 BIT 第 10 条；香港—英国 BIT 第 9 条；香港—比利时与卢森堡 BIT 第 10 条；香港—泰国 BIT 第 9 条。

　　[2]　香港—荷兰 BIT 第 11(5)条规定："仲裁庭应基于尊崇法律作出裁决。在仲裁庭作出裁决之前，在该程序的任何阶段，建议缔约各方友好解决该争端。"

　　[3]　香港—澳大利亚 BIT 第 11(2)(a)条。

　　[4]　香港—澳大利亚 BIT 第 11(8)条规定："然而，仲裁庭可裁决，由缔约一方承担较高比例的仲裁费用。"在香港—瑞典 BIT 第 10(8)条、香港—新西兰 BIT 第 10.8 条和香港—比利时与卢森堡 BIT 第 10(8)条也有类似规定。

　　[5]　香港—奥地利 BIT 第 10(7)条和香港—比利时与卢森堡 BIT 第 10(7)条规定："仲裁庭应基于国际承认的法治(on the basis of internationally recognized rules of law)作出其裁决。"

　　[6]　香港—法国 BIT 第 11(2)(a)条规定："不具有法国国籍和负责香港外交事务的国家之国籍及香港地区居留权的自然人可作为仲裁庭庭长。"

三、香港签订双边投资条约的法律依据问题

传统国际法认为,主权是缔约权的唯一依据,即只有主权国家才是条约的缔约主体。然而,在现代国际实践中,越来越多的非主权实体参与缔结条约,并且为国际社会所承认。一些实例表明,条约的缔结主体除主权国家外,还有国际组织、联邦制国家的成员、交战团体和区域性实体等。上述非主权实体签订条约的法律依据各不相同:一般而言,国际组织,是基于条约法和国际组织的基本文件;联邦制国家的成员,是基于联邦制国家宪法和国际社会的承认;交战团体,是基于条约或国际惯例;区域性实体,是基于主权国家授予的自治权和国际社会的承认。[1] 香港作为区域性实体,亦不例外。在此,香港缔约权的授权性质及其国际承认的依据问题值得进一步探讨。

（一）香港缔约权的授权性质

香港特区自治权的授权性质决定了香港特区缔约权的授权性质。在现代国际实践中,享有自治权的区域性实体可能成为国际条约的主体。然而,其前提是,该区域性实体应取得主权国家的缔约授权。香港与外国间经济协定的授权安排和规定进一步明确表明了香港单独缔约权的授权性质。

在过渡期,香港的国际实践不仅依据其事实上(*de facto*)自治权,而且受到《中英联合声明》的精神和有关规定的重要调整和影响。根据《中英联合声明》第4条规定,在过渡期,英国政府负责香港的行政管理,以维护和保持其经济繁荣和社会稳定,中国政府对此予以合作。《中英联合声明》附件二第4、5条进一步规定了中英两国政府通过中英联合联络小组在国际关系领域的合作。保持和发展香港与世界各国、各地区的双边经济关系,是需要中英两国政府合作的重要行政管理工作之一。因此,《中英联合声明》的上述规定可被视为中国参与香港过渡期双边经济协定实践的法律依据。事实上,1985年以来,在谈判和签署香港与外国间经济协定过程中,中英两国政府通过中英联合联络小组进行合作,英方承担了通知中方有关香港与外国间经济协定发展的义务,并在某种程度上与中方沟通和协商。中方则同意这些条约的效力将跨越1997年。[2]

从实践上看,在过渡期,香港与外国间经济协定的共同特征是,尽管对香港而言,缔约的权力来源于主权国家的授权,但条约文本并未表明授予香港缔约权的主权国家。香港与荷兰BIT序言指出:"香港政府,经负责其外交事务的主权政府正式

---

〔1〕 参见李浩培:《条约法概论》,法律出版社1988年版,第240页。

〔2〕 参见《英方将在联络小组会上向中方解释香港政府拟定双边航空协议方案》,载《信报》1986年8月2日。

授权签订本协定。"香港 BIT 范本[1]和其他香港 BITs 均采取相同的用语。这是故意的含糊其辞。由于《中英联合声明》指出，直至 1997 年 6 月 30 日，英国负责香港的行政管理；1997 年 7 月 1 日，中国对香港恢复行使主权。考虑到香港作为 BITs 缔约一方在上述日期前后并未改变其认同（identity），对于缔约对方而言，上述"负责其外交事务的主权政府"可理解为在不同时期的两个政府，即 1997 年 6 月 30 日之前指英国政府，1997 年 7 月 1 日之后指中国政府。

1997 年 7 月 1 日香港回归以后，香港特区与外国间经济协定明确表明了中华人民共和国的授权。在香港特区签署的所有 BITs 中，均在序言中明确载明："香港特别行政区政府，经中华人民共和国中央人民政府正式授权与……签订本协定"。

（二）国际承认的依据问题

一般认为，自治实体的自治权地位需要得到国际社会的承认。因此，香港特区高度自治权的地位不仅取决于香港特区本身、中国政府的单方面愿望，也取决于国际社会是否承认这一地位。[2]事实上，如果没有国家或国际组织与香港保持和发展双边关系的实践，香港特区在对外事务方面的自治权就毫无意义。根据国际法的基本原则，国家和国际组织被视为国际法主体的正常形态，符合某些条件即可取得国际法律人格。与国家和国际组织不同，香港特区的高度自治权和国际法律地位不仅取决于中国中央人民政府的授权，而且需要已有国际法主体的承认和接受。[3]香港BITs 的实践表明，香港特区的高度自治权和缔约主体地位已得到众多国际法主体的承认和接受。进一步的问题是，已有国际法主体承认和接受香港特区缔约主体地位的法律依据是什么？在香港 BIT 实践中，缔约对方如何认识香港特区高度自治权的法律依据或来源？

在国际实践中，有的自治实体、如所谓"国际领土"（international territories）的地位及其自治权是由条约确立的。[4]鉴此，有西方学者主张，《中英联合声明》产生了一个权利与义务由国际法调整的"客观国际实体"（objective international entity），该声明创设和保障了香港的特殊地位，并保留了香港的自治权利；作为国际法的产物，

---

[1] 《香港 BIT 范本》序言第 1 节，参见 Rudolf Dolzer, Margrete Stevens, *Bilateral Investment Treaties*, Martinus Nijhoff Publishers, 1995, p. 200。

[2] See Albert H. Y. Chen, Some Reflections on Hong Kong's Autonomy, *Hong Kong Law Journal*, Vol. 24, 1994, pp. 179-180; Roda Mushat, Foreign, External, and Defence Affairs, in Peter Wesley Smith, Albert H. Y. Chen (ed.), *The Basic Law and Hong Kong's Future*, Butterworths, 1988, p. 264.

[3] See Xiaobing Xu, George D. Wilson, The Hong Kong Special Administrative Region as a Model of Regional External Autonomy, *Case W. Res. J. Int'l L.*, Vol. 32, 2000, p. 31.

[4] 例如，根据《但泽自由条约》（Free Treaty of Danzig），但泽（Danzig）在 1920—1939 年被视为由国际法原则和规则调整的享有法律人格的自由城市。See Roda Mushkat, Hong Kong as an International Legal Person, *Emory International Law Review*, Vol. 6, 1992, pp. 109-110.

香港特区的存在或其"生存权"(right to life)应受到国际保护,其居民的"民族状态"(peoplehood)应受到尊重。[1] 还有西方学者主张,香港特区类似欧洲中世纪具有经济、政治和法律独立性的"自由城市"(free cities)。[2] 此类观点显然是片面的,因为它不适当地夸大《中英联合声明》的作用,而忽略了《中英联合声明》有关规定的法律根据或法律根源。

诚然,香港特区高度自治权的法律依据包括了国内法和国际法。但在双重法律依据中,有主从之分,层次之分。应当明确,香港特区高度自治权的法律根据首先是1982年《中华人民共和国宪法》(简称《中国宪法》)。该法第31条规定:"国家在必要时得设立特别行政区。在特别行政区内实行的制度按照具体情况由全国人民代表大会以法律规定。"《中国宪法》作为国家的根本大法,是中国条约实践和国内立法的基础和根据。《中英联合声明》第3条第1款规定,"为了维护国家的统一和领土完整,并考虑到香港的历史和现实情况,中华人民共和国决定在对香港恢复行使主权时,根据中华人民共和国宪法第31条的规定,设立香港特别行政区"。《中英联合声明》的一系列关于香港特区高度自治权的规定均为中国基于宪法第31条所作的政策声明和国际承诺。[3] 在国内立法方面,《基本法》在序言中重申了设立香港特区的宪法根据,[4]并进一步对香港特区享有的自治权范围作了具体明确的规定。

显然,香港特区首先是《中国宪法》的产物,[5]同时也由《中英联合声明》予以国际法层面的确认和保障。在理解香港特区高度自治权时,特别需要认识《中国宪法》作为决定性的第一级法律根据或法律根源的重要作用。《中英联合声明》有关规定尽管也可援引为香港特区高度自治权的法律根据,但毕竟是属于第二级的,并且明确属于"中国对香港的基本方针政策"的声明内容。在此双重法律结构中,《中国宪法》是第一级法律根据;《中英联合声明》和《基本法》是根据宪法制定的,属第二级法律根据。在这个意义上,香港特区高度自治权的决定性法律基础是中国国内法。如果将《中英联合声明》有关规定作为香港特区高度自治权的唯一根据,并据此强调香

〔1〕 See Roda Mushkat, id, pp. 110, 169; Brian Z. Tamanaha, Post-1997 Hong Kong: A Comparative Study of the Meaning of "High Degree of Autonomy" with a Specific Look at the Commonwealth of the Nothern Mariana Islands, *China Law Reporter*, Vol. 5, 1989, p. 168.

〔2〕 See Eric Johnson, Hong Kong after 1997: A Free City?, *German Yearbook of International Law*, Vol. 40, 1997, pp. 402-404.

〔3〕 参见《中英联合声明》第3条第1款和《中英联合声明》附件一第1条。

〔4〕 《基本法》序言指出:"为了维护国家的统一和领土完整,保持香港的繁荣和稳定,并考虑到香港的历史和现实情况,国家决定,在对香港恢复行使主权时,根据中华人民共和国宪法第三十一条的规定,设立香港特别行政区,并按照'一个国家,两种制度'的方针,不在香港实行社会主义制度和政策。"

〔5〕 See Albert H. Y. Chen, Further Aspects of the Autonomy of Hong Kong under the PRC Constitution, 14 *Hong Kong Law Journal*, Vol. 14, 1984, p. 343.

港特区的"国际化",将香港特区混同于主要依条约产生的所谓"国际领土"或"自由城市",[1]实属牵强附会,是违背客观现实的。进而言之,香港特区与享有自治权的所谓"国际领土"或"自由城市"的本质区别在于:前者是直辖于中国中央人民政府的地方行政区域,是主权国家宪政体制中不可分割的组成部分,其权利和义务主要由中国国内法确立和调整;而后者则是在特定历史条件下,主权归属或国内法地位尚未确定的区域实体,其权利和义务主要由条约确立和调整。因此,在香港 BIT 实践中,缔约对方和国际社会承认和接受香港特区缔约主体地位的法律依据,只能是《中国宪法》《中英联合声明》和《基本法》有关香港特区自治权的规定,而不是所谓香港特区本身的"客观国际实体"地位。[2]

四、香港双边投资条约衍生的条约适用问题

根据《中英联合声明》附件一第 11 条第 2 款和《基本法》第 153 条第 1 款的规定,中国缔结的国际协定,中央人民政府可根据香港特区的情况和需要,在征询香港特区政府的意见后,决定是否适用于香港特区。[3] 上述规定显然排除了将中国缔结的所有国际协定不加分析地适用于香港特区的可能,表明了中国采取的有选择、有条件适用的立场。[4] 这是因为考虑到,由于香港的历史和现状,特别是香港特区与中国内地社会经济和法律制度的重大差异,中国缔结的国际协定不一定适合于香港特区的情况和需要。为了遵循和体现"一国两制"和香港特区高度自治的原则,中央人民政府庄严承诺,在决定中国缔结的国际协定是否适用于香港特区时,需要从实体内容上考察,以该协定符合香港的情况和需要为依据;在程序上,需要正式征询香港特区政府的意见。

另外,根据《中英联合声明》附件一第 11 条第 1 款和《基本法》)第 151 条规定,香港具有在经济等领域的单独缔约权。在香港与中国分别与同一缔约对方签订 BITs

---

〔1〕 See Roda Mushkat, Hong Kong as an International Legal Person, *Emory International Law Review*, Vol. 6, 1992, pp. 109-111.

〔2〕 关于港外经济协定的法律依据及其意义,参见曾华群:《港外经济协定的实践及其法律依据》,载《厦门大学学报》(哲社版)2009 年第 2 期。

〔3〕 外国学者 Yash Ghai 认为,通过基本法第 153 条,香港特区本身的条约体制已构建,这是香港特区自治权行使的更具逻辑性和合理的方式。Anthony Aust 进一步认为,基本法这一规定允许中华人民共和国接受"其代表香港特区接受不同于中国其他地区"的条约责任。果真如此,中央政府须实施有关条约适用于香港特区的单独程序(formalities),尽管对于"属于外交事务或国防,或由于其性质和规定须适用于国家全部领土的条约",中央政府无须实施单独程序。See P. Y. Lo, *The Hong Kong Basic Law*, LexisNexis Butterworths, 2011, p. 771.

〔4〕 上述规定中的"国际协定"包括 1997 年 7 月 1 日之前和之后中国缔结的国际协定。对上述日期之前中国缔结的国际协定而言,可分为三类:一是中英两国都是缔约国,但目前并不适用于香港的国际多边条约,如 1979 年《联合国工业发展组织宪章》;二是中国已经参加但英国尚未参加的多边协定,如 1980 年《联合国国际货物买卖合同公约》;三是中国与外国签订的双边协定。

的情况下,可能产生香港 BITs 和中国 BITs 如何适用的问题。如前所述,迄今,香港特区以其名义与 18 个国家签订了 17 个 BITs,初步形成了香港系列 BITs。自 1982 年以来,中国与 128 个国家签署了 BITs,[1]形成了中国系列 BITs。两个系列 BITs 的主要条款存在明显不同。[2] 除中国—俄罗斯 BIT 外,中国 BITs 本身未对条约是否适用于香港特区作出明确规定。[3]

在此情况下,值得考虑的问题首先是,尽管有《中英联合声明》附件一第 11 条第 2 款和《基本法》第 153 条第 1 款的规定,在中国香港与中国分别与同一外国签订 BIT 的情况下,中国香港 BIT 与中国 BIT 如何适用? 对香港"投资者"(具有中国国籍的香港永久居民等)和香港特区而言,香港 BIT 是否当然优先? 依据何在?

鉴于香港签订 BIT 是经中国授权的,可以认为,中国授权香港缔约和香港单独缔约的法律事实本身清楚表明了中国和香港的"分别适用"的意愿和立场,即对香港"投资者"和香港特区适用香港 BITs,对中国"投资者"(不包括香港"投资者")和中国领土(不包括香港特区)则适用中国 BITs。对缔约对方而言,由于与香港和中国分别签订香港 BITs 和中国 BITs,也清楚表明了其"分别适用"的意愿和立场。然而,缔约双方"分别适用"的意愿和立场并不当然具有"排除对香港适用中国 BITs"的法律后果。《维也纳条约法公约》第 29 条确立的规则是,条约是否适用于各缔约国的全部领土,可由各缔约国依据意思自治原则协商确定,但如无明示或默示的相反意思,应认为条约适用于各缔约国的全部领土。[4] 由于中国 BITs 本身未规定中国"排除对香港适用中国 BIT"的意思,对缔约双方国民、国际司法机构或仲裁机构等第三方而言,出于特定因素考虑,仍然存在"挑选条约"(treaty shopping)的可能。

第二个问题是,在中国与特定外国签订 BIT,而香港与该国尚未签订 BIT 的情况下,中国 BIT 是否自动适用? 依据何在?

"谢业深诉秘鲁共和国案"(Mr. Tza Yap Shum v. The Republic of Peru,简称"谢业深案")[5]引发了中国 BITs 是否自动适用于香港特区的现实问题。

---

[1] United Nations Conference on Trade and Development, *World Investment Report 2012*, United Nations, 2012, p. 199.

[2] 关于香港系列 BITs 与中国系列 BITs 主要条款的区别,参见陈安:《对香港居民谢业深诉秘鲁政府案 ICSID 管辖权裁定的四项质疑——〈中国—秘鲁 BIT〉适用于"一国两制"下的中国香港特别行政区吗》,载《国际经济法学刊》第 17 卷第 1 期,北京大学出版社 2010 年版,第 14—17 页。

[3] 2006 年中国—俄罗斯 BIT 议定书规定,除非缔约双方另有约定,该协定不适用于中华人民共和国香港特别行政区和中华人民共和国澳门特别行政区。

[4]《维也纳条约法公约》第 29 条规定:"除该条约显示或另经确定有不同意思外,条约对每一当事国的拘束力及于其全部领土。"中国于 1997 年 5 月 9 日加入《维也纳条约法公约》。

[5] Mr. Tza Yap Shum v. The Republic of Peru, ICSID Case No. ARB/07/6, Decision on Jurisdiction and Competence, dated June 19, 2009.

主张中国 BITs 自动适用于香港特区的主要理由是：(1) 中国 BITs 的领土适用范围涵盖香港特区。中国 BITs 中一般规定，"领土"一词系指中华人民共和国的领土以及毗连本国海岸并按国际法对其拥有主权、主权权利或管辖权的海域。这一规定表明，中国 BITs 的适用范围是包括香港特区、澳门特区及台湾地区在内的中国全部领土；(2) 中国 BITs 的"投资者"定义包括具有中国国籍的香港永久居民。中国 BITs 通常规定，"自然人投资者"在中华人民共和国方面，系指具有其国籍的自然人。在"谢业深案"中，ICSID 仲裁庭认为，没有任何证据能够有效证明缔约方的意图是把香港永久居民排除在中国—秘鲁 BIT 的适用范围之外，该 BIT 也缺乏显示这种意图的明确规定。[1]

反对中国 BITs 自动适用于香港特区的主要理由是：(1) 中国 BITs 自动适用于香港特区有违《中英联合声明》和《基本法》的规定。根据《中英联合声明》附件一第11 条第 2 款和《基本法》第 153 条第 1 款的规定，中国缔结的国际协定并不自动适用于香港，只有在中央人民政府征询香港特区政府意见并作出正式决定后方可适用；(2)《中英联合声明》附件一第 11 条第 1 款和《基本法》第 151 条确认了香港特区在经济等领域的单独缔约权，中国 BITs 自动适用于香港特区可能造成与香港特区 BIT 实践的重叠或冲突。

1997 年 6 月 20 日，中国常驻联合国代表向联合国秘书长递交外交照会，全面阐述了中国政府关于香港特区适用国际条约的原则立场。[2] 然而，对于中国双边协定对香港的适用问题只是在《中英联合声明》这一双边条约层面和《基本法》这一国内法层面作原则性规定。上述规定可能被国际社会所忽略。

鉴此，有学者建议从国际法层面进一步明确中国 BITs 对香港特区的适用问题，可采取的方式包括：(1) 单方发出外交照会，申明中国 BITs 不自动适用于香港特区。我国可采取外交照会的形式，向缔约对方申明相关中国 BITs 并不自动适用于香港特区，并告知《中英联合声明》和《基本法》的相关规定，从而使我国"一国两制"下条约适用的特殊程序获得缔约对方的理解、认可和支持；(2) 启动条约修订程序，可考

---

〔1〕　参见陈安：《对香港居民谢业深诉秘鲁政府案 ICSID 管辖权裁定的四项质疑——〈中国—秘鲁 BIT〉适用于"一国两制"下的中国香港特别行政区吗》，载《国际经济法学刊》第 17 卷第 1 期，北京大学出版社 2010 年版，第 32 页。

〔2〕　即《中华人民共和国常驻联合国代表秦华孙大使就多边国际条约适用于香港特别行政区事项致联合国秘书长的照会》。照会的两个附件列明了自 1997 年 7 月 1 日起适用于香港特别行政区的 214 项国际条约。照会特别提到，《公民权利和政治权利国际公约》和《经济、社会与文化权利的国际公约》适用于香港的规定，自 1997 年 7 月 1 日起继续有效。照会指出，未列入照会附件的、中国是当事方或将成为当事方的其他条约，如决定将继续适用于香港特别行政区，中国政府将另行办理有关手续。对属于外交、国防类或根据条约的性质和规定必须适用于国家全部领土的条约，中国政府无须办理有关手续。参见王子珍：《就香港特别行政区适用的国际条约中国向联合国递交照会》，载《人民日报》(海外版)1997 年 6 月 23 日第 6 版。

虑作"投资者"和"领土适用范围"两方面的修订，明确中国 BITs 不自动适用于香港"投资者"和香港特区；(3) 依据《解决国家与他国国民间投资争端公约》第 25 条第 4 款有关"授权缔约国自行决定提交 ICSID 仲裁的争端类型"的规定，通知 ICSID 秘书处，中国 BITs 不自动适用于香港"投资者"和香港特区。[1]

笔者以为，在"谢业深案"中，ICSID 仲裁庭有关中国—秘鲁 BIT 适用于该案的管辖权裁决的明显缺失是，片面采取和强调了上述《维也纳条约法公约》第 29 条规定中"条约显示有不同意思"的单一标准，完全忽略或无视"另经确定有不同意思"的规定。《中英联合声明》附件一第 11 条第 2 款和《基本法》第 153 条第 1 款当可作为中国 BITs 不能自动适用于香港"投资者"和香港特区的法律依据，仲裁庭却视而不见。特别是，在秘鲁共和国政府提供了专家意见，明确指明相关法律依据的情况下，仲裁庭仍固执己见。由此可见，在国际仲裁实践中，在中国 BITs 不符合"条约显示有不同意思"标准的情况下，"另经确定有不同意思"的条约解释权属于仲裁庭，而不属于缔约方。由于当前国际仲裁实践缺乏有效的纠错机制，缔约方如不主动采取相应措施，发生类似缺憾在所难免。为防患于未然，在中国 BITs 中似应明确规定，该协定不自动适用于香港"投资者"和香港特区，以符合"条约显示有不同意思"的标准。

五、结语

实践表明，香港特区享有高于历史上和现实中的任何其他自治实体的自治权。在这个意义上，它确立了自治实体自治权的典范。[2]

过渡期以来，香港实现了从享有事实上自治权向享有法律上（*de jure*）自治权的重要转变。根据《中英联合声明》和《基本法》，香港特区享有法律上自治权。香港 BITs 的成功实践表明，香港特区的高度自治权和缔约主体地位已得到众多国际法主体的承认和接受。应当明确，《中国宪法》是缔约对方和国际社会承认香港特区缔约主体地位的第一级法律根据；而《中英联合声明》和《基本法》是根据《中国宪法》签订和制定的，属第二级法律根据。

进而言之，香港 BIT 实践对国际法特别是国际投资法和国际条约法作出了重要贡献。首先，从总体上看，过渡期香港 BIT 实践创造了在特殊历史条件下条约实践的新模式，它简化甚至避免了条约继承或续订的复杂问题。香港特区政府，作为过渡期香港 BITs 权利和义务的享有和承担者，保持香港区域性实体地位的认同，承认

---

〔1〕 参见高成栋：《中外 BITs 对香港特区的适用争议及其解决——以谢业深诉秘鲁政府案为例》，载《国际经济法学刊》第 17 卷第 1 期，北京大学出版社 2010 年版，第 68—72 页。

〔2〕 See Xiaobing Xu, George D. Wilson, The Hong Kong Special Administrative Region as a Model of Regional External Autonomy, *Case W. Res. J. Int'l L.*, Vol. 32, 2000, p. 6.

此类协定持续有效。其次,在 BITs 历史上,香港与荷兰 BIT 是第一例由非主权实体与主权国家签订的此类协定,是 BITs 缔约主体方面的重大突破。最后,一些新的法律概念、原则和新的程序安排由香港 BITs 的缔约双方共同创造或接受,构成新的国际实践,也提出了国际法研究的新课题,必将进一步丰富国际法学的内容和促进国际法学的发展。

On Hong Kong's Bilateral Investment Treaty Practice

Abstract: On the basis of some brief illustrations of Hong Kong's bilateral investment treaty（BIT）practice and evolutions, this Article meticulously analyzes main clauses in such BITs, including the scope of application, investment treatment, "deprivation" and related standards of compensation, and dispute settlement. It further discusses the nature of the authorization of Hong Kong's treaty-making competence, along with its grounds for international recognition. The Article points out that: Hong Kong's BIT practice follows the traditional model in general, and takes on certain critical features due to Hong Kong's unique status as a non-sovereign entity; the authorization statements in Hong Kong's BITs explicitly demonstrate the authorization nature of Hong Kong's treaty-making competence, and the Constitutional Law of P. R. C. is the decisive legal basis for Hong Kong's counterparts and international society to recognize Hong Kong's status as a contracting party; and issues on treaty applications derived from Hong Kong's BIT practice have already become realistic problems, which require cautious prevention.

第二节　Initiative and Implications of Hong Kong's Bilateral Investment Treaties[*]
（香港双边投资条约的创新与意涵）

Ⅰ. Introduction

In late 1950's, the first bilateral investment treaty (hereinafter BIT) was concluded between the Federal Republic of Germany and Pakistan, aiming at promotion and protection of international investment.[1] The Contracting Parties to the BITs are typically European countries and developing countries. Germany and other European States took the lead in this regard.[2] Gradually BITs are widely accepted by States around the world and have become the most popular form of investment treaty regime.[3]

In general a BIT is defined as an agreement concluded between two States in which each State agrees to offer certain protections to investors and investment from

---

[*] Initiative and Implications of Hong Kong's Bilateral Investment Treaties, *The Journal of World Investment & Trade*, ISSN 1660-7112, Vol. 11, No. 5, 2010.

This article is one of the achievements of researching project "the Legal Regime for Encouragement and Protection of China's Overseas Investment" [No. 09&ZD032] sponsored by the National Social Science Fund of China.

[1] The Treaty between the Federal Republic of Germany and Pakistan for the Promotion and Protection of Investments was concluded in 1959. It contains many substantive provisions that have become common in subsequent BITs. See Andrew Newcombe, Lluis Paradell, *Law and Practice of Investment Treaties*, *Standards of Treatment*, Wolters Kluwer, 42 (2009); Jason Webb Yackee, "Conceptual Difficulties in the Empirical Study of Bilateral Investment Treaties", 33 *Brooklyn J. Int'l L*. 405 (2008).

[2] Switzerland, France, Italy, United Kingdom, the Netherlands, and Belgium followed Germany's BIT practice in a relatively short time. See Jeswald W. Salacuse, "BIT by BIT: The Growth of Bilateral Investment Treaties and Their Impact on Foreign Investment in Developing Countries", 24 *The International Lawyer* 656-657 (1990).

[3] According to statistics of UNCTAD, there are 2750 BITs by the end of 2009. United Nations Conference on Trade and Development, *World Investment Report 2010*, 81. www. unctad. org 03/08/2010. For general picture of BIT practice, see UNCTAD, *Bilateral Investment Treaties 1995-2006*; *Trends in Investment Rulemaking*, United Nations (2007). Latin American States, home of the Calvo Doctrine, shifted their position on BITs and began signing BITs in the late 1980s. Over the past two decades, they have signed more than 500 BITs with countries around the world. See Mary H. Mourra (ed.), *Latin American Investment Treaty Arbitration*, *the Controversies and Conflicts*, Wolters Kluwer, 1 (2008).

the other State. [1] In the more than half century, most BITs mimic, at least in broad strokes, the 1959 Draft International Convention on Investments Abroad (commonly known as the Abs-Shawcross Convention) and the Organization for Economic Cooperation and Development (OECD) 1967 Draft Convention on the Protection of Foreign Property. [2] Due to their common origins, the terms used and subjects covered in different BITs appear remarkably similar over time and across countries. [3] In addition the Contracting Parties to the BITs are all sovereign States before the emergence of Hong Kong (HK) on its own as a new comer in this scene.

According to provisions of the Sino-British Joint Declaration on the Question of Hong Kong (hereinafter the JD)[4] and the Basic Law of Hong Kong Special Administrative Region of the People's Republic of China (hereinafter the BL), the Hong Kong Special Administrative Region (hereinafter HKSAR) may on its own, using the name "Hong Kong, China", maintain and develop relations and conclude and implement agreements with foreign States and regions and relevant international organizations in the appropriate fields, including the economic, trade, financial and monetary, shipping, communications, tourism, cultural and sports fields. [5]

In the period of British rule, HK's international investment relations were conducted within the framework of the United Kingdom (UK)'s BITs. [6] UK had covered HK under a number of its BITs by way of territorial extension in exchange of notes. The legal effect of these UK's BITs in HK only continued until 30 June

---

[1] Paul E. Comeaux, N. Stephan Kinsella, *Protecting Foreign Investment under International Law*, *Legal Aspects of Political Risk*, Oceana Publications Inc., 101 and note 7 (1997).

[2] For the brief history of the BITs, see Jeswald W. Salacuse, "BIT by BIT: The Growth of Bilateral Investment Treaties and Their Impact on Foreign Investment in Developing Countries", 24 *The International Lawyer*, 656-661 (1990).

[3] Jason Webb Yackee, "Conceptual Difficulties in the Empirical Study of Bilateral Investment Treaties", 33 *Brooklyn J. Int'l L.* 415-416 (2008).

[4] Joint Declaration of Government of the United Kingdom of Great Britain and Northern Ireland and the People's Republic of China on the Question of Hong Kong was formally signed on 19 December 1984 and came into force on 27 May 1985. The agreement was reprinted in 23 *ILM* 1371-1380 (1984).

[5] Art. 3, 9, 10, the JD; Section XI of Annex I of the JD; Art. 151, the BL. The key to the scope of HK's treaty-making power is the concept of "appropriate fields". The term itself is not defined, and it is necessary to examine all the provisions of the BL to determine in what areas Hong Kong may have capacity for external relations. See Yash Ghai, *Hong Kong's New Constitutional Order*, *The Resumption of Chinese Sovereignty and the Basic Law*, Hong Kong University Press, 435-436 (1997).

[6] For general picture of UK's BITs practice, see Eileen Denza & Shelagh Brooks, Investment Protection Treaties: United Kingdom Experience, 36 *Int'l & Com. L. Q.*, 908-923 (1987).

1997. In order to maintain and develop HK's international investment relations after 1997, HK had two choices in the transition period (from 27 May 1985 to 30 June 1997): one was that HK negotiate and conclude BITs in its name with foreign countries in accordance with above provisions of the JD and the BL, and the other was that HK's international investment relations were covered by the framework of Chinese BITs. [1] HK chose the first one then. Considering the different economic and legal systems as well as different status in the international investment context between HK and Mainland China, the choice may better meet the specific needs of HK and serve the purpose of promoting and protecting international investment for HK.

On 19 November 1992, Agreement between Government of Hong Kong and Government of Kingdom of Netherlands on Promotion and Protection of Mutual Investment (hereinafter HK-Netherlands BIT) was signed and entered into force on 1 September 1993. [2] As the first HK's BIT, HK-Netherlands BIT plays an important role of "*de facto* Model" in HK's earlier BIT practice for HK itself and its counterparts. The "*de jure* Model BIT", Model Agreement between the Government of Hong Kong and the Government of… For the Promotion and Protection of Investments (hereinafter HK Model BIT) was published in 1995, [3] following the traditional framework and general rules of BITs. [4] Comparing with "Treaty

---

[1] China has participated actively in negotiating BITs with foreign countries since earlier 1980's and there are 125 China-foreign BITs by the end of 2009, ranking only second to Germany (135 BITs) in the numbers of BITs concluded. United Nations Conference on Trade and Development, *World Investment Report 2010*, p. 81. www. unctad. org 03/08/2010.

[2] Texts published in *Special Supplement No. 5 to the Hong Kong Government Gazette*, E27-53 (1992).

[3] The whole text of HK Model BIT published in Rudolf Dolzer, Margrete Stevens, *Bilateral Investment Treaties*, Martinus Nijhoff Publishers, 200-208 (1995).

[4] It seems that there are two types of BIT models: one is the European model, the traditional one; the other is the US model, including provisions on some new elements and complicated dispute settlement regime. There are 11 Articles in the HK Model BIT: Article 1: Definition; Article 2: Promotion and Protection of Investment and Returns; Article 3: Treatment of Investments; Article 4: Compensation for Losses; Article 5: Expropriation; Article 6: Transfer of Investments and Returns; Article 7: Exceptions; Article 8: Settlement of Investment Disputes; Article 9: Disputes between Contracting Parties; Article 10: Entry into force; Article 11: Duration and Termination. It is evident that the HK Model BIT follows European model. See also the typical European BIT Models: German Model Treaty-2008; Treaty between the Federal Republic of Germany and […] concerning the Encouragement and Reciprocal Protection of Investments (13 Articles in total); and Draft Agreement between the Government of the Republic of France and the Government of the Republic of […] on the Reciprocal Promotion and Protection of Investments (2006) (11 Articles in total). For the preparation and purposes of the Model BITs, see Jeswald W. Salacuse, "BIT by BIT: The Growth of Bilateral Investment Treaties and Their Impact on Foreign Investment in Developing Countries", 24 *The International Lawyer*, 662-663 (1990).

between the Government of the United States of America and Government of [Country] Concerning the Encouragement and Reciprocal Protection of Investment" (2004) (hereinafter 2004 US Model BIT),[1]HK's two BIT Models are succinct and fulfill the basic functions for its BIT practice.[2]

Upon the positive practice in accordance with the two Models, HK has concluded 14 BITs in its name with 15 foreign countries by 25 June 2010.[3] All of HK's counterparts to BITs are developed countries except Thailand.[4] HK's successful BIT practice demonstrates remarkable achievements in practice of its external autonomy[5] and indicates an important breakthrough and initiative in the history of BITs and international law.

Due to HK's status of non-sovereign entity, HK's BITs have constituted a

---

[1] For the evolution of US Model BIT, see Kenneth J. Vandevelde, *U. S. International Investment Agreements*, Oxford University Press, 91-112 (2009).

[2] There are 37 Articles in the 2004 US Model BIT: Article 1: Definitions; Article 2: Scope and Coverage; Article 3: National Treatment; Article 4: Most-Favored-Nation Treatment; Article 5: Minimum Standard of Treatment; Article 6: Expropriation and Compensation; Article 7: Transfers; Article 8: Performance Requirements; Article 9: Senior Management and Boards of Directors; Article 10: Publication of Laws and Decisions Respecting Investment; Article 11: Transparency; Article 12: Investment and Environment; Article 13: Investment and Labour; Article 14: Non-Conforming Measures; Article 15: Special Formalities and Information Requirements; Article 16: Non-Derogation; Article 17: Denial of Benefits; Article 18: Essential Security; Article 19: Disclosure of Information; Article 20: Financial Services; Article 21: Taxation; Article 22: Entry into Force, Duration and Termination; Article 23: Consultation and Negotiation; Article 24: Submission of a Claim to Arbitration; Article 25: Consent of Each Party to Arbitration; Article 26: Conditions and Limitations on Consent of Each Party; Article 27: Selection of Arbitrators; Article 28: Conduct of the Arbitration; Article 29: Transparency of Arbitral Proceedings; Article 30: Governing Law; Article 31: Interpretation of Annexes; Article 32: Expert Reports; Article 33: Consolidation; Article 34: Awards; Article 35: Annexes and Footnotes; Article 36: Service of Documents; Article 37: State-State Dispute Settlement. The text is divided into three sections: Section A (Article 1 to Article 22), Section B (Article 23 to Article 36) and Section C (Article 37).

[3] www. legislation. gov. hk 08/07/2010.

[4] 15 out of the 16 counterparts of HK's BITs are member States of Organization for Economic Co-operation and Development (OECD), only one is developing country. The counterparts, the dates of entry into force and the texts available of the agreements are: Netherlands (1. 9. 1993), *Special Supplement No. 5 to the Hong Kong Government Gazette*, 134, no. 50 (1992): E25-E53; Australia (15. 10. 1993), Ibid, 135, no. 37 (1993): E103-E123; Denmark (4. 3. 1994),136, no. 6 (1994): E19-E48; Sweden (26. 6. 1994), 136, no. 23 (1994): E51-E78; Switzerland (22. 10. 1994), 136, no. 48 (1994): E85-E116; New Zealand (5. 8. 1995), 137, no. 34 (1995): E95-E115; France (30. 5. 1997), 2, no. 26 (1998): E215-E240; Japan (18. 6. 1997), 2, no. 26 (1998): E241-E281; Korea (30. 7. 1997), 2, no. 26 (1998): E283-E316; Austria (1. 10. 1997), 2, no. 26 (1998): E317-E351; Italy (2. 2. 1998), 2, no. 6 (1998): E3-E35; Germany (19. 2. 1998), 2, no. 10 (1998): E39-E66; UK (12. 4. 1999), 3, no. 15 (1999): E391-E414; Belgium and Luxembourg (18. 6. 2001), 5, no. 25 (2001): E175-E222; Thailand (12. 4. 2006), 10, no. 18 (2006): E41-E65.

[5] For general picture of HK's practice on external autonomy, see Zeng Huaqun, "Unprecedented International Status: Theoretical and Practical Aspects of the HKSAR's External Autonomy", 9 (3) *The Journal of World Investment & Trade*, 275-297 (2008).

series of its characteristics. Based on the provisions of HK's two BIT Models and relevant treaty practice, the following will discuss and analyze some key provisions of HK's BITs, such as provisions relating to authorization, scope of application, investment treatment, deprivation and compensation, dispute settlement, focusing on initiatives and implications of HK's BIT practice.

II. Authorization

The first unique feature of HK's BIT practice is the authorization statements, which is totally new content in the preamble of BITs. It is obvious that as HK is a non-sovereign entity, the source of authorization for HK's treaty-making power should be established and indicated clearly as a prerequisite.

According to traditional international law, only sovereign States may be Contracting Parties of treaties. In the development of modern international practice, more and more non-sovereign entities have become the Contracting Parties of treaties. In addition to sovereign States, international organizations, member States of federal States, belligerent, and regional entities with high autonomy, etc, have become the new comer for negotiating and concluding treaties. The legal grounds for these non-sovereign entities are different. The source of their treaty-making power comes from basic instruments for international organizations, from federal constitutions for member States of federal States, from customary international law for belligerent, and from authorization by sovereign States for regional entities. [1]

In the BIT practice before 1992, like other traditional treaty practice, all the Contracting Parties to BITs are sovereign States. HK-Netherlands BIT is the first one which is concluded between a non-sovereign entity and a sovereign State in the BIT history. It is an important breakthrough in terms of Contracting Parties of BITs.

One of the common features of HK's BITs concluded in the transition period is that the treaties do not indicate the name of the authorizing government in the texts though the treaty-making power of HK has actually been duly authorized by a sovereign government. The preamble of HK-Netherlands BIT states that: "the Govern-

---

[1] See Li Haopei, *On the Laws of Treaties* (in Chinese), Law Press, 240 (1988).

ment of Hong Kong, having been duly authorized to conclude this agreement by the sovereign government which is responsible for its foreign affairs, and the Government of the Kingdom of the Netherlands…" The HK Model BIT[1] and other HK's BITs follow the same terms. This description might be regarded as an intentional vague. Article 4 of the JD indicates that UK is in charge of HK's administration until 30 June 1997 and China resumes exercising its sovereignty from 1 July 1997. Therefore, for the counterparts to the HK in these BITs, the terms "the sovereign government which is responsible for its foreign affairs" might refer to two governments in different periods of time, namely UK before 30 June 1997 and China after 1 July 1997. In fact, the authorization of HK's BITs concluded in transition period have been transferred from UK to China after 1 July 1997 even the terms on authorization in HKs BITs remain unchanged.

HK's BITs concluded after 1 July 1997 clearly indicate the source of authorization for treaty-making power of HK. HK-UK BIT, the first HK's BIT concluded after 1 July 1997, states in the preamble that "the Government of Hong Kong Special Administrative Region of the People's Republic of China having been duly authorized to conclude this agreement by the Central People's Government of the People's Republic of China, and the Government of the United Kingdom of Great Britain and Northern Ireland…"

As for as legal status of HKSAR,[2] Article 12 of the BL provides distinctly that "Hong Kong Special Administrative Region shall be a local administrative region of People's Republic of China, which shall enjoy a high degree of autonomy and come directly under the Central People's Government." The provisions clarify the legal status of the HKSAR, which is a key to understand the nature of the HKSAR's external autonomy. The authorization arrangements and provisions in the preamble of HK's BITs further confirm the authorization nature of the HKSAR's external autonomy and its treaty-making power in the specified fields. Although this

---

[1] Preamble of HK model BIT, in Rudolf Dolzer, Margrete Stevens, *Bilateral Investment Treaties*, Martinus Nijhoff Publishers, 200 (1995).

[2] There are some comments on the HK/HKSAR's legal status before and after 1997, typically see Roda Mushkat, Hong Kong as an International Legal Person, 6 *Emory International Law Review*, 105-170 (1992); Xiaobing Xu, George D. Wilson, "The Hong Kong Special Administrative Region as a Model of Regional External Autonomy", 32 *Case W. Res. J. Int'l L.*, 1-38 (2000).

kind of formulation has not yet acquired popular usage in international law, its form clearly constituted HK as an entity with the capacity to enter into BITs and other treaties. [1]

Ⅲ. Scope of Application

The scope of application of BITs firstly is defined by definition clause. [2] The purpose of definitions in BITs is to determine the objects to which the rules of the agreement shall apply and the scope of their applicability. The typical BIT protects investments made by investors of one Contracting Party in the territory of the other Contracting Party. The scope of the subject matter of BIT thus depends on the definitions of certain key terms, in particular "investments" and "investors". [3] The clause also often define the notion of territory of a Contracting Parties, so that "investments" made in that territory of a Contracting Party by "investors" of another Contracting Party qualify as protected "foreign" investments. [4] In addition, duration and termination clause of BIT also define the scope of their applicability in time. Following the general practice of BITs in this regard, HK has made some new and different provisions with its counterparts due to its non-sovereign status, especially the provisions on "investors" and geographical application.

1. Investment

BITs usually provide a definition of what constitutes an investment protected by the treaty in their "definition" clause. The definitions of "investment" are very broad, typically referring to "every kind of asset", and then adding a specific non-exhaustive list of examples. [5] The broad definition of "investment" is particularly drafted by US and other capital-exporting States in their Model BITs. The objective behind this is to ensure that treaty protection could be given to a wide variety of

[1] See Anthony Neoh, Hong Kong's Future: The View of a Hong Kong Lawyer, 22 *Cal. W. Int'l L. J.* 351-352 (1992).

[2] Michael R. Reading, "The Bilateral Investment Treaty in ASEAN: a Comparative Analysis", 42 *Duke Law Journal*, 695 (1992).

[3] UNCTAD, *Bilateral Investment Treaties 1995-2006: Trends in Investment Rulemaking*, United Nations, 7 (2007).

[4] Andrew Newcombe, Lluis Paradell, *Law and Practice of Investment Treaties, Standards of Treatment*, Wolters Kluwer, 65 (2009).

[5] Andrew Newcombe, Lluis Paradell, *Law and Practice of Investment Treaties, Standards of Treatment*, Wolters Kluwer, 65-66 (2009).

activities associated with foreign direct investment (hereinafter FDI). [1]

Following general practice of most BITs, [2] Article 1 (e) of HK Model BIT provides that:

> "'investment' means every kind of asset, and in particular, though not ex-clusively, includes:
>
> (i) movable and immovable property and any other property rights such as mortgages, liens or pledges;
>
> (ii) shares in and stock and debentures of a company and any other form of participation in a company;
>
> (iii) claims to money or to any performance under contract having a finan-cial value;
>
> (iv) intellectual property rights and goodwill;
>
> (v) business concessions conferred by law or under contract, including concessions to search for, cultivate, extract or exploit natural resources;
>
> A change in the form in which assets are invested does not affect their char-acter as investments…"

The above provisions are followed by HK's BITs with minor revisions and/or supplement. [3] It seems that HK adopts the broad "asset-based" definition of "investment", the scope of which goes beyond covering only FDI. [4]

It should be pointed out that the provisions that "a change in the form in which assets are invested does not affect their character as investments" have very impor-tant practical implications. According to the provisions, the character of investments

---

[1] M. Sornarajah, *The International Law on Foreign Investment*, second edition, Cambridge University Press, 9 (2004).

[2] UNCTAD, *Bilateral Investment Treaties 1995-2006: Trends in Investment Rulemaking*, United Na-tions, 8 (2007).

[3] See Art. 1(3), HK-Netherlands; Art. 1(e), HK-Australia; Art. 1(3), HK-Denmark; Art. 1(3), HK-Sweden; Art. 1(5), HK-Switzerland; Art. 1.5, HK-New Zealand; Art. 1(2), HK-France; Art. 1.3, HK-Ja-pan; Art. 1(4), HK-Korea; Art. 1(c), HK-Austria; Art. 1(5), HK-Italy; Art. 1(2), HK-Germany; Art. 1(e), HK-UK; Art. 1(4), HK-Belgium and Luxembourg; Art. 1(3), HK-Thailand. Article 1(4)(f) of HK-Korea BIT adds a category of investment, providing that "goods that, under a leasing agreement, are placed at the disposal of a leasee in the area of a Contracting Party in accordance with its laws and regulations".

[4] In addition to the broad "asset-based" definition, there are tautological or circular definition, and closed-list definition for "investment" in BIT practice. See UNCTAD, *Bilateral Investment Treaties 1995-2006: Trends in Investment Rulemaking*, United Nations, 8-13 (2007).

is "freezed" at the time of making investment. Even the form of the investments changes afterwards, their character as investments is indisputable. The "precaution" provision might prevent or decrease the potential disputes concerning the character of investments.

2. Investors

BITs provide in general that "investors" means physical persons who are nationals of Contracting Parties[1] and companies incorporated or constituted under the law of Contracting Parties. In HK's BITs, while provisions for defining "companies" as "investors" follow the general practice of most BITs,[2] the provisions for defining "physical persons" as "investors" are unique due to HK's non-sovereign status and specific needs for protection to certain people.

Traditionally two different approaches have been taken in the drafting of the definition of the term "physical persons". One is to set forth a single definition for applying to both parties. The other is to offer two definitions, one relating to one Contracting Party, and the other to the second Contracting Party.[3] HK Model BIT creates the third approach. According to the Model, "'investors' means: (i) in respect of either Contracting Party: physical persons who have the right of abode in the area of that Contracting Party… (ii) in respect of [HK's counterpart]: physical persons who are its nationals".[4] It seems that the HK Model BIT adopts two standards-permanent resident standard and/or national standard[5]—for two Contracting Parties in different ways: only permanent resident standard for HK; both

---

[1] Most BITs protect physical persons who have the nationality of one of the Contracting Parties. Thus the typical definition of a national of a party is a physical person recognized by that party's internal law as a national or citizen. In some cases, the definition of "investor" is even broader to include not only citizens but also individuals, who qualify as permanent residents under domestic law. See UNCTAD, *Bilateral Investment Treaties 1995-2006: Trends in Investment Rulemaking*, United Nations, 13 (2007).

[2] BITs have essentially relied on three basic criteria to determine the nationality of a "company": (i) the concept of incorporation or constitution; (ii) the concept of the seat; and (iii) the concept of control. See Rudolf Dolzer, Margrete Stevens, *Bilateral Investment Treaties*, Martinus Nijhoff Publishers, 35-36 (1995).

[3] Rudolf Dolzer, Margrete Stevens, *Bilateral Investment Treaties*, Martinus Nijhoff Publishers, 31-32 (1995).

[4] Art. 1(f)(i), HK Model BIT.

[5] There is key difference between "national" and "citizen" in the legal implication in some countries. Under US law, the term "national" is broader than the term "citizen". For example, a native of American Samoa is a national of the US, but not a citizen. See Kenneth J. Vandevelde, *U. S. International Investment Agreements*, Oxford University Press, 144 (2009).

permanent resident standard and national standard for HK's counterparts. [1]

In a more clear way, HK-Netherland BIT provides that: "'investors' means: (a) in respect of Hong Kong: (i) physical persons who have the right of abode in its area…(b) in respect of the Kingdom of the Netherlands: (i) physical persons who are its nationals…"[2] These provisions have become general practice in most of HK's BITs. [3] The key difference between these provisions and those of the HK Model BIT is that only national standard is applied for the HK's counterparts.

It is evident that due to its non-sovereign status, HK can not adopt the national standard for defining "physical persons" as "investors". The simple reason is that apart from complicated nationality issue of HK residents before 30 June 1997, even after 1 July 1997 when China resumes exercising its sovereignty on HK, the protection of HK's BITs can not cover the Chinese nationals who have not the right of abode in HK, including Chinese nationals of Mainland, Macao and Taiwan. On contrary, the protection of HK's BITs might cover physical persons who are nationals of foreign States and permanent residents of HK.

However, the application of different standards for defining "physical persons" as "investors" may raise a "double BIT protection" issue. As the result of the application of permanent resident standard, HK's permanent residents who seek for protection from HK's BITs may cover all foreigners who have the right of abode in HK, including nationals of HK's counterparts. In this case, as qualified "investor" from both Contracting Parties, he or she may seek for BIT protection from HK and/or from HK's counterpart at will. Both of the Contracting Parties of HK's BIT therefore have to face and tackle the awkward "investor identity" issue.

For dealing with this issue, HK-UK BIT provides that "investors" means: in respect of HK, "physical persons who have the right of abode in the area of the Hong Kong Special Administrative Region but who are not British nationals"; in

---

[1] In practice only two HK's BITs adopt the provisions on "both permanent resident standard and national/citizen standard for HK's counterparts". Article 1(f) of HK-Australia BIT provides that: "in respect of Australia: (A) physical persons possessing Australia citizenship or who are permanently residing in Australia in accordance with its law…"Article 1(2)(b)(i) of HK-New Zealand BIT has similar provisions.

[2] Art. 1(2), HK-Netherlands.

[3] Art. 1(2), HK-Denmark; Art. 1(2), HK-Sweden; Art. 1(2), HK-Switzerland; Art. 1(3), HK-France; Art. 1.4, HK-Japan; Art. 1(5), HK-Korea; Art. 1(d), HK-Austria; Art. 1(6), HK-Italy; Art. 1(4), HK-Germany; Art. 1(f), HK-UK; Art. 1(5), HK-Belgium and Luxembourg; Art. 1(4), HK-Thailand.

respect of the UK, "physical persons who are British nationals but who do not have the right of abode in the Hong Kong Special Administrative Region". [1] This is a good example for clarification and establishment of the "investor identity". However, as a result of these provisions, "physical persons who are British nationals and who have the right of abode in the Hong Kong Special Administrative Region" cannot seek for HK-UK BIT protection from either side of the Contracting Parties. A new issue of "vacuum BIT protection" occurs.

3. Geographical application

The geographical scope of application of a BIT depends on the definition of the term "territory". The purpose of defining this term is not to delimit the territory of the Contracting Parties; that is an aspect normally dealt with in national constitutions. Rather, the rationale derives from the objective of investment protection, in particular to provide that investments located in maritime areas beyond the boundaries of the territorial waters are deemed to be within the Parties' territory for the purposes of the agreement. [2]

According to Article 1 (a) (i) of HK Model BIT, "area: (i) in respect of Hong Kong includes Hong Kong Island, Kowloon and the New Territories". [3] For the HK's counterpart, the geographical scope covers the whole territory of the sovereign State including the specified maritime areas. [4]

It is noticeable that in HK's BITs the Contracting Parties firstly use the term of "area" instead of "territory" for both Parties in the BIT history. The term "territory" is usually used for description of geographical scope of sovereign States. [5] Comparing with definition of "territory", "area" is broader and may be equally used for both non-sovereign entities and sovereign States. As HK is a non-

---

[1] Art. 1(f)(i), HK-UK BIT.

[2] UNCTAD, *Bilateral Investment Treaties 1995-2006: Trends in Investment Rulemaking*, United Nations, 17 (2007).

[3] Art. 1(a)(i), HK Model BIT. This is general practice without exception in all HK's BITs.

[4] For example, Art. 1.1 of HK-Netherlands BIT provides that "in respect of the Kingdom of the Netherlands, is the territory of the Kingdom including the maritime areas adjacent to the coast of the territory concerned, to the extent to which the Kingdom of the Netherlands exercises sovereign rights or jurisdiction in those areas according to international law".

[5] The general definition of territory is that: "a geographical area included within a particular government's jurisdiction; the portion of the earth's surface that is in a State's exclusive procession and control." Bryan A. Garner, *Black's Law Dictionary*, Eighth Edition, Thomson, 1512 (2004).

sovereign entity, the term "area" is more precise for description of HK's geographical scope than the term "territory". Moreover unlike the definition for its counterpart, the definition that in respect of HK, "area" "includes Hong Kong Island, Kowloon and the New Territories" indicates only land area, clearly excluding the maritime area, is covered by the treaty. [1]

4. Application in time

Regarding the issue of application in time, two main questions have traditionally arisen in BIT negotiations: one is application to existing investments; the other is the duration and determination of the period of application. [2]

4.1 Application to existing investments

In accordance with the Vienna Convention on the Law of Treaties, a treaty does not in general have retroactive effects. [3] Therefore the rights and obligations derived from a treaty apply only after the treaty has entered into force and with respect to acts or facts occurring thereafter. There is the issue of whether BITs should apply after their entry into force to investments already existing at that time. There are three approaches in recent BIT practice: (1) to provide protection to both future investments and existing investments, but not apply to any investment-related dispute or claim that arose or was settled before the entry into force of the BIT; (2) to provide protection only to future investments; and (3) not to address the issue. [4]

According to Article 1(e) of the HK Model BIT, "the term 'investment' includes all investments, whether made before or after the date of entry into force of this Agreement". This provision is followed by all HK's BITs. [5] It seems that

[1] Recent BITs of coastal nations generally include a reference to such maritime areas in the BIT. Rudolf Dolzer, Margrete Stevens, *Bilateral Investment Treaties*, Martinus Nijhoff Publishers, 43-44 (1995).

[2] UNCTAD, *Bilateral Investment Treaties 1995-2006: Trends in Investment Rulemaking*, United Nations, 19 (2007).

[3] Art. 28 of Vienna Convention on the Law of Treaties provides that: "Unless a different intention appears from the treaty or is otherwise established, its provisions do not bind a party in relation to any act or fact which took place or any situation which ceased to exist before the date of the entry into force of the treaty with respect to that party."

[4] UNCTAD, *Bilateral Investment Treaties 1995-2006: Trends in Investment Rulemaking*, United Nations, 20 (2007).

[5] HK Model BIT. See Art. 9, HK-Netherlands; Art. 1(e), HK-Australia; Art. 12(1), HK-Denmark; Art. 11, HK-Sweden; Art. 9, HK-Switzerland; Art. 2.2, HK-New Zealand; Art. 12, HK-France; Art. 10, HK-Japan; Art. 12, HK-Korea; Art. 11, HK-Austria; Art. 9, HK-Italy; Art. 9, HK-Germany; Art. 1(e), HK-UK; Art. 11, HK-Belgium and Luxembourg; Art. 1(3), HK-Thailand.

HK's BITs take a most opening-up attitude to the issue, namely indicating "to provide protection to both future investments and existing investments", and without excluding "any investment-related dispute or claim that arose or was settled before the entry into force of the BIT".

4.2 Duration and termination

Unlike other international agreements, BITs usually specify that they shall remain in force for a minimum fixed period. The rationale for this approach is to provide investors of the Contracting Parties with a high level of certainty and predictability regarding the international legal framework applicable to their investments. Among the BITs under UNCTAD's recent review, the prevailing trend has been to specify that the initial period for which the treaty shall be in force will be 10 years. A significant number of BITs provide for longer initial period of application such as 15 years. Other BITs provide in principle that BIT shall remain in force indefinitely until one Contracting Party notifies the other of its intention to terminate it. [1]

According to Article 11 of HK Model BIT:

> "This Agreement shall remain in force until the expiration of twelve months from the date on which either Contracting Party shall given written notice of termination to the other."

It seems that from the above provision there is not definite duration for the application of HK's BITs. The only way for termination of the treaties is by written notice of termination unilaterally.

However Article 13.1 of HK-Netherlands BIT set up another model, providing that:

> "This Agreement shall remain in force for a period of fifteen years. Unless notice of termination has been given by either Contracting Party at least twelve months before the date of expiry of its validity, the Agreement shall be extended tacitly for periods of ten years, each Contracting Party reserving the

---

[1] UNCTAD, *Bilateral Investment Treaties 1995-2006: Trends in Investment Rulemaking*, United Nations, 20 (2007).

right to terminate the Agreement upon notice of at least twelve months before the date of expiry of the current period of validity. "[1]

The model has become general practice in HK's BITs. (see Table 1)

Table 1　Provisions on Duration and Termination in HK's BITs[2]

BITs	Dates of entry into force	Duration	Extended periods
HK-Netherlands	1. 9. 1993	15	10
HK-Australia	15. 10. 1993	15	indefinitely
HK-Denmark	4. 3. 1994	15	indefinitely
HK-Sweden	26. 6. 1994	15	indefinitely
HK-Switzerland	22. 10. 1994	15	10
HK-New Zealand	5. 8. 1995	15	indefinitely
HK-France	30. 5. 1997	20	10
HK-Japan	18. 6. 1997	15	indefinitely
HK-Korea	30. 7. 1997	15	indefinitely
HK-Austria	1. 10. 1997	15	indefinitely
HK-Italy	2. 2. 1998	15	10
HK-Germany	19. 2. 1998	15	indefinitely
HK-UK	12. 4. 1999	15	indefinitely
HK-Belgium and Luxembourg	18. 6. 2001	15	10
HK-Thailand	12. 4. 2006	15	indefinitely

It is worth noticing that all HK's BITs provide longer initial period (15 years) of application with flexible extended period of application. The significance of the provisions on termination of HK's BITs concluded in transition period is that these BITs shall remain in force after 1 July 1997, reflecting that the Contracting Parties of HK's BITs believe that HK's international status would remain unchanged after 1 July 1997. These provisions certainly enhance the confidence of foreign investors to HK's investment environment.

---

〔1〕　Art. 13. 1, HK-Netherlands.

〔2〕　See Art. 13, HK-Netherlands; Art. 14, HK-Australia; Art. 14, HK-Denmark; Art. 13, HK-Sweden; Art. 14, HK-Switzerland; Art. 13, HK-New Zealand; Art. 14, HK-France; Art. 15, HK-Japan; Art. 14, HK-Korea; Art. 13, HK-Austria; Art. 13, HK-Italy; Art. 13, HK-Germany; Art. 15, HK-UK; Art. 13, HK-Belgium and Luxembourg; Art. 12, HK-Thailand.

Ⅳ. Investment Treatment

BITs aims at decreasing the political or non-commercial risks[1] by establishing the standards of treatment relating to transnational investments with legal effect.[2] They usually include one or several general principles that, together or individually, are intended to provide overall criteria by which to judge whether the treatment given to an investment and/or investor is satisfactory, and to help interpret and clarify how more specific provisions should be applied in particular situations. These provisions are typical substantive protection for covered investment and investors of BITs.[3]

1. Categories of investment treatment standards

There are a variety of standards of treatment provided for in BITs. They would usually contain one article on treatment standards but that article would identify several different treatment standards.[4]

There are two broad categories of standards in general practice of BITs.

One is absolute standards, including fair and equitable treatment, full protection and security, and the minimum standard of treatment according to customary international law.[5]

The second is relative standards, mainly referring to national treatment and

---

[1] Typical political risks includes risk of expropriation, currency risk, risk of political violence and breach of contract, for detailed discussion of political risks, see Paul E. Comeaux, N. Stephan Kinsella, *Protecting Foreign Investment under International Law*, *Legal Aspects of Political Risk*, Oceana Publications Inc. , 1-22 (1997).

[2] Michael R. Reading, "The Bilateral Investment Treaty in ASEAN: a Comparative Analysis", 42 *Duke Law Journal*, 684 (1992).

[3] UNCTAD, *Bilateral Investment Treaties 1995-2006*: *Trends in Investment Rulemaking*, United Nations, 28 (2007); Mary H. Mourra(ed.), *Latin American Investment Treaty Arbitration*, the Controversies and Conflicts, Wolters Kluwer, 169-171 (2008).

[4] M. Sornarajah, *The International Law on Foreign Investment*, second edition, Cambridge University Press, 233 (2004). US 2004 Model BIT takes a new approach that includes four Articles on investment treatment, namely Article 3: National Treatment, Article 4: Most-Favored-Nation Treatment, Article 5: Minimum Standard of Treatment and Article 8: Performance Requirement. The prohibition on performance requirement attempts to ensure that investments are made in accordance with commercial aims, not a State's promotion of protectionist or other policy goals. See Mary H. Mourra(ed.), *Latin American Investment Treaty Arbitration*, the Controversies and Conflicts, Wolters Kluwer, 170 (2008).

[5] There are many comments and related practice on these absolute standards, especially on fair and equitable treatment. See Alberto Alvarez-Jimenez, Minimum Standard of Treatment of Aliens, Fair and Equitable Treatment of Foreign Investors, Customary International Law and the Diallo Case before the International Court of Justice, 9 (1) *The Journal of World Investment & Trade*, 51-70 (2008); Mary H. Mourra(ed.), *Latin American Investment Treaty Arbitration*, the Controversies and Conflicts, Wolters Kluwer, 170-171, 188-190 (2008).

most-favoured-nation (MFN) treatment. Both impose an obligation to provide "non-discriminatory" treatment. [1]

National treatment is one of the core guarantees regularly endorsed in BIT practice. [2] In a BIT context it means the obligation of Contracting Parties to grant investors of the other Contracting Party treatment no less favourable than the treatment they grant to investments of their own investors. The standard is an empty shell that obtains substantive content in relation to the treatment afforded to someone or something else. The effect of the standard is to create a level playing field between foreign and domestic investors in relevant market. [3] The legal analysis involves a comparison between the host State's treatment of domestic and foreign investors or domestic and foreign investments. [4]

As with national treatment, MFN treatment is also a relative standard. The MFN treatment means that investments or investors of one Contracting Party are entitled to treatment by the other Contracting Party that is no less favorable than the treatment the latter grants to investments or investors of any other third country. The MFN standard ensures that investments or investors of Contracting Parties to a BIT receive the best treatment that each of them has granted to the investments or investors of any other third country. Thus the MFN standard establishes, at least in principle, a level playing field between all foreign investors protected by a BIT. [5] MFN treatment obligations require that State conduct does not discriminate between similarly situated persons, entities, goods, service or investments of different foreign nationalities. [6] In recent years the interpretation of MFN clauses by

---

[1] Mary H. Mourra(ed.), *Latin American Investment Treaty Arbitration*, *the Controversies and Conflicts*, Wolters Kluwer, 169-170 (2008).

[2] Stephan W. Schill, Tearing Down the Great Wall: the New Generation Investment Treaties of the People's Republic of China, 15 *Cardozo J. Int'l & Comp. L.* 94 (2007).

[3] UNCTAD, *Bilateral Investment Treaties 1995-2006: Trends in Investment Rulemaking*, United Nations, 33 (2007).

[4] Andrew Newcombe, Lluis Paradell, *Law and Practice of Investment Treaties*, *Standards of Treatment*, Wolters Kluwer, 148-149 (2009).

[5] UNCTAD, *Bilateral Investment Treaties 1995-2006: Trends in Investment Rulemaking*, United Nations, 38 (2007).

[6] Andrew Newcombe, Lluis Paradell, *Law and Practice of Investment Treaties*, *Standards of Treatment*, Wolters Kluwer, 193 (2009).

investment arbitration tribunals has attracted considerable attention. [1]

It is pointed out that though the BITs contemplate a two-way flow of invest-ments between Contracting Parties to the treaties, it is usually only a one-way flow that is contemplated and feasible in reality in the context of disparities of wealth and technology between the two parties. [2] As a result of the "one-way flow", only capital-exporting States and their overseas investors gain benefit from the high level of standards on treatment of investment in BITs. As HK is a developed region and most of its counterparts are also developed State, the provisions on treatment of the "two-way flow" investment in HK's BITs might be expected to bring the mutual benefit for both Contracting Parties.

2. Models of HK's BITs on treatment of investment

There are two main models of HK's BITs on treatment of investment: HK Model BIT and HK-Netherlands BIT Model.

2. 1 HK Model BIT

Article 3 of HK Model BIT provides that:

"(1) Neither Contracting Party shall in its area subject investments or returns of investors of the other Contracting Party to treatment less favourable than that which it accords to investments or returns of its own investors or to investments or returns of investors of any other State.

(2) Neither Contracting Party shall in its area subject investors of the other Contracting Party, as regards their management, maintenance, use, en-joyment or disposal of their investments, to treatment less favourable than that which it accords to its own investors or to investors of any other State. "

It seems that the provisions of HK Model BIT on treatment of investments take the form of combination of national treatment and MFN treatment in a clause. 9 of

---

〔1〕 For detailed comments on the issue, see Okezie Chukwumerije, Interpreting Most-Favoured-Nation Clau-ses in Investment Treaty Arbitrations, 8 (5) *The Journal of World Investment & Trade*, 597-646 (2007); Mary H. Mourra(ed.), *Latin American Investment Treaty Arbitration*, *the Controversies and Conflicts*, Wolters Kluw-er, 187-188 (2008).

〔2〕 M. Sornarajah, *The International Law on Foreign Investment*, second edition, Cambridge University Press, 207 (2004).

the HK's BITs follow this model with minor revisions and/or supplements. [1]

Although express national treatment obligations appear in almost all BITs, there are significant variations between clauses. [2] The national treatment clauses of HK Model BIT and most of HK's BITs show that the obligation appears in the same clause with MFN clause, applies to both investors and investments and specifies the types of activities to which it applies. They contain no express comparator, such as "in like circumstances". [3] Moreover the obligation is not expressly subject to national law except for HK-New Zealand BIT. [4]

2.2 HK-Netherlands BIT Model

Article 3 of HK-Netherlands BIT provides that:

"(1) Investments and returns of investors of each Contracting Party shall at all times be accorded fair and equitable treatment. Neither Contracting Party shall in any way impair by unreasonable or discriminatory measures the management, maintenance, use, enjoyment or disposal of investments in its area of investors of the other Contracting Party.

(2) Each Contracting Party shall in its area accord investments or returns of investors of the other Contracting Party treatment not less favourable than that which it accords to investments or returns of its own investors or to invest-

---

[1] Art.3(1)(2), HK-Australia; Art.3, HK-Denmark; Art.3, HK-Sweden; Art.4, HK-New Zealand; Art.3, HK-Korea; Art.3, HK-Austria; Art.3 (1) (2), HK-Germany; Art.3, HK-Belgium and Luxembourg; Art.3, HK-Thailand. Minor revisions and/or supplements such as: Article 3 of HK-Australia BIT refers to "employment" issue; Article 3 of HK-Korea BIT and Article 3 of HK-Thailand BIT provide that: "fair and equitable and no less favourable than…"

[2] The variations of national treatment of BITs include whether the obligation: (1) is expressly subject to national law; (2) appears in the same clause with MFN treatment; (3) applies to establishment; (4) applies to both investors and investments; (5) specifies the types of activities to which it applies; (6) contains an express comparator, such as "in like circumstances". See Andrew Newcombe, Lluis Paradell, *Law and Practice of Investment Treaties*, *Standards of Treatment*, Wolters Kluwer, 156 (2009).

[3] Article 3.1 of 2004 US Model BIT provides that: "Each Party shall accord to investors of the other Party treatment no less favorable than that it accords, in like circumstances, to its own investors with respect to the establishment, acquisition, expansion, management, conduct, operation, and sale or other disposition of investments in its territory." The inclusion of "in like circumstances" has led arbitral panels to adopt a "two-step" approach when determining whether a particular measure violates national treatment standard. The approach is that first the tribunal verified whether there were in fact differences in treatment between domestic and foreign investors or their investments; second, if a difference was found, the tribunal then addressed the issue of whether investors or investments were "in like circumstances". UNCTAD, *Bilateral Investment Treaties 1995-2006: Trends in Investment Rulemaking*, United Nations, 36 (2007).

[4] Article 4 of HK-New Zealand BIT provides that national treatment for investments and investors of the other Contracting Party is "subject to its laws and regulations".

ments or returns of investors of any other State, whichever is more favourable to the investor concerned.

(3) Each Contracting Party shall in its area accord investors of the other Contracting Party, as regards their management, maintenance, use, enjoyment or disposal of their investments, treatment not less favourable than that which it accords to its own investors or to investors of any other State, whichever is more favourable to the investor concerned.

(4) Each Contracting Party shall accord to such investments and returns full physical protection and security in their respective areas which in any case shall not be less than that accorded either to investments and returns of their own investors or to investors of any other State, whichever is more favourable to the investor concerned.

(5) Each Contracting Party shall observe any obligation it may have entered into with regard to investments of investors of the other Contracting Party."

In HK-Netherlands BIT Model, there is a combination of absolute standards and relative standards in a same clause. Firstly as a general principle, fair and equitable treatment has been applied to investments and returns of investors of each Contracting Party at all time. Though the meaning of fair and equitable treatment is contentious, the obligation of Contracting Party in HK-Netherlands BIT Model is not to "in any way impair by unreasonable or discriminatory measures the management, maintenance, use, enjoyment or disposal of investments in its area of investors of the other Contracting Party". Secondly the Model provides specifically the main aspects of the treatment of investments accorded to national treatment and MFN treatment with the "whichever is more favorable" rule, including: (1) investments and returns of investors; (2) the management, maintenance, use, enjoyment or disposal of investments; (3) full physical protection and security to investments and returns; [1] 3 of the HK's BITs adopt the HK-Netherlands BIT Model in this regard to some extent, especially the "whichever is more favorable" rule. [2]

---

[1] Art. 3, HK-Netherlands.
[2] Art. 3 (1) (2) (3), HK-Switzerland; Art. 4(1)(2), HK-France; Art. 3(1)(2), HK-Italy.

In general practice of BITs relating to treatment of investments, each Contracting Party shall in its area accord investments and/or returns of investors of the other Contracting Party national treatment and/or MFN treatment. HK's BITs follow the general rule. Still remains the issue on the relations between these two treatments. It is noticeable that the provision on "whichever is more favourable to the investor concerned" in HK's BITs, indicates the relations between these two treatment standards, demonstrating the policy approach of "more favourable to the investor".

In general, national treatment is more favourable than that of MFN treatment. However in practice, some host countries provide more favourable treatment for foreign investors and investments than that of domestic investors and investment by treaties and/or domestic legislations. Accordingly MFN treatment is more favorable than that of national treatment. The "whichever is more favorable" rule of HK's BITs therefore gives foreign investors and investments the best option.

It is worth noticing that HK's BITs do not adopt "the right of establishment clause". Aiming at liberalizing investment flows, this approach consists in providing foreign investors with national treatment and MFN treatment not only once the investment has been established, but also with respect to the establishment. The use of this approach was traditionally limited to BITs concluded by US[1] and after the mid-1990s when the North American Free Trade Agreement had entered into force, to agreements concluded by Canada. In recent years other States, such as Japan, have also adopted this method. According to customary international law, States have the right to regulate the admission of foreign investors and their investments in their territories. General practice of BIT indicates that States admit investments of investors of the other Contracting Party only if such investments conform to the host State's legislation. The so-called "admission clause" allows the host State to apply any admission and screening mechanism for FDI that it may have in

---

[1] US BITs, unlike the BITs of other capital-exporting countries, consistently extend promises of national treatment and MFN treatment to investors at the pre-establishment stage of the investment process. Generally, this means that host States entering into BITs with US promise to allow US investors to enter the country and make an investment under the same procedures and on the same terms as domestic investors or as the investors of other States. See Jason Webb Yackee, "Conceptual Difficulties in the Empirical Study of Bilateral Investment Treaties", 33 *Brooklyn J. Int'l L.* 417 (2008).

place and therefore to determine the conditions on which FDI will be allowed to enter the State. [1] Following the said customary international law and general practice of BITs, all of HK's BITs adopt the "admission clause" entitled "Promotion of Investments", "Applicability of this Agreement" or "Promotion and Protection of Investment and Returns". [2]

3. Exceptions for investment treatment

In the HK Model BIT, there is only taxation exception for treatment of investments. [3] In HK's BIT practice only HK-Korea BIT follows this provision. [4] In most of HK's BITs there are two exceptions for treatment of investments: taxation exception and regional trade agreement (RTA) exception. [5]

There are some other exceptions in HK's BIT practice, such as that "regulations to facilitate the frontier traffic between Austria and her neighbours shall not be invoked as the basis of most favored nation treatment under this Agreement"; [6] and "the grant to a particular person or company of the status of 'promoted person'

---

[1] UNCTAD, *Bilateral Investment Treaties 1995-2006*: *Trends in Investment Rulemaking*, United Nations, 21-26 (2007).

[2] Art. 2, HK-Netherlands; Art. 2(1), HK-Germany; Art. 2(1), HK-Australia; Art. 2(1), HK-Denmark; Art. 2(1), HK-Sweden; Art. 2(1), HK-Switzerland; Art. 2. 1, HK-New Zealand; Art. 2(1), HK-France; Art. 2. 1, HK-Japan; Art. 2(1), HK-Korea; Art. 2(1), HK-Austria; Art. 2(1), HK-Italy; Art. 2(1), HK-Germany; Art. 2(1), HK-UK; Art. 2(1), HK-Belgium and Luxembourg; Art. 2(1), HK-Thailand.

[3] Article 7 of HK Model BIT provides that: "the provisions in this Agreement relative to the grant of treatment not less favorable than that accorded to the investors of either Contracting Party or to investors of any other State shall not be construed so as to oblige one Contracting Party to extend to the investors of the other the benefit of any treatment, preference or privilege resulting from any international agreement or arrangement relating wholly or mainly to taxation or any domestic legislation relating wholly or mainly to taxation."

[4] Art. 4, HK-Korea.

[5] For example, Article 7 of HK-Netherlands BIT provides that:

"Without prejudice to Article 3(1), the provisions in this Agreement relative to the grant of treatment not less favorable than that accorded to the investors of either Contracting Party or to investors of any other State shall not be construed so as to oblige one Contracting Party to extend to the investors of the other the benefit of any treatment, preference or privilege resulting from:

(1) any international agreement or arrangement relating wholly or mainly to taxation or any domestic legislation relating wholly or mainly to taxation;

(2) its participation in any existing or future customs union, economic union or similar international agreement; or

(3) reciprocal arrangements with any other State."

These provisions have become general practice in HK's BITs. See Art. 7, HK-Australia; Art. 7, HK-Denmark; Art. 7, HK-Sweden; Art. 7, HK-Switzerland; Art. 8. 1, 8. 2, HK-New Zealand; Art. 4(3)(4), HK-France; Art. 4(1), HK-Austria; Art. 7, HK-Italy; Art. 3(3)(4), HK-Germany; Art. 7, HK-UK; Art. 8, HK-Belgium and Luxembourg; Art. 7(a)(b), HK-Thailand.

[6] Art. 4(2), HK-Austria.

under the law of Thailand."[1]

V. Deprivation and Compensations

The validity of nationalization or expropriation of FDI by host States and the standard of compensation have been the most controversial issues in theoretic and practical aspects of international law since late 1930s.[2] Accordingly protections upon nationalization or expropriation and the standard of compensation are most important provisions in BITs. Following the traditional practice of developed States in general, the provisions of HK's BITs have some technical developments in this regard.

1. "Deprivation" and requirements

Expropriation or nationalization is one of the major political or non-commercial risks in international investments. Aiming at preventing or decreasing the risk, BITs almost uniformly establish four requirements or conditions for expropriation: (1) for a public purpose; (2) in accordance with due process of law; (3) non-discriminatory and (4) accompanied by compensation.[3] HK's BITs in general follows the traditional practice.

According to Article 5 (1) of HK Model BIT:

"Investors of either Contracting Party shall not be deprived of their investments nor subjected to measures having effect equivalent to such deprivation in the area of the other Contracting Party except lawfully, for a public purpose related to the internal needs of that Party, and against compensation. Such compensation shall amount to the real value of the investment immediately before the deprivation or before the impending deprivation became public knowledge whichever is the earlier, shall include interest at a normal commercial rate

[1] Art. 7(c), HK-Thailand.

[2] The disagreement between capital exporting and importing States over the minimum standard of treatment came to a head in an exchange of correspondence between Mexico and the US in 1938 regarding the standard of compensation for expropriation. See Andrew Newcombe, Lluis Paradell, *Law and Practice of Investment Treaties, Standards of Treatment*, Wolters Kluwer, 369 (2009).

[3] Andrew Newcombe, Lluis Paradell, *Law and Practice of Investment Treaties, Standards of Treatment*, Wolters Kluwer, 18 (2009). For detailed analysis on expropriation of foreign property, see M. Sornarajah, *The International Law on Foreign Investment*, second edition, Cambridge University Press, 344-401 (2004).; Paul E. Comeaux, N. Stephan Kinsella, *Protecting Foreign Investment under International Law, Legal Aspects of Political Risk*, Oceana Publications Inc., 57-81 (1997).

until the date of payment, shall be made without undue delay, be effectively realizable and be freely convertible. The investor affected shall have a right, under the law of the Contracting Party making the deprivation, to prompt review by a judicial or other independent authority of that Party, of the investor's case and of the valuation of the investment in accordance with the principles set out in this paragraph."

In practice 4 of the HK's BITs provide three requirements or conditions for deprivation: (1) lawfully; (2) for a public purpose related to the internal needs of that Party, and (3) against compensation.[1]These provisions conform to the provisions of HK Model BIT.

In addition to the above three conditions for deprivation, Article 5 (1) of HK-Netherlands BIT adds a condition of "on a non-discriminatory basis". These "four conditions" provisions are followed by 11 of HK's BITs.[2] These provisions are consistent with the general stance of the developed States.[3]

It should be noticed that though the title of the clause still remains the term of "expropriation", Contracting Parties of HK's BITs carefully choose the term of "deprivation" instead of "expropriation" and "nationalization" in the content of the clause. It is evident that HK cannot use the concept of "nationalization" due to its non-sovereign status. Comparing with the concepts of "deprivation" and "expropriation", the meaning of the former is broader than the latter. "Deprivation of property" can probably include circumstances where title to the property has not been acquired by the government and neither has the government entered into possession of, obtained the control of or used the property concerned, but government action has resulted in a serious interference with the enjoyment of the property, a significant reduction in the value of the property, or the destruction or disappearance

---

[1] Art. 6(1) HK-Austria; Art. 4(2), HK-Germany; Art. 5(1), HK-Belgium and Luxembourg; Art. 5(1), HK-Thailand.

[2] Art. 5(1), HK-Netherlands; Art. 6(1), HK-Australia; Art. 5(1), HK-Denmark; Art. 5(1), HK-Sweden; Art. 5(1), HK-Switzerland; Art. 6.1, HK-New Zealand; Art. 5(1), HK-France; Art. 5.1, HK-Japan; Art. 6 (1), HK-Korea; Art. 5(1), HK-Italy; Art. 5(1), HK-UK.

[3] As a number of developing States denied that such conditions were part of customary international law, developed States turned to conventional international instruments-mostly BITs-to specifically provide for investment protection against expropriations. UNCTAD, *Bilateral Investment Treaties 1995-2006: Trends in Investment Rulemaking*, United Nations, 47 (2007).

of existing property rights.[1] Therefore that HK's BITs adopt the concept of "deprivation", not only adapts its status of non-sovereign entity, but also provides more comprehensive legal protection for foreign investors.

2. Standard of compensation for deprivation

The standard of compensation for expropriation continued to be a source of significant disagreement in the post world war II era. The most important, and historically the most contested requirement, is the standard of compensation. Hull rule, representing the stance of most developed countries, insists that "adequate, effective and prompt payment for the properties seized" are required under international law, while developing countries propose the standard of "appropriate" compensation.[2]

In practice the provisions on compensation for expropriation of BITs typically address four issues: (1) the standard of compensation and valuation methods; (2) the date for determining compensation; (3) convertibility and transferability; and (4) payment of interest. In addition, some BITs have provisions for a right to judicial review of expropriations.[3]

Following the provisions of HK Model BIT, HK's BITs provide in general that the standard of compensation for deprivation as follows:

(1) be amount to the real value of the investment immediately before the deprivation or before the impending deprivation became public knowledge whichever is the earlier, including interest at a normal commercial rate until the date of payment;

(2) be made without undue or unreasonable delay; and

(3) be effectively realizable and be freely convertible.[4]

---

[1] See Albert H. Y. Chen, "The Basic Law and the Protection of Property Rights", 23 (1) *HKLJ*, 60 (1993). In this sense, the term "deprivation of property" also covers the situations of "indirect expropriation" or "creeping expropriation".

[2] For the history and the competing norms on the standards of compensation, see M. Sornarajah, *The International Law on Foreign Investment*, second edition, Cambridge University Press, 435-488 (2004); Paul E. Comeaux, N. Stephan Kinsella, *Protecting Foreign Investment under International Law*, *Legal Aspects of Political Risk*, Oceana Publications Inc., 81-98 (1997); Andrew Newcombe, Lluis Paradell, *Law and Practice of Investment Treaties*, *Standards of Treatment*, Wolters Kluwer, 18, 369 (2009); Mary H. Mourra(ed.), *Latin American Investment Treaty Arbitration*, *the Controversies and Conflicts*, Wolters Kluwer, 23-28 (2008).

[3] Andrew Newcombe, Lluis Paradell, *Law and Practice of Investment Treaties*, *Standards of Treatment*, Wolters Kluwer, 377 (2009).

[4] Art. 5(1), HK Model BIT; Art. 5(1), HK-Netherlands; Art. 6(1), HK-Australia; Art. 5(1), HK-Denmark; Art. 5(1), HK-Sweden; Art. 5(1), HK-Switzerland; Art. 6. 1, HK-New Zealand; Art. 5(1), HK-France; Art. 5. 1, HK-Japan; Art. 6(1), HK-Korea; Art. 6(1) HK-Austria; Art. 5(1), HK-Italy; Art. 4(2), HK-Germany; Art. 5(1), HK-UK; Art. 5(1), HK-Belgium and Luxembourg; Art. 5(1), HK-Thailand.

There are further provisions on interpretations on Hull rule in HK's BITs. For the term "adequate", 4 of the HK's BITs further deal with the valuation of the compensation, providing that: "where that value cannot be readily ascertained, the compensation shall be determined in accordance with generally recognized principles of valuation and equitable principles taking into account the capital invested, depreciation, capital already repatriated, replacement value, currency exchange rate movements and other relevant factors. "[1]

For the term "prompt", Article 5 (1) of HK-Denmark BIT refers to the limitation of "undue delay", indicating that: "in any event, shall not extend a period of 3 months". Though using the term "against appropriate compensation" as one of the four conditions for deprivation, Article 5 (1) of HK-France BIT provides that: "compensation…shall be made without delay", which is stricter than relevant provisions in other HK's BITs.

Article 5 of HK-Thailand BIT also refers to the applicable law for the compensation. [2] In addition to the provisions of standards of compensation, the relevant provisions of HK's BITs also deal with the investors' right to judicial review of expropriations. [3]

Another character of HK's BITs in this regard is the provisions on the expropriation and compensation for the foreign shares in international joint venture corporations (IJVCs). Article 5(2) of HK Model BIT provides that:

"Where a Contracting Party expropriates the assets of a company which is

---

[1] Art. 6(1), HK-Australia; Art. 6. 1, HK-New Zealand; Art. 5(1), HK-Italy; Art. 5(1), HK-Belgium and Luxembourg.

[2] According to Article 5 (1),(2) of HK-Thailand BIT, "subject to the provisions of paragraph (2) of this Article, such compensation shall amount to the real value of the investment immediately before the deprivation or before the impending deprivation became public knowledge whichever is the earlier, shall include interest at the rate applicable under the law of the Contracting Party making the deprivation until the date of payment…"; "where a Contracting Party expropriates investments which consist only of immovable property, the provisions of paragraph (1) of this Article shall apply, except that the moment at which the real value of such property is determined shall be governed by the laws and policies of the Contracting Party which is expropriating that immovable property."

[3] Article 5(1) of HK Model BIT provides that: "The investor affected shall have a right, under the law of the Contracting Party making the deprivation, to prompt review by a judicial or other independent authority of that Party, of the investor's case and of the valuation of the investment in accordance with the principles set out in this paragraph." Similar provisions also in Art. 5 (1), HK-Netherlands; Art. 6 (1), HK-Australia; Art. 5 (1), HK-Denmark; Art. 5(1), HK-Sweden; Art. 5(1), HK-Switzerland; Art. 6. 1, HK-New Zealand; Art. 5(1), HK-France; Art. 5. 2, HK-Japan; Art. 6(2), HK-Korea; Art. 6(2) HK-Austria; Art. 5(2), HK-Italy; Art. 4(2), HK-Germany; Art. 5(1), HK-UK; Art. 5(1), HK-Belgium and Luxembourg; Art. 5(1), HK-Thailand.

incorporated or constituted under the law in force in any part of its area, and in which investors of the other Contracting Party own shares, it shall ensure that the provisions of paragraph (1) of this Article are applied to the extent necessary to guarantee compensation referred to in paragraph (1) in respect of their investment to such investors of the other Contracting Party who are owners of those shares. "

In practice HK's BITs follow the rule for ensuring compensation to foreign shareholders in IJVCs. [1] Though some other BITs refer to share of IJVCs in "definition" clause, HK's BITs precisely deal with the protection for investors who own shares of IJVCs in the context of expropriation.

VI. Dispute Settlement

An efficient and comprehensive dispute resolution mechanism is considered as one of the key elements for constituting mutual confidence between Contracting Parties of the BITs. [2] Therefore dispute resolution mechanisms both for investment disputes and disputes between the Contracting Parties are main contents of the BITs. [3] International Centre for Settlement of Investment Disputes (ICSID) regime is the most popular dispute resolution mechanism provided in BITs. The major feature of provisions in this regard of HK's BITs is not to use the ICSID regime in addition to some other technical provisions.

1. Investment disputes

In the BIT context, investment dispute refers to a dispute between an investor of one Contracting Party and the other Contracting Party concerning an investment of the former in the area of the latter. Many BITs make significant progress in the area of the resolution of investment disputes by specifying arbitration in a neutral

---

〔1〕 Art. 5 (2), HK-Netherlands; Art. 6 (2), HK-Australia; Art. 5 (2), HK-Denmark; Art. 5 (2), HK-Sweden; Art. 5(2), HK-Switzerland; Art. 6. 2, HK-New Zealand; Art. 5(2), HK-France; Art. 5. 3, HK-Japan; Art. 6(3), HK-Korea; Art. 6(3) HK-Austria; Art. 5(3), HK-Italy; Art. 4(3), HK-Germany; Art. 5(2), HK-UK; Art. 5(2), HK-Belgium and Luxembourg; Art. 5(3), HK-Thailand.

〔2〕 Li Shishi, "On Bilateral Investment Agreements concluded by China" (in Chinese), 1990 *the Yearbook of Chinese International Law*, 121-122.

〔3〕 Andrew Newcombe, Lluis Paradell, *Law and Practice of Investment Treaties, Standards of Treatment*, Wolters Kluwer, 65 (2009).

forum as the method of resolution of these disputes. There are several different types of clauses creating different obligations as to such arbitration. At the lowest level, the clauses merely direct the parties to arbitration as a way of dispute settlement. At the highest level, the clauses entitle the foreign investor to initiate proceedings by himself before an ICSID tribunal. [1]

The latter is a breakthrough in international law in term of individual in international tribunals. Compared to traditional means of enforcing public international law through diplomatic protection granted by the investor's home State, this empowerment of private investor has accurately been described as a "change in paradigm in international investment law." Instead of depending on the discretion of its home State to grant diplomatic protection, these BITs provide the covered investors with a unilateral right to initiate arbitral proceedings against the host State which usually gives general and advance consent to ICSID regime. [2] In standard international practice, investor-State arbitration is most often conducted under the rules of the ICSID. [3]

According to Article 8 of HK Model BIT, an investment disputes shall be:

(1) settled by the parties amicably;

(2) submitted to such procedures for settlement as may be agreed between the parties after a period of six months from written notification of the claim; or

(3) submitted to arbitration under the Arbitration Rules of the United Nations Commission on International Trade Law as then in force if no procedures (2) have been agreed within that six month period. The parties may agree in writing to modify those Rules.

---

[1] M. Sornarajah, *The International Law on Foreign Investment*, second edition, Cambridge University Press, 249-250 (2004). Until 1993, a majority of capital-importing States had not enter into a strong BIT—which contains dispute settlement provisions that allow foreign investors to initiate binding international arbitration against host State—with a major capital-exporting State. But by the end of the sample (2002), 117 out of the 149 developing countries—seventy-nine percent—had at least one strong BIT in force. See Jason Webb Yackee, "Conceptual Difficulties in the Empirical Study of Bilateral Investment Treaties", 33 *Brooklyn J. Int'l L.* 432-433 (2008).

[2] ICSID established by Convention on the Settlement of Investment Disputes between States and Nationals of other States (hereinafter the Washington Convention) has been an international institution for settlement of investment disputes and widely accepted by Contracting Parties of BITs.

[3] Stephan W. Schill, Tearing Down the Great Wall: the New Generation Investment Treaties of the People's Republic of China, 15 *Cardozo J. Int'l & Comp. L.* 87-88 (2007). For the latest development of investor-State arbitration under ICSID regime, see Mary H. Mourra(ed.), *Latin American Investment Treaty Arbitration, the Controversies and Conflicts*, Wolters Kluwer, 163-166 (2008); Andrew Newcombe, Lluis Paradell, *Law and Practice of Investment Treaties, Standards of Treatment*, Wolters Kluwer, 58-59 (2009).

In general HK's BITs follow the procedures.[1] There are some revisions or supplements for the procedures, such as emphasis of investors' right to initiate arbitrations[2] and shorter timing for amicable settlement.[3] Some HK's BITs also indicate the character of arbitration and the effect of the arbitration awards.[4]

It should be pointed out that in contrast to popular provisions on investment dispute settlement in BITs,[5] the above provisions indicate that the Contracting Parties of HK's BITs have not adopted the regime of ICSID.[6] Investors covered by protection of HK's BITs therefore have not direct right to ICSID. The reason is firstly due to HK's non-sovereign status. As HK is not a Contracting Party of the Washington Convention, it can not be a party of mediation and arbitration proceedings under ICSID without designation and approval of a Contracting Party of the Washington Convention.[7] The second reason is that the investors as respect of HK

---

[1]　Art. 10, HK-Netherlands; Art. 10, HK-Australia; Art. 9, HK-Denmark; Art. 9, HK-Sweden; Art. 11, HK-Switzerland; Art. 9, HK-New Zealand; Art. 9, HK-France; Art. 9. 2, HK-Japan; Art. 9(3), HK-Korea; Art. 9, HK-Austria; Art. 10, HK-Italy; Art. 10, HK-Germany; Art. 8, HK-UK; Art. 9, HK-Belgium and Luxembourg; Art. 8, HK-Thailand.

[2]　Article 10 of HK-Netherlands BIT provides that: "…If no such procedures have been agreed within that six month period, the dispute shall at the request of the investor concerned be submitted to arbitration…" Article 11 of HK-Switzerland and Article 9. 2 of HK-Japan have similar provisions.

[3]　Article 10 of HK-Australia states that: "a dispute…has not been settled amicably, shall, after a period of three months from written notification of the claim, be submitted to such procedures for settlement as may be agreed between the parties to the dispute." There is similar provision in Article 8 of HK-UK BIT.

[4]　Article 9 (4) of HK-Korea BIT provides that: "The arbitration award shall be final and binding on the parties to the dispute. Each Contracting Party shall ensure the recognition and enforcement of the award in accordance with its relevant laws and regulations." Article 10 of HK-Germany BIT states that: "The arbitration award shall be final and binding on the parties to the dispute and shall be enforced in accordance with relevant domestic law."

[5]　These provisions have caused practical consequence. Over the past ten years, there has been a surge of investor-State arbitrations based on BITs. At least 42 new cases were registered in the first eleven months of 2005. By the end of 2006, the total number of treaty-based arbitrations has risen to 259, 161 of which were brought before the ICSID. See Mary H. Mourra(ed.), *Latin American Investment Treaty Arbitration, the Controversies and Conflicts*, Wolters Kluwer, 17-18 (2008). China became a Contracting Party of the Washington Convention on 1 July 1992 and accepts the jurisdiction of the ICSID in an increasing number of BITs. The first claim of Chinese investor registered on 12 February 2007, Tza Yap Shum v. Republic of Peru, will be just the beginning of ICSID disputes with Chinese participation. See Monika C. E. Heymann, International Law and the Settlement of Investment Disputes Relating to China, 2008 *Journal of International Economic Law*, 507 (2008).

[6]　It is interesting to note that the first ICSID case, Asian Agricultural Products Ltd. (AAPL) v. Republic of Sri Lanka, involves a Hong Kong corporation which invested in Sri Lanka. See Rudolf Dolzer, Margrete Stevens, *Bilateral Investment Treaties*, Martinus Nijhoff Publishers, 43, 127 (1995).

[7]　Article 25 of the Washington Convention provides that: "(A) The jurisdiction of the Centre shall extend to any legal dispute arising directly out of an investment, between a Contracting State (or any constituent subdivision or agency of a Contracting State designated to the Centre by that State) and a national of another Contracting State, which the parties to the dispute consent in writing to the Centre. When the parties have given their consent, no party may withdraw its consent unilaterally…(C) Consent by a constituent subdivision or agency of a Contracting State shall require the approval of that State unless that State notifies the Centre that no such approval is required."

in HK's BITs may include the foreigners who have the abode of right in HK. Those investors who have not nationalities of the Contracting Parties of the Washington Convention also can not be a party of mediation and arbitration proceedings under ICSID. [1]In this case the investment dispute settlement mechanism still remains as an open issue for Contracting Parties to HK's BITs if no conforming with special requirements. This practice also indicates that the application of the provisions on "entitling the foreign investor to initiate proceedings by himself before ICSID" have some objective limitations for investment dispute settlement in certain BITs. [2]

2. Disputes between Contracting Parties

In BIT context, disputes between Contracting Parties refer to disputes between the Contracting Parties relating to the interpretation or application of BITs.

According to Article 9 of HK Model BIT, if any dispute between Contracting Parties arises, the Parties shall in the first place try to settle it by negotiation. If the Parties fail to settle the dispute by negotiation, it may be referred by them to such person or body as they may agree on or, at the request of either Party, shall be submitted for decision to a tribunal of three arbitrators.

The provisions on establishment, hearings and decisions of the *ad hoc* tribunal for the disputes between Contracting Parties in Article 9 of HK Model BIT consist with general practice of international arbitration, with following characteristics:

(1) emphasizing the capacity of the President of the International Court of Justice (ICJ). If within the time limits any appointment has not been made, either Party may request the President of the ICJ, in a personal and individual capacity, to make the necessary appointment within thirty days. [3] The provision on the President of the ICJ "in a personal and individual capacity" also relates to HK's non-sovereign status. According to the Statute of International Court of Justice, the

---

[1] Art. 25, the Washington Convention.

[2] World Bank advice to developing countries typically emphasizes the importance of signing BITs with pre-consents to ICSID arbitration. See Jason Webb Yackee, "Conceptual Difficulties in the Empirical Study of Bilateral Investment Treaties", 33 *Brooklyn J. Int'l L.* 405 (2008). HK's BIT practice in this regard demonstrates that there are some alternatives dispute resolutions for investment disputes.

[3] The exception for this appointment is Art. 11 (2)(b) of HK-France BIT, which provides that: "if within the time limits specified above any appointment has not been made, either Contracting Party may request the President of the International Chamber of Commerce, in a personal and individual capacity, to make the necessary appointment within thirty days."

qualified parties before ICJ are limited to States only.[1] In general practice of BIT, the President of ICJ acts as appointing authorities of arbitration in the context of disputes between States, also conforming to his capacity in ICJ. Considerately the emphasis of the President of ICJ "in a personal and individual capacity" in the context of disputes between a State and a non-sovereign entity, might prevent and avoid the controversy on the qualification of the appointing authorities.[2]

(2) providing the specific timetable for arbitration (see Table 2). These provisions are remarkable in several respects. First, it appears that no other BIT has attempted to lay down time limits for the conduct of an arbitral proceeding with such specificity. Second, this procedure would take a mere five and a half months from the constitution of the tribunal until the decision is rendered regardless of the complexity of the dispute.[3] These provisions may prevent the delay of *ac hoc* arbitration due to having no existing arbitration rules.

HK's BITs in principle follow the above main provisions of HK Model BIT.[4] However there are some important provisions different from HK Model BIT, like applicable law,[5] further provisions on successor arbitrators,[6] allocation of the costs,[7] the basis of the decision,[8] and further provisions on "a national of a State which can be regarded

---

[1] According to Article 34 (1) of Statute of International Court of Justice, "Only States may be parties in cases before the Court."

[2] There are not terms like "in a personal and individual capacity" in other model BITs. For example, Article 9 (4) of Germany Model Treaty 2008 states that "…either Contracting State may, in the absence of any other relevant agreement, invite the President of the International Court of Justice to make the necessary appointments."

[3] Rudolf Dolzer, Margrete Stevens, *Bilateral Investment Treaties*, Martinus Nijhoff Publishers, 43, 127 (1995).

[4] Art. 11, HK-Netherlands; Art. 10, HK-Australia; Art. 10, HK-Denmark; Art. 10, HK-Sweden; Art. 12, HK-Switzerland; Art. 10, HK-New Zealand; Art. 11, HK-France; Art. 11, HK-Japan; Art. 10, HK-Korea; Art. 10, HK-Austria; Art. 11, HK-Italy; Art. 10, HK-Germany; Art. 9, HK-UK; Art. 10, HK-Belgium and Luxembourg; Art. 9, HK-Thailand.

[5] Article 11 (5) of HK-Netherlands BIT states that: "The tribunal shall decide on the basis of respect for the law. Before the tribunal decides, it may, at any stage of the proceedings, propose to the Contracting Parties that the dispute be settled amicably."

[6] Art. 11(2)(a), HK-Australia.

[7] Article 11(8) of HK-Australia BIT provides that: "The tribunal may decide, however, that a higher proportion of costs shall be borne by one of the Contracting Parties." There are similar provisions in Art. 10(8), HK-Sweden; Art. 10. 8, HK-New Zealand; Art. 10(8), HK-Belgium and Luxembourg.

[8] Article 10(7) of HK-Austria and Article 10(7) of HK-Belgium and Luxembourg provide that: "The arbitral tribunal shall reach its decision on the basis of internationally recognized rules of law."

Table 2　Major Provisions on Time Limit (days) for Disputes between Contracting Parties in HK's BITs

Counterparts	Appointing Arbitrators by Parties	Appointing third Arbitrators by Arbitrators	Appointing Third Arbitrators by President of ICJ/ICC *	Submitting a Memo	Reply	Holding a Hearing	Giving a Written Decision	Requests for Clarification	Issuing Clarification
[Model]	30	60	30	45	60	30	30	15	15
Netherlands	60	60	30	45	60	30	30	15	15
Australia	30	60	30	45	60	30	30	15	15
Denmark	30	60	30	45	60	30	/	15	15
Sweden	30	60	30	45	60	30	30	15	15
Switzerland	60	60	30	60	60	30	30	30	30
New Zealand	60	60	30	45	60	30	30	15	15
France	30	60	30 *	/	/	/	/	/	/
Japan	30	60	30	/	/	/	60	/	/
Korea	30	60	30	45	60	30	30	15	15
Austria	30	60	30	45	60	30	30	15	15
Italy	60	60	30	45	60	30	30	15	15
Germany	30	60	30	/	/	/	/	/	/
UK	30	60	30	45	60	30	30	15	15
Belgium and Luxembourg	30	60	30	45	60	30	30	15	15
Thailand	30	60	30	45	60	30	30	15	15

by both Contracting Parties as neutral in relation to the dispute". [1]

Ⅶ. Significance of HK's BIT Practice

Due to HK's non-sovereign status, HK's BITs have gradually become a series of BITs with its Characteristics. HK's successful practice of BITs has tackled the specific issues on international investment relations between HK and its counterparts since 1992 when HK-Netherlands BIT was concluded. Also it has great implications from practical and theoretic aspects.

1. Providing the model for HKSAR, Macao SAR and Chinese Taipei

As for the BIT development of HK itself, HK's BITs concluded in the transition period have become the *de facto* precedents followed by HKSAR since 1 July 1997. [2]The first ground is that according to the provisions of these BITs, they maintain their effect beyond 1 July 1997. Second, basing on provisions of the JD and the BL as well as the specific situations of HK, the substantial and procedural provisions of these BITs are different from the China's BIT practice with the same counterparts to HK, [3] therefore provide unique and valuable experience for the HKSAR's BIT practice. In the procedural aspects these BITs also provide important reference for HKSAR. HK's BIT practice in transition period, as involved positively by many key capital exporting countries, sets the good examples for the international community and smoothes the way for negotiations by HKSAR with States more likely to hesitate before entering in to bilateral treaties with a non-sovereign entity. [4] Following the precedents established in transition period, HKSAR has continued its BIT practice successfully since 1 July 1997.

Furthermore the HKSAR is the first special administrative region in China.

---

〔1〕 Article 11(2)(a) of HK-France states that: "A physical person possessing neither French nationality nor the nationality of the State which is responsible for the foreign affaires of Hong Kong nor having the right of abode in Hong Kong area shall act as President of the tribunal."

〔2〕 See Gary N. Heilbronn, "Hong Kong's First Bilateral Air Service Agreement: A Milestone in Air Law and an Exercise in Limited Sovereignty", 18 *HKLJ*, 64-65 (1988).

〔3〕 For the characteristics and new development of China's BIT practice, see Stephan W. Schill, Tearing Down the Great Wall: the New Generation Investment Treaties of the People's Republic of China, 15 *Cardozo J. Int'l & Comp. L.* 73-118 (2007); Monika C. E. Heymann, International Law and the Settlement of Investment Disputes Relating to China, 2008 *Journal of International Economic Law*, 507 (2008).

〔4〕 Gary N. Heilbronn, The Changing Face of Hong Kong's International Air Transport Relations, 20 *Case W. Res. J. Int'l L.*, 223 (1988).

One direct outcome of granting external autonomy to HKSAR is that China has to tolerate additional "Chinese" representation in certain international institution and international activities.[1] In broad sense, HK's BIT practice can be regarded as realization of "one country two systems" policy in international investment fields. It has great significance for Macao Special Administrative Region (hereinafter Macao SAR) established on 20 December 1999. Following the HK's BIT models and practice, Macao SAR concluded BITs with Portugal and Netherlands on 17 May 2000 and on 22 May 2008 respectively and became the second non-sovereign Contracting Party to BITs.[2] HK's BIT practice might also provide an important reference of legal model for so called "international space" of Chinese Taipei before and/or after China's great reunification.[3]

2. Strengthening the high autonomy of HKSAR

According to general international law and practice, external autonomy of autonomous entity should be recognized by the international society. Actually the HK's external autonomy could become meaningless if few States and international organizations were interested in developing and maintaining separate relations with it. According to general principle of international law, unlike States and international organizations, which are regarded as the normal types of international legal persons and can acquire their international personalities by meeting fixed conditions, the HKSAR's external autonomy and international legal status relies not only

---

[1] See Xiaobing Xu, George D. Wilson, "The Hong Kong Special Administrative Region as a Model of Regional External Autonomy", 32 *Case W. Res. J. Int'l L.*, 18-19 (2000).

[2] Agreement on Mutual Encouragement and Protection of investments Between the Macao Special Administrative Region of the People's Republic of China and the Republic of Portugal(effective by exchange of notes on 2 April 2002 and 17 April 2002) and Agreement between the Macao Special Administrative Region of the People's Republic of China and the Kingdom of the Netherlands on Encouragement and Reciprocal Protection of Investments (effective by exchange of notes on 31 October 2008 and 9 March 2009) are available from http://cn.io.gov.mo/Legis/International/2/22.aspx

[3] The economic relations across the Taiwan Strait have developed rapidly since May 2008 when Kuomintang regained its power in Taiwan. The Economic Cooperation Framework Agreement across the Taiwan Strait (ECFA) signed on 29 June 2010 is the latest development of China's RTA practice. Furthermore ECFA is considered by Taiwan authorities as first step for Chinese Taipei's RTA practice with third parties. According to Xinhua News Agency, Press Release from Taipei Representative Agency in Singapore and Singapore Commerce Office in Taipei on 5 August 2010, states that Chinese Taipei and Singapore agree to conduct a research on the feasibilities for concluding an economic cooperation agreement and will discuss the issue late this year. See "Singapore and Taiwan Will Explore the Feasibility for Concluding Economic Agreement", *Xiamen Daily*, 6 August 2010, 18. It might indicate a coming breakthrough for Chinese Taipei's bilateral economic relations with third parties.

China's authorization but also on the recognition and acceptance of other existing international persons.[1] The HK's external autonomy therefore does not solely depend on the unilateral desire of HK, China or UK—it also depends on whether other countries are willing to recognize this status.[2]

As a matter of fact, China has kept its commitment on high external autonomy of HK under the provisions of the JD and the BL since 1985. The exercising of external autonomy of HK has been widely understood, received and supported by international society. Gradually HK has extended the network of bilateral agreements, including BITs, to cover relations in broad areas with many countries and will examine new multilateral treaties that may be relevant to HK. These multifarious external legal relations have helped to strengthen HKSAR's international status.[3] Since HK's BITs link to many foreign countries, especially the major capital-exporting countries, HK's external autonomy on international investment is subject to continual international oversight, which in turn will enhance its unique international status. In fact, HK's BITs, together with HK's bilateral air service treaties, HK's bilateral taxation treaties, constitute the major picture of HK's high external autonomy in international economic fields.[4] Today, the HKSAR's key international legal relations are covered and established by a number of multilateral treaties and bilateral treaties. With the further development of practice of external autonomy of HKSAR, once international network of the HKSAR constituted by its bilateral and multilateral treaties has been well set up, the HKSAR's external autonomy will be fully guaranteed by international law.

3. Making important contributions to the development of international law

In recent years BITs have emerged as one of the most remarkable recent developments in international law and received great attraction from international

---

[1]　Xiaobing Xu, George D. Wilson, "The Hong Kong Special Administrative Region as a Model of Regional External Autonomy", 32 *Case W. Res. J. Int'l L.*, 31 (2000).

[2]　Albert H. Y. Chen, "Some Reflections on Hong Kong's Autonomy", 24 *HKLJ*, 179-180 (1994).

[3]　Elsie Leung, "The Rule of Law and Its Operation in Hong Kong after Reunification", 6 *Policy Bulletin* 9-10 (1998).

[4]　See Zeng Huaqun, "Unprecedented International Status: Theoretical and Practical Aspects of the HKSAR's External Autonomy", 9 (3) *The Journal of World Investment & Trade*, 283-287 (2008).

lawyers.[1] It might be pointed out that as new development of BITs, HK's BIT practice has also made important contributions to the development of international law, especially laws of treaties.

First, HK's BIT practice in transition period creates a new model of treaty practice under special historical context. It simplifies and even prevents the complicated issues of succession or renewing of treaties.[2] As in the texts of HK's BITs concluded in transition period do not indicate the sovereign State which is responsible for HK's foreign affairs, it is unnecessary for HKSAR to make any revision on authorization in these agreement after 1 July 1997. HKSAR, as a Contracting Party of taking the powers, rights and obligations of HK under these BITs, maintains the identity of HK's status as a regional entity with high external autonomy and recognizes the continuing effect of these BITs.

Second, BITs traditionally are agreements between sovereign States. In the BIT history, HK-Netherlands BIT is the first BIT between a non-sovereign entity and a sovereign State. This is a big breakthrough of BIT in terms of Contracting Parties.[3] Since then the continuing HK/HKSAR's BIT practice has followed and enhanced the precedent. It is obvious that the traditional definition of BIT has to be rewritten on the Contracting Parties as the non-sovereign entity becomes the Contracting Party of BITs.

Third, some new concepts, principles and procedures established and received by the Contracting Parties of HK's BITs, constitute new international practice. For example, the special considerations and provisions on scope of application, investment treatment, deprivation and compensations, dispute settlement mechanism, authorization for a non-sovereign entity to conclude a BIT, treaty succession, etc., have gradually evolved new international practice.

Fourth, BITs typically are made between unequal partners. They are usually agreed between a capital-exporting developed State and a capital-importing develo-

---

[1] Jason Webb Yackee, "Conceptual Difficulties in the Empirical Study of Bilateral Investment Treaties", 33 *Brooklyn J. Int'l L.* 405 (2008).

[2] For comments on succession of governments and BITs, see M. Sornarajah, *The International Law on Foreign Investment*, second edition, Cambridge University Press, 258-259 (2004).

[3] Gary N. Heilbronn, "Hong Kong's First Bilateral Air Service Agreement: A Milestone in Air Law and an Exercise in Limited Sovereignty", 18 *HKLJ*, 64-65, 75 (1988).

ping State. There are imbalance on powers, rights and responsibilities between two partners to these treaties due to inequality of their bargaining power, economic strength and political positions. [1] Since most HK's BITs are concluded by relatively equal partners, namely developed States and developed HK, more balanced provisions on powers, rights and responsibilities of both Contracting Parties have been concluded, like clauses on investment treatment, dispute settlement, etc., in HK's BITs. In this sense, HK's BITs as a whole may offer important reference or direction for the sustainable development of BIT practice. [2]

Finally it should be pointed out that due to special status of non-sovereign entity in respect of HK, HK's BITs also have raised some relevant new issues, like the recent practical issues on application of China's BITs to HK in first Chinese ICSID case, [3] etc. Further studies on these issues might definitely enrich the content of modern international law and promote the development of international law.

---

〔1〕　For further discussion on this issue, see M. Sornarajah, *The International Law on Foreign Investment*, second edition, Cambridge University Press, 204-208 (2004).

〔2〕　Some scholars emphasize the importance of liberalization in BITs. See Kenneth J. Vandevelde, "The Political Economy of a Bilateral Investment Treaty", 92 *American Journal of International Law*, 621-641 (1998).

〔3〕　The application of China's BITs to HKSAR is an issue of first Chinese ICSID case Tza Yap Shum v. Republic of Peru. The development of HK's BITs has clear indicated HK's will, position and practice for concluding its own BITs with foreign States. In general China's BITs are not applied to HK according to the relevant provisions of the JD, the BL and HK's BITs. For further comments on the issue, see An Chen: "Queries to the Recent ICSID Decision on Jurisdiction Upon the Case of Tza Yap Shum v. Republic of Peru: Should China-Peru BIT 1994 Be Applied to Hong Kong SAR under the 'One Country Two Systems' Policy", 10 (6) *The Journal of World Investment & Trade*, 829-864 (2009).

第三节　香港双边投资条约实践的适用问题评析[*]

【摘要】　本文在分析香港双边投资条约（BITs）有关适用范围特殊规定的基础上，探讨香港 BIT 实践衍生的"特殊条约适用"问题，指出中国香港系列 BITs"优先适用"和中国系列 BITs"不自动适用于中国籍的香港投资者和香港特区"的依据，进而主张在中国系列 BITs 与中国香港系列 BITs 长期并存的情况下，亟须确立和遵循香港 BIT 实践重点发展、中国香港系列 BITs 优先适用及中国系列 BITs 明确适用安排等三项原则，建构中国系列 BITs 与中国香港系列 BITs 密切衔接、相辅相成的适用机制。

【关键词】　双边投资条约；适用范围；条约适用

《中华人民共和国政府和大不列颠及北爱尔兰联合王国政府关于香港问题的联合声明》（简称《中英联合声明》）附件一第 11 条第 1 款和《中华人民共和国香港特别行政区基本法》（简称《基本法》）第 151 条明确规定，香港特别行政区（简称"香港特区"）可以"中国香港"的名义，在经济、贸易、金融、航运、通讯、旅游、文化和体育等有关领域单独地同世界各国、各地区及有关国际组织保持和发展关系，并签订和履行有关协议。截至 2018 年 11 月 9 日，香港以其名义与 19 个国家签订的 18 个双边投资条约（bilateral investment treaties，BITs）已正式生效。[1] 香港 BIT 实践是香港特区在对外事务领域的重要条约实践，[2] 也反映了国际法特别是国际投资法发展的重要突破和创新。[3] 本文在简析香港 BIT 实践有关适用范围的特殊规定的基础上，对其衍生的"特殊条约适用"问题及其适用原则作初步探讨。

一、香港 BITs 有关适用范围的特殊规定

广义上，BITs 的适用范围主要指适用的地域、期限和对象，一般由协定的定义、

＊　原载《紫荆论坛》（香港）2019 年 1—2 月号，第 43 期。

〔1〕　https://www.doj.gov.hk/sc/laws/table2ti.html，2018 年 12 月 3 日访问。在 19 个香港 BITs 的缔约对方中，17 个是经济合作开发组织（OECD）的成员国，只有泰国、科威特是发展中国家。

〔2〕　关于香港对外事务实践的概况，参见 Zeng Huaqun, Unprecedented International Status：Theoretical and Practical Aspects of the HKSAR's External Autonomy, *The Journal of World Investment & Trade*, Vol. 9, No. 3, 2008, pp. 275-297。

〔3〕　香港 BIT 实践的特征主要体现于授权性质和适用范围、投资待遇、"剥夺"及赔偿标准、争端的解决等条款。See Zeng Huaqun, Initiative and Implications of Hong Kong's Bilateral Investment Treaties, *The Journal of World Investment & Trade*, Vol. 11, 2010, pp. 669-696.

期限等条款确定,对协定的效力具有重要意义。[1] BITs 定义条款的目的是确定协定的适用对象及其范围。典型的 BITs 保护缔约一方投资者在缔约另一方境内的投资。因此,BITs 的适用范围取决于某些关键术语,特别是"投资"和"投资者"的定义。[2]定义条款通常还对缔约双方的"领土"(territory)概念作出定义,使缔约一方"投资者"在缔约另一方"领土"之内的"投资"得以保护。[3]

（一）典型条文

香港遵循 BITs 有关适用范围的普遍实践,同时,由于其非主权实体地位等因素,也有一些特殊的规定,尤其在"自然人投资者"和"地域范围"等方面。

1. 自然人投资者

关于"投资者"的定义,BITs 通常规定,"投资者"指缔约双方的具有国民身份的自然人[4]和依据缔约双方法律设立的公司。香港 BITs 有关"公司"作为"投资者"的定义遵循 BIT 的普遍实践,[5]而由于香港的非主权实体地位及其保护特定人群的需要,有关自然人作为"投资者"的定义则具有明显特征,即以永久居民标准取代国民标准。

传统上,对"自然人投资者"的定义一般采取两种方式:一是采取单一定义,适用于缔约双方;二是采取两种定义,分别适用于缔约双方。[6]"香港政府与……政府关于促进和保护投资的协定范本"(简称"香港 BIT 范本")[7]采取第三种方式。根据该范本的规定,"投资者"指:"(i) 对于缔约各方:在该缔约方领域具有居留权的自然人……(ii) 对于【香港的缔约对方】:具有国民身份的自然人"。[8] 可见,香港 BIT 范

---

〔1〕　Michael R. Reading, The Bilateral Investment Treaty in ASEAN: a Comparative Analysis, *Duke Law Journal*, Vol. 42, 1992, p. 695.

〔2〕　UNCTAD, *Bilateral Investment Treaties 1995-2006: Trends in Investment Rulemaking*, United Nations, 2007, p. 7.

〔3〕　Andrew Newcombe, Lluis Paradell, *Law and Practice of Investment Treaties, Standards of Treatment*, Wolters Kluwer, 2009, p. 65.

〔4〕　绝大多数 BITs 保护具有缔约一方国籍的自然人。因此,缔约一方国民的典型定义是,根据该缔约方国内法承认为国民或公民的自然人。在一些情况下,"投资者"的定义更为宽泛,不仅包括公民,也包括根据内国法作为永久居民的自然人。参见 UNCTAD, *Bilateral Investment Treaties 1995-2006: Trends in Investment Rulemaking*, United Nations, 2007, p. 13.

〔5〕　BITs 通常依据三个基本标准决定"公司"的国籍:(1) 设立地标准;(2) 住所地标准;(3) 控制标准。See Rudolf Dolzer, Margrete Stevens, *Bilateral Investment Treaties*, Martinus Nijhoff Publishers, 1995, pp. 35-36.

〔6〕　Rudolf Dolzer, Margrete Stevens, *Bilateral Investment Treaties*, Martinus Nijhoff Publishers, 1995, pp. 31-32.

〔7〕　香港 BIT 范本发表于 Rudolf Dolzer, Margrete Stevens, *Bilateral Investment Treaties*, Martinus Nijhoff Publishers, 1995, pp. 200-208.

〔8〕　香港 BIT 范本第 1(f)(i)条。

本采取永久居民和国民两种标准[1]，对香港仅适用永久居民标准，对香港的缔约对方则适用永久居民和国民两种标准。[2]

1992 年《香港政府与荷兰王国政府关于鼓励投资和保护投资协定》（简称"香港—荷兰 BIT"）规定，"投资者指：(i) 对于香港：在该领域具有居留权的自然人……(ii) 对于荷兰王国：具有国民身份的自然人"。[3] 如此规定已成为香港 BITs 的普遍实践。[4] 此类规定与香港 BIT 范本的区别在于，对香港的缔约对方仅适用国民标准。

显然，由于其非主权实体地位，香港不能采用国民标准定义作为"投资者"的自然人。其原因在于，除了 1997 年 6 月 30 日之前香港居民复杂的国籍问题外，即使在 1997 年 7 月 1 日中国对香港恢复行使主权之后，香港 BITs 的保护范围也不能涵盖不具有香港永久居留权的中国国民，包括中国内地、澳门地区和台湾地区的中国国民。而香港 BITs 的保护范围则可能涵盖具有香港永久居留权的外国国民。

然而，对作为"投资者"的自然人适用不同的定义标准，可能产生"双重 BIT 保护"问题。因为，作为适用永久居民标准的后果，寻求香港 BITs 保护的香港永久居民可能是具有香港永久居留权的外国国民，甚至包括香港 BITs 缔约对方的国民。在此情况下，具有香港永久居民和香港 BITs 缔约对方国民双重身份的自然人，可按其意愿寻求或挑选来自香港或缔约对方的 BIT 保护。例如，根据 1993 年香港—澳大利亚 BIT 规定，具有香港永久居民和澳大利亚国民双重身份的自然人，可按其意愿寻求或挑选来自香港或澳大利亚的保护。香港 BITs 缔约双方则不得不面临此种棘手的"投资者认同"问题。

为解决这一问题，1999 年香港—英国 BIT 第 1(f)(i)条明确规定，"投资者"指：对于香港："具有香港特别行政区永久居留权且非英国国民的自然人"；对于英国："英国国民且不具有香港特别行政区永久居留权的自然人"。该规定试图澄清和解决"投资者认同"问题，却产生了"BIT 保护真空"的新问题。显然，"具有香港特别行

---

〔1〕 在一些国家中，"国民"（national）和"公民"（citizen）在法律意义上存在重要区别。根据美国法，"国民"的用语比"公民"更为宽泛。例如，美国萨摩（American Samoa）土著是美国国民，但不是美国公民。See Kenneth J. Vandevelde, *U. S. International Investment Agreements*, Oxford University Press, 2009, p. 144.

〔2〕 实践中，只有 3 个香港 BITs 采用"永久居民标准和国民/公民标准均适用于缔约对方"的规定。香港—澳大利亚 BIT 第 1(f)条规定："投资者"指"在澳大利亚方面：(A) 根据澳大利亚法律具有澳大利亚公民身份或永久居留于澳大利亚的自然人……"香港—新西兰 BIT 第 1(2)(b)(i)条和香港—加拿大 BIT 第 1 条也有类似规定。

〔3〕 香港—荷兰 BIT 第 1(2)条。

〔4〕 香港—丹麦 BIT 第 1(2)条；香港—瑞典 BIT 第 1(2)条；香港—瑞士 BIT 第 1(2)条；香港—法国 BIT 第 1(3)条；香港—日本 BIT 第 1.4 条；香港—韩国 BIT 第 1(5)条；香港—奥地利 BIT 第 1(d)条；香港—意大利 BIT 第 1(6)条；香港—德国 BIT 第 1(4)条；香港—英国 BIT 第 1(f)条；香港—比利时与卢森堡 BIT 第 1(5)条；香港—泰国 BIT 第 1(4)条；香港—科威特 BIT 第 1(6)条；香港—芬兰 BIT 第 1(4)条。

政区永久居留权的英国国民"无法从香港—英国 BIT 的缔约任何一方寻求 BIT 保护。

2. 地域范围

在 BITs 实践中,有关地域范围的规定一般采用"领土"的概念。BITs 适用的地域范围取决于"领土"的定义。定义该用语的目的并非划定缔约双方的领土范围。其重要意义在于,为 BITs 保护投资的目的,将位于缔约方领海之外海域的投资,视为位于缔约方"领土"之内。[1]

值得注意的是,在香港 BITs 中,采用"地区"(area)而不是"领土"的概念。根据香港 BIT 范本第 1(a)(i)条规定,所谓"地区",在香港方面,包括香港岛、九龙和新界;[2]在香港的缔约对方方面,系指包括该主权国家的全部领土,包括特定海域。[3]以"地区"概念取代"领土",在 BIT 历史上是第一次,也是由香港的非主权实体地位所决定的。"领土"通常用于表述主权国家的地域范围。[4]"地区"的涵义更广,可用于表述非主权实体和主权国家的地域范围。鉴于香港的非主权实体地位,"地区"的概念比之"领土",更能准确表述香港的地域范围。同时应当指出,根据香港 BITs 有关"地域范围"的规定,对缔约一方(香港)而言,香港 BITs 的适用范围是非主权实体香港地区。这是 BITs 有关适用范围实践的又一重要创新。

(二) 重要启示

在香港 BITs 适用范围的规定中,有关"自然人投资者"的定义最为特殊。其重要特征是,以永久居民标准取代国民标准,即香港 BITs 的"自然人投资者"保护范围涵盖具有香港永久居留权的中国国民(未涵盖不具有香港永久居留权的中国国民)和外国国民。由此相继产生的"双重 BIT 保护"和"BIT 保护真空"两大难题,是 BIT 实践前所未有的问题,对香港 BITs 的适用实践提出了新挑战。

由于香港的非主权实体地位,香港 BITs 有关适用范围的"自然人投资者"和"地域范围"等特殊规定,迥然有别于传统 BIT 实践(包括中国的 BIT 实践),从一个侧面反映了香港 BITs 本身的"内在特色"和"不可替代性",客观上成就了香港 BIT 实践的"自成体系",也预示其衍生的条约适用问题的独特性和复杂性。

---

〔1〕　UNCTAD, *Bilateral Investment Treaties 1995-2006*: *Trends in Investment Rulemaking*, United Nations, 2007, p. 17.

〔2〕　这是所有香港 BITs 的实践。

〔3〕　例如,香港—荷兰 BIT 第 1.1 条规定:"在荷兰王国方面,指荷兰王国的领土,包括与该领土海岸相邻的海域,及荷兰王国根据国际法行使主权权利或管辖权的海域。"

〔4〕　"领土"的一般定义是:"属特定政府管辖权内的地域;该地球表面部分由一国专属占有和控制。"See Bryan A. Garner, *Black's Law Dictionary*, 8th ed., Thomson Press, 2004, p. 1512.

二、香港 BIT 实践衍生的"特殊条约适用"问题

香港 BIT 实践衍生了国际法实践史无前例的"特殊条约适用"问题,需要在理论和实践层面予以探讨和解决。

（一）"特殊条约适用"问题的产生

根据《中英联合声明》附件一第 11 条第 2 款和《基本法》第 153 条第 1 款的规定,中国缔结的国际协定,中央人民政府可根据香港特区的情况和需要,在征询香港特区政府的意见后,决定是否适用于香港特区。上述规定显然排除了将中国缔结的所有国际协定不加分析地适用于香港特区的可能,表明了中国采取的"有选择、有条件适用"的立场。这是因为考虑到,由于香港的历史和现状,特别是香港特区与中国内地社会经济和法律制度的重大差异,中国缔结的国际协定不一定适合于香港特区的情况和需要。为了遵循和体现"一国两制"和香港特区高度自治的原则,中央人民政府庄严承诺,在决定中国缔结的国际协定是否适用于香港特区时,需要从实体内容上考察,以该协定符合香港的情况和需要为依据;在程序上,需要正式征询香港特区政府的意见之后再作决定。另外,根据《中英联合声明》附件一第 11 条第 1 款和《基本法》第 151 条规定,香港具有在经济等领域的单独缔约权。

如前所述,迄今,香港特区以其名义签订了 18 个 BITs,初步形成了"中国香港系列 BITs"。自 1982 年以来,中国的 BIT 实践迅速发展,迄今已签订 127 个 BITs,位居全球次席,[1]形成了"中国系列 BITs"。两个系列 BITs 的缔约主体和主要条款存在差异。除中国—俄罗斯 BIT 外,中国系列 BITs 本身未对"协定是否适用于香港特区"作出明确规定。[2]

由于中国香港系列 BITs 与中国系列 BITs 的并存,就可能产生两个特殊的条约适用问题:一是在中国香港和中国分别与同一外国签订 BIT(例如,中国香港—荷兰 BIT 和中国—荷兰 BIT)的情况下,何者"优先适用"的问题;二是在缺乏中国香港 BIT 的情况下,中国 BIT 是否"自动适用"于中国籍的香港投资者和香港特区的问题。之所以称之为"特殊条约适用"问题,其特殊性在于:(1) 在国际法实践中,与"条约适用"密切相关的"挑选条约"(treaty shopping)问题,通常指不同国家组合作为缔约双方的两个或两个以上条约(例如,中国—荷兰 BIT 和英国—荷兰 BIT)之间的选

---

〔1〕 截至 2018 年 11 月底,德国签署 132 个 BITs,居全球首位。参见 UNCTAD, http://investmentpolicyhub. unctad. org/IIA,2018 年 12 月 3 日访问。

〔2〕 2006 年中国—俄罗斯 BIT 议定书规定,除非缔约双方另有约定,该协定不适用于中华人民共和国香港特别行政区和中华人民共和国澳门特别行政区。

择适用问题,而香港 BIT 实践衍生的"挑选条约"问题,则是国家主体(中国)和其区域性实体(中国香港)分别与同一外国签订的两个不同条约(例如,中国—荷兰 BIT 和中国香港—荷兰 BIT)之间的选择适用问题;(2) 依《维也纳条约法公约》确立的原则,如无明示或默示的相反意思,条约适用于缔约国的全部领土。尽管《中英联合声明》附件一第 11 条第 2 款和《基本法》第 153 条第 1 款有此"相反意思"的一般规定,由于中国系列 BITs 本身(除中国—俄罗斯 BIT 外)无此具体明文规定,仍然引发了中国系列 BITs 是否"自动适用"于中国籍的香港投资者和香港特区的问题。

(二) 中国香港系列 BITs 是否"优先适用"问题

尽管有《中英联合声明》附件一第 11 条第 2 款和《基本法》第 153 条第 1 款的规定,仍然存在的问题是,在中国香港和中国分别与同一外国签订 BIT 的情况下,中国香港 BIT 和中国 BIT 如何适用? 对香港投资者和香港特区而言,中国香港 BIT 是否当然优先? 依据何在?

首先需要明确,在中国香港和中国分别与同一外国签订 BIT 的情况下,并不必然意味着由于两个条约的分立,产生了何者优先的问题。严格意义上,在两个条约有关适用范围(包括投资、投资者、地域范围和适用期限)的规定相同或重合的情况下,才会产生条约的"优先适用"问题。如规定不一,则另当别论。以"自然人投资者"为例,中国香港系列 BITs 对"自然人投资者"的保护采取永久居民标准,即不包括不具有香港永久居留权的中国国民,而包括具有香港永久居留权的外国国民;而中国系列 BITs 对"自然人投资者"的保护采取国民标准,即"对于中国,指中国国民"。显然,即使主张中国系列 BITs 适用于香港投资者和香港特区,"自然人投资者"也只能包括具有中国国籍的香港永久居民,不能包括具有香港永久居留权的外国国民。换言之,对具有香港永久居留权的外国国民而言,只能适用中国香港系列 BITs,不能适用中国系列 BITs,因而不存在中国香港系列 BITs 与中国系列 BITs 何者优先的问题。

鉴于中国香港签订 BITs 是经中央人民政府授权的,可以认为,中央人民政府授权中国香港缔约和中国香港单独缔约的事实本身,清楚表明了中国和中国香港"分别适用"两个系列 BITs 的意愿和立场,即对香港投资者和香港特区适用中国香港系列 BITs,对中国投资者(不包括香港投资者)和中国领土(不包括香港特区)则适用中国系列 BITs。对同一缔约对方(例如,荷兰)而言,由于同中国香港和中国分别签订中国香港系列 BIT(例如,中国香港—荷兰 BIT)和中国系列 BIT(例如,中国—荷兰 BIT),也清楚表明了其"分别适用"两个系列 BITs 的意愿和立场。

由于中国香港、中国及其缔约对方表明了"分别适用"中国香港系列 BITs 与中国系列 BITs 的意愿和立场,对缔约各方而言,本无何者"优先适用"的问题。然而,缔约各方"分别适用"的意愿和立场并不当然具有"排除对中国籍的香港投资者和香港特区适用中国系列 BITs"的法律后果。《维也纳条约法公约》第 29 条规定:"除该条约显示或另经确定有不同意思外,条约对每一当事国的拘束力及于其全部领土。"[1]由于中国系列 BITs(除中国—俄罗斯 BIT 外)本身未规定中国"排除对中国籍的香港投资者和香港特区适用中国系列 BITs"的意思,对缔约双方的投资者、国际仲裁机构或司法机构等第三方而言,出于特定因素考虑,仍有可能依《维也纳条约法公约》第 29 条确立的规则,主张或判断中国系列 BITs 适用于中国籍的香港投资者和香港特区,因而无视或忽略中国香港系列 BITs 的适用或优先适用。

笔者以为,在中国香港和中国分别与同一外国签订 BIT 的情况下,第三方理应基于该客观事实,理解或依据《中英联合声明》附件一第 11 条第 2 款和《基本法》第 153 条第 1 款的规定,尊重中国香港系列 BITs 与中国系列 BITs 缔约各方"分别适用"的意愿和立场,对香港投资者和香港特区适用中国香港系列 BITs。即使主张中国系列 BITs 适用于中国籍的香港投资者和香港特区,参照"特别法优先"的一般法律原则,也应对香港投资者(包括中国籍的香港投资者)和香港特区优先适用中国香港系列 BITs。

(三) 中国系列 BITs 是否"自动适用"问题

在中国与特定外国签订 BIT,而中国香港与该国尚未签订 BIT 的情况下,需要明确的问题是,中国 BIT 是否自动适用于中国籍的香港投资者和香港特区? 依据何在?

"谢业深诉秘鲁共和国案"(Mr. Tza Yap Shum v. The Republic of Peru,简称"谢业深案")[2]引发了中国系列 BITs 是否自动适用于中国籍的香港投资者和香港特区的现实问题。笔者以为,在该案中,"解决投资争端国际中心"(ICSID)仲裁庭有关中国—秘鲁 BIT 适用于该案的管辖权裁决的明显缺失是,片面采取和强调了上述《维也纳条约法公约》第 29 条规定中"条约显示有不同意思"的单一标准,完全忽略或无视"另经确定有不同意思"的规定。《中英联合声明》附件一第 11 条第 2 款和《基本法》第 153 条第 1 款当可作为中国系列 BITs 不自动适用于中国籍的香港投资者和香港特区的法律依据,而仲裁庭却视而不见。特别是,在秘鲁共和国政府提供了专家意见,明确指明相关法律依据的情况下,仲裁庭仍置若罔闻,固执己见。由此可见,

---

〔1〕 中国于 1997 年 5 月 9 日加入《维也纳条约法公约》。

〔2〕 Mr. Tza Yap Shum v. The Republic of Peru, ICSID Case No. ARB/07/6, Decision on Jurisdiction and Competence, dated June 19, 2009.

在国际仲裁实践中,在中国系列 BITs 不符合"条约显示有不同意思"标准的情况下,"另经确定有不同意思"的条约解释权属于国际仲裁庭等第三方,而不属于缔约方。[1] 由于当前国际仲裁实践缺乏有效的监督和矫正机制,缔约方如不主动采取相应措施,发生类似的"条约解释失控"局面在所难免。为防患于未然,建议在新签或修订中国系列 BITs 中作明文规定,清晰表明"协定不自动适用于中国籍的香港投资者和香港特区"和"经适当程序后协定适用于中国籍的香港投资者和香港特区"两层含义,以利明确符合《维也纳条约法公约》第 29 条确立的"条约显示有不同意思"的标准。应当进一步指出,"协定不自动适用于中国籍的香港投资者和香港特区"并不等于"协定不能适用于中国籍的香港投资者和香港特区"。一般而言,主张"协定自动适用于中国籍的香港投资者和香港特区"是依国际法明确中国系列 BITs 的适用范围,有利于保护中国投资者(包括中国籍的香港投资者)的海外投资权益和中国(包括香港特区)的国家利益。之所以"自我设限",主张"协定不自动适用于中国籍的香港投资者和香港特区",是中国恪守《中英联合声明》附件一第 11 条第 2 款和《基本法》第 153 条第 1 款的庄严法律承诺,即中国缔结的国际协定只有在中央人民政府征询香港特区政府意见并作出正式决定后方可适用。在履行上述程序后,中国系列 BITs 当然可以适用于中国籍的香港投资者和香港特区。

三、中国系列 BITs 与中国香港系列 BITs 的关系及其适用原则

实践表明,为妥善解决香港 BIT 实践衍生的"特殊条约适用"问题,需要在分析和明确中国系列 BITs 与中国香港系列 BITs 之间关系的基础上,在缔约实践和条约规范本身确立两者的适用原则。

(一) 中国系列 BITs 与中国香港系列 BITs 的关系

如所周知,中国系列 BITs 是中国改革开放实践的标志性成果。中国内地经历 40 年来的改革开放实践,社会主义市场经济制度和法律制度逐步建立和完善,经济发展成就举世瞩目。在国际投资领域,中国现已兼具重要资本输入国与资本输出国双重身份,BIT 实践后来居上,迅速形成规模高达 127 个的中国系列 BITs。

而中国香港系列 BITs 则是特定历史发展阶段的产物。回望历史,香港回归前的涉外投资关系是由英国与有关国家签订的 BITs(简称"英外 BITs")调整的。[2] 英

---

[1]　在 2012 年"澳门世能投资公司诉老挝人民民主共和国政府案"再次引发由国际仲裁庭和法院等第三方解释和裁决此类条约适用问题。参见何志鹏、刘力瑜:《中外 BITs 对香港、澳门特别行政区适用问题研究—从"谢业深案""世能案"引起的国际法思考》,载《国际经济法学刊》第 22 卷第 2 期,北京大学出版社 2015 年版,第 113—136 页。

[2]　关于英国 BIT 实践概况,参见 Eileen Denza, Shelagh Brooks, Investment Protection Treaties: United Kingdom Experience, *Int'l & Com. L. Q.*, Vol. 36, 1987, pp. 908-923.

国通过"领土延伸"的换文将一些英外 BITs 延伸适用于香港。此类协定在香港的法律效力仅延续至 1997 年 6 月 30 日。在过渡期，为了保持和发展香港的涉外投资关系，香港面临两种选择：一是香港以其名义单独同外国签订 BITs，二是中国签订的 BITs 的适用范围在 1997 年 7 月 1 日后扩及香港。香港选择前者。鉴于当时香港与中国内地之间经济和法律制度的重大差异以及在国际投资活动中的不同地位和角色，这一选择显然更能适应香港的实际需要，并且更能有效地服务于促进和保护香港与外国相互投资的目标。1992 年 11 月 19 日，香港—荷兰 BIT 在香港签署，1993 年 9 月 1 日生效，首开由非主权实体参与签订 BITs 的先河。[1] 之后历经 20 多年的发展，逐渐形成规模达 18 个的中国香港系列 BITs。

国际实践表明，自 20 世纪 50 年代末以来，多数 BITs 都模仿或至少广泛地照搬 1959 年《海外投资国际公约草案》（Draft International Convention on Investments Abroad）和经济合作开发组织（OECD）1967 年颁布的《保护外国财产的公约草案》（Draft Convention on the Protection of Foreign Property）。[2] 由于来源相同，不同 BITs 的主题、结构和用语，在不同的时期、不同的国家实践仍显得非常相似。[3] 中国和中国香港的 BIT 实践也不例外。由于中国系列 BITs 与中国香港系列 BITs 均遵循德国 BIT 模式，[4] 两者的主要内容和形式基本相同，就一般目标和功能而言，存在前者相当程度上替代后者的可能性。特别是，中国近年已发展为具有资本输入国和资本输出国双重身份，中国系列 BITs 与中国香港系列 BITs 的目标和功能更为趋同。对中国籍的香港投资者和香港特区而言，中国系列 BITs 可能为其提供与中国香港系列 BITs 同等或类似的国际法保护。

另外，中国系列 BITs 与中国香港系列 BITs 也存在重要区别。主要表现在，中国香港系列 BITs 可根据香港特区的具体情况和需要，作出符合非主权实体地位、维护本地区权益或迎合缔约对方"重要关切"的特别规定。例如，其保护范围可涵盖具有香港永久居留权的外国国民。在这个意义上，中国香港系列 BITs 有其超越传统 BIT 实践的"锦上添花"的特殊目标和功能，是中国系列 BITs 所无法替代的。因此，中国香港系列 BITs 有其长期存在的必要性和合理性。

---

〔1〕 该文本发表于 *Special Supplement No. 5 to the Hong Kong Government Gazette*，E27-53（1992）。

〔2〕 关于 BITs 的历史，参见 Jeswald W. Salacuse, BIT by BIT: The Growth of Bilateral Investment Treaties and Their Impact on Foreign Investment in Developing Countries, *The International Lawyer*, Vol. 24, 1990, pp. 656-661。

〔3〕 Jason Webb Yackee, Conceptual Difficulties in the Empirical Study of Bilateral Investment Treaties, *Brooklyn J. Int'l L.* Vol. 33, 2008, pp. 415-416。

〔4〕 关于 BITs 的模式及其新发展，参见曾华群:《论双边投资条约范本的演进与中国的对策》，载《国际法研究》2016 年第 4 期，第 65—72 页。

似可主张,中国系列 BITs 是调整中国(可包括香港特区)与外国(现有 127 个国家)之间投资关系的主要国际法规范,而中国香港系列 BITs 是调整香港特区与外国(现有 19 个国家)之间投资关系的主要国际法规范。就法律形式而言,中国系列 BITs 与中国香港系列 BITs 各有其特定的缔约主体组合和调整对象,是分立的,互不交集的;而就实质内容而言,两者同是以促进和保护国际投资为目标,经适当的法律安排,是可相互衔接的,可望相辅相成的。

(二)确立中国系列 BITs 与中国香港系列 BITs 的适用原则

在新的国际国内形势下,亟须适时确立中国系列 BITs 与中国香港系列 BITs 的适用原则。从行政资源配置和条约效益等实务角度,长远看来,值得认真思考的重要问题是,香港特区是否需要与中国"并驾齐驱",以其名义分别再同 100 多个国家逐一签订 BITs,以形成更具规模的中国香港系列 BITs?中国香港系列 BITs 的"优先适用"问题是否仍然保持"语焉不详"的现状?中央人民政府是否继续主张中国系列 BITs "不自动适用于中国籍的香港投资者和香港特区",且在实践中也不履行促成中国系列 BITs "可适用"的必要程序?

笔者以为,中国系列 BITs 与中国香港系列 BITs 的适用原则需要由缔约实践和条约规范本身来确立。回应上述重要问题,如下三项原则或可参考。

一是香港 BIT 实践重点发展原则。香港特区宜根据《中英联合声明》附件一第 11 条第 1 款和《基本法》第 151 条规定,从实际需要出发,继续重点发展中国香港系列 BITs。所谓"重点发展",意为谨慎选择重要的潜在缔约方开展缔约实践,而不是"全线出击"。事实上,现有中国香港系列 BITs 本身已体现了重点发展原则,其缔约对方多为发达国家,均为香港特区的重要投资目的国和/或重要投资来源国。建议香港特区适时客观评估中国香港系列 BITs 扩展的潜在缔约方,制订"香港特区双边投资条约规划"。从务实的角度,中国香港系列 BITs 扩展的潜在缔约方当限于同香港相互投资关系尤为密切的国家或地区(例如,香港特区的前 30 位投资目的国/地和前 30 位投资来源国/地),且相互有缔约意愿者。与此同时,考虑和明确中国系列 BITs 对中国籍的香港投资者和香港特区的可适用性。

二是中国香港系列 BITs 优先适用原则。对香港特区和香港投资者、特定缔约对方或相关第三方而言,在中国系列 BITs 与中国香港系列 BITs 并存(就个案而言,例如,中国—荷兰 BIT 与中国香港—荷兰 BIT 并存)的情况下,中国香港系列 BITs(例如,中国香港—荷兰 BIT)优先适用。在中国系列 BITs 和/或中国香港系列 BITs 中,可考虑作此明文规定。中国系列 BITs 中的特定 BIT 即使经《中英联合声明》附件一第 11 条第 2 款和《基本法》第 153 条第 1 款规定的程序而适用于中国籍的香港投资者和香港特区,一旦香港特区与该特定 BIT 缔约对方另行签订 BIT,后者仍然优先适用。

三是中国系列 BITs 明确适用安排原则。对香港特区和中国籍的香港投资者、特定缔约对方或相关第三方而言,在有中国系列 BITs、无中国香港系列 BITs 的情况下,中国系列 BITs“不自动适用于中国籍的香港投资者和香港特区”。在履行《中英联合声明》附件一第 11 条第 2 款和《基本法》第 153 条第 1 款规定的程序之后,中国系列 BITs 可适用于中国籍的香港投资者和香港特区。在中国与特定国家已签有BIT,而香港特区无意或尚未与该国另行签约的情况下,鉴于中国系列 BITs 的适用显然有利于维护国家、香港特区及中国籍的香港投资者的权益,中央人民政府和香港特区当可未雨绸缪,主动联络协作,适时履行上述《中英联合声明》和《基本法》规定的程序,在相关 BIT 作出明文规定,以利明确中国系列 BITs 对中国籍的香港投资者和香港特区的适用问题。

四、结语

根据《中英联合声明》和《基本法》的有关规定,本文从三个层面初步探讨香港BIT 实践的适用问题:一是香港 BITs 有关适用范围的特殊规定。由于香港的非主权实体地位,香港 BITs 缔约双方创设了不同于传统 BIT 实践的有关“自然人投资者”和“地域范围”等特殊规定。这是香港 BITs 适用实践的“内在特色”,客观上决定了香港 BIT 实践的“自成体系”;二是香港 BIT 实践衍生的“特殊条约适用”问题。由于两个系列 BITs 的并存,产生了中国香港系列 BITs 是否“优先适用”和中国系列BITs 是否“自动适用”的问题。这是香港 BITs 适用实践特有的“条约解释”问题,涉及相关条约的选择适用和履行。典型案例表明,由于国际仲裁机构或司法机构在审案中拥有最终解释权,相关条约本身的明文规定尤为重要;三是中国系列 BITs 与中国香港系列 BITs 之间的关系及其适用原则。这是香港 BITs 适用实践的“机制建构”问题,涉及两个系列 BITs 的相互衔接和机制化。笔者主张,在两个系列 BITs 长期并存的情况下,基于上述“内在特色”和“条约解释”的认知和关切,亟须确立和遵循香港 BIT 实践重点发展、中国香港系列 BITs 优先适用及中国系列 BITs 明确适用安排等三项原则,以利建构中国系列 BITs 与中国香港系列 BITs 密切衔接、相辅相成的适用机制,为中国籍的香港投资者和香港特区提供可预期的、更为务实有效的国际法保护。

第五编

中国特色国际经济法学科的创建

导　言

本编主要介绍本人参与创建中国特色国际经济法的经历和感悟,期望在论文交流的基础上,与学界同行和广大读者在实践层面进一步交流互勉。第十一章概述本人参与的学科建设实践。首先简述厦门大学国际法学科(本学科)的发展(第一节)。适应改革开放新形势之需,40多年来,本学科从无到有,逐步发展为特色鲜明的国家重点学科。本学科的创建经验和优良传统对学界同行或有借鉴意义。其次是教学改革实践,谨以国际经济法研究生培养方式的改革与实践(第二节)和国际法学科"国际化"教学模式的创建与发展(第三节)为例,探讨国际法研究生培养模式的改革创新。第十二章在回顾学会历史的基础上(第一节),感念学会前辈的家国情怀和治学精神(第二、三节),进而借由学会平台致辞(第四节)和《国际经济法学刊》再出发(第五节),展现学会常规学术交流活动之一二。学会关于"中国特色国际经济法学的使命担当和创新发展"的共识(第六节)则表达了学会广大同仁继往开来的庄严承诺。第十三章从学术成果推介(第一节)和创新平台感言(第二节)两个方面,反映学界同仁开展国际法研究交流的不懈努力,也分享本人有关治学理念和方法的点滴体会。

作者的主要体会:

(1) 厦门大学国际法学科的传统特色。创业难,守成和发展更难。在一定意义上,学科的生命力在于优良传统特色的形成、传承和发扬光大。本学科的优良传统特色主要表现在:志存高远,铭记中国国际法学人的使命担当;淡泊明志,传承严谨治学的优良学风;自强不息,创建学科建设的"铁打营盘";开拓创新,促进教学研究的"国际化";敬业奉献,凝聚学科建设的同心合力。

(2) 国际经济法人才培养模式的改革和实践。主要创新成果是,充分开拓和利用国内外学术资源,形成开放性的研究生培养模式;改革教学内容和方式,逐步形成"教研交融,师生互动"和"国际化"的教学方式。在指导和组织学生参加国际性国际法专业辩论赛中,注重传承敬业奉献精神,具有"中国队"的自信、立场及实力。

（3）中国国际经济法学者的学术使命。创建和发展中国特色国际经济法学，是中国国际经济法学者的学术使命。这是一项宏大、艰巨、长期的理论工程，需要我国一代又一代国际经济法学者矢志不移、持之以恒的艰苦奋斗。我们应增强使命感，潜心治学，勇于探索国际经济法的发展规律和现实课题。我们应增强"道路自信、理论自信、制度自信、文化自信"，更积极主动地开展国际经济法领域的学术研究、交流和合作，提出国际经济法理论和实践的"中国主张"和"中国方案"，为中国特色国际经济法学的发展和繁荣做出应有的贡献。

第十一章
学科建设实践

第一节　厦门大学国际法学科的发展[*]

自 1926 年厦门大学创建法科以来,国际法学人秉持"自强不息,止于至善"的校训,勠力同心,不懈开拓进取,已然创建了海内外知名、特色鲜明的国家重点学科。学海洋洋,关山重重,景象万千,谨记其要。

一、历史发展

(一)沿革

厦门大学国际法的教学研究,可追溯至创立法科初期。1935 年 4 月 15 日,厦门大学法律学会(学生自治组织)为废除西方列强在中国的领事裁判权而通电全国,指出:"诚以任何国家,应有独立自主之全权,此为国际公法确定之原则,亦吾民族合理之要求,各国基于法律正谊最高点之观念,自应予以同情也。"这可视为厦门大学法科早期师生基于国际公法原则维护国家主权的铿锵呐喊。

厦门大学法律系在 1979 年复办之初,适应改革开放新形势的迫切需要,确立国际经济法为发展重点,成为国内最早开展国际经济法教学研究的法律院系之一。42 年来,厦门大学法律系/法学院国际法学科(简称"本学科")广大师生筚路蓝缕,勠力同心,学科建设持续发展,成效显著。经原国家教委批准,厦门大学法律系 1981 年在全国率先招收国际法专业硕士研究生,1985 年在全国率先招收国际经济法专业本科生,1986 年开始招收国际经济法专业(1997 年后调整扩大为国际法学专业)博士研

---

　* 为庆贺厦门大学百年华诞而作,曾华群执笔,学科同仁集体完成附录。2020 年 8 月完成初稿,经学科同仁审阅,2020 年 10 月定稿。

究生。1987 年 10 月,成立厦门大学国际经济法研究所。2005 年 4 月,参与创建厦门国际法高等研究院。1995、2002、2008 年,本学科先后由教育部批准为全国高校"211工程"重点建设项目第一、二、三期项目。2002、2007 年,本学科由教育部连续评定为国家重点学科。2005—2008 年,经《中国大学评价》课题组评估,本学科连续评为"A＋＋"级。2010 年,厦门大学法学院入选由联合国贸易和发展会议（UNCTAD）主持遴选的"国际投资法研究领航法学院 15 强"。1987 年和 2011 年,本学科两次荣获厦门大学最高奖教荣誉"南强奖"集体一等奖。

（二）现状

本学科现已发展成为我国国际法教学、科研和学术交流的重要基地之一。

在教学方面,本学科积极开展教学改革,教学与科研相互促进,"出成果"与"出人才"并举,创新国际法人才的"国际化"培养模式。本学科的教学成果获得国家主管部门和海内外学界同行的重视和肯定。本科主干课程"国际经济法"入选"国家精品课程"（2004）和"国家级精品资源共享课"（2013）。厦门大学法学院入选教育部"涉外法律人才教育培养基地"（2012）。本学科组织和指导学生参加"Jessup 国际法模拟法庭竞赛"等国际性国际法模拟庭审（法庭或仲裁庭）竞赛,获得该赛事"Hardy C. Dillard Award 最佳书状全球第一名"（2006）等优异成绩。

在科研方面,本学科紧密联系改革开放实际,形成了以国际经济法为重点,促进国际法新领域发展的优势突出、特色鲜明的学科发展格局。本学科承担和完成国家社会科学基金重大项目和教育部重大攻关项目等 143 项主要研究项目,在海内外重要学术期刊和主流出版社持续发表论文和出版专著,荣获"全国高等学校人文社会科学研究优秀成果奖"11 项等科研成果奖。

在学术交流方面,借助厦门大学国际经济法研究所、中国国际经济法学会秘书处、《国际经济法学刊》、厦门国际法高等研究院及厦门大学陈安国际法学发展基金会等学术平台的创建和发展,本学科积极组织和开展海内外学术交流活动,包括主办和参与主办 77 次全国性学术研讨会和 40 次国际性学术研讨会或项目,在海内外国际法学界赢得了学术声誉。

本学科的目标是争取建成国内外知名、有特色、高水平的国际法领域教学、研究和学术交流的重要基地。

二、学科建设

（一）师资队伍建设

师资队伍建设,是学科建设的首要任务,也是学科发展的必要基础和持续保障。

法律系 1979 年复办后,1984 年设立国际经济法教研室。历任教研室主任为廖益新、曾华群、陈小敏、罗伟、杜震农、徐崇利、李国安和韩秀丽。在不同的发展时期,先后加盟本学科的教师达 60 人,为本学科的创建和发展奉献心力。一直以来,诸多原同事心系母校,以不同方式关心和支持本学科的发展。

在本学科创建和发展的重要时期,逐渐形成和保持一支以中青年为主、研究特色明显、教学研究能力强的师资队伍。学术带头人陈安教授是享誉海内外的国际经济法学家,2012 年被评为"全国杰出资深法学家";曾华群、廖益新、徐崇利、李国安教授学有专长,在国际经济法学界具有较大学术影响,分别入选国家首批"百千万人才工程第一、二层次人选"(1996)、教育部"跨世纪优秀人才培养计划"(1997)、教育部"新世纪优秀人才培养计划"(2004)和福建省"新世纪优秀人才培养计划"(2007)。中青年学术骨干陈辉萍教授和蔡从燕教授、韩秀丽教授分别入选福建省"新世纪优秀人才培养计划"(2006)和教育部"新世纪优秀人才培养计划"(2009、2011)。2011 年,本学科引进分别来自英国、德国和我国台湾地区的三位"千人计划学者",开拓了国际水法等新领域的研究。目前,本学科有 9 位教授、4 位副教授、6 位助理教授、1 位行政秘书,合计 20 人(其中 17 位法学博士)。比之海内外综合性大学同类学科的师资队伍,本学科具有一定的优势。(附表 1)

（二）学科建设项目

学科建设项目是学科建设的"目标性"任务,也是学科发展的"加速器"和强劲动力。

本学科申请的学科建设项目先后由教育部批准为全国高校"211 工程"重点建设项目第一、二、三期项目。

1995 年,原国家教委批准厦门大学"国际经济法及台港澳法研究"学科点为全国高校"211 工程"重点建设项目。

2002 年,教育部批准厦门大学"国际经济法与海洋法"学科点为全国高校"十五""211 工程"重点建设项目。

2008 年,教育部批准厦门大学"国际法律制度、两岸法律问题及和平发展研究"学科点为全国高校"十一五""211 工程"重点建设项目。

在本学科教师的共同努力下,认真完成了国家"211 工程"连续三期项目的各项任务,达到了预期发展目标。本学科的建设获得了长足的发展,也带动和促进了法学院和学校其他学科领域特别是台港澳法、海洋法及两岸法律问题的研究。曾华群教授担任上述各期项目的主要负责人,具体负责项目的申报论证、具体实施及总结报告等工作。

（三）学术平台建设

学术平台建设，是学科建设的重要内容和成果，更是学科可持续发展的"铁打营盘"。

30 多年来，本学科开拓创新，积极参与创建和发展国际法领域的学术平台，成效显著。

1. 厦门大学国际经济法研究所

1987 年，厦门大学国际经济法研究所（简称"研究所"）经学校批准成立。研究所是本学科开展教学、研究、学术交流及咨询服务的常设学术机构。其主要职能包括：组织商定本学科发展规划等重要事项，负责实施本学科建设项目；组织开展本学科重要集体研究项目；开展海内外学术交流活动等。

陈安教授为首任所长（1987—2000）。之后历任所长为曾华群教授（2000—2016）、蔡从燕教授（2016—2019）和陈辉萍教授（2019—　）。

2. 中国国际经济法学会秘书处

中国国际经济法学会（简称"学会"）创建于 1984 年"庐山国际经济法讲习班"，是国际经济法领域的全国性学术团体，业务主管单位原为国家教委。2006 年，学会在民政部正式登记为社会团体法人，业务主管单位为司法部。学会历任会长为姚梅镇教授（第一届，1984—1993）、陈安教授（第二、三、四届，1993—2011）和曾华群教授（第五、六、七届，2011—　）。

学会秘书处原设于江西大学（1984—1987）和武汉大学（1987—1993）。自 1993 年以来，学会秘书处设于我校，由本学科具体承担学会秘书处工作，曾华群（1993—2006）、徐崇利（2006—2011）、李国安教授（2011—2019）和房东副教授（2019—　）先后任学会秘书长。这是我国国际经济法学界对本学科的信任和支持，更是本学科与海内外学界密切交流的重要学术平台。

3.《国际经济法学刊》

《国际经济法学刊》（集刊）（简称《学刊》）创办于 1998 年，由陈安教授担任主编，中国国际经济法学会组织编辑委员会，厦门大学国际经济法研究所作为编辑部所在单位，先后由法律出版社和北京大学出版社出版发行。

2005 年，《学刊》成为"中文社会科学引文索引数据库"（CSSCI）首批收录的来源集刊之一（法学类共 5 种），并在之后两年一度的历次 CSSCI 遴选中连续五度入选。2017 年，《学刊》获国家级期刊号。自 2018 年起，《国际经济法学刊》（季刊）正式出版发行，陈安教授任主编，曾华群、李国安教授为副主编。

4. 厦门大学陈安国际法学发展基金会

2011 年，厦门大学陈安国际法学发展基金会（简称"基金会"）经福建省民政厅审批登记成立,成为基金会法人。曾华群教授任理事长(第一、二届,2011——　),李国安教授、徐崇利教授和傅明博士任副理事长(第一、二届,2011——　)。

基金会先后开展了一系列资助国际法教学、科研及学术交流的活动,主要项目包括"陈安国际法学讲座教授""中国国际经济法学会青年优秀论文奖"和"国际组织实习生资助"等,为培养我国国际法人才和推动我国国际法学的发展作出了积极贡献。

5. 厦门国际法高等研究院

厦门国际法高等研究院(简称"研究院")成立于 2005 年,是本学科积极参与创建的亚太地区唯一的国际法学高等研究机构。研究院设立董事会,由国际著名的国际法学家、法官和外交官等专业人士组成,联合国国际法院时任院长史久镛大法官担任首届董事会主席。本学科陈安教授连任董事会董事,曾华群、廖益新教授连任董事兼联席院长,陈辉萍教授连任行政理事会秘书长,池漫郊教授、张膑心助理教授先后担任副秘书长。

研究院借鉴海牙国际法高等研究院(The Hague Academy of International Law)的模式,其宗旨是促进国际法领域的国际学术研究、交流与合作。其主要职能之一是举办国际法前沿问题研修班。历经 15 年的发展,研究院在海内外国际法学界已享有较高学术声誉,成为我国国际法领域重要的国际性学术交流平台。

长期以来,研究所、学会秘书处、《学刊》、基金会及研究院,同为本学科的学术平台,各司其职,同心协力,共襄学科建设盛举。近年来,为适应新形势发展的需要,本学科相继成立了国际法领域的研究中心,包括"国际水法研究团队""解决国际投资争端研究中心""网络空间国际法研究中心"和"海洋和军事国际法研究中心"等,学术平台建设出现了可喜的新局面。

三、人才培养

(一)教材建设

教材建设,是本学科人才培养的基础性工作,也是本学科成为我国国际法教学基地之一的重要标志。

陈安教授主编的国际经济法系列专著(即《国际贸易法》《国际投资法》《国际货币金融法》《国际税法》和《国际海事法》,鹭江出版社 1987 年出版),是我国第一套国际经济法系列专著,也成为当时本校和国内其他高校的国际经济法专业本科教材。

1988—1991 年和 1996—1998 年,司法部法学教材编辑部先后组织编写两套高校法学教材"国际经济法系列",陈安、曾华群、廖益新教授等分别担任《国际经济法总论》、《国际经济法导论》和《国际税法》的主编。

陈安教授总主编的"国际经济法学系列专著"（即《国际贸易法学》《国际投资法学》《国际货币金融法学》《国际税法学》和《国际海事法学》，北京大学 1999—2002 年出版）和主编的全国首批统编研究生教材《国际经济法学专论》（高等教育出版社2002 年第一版、2007 年第二版）是系统研究国际经济法各分支理论与实务问题的重要研究成果和教材建设，国内高校广泛采用为本科教材和研究生教材。

2020 年，陈安教授主编《国际经济法学》（北京大学出版社，第八版）、《国际经济法新论》（高等教育出版社，第五版）和曾华群教授著《国际经济法导论》（法律出版社，第三版）的出版，反映了本学科在国际经济法教材建设的持续贡献和学术影响力。

（二）"国际化"培养模式

国际法人才的"国际化"培养模式的探索和形成，是本学科人才培养的创新性工作，也是本学科成为我国国际法教学基地之一的显著特色。

1. 开设外语教学系列课程

本学科根据教学需要，持续开展全外语和双语专业课程的教学。先后有 10 多位教师以英语或日语开设 20 多门全外语和双语专业课程。在全外语和双语专业课程教学中，本学科教师借鉴国外先进的培养方案、教学内容及教学方法，结合各自的外文研究成果和国际学术交流体会，取得了优良的教学效果。

全外语和双语专业课程教学为广大学生提供了专业学习的外语环境，为学生进一步参与国际学术交流，包括出国留学、参加厦门国际法高等研究院"国际法前沿问题研修班"及国际性国际法模拟庭审竞赛等打下了必要的基础。在这个意义上，全外语和双语专业课程是本学科"国际化"教学模式的重要支柱。

2. 创建"国际化"教学环境

历经 15 年的持续努力，厦门国际法高等研究院（简称"研究院"）已成为本学科国际性教学和学术交流的常设性平台，也是本学科国际合作办学的创新性成果。

研究院举办一年一度的"国际法前沿问题研修班"（简称"研修班"），由本学科承担全部行政管理工作并参与部分教学工作。经教育部批准，2008、2011 年两届研修班同时作为"国际法全国研究生暑期学校"。自 2010 年起，研修班课程列为本学科硕士生的必修课程和博士生的选修课程。近年来，研修班课程也列为我院"卓越法律人才（涉外法律人才）教育培养基地"的选修课程。

研究院教授和学员的"国际化"，使我国学员未出国门、我校学生不出校门，就能在"国际化"教学环境中学习，与来自海外的学员共享优质的国际学术资源，很有利于把握国际法的学术前沿和最新研究成果,拓宽国际学术视野和提高创新研究能力。

3. 指导学生参加各类国际法模拟庭审竞赛

自 2002 年以来,本学科教师认真组织和指导学生参加 Willem C. Vis 模拟国际商事仲裁竞赛、Jessup 国际法模拟法庭竞赛、ICRC 国际人道法模拟法庭竞赛、国际刑事法院(ICC)模拟法庭竞赛、WTO 模拟法庭竞赛和国际海洋法模拟法庭竞赛等国际性国际法模拟庭审竞赛。

2006 年以来,本学科陈辉萍、池漫郊、龚宇、于湛旻、陈喜峰、张膑心、苏宇、杨帆等老师以国际法模拟庭审竞赛为教学平台,相继开设"国际商事仲裁案例研究""国际公法案例研究""国际人道法案例研究""国际贸易法案例研究""国际海洋法案例研究"等课程,以反映国际法前沿问题的竞赛案例为研究对象,全程指导学生掌握关于案例分析、资料检索、诉状写作、口头辩论的方法和技巧,培养学生对国际法的兴趣及发现、分析和解决问题的能力,有效提高了学生的专业水平和英语技能。此类课程使更多的学生参与国际法案例的研究和实践,在专业和外语两方面得到扎实的锻炼。

4. 实现生源的"国际化"

招收外国留学生前来我院攻读学位,实现生源的"国际化",直接创造了不同国籍学生日常密切交流的学习环境。我院自 2007 年起设立中国民商法专业国际硕士学位项目,自 2016 年起设立国际法专业国际硕士学位项目,专门面向海外招生,本学科教师积极参加全英文授课和外国留学生的博士/硕士学位论文(英文)指导等工作。

(三)主要教学成果

在课程建设方面,本学科负责的本科主干课程"国际经济法学"被教育部评为"国家级精品课程"(2004),并入选"国家级精品资源共享课"(2013);硕士研究生学位课程"国际经济法研究"入选"福建省优质研究生课程"(2004)。

在教学改革方面,本学科"教学与科研互相交融,出人才与出成果同时并举——厦门大学国际经济法专业研究生教学方式"(1996)和"国际法学科'国际化'教学模式的创建与发展"(2014)先后荣获"福建省高等学校优秀教学成果奖"一等奖,反映了本学科在研究生培养工作中"教学与科研相结合"和"国际化教学模式"的鲜明特色。(附表 2)

在学术交流方面,2002 年以来,本学科教师指导我院代表队参加各类全国性、国际性国际法模拟庭审竞赛,与国内外名校佼佼者同台竞技,并屡获佳绩,从一个侧面

反映了本学科"国际化"教学模式的优秀成果。（附表 3）

在基地建设方面，在第二届"世界投资论坛"暨 2010 年国际投资协定年会的闭幕式上，UNCTAD 秘书长素帕猜·巴尼巴蒂博士宣布，为推动全球范围内国际投资法律与政策的发展，该组织正式发起成立"全球 15 所法学院领航项目"（G-15 Law School Pilot Project）。经严格遴选，我院由于在国际投资法教学研究的显著成果，从全球众多法律院校中脱颖而出，入选并成为该项目在中国大陆地区的唯一院校。2012 年，我院入选教育部"卓越法律人才（涉外法律人才）教育培养基地"项目。

四、科学研究

（一）主要研究领域及项目

主要研究领域及项目集中反映本学科研究工作的重点，也是本学科成为我国国际法研究基地之一的重要标志。

长期以来，本学科主要研究领域包括国际经济法理论、国际投资法、国际贸易法、国际货币金融法及国际税法等，形成学界广泛认同的传统学科优势和特色。近年来，适应新形势发展的需要，本学科注重拓展新领域，涉及国际法理论、国际水法、网络空间国际法、国际海洋法等。

本学科教师先后承担和完成国家社会科学基金、教育部、司法部、福建省等专题研究项目和商务部、外交部等咨询研究项目合计 144 项，包括国家社会科学基金项目 28 项，教育部项目 36 项，司法部项目 14 项，商务部项目 10 项，外交部项目 8 项，国家海洋局项目 9 项，福建省项目 22 项及其他机构项目 17 项。其中，曾华群教授负责的"促进与保护我国海外投资的法律体制研究"和徐崇利教授负责的"全球金融危机后国际经济秩序重构与中国的法律对策研究"分别入选国家社会科学基金重大项目和教育部重大攻关项目，反映了本学科在国际经济法领域的研究积淀和实力得到了学界的充分认可。（附表 4）

（二）代表性科研成果

代表性科研成果反映本学科科学研究工作的实力和水平，也是本学科成为我国国际法研究基地之一的重要标志。

长期以来，本学科教师持续在国内外出版和发表国际法领域的专著和论文，在海内外产生了较大的学术影响。

本学科集体完成的代表性科研成果包括：陈安教授主编的国际经济法系列专著（即《国际贸易法》《国际投资法》《国际货币金融法》《国际税法》和《国际海事法》，鹭江出版社 1987 年出版），是我国第一套国际经济法系列专著；陈安教授总主编的"国际经济法学系列专著"(即《国际贸易法学》《国际投资法学》《国际货币金融法学》《国际税法学》和《国际海事法学》,北京大学出版社 1999—2002 年出版),是系统研究国际经济法各分支理论与实务问题的重要研究成果;陈安、曾华群教授总主编的"WTO 法律制度系列专著"(即《WTO 与中国外贸法的新领域》《WTO 服务贸易的多边规则》《发展中国家与 WTO 法律制度研究》《WTO〈服务贸易总协定〉法律约束力研究》和《WTO 司法哲学中的能动主义之维》,北京大学出版社 2005—2006 年出版),反映了本学科 WTO 法研究的新成果及其特色,对推动我国 WTO 法的深入研究具有重要意义。应中国大百科全书编辑委员会聘请,本学科陈安教授担任《中国大百科全书. 法学》卷(修订版)(中国大百科全书出版社 2006 年版)"国际经济法"主编,曾华群、徐崇利教授担任副主编,主持和组织全国国际经济法学者撰写国际经济法学科的全部条目,从一个侧面反映了学界对本学科国际经济法研究的高度认可。曾华群教授主持的"厦门大学国际经济法文库"(厦门大学出版社出版,2003 年启动)和蔡从燕、陈辉萍教授主持的"厦门大学国际法名著译丛"(法律出版社出版,2009 年启动)展现了本学科青年学者的优秀成果和治学潜力。

学术带头人陈安教授的代表作有《中国特色话语:陈安论国际经济法学》《国际经济法学刍言》和 *The Voice from China：An CHEN on International Economic Law*(《中国的呐喊:陈安论国际经济法学》)等。2018 年 12 月,由中国法学会主办,中国国际经济法学会、厦门大学和北京大学出版社合办的"《中国特色话语:陈安论国际经济法学》发布会"在北京隆重召开。这是中国法学会第一次为中国法学者专门召开新书发布会,是中国法学界对陈安教授道德文章的充分肯定。

本学科教师在《中国社会科学》《法学研究》《中国法学》《世界投资与贸易学刊》(*The Journal of World Investment ＆ Trade*)、《国际经济法学刊》(*Journal of International Economic Law*)和《中国国际法学刊》(*Chinese Journal of International Law*)等海内外重要学术期刊持续发表论文,在海内外重要学术出版社出版专著。这些学术成果的主要特色是,具有开阔的国际视野和鲜明的"中国特色",治学严谨,开拓创新,在海内外产生了重要的学术影响。作者中既有以身作则的学术带头人,又有年富力强的学术骨干,更有朝气蓬勃的青年才俊,充分显示了本学科优良的学术传承和持续发展势头。(附表 5)

(三) 主要科研成果奖

本学科取得了一系列重要的科学研究成果奖,包括全国高校人文社会科学研究成果奖 11 项、福建省社会科学优秀成果奖 52 项。其中,全国高校人文社会科学研究成果奖是我国人文社会科学领域的重要奖项,本学科荣获 11 项,殊为不易。陈安教授还荣获"第五届吴玉章人文社会科学奖"一等奖（2007）、中国国家图书奖（2002）、"安子介国际贸易研究奖"一等奖（2004）等。（附表6）

五、学术交流

（一）国内学术交流

1. 主办和参与主办全国性学术会议

举办全国性国际经济法学术研讨会，是中国国际经济法学会（简称"学会"）持之以恒的重要学术活动。自1993年起，学会每年召开中国国际经济法学会年会暨国际经济法学术研讨会。自2007年和2010年起，学会每年与商务部条约法律司相继联合主办"国际投资法专题研讨会"和"WTO法专题研讨会"，成为学界与政府主管部门、涉外法律实务界沟通、互动和合作的重要平台。本学科作为学会秘书处，每年负责组织我国国际经济法学界的上述研讨会，也和学界同行保持密切的学术联系。此外，本学科还积极参与主办和联合主办全国性学术会议，学术领域包括国际经济法、国际法理论、国际私法、网络空间国际法、国际海洋法等。（附表7）

2. 主办《国际经济法学刊》及网站

《国际经济法学刊》（集刊，1998—2016；正式期刊，2018—　）由陈安教授担任主编（1998—　），本学科教师负责学术编辑工作。该刊承载发展和繁荣中国特色国际经济法学的重任，是中国国际经济法学者勇于担当、精耕细作的学术园地，也是中国国际经济法学者与各国同行交流互鉴、平等对话的学术平台。

本学科还相继创建和长期负责维护"中国国际经济法学会"网站（http://www.csiel.org）、"陈安国际法学发展基金会"网站（http://www.chenanfoundation.org）和"厦门国际法高等研究院"网站（http://www.xiamenacademy.org），为我国国际经济法学界提供了重要的信息交流平台，也促进了我国、我校国际法研究信息和成果在海内外学界的传播。

（二）国际学术交流

1. 主办、联合主办和应邀参加国际学术会议

自2005年起，中国国际经济法学会与韩国国际经济法学会轮流在韩国和中国举办国际学术研讨会，重点研讨WTO与中韩经贸法律问题等，迄今已召开8届。此外，本学科还积极参与主办和联合主办国际学术会议，学术领域包括国际经济法、国际水法、国际海洋法等。（附表8）

2005年12月和2010年12月，陈安教授和曾华群教授先后应邀参加OECD和UNCTAD联合主办的第一、二届国际投资协定研讨会，并作大会报告。近年来，本

学科教师特别是青年教师多次应邀在国际学术会议上作学术报告,显示出与国际同行开展学术对话的实力和潜力。

2. 举办"国际法前沿问题研修班"

创建厦门国际法高等研究院(简称"研究院")为本学科与相关国际组织及国际学术机构建立和加强学术联系提供了重要契机。历经15年的持续努力,研究院已成为本学科国际性学术交流的常设性平台。

迄今,研究院已连续成功举办十四届(2006—2019年)"国际法前沿问题研修班"。历届研修班均邀请世界一流的国际法学家、国际组织高级官员、国际司法界权威人士(包括联合国国际法院9位大法官)前来讲授国际法的前沿问题。联合国国际法院四任院长史久镛大法官、小和田恒(Hisashi Owada)大法官、彼得·汤卡(Peter Tomka)大法官和优素福(Abdulqawi A. Yusuf)大法官分别于2006年和2011年、2009年和2015年、2012年、2019年亲临研究院讲学,充分反映了国际社会和国际法学界同行对研究院的高度认同和鼎力支持。研究院每年均招收来自约30个国家及中国大陆地区、港澳台地区的100—120名学员参加研修班,在海内外产生了重要而深远的学术影响。

3. 与国际机构的学术合作与交流

经我国外交部推荐,2001年联合国有关机构批准在厦门大学国际经济法研究所设立"联合国托存图书馆"。

2008年以来,世界著名学术出版社 Martinus Nijhoff Publishers 出版《厦门国际法高等研究院演讲集》(The Collected Courses of the Xiamen Academy of International Law),迄今已出版11卷。由于《演讲集》汇辑国际法权威学者的最新研究成果,必将成为国际法领域最重要的研究文献之一。

长期以来,本学科与 UNCTAD、MIGA、ICSID 等国际组织建立信息交流、互访等学术联系。2012—2016年,陈辉萍教授接受 UNCTAD 的邀请,带领本学科学生全程参与"国际投资协定解析项目"(The Mapping Projects of International Investment Agreements),所提交的项目成果受到 UNCTAD 的高度评价。

六、社会服务

(一) 承担咨询研究工作

本学科与商务部、外交部等政府部门建立制度性、经常性联系,承担和完成了一系列有关缔约和立法的咨询研究任务。经过长期的合作,本学科已发展成为我国相关条约实践的主要咨询机构之一。

早在 80、90 年代，陈安、曾华群、徐崇利、陈辉萍教授等就接受原外经贸部/商务部的专题委托或咨询，为我国签订双边投资条约、加入《解决国家与他国国民间投资争端公约》（即《华盛顿公约》）和《建立多边投资担保机构公约》等提供理论支持和决策依据。2000 年 3 月，原对外经贸部条约法律司与厦门大学签订《共建国际经济法重点研究基地的协议》。2005 年，商务部条约法律司专函赞赏与我院的合作"堪称学术研究机构与政府决策部门互相配合、互相支持的典范"（2005 年 9 月 27 日商务部条法司致陈安教授专函）。

2011 年 11 月，外交部条约法律司与厦门大学签订《合作研究协议》，为本学科瞄准实践前沿课题、有的放矢地开展国际法理论和实践研究奠定了制度化基础。如针对"ICSID 公约适用于香港特区""中美双边投资条约谈判""南海仲裁案"等重要议题，本学科曾华群、蔡从燕、韩秀丽教授和陈喜峰副教授等分别提供了相关咨询研究意见。

近年来，在国际法新领域，如网络空间国际法问题，杨帆、张膑心助理教授等为中央网信办提供的咨询研究意见也得到重视和肯定。（附表 9）

（二）联办专业会议和国际项目

自 2007 年和 2010 年起，商务部条约法律司决定与中国国际经济法学会、厦门大学国际经济法研究所合作每年举行"国际投资法专题研讨会"和"WTO 法专题研讨会"，邀请国内相关领域专家就国际投资法和 WTO 法的前沿问题及我国面临的新问题进行深入交流。

厦门国际法高等研究院的工作得到了外交部的高度重视和鼎力支持。外交部条约法律司历任领导黄惠康司长、徐宏司长和贾桂德司长先后于 2013、2014、2019 年亲临研究院"国际法前沿问题研修班"作"开学演讲"。2015 年 7 月，受外交部委托，研究院参与承办"中国—亚非法律协商组织国际法研究交流项目"（China-AALCO Research and Exchange Program on International Law），来自亚非国家、地区的 29 位高级官员参加研究院第 10 届"国际法前沿问题研修班"。

（三）法律专业服务

经商务部研究决定，2003 年，陈安教授成为中国政府根据《华盛顿公约》向"解决投资争端国际中心"（ICSID）指派的首席仲裁员（2003—2017）；2017 年，曾华群教授成为我国政府向 ICSID 指派的调解员。同年，曾华群教授受聘为外交部国际法咨询委员会委员。

曾华群教授 1990 年任福建省代表团副团长，参加在北京召开的"第 14 届世界法律大会"；2000、2001 年先后为福建省委学习中心组作《澳门特别行政区基本法》辅导讲座和《世贸组织体制与中国"加入世贸组织"的准备》专题讲座。曾华群教授（2001—　）和徐崇利教授（2009—　）受聘为福建省人民政府顾问，李国安教授（2015—　）受聘为福建省人民政府立法咨询专家，长期提供政策和法律咨询服务等。曾华群教授还兼任厦门市人民代表大会法制委员会副主任委员（1998—2002）和内务司法委员会副主任委员（2002—2012），实际参与厦门市人大立法及对"一府两院"的法律监督工作。

本学科多位教师兼任中国国际经济贸易仲裁委员会仲裁员、律师、企业法律顾问等，参与处理涉外经贸争议，提供法律专业服务。

七、学科特色

创业难，守成和发展更难。在一定意义上，学科的生命力在于优良传统特色的形成、传承和发扬光大。经过 42 年来的创建和发展，本学科逐渐形成其优良传统特色。主要表现在：

（1）志存高远，铭记中国国际法学人的使命担当。本学科以马克思主义为指导思想，立足中国国情，紧密联系改革开放实际，与商务部、外交部等政府部门和涉外实务界保持密切的合作关系，重点研究我国在国际投资、国际贸易、国际货币金融和国际税务等方面的法律问题，适时拓展国家急需的国际水法、网络空间国际法、国际海洋法等新领域的研究。同时，坚定站在中国和广大发展中国家的立场，坚持改革国际经济旧秩序、建立国际经济新秩序的目标，重视研究国际经济法基本理论，特别是经济主权、公平互利和合作发展等国际经济法基本原则的理论和实践问题，勇于开拓创新，努力维护中国和广大发展中国家的合法权益。"知识报国，兼济天下"已然成为本学科广大教师的共识、志向和使命担当。

（2）淡泊明志，传承严谨治学的优良学风。本学科教师重视学术道德修养，深知为人师表，道德文章须经得起历史的检验。长期以来，学术带头人言传身教，广大教师潜心治学，精益求精，蔚然成风。本学科教师在海内外发表和出版的学术成果、《国际经济法学刊》的创办历程及本学科参与组织的学术交流活动等，均体现本学科教师严守学术规范、扎实严谨治学的优良学风。

（3）自强不息，创建学科建设的"铁打营盘"。本学科创建和借重的厦门大学国际经济法研究所、中国国际经济法学会秘书处、《国际经济法学刊》、厦门国际法高等研究院和厦门大学陈安国际法学发展基金会等学术平台，是本学科自强不息、来之不易的学科建设成果，也是本学科可持续发展的重要基础和"铁打营盘"。特别是，学会的"年会＋专题研讨会"、《国际经济法学刊》和研究院的"国际法前沿问题研修班"，是本学科居于全国性、国际性学科前沿的重要标志和基本保障。

（4）开拓创新，促进教学研究的"国际化"。 由于国际法有其"国际话语体系"，国际法教学研究"国际化"的重要性不言而喻。本学科教师"国际法学科'国际化'教学模式的创建与发展"的教学成果，持续在国际性专业期刊和出版社发表学术论著，参与创建厦门国际法高等研究院的不懈努力，连年指导参加国际性国际法模拟庭审竞赛并屡获佳绩等，均反映了本学科师生"走向国际"的重要特色，也是本学科践行改革"国际话语体系"、发出国际法领域"中国强音"的必要前提和能力建设。

（5）敬业奉献，凝聚学科建设的同心合力。 长期以来，本学科建设的许多工作，如中国国际经济法学会秘书处事务、《国际经济法学刊》学术编辑事务、国际性国际法模拟庭审竞赛的指导工作及厦门国际法高等研究院行政事务等，均属"公共事务"。本学科师生基于共同的世界观和价值观，长期甘当"义工"，勇挑重担，无私奉献，体现了强烈的事业心、责任感和团队意识。这是本学科最可宝贵的优良传统，也是本学科建设事业得以不断推进的决定性因素。长远看来，亟须促进解决相关机制问题，为本学科的可持续发展提供必要的制度保障。

当下，中国特色国际法学进入了新时代。我国改革开放和推动构建人类命运共同体的伟大实践，为我国国际法学界提供了知识报国的最佳时代背景和学术环境。本学科广大教师必将秉承"自强不息，止于至善"的校训和本学科的优良传统，继往开来，砥砺前行，为培养我国国际法人才和创建发展中国特色国际法学作出新的贡献。

附表目录（略）：
表1：厦门大学法学院国际法学科（国际法教研室）教师一览表
表2：国际法学科主要教学成果奖
表3：国际法学科指导参与国际法专业赛事获奖一览表
表4：国际法学科主要科研项目一览表
表5：国际法学科代表性科研成果一览表
表6：国际法学科主要科研成果奖
表7：国际法学科参与主办全国性学术会议一览表
表8：国际法学科参与主办国际性学术会议一览表
表9：国际法学科代表性咨询研究报告一览表

第二节　国际经济法研究生培养方式的改革与实践 [*]

【摘要】　近年来,厦门大学国际法学科点对国际经济法研究生的培养模式进行了改革和实践,主要内容包括:发挥学术梯队的整体优势,充分开拓和利用国内外学术资源,基本形成了开放性的研究生培养模式;改革教学内容和方式,逐步形成了"教研交融,师生互动"的教学方式;指导和组织研究生独立承担或参与科研项目,加强培养研究生的科研能力和创新能力;积极组织和推动研究生参加国际性专业赛事和国际学术会议等学术交流活动,培养研究生的国际观和学术交流能力;重视教材建设,形成国际经济法研究生教材和参考资料的系列化和立体化。

【关键词】　培养模式;互动教学;国际交流;教材建设

国际经济法学是一门综合性、边缘性的新兴学科。厦门大学分别于 1981 年和 1986 年开始招收国际经济法专业(1998 年调整为国际法专业)硕士研究生和博士研究生,是我国最早培养国际经济法专门人才的基地之一。1995 年 6 月和 2002 年 10 月,本学科点经教育部批准为全国高校"211"工程重点建设第一、二期项目。2002 年 1 月,我校国际法学(含国际经济法学)专业由教育部评为国家重点学科。由学科特点所决定,国际经济法专门人才需要具备"法律、经济、外语"三方面的技能,培养方式的改革尤为重要。近年来,在我校、法学院的关心和支持下,本学科点充分发挥师资力量较雄厚,教学、科研基础较扎实的优势,对国际经济法研究生培养模式进行了改革和实践,初见成效,形成了一定的特色。

一、开放性的研究生培养模式

国际经济法专门人才应具备良好的综合素质和开阔的学术视野。鉴此,本学科点注意改变传统的"师傅带徒弟"的研究生培养模式,发挥学术梯队的整体优势和团队精神,加强集体教学和研究工作,充分开拓和利用国内外学术资源,使研究生培养工作逐步走上了开放、多元和国际化的道路。

在研究生培养过程中,本学科点有意淡化各位导师与其指导的研究生之间的"师徒"关系,避免人为的学术封闭。主要表现在:各位导师充分尊重其指导的研究

* 原载《学位与研究生教育》2006 年第 4 期,作者:曾华群、龚宇、池漫郊。

生的研究兴趣和方向；各位导师开设和主持的课程、专题讲座和专题讨论会一般都向本学科点全体研究生开放，博士生课程亦允许硕士生旁听；各位导师主持的研究项目也向本学科点全体研究生开放，择优组成课题组；研究生在学习和研究过程中，可自由向导师以外的其他老师请教；研究生的学位论文开题报告，须经导师组审议通过。在博士生培养方面，坚持"博士生导师组"这一组织形式，实行集体教学与个别辅导相结合，充分发挥各位导师的学术专长，同时有效整合学术指导力量，提高了指导的综合质量和效率。

为进一步拓宽研究生的学术视野和信息渠道，本学科点积极组织国内外同行之间的互访、合作研究等学术交流活动，尽可能扩大教学和研究的开放度。本学科点与国内外著名高校、科研机构以及"多边投资担保机构（MIGA）"、"解决投资争端国际中心"（ICSID）、"南方中心"（South Centre）、"第三世界网络中心"（TWN）等国际组织建立了经常性的资料信息交流和学术交流关系，并定期邀请本学科领域的国内外专家学者来本校为研究生开设学术讲座或短期课程。频繁的国内外学术交流为研究生带来了重要的学术资源，更重要的是，研究生在实际接触和掌握本学科前沿研究动态的同时，拓宽了国际学术视野。

二、互动式的研究生教学方式

研究生教学绝非本科教学的简单延伸，其重点在于通过教学提高研究生的研究能力，并激发其研究兴趣和潜能。在借鉴国内外先进法学教育理念的基础上，本学科点从实际出发，在研究生教学中，注重发挥学生学习的主动性和创新性，逐步形成了"教研交融，师生互动"的教学方式，实现了教学内容和教学方法的革新。

在教学内容方面，考虑到研究生学习的目的和特点，本学科点舍弃了"大而全"的课程体系，转为重点开设更有深度和更适合研究生学习特点的专题研究，如曾华群教授的"国际经济法研究"（2004 年入选为"福建省优质硕士学位立项建设课程"）、廖益新教授的"国际税法研究"、徐崇利教授的"国际投资法研究"和李国安教授的"国际金融法研究"等，均是各位导师在其长期研究积累的基础上，为研究生开设的专题研究课。这些课程有助于研究生深入了解有关领域的重点、热点问题及最新研究成果，并在学习过程中找到自己的研究兴趣和方向。

在教学方法方面，在强调研究生自主学习的同时，本学科点注重集体教学，并使之制度化、规范化。在集体教学中，采用"互动式"和"案例分析"的教学方法。

"互动式"教学一改过去研究生"只听不讲、学而不思"的被动状况，强调导师与研究生之间、研究生相互之间的互动，强调研究生对教学过程的主动参与以及研究生研究能力的培养。

在硕士生教学中，"互动式"教学方式主要体现在：一是课堂讨论，即导师讲授某一专题后，提出难点或问题，留下一定时间让研究生即席提问和讨论；二是学习交流会，即导师在阐述某一专题后，提出需作进一步思考的问题，由研究生在课后查阅和研究相关专业文献资料，在随后课堂上，由导师主持，组织研究生就各自思考和研究心得进行交流，并在此基础上提交研究报告或论文。

在博士生教学中，本学科点逐渐形成了"专题学术报告会""分组学术交流会"和"博士生学术沙龙"三种主要的集体教学方式。这些方式均体现了"互动式"教学方法：在"专题学术报告会"上，通常是前半段由一位导师作学术报告，后半段由各位导师和博士生一起讨论；在"分组学术交流会"上，由各位导师分别选题和主持，组织其指导的博士生对本学科的前沿问题、难点或热点问题以及研究方法等开展讨论和交流；在"博士生学术沙龙"上，由博士生主持，组织博士生自由讨论专题学术报告或共同感兴趣的本学科点的理论、实践问题以及研究方法等，必要时邀请导师参与讨论。"互动式"的教学方法在激发研究生的研究兴趣、培养研究能力方面取得了明显的成效。作为课程作业提交的一些论文，经导师指导修改后，相继发表于各类学术刊物。一些研究生在思考和讨论过程中，确定了具有理论或实践研究价值的毕业论文选题。

鉴于国际经济法学的实践性，本学科点在教学过程中尽可能采用案例分析的教学方法。在博士生教学中，特别注重案例原始文档的翻译、研读和分析。在导师指导下，研究生对"解决投资争端国际中心"（ICSID）和"世界贸易组织"（WTO）等国际体制的案例研究，取得了重要的研究成果，得到国内外学术界的重视和肯定。案例分析的教学方法加深了研究生对相关法律问题的理解，同时培养了研究生分析和解决实务问题的能力。

三、创新性、自主性的研究生科研活动

加强研究生科研能力的培养是研究生教育与本科生教育的一大区别，也是本学科点一向坚持的优良传统。本学科点紧密联系我国改革开放的实际，积极组织研究生参加各种学术活动，注重培养研究生分析和解决涉外法律问题的能力。

近年来，在导师指导下，本学科点研究生参与承担的科研任务包括"WTO 法律制度专题研究""WTO 与我国对外贸易法律制度的改革""'入世'后中国外资法体系和内容研究"和"WTO 经典案例编译"等多项国家和省部级课题。在研究工作中，导师对研究生既委于重任，又悉心指导，严格把好学术质量关。同时，为进一步强化博

士生独当一面的科研能力，本学科点还鼓励和支持博士生独立申请科研项目，开展
自主性的科研活动，取得了显著的成效。如在上海 WTO 事务咨询中心"2003 年度
在读博士生与博士后研究课题定向招标"中，本学科点 3 位博士生在全国众多竞争者
中脱颖而出，中标 3 项课题，获得总额 9 万元的科研经费。

导师在指导研究生科研活动中，特别注重选题的创新性，鼓励研究生瞄准学科
前沿课题，刻苦攻关，开展创新性研究工作。近年来，本学科点博士生在《中国法学》
《现代法学》《世界政治与经济》《国际贸易问题》《厦门大学学报》等权威和核心学术
期刊上相继发表较高质量的学术论文。研究生学位论文的学术水平受到海内外学
术界的充分肯定。如陈辉萍同学的博士学位论文（英文版）《经合组织多边投资协
定：中国学者的观点》（*OECD's Multilateral Agreement on Investment：A Chinese
Perspective*），2002 年由国际性权威法律出版社 Kluwer Law International 出版，
2003 年获"福建省第五届社会科学优秀成果"二等奖。2002 年，陈东同学的博士学
位论文《论跨国公司治理中的责任承担机制》获"福建省优秀博士论文"一等奖。研
究生完成的科研项目受到学术界和实务界的充分肯定。如博士生郭俊秀、李万强和
朱炎生等同学担任《国际投资争端仲裁——"解决投资争端国际中心"机制研究》（复
旦大学出版社 2001 年出版）的副主编和主要撰稿人，该专著 2003 年获"司法部法学
教材与法学优秀科研成果"一等奖。2003 年 6 月，博士生蔡从燕同学的研究报告《中
欧贸易壁垒立法比较研究》受到商务部进出口公平贸易局采纳并给予高度评价。本
学科点教师指导的研究生多次荣获历届全国"挑战杯"大学生业余科技作品竞赛奖。

组织研究生参与学术刊物的编辑和翻译工作，是本学科点提高研究生研究能力
和学术素质的重要措施之一。本学科点编辑的《国际经济法学刊》（原《国际经济法
论丛》）是全国性国际经济法学领域的学术园地，现由北京大学出版社出版，自 1998
年创刊迄今已连续出版 12 卷，每卷约 45—50 万字，获得国内外学术同行的重视和好
评。该刊的编辑工作主要由研究生具体承担，导师负责指导和把关。研究生通过参
与编辑工作，及时了解最新学术动态，且锻炼了学术研究基本功，培养了严谨的学
风。本学科点还积极支持研究生参加《美国法通讯》（国际合作的学术刊物，由美中
律师协会、美国康奈尔大学法学院和中国 5 所法律院校联合主办）的编辑工作。2003
年，本学科点专门成立了由研究生为主体的《美国法通讯》翻译编辑组。博士生陈延
忠同学由于翻译编辑及组织工作的出色表现，被聘为该刊编委。

四、富于进取性的研究生国际学术交流

培养具有国际观，精通法律、经济、外语的高层次国际经济法人才，是本学科点

孜孜以求的目标。在研究生教学中,本学科点尽可能为研究生提供参加国际国内学术交流的各种机会,特别表现在积极组织研究生参加国际性专业赛事和国际学术会议。

2001—2002年,在曾华群教授和陈辉萍副教授的组织和指导下,以本学科点研究生为主组成的厦门大学代表队赴京参加由中国国际经济贸易仲裁委员会主办的第二届"贸仲杯国际商事仲裁辩论赛",获得亚军,并代表中国高校赴奥地利维也纳参加由联合国国际贸易法委员会、维也纳大学和美国佩斯大学共同主办的第九届"Willem C. Vis 国际商事仲裁辩论赛"。曾教授和陈副教授还先后受聘为该赛事仲裁员,首开中国高校教师担任该赛事仲裁员之先例。我校代表队的突出表现给比赛主办方、来自各国的仲裁专家和其他参赛队留下了深刻的印象。本学科点2003—2005年继续组队赴维也纳参加该项国际赛事,并逐年取得显著进步。2005年,在参加该赛事的代表各国诸多名校的154支代表队中,我校代表队进入前32强复赛,关晶同学荣获"最佳辩手提名奖"。

2003年,本学科点研究生组队参加了由美国国际法学生联合会主办的首届"Philip C. Jessup 国际法模拟法庭辩论赛(中国赛区)"。该赛事是国际法学界历史最悠久,影响力最广泛的国际性专业赛事。在该项比赛中,我校代表队获中国赛区季军。2005年,我校代表队取得了中国赛区亚军的成绩,并代表中国高校赴美国华盛顿参加第46届"Philip C. Jessup 国际法模拟法庭辩论赛"。在代表90多个国家和地区的108支代表队中,我校代表队首次参赛就取得了口头辩论第27名、书面诉状第9名的优异成绩。

2004年,以本学科点硕士生为主的我校代表队参加了由联合国主办、在北京举行的"第二届模拟联合国辩论赛",取得了"友谊奖"与"鼓励奖"两项奖励。在"2005年西安模拟联合国辩论赛"中,我校代表队荣获"优秀代表队",本学科点硕士生樊丹同学荣获个人奖项的最高奖"最高领导才能奖"。

参赛研究生在备战和实战过程中,实际运用所学专业知识和专业外语,强化和提高了从事国际经济法实践的综合素质和能力。上述国际性专业赛事,给参赛研究生提供了参与国际专业竞争的高层次平台和国际学术交流的宝贵机会,也向世人展示了中国法学教育的显著成果,赢得了良好声誉。

在参加各项国际性专业赛事之后,本学科点注意因势利导,以点带面,在校内积极主办类似比赛,充分发挥参赛队员的示范作用和辐射效应,以利在更大范围培养研究生的国际竞争素质,包括法律研究、法律实践以及外语交流能力,同时选拔新一届参赛队员,初步形成了"人才辈出"的良好发展势头。迄今,本学科点已连续举办了四届"南强杯国际法律辩论赛"。以参与国际性专业赛事为契机,本学科点还专门开设国际法案例研究课程,使更多的学生参与有关案例的研究,提高专业研究能力和英语"四会"能力。2005年10月,在我校、法学院的支持下,以本学科点研究生为主体,成立了"厦门大学国际法辩论与交流协会"。这标志本学科点研究生参加国际性专业赛事由"自在"阶段向"自为"阶段的飞跃。

本学科点还积极组织和鼓励研究生参加国际学术会议,为其提供更高的学习和交流平台。2004年4月,本学科点研究生李璇等5名同学在参加国际商事仲裁辩论赛期间,出席了由联合国国际贸易法委员会在维也纳举办的"国际商事仲裁临时保全措施研讨会",他们在会上流利的英文提问和发言引起与会专家学者的关注和热烈回应。2004年11月,本学科点研究生还参加了由中国国际经济法学会、厦门大学法学院和厦门大学国际经济法研究所联合主办的"国际经济法与经济转型期的中国"国际学术研讨会,研究生以英文积极发言,得到了各国专家学者的高度评价。2005年8月,本学科点博士生陈延忠同学参加在北京举行的由北京大学财经法研究中心、国家税务总局税收科学研究所和世界税法协会(ITLA)共同主办的"首届中美税法高级论坛",其在发言中显示的国际税法专业水平和流利的英文表达能力深受与会专家学者赞赏。

五、系列化、立体化的研究生教材建设

鉴于研究生教材建设是研究生培养的基础性工作,本学科点一向重视国际经济法研究生的教材建设。

由陈安教授任总主编、本学科点教授为主撰写的"国际经济法系列专著",含《国际投资法学》《国际贸易法学》《国际货币金融法学》《国际税法学》和《国际海事法学》一套5部,总字数约300万字,北京大学出版社1999—2001年出版,被国内高校广泛选为国际经济法研究生的系列教材。由陈安教授主编、本学科点教授为主撰写的《国际经济法学专论》,总字数为117万字,被评选为全国首批研究生教材之一,高等教育出版社2002年7月出版,由教育部研究生工作办公室推荐为全国性研究生教材,并获得广泛好评。

2002年,高等教育出版社首次在国内提出了"立体化教材"的新概念。其主要含义是,突破以往以纸介质为知识传播载体的局限,利用现代教育技术来完善教材建设工作。2001—2002年本学科点陈安、李国安教授承担了高等教育出版社"新世纪网络课程建设项目——《国际经济法》(网络课程)"。2002年8月,该项目成果提交教育部主管部门鉴定,目前已通过验收。该成果的内容除丰富的文字资料外,辅以

图片、动画等音频文件,生动立体地对国际经济法学内容作了深入浅出的讲解。特别重要的是,该网络教材还设计了功能强大的全文搜索系统以及数个内容丰富的专业数据库,包括国际经济法条约法律数据库、国际经济法专业英语数据库、国际经济法教学案例数据库等,形成了一部内容丰富的立体化国际经济法学教材和参考资料,可较充分地满足研究生独立学习和研究的需要。

参考文献

1. 陈安主编:《国际经济法学专论(上编 总论)》,高等教育出版社 2002 年版。

2. 刁承湘:《实施研究生教育创新是系统工程》,载《学位与研究生教育》2004 年第 1 期。

第三节　国际法学科"国际化"教学模式的
创建与发展（2002—2013）[*]

厦门大学国际法学科经过12年的发展,创建和发展了"国际化"教学模式,其主要内容是,以师资队伍的"国际化"为基础,开设全外语和中外双语教学系列课程,创建厦门国际法高等研究院为教学和学术交流平台,指导学生参加国际性专业大赛等国际学术交流活动,各项教学创新措施及实践相辅相成,逐渐形成了可持续发展的"国际化"教学模式。该创新性教学模式的创建和发展,是新形势下研究生教育"国际化"的实践,显著提升了我校国际法人才的"国际化"培养水平,也惠及海内外其他法学院校师生,在国际法学领域产生了重要而深远的学术影响。

一、师资队伍的"国际化"努力是创建和发展"国际化"教学模式的基础

（一）本学科和师资队伍概况

厦门大学1926年开始设立法科。自1979年复办以来,学科建设成果显著。在2005、2009年教育部学位与研究生教育发展中心组织的学科评估中,厦门大学法学学科在全国综合性大学中分别名列第五、第六。适应改革开放形势的迫切需要,厦门大学法律系在我国较早开展国际经济法的教学和研究。经原国家教委批准,1981年在全国率先招收国际法专业硕士生,1985年在全国率先招收国际经济法专业本科生,1986年开始招收国际经济法专业（1997年后调整扩大为国际法学专业）博士生。1987年10月,成立厦门大学国际经济法研究所。2005年4月,成立厦门国际法高等研究院。1995、2002、2007年,本学科先后由教育部批准为全国高校"211"工程重点建设项目第1—3期项目。2002、2007年,本学科由教育部连续评定为国家重点学科。本学科的目标是争取建成国内外知名、有特色、高水平的国际法领域的重要研究基地、咨询机构和国际法高层次人才的培养基地。

目前,本学科已形成和保持一支以中青年为主、研究特色明显、教学研究和外语能力强的可持续发展的学术团队。其中,学科带头人陈安教授在海内外具有较大的学术影响,曾华群、廖益新、徐崇利和李国安教授分别入选国家首批"百千万人才工程第一、二层次人选"、教育部"跨世纪优秀人才培养计划"、教育部和福建省"新世纪

---

　　* 本文是教学成果《国际法学科"国际化"教学模式的创建与发展》的总结报告,曾华群执笔。该教学成果获福建省第七届高等教育教学成果奖一等奖（2014年）。

优秀人才培养计划"。青年学术骨干蔡从燕教授、韩秀丽副教授入选教育部"新世纪优秀人才培养计划",陈辉萍教授入选福建省"新世纪优秀人才培养计划"。廖益新、徐崇利、陈辉萍和蔡从燕教授相继入选美国"富布赖特基金会项目"。本项目 19 位主要完成者中,有 8 位教授、6 位副教授、4 位助理教授(其中 15 位法学博士)。(附表 1)

2011 年和 2012 年,本学科成功引进分别来自英国、德国和我国台湾地区的三位"千人计划学者",与他们签订长期工作合同,具体商定了工作目标、教学计划和研究项目,及时组织本学科教师参与相关研究,形成"国际公法新领域"教学和研究团队。三位"千人计划学者"的加盟,从学科团队人员构成方面进一步提升了本学科的"国际化"水平。

(二) 在国外发表研究成果情况

本学科教师积极向《世界投资与贸易学刊》(*The Journal of World Investment & Trade*)、《国际经济法学刊》(*Journal of International Economic Law*)和《中国国际法学刊》(*Chinese Journal of International Law*)等国际性学术期刊投稿,与国际同行开展较深入的学术交流。

2002—2013 年,本学科教师在外国著名出版社出版专著 6 部,在国际性学术期刊发表学术论文 63 篇,在国内同类学科中名列前茅(附表 2)。这些学术成果的主要特色是,具有开阔的国际视野和鲜明的"中国特色",产生了重要的国际学术影响。作者中既有以身作则的学术带头人,又有年富力强的学术骨干,更有朝气蓬勃的青年才俊,充分显示了本学科优良的学术传承和可持续的发展势头。

(三) 主办和应邀参加国际学术会议情况

本学科以中国国际经济法学会秘书处、厦门大学国际经济法研究所和厦门国际法高等研究院等为重要学术交流平台,积极开展国内外学术交流活动,与国际组织、外国高等院校和研究机构建立和保持密切的学术联系。

2002—2013 年,本学科主办和联合主办国际学术会议 11 次(附表 3)。更为可喜的是,本学科教师特别是青年教师应邀在国际学术会议上作学术报告达 41 人次(附表 4),显示出与国际同行开展学术对话的实力和潜力。

"打铁还需自身硬"。创建和发展"国际化"的教学模式,首先需要造就具有高远目标、敬业精神和学有专长的"国际化"师资队伍。实践表明,本学科师资队伍建设"国际化"的持续努力及成效,是从事"国际化"教学实践的基本条件和保障。

二、全外语和双语教学系列课程是"国际化"教学模式的重要支柱

本学科多数教师都有国外留学经历,学有专长,具有开设全外语和双语专业课程的扎实专业能力和外语基础。在各门本科和研究生国际法专业课程的教学中，本学科教师特别注重指导学生研读外文专业文献。硕士生学位课程"法学研究方法"的主要教学内容之一是翻译相关专业文献。

与此同时，本学科根据教学需要，持续开展全外语和双语专业课程的教学。目前，本学科有 11 位教师以英语或日语开设 18 门全外语和双语专业课程，加盟的"千人计划学者"也参与全英语课程教学。本学科开设的全外语和双语专业课程包括：

法学硕士/本科生专业课程（9 门）：国际经济法研究、国际法、国际投资法、国际电子商务法、国际人权法、国际水法与政策、跨国水法、英美法导论、国际仲裁法；

法学硕士/本科生案例研究课程（4 门）：国际商事仲裁案例研究、国际公法案例研究、国际人道法案例研究、国际合作法案例研究；

国际硕士专业课程（5 门）：中国法律制度、中国民法、中国外资法、中国税法、中国金融法。（附表 5）

在全外语和双语专业课程教学中，本学科教师采用国外优秀教材，借鉴国外先进的培养方案、课程体系、教学内容、教学方法及教学评价体系，同时，结合各自的外文研究成果和国际学术交流体会，取得了优秀的教学效果。全外语和双语专业课程教学为本学科研究生提供了专业学习的外语环境，为研究生进一步参与国际学术交流，包括出国留学、参加厦门国际法高等研究院国际法前沿问题研修班及国际性国际法专业辩论大赛等打下了必要的优良基础。在这个意义上，全外语和双语专业课程是本学科"国际化"教学模式的重要支柱。

三、厦门国际法高等研究院是"国际化"教学模式的重要平台

（一）厦门国际法高等研究院的创建

厦门国际法高等研究院（http://www.xiamenacademy.org，简称"研究院"）成立于 2005 年 4 月 6 日，是本学科教师积极参与创建的亚太地区唯一的国际法学高等研究机构。研究院设立董事会，由国际著名的国际法学家、法官和外交官等专业人士组成，联合国国际法院前任院长史久镛大法官担任首届董事会主席。研究院的目标是建成自主性常设国际法学术机构，旨在促进国际法领域的国际学术研究、交流与合作；培训各国特别是亚太地区各国的国际法专业人才；加强国际法在规范国际关系和建立国际新秩序方面的功能。研究院的主要职能之一是举办国际法前沿问题研修班，即邀请世界一流的国际法专家、学者授课，学员主要是各国高等院校教师、研究生、涉外事务官员、律师等。

为扩大研究院在海内外的学术影响,研究院联系世界著名学术出版社 Martinus Nijhoff Publishers 出版《厦门国际法高等研究院演讲集》(*The Collected Courses of the Xiamen Academy of International Law*),2008 年出版第 1 卷,迄今已出版 4 卷。《演讲集》将成为国际法领域最重要的研究文献之一。

创建研究院是本学科迈向国际化的重大举措,为本学科与相关国际组织及国际学术机构建立和加强学术联系提供了重要机遇。历经八年的持续努力,研究院已成为本学科国际性教学和学术交流的常设性平台。

(二)厦门国际法高等研究院的"国际化"教学功能

研究院不仅是闻名海内外的国际法领域的重要学术交流平台,也是本学科国际合作办学的创新性成果。举办一年一度的国际法前沿问题研修班,是研究院的主要工作,本学科教师承担了办学的全部行政管理工作。借鉴海牙国际法高等研究院的经验,研究院建立了邀请教授、招收学员、教学安排及宣传推广等一系列办学规则和运作规程。迄今,研究院已连续成功举办八届(2006—2013 年)国际法前沿问题研修班,其中,经教育部批准,2008 年、2011 年两届国际法前沿问题研修班同时作为国际法全国研究生暑期学校。历届研修班均邀请世界一流的国际法学家、国际组织的高级官员、国际司法界的权威人士前来讲授国际法的前沿问题。联合国国际法院三任院长史久镛大法官、小和田恒(Hisashi Owada)大法官和彼得·汤卡(Peter Tomka)大法官分别于 2006 年和 2011 年、2009 年、2012 年亲临研究院讲学,充分反映了国际社会和国际法学界同行对研究院的高度认同和鼎力支持。(附表 6)研究院每年均招收来自约 30 个国家及中国大陆地区、港澳台地区的 120—150 名学员参加,在海内外产生了重要的学术影响。

研究院教授和学员的"国际化",使大陆地区学员未出国门、我校学生不出校门,就能在"国际化"教学环境中学习,与来自海外的学员共享优质的国际学术资源,很有利于把握国际法的学术前沿和最新研究成果,拓宽国际学术视野和提高创新研究能力。自 2010 年起,研修班课程正式列为我校法学院国际法专业硕士生的必修课程、博士生的选修课程。

为进一步办好研究院,2010 年 12 月,本学科曾华群、陈辉萍、池漫郊老师访问海牙国际法高等研究院,与该院建立合作交流关系;2012 年,陈辉萍老师以特邀学员身份参加海牙国际法高等研究院暑期班,虚心取经。

四、学生国际学术交流是"国际化"教学模式的重要形式及检验

(一)出国留学与生源"国际化"

2002 年以来,法学院积极开展国际交流与合作,鼓励学生充分利用校、院渠道参

与国际学术交流活动。目前,我院除校际层面的合作学校以外,还与荷兰马斯特里赫特大学法学院、法国巴黎第十大学法学院、美国威斯康星大学麦迪逊法学院、美国伊利诺伊州立大学香槟分校法学院、美国东北大学刑事司法学院、日本东洋大学法学院和韩国仁荷大学法学院等建立了院际交流关系。我院每年均选派优秀学生赴国外学习,2007年以来,已有11位博士生、17位硕士生出国深造。(附表8)本学科还特别出台"国际组织实习资助项目",支持学生申请参与国际组织的实习活动。

招收外国留学生前来我院攻读学位,实现生源的国际化,直接创造了不同国籍学生日常密切交流的学习环境。我院自2007年起设立"中国民商法"专业国际硕士学位,专门面向海外招生,本专业5位教师参加全英文授课和论文指导。2002年以来,在我院攻读法学博士的外国留学生达15人(附表7)。

(二) 国际性专业辩论赛

自2002年以来,本学科教师认真组织和指导学生参加Willem C. Vis国际商事模拟辩论赛(英文、维也纳)、Jessup国际法模拟法庭辩论赛(英文、华盛顿 D. C.)、国际人道法模拟法庭辩论赛(英文、香港)和ELSA-WTO模拟法庭竞赛等四项全国性和国际性专业大赛。

Willem C. Vis国际商事模拟仲裁辩论赛由联合国国际贸易法委员会(UNCI-TRAL)主办,是国际法领域最重要的国际模拟法庭大赛之一,也是联合国机构在全球范围唯一举办的学生比赛。该比赛是各国知名法学院展现实力、锻炼人才的重要赛事,也是各参赛学校进行学术交流的国际平台。2002年以来,我院代表队连年参加该赛事。

Jessup国际法模拟法庭辩论赛由美国国际法学生联合会(International Law Students Association,ILSA)主办。自1959年首次举办,至今已有54年的历史,参赛国已经将近100个,参赛学校也已经达800多个,是目前国际上规模最大、历史最悠久的专业性辩论赛,被誉为国际法学界的"奥林匹克竞赛""诺贝尔奖""奥斯卡奖"。2003年以来,我院代表队连年参加该赛事。

红十字国际人道法模拟法庭竞赛由红十字国际委员会(ICRC)主办。作为ICRC主办的全球性国际人道法系列赛事的重要组成部分,该比赛旨在推广国际人道法的教学与研究。每年在瑞士举行的Jean-Pictet国际人道法模拟法庭竞赛已有20多年的历史;中国香港自2002起举办(亚太区)国际人道法模拟法庭竞赛。2009年以来,我院代表队连年参加该赛事。

ELSA-WTO模拟法庭竞赛由欧洲法律学生联合会(ELSA)主办,旨在通过模拟重现WTO争端解决程序,培养学生参与国际贸易争端解决的实务能力。比赛分为亚太、美洲、欧洲和非洲区域赛,通过各区域赛选拔的 20 支队伍将晋级在日内瓦举行的总决赛。我院代表队自 2012 年起参加该赛事。

2006 年以来,本学科陈辉萍、池漫郊、龚宇和于湛旻老师专门开设"国际商事仲裁案例研究"和"国际法案例研究"两门双语案例分析课程,以反映国际法前沿问题的辩题为研究对象,全程指导学生案例分析、资料检索、诉状写作、口头辩论等研究方法与技巧,培养学生对国际法的兴趣及发现、分析和解决问题的能力,有效提高了学生的专业水平和英语技能。这两门课程使更多的学生参与国际法案例的研究,在专业和外语两方面得到扎实的锻炼。

事实上,参加全国性、国际性国际法专业辩论大赛不仅是创新性教学模式及学生层面国际学术交流的重要形式,也是本学科"国际化"教学模式的重要检验。经过实践,由本学科教师担任教练的我院代表队已形成参加国际性专业大赛的基本流程:开设案例研究课程/举办辩论选拔赛—选拔队员—案例研究和写作—口头辩论训练—参加全国赛—参加国际赛。同时,我院代表队还形成了"潜心研究、刻苦训练、勇于拼搏"的优良传统。参赛学生在备战和实战过程中勤学苦练,实际运用所学专业知识和专业外语,极大提高了从事国际法实践的综合素质和能力。同时,参赛期间,我院代表队还与世界著名法学院师生广泛交流。参赛学生普遍反映,参赛经历是其多年法学学习研究中强度最大、收获也最大的国际化专业培训。在 2002—2013 年历届全国性、国际性国际法专业辩论大赛中,我院代表队与国内外名校佼佼者同台竞技,取得了 Jessup 国际法模拟法庭辩论赛"书状世界冠军"(2006、2011 年)等一系列优异成绩,从一个侧面反映了本学科"国际化"教学模式的丰硕成果。(附表 9)

五、创建"国际化"教学模式的初步体会

(一)同心协力,共同创建和发展"国际化"教学模式

本学科在创建和发展"国际化"教学模式中,一向倡导和践行敬业精神、创新精神和奉献精神。本学科教师达成共识,凝聚学科建设合力,是取得成效的最重要因素。

本学科持续在国际性专业刊物和出版社发表学术论著,开设全外语和双语专业课,创建厦门国际法高等研究院并连年举办国际法前沿问题研修班,连续参加四项国际性专业大赛并屡获佳绩等,均反映了本学科教师勇于开拓创新的精神。在创建和发展"国际化"教学模式的各项工作中,本学科教师基于共同的目标,勇挑重担,发挥专长,有 11 位老师主讲全外语和双语课程,11 位老师参与研究院的行政事务性工

作,8位老师承担国际法专业辩论队的教练工作,体现了强烈的事业心、责任感和团队意识。

（二）持之以恒,促进"国际化"教学模式逐步发展

创业难,可持续发展更难。本学科"国际化"教学模式是在加强师资"国际化"建设的基础上,因势利导,循序渐进,逐步发展起来的。

就"参加国际性专业大赛"和"创建厦门国际法高等研究院"两项创新模式而言,本学科自2002年开始指导学生参加国际性专业大赛,在此项工作逐步上轨道后,为进一步促进和深化"国际化"教学模式,2005年即开始创建厦门国际法高等研究院的工作。两项工作相继启动后,本学科教师克服重重困难,持之以恒,并争取不断发展。例如,本学科教师于2002年和2003年指导学生参加Willem C. Vis国际商事模拟辩论赛和Jessup国际法模拟法庭辩论赛;为适应形势发展和培养人才的需要,又于2009年和2012年指导学生参加国际人道法模拟法庭辩论赛和ELSA-WTO模拟法庭竞赛。

（三）措施互动,保障"国际化"教学模式可持续发展

本学科有关创建"国际化"教学模式的各项措施互补互动,相辅相成。

本学科师资队伍"国际化"是创建"国际化"教学模式的必要条件,是开设全外语和双语专业课程、创建国际性学术平台和开展学生层面国际学术交流的基础性保障。

全外语和双语专业课程是创建"国际化"教学模式的重要支柱。教学相长。本学科教师讲授全外语和双语专业课程,提高了本身的专业水平及国际学术交流能力。而学生选修全外语和双语专业课程,则为参加研究院国际法前沿问题研修班的学习、出国留学、参加国际性专业大赛等国际学术交流活动创造了必要的基础条件。

研究院不仅是国际性学术交流平台,其主办的国际法前沿问题研修班也是全外语和双语专业课程的组成部分。研究院还促进了本学科师资队伍和生源的"国际化"。前来研究院讲学的著名教授专家大多与本学科建立了学术交流合作关系。本学科引进的两位分别来自英国、德国的"千人计划学者"是研究院研修班的授课教授。研究院研修班的多名外国学员结业后申请成为攻读本学科博士学位的留学生。

在一定意义上,本学科教师指导学生参加全国性、国际性国际法专业辩论大赛,是全外语和双语专业课程的延伸和深化。国际法专业辩论大赛不仅是学生层面国际交流的重要形式,也是"国际化"教学模式的重要检验。2005年10月,我院学生成立了"厦门大学国际法辩论与交流协会"。这标志着参与国际法案例的研究和辩论活动,已成为我院广大学生自觉的行动。

（四）十年一剑，"国际化"教学模式的发展任重道远

12年来，经过广大师生的不懈努力，本学科"国际化"教学模式的创建和发展取得了初步的成果，得到教育部、国际同行及社会各界的充分肯定，包括：

（1）入选教育部"涉外法律人才教育培养基地"。2012年7月，经评审，厦门大学法学院入选教育部"卓越法律人才教育培养基地"计划的"涉外法律人才教育培养基地"。

（2）入选联合国贸发会议"国际投资法研究领航法学院15强"。2010年6月，基于本学科在国际投资法领域显著的教学研究成果，厦门大学法学院入选由联合国贸发会议主持遴选的"国际投资法研究领航法学院15强"，是中国大陆唯一入选的法学院（附件10）。2012年10月，联合国贸发会议邀请陈辉萍教授承担该组织研究项目（附件11）。

（3）本学科研究生广受海内外同行及社会各界的重视和好评。近年来，本学科研究生由于法学专业和外语能力突出，且具有国际视野，顺利通过各种考核方式进入国家机关、涉外企事业单位等，普遍取得了优良的工作业绩。还有部分研究生分别获得哈佛大学、纽约大学、海德堡大学、莱顿大学等国际顶级名校法学院奖学金，继续深造，获得在统一国际私法协会、新加坡国际仲裁中心等国际机构研修或实习的机会，或获得在美国仲裁协会和金杜律师所、君合律师所、史密夫律师所等顶尖国内、国际律师事务所的工作机会。这些成就增强了我院研究生的竞争力与美誉度，扩大了我院尤其是本专业的国际影响力。

我们深知，"十年磨一剑"，本学科"国际化"教学模式尚处于初级阶段，发展之路任重道远，当戮力同心，继续奋斗，同时也亟须各级政府主管部门、学校及社会各界继续关心、指导和支持。

附件（略）：

1. 本项目主要完成者简况一览表
2. 本项目主要完成者发表的外文学术成果
3. 本学科参与主办的国际学术会议
4. 应邀在国际学术会议报告
5. 本项目主要完成者开设双语课程情况
6. 厦门国际法高等研究院课程表
7. 法学院招收外国博士生情况
8. 法学院研究生出国留学情况一览表

9. 法学院代表队参加全国性、国际性专业赛事获奖一览表

10. 国际投资法研究领航法学院 15 强入选通知（中英文）

11. 联合国贸发会议邀请陈辉萍教授承担组织其研究项目"Mapping Project of IIAs"（中英文）

12. 法学院代表队队员就业、升学情况

附：第一次搏击[*]

这次作为指导老师赴维也纳参赛，与世界诸多名校代表队同场竞技，是我教学生涯中的难得机遇，也使我加深理解了日常平凡工作的意义。在赛场上，我方队员面对以英语为母语的强手，慷慨陈词，沉着答辩，或势均力敌，或略占上风。我们自己培养的法律人才在国际商事仲裁或诉讼中的风采已隐约可见。赛场内外，Chinese teams（中国队）的出色表现一时成为各国仲裁员的热门话题。初出茅庐，首次参加法律学子的"奥林匹克"，就让世界对中国的法学教育和法律学子刮目相看，我以为我队已不辱使命。

人生能有几回搏，队员们为了赛场的这一搏，6 个多月来付出了几多心血，个中甘苦辛酸，只有当事人才能真切感知。这一体验的重要启示是，在参与激烈的国际竞争时，无论是模拟或实战，我们不仅要有更强的自信心、更好的法律功底和更高的英语水平，还要有淡泊名利的平常心、处变不惊的心理素质以及众志成城的团队精神。由于日常工作繁忙，我们指导老师对大赛的投入和奉献还远远不够，深以为憾！我们法学院的整体法学教育水平和设施也还有待进一步提高。

不争的事实是，在大赛中名列前茅的代表队，都有一支学识渊博的法学师资队伍和一个信息丰富的法学图书馆作为后盾。因此，扎扎实实从基础工作做起，卧薪尝胆，假以时日，中国队的冠军梦一定能够实现。

---

[*] 原载《厦门日报》2002 年 4 月 15 日第 13 版。

第十二章
学会工作感悟

第一节　学术办会 知识报国
—— 中国国际经济法学会成立 30 周年述略[*]

　　1978 年以来,应改革开放之运,我国国际经济法学蓬勃兴起,迅速发展。1984
年,我国国际经济法学者在庐山创建全国性国际经济法学术团体"国际经济法研究
会"(即"中国国际经济法学会"的前身),迄今已届"而立"之年。作为学会活动的参
与者和见证人,回望历史,思绪万千,谨记其要以励志共勉。

一、庐山论道 共襄创会盛举

　　1984 年 5 月 8 日至 6 月 5 日,经武汉大学法律系、南开大学经济研究所、上海社
会科学院法学研究所、厦门大学法律系、安徽大学法律系、中山大学法律系和江西大
学法律系发起组织,在庐山举办了"国际经济法讲习班",来自全国 53 个单位的 90 多
名代表参加。这是全国国际经济法学者的第一次学术盛会。5 月 27 日下午,讲习班
学者、学员倡议和一致通过成立"国际经济法研究会"(简称"研究会"),并通过了《国
际经济法研究会章程》。经充分协商,选举产生了研究会理事会,武汉大学姚梅镇教
授当选为会长,李庆轩、夏焕瑶先生为副会长,陈安、董世忠、高尔森、盛愉教授为常
务理事,聘请周子亚教授为顾问,王国良老师担任干事长。[1] 1993 年 11 月 17 日,研
究会在珠海召开中国国际经济法学术研讨会暨研究会会员代表大会,选举产生第二
届理事会,并一致通过决议将研究会更名为"中国国际经济法学会"(简称"学会"),

　　* 原载《国际经济法学刊》第 21 卷第 4 期,北京大学出版社 2015 年版。
　　〔1〕 据国际经济法研究会编:《简报》第 1 期,1984 年 5 月 28 日。

厦门大学陈安教授当选为会长。

学会的宗旨是团结全国从事国际经济法教学研究和实务工作的人员，积极开展国际经济法学术活动，促进国际经济法学科的发展，为我国对外经济交往和社会主义现代化建设事业服务。

学会的业务主管单位原为国家教委/教育部(1994—2005)。2006 年 7 月 19 日，学会完成了在民政部的正式登记手续，成为社会团体法人（社证字第 4797 号），业务主管单位为司法部。

创业难。成立全国性国际经济法学术团体，是姚梅镇、周子亚、陈安和董世忠教授等老一辈国际经济法学者对我国国际经济法学创建和发展的历史性贡献，也是世界范围国际经济法学界的一大创举。

二、神州万里 构建学术平台

创会以来，学会逐渐形成"以文会友，以友辅仁，知识报国，兼济天下"的共识。学会的主要活动包括举办和参与国内外学术研讨会、创办《国际经济法学刊》及创建"中国国际经济法学会"网站。三者相辅相成，共同目标是构建国际经济法学术交流平台，促进我国国际经济法教学研究的发展及服务于我国改革开放事业。

（一）举办和参与国内外学术研讨会

举办全国性国际经济法学术研讨会，是研究会/学会持之以恒的重要学术活动。1987、1989、1992、1993 年，研究会先后在武汉、大连、厦门和珠海举办国际经济法学术研讨会。1994—2014 年，学会分别在重庆、上海、昆明、杭州、深圳、海口、北京、上海、大连、兰州、厦门、长沙、黄山、湛江、天津、杭州、南京、厦门、上海、西安和武汉召开国际经济法学术研讨会。在历届研讨会上，对外经贸部/商务部条约法律司领导均应邀莅临报告我国国际经济交往的最新实践和面临的重要法律问题。来自全国高等院校和科研机构的国际经济法学者及来自涉外经贸部门管理和实务工作者聚集一堂，相互交流国际经济法学术研究成果和讨论我国国际经济法领域的重要理论和实践问题。以文会友，百家争鸣，蔚为风气。

近年来，学会与商务部条约法律司联合主办国际经济法专题研讨会，成为政界与学界、实务界沟通、互动和合作的重要平台。2007—2013 年，"国际投资法专题研讨会"连续在厦门召开；2010—2014 年，"WTO 专题研讨会"连续在南京、厦门、上海、西安和武汉召开，逐渐形成其鲜明特征：一是"三结合"的参与者。为了共同的"知识报国"目标，官员、学者、律师积极参与，相互给力，互补共赢。二是研讨"当下"的课题。重点关注和研讨最新国际投资、贸易案例及国际投资条约、WTO 体制的最新发展。三是取得"实践性"研讨成果。由"三结合"的参与者共同探讨"当下"的课题,集思广益,建言献策,为我国相关国际实践提供了重要的对策性建议。

学会与联合国国际贸易和发展会议(UNCTAD)、经济合作开发组织(OECD)、世界贸易组织(WTO)、多边投资担保机构(MIGA)、解决投资争端国际中心(ICSID)等国际组织长期保持较密切的学术联系,应邀参加国际组织举办的国际学术研讨会,包括 UNCTAD、OECD、ICSID 联合主办的第一、二届国际投资条约研讨会(2005,2010)等,并作大会报告。在国际学术交流方面,学会与韩国国际经济法学界之间的交流尤为突出。早在 1988 年,陈安教授、董世忠教授和王贵国教授曾应邀访问韩国,与韩国同行探讨中韩经济交流的法律问题。这在当时的政治环境下殊为不易。2004 年,韩国国际经济法学会会长朴鲁馨教授应邀到厦门参加国际经济法学术研讨会,揭开了两国学会交流的历史新页。2005、2008、2010、2011、2013 年,两国学会轮流在韩国首尔和中国天津、厦门联合举办五届国际学术研讨会,重点研讨中韩贸易关系,特别是中韩自由贸易区的法律与实践问题等,取得了重要的学术交流成果。

(二)创办《国际经济法学刊》

学会和厦门大学国际经济法研究所联合主办的《国际经济法学刊》(原名《国际经济法论丛》,简称《学刊》)创办于 1998 年,由陈安教授担任主编。《学刊》先后由法律出版社和北京大学出版社编辑出版,初期每年一卷一册,自 2005 年起每年一卷四期。迄今,已精心编辑出版 21 卷。

《学刊》创办十六年来,始终践行学会宗旨,立足我国改革开放与建立社会主义市场经济体制的实践,借鉴国外先进立法经验和最新研究成果,深入研究国际经济关系各领域的重要法律问题,积极开展国内外学术交流,推动我国国际经济法教学研究的发展,并为我国国际经济法实践提供法理依据或实务参考。春风化雨,润物无声。《学刊》每卷每期每篇佳作,均凝聚着作者、编者的心血和智慧。在海内外学界同仁和各界人士的热情关心、倾心支持和通力合作下,《学刊》逐渐赢得学术声誉,跻身学术之林,成为国际经济法领域学术交流互动的重要平台。2005 年,经南京大学中国社会科学研究评价中心主持的"中文社会科学引文索引数据库"(CSSCI)指导委员会组织专家遴选,《学刊》成为 CSSCI 首批收录的来源集刊之一(法学类共 5种),并在之后两年一度的历次 CSSCI 遴选中持续入选。这是学术界对《学刊》学术成就的连续认同,更是国际经济法学界广大同仁长期不懈努力的成果。

(三)创建"中国国际经济法学会"网站

2008 年以来,学会创建和维护"中国国际经济法学会"网站(http://www.csiel.

org），设"学会概况""组织机构""会议信息""资料下载"和"中国之声"等栏目，为我国国际经济法学界提供了重要的信息交流平台，也促进了我国国际经济法研究成果在海内外的传播。

三、自强不息 传承优良传统

30年来，学会广大同仁努力践行学会宗旨，逐渐形成了学会的优良传统，亟须认真总结，发扬光大。

（一）"专注学术，知识报国"的传统

学会创会会长姚梅镇教授和连选连任长期担任学会会长的陈安教授等前辈学者，均为海内外享有学术盛誉的国际经济法学家，一向严谨治学，学术办会，奠定了学会"专注学术，知识报国"传统的基石。学会以"学术"为第一要务，以构建学术交流平台为工作重心。学会广大同仁身体力行，兢兢业业，承担国际经济法领域的教学研究工作，为创建和发展中国特色的国际经济法学作出了积极贡献。

长期以来，学会与商务部条约法律司等政府主管部门建立了密切的联系，积极研究我国面临的重要国际经济法问题，力争成为国际经济法领域的民间智库。事实上，"专注学术，知识报国"已然成为学会广大同仁的自觉行动和学会的优良传统。学会诸多学者已担当国际经济法专家重任。陈安、余劲松、王传丽教授是我国政府连续遴选向ICSID指派的仲裁员/调解员，张月姣教授是WTO上诉机构成员，董世忠、张玉卿、朱榄叶、曾令良、韩立余教授等是我国政府遴选向WTO推荐的专家组指示名单成员。学会广大同仁在各自岗位上，通过承担商务部、外交部研究课题和"挂职"等多种形式，深度参与我国国际经济法实践问题的研究，实现"知识报国"之志。

（二）"五湖四海，团结奋斗"的传统

学会作为全国性国际经济法领域的学术团体，其生命力首先在于学界、政界和实务界的普遍关心、认同、参与和奉献。"五湖四海"的涵义首先是，学会与各界各方的团结一心和相互支持。在学会组织的各项学术活动中，均得到商务部和各级政府部门的亲切关心、悉心指导和鼎力支持，亦得到各高等院校、研究机构及实务部门的密切合作和全力协助。仅以学术研讨会为例，有25任东道主倾心倾力的奉献，[1]才

---

〔1〕 25任东道主依次为武汉大学（1987）、大连海事学院（1989）、厦门大学和厦门市国际经济贸易学会（1992）、广东省对外经济贸易委员会（1993）、西南政法学院和重庆市对外经济贸易委员会（1994）、上海法学会、复旦大学、上海对外贸易学院、华东政法学院和上海大学（1995）、云南大学（1996）、杭州大学（1997）、深圳大学法学院和深圳市贸易服务中心（1998）、海南大学（1999）、对外经济贸易大学和中国国际经济贸易仲裁委员会（2000）、复旦大学（2001）、大连海事大学（2002）、甘肃政法学院（2003）、厦门大学（2004）、湖南师范大学（2005）、安徽财经大学（2006）、中国政法大学和广东省律师协会（2007）、南开大学（2008）、浙江工商大学（2009）、南京大学（2010）、厦门大学（2011）、华东政法大学（2012）、西安交通大学（2013）和武汉大学（2014）。

有学会 25 次全国性国际经济法学术研讨会的成功举行！

"五湖四海"的进一步涵义是，学会是全国国际经济法学界和实务界广大同仁的共同事业，志同道合，同舟共济，无高下之分，更无门户之见。学会是民间社会团体，白手起家，民主持家。学会全体会员是学会的主体，理事会全体成员是学会的"义工"，秘书处是学会全体会员的服务机构。"众人拾柴火焰高"。学会在创建和发展过程中形成的"五湖四海，团结奋斗"的优良传统弥足珍贵，是学会的活力所在和精神源泉。

（三）"坚信法治，依法维权"的传统

学会作为全国性国际经济法领域的学术团体，具有独立法律人格，依法享有权利和承担义务。学会 1999—2006 年依法申请登记之路及 2013 年以来依法维权之诉从一个侧面反映了我国的国情和法治发展现状。虽历经坎坷，学会秉持法治信念，永葆"草根"本色，依法维护学会合法权益，为我国法治目标的实现而孜孜以求，不懈奋斗。学会当为最富有"书生气"的全国性法学社团之一。"坚信法治，依法维权"不仅是学会的优良传统，也是维护学会生存和发展的基本保障，更是学会对我国法治建设的应有贡献。

在学会成立 30 周年之际，饮水思源，我们对我国国际经济法学科的奠基人、学会的创建人和各位先贤、前辈学者筚路蓝缕，艰苦创业充满敬意和感恩！满怀感恩的心，我们感谢长期关心、指导和支持学会工作的商务部条约法律司和历任领导，特别是长期亲自参与学会工作，作出卓越奉献的张月姣司长、张玉卿司长、李玲司长和李成钢司长、杨国华副司长！我们感谢长期关心、支持和协助学会工作的全国各高等院校、研究机构及实务部门，特别是为学会学术活动作出重要贡献的历任东道主！我们感谢长期以各种方式关注、关心、支持和帮助学会工作的海内外相关机构和各界人士！由于大家的共同努力，成就了学会的今天，必将成就学会更美好的明天！

第二节　姚梅镇老师三会之缘[*]

武汉、庐山、厦门，有幸与姚梅镇老师有三次千里相会之缘，悠悠往事历久弥新。

武　汉

初访姚老师是在武汉大学。

1982年2月，我考入厦门大学法律系国际法专业硕士研究生，属81级。素仰武汉大学国际法学术渊源深远，师资实力雄厚，1983年春季学期，我校81、82级国际法专业研究生五位同学一起赴武汉大学法律系"留学"，主修李双元老师的"国际私法"、梁西老师的"国际组织法"和美国琼斯教授的"国际商法"（英文）等研究生课程。记得李老师讲课生动激昂，声如洪钟；梁老师则温文尔雅，娓娓道来。那时梁老师刚从北京大学调回母校，天天晨练，意气风发，授课教材就是其大作《国际组织法》的第一稿。两位老师博学敬业、传道授业解惑，令我们视野顿开，受益匪浅。琼斯教授的授课则让我们初尝"国际化"的教学氛围。

我们还慕名登门拜访了国际法大家韩德培老师、姚梅镇老师和黄炳坤老师，请教学问之道。各位老师热情欢迎我等"不速之客"，悉心传授治学经验，还嘘寒问暖，亲切招待喝茶吃糖。之前，我们拜读了姚老师的系列国际经济法论文和译文，对姚老师做学问的旁征博引、论证缜密印象殊深。文如其人。谈及如何治学，姚老师谦逊地说，由于种种原因，岁月蹉跎，近年才有重新做学问的环境；个人经验是尽可能广泛收集中外相关专业文献资料，及时记录所学所思，日积月累，水到渠成。姚老师还特别称羡我们赶上了改革开放的新时代，是学习和研究国际经济法的最好时机，嘱咐我们好好珍惜，多下功夫。姚老师平易近人，一席话言简意赅，语重心长。我们深切感受到姚老师虚怀若谷、宁静致远的大家风范。

庐　山

时隔一年，上庐山又见姚老师。

1984年5月8日至6月5日，我在庐山参加了"首届国际经济法讲习班"。讲习班的发起单位是武汉大学法律系、南开大学经济研究所、上海社会科学院法学研究

---

[*]　原载余劲松、许前飞主编：《姚梅镇先生百年诞辰纪念文集》，武汉大学出版社2014年版。

所、厦门大学法律系、安徽大学法律系、中山大学法律系和江西大学法律系。90多位学员来自全国53个单位，不经意间参与了我国国际经济法学界的首届学术盛会，也见证了我国国际经济法学术团体的诞生。

在庐山课堂上，我们领略了我国早期国际经济法学者周子亚、姚梅镇、陈安、董世忠、高尔森、朱学山、盛愉、江振良、卢绳祖、方之寅等老师的风采和学识。授课内容涵盖国际经济法理论、国际投资法、国际贸易法、国际税法和国际经济争端的解决等，大致构建了我国国际经济法学的基本框架。5月20日、22—24日和25—28日，姚老师讲授"国际经济法概论""国际投资的法律保护"和"外资立法的比较研究"等三门课程，涉及国际经济法特别是国际投资法的基本理论和主要内容。姚老师精神矍铄，讲课严谨认真，内容丰富翔实，课后还提供亲自编撰的《国际经济法的理论与实践》（武汉大学国际法研究所，1984年），作为学员进一步学习的参考资料。当时姚老师已年近古稀，9天连讲8堂课，合计24课时，是所有任课教师中承担任务最繁重者。

5月27日下午，讲习班学者、学员倡议和一致通过成立"国际经济法研究会"（简称"研究会"，即中国国际经济法学会的前身），并通过了《国际经济法研究会章程》。经充分协商，选举产生了研究会理事会。当晚，在庐山宾馆召开理事会第一次全体会议，选举姚老师为会长，李庆轩、夏焕瑶老师为副会长，陈安、董世忠、高尔森、盛愉老师为常务理事，聘请周子亚老师为顾问，王国良老师担任干事长。成立全国性国际经济法学术团体，是姚老师等老一辈国际经济法学者对我国国际经济法学创建和发展的历史性贡献，也是世界范围国际经济法学界的一大创举。事实上，尽管欧美国家国际经济法学研究早于我国，当时均尚未成立全国性国际经济法学术团体。

创业难。1984年至1992年，时值研究会创建初期，姚老师肩负创会会长重任，筚路蓝缕，以身作则，奠定了"学术办会"传统的根基。30年来，中国国际经济法学会先后在姚老师、陈安老师、董世忠老师和吴焕宁老师等的领导下，团结全国高校、科研机构广大国际经济法学者，积极开展国际经济法领域的教学、研究和交流，逐渐形成"以文会友，以友辅仁，知识报国，兼济天下"的共识，为促进我国国际经济法学的发展作出了重要贡献。同时，学会与商务部条约法律司等政府主管部门建立了密切的联系，积极研究我国面临的重要国际经济法问题，建言献策，力争成为国际经济法领域的民间智库。当前，我国国际经济法学成为法学各分支学科中最富有朝气的学科之一，学会亦成为最富有"书生气"的全国性学术团体之一。饮水思源，我们对我国国际经济法学科的奠基人、学会的创建人和各位前辈学者充满敬意和感恩！

厦　　门

庐山惜别六年之后，在家乡母校喜迎姚老师。

1984年12月，我毕业留校任教；1987年2月，荣幸成为我校第一位国际经济法专业博士生，师从陈安老师。1990年2月，我完成了学位论文《中外合资企业法律问题研究》，呈送韩德培老师和姚老师评阅。近日经批准，我从校档案馆查到姚老师当年的亲笔评语。姚老师充分肯定论文的选题意义、研究主题、方法及特点，同时也指出不足及可商榷之处。历时24年，得见姚老师精心谋篇、力透纸背的苍劲字迹和篆体印章，十分感慨和赞叹姚老师治学做事的严谨认真、一丝不苟！

1990年4月10日，在我校举行了首届法学博士学位论文答辩会，韩德培老师和姚老师应邀亲临主持。韩老师笑容可掬，举重若轻，建议每位答辩委员会成员只提一个问题，营造了温馨的评审切磋气氛，亦彰显仁厚长者风范。两位老师当时年逾古稀，千里迢迢专程来厦，令人感动。我深切体会两位老师对后学的关爱和厚望，更深切感受两位老师对创建中的我校国际法学科的倾心关怀和鼎力支持。

姚老师淡泊明志，"面壁坐冷"，物我两忘，数十年如一日。答辩会之后，我陪同参访，才感知姚老师的幽默风趣和洞察力。姚老师笑谈厦门之行创下的多项"第一次"记录，连连赞赏中山路骑楼的特色、沿街店铺的精致和鹭岛的海阔天空。翌日，姚老师心系武汉大学的教学工作，匆匆返校。原以为总还有机会再尽地主之谊，竟成永远之憾！

1991年初，我将学位论文修订成书稿《中外合资企业法律的理论与实务》，敬请姚老师作序。姚老师欣然应允，序文长达千余言，详细评析书稿的内容特点、研究方法及意义，字里行间洋溢对后学的关爱提携和殷殷期待之情。尤其令我感动的是，姚老师胸怀五湖四海，对学生不问门户出身，一视同仁，对外校学生显然更为优待。姚老师对我学习成果的肯定，实际上也蕴含着对广大国际经济法初学者的关怀、鼓励和期盼。

感　　悟

八年之间，有缘与姚老师三次相会，如沐春风，感悟万千。

姚老师最可贵的是爱国精神。姚老师长期蒙冤，历经磨难，仍始终怀有"先天下之忧而忧，后天下之乐而乐"的传统知识分子情怀，始终怀有"天下兴亡，匹夫有责"的拳拳报国之心。"文革"后重返教职以来，姚老师以花甲古稀之年，惜时如金，殚精竭虑，教书笔耕不辍，勉力创建研究会，报效国家和人民，竟至积劳成疾，鞠躬尽瘁。

姚老师最可贵的是学术精神。姚老师潜心学术，心无旁骛，不求名利。在国际经济法领域的开拓性教学研究中，姚老师始终站在我国和发展中国家立场，紧密联系实际，坚持和发扬"扬弃"精神，独立思考，严谨治学，维护和发展普遍认同的国际经济法原则和规范，创建和发展中国特色的国际经济法学，充分体现了我国老一辈知识分子"自尊、自信、自强"的学术风骨。

姚老师最可贵的是育人精神。姚老师献身教育，甘为园丁，敬业勤业乐业凡53年，桃李满天下。姚老师培养的诸多毕业生在各自岗位上为国家和人民效力，业绩斐然。其中，姚老师培养的武汉大学首届国际经济法专业博士生余劲松、王传丽和许前飞分别成为著名的学术领军人物和"学者型"司法领导。

初访姚老师至今已31年，平淡是真，上善若水，时常感念师德师恩师情！我亲聆姚老师教诲授课，亲蒙姚老师栽培勉励，长期从事国际经济法教学研究，又长期参与中国国际经济法学会工作，何其有缘幸运！寸草春晖，唯有学习和传承姚老师的高尚精神和品格，兢兢业业，努力为我国国际经济法学事业的发展作出应有的一份奉献。

第三节　《中国特色话语：陈安论国际经济法学》发布会感言[*]

尊敬的各位领导，各位学界同行，各位朋友：

今天的新书发布会气氛非常热烈。首先，我谨代表中国国际经济法学会向"《中国特色话语：陈安论国际经济法学》发布会"的隆重召开表示热烈祝贺！向商务部、外交部等政府部门、学界和媒体代表的关心、关注和支持表示衷心的感谢！陈安教授的新书出版，是中国国际经济法学界的学术盛事，更是中国法学界、中国知识分子向改革开放40周年的隆重献礼！

刚才各位发言者已从各个方面谈了陈安老师的不凡业绩、治学理念和家国情怀，我想在这里谈两点感想。

第一，中国国际经济法学与改革开放紧密联系。

如所周知，中国国际经济法学是适应改革开放新形势的需要而产生和发展起来的。随着我国实行改革开放政策，20世纪70年代末，我国最早一批国际经济法学者深切感受到改革开放需要研究国际经济法，当时陈安老师，武汉大学姚梅镇老师等发表了最早一批国际经济法的著述。1984年5月8日至6月5日，在庐山举办的"第一期国际经济法讲习班"上，陈安老师、姚梅镇老师、上海社会科学院周子亚老师、安徽大学朱学山老师、复旦大学董世忠老师、南开大学高尔森老师和中国社会科学院盛愉老师等，分别讲授国际经济法的基本原理和重要专题。当时王传丽老师和我同是学员。5月27日，来自全国53个单位的90多位讲习班代表发起创立了国际经济法研究会（即中国国际经济法学会的前身），选举姚梅镇老师为会长，陈安老师、董世忠老师、高尔森老师和盛愉老师为常务理事，聘请周子亚老师为顾问。自1993年起，陈安老师连选连任中国国际经济法学会会长。34年来，学会团结全国学界和实务界同仁，积极开展国际经济法领域的国内外学术交流，逐渐形成和确立了"以文会友，以友辅仁，知识报国，兼济天下"的学会宗旨和共识。回想起来，学会紧密联系改革开放实际，主要做了三项工作：

一是组织召开学术会议。迄今我们开了29届"中国国际经济法学术研讨会"，从1993年开始，是作为学会年会召开。我们还与商务部条约法律司从2007年开始联合主办"国际投资法专题研讨会"，迄今召开12届；从2010年开始，联合主办"世界贸

---

[*] 摘自"改革开放四十周年献礼——《中国特色话语：陈安论国际经济法学》发布会实录"，原载《国际经济法学刊》2019年第2期。

易组织法专题研讨会",迄今召开 9 届,都是"一年一度"的制度性安排。

二是创办了《国际经济法学刊》,1998 年创刊(集刊),陈安老师担任主编,厦门大学国际经济法研究所负责编辑部工作,20 年间编辑出版 57 期。2017 年经国家新闻出版广电总局批准,《国际经济法学刊》成为国家级正式期刊,2018 年创刊"再出发",有一个质的飞跃。

三是服务国家改革开放实践,承担商务部、外交部的咨询研究任务和参与国际经济法律实践。如张月姣教授,出任世界贸易组织(WTO)上诉机构成员,本月 18 日获"改革先锋"殊荣;董世忠、张玉卿、朱榄叶、曾令良、韩立余教授等是我国政府遴选向 WTO 推荐的专家组成员。还有 9 位学会同仁受国家或国际组织委派,成为世界银行集团"解决投资争端国际中心"(ICSID)的仲裁员和调解员。陈安教授是我国政府连续委派的 ICSID 仲裁员。张月姣教授是现任 ICSID 仲裁员,由行政理事会指派。还有陈治东、余劲松、王传丽、张玉卿、单文华、石静霞教授和我都是我国政府先后委派的 ICSID 仲裁员或调解员。

第二点感想是,中国国际经济法学需要有中国特色。

新书是陈安老师积四十年之功的呕心沥血之作。从作者的治学立场、理念、追求及对中国特色国际经济法学的杰出贡献,我们看到了老一辈知识分子的命运是如何与国家的命运紧密相连,更感受到老一辈知识分子"知识报国,兼济天下"的历史责任感、宽广襟怀、坚定的政治立场和鲜明的价值取向。

当前,中国特色社会主义进入了新时代,中国特色国际经济法学也进入了新时代。所谓中国特色国际经济法学,我理解,包括陈安老师这部新书的特色,最重要的是以马克思主义为指导思想,站在中国和广大发展中国家的立场,坚持建立国际经济新秩序的目标,坚定维护和发展国际社会普遍认同的经济主权、公平互利和合作发展三大国际经济法基本原则。这是最基本的中国特色,是我们与西方国际经济法学截然不同的,或者凸显中国特色的方面。我国国际经济法学界老一辈学者曾亲身经历过"三座大山"压迫下的旧社会,他们的沧桑历练、关注焦点、观察视角、敏感程度及精神境界很值得中青年学者借鉴和学习。我们要学习陈安老师坚持马克思主义指导地位,坚持中国和发展中国家的立场,坚持国际经济法基本原则的精神。这个"接力棒"我们一定要接好,要一代一代传承下来。陈安老师刚刚谈了他的治学历程,是很坎坷的。到了我们这一代,我自称是"农民工学者"或"知识青年学者",也经历了一些曲折。适逢更好的时代、更好的机会,是像石静霞、单文华教授这一代。他们有机会分别获得武汉大学、厦门大学的法学博士学位,又分别赴美国和英国留学,获得耶鲁大学、剑桥大学法学博士学位。他们有这么好的机遇,希望更注重学习老一辈知识分子,继承和发展"中国特色话语",紧密联系中国和国际实践,在汲取国际社会长期积淀的国际经济法学精华的同时,开拓创新,丰富和革新国际经济法学的"国际话语体系"。

这是我的两点感想。我想,感恩、感动和传承是我们这次会议的主题词,也表达了我们此时此刻的心情。当下,国际经济法处于迅速发展之中。我国改革开放和推动构建人类命运共同体的伟大实践,为我国国际经济法学界提供了知识报国的最佳时代背景和学术环境。我们感恩这个伟大的时代,改革开放的新时代,给我们这么多的发展机遇,给我们这么多的幸福感。对知识分子来说,有这么好的学术环境,中国特色法学、中国特色国际经济法学迎来了蓬勃发展的春天。我们感动,面对陈安老师这部新书,我们感动于老一辈知识分子的敬业奉献精神！我注意到,吴志攀教授在新书序言中,是在描述老一辈知识分子共同的敬业奉献精神。刚刚陈安老师也谈到他的治学历程,自言"半生蹉跎,韶华虚掷"。我并不这样认为,他一直都在努力,我感动于他的"板凳甘坐七十年"。在改革开放之前,他也一直在治学,包括钻研马克思主义,还有世界历史。老一辈知识分子的这种敬业奉献精神,很值得我们学习和传承,这也正是我们这次新书发布会重大而深远的意义。我们要把这种精神传承下来,发扬光大,为促进国际经济法理论和实践的发展,为推动构建人类命运共同体做出积极的贡献。

我就谈到这里,谢谢大家！

第四节　学会平台致辞

一、中国国际经济法学会 2018 年年会致辞 *

尊敬的各位领导、嘉宾,各位国际经济法学界同仁:

党的十九大和改革开放四十周年的东风浩荡,在中国政法大学同仁和中国国际经济法学会的共同努力下,"2018 年中国国际经济法学术研讨会"在北京隆重召开了! 我谨代表中国国际经济法学会对会议的召开表示热烈的祝贺! 对来自全国各地的学界和实务界同仁表示热烈的欢迎,感谢各位的积极参与和奉献! 感谢商务部条法司、外交部条法司长期以来对本会的亲切关心和鼎力支持!

回顾学会历史,这是第二次在北京开年会。第一次是 2000 年,由对外经济贸易大学和中国国际经济贸易仲裁委员会联合主办。1984 年以来,学会在大江南北开年会,在北京开年会尤为难得。中国政法大学对学会的发展做出了重大贡献。这是中国政法大学第二次举办学会年会。第一次是在 2007 年,在广东湛江与广东省律师协会联合主办年会。学会的发展全靠全国学界和实务界同仁的共同努力,同时得到了我国政府相关部门,特别是商务部条法司和外交部条法司的指导和支持。学会力争成为我国国际经济法领域的民间智库,一直在朝这个目标努力奋斗。

当前,中国特色社会主义进入了新时代,中国特色国际经济法学也进入了新时代。在此,和各位同行分享三点感想,和大家共勉。

第一,要坚定中国特色国际经济法学的方向、立场和原则。所谓中国特色国际经济法学,就是要坚持马克思主义,坚持中国和广大发展中国家的立场,坚持经济主权、公平互利、合作发展的国际经济法基本原则。要汲取世界各国国际经济法学的精华,创新发展,为国家和国际社会的共同发展做出我们的学术贡献。在创建和发展中国特色国际经济法学需要注意处理的关系包括:一是"中国特色"与"国际话语体系"之间的关系,不能为了追求"中国特色"而自说自话,忽略了"国际话语体系";二是"国家利益"与"人类命运共同体利益"之间的关系,要认识国家利益的重要性,但不能奉行"国家利益至上"的主张,而是要践行"义利兼顾,以义为先",严格区别于美国现政府的"美国优先"政策。

---

* 2018 年 11 月 16—18 日,中国国际经济法学会年会暨学术研讨会在北京召开,主题为"'一带一路'法治建设与国际经济法的新发展",东道主为中国政法大学。

第二，"一带一路"国际合作是中国特色国际经济法的伟大实践。时代给了中国国际经济法学人实现"知识报国"学术抱负的机遇。自2013年习近平主席提出"一带一路"倡议以来，学会持续重视和研讨这一时代主题。学会2013年"西安年会"大会专题报告就涉及"丝绸之路经济带"议题。之后三届年会主题不断深化对"一带一路"的认识，不断凸显中国特色国际经济法理论和实践在"一带一路"国际合作的重要作用。我们在2015年"昆明年会"提出的大会主题是"'一带一路'战略背景下的中国国际经济法的新发展"，2017年"广州年会"的大会主题是"'一带一路'法律框架的构建与国际经济法的新发展"，今年的大会主题是"'一带一路'法治建设与国际经济法的新发展"。应当进一步指出，"一带一路"是我国推动构建人类命运共同体和构建新型国际关系的伟大实践。"一带一路"给我国学界提出了重大的理论课题。"一带一路"法治建设当是中国国际经济法学人在今后一段时期甚至长期需要研究的重大课题。

第三，要发扬学会优良传统，不忘初心，知识报国。刚才黄进校长的讲话全面、专业而深刻，富有指导意义，也回顾了学会的历史。武汉大学是国际法领域的领军大学。1990年，国际法大家武汉大学韩德培教授、姚梅镇教授曾亲临厦门大学指导国际法学科建设和主持博士生论文答辩，历历在目，永志不忘。学会创会会长姚梅镇教授、连选连任长期担任学会会长的陈安教授、副会长董世忠教授和吴焕宁教授等，均为享誉海内外的国际经济法学家，一向严谨治学，学术办会，奠定了学会"专注学术，知识报国"传统的基石，也给我们树立了优秀的榜样。在本届年会上，吴焕宁老师将作大会主题报告。董世忠老师心系学会，希望我向学会同仁转达他的问候和祝愿，祝本届年会顺利举办，学会同仁学术更上层楼。陈安老师迄今笔耕不辍，著书立说，向海内外传播中国学术强音。本届年会的纸质资料中有一份陈老师即将出版的大作《中国特色话语——陈安论国际经济法学》简介，新书发布会将于近期举办。中国特色国际经济法学的创建和发展需要一代又一代国际经济法学人坚定立场，勇于担当，扎实治学，借助学会和各种学术平台加强交流，相互促进，共襄盛举。

谨此预祝在各位共同努力下，本届年会取得圆满成功！

二、第十二届国际投资法专题研讨会致辞[*]

尊敬的各位领导、专家，各位国际经济法学界同仁，女士们，先生们：

在商务部条约法律司、中国国际经济法学会、厦门大学国际经济法研究所、国际

---

[*] 2018年7月30日，第十二届国际投资法专题研讨会在厦门召开，东道主为厦门大学。

投资争议解决研究中心、昊理文律师事务所同仁的共同努力下，"第十二届国际投资法专题研讨会"今天隆重召开了，我谨代表中国国际经济法学会对会议的召开表示热烈的祝贺！向来自各地的嘉宾和专家学者，特别是来自香港特区的政府官员和法律专家表示热烈欢迎！香港特区同行参与国际实践的经验丰富，希望将来继续参与交流。

国际投资法专题研讨会是中国国际经济法学会一年一度的重要学术活动。1984 年，学会成立于庐山国际经济法讲习班。34 年来，学会的主要工作是创建国际经济法领域的交流平台。经过长期的发展，逐渐形成"以文会友，以友辅仁；知识报国，兼济天下"的宗旨，已然成为中国广大国际经济法学者的共识，且付诸实践。学会一直努力争取成为我国国际经济法领域的民间智库。

第一届国际投资法专题研讨会创办于 2007 年，是国际投资贸易洽谈会（即厦门98 投洽会）的论坛之一，定位为国际投资法领域的专家会议，是我国国际投资法专家的重要交流平台。历经十二年，已形成政、产、学三结合的优良传统，需要继续共同珍惜，共同建设。适应改革开放新形势的需要，厦门不断发展，承担的使命和任务日趋重要，从经济特区、自由贸易试验区、"一带一路"节点城市到"金砖国家领导人峰会"举办城市，也义不容辞地成为国际投资法专题研讨会的长期东道主。

如所周知，国际投资法是近年来国际经济法的重点和热点研究领域。"投资者—国家间争端解决机制"（ISDS）更是该研究领域的重中之重。本次会议主题是ISDS 的改革问题。当前，我国面临与此密切相关的两个问题：一是 ISDS 改革的中国方案；二是"一带一路"国际合作的争端解决机制。本月 2—3 日，外交部和中国法学会在北京主办的"'一带一路'法治合作国际论坛"，对"一带一路"争端解决机制也作了专题研讨。在我国参与国际经济规则制定和实施"一带一路"法治合作的背景下，召开本次研讨会，具有重要的现实意义。

ISDS 是双边投资条约（BITs）的核心内容，也是国际社会创建"解决投资争端国际中心"（ICSID）的"初心"。ISDS 改革的动因是投资者保护与东道国管制权力的矛盾冲突。当前学界的一般研究路径是，分析面临的问题——比较不同的改革方案——提出中国立场和中国方案。我以为，在 ISDS 的改革问题研究中，表面上是实务性、技术性的问题，仍需要历史的考察和理论的探讨，特别是需要重视联系问题的产生原因、实质及时代背景；在探讨具体条款、具体制度的改革时，结合探讨结构性、体制性、全局性的改革问题。这样，才可望有的放矢，深化研究，提出符合各国共同利益、为国际社会普遍认同的改革建议。

希望各位在本次会议上，充分利用"政、产、学三结合"平台，加强互动交流。希望各位进一步深化专题研究，贡献学术成果。令人振奋的喜讯是，学会《国际经济法学刊》近日获准成为正式期刊，可发表会议的研究成果。

谨此预祝本次研讨会取得圆满成功！

祝与会各位同仁阖家幸福安康，事业发达！

厦门是个喜欢"泡功夫茶"的城市，希望各位在厦门轻松愉快！

三、第三届 WTO 法专题研讨会致辞 *

尊敬的各位来宾，各位国际经济法学界同仁，女士们，先生们：

在商务部条法司、中国国际经济法学会和华东政法大学同仁的共同努力下，"第三届 WTO 法专题研讨会"今天在上海隆重召开了。一年一度，在短期内组织会议，对会议组织者、参与者都是考验。会议组织者高效工作，各位专家积极配合，在百忙中专心研究，及时准备报告和评论，殊为不易。我谨代表中国国际经济法学会对会议的召开表示热烈的祝贺！对精心筹备和参加本次会议的各位同仁表示由衷敬意和感谢！

迄今，我国"入世"已有 11 周年，面临许多新问题新挑战。在实务层面，涉华 WTO 案例逐渐增多，需要及时研究，更需要注重培养精通 WTO 法的专门人才。

2010 年，南京会议创办的"WTO 法专题研讨会"经历 2011 年厦门会议的沿袭，现已是第三届，已然成为我国制度化的理论紧密联系实践的 WTO 专家会议，形成了三个重要的特征：

一是"三结合"的参会者。为了共同的目标，官员、律师、学者"三结合"出席，相互给力，互补性很强。在本次会议六位报告人中，张玉卿前司长和冯雪薇律师具有长期在我国商务部和 WTO 工作的丰富经验，三位参与办理涉华 WTO 案件的专职律师，还有一位长期研究 WTO 法的教授。在评议人中，有两位政府官员，18 位教授。在本次会议参会者中，我国政府选派的 WTO 专家组成员有八位，充分反映了与会专家的高级别。这一典型的官产学"三结合"的 WTO 法高端论坛，来之不易！

二是研讨"当下"的问题。会议研讨重点在"当下"特别是本年度的重要问题和 WTO 法的具体实践问题。议题集中，法律技术性强。本次会议的主要议题是关注今年涉华 WTO 案例和 WTO 体制的最新发展。

三是产出"实践性"的成果。"三结合"的参会者共同探讨"当下"的问题，集思广

---

* 2012 年 11 月 2 日，第三届 WTO 法专题研讨会在上海召开，东道主为华东政法大学。

益,相辅相成。在会议筹备、进行和后续研究中,政府主管部门官员主导和组织,运筹帷幄,把握全局和方向;实务界专家报告最新案例,与学界专家讨论重要法律问题,拓宽和深化办案思路;学界专家有机会第一时间接触最新实践和第一手资讯,很有利于理论联系实际、有的放矢地开展 WTO 法专题研究。

从议程可以看出,本次会议研讨的主题紧密联系实际,切合时需,具有重要的理论和现实意义。本人笃信,各位同仁在本次会议的研究与交流成果,必将对我国政府部门的 WTO 法实践和有关决策有所促进,有所裨益!

谨此预祝本次研讨会取得圆满成功!

祝与会各位同仁身体健康,家庭幸福,事业顺利!

四、Speech at the 5ᵗʰ Session of Korea-China Symposium(第五届中韩学术研讨会致辞)*

Good morning, distinguished guests, dear colleagues and students, ladies and gentlemen,

Warm Congratulations for the opening of the 2013 international symposium on China-Korea FTA!

At this great moment, on behalf of Chinese Society of International Economic Law (CSIEL), I like to extend my heartfelt thanks to all the Korean colleagues and friends of Korea Society of International Economic Law, for your kind invitation and great efforts and contributions!

As we all know, the exchange of China and Korea in every aspect has a very long history. As for the International Economic Law circle, 25 years ago happens the first contact. In 1988, former president and vice president of CSIEL, Professor Chen An and Professor Dong Shizhong visited Korea. They were invited by Seoul National University and Federation of Industries of Korea to give lectures at the Seminar on Far-East Asia Economic Exchange. The first contact is not easy considering the politic relation between China and Korea at the period of time.

In 2004, Professor Nohyoung Park, former president of International Economic Law Association of Korea attended the International Conference on International E-

---

* 2013 年 7 月 17 日,由中国国际经济法学会和韩国国际经济法学会联合主办的第五届中韩学术研讨会在韩国首尔召开,主题为"中韩自由贸易协定:前景展望与法理"(Korea-China FTA: Prospects and Jurisprudence)。

conomic Law and China in Transition held in Xiamen, opening the first page of exchanges between our two societies.

In 2005, we had first joint conference held by two societies in Seoul, the topic was "China-Korea Trade Relations in WTO First 10 Years". The 2nd session of the conference "WTO Regime and Regional Trade Groups: Law and Practice of China, Korea FTA" was held in Tianjin in 2008. The 3rd session "Korea-China FTA: Seeking Ways to Reduce Barriers for the Special Partnership" came again in Seoul in 2010. The 4th session "China-Korea FTA: The Main Issues and Promoting Path of China-Korea FTA" was held in Xiamen in 2011. This is the 5th session, focusing on "Korea-China FTA: Prospects and Jurisprudence".

We might see that last 10 years we focus on the China-Korea Trade Relation in the context of WTO and RTAs, the two main systems of international trade law, meeting the needs of both sides in theoretic and practical aspects. Though the China-Korea FTA has not been concluded yet, the continuing researching on this topic has substantially promoted the development of negotiation on this agreement. Some of the results of the conferences publishes in both domestic and international journals, and produced important impacts on the decision-making of both sides.

Ladies and gentlemen, we need platform for international exchanges. The joint conference held by our two societies is one of the idea platform of international exchanges.

One world one dream! For international lawyers, our dream is to achieve the rule of law in international society! As international lawyers, we all recognize our mission for each country and the whole world. At a highest level, justice and rule of law have universal value. We also pursue Peace, Development, Harmony and Happiness of all peoples by rule of law. At the practical level, we should serve our people and States with professional spirit and technique!

I firmly believe that with our common efforts, we will achieve great success of this symposium!

五、学会第五届理事会第一次会议致辞*

各位理事：

大家好！首先，十分感谢国际经济法学界各位同仁对学会工作的积极参与和鼎力支持！学会自1984年庐山讲习班创建以来，已有28年的历史了。学会的历史，是专注学术，"知识报国，兼济天下"的历史。学会为我国国际经济法学科的建设，为促进国际经济法学界的交流，服务国家的改革开放事业做出了重要的贡献。学会的历史，是坚持法治理念，艰苦奋斗，自强不息的历史。在一定意义上，学会的历史验证了中国法治的发展。

在学会第五届理事会成立之际，我们深切缅怀创建学会的先贤！创业艰难。我们永远铭记学会创会会长姚梅镇教授、副会长冯大同教授和学会顾问周子亚教授等为学会的创建和早期发展鞠躬尽瘁的历史功绩！

我们由衷感谢学会顾问朱学山教授、郭寿康教授等长期关心、支持和指导学会的工作！他们言传身教，是广大国际经济法学者特别是中青年学者的楷模。

我们由衷感谢以张玉卿司长为代表的商务部条约法律司领导对学会工作长期的关怀、指导和支持！

我们由衷感谢学会创建人、连选连任学会第二、三、四届会长陈安教授，副会长董世忠教授、吴焕宁教授！他们长期主持学会工作，呕心沥血，筚路蓝缕，为学会的创建和可持续发展做出了无可比拟的杰出贡献！

我们由衷感谢全国国际经济法学界同仁一直以来的风雨同舟，共襄盛举！

当下，历史将我们这一代学者推到学会工作的前排，深感责任重大。我们受老一辈学者影响尤深，又具有"老三届""知识青年"和"77、78级"的特质，是"农工知识分子"，常怀感恩之心、公益心和责任心。

学会人才济济，国际经济法学界学者、政界学者型官员、实务界专家型律师等源源加盟。因缘际会。各位同仁选举我承担会长工作，主要是对厦门大学国际经济法团队多年承担学会秘书处工作的认同，我需要比以往有更多的投入，有更直接的担当。学会是全国性学术社团，会员代表大会是权力机构，理事会是执行机构，秘书处是服务机构。会长是学会决议的执行者和学会活动的责任人，是学术义工。"专注学术，无私奉献"，是学会历届理事会的优良传统，新一届理事会必将发扬光大。

新一届理事会有决心和信心做好学会工作。经过28年的发展，学会已具有优良的发展基础。学会具有很强的学术凝聚力，从新一届理事会理事名单可以看出，来

---

* 2011年10月28—30日，中国国际经济法学会在厦门举行2011年中国国际经济法学术研讨会暨会员代表大会，选举产生了第五届理事会。

自国际经济法学界、实务界和政界的专家学者云集，能量和潜力无限。学会顾问、荣誉会长等老一辈学者继续参与和指导学会工作，是学会工作继续发展的重要保障。学会还有国家主管部门，特别是司法部、商务部一如既往的关怀、指导和支持。更为根本的是，学会有全国国际经济法学界同行的积极参与和倾心投入。

新一届理事会必将牢记和践行"以文会友，以友辅仁，知识报国，兼济天下"的学会宗旨，明确学会作为全国性学术社团的性质，注重学会工作的学术性、自主性和民主性。特别是，在学会工作中必须坚持"五湖四海"，集思广益，群策群力。

依我理解，学会的职能主要有三：

第一，学会是国际经济法领域学术交流的平台。学会每年举办中国国际经济法学会年会暨学术研讨会、全国性国际经济法专题研讨会和国际性学术研讨会，促进国际、国内学术交流；学会与厦门大学国际经济法研究所联合出版《国际经济法学刊》（每年一卷四期），作为国际经济法领域的学术园地；学会创建和维护中国国际经济法学会网站（www.csiel.org），为全国国际经济法学界同仁提供学术成果、学术活动等信息，理事、会员提供的专业信息，可作为学会组织课题研究和专题会议的重要参考。

第二，学会是服务国家改革开放事业的民间智库。学会与商务部条法司长期合作，已形成了较密切的学术联系和制度性安排。目前，学会每年与商务部条法司联合主办两个专题研讨会：一是每年9月作为"中国投资贸易洽谈会"论坛召开的"国际投资协定研讨会"，已连续召开5届；另一是每年10月或11月学会年会之前召开的"WTO法专题研讨会"，已连续召开2届。多年来，学会会员还承担了商务部条法司委托的多项研究课题。学会拟根据各位会员的研究领域、研究成果编制专家学者名单，供国家相关部门参考。

第三，学会是培养国际经济法人才的基地。学会通过组织国际、国内学术研讨会，为青年学者创造更多更好的学术研究和交流机会。学会通过一年一度的"中国国际经济法学会青年优秀论文"评选活动，鼓励和促进青年学者潜心治学，脱颖而出。作为学会秘书处所在单位，厦门大学国际法学科一直在努力，争取更好地为学会服务。2010年，厦门大学法学院入选由联合国贸发会议主持遴选的国际投资法研究"领航法学院15强"（Pilot Project—the "G15 of law schools"）。后生可畏。2006、2011年，厦门大学法学院辩论队在美国华盛顿特区举行的"Jessup国际法模拟法庭辩论赛"中先后获得书状奖第一名（即2006 The Hardy C. Dillard Award和2011 Best Respondent Memorial），给国人莫大的鼓舞和深刻的启迪。

我相信，各位同仁同心协力，新一届理事会必定能承前启后，开拓进取，有新的作为和奉献！

第五节　《国际经济法学刊》再出发

一、《国际经济法学刊》创刊词 *

在经济全球化趋势下,国际经济秩序和全球治理体系变革加速推进,各国在国际贸易、国际投资、国际货币金融、国际税务等领域面临挑战和机遇。我国改革开放和推动构建人类命运共同体的伟大实践,为我国国际经济法学界提供了知识报国的最佳时代背景和学术环境。当前,中国特色社会主义进入了新时代,中国特色国际经济法学也进入了新时代。其重要标志之一是,《国际经济法学刊》(国家级期刊)(简称"本刊")正式面世了!这是我国国际经济法学界砥砺奋进、梦想成真的学术盛事!

回望历史,创业维艰,春华秋实。在世界范围,国际经济法是第二次世界大战后产生和发展的新兴学科。自1978年实行改革开放政策以来,我国国际经济法学应运而生,蓬勃发展。1998年创办的《国际经济法学刊》(集刊)(简称《学刊》),由我国国际经济法学科奠基人之一、厦门大学陈安教授担任主编,中国国际经济法学会组织编辑委员会,厦门大学国际经济法研究所作为编辑部所在单位,先后由法律出版社和北京大学出版社出版发行。二十年来,秉持"知识报国,兼济天下"的办刊宗旨,学界同仁筚路蓝缕,自强不息,《学刊》获得了我国政府部门和海内外国际经济法学界的高度评价和广泛认同。2005年,《学刊》入选为"中文社会科学引文索引数据库"(CSSCI)首批收录的来源集刊,并在历次CSSCI遴选中持续入选。2017年,《学刊》"二十而冠",我国政府主管部门授予国家级期刊号,表达了国家对《学刊》的充分肯定和殷切期许。《学刊》实现了由"集刊"到"期刊"的成功"转型",是质的重大飞跃,必将以更高的学术水平、创新的内容和形式跻身海内外重要学术期刊之林。

展望未来,使命光荣,任重道远。国际经济法处于迅速发展之中。中国特色国际经济法学的历史使命是,站在中国和广大发展中国家立场,以马克思主义为指导思想,紧密联系中国和国际实践,坚持建立国际经济新秩序的目标,汲取国际社会长期积淀的国际经济法学精华,开拓创新,丰富和革新"国际话语体系",坚定维护和发展国际社会普遍认同的经济主权、公平互利、合作发展等国际经济法学基本原则,为促进国际经济法实践的健康发展,为推动构建人类命运共同体做出积极的学术贡

---

* 原载《国际经济法学刊》2018年第1期,曾华群执笔。

献。本刊承载发展和繁荣中国特色国际经济法学的重任，是中国国际经济法学者勇于担当、精耕细作的学术园地，也是中国国际经济法学者与各国同行交流互鉴、平等对话的学术平台。本刊必将坚持"百花齐放，百家争鸣"方针，必将增强"道路自信、理论自信、制度自信、文化自信"，为国际经济法领域的学术研究、交流和合作做出应有的贡献。

"合抱之木，生于毫末。九层之台，起于累土。千里之行，始于足下。"值此本刊创办"再出发"之际，谨望海内外国际经济法理论界和实务界广大学者一如既往，源源惠赐佳作，以弘扬中华学术精神，共襄发展和繁荣中国特色国际经济法学之盛举！

《国际经济法学刊》编辑委员会
2017 年 12 月 19 日

二、不忘初心，自信自强"再出发"[*]

作为《国际经济法学刊》（简称《学刊》，2018 年创刊）的副主编，有机会参加本次培训班，开阔视野，增长知识，获益颇丰。培训班涉及的主题，引发了一些初步思考，略述一二。

不忘初心，创建具有中国特色的《学刊》

在世界范围，国际经济法是第二次世界大战后产生和发展的新兴学科。我国改革开放和推动构建人类命运共同体的伟大实践，为我国国际经济法学界提供了知识报国的最佳时代背景和学术环境。自 1978 年实行改革开放政策以来，我国国际经济法学应运而生，蓬勃发展。1998 年《学刊》（集刊）创办，秉持"知识报国，兼济天下"的办刊宗旨，学界同仁筚路蓝缕，自强不息，《学刊》（集刊）获得了我国政府部门和海内外国际经济法学界的高度评价和广泛认同。2005 年以来持续入选 CSSCI 的来源集刊。

2017 年，我国政府主管部门授予《学刊》国家级期刊号，表达了国家对《学刊》的充分肯定和殷切期许。《学刊》实现了由"集刊"到"期刊"的成功"转型"，是质的重大飞跃，必将以更高的学术水平、创新的内容和形式跻身海内外重要学术期刊之林。值此《学刊》"再出发"之际，当不忘出版业"为读者选择内容"的初心，不忘《学刊》"创建和发展中国特色国际经济法学"的初心。

自信自强，努力创建海内外国际经济法领域的一流期刊

当前，传统媒体面临互联网时代和新媒体的种种挑战。《学刊》应如何应对和发

---

[*] 2018 年 9 月 21 日，在第 55 期中央单位在京社科类期刊主编岗位培训班交流会的发言。

展,是面临的重大课题。

本人认为,首先,应"知己知彼",对自己有客观、准确的定位,增强自信,承担起历史使命和社会责任。可从以下三方面理解"定位"问题:

(1)传统媒体(出版)的本质功能包括注册登记、质量控制、生产传播和长期保存,这是新媒体所无法全面覆盖或取代的;

(2)传统媒体是"内容"特别是"原始内容"的主要提供者。"内容为王"或有争议,"内容为本"当能得到普遍赞同。在这个意义上,"内容"特别是"原始内容"和"优质内容"是传统媒体的最大优势;

(3)传统媒体因其长期积淀的品牌效应,一般具有较强的公信力。学术期刊的评价标准主要是社会效益、社会影响力。特别是,专业性学术期刊,还承载促进学术交流和学科发展的重任。

在增强自信的基础上,应具有自强不息的精神,敬业爱岗,把本职工作做到极致。"华西口腔"编辑部就是很好的示范。

《学刊》作为我国国际经济法领域唯一的学术期刊,力争优质创办。在《学刊》2018年第1—4期,发表《论中国特色国际经济法学》,设立"中非合作的法治"和"单边贸易措施与WTO规则"两个紧密联系实际的专栏,初步展现了内容和形式方面的"高标准"。

量力而行,借助新媒体新技术促进《学刊》新发展

当下,新媒体新技术的快速发展,对传统媒体是现实的挑战,也冲击了某些传统媒体的生存和发展环境。同时,也应当看到,传统媒体获得了借助新媒体新技术"再出发"的发展机遇。在此新形势下,传统媒体人应具备和增强"互联网思维",认清大势,根据本单位实际情况,量力而行,主动采取适应或改革的举措,积极融入"融媒体""全媒体"的大趋势。

事实上,当前的发展环境对传统媒体"互联网思维"的实践是很有利的。例如,"中国知网"的一系列研发项目和平台建设已为期刊的"数据化"建设提供了"搭便车"的机遇。

《学刊》借助新媒体新技术的初步考虑:

(1)《学刊》需要高质量开展网站建设;

(2)积极参与"中国知网"向期刊开放的媒体融合项目;

(3)探索适合《学刊》发展和社会需求的"数据化"建设模式。例如,《学刊》中紧密联系我国国际实践的论文电子版在第一时间"精准推送"商务部条约法律司、外交

部条约法律司等，更好地发挥"民间智库"作用。

《学刊》承载发展和繁荣中国特色国际经济法学的重任，是中国国际经济法学者勇于担当、精耕细作的学术园地，也是中国国际经济法学者与各国同行交流互鉴、平等对话的学术平台。《学刊》必将坚持"百花齐放，百家争鸣"方针，必将增强"道路自信、理论自信、制度自信、文化自信"，为国际经济法领域的学术研究、交流和合作做出应有的贡献。

第六节 关于"中国特色国际经济法学的使命担当和创新发展"的共识[*]

2019 年 10 月 25—27 日,正值纪念五四运动 100 周年和庆祝中华人民共和国成立 70 周年之际,在革命圣地西柏坡,中国国际经济法学会隆重召开了第 30 届中国国际经济法学术研讨会暨第七届会员代表大会。与会全体同仁追忆历史,感悟当下,展望未来,深入研讨大会主题"中国特色国际经济法学的使命担当和创新发展",达成如下共识:

一、中国特色国际经济法学的历史使命

当今世界处于百年未有之大变局,国际经济法学的改革发展适逢其时。中国特色国际经济法学的历史使命是,站在中国和广大发展中国家立场,以马克思主义为指导思想,紧密联系中国和国际实践,坚持建立国际经济新秩序的目标,汲取国际社会长期积淀的国际经济法学精华,开拓创新,改革和丰富"国际话语体系",坚定维护和发展国际社会普遍认同的经济主权、公平互利、合作发展等国际经济法基本原则,为促进国际经济法实践的健康发展,为推动构建人类命运共同体做出积极的学术贡献。

二、中国国际经济法学者的学术使命

创建和发展中国特色国际经济法学,是中国国际经济法学者的学术使命。这是一项宏大、艰巨、长期的理论工程,需要我国一代又一代国际经济法学者矢志不移、持之以恒的艰苦奋斗。我们应增强使命感,潜心治学,勇于探索国际经济法的发展规律和现实课题。我们应增强"道路自信、理论自信、制度自信、文化自信",更积极主动地开展国际经济法领域的学术研究、交流和合作,提出国际经济法理论和实践的"中国主张"和"中国方案",为中国特色国际经济法学的发展和繁荣做出应有的贡献。

---

* 中国国际经济法学会《关于"中国特色国际经济法学的使命担当和创新发展"的共识》(2019 年 10 月 27 日中国国际经济法学会第七届会员代表大会通过),曾华群执笔。

三、中国国际经济法学会的服务使命

本会成立于 1984 年庐山"第一期国际经济法讲习班"，是我国国际经济法学界普遍认同、正式登记于民政部的全国性学术社团法人，服务于中国特色国际经济法学和中国国际经济法学者的使命担当。本会一向努力践行"知识报国，兼济天下"的宗旨，严格遵守法律法规和本会章程，团结全国高校、科研机构和相关部门广大国际经济法学者和实务工作者，专心致志，积极开展国际经济法领域的研究和交流；同时，与商务部、外交部等保持密切联系和合作，力争成为我国国际经济法领域的民间智库。任重道远，使命光荣。本会必将发扬"专注学术，知识报国""五湖四海，团结奋斗"和"崇尚法治，勇于实践"的优良传统，加强思想、组织和能力建设，不忘初心，砥砺奋进！

第十三章
治学心得分享

第一节　学术成果推介

一、"厦门大学国际经济法文库"序言 *

　　国际经济法是新兴的边缘性法学学科。在世界范围,国际经济法作为独立的法学学科,直至第二次世界大战后才逐渐形成和发展起来。1978 年我国实行改革开放政策以来,国际经济法在我国应运而生,迅速发展成为我国法学各学科中理论研究最活跃、实践性最强的学科之一。当前,在经济全球化和中国加入 WTO 的新形势下,国际经济法更呈现其鲜明的时代性和蓬勃的生命力。

　　得改革开放风气之先,厦门大学在我国较早开展国际经济法的教学和研究。经原国家教委批准,1981、1985 年在全国率先招收国际经济法专业硕士生和本科生,1986 年开始招收国际经济法专业(1997 年后调整扩大为国际法学专业)博士生。1987 年成立厦门大学国际经济法研究所。1995 年,厦门大学"国际经济法及台港澳法研究"学科点列为全国高校"211"工程重点建设项目。2002 年,厦门大学国际法专业获教育部批准为国家重点学科,目标是建成我国国际法领域的重要研究基地和人才培养基地之一。20 多年来,秉承"自强不息,止于至善"的校训,厦门大学国际法专业学者囊萤映雪,专心治学,开展了一系列国家急需的国际经济法理论和实务研究工作,为我国的法治建设和学科发展作出了应有的贡献。同时,经过不断探索,本专业逐渐形成"出人才"和"创成果"相互促进、相辅相成的研究生培养模式,培养了大

---

　　* 原载"厦门大学国际经济法文库",即陈东著《跨国公司治理中的责任承担机制》(厦门大学出版社 2003 年出版)等,曾华群执笔。

批"懂法律,懂经济,懂外语"的国际经济法专门人才。历届毕业生在成才过程中,也为学术发展奉献出青春才华。

"厦门大学国际经济法文库"(文库)的编辑出版,是本专业学科建设和发展的长期性工作之一。文库的宗旨是以系列学术专著的形式,集中展现国际经济法领域的专题研究成果,促进学术和社会发展。文库立足出版厦门大学学者、校友国际经济法领域的新成果,更欢迎海内外国际经济法学者惠赐佳作。文库坚持作品的原创性标准,崇尚严谨治学,鼓励学术创新和争鸣。在出版国际经济法专家学者力作的同时,尤其关注国际经济法学界的新人新作,包括在优秀博士学位论文基础上发展的学术专著。我们期望文库成为国际经济法专家学者耕耘的园地,源源不断地产出智慧之果,启迪思想,弘扬学术。同时,更希望文库发挥国际经济法"智库"的功能,为我国参与缔结国际经济条约的实践、涉外经济立法以及对外经贸实务提供有益的理论指导或实务参考。

"厦门大学国际经济法文库"编委会

2003 年 6 月 2 日

二、"厦门大学国际法名著译丛"总序 *

在厦门大学国际法学科和法律出版社的共同努力和通力合作下,"厦门大学国际法名著译丛"问世了。这是厦门大学国际法学科发展史上值得祝贺和鼓励的学术盛事。

近年来,厦门大学国际法学科重视开展教师和学生两个层面的国际学术交流。创建厦门国际法高等研究院并连年举办"国际法前沿问题研修班",连续参加"Willem C. Vis 国际商事模拟仲裁辩论赛"(维也纳)和"Jessup 国际法模拟法庭辩论赛"(华盛顿哥伦比亚特区),持续在国际性专业刊物和出版社发表学术论著等,均反映了本学科师生走向国际的初步努力。翻译国际法名著,则是更为基础性的国际化努力。

众所周知,我国国际法学的发展亟须汲取世界各国国际法学的精华。与国内法学者比较而言,国际法学者更迫切需要了解和学习国际同行的名著,更迫切需要与国际同行对话和交流。国际法名著的翻译成果,为我国法学院校广大师生和相关实务工作者提供了与国际法学术大师更为便捷交流的中文语境,功德无量。

---

* 原载"厦门大学国际法名著译丛",即〔美〕杰克·戈德史密斯和埃里克·波斯纳著、龚宇译《国际法的局限性》(法律出版社 2010 年出版)等。

当下十分提倡和强调学术创新。学术创新自有其发展规律，需要经历对既有优秀学术成果的吸收、消化、扬弃、升华的过程。国际法名著的翻译工作，对译者而言，是超越时空向国际法学术大师的虚心求教，是优秀学术成果的吸收、消化的过程，也是创新的酝酿或前奏。进而言之，翻译工作是对原作融会贯通之后的再创作。在这个意义上，翻译工作也是创新。虽然，在现行各种学术成果评估体系中，译作并未受到应有的重视，令人感佩的是，本译丛的译者能有"上善若水"的感悟与追求。

翻译的"信、达、雅"是学界一向追求和普遍认同的理想境界。对译者而言，"雅"是取决于已有文化积淀和文字功底的高标准，一时难以企及；而"信""达"则是不遗余力、必须达到的基本标准。国际法名著最理想的译者自然是学贯中西、潜心治学的年长国际法学者。由于历史和现实的种种原因，殊难如愿。值得庆幸的是，在本译丛第一批译者中，蔡从燕教授、陈辉萍教授、池漫郊副教授、韩秀丽副教授和龚宇博士等都曾在国际性专业刊物或出版社发表学术论著，或有翻译法学论著的经验。其他译者是莘莘学子中的佼佼者，后生可畏。2006 年，厦门大学法学院代表队在美国举行的"第 46 届 Jessup 国际法模拟法庭辩论赛"荣获"最佳书状奖第一名"（The Hardy C. Dillard Award），展现了我国新一代国际法学者的专业研究能力和英语运用能力，给国人莫大的自信与启迪。该最佳书状作者之一季烨博士生也忝列为本译丛译者。

"人之云，非知之难，行之惟难；非行之难，终之斯难。"本译丛作为厦门大学国际法学科建设的重要组成部分，持之以恒，当为我国国际法学的发展和繁荣作出应有的一份贡献。本译丛的生命力在于质量，希望得到国际法学界的持续关注和指导，更希望广大读者对译作多提批评意见，以利修订完善。

曾华群　谨识

2009 年 3 月 9 日

三、《国际经济新秩序与国际经济法的新发展》前言[*]

为祝贺陈安老师八十华诞和从教五十九周年，厦门大学国际经济法研究所向我校国际经济法学科同事和校友征稿出版文集。一呼百应，遂成巨篇。

八十年岁月峥嵘。在民不聊生、战乱频仍的旧中国，陈老师少年立振兴中华之志，勤奋用功。战后考入厦门大学，修习法学之余，开始接触和接受马克思列宁主义

---

　　* 原载曾华群主编：《陈安教授八十华诞祝贺文集/国际经济新秩序与国际经济法的新发展》，法律出版社 2009 年出版。

的启蒙和陶冶。1951年以来,陈老师任教于厦门大学,法律系停办期间,由法学转为马克思列宁主义领域。改革开放三十年,是陈老师学术生涯的黄金时期。1981年,陈老师以"知天命"之年,远赴重洋,求学和讲学于哈佛大学,开始了专攻国际经济法的漫漫征程。

陈老师是厦门大学国际经济法学科的创建人和学术带头人。1979年我校法律系复办伊始,与陈朝璧教授、盛新民教授、胡大展教授等同仁,为适应改革开放形势之急需,及时确立了以国际经济法专业为重点的学科发展战略。先后于1982年、1985年和1986年获教育部批准招收国际经济法专业硕士生、本科生和博士生,并于1987年主编出版了国内第一套国际经济法系列著作,为我校国际经济法学科的发展奠定基石。

陈老师是中国国际经济法学会的创建人之一。在1984年庐山国际经济法讲习班讲学期间,与上海市社会科学院周子亚教授、武汉大学姚梅镇教授、复旦大学董世忠教授、南开大学高尔森教授和中国社会科学院盛愉教授等发起创立了国际经济法研究会(即中国国际经济法学会的前身)。1993年起,陈老师连选连任中国国际经济法学会会长。25年来,作为国际经济法领域的全国性民间学术团体,学会发展之路关山重重。陈老师身先士卒,筚路蓝缕,团结全国学界和实务界同仁,积极开展国际经济法领域的国内外学术交流,逐渐形成和确立了"以文会友,以友辅仁,知识报国,兼济天下"的学会宗旨和共识。

陈老师是中国特色国际经济法学的奠基人之一。在潜心治学中,一向坚持马克思列宁主义,追求公平正义的法治精神,积极倡导"知识报国,兼济天下"的治学理念。一介书生,位卑未敢忘忧国,为振兴中华竭尽心力。一介书生,时刻关注天下大势,始终不渝地坚持改革国际经济旧秩序、建立国际经济新秩序的目标和立场,奋力为饱受欺凌压迫的广大发展中国家摇旗呐喊。天道酬勤。陈老师创办和主编的《国际经济法学刊》,鸿篇巨制《国际经济法学刍言》和《陈安论国际经济法学》以及发表于海内外权威学术刊物的中英文学术论文,忠实记录了其"板凳甘坐卅年冷"的执着和对中国特色国际经济法学的杰出奉献。

陈老师还是中国国际经济法律实践的先行者之一。在教学研究百忙之中,承办了一系列重要的国策咨询和典型国际经贸仲裁、司法案件,是中国政府根据《华盛顿公约》遴选向"解决投资争端国际中心"(ICSID)指派的国际仲裁员。

艰难困苦,玉汝于成。陈老师在长达五十九年的执教生涯中,以其坚韧不拔的精神和持之以恒的努力,成就了利国利民的不平凡业绩,实现了其报效国家人民之志,亦成为后学之师范。

得益于陈老师的言传身教,经过近三十年的发展,厦门大学国际经济法学科及学术团队逐渐形成其传统和特色。主要表现在:

第一,立足中国国情,理论紧密联系实际。与商务部等政府部门和涉外经贸实务界长期保持密切的合作关系,结合改革开放实际,力图较全面、深入研究我国在国际投资、国际贸易、国际货币金融和国际税务等方面的法律问题,为我国法治建设和改革开放事业作出应有贡献。

第二,关注南北问题,坚持第三世界立场。在全球化背景下,铭记作为中国学者的历史责任和使命,坚持改革国际经济旧秩序、建立国际经济新秩序的目标和立场,重视研究国际经济法基本理论,特别是经济主权、公平互利和合作发展等国际经济法基本原则的理论和实践问题,努力维护发展中国家的权益。

第三,追求严谨学风,重视学术道德修养。深知为人师表,道德文章须经得起历史的检验。潜心钻研学问,崇尚淡泊明志,宁静致远。提倡学术民主,博采众长,百家争鸣。注重学术规范,严格自律,以身作则。

第四,勇于开拓创新,促进国际学术交流。创建厦门国际法高等研究院并连年举办“国际法前沿问题研修班”,连续参加“Willem C. Vis 国际商事模拟仲裁辩论赛”(维也纳)和“Jessup 国际法模拟法庭辩论赛”(华盛顿哥伦比亚特区)并屡获佳绩,持续在国际性专业刊物和出版社发表学术论著等,均反映了本学科师生走向国际的初步努力。

第五,强化团队意识,凝聚学科建设合力。在本学科建设的各项工作中,如《国际经济法学刊》的编辑、中国国际经济法学会秘书处事务、国际专业大赛辩论队的指导,厦门国际法高等研究院行政事务等,本学科师生基于共同的世界观和价值观,甘当“义工”,勇挑重担,体现了强烈的事业心、责任感和团队意识。

自 1981 年以来,厦门大学国际经济法专业已逐渐发展成为我国培养国际经济法专才的重要基地之一。本专业的毕业生,无论身在国内或海外,无论服务于学界或实务界,均秉承“自强不息,止于至善”的校训和本专业的传统,兢兢业业,勉力回馈母校和老师,报效祖国和人民。

本文集汇辑了本学科部分同事和校友的最新研究成果,涉及国际经济法基本理论、国际贸易法、国际投资法、国际货币金融法、国际税法和国际经济争端处理法等领域,从一个侧面反映了国际经济新秩序和国际经济法专题研究的新发展。文集的每一篇文章,都蕴含着作者对厦门大学国际经济法学科的热忱挚爱与支持,更蕴含着作者对陈老师八十华诞和从教五十九周年的由衷祝贺与敬意。文集还附上陈安老师简介、陈安老师主要著述、陈安老师主要获奖成果和中国国际经济法学会大事记，以利查阅。

光阴荏苒，时不我待。祈望同行学者特别是青年学者不仅从本文集获得国际经济法研究的最新信息和成果，更从陈安老师的艰辛奋斗历程获得人生启迪和感悟。

曾华群　谨识

2009 年 1 月 18 日

四、《WTO 与中国：法治的发展与互动——中国加入 WTO 十周年纪念文集》序言一 [*]

2001 年 12 月 11 日，中国正式成为世界贸易组织（WTO）的第 143 个成员。这是 WTO 在成员构成方面的重要发展，也是中国与多边贸易体制接轨的重要里程碑。

如所周知，实行市场经济和法治是中国改革开放的应有之义。WTO 以市场经济为基础，以法治（规则）为取向，契合了中国改革开放的发展方向。中国加入 WTO 的重要后果是，实行市场经济和法治不仅是中国自主决定的大政方针，也是必须恪守的国际义务。在这个意义上，加入 WTO 推动了中国法治的发展。

毋庸讳言，关税及贸易总协定（GATT）与国际货币基金组织（IMF）、世界银行（IBRD）是战后由发达国家建立的支撑国际经济秩序的三大支柱。作为 GATT 的继承者，1995 年成立的 WTO 仍然由发达国家主导构建，服务于发达国家促进经济自由化、全球化的目标。尽管 WTO 体制已由 GATT 的"实力取向"发展为某种程度的"规则取向"，对广大 WTO 成员特别是发展中成员而言，该体制远非完美的法治。实践表明，WTO 体制的生命力在于其本身法治的持续发展和广大成员的普遍认同。鉴此，中国作为 WTO 成员，在履行 WTO 义务的同时，也承担了参与促进 WTO 法治发展的责任和使命。

WTO 作为普遍接受的多边贸易体制，中国作为发展中大国和 WTO 成员，两者法治的发展与互动，具有重大而深远的意义。2010 年 10 月 14 日，中国国际经济法学会与商务部条约法律司在南京联合举办了"WTO、法治与中国——中国加入WTO 十年专题研讨会"，集中探讨有关 WTO 与中国法治发展的理论和实践问题，成果甚丰。本书以该研讨会的交流成果为基础，荟集了 30 篇代表性论文，力图反映"中国与 WTO：法治的发展与互动"这一主题。

---

[*]　原载曾华群、杨国华主编：《WTO 与中国：法治的发展与互动——中国加入 WTO 十周年纪念文集》，中国商务出版社 2011 年出版。

尽管见仁见智，文风各异，本书各篇文章呈现出如下共同特点：

一是鲜明的"中国特色"。各篇文章或以中国的立场考察 WTO 法治和规则，或直接研究涉及中国的特殊 WTO 规则或典型案例，表明了作者以"中国特色"问题为重心的治学态度。

二是理论紧密联系实践。各篇文章如侧重理论问题研究，则言之有据，来源于实证分析或实践经验；如侧重实务问题研究，则条分缕析，援引或提炼相关法律依据或法理原则。有的作者直接从事 WTO 法律实务，更奉献出来自切身实践的真知。

三是可贵的创新精神。各篇文章在不同程度上反映了作者选题的独具匠心和研究内容的原创性。例如，有关 WTO 法治模式和推动 WTO 变法的研究，论证缜密，具有重要的理论和实践价值。

为促进"中国与 WTO：法治的发展与互动"的专题研究，本书谨附部分外文相关研究成果目录，供查阅参考。

在南京会议的组织和本书的编辑中，厦门大学法学院蔡从燕教授全程参与，奉献颇多心力；国际法学专业博士生陆以全、陈丹艳、李庆灵、朱晓丹、徐丽碧、张美红、李金旺、李任远同学共同参与中外有关"中国与 WTO"研究成果的查阅整理工作，谨此表达由衷谢忱！

本书编辑出版之际，适逢中国加入 WTO 十周年。本人期望，本书的出版有助于学界同行和广大读者加深了解中国的 WTO 实践及其对中国和 WTO 法治发展的重要意义，也有助于推动"中国特色"WTO 法研究的进一步发展。

曾华群
2011 年 6 月 2 日

五、当前国际投资政策趋向与我国的应有作为 *

2010 年 12 月，由联合国贸易和发展会议（UNCTAD）和经济合作与开发组织（OECD）联合主办的第二届国际投资协定研讨会，提出了"国际投资协定向何处去"的严峻问题；UNCTAD《2012 年世界投资报告》题为"迈向新一代投资政策"，制定了"可持续发展的投资政策框架"（IPFSD）。这表明国际社会对国际投资政策的"共同

---

* 2012 年 9 月 9 日，联合国贸易和发展会议（UNCTAD）和中国商务部在第 16 届中国国际投资贸易洽谈会（厦门）期间共同举行了《2012 年世界投资报告》中文版发布暨新一代投资政策研讨会，主题为"促进国际投资 实现可持续发展"。曾华群应邀作大会发言（英文），进而发表此文，原载《光明日报》2013 年 8 月 7 日第 11 版。

路径"取得了初步共识和成就。我国作为发展中大国，兼有资本输入国和资本输出国双重身份，亟须对上述问题确立相应的立场和对策。

国际投资政策从"传统"到"新一代"的发展趋向

《2012 年世界投资报告》第一次高度关注投资决策和决策者。值得注意的是，在此语境中，"投资政策"包括国内法方面的外国投资立法和国际法方面的国际投资条约实践。而"新一代"的用语非常重要，我们需要回顾"投资政策"的传统特征并考虑新旧"投资政策"之区分。

投资政策的传统特征如下：一是偏重对外资和外国投资者的保护。长期以来，在经济全球化趋势下，为吸引外资，发展中国家的外资法律政策普遍偏重对外资和外国投资者的保护和优惠，缺乏或放松对外资必要的管制或制约。在双边投资条约实践中，片面强调对外资和外国投资者的自由开放（如"设立权"条款等）、高水平待遇（如国民待遇、最惠国待遇、公平与公正待遇等）、高水平保护（如征收赔偿的"赫尔"规则等）及投资者直接诉诸国际仲裁的权利等。二是未重视"可持续发展"。作为偏重保护外资和外国投资者的后果，传统投资政策未能充分顾及东道国的需要和发展，尤其是在"可持续发展"方面缺少作为。三是保护和管制外资的两种努力各行其道。一般而言，保护外资的法律，无论国内立法或国际条约，均属"硬法"，具有法律效力，而管制外资、跨国公司的国际规范，则大多属于"软法"，成效甚微。

在很大程度上，"新一代"投资政策试图解决上述三个问题，提出了 11 项"可持续发展投资决策的核心原则"。对此，可以用三个关键词来概括其解决思路或方式：其一是"平衡"，其二是"可持续发展"，其三是"全面"。可持续发展投资决策的核心原则是全方位的，强调保护外资和管制外资同等重要，力图连接上述"各行其道"的保护外资和管制外资的两种努力。

总体上，"可持续发展投资决策的核心原则"是 UNCTAD 关于国际投资方面国际治理的重大贡献。其特别强调投资决策中的发展中国家权益，是发展中国家长期斗争的重大成果，也获得发达国家有识之士的支持。在一定意义上，可持续发展投资决策的核心原则可视为"南北合作"的新共识和新成就，奠定了国际投资新秩序的基石。

我国在建构国际投资新秩序中的应有作为

"可持续发展的投资政策框架"旨在建构资本输入国与资本输出国"可持续发展""和谐共赢"的国际投资新秩序，符合我国和广大发展中国家的共同目标和长远利益。我国作为发展中大国，兼具资本输入国与资本输出国双重身份，在基于IPFSD 的国家和国际实践中任重道远，大有可为。

第一，促进"平衡""可持续发展""全面"成为国际共识。"平衡""可持续发展"和"全面"是"公平互利"原则的体现，具有普遍性价值。然而，UNCTAD制定了"可持续发展的投资政策框架"，并不意味着国际社会对此已经达成共识。我国国际法学界、政府主管部门在国际论坛和国际实践中，应通过各种努力，促进各国真正达成"平衡""可持续发展"和"全面"的共识。这不仅符合国际经济法的"公平互利"原则，也符合我国的国家利益。从解决"南北问题"的角度看，"平衡""可持续发展"和"全面"是改革国际经济旧秩序、建立国际经济新秩序的基本理念，我国应始终坚持并积极实践。

第二，及时制定我国"可持续发展友好型"双边投资条约范本。双边投资条约范本可分为欧洲范本和美国范本。欧洲范本是传统范本，条文与投资密切相关；美国范本内容繁杂，涉及国家安全例外、金融审慎、税务等新内容和复杂的争端解决机制。美国双边投资条约范本（2012版）更是在"传统特征"方面不断升级和强化。我国现行双边投资条约范本主要借鉴欧洲范本。当前，需要认真总结我国30多年来的双边投资条约实践经验，研究相关国际实践和案例，遵循"可持续发展的投资政策框架"和"可持续发展投资决策的核心原则"，参考UNCTAD的"国际投资协定要素：政策选项"，选择和采用体现"平衡""可持续发展"和"全面"的要素，及时制定我国"可持续发展友好型"双边投资条约范本。

第三，积极开展"可持续发展友好型"双边投资条约实践。"可持续发展友好型"双边投资条约实践的重要特征，是增加了"可持续发展""东道国权益"及"投资者责任"等创新因素，以求平衡资本输入国与资本输出国之间的权益。在当前的国际体制下，期望发达国家主动遵循"可持续发展的投资政策框架"开展"可持续发展友好型"双边投资条约实践是不现实的。在发达国家基于国家利益考虑而固守传统的情势下，发展中国家相互之间的双边投资条约实践如何发展，至关重要。我国与其他发展中国家作为平等的缔约双方，具有建立国际经济新秩序的共同历史使命，可遵循"可持续发展的投资政策框架"和"可持续发展投资决策的核心原则"，选择"国际投资协定要素：政策选项"中的创新因素，形成和确立共同的价值取向和基本立场，在强调"平衡""可持续发展"和"全面"等方面形成和发展新的规则和标准，逐渐形成"可持续发展友好型"双边投资条约的普遍实践，进而影响发达国家与发展中国家之间双边投资条约实践及双边投资条约的总体发展趋势。（作者为国家社科基金重大项目"促进与保护我国海外投资的法律体制研究"首席专家、厦门大学教授）

第二节　创新平台感言

一、"厦门国际法高等研究院"的使命

（一）Speech at the Opening Ceremony of 2019 Summer Program（厦门国际法高等研究院 2019 年"国际法前沿问题研修班"开学典礼致辞）*

Good morning，distinguished guests，dear professors and participants，ladies and gentlemen，

Congratulations and Thanks

Warm welcome to Xiamen Academy of International Law！Welcome to Xiamen，China！

Warm congratulations for the opening of the 14th Session（2019）Summer Program of Xiamen Academy！

At this great moment，firstly，on behalf of Administrative Council of the Academy，I like to extend my heartfelt thanks to all the professors and all the participants from home and abroad！

Heartfelt thanks for all the relevant international institutions，in particular the International Court of Justice（ICJ）．We have received great support from ICJ，and law schools around the world！We hold the first curatorium meeting of Xiamen Academy in ICJ in 2005，and since then 9 Judges and the Registrar of ICJ came to Xiamen for lectures．This year Judge Yusuf is the fourth president of ICJ to come to Xiamen Academy，following President SHI Jiuyong，President Owada and President Tomka．It demonstrates the continuing great support from ICJ！I believe this is a very exceptional case in any summer program around the world！

Heartfelt thanks also for the Ministry of Foreign Affairs，PRC！We have received great support from the Ministry，Director Huang Huikang and Director Xu Hong made opening speeches here in 2013 and 2014，and China-AALCO International Law Programme was held in the Academy in 2015！Today Director Jia Guide

---

will give us an important opening speech on China International Law Practice in Last Seventy Years.

Great thanks for the Xiamen Municipal Government, the heads of the city, Dr. Zhong Xingguo, Mr. Chen Bingfa and Mr. He Qingqiu, give us their strong support in various aspects!

Many thanks for my colleagues and volunteers from Xiamen University Law School, for their great support and great contributions!

I firmly believe that with our joint efforts, we will achieve great future of Xiamen Academy!

Aim of the Xiamen Academy

For my understanding, this is great time for the development of international law. Currently, international law, or existing international legal regime is confronted with great challenges. We are facing three conflicts: (1) the conflict between multilateralism and unilateralism; (2) the conflict between rule orientation and power orientation; (3) the conflict between common interest of international society and interest of a state (like "American First" policy). The international society needs international law than ever before!

Why we are gathering here? What is the aim of Xiamen Academy?

In short, to promote the rule of law in international society. For this aim, we set up the Academy to conduct and promote international law education and training for young international lawyers; to conduct and promote international exchanges among international lawyers from different States, different cultures. We shall always bear these in mind and try our best. Surely the Academy is an important forum for international law circles.

Suggestions

I have indicated three elements to promote and guarantee the success of this summer program: leading professors, excellent participants and good location. I have further three suggestions for you.

1. Concentrating on your international law studies

(1) Learning from leading professors. We have invited leading international law professors, not only from leading academic institutes around the world, but also from ICJ and other key international institutions. The professors all have rich expe-

rience for teaching, researching and practicing international law. As great masters they offer you great knowledge and researching methods on international law. By attending the course, you might also learn some other things from them as gentlemen and gentlewomen, for example, the outlook of the world, the attitude to life, family and society, etc. I also like to indicate that looking back to the history, international law is developing and changing. We need exchanging ideas and promoting initiative. We need diversity and different voice, especially the voice of professors from developing states.

(2) Learning from excellent participants. We have a very good participant-structure in this program. I believed that Xiamen Academy is an idea platform for international exchanges in international law circles, for international lawyers with different backgrounds, especially for young generation from different countries. As for professional aspect, there are young university professors, lawyers, and graduate students as a main part. As for geographical aspect, the total 100 participants come from around 20 countries and regions. Comparing with Hague Academy, the size of participants is smaller, which is good for discussion and Q & A.

2. Setting up the academic links and "friend circles"

Nowadays we have more and more new teaching methods. However, the face-to-face teaching is first choice since it provides the best direct and closer way for exchanging ideas.

We need platform for international exchanges. Xiamen Academy is one of the idea platforms for international exchanges. We have two levels of exchanges: professor to participants, and participants to participants. I am very glad to see that excellent participants come from famous institutions around the world. You are the main actors in the platform. You might learn from each other, exchange ideas on international law, cultures and social issues relating China, other countries and the world. To large extent your performance decides the success of the program.

3. Exploring China's development from the unique location

For overseas participants especially, we have two classrooms in this program: one is here, main classroom for international law studies. The other is a great classroom for China studies through Xiamen.

I like you to pay attention to some profiles of Xiamen: (1) one of the four special economic zones since 1980s; (2) supporting city for "Belt & Road" initiative; (3) host of BRICS Summit in 2017 when President Xi recalled his work in Xiamen from1985 to 1988. In addition, Gulangyu (Kulangsu) was listed in "UN world cultural heritage list" in 2017. By the history of Xiamen (Amoy), you might see a good example of the conflict, coexistence and harmony between East and West in China.

Our Dream

Ladies and gentlemen,

This is time for international lawyers! As international lawyers, our dream is to achieve the rule of law in international society! One of the key issues is the participation of law making. As all states are subjects of international law, they should join the law making equally. In particular, we need voice, participation and contribution on international law from developing states.

One world one dream! As international lawyers, we are seeking for the common value and common professional sprite. We all recognize our mission for our motherlands and the whole world. At a highest level, justice and rule of law have universal value. We also pursue peace, development, harmony and happiness for all peoples by rule of law. Peace and development of the world first! At the practical level, we should serve our people and states with professional spirit and technique!

As a Xiamenese, I am very proud of my hometown and wish you a very happy time here. I wish you firstly, to concentrate on international law studies. Secondly, wish you enjoy and cherish every sunrise and sunset in this modern city and beautiful island!

（二）Speech at the Closing Ceremony of 2015 Summer Program（厦门国际法高等研究院 2015 年"国际法前沿问题研修班"闭学式致辞）*

Good afternoon, ladies and gentlemen!

Thank you and Congratulations

At this great moment, on behalf of Administrative Council of the Xiamen Academy, I like to express my heartfelt gratitude to all the leading professors, and all the participants came from home and abroad! Also extend my heartfelt thanks to

---

* 2015 年 7 月 31 日，在厦门国际法高等研究院 2015 年"国际法前沿问题研修班"闭学式致辞。

all my colleagues, students and especially the volunteers from Xiamen University Law School!

With our joint effort, we have celebrated the 10th anniversary of Xiamen Academy and achieved the great success of the 2015 Summer Program! I think this is the most successful summer program in the 10-year history of Xiamen Academy!

Warm Congratulation for the success of China-AALCO International Law Program!

At this great moment, I would also like to extend my warm congratulations for all the participants! For your completing the studies and excellent performance in this program!

Three Great Achievements in the Program

What happens in these three weeks?

I found we are so fortunate and at least we have three achievements needed to be celebrated:

1. We set a new record in all the international law program around the world.

In addition to three distinguished professors, i. e. Professor Ernst-Ulrich Petersmann, Professor Photini Pazartzis and Professor Chia-Jui Cheng, three ICJ Judges, i. e. Judge Hisashi Owada, Judge James Crawford and Judge Hanqin Xue have given lectures here! The great record of high-class lecturers for international law programs is very difficult to break out in the coming years!

I firmly believe that you received great reward in these three weeks. The topics of the lectures involve basic theory and hot topics on development of international law: State Responsibilities, Procedural Justice and Jurisdiction of ICJ, Arbitration in International Law, International Agriculture Law, Methodological Problem in IEL etc. Every professor offers his/her own researching focus and achievements, and valuable experience on international law practice. We have heard different voices, opinions and comments coming from different part of the world.

I firmly believe that face to face, you learn a lot from the great professors and great masters in international law fields, not only the academic aspect, but also the great thought on the world and human being, working-hard spirit, and career development as great masters and international lawyers. You might enhance the basis and expend the fields of international law through this program, and might also develop or find some interesting subjects for your future studies.

2. We have great participants with excellent performance.

We set another good record for the Academy that all seats are almost fully occupied all the time in the classroom. We have very good international exchanges at both the professors to participants level and the participants to participants level.

Thank for the China-AALCO International Law Program, we have more participants with rich working experience, especially on practicing international law than ever before! Due to the working experience, they raise practical questions and make great comments.

I am very glad to learn that all of the participants concentrate on and enjoy the lectures, asking questions, and making comments vividly. I found that the participants work very hard, and cherish the great opportunity to every minute, therefore professors have to answer many questions in and after class. Professors often extend their courses due to the questions, almost more than 30 minutes after class.

In addition to the fascinating lectures, we held two participant-salons, discussing the legal issues, systems and cultures in different home countries, exchanging ideas on rule of law particularly.

The gala party this year might not be the most colorful one in the history of the Academy, but it definitely reaches the highest-class, as our distinguished professor Judge Owada teach Chinese participant to sing a Japanese song. What a warm picture! Judge Owada also sing a song for us, so wonderful and touch everyone's heart! We learn that a great international lawyer is so easy-going and friendly.

3. We have good experience to learn China

For all the participants, especially foreign participants, the very important thing is that you learn something on China from your personal experience. I think you have wonderful free time after class in last three weeks.

I like to give you some information relating to Xiamen for you: (1) the Maritime Silk Road started from Quanzhou and Xiamen in ancient times; (2) the New Land Silk Road established currently (the new China-Europe train start from Xiamen to Poland); and (3) the New Air Silk Road achieved last week. Xiamen Airlines has opened its first airline to Amsterdam, and just follow the Beijing, Shanghai and Guangzhou in terms of frequency of flight to European.

Future of International Law

Ladies and Gentlemen, young lawyers,

I like to ask you a basic question: We study international law for what? The simple answer might be: "To make the world a better place to live!"

As international lawyers, we have to always to keep the following questions in mind:

(1) Where is international law in the current international society?

(2) Who and how to decide the development of international law?

(3) What is the most important right among human rights?

We may find that we face great challenges on international law these days and we need the rule of international law than ever before!

I believe that we are gathering here for our dream, our mission and future.

As international lawyers, we have the same objectives, same missions and same responsibilities for the rule of law in our home countries and international society, for the world peace, right to life, safety, security, development and happiness of the human being by means of international law. As young generation in international law field, having the beautiful dream in mind we have to study hard, work hard, to bear our responsibilities for our countries and the whole world.

For all the young participants, I like to indicate that you have met great master here. You might learn great thought from them. You might learn something from their career. You might learn how to step by step, lead to the excellence!

I also like to indicate that something should be changed, and you should have innovative idea. You are new generation of international lawyers. You might decide the trend and direction of international law. You might decide the role of rule of law in international society. Therefore, you are the future of international law! You might further study, rethink and reconsider international law independently, learning from not only Western scholars, but also scholars from China and other developing countries. Most importantly you have more confident, and have to learn and think independently.

Keep in Touch

Comparing with Hague Academy of International Law with long history, Xiamen Academy is a very young and a developing one. Xiamen Academy is an autonomous international institute on international law, located in Xiamen University and supported by Xiamen University, Xiamen city and international law circles around the world. The Academy is only 10 years old. In this sense you are the pioneers of Xiamen Academy. We have set up the platform for international exchanges and have achieved encouraging result. We have to work hard for better future of the platform.

The 2015 Summer Program is coming to the end. I like to emphasize that this is only the end of beginning of your relation with Xiamen Academy. After the program, you will become the alumni of Xiamen Academy. We have a list of participants for future communications, more than 1000 members with great potential. This summer program is our new starting point! Therefore, we might keep in touch and work together more closely. You may see that many professors involved in this program are good friends, coming from every corner of the world. The world is small, and the international law circle is smaller. I hope in the near future, you might become close colleagues and a strong team in practical and/or academic fields of international law.

Though the sentimental feeling for leaving always occurs to me at this moment, as Chinese saying: "meeting together is not easy and saying goodbye is even harder" (相见时难别亦难), there are also some encouraging examples. I remember that a girl student from Brazil who attends 2011 Summer Program decides to come back as a professor in Xiamen University Law School and Xiamen Academy of International Law. I firmly believe it and wish her dream comes true in the near future. Some participants are planning to apply for scholarship of Ph. D. candidates or LL. M. candidates in Xiamen Law School.

In conclusion, I hope that the program is meaningful for all of you and may made some positive impacts on the track of your life. I wish all of you have a great success and happy life! I will miss you all!

二、"厦门大学陈安国际法学发展基金会"的初心 *

尊敬的各位领导,亲爱的校友、同事和同学们:

大家好!"感恩、责任、奉献"是庆祝我校 90 周年华诞的主题,也是今天大会的主

---

* 2011 年 4 月 9 日,在"陈安国际法学发展基金会成立大会"致辞。

题，更表达了我们此时此刻的心情。

首先，我谨代表"陈安国际法学发展基金会筹备委员会"，热烈祝贺基金会正式成立！向关心和支持创建基金会的各级领导和广大校友、师生和各界人士表示由衷的感谢！向一年多来参与创建基金会的众多志愿者（我院博士生、硕士生和本科生）倾心倾力的奉献表示衷心的感谢！

在此，我向各位简要报告基金会筹组情况和感想。

（一）基金会筹组情况

1. 资金筹集

根据 2004 年《基金会管理条例》第 8 条规定，"非公募基金会的原始基金不低于200 万元人民币"。自 2009 年 10 月 9 日本会发出《关于成立"陈安国际法学发展基金会"的倡议书》以来，承蒙广大校友、师生和各界人士的热情关心和鼎力相助，人民币 200 万元已足额到位。

本会倡导和遵循的原则是，"捐赠不分先后，款项不分巨细，重在参与，共襄盛举"。各人情况不同，心相同。各笔捐款都是宝贵的奉献，都是基金会成立的基石。各笔捐款同样表达了报答师恩、回馈母校和社会的拳拳之心，为基金会的成立奠定了坚实的基础，更为我国国际法事业的发展作出了宝贵的贡献。在此，我谨代表本会向各位捐赠者表示崇高的敬意和由衷的谢忱！

在衷心感激各位"给力"共襄盛举的同时，很有必要特别感激：

最突出的"给力"：资深校友傅明、何培华、林忠、苏启云、谢岚、郑明芳、赵德铭给予基金会最突出的"给力"。

最及时的"给力"：资深校友张昕和邓德雄在第一时间响应倡议，给予基金会最及时的"给力"。

最年轻的"给力"：众多年轻校友的各笔捐款同样令人感动。一位年轻校友捐款附言："此款两千元系为基金会捐款，弟子财力有限，贡献微薄，待日后努力，再报答母校与师恩"。

最持续性的"给力"：肖彬老师及其领导的志愿者团队认真细致的行政联络和财务管理工作将持之以恒。

2. 组织机构

经初步酝酿，本会提出基金会第一届理事会理事建议名单。主要考虑工作需要，并兼顾地区分布因素。建议名单如下：

北京：洪艳蓉、张昕、邓德雄；

上海：傅明、林忠、赵德铭、郭俊秀；

深圳：邱永红、苏启云、赵俊荣；

西安：单文华、李万强；

广州：何培华；

香港：谢岚；

厦门：曾华群、廖益新、徐崇利、李国安。

本会还建议成立基金会秘书处。秘书处主要成员建议名单如下：

蔡从燕、陈辉萍、肖彬、房东。

理事会理事和秘书处人员都是"义工"性质，希望各位在百忙中接受这份"义工"，奉献社会。

3. 网站

在本会的筹划下，经网络工程师李璞先生精心制作，基金会网站已开通试运行。网站的主要功能是：(1) 宣传平台，及时发布基金会的各类信息；(2) 互动平台，便利基金会与公众特别是捐赠者和广大校友沟通互动；(3) 工作平台，设有"捐赠""资助"两个栏目，可直接在网上办理相关事务。

网站的开通，将有助于基金会增强运作的透明度。

（二）基金会的共识、宗旨和主要活动

1. 共识

基金会网站题词是："报师恩，济天下"。捐赠证书题词为："感念师恩，振兴中华"。上述题词表达了各位感念和报答陈安老师、法学院老师和厦门大学老师的培育之恩及回馈社会、报效国家的情怀，也是基金会全体创建者、贡献者和参与者的共识。

2. 基金会的宗旨和主要活动

根据《基金会章程》规定，基金会的宗旨是，"支持和促进开展国际法学领域的教学、研究和交流活动，促进中国国际法学特别是国家重点学科厦门大学国际法学科的发展。"基金会的主要活动范围是：(1) 资助国内外国际法专家学者前来厦门大学讲学；(2) 促进厦门大学国际法学科发展的活动；(3) 促进中国国际法学发展的活动。

基金会近期拟先开展"陈安国际法讲座"活动，邀请国际法学界学有专长的中青年学者来我院讲学。基金会将量力而行，逐步拓展支持学科建设的其他活动。

我谨代表基金会表示，本会的活动一定遵守相关法律法规，规范运作，讲求实效，实现各位捐赠人"捐资兴学，培育英才"的美意。

（三）基金会成立的意义

我们认为，基金会的成立具有十分重要的历史和现实意义。

本会是第一个以法学院教师命名的基金会。刚才，各位发言者对陈安老师的贡献作了高度评价。我想说的是，厦大建校90周年，陈安老师为厦大服务了60年，为学科建设作出了卓越贡献，目前还在继续奉献。就此而言，常人难以企及。以陈安老师命名的基金会的成立，具有精神和文化传承的深远意义。

本会是第一个由法学院校友发起的基金会。厦大法科建于1926年，老一辈校友为厦大法学的发展作出了历史性贡献。1979年复办、1980年后入学的新一代校友在海内外奋发有为，业绩显著，具有回馈母校和社会的使命感和公益心。基金会的成立，为广大校友提供了与我院加强联系、支持学科发展的重要平台。

本会是法学院第一个以支持学科建设为宗旨的基金会。近年来，国家对教育的投入虽不断加大，仍不能适应新形势发展的需要，特别是一些开拓性、创新性的工作，由于不在"预算内"，常有"兵马已动，粮草未备"的情况，急需开拓和借助社会资源。90周年校庆之际，我院国际法学科荣获我校最高学术奖"南强奖（集体）"一等奖。在美国华盛顿哥伦比亚特区举行的2011年"Jessup国际法模拟法庭辩论赛"中，我院辩论队荣获"反方诉状第一名"和"诉状总分第三名"，展现了我院教学科研的综合实力和水平，也反映了同学的勤奋有为、教师的敬业奉献。我们相信，基金会的成立，必将进一步促进我院国际法学科的发展，也必将为我国国际法学的发展作出应有的贡献。

三、勇于担当网络空间国际法研究的新使命 *

很感谢周宏仁主任专业的、跨学科的精彩报告。周主任的报告开阔了我们的学术视野，拉近了网络空间与法学、国际法学的距离，为网络空间法学研究提供了重要的指导意见。作为网络空间法学的初学者，我和大家分享三点体会：

第一，网络空间法学者需要准确理解网络空间技术的相关概念和原理。网络空间是一个不断发展的领域，需要我们持续跟踪网络空间技术实践的变化，时时关注和了解网络空间技术发展的前沿。作为网络空间法学者，我们需要准确理解网络空间技术的相关概念和原理。由于网络技术的飞速发展，网络空间技术的相关概念是

---

* 2019年4月11日，国家信息化专家委员会网络空间国际治理研究中心第二届学术研讨会在厦门召开，主题为"网络空间国际法的理论与实践"，由厦门大学法学院网络空间国际法研究中心承办。曾华群应邀作为主旨报告与谈人作大会发言。

动态、发展的。由于网络空间领域具有极强的专业性，为全面和准确了解网络空间领域的基本情况和技术原理，我们需要与网络空间技术专家保持密切联系，主动求教，加强跨学科研究、交流和合作。只有这样，我们才能准确认识和把握网络空间法学的研究对象，有的放矢地开展相关的规范性研究。

第二，网络空间法学、国际法学研究是网络空间领域研究的重要组成部分。周主任在报告中提出了由"领域维"和"功能维"构成的观察网络空间的模型。"领域维"包括政治、经济、社会、文化、军事、科技等六个维度。"功能维"包括综合治理、公共安全、网络情报、网络国防等四个维度。这些维度都是我们法学者所关注和理解的，与我们法学者的研究思维方式非常契合。这个模型具有很重要的指导意义。进而言之，无论哪个维度，都离不开法律，包括各国国内法和国际法的调整、规范和保障。由于网络空间的"跨境""全球"特征，比之国内法，国际法在调整、规范和保障方面的重要性显然更为突出。与物理空间的陆、海、空领域相比，网络空间更具"全球"特征，国际法规范层面的研究也更为重要。周主任的报告还强调指出，需要借鉴物理空间领域的既有研究经验来促进网络空间领域法学研究的发展。温故知新。在法学领域，我们也常采用以传统学科既有原则和经验指导新兴学科的创建发展。对网络空间法学这一新兴研究领域，我们同样需要借鉴和吸收法学传统学科的基本原则和基本方法。在实践中，法学传统学科（如民商法、刑法、金融法等）的研究，已在不同程度上渗透或扩及网络空间领域。

第三，中国国际法学者需要担当网络空间国际法研究的新使命。历史上，相继出现大国的"制海权之争"和"制空权之争"。当前，网络空间战略地位不断上升，在国际议程中的位置加速前移，"制网权之争"的时代已然来临。"制网权之争"的核心是网络技术和网络空间秩序的主导权之争。由于"制网权"这一新兴权力场域的出现，我国面临严峻的挑战和难得的机遇，相应地，也需要我国国际法学者攻坚克难，担负起网络空间国际法研究的新使命。我国亟须抓住机遇，凭借网络技术发展的优势条件，力争增强我国和广大发展中国家在这一新领域中的国际话语权，积极参与和引导网络空间国际立法活动。我国的基本立场是，各国基于"人类命运共同体"的理念，在相互尊重、相互信任的基础上，加强对话合作，推动全球网络空间治理体系变革，共同构建和平、安全、开放、合作的网络空间，推动建立多边、民主、透明的全球网络空间治理体系。我国国际法学者理应坚持和发展以《联合国宪章》宗旨和原则为基础的、各国普遍接受的国际法原则，积极参与研究网络空间国际治理的中国方案，为网络空间的国际法治作出应有的贡献。

四、适时推进"当代中国与国际经济法"英文系列专著项目 *

近期，中国国际经济法学会荣誉会长、厦门大学法学院陈安教授向学界部分术业有专攻的学者发出"通告信"并逐一沟通，诚邀他们积极参加撰写"当代中国与国际经济法"(Modern China & International Economic Law)英文系列专著，申请"国家社科基金中华学术外译项目"立项，并将英文专著交由德国 Springer 出版社向全球推出，以对外弘扬中华法学文化，增强"中国特色话语"在国际法学论坛上的发声量和影响力。截至 2020 年 7 月 6 日，已有 22 位知名教授和中青年学者明确表示参与该项目的意愿。中国国际经济法学会拟利用年会期间或其他时机，邀请 Springer 出版社李琰、王磊编辑与各位参撰作者面商出版合同事宜，力争后续各部专著早日相继问世。

"当代中国与国际经济法"英文系列专著项目的起源可追溯至 2012 年。当年，陈安教授的专著《中国的呐喊：陈安论国际经济法学》(*The Voice from China：An CHEN on International Economic Law*)获得"国家社科基金中华学术外译项目"立项批准。次年，陈安教授将英文专著交由 Springer 出版社在全球出版发行。该专著出版后，海内外学界纷纷撰文予以评论和回应，共同向世界传达中华学术正气和中华正义之声。鉴于该专著广泛的学术影响，Springer 出版社主动建议开展进一步学术合作，邀请陈安教授主编题为"当代中国与国际经济法"的英文系列专著，遴选和邀请学有专长的中国学者围绕这一主题，撰写创新性著作，提交该出版集团免费出版。2015 年初，陈安教授应邀与 Springer 出版社签订了长期的出版合同。2015 年，武汉大学曾令良教授应陈安教授邀请，在其长期研究成果的基础上，撰写专著《当代国际法与中国的和平发展》(*Contemporary International Law and China's Peaceful Development*)中文稿，继而由其弟子张皎博士等承担翻译重任。近日该专著英文稿已提交 Springer 出版社，将于 2021 年年初在全球发行。这是"当代中国与国际经济法"系列专著的第一部专著，由两代学人"接力"完成，令人感佩。

鉴于"当代中国与国际经济法"系列专著项目的适时推出关系到"知识报国，向世界发出中国强音"的大业，陈安教授连日来就相关事宜与曾华群、车丕照、陈辉萍、韩秀丽和朱晓勤教授等进行了多次协商和讨论，并拟订相关执行方案。其后，陈安教授亲自邀请部分知名同行专家学者（如中国政法大学孔庆江教授，中国人民大学韩立余教授，香港大学赵云教授，西安交通大学李万强教授，厦门大学法学院基金讲

---

* 原载《国际经济法学刊》2020 年第 4 期，张金矜撰稿，曾华群修订。

座教授何培华博士、赵德铭博士和张昕博士等)积极参与该项目。同时,陈安教授也联络部分优秀同行青年学者,邀请他们积极参与系列专著的撰写,勉励他们要敢于并善于给自己施加"压力",在学术上及时"更上一层楼"。在陈安教授的精神感召下,反响热烈。陈安教授随即向 Springer 出版社李琰、王磊编辑发送了"当代中国与国际经济法"系列专著的作者推荐名单,同时也向各位作者传达在 Springer 出版社出版著作的程序和质量要求,为出版社和作者之间的后续合作搭建起沟通的桥梁。

中国国际经济法学会全力支持"当代中国与国际经济法"系列专著项目的适时推进。为践行学会"知识报国,兼济天下"的宗旨,促进中国特色国际经济法学走向世界,耄耋之年的陈安教授以身作则,笔耕不辍,并竭力为后学搭桥铺路。该项目的适时推进不仅具有精神和文化传承的深远意义,而且蕴含着陈安教授等老一辈国际经济法学者对广大中青年学者的关怀和期盼。应当说明,该项目是长期向广大国际经济法学人开放的项目。本学会在密切跟踪现有申报专著进展情况的同时,热诚鼓励国际经济法领域的专家学者撰写、推荐或自荐优秀书稿,积极参与"当代中国与国际经济法"系列专著项目,共襄"发出中国学术强音"之盛举。

中国国际经济法学会秘书处

附 编

惠风和畅 家国情感

导　言

"天朗气清,惠风和畅"是古今崇尚的自然景象和社会理想。本编是本书最为个性化的部分,披露点滴家事和本人经历,希望与广大读者特别是莘莘学子促膝谈心,共同感受个人和家庭的命运与国家的命运的密切关联。第十四章感念父母平凡而伟大的人生及其留下的珍贵精神财富(第一、二节),与治学主题相关,特别记录了我家追寻大学梦的百年之旅(第三节)。第十五章回顾本人的成长经历和社会实践。我们这一代学者亲历"困难时期""文革""上山下乡"和"改革开放",是时代"弄潮儿"中的"幸运儿",丰富多彩的人生体验带有鲜明的时代印记,包括"初一"少年不知愁(第一节)、在上杭的青春岁月(第二节)、农工学者本色(第三节)、人大代表履职事例(第四节)及漫漫法学之旅(第五节),概括了本人追求"自强不息,在服务社会中丰富人生"的持续努力。

作为本人感恩汇报的工作录和成绩单,本编附录包括指导的研究生和论文题目、主要研究项目、主要研究成果、主要学术交流活动、主要获奖成果和学术荣誉,一定程度上浓缩了且行且珍惜的"万水千山",体现了探索中国特色国际经济法学的"工匠"精神,更反映了知识报国的学术环境和社会各界持续给予的关爱勉励。

作者的感悟:

(1)人有生命、慧命、使命,贵有自知之明、感恩之心、奉献之志。感恩父母!人生茫茫,家风绵延。父母对我们的养育之恩永铭于心!感恩母校!学海洋洋,校风绵延。母校对我们的栽培之恩永铭于心!感恩改革开放的新时代!个人和家庭的命运总是与国家的命运息息相关。改革开放的新时代,给予我家追梦大学的现实机遇,更给予我们"知识报国,兼济天下"的广阔天地。寸草春晖!我们常怀感恩之心,且行且珍惜,必将继续担当使命,奉献社会。

(2)一直自认为是农工知识分子。在知识分子群中,常想起上杭的日子,常想起田野、工地上可亲可敬的农友工友。青春年华在"社会大学"的求索在很大程度上塑造了我做人的品格和意志，也使我时时记起对社会和民众的一份应尽的责任。

（3）"自强不息，在服务社会中丰富人生"，是我的人生追求。回望来时路，是记录特定年代一位"50后"学者的成长历程，更是一位"知青"学者或"农民工"学者向国家和人民的感恩汇报。"路漫漫其修远兮"，永葆"法治"的美好愿景，我的法学之旅还在继续探索和坚定前行中。

第十四章
家事依依　感念感恩

第一节　父亲的传奇[*]

去年初冬，敬爱的父亲曾国琛坚定走过其沧桑百年人生，平凡之中亦有传奇，谨录一二。

父亲勤学慎思，永葆艺文之心。父亲 9 岁在安海曾家祠堂拜孔"破笔"。在安海养正小学读书时，曾以"学业第一"而入选《养正大观》。因家境贫寒，父亲小学毕业后就离乡背井，到石码碾米厂当学徒。之后，为避"抽壮丁"而入养正中学复读一年。1939—1945 年，父亲先后在晋江岱峰、成美小学及同安双溪、洗墨池小学等任教，初露才华。时值抗战艰难时期，父亲因陋就简，讲授"砖刻"（类似"木刻"，以闽南红砖代替木头作为雕刻材料）课程，还编辑出版"砖刻"作品，反映抗战等社会现实题材。惜岁月蹉跎，父亲长期无暇顾及艺文。及至退休，父亲才得以"重操旧业"，修习书法篆刻，聊以自娱。

父亲外柔内刚，担当匹夫之责。1945 年 8 月，父亲在同安教书时因"共党嫌疑"而被国民党当局逮捕，从同安经泉州徒步押解往莆田监狱。途经安海时，父亲要求将其斗笠脱下以掩其背后的"五花大绑"，尽可能保持其书生风度。长达八个月的铁窗生活九死一生。受狱中地下党人影响，父亲更坚定其理想信念。在厦门解放前夕的"白色恐怖"中，父母一起掩护和留宿从南洋途径厦门的地下党人张木生、张玉、沈保良和许金越；父亲还曾带领地下党人登门向在厦门的晋江籍商人募集活动经费。解放后，父亲放弃私营企业高薪待遇，服从工作需要，曾任国营企业会计、业务科长

＊ 本文主要内容原载《厦门日报》2017 年 4 月 24 日 B08 版（城市副刊），《厦门日报》（电子版）http://epaper. xmnn. cn/xmrb/20170424/16. pdf

等职，一向敬业清廉。曾在胃痛时坚持值夜班，突发"胃穿孔"而送医急救。久经组织考验，父亲于1958年实现入党夙愿，更以党员标准严格律己。

父亲忠厚仁爱，传承"耕读"家风。2008年汶川大地震，父亲年近九十，亲自前往镇海路农业银行，以其恩人"曾瀛洲"名义捐款6000元。平时捐资助学更是不遗余力。父亲与母亲陈秀叶1949年初结为连理，相濡以沫凡66年。1959—1978年母亲蒙冤离职期间，父亲在历次政治运动中亦受牵连。父母患难与共，悉心培养五子女成长。我和大哥1969年下乡上杭，父亲专程翻山越岭前来探望和鼓励。父亲常称羡其一位小学同学有机会一直读书，成为大学教授。借改革开放春风，父母言传身教，竟成就"厦门一家人"走出四位博士、教授的佳话。

父爱如山，母爱似海！父母倾其毕生所能所有，奉献国家、社会和家庭，留下了珍贵的精神财富。父母的美德和精神永存！父母未竟的梦想我们继续追寻！

第二节 母爱长青
——感念母亲陈秀叶[*]

追思依依往事,平凡的母亲,度过了不平凡的一生,留下了珍贵的精神财富,令人感念万千。

一、大爱无疆

母亲充满爱心,是有大爱的人。

母亲深爱小家。1925 年 2 月,母亲出生于晋江县安海镇一个传统的家庭。她自幼聪慧好学,孝敬父母长辈,在安海养正中学初中毕业后,就下乡当小学教员,帮助维持家庭生计,勉力尽长女之责。1949 年婚后定居厦门,工作之余,她相夫教子,是典型的贤妻良母,心中只有家人,唯独没有自己。20 世纪六七十年代是家境最艰难时期,母亲积极达观,坦然面对生活的甘苦。至今,我们仍念念不忘当年在家里和母亲一起制作信封纸盒的"勤工"情景,特别是母亲以糯米饭、菜头粿"奖赏"我们的"拜六晚"。

母亲深爱大家。抗战时期,厦门沦陷,安海不时遭受日机侵扰轰炸。母亲 17 岁就参加安海妇女抗日救护队的培训。解放战争时期,大舅在安海以"文化书店"为名行"地下党交通站"之实,母亲参与送情报等工作。新中国成立前夕,在"白色恐怖"中,父母亲在厦门继续与安海地下党组织保持联系,曾奉命一起迎送和掩护过往地下党员。这些在当时是生死攸关的事,母亲淡定处之,认为理所应当。新中国成立后,母亲热心公益,以感恩博爱之心,长期服务社会。

二、敬业奉献

母亲毕生从事两个平凡的职业,都全身心投入,做到极致。

第一个职业是小学教员。母亲初中毕业后在晋江乡村多所"国民学校"任教。"国民学校"是为普及偏远农村小学教育而设,全校师资配备为一校长一教员。教学任务繁重,生活条件艰苦,自办伙食,借宿民居。母亲专心致志,当语文、算术、音乐"全科"教师,上不同年级学生同聚一教室的"复式"课,经常家访劝学,深受学生和家

---

[*] 原载《厦门大学报》2015 年 4 月 10 日第 16 版。参见曾华群:《母亲的敬业奉献》,载《厦门日报》2015 年 4 月 10 日 C08 版(城市副刊),《厦门日报》(电子版),http://epaper.xmnn.cn/xmrb/20150410/28.pdf。

长好评。1948 年在安海养正小学任教时,母亲教学精益求精,所教的学生一举囊括晋江县小学算术抽考第一、三名。

母亲的第二个职业是妇联干部。自 20 世纪 50 年代以来,母亲长期在厦门市妇联做"人民来信来访"工作,主要处理婚姻、家庭纠纷、家庭暴力等关系妇女权益的事务。每周来访接待日,她满怀爱心,亲切接待每位来访者。"事事有交代,件件有着落",是她的工作准则。其他工作日甚至节假日,不分昼夜,她奔波于鹭岛内外。"哪里有受苦的姐妹,那里就有老陈瘦弱的身影",是她日常工作的真实写照。她经常配合法院工作,参与离婚诉讼中的调解工作。在她苦口婆心的调解下,许多濒临破裂的家庭重归于好。在她坚持不懈的努力下,许多特困家庭的生计或住房等难题得到了妥善解决。在她倾尽心力的救助下,轻生的姑娘、被遗弃的婴儿获得了新生。母亲的敬业奉献受到了广大妇女群众的高度赞誉和组织的充分肯定。她多次获市政府授予的"厦门市信访工作先进个人"荣誉。1989 年和 1990 年,全国妇联、福建省妇联和厦门市妇联分别向母亲颁发荣誉证书,表彰她"长期从事妇女工作,为妇女解放事业做出了积极贡献"。

三、坚忍不拔

很难想象,母亲的柔弱之躯长期承载着万钧重负。

1959 年,母亲蒙冤离职,延至 1978 年才平反复职。漫漫十九年,正值母亲风华正茂之年,也是我们成长的重要时期。母亲以"舍我其谁"的勇气,承受巨大的、多重的压力和苦难。由于担心影响我们的成长,她表面上若无其事,严守"秘密"。"文革"前,作为"监督改造"的安排,她每天要负责我家所在小巷和所住楼房天台的清洁卫生工作。为了保守"秘密",她天天要赶在天亮之前完成这一艰难任务。历时六年,母亲在我们睡梦之中忍受的苦痛和辛劳,我们竟然一无所知!"文革"期间,"秘密"无从保守,"监督改造"的安排也升级了。她时常被派去参加篔筜港围海造地、人防工程等重体力劳动。当时,我们也已长大,坚信母亲是最好的,力争分担她的身心重负。

不言而喻,正是母亲长期严守"秘密"和独力应对苦难,我们才有无忧无虑、天天向上的童年和少年。我们感念她伟大的母爱和非凡的品格。我们深知,是对未来的信念,对家人的热爱和担当,支撑她坚定走过人生这段最坎坷的漫长旅程。

四、教子有方

父母亲悉心培养我们五个兄弟姐妹健康成长,是我们的启蒙老师。

母亲经常回忆年少读书的艰难。当时,因家境贫寒,她买不起课本,只能靠逐字逐页抄书,连历史书上史可法画像等也用毛边纸细致临摹。她还常谈起当年作为"新女性"所推崇的"精神胜于物质"和"反对拜金主义"等新风尚。母亲刻苦勤奋、追求卓越的精神潜移默化,一直是激励我们奋发前行的动力。我们在中、小学期间均品学兼优,还各有"一技之长"。

母亲向来鼓励我们到艰苦环境中锻炼成长。1969 年 3 月和 6 月,她支持民哥和我分赴老区上杭县中都公社和溪口公社插队落户。1976 年 8 月,又支持琦妹赴厦门郊区灌口公社下乡。我们在上杭期间,家里节衣缩食,不时寄来巴浪鱼干、面茶、猪油和粮票等,为我们提供了"久旱甘霖"般的"物质援助"。一封封充满亲情励志的家书,更是我们源源不断的精神源泉。我们兄妹三人在农村均能吃苦耐劳,较快适应和融入当地主流。

1977 年恢复高考制度后,我和淳弟、琦妹、伟弟先后考上厦门大学历史系、化学系和生物系,分属 77 级、78 级和 80 级。毕业后,又分别在厦门大学、加拿大不列颠哥伦比亚大学、新加坡国立大学和美国怀俄明州立大学获得博士学位。学成之后,我们秉承"自强不息,止于至善"的校训,在海内外高校和科研机构努力工作,回馈社会。母亲一向十分关心我们的学习、工作和生活,给予最及时、最温馨的教导和勉励。

2005 年,母亲获厦门市"杰出母亲"殊荣,可谓实至名归。

感念绵长,寸草春晖! 母亲之爱、母亲之德、母亲之恩永在我们心中!

第三节　百年追梦录[*]

"大学"的涵义见仁见智。对我家而言，"大学"是百年追梦，是一种家国情怀，一种精神传承。

一、心驰神往

对父亲曾国琛、母亲陈秀叶而言，读书难，上大学更是遥不可及的梦想。

20 世纪初期，父母出生于晋江安海。父亲 9 岁在曾家祠堂拜孔圣人"破笔"。因家境贫寒，父亲养正小学毕业后就离乡背井，到石码碾米厂当学徒。之后，为避"抽壮丁"而复读养正中学。因生计无着，心有旁骛，仅读一年又辍学了。抗战艰难岁月，父亲以"初一"学历，先后在晋江岱峰、成美小学及同安双溪、洗墨池小学等任教，初露艺文才华。当年弘一法师云游晋江，父亲曾慕名求字一幅。上美术课时，父亲因陋就简，讲授"砖刻"（类似木刻，以闽南红砖代替木头作为雕刻材料）技能，还编辑出版砖刻作品，反映抗战等社会现实题材。父亲外柔内刚，生性率真，不满社会现状或有流露。1945 年，父亲在双溪小学因"共党嫌疑"而被捕，身陷囹圄八个月，九死一生，也由此彻底阻断了"文青"之梦。

母亲上学时，家道中落，是外祖母极力坚持，才有勤工俭学的机会。她买不起课本，只能靠逐字逐页照抄，连历史书上史可法画像等也用毛边纸细致临摹，课余兼做手工贴补家用。锲而不舍，母亲竟读到养正中学初中毕业。作为"新知识女性"，母亲先当多年乡村"国民学校"教员，后获聘为养正小学教员，一向敬业勤勉，精益求精。1948 年，她的学生一举获得晋江县算术抽考第一、三名，载入学校史册《养正大观》。母亲时年 23 岁，如有机会，正是读大学的青春年华。

"爱读书"还是促成父母长达 66 年"超钻石"姻缘的红线。父亲在小学读书时，曾以"学业第一"入选《养正大观》。当年养正小学校长得知父母相恋后，特向母亲展示了《养正大观》中父亲的少年照并大加赞赏。

尽管大学遥不可及，父母心向往之。父亲常称羡一位小学同学有机会一直读到大学，成为厦门大学教授。母亲也多次提起，当年算术抽考获奖的两位学生后来都上了大学，一位还留学苏联。

---

* 原载厦门大学校友总会认证公众号：厦大人"群贤文苑"专栏，2021 年 5 月 28 日；厦门大学校友总会网站 https://alumni.xmu.edu.cn，"校友风采——群贤文苑"专栏，2021 年 5 月 31 日。

令人感佩的是,"读书难"的父母在青年时代直面现实,努力奋斗,特别是毅然决然投身振兴中华的时代潮流,勇担"匹夫之责"。

二、梦想成真

对我们兄弟妹而言,读书不难,上大学确属不易。

由于深知父母的"读书难",我们兄弟妹中、小学期间都很珍惜"有书读"的幸运,上大学原本是可预期实现的共同目标。1966年,"文革"狂飙突起,中断了我们的升学之路。1969年,民兄和我分赴上杭县中都公社和溪口公社插队落户。

70年代初,推荐工农兵学员上大学,家里一度燃起"上大学"的希望。父亲不辞辛劳,翻山越岭,专程前来上杭山区探望鼓励。我利用工余时间自学了中学课程,以增强求学实力。1972、1973年,我曾连续两次被工厂推荐到县里,均折戟而返。

1977年高考制度恢复后,我和淳弟、琦妹、伟弟相继考入厦门大学。入学时经历迥异、年龄不同,反映了不寻常年代的特征。我1965年读初一,自1966年夏天起,就在社会上"闯荡",历经"文革"、上山下乡、招工和对调工作,成为交通部第四航务工程局工人,1978年2月考入历史系,年已25岁。淳弟74届高中毕业,"留城"在厦门市医药站工作,1978年9月考入化学系,22岁。琦妹77届高中毕业,赴厦门灌口公社铁山大队下乡,也在1978年9月考入生物系,19岁。伟弟80届高中毕业,即考入生物系,年方16岁。我与伟弟年龄相差12岁,伟弟报名读小学时我已是上杭县瓷厂工人,居然还能成为大学同学。历尽艰辛的普通人家出了四位大学生,一时传为佳话。当时厦门电视台以此事例制作成《厦门一家人》的首期节目,中央电视台(四套)转播,向海内外展现我国改革开放的新气象。

上大学期间,我们有幸走进梦想中的校园"大厦",囊萤映雪,刻苦攻读。有幸聆听博学勤业的老师授课,如沐春风。与"大师"也有缘交集,铭感于心。学部委员蔡启瑞教授是淳弟的老师,淳弟擅长书画,常为蔡教授精心绘制赴海内外讲学的示意图。父女学部委员唐仲璋、唐崇惕教授和著名生物学家汪德耀教授是琦妹、伟弟的老师,唐崇惕教授成了伟弟的硕士生导师,汪德耀教授曾力荐琦妹留校任教。傅衣凌、韩国磐教授是享誉海内外的明清史、隋唐史大师,悉心传授学问之道。临别依依,两位大师还专为我们历史1977级的《毕业纪念册》题词并逐一赠言鼓励。

上大学期间,是我家最美好的时光。饱经沧桑的父母抚今忆昔,扬眉吐气,为我们大学梦的实现而欢欣鼓舞。有老友戏问:"厦门大学可是你家办的吗?"父亲妙答:"是啊!校长是曾鸣。"

因缘际会,我们兄弟妹四人同时在厦门大学攻读本科课程。这在厦门大学历史上，当属百年一遇。就中外大学史而言，亦属罕见。

三、自强不息

本科毕业后，我们秉持"自强不息，止于至善"的校训，在不同的专业领域，专心致志，勇于拼搏。

淳弟本科毕业后留在化学系任助教。1984 年赴加拿大不列颠哥伦比亚大学留学，1989 年获理学博士（物理化学）学位，随后在多伦多大学从事博士后研究。1991年起，他受聘于新加坡国立大学工学院，长期从事物理化学的教学研究工作，近年主要从事纳米科学技术研究。现任化学与生物分子工程系教授、纳米材料研究项目负责人，新加坡国立大学苏州研究院首席研究员，还受聘为国际组织"智能制造系统"制造业纳米技术程序委员会委员等。2011 年，作为联合国"国际化学年"的项目，汤森路透集团（Thomson Reuters）依据全球化学领域论文的影响因子确定和发布了"2000—2010 年全球顶尖一百化学家名人堂榜单"（Top 100 Chemists，2000—2010），淳弟位列第 49 名。

琦妹本科毕业后分配到福建医学院任助教。之后赴海外留学，1989、1993 年先后在美国罗斯韦尔-帕克纪念研究所（Roswell Park Memorial Institute）和新加坡国立大学获得科学硕士（生物学）和理学博士（生物学）学位。1989 年起，琦妹在新加坡国立大学分子细胞生物学研究院工作，主要从事基因研究。她开发的转基因鼠技术，创制了亚洲第一例转基因鼠。美国《财富》（Fortune）杂志（Oct. 7，1991）专文报道，以此作为亚洲产业转型的典例。琦妹现任教授级研究主任、新加坡国立大学生物化学系兼职教授，有关 PRL-3 的持续研究成果（包括 PRL-3 磷酸酶与癌症治疗的创新理论）受到国际学术同行的高度重视，并获多项国际专利。

伟弟本科毕业后考取我校硕士研究生，1987 年获理学硕士（生物学）学位，学位论文发表于《厦门大学学报》（第 28 卷第 3 期，1989）。毕业后分配在厦门市水产研究所工作。1989 年赴美国访问留学，1996 年获美国怀俄明州立大学理学博士（生物学）学位，随后进入美国国家健康研究院（National Institutes of Health）从事博士后研究。1999 年起，在美国格兰德福克斯营养学研究中心工作，主要从事生物学与营养学的跨学科研究。现任高级研究员、实验室负责人、北达科他州立大学生物系兼职教授，在基因与健康等领域的创新研究中取得了显著成果。

我本科毕业后，考取我校国际法专业硕士研究生，1984 年毕业后留校任教。1987 年又考取我校国际经济法专业博士研究生，1990 年成为我校培养的第一位法学博士，1996 年入选为国家"百千万人才工程首批第一、二层次人选"。我主要从事国际经济法的教学研究,长期任国际经济法研究所所长,负责国家重点学科厦门大学国际法学科的创建发展工作,曾赴美国、瑞士、英国、新加坡等研修和讲学。还兼任厦门市人民代表大会法制委员会副主任委员(第十一届)、内务司法委员会副主任委员(第十二、十三届)。现任中国国际经济法学会会长、厦门国际法高等研究院联席院长和世界银行集团"解决投资争端国际中心"(ICSID)调解员等。

有志事成,爱拼会赢。我们兄弟妹同窗求学,同为博士,同为教授,同行专业奉献之路,涉及纳米科学、生物医学、生物营养学、国际法学等研究领域,已然创造了我家追梦大学的"超级"境界。

四、感恩奉献

人有生命、慧命、使命,贵有自知之明、感恩之心、奉献之志。

我们感恩父母! 父母对我们的养育之恩永铭于心! 父母是我们的最佳启蒙老师。人生茫茫,家风绵延。父母刻苦勤奋、敬业奉献、坚忍乐观的精神潜移默化,一直是激励我们奋发前行的源泉。

我们感恩母校! 母校对我们的栽培之恩永铭于心! 厦门大学是我们的共同母校,是我们梦想成真的大学,更是我们学术发展的"根据地"。学海洋洋,校风绵延。得益于母校玉成的"书香门第",我家新一代继往开来,续写追梦华章。子女们本科入读清华大学、加州理工学院等中外大学,品学兼优。蓓斯率先毕业,已成长为外贸人才。迄今,弘毅获斯坦福大学博士(计算机科学)学位,洪程、洪明分获克利夫兰医学院博士(医学)学位、伦敦大学帝国学院和新加坡南洋理工大学学士(医学)学位。佳瓦、凯闻正在耶鲁大学、威斯康星大学攻读博士(化学工程)学位,凯妮正准备报考大学。

我们感恩改革开放的新时代! 个人和家庭的命运总是与国家的命运息息相关。改革开放的新时代,给予我家追梦大学的现实机遇,更给予我们"知识报国,兼济天下"的广阔天地。寸草春晖! 我们常怀感恩之心,且行且珍惜,必将继续担当使命,奉献社会。

第十五章
征途漫漫　且行且享

第一节　"初一"少年不知愁 *

　　蓦然回首,我进入中学已是半个世纪之前的事了。尽管所受的正规中学教育只有"初一",还是很值得留恋和回味的。

　　1965年初夏,我面临求学的一个重要节点,小学要毕业了,考哪个中学,一中还是八中?八中优势明显,试行中学五年一贯制,免考高中,还可节省一年。而一中仍按部就班,初、高中各读三年,还要考高中。小伙伴们大多决定报考八中,我决定实地考察后再说。经考察发现,一中校园够大,有大运动场,设有一个正规足球场,还一分为二,再设两个小足球场,总共三对球门,如不怕冲撞,可同时安排三场足球赛。一中乒乓球室也够大,摆了10多张乒乓球桌。我在小学深受乒乓球桌紧缺之苦,放学后常要等天色黑到大同学看不见球了,才有机会上阵。天道酬勤,我一路摸黑苦练,成为校队主力,还曾参加市少体校(设于中山公园妙释寺)的培训,比世界冠军郭跃华更早拜汤教练为师。受到一中体育设施的强力诱惑,我毅然报考一中,如愿以偿,可惜不能再与一起快乐成长于第五幼儿园(设于泰山礼拜堂)和民立小学的多数小伙伴继续"斗阵"了。

　　不知是由于"山雨欲来"的政治背景,或是由于一中"素质教育"的光荣传统,新生入学报告会上,学校请来两位校友作报告,主题当是革命英雄主义。报告人一位是杰出校友倪志钦,当年的全运会跳高冠军,开讲如何刻苦拼搏,为国争光。我们在台下仰视,觉得他很高很帅,也为学校能培养出这么伟大的运动员而欢欣鼓舞。另

　　＊　原载《厦门大学报》2015年11月27日第8版和厦门知青文化活动组委会编:《永远的初一》,2015年12月出版,第3—5页。

一位报告人是杰出校友黄美妙的同学。60 年代初黄美妙高中毕业后,响应党的号召上山下乡,不幸在一次扑灭山火的战斗中牺牲了。她的同学回忆烈士生前的点点滴滴,谈及困难时期她在家煮饭时,每次抓一小把米藏起来,积少成多,在家里断粮时聊补无米之炊。两个报告的重要启迪是,学校不欣赏只会读书考试的"书呆子",而是鼓励学生成为德智体全面发展的社会主义事业接班人。为体验农村生活,1966 年暑假,我们班 10 多位同学自发组织到五通下乡,白天干农活,夜间巡水路,吃菜饭咸粥,睡地板"饲"蚊子。1969 年 6 月,我赴上杭县溪口公社大丰大队插队落户。和黄美妙校友一样,从厦门到山区,也经历过山火考验,一切似曾相识,有些许"历史重演""前仆后继"的意味。

难忘当年初一(5)班的课堂。我们班的老师是清一色的年轻人,朝气蓬勃,富有敬业精神。语文课叶国华老师戴着黑框眼镜,笑容可掬,性情忠厚,后来一直兢兢业业从事"园丁"工作,曾任职厦门师范学校。80 年代初,我们班一位同学从福建师范大学毕业后成为他的同事,才有了他的最新信息。相比之下,数学课蔡由利老师较为严格,违规同学总能感受他那透过厚厚镜片的威严目光,"要自爱点"是他经常对违规同学的告诫,语重心长。他是我们的班主任,一向关注各位同学的成长,保持较密切的联系。近年春节期间偶有聚会,还认得出各位"老得好样"(我班女同学对男同学的恭维语)的同学。英语课林辉老师,身材魁梧,一看就是侨生出身,普通话带印尼腔。第一节课就要求我们"口要洋,心要红",又红又专。林老师讲课十分投入,表情手势生动活泼。我们早在小学二年级就学俄语,后因中苏关系恶化而中断,五、六年级改学英语,初一还学相同的课本,驾轻就熟。与其他学校不同,一中还专设书法课,请擅长楷书的陈美祥老师讲授。翩翩一介书生,大毛笔蘸白粉浆在黑板上行云流水,印象殊深。陈老师锲而不舍,已成为书法名家多年,南普陀等名胜可见其秀美字迹。

课余,我们自然不会辜负学校及周边的体育设施,努力锻炼身体。常规安排是,中午游泳,下午踢球。从学校篮球场往上走三五分钟,就到了市游泳池,门票五分钱。我们中午吃学校食堂。自带米,便当蒸饭,蒸饭票两分钱。母亲给我的午餐菜钱一角,属中等水准,我从中省五分钱买游泳池门票。午餐三分钱可选购一份素菜(青菜、豆腐或芋头等),相当可口,两分钱再买一份鱼丸汤(二个鱼丸),常把饭团翻在便当盖,用便当盛汤。"汤足饭饱"之后,就到游泳池开练了,各式跳水、泳姿,无师自通。个别同学解决不了门票费问题,只得冒险偷游或垂钓万石岩水库。每天下午放学后,我们班男同学占据一个小足球场,分成两队,大多光脚,踢球到天黑。顺应"民意",我竟然放弃乒乓球,改练对抗性更强、更需要团队精神的足球。一中当年还实施高年级同学全方位帮助低年级同学的"一帮一"制度。我们班与高一（五）班结成对子，常邀该班老大哥来踢球。自定的规则是，我们班人数占优（如我方 11 人：对方 9 人），高一（五）班个头占优，激烈混战，不打不相识。

感谢一中，感谢一中亲爱的老师，给了我们潇洒自如的"初一"，让我们不经意间也蓄积了搏击"文化大革命"和"上山下乡"风浪的勇气和体魄！

第二节 在上杭的青春岁月[*]

1969 年 6 月至 1976 年 12 月，年方 17 至 24 岁，我在老区上杭县度过了丰富多彩的青春岁月，往事历历，心驰神往。

一、溪口务农

1965 年 9 月，我读厦门一中，属"老三届"中的"初中 68 届毕业生"。1969 年 6 月 2 日，响应毛主席"知识青年上山下乡"的号召，我们 18 位同学一起乘火车到龙岩，转乘大卡车赴老区上杭县溪口公社大丰大队插队落户。

由于当地男人大多去割松香或伐木，我们男知青很快成为作业组的强劳力。日出而作前的温馨时刻是在作业组长陈代英家的集合，大家边聊天边享用陈家的小番薯或其他"小吃"，我借机操练客家话，以利尽快融入当地主流。陈组长是位精瘦的"女强人"，慈祥豪爽，笑声震天，传说是土地革命时期的赤卫队员。在她的带领下，我们天天耕作于层层梯田。春雨绵绵，穿蓑衣戴斗笠插秧忙。夏日炎炎，戴着"伐木小帽"光膀挥汗甩谷，芒刺浑身，收工再挑一担谷饥肠辘辘硬撑下山。令人惬意或不平的是出工的"烟歇"惯例，一声"食烟了"，男人立马"脱岗"，在田头吹起"大喇叭"，吞云吐雾，尽显爷们风范，女人则得照干不误。男女知青亦不例外。也许是得益于"文革""串联"的磨炼，我较快适应了山区的生活，学会了春耕、夏收夏种和秋收的多种农活，一年内工分从 4 工分提升为 6 工分（每个工分值 0.048 元），并列所在宫下村知青的最高分。

二、泮境做工

在同批下乡的知青中，我是特别幸运的。1970 年 8 月，下乡刚满一年两个月，我就第一个被分配工作，成为国营上杭县瓷厂的学徒工，实现农转"非"，月薪 18 元整，经济上自给自足。

工厂坐落在上杭县泮境公社院康大队境内的大山深处，不通公路，山路离县城 30 里，离公社 10 里。瓷土矿就在后山。烧制瓷器的松木也取自附近山头，当地农民由近及远砍伐，源源供应。碗、茶壶、杯子等产品由农民挑到城里，大多销售本县。

---

* 原载《厦门大学报》2013 年 6 月 28 日第 4 版。

我当原料班工人，和工友承担瓷土加工一整套工序的劳作，包括在水碓房的挥锹起落泥、长柄锄头在大水池的搅拌"洗"泥、人力压榨机的旋转"榨"泥及肩挑加板车的运泥等，全凭汗马实力。梁兰芬班长身先士卒，不让须眉，众工友共苦同甘。工歇时常聚餐自产的南瓜、木薯，亲如一家。

当年"工业学大庆""人定胜天"深入人心，晚饭后的义务劳动习以为常。我们挖鱼塘，种油茶……屡败屡战。最雄心勃勃的是学愚公，力图靠精神和锄头开出通往公社的 10 里公路，奋战数月，无奈缺乏爆破技术和专业人才，面对比锄头更硬朗的岩石，结局可想而知。

作为厂里的"知青"，我得到了许多重用机会。厂里将最为先进贵重、耗电量最大的真空炼泥机交由我操作，每晚加班 3 小时炼泥。曾奉派到尤溪县电瓷厂学制作电工瓷技术，到连城县瓷厂、大浦县瓷厂学制作出口瓷技术，到湖南醴陵陶瓷轻工机械厂学维修真空炼泥机技术。还曾不自量力地绘制图纸，送到县农业机械厂制造简易炼泥机。

三、山火考验

青春年少，有时会翘首企盼"壮怀激烈"的事情发生。两次迎战山火，算是平凡农工生活中的严峻考验。

在泮境的一天深夜，山林突发大火，全厂民兵紧急集合，人手一筒 10 个大饼，向火场方向出发。伸手不见五指，一路急行军。远处火光冲天，还隐约传来竹子燃烧爆裂声。在大山里左冲右突，却无法接近火场，连向导也迷了路，只能宣布就地等待天明。一夜折腾，一筒饼不知何时已消灭殆尽。天蒙蒙亮，找到了通往火场的小路，士气大振。逼近火场时，烧了一整夜的大火已显颓势，大家砍下树枝作灭火工具，连线成一长排，顺着风势一路扑将下去。兵不血刃，终于在中午时分扑灭了残余的山火。大功告成，一身轻松，顿觉筋疲力尽。回厂路上，大多跌跌撞撞，三五十步一歇，十多里山路走了三四个钟头。

在连城县瓷厂学习期间，又巧遇一场夜间山火。"火光就是命令"，我们一行五位来自上杭的"进修生"义无反顾地加入当地的灭火大军，可谓"将在外，无君命也自战"。

四、泉酒绵延

下乡后，我们的生活有了很大的改变，毕竟是从"中山路"来到"山中路"。所幸溪口公社通公路，山清水秀，别有洞天。宫下村口就有一眼温泉，简易搭盖，石板池，温泉真真切切从池底的石缝冒出来,气泡连连。以天色明暗为界,男女分时段共享一池水,男士优先。收工回来,一身汗水泥巴直接泡入温泉,有时还洗出附体蚂蟥,不亦乐乎。夏夜我们时常躺在溪边瓜棚架上,仰望满天繁星,浮想联翩。明月当空,万籁俱寂,我喜欢独自在大山深处练太极拳,感受出神入化的意境。

闽西家家自酿糯米酒,温热了一人一锡壶,不醉不休不散。我落户范大富大哥家,熟米饭,南瓜芥菜,亲情浓浓,还很快练出了好酒量。父母那时常寄来巴浪鱼干,本是给范大哥添为家常菜,他却舍不得与妻儿分享,专作每晚邀我对饮的下酒菜。世事倥偬。30年后我带儿子重返宫下村与范大哥家团聚,当年坐在饭桌对面拨弄干菜的小孩恍惚依然,定睛查询,已是当年小孩生的小孩了。那年返乡时范大哥在村头整日等候,各家农友连环酒宴,离别相拥紧握,男儿泪轻弹,此农友之情至纯至真!

1978年2月以来在厦门大学学习工作,不觉已有35年。一直自认为是农工知识分子。在知识分子群中,常想起上杭的日子,常想起田野、工地上可亲可敬的农友工友。青春年华在"社会大学"的求索在很大程度上塑造了我做人的品格和意志,也使我时时记起对社会和民众的一份应尽的责任。

第三节　农工学者本色*

曾华群　男，1952年7月出生于厦门。1969年6月参加工作，1979年11月加入中共。毕业于厦门大学，获历史学学士（1982年）、法学硕士（1984年）和法学博士（1990年）学位。

1984年12月以来在厦门大学法律系/法学院任教，历任讲师、副教授，1991年12月晋升为教授，1994年12月评为博士生导师，1997年入选国家"百千万人才工程首批第一、二层次人选"。现任厦门大学国际经济法研究所所长、厦门国际法高等研究院联席院长。兼任中国国际经济法学会常务副会长、中国国际法学会常务理事、中国国际经济贸易仲裁委员会仲裁员、福建省人民政府法律顾问、厦门市第十一、十二、十三届人民代表大会法制委员会和内务司法委员会副主任委员等。曾赴美国威拉姆特大学法学院、香港大学法学院、瑞士比较法研究所、伦敦大学亚非学院、新加坡国立大学东亚研究所、台湾东吴大学法学院和澳门大学法学院研修和讲学。

主要从事国际经济法领域的教学和研究工作。讲授多门本科生主干课程和研究生学位课程。先后承担"霍英东教育基金会第三次高等学校青年教师基金"项目、国家社会科学基金重大项目等。其代表作有：《国际经济法导论》（第二版）（法律出版社，2007年）；《WTO与中国外资法的发展》（厦门大学出版社，2006年）；《国际投资法学》（主编，北京大学出版社，1999年）；《中外合资企业法律的理论与实务》（厦门大学出版社，1991年）；Initiative and Implications of Hong Kong's Bilateral Investment Treaties，*The Journal of World Investment & Trade*（*JWIT*），Vol. 11，No. 5，2010；Unprecedented International Status：Theoretical and Practical Aspects of the HKSAR's External Autonomy，*JWIT*，Vol. 9，No. 3，2008；"One China Four WTO Memberships"：Legal Grounds，Relations and Significance，*JWIT*，Vol. 8，No. 5.，2007等。获"全国高等学校人文社会科学研究优秀成果奖著作类二等奖"（1995）等多项国家和省部级科研和教学成果奖。

我们是厦门东渡港口最早的建设者，第一步是移山填海，开辟建造水泥预制块的场地。我当风钻工，上夜班，在殿前工地打炮眼。我有些近视，打炮眼是

---

*　原载何勤华主编：《中国法学家访谈录（第四卷）》，北京大学出版社2013年版。本文记者为李秋实，文稿由曾华群修订。

一项有点危险的工作，钢钎必须持续对准炮眼，否则钢钎撞断可能出事，在作业面复杂的情况下，还要提防炮眼周边的石头震动坠落。炮眼打好后，通常是下半夜了，爆破组上，实施爆破。第二天，由搬运工来搬运碎石填海。上大学之前九年，我一直和农民、工人朝夕相处，同甘共苦，有较深厚的感情，也深受他们朴实人生观的影响，我一直自认为是"农工知识分子"。

记者（以下简称"记"）：老师，您好，我们得知，您在上大学之前曾经工作过一段时间，能谈谈当时的一些情况吗？

曾华群（以下简称"曾"）：我们这一代跟老一辈比起来算是很幸运了。我是1965年9月上中学，属于"老三届"，是"文化大革命"期间中学六个年级的最低年级"初中68届"，最高是"高中66届"。1969年6月下乡时，我们算是1968届初中毕业生。其实，我们只是在1965年9月到1966年5月读了一学年的书，1966年5月，"文革"就开始了。

1969年6月，我就到闽西老区上杭县溪口公社大丰大队宫下生产队下乡。虽然是省内，但因为当时交通不便，也算是遥远的。现在从厦门到上杭大约三个多小时车程，当年要花上两天时间。先乘火车或汽车到龙岩，在那里过夜后，第二天才有开往上杭的班车。下乡后，我们的生活有了很大的改变，毕竟是从城市到了山区。得益于"文革"的锻炼，我还是较快适应了山区的生活，和农民同吃同住同出工，较快学会了春耕、夏收夏种和秋收的各种农活，一年内工分从4工分升为6工分（每个工分值4.8分人民币），当时是全生产队知青的最高分。

在知青中，我又是特别幸运的。下乡才一年多，即1970年8月，我就第一批被选调到工厂工作，实现了农转"非"，月工资18元，经济上实现了独立，还略有节余。当时选调工作是民主的，我们大队分配到一个名额，据说是让农民评选，评选的标准主要是劳动表现。选上后，我从上杭县溪口公社调到位于上杭县泮境公社的国营县办工厂"上杭县瓷厂"。工厂坐落在泮境公社院康大队附近的大山里，不通公路，瓷土矿就在后山，烧制瓷器的松木也取自附近山头，当地农民由近及远砍伐，源源供应，瓷器生产出来后由农民挑到城里，大多销售本地。我那时干的是体力活，当原料车间工人，承担瓷土加工一整套工序的劳作，包括碓泥、洗泥、榨泥、炼泥及板车运输等。我下乡的溪口公社通公路，山清水秀，还有温泉。我从农村调到工厂，劳动强度更大，生活环境远不如溪口。溪口的农友来看我时，不免一番感叹，劝我"打道回府"。

我在上杭县瓷厂待到1976年12月。1972、1973年我曾连续被工厂推荐为工农兵学员候选人，上报县里，可惜因名额限制，两次都落选了。1974年以后，连被推荐的机会也没有了。1976年春节我回厦门探亲时，同学提供了一个重要信息，说厦门在兴建港口，建港的工程队里有上杭人，可以争取对调工作。生活忽然有了新的目标，我决定试试。经过了近一年的联络和申请，在1976年的最后一天，我如愿回到了厦门。1977年元旦过后，我开始在厦门上班。

我在厦门的单位是交通部第四航务工程局第四工程处第八中队第一小队。厦门港早就有了，但现代化港口是20世纪70年代中期才开始兴建的。我们是厦门东渡港口最早的建设者，第一步是移山填海，开辟建造水泥预制块的场地。我当风钻工，上夜班，在殿前工地打炮眼。我有些近视，打炮眼是一项有点危险的工作，钢钎必须持续对准炮眼，否则钢钎撞断可能出事，在作业面复杂的情况下，还要提防炮眼周边的石头震动坠落。炮眼打好后，通常是下半夜了，爆破组上，实施爆破。第二天，由搬运工来搬运碎石填海。

上大学之前九年，我一直和农民、工人朝夕相处，同甘共苦，有较深厚的感情，也深受他们朴实人生观的影响，我一直自认为是"农工知识分子"。

记：您经历过"文革"，能谈一下您对"文革"的记忆和看法吗？

曾：不容否认，总体上，"文革"给我们国家和人民带来了灾难性后果。在我看来，各地、各个时期情况不同，危害程度不能一概而论。有一些情况并非后来的某些描述或想象那么糟。印象中，由于当时厦门地处"海防前线"，军队影响力大，局势相对较稳定。当然，对我们这一代人的切身影响是，大多数人失去了上大学的机会，改变了命运。当时的年轻人单纯而富有理想和激情，积极响应毛主席的号召，投身"革命"洪流参加各种活动，是自然而然的。"文革"开始时我14岁，也参加了抄大字报、批判会及"大串联"等活动，经受了许多风雨考验。我希望，历史会给参加"文革"的年轻人一个公正的评价。

记：您怎么了解到恢复高考的消息？

曾：我是回厦门工作后听说的，大约是1977年7、8月，社会上风传要恢复高考了。当时，我们工程队要抽调一个中队参加"汕头市燃料油库码头工程会战"，我所在的第八中队中选。我找到工程队领导，说我是厦门人，对调回来工作的目的就是想照顾家人，能不能让我留在厦门上班。队领导答复，你们中队闽南人多，你要是留下来，很多人也会申请，特别是已成家的工人，照顾家庭的理由更充足，队里不好办。我服从工程队的工作需要，同时提了一个要求，请队领导在高招开始时帮我报个名。我们当时在汕头的一个海岛施工，交通不便，两天才由小船送一次信。高招开始报名时，队领导信守诺言，发了一个电报让我赶回厦门，说不懂得如何帮我填报志愿。报名之后，队领导让我留在厦门，说等高考结果出来后，再回汕头继续上班或打点行李上大学。我很幸运地及时报了名，参加了"文革"后恢复的第一次高考，竟然考上了。

岁月蹉跎，大家都很珍惜失而复得的学习机会，一心一意读书，经常白天黑夜连轴转。临近毕业，我们班67名同学中，有29名准备报考研究生。

记：您工作那么多年，平时一直都有坚持学习吗？

曾：1972年、1973年两次被推荐为工农兵学员候选人期间，我就让弟妹把学过的中学课本寄给我。工作之余，我抓紧时间学习备考。那时"工业学大庆"，学"铁人精神"，八小时上班以外的时间经常义务加班加点。我们厂地处山区，有许多加班的特色，曾为改善生活而开路、挖鱼塘、种油茶树等，更经常性的加班是堆放收购来的木柴，以节省人工成本。我还上夜班，负责真空炼泥机的操作，那时其他机器停开，才有充足的电力供应那台机器。那两年，自己能把握和利用的只有午休时间，刻苦自学，大致补上了中学的全部课程。可惜没有实验的机会，物理、化学只是书上看看，底气不足。高考报名时，为求成功率大些，就选报了文科类。

记：我们得知您高考报考的是历史学专业，您选择历史学有什么个人原因吗？

曾：1977年报考时，厦门大学还没有法学专业，1979年才复办法学专业，1980年开始招收本科生。我当时报考文科类专业，文科中最难的大概是中文专业，似乎上中文系就能当作家了。我的想法是能上大学就谢天谢地了，哪能凭兴趣挑专业！出于现实的考虑，我选择了相对"冷门"的历史学专业。总体上，那时的考生普遍对专业了解很少，也没有太多的考虑。

记：那么，您后来为什么选择攻读法学专业的研究生呢？

曾：我们历史学专业77级是很优秀的集体，1979年曾荣获共青团中央授予的"全国新长征突击队"称号。班上同学的年龄最大差别为14岁，许多是经历过社会实践的"老三届"。相对而言，那时外文系、中文系的学生较年轻，我们班平均年龄较大。岁月蹉跎，大家都很珍惜失而复得的学习机会，一心一意读书，经常白天黑夜连轴转。临近毕业，我们班67名同学中，有29名准备报考研究生。大家商量，应分散报考，不要"扎堆"报考本校历史学专业，才会有更多的机会。结果，我们29个同学分别报考了本校和外校的历史、经济、法律、外交等专业。我选择报考本校法学专业。决定后，我开始到法律系选修一些专业课程。当时，只是隐约觉得，法律与现实联系较密切，对社会的发展是重要的。这也可算是我报考法学专业研究生的一个动因。我们班有3个同学同时考上了厦门大学法律系。

记：您是厦门大学复办法学专业后培养的第一届硕士研究生和第一位博士研究

生，能谈一下求学经历和您印象比较深刻的老师吗？

曾：厦门大学1926年就创办法科，20世纪50年代初全国院系调整时，厦门大学法律系合并到华东政法学院。1979年，厦门大学决定复办法律系之后，由陈朝璧、何永龄和盛辛民先生等先后主政，把法律系原来的老师和早期毕业生招回来，并招收了一些非法学专业的年轻本科毕业生，让他们边学边教，组建了复办后的第一支师资队伍。出于培养法律系师资的考虑，盛辛民老师等力主尽快招收法学专业研究生。1981年经国家教委批准，法律系设立了国际法专业和外国法制史专业两个硕士点。1982年初，我们10个非法学专业的本科毕业生考上了法律系的研究生，7个是国际法专业，3个是外国法制史专业。当时，法律系师资紧缺，就采取开门办学的方式，一方面邀请外校老师前来讲学，另一方面也让我们到外校上课。

1983年春季学期，我们在武汉大学法学院"留学"，上了梁西老师的"国际组织法"、李双元老师的"国际私法"和美国琼斯教授的"国际商法"等研究生课程，还登门拜访了韩德培老师、姚梅镇老师和黄炳坤老师等，请教学问之道。各位老师虚怀若谷，悉心传授治学经验，还亲切招待我们喝茶、吃糖。

1984年初，我们开始收集专业资料，准备写毕业论文，也有机会在全国各地跑，曾到深圳、上海等地调研，在武汉大学法学院、北京图书馆等收集资料。那年5月8日至6月5日，我在庐山参加"首届国际经济法讲习班"，领略了我国早期国际经济法学者周子亚、姚梅镇、陈安、高尔森、朱学山、江振良、盛愉、卢绳祖、董世忠、方之寅等老师的风采，也见证了"中国国际经济法研究会"（即"中国国际经济法学会"的前身）的产生。

1986年，国家教委批准厦门大学设立国际经济法专业博士点。通过入学考试，我荣幸地成为厦门大学的第一位法学专业博士生，师从陈安老师。1987年2月入学，1990年4月毕业。我的博士学位论文由武汉大学韩德培老师和姚梅镇老师评阅。两位老师当时已年逾古稀，还千里迢迢专程来厦门主持我的论文答辩会，令我感动万分。

在厦门大学法律系/法学院长期的学习和工作中，系主任盛辛民老师在学潮中希望师生"谨言慎行"的谆谆教诲和温文宽厚的长者风范，陈安老师创建国际经济法学科的强烈事业心、坚忍不拔精神和身体力行，对我的影响尤为深刻。

记：您在读本科和研究生时对国际法有一些了解吗，您怎样看待当时国内国际法专业的状况？

曾：改革开放之前，中国的国际法研究中断或停滞了相当长的一段时间。特别是在"文革"期间，搞"法律虚无主义"，国际法更是乏人关注。读本科时，我对国际法也没有什么了解，只知道是法学的一个分支学科。国际法的研究与时代密切相关。1978年以来，我国实行改革开放政策，厦门作为经济特区，引进外资，促进外贸，需要研究相关国际法和国内法问题，国际法、国际经济法的重要性日益凸显。在这种背景下，我学习国际法、国际经济法的目标就比较明确了。我的硕士学位论文选题是"中外合资企业管理权分享问题"，具有鲜明的时代特点，也有较强的实践性。为取得第一手资料，我还到厦门特区外资处和深圳特区的中外合资企业调研，受到政府机关负责人和企业老总的认真接待。

记：您在大学期间，哪些事情使您印象深刻？

曾：大学生活丰富多彩，当是人生最美好、最值得留恋的时光之一。学习之余，军训和班级集体活动特别令人难忘。当年的大学生活与现在有很大的不同，厦门大学更有特色。现在新生一般在校园军训。我们当时是到部队军训，与战士同吃同住。在军营练实弹射击后，我们回学校后还在校园后山加练步枪、冲锋枪的实弹射击，在白城山坡演练匍匐前进和爆破。厦门岛与金门岛隔海相望，那时厦门大学白城以北就是军事禁区，专门设有一个军事岗哨，未经许可不准逾越。本科学习期间，我们是真正的"民兵"，晚上荷枪实弹，在白城一带海边执勤巡逻，或潜伏在坑道里观察海面"敌情"，一班两个小时，轮值通宵达旦。当年，我们在宿舍还能听到随风飘来的金门广播，有邓丽君的"靡靡之音"，也有对"共军官兵弟兄们"的喊话。后来两岸局势逐渐缓和，我们的军事行动也取消了。时间久了，很多事都淡忘了。有一次，我在翻书的时候，发现里面夹着一张历史系民兵营的通知，才记起我暑假守卫弹药库的往事。当时，弹药库就在我们宿舍楼的一个房间，我在那里守了整整一个暑假，责任重大，真正是亦民亦兵，亦文亦武。当然，这些往事与特定的年代和厦门大学的特殊地理位置有关，其他地方的大学生难有这种"前线民兵"的体验。

国内有的学者对西方国际法的历史发展不够了解，在学习西方国际法理论中缺乏独立思考和"扬弃"精神，难以深刻认识西方国际法的霸权主义实质。我国老一辈国际法学者对创建中国特色的国际法理论有强烈的意识……这从一个侧面反映了历史学，特别是法制史学的重要性，我们需要更深入地了解西方国际法的缘起、发展及其实质，从中探求中国特色国际法学的历史使命和发展方向。

记：老师，请您谈谈您的主要学术观点？

曾：我主要的研究领域是国际法，特别是国际经济法。我国国际法学主要是从西方传来的，国际法学的概念、术语、原则、规则等大多来自西方。我认为，西方国际法理论中具有普世价值的部分值得汲取和借鉴,但我们更应该注重发展中国特色的国际法理论,这需要长期的、坚持不懈的努力。国内有的学者对西方国际法的历史发展不够了解,在学习西方国际法理论中缺乏独立思考和"扬弃"精神,难以深刻认识西方国际法的霸权主义实质。我国老一辈国际法学者对创建中国特色的国际法理论有强烈的意识,如陈安老师,十分推崇和坚决主张建立国际经济新秩序的理论和原则。然而,这一主张在学界尚不能被广为认同。我认为,这从一个侧面反映了历史学,特别是法制史学的重要性,我们需要更深入地了解西方国际法的缘起、发展及其实质,从中探求中国特色国际法学的历史使命和发展方向。我赞成追求公平正义,特别是实质上的公平正义,而不仅仅是表面的、形式的公平正义。长期以来,西方国际法奉行弱肉强食的原则,强调强者主宰世界,历史上比较典型的是"先占原则",当前是所谓"先发制人"和某些"人道主义干预"。本质上,西方国际法理论的一些所谓"新发展"也是为推行其霸权主义服务的。

当前,我国的国际法理论研究还是很不够的。就国际投资法而言,最重要的国际法规范如《解决国家与他国国民之间投资争端公约》《多边投资担保机构公约》及双边投资条约等,都需要我们进一步深入研究。当前,国际投资法发展迅速,其趋向值得密切关注。近来,双边投资条约普遍规定接受"解决投资争端国际中心"(ICSID)的管辖,甚至规定投资者可以单方面启动 ICSID 程序。传统国际投资法本来就是发达国家为保护其海外投资者的产物,带有与生俱来的片面维护资本输出国权益的烙印,其新近发展并未起到平衡发达国家与发展中国家之间和东道国与外国投资者之间的权利和利益关系,而是更加片面强调保护发达国家和外国投资者的权益,进一步限制东道国的主权。通过此类规范的不断强化,发达国家推动投资自由化,以实现其国家利益。在坚持和维护国家主权原则方面,中国国际法学界的声音是不够的,主要是缺乏原创性的理论研究。由于理论研究的欠缺,也影响了我国的国际实践层面,在所谓"经济全球化"趋势下,我国的某些国际实践顺应了西方国家主导和推波助澜的所谓"时代潮流"。

我认为,我国的国际法理论研究应有自己的原则和立场,应有自己的原创性学术成果。在这方面,厦门大学国际法学者一直在努力。作为第一步,是争取在国际性学术刊物发表文章,表达中国国际法学者的立场和观点。

记:随着我国经济的迅速发展,我国很多公司企业也开始到海外投资,在我国国际经济地位发生转变的情况下,我国国际投资法的研究应把握怎样的立场呢?

曾:我向来主张,无论我国国际经济地位发生怎样的改变,无论是净资本输入国,还是成为资本输入国兼资本输出国,甚至是净资本输出国,我国应该有始终如一的、坚定的原则和立场。这或许是天真的书生之见。我以为，我国必须坚持和强调经济主权原则和公平互利原则，不能因为居于资本输出国地位就片面强调资本输出国的权益，要求资本输入国限制其主权。我国一向反对发达国家"以邻为壑""损人利己"，同样，也要引以为戒，严格自律。有学者认为，随着我国国际经济地位的改变，我国对外经济政策和立场也要相应调整。我赞同政策可以根据形势的变化而调整，但立场要坚定，不因地位的转变而变化，不因利益的诱导而变化。学者进行学术研究要有"立场"意识，政府主管部门在国际经济实践中也应当有坚定的立场。

记：我们知道，您曾在国外的许多大学和研究机构研修与讲学，有哪些较深刻的体会？

曾：我第一次出国留学是在美国俄勒冈州的威拉姆特大学法学院（Willamette University College of Law），从 1987 年 11 月到 1988 年 12 月。虽然是作为访问学者，我在那里正式选修法律博士（JD）课程，参加期末考试，体验了美国法学院的学习生活。法学院教授认可我的表现，为我提供全额奖学金，希望我能在那里攻读 JD 学位，而厦门大学则希望我早日回校教学。出于责任心，我婉拒了美方资助，服从学校的工作需要。当时的另一个考虑是，我已是厦门大学的法学博士生，应回国完成学业。留美期间，最深刻的感受是教学的自由和生动活泼，不同老师教学风格各异，共同的特点是注重调动学生学习的主动性和积极性。学生的规则意识很强，期末考试不需要监考老师。各门课程的考卷放在法学院大楼的大厅桌上，学生各取所需，到指定的教室考试。一年多的留美经历受益匪浅。后来，我有机会先后到瑞士比较法研究所、英国伦敦大学亚非学院和新加坡国立大学东亚研究所等访问研修，体验了不同的教学和研究风格。

1996 年 2 月，在瑞士比较法研究所作了半年研究后，研究所邀请我作学术报告。经过认真准备，我以《香港过渡期的双边条约实践》为题，第一次以英文向国外同行作专题报告，获得好评。在英国伦敦大学亚非学院、新加坡国立大学东亚研究所访问期间，我应邀作过多场与中国相关的国际法专题学术讲座。在同国外学者的交流中，对很多问题有了新的视野、新的思路。

记：在您多年的研究工作中，您比较倾向于采用何种研究方法？

曾：我向来比较侧重具体法律制度或实务问题的研究，也力图探讨相关理论问题，争取有创新性的成果。我主要采用历史与现实结合、国际法与国内法综合研究、比较研究和案例研究等方法，这些都是国际经济法学界较普遍采用的方法。跨学科的研究方法是值得提倡的，同时我觉得，跨学科的研究方法的运用有相当的难度。首先，对所跨的相关学科知识应有基本的掌握，才谈得上对该学科研究方法的适当运用。其次，法学研究主要是对法律规范本身的研究，跨学科的研究方法也要为此研究目的服务，而不是偏向所跨的其他学科，淡化甚至放弃了法学研究的本色。

记：您认为当下青年学者的研究状态是否存在浮躁的情况？

曾：从整体上看，当前我国学术研究是比较繁荣的。然而，毋庸讳言，当前的学术评价体系是亟待改革的，各种学术评估标准更多是关注数量而非质量，关注形式而非内容。国内高校普遍流行的对教师的考核制度是，重科研轻教学，只有科研是硬指标，一个统一的标准适用于各个专业，科研课题及经费、论文数量及刊物等级、获奖及等级是重要的评估依据。这种行政化管理科研的状况不利于学术的发展，也不利于人才的培养。

由于我国经济社会环境的急剧变化，青年学者面临着许多现实的问题与挑战，诸如职称晋升等实际问题，不得不努力适应现行体制的要求，迎合学术评估标准的各种量化指标，无法"十年磨一剑"，这是可以充分理解的。值得关注的是，在现行体制下，一些优秀青年学者，求"质"又求"量"，付出了超常的心力，甚至以健康为代价。也有少数优秀青年学者，超脱于现行体制，特立独行，即使教学研究业绩不凡，也得不到"体制内"的认可。两种不同的情况，都不利于优秀人才的"可持续发展"。

记：在您看来，一个良好的学术评价体系应该是怎样的呢？

曾：国内有学者专门研究教育学、高等教育学，现行学术评价体系的改革应是一个重要课题。国外高校一些先进经验值得研究借鉴。据了解，很多国外名校对教师实行综合的学术评价制度，更关注的是教师的综合素质，全面考察其教学、研究和社会服务等方面的能力和业绩，尤为重视工作质量和学术影响力。总体上，是一种宽松的以人为本、尊重教师、相信教师的学术评价机制。

当了多年的教师，我一直认为，教师应当是学校的主体，而不是被管理的客体。对教师不能用简单的、量化的行政方式来管理。记得我们当学生的年代，高校管理并不像今天这样程式化、精细化。老师敬业乐业，自由自在。我们的老师教学尽心尽力，备课非常认真，与我们的交流也很密切。在教学优先的情况下，老师的研究工作是自由的、自觉的。对老师来说，两年发表一篇文章还是三五年发表一篇文章都没关系。教师相互之间也不存在潜在的竞争关系。老师言传身教，要求我们"多读、多思、多记"，提倡"厚积薄发"。对研究生也没有发表论文的"硬指标"。我以为，当时"无为而治"的管理模式，更有利于学术的发展和人才的培养。

记：您能对中国法学当前的研究状态做一个整体的评价吗？

曾：我只能谈谈自己的一点感想。中国法学自改革开放以来取得了很大的发展，这是值得庆幸的。法学的发展与法治的建设是密切相关、相互促进的。只有我国的法治建设进一步得到重视,更好地实施法治,法学研究才能有更好的发展。法学研究为法治建设提供必要的理论基础,也能促进法治建设的发展。"百花齐放、百家争鸣"也是法学界所期待的学术环境和氛围。从国际经济法领域来说,研究基本上没有禁区,学术探讨是自由、开放的,法学其他领域,诸如民商法、经济法等领域的研究也是如此。

我以为,在从事法学研究中,应充分认识我国国情,立足于我国国情。中国法治建设的发展是一个长期的、渐进的过程,我国学者应更多地关注、研讨和创建适合我国国情的法学理论,而不能仅仅是"引进"和"移植"西方的法学理论和法律制度。西方的法学理论、法律制度远非完美,更不一定能适合于我国国情。例如,在金融法理论和制度建设方面,我国多年来主要借鉴美国金融法律制度,2007 年爆发的"美国次贷危机"暴露了该法律制度本身也存在诸多问题。

> 青年学者要有远大的理想,要有奋斗的目标。就国际法学习和研究而言,我们要有更强的国际意识。我们所处的时代要求我们更多地了解世界、认识世界,要有国际观和使命感。国际法的学习和研究特别需要国际化,我们特别需要积极参与国际学术交流。

记:您能通过您的经历给青年学者一些建议吗?

曾:青年学者要有远大的理想,要有奋斗的目标。就国际法学习和研究而言,我们要有更强的国际意识。我们所处的时代要求我们更多地了解世界、认识世界,要有国际观和使命感。国际法的学习和研究特别需要国际化,我们特别需要积极参与国际学术交流。

在这方面,厦门大学法学院一直在努力。近年来,我院一些青年教师积极向国外学术刊物投稿,在国际学术界崭露头角,显示出很强的学术发展潜力。

2002 年 3 月和 2003 年 4 月,我作为教练和领队,指导和率领我院辩论队参加在奥地利维也纳举行的第九、十届 Willem C. Vis 国际商事模拟辩论赛(英文),并应邀担任该赛事仲裁员。我院辩论队的首批队员是博士生池漫郊,硕士生陈延忠、黄哲和于湛旻,本科生邱冬梅和颜盈盈。在赛场上,我方队员面对以英语为母语的欧美名校强手,慷慨陈词,沉着答辩,或势均力敌,或略占上风,完成了我院辩论队在国际性专业大赛的第一次搏击,积累了宝贵的实战经验。

其后,我院辩论队由陈辉萍、池漫郊、龚宇、于湛旻等青年教师指导,连年参加Willem C. Vis 国际商事模拟辩论赛、Jessup 国际法模拟法庭辩论赛(英文)和国际人道法模拟法庭辩论赛(英文)等国际性专业大赛,形成优良传统,屡获佳绩,如 2006 年获得 Jessup 国际法模拟法庭辩论赛 Hardy C. Dillard 最佳书状奖第一名和 Willem C. Vis 国际商事模拟辩论赛书状奖一等奖（Top 10），为我国的法学教育赢得了国际声誉，也给国人莫大的启示和鼓舞。与西方比较而言，我国的法学教育历史不够悠久，教学设施不够先进，英语不是母语，我国也不是典型的英美法系或大陆法系国家，由于我院指导老师的敬业奉献和学生的全心投入，我们还是具备了与世界强校一争高下的实力。

相比我们这一代"老三届""农工知识分子"，青年学者和学生后来居上，具有很好的基础，很高的起点，更好的发展环境和机会，专心致志，自强不息，在国际法理论和实践方面当有更大的作为。

记：请您对有志于学习国际经济法的学子们推荐有利于他们学习的书籍？

曾：我认为，陈安老师的《陈安论国际经济法学》（5 卷本）（复旦大学出版社，2008 年）是值得认真研读的。作为老一辈国际经济法学者，陈安老师无论在理论方面还是在实务方面都有其独特的建树，其鲜明的"中国特色"立场、缜密的思辨和犀利的文风独树一帜，我想青年学子当可从中得到启发和教益。

第四节 人大代表履职事例

1997—2012 年,本人作为厦门市第十一、十二、十三届人民代表大会代表,认真履行职责,注重反映民意,积极提出有关专业和其他领域的建议、议案。谨举三例。

一、关于厦门大学与厦门市共建"厦门国际法高等研究院"的建议 *

在海内外国际法专家学者的关心和支持下,有关"厦门国际法高等研究院"(The Xiamen Academy of International Law,简称"研究院")的各项筹备工作正在顺利进行之中。有关研究院的筹建情况和建议简述如下:

(一)研究院简介及筹建情况

研究院的目标是建成享誉国际的自主性常设国际法学术机构,旨在促进国际法领域的国际学术研究、交流与合作;培训各国特别是亚太地区各国的国际法专业人才;加强国际法在规范国际关系和建立国际新秩序方面的功能。

借鉴在全球享有学术盛誉的海牙国际法高等研究院的模式,研究院的主要职能包括:举办国际法高等研修班,即邀请世界一流的国际法专家、学者授课,学员主要是各国青年外交官、涉外官员、高等院校教师、法官、律师以及研究生等;组织和主办国际法领域的国际学术研讨会;组织出版国际法高等研修班的讲演集和其他国际法论著;建立国际法专业图书馆;提供从事国际法研究的学术环境。

研究院设立董事会,由国际著名的国际法学家、法官和外交官等专业人士组成。目前,研究院的建设已得到国际社会和国际法学界同行的鼎力支持。2005 年 7 月 12 日,在荷兰海牙和平宫国际法院会议厅,隆重召开了研究院首届董事会成立会议暨第一次董事会会议。来自国际组织和各国的法官、国际法学者出席会议,共商研究院发展大计。会议产生了研究院首届董事会,联合国国际法院现任院长史久镛大法官担任首届董事会主席。

(二)共建研究院的建议及其意义

我们建议,将研究院的建设列入厦门市与厦门大学"985 工程"二期建设项目地方政府资金支持的具体项目之一。厦门市在成立研究院的审批手续、建设经费等方

---

* 厦门市第十二届人民代表大会第四次会议建议(2006 年 2 月),建议人:曾华群。

面予以支持,并参与研究院的行政管理。

研究院的运作主要借重我校的国际法学术资源。我校具有国际法教学研究的优良基础,自 1926 年设立法科以来,一向重视国际法的教学和研究,2002 年我校国际法学专业被教育部批准为国家重点学科(全国共有 3 家,另外两家分别是武汉大学和对外经济贸易大学)。我校法学院和国际经济法研究所在国内具有相当的学术地位和学术影响力,将与研究院相辅相成,共同发展。目前,我校已将研究院的建设定为"十一五"重点建设项目之一,将从各方面予以全力支持。

我们认为,由我校和厦门市共建研究院是一项具有深远历史意义的重要工程。

第一,研究院应"改革开放"之运而生,顺应"和平发展"之时代潮流而发展。经过不懈的努力和长期的发展,研究院将成为我国国际法教育和国际交流的重要平台,必将为提升我国国际法教育和研究水平,推动当代国际法的健康发展及建立新国际秩序作出重要的贡献。

第二,研究院的成立及其成功运作,必将进一步丰富厦门作为"全国文明城市"的内涵,进一步提升厦门的核心竞争力和在海内外的影响力和知名度。在市委、市政府的领导下,厦门目前已发展为国际化程度较高的"全国文明城市"。荷兰海牙由于是国际法院和海牙国际法高等研究院的所在地而闻名于世,旨在与海牙国际法高等研究院并驾齐驱的厦门国际法高等研究院的发展,也将为厦门的国际化作出重要的贡献。

第三,研究院的成立及其成功运作,必将进一步促进厦门"教育之城"的建设。为建设"教育之城",厦门近年积极引进国内高等院校来厦门办学,取得了显著的成效。研究院是高起点的国际性学术机构,建设研究院的工作本身,是推动厦门"教育之城"建设迈向国际化的重要举措。

二、关于加强城市规划工作的建议 *

在我市经济高速发展和迈向国际化都市的形势下,城市规划工作的重要性不言而喻。建议各级政府:

一、坚持依法行政,严格遵守有关城市规划和环境保护的全国性法律和地方法规。

二、确实发挥市城市规划委员会的作用。《厦门市城市规划条例》第二章规定了

---

* 厦门市第十三届人民代表大会第三次会议建议(2008 年 2 月),建议人:曾华群。该建议被评为"2007—2008 年度优秀代表建议"(2009 年 2 月,厦门市人大常委会办公厅颁发荣誉证书)。

市城市规划委员会的设立、职能和议事规则等。该委员会由公务员、有关专家学者及社会人士组成,其中,非公务员不得少于委员总数的二分之一。这在一定程度上从组织上保障了决策的专业性,应特别重视和确实发挥该委员会的作用。

三、在城市规划工作中以人为本,尊重民意,体察民情,民主决策。《厦门市城市规划条例》第四条第二款规定,"制定城市规划应当充分发扬民主,保障人民通过多种渠道参与城市规划制定活动"。对涉及环境景观和广大市民利益的重大项目,如BRT,应充分论证,科学决策,民主决策,包括举行听证会等。目前 BRT 第一期已在建,建议缓建第二期。在进一步调研、论证和分析 BRT 第一期实际运作情况的基础上再作决定。

三、关于维护鼓浪屿人文社会环境的建议和议案

（一）关于尽快恢复鼓浪屿就医条件的建议 *

近年,按市政府有关厦门医疗资源整合的部署,位于鼓浪屿的厦门第二医院现已取消妇产科病房、外科病房和小儿科门诊(目前由内科医生兼小儿科急诊),部分医务人员调往海沧、集美,原有较好的设备如 X 光机、彩色 B 超等相继搬迁海沧,鼓浪屿居民的就医条件明显下降,且有继续下降的发展趋势。

鼓浪屿是老市区,居民中老年人比例甚高,在全市其他地区普遍提高医疗水平的情况下,鼓浪屿居民需要维持原有的就医条件。另外,鼓浪屿作为国家级风景名胜区,也需要有较高水平的医疗保障。

我们认为,整合医疗资源是为人民谋利益之举,不应以鼓浪屿就医条件倒退、人民权益受损为代价。建议市政府本着对人民高度负责的态度,调整有关部署,采取必要措施,尽快恢复鼓浪屿原有的就医条件。

（二）关于开展鼓浪屿定位及对策专题研究的建议 **

近年来,随着我市旅游事业的发展,市政府在强调发展鼓浪屿旅游事业时,在一定程度上忽略了鼓浪屿首先是居民区这一基本情况。鼓浪屿之所以成为世界闻名的旅游区,在很大程度上是因为中西文化在这里的碰撞、交融及具有一定数量较高文化素质的本地居民。

由于"鼓浪屿是旅游区"的政策导向,近年来,随着厦门第二医院、第二中学等的

---

　* 厦门市第十二届人民代表大会第三次会议建议(2005 年 2 月),建议人:曾华群。
　** 厦门市第十二届人民代表大会第四次会议建议(2006 年 2 月),建议人:曾华群。

搬迁,鼓浪屿的医疗、教育水平急剧下降,导致鼓浪屿居民人口锐减,岛上居民成分也发生很大变化,外来人口占了相当比例。岛上一些历史风貌建筑甚至成为流浪人员的"避难所"。事实表明,鼓浪屿的"人居环境"已日趋恶化。照此发展,随着岛上居民的外迁,"琴岛"和"音乐之岛"的美誉也将失去岛上广大"音乐人家"的基础性支撑。

建议市政府及时组织力量,调查研究如下主要问题:

1. 居民情况,现有人口规模、构成及素质;

2. 医疗条件,与过去的对比;

3. 教育条件,与过去的对比;

4. 旅游对鼓浪屿人居环境的冲击或影响。

在此基础上,开展鼓浪屿定位及对策的专题研究。

（三）关于尽快重建鼓浪屿宜居环境的建议 *

厦门是联合国人居城市,鼓浪屿是厦门的精华所在,理应是宜居的典范。

近年来,由于未能适当处理"旅游"与"人居"的关系,鼓浪屿人居环境已遭受"旅游"的严重负面影响。特别是,自厦门市第二医院迁出鼓浪屿后,岛上居民得不到100多年来一直享有的"全科医院"的医疗保障。随着鼓浪屿居民的不断外迁,基础教育因生源减少而日渐萎缩,亦导致优质师资的流失。由于存在医疗和基础教育两大问题,鼓浪屿事实上已成为"相对不宜居"的地方。其产生的直接后果是,鼓浪屿原住居民不断外迁,外来农民工不断涌入定居,岛上居民结构已然发生重大转变。

众所周知,鼓浪屿成为国家级旅游区是缘于其人文特色与自然环境相得益彰,其人文特色又是靠鼓浪屿原住居民的世代传承。例如,"琴岛"的美誉源于众多"音乐之家"的支撑。"皮之不存,毛将焉附"? 要保护鼓浪屿的人文特色,当务之急是重建鼓浪屿宜居环境,留住鼓浪屿原住居民。近年的经验表明,片面追求旅游的经济效益,忽略甚至影响人居环境,旅游经济发展的空间和品位也颇受局限。对大多数游客来说,鼓浪屿目前只是一个供白天走马观花的风景点,其深厚的历史文化底蕴和活生生的人文特色难以甚至无从感受。

建议政府以人为本,将鼓浪屿"人居"问题摆在首要地位。在充分研究论证的基础上,制定相关政策措施,投入必要的经费,尽快重建鼓浪屿宜居环境。当前急需研究解决的两大问题一是恢复有百年历史的厦门市第二医院在鼓浪屿的"全科医院"建制;二是优化鼓浪屿的基础教育事业。

---

* 厦门市第十三届人民代表大会第三次会议建议(2008 年 2 月),建议人:曾华群。

（四）关于加强组织协调，完善管理体制，积极推进鼓浪屿"申遗"进程的议案[*]

案由：加强组织协调，完善管理体制，积极推进鼓浪屿"申遗"进程。

案据：

鼓浪屿自然风光优美，历史文化积淀丰厚，全岛建筑与格局深具中西文化交融特色，素有"万国建筑博物馆"的美誉。开展申请确认鼓浪屿为"世界文化遗产"（"申遗"）的工作，争取将鼓浪屿纳入国际法和国内法的双重保护范围，对于进一步做好鼓浪屿风景区历史文化资源的保护工作，对于鼓浪屿人居环境的恢复和改善，具有十分重要的意义。"申遗"成功，必将极大地提升厦门的知名度和城市影响力。

当前，鼓浪屿"申遗"工作面临很多困难和问题，严重影响了该项工作的顺利进行。主要有：

一、缺乏专门的协调机构。"申遗"工作是一项系统工程，涉及文化、规划设计、建设、市政园林等多方面的事务，仅仅依靠一个单位、一个部门难以启动和统筹开展"申遗"工作，而目前我市没有专门的统筹整个"申遗"工作的协调机构。

二、现有体制不能适应"申遗"的需要。鼓浪屿风景区管委会作为鼓浪屿风景区的行政主管部门，但涉及鼓浪屿内保护与管理的许多事务又同时由市政府其他职能部门管理，存在一定程度的政出多门、多头管理的问题。

三、经费投入与人员编制未获基本保障。"申遗"工作需要划拨专项经费和配备专职工作人员，而目前经费和人员都尚未得到基本的保障。

四、"申遗"工作的相关调研未能启动。"申遗"工作是关系鼓浪屿发展和民生问题的重大决策，需要在广泛征求民意、深入调查研究的基础上，制订工作计划和编制可行性研究报告，以供市政府决策参考。

方案

一、市政府牵头，成立专门的组织协调机构，例如可以采取协调办、指挥部的形式，统筹"申遗"中文化、规划设计、建设等多方面的工作。

二、以人为本，执政为民。鼓浪屿建筑群的有效、长远的保护的前提是人居环境的恢复和改善。考虑到鼓浪屿建筑群作为世界文化遗产的保护是整个社会形态的保护，而不仅仅是物质的保护，需要着手开展恢复原有社会形态的工作，特别是恢复医疗和基础教育事业。同时，应尽快改变"只出不进"的户籍政策。创造条件，鼓励原住民返迁。同时，鼓励从事文艺、文教工作者定居鼓浪屿。事实上，没有居民，鼓浪屿建筑群也无从保护。

---

[*]　厦门市第十三届人民代表大会第四次会议议案（2009 年 2 月），议案领衔人：曾华群。

三、充实专门人员，配备专业能力强、业务素质高的人员到"申遗"相关工作机构，为"申遗"工作提供有力的人员保障。

四、针对鼓浪屿管理体制不完善的问题，市政府应组织进行专题调查研究，并在年内提出改革和完善方案，尽早加以实施。

五、保障"申遗"经费，如果保护规划、"申遗"文本等工作正式启动，资金会有一定缺口，政府应划拨专项资金保证"申遗"经费。

六、积极调研，并在此基础上进一步做好工作计划，有计划地做好遗产调查评估、开发利用的调研，做好申报材料编撰、保护和开发利用工作的规划编制。

（五）尽快重建鼓浪屿宜居环境、保护传统人文特色的议案*

案由：实践科学发展观，以人为本，及时调整相关政策，及时采取有效措施，尽快重建鼓浪屿宜居环境、保护鼓浪屿传统人文特色。

案据：

厦门是联合国人居城市，鼓浪屿是厦门的精华所在，理应是宜居的典范。

多年来，随着旅游事业的发展，我市在强调发展鼓浪屿旅游事业时，在一定程度上忽略了鼓浪屿首先是居民区这一基本情况。由于未能科学处理"旅游"与"人居"的关系，鼓浪屿人居环境已遭受"旅游"的严重负面影响。特别是，自厦门市第二医院迁出鼓浪屿后，岛上居民得不到100多年来一直享有的"全科医院"的医疗保障，医疗条件大不如前。随着鼓浪屿居民的不断外迁，鼓浪屿原有的基础教育事业因生源减少而日渐萎缩，亦导致优质师资的流失。由于存在医疗和基础教育两大民生问题，鼓浪屿事实上已成为"相对不宜居"的地方。其产生的直接后果是，鼓浪屿原住居民不断外迁，外来农民工则因租金低廉而不断涌入定居，岛上居民结构已然发生重大转变。

众所周知，鼓浪屿之所以成为世界闻名的旅游区，缘于其人文特色与自然环境的相得益彰。其人文特色主要体现于中西文化的共存与融合，而这一鲜明特色主要靠鼓浪屿原住居民的世代传承。例如，"琴岛"的美誉源于众多"音乐之家"的支撑。近年来，由于鼓浪屿原住居民人口锐减，"琴岛"的美誉已在很大程度上失去岛上广大"音乐人家"的基础性支撑。如不及时采取措施，鼓浪屿的人文特色势必丧失殆尽。

对鼓浪屿的上述问题，鼓浪屿原住居民、海内外各界人士从各种渠道反映多年，由于种种原因，一直未能得到应有的重视和解决。

---

* 厦门市第十三届人民代表大会第五次会议议案（2010年2月），议案领衔人：曾华群。

方案：

保护鼓浪屿的人文特色，当务之急是重建鼓浪屿宜居环境。建议我市以人为本，顺应民意，科学处理鼓浪屿"人居"与"旅游"的关系，及时调整和制定相关政策，及时采取有效措施，投入必要的经费，尽快重建鼓浪屿宜居环境。当前，急需研究解决的主要问题：

一是恢复有百年历史的厦门市第二医院在鼓浪屿的"全科医院"建制。鼓浪屿是老市区，居民中老年人比例甚高，在全市其他地区普遍提高医疗水平的情况下，鼓浪屿居民理应维持和提高原有的就医条件，而不是相反。另外，鼓浪屿作为国家级风景名胜区，也需要有较高水平的医疗保障。鼓浪屿"全科医院"的恢复和发展，可以考虑与我市高端医疗和疗养的建设规划衔接起来。

二是优化鼓浪屿的基础教育事业。在发展鼓浪屿高等教育、职业教育、特色教育的同时，积极采取有效措施，办好幼儿、小学、中学教育事业。在全民普遍重视子女成长环境的时代，优质基础教育是人居环境的关键甚至是决定性因素之一。

三是尽快改变鼓浪屿"只出不进"的户籍政策，制定"可进可出，鼓励长住"的新政策。积极采取有效措施，创造优良人居条件，特别是在解决医疗和教育问题的前提下，鼓励原住居民返迁。同时，鼓励各类人才，特别是从事文艺、文教、文化创意工作者定居鼓浪屿。可以考虑与我市解决引进人才住房问题的规划建设衔接起来，将鼓浪屿部分公管住房或新建住房作为"人才保障房"，供各类人才租住或购买。

四是与鼓浪屿"申遗"工作结合起来。鼓浪屿建筑群的有效、长远保护的基础和前提是人居环境的恢复和改善。考虑到鼓浪屿建筑群作为世界文化遗产的保护是整个社会形态的保护，而不仅仅是物质的保护，需要及时着手开展恢复原有社会形态的工作，特别是通过恢复医疗和优质基础教育事业吸引原住居民和各类人才长住鼓浪屿。事实上，没有适当规模的居民，没有人文特色的维系，鼓浪屿建筑群也无从保护。

第五节　漫漫法学之旅[*]

由工转学，近 40 年。由史学转法学，也有 35 年了。漫漫法学之旅，山重水复，甘苦自知，纪实一二。

一、初入"法门"

1981 年秋季，毕业在即，我所在厦门大学历史系 77 级全班 65 位同学中，有 29 位拟报考研究生，相约分散报考以求提高升学率。时值厦门大学法律系复办之初，系领导陈朝璧、盛辛民、何永龄老师高瞻远瞩，及时向国家教委申办并获准招收法学硕士研究生，为我们开启了一扇"法门"。

经突击备考，我和历史系 78 级廖益新、哲学系 77 级傅宁、外文系 77 级秦向明有幸成为法律系 81 级国际法专业硕士生，1982 年 2 月入学，师从当时负笈海外的陈安老师。得益于法律系"请进来走出去"的开放教学模式，我们在校修读应邀前来讲学的中国人民大学林榕年老师的"法制史"等课程，还"留学"武汉大学一学期，主修李双元老师的"国际私法"、梁西老师的"国际组织法"和美国琼斯教授的"国际商法"（英文）等研究生课程。第三学年，为撰写硕士学位论文，我先后在厦门和深圳经济特区调研，访问主管外资工作的官员及中外合资企业的高管，在武汉大学、北京图书馆收集专业文献资料，还上庐山参加"第一期国际经济法讲习班"。1984 年底，如期完成了法学硕士学位论文《中外合资企业管理权分享探索》。该论文"一分为三"，分别发表于《南开经济研究》《法学评论》和《法学研究》，或可佐证学界对我系首届硕士学位论文质量的认可。

1986 年，国家教委批准我校设立国际经济法专业博士点，陈安老师为指导老师。年底，我通过入学考试，荣幸成为法律系第一位博士生，1987 年 2 月入学。同年 11 月，赴美国威拉姆特大学（Willamatte University）法学院研修，属校际学术交流项目。旅美期间，选修"国际商事交往""比较法"等法律博士（JD）课程，通过课程考试；还入选"美中关系全国委员会"组织的"学者考察团"，参访国会、法院等法律相关机构，大开眼界。1988 年底，应学校工作之需，我婉拒美方提供的 JD 全额奖学金待遇，毅然回国。1990 年初，完成法学博士学位论文《中外合资企业法律问题研究》。武汉大学

---

　　* 原载"厦门大学法学院 90 周年院庆"专题网站（www.law90.xmu.edu.cn），2016 年 8 月 6 日发布；主要内容以"曾华群的法学之旅"为题，载《厦门大学报》2018 年 4 月 1 日第 8 版。

韩德培老师和姚梅镇老师为论文评阅人,亲临我校主持论文答辩会,我深感学术大家对后学的鼎力奖掖和殷切期望。该论文 1991 年修订出版,题为《中外合资企业法律的理论与实务》,获首届"全国高等学校人文社会科学研究优秀成果奖著作类二等奖"。

二、潜心教研

1984 年 12 月毕业留校以来,主要从事国际经济法的教学和研究。

"得天下英才而教之",是教师追求的理想。先后讲授本科生、硕士生、博士生及留学生多门课程。教学相长。主持讲授的本科生学位课程"国际经济法学"由教育部评为国家级精品课程,主讲的研究生学位课程"国际经济法研究"入选为"福建省优质研究生课程"。作为研究生指导教师,兢兢业业,迄今指导毕业的硕士生已逾百名、博士生达 36 名。指导的两篇博士学位论文荣获"福建省优秀博士学位论文一等奖",参与主持的教学成果两次荣获"福建省高等学校优秀教学成果一等奖",忝列为"福建高等学校教学名师"和"福建省优秀教师",还主持完成了教育部教学改革项目"国际经济法人才的国际化培养模式"。

一直以来,努力践行"知识报国,兼济天下"的治学理念。作为项目负责人和主要承担人,主持完成国家社会科学基金重大项目"促进与保护我国海外投资的法律体制研究"等各级研究课题及商务部条法司的委托研究课题等。面壁坐冷,勤于笔耕。迄今,独立完成《WTO 与中国外资法的发展》《国际经济法导论》等专著、教材 5 部,独撰的论文亦持续发表于中外重要学术期刊,紧密联系中国实际,对国际经济法理论、国际投资法及 WTO 体制等领域作了较深入的探讨。中英文代表作曾三次获"全国高等学校人文社会科学研究优秀成果奖"。

在学术研究和国际交流中,坚定站在中国和发展中国家的立场,自信自强,在国际学术论坛发出"中国之声"。曾在美国乔治城大学法律中心主办的"中国加入WTO 研讨会"上(华盛顿哥伦比亚特区,2002),质疑美国国会"监督"中国履行 WTO义务的合法性。应邀参加 OECD 和 UNCTAD 主办的"第二届国际投资协定研讨会"(巴黎,2010),以"南北问题"为视角,作题为"国际投资协定的革新之路"的大会报告,引起热烈讨论。之后,撰写论文《平衡、可持续发展与一体化:双边投资条约实践的创新之路》,发表于《国际经济法学刊》(牛津),进一步予以论证。

三、奉献学科

因工作需要,留校不久即任系主任助理、国际经济法教研室主任。1991—1999

年,任法律系副系主任,分管科学研究及研究生工作。还兼任我校学术委员会委员、教学委员会委员及《厦门大学学报》(哲社版)编委会委员等职。1997年入选为国家"百千万人才工程首批第一、二层次人选"。

2000年初,为申报教育部人文社会科学重点研究基地,陈传鸿时任校长聘我为国际经济法研究所所长。作为学术带头人之一,具体主持国际法学科参与的"211工程"一、二、三期项目,亲力亲为,负责论证、组织实施及总结报告全过程。经学科同仁的共同努力,学术团队和学术平台建设成效显著。

为创建可持续发展、治学严谨的学术团队,一向以身作则,勉力当好"学术义工"。为维护优良学风,曾一再挺身而出,坚决反对学术不端行为,凸显无私无畏、纯朴率真的"工农本色"。关键时刻,幸遇"路人甲"相助,成就"力挽狂澜"之传奇。

学术平台是学科建设的重要基础。1993年以来,中国国际经济法学会秘书处设于我校,成为国际法学科的重要学术平台。我历任学会秘书长、副会长和会长(2011—)。迄今,参与组织和主持22届"中国国际经济法学会年会暨学术研讨会"、10届"国际投资法专题研讨会"、7届"WTO法专题研讨会"及6届"中韩国际经济法学术研讨会"等,为促进海内外学术交流而筹划和奔波于大江南北。还参与主持处理学会的"申请登记"和"业务主管单位调整"问题,为依法维护学会的生存权和发展权而不懈奋斗。

自1998年《国际经济法学刊》创办以来,我长期担任编委会委员,参与审稿工作等。《学刊》2005年入选为中国社会科学研究评价中心(CSSCI)首批来源集刊,迄今连续五度入选,已成为国际经济法领域的重要学术交流平台。

作为发起人之一,我还参与创建2005年成立的厦门国际法高等研究院和2011年成立的厦门大学陈安国际法学发展基金会,为国际法学科提供了新的学术平台。

四、服务社会

法学是经世致用之学。20世纪80年代,因法律实务人才缺乏,留校即任兼职"律师工作者"。1986年通过国家第一次律师资格考试后,成为兼职律师。担任多家涉外企业法律顾问,主要承办涉外经济案件,力求与教研相结合。1995年以来,应聘为中国国际经济贸易仲裁委员会仲裁员,在北京、上海和深圳参与审理仲裁案件。

自1997年起,连选连任三届市人大代表,并以专业人士身份,先后兼任市人大法制委员会副主任委员和内务司法委员会副主任委员,实际参与市人大立法及对"一府两院"的法律监督工作。在其位谋其政。富有"人大意识"和专业精神,勇于担当,务求实效。曾在相关会议上针对现状,尖锐提出"市委书记不适合当市土地管理委员会主任";"拆迁纠纷中,公安部门应站在保护被拆迁人的立场"等专业意见。也曾为《监督法》的出台发表专文《一部推进社会主义民主与法治的重要法律》,并应邀为人大代表培训班作《监督法》的辅导讲座。

作为人大代表,肩负反映民意、促进民主决策的责任。我关注国情民生,积极建言献策。先后向市人大提交的建议和议案涉及"厦门地铁建设""支持民间戏团""知青特殊政策""开展两岸警务合作""共建厦门国际法高等研究院""重建鼓浪屿人居环境"及"鼓浪屿'申遗'"等议题。其中,"关于加强城市规划工作的建议"(包含"反对在老市区建设高架 BRT"等内容)获评"优秀代表建议",多项建议和议案被采纳。2007 年底,在市民代表及部分市人大代表、市政协委员参加的"PX 项目座谈会"上,我在市人大代表中率先"呛声",从城市发展定位、环评报告结论及海沧污染现状三方面论证,明确反对在海沧投资建设 PX 项目。

1990 年曾任福建省代表团副团长,参加在北京召开的"第 14 届世界法律大会"。先后为省委学习中心组作《澳门特别行政区基本法》辅导讲座(2000)和《世贸组织体制与中国"加入世贸组织"的准备》专题讲座(2001)。自 2001 年 9 月起,应聘为省政府法律顾问。在聘任仪式上,习近平时任省长强调,聘任法律顾问的意义在于"以宪法、法律为依据","促进政府行政管理规范化、法制化",尤为深刻。

五、走向国际

20 世纪 80、90 年代,我海外访学累计三年多。北美、欧陆、英伦、南洋及港澳,均留游学足迹,也结识了学术同行和朋友。

旅外期间,海阔天空,尽可"潇洒走一回"。在瑞士比较法研究所,第一次作英文学术报告,题为"过渡期香港的双边条约实践"。在伦敦国际法教授 96 年度酒会上,第一次用英文即席发言,提出香港回归的国际法问题。在伦敦大学亚非学院,第一次用英文讲授研究生专题课程"厦门的环境保护法制"。在新加坡国立大学东亚研究所,第一次撰写和发表英文学术论文《中国外资法:迈向"市场经济型"的新发展》。

海外归来,我身体力行,积极推动国际法学科建设的"国际化"。开设国际硕士课程"中国外资法"(英文),还因材施教,悉心指导外国研究生。迄今,已指导毕业的外国硕士生 12 名、博士生 4 名,分别来自亚、欧、非、澳四大洲 12 国。在《国际经济法学刊》(牛津)、《世界投资与贸易》(日内瓦)等国际性学术期刊发表多篇英文论文;作为联合主编,出版了《中国与东盟关系:经济与法律问题》(英文,世界科学出版社)。还应邀担任《中国国际法学刊》(牛津)编委会委员和《中国比较法学刊》(牛津)咨询委员会委员。

　　2001 年，作为领队和主教练，指导我院辩论队参加中国国际经济贸易仲裁委员会主办的第二届"贸仲杯"仲裁辩论赛，荣获亚军。2002 年，指导我院辩论队参加在维也纳举行的第九届 Willem C. Vis 国际商事模拟辩论赛。2003 年，再次率队参加该赛事，还应聘担任"仲裁员"。当时，与辩论队同学同宿青年旅馆，一起应对"非典"危机，其乐融融。有感于我院辩论队与欧美名校同台竞技的精彩表现，曾在媒体放言"假以时日，中国队的冠军梦一定能够实现"。之后，我院辩论队由年轻教师陈辉萍、池漫郊、龚宇、于湛旻、张膑心、陈喜峰、苏宇和张璜指导，连年参加五大国际性专业赛事，形成优良传统，荣获"Jessup 国际法模拟法庭辩论赛书状世界冠军（2006）"等优异成绩，为我国法学教育赢得国际声誉。

　　我还参与厦门国际法高等研究院的创建和发展工作。2005 年 4 月，在海内外国际法同行的共同努力下，研究院在我校宣告成立。同年 7 月，在海牙和平宫举行该院董事会第一次会议，联合国国际法院前任院长史久镛大法官出任首届董事会主席。作为研究院董事兼联席院长，我具体负责行政工作，参与组织和主持 2006—2016 年历届"国际法前沿问题研修班"，还讲授专题课"国际经济条约的新发展与中国的实践"等。作为中国国际法学者，有机会在我校接待应邀前来讲学的国际法院八位大法官（包括三任院长）和 60 多位权威国际法学家，有机会向来自世界各国的教授和学员传播中国法治的发展和国际法领域的"中国之声"，深感自豪和荣幸！研究院历经十一年的发展，在海内外已享有学术声誉，亦成为我国国际法领域重要的国际性学术交流平台。

　　"自强不息，在服务社会中丰富人生"，是我的人生追求。上述实录反映了一位"资深"法律系学生的成长历程，更是一位"知青"或"农民工"学者向国家和人民的感恩汇报。"路漫漫其修远兮"，永葆"法治"的美好愿景，我的法学之旅还在继续探索和坚定前行中。

附录一　指导的研究生名单和论文题目

附表 1.1　指导的硕士研究生名单和论文题目(1988—　　)

序号	姓名	国籍	届别	论文题目
1	赵德铭	中国	1991	《涉外经济合同效力之影响因素论》
2	钟诚	中国	1991	《关于涉外经济合同履行的法律研究》
3	罗奇志	中国	1993	《论协调东道国与跨国公司之间法律关系的有效途径》
4	蒋武军	中国	1994	《美国反倾销立法与实践研究——兼论我国应采取的对策》
5	赵俊荣	中国	1995	《论香港证券自律制度——兼论中国证券监管制度的健全与完善》
6	陈海晖	中国	1996	《证券市场的全球化与内幕交易的法律制度研究》
7	叶兰昌	中国	1996	《母子公司关系若干法律问题研究》
8	周奋强	中国	1996	《欧盟反倾销法与我国的对策初探——兼论中国的反倾销立法》
9	石劲磊	中国	1997	《论外资并购的法律调整》
10	陈东	中国	1999	(提前攻博)
11	林文生	中国	2000	《英国公司重整制度研究》
12	蔡奕	中国	2000	(提前攻博)
13	张乃菲	中国	2001	《跨国电子合同基本法律问题研究》
14	涂晴	中国	2001	《现代商人法在国际商事仲裁中的适用》
15	林瑞云	中国	2001	《略论托运人和提单持有人诉权》
16	吴丽雪	中国	2001	《论我国〈公司法〉对股东权的保护》
17	戴绍业	中国	2002	《欧共体反倾销法中的市场经济地位问题》
18	简丽丽	中国	2002	《WTO 争端解决机制及发展中国家的有效利用问题》

（续表）

序号	姓名	国籍	届别	论文题目
19	王宁宁	中国	2002	《论船舶抵押权人利益的保险保障》
20	谢静波	中国	2002	《略论中国股票发行强制信息披露制度的健全和完善》
21	骆旭旭	中国	2003	《竞争法的冲突与解决》
22	王玲	中国	2003	《论〈联合国国际货物销售合同公约〉中的活价条款问题》
23	王巍	中国	2003	《我国金融混业经营的发展趋势及过渡模式的法律思考》
*24	Ndongou Alain A.	中非	2003	International Legal Control on Investment by Multinational Corporations in the Developing Countries（《对跨国公司在发展中国家投资的国际法律管制》）
25	洪涛	中国	2004	《国际信用证的法律适用问题》
26	刘欣	中国	2004	《WTO体制下的反倾销争端解决机制研究》
27	张吉	中国	2004	《TRIPS协定"植物新品种保护制度"评析》
28	苏文颖	中国	2005	《药品专利权保护与公共健康的博弈》
29	衣淑玲	中国	2005	《与环境有关的单边贸易措施在GATT/WTO体制中的地位》
30	章明	中国	2005	《NAFTA征收条款研究》
31	张旭东	中国	2005	《外资并购反垄断法律制度的研究》
*32	罗荣强	马来西亚	2005	《论东盟—中国自由贸易协定的性质与特征》
33	刘焕礼	中国	2006	《WTO体制下补贴界定研究》
34	许莹姣	中国	2006	《美国公司型投资基金治理结构法律研究及借鉴》
35	刘红	中国	2006	《美欧倾销幅度确定方法之比较》
*36	山磨里	老挝	2006	《中老外国投资法比较研究》
37	陈钟	中国	2007	《美国受控外国公司立法初探》
38	柳进喜	中国	2007	《论WTO体制下之透明度原则：从WTO成员义务的角度分析》
39	杨逢柱	中国	2007	《美国对跨国并购的国家安全法律审查制度研究》
40	刘巍	中国	2007	《双边投资协定中的保护伞条款研究》
41	朱彤	中国	2007	《美国反倾销法中信息保密制度研究》
42	李敏	中国	2007	《〈联合国国际货物销售合同公约〉免责制度研究》
43	陈小荣	中国	2007	《论我国强制部分要约收购制度的确立和完善》
44	徐进伟	中国	2007	《〈2004年约克-安特卫普规则〉评述》
45	赵业新	中国	2007	《欧美反垄断法的相关市场界定问题研究》
46	胡红春	中国	2008	《欧盟版权管理制度研究》
47	王南	中国	2008	《试论美国有关审查企业合并的实质性标准的制度》
48	梁涛	中国	2008	《保障措施"未预见的发展"问题研究》

（续表）

序号	姓名	国籍	届别	论文题目
49	刘蓓	中国	2008	《我国对外直接投资管理法律制度研究》
50	梁忠	中国	2008	《论反倾销法中的正常价值》
51	吴江辉	中国	2008	《对业主委员会法律地位的探析——从"小区架空层权属的争夺"论起》
52	刘璞	中国	2009	《投资仲裁透明度问题研究》
53	蒋健	中国	2009	《论 WTO 特殊与差别待遇的法理基础》
54	黄晓晴	中国	2009	《国际能源合作机制的法律原则探析》
55	连煜雄	中国	2009	《〈联合国国际合同使用电子通信公约〉电子通信错误制度研究》
56	张林	中国	2009	《论我国对外资并购的反垄断法律规制》
57	杨文霞	中国	2009	《我国劳动力派遣中的雇主替代责任分担制度研究》
58	李婧	中国	2009	《中国 FTA 实践的原产地规则评析》（提前攻博）
59	王雨	中国	2010	《作为一般法律原则的公平与公正待遇——国际投资法中公平与公正待遇的性质与含义新解》
60	徐丽碧	中国	2010	《TRIPS 框架下中美知识产权争端解决方式初探——以 DS362 案为主要分析对象》
61	付潇	中国	2010	《CAFTA 与 CEPA 服务贸易规范比较研究》
62	钟盈	中国	2010	《国际投资中间接征收认定的多维度思考》
* 63	Chen Si	澳大利亚	2010	Legal Consideration on Mergers and Acquisitions in China by Australian Investors（《试析澳大利亚投资者在华并购企业的法律问题》）
* 64	Josephyiey lam Both	埃塞俄比亚	2010	The Regulations of Chinese Environmental Law on Foreign Direct Investment（《中国环境法对外商直接投资的调整》）
65	黄晓颖	中国	2011	《国际投资法律框架下的环境保护问题研究》
66	王丽菊	中国	2011	《国际投资协定例外条款的适用及完善》
67	徐佳茵	中国	2011	《引渡中的人权保护——以〈公民权利与政治权利国际公约〉为视角》
68	张琪	中国	2011	《区域贸易协定投资规范比较研究》
* 69	Imran Lakho	巴基斯坦	2011	Cross Border Merger & Acquisition in China—Legal Framework & Regulatory Control（《中国的跨国并购——法律框架与管制》）
* 70	Lusekelo Elisha Mwamkinga	坦桑尼亚	2011	Legal Implications of Umbrella Clauses under Bilateral Investment Treaties—A Closer Look into the Role of ICSID's Awards on the Semantic Evolution of Umbrella Clauses（《双边投资条约保护伞条款的法律涵义——考察"解决投资争端国际中心"有关保护伞条款语义演进的裁决之作用》）

（续表）

序号	姓名	国籍	届别	论文题目
71	郑佳宝	中国	2012	《论 ICSID 仲裁实践中的 NGO 参与》
72	柯玲玲	中国	2012	《"间接征收"与"不予补偿的管制措施"辨析》
73	马寅	中国	2012	《我国外资并购反垄断审查制度研究》
74	刘盛宇	中国	2012	《国际投资条约对环境问题的规制研究》
75	黄佳	中国	2012	《论国际投资法中"投资"的定义》
76	强之恒	中国	2012	《论双边投资条约中重大安全例外条款的适用》
77	付凌岳	中国	2012	《ECFA 背景下厦门相关法制的发展研究》
78	陈隽洁	中国	2012	《论新形势下我国海外投资保险制度的重构》
79	徐涵	中国	2012	《国际投资法的"管制性征收"初探》
80	岳川	中国	2012	《浅论中国企业跨国并购的法律风险及对策》
81	张越	中国	2013	《中国百年流失文化财产返还的国际法依据问题研究》
82	张伟华	中国	2013	《中德 BIT 与港德 BIT 比较研究》
83	魏莎莎	中国	2013	《ICSID 仲裁裁决的承认与执行机制研究》
84	张莉敏	中国	2013	《论 WTO 争端解决机制专家意见程序及其完善》
85	赵惠琳	中国	2013	《论构建 WTO 争端解决机制"法庭之友"制度的法律依据》
* 86	Clément Hervelin	法国	2013	The "Rule of Law" with Chinese Characteristics and Its Impact on China's Economic Development（《中国特色的"法治"及其对中国经济发展的影响》）
* 87	Ozue Vivian Adaeze	尼日利亚	2013	Impact of Economic Globalisation and WTO Accession on Development of Chinese Laws（《经济全球化与"入世"对中国法律发展的影响》）
* 88	Nelly Urni	意大利	2013	Development and Implication of the Chinese Foreign Investment Law（《中国外商直接投资法的发展和成效》）
89	黄丹	中国	2014	《WTO 争端解决机构对 GATS 具体承诺表的解释方法及其新发展》
90	袁颖	中国	2014	《竞争法域外适用法律冲突的解决方法》
91	王春燕	中国	2014	《我国国际板推出背景下跨境证券监管合作进路研究》
* 92	Kristjansson Dagurkristjanss	冰岛	2014	Studies on Safeguard Clauses of Iceland-China Free Trade Agreement（《冰岛与中国间自由贸易协定的保障条款研究》）
* 93	Nakhasen Siharath	老挝	2014	Comparative Studies on FDI Policy and Law in Lao People's Democratic Republic（《老挝人民民主共和国外国直接投资政策与法律比较研究》）
94	莫元媛	中国	2015	《WTO 和 TBT 协定中的国民待遇原则及其选择适用问题研究》
95	李恒学	中国	2015	《国际投资法的负面清单问题研究》

（续表）

序号	姓名	国籍	届别	论文题目
＊96	Saeid Shabani Boroujeni	伊朗	2015	A Comparative Study of Legal Affairs on Management of Joint Venture between Iran and China(《伊朗—中国合营企业管理法律实务的比较分析》)
97	李雅琳	中国	2016	《论国际投资规则的环境条款与中国的对策》
98	林惠雅	中国	2016	《国际投资条约的拒绝授惠条款》
99	林婷婷	中国	2016	《论补充性解释方法在 WTO 争端解决中的适用》
＊100	Bjorn Leif Brauteseth	美国	2016	A Legal Study of Chinese FDI in Water Resource Development in Africa(《中国投资开发非洲水资源的法律问题》)
101	黄惠娥	中国	2017	《上海自贸区仲裁制度创新的比较研究》
102	张艺鸣	中国	2017	《国际投资仲裁中投资腐败法律后果认定研究》
103	吉克	中国	2017	《跨境电子商务的法律风险及对策》(澳门科技大学)
104	牛贺明	中国	2017	《中美药品专利链接制度之比较研究》(澳门科技大学)
105	赵晨光	中国	2017	《GATS 的市场准入制度研究》(澳门科技大学)
106	刘雨婷	中国	2017	《浅析中国企业国际贸易中知识产权纠纷及其对策》(澳门科技大学)
107	汪迪茜	中国	2017	《我国外资银行监管法律制度研究》(澳门科技大学)
108	谭裕彬	中国	2017	《信用证若干法律问题研究》(澳门科技大学)
109	许琼露	中国	2017	《澳门仲裁制度的新发展研究》(澳门科技大学)
110	施晓晓	中国	2018	《区域贸易协定中服务贸易紧急保障措施条款研究》
111	邱明飞	中国	2018	《国际投资协定的缔约国解释问题研究》
112	王语惜	中国	2019	《ISDS 机制改革与中国对策研究》(澳门城市大学)
113	李岩	中国	2019	《国际投资协定的环境保护条款研究》(澳门城市大学)

注：

1. 序号加"＊"者为外国留学生，合计 14 位，分别来自中非、马来西亚、老挝（2 人）、澳大利亚、埃塞俄比亚、巴基斯坦、坦桑尼亚、法国、尼日利亚、意大利、冰岛、伊朗、美国等 13 个国家。其中，分别来自马来西亚、尼日利亚的两位留学生获法学硕士学位后，申请由本人指导，继续攻读厦门大学法学博士学位。

2. 未特别注明者，均为厦门大学硕士研究生。

附表 1.2　指导的博士研究生名单及论文题目(1994—　　)

序号	姓名	国籍	届别	论文题目
1	郭俊秀	中国	1999	《美国外资银行管理法研究》
2	李万强	中国	1999	《ICSID 仲裁机制研究》
3	孟国碧	中国	2000	《略论经济主权原则的理论与实践》
4	陈东	中国	2001	《论跨国公司治理中的责任承担机制》

序号	姓名	国籍	届别	论文题目
5	蔡奕	中国	2001	《国际金融一体化和金融自由化背景下跨国银行监管的主要法律问题研究》
6	张照东	中国	2001	《政府采购制度研究》
7	肖冰	中国	2003	《〈SPS 协定〉研究》
8	林秀芹	中国	2003	《TRIPs 体制下的专利强制许可制度研究》
9	张东平	中国	2003	《WTO 争端解决中的条约解释研究》
10	张亮	中国	2005	《反倾销法损害确定问题研究》
11	蔡从燕	中国	2005	《私人结构性参与多边贸易体制》
12	韩秀丽	中国	2006	《论 WTO 法中的比例原则》
13	丁明红	中国	2006	《WTO 体制下贸易与环境政策之法律协调问题研究——可持续发展的视角》
14	徐运良	中国	2007	《论 WTO 争端解决机制与 RTAs 争端解决机制的冲突与协调》
15	陈海波	中国	2007	《WTO 对 RTAs 的法律约束》
16	常景龙	中国	2007	《DSB 报告执行制度论——从建构走向变革》
17	衣淑玲	中国	2008	《国际人权法视角下〈TRIPS 协定〉的变革研究》
18	骆旭旭	中国	2009	《区域竞争法机制研究》
19	赖燕雪	中国（台湾地区）	2009	《国际投资法制下的衡平原则研究——以东盟国际投资条约实践为中心》
*20	罗荣强	马来西亚	2009	《马来西亚与中国外资法律问题比较研究》
21	杨小强	中国	2010	《国际投资条约多功能化研究》
22	徐昕	中国	2010	《NGOs 制度性参与 WTO 事务研究》
23	陈海明	中国	2010	《国际社会利益影响下的国际法结构变迁研究》
24	邓丽娟	中国	2011	《GATS 海运服务贸易规则研究》
25	孙蕾	中国	2011	《ICSID 管辖权确立的实证研究》
26	张建邦	中国	2011	《国际投资条约中的知识产权保护问题研究》
27	朱明新	中国	2012	《国际投资争端赔偿的法律问题研究》
28	李婧	中国	2012	《FTA 争端解决机制研究》
29	廖湖中	中国（台湾地区）	2012	《两岸经贸仲裁之合作机制研究》
*30	Maziyar Shokrani	伊朗	2013	Analysis on the Role of the United Nations Security Council in the Strengthening of Article II of the NPT(《〈不扩散核武器条约〉的不扩散条款及联合国安理会的作用》)
31	于湛敏	中国	2014	《国际商事仲裁司法化问题研究》
32	林静	中国	2014	《WTO 食品安全规制研究》

序号	姓名	国籍	届别	论文题目
33	刘佳	中国	2014	《WTO 下私人国际贸易自由权利救济机制之构建》
34	强之恒	中国	2016	《论国际投资条约的"人本化"趋势》
＊35	Kate Melinda Deere	澳大利亚	2016	Empirical Analysis of "New Issues" in China's Free Trade Agreement Practice(《中国自由贸易协定实践中的"新议题"之实证分析》)
＊36	Khasan Sayfutdinov	乌兹别克斯坦	2016	Legal Analysis on the Effectiveness of China's Bilateral Investment Treaties in Attracting Foreign Direct Investment (《中外双边投资条约吸引外国直接投资有效性的法律分析》)
37	郑旸	中国	2017	《国际投资条约中的绝对待遇标准研究》
38	陈丹艳	中国	2017	《"投资者——国家争端解决"中的国家责任问题研究》
＊39	Kenneth Way Shiong Kang	英国	2017	Embracing the Study of Paradoxes：A Social Systems Perspective of International Law's Regulation of Transboundary Waters(《关于悖论的研究：从社会系统论角度探讨国际法对跨界水问题的调整作用》)(曾华群为第一导师,合作)
＊40	Ozue Vivian Adaeze	尼日利亚	2017	The Decision-making Process of the WTO in Relation to Developing Countries(《论 WTO 适用于发展中国家的决策程序》)
41	曾建知	中国	2018	《国际投资法中的规制权研究》
42	李冬冬	中国	2018	《论〈技术性贸易壁垒协定〉对成员方规制权的制衡》
＊43	Md Mehedi Hasan	孟加拉国	2019	On the Effectiveness of Special and Differential Treatment Clauses and Its Mechanism for Development in WTO Regime(《论 WTO 体制特殊与差别待遇条款的有效性及其促进发展的机制》)
44	陆以全	中国	2020	《南南合作型经济一体化协定的投资条款研究》
45	李妍婷	中国	2021	《基于"共同法"理念的澳门特别行政区海洋环境保护法制之创新》(澳门科技大学)
附:博士后合作研究人员				
1	张膑心	中国	2013	《国际刑事法院的被害人赔偿制度研究》

注:

1. 序号加"＊"者为外国留学生,合计 7 位,分别来自马来西亚、伊朗、澳大利亚、乌兹别克斯坦、英国、尼日利亚和孟加拉国等 7 个国家。

2. 未特别注明者,均为厦门大学博士研究生。

附录二　主要研究项目

附表 2　主要研究项目(1990—　　)

序号	研究期间/项目编号	课题名称	课题来源	承担任务
1	1990—1992	国际合营企业法律问题的比较研究	国家社会科学基金青年项目	课题负责人及承担人
2	1992—1997	中国大陆、香港、澳门、台湾涉外经济法律的比较研究	霍英东教育基金会第三次高等学校青年教师基金项目	课题负责人及主要承担人之一
3	1993—1996	外资企业法律的理论与实务研究	国家教委"八五"博士点基金项目	课题负责人及主要承担人
4	1997—2000	中欧相互直接投资的新法律框架与实务问题研究	中欧高等教育合作项目	课题负责人及主要承担人
5	2002—2003	WTO 经典案例编译	上海 WTO 事务咨询中心	课题负责人及主要承担人之一
6	2002—2005 (02SFB1015)	WTO 与我国对外贸易法律制度的改革	司法部法治建设与法学理论研究部级重点项目	课题负责人及主要承担人之一
7	2002—2005 (01JB820002)	"入世"后的中国外资法体系和内容研究	教育部博士点人文社会科学研究基金项目	课题负责人及主要承担人之一
8	2005—2008	国际经济法人才的国际化培养模式	教育部"经济学类、管理学类和法学专业人才培养教学改革项目"	课题负责人及主要承担人之一
9	2008	新形势下中国双边投资保护协定范本研究	商务部委托研究项目	课题负责人及主要承担人之一
10	2009	双边投资协定中国范本及国际仲裁案例研究	商务部委托研究项目	课题负责人及主要承担人之一
11	2009—2011 (09SFB1008)	两岸经济合作框架协议研究	司法部国家法治与法学理论研究项目重点课题	课题负责人及主要承担人之一
12	2009—2015 (09&ZD032)	促进与保护我国海外投资的法律体制研究	国家社会科学基金重大项目	项目联合首席专家及主要承担人之一
13	2011—2014	香港特别行政区的对外事务权(二)	教育部人文社科规划项目	课题负责人及承担人
14	2012	香港政制发展研究	全国人大港澳基本法委员会	课题负责人及承担人
15	2020—2022 (20FFXA005)	中国特色国际经济法的创新	国家社科基金后期资助重点项目	课题负责人及承担人

附录三　主要研究成果

【著作/译作】

(1)《促进与保护我国海外投资的法制》,北京大学出版社 2017 年出版,ISBN 978-7-301-27869-7,全书 61 万字,联合主编,撰写第一章,第八章第一、二节及第九章第四、五节。

(2)《WTO 与中国:法治的发展与互动——中国加入 WTO 十周年纪念文集》,中国商务出版社 2011 年出版,ISBN 978-7-5103-0575-7,全书 41.6 万字,联合主编。

(3)《国际经济新秩序与国际经济法新发展》,法律出版社 2009 年出版,ISBN 978-7-5036-9325-0,全书 87 万字,主编。

(4) WONG John,ZOU Keyuan,ZENG Huaqun (ed.),*China-ASEAN Relations: Economic and Legal Dimensions*,World Scientific Publishing Co. Pte,Ltd,ISBN 981-256-657-0,2006.

(5)《WTO 规则与中国经贸法制的新发展》,厦门大学出版社 2006 年出版,ISBN 7-5615-2528-1/D.297,全书 35.8 万字,主编,撰写第一、二、五章。

(6)《WTO 与中国外资法的发展》,厦门大学南强丛书第四辑,厦门大学出版社 2006 年出版,ISBN 7-5615-2541-9/D.299,全书 36.3 万字,独立完成。

(7)《WTO 与中国外贸法的新领域》,北京大学出版社 2006 年出版,ISBN 7-301-10195-3/D,全书 39.3 万字,主编,撰写第一、九、十章。

(8)《中国大百科全书》[法学(修订版)],中国大百科全书出版社 2006 年出版,ISBN 7-5000-7409-3,国际经济法学科副主编,撰写部分条目。

(9)《美国——〈1974 年贸易法〉第 301—310 节案》,上海人民出版社 2005 年出版,ISBN 7-208-05514-9,全书 78.1 万字,主编,审订文稿、校对部分译文及统稿。

(10)《国际投资法学》,北京大学出版社 1999 年出版,ISBN 7-301-03998-0/D.404,全书 60 万字,主编,撰写绪论、第一、二、三、八、九、十章,约 20 万字。

(11)《香港经贸法》,中国政法大学出版社 1996 年出版,ISBN 7-5620-1391-8D.1351,全书 21 万字,独立完成。

(12)《国际投资法概论》,厦门大学南强丛书,厦门大学出版社 1995 年出版,ISBN 7-5615-1022-5/D.73,全书 22.1 万字,独立完成。

(13)《中港公司法律实务》,商务印书馆(香港)1994 年出版,ISBN 962-07-6176-

6，第一作者，撰写引言和第一、二、三、七章，约 10 万字。

（14）《欧洲单一市场法律制度》，中国大百科全书出版社 1994 年出版，ISBN 7-5000-5297-9/D.11，米健主编，本人完成第四章，约 5 万字。

（15）《中外合资企业法律的理论与实务》，厦门大学出版社 1991 年出版，ISBN 7-5615-0373-3/D.15，全书 24 万字，独立完成。

（16）《国际投资法》，鹭江出版社 1987 年出版，ISBN 7-80533-051-4/D.7，陈安主编，全书 29.3 万字，本人为主要撰稿人之一。

【教材】

（1）《国际经济法导论》（第三版），法律出版社 2020 年出版，ISBN 978-7-5197-4370-3，全书 47.3 万字，独立完成。

（2）《国际经济法学》（第一至八版），高等学校法学教材，北京大学出版社 1994、2001、2004、2007、2011、2013、2017、2020 年出版，ISBN 978-7-301-31574-3（第八版），陈安主编，本人撰写第十、十一章，约 7 万字。

（3）《国际经济法学新论》（第一至五版），高等教育出版社 2007、2010、2012、2017、2020 年出版，ISBN 978-7-04-055116-7（第五版），陈安主编，本人撰写第九、十章，约 6 万字。

（4）《国际经济法导论》（第二版），普通高等教育"十一五"国家级规划教材，法律出版社 2007 年出版，ISBN 7-5036-7369-6，全书 44.8 万字，独立完成。

（5）《国际经济法学专论》（第一、二版），研究生教学用书，高等教育出版社 2002、2007 年出版，ISBN 7-04-008299-3，ISBN 978-7-04-021631-8，陈安主编，全书第一版 117 万字，第二版 134 万字。本人撰写第一章第七节；第二章第二、四、六节；第三章第一、二节，第三节第一、二目；第七章第一节第一、二目，第五、七、八节，约 20 万字。

（6）《国际经济法导论》，"九五"规划高等学校法学教材，法律出版社 1997 年出版，ISBN 7-5036-1995-3/D.1629，全书 27.5 万字，独立完成。

（7）《国际经济法学》，高等学校法学教材，高等教育出版社 1994 年出版，ISBN 7-04-004714-4，余劲松主编，本人为副主编，撰写第九章第三、四节和第十三章，约 5 万字。

（8）《国际经济法总论》，高等学校法学试用教材，法律出版社 1991 年出版，ISBN 7-5036-0635-5/D.503，陈安主编，本人完成第六（二稿）、七、九章，约 7 万字。

【论文/评论】

（除特别注明者外，均为本人独立完成）

（1）《关于国际法"国际话语体系"的思考》，《国际经济法学刊》，ISSN 2096-5273

CN10-1533/D,2021 年第 3 期。

（2）《共同发展：中国与"一带一路"国家间投资条约实践的创新》,《国际经济法学刊》,ISSN 2096-5273 CN10-1533/D,2019 年第 1 期。

（3）《香港双边投资条约实践的适用问题评析》,《紫荆论坛》（香港）,ISSN 2224-7793,2019 年 1—2 月号,第 43 期。

（4）《论中国特色国际经济法学》,《国际经济法学刊》,ISSN 2096-5273 CN10-1533/D,2018 年第 1 期。

（5）《论双边投资条约范本的演进与中国的对策》,《国际法研究》,ISSN 2095-7610 CN10-1216/D,2016 年第 4 期。

（6）《论我国"可持续发展导向"双边投资条约的实践》,《厦门大学学报》（哲学社会科学版）,ISSN 0438-0460 CN35-1019/C,2015 年第 1 期。

（7）Balance, Sustainable Development, and Integration：Innovative Path for BIT Practice, *Journal of International Economic Law*,（Oxford）ISSN 1369-3034, Vol. 17, No. 2, 2014.

（8）《"可持续发展的投资政策框架"与我国的对策》,《厦门大学学报》（哲学社会科学版）,ISSN 0438-0460 CN35-1019/C,2013 年第 6 期。

（9）《当前国际投资政策趋向与我国的应有作为》,《光明日报》2013 年 8 月 7 日第 11 版。

（10）《中国特色国际经济法学的理念与追求——〈陈安论国际经济法学〉的学术创新与特色贡献》,《西南政法大学学报》,2012 年第 2 期。

（11）《ECFA：两岸特色的区域贸易协定》,《厦门大学学报》（哲学社会科学版）, 2011 年第 4 期。

（12）《论香港双边投资条约实践》,《国际经济法学刊》第 19 卷第 3 期,ISBN 978-7-301-21424-4,2012 年。

（13）《ECFA：两岸特色的区域贸易协定》,《厦门大学学报》（哲社版）,2011 年第 4 期。

（14）Characteristics and Implications of ECFA, *Korean Journal of International Economic Law*, ISSN 2005-9949, Vol. 8, No. 2, 2010.

（15）ECFA：Internal RTA with Cross-Strait Characteristics, *Sungkyunkwan Journal of Science & Technology Law*, Vol. 4, ISSN 1976-1422, 2010.

（16）《多边投资协定谈判前瞻》,《国际经济法学刊》第 17 卷第 3 期,ISBN978-7-301-18034-1,2010 年。

（17）《论双边投资条约实践的"失衡"与革新》，《江西社会科学》，ISSN 1004-518X，2010 年第 6 期。

（18）ZENG Huaqun, Initiative and Implications of Hong Kong's Bilateral Investment Treaties, *The Journal of World Investment & Trade*, ISSN 1660-7112, Vol. 11, No. 5, 2010.

（19）《南北矛盾与双边投资条约的发展趋向》，载于曾华群主编、李国安副主编：《国际经济新秩序与国际经济法新发展》，ISBN 978-7-5036-9325-0，法律出版社 2009年出版。

（20）《港外经济协定实践及其法律依据》，《厦门大学学报》（哲社版），ISSN 0438-0460 CN35-1019/C，2009 年第 1 期。

（21）ZENG Huaqun, Unprecedented International Status: Theoretical and Practical Aspects of the HKSAR's External Autonomy, *The Journal of World Investment & Trade*, ISSN 1660-7112, Vol. 9, No. 3, 2008.

（22）Zeng Huaqun, "One China Four WTO Memberships": Legal Grounds, Relations and Significance, *The Journal of World Investment & Trade*, ISSN 1660-7112, Vol. 8, No. 5., 2007.

（23）《论 WTO 体制与国际投资法的关系》，《厦门大学学报》（哲社版），ISSN 0438-0460 CN35-1019/C，2007 年第 6 期。

（24）《变革期双边投资条约实践述评》，《国际经济法学刊》第 14 卷第 3 期，ISBN 978-7-301-12736-0/D. 1864，2007 年。

（25）John WONG, ZOU Keyuan, ZENG Huaqun, New Dimensions in China-ASEAN Relations, in John WONG, ZOU Keyuan, ZENG Huaqun (ed.), *China-ASEAN Relations: Economic and Legal Dimensions*, World Scientific Publishing Co. Pte, Ltd, ISBN 981-256-657-0, 2006.

（26）ZENG Huaqun, WTO Rules and the Development of China-ASEAN FTA Agreement, in John WONG, ZOU Keyuan, ZENG Huaqun (ed.), *China-ASEAN Relations: Economic and Legal Dimensions*, World Scientific Publishing Co. Pte, Ltd, ISBN 981-256-657-0, 2006.

（27）《国际经济法研究生培养模式的改革与实践》，《学位与研究生教育》，ISSN 1001-960X，2006 年第 4 期，第一作者。

（28）《外资征收及其补偿标准：历史的分野与现实的挑战》，《国际经济法学刊》第 13 卷第 1 期，ISBN 7-301-10644-0/D. 1483，2006 年。

（29）《WTO 规则与中国东盟自由贸易区的发展》,《厦门大学学报》(哲社版),ISSN 0438-0460 CN35-1019/C,2005 年第 6 期。

（30）《香港单独缔约权的实践及其法律依据》,载于饶戈平编:《山高水长——王铁崖先生纪念文集》,ISBN 7-301-08401-3/D1049,北京大学出版社,2004 年。

（31）《CEPA:两岸四地经合模式之展望》,载于王贵国主编:《区域安排法律问题研究》,ISBN 7-301-08619-9/D1083,北京大学出版社,2004 年。

（32）《论内地与香港 CEPA 之性质》,《厦门大学学报》(哲社版),ISSN 0438-0460 CN35-1019/C,2004 年第 6 期。

（33）Promoting a New Bilateral Legal Framework for China-EU Economic Relations,*Chinese Journal of International Law*,ISSN 1540-1650,Vol. 3,No. 1,2004.

（34）《我国国际法学当前应当重点研究的若干问题》,《法学研究》,ISSN 1002-896X,2004 年第 2 期,合著者之一。

（35）《从中国内地与中国香港之间的 WTO 成员关系看"一国四席"问题》,载于孙琬锺主编:《中国经贸法律的热点问题》(世界贸易组织法研究文丛第 1 卷),ISBN 7-81087-494-2/D. 397,中国人民公安大学出版社,2004 年。

（36）《关于内地、香港、澳门地区更紧密经贸关系的法律思考》,载于孙琬锺主编:《中国经贸法律的热点问题》(世界贸易组织法研究文丛第 1 卷),ISBN 7-81087-494-2/D. 397,中国人民公安大学出版社,2004 年。

（37）《论"特殊与差别待遇条款"的发展及其法理基础》,《厦门大学学报》(哲社版),ISSN 0438-0460 CN35-1019/C,2003 年第 6 期。

（38）Hong Kong's Autonomy:Concept,Developments and Characteristics,*China:An International Journal*,ISSN 0219-7472,Vol. 1,No. 2,2003.

（39）《两岸四地建立更紧密经贸关系的法律思考》,《国际经济法论丛》第 7 卷,ISBN 7-5036-4265-3/D. 3983,2003 年。

（40）《新型自由贸易区:"更紧密经贸关系"的法律模式》,《广西师范大学学报》(哲社版),ISSN 1001-6597 CN45-1066/C,2003 年第 3 期。

（41）《略论 WTO 体制的"一国四席"》,《厦门大学学报》(哲社版),ISSN 0438-0460 CN35-1019/C,2002 年第 5 期。

（42）《国际经济法涵义再探——由杨紫烜教授的"国际经济协调论"引发的思考》,《国际经济法论丛》第 5 卷,ISBN 7-5036-3715-3/D. 3350,2002 年。

（43）《WTO 体制下中国与中国香港之间的成员关系初探》,载于香港法律教育信托基金编:《中国入世与中国法治——内地、香港法制比较》,ISBN 7-208-0421-0/D.719,上海人民出版社,2002 年。

(44)《TRIPS 对我国技术市场的影响和对策》,《开放潮》,ISSN 1006-6098 CN35-1181/F,2002 年第 5 期。

(45)《香港特别行政区高度自治权刍议——对外事务实践的视角》,《比较法研究》,ISSN 1004-8561 CN11-3171/D,2002 年第 1 期。

(46)《略论国际经济法的合作发展原则》,《对外经济贸易大学学报》,ISSN 1002-4034 CN11-3645/F,2002 年第 1 期。

(47)《中国政府"入世"的法制保障》,《开放潮》,ISSN 1006-6098 CN35-1181/F,2002 年第 1 期。

(48)《加入 WTO 与中国法制建设》,《宣传半月刊》,ISSN 1008-195X CN35-1024/D,2002 年第 3、4 期。

(49)《调整中欧经济关系的法律框架初探》,《欧洲》,ISSN 1004-9789 CN11-3211/C,2001 年第 4 期。

(50)《我国对外资实行国民待遇原则的法律实践》,《厦门大学学报》(哲社版),ISSN 0438-0460 CN35-1019/C,2001 年第 4 期。

(51)《中国仲裁机构的新发展与国际商事仲裁实务》,《厦门大学法律评论》,ISBN 7-5615-1736-X,2001 年第 1 期。

(52) Legal Development of FDI Admission into China, *China Mail*, ISSN 0218-1517,Vol. 13, No. 1, 2000, TWL Publishing (Singapore) Pte Ltd.

(53)《欧共体明示与隐含缔约能力浅析》,《厦门大学学报》(哲社版),ISSN 0438-0460 CN35-1019/C,2000 年第 1 期。

(54)《试论香港特区高度自治权的基本特征及其对外事务实践》,载于《中国内地、香港法律制度研究与比较》,ISBN 7-301-04630-8/D. 484,北京大学出版社,2000 年。

(55)《论国际经济法学的发展》,《国际经济法论丛》第 2 卷,ISBN 7-5036-2692-5/D. 2399,1999 年。

(56)《邓小平对"一国两制"理论及其法律化的贡献》,载于陈传鸿、王豪杰主编:《邓小平理论学习与研究》,ISBN 7-5615-1478-6/B. 55,厦门大学出版社,1999 年。

(57)《仲裁解决中外投资争议的新发展》,《中国外资》,ISSN 1004-8146 CN11-3073/F,1999 年第 5 期。

(58)《仲裁解决中外投资争议:法制的发展与实践的考虑》,《东亚论文》(新加坡国立大学东亚研究所），ISSN 0219-1415 ISBN 981-04-1810-8,第 16 期,1999 年。

(59)《中国外商投资法律的"市场经济型"发展及其意义》,《东亚论文》(新加坡国立大学东亚研究所),ISSN 0219-1415 ISBN 981-04-1319-1,第 12 期,1999 年。

(60) *Chinese Foreign Investment Laws：Recent Developments towards a Market Economy*, East Asian Institute Contemporary China Series No. 29, World Scientific and Singapore University Press, ISBN 981-02-4224-7 (pbk), 1999.

(61) On the Legal Framework of China-EU Economic Relations：Historical Developments, Political Issues and Legal Considerations, *EAI WORKING PAPERS*, ISSN 0219-1318 ISBN 981-04-1896-5,No. 29,1999.

(62) Towards National Treatment Principle：Recent Developments of Chinese Foreign Investment Laws, *China Mail*, ISSN 0218-1517, Vol. 12, No. 4, 1999, TWL Publishing (Singapore) Pte Ltd.

(63) The Major Developments of China-EU Economic Relations, *China Mail*, ISSN 0218-1517, Vol. 12, No. 3, 1999, TWL Publishing (Singapore) Pte Ltd.

(64) Resolving China-foreign Investment Disputes by Arbitration, *China Mail*, ISSN 0218-1517, Vol. 12, No. 3, 1999, TWL Publishing (Singapore) Pte Ltd.

(65)《中国国际经济法学的创立与发展》,《中国法学》,ISSN 1003-1707 CN11-1030/D,1998 年第 5 期,第一作者。

(66)《略论香港特别行政区的高度对外自治权》,《厦门大学学报》(哲社版),ISSN 0438-0460 CN35-1019/C,1998 年第 1 期。

(67)《过渡期香港双边条约实践初探》,《国际经济法论丛》第 1 卷,ISBN 7-5036-2371-9/D. 1934,1998 年。

(68)《当代经济主权问题纵横谈》,《法制日报》1997 年 3 月 22 日第 8 版(国外法坛),本人为执笔人。

(69)《关于国际经济法概念的分歧与共识》,《厦门大学学报》(哲社版),ISSN 0438-0460 CN35-1019/C,1997 年法学专号。

(70)《试析"港荷投资协定"的特征》,《比较法研究》,ISSN 1004-8561 CN11-3171/D,第 9 卷第 3 期,1995 年。

(71)《香港与外国民航协定刍议》,《厦门大学学报》(哲社版),ISSN 0438-0460 CN35-1019/C,1994 年第 2 期。

(72)《欧共体"单一银行执照制"初探》,《欧洲》,ISSN 1004-9789 CN11-3211/C,1993 年第 4 期。

（73）《香港股份有限公司董事会的若干法律特征》，《厦门大学学报》（哲社版），ISSN 0438-0460 CN35-1019/C，1992 年法学专号。

（74）《中外合营者之间争端的解决方式评析》，《厦门大学学报》（哲社版），ISSN 0438-0460 CN35-1019/C，1992 年第 1 期。

（75）《普通法系国家合营企业的法律概念与特征》，《厦门大学学报》（哲社版），ISSN 0438-0460 CN35-1019/C，1991 年法学专号。

（76）《跨国公司参与合营企业的股权策略浅析》，《南开经济研究》，ISSN 1001-4691，1990 年第 5 期。

（77）《中外合资企业技术转让条款探讨》，《厦门大学学报》（哲社版），ISSN 0438-0460 CN35-1019/C，1990 年第 1 期。

（78）《合营公司的管理机构：中美日有关法制的比较》，《比较法研究》，北京新闻出版局内部准印证号：891051，1989 年第 3—4 期。

（79）《事实上控制的预防——与跨国公司签订中外合资经营企业合同的考虑》，《厦门大学学报》（哲社版），ISSN 0438-0460 CN35-1019/C，1987 年增刊。

（80）《合资企业的事实控制问题》，《法学研究》，代号：2-528；国外代号：Bm164，1987 年第 2 期。

（81）《中外合营企业管理权分享探讨》，《法学评论》，湖北省报刊登记证第 146 号，1985 年第 5 期。

附录四　主要学术交流活动

附表 4.1　主要国内学术交流活动(1984—　　)

序号	时间地点	会议名称/交流活动	主办机构	参与情况
1	1984.05.08—06.05 庐山	第一期国际经济法讲习班和国际经济法研究会(中国国际经济法学会前身)成立大会	武汉大学法律系、南开大学经济研究所、上海社会科学院法学研究所、厦门大学法律系、安徽大学法律系、中山大学法律系和江西大学法律系	参加第一期国际经济法讲习班全部课程学习和国际经济法研究会成立大会。
2	1992.10.16—20 厦门	1992 年中国国际经济法学术研讨会	中国国际经济法研究会、厦门大学法律系、厦门大学国际经济法研究所、厦门市国际经济贸易学会	参与会务组织,提交论文《欧共体"单一银行执照制"初探》并作专题发言。
3	1993.11.15—19 珠海	1993 年中国国际经济法学术研讨会	中国国际经济法研究会、广东省对外经济贸易委员会	参与会务组织,提交论文《香港与外国民航协定刍议》并作专题发言。
4	1994.11.14—17 重庆	1994 年中国国际经济法学术研讨会	中国国际经济法学会、西南政法学院、重庆市对外经济贸易委员会	参与会务组织,提交论文《试析"港荷投资协定"的特征》并作专题发言。
5	1997.10.24—28 杭州	1997 年中国国际经济法学术研讨会	中国国际经济法学会、杭州大学法律系	参与会务组织,提交论文《略论香港特别行政区的高度对外自治权》并作专题发言。
6	1999.11.12—14 海口	1999 年中国国际经济法学术研讨会	中国国际经济法学会、海南大学法学院、海口市中级人民法院	参与会务组织,提交论文《欧共体明示与隐含缔约能力浅析》并作专题发言。
7	1999.11.19—20 香港	中国内地、香港法律制度比较研讨会	香港法律教育基金	提交论文《试论香港特区高度自治权的基本特征及其对外事务实践》并作专题发言。
8	2000.01.06 福州	中共福建省委学习中心组学习会	中共福建省委	应邀作《澳门特别行政区基本法》辅导讲座。
9	2000.10.19—23 北京	2000 年中国国际经济法学术研讨会,主题为"经济全球化与国际经济法学"	中国国际经济法学会、对外经济贸易大学法学院、中国国际经济贸易仲裁委员会	参与会务组织,提交论文《我国对外资实行国民待遇原则的法律实践》并作专题发言。

（续表）

序号	时间地点	会议名称/交流活动	主办机构	参与情况
10	2001.07.16 福州	中共福建省委学习中心组学习会	中共福建省委	应邀作题为"世贸组织体制与中国加入世贸组织的准备"的专题讲座。
11	2001.11.08—10 上海	中国内地、香港法律制度比较研讨会	香港法律教育基金	提交论文《WTO体制下中国与中国香港之间的成员关系初探》并作专题发言。
12	2001.11.02—04 上海	2001年中国国际经济法学术研讨会，主题为"全球化与区域一体化中的国际经济法"	中国国际经济法学会、复旦大学法学院	参与会务组织，提交论文《略论WTO体制的"一国四席"》并作专题发言。
13	2001.11.15—16 厦门	中国"入世"后海峡两岸经贸法律新问题研讨会	中国法学会、厦门大学WTO中心、厦门大学国际经济法研究所	参与会务组织，提交论文《从中国内地与中国香港之间的WTO成员关系看"一国四席"问题》并作专题发言。
14	2002.09.18—20 大连	2002年中国国际经济法学术研讨会	中国国际经济法学会、大连海事大学法学院	参与会务组织，提交论文《两岸四地建立更紧密经贸关系的法律思考》并作专题发言。
15	2003.09.27—30 兰州	2003年中国国际经济法学术研讨会	中国国际经济法学会、甘肃政法学院	参与会务组织，提交论文《论"特殊与差别待遇条款"的发展及其法理基础》并作专题发言。
16	2004.05.29—30 厦门	"坎昆会议后WTO法制的走向和中国的对策"专家研讨会	中国法学会世界贸易组织法研究会、厦门大学国际经济法研究所	参与会务组织，提交论文《关于内地、香港、澳门地区更紧密经贸关系的法律思考》并作专题发言。
17	2004.07 长沙	"区域安排法律问题"研讨会	湖南师范大学法学院	提交论文《CEPA：两岸四地经合模式之展望》并作专题发言。
18	2004.11.05—08 厦门	2004年中国国际经济法学术研讨会	中国国际经济法学会、厦门大学国际经济法研究所	参与会务组织，提交论文《论内地与香港CEPA之性质》并作专题发言。
19	2005.03.10—11 香港	WTO与大中华经济圈法律研讨会	香港城市大学法学院	提交论文《WTO规则与中国东盟自由贸易区的发展》并作专题发言。

（续表）

序号	时间地点	会议名称/交流活动	主办机构	参与情况
20	2005.08 井冈山	中国国际经济法学会专题研讨会	中国国际经济法学会、南昌大学法学院	参与会务组织，提交论文《关于建立中国—韩国自由贸易区的法律思考》并作专题发言。
21	2005.10.13—16 长沙	2005 年中国国际经济法学术研讨会	中国国际经济法学会、湖南师范大学法学院	参与会务组织，提交论文《外资征收及其补偿标准：历史的分野与现实的挑战》并作专题发言。
22	2006.02.26 厦门	中国国际经济法学会会员代表大会（履行民政部登记程序）	中国国际经济法学会	参与会务组织，作学会工作报告。
23	2006.10.20—22 黄山	2006 年中国国际经济法学术研讨会	中国国际经济法学会、安徽财经大学法学院	参与会务组织，提交论文《变革期双边投资条约实践述评》并作专题发言。
24	2007.05.24—25 北京	中国国际法学会 2007 年学术年会，主题为"世界多极化、经济全球化与中国国际法学"	中国国际法学会	提交论文《双边投资条约实践的新发展》并作专题发言。
25	2007.09.09 厦门	第十一届中国国际投资贸易洽谈会/第一届国际投资保护协定研讨会	商务部条约法律司、中国国际经济法学会、厦门大学国际经济法研究所	参与会务组织，提交论文《双边投资条约实践的新发展》并作大会发言。
26	2007.11.02—05 湛江	2007 年中国国际经济法学术研讨会，主题为"结构变化与国际经济法的新问题、新挑战"	中国国际经济法学会、中国政法大学国际法学院、广东省律师协会、广东环宇京茂律师事务所	参与会务组织，提交论文《论 WTO 体制与国际投资法的关系》并作专题发言。
27	2007.11.25 北京	中国法学会审判理论研究会成立大会暨第一届年会	最高人民法院、中国法学会	应邀参会并担任审判理论研究会首届理事会理事。
28	2008.05.29—30 北京	中国国际法学会 2008 年学术年会，主题为"机遇与挑战：中国和平发展面临的国际法问题"	中国国际法学会	提交论文《南北矛盾与国际投资条约实践的新发展》并作专题发言。
29	2008.09.09 厦门	第十二届中国国际投资贸易洽谈会/第二届国际投资保护协定研讨会	商务部条约法律司、中国国际经济法学会、厦门大学国际经济法研究所	参与会务组织，致辞，提交论文《南北矛盾与 BITs 实践的新发展》并作大会发言。

（续表）

序号	时间地点	会议名称/交流活动	主办机构	参与情况
30	2008.10.25—27 天津	2008年中国国际经济法学术研讨会	中国国际经济法学会、南开大学法学院	参与会务组织，提交论文《港外经济协定实践及其法律依据》并作专题发言。
31	2008.12.13—14 广州	"外国仲裁裁决在中国的承认与执行"专题研讨会	中国国际经济法学会、广东省律师协会、厦门大学国际经济法研究所、广东环宇京茂律师事务所	参与会务组织，作专题报告评论。
32	2008.11.21—22 香港	两岸四地法律发展学术研讨会	香港城市大学法学院	提交论文《两岸经济合作机制的模式选择及法律对策》并作专题发言。
33	2009.03.01—07 澳门	应邀开展学术交流活动	澳门大学法学院	开设"国际经济法研究"专题讲座。
34	2009.05.10 厦门	"中国国际经济法的研究方法暨陈安教授学术思想"研讨会	厦门大学法学院、厦门大学国际经济法研究所	参与会务组织和研讨。
35	2009.09.09 厦门	"中国海外投资法律问题"专题研讨会	中国国际经济法学会、广东省律师协会、厦门大学国际经济法研究所、广东环宇京茂律师事务所	参与会务组织和主持研讨。
36	2009.09.10—11 厦门	第十三届中国国际投资贸易洽谈会/第三届国际投资保护协定研讨会	商务部条约法律司、中国国际经济法学会、厦门大学国际经济法研究所	参与会务组织及专题报告评议。
37	2009.10.31—11.01 杭州	2009年中国国际经济法学术研讨会，主题为"国际金融危机与国际经济法的变革"	中国国际经济法学会、浙江工商大学法学院、浙江泽厚律师事务所	参与会务组织，提交论文《论双边投资条约实践的"失衡"与革新》并作专题发言。
38	2009.12 北京	双边投资保护协定专家研讨会	商务部条约法律司	参与研讨发言。
39	2010.03.28 台北	海峡两岸法学交流廿周年纪念研讨会	台湾东吴大学法学院暨法律系	分组会发言。
40	2010.09.09—10 厦门	第十四届中国国际投资贸易洽谈会/第四届国际投资保护协定研讨会	商务部条约法律司、中国国际经济法学会、厦门大学国际经济法研究所	参与会务组织，提交论文《两岸特色的RTA》并作专题发言。
41	2010.10.15 南京	"WTO、法治与中国——中国加入WTO十年"研讨会	商务部条约法律司、中国国际经济法学会、厦门大学国际经济法研究所、南京大学法学院	参与会务组织，致辞。

序号	时间地点	会议名称/交流活动	主办机构	参与情况
42	2010.10.15—17 南京	中国国际经济法 2010 年年会暨学术研讨会，主题为"国际经济法面临的新格局与新挑战：中国视角"	中国国际经济法学会、南京大学法学院	参与会务组织，致辞，提交论文《ECFA：两岸特色的 RTA 实践》并作专题发言。
43	2010.10.21—30 澳门	应邀开展学术交流活动	澳门大学法学院	开设"国际经济法研究"专题讲座。
44	2011.03.21—22 北京	"反倾销措施 WTO 争端解决案件"专题研讨会	商务部条约法律司	参与研讨。
45	2011.04.09 厦门	"陈安国际法学发展基金"成立大会暨国际法学研究方法研讨会	厦门大学法学院、厦门大学国际经济法研究所	代表陈安国际法学发展基金会筹备委员会作报告。
46	2011.09.09 厦门	第十五届中国国际投资贸易洽谈会/第五届国际投资保护协定研讨会	商务部条约法律司、中国国际经济法学会、厦门大学国际经济法研究所	参与会务组织，作专题报告《国际投资协定中国民待遇"负面清单及其影响"》。
47	2011.10.09—15 澳门	应邀开展学术交流活动	澳门大学法学院	开设"国际经济法研究"专题讲座。
48	2011.10.28 厦门	第二届 WTO 法专题研讨会，主题为"中国加入 WTO 十年的争端解决实践"	商务部条约法律司、中国国际经济法学会、厦门大学国际经济法研究所	参与会务组织，致辞等。
49	2011.10.28—30 厦门	中国国际经济法 2011 年年会暨学术研讨会，主题为"'入世'十年与国际经济法的改革与发展"	中国国际经济法学会、厦门大学国际经济法研究所	参与会务组织，致辞，提交论文《BIT 范本：缘起、发展与中国的创新》并作专题发言。
50	2011.11.24 汕头	参加汕头大学法学院 30 周年院庆	汕头大学法学院	作专题报告《双边投资条约的新发展与中国的实践》。
51	2012.03.30 厦门	第一届海峡两岸国际经济法论坛："WTO 贸易及与贸易有关的新问题"学术研讨会	厦门大学法学院、台湾政治大学法学院、厦门大学国际经济法研究所	作专题报告《ECFA："两岸特色"的区域贸易协定实践》。
52	2012.07.04 北京	"一国两制"与香港特区的对外法律事务研讨会	外交部条约法律司、北京大学港澳研究中心	提交论文《论香港的双边经济协定实践》并作专题发言。

（续表）

序号	时间地点	会议名称/交流活动	主办机构	参与情况
53	2012.09.10 厦门	第十六届中国国际投资贸易洽谈会/第六届国际投资协定研讨会"国际投资协定的新发展：以美国2012年投资协定范本和中国缔约新实践为中心"	商务部条约法律司、中国国际经济法学会	参与会务组织，致辞及专题报告评议。
54	2012.09.10—15 澳门	应邀开展学术交流活动	澳门大学法学院	开设"国际经济法研究"专题讲座。
55	2012.09.27—28 昆明	跨境经济合作区法律问题研讨会	云南省高级人民法院、云南大学	提交论文《WTO规则、FACEC与"跨境经济合作区"的发展》并作专题发言。
56	2012.11.02 上海	第三届WTO法专题研讨会	商务部条约法律司、中国国际经济法学会、华东政法大学国际法学院	参与会务组织，致辞。
57	2012.11.02—04 上海	中国国际经济法2012年年会暨学术研讨会，主题为"国际经济新秩序与中国特色国际经济法学"	中国国际经济法学会、华东政法大学国际法学院	参与会务组织，致辞，提交论文《中国特色国际经济法学的理念与追求》并作专题发言。
58	2012.12.07—09 台北	现代国际法与超国界法学术研讨会	台湾政治大学法学院	作专题报告《ECFA的创新实践及国际意义》。
59	2012.11.15—18 厦门	"两会协议的理论与实务"学术研讨会	厦门大学台湾研究院	提交论文《ECFA："两岸特色"的区域贸易协定实践》并作专题发言。
60	2013.09.08—09 厦门	第十七届中国国际投资贸易洽谈会/第七届国际投资保护协定研讨会	商务部条约法律司、中国国际经济法学会、厦门大学国际经济法研究所	参与会务组织，致辞，作为"'可持续发展的投资政策框架'与我国外资法的创新"的专题发言。
61	2013.10.25 西安	第四届WTO法专题研讨会	商务部条约法律司、中国国际经济法学会、西安交通大学法学院、丝绸之路国际法与比较法研究所、厦门大学国际经济法研究所	参与会务组织，致辞等。

（续表）

序号	时间地点	会议名称/交流活动	主办机构	参与情况
62	2013.10.26—27 西安	2013 年中国国际经济法学会年会暨学术研讨会",主题为"后危机时代国际经济法的新发展与中国的实践"	中国国际经济法学会、西安交通大学法学院、丝绸之路国际法与比较法研究所	参与会务组织,致辞,提交论文《"可持续发展的投资政策框架"与我国的对策》并作专题发言。
63	2013.11.26 北京	中国法学会香港基本法澳门基本法研究会成立大会	清华大学	作为创会会员参加并任该会首届理事会理事。
64	2013.11.26—27 北京	政学结合研讨会	外交部条约法律司	参与研讨发言。
65	2014.02.26 北京	《国际法研究》期刊座谈会	中国社会科学院国际法研究所	参与研讨发言。
66	2014.10.31 武汉	第五届 WTO 法专题研讨会	商务部条约法律司、中国国际经济法学会、武汉大学法学院、厦门大学国际经济法研究所	参与会务组织,致辞等。
67	2014.10.31—11.02 武汉	2014 年中国国际经济法学术研讨会暨姚梅镇先生百年诞辰纪念会	中国国际经济法学会、武汉大学法学院	参与会务组织,致辞和总结,提交论文《论我国"可持续发展导向"BITs 的实践》并作专题发言。
68	2014.12.27 厦门	第八届国际投资法专题研讨会:国际投资法的新发展与中国的对策	中国国际经济法学会、商务部条约法律司支持	参与会务组织,致辞和总结,作题为"我国 BIT 实践的目标与规则取向"的专题报告。
69	2015.10.23 昆明	第六届 WTO 法专题研讨会	中国国际经济法学会、商务部条约法律司支持	参与会务组织,致辞和总结。
70	2015.10.23—25 昆明	2015 年中国国际经济法学会年会暨学术研讨会,主题为"'一带一路'战略背景下中国国际经济法的新发展"	中国国际经济法学会、云南大学法学院	参与会务组织,致辞和总结,提交论文《论双边投资条约范本的演进与中国的对策》并作专题发言。
71	2015.12.12 厦门	第九届国际投资法专题研讨会:"一带一路"战略下我国国际投资条约面临的机遇与挑战	中国国际经济法学会、商务部条约法律司支持	参与会务组织,致辞和总结,作题为"关于我国 BIT 实践发展趋向的思考"的专题报告。
72	2016.11.03 厦门	第七届 WTO 法专题研讨会	中国国际经济法学会、商务部条约法律司支持	参与会务组织,致辞和参与研讨。

（续表）

序号	时间地点	会议名称/交流活动	主办机构	参与情况
73	2016.11.04—05 厦门	2016 年中国国际经济法学会年会暨学术研讨会,主题为"重构国际经济秩序与中国的贡献"	中国国际经济法学会、厦门大学法学院、厦门大学国际经济法研究所	参与会务组织,致辞和总结,提交论文《论中国特色国际经济法学》并作专题发言。
74	2016.12.17—18 珠海	2016 年香港基本法澳门基本法研究会年会暨"基本法与国家统合"高端论坛	香港基本法澳门基本法研究会	作题为"香港双边投资条约实践的依据及适用"的大会报告。
75	2016.12.10 厦门	第十届国际投资法专题研讨会	中国国际经济法学会、商务部条约法律司支持、厦门大学国际经济法研究所、厦门大学法学院国际投资争议解决研究中心、昊理文律师事务所、环球律师事务所	参与会务组织,致辞和总结。
76	2017.01.21—22 澳门	两岸四地法律发展——法治与权利研讨会	澳门大学法学院高级法律研究所	作题为"两岸经贸关系发展的法治化及其特征"的发言。
77	2017.03.29 澳门	纪念澳门基本法颁布 24 周年研讨会	澳门基本法推广协会	作题为"香港特别行政区的双边经济协定实践"的发言。
78	2017.11.30 厦门	第十一届国际投资法专题研讨会,主题为"中国与变革中的国际投资争端解决机制"	中国国际经济法学会、厦门大学国际经济法研究所、厦门大学法学院国际投资争议解决研究中心	参与会务组织,致辞和总结,作题为"新形势下中国在投资者—东道国争端解决机制改革中的贡献"的发言。
79	2017.11.17 广州	第八届 WTO 法专题研讨会	中国国际经济法学会、商务部条约法律司支持	参与会务组织,致辞和总结。
80	2017.11.17—19 广州	2017 年中国国际经济法学会年会暨学术研讨会,主题为"'一带一路'法律框架的构建与国际经济法的新发展"	中国国际经济法学会、华南理工大学法学院、华南理工大学社科处、华南理工大学中国对外开放法治研究中心	参与会务组织,致辞和总结,提交论文《论中国特色国际经济法学》并作专题发言。
81	2017.12.08—10 香港	"基本法的理论与实践:20 年的回顾与前瞻"法律研讨会	香港基本法澳门基本法研究会和香港大学法律学院、香港大学法律学院中国法中心、深圳大学港澳基本法研究中心	提交论文《香港双边投资条约实践的创新》并作专题报告。

（续表）

序号	时间地点	会议名称/交流活动	主办机构	参与情况
82	2018.03.24 佛山	香港法律教育基金有限公司三十周年会庆暨学术研讨会	香港法律教育基金有限公司（法律教育信托基金）	提交论文《香港双边投资条约实践的创新》并作专题报告。
83	2018.07.31 厦门	第十二届国际投资法专题研讨会	中国国际经济法学会、商务部条约法律司支持	参与会务组织，致辞和总结，作题为"'一带一路'国际合作的 ISDS 机制"的专题报告。
84	2018.08.11—12 平潭	2018 年中国法学会香港基本法澳门基本法研究会年会暨"新时代港澳基本法研究的新课题"学术论坛	香港基本法澳门基本法研究会、平潭管委会，福州大学法学院、福建师范大学法学院	提交论文《论香港双边投资条约实践的适用问题》并作大会报告。
85	2018.11.16 北京	第九届 WTO 法专题研讨会	中国国际经济法学会、商务部条约法律司支持	参与会务组织，致辞和总结。
86	2018.11.16—18 北京	2018 年中国国际经济法学会年会暨学术研讨会，主题为"'一带一路'法治建设与国际经济法的新发展"	中国国际经济法学会、中国政法大学	参与会务组织，致辞和总结，提交论文《共同发展：中国与"一带一路"国家间投资条约实践的创新》并作专题发言。
87	2018.12.23 北京	庆祝中国改革开放四十周年献礼——《中国特色话语:陈安论国际经济法学》新书发布会	中国法学会、中国国际经济法学会、厦门大学、北京大学出版社	参与会务组织，代表中国国际经济法学会作大会致辞。
88	2019.04.11—12 厦门	国家信息化专家委员会网络空间国际治理研究中心第二届学术研讨会:网络空间国际法的理论与实践	国家信息化专家委员会网络空间国际治理研究中心、厦门大学法学院网络空间国际法研究中心	作为主旨报告与谈人，作题为"勇于担当网络空间国际法研究的新使命"的大会发言。
89	2019.05.11 厦门	祝贺陈安教授从教六十九周年暨中国特色国际经济法学研讨会	厦门大学法学院、中国国际经济法学会	参与会务组织，代表中国国际经济法学会致辞，提交评论《国际法领域"中国特色话语"平台的创建与发展——厦门大学国际法学科的奉献》并作专题报告。
90	2019.10.25 西柏坡	第十届 WTO 法专题研讨会	中国国际经济法学会、商务部条约法律司支持	参与会务组织，致辞和总结。

（续表）

序号	时间地点	会议名称/交流活动	主办机构	参与情况
91	2019.10.25—27 西柏坡	2019 年中国国际经济法学会年会暨学术研讨会，主题为"中国特色国际经济法的使命担当和创新发展"	中国国际经济法学会、河北经贸大学	参与会务组织，致辞和总结，提交论文《论国际法"国际话语体系"》并作专题发言。
92	2019.11.09 厦门	第十三届国际投资法专题研讨会，主题为《ICSID 仲裁规则》修订和《外商投资法实施条例》(征求意见稿)研讨"	中国国际经济法学会、商务部条约法律司支持、厦门大学国际经济法研究所、厦门大学法学院国际投资争议解决中心	参与会务组织，致辞、参与研讨及总结。
93	2019.11.12 澳门	澳门回归 20 周年对外法律事务研讨会	外交部	提交论文《WTO"一国四席"的创新实践》并作专题报告。
94	2020.10.30—11.01 上海	2020 年中国国际经济法学会年会暨学术研讨会，主题为"高水平开放型经济建设与国际经济法的创新发展"	中国国际经济法学会、上海对外经济贸易大学	参与会务组织，致辞和总结，提交论文《论"一国两制"下香港双边投资条约实践的适用问题》并作专题发言。
95	2021.06.04 厦门	第三届网络空间国际法专题研讨会，主题为"跨境数据流动的政策、法律与实践"	厦门大学法学院、厦门大学法学院网络空间国际法研究中心	参与会议并作总结。
96	2022.06.09 北京、深圳 (线上＋线下)	"一国两制"视角下的涉外法治：机遇和展望——纪念香港回归二十五周年涉外法律事务研讨会	外交部、深圳大学	作题为"发挥香港特区独特优势，创建国际法的'东方之珠'"的专题发言。

附表 4.2 主要国际学术交流活动(1990—   )

序号	时间地点	会议名称/交流活动	主办机构	参与情况
1	1990.04.22—27 北京	第 14 届世界法律大会	通过法律维护世界和平中心	任福建省代表团副团长，参与会议讨论。
2	1996.02 瑞士洛桑	瑞士比较法研究所学术报告会	瑞士比较法研究所	讲题为 The Development of Hong Kong's Bilateral Treaties in the Period of Transition（过渡期香港双边条约的发展）。

序号	时间地点	会议名称/交流活动	主办机构	参与情况
3	1996.06 英国伦敦	伦敦大学亚非学院学术报告会	伦敦大学亚非学院、伦敦律师协会中国组	讲题为 May Hong Kong Maintain Her International Status after 1997?（香港1997年后能保持其国际地位吗?）
4	1998.11.09 英国伦敦	伦敦大学亚非学院法律系专题报告会	伦敦大学亚非学院法律系	讲题为 The New Development of China's Foreign Investment Law and the New Opportunities for European Investors（中国外商投资法律的新发展与欧洲投资者的新机会）。
5	1999.03.20 新加坡	新加坡国立大学国际企业研究所专题报告会	新加坡国立大学国际企业研究所	讲题为《仲裁解决对华投资争议的新发展》。
6	1999.03.29 新加坡	接受新加坡电视机构（Television Corporation of Singapore，TCS）直播采访	新加坡电视机构	接受有关中国投资环境的直播采访并现场回答新加坡公众通过电话提出的有关投资中国的法律问题。
7	1999.04.09 新加坡	新加坡国立大学东亚研究所学术报告会	新加坡国立大学东亚研究所	讲题为 Legal Framework on China-EU Economic Relations（中国—欧盟经济关系的法律框架）。
8	1999.05.04 新加坡	新加坡国立大学东亚研究所学术报告会	新加坡国立大学东亚研究所	讲题为 External Autonomy of Hong Kong Special Administrative Region（香港特别行政区的对外自治权）。
9	1999.08 新加坡	新加坡国立大学东亚研究所学术报告会	新加坡国立大学东亚研究所	讲题为 The Development of Supervisory Power of People's Congress of PRC-Case Studies（中国人大监督权的发展——案例研究）。
10	1999.10 上海	第一届中国—北欧国际法研讨会	瑞典隆德大学瓦伦堡研究所等	会议发言。
11	2000.02 北京	第二届中国—北欧国际法研讨会	瑞典隆德大学瓦伦堡研究所等	会议发言。
12	2000.05 北京	反倾销专题研讨会	对外贸易经济合作部、欧洲联盟执行委员会	大会发言讨论。

（续表）

序号	时间地点	会议名称/交流活动	主办机构	参与情况
13	2000.10 上海	第三届中国—北欧国际法研讨会	瑞典隆德大学瓦伦堡研究所等	会议发言。
14	2001.03 厦门	第四届中国—北欧国际法研讨会	瑞典隆德大学瓦伦堡研究所、厦门大学国际经济法研究所	提交论文《国际经济法的合作发展原则》，参与主持会议和发言。
15	2001.07.10—13 北京	中国—欧盟高等教育合作项目参加人员学术交流大会	中国—欧盟高等教育合作项目	在分组会议发言。
16	2001.09.20—21 北京	中国—欧盟高等教育合作项目参加人员第二次学术交流大会	中国—欧盟高等教育合作项目	在分组会议发言。
17	2001.10.22—24 北京	《货物进出口条例》国际研讨会	亚洲开发银行、对外贸易经济合作部	提交论文《WTO 基本法律原则与中国货物进出口管理法制的革新》并作大会发言。
18	2002.10 美国华盛顿哥伦比亚特区	Symposium on International Economic Law and Developing Countries（"国际经济法与发展中国家"研讨会）	美国国际法学会国际经济法研究分会	提交论文 Political Elements and International Economic Law（政治因素与国际经济法）并作大会发言。
19	2002.10 美国华盛顿哥伦比亚特区	Symposium on PRC's Accession to WTO（"中华人民共和国加入世界贸易组织"研讨会）	美国乔治城大学法律中心	作题为 On the "One Country, Four Memberships" in WTO Regime（WTO 体制的"一国四席"问题）的大会报告。
20	2003.09 新加坡	新加坡国立大学东亚研究所学术讲座	新加坡国立大学东亚研究所	讲题为 One China, Four WTO Members: Legal Ground, Relations and Perspectives（一个中国，四个WTO成员：法律依据，相互关系与展望）。
21	2004.11.04—05 厦门	Symposium on International Economic Law and China in Transition（"国际经济法与转型期的中国"学术研讨会）	中国国际经济法学会、厦门大学国际经济法研究所、厦门大学法学院	参与会务组织，提交论文 WTO Rules and the Development of FTA Agreement between China and ASEAN（WTO 规则与中国—东盟自由贸易协定的发展）并作大会报告。

（续表）

序号	时间地点	会议名称/交流活动	主办机构	参与情况
22	2004.12 新加坡	Symposium on China-ASEAN Relations：New Dimensions（"中国—东盟关系：新领域"学术研讨会）	新加坡国立大学东亚研究所、厦门大学国际经济法研究所	参与会务组织，提交论文 WTO Rules and the Development of FTA Agreement between China and ASEAN（WTO 规则与中国—东盟自由贸易协定的发展）并作大会报告。
23	2005.06 厦门	东亚数据传媒的合一，数据内容与韩流	韩国信息传播学会、韩国仁荷大学、厦门大学法学院	参会交流。
24	2005.06.17—18 韩国首尔	第一届中韩国际学术研讨会，主题为 China-Korea Trade Relation in Ten Years of WTO（"WTO 十年的中韩贸易关系"研讨会）	中国国际经济法学会、韩国国际经济法学会	参与会务组织，提交论文 Legal Considerations on the China-Korea FTA（关于建立中国—韩国自由贸易区的法律思考）并作大会报告。
25	2005.07.12 荷兰海牙	厦门国际法高等研究院董事会成立会议暨第一次会议	厦门国际法高等研究院	参与会务组织，参加会议及相关访问交流活动。
26	2006.01 厦门	Seminar on Legal and Economic Development in Northeast Asia（"东北亚地区的法律与经济发展"专题研讨会）	美国威斯康星州立大学法学院、厦门大学法学院	参与联络组织和研讨活动。
27	2006.08.27—09.15 厦门	The 1st Summer Session on International Law（第一届国际法前沿问题研修班）	厦门国际法高等研究院	参与组织，代表行政理事会致辞和总结。
28	2006.11 韩国仁川	中韩法学教育以及中韩贸易的法律问题	厦门大学法学院、厦门大学国际经济法研究所、韩国仁荷大学法学院	作专题报告，参与相关交流活动。
29	2007.07.09—27 厦门	The 2nd Summer Session on International Law（第二届国际法前沿问题研修班）	厦门国际法高等研究院	参与组织，代表行政理事会致辞和总结。讲授专题课程 The New Development of International Economic Treaties and China's Practice（国际经济条约的新发展与中国的实践）。

（续表）

序号	时间地点	会议名称/交流活动	主办机构	参与情况
30	2008.01 厦门	全球化下中韩知识产权与经贸法律的新发展	厦门大学法学院、厦门大学国际经济法研究所、韩国仁荷大学法学院	作专题报告，参与相关交流活动。
31	2008.07.07—25 厦门	The 3rd Summer Session on International Law & 2008 National Post-Graduate Summer School on International Law（第三届国际法前沿问题研修班暨2008年国际法全国研究生暑期学校）	厦门国际法高等研究院 厦门大学法学院、厦门大学国际经济法研究所	参与组织，代表行政理事会致辞和总结。
32	2008.10.24 天津	第二届中韩国际学术研讨会，主题为 The WTO Regime and Regional Trading Blocs: Laws and Practices of the Free Trade Agreements（FTAs）in China and Korea（WTO体制与区域贸易集团：中国、韩国自由贸易协定的法律与实践）	中国国际经济法学会、韩国国际经济法学会	参与会务组织，作专题报告 China's FTA practice and Potentials for China-Korea FTA（中国的自由贸易协定实践及中韩自由贸易协定展望）。
33	2009.07.06—24 厦门	The 4th Summer Session on International Law（第四届国际法前沿问题研修班）	厦门国际法高等研究院	参与组织，代表行政理事会致辞和总结。
34	2010.06 加拿大维多利亚	Three Decades of Chinese SEZ's: Old Roads and New Roads（中国经济特区30年：新旧交替）专题研讨会	加拿大维多利亚大学法学院	作题为 New Profile and Role of Xiamen SEZ—Economic-plus Aspects（厦门经济特区的新形象与新功能——超经济方面）的大会主题报告。
35	2010.07.05—23 厦门	The 5th Summer Session on International Law（第五届国际法前沿问题研修班）	厦门国际法高等研究院	参与组织，代表行政理事会致辞和总结。
36	2010.08.19—21 韩国首尔	第三届中韩国际学术研讨会，主题为 Korea-China FTA—Seeking Ways to Reduce Trade Barriers for the Special Partnership（中韩自由贸易区——寻求削减贸易壁垒以建立特殊伙伴关系之路）	中国国际经济法学会、韩国国际经济法学会、韩国外交通商部	提交论文 Characteristics and Implications of ECFA（ECFA的特征与意涵）并作大会报告和评论。

（续表）

序号	时间地点	会议名称/交流活动	主办机构	参与情况
37	2010.08.22 韩国首尔	韩国成吉馆大学法学院学术报告	韩国成吉馆大学法学院（Sungkyunkwan University Law School）	讲题为 ECFA：Internal RTA with Cross-Strait Characteristics（ECFA：具有两岸特色的国内区域贸易协定）。
38	2010.12.14 法国巴黎	Second Symposium on International Investment Agreements/International Investment Agreements and Investor-State Dispute Settlement at a Crossroads：Identifying Trends，Differences and Common Approaches（第二届国际投资协定研讨会/处于十字路口的国际投资协定与投资者—国家间争端的解决：确认趋向、分歧与共同取向）	"经济合作与开发组织"（OECD）和"联合国贸易与发展会议"（UNCTAD）	作题为 Innovative Path for International Investment Agreements（国际投资协定的革新之路）的大会报告。
39	2010.12.15—18 荷兰海牙	访问联合国国际法院、海牙国际法高等研究院、荷兰莱顿大学、博睿出版社（Koninklijke Brill NV）	厦门大学国际经济法研究所、厦门国际法高等研究院	参与访问交流活动。
40	2011.07.04—22 厦门	The 6th Summer Session on International Law & 2011 National Post-Graduate Summer School on International Law（第六届国际法前沿问题研修班暨2011年国际法全国研究生暑期学校）	厦门国际法高等研究院 厦门大学法学院、厦门大学国际经济法研究所	参与组织，代表行政理事会致辞和总结。
41	2011.10.28 厦门	第四届中韩国际学术研讨会，主题为 Main Issues and Promoting Path of China-Korea FTA（中韩自由贸易协定的主要问题与促进路径）	中国国际经济法学会、韩国国际经济法学会、厦门大学国际经济法研究所	参与会务组织，致辞和主持研讨。
42	2012.01 厦门	国际学术研讨会：法律全球化—韩国与中国的视角	厦门大学国际经济法研究所、韩国成均馆大学校	作题为 China's Representation in International Stage（中国在国际舞台的代表权）的专题报告。
43	2012.07.02—20 厦门	The 7th Summer Session on International Law（第七届国际法前沿问题研修班）	厦门国际法高等研究院	参与组织，代表行政理事会致辞和总结。

（续表）

序号	时间地点	会议名称/交流活动	主办机构	参与情况
44	2012.09.09 厦门	《2012年世界投资报告》中文版发布暨新一代投资政策研讨会，主题为"促进国际投资实现可持续发展"	联合国贸易和发展会议（UNCTAD）、中国商务部	应邀出席并就会议主题作大会评论。
45	2013.04.26—27 厦门	"国际经济法和纠纷解决程序：问题与改革"国际学术研讨会（International Conference on International Economic Law and Dispute Resolution Processes: Issues and Reforms）	厦门大学法学院、汕头大学法学院、厦门大学国际经济法研究所	参与会务组织，主持，提交论文 Balance, Sustainable Development and Integration: Innovative Path for BIT Practice（平衡，可持续发展与一体化：双边投资条约实践的创新路径）并作大会报告。
46	2013.06—07 美国斯坦福	访问美国斯坦福大学法学院		与斯坦福大学法学院国际法与比较法项目 Allen Weiner 主任交流。
47	2013.07.08—26 厦门	The 8th Summer Session on International Law（第八届国际法前沿问题研修班）	厦门国际法高等研究院	参与组织，代表行政理事会致辞和总结。
48	2013.07.17 韩国首尔	第五届中韩国际学术研讨会，主题为 Korea-China FTA: Prospects and Jurisprudence（中韩自由贸易协定：前景展望与法理）	中国国际经济法学会、韩国国际经济法学会	致辞和主持研讨。
49	2013.07.18—19 韩国首尔	第三届亚洲国际经济法学界双年会，主题为 The WTO at 20 and the Future of the International Law on Trade, Investment and Finance（WTO 20周年与有关贸易、投资和金融的国际法之未来）	亚洲国际经济法学界（Asian International Economic Law Network, AIELN），Ewha Womans University	参与研讨和相关交流活动。
50	2013.09.10 厦门	Seminar on the China-EU Investment Rule-Making and the Future of International Investment Law（"中欧投资规则制定与国际投资法的未来"研讨会）	厦门大学法学院、厦门大学国际经济法研究所、德国发展研究所、Siegen University	参与会务组织，提交论文 Balance, Sustainable Development and Integration: Innovative Path for BIT Practice（平衡，可持续发展与一体化：双边投资条约实践的创新路径）并作大会报告。
51	2014.06—07 美国伯克利	访问美国加州大学伯克利法学院		访问交流。

（续表）

序号	时间地点	会议名称/交流活动	主办机构	参与情况
52	2014.07.07—25 厦门	The 9th Summer Session on International Law（第九届国际法前沿问题研修班）	厦门国际法高等研究院	参与组织，代表行政理事会致辞和总结。
53	2014.12.08 新加坡	Workshop on China, S. E. Asia and International Economic Law（"中国、东南亚与国际经济法"研讨会）	厦门大学国际经济法研究所、新加坡国立大学法学院亚洲法律研究中心（Centre for Asian Legal Studies，CALS）	作题为 China's Position in IIA Practice(中国国际投资条约实践的立场)的专题报告。
54	2015.05—06 美国旧金山	访问美国旧金山大学法学院		访问交流。
55	2015.07.13—31 厦门	The 10th Summer Session on International Law(第十届国际法前沿问题研修班)	厦门国际法高等研究院	参与组织，代表行政理事会致辞和总结。
56	2016.07.04—22 厦门	The 11th Summer Session on International Law(第十一届国际法前沿问题研修班)	厦门国际法高等研究院	参与组织，代表行政理事会致辞和总结。
57	2017.02.20—22 新加坡	亚洲法学院院长论坛	新加坡国立大学、中国人民大学	作题为"发展中法学院跨学科教学的初步实践"的大会报告。
58	2017.05 美国旧金山	访问美国旧金山大学法学院		签署澳门科技大学法学院与美国旧金山大学法学院合作协议。
59	2017.06.16—17 厦门	第五届亚洲国际经济法学界双年会，主题为 International Investment Law in Asian Perspective（亚洲视角下的国际投资法）	亚洲国际经济法学界（Asian International Economic Law Network，AIELN）、中国国际经济法学会、厦门大学法学院	致辞和总结。
60	2017.07.03—22 厦门	The 12th Summer Session on International Law(第十二届国际法前沿问题研修班)	厦门国际法高等研究院	参与组织，代表行政理事会致辞和总结。 作开学讲座：International Legal Perspective on China's "Belt and Road" Initiative（中国"一带一路"倡议的国际法观察）。
61	2017.10.14 韩国首尔	第七届中韩国际学术研讨会，主题为 Current Issues and Prospect(当前问题与展望)	中国国际经济法学会、韩国国际经济法学会、韩国外交部支持	致辞和主持研讨。

（续表）

序号	时间地点	会议名称/交流活动	主办机构	参与情况
62	2017.11.02 厦门	International Legal Order for Investment：What Role the BRICS Can Play?（国际投资法律秩序：金砖国家的作用）	厦门大学法学院	致辞和提交论文 China's Initiative on Bilateral Investment Treaty Practice（中国双边投资条约实践的创新）。
63	2017.12.11—12 澳门	第五届葡语国家法律大会	澳门城市大学	提交论文《一带一路倡议下中国与亚非葡语国家之间投资条约实践的创新》并作大会报告。
64	2018.04.23—24 德清、杭州	The 9th International Conference on the New Haven School of Jurisprudence（第九届纽黑文学派国际学术会议）	浙江大学国际战略与法律研究院、耶鲁大学法学院、杜兰大学法学院	作题为 Towards the "Common Development" Model：China's Initiative on BIT Practice（"共同发展"模式：中国双边投资条约实践的创新）的大会报告。
65	2018.07.02—03 北京	"一带一路"法治合作国际论坛	外交部、中国法学会	参与讨论发言。
66	2018.07.09—27 厦门	The 13th Summer Session on International Law（第十三届国际法前沿问题研修班）	厦门国际法高等研究院	参与组织，代表行政理事会致辞和总结。
67	2018.08.03—04 澳门	澳门海洋管理、利用与发展国际研讨会	澳门特区政府政策研究室	提交论文《创建海洋经济协同发展的"两门"（厦门—澳门）合作机制——以"海洋旅游"为优先领域》并作大会报告。
68	2019.05.25 杭州	第八届中韩国际学术研讨会，主题为 New Development of International Economic Law in China & Korea（中韩国际经济法的最新发展）	中国国际经济法学会、韩国国际经济法学会	致辞，参与研讨和总结。
69	2019.05.31—06.01 杭州	The 10th International Conference on the New Haven School of Jurisprudence and International Law（第十届纽黑文学派与国际法国际学术会议）	浙江大学国际战略与法律研究院、耶鲁大学法学院、杜兰大学法学院和中国国际贸易促进委员会法律事务部	作题为 Legal Initiative on the Belt and Road International Cooperation（一带一路国际合作的法制创新）的大会报告。

（续表）

序号	时间地点	会议名称/交流活动	主办机构	参与情况
70	2019.07.08—26 厦门	The 14th Summer Session on International Law（第十四届国际法前沿问题研修班）	厦门国际法高等研究院	参与组织,代表行政理事会致辞和总结。讲授专题课程 China's Contributions and Initiative to International Economic Law（中国对国际经济法的贡献与创新）。
71	2021.04.06 厦门	International Forum on Humanities and Social Science: Theory and Practice of International Rule of Law & Governance（人文社会科学国际论坛:国际法治的理论与实践研究国际研讨会）	厦门大学法学院	提交论文《共同发展:国际投资条约体制的目标创新》（Common Development: the Objective Initiative of International Investment Treaty Regime）并作大会发言。
72	2021.06.25 （线上）	第九届中韩国际学术研讨会,主题为 Multilateralism and New Development in International Economic Law（多边主义与国际经济法的新发展）	中国国际经济法学会、韩国国际经济法学会	致辞,参与研讨和总结。

附录五　主要获奖成果和学术荣誉

附表 5.1　主要教学成果奖

序号	获奖者	教学成果	奖项	获奖时间
1	余劲松、王传丽、曾华群等	《国际经济法学》（高等教育出版社 1994 年版,曾华群任副主编）	国家教委第三届普通高等学校优秀教材中青年奖	1995
2	陈安、曾华群、廖益新、徐崇利、李国安	"教学与科研相互促进,出人才与出成果共同并举"的研究生培养模式	福建省教学成果一等奖	1997
3	曾华群（指导教师）	张昕:《九七后 MIGA 公约在香港特别行政区适用的若干问题》	全国"挑战杯"大学生业余科技作品竞赛三等奖	1997
4	曾华群、陈辉萍	指导法学院国际法辩论队	第二届"贸仲杯"模拟国际商事仲裁竞赛亚军	2001
5	曾华群（指导教师）	陈东:《论跨国公司治理中的责任承担机制》	福建省优秀博士学位论文一等奖	2002
6	曾华群（负责）	本科生"国际经济法学课程"	教育部国家级精品课程	2004
7	曾华群（负责）	国际经济法研究生培养模式的改革与实践	福建省优秀教学成果奖二等奖	2005
8	曾华群（指导教师）	蔡奕:《跨国银行监管的主要法律问题研究》	福建省优秀博士学位论文二等奖	2005
9	曾华群（负责）	硕士学位课程"国际经济法研究"	福建省优质硕士学位课程	2006
10	曾华群（指导教师）	蔡从燕:《私人结构性参与多边贸易体制——对变动着的国际法结构的一种考察》	福建省优秀博士学位论文奖一等奖。	2007
11	曾华群、陈辉萍、李国安、蔡从燕、池漫郊、肖彬、于湛旻、龚宇	国际经济法人才的国际化培养模式	福建省教学成果奖二等奖	2009
12	曾华群、陈安、廖益新、徐崇利、李国安、陈辉萍、于飞、蔡从燕、池漫郊、韩秀丽、蔡庆辉、陈喜峰、房东、龚宇、陈欣、于湛旻、邱冬梅、张膑心、肖彬	国际法学科"国际化"教学模式的创建与发展	福建省教学成果奖一等奖	2014
13	曾华群（负责）	本科课程"国际经济法学"	教育部首批"国家级精品资源共享课"	2016

附表 5.2　主要科研成果奖

序号	获奖者	获奖论著名称	奖励名称	获奖时间
1	曾华群	中外合资企业法律的理论与实务	首届全国高等学校人文社会科学研究优秀成果奖著作类二等奖	1995
2	曾华群	WTO 与中国外资法的发展	第五届高等学校科学研究优秀成果奖（人文社会科学）著作类三等奖	2009
3	曾华群	Initiative and Implications of Hong Kong's Bilateral Investment Treaties	第六届高等学校科学研究优秀成果奖（人文社会科学）论文类三等奖	2013
4	陈安、曾华群等	"国际经济法系列专著"(含《国际投资法》《国际贸易法》《国际货币金融法》《国际税法》《国际海事法》)	福建省 1979—1987 年社会科学优秀成果一等奖	1988
5	曾华群	中外合资企业法律的理论与实务	福建省第二届社会科学优秀成果奖二等奖	1994
6	曾华群	国际经济法导论	福建省第四届社会科学优秀成果奖二等奖	2000
7	陈安、曾华群等	国际经济法学专论（两卷本）	福建省第五届社会科学优秀成果奖二等奖	2003
8	曾华群	论"特殊与差别待遇"条款的发展及其法理基础	福建省第六届社会科学优秀成果奖二等奖	2005
9	曾华群	香港经贸法	福建省第三届社会科学优秀成果奖三等奖	1998
10	曾华群、徐崇利、林忠	国际投资法学	福建省第四届社会科学优秀成果奖三等奖	2000
11	曾华群（主编）	WTO 与中国外贸法的新领域	福建省第七届社会科学优秀成果奖三等奖	2007
12	曾华群	WTO 与中国外资法的发展	福建省第七届社会科学优秀成果奖三等奖	2007
13	曾华群、陈辉萍（主编）	美国《1974 年贸易法》第 301—310 节案	福建省第八届社会科学优秀成果奖三等奖	2009
14	曾华群	共同发展：中国与"一带一路"国家间投资条约实践的创新	福建省第十四届社会科学优秀成果奖三等奖	2021
15	曾华群、徐崇利、林忠	国际投资法学	司法部 2002 年度法学教材和研究优秀成果奖优秀奖	2003
16	曾华群（主编）	WTO 与中国外贸法的新领域	第十五届"安子介国际贸易研究奖"三等奖	2008
17	曾华群	论香港双边投资条约实践的适用问题	中国法学会香港基本法澳门基本法研究会优秀论文一等奖	2018

附：高等学校科学研究优秀成果奖获奖成果简介

1. 曾华群：《中外合资企业法律的理论与实务》（厦门大学出版社 1991 年出版）

本书主要采取综合比较的研究方法，在探讨有关合营企业一般理论问题的基础上，从法理和实践两方面，对中外合资企业的重要法律问题进行了较系统的论述。其主要学术价值：一是对合营企业的法律概念与特征、国际合营公司的组织结构及调整国际合营公司的法律框架等一般理论问题和共同投资、共同管理、共负盈亏、所得税、技术转让、国有化和征收、反托拉斯及争端解决方式等法律实务问题进行了较深入的分析论证；二是将中外合资企业的法律问题作为一个整体进行综合研究，注重论证相关国内法和国际法规范的相互联系。

Zeng Huaqun, Theory and Practice on Chinese-foreign Joint Venture Law, *Xiamen University Press,* *1991.*

Based on the studies on theoretic issues of joint venture in general, the work deals with systematically the theoretic and practical legal issues on China-foreign joint ventures by comprehensive and comparative researching methods. The main academic achievements of the work are firstly, to explore the general theoretic issues (i. e. legal concepts and characteristics of joint ventures, structures of international joint ventures, and legal framework for governing international joint ventures) of joint ventures, and the practical legal issues (i. e. common investment, common control, sharing profit and loss, income taxation, technology transfer, nationalization and expropriation, antitrust and dispute resolutions) of China-foreign joint ventures in depth; and secondly, to make comprehensive studies on the legal issues of China-foreign joint ventures as a whole, and stress the link between relative national law and international law.

2. 曾华群：《WTO 与中国外资法的发展》（厦门大学出版社 2006 年出版）

基于国际投资法与 WTO 体制形成联系和中国"入世"后需要创设更优良投资环境的认识，本书从理论和实践两个方面，分别对 WTO 与多边投资体制、WTO 与中国的区域贸易协定实践、双边投资条约的发展与中国的实践、中国外资法的"转型"发展等专题作较深入、细致的研究，提出我国有关国际投资的条约实践和国内立法的建议。其主要学术价值：一是较深入探讨和论证 WTO 体制与国际投资法的相互关系；二是较全面研究"入世"以来中国外资法（含国际法和国内法规范）的新发展；三是拓展了国际法视野下中国外资法研究的新领域。

Zeng Huaqun, WTO and Development of Chinese Foreign Investment Law, *Xiamen University Press*, 2006.

Considering the link between international investment law and WTO regime, and the needs for creating better investment environment after China's WTO accession, the work deals with in depth the issues on WTO and multilateral investment regime, WTO and China's regional trade agreement practice, development of bilateral investment treaties and China's practice, and the "transition" development of Chinese foreign investment law, and provides suggestions for China's international investment treaty practice and foreign investment legislations. The main academic contributions of the work are firstly, to explore the issue on the relationship between WTO regime and international investment law; and secondly, to study comprehensively the development of Chinese foreign investment law, including national law and international law after China's WTO accession; and thirdly, to expand the fields of Chinese foreign investment law studies in the international law perspective.

3. 曾华群:《香港双边投资条约的创新与意涵》(英文)(《世界投资与贸易学刊》2010 年第 11 卷第 5 期)

自 1992 年以来,香港以其名义签订了 15 项双边投资条约(BITs)。这一新发展显示了香港对外自治权实践的显著成就,也反映了 BIT 历史的重要突破和创新。基于香港 BIT 范本条款和相关条约实践,本文研析香港 BITs 的重要条款,如授权、适用范围、投资待遇、剥夺与补偿、争端解决等条款。作者指出,一般而言,香港的 BIT 实践遵循了传统模式,因其非主权实体地位,也具有一些特征;香港 BIT 实践的重要意义是,为香港特别行政区、澳门特别行政区和中国台北提供了相关模式,加强了香港特别行政区的高度自治权,为国际法的发展做出了重要贡献。

Zeng Huaqun, Initiative and Implications of Hong Kong's Bilateral Investment Treaties, *The Journal of World Investment & Trade*, *Volume 11 Number 5*, 2010.

Hong Kong (HK) has concluded 15 bilateral investment treaties (BITs) in its name since 1992. The new development demonstrates remarkable achievements in practice of HK's external autonomy and indicates an important breakthrough and initiative in the history of BITs. Based on the provisions of HK Model BIT and relevant treaty practice, the article discusses and analyses some key provisions of HK's BITs, such as provisions on authorization, scope of application, investment treatment, deprivation and compensation, and dispute settlement. The author points out that though HK's BIT practice in general follows the traditional practice it has some characteristics due to its non-sovereign status. The great implications of HK's BIT practice are to provide the model for HKSAR，Macao SAR and Chinese Taipei，to strengthen the high autonomy of HKSAR，and to make important contributions to the development of international law.

附表5.3　主要学术荣誉

序号	获奖者	学术荣誉	颁授部门	授予年份
1	曾华群	享受国务院政府特殊津贴	国务院	1993
2	曾华群	入选为国家"百千万人才工程首批第一、二层次人选"	人事部、科技部、教育部、财政部、国家计划委员会、中国科学技术协会、国家自然科学基金委员会	1996
3	曾华群	福建省优秀专家	中共福建省委福建省人民政府	2002
4	曾华群	第二届福建省高等学校教学名师	福建省教育厅	2006
5	曾华群	福建省优秀教师	福建省人事厅福建省教育厅	2007
6	曾华群	入选为"当代中国法学名家"	《当代中国法学名家》编委会	2009
7	曾华群	入选为"影响中国法治建设的百位法学家"	《今日中国》(中国法治建设特刊)编委会	2016